A Dictionary for the Modern Conductor

DICTIONARIES FOR THE MODERN MUSICIAN

Series Editor: David Daniels

Contributions to **Dictionaries for the Modern Musician** offer both the novice and the advanced artist lists of key terms designed to fully cover the field of study and performance for major instruments and classes of instruments, as well as the workings of musicians in areas from conducting to composing. Focusing primarily on the knowledge required by the *contemporary* musical student and teacher, performer, and professional, each dictionary is a must-have for any musician's personal library!

A Dictionary for the Modern Singer by Matthew Hoch, 2014
A Dictionary for the Modern Clarinetist by Jane Ellsworth, 2014
A Dictionary for the Modern Trumpet Player by Elisa Koehler, 2015
A Dictionary for the Modern Conductor by Emily Freeman Brown, 2015

A Dictionary for the Modern Conductor

Emily Freeman Brown

ROWMAN & LITTLEFIELD
Lanham • Boulder • New York • London

Published by Rowman & Littlefield
A wholly owned subsidiary of The Rowman & Littlefield Publishing Group, Inc.
4501 Forbes Boulevard, Suite 200, Lanham, Maryland 20706
www.rowman.com

Unit A, Whitacre Mews, 26-34 Stannary Street, London SE11 4AB

British Library Cataloguing in Publication Information Available

Library of Congress Cataloging-in-Publication Data
Brown, Emily Freeman.
A dictionary for the modern conductor / Emily Freeman Brown.
  pages cm. — (Dictionaries for the modern musician)
Includes bibliographical references.
ISBN 978-0-8108-8400-7 (cloth : alk. paper) — ISBN 978-0-8108-8401-4 (ebook)
1. Conducting—Dictionaries.   I. Title.
ML102.C64B76 2015
781.4503—dc23   2015008615

♾️™ The paper used in this publication meets the minimum requirements of American National Standard for Information Sciences—Permanence of Paper for Printed Library Materials, ANSI/NISO Z39.48-1992.

Printed in the United States of America

Contents

Preface

Why a *Dictionary for the **Modern** Conductor*? Simply put, because the world of today's conductor has changed to such an extent that it is time for a new look, a new perspective. Gone are the days of the great maestros who ruled with an iron fist, who hired and fired of their own accord, and who garnered enormous recording contracts but didn't have to be involved in fundraising, community outreach, social media, or education. Today's conductors, like those before, must have all the same skills. But they must also have much more.

This dictionary is an attempt to meet a unique need in defining the new conducting world by touching upon as many aspects as possible in a single volume.

It provides an observer's perspective at a given point in history. It is a book that the reader can dip into at any point and find something interesting or look things up to get a quick definition, a short biography, or a description of a specific conducting technique. My hope is that it will be as fascinating to read as it was to write.

Acknowledgments

Many excellent and extremely intelligent people have helped me to write this book. I would like to begin by thanking Bennett Graff, who originally contacted me about the project, and Monica Savaglia and Kellie Hagan from Roman & Littlefield, who have been very generous with their time.

I am indebted to Bowling Green State University for allowing me a semester's leave to begin the research, especially Dr. Jeffrey Showell, dean of the College of Musical Arts, Dr. William Mathis, chair of performance studies, and Michelle Paul, departmental secretary. Numerous current and former conducting students helped along the way. They include, but are not limited to, Vicente Larrañaga, Octavio Màs-Arocas, and Sanitago Piñeros-Serrano, who helped especially with definitions of Spanish terms, and Iwona Sowinska. Other BGSU colleagues who provided invaluable assistance include music librarian Susannah Cleveland, author and musicologist Mary Natvig, hornist extraordinaire Andrew Pelletier, the beautiful oboist Nermis Mieses, intrepid violin professor Penny Thompson Kruse, incredible flutist Conor Nelson, lover of all things cello professor Alan Smith, and director of the Mid-American Center for Contemporary Music at Bowling Green State University Kurt Doles. Special thanks to Andrew Martin Smith for creating the musical examples and symbols and Derek Brennan for the drawings. Heather Strohstein and Lydia Dutciuc helped with initial editing work. Professor at the Juilliard School Samuel Zyman, Berlin Philharmonic bassist Ulrich Wolff, composer Alexander Liebermann, conductor and Laban expert Harlan Parker, conductor Stefan Sanderling, and author David Daniels all provided valuable help and insights. I would also like to thank numerous family members, friends, and colleagues who have encouraged me throughout this process. And saved for last, my gratitude to Samuel Adler: a better partner in life could not be found.

THE DICTIONARY

A. The pitch that is sounded for the tuning of the orchestra. Can also designate a key of a composition, as in Symphony in A.

A=440 Hz (Hertz). The standard tuning pitch for most ensembles today except in continental Europe, where that pitch can be as high as A=444 Hz. "Hz" stands for the measurement of the frequency of vibrations per second. This system was invented by the German physicist **Heinrich Hertz** (1857–1894).

Abbado, Claudio. (1933–2014.) Italian conductor who succeeded **Herbert von Karajan** as music director of the **Berlin Philharmonic** (1989–2002). Music director at the **La Scala Milan Opera** (1968–1986), principal conductor of the **London Symphony Orchestra** (1979–1987), principal guest conductor of the **Chicago Symphony** (1982–1986), music director of the **Vienna State Opera** (1986–1991), and founding conductor of the **Lucerne Festival Orchestra** (2003). His legacy is evident in his support of young musicians: he founded the **European Youth Orchestra** in 1978 and the **Gustav Mahler Youth Orchestra** in 1986. With a long list of exceptional recordings, he is known as a conductor of subtle, expressive gestures and insightful interpretations.

abbassare l'intonazione, abbassare l'accordatura. (It.) A term used to call for a lowering of the pitch or tuning. (Fr. *baisser l'accord, baisser l'intonation*; Ger. *herunterstimmen, erniedrigen*; Sp. *bajar la afinación.*)

abierto. (Sp.) Open. An indication that is seen in brass parts after the notation "closed" when the player mutes the sound by inserting his or her hand partway into the bell of the instrument or by using a mute. When stopping the horn with the hand, the pitch rises by a half step and the player must adjust. When using the mute, the pitches don't change. See **brass mutes, stopped**. (Fr. *ouvert*; Ger. *offen*; It. *aperto, sfogato.*)

à bouche fermée. (Fr.) with the mouth closed, humming. (Ger. *summen*, It. *a bocca chiusa*, Sp. *boca cerrada.*)

Abravanel, Maurice. (1903–1993.) Greek-born American conductor, music director of the **Utah Symphony Orchestra** from 1947 to 1979. He built the orchestra into a full-time ensemble and released several significant recordings with them on the **Vanguard** and later **Vox** labels, including a complete cycle of the symphonies of **Gustav Mahler**. Under his leadership, the orchestra made an important contribution to the cultural life of the state of Utah and the United States. Abravanel worked in opera in Berlin from 1922 to 1933 and moved to Paris in 1933, where he studied with and assisted **Bruno Walter**. After a short time in Australia conducting the Melbourne and Sydney operas, he accepted a position with the **Metropolitan Opera** in New York.

abreissen. (Ger.) A way of playing a note; to break, break off, to sever, to tear off. Example: *Ganzes Orchester scharf abreissen.* The whole orchestra cut off sharply. **Gustav Mahler**, Symphony No. 1, mvt. 2. (Fr. *arracher*, It. *strappare*, Sp. *dejar un lado el arco.*)

Abreu, José Antonio. (b. 1939.) Venezuelan pianist, economist, educator, activist, and politician. Founder of **El Sistema**, a musical program for youth in Venezuela now known as the Fundación Musical Simón Bolívar. It was designed to compensate for inadequate academic and economic opportunities among the poor by providing music education to thousands of children from mostly impoverished neighborhoods. El Sistema now reaches hundreds of thousands of children. The **Simon Bolivar Orchestra** (Orquesta Sinfónica Simón Bolívar), its most famous and professional ensemble, can be heard on tour in cities across the globe, led by its most famous alumnus, **Gustavo Dudamel**. El Sistema was brought to the attention of Americans when it was featured in a story broadcast multiple times on CBS's *60 Minutes.*

Similar programs have arisen in towns and cities across the United States. See Tunstall, Tricia. *Changing Lives: Gustavo Dudamel, El Sistema, and the Transformative Power of Music*. New York: W. W. Norton & Co., 2012.

Abschluss. (Ger.) Conclusion, end. (Fr. *conclusion*, It. *conclusione*, Sp. *conclusión*.)

absolute music. Music that is free from any programmatic association, that has no theme or narrative associated with it; music that stands on its own, that is without links to specific emotions, events, or characters. The opposite of a **symphonic poem**. Sometimes referred to as **abstract music**. (Ger. *absolute Musik, absolute Tonkunst*; Sp. *música absoluta*.)

absolute pitch. The ability to recall any pitch without reference to any instrument or tuning device. See also **perfect pitch**. (Fr. *oreille absolue*, Ger. *absolutes Gehör*, It. *orecchio assoluto*, Sp. *oído absoluto*.)

absolutes Gehör. (Ger.) **Absolute pitch**. The ability to recall any pitch without reference to any instrument or tuning device. See also **perfect pitch**. (Fr. *oreille absolue*, It. *orecchio assoluto*, Sp. *oído absoluto*.)

abstract music. See **absolute music**.

Abstrich. (Ger.) Down-bow, a downward stroke of the bow in the direction from the **frog** to the tip. (Fr. *tiré*, It. *arcata in giù*, Sp. *arco abajo*.) See **Aufstrich**.

Abtakt. (Ger.) **Downbeat**. Most often the first beat of the bar as indicated by the conductor with a downward gesture and an **ictus** on the pulse. (Fr. *temps fort, frappé*; It. *battuta in terra*; Sp. *primer tiempo, tiempo fuerte*.)

abwechselnd. (Ger.) To alternate, as in between two instruments, such as the piccolo and the flute or the clarinet in B-flat and the clarinet in A.

Academy for Ancient Music Berlin (Akademie für Alte Musik Berlin). Established in 1982 and also known as *Akamus*, it is a widely recorded chamber orchestra that specializes in the performance of early music. The ensemble offers its own concerts but also performs regularly with the **Berlin State Opera**, the **RIAS Chamber Choir**, the Netherlands Opera, and others.

Academy of Music. Built as a concert hall in 1857 and designed by architects Napoleon LeBrun and Gustavus Runge, the academy served as the home for the **Philadelphia Orchestra** from the orchestra's founding in 1900 until it moved to the Kimmel Center in 2001. Still owned by the Philadelphia Orchestra, the academy is also the home of the Pennsylvania Ballet and the Opera Company of Philadelphia. The academy has hosted the most famous musicians in the world, including Marian Anderson, Enrico Caruso, **Gustav Mahler**, Isaac Stern, **Richard Strauss**, and Pyotr Tchaikovsky.

Academy of St. Martins in the Fields. A chamber orchestra founded by **Sir Neville Marriner** in 1958, which originally gave its concerts in the London church of the same name. The ensemble started as a "conductorless" group of eleven string players. Marriner, a violinist in the **London Symphony** at the time, played concertmaster, playing solos and leading the orchestra from the first stand of violins. In 1970, he switched to the position of conductor. The orchestra grew to include winds, and its repertoire gradually expanded to include modern works. Marriner served as music director until 1978 when the position was taken over by its **concertmaster**, Iona Brown. In 2000, pianist Murray Perahia became principal guest conductor, leading many recordings as conductor and pianist. In 2011, violinist Joshua Bell was appointed as music director. The ensemble has recorded widely on the **L'Oiseau-Lyre**, **Chandos**, **Decca**, **EMI**, **Philips**, **Hyperion**, and other labels under its own name and also as the "Argo Chamber Orchestra" and the "London Strings" or "London String Players." They performed the soundtrack of the movie *Amadeus* (1984) and *The English Patient* (1996). Marriner is life president.

a cappella. (It.) choral music performed without instruments, unaccompanied.

Accademia Musicale Chigiana. International Summer Music Institute in Siena, Italy. Founded in 1932, students may study all standard orchestral instruments, guitar, and piano as well as chamber music, singing, composition, film music composition, and orchestral conducting. The faculty is highly regarded and comes mainly from Europe. The distinguished conductor **Franco Ferrara** taught there for many years. His students included **Daniel Barenboim**, **Carlo Maria Giulini**, **Zubin Mehta**, **Claudio Abbado**, **Riccardo Chailly**, and **Giuseppe Sinopoli**.

accelerando. (It.) Getting faster; commonly used in this Italian form. (Fr. *accélérant, en*; Ger. *beschleunigend*; Sp. *acelerador, acelerar el tiempo*.)

accélérant, en. (Fr.) Getting faster; commonly used in the Italian form, *accelerando*. (Ger. *beschleunigend*, It. *accelerando*, Sp. *acelerador, acelerar el tiempo*.)

accelerare. (It.) To get faster, accelerate. (Fr. *accélérer*, Ger. *beschleunigen*, Sp. *acelerar*.)

accélérer. (Fr.) To get faster, accelerate. (Ger. *beschleunigen*, It. *accelerare*, Sp. *acelerar*.)

accent. To emphasize a note or chord with a stress; to heighten, sharpen, or intensify a note or chord; to make a note distinct from others by accenting it. (Fr. *accent*, Ger. *Akzent*, It. *accento*, Sp. *acento*.) See **conducting technique**.

accent. (Fr.) **Accent**. (Ger. *Akzent*, It. *accento*, Sp. *acento*.)

accent agogique. (Fr.) **Agogic accent**. (Ger. *Akzent agogik*, It. *accento agogica*, Sp. *acento agógico*.)

accent mark. The notation device used to mark an accent in music.

Accent mark. *Courtesy Andrew Martin Smith.*

accento. (It.) **Accent**, played in an accented manner. (Fr. *accent*, Ger. *Akzent*, Sp. *acento*.)

accento agogica. (It.) **Agogic accent**. (Fr. *accent agogique*, Ger. *Akzent agogik*, Sp. *acento agógico*.)

accentuate. (It.) Accented, accentuated, stressed. (Fr. *accentué*, Ger. *akzentuiert*, Sp. *acentuado*.) See **accent**.

accentué. (Fr.) Accented, accentuated, stressed. (Ger. *akzentuiert*, It. *accentuate*, Sp. *acentuado*.) See **accent**.

accident. (Fr.) **Accidental** (lit. "accidental sign"). (Ger. *Versetzungszeichen*, It. *accidente*, Sp. *alteración*.)

accidental. A notation symbol used to raise, lower, or, in the case of the **natural sign**, neutralize a previous accidental.

accidente. (It.) **Accidental**. (Fr. *accident*, Ger. *Versetzungszeichen*, Sp. *alteración*.)

accompagnant, en. (Fr.) Accompanying, in the style of an accompaniment, to play with flexibility and sensitivity to another musician, to allow interpretive freedom while playing with another musician who has a primary role.

accompagnare. (It.) To accompany, as in a concerto or other work with a soloist. (Fr. *accompagner*, Ger. *begleiten*, Sp. *acompañar*.)

accompagner. (Fr.) To accompany, as in a concerto or other work with a soloist. (Ger. *begleiten*, It. *accompagnare*, Sp. *acompañar*.)

accompaniments, conducting. See **conducting accompaniments**.

accompany. To perform a supporting role on the piano or in an ensemble with a soloist. One can also accompany a choir or even a dance group. Conductors who are known as being good accompanists are particularly flexible and sensitive to the soloist(s).

accord. (Fr.) Chord, a group of notes played simultaneously. Example: *très rapide presque en accord*, very quick close to the chord. A note in the first harp part of *Rapsodie Espagnole* by Maurice Ravel. (Ger. *Akkord*, It. *accord*, Sp. *acorde*.)

accord. (It.) **Chord,** a group of notes played simultaneously. (Fr. *accord*, Ger. *Akkord*, Sp. *acorde*.)

accordare. (It.) To tune, as in to tune an instrument. (Fr. *accorder*, Ger. *stimmen*, Sp. *afinar*.) See **tuning practices**.

accordato. (It.) Tuned, true, tempered. (Fr. *accordé*, Ger. *gestimmt*, Sp. *afinado*.) See **tuning practices**.

accordé. (Fr.) Tuned, true, tempered. (Ger. *gestimmt*, It. *accordato*, Sp. *afinado*.) See **tuning practices**.

accorder. (Fr.) To tune, as in to tune an instrument. (Ger. *stimmen*, It. *accodare*, Sp. *afinar*.) See **tuning practices**.

accordo. (It.) Chord, a group of notes played simultaneously. (Fr. *accord*, Ger. *Akkord*, Sp. *acorde*.)

acelerador. (Sp.) Getting faster; commonly used in the Italian form, **accelerando**. Also *acelerar el tiempo*. (Fr. *accélérant, en*; Ger. *beschleunigend*; It. *accelerando*.)

(L to R): accidental sharp, accidental flat, accidental natural, accidental double sharp, and accidental double flat.
Courtesy Andrew Martin Smith.

acelerar. (Sp.) To get faster, to accelerate. (Fr. *accélérer*, Ger. *beschleunigen*, It. *accelerare*.)

acento. (Sp.) An **accent**, stress, played in an accented manner. (Fr. *accent*, Ger. *Akzent*, It. *accento*.)

acento agógico. (Sp.) **Agogic accent.** (Fr. *accent agogique*, Ger. *Akzent agogik*, It. *accento agogica*.)

acentuado. (Sp.) Accented, accentuated, stressed. (Fr. *accentué*, Ger. *akzentuiert*, It. *accentuate*.)

à chaque fois. (Fr.) every time. A directive heard in rehearsal. Also *toutes les fois*. (Ger. *jedesmal*, It. *ogni volta*, Sp. *cada vez*.)

Achtel, Achtelnote. (Ger.) Eighth note. (Fr. *croche*, It. *croma*, Sp. *corchea*.) See **appendix 7: "Rhythmic Terms and Their Translations."**

Achtelpause. (Ger.) Eighth-note rest. (Fr. *demi-soupir*, It. *pausa di croma*, Sp. *silencio de corchea*.) See **appendix 7: "Rhythmic Terms and Their Translations."**

acompañar. (Sp.) To accompany, as in a concerto or other work with a soloist. (Fr. *accompagner*, Ger. *begleiten*, It. *accompagnare*.)

acorde. (Sp.) **Chord**, a group of notes played simultaneously. (Fr. *accord*, Ger. *Akkord*, It. *accord*.)

acoustics. An interdisciplinary science that includes the production, propagation, and perception of sound. Its application to the field of music is multifaceted, ranging from the generation of sound by instruments to how the sounds are heard in performance, rehearsal, and practice spaces and on recording and through broadcast, in addition to the study and science of human hearing. A scientist in the field is an acoustician or acoustical engineer. In the music field, these professionals design the spaces where music is heard, and instrument makers and repair professionals deal with the intricate and specialized production of sound by the instruments. Good acoustic properties in a performance or rehearsal space can change the public's perception of the quality of an ensemble and also have an impact on how the members of the ensemble hear each other, as well as themselves.

acoustic scale. A seven-note scale described by the musicologist Erno Lendai and stemming from his study of the music of Béla Bartók. It is based on the series of pitches C, D, E, F-sharp, G, A, and B-flat. The acoustic scale is the fourth mode of the melodic minor ascending scale, sometimes called the **Lydian** dominant scale. The name "acoustic scale" is used because of the scale's similarity to the notes beginning with the eighth and going to the fourteenth pitch of the **harmonic series**. From low to high, it reads C4, D4, E4, F-sharp4, G4, A4, B-flat4.

acte. (Fr.) An act in an **opera**. (Ger. *Aufzug, Akt*; It. *atto*; Sp. *acto*.)

active gestures. In **conducting**, this applies to gestures that have an intention, an **impulse of will**, to evoke a specific musical reaction as opposed to **neutral gestures** that simply mark a beat within a bar or passage. Active gestures usually come with a preparatory breath in the tempo, dynamic, and character of the music to follow. See **conducting technique.**

acto. (Sp.) An act in an **opera**. (Fr. *acte*; Ger. *Aufzug, Akt*; It. *atto*.)

adagietto. (It.) A tempo marking that is slightly faster than **adagio**.

adagio. (It.) A tempo marking that means slowly, slower than **andante** but not as slow as **largo**. It was regarded as the slowest possible tempo during the eighteenth and nineteenth centuries.

adagissimo. (It.) A tempo marking that means very slow, slower than **adagio**.

Adams, John. (b. 1947.) Significant American composer and conductor. Adams was born in Worcester, Massachusetts, and is most well known for his work *Short Ride on a Fast Machine*. He is also the composer of many orchestral and operatic works such as the operas *Nixon in China, Doctor Atomic, Harmonium, Grand Pianola Music, The Chairman Dances*, the *Chamber Symphony*, the *Violin Concerto*, and many others. Adams is also known as an excellent conductor, especially of his own music. See Adams, John. *Hallelujah Junction: Composing an American Life*. New York: Picador, 2008.

adaptación. (Sp.) An adaptation of a piece of music to make it easier to play for a younger ensemble. Also *arreglo*. (Fr. *arrangement, adaptation*; Ger. *Bearbeitung*; It. *adattamento*.)

adaptation. (Fr.) An adaptation of a piece of music to make it easier to play for a younger ensemble. Also *arrangement*. (Ger. *Bearbeitung*; It. *adattamento*; Sp. *adaptación, arreglo*.)

adattamento. (It.) An arrangement of a piece of music for another kind of ensemble, such as an orchestral work arranged for band. (Fr. *arrangement, adaptation*; Ger. *Bearbeitung*; Sp. *arreglo, adaptación*.)

added-note chord. A chord of thirds, a tertian chord, such as a major chord with one or more pitches added that change the intervallic structure. The so-called **Copland chord**, C E G with an F as the bass note, is an example. Others are C E G plus A or C E G plus D. See **Iconic chords**.

additive meter. Meter that is constructed by adding small metric units into groups that form measures. Examples: 8/8 written as 3 + 3 + 2, 2 + 3 + 3, or 3 + 2 + 3.

adelante. (Sp.) To keep going, carry on. Also as an expression: "Come in!" "Keep going!" "Go ahead!"

à demi-voix. (Fr.) an expression seen not only in vocal music meaning half-voice or quietly. Also *à mi-voix.* (Ger. *mit halber Stimme,* It. *mezza voce,* Sp. *a media voz.*)

Adès, Thomas. (b. 1971.) English composer, conductor, and pianist. A prolific composer, Adès serves on the composition faculty of the Royal Academy of Music, London. He was artistic director of the **Aldeburgh Festival** (1999–2008). He has conducted the Los Angeles Philharmonic and associated ensembles in performances of his own and others' compositions. He is an active pianist.

à deux. (Fr.) an indication that two players are to play the same part. Also à 2. (Ger. *zu zweit,* It. *a due,* Sp. *a dos.*)

Adler, Samuel. (b. 1928.) German-born American composer and author, he immigrated to America in 1939. Adler's teachers included Herbert Fromm, Paul Hindemith, and Walter Piston. He studied with **Aaron Copland** and **Serge Koussevitsky** at the **Berkshire Music Center** at **Tanglewood** (1949–1950). Adler was drafted into the U.S. Army in 1950 and founded the **Seventh Army Symphony Orchestra**. The ensemble performed throughout Germany and Austria in order to reestablish cultural ties between America and Germany. He served as professor of composition at the University of North Texas (1957–1966), **Eastman School of Music** (1966–1995), and the **Juilliard School** (1997). He is the author of several books, including *Choral Conducting* and *The Study of Orchestration.* Adler has conducted many orchestras throughout the world.

ad libitum. (It., Latin.) At will, freely, at the performer's discretion. (Fr. *à volonté, à votre gré;* Ger. *nach Belieben;* It. *a piacere, a volonta;* Sp. *a placer, a gusto.*)

Adorno, Theodor W. (1903–1969.) German writer and philosopher of music. Adorno studied **piano** with Bernhard Sekles in Frankfurt and Alban Berg in Vienna (1925–1927). He returned to Frankfurt in 1927 to study philosophy and from 1928 to 1931 was editor of the journal *Anbruch,* where his writings included extensive articles on music. He taught philosophy at the Frankfurt University (1931–1934) but was removed during the rise of the Nazi regime. He moved to Oxford in 1934 and then to the United States in 1938 with an invitation from philosopher Max Horkheimer, who had brought his Institute for Social Research from Frankfurt to New York. Adorno worked at Princeton for the Radio Research Project (1938–1940) and moved to Southern California in 1941 along with Horkheimer and his institute. In Los Angeles, he collaborated with German writer Thomas Mann on his novel *Doctor Faustus,* which includes detailed descriptions of twelve-tone compositional techniques. After World War II (1949), Adorno returned to Frankfurt with Horkheimer, reestablishing the institute there and teaching again at the university. Eventually he succeeded Horkheimer as head of the institute, where he was known for developing a line of Marxist reasoning. Adorno promoted a sociology of music that advocated on behalf of the **Second Viennese School** composers, especially **Arnold Schoenberg**. He was also a scathing critic of contemporary mass culture and a prolific author (see the **bibliography**).

a dos. (Sp.) an indication that two players are to play the same part. (Fr. *á deux, à 2*; Ger. *zu zweit*; It. *a due.*)

a due. (It.) an indication that two players are to play the same part. (Fr. *á deux, à 2*; Ger. *zu zweit*; Sp. *a dos.*)

aeolian mode. See **church modes**.

aesthetics. (fr. Greek.) The branch of philosophy dealing with the study of the nature of beauty and art; a particular taste for, or approach to, creating art that is appealing to the senses.

afectuoso. (Sp.) Fondly, longingly. (Fr. *affectueux,* It. *affettuoso.*)

affaiblissez. (Fr.) Becoming softer and weaker. Also *affaibli.* (Ger. *schwächen,* It. *indebolire,* Sp. *debilitándose.*)

affectueusement. (Fr.) Tenderly, affectionately. (It. *affettuosamente,* Sp. *afectuosamente.*)

affectueux. (Fr.) Fondly, longingly. (It. *affettuoso,* Sp. *afectuoso.*)

affettuoso. (It.) Fondly, longingly, affectionate. (Fr. *affectueux,* Sp. *afectuoso.*)

Affiliate Artists. A program that existed from the 1960s to 1990s to support young performers, in particular the **Exxon-Arts Endowment Conductors Program**, the Texaco Affiliate Artist program, and the Affiliate Artists

Xerox Pianist Program. Conductors who were selected were supported in getting auditions for jobs with orchestras and given special professional training opportunities. Winners included Myung-whun Chung, Andrew Litton, Kent Nagano, and **Hugh Wolff**.

affrettando, affrettato. (It.) Hurrying, hurried. (Fr. *presser, pressé*; Ger. *eilen; eilte*; Sp. *apresurándose, apresurando*.)

affrettare. (It.) To hurry. (Fr. *se dépêcher*, Ger. *zu beeilen*, Sp. *prisa*.)

affrettato. (It.) Hasty. (Fr. *hâtif*, Ger. *hastig*, Sp. *apresurado*.)

afinación. (Sp.) To tune, as in to tune an instrument. (Fr. *accordé*, Ger. *stimmen*, It. *accordare*.) See **tuning practices**.

afinado. (Sp.) Tuned, true, tempered. (Fr. *accordé*, Ger. *gestimmt*, It. *accordato*.)

afinar. (Sp.) To tune, as in to tune an instrument. Example: *Cellos deben afinar hacia abajo la cuerda do a un si.* Cellos have to retune the C string down to a B natural. (Fr. *accorder*, Ger. *stimmen*, It. *accordare*.) See **Tuning practices**.

aggregate. Any vertical combination of pitches; in set **theory**, a term used for vertical combinations of **hexachords** or smaller units of **pitch sets**. Example: In set theory, the pitches of one hexachord create a twelve-note aggregate with the pitches of another hexachord as long as there are no duplicate pitches between the two.

ágil. (Sp.) Nimble, fast, light. (Fr. *agile, agilement*; Ger. *Behände*; It. *agile*.)

agile. (It.) Nimble, fast, light. (Fr. *agile, agilement*; Ger. *Behände*; Sp. *ágil*.)

agile, agilement. (Fr.) Nimble, fast, light. (Ger. *Behände*, It. *agile*, Sp. *ágil*.)

agitado. (Sp.) Agitated, excited. (Fr. *agité*; Ger. *erregt*; It. *agitato, concitato*.)

agitato. (It.) Agitated. Also *concitato*, excited. (Fr. *agité*, Ger. *erregt*, Sp. *agitado*.)

agité. (Fr.) Agitated, excited. (Ger. *erregt*; It. *agitato, concitato*; Sp. *agitado*.)

agogic accent. A particular kind of accent having to do with the length of a note. That is, when a long note appears after a series of shorter notes, it creates an agogic accent, an accent of time. Agogic accents may describe the slight lengthening of a note or notes that occurs when a heightened expression is desired. (Ger. *Akzent agogik*, Fr. *accent agogique*, It. *accento agogica*, Sp. *acento agógico*.)

agradable. (Sp.) Pleasant, agreeable. Also *amable*. (Fr. *agréable, plaisant*; Ger. *angenehm*; It. *gradevole, piacevole*.)

agrandissant, élargir, en. (Fr.) See ***élargir, en agrandissant***.

agréable. (Fr.) Agreeable. Also *plaisant*, pleasant. (Ger. *angenehm*; It. *gradevole, piacevole*; Sp. *agradable, amable*.)

Agreement on Trade-Related Aspects of Intellectual Property Rights (TRIPS). Negotiated as part of the **General Agreement on Tariffs and Trade (GATT)** in 1994 as an international consensus covering minimum standards for intellectual property for all members of the World Trade Organization (WTO). **TRIPS** requires that all signatories have laws that meet common standards for copyright, including performers and producers of sound recordings. The advent of the Internet and new electronic means of distributing music have brought many challenges to the agreement. New legal standards have yet to be established.

air, à l'. (Fr.) In the air, up. Example: *pavillon à l'air*, bell of the horn in the air.

Akiyama, Kazuyoski. (b. 1941.) Japanese conductor. Akiyama studied at the **Toho Gakuen School of Music** in Tokyo with **Hideo Saito**. He served as music director of the Tokyo Symphony Orchestra (1974–2004) Syracuse Symphony (1985–1992), and **Vancouver Symphony Orchestra** (1972–1985), and he remains in laureate positions with all three ensembles. He conducted the Japanese premiere of Schoenberg's *Moses and Aron* and was awarded Japan's Emperor's Purple Ribbon Medal for outstanding contribution to musical culture. Along with **Seiji Ozawa**, he influenced many young American and Japanese conductors through the teaching and promotion of the techniques of **Hideo Saito**.

Akkord. (Ger.) **Chord**, a group of notes played simultaneously. (Fr. *accord*, It. *accordo*, Sp. *acorde*.)

Akron Symphony Orchestra, Ohio. Established by Mabel Lamborn Graham in 1949 with a $500 grant from the *Akron Beacon Journal*. The first concert season was offered in 1953. Run by the Greater Akron Musical Association, the partner organizations include the Akron Symphony, Youth Orchestra, Symphony Chorus, and the Gospel Meets Symphony Choir. The orchestra offers both classics and pops concert series in addition to educational programming. The current music director is Christopher Wilkins, appointed in 2006. Previous music directors include John Francis Farinacci (1953–1954), Laszlo Krauz (1954–1959), **Louis Lane** (1959–1982), Alan Balter (1983–1998), and Ya-Hui Wang (2000–2005). Concerts are rebroadcast on WKSU 89.7FM.

Akzent. (Ger.) **Accent**, stress, played in an accented manner. (Fr. *accent*, It. *accento*, Sp. *acento*.)

Akzent agogik. (Ger.) **Agogic accent**. (It. *accento agogica*, Fr. *accent agogique*, Sp. *acento agógico*.)

akzentuiert. (Ger.) Accented, emphasized, marked. See **accent**.

Alabama Symphony Orchestra. Officially formed in 1933 in Birmingham, by 1935 the orchestra had as many as eighty members when needed. After a temporary cessation during World War II, the orchestra began presenting concerts again in 1949. In 1957, it changed its name to the Birmingham Symphony Orchestra and became fully professional. With a number of reorganizations over the years, the orchestra's name was changed back to the Alabama Symphony Orchestra. The orchestra employs fifty-four full-time musicians. Previous music directors include Dorsey Whittington (1933–1942), Arthur Bennett Lipkin (1949–1960), Arthur Winograd (1960–1964), Amerigo Marino (1964–1984), Paul Polivnick (1985–1993), Richard Westerfield (1997–2004), and Justin Brown (2006–2013), who is now conductor laureate. The orchestra presents classics, pops, young people's, and holiday concerts. In 2020, the orchestra launched a new initiative to promote music by living composers and won an ASCAP Award for adventurous programming in 2010 and 2011.

à la blanche. (Fr.) In two beats per measure, also called ***alla breve***. (Ger. *in halben Noten*, It. *alla breve*, Sp. *compás alla breve*.)

à la corde. (Fr.) a direction to play on the string, not off. (Ger. *an der Saite*, It. *alla corda*, Sp. *a la cuerda*.)

a la cuerda. (Sp.) a direction to play on the string, not off. (It. *alla corda*, Ger. *an der Saite*, Fr. *á la corde*.)

à la fin. (Fr.) To the end. A direction to play to the end or to skip to the end. (Ger. *am Ende, am Schluss*; It. *al fine*, Sp. *al final*.) Also a directive sometimes used in pieces with multiple repeated sections to indicate the section that finishes the piece. (Ger. *zum Ende*, It. *alla fine*, Sp. *hasta el fin*.)

à la hausse. (Fr.) An indication for string players to play with the bow at the **frog** or at the heel (British usage). (Ger. *am Frosch*, It. *al talone*, Sp. *al talón*.)

à l'aise. (Fr.) Comfortable. Seen in the score to the ballet *Jeux* by Claude Debussy.

alangui. (Fr.) Slowed down, weaker, softer. Also *en alanguissant*.

à la pointe. (Fr.) A bowing term that directs the player to play at the point or tip of the bow. Also ***avec la pointe de l'archet***. (Ger. *an der Bogenspitze, an der Spitze, mit der Bogenspitze, mit Bogenspitze*; It. *alla punta d'arco, con la punta d'arco*; Sp. *con la punta del arco, en la punta del arco*.)

a la punta d'arco. (It.) a bowing term that directs the player to play at the point or tip of the bow. (Fr. *à la pointe*, Ger. *an der Sptize*, Sp. *en el punta del arco*.)

alargar, ampliar, expandir. (Sp.) To broaden or slow down the tempo. An expression used to describe an interpretation of the pacing of a passage: to amplify, broaden, expand. (Fr. *élargir, en agrandissant*; Ger. *erweitern*; It. *allargare, ampliando, espandere*.)

a la señal. (Sp., lit. "to the sign.") An indication to a player to go back to a spot specified by a sign. Usually used in a piece that has a series of repeats and **da capo** markings, such as a waltz by Johann Strauss Jr. (Fr. *au signe*; Ger. *zum Zeichen*; It. *dal segno, al segno*.) See also ***dal segno***.

Albany Records. An American record company founded and run by Peter Kermani and located in Albany, New York. It specializes in contemporary American music and serves as a distributor for many other CD companies. Also known as Albany Music.

Albany Symphony Orchestra, New York. Founded in 1930, the orchestra is a fully professional ensemble. Its current music director is David Alan Miller, who has served since 1992. The orchestra, which has in its mission the performance of new works by living composers, has made more than sixty recordings on the New World Recordings, **CRI**, **Albany Records**, Argo, **Naxos**, and **London/Decca** labels. Many of the music world's top solo artists have performed with the orchestra. Past music directors include Julius Hegyi (1965–1988), Geoffrey Simon (1987–1991), and George Lloyd (1990–1991).

Aldeburgh Festival, England. Founded in 1948 by composer **Benjamin Britten**, Peter Pears, and Eric Crozier, it has grown into a major music institution—**Aldeburgh Music**, of which the festival is but one entity—that presents programming all year.

Aldeburgh Music. The organization that runs the **Alde-burgh Festival** and other performing centers associated with the festival, including the Snape Maltings Concert Hall, the principal performing space, and the Hoffman Building. Aldeburgh runs young artist training programs, including the long-running Britten-Pears Young Artist Programme; the Jerwood Opera Writing Programme; Faster Than Sound, an experimental program that crosses boundaries of music and the digital arts; Group A, an unauditioned vocal and performance group for teenagers; and more.

aleatoric music. (Fr. Latin, alea.) A piece of music that uses elements of chance, randomness, or indeterminacy. Music in which the composer presents a set of choices, giving the performer or conductor a role in the construction of the work. Elements that may be left up to the performer can be rhythm, duration, pitch, dynamic, and in some cases the actual form of the work. Such a composition may not be entirely aleatoric but may contain some passages of aleatoric procedures. Music notation techniques such as **graphic notation** and **open forms** have been developed to facilitate aleatoric procedures. Some composers of aleatoric music are **Pierre Boulez**, Earle Brown, John Cage, Jacob Druckman, Witold Lutoslawski, and **Krzysztof Penderecki**.

aleatory. (fr. Latin, alea.) The practice of using elements of chance or indeterminacy in a piece of music or other art form. The element of chance is manifested in choices set up by the composer using various techniques, such as the throw of dice or in the case of American composer John Cage, the I Ching. Aleatory as a concept continues to have a great influence on the music of today. Elements of or individual passages of aleatoric music are not at all uncommon in modern composition. See the **bibliography.**

alegre. (Sp.) Happy, cheerful, gay. Also *con alegría*, with a happy spirit. (Fr. *gai, gaiement*; Ger. *frölich, lustig*; It. *gaio, giocoso*.)

alegremente. (Sp.) Merrily, rejoicing. (It. *allegramente*.)

alegría, con. (Sp.) With a cheerful spirit, happily, with pleasure. (Fr. *volontiers*, Ger. *gerne*, It. *volentieri*.)

alejándose. (Sp.) Going away, becoming distant. Also *alejar*.

alerte. (Fr.) Bold. Seen in its German form in scores of **Gustav Mahler**. Also **dégagé**. (Ger. *keck*; It. *spigliato*; Sp. *audaz, atrevido*.)

Alexander technique. A technique developed in the 1890s by the actor Frederick Matthias Alexander. Alexander developed ways of using the body to improve balance and efficiency of motion. The technique has been often applied to the physical work of musicians, actors, and others. Good, informative texts are *How to Learn the Alexander Technique: A Manual for Students* by Barbara and William Conable; *Body Learning: An Introduction to the Alexander Technique* by Michael Gelb; and *The Alexander Technique* by Wilfred Barlow. See also *The Alexander Technique: The Essential Writings of F. Matthias Alexander* selected and introduced by Edward Maisel. Alexander Technique instructors who specialize in working with musicians exist throughout the United States.

algo. (Sp.) A little, a bit (lit. "something"). Example: *algo más*, a little more.

a libro aperto. (It.) Play at sight, sight read. Also *suonare a prima vista*. (Fr. *jouer à vue, déchiffrer*; Ger. *vom Blatt spielen*; Sp. *tocar a primera vista*.)

alla breve. (It.) Conducted in two beats per measure. (Fr. *à la blanche*, Ger. *in Halben noten*, Sp. *compás alla breve*.)

Alla breve. *Courtesy Andrew Martin Smith.*

alla corda. (It.) A directive to string players to play with the bow on the string. (Fr. *à la corde*; Ger. *auf der Saite, an der Saite*; Sp. *a la cuerda*.)

alla fine. (It.) To the end. A directive sometimes used in pieces with multiple repeated sections to indicate the section that finishes the piece. (Fr. *à la fin*, Ger. *zum Ende*, Sp. *hasta el fin*.) Also finally, lastly. (Fr. *à la fin*, Ger. *zuletzt*, Sp. *por fin*.)

allant. (Fr.) Lively. Example: *Un peu plus "allant,"* a little more lively, from "Gigues" of *Images* by Claude Debussy.

alla punta d'arco. (It.) An indication for a string player to play at the point or tip of the bow. (Fr. *avec la pointe del'arche, à la pointe*; Ger. *an der Bogenspitze, mit Bogenspitze, an der Spitze*; Sp. *en la punta del arco, con la punta*.)

allargando. (It., Sp.) The process of becoming slower or more drawn out, broadening. (Fr. *en élargissant*, Ger. *breiter werden*.)

allargare, ampliando, espandere. (It.) To broaden or slow down the tempo. An expression used to describe an interpretation of the pacing of a passage: to amplify, broaden, expand. (Fr. *élargir, en agrandissant*; Ger. *erweitern*; Sp. *alargar, ampliar, expandir*.)

allargare, ampliando, espandere. (It.) To broaden or slow down the tempo. An expression used to describe an interpretation of the pacing of a passage, to amplify, broaden, expand. (Fr. *élargir, en agrandissant*; Ger. *erweitern*; Sp. *alargar, ampliar, expandir*.)

all-combinatorial set. A twelve-tone **row** created in such a way that the first six pitches, or **hexachord**, of any of its transformations at any level of transposition do not duplicate any of the first six notes of the original row. Some of the transformation forms (versions) of a hexachord include retrograde, transposition up or down at a specific interval, inversion at a specific interval, and retrograde inversion. For each set, only a select few of the variation forms will generate the all-combinatorial characteristic.

alegremente. (Sp.) Lively, cheerfully. (Fr. *allégrement, gaiement*, Ger. *frolic*, It. *allegramente*)

alle. (Ger.) All, everyone. An indication used to tell everyone in a section to play after a period where only single instruments played. Also *fast alle*, almost all. (Fr. *tout*; It. *tutte, tutti*; Sp. *todos*.)

allegramente. (It.) Lively, cheerfully. (Fr. *allègrement, gaiement*; Ger. *frölich*; Sp. *alegremente*.)

allègre. (Fr.) Happy, cheerful, in the style of an **allegro**. Also *gai*. (Ger. *fröhlich*, It. *allegro*, Sp. *alegre*.)

allègrement. (Fr.) Lively, cheerfully. (Ger. *frölich*, It. *allegremente*, Sp. *alegremente*.)

allegro. (It.) Happy, cheerful, in the style of an allegro. (Fr. *gai, allègre*; Ger. *fröhlich*; Sp. *alegre*.)

allegro aperto. (It.) An **allegro** that is open or frank in nature and feeling. Used in the Mozart flute and oboe concertos.

allegro assai. (It.) Very fast, faster than **allegro**.

allegro giusto. (It.) A steady or stict **allegro**.

aller. (Fr.) To go, walk, proceed. (Ger. *gehen*, It. *andare*, Sp. *ir*.)

Allgemeine musikalische Zeitung (**general music journal**). A music journal published in the nineteenth century between 1798 and 1848. Founded by publisher **Breitkopf & Härtel** in Leipzig. From 1866 to 1868 it oper-

ated under the title *Leipziger Allgemeine musikalische Zeitung* (AmZ of Leipzig). Its first editor, Friedrich Rochlitz, established the journal as the leading periodical of its time. It was divided into essays, biographical information, reviews of theoretical works and music, descriptions of instruments, news items, and other items, a system that set it as a model for future journals.

Among its most important articles were **Ludwig van Beethoven**'s submission of metronome markings for his symphonies in 1817, a serialized version of Georg August Griesinger's biography of Joseph Haydn, articles by Gustav Nottebohm, and critics Eduard Hanslick and E. T. A. Hoffmann. Composers Robert Schumann and **Franz Liszt** both wrote for the journal. While some of the material that appeared has proven to be spurious, it remains an important resource for the study of the music of the nineteenth century. Issues of the *Allgemeine musikalische Zeitung* are now available online. See also **Neue Zeitschrift für Musik**.

all-interval set. A **twelve-tone row** constructed so that it has the eleven possible interval relations without any repetition.

allmählich. (Ger.) Bit by bit, by degrees, gradually, little by little. Examples: *Allmählich und unmerklich in das Hauptzeitmass übergehen*, Gradually and unnoticeable moving back to the main tempo; *Allmählich immer starker*, Gradually getting stronger, from *The Prelude to Die Meistersinger von Nürenberg* by **Richard Wagner**. (Fr. *graduel, coup sur coup*; It. *gradamente*; Sp. *graduado, poco a poco*.)

allonger. (Fr.) To slow down, hold back, delay forward motion.

allora. (It.) Then. Also *poi*. (Fr. *ensuite, puis*; Ger. *dann*; Sp. *entonces*.)

all'ottava. (It.) A direction in music to play a passage at the octave. (Fr. *á l'octave*, Ger. *in der Oktave*, Sp. *a la octava*.)

all-state orchestra. Each state in the United States has its own honors **orchestra**, **band**, and chorus program. Most often states are divided into regions that have their own ensemble festivals sometime each fall. Students who are selected for a regional ensemble are then further selected for the appropriate all-state ensemble. All-state ensembles often gather, rehearse, and perform at an annual statewide music educators' convention. Some states organize these ensembles according to different priorities and on different schedules. Some will meet for extended rehearsals the summer in advance and then come back together for the conference later in the year. Some states select students based entirely upon talent, others opt for geographical parity, allowing each region to forward a minimum allotment of students. Conductors for these ensembles are selected from across the country. It is considered a high honor in the field to lead such an ensemble.

all'unisono. (It.) In unison. (Fr. *a l'unisson*, Ger. *Unisono*, Sp. *al unísono*.)

al luogo, loco. (It.) A directive used after a passage of change or transposition, to indicate sounding as written. (Fr. *à sa place*, Ger. *an seinem Platz*, Sp. *como escrita*.)

alma. (Sp.) The sound post of a string instrument. (Fr. *âme*, Ger. *Stimmstock*, It. *anima*.)

al mismo tempo. (Sp.) The same tempo. (Fr. *le même mouvement*; Ger. *im gleichen Tempo, dasselbe Zeitmaß*; It. *lo stesso tempo, l'istesso tempo*.)

alpha chord. Sometimes called the "alpha-chord collection," it is a chordal presentation of the two diminished seventh chords that make up the **octatonic scale**. Can be spelled vertically beginning with the lowest note, C-sharp, E, G, B-flat, C, E-flat, F-sharp, A.

alpha scale. A scale derived from the diminished seventh chords created by the **octatonic scale**. See **alpha chord**.

al segno or ***dal segno.*** (It., lit. "to the sign.") An indication to a player to go back to a spot specified by a sign. Usually used in a piece that has a series of repeats and *da capo* markings, such as a waltz by Johann Strauss Jr. (Fr. *au signe*, Ger. *zum Zeichen*, Sp. *a la señal*.)

Alsop, Marin. (b. 1956.) American **conductor** and violinist, the first woman to lead a major American orchestra. She was appointed music director of the **Baltimore Symphony Orchestra** in 2007. Alsop served as music director of the **Colorado Symphony Orchestra** from 1993 to 2005 and the **Cabrillo Festival of Contemporary Music** since 1992. She is the principal guest conductor of the Royal Scottish National Orchestra and the City of London Sinfonia and was principal conductor of the **Bournemouth Symphony Orchestra** (2002–2008). Alsop was appointed music director of the Sao Paulo State Symphony Orchestra, Brazil, in 2013. She is known for innovative **outreach programs** such as the **Rusty Musicians Program, OrchKids**. She also heads the **Taki Concordia Conducting Fellowship** to support young women conductors. Alsop is the recipient of the prestigious MacArthur Fellowship, was made a fellow of the American Academy of Arts and Sciences in 2008, and was chosen as **Musical America's** Conductor of the Year in 2009.

Marin Alsop. *Courtesy Grant Leighton.*

al tallone. (It.) A bowing term that calls for playing with the bow at the frog or at the heel (British usage). (Fr. *à la hausse*, Ger. *am Frosch*, Sp. *al talón*.)

al talón. (Sp.) A bowing term that calls for playing with the bow at the frog or at the heel (British usage). (Fr. *à la hausse*, Ger. *am Frosch*, It. *al tallone*.)

alteración. (Sp.) Accidental, accidental sign. (Fr. *accident*, Ger. *Versetzungszeichen*, It. *accidente*.) See **accidental**.

altered chord. A chord in tonal harmony with one or more pitches foreign to the key, such as the Neapolitan and augmented sixth chords. An altered chord can also be a dominant of a degree in the prevailing scale. Example: A D-major chord in the key of C would be a V of v. An A-major chord in C would be a V of ii.

alternative scales. Unusual scales, other than the traditional major and minor, such as ethnic scales (Hungarian minor, C D E-flat F-sharp G A-flat B-natural C; Hungarian major, C D-sharp E F-sharp G A B-flat; Algerian scale, C D E-flat F-sharp G A-flat B-natural C D E-flat F-natural, as used by Ibert in *Escales*; a Jewish scale called Adonai Malach, C D E F G A B-flat D); alpha, beta, delta, and gamma scales occurring in the music of **Wendy Carlos**; the forty-three-note scale of Harry Partch; and the **Lambda scale**, also called the **Bohlen-Pierce scale**. See the **bibliography**.

alto. (It.) A women's voice of middle range. The clef used for the viola. A term used to indicate a medium-ranged instrument such as alto flute or alto saxophone. See **C clefs**.

alto. (Fr.) Viola. (Ger. *Bratsche*, It. *viola*, Sp. *viola*.) See also **alto** (It.)

alto. (It., Sp.) High. (Fr. *haut*, Ger. *hoch*.) Also a female voice classification that lies between **mezzo soprano** and **contralto**. See **voice classifications**.

alto clarinet in E-flat. While it is more or less a standard in the concert **band** or **wind ensemble**, the alto clarinet is almost never used in the orchestra. It does appear in some important pieces of the twentieth century, including the original version of **Igor Stravinsky**'s *Symphonies of Wind Instruments*. Its written range is from a low E3 up to an E6, but it sounds at G2 up to G5. (Fr. *Clarinette alto*; Ger. *Altklarinette*; It. *Clarinetto alto*; Sp. *clarinete alto, clarinet contralto*.) See **clarinet, clarinet in E-flat or D, bass clarinet, basset horn, contrabass clarinet, appendix 3: "Instrument Names and Their Translations."**

Alto clarinet in E-flat as it sounds. *Courtesy Andrew Martin Smith.*

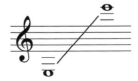

Alto clarinet in E-flat as written. *Courtesy Andrew Martin Smith.*

alto flute. Sometimes called the **bass flute**, it is a transposing instrument in G; consequently, it sounds a fourth lower than written. The instrument came to prominence in the work of **Igor Stravinsky** and Maurice Ravel. The written range is from C4 up to C7, but it sounds G3 to G6. (Fr. *Flûte en sol*; Ger. *Altflöte*; It. *Flauto contralto*; Sp. *flauto contralto, flauto en sol*.) See **flute, piccolo, bass flute, appendix 3: "Instrument Names and Their Translations."**

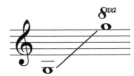

Alto flute range as it sounds. *Courtesy Andrew Martin Smith.*

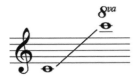

Alto flute range as written. *Courtesy Andrew Martin Smith.*

alto trombone. The alto trombone is a nontransposing brass instrument, the highest of the trombone family. It has seven playing positions, each named after the second partial of its harmonic series. Each position allows pitches up to the tenth or twelfth partial. The instrument has a range from A3 to E-flat5 and is usually notated in the alto clef. The alto trombone came into prominence in the eighteenth and nineteenth centuries. It fell into disuse when it became easier to play in the higher register on the **tenor trombone.** It is now coming back into favor as players and conductors have begun to prefer its soft, pure tone. See **trombone.**

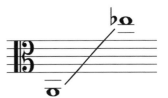

Alto trombone range. *Courtesy Andrew Martin Smith.*

al unísono. (Sp.) In unison. (Fr. *a l'unisson*, Ger. *Unisono*, It. *all'unisono*.) Example: *al unísono hasta*, in unison until . . . (Fr. *á l'unisson jusqu'à . . .*, Ger. *Unisono bis . . .*, It. *unisono all'. . .*)

à l'unisson. (Fr.) in unison. (Ger. *Unisono*, It. *all'unisono*, Sp. *al unísono*.)

à l'unisson jusqu'à . . . (Fr.) "in unison until . . ." An expression seen in music and heard in rehearsal used to clarify how a given passage is to be played. (Ger. *Unisono bis*, It. *unisono all'*, Sp. *al unísono hasta*.)

al votro servizio. (It.) At your service. (Fr. à *votre service*, Sp. *a sus órdenes*.)

alzada. (Sp.) The upbeat, one or more notes that occur before the first measure of a work or phrase, anacrusis, the conductor's pick-up. Also *anacrusa*. (Fr. *levée*; Ger. *Auftakt*; It. *in levare, levata*.)

amable. (Sp.) Pleasant, agreeable. Also *agradable*. (Fr. *plaisant, agréable*; Ger. *angenehm*; It. *piacevole, gradevole*.)

ambidextrous conducting. The ability to conduct equally well with both hands. Will develop flexibility and coordination and reduce awkwardness, especially when both hands are needed for **cues, dynamic gestures,** and any time the conductor has to execute more than one **conducting technique** simultaneously.

âme. (Fr.) The sound post of a string instrument. (Ger. *Stimmstock*, It. *anima*, Sp. *alma*.)

a media voz. (Sp.) an expression seen not only in vocal music meaning half-voice or quietly. (Fr. *à demi-voix, à mi-voix*; Ger. *mit halber Stimme*; It. *mezza voce*.)

American Academy of Arts and Letters. Originally named the National Institute of Arts and Letters, the academy was founded by an act of Congress in 1898. Since its founding, the honorary academy has maintained its total membership at only 250 individuals in the areas of visual arts, architecture, literature, and music. The academy gives away thousands of dollars in awards each year to support younger creative artists in their work. Major donations to the academy have included the estate of American composer Charles Ives.

American Academy of Conducting at Aspen (AACA). Founded by **David Zinman**, a summer training program that is part of the **Aspen Music Festival and School** (AMFS). Conductor **Robert Spano**, music director of the **Atlanta Symphony**, is the current music director of the academy. Students who are accepted into the conducting program receive fellowships to attend and play an instrument in the AACA orchestra. It acts as a reading orchestra for the conducting program. Performance opportunities exist with orchestras and chamber ensembles and awards to conductors each year.

American Bandmasters Association (ABA). A professional organization founded in 1929 with John Phillip Sousa was its first honorary life president. Its objective is to promote concert band conductors and composers. Membership is by invitation only and is currently comprised of three hundred North American conductors and composers. Associate members, of which there are eighty, are businesses and corporations that support bands and the publication of band music. One of its major projects is its Sousa/Ostwald Composition Contest.

American Boychoir and School. Founded as a boys' choir in 1937 in Columbus, Ohio, the choir moved to Princeton, New Jersey, in 1950, where the school was added. Its mission is to promote and sustain a distinctively American voice within the thousand-year-old tradition of boys' choir schools. Its main focus is a commitment to being one of the finest boys' choirs in the world while combining intense musical training with a high standard of academics and teaching of traditional values such discipline, self-reliance, hard work, and teamwork.

American Choral Directors Association (ACDA). Founded as a professional organization in 1959 to promote choral singing, choral music, high standards, the composition of choral music of superior quality, and the development of choruses in cities and towns across the country in an effort to create a culture of choral music in America. There are seven divisions within the United States and fifty state chapters. The ACDA publishes the *Choral Journal* and the *International Journal of Research in Choral Singing* and maintains several Internet sites, including ChoralNet.com.

American Choral Foundation. Founded by **Margaret Hillis** in 1954, it is now known as **Chorus America**.

American Classical Music Hall of Fame. Established in Cincinnati in 1996, the Hall of Fame supports classical music by celebrating the achievements of American musicians. The Hall of Fame has inducted many significant American individuals and organizations since 1997.

American Composers Alliance, Inc. (ACA). A nonprofit, alternative publisher of American concert music associated with **Broadcast Music International** (BMI). Its aims include the performance of American music of all genres in concert programs across the country and internationally. The organization maintains an active website at Composers.com. It was established in 1937 by **Aaron Copland**, Milton Adolphus, Otto Luening, and others.

American Composers Forum (ACF). Founded in 1973 as the **Minnesota Composers Forum**, the ACF promotes performances of new music throughout America. The organization supports composers though its programs and services of commissions, performances, readings of new works, and fellowships. Membership is open and includes composers, performers, presenters, and organizations that share its goals. The ACF maintains an active Internet site.

American Conservatory of Fontainebleau (Conservatoire américain de Fontainebleau). Started in 1921, the conservatory provides a French-style music education to young musicians and is now run under the umbrella organization, Fontainebleau Schools. The faculty has included some of France's most distinguished musicians and educators, such as **Nadia Boulanger**, who worked at Fontainebleau until her death in 1979. Many important American composers, such as **Aaron Copland**, Virgil Thompson, Louise Talma, and Elliott Carter, studied there.

American Federation of Musicians (AF of M). Founded in 1896 at a gathering initiated by the American Federation of Labor, the AF of M is a musicians' trade union. It serves professional musicians in Canada and the United States. The *International Musician* is the official journal of the AF of M. Both the journal and the federation maintain active websites.

American Guild of Music. Founded in 1901, a nonprofit national organization that organizes music competitions for students and an annual national convention and contest.

American Guild of Organists (AGO). Established in 1896, a national educational and service organization for academic, church, and concert organists with 9 regions and 330 chapters nationwide. The AGO publishes a monthly journal, *The American Organist*; runs a national convention in even-numbered years and regional conventions in odd-numbered years; and sponsors educational programs.

American Institute of Musicology, Inc. (AIM). Founded in 1946, AIM supports interest in Medieval, Renaissance, and early Baroque music. The institute publishes several journals including *Musica Disiplina* (MD), an annual yearbook of articles; *Corpus Mensurabilis Musicae* (CMM), a journal of fourteenth- to sixteenth-century polyphonic music; *Corpus of Early Keyboard Music* (CEKM), a journal focusing on keyboard music written from the fourteenth to seventeenth century; *Musicological Studies and Documents* (MSD), a series presenting a variety of musicological studies; and more. All are published by **A-R Editions, Inc.**

American Music Center (AMC). Founded in 1940 by Marion Bauer, **Aaron Copland**, **Howard Hanson**, **Otto Luening**, and Quincy Porter to support the creation and performance of American music. The center has now merged with the organization **Meet the Composer** (MTC) and is called **New Music USA**.

American Musicological Society (AMS). Founded in 1934 to support various areas of music research and scholarship. AMS has an annual conference in various locations in the United States. AMS sponsors fellowships, grants, awards, and prizes and publishes a journal and a regular newsletter.

American Music Publishers Association. Founded the **Harry Fox Agency** in 1927 to collect and distribute recording licensing fees on behalf of American music publishers.

American Record Guide (*ARG*). A classical music magazine founded in 1935 to review recordings. In 1992, when *Musical America* ceased publication, *ARG* adopted its subscribers, writers, and editorial content, and it began covering concerts, musicians, ensembles, and orchestras in the United States. *ARG* is now available primarily through subscription. See **music magazines**.

American Society of Composers, Authors and Publishers (ASCAP). New York. Founded in 1914 by composer Victor Herbert to protect the copyrighted musical compositions of its members. ASCAP collects licensing fees from music users such as restaurants and distributes them to its members. See **ASCAP Award for Adventurous Programming**.

American Society of University Composers (ASUC). See **Society of Composers, Inc., The.**

American String Teachers Association (ASTA). Founded in the early 1950s, ASTA is an organization of string teachers and string orchestra directors dedicated to the education and encouragement of string players in America. ASTA has an annual conference, sponsors competitions for young string players, and publishes the *American String Teacher* and the *String Research Journal*. Its website, Astaweb.com, has a member resources center and calendar of events.

American Symphony Orchestra (ASO). Founded in 1962 by **Leopold Stokowski** in an effort to bring classical music to all audiences. The ASO continues the effort under the current music director, **Leon Botstein**. Other conductors have included **Kazuyoshi Akiyama** (1973–1978), John Mauceri, and Catherine Comet.

American Symphony Orchestra League (ASOL). Now known as the **League of American Orchestras** (LAO).

am Frosch. (Ger.) An indication to string players to play with the bow at the frog or the heel (British usage). (Fr. *à la hausse*, It. *al tallone*, Sp. *al talón*.)

am Griffbrett. (Ger.) An indication to play with the bow on the fingerboard of a string instrument. (Fr. *sur la touche*, It. *sul tasto*, Sp. *sobre el diapasón*.)

à mi-voix. (Fr.) an expression seen not only in vocal music meaning half-voice or quietly. Also *à demi-voix*. (Ger. *mit halber Stimme*, It. *mezza voce*, Sp. *a media voz*.)

ample. (Fr.) Broadly, with dignity. Also *amplement*, *avec ampleur*.

ampliar, expandir, en expansion. (Sp.) To broaden or slow down the tempo. An expression used to describe an interpretation of the pacing of a passage, to amplify, broaden, expand. (Fr. *élargir*, *en agrandissant*; Ger. *erweitern*; It. *allargare, ampliando, espandere*.)

amplio. (Sp.) A broad, very slow tempo, as with any tempo name, sometimes used as a movement title. (Fr. *large*, Ger. *breit*, It. *largo*.)

am Steg. (Ger.) An indication to play with the bow on or near the bridge of a string instrument. (Fr. *prés du chevalet*, *au chevalet*; It. *sul ponticello*; Sp. *sobre el puente*.)

Amsterdam Concertgebouw Orchestra. See **Royal Concertgebouw Orchestra.**

Amy, Gilbert. (b. 1936.) French composer, conductor, and author who specialized in performances of contemporary music. He studied with **Oliver Messiaen** and Darius Milhaud, succeeded **Pierre Boulez** as music director of the Odéon Theater in Paris in 1962, was the director of Domain Musical (1967–1973), and was the music director of the Nouvel Orchestre Philharmonique of the French Radio (1976–1981). Amy's early compositional style was influenced by Boulez, especially during his studies at **Darmstadt**, and later it became more continuous, flowing, and romantic. Some of his early works incorporate electronically recorded sound.

anacrouse. (Fr.) One or more notes that occur before the first measure of a work or phrase, anacrusis, a conductor's pickup or upbeat gesture. Also *levée.* (Ger. *Anakrusis*, It. *anacrusis*, Sp. *anacrusa, alzada.*)

anacrusa. (Sp.) One or more notes that occur before the first measure of a work or phrase, anacrusis, a conductor's pickup or upbeat gesture. Also *alzada.* (Fr. *anacrouse, levée*; Ger. *Anakrusis, Auftakt*; It. *anacrusis, in levare, levata.*)

anacrusis. (Fr. Greek.) One or more notes that occur before the first measure of a work or phrase, anacrusis. Also, a conductor's pickup gesture or beat that happens just before the downbeat. (Fr. *anacrouse, levée*; Ger. *Anakrusis, Auftakt*; It. *anacrusis, in levare, levata.*)

Anakrusis. (Ger.) One or more notes that occur before the first measure of a work or phrase, anacrusis, a conductor's pickup. Also *Auftakt.* (Fr. *anacrouse, levee*; It. *anacrusis, in levare, levata.*)

Ancerl, Karel. (1908–1973.) Czech conductor, he studied with **Hermann Scherchen** and **Václav Talich**. Early in his career he worked for Czech radio orchestras (1933–1939). Ancerl and his family were interned at the Theresienstadt concentration camp in 1942 where he led the Terezín String Orchestra, organizing musical events in the ghetto. Having lost his wife and son, he survived a move to Auschwitz. After World War II, Ancerl served as artistic director of the **Czech Philharmonic Orchestra** (1950–1968). Following the 1968 invasion of Prague, he immigrated to Toronto and became the conductor of the **Toronto Symphony Orchestra** (1968–1973). Known as the next greatest Czech conductor of his generation after **Rafael Kubelik**, his legacy includes many recordings of Czech music and performances that were full of rhythmic life and lyrical warmth.

anche. (Fr.) Reed, as used by wind instruments. (Ger. *Rohrblatt*, It. *ancia*, Sp. *caña.*)

anche double. (Fr.) The **double reed** used by the double reed instruments in the oboe and bassoon families. (Ger. *Doppelrohrblatt*, It. *ancia doppia*, Sp. *doble caña.*)

Anchorage Symphony Orchestra, Alaska (ASO). Founded in 1946, the orchestra's membership is a combination of professionals and amateurs. The current music director, Randall Craig Fleischer, was appointed in 1999. The orchestra is run by a **board of directors** and supported by a **symphony league**. It performs a five-concert classics series in addition to pops and educational concerts.

ancia. (It.) Reed, as used by wind instruments. (Fr. *anche*, Ger. *Rohrblatt*, Sp. *caña.*)

ancia doppia. (It.) The **double reed** used by the double reed instruments in the oboe and bassoon families. (Fr. *anche double*, Ger. *Doppelrohrblatt*, Sp. *doble caña.*)

ancora. (It.) An Italian expression heard in rehearsal meaning again, still more, as in *acora più forte*, again louder, *ancora una volta*, again one more time. See **encore**.

andante. (It.) A tempo indication usually interpreted as a walking tempo, slower than **allegro** but faster than **adagio**. From the Italian verb **andare**, to walk, to go.

andante con moto. (It.) *Andante* with motion, moderately faster than *andante.*

andantino. (It.) The diminutive of **andante**, currently considered a little bit quicker than andante, the meaning being "less" slow, so faster. In the eighteenth century, the meaning was also considered a diminutive but with the opposite interpretation: slower. Scholars have shown that to Mozart, andantino was slower than andante and that the definition was in dispute for Beethoven. The switch took place gradually during the nineteenth century, with Brahms defining the andantino tempo in the third movement of his first symphony as close to an **allegretto**.

andare. (It.) To go, walk, proceed. The verb form of the commonly used tempo indication **andante**. (Fr. *aller*, Ger. *gehen*, Sp. *ir.*)

an der Bogensptize. (Ger.) An indication for string players to play at the point or tip of the bow. Also *mit Bogenspitze, an der Spitze.* (Fr. *à la pointe, avec la pointe de l'archet*; It. *alla punta d'arco, con la punta d'arco*; Sp. *con la punta del arco, en la punta del arco.*)

an der Saite. (Ger.) A directive to string players to play with the bow on the string. (Fr. *à la corde*, It. *alla corda*, Sp. *a la cuerda.*)

an der Sptize. (Ger.) At the point of the bow, an indication to play at the point or tip of the bow. Also *mit der Bogenspitze*, *an der Bogenspitze*. (Fr. *à la pointe, avec la pointe de l'archet*; It. *a la punta d'arco, con la punta d'arco*; Sp. *en el punta, con la punta del arco*.)

Andrew W. Mellon Foundation. Located in New York City and Princeton, New Jersey, it is a private foundation endowed with wealth accumulated by Andrew W. Mellon and is the result of a merger of the Avalon Foundation and the Old Dominion Foundation, set up by two of Mellon's children, Paul and Ailsa Mellon-Bruce. It has five areas of interest: higher education, museum and art conservation, performing arts, conservation, and the environment and information technology. In 2004, the Mellon Foundation was awarded the National Medal of Arts.

For ten years, ending in 2009, the foundation's Performing Arts program ran a study investigating four areas of concern for the modern American orchestra: leadership, the role of the musicians, changing community expectations, and programming. Participating orchestras received direct grants, were part of an orchestra forum, and attended semiannual retreats that created a model for discussion among musicians, trustees, and the administrative staff of the orchestras that was designed to encourage communication and relationship development both within and among the participating ensembles. A subgroup of the forum, the **Elephant Task Force** (ETF), studied the relationships between orchestras' economic strategies and missions while developing financial modeling tools for future use. Its final report may be accessed on its Internet website. The foundation continues to support direct grants to orchestras for strategic initiatives in order to develop diverse, artistically ambitious models of performance; new technologies to increase the orchestra's reach; new wide-range roles for orchestra musicians; and participatory experiences for audiences in an effort to test models that may serve other orchestras in a sustaining way in the future. The Mellon Foundation also supports **Meet the Composer** residencies and the **League of American Orchestras**' Learning and Leadership Program.

Anfang. (Ger.) Beginning. (Fr. *commencement, début*; It. *inizio, principio*; Sp. *comienzo, principio*.) Example: *Im Anfang sehr gemächlich*, In the beginning very leisurely, from *Symphony No. 1*, mvt. 1, by **Gustav Mahler**.

angenehm. (Ger.) Pleasant, pleasing, agreeable. (Fr. *agréable, plaisant*; It. *gradevole, piacevole*; Sp. *agradable, amable*.)

Anhang. (Ger.) Coda, end, the final part of a piece. Also *Schlussteil*. (Fr. *partie finale*, It. *coda*, Sp. *coda*.)

anima. (It.) The sound post of a string instrument. (Fr. *âme*, Ger. *Stimmstock*, Sp. *alma*.)

anima (con). (It.) With feeling. (Fr. *avec âme*, Ger. *gemütvoll*, Sp. *con sentimiento*.)

animado. (Sp.) Lively, in an animated character. (Fr. *animé*, Ger. *belebt*, It. *animato*.)

animando. (It., Sp.) Becoming livelier, animated. (Fr. *en animant*, It. *animando*, Sp. *animando*.)

(en) animant. (Fr.) Becoming livelier, animated. Example: *En animant beaucoup*, becoming very lively, from *Jeux du vagues*, mvt. 2 of *La Mer* by Claude Debussy. (Ger. *lebhafter werdend*, It. *animando*, Sp. *animando*.)

animato. (It.) Lively, in an animated character. (Fr. *animé*, Ger. *belebt*, Sp. *animado*.)

animé. (Fr.) Lively, in an animated character. Examples: *en laissant aller jusqu'au très animé*, relax the tempo a little until the *très animé*, from *Dialogue du vent et de la mer*, mvt. 3 of *La Mer* by Claude Debussy; *animé et très rythmé*, animated and very rhythmic, *un peu plus animé*, a little more animated, from "Fêtes," mvt. 2 of *Nocturnes* by Debussy. (Ger. *belebt*, It. *animato*, Sp. *animado*.)

Anmerkung. (Ger.) Comment, annotation, note. Also *Notiz*. Example: *Anmerkung für den Dirigenten*, Note for the conductor. Seen often in scores of **Gustav Mahler** with various specific directions following. (Fr. *annotation, notice*; It. *annotazione*.)

an seinem Platz. (Ger.) A directive used after a passage of change or transposition to indicate sounding as written. (Fr. *à sa place*; It. *al luogo, loco*; Sp. *como escrita*.)

Ansermet, Ernest Alexandre. (1883–1969.) Swiss conductor, he studied composition with Ernest Bloch and conducting with **Felix Weingartner** and **Arthur Nikisch** during a year spent in Berlin. Ansermet conducted his first concerts in Lausanne and Montreux in 1910. **Igor Stravinsky** recommended him to the impresario **Sergei Diaghilev**, who appointed him conductor for the **Ballet Russes** (1915–1923). Ansermet came in contact with Claude Debussy, Maurice Ravel, and Manuel de Falla and conducted premieres of *La Valse*, *The Three Cornered Hat*, and Stravinsky's *Soldier's Tale*, *Pulcinella*, *Renard*, and *Les Noces*. He also conducted the German premiere of *The Rite of Spring* (1922). He was most famous for his long association with the **L'Orchestre de la Suisse Romande**, which he founded in 1918. For more than fifty years he cultivated the ensemble and brought it to international prominence, mostly through a lengthy recording contract with **Decca**. Ansermet left a legacy of devotion to the music of the early twentieth century through his many definitive recordings and premieres. The list of these important composers includes Stravinsky, Ravel, Debussy, Albert Roussel, Emmanuel Chabrier, Édouard Lalo, Béla Bartók, Benjamin Britten, Ernest Bloch, Witold Lutosławski, Bohuslav Martinů, William Walton, the Russian nationalists, and his Swiss compatriots Arthur Honegger and Frank Martin.

In America, Ansermet guest conducted the **NBC**, **Chicago**, **Dallas**, **Cleveland**, and **Philadelphia** orchestras, premiering works of American composers such as those of **Aaron Copland**. He was known for having a reserved conducting technique and being very precise in his comments in rehearsal.

anstimmen. (Ger.) To pitch or tune. (Fr. *entonner*, It. *intonare*, Sp. *afinar*.)

anterior. (Sp.) Preceding, former, previous. Examples: *ritmo anterior*, the preceding rhythm, *movimiento anterior*, previous movement, *compás anterior*, the bar before. (Ger. *vorergehend, im Vorigen*; It. *anteriore, precedente*; Fr. *précédent*.)

antes. (Sp.) Before. Commonly heard in rehearsal when telling the ensemble where to being playing. Example: *Cuatro antes D*, Four before D. (Fr. *avant*, Ger. *vor*, It. *prima*.)

antique cymbals. See **Crotales**; See **appendix 4: "Percussion Instruments and Their Translations."**

anvil. A large, heavy metal block originally used by blacksmiths. It is unpitched and has a bright, hard tone. Used in the *Symphony No. 3* of **Aaron Copland**. (Fr. *enclume*, Ger. *Amboss*, It. *incudine*, Sp. *yunque*.) See **appendix 4: "Percussion Instruments and Their Translations."**

apagado. (Sp.) Muffled, muted. Used with percussion instruments and timpani.

apaisé. (Fr.) Calm, quiet. Also, *en s'apaisant*.

apasionado. (Sp.) Impassioned. (Fr. *passionné*, Ger. *leidenschaftlich*, It. *appassionata*.)

aperto, sfogato. (It.) Open. An indication that is seen in brass parts after the notation "closed" when the player mutes the sound by inserting the hand partway into the bell of the instrument or by using a mute. When stopping the horn with the hand, the pitch rises by a half step and the player must adjust. When using the mute, the pitches don't change. See **brass mutes, stopped**. (Fr. *ouvert*, Ger. *offen*, Sp. *abierto*.)

a piacere. (It.) an expression seen in music that indicates the player has freedom in executing a passage; at your pleasure, as you like. Also *a volonta*. (Fr. *à volonte, à votre gré*; Ger. *nach Belieben*; Sp. *a placer, a gusto*.) See **piacere, a.**

a placer. (Sp.) an expression seen in music that indicates the player has freedom in executing a passage; at your pleasure, as you like. Also *a gusto*. (Fr. *à volonté, à votre gré*; Ger. *nach Belieben*; It. *a piacere, a volonta*.)

a placer. (Sp.) At will, freely, at the performer's discretion. Also *a gusto*. (Fr. *à volonté, à votre gré*; Ger. *nach Belieben*; It. *ad libitum, liberamente*.)

aplauso. (Sp.) Applause. (Ger. *Beifall*, Fr. *applaudissement*, It. *applauso*.)

apoyado. (Sp.) With emphasis. Also *con emfasis*.

Appalachian Spring. (1944.) A ballet with music by **Aaron Copland**. See **appendix 1: "Six Pieces That Changed Conducting."**

appassionata. (It.) Impassioned. (Fr. *passionné*, Ger. *leidenschaftlich*, Sp. *apasionado*.)

appena. (It.) Scarcely, very slightly. Example: *appena ritardando*, slowing down only slightly, *appena toccato*, scarcely played, very soft.

applaudissement. (Fr.) Applause. (Ger. *Beifall*, It. *applauso*, Sp. *aplauso*.)

applause. (Fr. *applaudissement*, Ger. *Beifall*, It. *applauso*, Sp. *aplauso*).

applauso. (It.) Applause. (Fr. *applaudissement*, Ger. *Beifall*, Sp. *aplauso*.)

appoggiatura. (It.; Fr., from *appoggiare*, "to lean.") A dissonant note that "leans" on a consonant note, taking part of its rhythmic value; usually a step or half step above or below that note. The appoggiatura adds expression through the harmonic stress and release of the dissonance. The rhythmic value of the appoggiatura was not codified until the late Baroque and early Classical period. However, practices of the use of appoggiaturas have continued to change throughout music history. (Ger. *Vorschlag*, Sp. *appoyatura*.)

appoyatura. (Sp.) From *appoggiare* (It., Fr.), "to lean." See *appoggiatura.*

apprenticeship. The study of conducting was long handed down not in music academies but through private instruction in which a student would work as an assistant to a master conductor over a period of years.

appuyant. (Fr.) A term used to indicate pressing the tempo forward. (Ger. *drängend*, It. *incalzante*, Sp. *empujar*.)

appuyé. (Fr.) Stressed, emphasized. Example: *expressif et appuyé dans la doucer*, expressive and stressed within the sweetness (softness), from *Les parfums de la nuit*, from "Ibéria" of *Images pour orchestre* by Claude Debussy.

après. (Fr.) After, behind. Also *ensuite*. (Ger. *nach*; It. *dopo, poi*; Sp. *después*.)

apresurado. (Sp.) Hasty, hurried. A character word. (Fr. *hâtif*; Ger. *drängend, eilend, Hastig*; It. *affrettando, precipitoso*.)

apresurándose. (Sp.) Hurrying, hurried. Also *apresurando*. (Fr. *presser, pressé*; Ger. *eilen, eilte*; It. *affrettando, affrettato*.)

apuro. (Sp.) Hurrying, pressing forward. Also *apurando*. Example: *No hay apuro*, no need to rush.

arcata. (It.) The bow stroke, bowing. Also *colpo d'arco*. (Fr. *coup d'archet*; Ger. *Bogenführung, Bogenstrich, Strichart*; Sp. *golpe de arco*.)

arcata in giú. (It.) Down-bow, a downward stroke of the bow in the direction from the **frog** to the tip. (Fr. *tiré*, Ger. *Abstrich*, Sp. *arco abajo*.)

arcata in su. (It.) Up-bow. (Fr. *poussé*; Ger. *Anstrich, Aufstrich*; Sp. *arco arriba*.)

archet. (Fr.) The bow, as used with string instruments. (Ger. *Bogen*; It. *arco, archetto*; Sp. *arco*.)

archi. (It.) The string section, string players. (Fr. *cordes*, Ger. *Streicher*, Sp. *sección de cuerdo*.)

ARCHI magazine. A magazine published every two months by the Italian Strings Society (Accademia Italiana degli Archi), a national organization of more than one thousand members. *ARCHI* is devoted to promoting all aspects of classical bowed string instruments. Each volume includes features that cover concerts, accessories, music, articles about famous players of the past, orchestra audition announcements, competition listings, CD reviews, and more. It is available primarily to members of the Italian Strings Society and by subscription. See **music magazines**.

arco. (It., pl. *archi*.) The bow, as used with string instruments. Also *archetto*. (Fr. *archet*, Ger. *Bogen*, Sp. *arco*.)

arco. (Sp.) The bow, as used with string instruments. (Fr. *archet*; Ger. *Bogen*; It. *arco, archetto*.)

arco abajo. (Sp.) Down-bow, a downward stroke of the bow in the direction from the **frog** to the tip. (Fr. *tiré*, Ger. *abstrich*, It. *arcata in giú*.)

arco arriba. (Sp.) Up-bow, an upward stroke of the bow, the stroke in the direction from tip to **frog**. (Fr. *poussé*, Ger. *Aufstrich*, It. *arcata in su*.)

argentin. (Fr.) Silvery, clear, bell-like. A character word, sometimes heard in rehearsal to describe a certain quality of sound.

ärgerlich. (Ger.) Angrily. A character word sometimes heard in rehearsal to evoke a certain style of playing.

arioso. (It.) Cantabile, singing, play in a singing manner.

Arkansas Symphony Orchestra. Founded in 1966 in Little Rock, the orchestra gives masterworks, pops, chamber music, and educational concerts in addition to other outreach programs and sponsors its own youth orchestra program. Its current music director is Philip Mann. Past music directors include David Itkin (1993–2010).

armadura. (Sp.) Key signature. (Fr. *armure de la clé*; Ger. *Tonartvorzeichnung, Vorzeichen*; It. *armatua di chiave*.)

armatua di chiave. (It.) Key signature. (Fr. *armure de la clé*; Ger. *Tonartvorzeichnung, Vorzeichen*; Sp. *armadura*.)

armonia. (It.) Harmony, chords. (Fr. *harmonie*, Ger. *Harmonie*, Sp. *armonía*.)

armonía. (Sp.) Harmony, chords. (Fr. *harmonie*, Ger. *Harmonie*, It. *armonía*.)

armonico. (It.) Harmonic. (Fr. *flageolet, harmonique, sons harmonique*; Ger. *Flageolett*; Sp. *armónico*.) See **string harmonics**.

armónicos. (Sp.) **Harmonics.** (Fr. *flageolet, sons harmoniques*; Ger. *Flageoletöne, Flageolett*; It. *suoni armonici, zufolo*.) See **harmonic series**, **string harmonics**.

armure de la clé. (Fr.) Key signature. Also *armature*. (Ger. *Tonartvorzeichnung, Vorzeichen*; It. *armatua di chiave*; Sp. *armadura*.)

arpa. (It., Sp.) **Harp**. (Fr. *harpe*, Ger. *Harfe*.) See **appendix 3: "Instrument Names and Their Translations."**

arpégé. (Fr.) A broken chord or the notes of a chord played in succession instead of simultaneously. Also *arpéges*. (Ger. *Arpeggio*, *Arpeggiert*; It. *arpeggio*, *arpeggiando*, *arpeggiato*; Sp. *arpegio*, *arpegiando*, *arpegiado*.)

arpeggiate. A manner of playing chords broken, one note after another, not simultaneously. See **arpeggio**, **cassant**.

arpeggio. (It.) A broken chord or the notes of a chord played in succession instead of simultaneously. Also *arpeggiando*, *arpeggiato*. (Fr. *arpégé*; Ger. *Arpeggio*, *Arpeggiert*; Sp. *arpegio*, *arpegiando*, *arpegiado*.)

Arpeggio. (Ger.) A broken chord or the notes of a chord played in succession instead of simultaneously. Also *Arpeggiert*. (Fr. *arpégé*; It. *arpeggio*, *arpeggiando*, *arpeggiato*; Sp. *arpegio*, *arpegiando*, *arpegiado*.)

arpegio. (Sp.) A broken chord or the notes of a chord played in succession instead of simultaneously. Also *arpegiando*, *arpegiado*. (Fr. *arpégé*; Ger. *Arpeggio*, *Arpeggiert*; It. *arpeggio*, *arpeggiando*, *arpeggiato*.)

arrabbiato. (It.) Raging, furious. Also *rabbioso*. Seen in its German form in the scores of **Gustav Mahler**. (Fr. *enragé*, *rageur*; Ger. *wütend*; Sp. *furioso*.)

arraché. (Fr.) Forceful, torn. Used for the **bass pizzicato** notes in the last bars of *De l'aube à midi sur la mer*, mvt. 1 of *La Mer* by Claude Debussy. (Ger. *gerissen*; It. *strappato*; Sp. *rasgado*, *arrancar*.)

arrangement. (Fr.) An arrangement of a piece of music for another kind of ensemble, such as an orchestral work arranged for **band**. Also *adaptation*. (Ger. *Bearbeitung*; It. *arrangiamento*, *adattamento*; Sp. *arreglo*, *adaptación*.)

arrangiamento. (It.) An arrangement of a piece of music for another kind of ensemble, such as an orchestral work arranged for **band**. Also *adattamento*. (Fr. *arrangement*, *adaptation*; Ger. *Bearbeitung*; Sp. *arreglo*, *adaptación*.)

array. An arrangement in the form of a **matrix** of a numerical series representing musical elements such as pitch, transposition, dynamics, and articulation as presented in a particular order or pattern. Example: *Structures 1a* by Pierre Boulez (1952).

arreglo. (Sp.) A modification of a piece of music for another ensemble, similar to an arrangement. (Fr. *arrangement*, *adaptation*; Ger. *Bearbeitung*; It. *arrangiamento*, *adattamento*.)

arriver. (Fr.) Arrive. Example: *Peu à peu animé pour arriver à 138 = ♪ au No. [32]*, Getting faster little by little so as to be at ♩ = 138 at No. [32], from *Jeux de vagues*, mvt. 2 from *La Mer* by Claude Debussy.

art. (Fr., Latin.) Skill in doing something as the result of acquired knowledge and practice as opposed to that which comes naturally; that which is created, composed, or written with conscious skill; the skillful application of artistic principals to the production of a work of expression in audible or visible forms. Is also used to mean something that is designed to have an artistic effect. In recent years, the definition has been turned on its head, gradually coming to mean something done without training or skill but simply through inspiration or "natural" talent.

articolando. (It.) Articulating. (Fr. *en articulant*, Ger. *artikulierend*, Sp. *articulando*.)

articolare. (It.) To articulate. (Fr. *articuler*, Ger. *zu artikulieren*, Sp. *articular*.)

articolato. (It.) Articulated. (Fr. *articulé*, Ger. *artikuliert*, Sp. *articulado*.)

articulación con la lengua. (Sp.) Articulate with the tongue, **tonguing**. The technique of attacking at the beginning of a note with the tongue to start the airflow on wind and brass instruments. Also *ataque con la lengua*, or simply *articular*, articulate. (Fr. *coup de langue*; Ger. *Zungenstoß*, *Zungenschlag*; It. *colpo di lingua*.)

articulación doble. (Sp.) Double tonguing. A technique used by wind and brass players for articulating faster passages. The player uses the two consonants *t-k, t-k* repeatedly. (Fr. *double articulation*, Ger. *Doppelzunge*, It. *doppio colpo di linqua*.) See **tonguing**, **triple tonguing**, **flutter tonguing**.

articulado. (Sp.) Distinct, articulated. (Ger. *artikuliert*, It. *articolato*, Fr. *articulé*.)

articulando. (Sp.) Articulating. (Fr. *en articulant*, Ger. *Artikulierend*, It. *articolando*.)

articulant. (Fr.) Articulating. (Ger. *artikulierend*, It. *articolando*, Sp. *articulando*.)

articular. (Sp.) To articulate. (Ger. *zu artikulieren*, It. *articulare*.)

articulate, articulation. The clear execution of individual pitches and rhythms so as to be distinct, clear. When played by strings, this means playing the notes separately as opposed to slurred or smoothly. When played by winds or brass, this means that notes should be separated by tonguing.

articulate more. A common expression used to achieve clarity and precision. (Fr. *plus d'articulation*; Ger. *mehr articulation, mehr articulieren, etwas präziser*; Sp. *articulación clara, articulación más clara*.)

articulation marks. See the associated figures.

Articulation staccato. *Courtesy Andrew Martin Smith.*

Articulation wedge. *Courtesy Andrew Martin Smith.*

Articulation wedge staccato. *Courtesy Andrew Martin Smith.*

articulé. (Fr.) Distinct, articulated. (Ger. *artikuliert*, It. *articolato*, Sp. *articulado*.)

articuler. (Fr.) To articulate. (Ger. *zu artikulieren*, It. *articolarae*, Sp. *articular*.)

artificial harmonics. Harmonics generated on string instruments by solidly holding down one pitch and then lightly touching a pitch above it. The most commonly used artificial harmonic is the one at the fourth, where the note touched above is at the interval of one fourth above the bottom, held note. (Fr. *harmoniques artificielles*, Ger. *künstliches Flageolett*, It. *harmonici arificiali*, Sp. *armónicos artificiales*.) See **string harmonics**.

artikuliert. (Ger.) Articulated. (Fr. *articulé*, It. *articolato*, Sp. *articulado*.)

art of interpretation. Based on the study of established and ever-changing principles of musical execution. This includes the study of musical styles; performance practice; well-reasoned artistic choice within the parameters of an individual piece as understood in its historic, social, and poetic context; and the known output of the composer. See **interpretation, conductor as interpreter**.

A-Saite. (Ger.) On the A-string, an indication for string players to play on the A-string. See *Saite*.

à sa place. (Fr.) A directive used after a passage of change or transposition to indicate sounding as written. (Ger. *an seinem Platz*; It. *al luogo, loco*; Sp. *como escrita*.)

ASCAP. See **American Society for Composers, Authors and Publishers**.

ASCAP Award for Adventurous Programming. An annual award administered by the **League of American Orchestras** (LAO) and presented to orchestras in three categories: contemporary music, educational programming, and American programming on foreign tours.

Aspen Music Festival and School (AMFS). Founded in 1949, a summer music festival and training program for young musicians located in Aspen, Colorado. Its current music director is **Robert Spano**, who also serves as music director of the **Atlanta Symphony**. See also **American Academy of Conducting at Aspen**.

áspero. (Sp.) Harsh, rough, rude; A character word sometimes heard in rehearsal. Used by Maurice Ravel in the score to his ballet *Daphnis et Chloé*. (Fr. *rude*, Ger. *rau*, It. *grezzo*.)

assai. (It.) Very. Often seen in music and heard in rehearsal as a part of various phrases. Examples: *Allegro assai*, very **allegro**. (Fr. *très*, Ger. *sehr*, Sp. *muy*.)

assez. (Fr.) Pretty, rather, plenty. A common French tempo marking is *assez animé*, pretty animated. Example: *Assez lent ♩= ♪ de la mesure précédente*, Rather slow, quarter note = the eighth note of the preceding measure. Seen in *Daphnis et Chloé* by Maurice Ravel.

assistant conductor. A conductor within an organization with the rank of assistant (lower than associate). The assistant conductor usually acts as a cover conductor for the music director and any guest conductor, may conduct young peoples' and run-out or community concerts, and may also conduct the local youth orchestra. The larger the organization, the more likely it is that there will also be an **associate conductor**, whose rank is higher and responsibilities greater. Depending on the orchestra, the assistant conductor may also help produce radio broadcasts. See **resident conductor**.

associate conductor. A conductor within an organization with the rank of associate (higher than assistant). An associate conductor has responsibilities for performances, rehearsals, and often conducts at least one subscription concert in each season. Depending on the size of the orchestra, the associate conductor will also conduct community and young peoples' concerts and may also serve as music director for the local youth orchestra. Some orchestras give the associate conductor responsibility for organizing special projects, such as a festival or series of contemporary music concerts. Depending on the orchestra, the associate conductor may also help produce radio broadcasts. See **resident conductor**.

Associated Councils of the Arts. See **National Assembly of State Arts Agencies**.

Association of California Symphony Orchestras (ACSO). An advocacy organization that is made up of orchestra managers, conductors, educators, trustees, and volunteers. The ACSO sponsors an annual conference, a newsletter, and events that support music in California.

assoupli. (Fr.) Relaxed. Example: *Conserver le rythme mais plus assoupli*, keep the rhythm but more relaxed, from *Rondes de Printemps* by Claude Debussy.

assuré. (Fr.) Certain, definite, a character word. Also *certain*. (Ger. *sicher*, It. *certo*, Sp. *cierta, cierto*.)

a sus órdenes. (Sp.) At your service. (Fr. à *votre service*, It. *al votro servizio*.)

asymmetrical meters. See **conducting asymmetrical meters** or **uneven meters** and **patterns**.

a talón. (Sp.) a bowing term calling for the string player to play at the **frog** of the bow or at the heel of the bow (British usage). (Fr. *au talon*, Ger. *am Frosch*, It. *al tallone*.)

ataque. (Sp.) Attack, as in a note, a piece of a beginning of a passage. (Fr. *attaque*, It. *attacca*.)

ataque con la lengua. (Sp.) Articulate with the tongue, **tonguing**. The technique of attacking at the beginning of a note with the tongue to start the airflow on wind and brass instruments. Also *articulación con la lengua* or simply *articular*, articulate. (Fr. *coup de langue*; Ger. *Zungenstoß, Zungenschlag*; It. *colpo di lingua*.)

Atem. (Ger.) A breath. Often heard in rehearsal as a directive, such as "breath with me," "breath in rhythm." (Fr. *souffle*, It. *respiro*, Sp. *respiración*.) See **rehearsal directives in English and their translations**.

a tempo. (It.) In tempo, suggesting "back in tempo" after a passage played at a different speed or to be played in one steady tempo without flexibility or pushing and pulling the tempo.

a tempo. (It.) in tempo, play in tempo; usually indicates the return of the original tempo after a passage of contrasting tempo.

Atemzeichen. (Ger.) **Breath mark**. A notation devise that indicates a breath is to be taken by the performer at a given moment in the music. See **breath mark**.

Athens State Orchestra. Greek orchestra traces its roots to the late nineteenth century and the founding of the Athens Conservatory Symphony Orchestra. It received its current name in 1943. The orchestra has worked with many of the great conductors of the past and presents symphonic, family, and chamber concerts and serves as the orchestra for the Greek National Opera. The current conductor is Vassilis Christopoulos.

Atherton, David. (b. 1944.) English conductor. As co-founder and music director of the **London Sinfonietta** he led first performances of many important contemporary works. He became conductor at the **Royal Opera House, Covent Garden**, at the invitation of **Sir George Solti** (1967), conducting over 150 performances; music director of the San Diego Symphony (1980–1987); principal conductor of the **Royal Liverpool Philharmonic**; and music director of the **Hong Kong Philharmonic** (1989–2000). He was particularly influential through his work organizing and conducting numerous festivals presenting the complete works of Maurice Ravel, **Igor Stravinsky**, Anton Webern, and Edgard Varèse with the **London Sinfonietta**, the **London Symphony Orchestra**, the **BBC Symphony Orchestra**, and the **Royal Opera House, Covent Garden**.

Atlanta Symphony Orchestra (ASO). One of the leading cultural institutions in the southeastern United States, the ASO and it choruses have a history of excellent performances and recordings under distinguished conductors. The orchestra was established in 1945 as the Atlanta Youth Orchestra, though only two years later the name was changed to the Atlanta Symphony Orchestra. Conductor Henry Sopkin was the music director until 1966. **Robert Shaw**, music director from 1967 to 1988, founded the reputable Atlanta Symphony Orchestra Chorus and led many important recordings. Conductor Joel Levi was the music director from 1988 to 2000, and in 2001, **Robert Spano** was appointed to the position. During a thirty-two-year association with **Telarc**, more than one hundred recordings have been made, with twenty-seven winning **Grammy** awards.

Atmung, die. (Ger.) Breathing, the. (Fr. *la respiration*, It. *la respirazione*, Sp. *la respiración*.)

atonal. Adjective for **atonality**.

atonality. Music without a tonal center achieved by avoiding cadential patterns. The most important being music written with the **twelve-tone** or **serial technique**. Also included are works using quarter-tone and other microtone techniques. **Arnold Schoenberg** disliked the term *atonality* because in its strictest translation it means "without tones." He instead preferred *pantonality*, implying a merging or sum of tonalities.

atrás. (Sp.) Back, as in to go back to a previous spot. Example: *Volvamos atrás a la letra A*, Let's go back to letter A (as in rehearsal letter A). (Fr. *derriere, en arriére*; Ger. *zurück*; It. *indietro.*) See **rehearsal letters**.

atrevido. (Sp.) Bold. Also *audaz*. Seen in its German form in the symphonies of **Gustav Mahler**. (Fr. *alerte*, dégagé; Ger. *keck*; It. *spigliato.*)

atril. (Sp.) Music stand, desk of a musician in an ensemble. String players sit in pairs (bass players sometimes prefer to have their own stand in order to see the music better), woodwind and brass players sit on their own, percussion players often have multiple stands in order to accommodate multiple instruments. (Fr. *pupitre*; Ger. *Notenpult, Pult*; It. *leggio.*)

attacca. (It.) Attack, as in a note, a piece of a beginning of a passage. May be used as a declarative: *"Attacca!"* (Fr. *attaque*, Sp. *ataque.*)

attacca subito. (It.) Start immediately, go on right away. May be used as a declaration: *"Attacca subito!"*

attack. The manner of beginning a note, piece, passage, or phrase; can mean with a sense of urgency. An attack can be hard, soft, or any other style as needed.

attaque. (Fr.) Attack, as in a note, a piece of a beginning of a passage. (It. *attacca*, Sp. *ataque.*)

attarder, s'. (Fr.) To delay, to linger. Also *attardé.* (Sp. *retardar.*)

attendez s'il vous plait. (Fr.) Wait one moment, please. A directive often heard in rehearsal. (Ger. *Warten, bitte*; It. *Attendere, prego*; Sp. *Esperar, por favor.*)

attention-getting gesture. A gesture described by **Sir Adrian Boult**, it is a gesture given before the preparatory beat that brings the ensemble's attention into focus for that preparatory beat. Boult described it as possibly beginning out of tempo, usually slower, and flowing into the tempo of the preparatory beat in a circular motion. Sometimes called a "free preparation gesture." See Boult, Adrian. *A Handbook of Conducting.* Oxford: Hall

the Printer, 1936. Boult, Adrian. *Boult on Music.* London: Toccata Press, 1983, a collection of essays. See also **conducting technique**.

at the frog (of the bow). Play at the **frog** of the bow or the heel of the bow (British usage). (Fr. *au talon*, Ger. *am Frosch*, It. *al tallone*, Sp. *al talón.*)

at the point (of the bow). Play at the point or tip of the bow. (Fr. à la pointe; Ger. *an der Bogenspitze, an der Spitze*; It. *alla punta d'arco*; Sp. *a la punta del arco.*)

atto. (It.) An act in an opera. (Fr. *acte*; Ger. *Aufzug, Akt*; Sp. *acto.*)

au chevalet. (Fr.) An indication to play with the bow on or near the bridge of a string instrument. (Ger. *am Steg*, It. *ponticello*, Sp. *sobre el puente.*)

aucun. (Fr.) No, not, none. (Ger. *keine, kein, keiner*; It. *niente*; Sp. *nada, ningún, ninguna.*)

audaz. (Sp.) Bold. Also *atrevido*. Seen in its German form in the symphonies of **Gustav Mahler**. (Fr. *alerte*, dégagé; It. *spigliato*; Ger. *keck.*)

audience. (Fr. Latin, *audientia*, to hear.) A group of listeners at a concert, ballet, opera, or theatrical production; the act or state of hearing; a formal hearing or interview.

audition. To play as a test for purposes of entry into a school or membership in an ensemble or orchestra, for example.

auf. (Ger.) On, over. Also *auf der, auf die*. (Fr. *sur, sur le, sur la*; It. *su, sul, sulla, sopra*; Sp. *en, sobre.*) Examples: *auf der G-Saite*, on the G string; *am Griffbrett*, on the fingerboard. (Fr. *Sur la touche*; It. *sulla tastiera, flautando*; Sp. *sobre el batidor.*) Variations: **auf I** indicates that a violinist should play the marked passage on the E string, **auf II** indicates that a violinist should play the marked passage on the A string, **auf III** indicates that a violinist should play the marked passage on the D string, and **auf IV** indicates that a violinist should play the marked passage on the G string. These four designations can used with any string instrument with the numbers associated with the four strings from the highest to the lowest, I down to IV.

Aufgage. (Ger.) Edition, as in an edition of a piece of music. (Fr. *edition*, It. *edizione*, Sp. *edición.*)

Auflösungszeichen. (Ger.) The natural sign (♮), often used to cancel a previous sharp or flat. Also *auflösen*, to cancel. (Fr. *bécarre*; It. *bequadro*; Sp. *bequadro, natural.*) See **accidental**.

Aufschwung. (Ger.) Momentum, upswing, similar to **schwung**. Example: *mit großem Aufschwung*, with a lot of momentum, upswing, from *Das Lied von der Erde* by **Gustav Mahler**.

Aufstrich. (Ger.) Up-bow, an upward stroke of the bow, the stroke in the direction from tip to **frog**. (Fr. *poussé*, It. *arcata in su*, Sp. *arco arriba*.)

Auftakt. (Ger.) Upbeat, one or more notes that occur before the first measure of a work or phrase, anacrusis, pickup. Example: *breiter Auftakt*, broad upbeat, from *Pierrot Lunaire* by **Arnold Schoenberg**. (Fr. *levée*; It. *in levare*, *levata*; Sp. *alzada*.)

Auftritt. (Ger.) A scene in an opera or theatrical play; can also mean an entrance, appearance, gig.

Aufzug. (Ger.) An act in an opera. Also *Akt*. (Fr. *acte*, It. *atto*, Sp. *acto*.)

Augenmusik. (Ger.) Eye music. Implies music that looks good to the eye on paper but may not sound good when heard. Its origin is often attributed to **Richard Wagner**.

augmentant, en. (Fr.) Becoming louder, increasing. Also *augmenter*, *augmentez*. Example: *Un peu moins vif en animant et en augmetant jusqu'à* [130], a little less lively, then animating and increasing (getting louder) until [130], from *Daphnis et Chloé* by Maurice Ravel.

augmentant. (Fr.) Increasing, getting louder. Example: *En animant et augmentant peu à peu avec une expression toujours plus passioné*, getting faster and louder little by little with more and always passionate expression, from the ballet *Jeux* by Claude Debussy.

augmentare. (It.) To increase, augment, heighten, **crescendo**. (Fr. *augmenter*, Ger. *steigern*, Sp. *aumentar*.)

augmentation. A compositional technique in which the durations of a given set of notes are increased proportionally, such as twice the value or half again the value. See **rhythmic augmentation**, **rhythmic diminution**, **diminution**.

augmenter. (Fr.) To increase, augment, heighten, **crescendo**. (Ger. *steigern*, It. *augmentare*, Sp. *aumentar*.)

aumentar. (Sp.) To increase, augment, heighten, **crescendo**. (Fr. *augmenter*, Ger. *steigern*, It. *augmentare*.)

au movement. (Fr.) In tempo, often indicates the return of the original tempo after a passage of contrasting tempo. See *a tempo*.

Ausdehnung. (Ger.) Compass; range, of an instrument, for instance. Also *Raum*, *Umfang*. (Fr. *ètendue*, It. *gamma*, Sp. *rango*.)

Ausdruck, mit. (Ger.) Expression, with. A commonly used phrase in rehearsal. (Fr. *avec expression*, It. *con l'espressione*, Sp. *con la expression*.)

Ausdrucksbezeichnung. (Ger.) Symbols, expression marks, words or phrases used in music to suggest a certain manner of playing. (Fr. *signe d'expression*, It. *segno d'espressione*, Sp. *signo de expresión*.)

ausdruckslos. (Ger.) Expressionless.

ausdrucksvoll. (Ger.) Full of expression. (Fr. *expressif*, It. *espressivo*, Sp. *expresivo*) Example: *P aber sehr ausdrucksvoll*, Quiet but very expressive; *Sehr ausdrucksvoll*, very expressive, molto expressive, from *The Prelude to Die Meistersinger von Nürenberg* by Richard Wagner. Also *PP aber sehr ausdrucksvoll und lang gestrichen*, PP but very expressive and full bows, from *Das Lied von der Erde*, mvt. 1, by **Gustav Mahler**.

Ausgabe. (Ger.) Edition. For example, the new Barenreiter critical editions of the works of Mozart are called the **Neue Ausgabe** (New Edition).

aushalten. (Ger.) To hold, hold on. Also *halten*. (Fr. *tenir*; It. *tenere*; Sp. *frenar*, *retener*.)

au signe. (Fr.) An indication to a player to go back to a spot specified by a sign (lit. "to the sign"). Usually used in a piece that has a series of repeats and **da capo** markings, such as a waltz by Johann Strauss Jr. (Ger. *zum Zeichen*; It. *al segno*, *dal segno*; Sp. *a la señal*.) See *dal segno*.

äussert. (Ger.) Extreme, extremely, utmost. (Fr. *extrèmement*, It. *estremamente*, Sp. *extremadamente*.) Example: *äussert kurz, wie Tropfen*, extremely short, like droplets, from *Pierrot Lunaire* by **Arnold Schoenberg**.

aussi . . . que. (Fr.) A French expression meaning "as . . . as." Example: *aussi pp que possible*, as pp as possible, from the movement *Feria*, from *Rapsodie Espagnole* by Maurice Ravel.

aussi . . . que possible. (Fr.) As . . . as possible. Examples: *aussi doux que possible*, as soft as possible; *aussi forte que possible*, as loud as possible.

Australian Opera Company. See **Opera Australia**.

auswendig spielen. (Ger.) To play by heart, to play by memory. (Fr. *jouer par coeur*, It. *suonare a memoria*, Sp. *tocar de memoria*.)

Auszug. (Ger.) Excerpt, extract. Also *Ausschnitt*. (Fr. *extrait*, It. *estratto*, Sp. *extracto*.)

au talon. (Fr.) At the **frog** (heel) of the bow. (Ger. *am Frosch*, It. *al tallone*, Sp. *al talón*.) See **bowing terms**.

autant que possible. (Fr.) As much as possible. A regularly used rehearsal expression. (Ger. *so viel wie möglich*, It. *tanto come possibile*, Sp. *tanto como possible*.) Examples: *Il più presto possibile* (It.), As fast as possible; *Los más pronto possible* (Sp.), As fast as possible.

autres. (Fr.) Others. Example: *les autres*, the others.

avant. (Fr.) Before, in front of. Also *avant que*. Commonly heard in rehearsal when telling the ensemble where to begin playing. (Ger. *vor*, It. *prima*.) Example: *Quatre avant D*, Four before D (Ger. *Vier vor Buchstabe D*, It. *Quattro prima D*.)

avantbras, avec l'. (Fr.) With the forearm, sometimes seen as a direction for a pianist to play a large cluster of notes with the whole forearm.

avant garde. (Fr.) That which is literally "in front" culturally or artistically at a given time. Avant garde artists are those with new ideas and methods beyond the norm.

avec. (Fr.) With. Example: *avec la pointe de l'archet*, at the point or tip of the bow, from *Sirénes*, mvt. 3 of *Nocturnes* by Claude Debussy. (Ger. *an der Bogensptize*, It. *col la punta d'arco*, Sp. *con la punta del arco*.)

avec elegance. (Fr.) With elegance. (Ger. *mit Eleganz*, It. *con eleganza*, Sp. *con elegancia*.)

avec l'âme. (Fr.) With feeling, sentiment. (Ger. *gemütvoll*, It. *con l'anima*, Sp. *con sentimiento*.)

avec la pointe de l'archet. (Fr.) An indication for a string player to play at the point or tip of the bow. Example: *avec la pointe de l'archet*, at the point or tip of the bow, from *Sirénes*, mvt. 3 of *Nocturnes* by Claude Debussy. (Ger. *an der Bogenspitze, mit Bogenspitze*; Sp. *en la punta del arco, con la punta*.)

avec le bois. (Fr.) An indication to play with the wood of the bow. (Ger. *mit dem Holz*, It. *col legno*, Sp. *con la vara*.)

avec les pouce. (Fr.) With the thumb. An indication used with the tambourine, a particular way to play the tambourine. (Ger. *mit dem Daumen*, It. *con il pollice*, Sp. *con el pulgar*.)

avec l'expression. (Fr.) A commonly used phrase in rehearsal meaning with expression. (Ger. *mit Ausdruck*, It. *con l'espressione*, Sp. *con la expresión*.)

avec movement. (Fr.) A term that is often seen in music and heard in rehearsal meaning with motion. (Ger. *mit bewegung, bewegt*; It. *con moto*; Sp. *con movimiento*.)

avec quelques licences. (Fr.) With some freedom. A directive seen in parts and heard in rehearsal. (Ger. *mit einiger Freiheit*, It. *con qualche licenza*, Sp. *con cierta licencia*.)

avec tendresse. (Fr.) With tenderness. (Ger. *mit zärtlichkeit*, It. *con tenerezza*, Sp. *con ternura*.)

avec verve. (Fr.) Full of life, excitement. Also *enlevé*. (Ger. *schwungvoll*; It. *brio, con brio*; Sp. *brío*.)

Avery Fisher Hall. Home of the **New York Philharmonic** in New York's **Lincoln Center**. The hall was designed by Max Abramovitz and opened in 1962 as Philharmonic Hall. It got its current name when Avery Fisher, then a member of the **board of directors**, made a $10.5 million donation. The hall seats 2,738.

avivando. (Sp.) Becoming livelier in tempo and/or feeling. (Fr. *en ranimant*, Ger. *neu belebend*, It. *avvivando*.)

à voix basse. (Fr.) quietly, subdued, in an undertone (lit. "under the voice"). (Ger. *unter der Stimme, mit leiser Stimme*; It. *sotto voce*; Sp. *en voz baja*.)

a volonta. (It.) A directive to play with freedom, at one's pleasure. Also *a piacere*. (Fr. à volonté, *à votre gré*; Ger. *nach Belieben*; Sp. *a placer, a gusto*.)

à volonté. (Fr.) A directive to play at will, freely, at the performer's discretion. Also *à votre gré*. (Ger. *nach Belieben*, It. *ad libitum*, Sp. *a placer, a gusto*.)

àvotre service. (Fr.) At your service. A polite phrase sometimes still heard in certain company. (It. *al votro servizio*, Sp. *a sus órdenes*.)

Avshalomov, Jacob. (b. 1919.) Chinese-born American conductor and composer. He had his greatest influence as the second music director, after **Jacques Gerhskovitch**, of the **Portland Youth Philharmonic** (1954–1995). During his forty years, he oversaw numerous international tours, commissions, several recordings, and an estimated 640 concerts. He had a profound influence on the youth orchestra movement in America.

avvivando. (It.) Becoming livelier in tempo and/or feeling. (Fr. *en ranimant*, Ger. *neu belebend*, Sp. *avivando*.)

axis relations. A term devised by Joseph Schillinger and used to describe the relationship between two or more independent musical lines such as in a polyphonic work. See *The Schillinger System of Musical Composition.* New York: Carl Fisher, 1946. See the **bibliography**.

axis system. A system of musical analysis developed by Ernö Lendvaï in his work with the music of Béla Bartók. His system describes a type of harmonic relationship between pitches and chords aiming to show that when they are related by intervals of a minor third or tritone they can function as tonal substitutes for one another and often do so in Bartók's music. See Lendvaï, Ernö. *Béla Bartók: An Analysis of His Music.* London: Kahn & Averill, 1971.

B. A pitch or note name. Example: B-natural. It is called "H" in German, with "B" in German meaning B-flat. See **appendix 5: "Pitch Names and Their Translations."**

B. (Ger.) B-flat.

Babbitt, Milton. (1916–2011.) American composer, theorist, and pedagogue. Babbitt contributed significantly to the understanding of what he called "twelve-note practice." His essay "The Function of Set Structure in the Twelve-Note System" (1946) remains unpublished but in 1992 Babbitt received his PhD at Princeton University as a result of it. Other important essays that formalize and facilitate the understanding of twelve-tone techniques are "Some Aspects of Twelve-Tone Composition" (1955, *The Score*), "Twelve-Tone Invariants as Compositional Determinants" (1960, *Musical Quarterly*), and "Set Structure as a Compositional Determinant" (1961, *Journal of Music Theory*). A prolific composer, Babbitt served on the faculty of Princeton University from 1938 to 1945 and again from 1948 until his retirement in 1986. He became a member of the composition faculty of the **Juilliard School** in 1973, served as the director of the **Columbia-Princeton Electronic Music Center** beginning in 1959, was on the editorial board of **Perspectives of New Music**, and was president of the American section of the **International Society for Contemporary Music** (ISCM).

bacchetta. (It.) Conductor's baton or a drumstick, beater, stick, as used with timpani or other drum. (Fr. *bâton*, Ger. *Taktstock*, Sp. *batuta*.) See **baton**.

bacchetta di spunga. (It.) A soft-headed stick as used by a timpanist; an indication in timpani parts for the timpanist to use a soft stick. (Fr. *baguette d'éponge*, Ger. *Schwanmmschlegel*, Sp. *baqueta blanda*.)

bacchette di legno. (It.) A hard, usually wooden-headed stick used by a timpanist; an indication in timpani parts for the timpanist to play with wooden sticks. (Fr. *baguettes en bois*, Ger. *Holzschlegeln*, Sp. *baqueta de madera*.)

Bach-Gesellschaft. Formed in 1850 to oversee the publication of the complete works of Johann Sesbastian Bach. Superseded by the Neue Bachgesellschaft (New Bach Society) in 1900. See *Gesellschaft*.

Bach Werkverzeichnis (BWV). The catalogue of works of Johann Sebastian Bach. It was created by Wolfgang Schmieder in the 1950s. See **thematic catalogue**.

backbeat. In conducting, a backbeat is a rebound off a pulse in which the energy of the beat is directed up and away from the **ictus** instead of down and into the beat. The backbeat may make the conductor's gesture appear to be before the actual sound of the music.

background. A term used in **Schenkerian analysis** to describe the overall melodic stepwise descent to the tonic supported by the bass progression of I–V–I arpeggiated and projected over the duration of the work. See **Schenkerian analysis**.

badin. (Fr.) Playful. A character word. (Ger. *spielerisch*, It. *giocoso*.)

baguette. (Fr.) A conductor's baton, the stick of the bow for a string instrument, or a mallet or stick, as used by a percussionist. Examples: *baguette de timb(ale)*, timpani stick; *baguette de bois*, wooden stick or mallet.

baguette d'éponge. (Fr.) A soft stick; an indication in timpani parts to use a soft-headed stick or mallet.

(Ger. *Schwanmmschlegel*, It. *bacchetta di spunga*, Sp. *baqueta blanda*.)

bacchette di legno. (It.) Hard, wooden-headed sticks; an indication in timpani parts for the timpanist to play with wooden sticks. (Fr. *baguettes en bois*, Ger. *Holzschlegeln*, Sp. *baqueta de madera*.)

baguettes de timbales. (Fr.) Specifically timpani sticks as opposed to sticks used by a snare drum player, for instance. Often seen as a directive to play a suspended cymbal with timpani sticks, which, unless otherwise specified, are soft, thus producing a soft tone.

baguettes en bois. (Fr.) Hard, often wooden-headed sticks; an indication in timpani parts for the timpanist to play with wooden sticks. (Ger. *Holzschlegeln*, It. *bacchette di legno*, Sp. *baqueta de madera*.)

baisser l'accord. (Fr.) A term used to call for a lowering of the pitch or tuning. Also *baisser l'intonation*. (Ger. *herunterstimmen, tiefer stimmen*; It. *abbassare l'intonature, abbassare l'accordatura*; Sp. *bajar la afinación, bemolar*.) See also ***scordatura***.

baja/o. (Sp.) Lower. A term seen in scores and parts. Example: *8a baja*, an octave lower. The bass part or voice, the lowest of the vocal ranges. (Fr. *basse*, Ger. *Bass*, It. *basso*.) Also under, below, as in pitch or tuning. Example: *un poco bajo*, a little low (flat). (Fr. *dessous, sous*; It. *sotto*; Ger. *unter*.)

bajar la afinación. (Sp.) A term used to call for a lowering of the pitch or tuning. Also *bemolar*. (Fr. *baisser l'accord, baisser l'intonation*; Ger. *herunterstimmen, erniedrigen*; It. *abbassare l'intonazione, abbassare l'accordatura*.) See also ***scordatura***.

bajón. (Sp.) **Bassoon.** (Fr. *basson*, Ger. *Fagott*, It. *fagotto*.) See **appendix 3: "Instrument Names and Their Translations."**

bajo ostinato. (Sp.) A compositional technique involving the constant repetition of a musical phrase or motive in the bass line of a piece. (Fr. *basse obstinée*, It. *basso ostinato*.) See ***ostinato***.

Baker's Biographical Dictionary of Musicians. First published by Theodore Baker in 1900 under the title *A Biographical Dictionary of Musicians*, the dictionary is now in its ninth edition. A comprehensive dictionary of musicians, the fifth through the eighth editions were written and edited by **Nicolas Slonimsky** (1894–1995). Slonimsky had a great influence on the style and content, creating a personal tone through his in-depth knowledge of many of the people he wrote about. For many years it was one of the only reference sources about American musicians and composers in particular.

While the eighth edition was a major expansion on previous versions, with an additional 1,100 entries covering women, Asian musicians, multimedia composers, performers, and musicologists, the ninth edition, edited by Laura Kuhn, appeared in 2001 and was the first to appear in multiple volumes.

balance. With any ensemble, conductors are concerned with achieving the best possible balance. Certain instruments are capable of playing much louder than others, while some can play significantly quieter. The conductor's goal is to make it possible to hear all parts or voices as clearly as possible. (Fr. *balance*, Ger. *Balance*, It. *bilancio*, Sp. *balance*.) Examples: The brass are too loud. (Fr.) *Moins de cuivre*. (Ger.) *Blässer, lieser, bitte*. (Sp.) *Los metales están muy fuerte*, or just *menos metales*. More second violin, please! (Fr.) *Plus deuxième violin, s'il vous plaît!* (Ger.) *Mehr zweite Violine, bitte!* (It.) *Più secondo violino, per favore!* (Sp.) *Más segundo violín, por favor!*

balanced. An expression heard in rehearsal that refers to the dynamic relationship between instruments, allowing all parts to be heard simultaneously. Also well balanced. (Fr. *balancé, bien balancé*; Ger. *klanglich ausgewogen*; It. *bilanciato*; Sp. *balanceado, bien balanceado*.)

balance point of the baton. Conductors who use batons often consider it important that there be a good **balance point** between the handle and the tip of the stick at the place where it is held between the index finger and the thumb. This allows the baton to feel as if it is practically floating in air. Some conductors prefer a baton with a heavier handle and possibly a heavier stick, which moves the balance point further out toward the tip.

ballet conducting. An art in itself, involving great sensitivity to the dancers on stage. Conducting ballet requires a regularity and predictability of tempo on which the dancers can rely. A ballet conductor will often receive a recording of the music in advance so as to replicate all tempos exactly. When ballet music is performed in concert—without the dancers—it is often done with greater tempo flexibility and freedom.

ballo. (It.) Dance. Also *danza*. Example: *tempo di ballo*, in a dance tempo. (Fr. *danse*, Ger. *Tanz*, Sp. *danza*.) See ***dansant***.

Baltimore Symphony Orchestra (BSO). Founded in 1916, the BSO is the only major American orchestra originally established as a branch of a municipal government; it is now a private institution. When **Marin Alsop** was appointed music director in 2007 she became the first woman to head a major American orchestra. The BSO performs in the Joseph Meyerhoff Symphony Hall, which was opened in 1982 and seats 2,443. The BSO has a very innovative community outreach series including **"Rusty Musicians,"** the **BSO Academy**, **OrchKids**, and **"BSO on the Go**."

bamboo wind chimes. Wooden wind chimes made of bamboo for its particular sound. Played by the hand stroking the chimes from side to side. See **appendix 4: "Percussion Instruments and Their Translations**."

band. An ensemble of woodwind, brass, and percussion instruments with the occasional addition of piano (and other keyboards), double bass, harp, and electronics; essentially any large ensemble without strings. Also known as the concert band. Other forms of the band are the wind ensemble, founded in 1952 at the **Eastman School of Music** by **Frederick Fennell**, with the makeup of the standard orchestra woodwind, brass, and percussion sections; the symphonic band, a much larger ensemble; and the marching band, which in its modern form serves as entertainment for American college football games. The history and tradition of the band is long standing. In most countries, the armed services have their own bands that perform at ceremonial occasions. The twentieth century has seen an enormous rise in the repertoire for the band as American composers in particular recognize the ensemble as a significant vehicle for musical expression. Some of the most important works are Gustav Holst's *Suite in E-flat*; Paul Hindemith's *Symphony in B-flat*; **Arnold Schoenberg**'s *Theme and Variations*, opus 43a; Igor Stravinsky's *Symphonies of Wind Instruments*; and works by Percy Grainger and Ralph Vaughan Williams, along with works by more contemporary composers such as **Samuel Adler**'s *Southwestern Sketches*, Warren Benson's *The Leaves Are Falling*, Joseph Schwantner's now-classic *" . . . And the Mountains Rising Nowhere"* (for wind ensemble), Karel Husa's *Music for Prague*, and **John Corigliano**'s *Circus Maximus*. In England, the expression "the band" is used as a nickname for the orchestra.

baqueta blanda. (Sp.) Soft-headed stick; an indication in timpani parts for the timpanist to use a soft-headed stick or mallet. (Fr. *baguette d'éponge*, Ger. *Schwanmmschlegel*, It. *bacchetta di spunga*.)

baqueta de madera. (Sp.) Hard, wooden-headed sticks; an indication in the timpani part for the timpanist to play with wooden sticks. (Fr. *baguettes en bois*, Ger. *Holzschlegeln*, It. *bacchette di legno*.)

bar. Measure; a dividing line in musical notation. (Fr. *mesure*, *barre*; Ger. *Takt*; It. *barra*; Sp. *barra*.)

Barbican Centre. Home to the **London Symphony Orchestra**, the **BBC Symphony Orchestra**, the Academy of Ancient Music, and other ensembles, the Barbican Centre in London is one of the largest arts venues in Europe. Conceived in the 1960s as a means of reinvigorating the city of London after the devastation of World War II, the center was opened in 1982 and is owned and principally funded by the City of London Corporation. Presenting a wide array of arts programming, the center has a concert hall, two theatres, cinemas, art galleries, a library, conference facilities, and restaurants. It also runs a creative-learning series that focuses on learning theories and practice. The **Guildhall School of Music and Drama** is also located next to the center and is part of the growing Barbican complex.

Barbirolli, Sir John. (1899–1970.) English conductor and cellist. Barbirolli had his greatest impact as conductor of the Hallé Orchestra when he took over after World War II and rebuilt the dwindling orchestra into a fine ensemble. He followed **Arturo Toscanini** as music director of the **New York Philharmonic** (1936–1943) and was chief conductor of the **Houston Symphony** (1961–1967). He was a great supporter of the music of Jean Sibelius, Vaughan Williams, Sir Edward Elgar, and Frederick Delius, introducing many new works, and he often programmed **Gustav Mahler** and Anton Bruckner when others had not. He had a reputation as a meticulous rehearsal conductor, sometimes to the extent of sacrificing a sense of the architecture or structure of a piece.

Bard College. A private, liberal arts institution with an excellent music conservatory and a college of liberal arts with eight graduate programs. Founded in 1860 as St. Stephen's College, it is located in Annandale-on-Hudson, New York. It is the host of the Bard Music Festival under the direction of Leon Botstein.

Barenboim, Daniel. (b. 1942.) Argentinean-born Israeli pianist and conductor who has performed and conducted on virtually every acclaimed stage in the world. Barenboim is the founder of the **West-Eastern Divan Orchestra** and Workshop that brings together young Palestinian and Israeli musicians in a professional training setting. The orchestra now tours internationally. He has been the music director of the **Staatsoper** in Berlin since 1992, and he was also the music director of the **Chicago Symphony Orchestra** (1991–2006). He was appointed music director of **La Scala**, Milan, in 2005. Known as a conductor of an enormous repertoire, from Wolfgang Amadeus Mozart and **Richard Wagner** to **Pierre Boulez** and composers of the younger generation, Barenboim believes in the tradition of the conductor as "maestro," an exponent and interpreter of musical taste.

Bärenreiter-Verlag. Also known simply as Bärenreiter, it is a German music publisher based in Kassel that specializes in the New Complete editions (**Neue Ausgabe**). Known as **Urtext** editions and based on available original scholarly and autographical materials, the series includes such composers as Johann Sebastian Bach, Gabriel Fauré, Christoph Willibald Gluck, George Frideric Händel, Leoš Janáček, Wolfgang Amadeus Mozart, Franz Schubert, Georg Philipp Telemann, and others. Of particular significance to conductors is the new edition of Beethoven symphonies edited by **Jonathan Del Mar.** Bärenreiter also published the major music encyclopedia *Die Musik in Geschichte und Gegenwart.* Bärenreiter is represented in the United States by **Theodore Presser.**

baritone. A brass instrument with three valves used almost exclusively in **bands**. The range is from E-natural below bass clef up to G1. Also a male voice classification that lies between the low **bass** and the high **tenor** ranges. See **vocal classifications**.

Baritonhorn. (Ger.) The German equivalent of the **euphonium**. (Fr. *euphonium*, Ger. *Baritonhorn*, It. *bombardino*, Sp. *bombardino*.) See **appendix 3: "Instrument Names and Their Translations."**

bar line. The bar line is the vertical line that separates each measure on the **stave** in a score or other piece of music. (Fr. *barre de mesure*; Ger. *Taktstrich, Notenbalken*; It. *stranghetta, barra*; Sp. *barra de compás*.)

bar number. The sequential number of a bar in a piece. Orchestra scores and parts usually contain bar numbers in order to facilitate rehearsal. They are often placed every ten bars, but in some cases, composers will put them at specific important structural moments. (Fr. *nombre de ensures*, Ger. *Taktzahl*, It. *numero di battute*, Sp. *número del compás*.)

barra. (It.) Bar line, the dividing line between measures or bars in printed music. (Fr. *barre de mesure*, Ger. *Taktstrich*, Sp. *barra de compás*.)

barra de compás. (Sp.) Bar line, the dividing line between measures or bars in printed music. (Fr. *barre de mesure*, Ger. *Taktstrich*, It. *barra*.)

barre de mesure. (Fr.) Bar line, the dividing line between measures or bars in printed music. (Ger. *Taktrstrich*, It. *barra*, Sp. *barra de compás*.)

barsch. (Ger.) Abrupt, harsh, brusque. A character word sometimes used to evoke a certain style of playing. Also *brüsk.* (Fr. *brusque, brusquement*; It. *brusco, bruscamente*; Sp. *brusco, bruscamente*.)

Bartók pizzicato. A pizzicato that involves the player pulling the string away from the fingerboard and releasing it so quickly that it snaps loudly back on the board. Its effect is very percussive. It is named after the Hungarian composer Béla Bartók, who often used it in his string writing. Also called the **snap pizz**.

Bartok pizzicato. *Courtesy Andrew Martin Smith.*

Barzin, Léon. (1900–1999.) Belgian-born American conductor and violinist. Barzin had an enormous impact on the musical life of the United States by founding and nurturing the **National Orchestral Association (NOA)**, a training orchestra for thousands of young musicians who passed through its doors and went on to play in professional orchestras. Barzin was born in Belgium and came with his family to New York. He played in the **Metropolitan Opera Orchestra** and later the **New York Philharmonic**, where he met **Arturo Toscanini**. It was the great maestro who advised Barzin to become a conductor and to accept a position as the assistant conductor of the **American Orchestral Society**, which he shortly thereafter reorganized into his **National Orchestral Association**.

basic conducting patterns for musical styles. See **heavy staccato, legato style, light staccato, marcato style, staccato style,** and **tenuto style**. See also **conducting compound beat patterns, conducting dynamic changes, conducting in four, conducting pattern styles, conducting technique, subdivided beat patterns**.

bass. See **double bass**.

Bass. (Ger.) Bass part or voice, the lowest of the vocal ranges. (Fr. *basse*, It. *basso*, Sp. *bajo*.) See **vocal classifications**.

bass clarinet. Most commonly used in its B-flat version, it also exists as an instrument in A. The bass clarinet is a transposing instrument. When it is in B-flat, its written range is from a low E3 up to an E6, sounding an octave and a step lower, D1 up to D5. Because many composers of the mid-twentieth century called for lower notes, the range of the instrument has extended down to a C2. Some instruments go as low as E-flat3, but this is not universal. Note that when the bass clarinet is notated in the bass clef, it is transposed (if in B-flat, a whole step lower; in A, a minor third lower); if notated in the treble clef, B-flat sounds a major ninth lower or if in A, a minor tenth lower. (Fr. *clarinette basse*; Ger. *Bassklarinette*; It. *clarinetto basso, clarone*; Sp. *clarinet bajo*.) See **clarinet, clarinet in E-flat or D, alto clarinet, basset horn, contrabass clarinet**. See **appendix 3: "Instrument Names and Their Translations."**

Bass clarinet range as it sounds. *Courtesy Andrew Martin Smith.*

Bass clarinet range as written. *Courtesy Andrew Martin Smith.*

bass clef. A figure of notation, placed on the second line down of the music stave in order to indicate the pitch name F and hence the names of those pitches on the other lines and spaces. See **clef, C clefs, treble clef**.

Bass clef. *Courtesy Andrew Martin Smith.*

bass drum. A large, double-headed drum with a deep sound. (Fr. *grosse caisse*; Ger. *Grosse Trommel*; It. *gran cassa, gran tamburo*; Sp. *bombo*.) See **appendxi 4: "Percussion Instruments and Their Translations."**

basse. (Fr.) Bass part or voice, the lowest of the vocal ranges. (Ger. *Bass*, It. *basso*, Sp. *bajo*.)

basse continue. (Fr.) **Ground bass, continuo**. A Baroque term for figured bass, that is, a bass line written with chord numbers below. Usually to be improvised by the performer. (It. *basso continuo*.)

basse marqueee, la. (Fr.) Literally "The bass part marked"; in other words, "mark (accentuate) the bass part."

basse obstinée. (Fr.) Ostinato bass, a compositional technique involving the constant repetition of a musical phrase or motive in the bass line of a piece. (Ger. *Basso ostinato, Ostinato*; It. *basso ostinato*; Sp. *bajo ostinato, ostinato*.)

basset horn. A transposing, clarinet-like single-reed instrument in F with a written range from C3 up to G6; it

sounds a fifth lower. During its history it has been made in different sizes and pitched in different keys. Invented in the 1760s, Mozart used it in at least twenty works, with **Beethoven, Spohr, Mendelssohn, Richard Strauss**, and many more recent composers also making use of it. For that reason, it is kept in production. It has the name "horn" because in its original form it had a curved metal body similar to today's bass clarinet. The modern basset horn is straight, with a metal bell that curves up. The set up of its keys is equivalent to the B-flat clarinet. (Fr. *cor de basset*, Ger. *Bassetthorn*, It. *corno di bassetto*, Sp. *corno di bassetto*.) See **clarinet, clarinet in E-flat or D, alto clarinet, bass clarinet, contrabass clarinet**. See **appendix 3: "Instrument Names and Their Translations."**

Basset horn range as it sounds. *Courtesy Andrew Martin Smith.*

Basset horn range as written. *Courtesy Andrew Martin Smith.*

Bassetthorn. (Ger). See **basset horn**.

Bassflöte. (Ger.) **Bass flute**.

bass flute. The first truly useable bass flute was only full developed in 1930 by Rudall, Carte & Co. based on **Theobald Boehm**'s system. It is a transposing instrument with a written range from C4 up to C7 but sounding an octave lower. See **flute, piccolo, alto flute**. (Fr. *flûte bass*, Ger. *Bassflöte*, It. *flauto basso*, Sp. *flauto bajo*.) See **appendix 3: "Instrument Names and Their Translations."**

Bass flute range as it sounds. *Courtesy Andrew Martin Smith.*

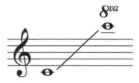

Bass flute range as written. *Courtesy Andrew Martin Smith.*

basso. (It.) Bass part or voice, the lowest of the vocal ranges. (Fr. *basse*, Ger. *Bass*, Sp. *bajo*.)

bass oboe. Sometimes called the baritone oboe, it has the same range as the **Heckelphone**, but since it has an oboe d'amore bell, it looks more like an English horn in shape. It is also generally easier to obtain than the Heckelphone. The instrument is used in Gustav Holst's *The Planets*. See **oboe**, **Heckelphone**, **oboe d'amore**, **English horn**.

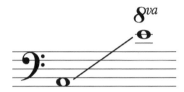

Bass oboe range as it sounds. *Courtesy Andrew Martin Smith.*

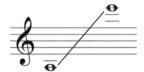

Bass oboe range as written. *Courtesy Andrew Martin Smith.*

basso continuo. (It.) **Ground bass, continuo**. A Baroque term for figured bass, that is, a bass line written with chord numbers below. Usually to be improvised by the performer. (Fr. *basse continue*.)

basson. (Fr.) The bassoon. (Ger. *Fagott*, It. *faggotto*, Sp. *fagot*.) See **appendix 3: "Instrument Names and Their Translations."**

bassoon. The bass instrument of the double-reed family in the woodwind section of the orchestra. A nontransposing instrument, it is made of wood, the keys and bocal (mouthpiece) are metal. The range of the instrument begins on the low B-flat1, but on extended new models the range begins on the A-natural a step below. The upper range has been constantly extended upward, especially since the initial solo of Igor Stravinsky's *The Rite of Spring*, which includes a high D5. Some bassoonists can even play as high as F5. The bassoon is notated in bass and tenor clef. It is abbreviated as "Bsn." or "bssn." (Fr. *basson*, Ger. *Fagott*, It. *faggotto*, Sp. *fagot*.) See **contra-bassoon** and **extensions**. See **appendix 3: "Instrument Names and Their Translations."**

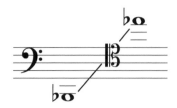

Bassoon range. *Courtesy Andrew Martin Smith.*

basso ostinato. (It.) Commonly called ostinato bass, a compositional technique involving the constant repetition of a musical phrase or motive in the bass line of a piece. Can be a passacaglia. (Fr. *basse obstinée*; Sp. *bajo ostinato*, *ostinato*.) See *ostinato*.

bass trombone. The lowest and largest of the trombone family, it has a darker sound than the tenor trombone due to the larger bore and mouthpiece. A nontransposing instrument with a range of B-flat1 to B-flat4, it can also produce pedal tones that extend the range by seven half steps. The bass trombone has six playing positions, the note name of each is the second partial of the harmonic series generated. It is notated in bass clef. See **trombone** See **appendix 3: "Instrument Names and Their Translations."**

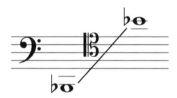

Bass trombone range. *Courtesy Andrew Martin Smith.*

bass trumpet. Often called a trombone with valves because it uses a trombone mouthpiece, it provides an extension to the lower range of the trumpet family. The bass trumpet exists in four different sizes: C, B-flat, D, and E-flat. The ranges are as follows: C from F-sharp3 to C6, sounding an octave lower; B-flat, from F-sharp3 to C6, sounding E2 to B-flat4; E-flat, F3 to C6, sounding A-flat2 to E-flat5; and D, F3 to C6, sounding G2 to D5. See **trumpet**. See **appendix 3: "Instrument Names and Their Translations."**

Bass trumpet B-flat range as it sounds. *Courtesy Andrew Martin Smith.*

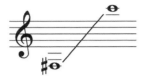

Bass trumpet B-flat range as written. *Courtesy Andrew Martin Smith.*

Bass trumpet C range as it sounds. *Courtesy Andrew Martin Smith.*

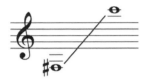

Bass trumpet C range as written. *Courtesy Andrew Martin Smith.*

Bass trumpet D range as it sounds. *Courtesy Andrew Martin Smith.*

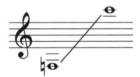

Bass trumpet D range as written. *Courtesy Andrew Martin Smith.*

Bass trumpet E-flat range as it sounds. *Courtesy Andrew Martin Smith.*

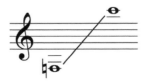

Bass trumpet E-flat range as written. *Courtesy Andrew Martin Smith.*

Bastille Opéra (*opera de la Bastille*). Paris. Built in 1989, it is the main building of the **Paris National Opera**. The new facility shares opera and ballet performances with the older Palais Garnier.

batería. (Sp.) The percussion section of the orchestra; a drum roll. (Fr. *batterie,* Ger. *Schlagzeug,* It. *batteria.*) See also **battery**.

batir el compas. (Sp.) To show with a regular gesture the beats of the music so as to keep the musicians together. (Fr. *batter la mesure,* Ger. *taktieren,* It. *battere la misure.*)

baton. A tapered, smooth stick used by conductors to keep a steady beat or pulse in a manner visible to a large ensemble. The stick or shaft of the baton may be made out of wood, graphite, fiberglass, or other materials. It is usually painted white but may also be a natural wood color or even lit from within by a small battery in the handle. The handle is made of cork or wood, or it may be of one piece with the stick shaped in such a way that it is rounder and thicker at the end that the conductor holds and thin at the tip. (Fr. *bâton,* Ger. *Taktstock,* It. *bacchetta,* Sp. *batuta.*) See **balance point of the baton**.

The length of a baton varies depending on several considerations: the size of the ensemble, height of the conductor, personal preference, desired musical effect, and sometimes tradition. Some conductors use the measurement of the distance between the center of the palm of the hand and the crook of the elbow as a guide for a suitable length, while others are successful without a baton at all. A few well-known nonbaton conductors are **Pierre Boulez**, **Valery Gergiev**, **Dimitri Mitropoulos**, and **Leopold Stowkowski**. Many choral conductors work without a baton. In the hands of an excellent conductor, the baton has developed as a tool of great expression. See **history of the baton, baton hold**.

bâton. (Fr.) A conductor's **baton**. (Ger. *Taktstock,* It. *bacchetta,* Sp. *batuta.*)

baton, history of the. See **history of the baton**.

baton hold or grip. Generally the baton is held in the right hand, between the thumb and the first knuckle of the forefinger while sometimes taking the support of the middle finger under the handle. Depending on the individual baton, the fingers should sit at the end of the handle where the balance point of the baton is usually found. Taking advantage of this spot will allow the conductor to hold the baton, which generally doesn't weigh more than a few ounces, with a practically weightless feel. Often conductors turn the palm of the baton hand down to the floor, while others hold the hand slightly open or rotated, with the thumb a bit on top. See **conducting technique**.

Baton grips may change during the course of a work depending on the weight or force of the music versus its light or fleetness. When force is desired, the baton hand can completely wrap around the baton. When delicacy is the option, the baton can be held in the fingertips. Whatever the basic baton hold or grip, it is often effective to develop flexibility in the fingers in order to amplify nuanced articulations to the tip.

Baton hold. *Courtesy Derek Brennan.*

baton makers. Well-known baton makers include Mollard, Newland Custom Batons, G. L. Custom Batons, and Grover-Trophy Batons.

baton technique. The technique of conducting with a baton; using the baton to give a precise pulse, indicate tempi, dynamics, articulations, style, and character of the music. The baton functions as an extension of the arm and is used to make gestures more visible and clear to the musicians. According to contemporary teaching, the motions of the baton, that is, the gestures of the baton, "should look like the music sounds." The development of the baton technique as a means of nuanced musical communication has progressed alongside the ability and high artistry of the musicians of the orchestra and the subtlety of the music being conducted. See **conducting technique**.

battere. (It.) To beat, as in to beat time. (Fr. *batter*, Ger. s*chlagen*.)

battere il tempo. (It.) To beat the time, show the tempo with regular gestures. (Fr. *battre la mesure*; Ger. *Takt schlagen*; Sp. *marcar el compás, llevar el compás*.)

battere la misure. (It.) To show with a regular gesture the beats of the music so as to keep the musicians together, to beat time. (Fr. *batter la mesure*, Ger. *taktieren*, Sp. *batir el compas*.)

batteria. (It.) The percussion section of the orchestra; a drum roll. (Fr. *batterie*, Ger. *Schlagzeug*, Sp. *batería*.)

batterie. (Fr.) The percussion section of the orchestra; a drum roll. (Ger. *Schlagzeug*, It. *batteria*, Sp. *batería*.)

batter la mesure. (Fr.) To show with a regular gesture the beats of the music so as to keep the musicians together.

To beat time. (Ger. *taktieren*, It. *battere la misure*, Sp. *batir el compas*.)

battery. A term sometimes used to refer to the percussion section of the orchestra.

Battisti, Frank. (b. 1931.) American **band conductor**. Battisti began his career at the most renowned high school **wind ensemble** in Ithaca, New York. He was then appointed to the faculty of the **New England Conservatory of Music**, where he founded and conducted the NEC Wind Ensemble for thirty years.

battre. (Fr.) To beat, as in to beat time. (Ger. s*chlagen*, It. *battere.*)

battre la mesure. (Fr.) To show with a regular gesture the beats of the music so as to keep the musicians together. To beat time. (Ger. *Takt schlagen*; It. *battere il tempo*; Sp. *marcar el compás, llevar el compás*.)

battuta. (It.) The beat or measure, as in the written subdivision of the music. Examples: *battuta composta*, compound time; *battuta semplice*, simple time.

battuta in aria. (It.) Upbeat, pickup, the conductor's pickup. (Fr. *levée*, Ger. *Auftakt*, Sp. *levare*.)

battuta in terra. (It.) Downbeat, the first beat of a bar as indicated by the conductor with a downward gesture and often an **ictus** on the pulse. (Fr. *frappé*; Ger. *Abtakt*; Sp. *primer tiempo, tiempo fuerte*.)

batuta. (Sp.) Conductor's **baton**. (Fr. *baton*, Ger. *Taktstock*, It. *bacchetta*.)

Bavarian Radio Symphony Orchestra, Munich (Symphonieorchester des Bayerischen Rundfunks). The official orchestra of the Bavarian radio, it was founded in 1949 by conductor **Eugen Jochum** and members of a previous orchestra in Munich. Jochum served as chief conductor until 1960 and was followed by **Rafael Kubelík** (1961–1979), **Sir Colin Davis** (1983–1992), **Lorin Maazel** (1993–2002), and **Mariss Jansons** (2003–present). Guest conductors include virtually all noted conductors of the day. The orchestra records for **Deutsche Grammophon**, **RCA**, and **EMI** and won a **Grammy Award** for Best Orchestral Performance for Dmitri Shostakovich's *Symphony No. 13* in 2006. The orchestra also produces recordings under its own BR-Klassik label.

Bavarian State Opera Munich (Bayerische Staatsoper). The company was established in 1653 as the court theater and is Germany's largest opera company. It has been the host of the internationally known Munich Opera Festival since 1875. The company includes the Bavarian State Ballet and its' resident orchestra, the **Bavarian State Orchestra**. The current music director is **Kirill Petrenko** (appointed in 2013). Past music directors include Franz Lachner (1836–1867), **Hans von Bülow** (1867–1869), Franz Wüllner (1870–1877), **Hermann Levi** (1872–1896), **Richard Strauss** (1894–1896), Max Ermannsdörfer (1896–1898), Bernhard Stavenhagen (1898–1902), Herman Zumpe (1901–1903), **Felix Mottl** (1904–1911), **Bruno Walter** (1913–1922), **Hans Knappertsbusch** (1922–1935 and 1945), **Clemens Krauss** (1937–1944), **Georg Solti** (1946–1952), **Rudolf Kempe** (1952–1954), **Ferenc Fricsay** (1956–1958), Joseph Keilberth (1959–1968), **Wolfgang Sawallisch** (1971–1992), Peter Schneider (1992–1998), **Zubin Mehta** (1998–2006), and **Kent Nagano** (2006–2013). The company is known for its large number of opera premieres and more recently its presentation of live streaming video free of charge for selected performances online at STAATSOPER.TV.

Bavarian State Orchestra Munich (Bayerisches Staatsorchester). The resident orchestra of the **Bavarian State Opera**. In addition to serving as the orchestra for the opera, the ensemble has been presenting a series of concerts called the Academy Concerts (*Akademiekonzerte*) since 1811. Among the conductors the orchestra worked with was **Carlos Kleiber** (1968–1997), though he was never the music director. The list of music directors may be seen above under **Bavarian State Opera Munich**.

Bay Area Women's Philharmonic, The. See **Women's Philharmonic, The**.

Bayreuth Festival (Bayreuther Festspiele). A music festival held every summer in Bayreuth, Germany, that presents the music of Richard Wagner. The site of the opera theater, the Bayreuth Festspielhaus, was specially designed by the composer to accommodate both the large orchestras he used in his operas and his ideas for staging. The festival opened in 1876 with a performance of *Das Rheingold* in the presence of Kaiser Wilhelm I; other nobles; composers Anton Bruckner, Edvard Grieg, Pyotr Tchaikovsky, **Franz Liszt**, and Arthur Foote; and the philosopher Friedrich Nietzsche. While it wasn't a financial success for several years, it has always attracted leading conductors and singers. **Hans Richter** conducted the first production of the **Ring Cycle** in 1876 and **Hermann Levi** the premiere of *Parsifal* in 1882 with the young Engelbert Humperdinck as his assistant.

BBC. See **British Broadcasting Corporation**.

BBC Music Magazine. A British monthly magazine. It first appeared in June 1992, published by BBC Worldwide. Since 2012, it has been published by Immediate Media Company. It is devoted mostly to classical music, though it has sections on jazz and world music. Each issue comes with a new audio CD. It features articles on the current classical music scene with features covering subjects such as the favorite conductor of professional conductors and articles asking composers to discuss trends in classical music. See **music magazines**.

BBC Proms (The Henry Wood Promenade Concerts presented by the BBC). An eight-week music festival that takes place in London's Royal Albert Hall. Founded in 1895, the title "Proms" refers to the tradition of promenade concerts offered outdoors in parks around London from the mid-nineteenth century. The music festival presents promenade concerts indoors. To this day "promenaders" or "prommers" can purchase inexpensive tickets on the day of the concert to stand (or sit, if the space is available) on an empty area in front of the stage or in the upper balcony. Now one of the longest music festivals in the world, the Proms were started as a way to draw in audiences with cheap tickets and popular repertoire. While the tickets remain inexpensive, the repertoire has expanded greatly and now often includes works of contemporary composers. The *Last Night at the Proms* is the culmination and the "winding down" of the festival with lighter repertoire and many popular British patriotic pieces. *Rule Britannia!* Edward Elgar's *Pomp & Circumstance March No. 1*, and Sir Henry Woods's *Fantasia on British Sea Songs* are always performed, and the concert is broadcast live.

BBC Scottish Symphony Orchestra (BBC SSO). The oldest full-time professional orchestra in Scotland and one of the five orchestras run by the **British Broadcasting Corporation** (BBC). Established in 1935 in Glasgow, the orchestra did over thirty hours of broadcasting a week during World War II on both BBC Home and World Services, broadcasting nearly any time of day or night so that it could be heard even in South America. The orchestra regularly performs at the Edinburgh Festival. The current chief conductor is Donald Runnicles (appointed 2009). He was preceded by Ilan Volkov (2003–2009), **Osmo Vänskä** (1996–2002), Jerzy Maksymiuk (1983–1993), Karl Anton Rickenbacher (1978–1980), Christopher Seaman (1971–1977), James Loughran (1965–1971), Norman Del Mar (1960–1965), Ian Whyte (1946–1960), and Guy Warrach (1935–1946). It was Norman Del Mar who brought public performances to the orchestra and broadened the repertoire to include more contemporary music. Since 1994, the orchestra has had a series of affiliated composers, including Tan Dun, Stuart MacRae, Jonathan Harvey, Anna Meredith, and Matthias Pintscher. The orchestra has made numerous recordings and won a Gramophone Award in 2009. Concerts can be heard on BBC Radio and on the Internet.

BBC Symphony Orchestra (BBC SO). Known for its mission of championing the works of contemporary composers, the BBC SO in London is the principal orchestra of the **British Broadcasting Corporation**, the state broadcasting system of Britain, and was founded in 1930. Most concerts are broadcast on BBC Radio 3 and are currently streamed online. Many broadcasts are also televised. **Sir Adrian Boult** was the first director of music, remaining in the position for twenty years. Boult was responsible for building and training the orchestra and conducting innumerable premieres. The main orchestra of the music festival the Proms, the "BBC" makes its home during the concert season at the **Barbican Centre** in London. It engages in many educational initiatives for students and families.

Bearbeitung. (Ger.) An arrangement or adaptation of a piece of music. (Fr. *arrangement, adaptation*; It. *arrangiamento, adattamento*; Sp. *arreglo, adaptación*.)

beat. The gesture given by the conductor that equates to the number of main rhythmic pulses in a measure. Early conductors beat time audibly with their hands, feet, or with a stick on the floor (see **Lully, Jean Baptiste**). In the nineteenth century, with the rise of professionalism in the music field, both musicians and audience members began to complain about the noise, and so the practice declined and was replaced by a conductor who led silently. See **conducting technique**.

beat conformation. A principal of conducting that refers to the regularity of the beats, the size and spacing of the beats within the conducting patterns. See **conducting technique**.

beat inevitability. The goal of clear conducting is to create a sense of inevitability and trust for the musicians of the ensemble. Clear, smooth, natural preparatory beats are the essence of beat inevitability. See **conducting technique**.

beat patterns. The pattern of the beats that the conductor uses to interpret a given metric pattern. See **conducting beat patterns**, **conducting pattern styles**, **subdivided patterns**, **conducting technique**.

beat placement. Where the beats are placed within the pattern as conducted. Clear conducting is dependent on clear beat placement. Separated spatially, the beats are clearer to the player who relies on peripheral vision. See **conducting technique**.

beat size. The size of the beat may reflect the size of an ensemble, although many conductors will be surprised at how a small but clear beat will be visible. Size can also reflect the musical dynamic or bring out climactic or otherwise important moments. Danger is upon us when a conductor fails to moderate the size of the beat while calling out "Quiet! Play quietly!" See **conducting technique**, **dynamics**, **dynamic changes**, **tempo changes**.

beat style. The goal of the conductor is to describe musical style through the gestures, beats, and motions between the beats. Sustained music is shown through a slowing or pulling of the motion between the beats. Sharper attacks are shown by a motion that stops and starts rapidly as it moves from pulse to pulse. See **basic conducting patterns for musical styles**, **conducting pattern style**, **conducting technique**.

beat time, to. To show with a regular gesture the beats of the music so as to keep the musicians together. (Fr. *batter la mesure*; Ger. *Takt schlagen, taktieren*; It. *battere la misure*; Sp. *batir el compass, llevar el compás*.)

beaucoup. (Fr.) Many, much. Often heard as part of directive phrases in rehearsals. Example: *Beaucoup moins vif*, much less fast, from *Daphnis et Chloé* by Maurice Ravel. (Ger. *viel, viele*; It. *molto*; Sp. *mucho*.)

bécarre. (Fr.) The natural sign, it often negates a previous sharp or flat. (Ger. *Auflösungszeichen*, It. *bequadro*, Sp. *natural*.) See **accidental**.

Becken. (Ger.) **Cymbal**, a curved metal plate available in varying sizes. Cymbals may be suspended and struck individually by various devices, including a wooden drumstick, a triangle beater, a wire brush or a marimba mallet, and more. They may also be played as crash cymbals, where two, held in the hands with a leather strap, can be played in any number of ways in order to generate a wide variety of sounds. (Fr. *cymbals*; It. *piatti, cinelle*; Sp. *platos*.) See **appendix 4: "Percussion Instruments and Their Translations."**

bedächtig. (Ger.) Deliberate, slow, thoughtful. A character word sometimes heard in German.

bedeckt. (Ger.) Covered, dampened, as is frequently done on timpani. (Fr. *couvert, sourd*; It. *coperto, velato*; Sp. *cubierto*.)

bedeutend. (Ger.) Meaningful, meaning. Also *bedeutet*. Example: *bedeutet **Hauptstimme***, main voice, from ***Pierrot Lunaire***, **Arnold Schoenberg**.

bedrohlich. (Ger.) Threating, forbidding, menacing. A character word sometimes used to evoke a particular style of playing.

Beecham, Sir Thomas. (1879–1961.) A self-taught English conductor and impresario, Beecham formed the New Symphony Orchestra (1905), the Beecham Symphony Orchestra (1906), and the Beecham Opera Company (later the **English National Opera**) in 1915, the year he was knighted. Born into a wealthy family, his father, Sir Joseph Beecham, was a manufacturing chemist who was responsible for the growth and expansion of *his* father's medicinal pill business (Beecham's Pills). Bankrupted when his father died in 1920, Sir Thomas withdrew for a time from musical life, but he went on to found the **London Philharmonic Orchestra** in 1932 and the **Royal Philharmonic Orchestra** in 1946. He conducted many opera premieres at the **Royal Opera House, Convent Garden**, and several Ring cycles. He appeared at the **Metropolitan Opera** in New York and was the conductor of the **Seattle Symphony** from 1941 to 1944.

Beecham was thought by some to be a conductor who strove to raise the standards of orchestra playing and by others as one who was far too spontaneous, even an "improviser" in performance. His sense of humor was infamous and beloved by orchestra players as a way of relieving the day-to-day stress of rehearsals. Even during his lifetime, musicians collected and retold "Beecham stories," and in 1978, a collection was published under that very title. His book, *A Mingled Chime:—Leaves from an Autobiography*, was published in 1959. In addition, he wrote a small biography of Frederick Delius. See the **bibliography**.

beeilen, zu. (Ger.) To hurry. (Fr. *se dépêcher*, It. *affrettare*, Sp. *prisa*.)

Beethoven, Ludwig van. (1770–1827.) German composer of great renown. See **appendix 1: "Six Pieces That Changed Conducting"**; *Symphony No. 9 in D minor (1824), Ludwig van Beethoven*.

begleiten. (Ger.) To accompany, as in a concerto or other work with a soloist. (Fr. *accompagner*; Ger. *begleiten*; Sp. *para acompañar, acompañamiento*.)

Begleitung. (Ger.) Accompaniment, as in a piano accompaniment or accompaniment by an orchestra. (Fr. *accompagnement*, It. *accoompagnamento*, Sp. *acompaãmiento*.)

Behände. (Ger.) Nimble, a character word. (Fr. *agile, agilement*; It. *agile*; Sp. *ágil*.)

Beifall. (Ger.) Applause. (Fr. *applaudissement*, It. *applauso*, Sp. *aplauso*.)

Beijing Central Conservatory of Music. Known in China as the Central Conservatory of Music, it was established in 1950. The conservatory offers undergraduate programs of four or five years in both Western music and traditional Chinese musical instruments. Degree programs include composition, performance, conducting, musicology, and more. It also has a six-year middle school program and special evening courses for younger students and adults. The conservatory has over five hundred pianos on site and an advanced electronic music studio. It sponsors the annual **Beijing Modern Music Festival** every May.

Beijing Modern Music Festival. Founded in 2004, a festival that takes place every May. The festival attracts composers and performers worldwide. It includes a Young Composers Competition and community projects that involve young school performers, and it has sponsored various forums on culture and new music. The director of the festival is Chinese composer Xiaogang Ye.

beinahe. (Ger.) Almost, nearly, as if. Also *fast, als ob*. (Fr. *presque*; It. *quasi*; Sp. *casi, cercano a, como, parecido*.) Examples: *Wir sind beinahe am Ende*, We are almost at the end; *Es klingt fast zu rau*, It sounds almost too rough; *Bitte, spielt das als ob es ein Tanz wäre*, Please play this as if it were a dance.

Beinum, Eduard van (1901–1959). Dutch conductor who grew up in a family of musicians. Beinum studied at the Amsterdam Conservatoire and entered the Arnhem Orchestra as a violinist in 1918. He first conducted the **Royal Concertgebouw Orchestra** in 1929, becoming the second conductor under **Willem Mengelberg** in 1931. He was promoted to coprincipal with Mengelberg in 1938. After World War II, when Mengelberg was dismissed because of his apparent disposition toward Nazi occupiers, Beinum became the Concertgebouw's sole principal conductor, becoming known as one of the greatest Dutch conductors of his generation. He conducted the **London Philharmonic Orchestra (LPO)** from 1947 to 1949 but left for health reasons. In 1954, Beinum made his U.S. debut with the **Philadelphia Orchestra** and led a U.S. tour with the Concertgebouw. In 1956, he became the music director of the **Los Angeles Philharmonic**, remaining there until his early death from a heart attack in 1959 while rehearsing Johannes Brahms's *Symphony No. 1*. Beinum's personality and style contrasted the flamboyance of Mengelberg. He was restrained, much less demonstrative, and believed in allowing the music to speak for itself. He saw himself as a member of the orchestra and cultivated relationships with the players based on mutual respect. Beinum was known to always conduct with the score, whether the work was familiar or not.

Beinum championed the music of Benjamin Britten, premiering the *Spring Symphony* with the Concertgebouw in 1949. He was a promoter of Dutch composers such as Louis Andriessen, Badins, Hans Henkemans, Léon Orthel, and others. He encouraged the LPO's first trumpet player, Malcolm Arnold, as a composer, conducting a premiere recording of his work *Beckus the Dandipratt*. Other contemporary composers whose music he promoted include Béla Bartók, Claude Debussy, Zoltán Kodály, Leoš Janáček, Maurice Ravel, Antoine Roussel, Karol Szymanowski, Dmitri Shostakovich, and **Igor Stravinsky**. Beinum's recordings, which were primarily with the Concertgebouw, are available on the **Philips** and **Decca** labels. Among the most notable are Bartók's *Concerto for Orchestra*, **Hector Berlioz's** *Symphonie fantastique*, Stravinsky's *Le Sacre du printemps*, **Gustav Mahler's** *Symphony No. 4*, and Anton Bruckner's *Symphonies Nos. 7, 8,* and *9*.

belebt. (Ger.) Lively, animated, a character word. (Fr. *animé*, It. *animato*, Sp. *animado*.)

Bell Laboratories. Experimental laboratories where early research was done into computer sound and tape recording. It was owned by the American Telephone and Telegraph Company and Western Electric. Originally named the **Bell Telephone Laboratory (BTL)**, it was later shortened.

Bell Telephone Laboratory (BTL). See **Bell Laboratories**.

bell tree. A percussion instrument consisting of multiple small bells mounted on a stand (tree) and struck by a metal beater either up, down, or both. See **appendix 4: "Percussion Instruments and Their Translations."**

Bělohlávek, Jiří. (b. 1946.) Czech conductor who studied with **Sergiu Celibidache**, he founded the Prague Philharmonia in 1994. Bělohlávek conducts orchestras throughout Europe and the United States and he is known as a proponent of Czech music, particularly that of Leoš Janáček, Bohuslav Martinů, Bedřich Smetana, and Antonín Dvořák.

bémol. (Fr.) **Flat**. (Ger. *B*, It. *bemolle*, Sp. *bemol*.) See **appendix 5: "Pitch Names and Their Translations," accidental**.

bemol. (Sp.) **Flat**. (Fr. *bémol*, Ger. *B*, It. *bemolle*.) See **appendix 5: "Pitch Names and Their Translations," accidental**.

bemolar, bajar la afinación. (Sp.) A term used to call for a lowering of the pitch or tuning. Also *bajar la afinación*. (Fr. *baisser l'accord, baisser l'intonation*; Ger. *herunterstimmen, erniedrigen*; It. *abbassare l'intonazione, abbassare l'accordatura*.) See also **scordatura**.

bemolle. (It.) Flat. (Fr. *bémol*, Ger. *B*, Sp. *bemol*.) See **appendix 5: "Pitch Names and Their Translations," accidental**.

ben. (It.) A term heard often in rehearsal meaning good, well done. Also *bene*. Example: *molto bene*, very good (as in "well done"). (Fr. *bien*; Ger. *gut, gut gemacht*; Sp. *bueno*.)

Ben-Dor, Gisele. (b. 1955.) Uruguay-born Israeli American conductor. Ben-Dor served as the music director of the Santa Barbara Symphony Orchestra (1994–2006), Boston Pro Arte Chamber Orchestra (1991–2000), Annapolis Symphony (1991–1997) and Shepherd School of Music Symphony (1988–1990). She was also the resident conductor of the **Houston Symphony** (1988–1991) and has been a guest conductor for orchestras worldwide, including the **New York Philharmonic**, **London Symphony**, **Los Angeles Philharmonic**, **Orchestre de la Suisse Romande**, **Israel Philharmonic**, and the **Jerusalem Symphony**. She is a champion of Latin American composers such as Alberto Ginastera, Silvestre Revueltas, Ástor Piazzolla, Heitor Villa-Lobos, and Luis Bacalov. Ben-Dor is the conductor laureate of the Santa Barbara Symphony and conductor emerita of the Boston Pro-Arte Chamber Orchestra.

bequadro. (It.) The **natural sign**, it often negates a previous sharp or flat. (Fr. *bécarre*, Ger. *Auflösungszeichen*, Sp. *natural*.) See **accidental**.

bequem. (Ger.) Comfortable, easy. (Fr. *commodément*; It. *comodamente*; Sp. *cómodo, cómodamente*.)

berceuse. (Fr.) Lullaby, cradle song. (Ger. *Wiegenlied*; It. *ninna nanna*; Sp. *nana, canción de cuna*.)

Berglund, Paavo. (1929–2012.) Finnish conductor and violinist. Berglund played the violin and conducted left-handed. His rehearsal manner was disciplined to the point of being called ruthless by some, while others appreciated his business-like approach. He often prepared every musician's part with his own bowings (for the strings), details of style, corrections, and, sometimes, actual changes in what the composer wrote. Berglund made over one hundred recordings and conducted all over Europe and in the United States.

Berkshire Music Center at Tanglewood. See **Tanglewood Music Center**.

Berlin Philharmonic Orchestra, Berlin, Germany. Founded in 1882, its chief conductors make up a list of great leaders in the field. Chief conductors include **Hans von Bülow**, **Arthur Nikisch**, **Wilhelm Furtwängler**, **Sergiú Celibidace**, **Herbert von Karajan**, **Claudio Ab-**

bado, and since 2002, **Sir Simon Rattle**. A partial list of guest conductors is no less impressive: Johannes Brahms, Edvard Grieg, **Gustav Mahler**, **Richard Strauss**, and **Felix Weingartner**. Grounded in a long, traditional musical culture, the current manifestation of the orchestra is forward looking and modern. Rattle made it a condition of signing his initial contract that the orchestra become self-governing, a restructuring that encouraged the participation of orchestra members in artistic decisions and more. In 2004, the orchestra engaged in an innovative educational outreach program, recruiting 250 children from Berlin schools to participate in a staging of **Igor Stravinsky's** *The Rite of Spring*. The project was documented in the video ***Rhythm Is It!*** directed by Thomas Grube and **Enrique Sanchez Lansch**. When it was released to movie theaters, it sold four hundred thousand tickets and won major awards. The success of this program, which was under the musical direction of Rattle, led to many other outreach initiatives. The orchestra is resident in the **Philharmonie**, a hall designed by architect Hans Scharoun and built between 1960 and 1963 in order to replace the original hall, which was destroyed in World War II. See Kleinert, Annemarie. *Music at Its Best: The Berlin Philharmonic: From Karajan to Rattle*. 2009.

Berlin Radio Symphony Orchestra. The name was used for two orchestras, the German Symphony Orchestra Berlin (*Deutsches Symphonie-Orchester Berlin*), which was known as the Radio Symphony Orchestra in West Berlin (*Rundfunk-Sinfonieorchester Berlin*) from 1956 to 1993, or the Berlin Radio Symphony Orchestra in East Berlin, which was founded in 1923. See **Radio Symphony Orchestra Berlin**; **German Symphony Orchestra, Berlin**.

Berlin State Opera (Staatsoper Unter den Linden). One of the most important opera companies in Germany today. King Frederick II had the first court opera building constructed in 1741, and the first performance took place one year later. The opera is also the site of the Staatskapelle Berlin, the state orchestra. The company presents opera, ballet, concerts, special workshops for children, and opera workshops with performances of chamber operas and other projects. The current music director is **Daniel Barenboim** (appointed in 1992). The list of past conductors includes some of Germany's most distinguished musicians: **Gaspare Spontini** (1820–1841), Giacomo Meyerbeer (1842–1846), Otto Nicolai (1848–1849), Robert Radecke (1871–1887), Joseph Sucher (1888–1899), **Richard Strauss** (1899–1913), Leo Blech (1913–1920), **Erich Kleiber** (1923–1934), Clemens Krauss (1935–1936), **Herbert von Karajan** (1941–1945), Joseph Keilberth (1948–1951), **Erich Kleiber** (1954–1955), Franz Konwitschny (1955–1962), and Otmar Suitner (1964–1990).

Berlin Symphony Orchestra (Berliner Symphoniker). Founded in 1967 as the **Symphonisches Orchester Berlin** and renamed in 1991, it originated with the merger of the Berliner Symphonisches Orchester (founded in 1949) and the Deutsches Symphonieorchester. The orchestra has made many international tours through Europe, Asia, South America, and Africa.

Berlioz, Louis Hector. (1803–1869.) French composer, conductor, critic, innovator, and author. Mostly known as a composer of such works as the *Symphonie Fantastique* (1830) and his massive *Requiem* (*Grand messe des morts*, 1837), Berlioz became a conductor for the same reasons that many composers before and after him had, that is, he was frustrated with the performances he was getting under the direction of others. Berlioz became one of the first baton conductors aside from **Felix Mendelssohn** to attain an international reputation and influence.

At the time, there were no schools nor teachers of conducting; learning was done by observing others (see **apprenticeship**). Berlioz began, as has been described by several sources, by "over-"conducting, that is, using very large, energetic gestures that lacked focus. Through years of organizing and leading concerts of his own, he became known as a conductor of the symphonies of Beethoven. He reportedly developed a concentrated, clear, and precise technique that became a tradition handed down through the generations to many of France's great conductors today.

To supplement his income and pay off debts, he wrote hundreds of journal articles about the musical life he observed. His orchestration book, ***Grand Traité d'instrumentation et d'orchestration modernes***, was later modernized by composer Richard Strauss and is still used in music schools today. Shortly after its initial publication, Berlioz added essays on the state of the orchestra in his day (poor) and **"On Conducting: Theory of the Art of Conducting."**

Berlioz was fascinated by the latest invention or gadget. In his essay on conducting, he describes a trip to Brussels where he came in contact with **Henri Verbrugghen**, the inventor of a contraption—Berlioz referred to it as an "electric metronome"—that would make it possible to communicate the beat via copper wires to an offstage or otherwise invisible subconductor. Berlioz was so convinced by it that he brought Verbrugghen and his metronome to Paris for a concert of "gargantuan" proportions requiring, in addition to himself, the participation of five subconductors.

Berlioz was awarded the coveted Prix de Rome only on his fourth attempt. During his stay in Rome, he met and befriended **Felix Mendelssohn**. A few years later he renewed this relationship and traveled to Germany, establishing connections that led to many performances. It was on this first trip to Germany that he and

Mendelssohn exchanged batons. From then on he would travel throughout Europe, including Russia more than once, expanding his reputation as a conductor and composer with performances in virtually every capital and musically important city. See the **bibliography**.

Hector Berlioz.

Bernstein, Leonard. (1918–1990.) American composer, conductor, pianist, and pedagogue. Bernstein is most likely the single most influential and versatile American musician of the twentieth century. The conductor of the New York Philharmonic from 1958 to 1969, Bernstein was, and may still be, beloved by audiences throughout the globe. He composed works that have been performed worldwide, including his most popular work, the musical *West Side Story*. Also important but less well known are his three symphonies, No. 1, "Jeremiah"; No. 2, "Age of Anxiety"; and No. 3, "Kaddish." His *Mass* was commissioned for the opening of the **Kennedy Center** in Washington, DC, but his most famous choral work was *Chichester Psalms*. His compositional style was eclectic, integrating influences of **Gustav Mahler**, Dmitri Shostakovich, **Igor Stravinsky**, and others with his Jewish and American background.

As a conductor, he was very supportive of contemporary American composers, conducting the premiere recordings of innumerable pieces. His recording list includes works of Mahler, Wolfgang Amadeus Mozart, Ludwig van Beethoven, and many, many more. He was a frequent guest conductor with the **Vienna** and **Berlin Philharmonic Orchestras**, the **London Symphony**, and many other ensembles in Europe. The first time he conducted the Berlin ensemble he is said to have spent the entire first rehearsal (out of only two) analyzing and explaining Mahler's *Symphony No. 9*, winning the orchestra over through his prodigious intellect and excellent German.

Aside from his active work as a conductor and composer, he taught at the **Tanglewood Summer Music Institute** for years. Many of the conductors he worked with are active as professionals now. He was the first conductor to give classical music lectures on television, usually with a live symphony orchestra on hand, influencing countless young Americans who grew up watching these programs. See the **bibliography**.

Leonard Bernstein. *Courtesy Library of Congress.*

Bertini, Gary. (1927–2005.) Israeli conductor and composer. Bertini founded the Israel Chamber Orchestra in 1965 and was its conductor for ten years. He was the conductor of the **Jerusalem Symphony** from 1978 to 1986 and the music director of the New Israeli Opera from 1994 until his death in 2005. He was the music director of the **Detroit Symphony** from 1981 to 1983, principal conductor of the **Cologne Radio Symphony** from 1983 to 1991, and other orchestras. He was known as a great exponent of Israeli music, receiving the Israel Prize for music in 1978.

beruhigen. (Ger.) To calm, soothe. Used in rehearsal to invoke a particular feeling or sound. (Fr. *calmer*, It. *calmare*, Sp. *calmar*.)

beruhigend. (Ger.) Soothing, calming, a character word used in rehearsal. (Fr. *en calmant*, It. *calmando*, Sp. *calamante*.)

beschleunigen. (Ger.) To get faster, accelerate. (Fr. *accélérer*, It. *accelerare*, Sp. *acelerar*.) Example: *Noch ein wenig beschleunigen*, still a little speeding up, from *Symphony No. 1*, mvt. 1 by **Gustav Mahler**.

besitzen. (Ger.) To have, own, or feature something as in an instrument having a specific note in its range. Example:

So lange das Engl. Horn diesen Ton nicht besitzt, mag es h statt b blasen, as long as the English horn doesn't have this note, play the B-natural instead of the B-flat, From *Das Lied von der Erde*, mvt. 1 by **Gustav Mahler**.

bestimmt. (Ger.) Decisive, decisively, a character word. (Fr. *determine*; It. *determinato*; Sp. *decidido, determinadamente*.)

betont. (Ger.) A term sometimes seen in scores meaning stressed or emphasized. A character word that evokes a certain style of playing.

Betonung. (Ger.) Emphasis, stress, a character word. Example: *Alle Betonungen zart*, all accents tender, from *Symphony No. 1*, mvt. 1 by **Gustav Mahler**.

bewegend. (Ger.) An expression seen in the scores of **Gustav Mahler** meaning, for example, moving along. (Fr. *en movement*, It. *movendo*, Sp. *movimiento*.)

bewegt. (Ger.) Movement, motion, moving. Examples: *Sehr mäßig bewegt*, Moving very moderately; *Bewegt, doch immer etwas breit*, Moving, but always somewhat broad, from *The Prelude to Die Meistersinger von Nürenberg* by **Richard Wagner**.

bewegter. (Ger.) Faster, with more motion. Example: *Noch bewegter*, even faster; *Immer bewegter im Vortrage*, always played with forward motion (lit. "always moving in its presentation"), from the prelude to *Die Meistersinger von Nürenberg* by Richard Wagner.

Bewegung. (Ger.) Movement, motion, a character or descriptive word seen in scores and parts of the late nineteenth and twentieth centuries. (Fr. *mouvement*; It. *moto, movimiento*; Sp. *movimiento*.) Also *mit Bewegung*, with motion. (Fr. *avec movement*, It. *con moto*, Sp. *con movimiento*.)

bichordal. A vertical sonority that consists of two identifiable chords from different keys. For instance, the simultaneous sounding of a D major against B major triad, or C7 against A7.

bien. (Fr.) A term heard often in rehearsal meaning good, well done. (Ger. *gut, gut gemacht*; It. *ben, bene*; Sp. *bueno*.)

Billings, William. (1746–1800.) American composer and teacher of choral singing. Perhaps the first American-born composer, Billings began teaching at singing schools as early as 1769. As his reputation grew, he was in demand at Boston's churches too.

He wrote over 340 works that appeared in various collections throughout his life. At the time, there were no copyright laws, so many of his most popular works also turned up in the collections of others. During the nineteenth century, his music declined in popularity but was "rediscovered" in the twentieth century, serving as source material for composers such as William Schuman in his orchestral *New England Triptych*.

Billings Symphony Orchestra. Established in 1950 in Billings, Montana, and adding a symphony chorale in 1955, the orchestra's current music director is **Anne Harrigan**. Past music directors include Robert Staffason (1950–1955), George Perkins (1955–1984), and its first full-time music director, Uri Barnea (1984–2004).

bimeter. The simultaneous use of two different meters. Examples: *String Quartet No. 3* by Béla Bartók, *Kammermusik No. 2* by Paul Hindemith.

bimodality. The simultaneous use of two modes. Example: Samuel Adler's *Capriccio for Piano* as cited in Leon Dallin, *Techniques of Twentieth Century Composition*, 2nd ed. (Dubuque, IA: William C. Brown, Dubuque, 1971). See **church modes**, **bibliography**.

Bindebogen. (Ger.) **Slur**, a music notation sign that connects two or more notes. Also *Bindung*. (Fr. *liaison*, It. *legatura*, Sp. *ligatura*.)

binden. (Ger.) To tie or **slur** two or more notes together. (Fr. *lier*, It. *legare*, Sp. *ligar*.)

Birmingham Symphony Orchestra. See **City of Birmingham Symphony Orchestra**.

Bis! (Fr., It., Sp.) An expression of approval cried out by the audience (mostly in Europe) when they want a performer to play an **encore**. Also (in French) ***encore!*** (Ger. *noch einmal! Zugabe!*)

bisbigliando. (It., Sp.) In harp playing, a light, rapid back-and-forth motion of the fingers creating a tremolo out of the notes of a chord; whispering. (Fr. *tremolo [harpe]*, Ger. *tremolo [Harfe]*.)

bischero. (It.) A tuning peg of a string instrument. (Fr. *cheville*; Ger. *Wirbel*; It. *bischero, pirolo*; Sp. *clavija*.)

biscroma. (It.) Thirty-second note, demisemiquaver (British usage). (Fr. *triple croche*, Ger. *Zweiunddreißigstel*, Sp. *fusa*.) See **rhythmic terms**.

BIS Records. A Swedish record company founded in 1973 by Robert von Bahr that focuses on classical music from early to contemporary periods.

bissig. (Ger.) Biting. A character word used to evoke a particular style of playing. Also *spitzig.* (Fr. *mordant*; It. *mordace, mordent*; Sp. *mordaz.*)

bis, zu. (Ger.) Until. Often used in phrases that appear in music and are heard in rehearsal. Also *zu.* (Fr. *jusque*; It. *sin, sino*; Sp. *hasta.*) Examples: *bis zum Ende*, to the end; *[accel.] bis zum Schluss*, [accel.] until the end, from **Pierrot Lunaire** by **Arnold Schoenberg**. (Fr. *à la fin*, It. *al fine*, Sp. *hasta el final.*)

bitonality. The simultaneous use of two keys, sometimes called *dual modality.* Examples: György Ligeti's *Etudes for Piano*, Béla Bartók's *Duos for Two Violins*, and Charles Ives's *67th Psalm for Chorus.*

blanca. (Sp.) Half note. (Fr. *blanche*; Ger. *Halbe*; It. *metà, minima.*) See **appendix 7: "Rhythmic Terms and Their Translations."**

blanche. (Fr.) Half note. (Ger. *Halbe*; It. *metà, minima*; Sp. *blanca.*) See **appendix 7: "Rhythmic Terms and Their Translations."**

Blasinstrumente. (Ger.) Wind instruments. (Fr. *instruments à vent, les bois*; Ger. *Blasinstrumente*; It. *strumenti a fiato, i legni*; Sp. *instrumentos de viento.*) See **appendix 3: "Instrument Names and Their Translations."**

Blatt. (Ger.) A sheet, leaf, or page of music. Also *Seite.* (Fr. *page, feuille*; It. *pagina, foglia*; Sp. *página, folio.*)

Blatter, Alfred. American composer and theorist. Blatter is the author of *Instrumentation and Orchestration* and *Revisiting Music Theory: A Guide to the Practice.* Known for his work in computer and electronic music, psychoacoustics, musical theater, and the music of **Harry Partch**, Blatter has been on the faculty of the **Curtis School of Music** since 1989.

Blechinstrumente. (Ger.) Brass instruments. (Fr. *les cuivres*; It. *strumenti a fiato di ottone, gli ottoni*; Sp. *instrumentos de metal.*)

Blechinstrumente. (Ger.) Instruments made out of brass; the section of the **orchestra** or **band** made up of brass instruments. (Fr. *cuivres*; It. *ottoni*; Sp. *instrumentos de metal, metals.*)

bleiben. (Ger.) To stay, remain. Seen and heard regularly as a part of directive phrases. Example: *im Tempo bleiben*, to stay in the same tempo. (Fr. *rester*; It. *restare, rimanere*; Sp. *permanecer.*)

block chords. Complex or dense chords that move mostly in parallel motion. Examples: Claude Debussy's "Nu-ages" from *Nocturnes* and *La cathédrale engloutie* for piano solo.

Blomstedt, Herbert. (b. 1927.) Swedish conductor. Born in Springfield, Massachusetts, when Blomstedt was two years old his family returned to their native Sweden. He was the music director of the **San Francisco Symphony Orchestra** (1985–1995) and the principal conductor of the **North German Radio Symphony** (1996–1998) and the **Leipzig Gewandaus Orchestra** (1998–2005). Blomstedt taught a summer course for young conductors at Loma Linda University in California for several years. Sought after as a guest conductor, he is known for always **conducting from memory**. Blomstedt has made a reputation for performances of German and Austrian composers and the Scandinavian composers Edvard Grieg, Carl Nielsen, Franz Berwald, and Jean Sibelius.

blue note. In jazz, a pitch of uncertain intonation; the third, fifth, or seventh notes of the scale, commonly flattened or sharpened to create a blues quality. See **blues scale**.

blues scale. A scale common to jazz. Example, spelled from low to high: C D E-flat E F F-sharp G A B-flat. See Fink, Robert, and Robert Ricci. *Twentieth Century Music: A Dictionary of Terms.* New York: Macmillan, 1975.

Blumlein, Alan Dower. (1903–1942.) Important British electronic engineer known for many inventions in the areas of telecommunications, radar, television, and especially sound recording. In 1931, Blumlein revolutionized recorded music with his invention of stereophonic sound, referring to it as "binaural sound." He held 128 patents in his lifetime.

Blu-ray disc (BD). A digital optical data storage format disc that was designed to improve upon DVD technology. The same size as DVDs and CDs, conventional Blu-ray discs contain 25 GB per layer. Dual-layer discs, with 50 GB per layer, are the current industry standard for feature-length videos. Triple- and quadruple-layer discs are also available. The Blu-ray disc is also associated with multimedia formats. Developed by the Blu-ray Disc Association and released by **Sony** in competition with Toshiba's HD DVD format in 2000, Toshiba accepted the superiority of Blu-ray technology in 2008 and released its own Blu-ray disc player in 2009. The storage capacity of the disc continues to increase exponentially.

BMI. Abbreviation for **Broadcast Music, Inc.**

boca. (Sp.) Mouth. Seen used in combination with various phrases and directives. See ***boca cerrada***. (Fr. *bouche*, Ger. *Mund*, It. *bocca.*)

boca cerrada. (Sp.) Humming, lit. "with the mouth closed." (Fr. *à bouche fermée*, Ger. *summen*, It. *a bocca chiusa.*)

bocal. The curved metal tube that connects the **double reed** of the **bassoon** to the body of the instrument.

bocca. (It.) Mouth. Seen used in combination with various phrases and directives. See *bocca chiusa, a.* (Fr. *bouche*, Ger. *Mund*, Sp. *boca.*)

bocca chiusa, a. (It.) Humming, lit. "with the mouth closed." (Fr. *à bouche fermée*, Ger. *summen*, Sp. *boca cerrada.*)

bocchino. (It.) Mouthpiece, as used with brass and wind instruments. (Fr. *embouchure*, Ger. *Mundstück*, Sp. *embocadura.*)

Bodansky, Artur. (1877–1939.) Austrian-born conductor who immigrated to the United States and conducted the German repertory at the **Metropolitan Opera** from 1915 to 1939. He was known for widely fluctuating tempi, some critics perceived them as too fast and others as too slow.

body language. Expressive elements communicated silently through posture, physical position, hand position, and facial expression to reflect the music. See **conducting technique**.

Boehm, Theobald. (1794–1881.) German flutist, composer, and instrument developer. While known as one of the greatest flutists of his day, Boehm is primarily remembered for the significant improvements he made to the flute that were then adapted to the oboe, clarinet, and bassoon. Self-taught as a child, he was appointed as a flutist in the Munich court orchestra in 1818 and established his first flute factory in 1828. In 1829, he received a patent for a conical-bore wooden flute. While on a concert tour in London, he heard a performance on an instrument that had distinctly larger holes capable of generating a much larger sound. Acknowledging that his own sound didn't measure up, he set about a redesign of his own flute's key mechanism. The new conical-bore flute, which was introduced in 1832, had tone holes that were placed to improve the tuning in addition to a system of interlocking keys with ring touch pieces that allowed the performer to open or close all of its fourteen holes. While awarded a silver prize in 1834 and 1835, it didn't garner much attention. Boehm promoted it but also continued to work on various improvements. In 1839, he sold his workshop and worked for several years in the steel industry studying various metals. From 1846 to 1847 he focused on the study of acoustics, and when he was ready, he opened a new workshop. There he produced his second-model

flute. This one was made of metal with a cylindrical bore, fifteen holes, twenty-three levers, and keys of a size and placement determined by acoustic principles. Made with his innovative 1832 key mechanism, Boehm's new flute became known for its strength, purity, and uniformity of tone. Boehm's writings include *Die Flöte und das Flötenspiel* (Munich, 1871; translated into English, 1922.) A critical edition of his complete works for flute was published by the Theobald-Böhm-Archiv (Munich) in 2010.

Bogen. (Ger.) Bow, as for a string instrument. (Fr. *archet*; It. *arco, archetto*; Sp. *arco.*) Examples: *Bogen wechseln*, change bows; *auf jede Note einen ganzen Bogen*, use the whole bow for every note, both from *Das Lied von der Erde* by **Gustav Mahler**.

Bogenspitze, mit der. (Ger.) An indication for string players to play "with the tip of the bow." (Fr. *avec la pointe de l'archet*, It. *alla punta d'arco*, Sp. *con la punta.*)

Bogenstrich. (Ger.) The bow stroke, bowing. Also *Strichart, Bogenführung.* (Fr. *coup d'archet*; It. *arcata, colpo d'arco*; Sp. *golpe de arco.*)

Böhm, Karl. (1894–1981.) Austrian conductor. Böhm read law at the University of Graz as a backup plan to music, as suggested by his father, who was an amateur musician and friend of the conductor **Hans Richter**, while simultaneously studying piano at the Graz Conservatory. From 1913 to 1914 he enrolled at the **Vienna Conservatory** and studied composition and theory with Eusebius Mandyczewski and music history with Guido Adler. After service in the Austrian army in World War I, Böhm completed his doctor of law degree (1919). He made his operatic conducting debut in 1917 while working as a rehearsal pianist and prompter at the Graz Opera. He was appointed chief conductor there in 1920. The same year, conductor **Karl Muck** attended a performance Böhm led of **Richard Wagner**'s *Lohengrin*. Muck had a great influence on the young conductor and soon recommended him to **Bruno Walter** at the **Munich Opera**, where he served as assistant from 1921 to 1927. Böhm was the music director in Darmstadt (1927–1931), where he conducted several contemporary operas, including Alban Berg's *Wozzeck* with Berg present at rehearsal, as well as in Hamburg (1931–1934) and Vienna (1943–1945). He served as the music director of the **Dresden Staatsoper** (1934–1943), where he conducted the premieres of **Richard Strauss**'s *Die schweigsame Frau* and *Daphne*, which Strauss dedicated to him. In this position, he led several recordings in the 78 rpm format that remain of great interest. They include Ludwig van Beethoven's *Symphony No. 9*, the *Violin Concerto*, and *Piano Concertos Nos. 3, 4*, and *5*; Johannes Brahms's Violin Concerto;

Bruckner Symphonies 4 and *5*; Richard Strauss's *Til Eulenspiegel* and *Don Juan*; and the complete act 3 of Richard Wagner's *Die Meistersinger*.

Böhm began a long association with the **Salzburg Festival** in 1938. The same year, he made his debut at the **Vienna State Opera** in a performance of *Der Rosenkavalier*. In 1942 and again from 1954 to 1956, he served as director of the opera. He continued to conduct there until 1980. Böhm made his London debut at the **Royal Opera House, Covent Garden**, in 1936 and his U.S. debut at the **Metropolitan Opera** in 1957 with a performance of Wolfgang Amdeus Mozart's *Don Giovanni*. His **Bayreuth Festival** debut came in 1962 with Wagner's *Tristan and Isolde*. Böhm maintained lifelong relationships with these opera houses and concert halls throughout a busy career.

In 1970, he received the Great Gold Medal for distinguished service to Viennese music and was named the general music director of Austria. Known as one of the finest interpreters of Mozart, Wagner, and Strauss, his conducting style has been described as economical but authoritative, tempered but expressive. While he addressed an orchestra quietly, he quickly gained their respect. He was said to achieve an enormous range of dynamics with minimal effort, and while he believed in allowing the score to speak for itself, he was demanding in terms of its details.

Böhm's recording legacy is substantial. For nearly fifty years he was a prolific recording artist, noted for his performances of Franz Schubert, **Wagner**, Anton Bruckner, **Strauss**, and Berg, but in particular of Mozart. While current performance practice has changed our expectations of Mozart's style, Böhm was known as having moved the style forward through steady tempos, clear textures, and beauty of sound.

bois. (Fr.) Woodwind instruments. Also *les bois*. See also *avec le bois*.

Boise Philharmonic. Founded in 1960 in Boise, Idaho, the seventy-member professional ensemble can trace its origins back to 1885 and the Boise City Philharmonic. The current orchestra performs fourteen classics concerts each season in addition to Casual Classics, family, and children's concerts. It also runs the Boise Philharmonic Youth Orchestra. The current music director is Robert Franz (appointed 2009). Past conductors include Jacques Brourman (1960–1966), Mathys Abas (1967–1974), Daniel Stern (1974–1986), and James Ogle (1987–2008). Boise State Public Radio broadcasts the classics concerts on KBSX 90.3 FM.

Boito, Arrigo. (1842–1928.) Italian poet, journalit, novelist, composer, and librettist. He is most famous for his librettos for Giuseppe Verdi's operas *Othello* and *Falstaff*.

Bolshoi Ballet. Founded in 1776 in Moscow and resident at the **Bolshoi Theater**, it is, along with the Mariinsky Ballet in St. Petersburg, one of the world's major ballet companies. It has been the site of numerous ballet premieres, and many of its dancers have been among the world's stars.

Bolshoi Theater. The origins of this Moscow theater date to the late eighteenth century. While the first building, known as the Petrovsky Theater, opened in 1780, it burned down in 1806. The new theater, called the Bolshoi—which means "big" in Russian and referred to the obvious size difference with its predecessor—was built between 1821 and 1824 and opened in 1825. It suffered the same fate as its earlier incarnation, burning down in 1853. A new, once again expanded theater was rapidly built and opened in 1856 in time for the coronation of Emperor Alexander II. Since that time, the theater has survived World War II bombings and Soviet era neglect. In 2002, the New Theater was added and in addition, from 2005– to 2011, the main theater was closed for a massive renovation reported to cost close to $1 billion. The Bolshoi is the major performance space in Moscow and the site of the Bolshoi Ballet and Opera companies in addition to the Bolshoi Orchestra. All three tour internationally.

Operas premiered in the theater include Pyotr Tchaikovsky's *Mazeppa*, Modest Mussorgsky's *Boris Godunov*, Mikhail Glinka's *A Life for the Tsar* and *Ruslan and Ludmilla*, Nikolai Rimsky-Korsakov's *The Maid of Pskov*, and the 1935 Moscow premiere, one year after the first performance in Leningrad in 1934, of Dmitri Shostakovich's *Lady Macbeth of the Mtsenek District*. The Bolshoi maintains a Young Artists Opera Program for the cultivation of future talent. Conductor **Turgan Sokhiev** was appointed music director in 2014.

bomba de afinación. (Sp.) Tuning slide, as used with a trombone. (Fr. *coulisse*, Ger. *Zug*, It. *pompa movile a coulisse*.)

bombardino. (It., Sp.) Euphonium. (Fr. *euphonium*, Ger. *Baritonhorn*.) See **appendix 3: "Instrument Names and Their Translations."**

bombo. (Sp.) The **bass drum**. (Fr. *grosse caisse*; Ger. *Grosse Trommel*; It. *gran cassa, gran tamburo*.) See **appendix 4: "Percussion Instruments and Their Translations."**

Bond, Victoria Ellen. (b. 1945.) American conductor and composer. The first woman to be awarded the doctorate in orchestral conducting from the **Juilliard School**, Bond was an **Exxon/Arts Endowment** conductor with the **Pittsburgh Symphony** and later the music director of the Roanoke Symphony Orchestra and artistic director for the Virginia Opera, the Harrisburg Opera, and the New Amsterdam Symphony. She conducted the premiere of her work *Ringing* with the **Houston Symphony** and runs a series of concerts in New York called Cutting Edge Concerts. She wrote an opera, *Mrs. President*, about Victoria Woodhall, the first woman to run for president, and is currently working on another about Clara Schumann, virtuoso pianist, wife of composer Robert Schumann, and friend to Johannes Brahms.

bongos. Single-headed Latin American drums that come in attached pairs with two sizes of drums. They are usually played by hand. See **appendix 4: "Percussion Instruments and Their Translations."**

Book of Changes, The. See ***I Ching***, **Chance Music**.

Boston Pops Orchestra. Established in 1885 in order to create a second identity for the **Boston Symphony Orchestra (BSO)**. The Pops orchestra is mostly made up of musicians from the **BSO**, though generally not the first-chair players, and performs popular repertoire at several times during the year, often when the BSO is on vacation. Among its most influential music directors were **Arthur Fiedler** (1930–1979) and John Williams (1980–1995). The current music director is **Keith Lockhart**, who was appointed in 1995. The Boston Pops Orchestra has recorded widely.

Boston Symphony Orchestra (BSO). Established in 1881 under the guidance of businessman and philanthropist Henry Lee Higginson. The first music director was Sir George Henschel (1881–1884). He was followed by Wihlem Gericke (1884–1889 and 1898–1905), **Arthur Nikisch** (1889–1993), Emil Paur (1893–1898), **Karl Muck** (1906–1908 and 1912–1918), Max Fiedler (1908–1912), Henri Rabaud (1918–1919), **Pierre Monteux** (1919–1924), **Serge Koussivitzky** (1924–1949), **Charles Munch** (1949–1962), **Erich Leinsdorf** (1962–1969), **William Steinberg** (1969–1972), **Seiji Ozawa** (1973–2002), and **James Levine** (2004–2011). The current music director is Andriss Nelsens. The initial years were known for the German influence, but with the appointment of Rabaud, the orchestra became known as an orchestra in the French tradition. The **Koussevitsky** years were important in the founding of the **Tanglewood Music Center** as the BSO's summer home.

Boston University School of Music. Founded in 1872, the school was the first degree-granting music program in the United States. In the forefront of online learning, the school offers music education master's and doctoral degrees entirely on the Internet. The school has a close connection with the **Boston Symphony Orchestra**, with thirty symphony members serving as faculty. The **Boston University** School of Music awarded one of the first DMA degrees in 1955. See **doctor of musical arts**.

Boston University Tanglewood Institute (BUTI). A summer program where high school students study at the Tanglewood Institute under the guidance of members of the **Boston Symphony Orchestra**. It is run by **Boston University** faculty and administration.

Boston Woman's Symphony Orchestra. Active from 1926 to 1930 and conducted by **Ethel Leginska**, the orchestra made two tours of the eastern United States in 1928 and 1929. The all-woman orchestra and its conductor had a great impact on future women musicians. They received much positive press while touring with substantial repertoire that included Ludwig van Beethoven's *Symphony No. 5*, **Richard Wagner**'s *Prelude to Die Meistersinger*, Franz Liszt's *Hungarian Fantasy* and *Les Preludes*, and more. See Bowers, Jane, and Judith Tick, eds. *Women Making Music: The Western Art Tradition, 1150–1950.* Urbana: University of Illinois Press, 1986.

bouche. (Fr.) Mouth. (Ger. *Mund*, It. *bocca*, Sp. *boca*.) Example: *bouchez ouvertes*, mouths open, a direction to the choir to sing with open mouths after a long passage of humming, from *Daphnis et Chloé* by Maurice Ravel. Also *bouches fermées*, mouths closed (from the same score).

bouché. (Fr.) **Stopped**. Also ***bouchez***. (Ger. *gestopft*, *gedeckt*; It. *chiuso*, *tappato*; Sp. *cubierto*, *tapado*.)

bouche fermée, à. (Fr.) With the mouth closed, humming. (Ger. *summen*, It. *a bocca chiusa*, Sp. *boca cerrada*.)

bouchés, sans sourdines. (Fr.) **Stopped**, without mute. Appears in the horn parts of the *Rapsodie Espagnole* by Maurice Ravel. See ***bouché***.

bouchez. (Fr.) Stop. The directive to stop a note, as played by a horn player. Also ***bouché***, *bouchés*. See also **stopped**.

Boulanger, Nadia Juliette. (1887–1979.) Influential French teacher, composer, and conductor. One of the first professional women conductors, Boulanger appeared with the **Boston Symphony Orchestra**, **New York Philharmonic**, **Philadelphia Orchestra**, the **BBC Symphony**, and the **London Philharmonic**. She was a founding member of the **American Conservatory at Fontainebleau** in 1921 and became its director in 1948. She had her greatest influence as a teacher, both at the conservatory and later in her life at home, where she continued to teach and lead master classes until her death. Among the Americans she taught were **Leonard Bernstein**, Elliott Carter, **Aaron Copland**, David Diamond, Roy Harris, and Virgil Thomson. She often visited the United States, teaching at Wellesley College, Radcliffe College,

Harvard University, the Peabody Conservatory, and the **Juilliard School**. She was a great promoter of contemporary music, especially that of her sister, Lili, who had died very young. Among the premieres she conducted was Igor Stravinsky's *Dumbarton Oaks*. In 1977, an excellent video was made about her life and work called *Mademoiselle*. It was directed by Bruno Monsaingeon.

Nadia Boulanger. *Courtesy Photofest.*

Boulez, Pierre. (b. 1925.) French conductor and composer. Boulez may be one of the rare musicians who has been equally influential as a composer and conductor. As a young man, he was a radical, writing provocative articles such as one under the title "Schoenberg Is Dead." He promoted the total serialization of music to include pitches, timbre, durations, and dynamics. He also came to use **aleatoric** procedures and **electronic music** in his compositions. As a kind of impresario and conductor of new music, he had a great impact at the **Darmstadt** and **Donaueschingen Festivals**, the **Domaine Musical** series of composers' concerts, and later when he founded **IRCAM** (Institut de Recherche et Coordination Acoustique/Musique) and its associated **Ensemble InterContemporain**. In these settings, he conducted his own works and many premieres of the music of other contemporaries. He served as the music advisor of the **Cleveland Symphony** (1971–1972), chief conductor of the **BBC Symphony** (1971–1975), music director of the **New York Philharmonic** (1971–1977), and he continues in the position of conductor emeritus of the **Chicago Symphony Orchestra**. In New York, he initiated a successful series of so-called **Rug Concerts** designed to bring in younger listeners. While Boulez has not produced many new compositions for several years, he continues with conducting projects, including a recent collaboration with the **Staatskapelle Berlin**. He never conducts with a baton and is known for conducting sets

of counter rhythms, one in each hand. See the **bibliography** for selected books by Boulez.

Boult, Sir Adrian Cedric. (1889–1983.) English conductor. Boult made the **BBC**'s orchestra, known as the "Wireless Symphony Orchestra," into a full-time ensemble in 1930 under the name **BBC Symphony Orchestra** (BBC SO) and served as its chief conductor until 1950. In that role, he introduced numerous works to the British public, including works by Béla Bartók, Alban Berg—in 1934, he conducted the first British performance of Berg's opera *Wozzeck*—**Igor Stravinsky**, **Arnold Schoenberg**, Anton Webern, and many of Britain's top composers, including Sir Arthur Bliss, **Sir Benjamin Britten**, Frederick Delius, Sir Michael Tippett, Ralph Vaughan Williams, and Sir William Walton. He also led the first performance of the *Symphonic Pieces*—excepts of Berg's opera *Lulu*, selected by the composer—which was left incomplete on the composer's death. Under his long tenure, the BBC SO became known as one of the finest ensembles in the world.

As a young conductor, he was greatly influenced by **Arthur Nikisch**, with whom he studied at the **Leipzig Conservatory** during 1912–1913. Boult not only emulated Nikisch's flexibility and nuanced gestures, he also appropriated his long baton. When he returned from his studies, he worked as a vocal coach at the **Royal Opera House, Covent Garden**, and conducted Sergei Diaghilev's **Ballets Russes**. In 1918, he led the premiere of Gustav Holst's *The Planets*. See the **bibliography** for selected books by Sir Adrian Boult.

Bournemouth Symphony Orchestra (BSO). Established in 1893, the BSO has developed a reputation as one of Britain's major orchestras. The orchestra's current principal conductor is the Ukrainian Kirill Karabits. Past principals include **Marin Alsop** (2002–2008), Yakov Kreizberg (1995–2000), **Andrew Litton** (1988–1994), Rudolf Barshai (1982–1988), Uri Segal (1980–1982), **Paavo Berglund** (1972–1979), Constantin Silvestri (1962–1969), Sir Charles Groves (1951–1961), and more. The orchestra has given several premieres and made many recordings.

bout. (Fr.) End, in this case, the point of the bow. Seen in string parts as an indication to play at the point of the bow. Example: *du bout de l'archet*, at the point of the bow, from *Nocturnes, Fêtes* by Claude Debussy.

bow. A specially shaped wooden device, sometimes called a stick, with hair (usually horsehair) drawn between both ends that is used to play a string instrument. The hair is tightened and loosened at the lower end, called the frog, by a metal screw. (Fr. *archet*; Ger. *Bogen*; It. *arco*, *archetto*; Sp. *arco*.)

bowing terms. See *à la pointe*; *a la punta d'arco*; *Abstrich*; *alla corda*; *al tallone*; *al talon*; *am Frosch*; *am Griffbrett*; *am Steg*; *an der Bogensptize*; *an der Saite*; *an der Sptize*; *Anstrich, Aufstrich*; *arcata in giú*; *arcata in su*; *archet*; *arco, archetto*; *arco*; *archi*; *arco abajo*; *arco arriba*; **at the frog**; **at the point**; *au chevalet*; *auf, auf der, auf die*; *Aufstrich, Anstrich*; *avec le bois*; *avec la pointe de l'archet*; *Bogen*; *Bogenspitze, mit der*; *Bogenstrich, Strichart, Bogenführung*; *bout*; *col legno*; *Collé*; *colpo d'archo, Arcata*; *con la punta del arco*; *con la punta d'arco*; *con la vara*; **contact point**; *corda vuota*; *corde à vide*; *coup d'archet*; *cuerda al aire*; *détaché*; **down-bow**; *en el punta*; *flautando*; *fliegendes Staccato*; **flying spiccato**; **frog**; *golpe de arco*; *grand détaché*; **hammered**; **hooked bow**; *jeté*; *lange bogen*; *lang gezogen*; *leere Saite*; **legato**; **L.H.**; *louré*; *marcado*; **marcato**; *martelé*; *martellato*; **M.B.**; *mit Bogenspitze*; *mit dem Bogen, mit dem Bogen geschlagen*; *mit dem Holtz des Bogens*; *mit der Bogenstange*; **nut**; *ondeggiando*; **nodule**; **point**; *ponticello*; *portato*; *poussé*; **ricochet**; *saltando, saltato*; *saltillo*; *sautillé*; **slurred**; *sobre el batidor*; *sobre el peunte*; **spiccato**; **spring bow arpeggio**; *Springbogen*; *springend*; **staccato**; *staccato volant*; *staccato volante*; *sul ponticello*; *sul tasto, sulla tastiera*; *sur le chevalet*; *sur la touché*; *Spitze, an der*; **talon**; **tip**; *tiré, tirer, tirez*; *tout l'archet*; **tremolo**; *tout l'archet*; **U.H.**; **up-bow**; **W.B.**

boxes. The squares used in the **graphic notation** system designed to accommodate aleatoric music. Boxes are used to isolate musical fragments to be played as directed by the composer. Example: " . . . And the Mountains Rising Nowhere" by Joseph Schwantner. See **graphic notation**, **frame notation**.

brake drum. Automobile brakes in varying sizes played with drumsticks or brushes, sometimes substituted with metal plates. Example: *Connotations* by **Aaron Copland** and *Phaeton* by Christopher Rouse. See **appendix 4: "Percussion Instruments and Their Translations."**

brass mutes. Made out of metal or fiberboard, the brass mute has two main purposes. The first is to soften the sound, the second to change its character or color. Shaped like a cone with pieces of cork on the sides that help gauge the fit in the bell of the instrument, there are several mutes designed for the trumpet and the trombone but only one that is suitable for the horn and one for the tuba. The most commonly used mute is the **straight mut**e. Unless otherwise noted by the composer, it is the mute that brass players use. The metal **Harmon mute** (sometimes called the **wa-wa mute**), mostly used with the trumpet, has a stem that can be adjusted in and out to create a variety of colors. The *wa-wa* effect is achieved by covering and uncovering the outer "bowl-shaped" indentation with the palm of the hand while playing. Well

named, the **Whispa mute** creates the softest sound of any brass mute. The **Solotone mute**, similar in function to the **Harmon mute**, generates a somewhat nasal sound. The **cup mute**, most often used in jazz bands, operates by opening or closing the cup; the more closed it is, the more muffled the tone will be. The **bucket mute** creates a particularly soft, warm tone.

Horn players often mute their instrument by inserting their hand into the bell. When they do this, the pitch goes up a half step, requiring the player to transpose the written notes appropriately. The standard horn mute (a **straight mute**) is nontransposing, that is, it is manufactured so that no adjustment is necessary. The tuba, euphonium, and the Wagner tuba all have their own specially designed mutes.

brass, the. The instruments made out of brass; the section of the **orchestra** or **band** made up of brass instruments. (Fr. *cuivres*; Ger. *Blechinstrumente*; It. *ottoni*; Sp. *instrumentos de metal, metales*.)

Bratsche. (Ger.) **Viola**, a string instrument. (Fr. *alto*, It. *viola*, Sp. *viola*.)

bravissimo! (It.) Very good! Excellent! (Fr. *Trés bien!* Ger. *Sehr gut!* Sp. *Muy bien! Genial! Excelente!*)

bravo! (It.) An Italian expression meaning "well done," often called out at the end of a performance. It is used in several countries, not just Italy.

bravura. (It.) *Bravura*, virtuosity (lit. "skill, bravery"). See *bravura, con*.

bravura, con. (It.) In a virtuosic manner, with *bravura*. Sometimes heard in rehearsal to evoke an energetic, exciting style of playing.

breathe, to. (Fr. *à respirer*, Ger. *zu atmen*, It. *per respirare*, Sp. *para respirar*.) Examples: Breathe with me (Fr. *respire avec moi*, Ger. *atmen mit mir*, It. *respirare con me*, Sp. *respirar conmigo*); Breathe in rhythm (Fr. *respirer en rythme*, Ger. *atmen im Rhythmus*, It. *respirare ritmo*, Sp. *respirar con ritmo*); Breathe in time (Fr. *respire dans le temps*, Ger. *atmen im tempo*, Sp. *respirar en el tiempo*).

breath mark. A notation devise that indicates a breath is to be taken by the performer at a given moment in the music.

Breath mark. *Courtesy Andrew Martin Smith.*

brechen. (Ger.) To break, arpeggiate. Also ***gebrochen***, broken; ***nicht gebrochen***, not broken, as in, don't arpeggiate in a harp part.

bref. (Fr.) Concise, brief. Also *brève, court.* (Ger. *kurz*; It. *breve, corto*; Sp. *breve, corto.*)

breit. (Ger.) Broad. Example: *breiter **Auftakt**,* broader upbeat, from **Pierrot Lunaire** by **Arnold Schoenberg**. (Fr. *large*; It. *largo*; Sp. *amplio, largo.*)

breiter werden. (Ger.) Becoming slower or more drawn out. German usage seen often in scores and parts. (Fr. *en élargissant*, It. *allargando*, Sp. *allargando.*)

breiter werdend. (Ger.) Slowing down, broadening. (Fr. *en élargissant*; It. *slargando, allargando*; Sp. *moderar el tiempo.*)

Breitkopf & Härtel. Located in Leipzig, Germany, and founded in 1719 by Bernhard Christoph Breitkopf, it is the oldest music-publishing firm in the world. The Härtel name was added in 1795 when Gottfried Christoph Härtel took over the company. The firm is known for having published the influential music journal the *Allgemeine musikalishce Zeitung* in the nineteenth century and for the first complete edition of the works of Wolfgang Amadeus Mozart, the *Alte Mozart-Ausgabe* (Old Mozart Edition), now mostly supplanted by the *Neue Ausgabe* (New Edition) published by **Bärenreiter-Verlag.**

breve. A rhythmic value used internationally that is equivalent to a **double whole note** (American usage), a note that is used to last for a whole bar, especially when the bar is longer than four beats. First used in medieval music. An excellent example of contemporary usage is *Adagio for Strings* by Samuel Barber. See **appendix 7: "Rhythmic Terms and Their Translations."**

breve. (It., Sp.) Short. (Fr. *bref, court*; Ger. *kurz*; It. *corto*; Sp. *corto.*)

breve, alla. (It.) In two beats per measure; conducted in two beats per measure. (Fr. *à la blanche*, Ger. *in halben Noten.*) See ***all breve.***

Brico, Antonia. (1902–1989.) Dutch-born American conductor and pianist. Brico was the first American to graduate in conducting from the Berlin State Academy of Music (1929). She studied with **Karl Muck**, who was the principal conductor of the **Hamburg Philharmonic Orchestra.** She made her professional debut with the **Berlin Philharmonic** in 1930, was the first woman to conduct the **New York Philharmonic** (1938), and in 1939, she was invited by Jean Sibelius to conduct the Helsinki

Symphony Orchestra in a concert of his music. In 1942, she moved to Denver, Colorado, where she founded a Bach society, the Denver Businessmen's Orchestra, which was renamed the Brico Symphony Orchestra in 1968. Brico became the conductor of the Denver Community Symphony in 1948, which became the **Denver Symphony Orchestra** (now the **Colorado Symphony**). A documentary, *Antonia: A Portrait of a Woman*, was made in 1974 by her former student Judy Collins and Jill Godmilow. The documentary led to further conducting invitations.

brillant. (Fr.) With a sudden burst, bright, brilliant, brilliantly. Character expression sometimes heard in rehearsal to evoke a quality of sound and style of playing. Also *avec éclat.* (Ger. *brillant, hell*; It. *brillante, brillantemente*; Sp. *brillante.*)

brillant. (Ger.) With a sudden burst, bright, brilliant, brilliantly. Character expression sometimes heard in rehearsal to evoke a quality of sound and style of playing. Also *hell.* (Fr. *avec éclat, brillant*; It. *brillante, brillantemente*; Sp. *brillante.*)

brillante. (It.) With a sudden burst, bright, brilliant, brilliantly. Character expression sometimes heard in rehearsal to evoke a quality of sound and style of playing. Also *brillantemente.* (Fr. *avec éclat, brillant*; Ger. *brillant, hell*; Sp. *brillante.*)

brillante. (Sp.) With a sudden burst, bright, brilliant, brilliantly. Character expression sometimes heard in rehearsal to evoke a quality of sound and style of playing. (Fr. *avec éclat, brillant*; Ger. *brillant, hell*; It. *brillante, brillantemente.*)

brindisi. (It.) A drinking song. For an example, see the opera *La Traviata* by Giuseppe Verdi.

brio. (It.) With vigor, energy, full of life, excitement. Also *con brio.* (Fr. *avec verve, enlevé*; Ger. *schwungvoll*; Sp. *brío.*)

British Broadcasting Corporation (BBC). Founded in 1922 as the first national public service broadcasting corporation. The BBC broadcasts on radio, television, and now the Internet via multiple stations. Out of a total budget of £4.896 million, orchestras and other performing ensembles sponsored by the BBC cost £29.2 million. These ensembles include the **BBC Symphony Orchestra**, BBC Singers, BBC Symphony Chorus, BBC Big Band, all in London; the **BBC Scottish Symphony Orchestra** in Glasgow; the BBC Philharmonic in Manchester; the BBC Concert Orchestra in Watford; and the BBC National Orchestra of Wales in Cardiff.

Britten, Sir Benjamin. (1913–1976.) English composer, conductor, and pianist. One of the most significant British composers of the twentieth century, Britten wrote important operas such as *Peter Grimes* (1945), works for chorus and orchestra such as the *War Requiem* (1962), works for orchestra alone such as the *Sinfonia da Requiem* (1941) and *The Young Person's Guide to the Orchestra* (1945), in addition to chamber music, songs, and more. Britten was also an accomplished conductor who led many of his own works, especially in recording. In the 1950s and 1960s, he conducted recordings of his complete operas; his ballet, *The Prince of the Pagodas*; *The Spring Symphony*; and many other works. His recording of the *War Requiem*, which was made in 1963, remains in the Decca catalogue. In 2013, celebrating the one hundreth anniversary of Britten's birth, Decca released a sixty-five CD and one DVD set titled *Britten: The Complete Works*.

broad. A descriptive term used to address tempo and style of bowing and breathing. (Fr. *large*, Ger. *breit*, It. *largo*, Sp. *largo*.) See **broaden, to**; **broadening**.

Broadcast Music Incorporated (BMI). Founded in 1939, BMI is an American performing-rights organization with a mission to protect the copyrights of its members and thus the value of the music they create and publish. BMI collects license fees from businesses that use music and distributes them to songwriters, composers, and music publishers of all types.

broadening. The process of becoming slower or more drawn out, stretching the tempo. (Fr. *en élargissant*, Ger. *breiter werden*, It. *allargando*, Sp. *allargando*.)

broaden, to. As in to broaden the tempo or style of playing with the bow and the breath. (Fr. *élargir*, Ger. *erweitern*, It. *allargare*, Sp. *alargar*.)

Brown, Beatrice. Conductor and violist. Born in England, Brown studied at Hunter College, where she conducted the orchestra, and studied conducting with **Serge Koussevitsky** at the **Tanglewood Institute**. As a young musician, Brown was first violist in **Leopold Stokowski**'s American Symphony Orchestra. She was awarded a **Fulbright** and Rockefeller grant in order to pursue her work in conducting, working for six years with **Herman Scherchen** in Europe. She served as the music director of the Scranton Symphony (1962–1971) and founded the Ridgefield Symphony in 1964.

Brown, Elaine. (1910–1997.) American choral conductor and founder of the one-hundred-voice amateur Singing City Choir of Philadelphia, which recorded with the **Philadelphia Orchestra**. She was only the second woman to conduct the **Philadelphia Orchestra** in a performance of **Igor Stravinsky**'s *Symphony of Psalms*. Brown taught at Temple University from 1945 to 1956 and again beginning in 1975.

Bruck, Charles. (1911–1995.) French conductor and pedagogue of Romanian birth, student of **Nadia Boulanger** and **Pierre Monteux**. Bruck succeeded Monteux as the director of the **Monteux School**, Hancock, Maine, in 1970 and taught there until his death. He had a great impact on the many young conductors and orchestral musicians who participated in the school, which ran every summer. As a conductor, he left an important legacy of premieres and performances of an enormous number of contemporary works. His flawless baton technique and notable analytical abilities made him a convincing advocate for the new music he promoted.

brummen. (Ger.) To hum. Also *Brummstime.* (Fr. *chantonner*; It. *canticchiare*; Sp. *cantar con la boca cerrada*; *boca chiusa*.)

Brunelle, Phillip. (b. 1943.) American choral conductor. Bruenelle was the founding artistic director of VocalEssence and the conductor of the Plymouth Music Series Chorus and Orchestra in Minneapolis. VocalEssence and the VocalEssence Ensemble Singers have commissioned and premiered dozens of new pieces. They have received six **ASCAP**/Chorus America Awards for the adventurous programming of new music.

brusco. (It., Sp.) Abrupt, harsh, brusque. A character word used to evoke a particular style of playing. (Fr. *brusque*; Ger. *barsch*, *brüsk*.) Also *bruscamente*, abruptly.

brusque. (Fr.) Abrupt, harsh, brusque. A character word used to evoke a particular style of playing. (It. *brusco*; Ger. *barsch*, *brüsk*; Sp. *brusco*.) Also *brusquement*, abruptly.

Brusilow, Anshel. (b. 1928.) American conductor, violinist, and pedagogue. Brusilow served as the concertmaster of the **Cleveland Orchestra** (four years) and the **Philadelphia Orchestra** (seven years). In 1970, he was appointed as the executive director and conductor of the **Dallas Symphony**. He was the director of orchestral studies and professor of conducting at the University of North Texas, Denton, Texas, from 1973 to 1982 and again from 1989 to 2008. From 1982 to 1989 he was the head of the orchestra program at Southern Methodist University.

Brussels Conservatory of Music. See **Royal Brussels Conservatory of Music**.

BSO on the Go. A **Baltimore Symphony Orchestra outreach program** to bring a BSO musician to your school or community. The program offers performances by individuals and small ensembles who visit schools and other settings within the community and address topics of conversation including musical careers, music history, and many aspects of musical education, such as learning the families of instruments. They do anything from single to multiday residencies and present to students and adults.

bucket mute. See **brass mutes**.

Budapest Philharmonic Orchestra. Hungary's oldest orchestra, the ensemble gave its first concert in 1853 under conductor Ferenc Erkel, who served as chief conductor until 1871. He was followed by his son Sándor Erkel (1875–1900), István Kerner (1900–1918), Ernö Dohnányi (1981–1960), János Ferencsik (1960–1967), András Kórodi (1967–1986), Erich Gergel (1989–1994), and Rico Saccani (1997–2005). The current conductor is György Györiványi-Ráth, appointed in 2011. The Budapest Philharmonic has given over one hundred premieres including Johannes Brahms's *Piano Concerto No. 1* with the composer at the piano in 1881, **Gustav Mahler**'s *Symphony No. 1* in 1889, and works by many other renowned composers of the nineteenth and twentieth centuries. The orchestra's musicians are from the Hungarian State Opera and National Theater.

Budapest Philharmonic Society. Established to oversee the **Budapest Philharmonic Orchestra**, the National Theater, and later the Hungarian State Opera House, where the orchestra often performs. The first concert was given in 1853 under the baton of conductor Ferenc Erkel.

Buena suerte! (Sp.) An expression used before a concert or performance to mean "Good Luck!" (Fr. *Trois fois merde!* Ger. *Toi, toi, toi! Hals und Beinbruch!* It. *In bocca al lupo!*)

bueno. (Sp.) A term heard often in rehearsal meaning "good," "well done." (Fr. *bien*; Ger. *gut, gut gemacht*; It. *ben, bene*.)

Buffalo Philharmonic Orchestra. Established in 1934 in Buffalo, New York. The orchestra's current music director is **JoAnn Falletta** (appointed in 1999). Past music directors include Lajos Shuk (1935–1946), Franco Auturi (1936–1945), **William Steinberg** (1945–1952), **Josef Krips** (1954–1963), Lukas Foss (1963–1971), **Michael Tilson Thomas** (1971–1979), **Julius Rudel** (1979–1985), **Semyon Bychkov** (1985–1989), and Maximiano Valdes (1989–1998). Under Falletta, the orchestra has released several CDs on the **Naxos label**. The BPO has many outreach initiatives for young people and adults, such as the Symphony Scholars program for teens.

Bügelhorn. (Ger.) The German equivalent of the **flugelhorn**. Also *Flügelhorn*. (Fr. *bugle à pistons*, It. *flicorno*, Sp. *flicorno*.)

bugle à pistons. (Fr.) The French equivalent of the **flugelhorn**. (Ger. *Bügelhorn, Flügelhorn*; It. *flicorno*; Sp. *flicorno*.)

Bühne. (Ger.) The stage, of an opera house for example. Also *Szene*. (Fr. *scène, planches*; It. *scena, palcoscenico*; Sp. *escena, etapa*.)

Bühnenmusik. (Ger.) Incidental music or stage music for a play or music played on stage in an opera. (Fr. *musique, de scène*; It. *musica di scena*; Sp. *música de escena*.)

buio. (It.) Dark. A term used to evoke a certain tone or character in the playing. (Fr. *sombre*, Ger. *dunkel*, Sp. *tenebroso*.)

Bülow, Hans von. (1830–1894.) Commonly known as a "Wagnerian," the German conductor Bülow also specialized in the works of Giacomo Meyerbeer, Mikhail Glinka, François-Adrien Boieldieu, Gaspare Spontini, and Daniel Auber and was praised for his interpretations of Wolfgang Amadeus Mozart, Ludwig van Beethoven. He was an active promoter of the music of Johannes Brahms. A student of Franz Liszt (he married his daughter Cosima, who eventually left him and married **Richard Wagner**), Bülow did much to modernize certain instruments of the orchestra by introducing the pedal timpani, the five-string bass, and Hermann Ritter's alto viola, a larger-sized instrument intended for use in works of Richard Wagner. One of the most influential conductors of his day, he conducted the Boston premiere of Pyotr Tchaikovsky's *Piano Concerto No. 1* in 1875 and conducted in Hanover (1878–1880) and Meiningen (1880–1885), where he is said to have raised the level of the orchestra to one of world class. His performances have been described as intellectually clear and well defined. Through his artistry as both conductor and pianist, he expanded the repertoire of his time, bringing many works into the standard repertory.

Burgin, Richard. (1892–1981.) Polish-born American violinist and conductor. Burgin served as the concertmaster of the **Boston Symphony Orchestra** (BSO) for forty-two years. As the associate conductor, he lead the BSO in over three hundred concerts, with seven world premieres and also many Boston premieres included. He was the head of the string department at the **New England Conservatory of Music** and also taught at **Boston University's School of Music**. An influential performer and pedagogue, he once said, "There are no bad bowings, only poor execution."

Burgos, Rafael Frühbeck de. (1933–2014.) Spanish conductor. Burgos served as the music director of the **Spanish National Orchestra** (1962–1978), **Montreal Symphony Orchestra** (1975–1976), **Rundfunkorchestrer Berlin**, and **Deutsche Oper Berlin** (1992–1997); as the principal conductor of the RAI National Symphony Orchestra, France (2001–2007); and as the music director of the Dresden Philharmonic (2004–2011) and **Danish National Radio Symphony Orchestra** (2012–2014).

burlesco. (It.) Jesting, light. A character word sometimes seen in scores and parts. (Fr. *de façon burlesque*; Ger. *scherzhaft*; Sp. *burlón, en broma*.)

burlón. (Sp.) Jesting, light. A character word sometimes seen in scores and parts. Also *en broma*. (Fr. *de façon burlesque*, Ger. *scherzhaft*, It. *burlesco*.)

BWV. See **Bach Werkverzeichnis, thematic catalogue**.

Bychkov, Semyon. (b. 1952.) Born in what was then Leningrad to Jewish parents, Bychkov immigrated to the United States in 1974 in order to study at the Mannes College of Music in New York. He served as the music director of Michigan's **Grand Rapids Symphony** (1980–1985), the **Buffalo Philharmonic Orchestra** (1985–1989), the **Orchestre de Paris** (1989–1998), and became the principal guest conductor of his hometown **Saint Petersburg Philharmonic Orchestra** in 1990. He was the chief conductor of the **WDR Symphony Orchestra** in Cologne, Germany (1997–2010), and made his debut at the **Royal Opera House, Covent Garden**, in 2003 with **Richard Strauss**'s *Elektra*. He has returned to conduct at the Royal Opera House many times and had his debut at the Metropolitan Opera in 2004. His recordings include works of Richard Strauss with the **WDR Symphony Orchestra**, **Richard Wagner**'s *Lohengrin*, Giuseppe Verdi's *Requiem*, and much more. He has guest conducted nearly all of the leading orchestras of the world, including the **Berlin** and **New York Philharmonic Orchestras** and the **Royal Concertgebouw Orchestra**. He currently holds the **Otto Klemperer** Chair in Conducting at the **Royal Academy of Music** in London.

C. The name of the first note of the C major scale, also called C in German, *Ut* in French, and *Do* in Italian. See **appendix 5: "Pitch Names and Their Translations into French, German, and Italian."**

Cabrillo Festival of Contemporary Music. A two-week summer festival in Santa Cruz, California. Founded in 1963 by the American composer Lou Harrison, the festival has hosted composers such as John Adams, John Cage, Carlos Chávez, **John Corigliano**, Michael Daugherty, and more. Under the direction of conductor **Marin Alsop** since 1992, the festival has also offered conductor/composer training workshops.

cada. (Sp.) Each. (Fr. *chaque*, Ger. *jeder*, It. *ogni*.)

cada vez. (Sp.) Every time. A directive heard in rehearsal. (Fr. *toutes les fois, à chaque fois que*; Ger. *jedesmal*; It. *ogni volta*.) See also *todas las veces*.

cadence. (Fr.) See *cadenza*. (Ger. *Kadenz*, It. *cadenza*, Sp. *candencia*.)

cadenza. (It.) An interlude in a concerto for the soloist of either improvised or previously composed music that allows the performer to display a level of virtuosity on their own. The cadenza usually occurs toward the end of the first and/or last movement when the music arrives harmonically on the dominant and will cadence immediately on the tonic, moving into either a coda or other concluding passage. (Fr. *cadence*, Ger. *Kadenz*, Sp. *cadencia*.)

caesura. (It.) A pause marked with an apostrophe or done as a matter of interpretation that allows a breath between phrases or sections in music. (Fr. *césure*, Ger. *Zäsur*, Sp. *cesura*.)

Caesura. *Courtesy Andrew Martin Smith.*

Cairo Symphony Orchestra. Founded in 1959 by Franz Litschauer, its first music director and conductor. Since 1990, the orchestra has been resident in the Cairo Opera House, though it gives only symphony concerts. Egyptian conductors Ahmed Ebeid and Youssef Elsisi led the orchestra after Litschauer. Other past conductors have included Sergio Càrdenas (2003–2004), Christoph Mueller (2004–2005), Steven Lloyd (2005–2007), Andreas Spörri (2007–2008), and Marcello Mottadell (2008–2011). The current music director, Jirí Petrdlík, was appointed in 2012. The Cairo Symphony Orchestra has hosted many international soloists and conductors, including Israeli-Argentinean **Daniel Barenboim**, who led Ludwig van Beethoven's Symphony No. 5 in 2009. The orchestra has also toured Europe and China.

caja. (Sp.) A two-headed drum used in Spain and Latin America. See also **appendix 4: "Percussion Instruments and Their Translations."**

calamante. (Sp.) Soothing, calming; a character word sometimes used in rehearsal to evoke a particular mood or quality of playing. (Fr. *en calmant*, Ger. *beruhigend*, It. *calmando*.)

calando. (It.) Waning, lowering. Also *calante*. (Fr. *en faisant descendre, en descendant*; Ger. *abnehmend*; Sp. *disminuyendo*.)

calderón. (Sp.) **Fermata**, pause. Also *corona*. (Fr. *point d'arrêt*; Ger. *Haltung, Fermate*; It. *fermata, corona*.)

caldo. (It.) Warm; a character word often used in rehearsal to evoke a certain sound quality. (Fr. *chaud*, Ger. *warm*, Sp. *cálido*.) See also *calore, con*.

Caldwell, Sarah. (1924–2006.) Important American opera conductor and director, as well as child prodigy violinist. Caldwell was the assistant to **Boris Goldovsky** for eleven years. She became head of the Boston University opera workshop (1952) and founded the Boston Opera

Group (later known as the Opera Company of Boston) in 1957. She was the first woman to conduct at the **Metropolitan Opera**. Caldwell conducted and staged operas for the **New York City Opera** and also conducted the **New York Philharmonic**, **Pittsburgh Symphony**, **Rochester Philharmonic**, **St. Paul Chamber Orchestra**, and **Boston Symphony Orchestra**.

calidez, con. (Sp.) With warmth or feeling; a character word often heard in rehearsal to describe the tone or sound. (Fr. *avec chaleur*, Ger. *mit Wärme*, It. *con calore*.)

calmando. (It.) Soothing, calming, becoming quiet; a character word sometimes heard in rehearsal to evoke a certain quality in the playing. Also *calmandosi, calmato*. (Fr. *en calmant*, Ger. *beruhigend*, Sp. *calamante*.)

calmant, en. (Fr.) Soothing, calming, becoming quiet; a character word sometimes heard in rehearsal to evoke a certain quality in the playing. (Ger. *beruhigend*, It. *calmando*, Sp. *calamante*.)

calmar. (Sp.) To calm. (Fr. *calmer*, Ger. *beruhigen*, It. *calmare*.)

calmare. (It.) To calm. (Fr. *calmer*, Ger. *beruhigen*, Sp. *calmar*.)

calme. (Fr.) Calm, tranquil, quiet; a character word seen in the works of Claude Debussy and others. Also *calmement*. (Ger. *ruhig*; It. *calmo, quieto*; Sp. *calmo*.)

calmer. (Fr.) To calm. (Ger. *beruhigen*, It. *calmare*, Sp. *calmar*.)

calore, con. (It.) With warmth, feeling; a character word often heard in rehearsal to describe the tone or sound. Also *caloroso*. (Fr. *avec la chaleur*, Ger. *mit Wärme*, Sp. *con calidez*.)

cambiar. (Sp.) To change, as when a player is asked to change from one instrument to another in the course of a piece or movement. See **Taktwechsel**. (Fr. *changer*, Ger. *wechseln*, It. *cambiare*.)

cambiare. (It.) To Change, as when a player is asked to change from one instrument to another in the course of a piece or movement. (Fr. *changer*, Ger. *wechseln*, Sp. *cambiar*.) See also **Taktwechsel**.

Cambreling, Sylvain (b. 1948). French conductor. Cambreling studied at the **Paris Conservatory** and took second prize in the **International Besançon Competition for Young Conductors** in 1974. He guest conducted at the **Ensemble Intercontemporain** at the invitation of

Pierre Boulez. He served as the music director of the Théâtre de la Monnaie, Brussel (1981–1991), was the general music director at the **Frankfurt Opera** (1993–1997), chief conductor of the **SWR Sinfonieorchester Baden-Baden und Freiburg** (1999–2011), and was appointed the music director of the Stuttgart State Opera in 2012 and **Yomiuri Nippon Symphony Orchestra**, Japan, in 2010.

caminando. (Sp.) See *cammindando*.

camisão. A Brazilian single-headed frame drum often played with a leather strap or whip. It comes in two sizes, large and small, and was used in Choros No. 6 by Heitor Villa-Lobos See also **appendix 4: "Percussion Instruments and Their Translations."**

caña. (Sp.) Reed, as used by wind instruments. (Fr. *anche*, Ger. *Rohrblatt*, It. *ancia*.) See also *doble caña*.

Canadian Broadcast Corporation Radio Orchestra (CBC). Established in 1938, the CBC performed and recorded until 2008. It was the longest surviving **radio orchestra** in North America.

Canadian Opera Company (COC). Established in 1950 in Toronto as the Royal Conservatory Opera Company by Nicholas Goldschmidt and Herman Geiger-Torel, the company became the Canadian Opera Company in 1977. Lofti Mansouri, the general director of the **San Francisco Opera** from 1988 to 2001, served as the general director from 1976 to 1988, followed by Brian Dickie (1988–1993). In 1983, the COC became the first opera company to offer surtitles at their productions. Richard Bradshaw was the chief conductor beginning in 1989, becoming the general director in 1998 and serving until his death in 2007. During his tenure, he raised funding for the new Four Seasons Centre, the company's current home in downtown Toronto. The current music director is Johannes Debus, and the current general director is Alexander Neef. The COC presents six main stage operas per season in addition to productions in its Ensemble Studio and numerous outreach programs for schools, youth, and adults. It publishes the magazine *Opera Canada* and offers discounted tickets to those under thirty, backstage tours, and pre-performance talks.

Canarina, John. (b. 1934.) American conductor and author. Canarina wrote *Uncle Sam's Orchestra: Memories of the Seventh Army Symphony* (1998); *Pierre Monteux, Maitre* (2003); and *The New York Philharmonic: From Bernstein to Maazel* (2010). He was the conductor of the Jacksonville (FL) Symphony Orchestra from 1962 to 1971 and the assistant conductor of the **New York Philharmonic** under **Leonard Bernstein**. He was also the conductor of the orchestra at Drake University, Des Moines, from 1971 to 2008.

canción. (Sp.) song. Also *canto*. (Fr. *chanson, chant*; Ger. *Lied, Gesang*; It. *canto*.)

canción de cuna. (Sp.) lullaby, cradlesong. (Fr. *berceuse*, Ger. *Wiegenlied*, It. *ninna nanna*.)

cantabile. (It., Sp.) in a singing style, a descriptive term often heard in rehearsal to inspire a certain quality of playing by instrumentalists. Abbreviation *cant.* (Fr. *chantant*, Ger. *gesangvoll*.)

cantando. (Sp.) singing, to sing. (Fr. *chantant*, Ger. *singend*, It. *cantando*.) See also **cantabile**.

cantando. (It.) singing. (Fr. *chantant*, Ger. *singend*, It. *cantando*.) See also **cantabile**.

cantar. (Sp.) to sing. (Fr. *chanter*, Ger. *singen*, It. *cantare*.)

cantar a primera vista. (Sp.) to sing at sight, to sight sing. (Fr. *chanter à vue*, Ger. *vom Blatt singen*, It. *cantare a prima vista*.)

cantar con la boca cerrada. (Sp.) to hum with the mouth closed. Also *boca chiusa*. (Fr. *chantonner*, Ger. *brummen*, It. *canticchiare*.)

cantare. (It.) to sing. (Fr. *chanter*, Ger. *singen*, Sp. *cantar*.)

cantare a prima vista. (It.) to sing at sight, to sight sing. (Fr. *chanter à vue*, Ger. *vom Blatt singen*, Sp. *cantar a primera vista*.)

canticchiare. (It.) to hum, with the mouth closed. (Fr. *chantonner*, Ger. *brummen*, Sp. *cantar con la boca cerrada, boca chiusa*.)

cantilena. (It.) lullaby, melodious, or in a singsong style.

canto. 1. (It., Sp.) Song. (Fr. *chanson, chant*; Ger. *Lied, Gesang*; Sp. *canción, canto*.)
  2. The principal form of division of a long poem as used in Dante's *Divine Comedy* and Ezra Pound's *The Cantos*.

canto de un pájaro. (Sp.) bird song. (Fr. *chant d'oiseau*, Ger. *Vogelstimme*.)

canzone. (It.) song. Also *canto*. (Fr. *chanson, chant*; Ger. *Lied, Gesang*; Sp. *canción, canto*.)

Capelle. (Ger.) out-of-date spelling for **Kapelle**.

Capellmeister. (Ger.) out-of-date spelling for **Kapellemeister**.

capo. (It.) the beginning, as in *da capo al fine*, play from the beginning to the end, or *da capo al segno*, from the beginning to the sign. Also part of the Abbreviation *D.C.* meaning *da capo* (lit. "head").

cappella. (It.) chapel or choral music sung without instrumental accompaniment. Also *a cappella*.

capriccioso. 1. (It.) fanciful, capricious; a character word often seen in Italian scores and parts. (Fr. *capricieux*; Ger. *kapriziös, launisch*; Sp. *capricho*.)
  2. A title for a piece in a virtuosic style.

capricho. (Sp.) fanciful, capricious. (Fr. *capricieux*; Ger. *kapriziös, launisch*; It. *capriccioso*.) See also **capriccioso**.

capricieux. (Fr.) fanciful, capricious. (Ger. *kapriziös, launisch*; It. *capriccioso*; Sp. *capricho*.) See also **capriccioso**.

caressant. (Fr.) caressingly, a directive seen in the works of Claude Debussy among others.

carezzevole. (It.) coaxing, caressing, an Italian character word used to evoke a particular quality in the playing. (Fr. *caressant, en caressant*.)

caricaturale. (It.) caricatured, exaggerated, a descriptive term used to express a particularly exaggerated character.

Carlos, Wendy. (b. 1939.) American composer and consultant to **Robert A. Moog** during the development of his synthesizer. Carlos is known for devising a method of creating electronic sounds that imitated those of the orchestra and then combining them with purely electronic sounds. This led to the hugely successful recording *Switched-On Bach* (1968), which was made on a **Moog synthesizer** and sold over one million copies. Other compositions by Carlos were used in the film *A Clockwork Orange* (1971) and *TRON* (1982). Her later projects included alternative tuning systems in combination with traditional tuning in music for *Beauty and the Beast* (1986). In 2000, she used the latest technology to create a reworking of her classic, *Switched-On Bach*.

Carnegie Hall. One of the most important concert halls in America and the world, it opened in 1891 with guest of honor Pyotr Tchaikovsky conducting his *Marche Solennelle*. Since then, virtually all of the most famous performers, soloists, ensembles, and chamber musicians have performed there. Located in New York City, Andrew Carnegie financed most of the cost—$1.1 million—at the instigation of conductor **Walter Damrosch**. William Tuthill, a cellist, was the architect. He made a study of the acoustics of European concert halls in preparation for the design and kept the materials simple and elegant in order to create an ideal acoustic. Carnegie Hall's first **Young People**'s concert was in 1891. See also **outreach programs**.

Carse, Adam. (1878–1958.) British author. Carse wrote many books of interest, including *The Orchestra in the XVIIIth Century* (1969); *18th Century Symphonies: A Short History of the Symphony in the 18th Century with Special Reference to the Works in the Two Series*; *Early Classical Symphonies and 18th Century Overtures* (republished by Hyperion Press, 1979); *The Orchestra from Beethoven to Berlioz: A History of the Orchestra in the First Half of the 19th Century, and of the Development of Orchestral Baton-Conduction* (Cambridge University Press, 1948; republished in the United States in 1976); *The School Orchestra: Organization, Training and Repertoire* (London, 1925); *Musical Wind Instruments: A History of the Wind Instruments Used in European Orchestras and Wind-Bands from the Later Middle Ages Up to the Present Time* (New York, 1975); *Musical Wind Instruments* (republished by Dover, 2002). See also the **bibliography**.

Casa Ricordi. See **Ricordi, Casa**.

casi. (Sp.) almost, nearly, as if. Also *cerano a, como, parecido a.* (Fr. *presque*; Ger. *beinahe, fast, als, ob*; It. *quasi*.) An expression used often in phrases in rehearsal. Examples: *Tocar como si fuera liviano*, play lightly; *Tocar como si fuera fácil*, play as if it were easy.

cassant. (Fr.) broken. A term that describes the manner of playing harp chords in an arpeggiated style. See **arpeggiate**.

cassette. A plastic, box-like container that holds 1/8–inch wide magnetic tape on two rolls so that it can be played forward and then run backward in order to start again, making manual threading unnecessary.

cassette recorder. A tape recorder that uses **cassette** tapes. (Fr. *cassettphone*, Ger. *Kassettenrekorder*, It. *registratori a cassetta*.) See also **reel to reel tape recorder**.

castanets. Made of two small, rounded wooden shells that are struck together. (Fr. *castagnettes*; Ger. *Kastagnetter*; It. *castagnette, nacchere*; Sp. *castañuelas*.) There are three kinds: the hand castanet that is played in pairs, one in each hand; the paddle castanet with a pair mounted on a paddle; and the concert castanet, which are mounted on a board with lower one stationary and the upper one struck with the hand or a drumstick. See also **appendix 4: "Percussion Instruments and Their Translations."**

Castleton Festival. Founded in 2007 by **Lorin Maazel** and Nietlinde Turban-Maazel as a part of the Chateauville Foundation with the goal of nurturing young artists. The site is the Maazel estate in Castleton, Virginia, and includes a space for opera performances. Specializing in the training of young singers with its Castleton Artists Training Seminar (C.A.T.S.), the festival has expanded to include a competition for young composers and orchestral and chamber music concerts.

ça suit. (Fr.) continue without a pause. A phrase heard often in rehearsal. (Ger. *es folgt*, It. *segue*, Sp. *sigue*.)

catégorique. (Fr.) exaggerated, pompous, emphatic. A character word. (Ger. *nachdrücklich*, It. *enfatico*, Sp. *enfático*.)

C attachment or extension. See **extensions**, **instrument**.

caxambu. A Brazilian large, single-headed drum. See also **appendix 4: "Percussion Instruments and Their Translations."**

caxixi. A Brazilian percussion instrument in the form of a woven basket rattle. See also **appendix 4: "Percussion Instruments and Their Translations."**

CBC Radio Orchestra. See **Canadian Broadcasting Corporation Radio Orchestra**.

C clefs. The clefs used where **"middle"** C is indicated by the shape of the clef: bass clef (Fr. *clé de fa quatroisiéme ligne*, Ger. *Bassschlüssel*, It. *chiave di basso*, Sp. *clave de fa en cuarta [línea]*), alto clef (Fr. *clé d'ut troisiéme ligne*, Ger. *Altschlüssel*, It. *chiave di contralto*, Sp. *clave de do en tercera [línea]*), mezzo-soprano clef (Fr. *clé d'ut seconde ligne*, Ger. *Mezzosopranschlüssel*, It. *chiave di mezzosoprano*, Sp. *clave de do en segunda [línea]*), soprano clef (Fr. *clé d'ut première ligne*, Ger. *Sopranschlüssel*, It. *chiave di soprano*, Sp. *clave de do en primera [línea]*), and tenor clef (Fr. *clé d'ut quatriéme ligne*, Ger. *Tenorschlüssel*, It. *chiave di tenore*, Sp. *clave de do en cuarta [línea]*).

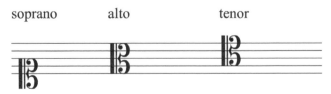

C clefs. *Courtesy Andrew Martin Smith.*

CD. Abbreviation for compact disc. (Fr. *disque compact*, Ger. *CD*, It. *supporti a letture ottica*.)

CD-ROM. A compact disk used to store large amounts of information including music, text, and images (photographs and film); often sold in combination with textbooks. The abbreviation stands for "compact disk–read only memory.")

C dur. (Ger.) C major. (Fr. *Ut majeur*, It. *Do Maggiore*.) See **appendix 5: "Pitch Names and Their Translations into French, German, and Italian."**

cédant. (Fr.) yielding, relaxing the tempo. A descriptive often seen in French music. Example: *En cédant et en diminuant*, relaxing the tempo and getting quieter, from "Gigues" of *Images* by Claude Debussy; *En cédant et plus libre*, relaxing the tempo and more free, from "Le matin d'un jour de fête" from "Ibéria" of *Images* by Claude Debussy.

cédé. (Fr.) held back. A term seen in the works of Claude Debussy and others. See also *cédant, cédez.*

cédez. (Fr.) slow down. Also *céder*. Example: *Cédez pendant ces 4 mesures*, slow down during these four bars, from "Dialogue du vent et de la mer," mvt. 3 of *La Mer* by Claude Debussy; *Cédez à peine*, slow a little, from "Habanera," *Rapsodie Espagnole*, by Maurice Ravel.

celermente. (It.) rapidly, quickly. A character word. (Fr. *rapidement*, Ger. *schnell*, Sp. *rápidamente*.)

celesta. A steel-bar keyboard instrument used in the orchestra. (Fr. *céleste*.) The tone is produced by felt hammers striking steel bars that lie on a wooden resonator. A well-known example of the use of the celesta is Pyotr Tchaikovsky's *The Nutcracker* ballet. See also **appendix 4: "Percussion Instruments and Their Translations."**

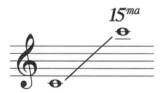

Celesta range as it sounds. *Courtesy Andrew Martin Smith.*

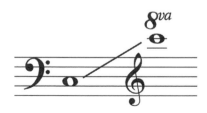

Celesta range as written. *Courtesy Andrew Martin Smith.*

céleste. (Fr., It.) heavenly, divine. 1. A character word sometimes used to evoke a particular way of performing a passage. (Ger. *himmlisch*, Sp. *celestial*.)
   2. The instrument the **celesta**.

Celibidache, Sergiu. (1912–1996.) Romanian conductor known as one of most exacting rehearsal conductors in the business, often demanding as many as twenty rehearsals per performance when the norm was no more than four. Though he studied and even advocated the principles of Zen Buddhism, Celibidache was also known to be capable of cruelty in rehearsal. While some felt he brought a spiritual insight to the music, others saw him as nothing but a self-promoter. Celibidache always conducted from memory and was known to have particularly expressive gestures. For most of his career he refused to record but did broadcasts on radio and television.
   Celibidache had the unusual good fortune of being named the principal conductor of the **Berlin Philharmonic** in 1946 when Leo Borchardt, who was about to become its music director, was shot at Checkpoint Charlie (1945). From 1947 to 1952 he shared conducting responsibilities with **Wilhelm Furtwängler**. He went on to serve as the music director of several orchestras, including the **Swedish** and **Stuttgart Radio Symphony Orchestras** and the Orchestre Nationale de France. In 1979, he was appointed to the **Munich Philharmonic Orchestra**, a position he held until his death.

cello. A commonly used nickname for the **violoncello**, a member of the string family. The cello is played in a sitting position with the instrument held between the knees and supported by an endpin that extends from the bottom to the floor. Its strings are C, G, D, and A, from low to high. See also **appendix 3: "Instrument Names and Their Translations."**

Cembalo. (Ger., It.) harpsichord. (Fr. *clavecin*, Sp. *cémbalo*.)

cent. A measurement used to determine the size of the interval between two pitches; it is 1/100 of a half step in the equal temperament tuning system. The octave in this tuning scheme is equal to 1,200 cents, with each of the twelve half steps equally tempered to 100 cents. Introduced by the German scientist **Hermann Helmholtz** in 1863, the system was adapted for practical use in 1885 by Alexander J. Ellis.

center point style. This approach to conducting puts every **ictus** in a point at the bottom center of the **beat plane**. Each **beat** is clarified by the direction up and out away from that ictus. Usually the **rebound** up from beat four is higher so as to distinguish the coming **downbeat** of each bar. Center point style can be particularly effective in recitative and some **aleatoric** music.

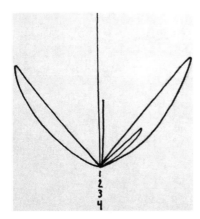

4/4 pattern in center point style.
Courtesy Derek Brennan.

centitone. A unit of measurement equal to 1/100 of a whole tone in the equal temperament tuning system, thus equaling to two cents. See also **tuning systems**.

centro, al. (It.) at the center, of a drum, for instance. A technique of playing drums that generates a particular sound.

cerca del puente. (Sp.) an indication for string players to play near or at the bridge. (Fr. *prés du chevalet*, Ger. *am Steg*, It. *sul ponticello*.)

cercle. (Fr.) circle. Example: *sur le cercle*, on the head of the tambourine, from "Gigues" of *Images* by Claude Debussy.

certo. (It.) certain, definite. A character word. (Fr. *assuré*, *certain*; Ger. *sicher*; Sp. *cierta*, *cierto*.)

Ces. (Ger.) C-flat. See also **appendix 5: "Pitch Names and Their Translations," accidental**.

Ceses. (Ger.) C double flat. See also **appendix 5: "Pitch Names and Their Translations," accidental**.

cesura. (It., Sp.) cutoff, break, *caesura*. (Fr. *césure*, Ger. *Zäsur*.)

césure. (Fr.) cutoff, break, *caesura*. (Ger. *Zäsur*, It. *cesura*, Sp. *cesura*.)

Chailly, Riccardo. (b. 1953.) Italian conductor. Chailly studied conducting with **Franco Ferrara** and was an assistant conductor to **Claudio Abbado** at **La Scala**, Milan. He served as the chief conductor of the **Berlin Radio Symphony Orchestra** (1982–1988) and the Bologna opera house (1986–1993) and was the principal guest conductor of the **London Philharmonic Orchestra** (1983–1986). He was the chief conductor of the **Royal Concertgebouw Orchestra** (1988–2004), where he led numerous recording projects and expanded the orchestra's repertoire by increasing performances of twentieth-century and contemporary music. He became the chief conductor of the **Leipzig Gewandhaus Orchestra** and general music director of the Leipzig opera in 2005. While he continues at the orchestra, his term at the opera was completed in 2008. Chailly also served as the music director of the Symphony Orchestra, Giuseppe Verdi, called "La Verdi," from 1999 to 2005 and was appointed the music director of **La Scala**, Milan, for a term from 2015 to the end of 2016. His recordings include complete symphony cycles of Johannes Brahms, Gustav Mahler, and Anton Bruckner on the **Decca** label.

chaleur. (Fr.) with warmth, feeling. A character word often heard in rehearsal to describe the tone or sound. Also *avec*. (Ger. *mit Wärme*, It. *con calore*.)

chalumeau. (Fr.) the low range of a modern **clarinet**.

chamber music. Music written for small ensembles such as duos, trios, quartets, quintets, and other groups up to the size of a **chamber orchestra**. These groups usually are not conducted. In recent years, because of the difficulty of some of the compositions written for them, a conductor is required.

chamber orchestra. A small orchestra. While its original definition was an orchestra small enough to perform in a smaller space, in its modern form, it often goes beyond a standard orchestra and consists of almost any combination of instruments. (Fr. *orchestra de chambre*, Ger. *Kammerorchester*, It. *orchestra da camera*, Sp. *orquesta de cámara*.) Examples of music: *La Creation du Monde* by Darius Milhaud. See also **Orpheus Chamber Orchestra** as an example of a chamber orchestra that operates without a conductor; **Chamber Orchestra of Europe**; **St. Paul Chamber Orchestra**.

Chamber Orchestra of Europe (COE). Founded in 1981 by a group of young musicians who were leaving the **European Youth Orchestra**. Members of the COE maintain parallel careers as members of full-time orchestras, soloists, and chamber musicians and teachers. The orchestra has performed throughout the world with many of the most distinguished conductors and soloists and has recorded more than 250 works on **CD** and **DVD**, winning two **Grammy Awards**. It also maintains a COE Academy that offers scholarships to postgraduate-level musicians who study with principal players.

chance music. See **aleatory**, **chance operations**, **I-Ching**.

chance operations. 1. Random processes such as the rolling of dice or tossing of a coin used to select and order musical materials in an **aleatoric** piece.

2. Free or controlled decisions made by the performer in an **aleatoric** piece during the performance. See also **I-Ching**.

changer, en. 1. (Fr.) change, as in to change to a different instrument, such as a different clarinet, or from the flute to the piccolo in the course of a piece or movement thereof.

2. (Fr.) to retune, for instance to retune the pitches of the timpani. (Fr. *changer*, Ger. *wechseln*, It. *cambiare*, Sp. *cambiar*.)

changing meters, conducting. See **conducting changing meters**.

changing the number of beats in a bar. There are four basic situations in which a conductor will choose to change the number of beats given in each bar: (1) When the tempo is getting gradually faster or slower. (2) When the metrical feel switches from, for example, four pulses in a bar to two or from three to one. (3) When there is a sudden change of tempo, for instance, going from a slow introduction to a fast allegro tempo. (4) When there are **mixed meters**.

In the case of a *ritardando*, or a slowing of the tempo, when the tempo gets too slow to control with fewer beats, the conductor will add beats or subdivisions of the beat. In the case of an *accelerando*, or an increase in the speed, beats or subdivisions will be removed and the number of beats decreased. In either case, it is clearer for the ensemble when the conductor signals the upcoming change by using a pivot point, where the tempo is at a stage when either pattern will fit, to make the switch. Usually this point is the last beat of a bar.

Changing the number of beats in a bar according to the metric feel is simply a matter of finding the right place. Usually the bar line tends to be clearest. In the case of an abrupt tempo change from one tempo to another, the conductor figures out the right beat pattern for the new tempo and signals the change at the pickup. If there is a tempo connection, for instance, when the new faster tempo is twice as fast or even four times as fast as the slower one, the conductor makes the switch by simply subdividing that final beat before the change.

chanson. (Fr.) song. Also *chant*. (Ger. *Gesang, Lied*; It. *canto, canzone*; Sp. *canción, canto*.)

chantant. (Fr.) in a singing style, a descriptive term often heard in rehearsal to inspire a certain quality of playing by instrumentalists. Also **chanté**. (It. *cantabile*.)

chantant. (Fr.) singing, to sing. Also *chanter*. Often used to address instrumentalists in order to evoke a particular manner of playing. (Ger. *singend, singen*; It. *cantando, cantare*; Sp. *cantando*.)

chant d'oiseau. (Fr.) bird song. (Ger. *Vogelstimme*, Sp. *canto de un pájaro*.)

chanter à vue. (Fr.) to sing at sight, sight sing. (It. *cantare a prima vista*, Ger. *vom Blatt singen*, Sp. *cantar a primera vista*.)

chanterelle. (Fr.) the highest string, on a violin, for instance.

chantonner. (Fr.) To hum with the mouth closed. (Ger. *brummen*; It. *canticchiare*; Sp. *cantar con la boca cerrada, boca chiusa*.)

chaque. (Fr.) each, every, any. A common word used in phrases and often heard in rehearsal. (Ger. *jede, jeder, jedes*; It. *chiascuno, ogni, tutto, tutta*; Sp. *cada, todo, toda*.)

charisma. A personal characteristic or quality of leadership that arouses feelings of enthusiasm and sometimes loyalty.

charme. (Fr.) charm. Also *avec charm*, with charm. Seen in the works of Claude Debussy and others.

Charry, Michael. (b. 1933.) American conductor and pedagogue and author of *George Szell: A Life of Music* (2011). Charry was the **assistant conductor** of the **Cleveland Orchestra** under **George Szell** for nine years. He also served as the **music director** of the Nashville and Canton Symphonies, with much guest conducting and opera work. A renowned teacher of conducting, he was the music director of the orchestras and head of orchestral conducting at the **Mannes School of Music** (1989–1999). See also **bibliography**.

charts. Graphs, line drawings, or other visual aids used to facilitate learning various aspects of a score. They can be used to focus on large scale structures, phrase and harmonic structures, cue sequences and orchestration, dynamics, or even, when learning them, conducting gestures. See also **score study**.

chatoyant. (Fr.) brilliant, showy, shimmering. (Ger. *schimmernd*, It. *scintillante*, Sp. *reluciente*.)

chaud. (Fr.) Warm, fervent, a character word often used to evoke a certain quality of playing. (It. *caldo*; Ger. *warm*; Sp. *caluroso, cálido*.)

chef d'attaque. (Fr.) historically the concertmaster or leader of a section in an ensemble who assisted all entrances. See also **history of conducting**.

chef d'orchestre. (Fr.) the "chief" of the orchestra, that is, the orchestra conductor. (Sp. *jefe de* + instrument name, *principal de* + instrument name.)

Chen, Mei-Ann. (b. 1973.) Taiwanese American conductor and violinist. Chen was the music director of the Memphis Symphony (2010) and the Chicago Sinfonietta (2011). She was awarded the Helen M. Thompson Award at the 2012 national conference of the **League of American Orchestras**. In 2005, Chen won the Malko Conducting Competition. She served as the assistant conductor of the **Atlanta** and **Baltimore Symphony Orchestras**. Chen received her **doctor of musical arts** degree in conducting at the **University of Michigan**. See also **conducting competitions**.

cheto. (It.) quiet, hushed, a character word used to evoke a certain quality of playing. Also *chetare*, to calm, pacify.

chevalet. (Fr.) the bridge of a string instrument. (Ger. *am Steg*, It. *ponticello*, Sp. *puente*.) See also *au chevalet*.

chevrotant. (Fr.) Quivering, trembling, a character word seen in French scores and parts. (Ger. *zittern*; It. *tremolando*; Sp. *tembloroso, temblando*.)

chiaro. (It.) clear. A commonly heard descriptive. (Fr. *clair*; Ger. *klar*; Sp. *clar, claramenteo*.) Also *chiaramente*, clearly.

chiascuno. (It.) each, every, any. A commonly used word in phrases that are often heard in rehearsal. Also *ogni, tutto, tutta*. (Fr. *chaque*; Ger. *jede, jeder, jedes*; Sp. *cada, todo, toda*.)

chiave. (It.) clef (lit. "key"). (Fr. *clé, clef*; Ger. *Schlüssel*, Sp. *clave*.) See also **clef** and **C clefs**.

Chicago Orchestra Hall. Built in 1904 for the **Chicago Symphony Orchestra** (CSO), the architect was Daniel Burnham. Following a multimillion-dollar renovation (1995–1997), it is now called Symphony Center and houses Orchestra Hall, Buntrock Hall, a rehearsal and performance space, and the Grainger Ballroom. It remains the home of the CSO.

Chicago Symphony Orchestra (CSO). Founded in 1891, the CSO is one of America's top five orchestras. Its first conductor was **Theodore Thomas**, who served for thirteen years. Subsequent music directors include **Frederick Stock** (1905–1943), Désiré Defauw (1943–1947), Artur Rodzinski (1947–1948), **Rafael Kubelik** (1950–1953), **Fritz Reiner** (1953–1962), Jean Martinon (1963–1968), **Sir Geog Solti** (1969–1991), **Daniel Barenboim** (1991–2006), and **Ricardo Muti** (2010–present). The CSO has recorded since its very early days. Stock recorded Felix Mendelssohn's *Wedding March* in 1916 and continued to record for **Columbia Records**, later known as **RCA** Victor. In 1951, Kubelik make the first high-fidelity recordings for **Mercury Records**, and in the 1950s and 1960s, Reiner made the first stereo recordings with RCA using their triple channel "Living Stereo" technology. Solti recorded with the orchestra on the **Decca** label, including a highly acclaimed Mahler series, and in 2007, the orchestra created its own recording label, **CSO Resound**, after reaching an agreement with the orchestra's musicians for these recordings to be released both online and on CD. See also **orchestra-owned recording labels**.

chimes. See **tubular bells**; **appendix 4: "Percussion Instruments and Their Translations."**

China National Symphony Orchestra. Founded as the Central Philharmonic Orchestra of China in 1956 in Beijing with conductor Li Delun, who is a graduate of the Shanghai Conservatory (1943) and the Moscow Conservatory (1957). Li Delun has guest conducted numerous orchestras, introducing many Chinese compositions across the globe. In 1996, the ensemble was reorganized under its new name. Its current music director is Michel Plasson (2010–present), the principal resident conductor is Xincao Li, Muhai Tang is conductor laureate, and En Shao is the principal guest conductor. The orchestra's executive director is the composer Xia Guan, a graduate of the **Central Conservatory of Music, Beijing**. His compositions have been performed internationally.

Chinese cymbals or china cymbals. With slightly inverted edges, these cymbals of various sizes produce a distinct tone. (Fr. *cymbals chinoise*, Ger. *chinesische Becken*, It. *piatti cinesi*, Sp. *platillos chinos*.) See **appendix 4: "Percussion Instruments and Their Translations."**

chin rest. A device made of wood and used by violinists and violists to support the lower body of the instrument under the chin of the player, making it easier to play.

chitarra. (It.) guitar. (Fr. *guitar*, Ger. *Gitarre*, Sp. *guitarra*.)

chiusa. (It.) stopped (lit. "closed"), to put the hand in the bell of a horn to create a muffled sound. When the hand is inserted into the horn, it raises the pitch one half step, and the player adjusts. While certain terms may be used to signify either stopped or muted, it should be noted that only the horn is stopped, other brass instrument can be muted but not stopped. It can also mean dampened, muted. Also *chiuso, tappato*. (Fr. *bouché, étouffé*; Ger. *gestopft, gedeckt*; Sp. *cubierto, tapado*.) See also **stopped**.

chocalho. A Brazilian metal or wooden tube shaker filled with pellets. Also called **xucalho**. See **appendix 5: "Percussion Instruments and Their Translations."**

choeur. (Fr.) **choir**. (Ger. *Chor*, It. *coro*, Sp. *coro*.)

chœur d'hommes. (Fr.) men's chorus. (Ger. *Männerchor*, It. *coro maschile*, Sp. *coro masculino*.)

choir, chorus. An ensemble consisting of singers. Usually made up of four voices: soprano, alto, tenor, and bass. These may be divided into any multitude of first sopranos, second sopranos (mezzo-soprano), first altos, second altos (contralto), tenor one (high), tenor two (low), bass one (high), and bass two (low). A chorus may be accompanied by piano or instrumental ensemble or perform **a cappella** (without accompaniment). There are also women's choruses, SSAA, male choruses, TTBB, and in some religious organizations, boys voices are substituted for sopranos and altos. The chorus is possibly the oldest ensemble in Western music and can vary in size from about twelve to hundreds of participants. (Fr. *choeur*, Ger. *Chor*, It. *Coro*, Sp. *coro*.)

Chopin University of Music. See **Frederick Chopin University of Music**.

Chor. (Ger.) **choir**. (Fr. *choeur*, It. *coro*, Sp. *coro*.)

Choral Symphony. The name often given to Ludwig van Beethoven's Symphony No. 9. Has also been used for other works for chorus and orchestra in the form of a symphony. See Kelly, Forrest. *First Nights: Five Musical Premieres.* New Haven, CT: Yale University Press, 2000.

chord cluster. Two or more chords, such as **polychords** or **tone clusters**, that sound simultaneously.

chord of resonance. A term coined by composer **Olivier Messiaen** for a chord built of all the notes of a harmonic series stacked above the fundamental pitch. Example from Messiaen, spelled from low to high: C E G B-flat E-flat G-flat A-flat B-natural.

choriste. (Fr.) a pitch pipe. A small device that when blown through sounds any of several pitches in order to give a choir a starting pitch when no accompaniment precedes the entrance. Also *flute d'accord, diapason à bouche.* (Ger. *Stimmpfeife*; It. *corista, diapason a fiato*; Sp. *diapasón de boca*.)

Chorus America (CA). Originally known as the **American Choral Foundation**. Founded in 1972, CA publishes *The Voice* magazine and sponsors an annual conference.

chromatic cluster. A tone cluster built entirely of minor seconds. See **tone cluster**.

chuchoter. (Fr.) to whisper, murmur. (Ger. *flüstern*, It. *sussurrare*, Sp. *susurrar*.)

chuchoté. (Fr.) whispered.

church modes. The scales based on the sequence of pitches that occur when playing only the white notes on the piano from one note to the same note an octave up. Examples are Dorian (D–D1), Phrygian (E–E1), Lydian (F–F1), Mixolydian (G–G1), Aeolian (A–A1), Ionian (C–C1). These scales were generally dropped over time in favor of the major and minor mode scales. However, some composers use them to create a modified sense of tonality in a work or to capture a folk music affect. (Fr. *éolien, dorien, ionien, mixo-lydien, phrygian*; Ger. *äolisch, dorisch, ionisch, mixolydisch, phrygisch*; It. *eolio, dorico, frigio, ionico, misolidio*; Sp. *dórico, dorio, eólico, eolio, frigio, lidio, mixolidio*.)

ciclo. (It., Sp.) cycle. (Ger. *Zyklus*.)

cierta, cierto. (Sp.) certain, definite, a character word. (Fr. *assuré, certain*; Ger. *sicher*; It. *certo*.)

cimbalom. An Eastern European folk instrument similar to a hammered dulcimer that lies flat, the metal strings struck by leather or wooden mallets. It is similar to a piano in that it has multiple strings for each pitch. It is often equipped with a foot-operated damper pedal and has a compass of four octaves with all chromatic pitches. Used in *Háry János* by Hungarian composer Zoltán Kodály, by **Igor Stravinsky** in his ballet *Renard* and in *Ragtime* and other works, by Frenchman Henri Dutilleux in his *Concerto for Violin* and *Mystère de l'Instant* for chamber orchestra, and many more. (Fr. *cymbalum*; Ger. *Zimbal, Cymbal*; It. *cimbalom*; Sp. *zimbalón*.)

Cimbalom range. *Courtesy Andrew Martin Smith.*

cimbalon. (It.) **cimbalom**.

cimbasso. (It.) **tuba**. Also *tuba*. (Fr. *tuba*, Ger. *Tuba*, Sp. *tuba*.) See also **appendix 3: "Instrument Names and Their Translations."**

Cincinnati May Festival. Founded in 1873 with **Theodore Thomas** conducting an orchestra of 108 musicians and combined choruses of nearly 800 singers with nearly 5,000 in attendance, the annual festival was conceived to enhance Cincinnati's reputation as a national cultural center. The May Festival Chorus, established in 1880 as the official resident chorus, is an all-volunteer choir that performs every year. The festival continues to be a vehicle for bringing together business and community leaders in an effort to boost civic pride. Throughout its history it has been a part of significant musical events in Cincinnati, attracting important conductors and soloists. In 1878, the new Music Hall was inaugurated during the festival and has remained its permanent home. The current music director, **James Conlon**, will step down in 2016.

Cincinnati Pops Orchestra. Founded in 1977 out of the Cincinnati Symphony with Erich Kunzel as its conductor. He conducted the famous **Eight O'Clock Pops** series and began the Concerts in the Parks series in 1967. He remained as the conductor until his death in 2009, making over ninety recordings on the **Telarc** label. The Cincinnati Pops consisted of the entire **Cincinnati Symphony**. John Morris Russell was appointed to replace Kunzel in 2011.

Cincinnati Symphony Orchestra. The orchestra gave its first concerts in 1895 and moved into its current home, the Music Hall, one year later. Its first conductor was Frank van der Stucken, a Texas-born musician. On his departure from the position in 1907, the orchestra temporarily disbanded, reforming in 1909 under the direction of **Leopold Stokowski**. The orchestra left the Music Hall 1911 but returned in 1936. During its early years, the orchestra gave the American premieres of **Gustav Mahler**'s Symphonies No. 3 and 5. Its music directors include **Leopold Stokowski** (1909–1912), Eugène Ysaye (1918–1922), and **Fritz Reiner** (1922–1933). Thor Johnson (1947–1958) led the orchestra in recordings for the **Remington Records** label. He was succeeded by **Max Rudolf** (1958–1970). Thomas Schippers took over in 1970 but died of cancer in 1977. Michael Gielen served in the post from 1980 to 1986 and Jesús López-Cobos from 1986 to 2001. Paavo Järvi led the orchestra for a ten-year period from 2001 to 2011 and was replaced by Louis Langrée in 2013. The Cincinnati Symphony supports a **youth orchestra** for musicians from grades 9 to 12. In 2010, the orchestra began its own record label, Cincinnati Symphony Orchestra Media, releasing its first **CD**, *American Portraits*, the next year. In November 2011, it became the first orchestra to have a **twitter zone** at its concerts.

cinelle. (It.) a curved metal plate available in varying sizes. Cymbals may be suspended and struck individually by various devices, including a wooden drumstick, a triangle beater, a wire brush, a marimba mallet, and more. They may also be played as crash cymbals, where two, held in the hands with a leather strap, can be played in any number of ways in order to generate a wide variety of sounds. Also *piatti*. (Ger. *Becken*, Fr. *cymbals*, Sp. *platos*.) See also **appendix 4: "Percussion Instruments and Their Translations."**

circle conducting. Conductors may conduct in **circle gestures** in passages that constitute a series of repeated rhythms, often in one beat to a bar. While it is possible that it may become dull, the gesture may remain exciting by being constantly modified or tempered to reflect changes in dynamic, phrasing, tempo, or energy. See also **conducting technique.**

circle gestures. See **circle conducting**.

circle of fifths. Often used as a teaching or memory device, a circular arrangement of the twelve pitches, their major and relative minor key signatures, and key names. When reading clockwise, they are a fifth apart. (Fr. *cycle de quintes*, Ger. *Quintenzirkel*, It. *circolo delle quinte*, Sp. *círculo de quintas*.)

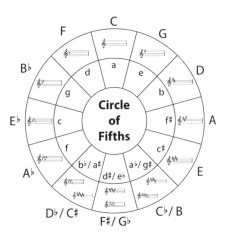

Circle of fifths. *Courtesy Andrew Martin Smith.*

circolo delle quinte. (It.) **circle of fifths**.

circulo de quintas. (Sp.) **circle of fifths**.

Cis. (Ger.) C-sharp. See also **appendix 5: "Pitch Names and Their Translations,"** **accidental**.

Cisis. (Ger.) C double sharp. See also **appendix 5: "Pitch Names and Their Translations,"** **accidental**.

Cité de la Musique (City of Music). Established in 1995 in Paris as a conglomeration of institutions dedicated to music. Home to an amphitheater, a concert hall, a museum (Musée de la Musique) with a large collection of musical instruments of historic interest, exhibition halls, workshops, and archives located in the La Villette quarter of the nineteenth arrondissement in Paris.

In 2014, a 2,400–seat concert hall, the Philharmonie de Paris, opened. The Conservatoire National Supérior de Musique et de Danse de Paris (**National Superior Conservatory of Paris for Music and Dance**), a separate institution from the Conservatoire de Paris (**Paris Conservatory**), is located next to the cité.

City of Birmingham Symphony Orchestra (CBSO). Established in 1920 by Neville Chamberlain, Appleby Matthews was its first chief conductor (1920–1924). He was followed by **Sir Adrian Boult** (1924–1930), who returned from 1959 to 1960 and was followed by Hugo Rignold (1960–1969), Louis Frémaux (1969–1978), **Simon Rattle** (1980–1998), Sakari Oramo (1998–2008), and **Andris Nelsons** (2008–2015). Simon Rattle made several impressive recordings with the CBSO during his tenure, including works of Jean Sibelius and **Gustav Mahler**. Under the leadership of the Finnish conductor Sakari Oramo, the orchestra began a festival of contemporary music. The orchestra runs a **youth orchestra** and has a CBSO chorus, and there are many chamber ensembles connected to the orchestra that are made up by its members.

City of Prague Philharmonic Orchestra (Filharmonici města Prahy). Established in 1947 with the name Czech Symphony Orchestra, its name was changed in 1992. The **orchestra** has become a leading recording orchestra with hundreds of sessions each year for companies such as **Decca**, **EMI**, and **Sony** and film studios such as Paramount, Lucasfilm, and others, in addition to television series, all kinds of CDs, DVDs, video games, and even ring tones. They have a partnership with Smecky Music Studios.

Civic Orchestra of Chicago. Founded by **Frederick Stock** in 1919, the Chicago Civic was the first training orchestra in America associated with a professional symphony orchestra. The Civic provides opportunities for talented young orchestra musicians to receive a high-level experience in preparation for positions with professional orchestras. It is often conducted by the **Chicago Symphony Orchestra**'s **associate conductor** and is sometimes guest conducted by its **music director**.

clair. (Fr.) Clear, distinct. A directive often heard in rehearsal. Also *claire.* (Ger. *klar, deutlich*; It. *chiaro*; Sp. *claro*.)

clairement. (Fr.) clearly.

clarinet. A single-reed woodwind instrument usually tuned in either B-flat or A. The range of the standard clarinet in B-flat with the "Boehm system" of keys and fingerings begins with the low-written E3 up to A6, sounding D3 up to G6. The upper register can be extended upward by individual players, but orchestral players prefer nothing above the G6. The overall compass is divided into four registers known as the chalumeau, throat, clarinet, and extreme. The chalumeau register, which begins at the lowest note and goes to about G4, is very distinct. With a prevalence of odd numbered partials in the sound, it is sometimes described as "hollow." The throat or break register occurs between the chalumeau and clarinet registers and is less distinct, if not plain, in sound. The clarinet or clarion register is made mostly from the overblown twelfths above the notes and extends from about B4 to C6. It is the unusual quality of these twelfths that give the instrument its distinctive color. From C-sharp6 up to F6, the notes are the fifth harmonics above the fingering for A to C-sharp in the chalumeau. Above that, in the extreme register, the manipulation of the lips is as important as the fingerings in producing the pitches.

What sets the clarinet apart from every other wind instrument is that it can play extreme *fortissimo* to extreme *pianissimo* on any note, from its lowest to its highest pitch. (Fr. *clarinette*, Ger. *Klarinette*, It. *clarinetto*, Sp. *clarineto*.) See also **clarinet in E-flat or D, bass clarinet (B-flat or A), alto clarinet, double bass clarinet, basset horn**, and **extensions**. See also **appendix 3: "Instrument Names and Their Translations."**

Clarinet B-flat range as it sounds. *Courtesy Andrew Martin Smith.*

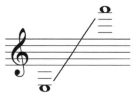

Clarinet B-flat range as written. *Courtesy Andrew Martin Smith.*

Clarinet A range as it sounds. *Courtesy Andrew Martin Smith.*

Clarinet A range as written. *Courtesy Andrew Martin Smith.*

clarinet in E-flat or D. Also called the "piccolo" clarinet, this single-reed transposing instrument extends the range of the clarinet upward. While one will see parts written for both instruments, only the E-flat instrument is regularly used now. The written range of the E-flat goes from a written E3 up to an A6 and sounds up a minor third. The sound pitches for the D-flat clarinet are up a whole step. (Fr. *petite clarinette*; Ger. *kleine Klarinette*; It. *clarinetto piccolo*; Sp. *clarinet soprano, clarinet requinto, clarinet sopranino, clarinet en mi bemol, clarinet en re*.) See also **appendix 3: "Instrument Names and Their Translations."**

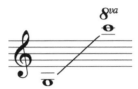

Clarinet E-flat range as it sounds. *Courtesy Andrew Martin Smith.*

Clarinet E-flat range as written. *Courtesy Andrew Martin Smith.*

Clarinet D range as it sounds. *Courtesy Andrew Martin Smith.*

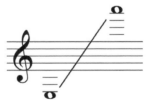

Clarinet D range as written. *Courtesy Andrew Martin Smith.*

clarineto. (Sp.) **clarinet**. (Fr. *clarinette*, Ger. *Klarinette*, It. *clarinetto*.) See also **appendix 3: "Instrument Names and Their Translations."**

clarinette. (Fr.) **clarinet**. (Ger. *Klarinette*, It. *clarinetto*, Sp. *clarineto*.) See also **appendix 3: "Instrument Names and Their Translations."**

clarinetto. (It.) **clarinet**. (Fr. *clarinette*, Ger. *Klarinette*, Sp. *clarineto*.) See also **appendix 3: "Instrument Names and Their Translations."**

clarino. (It.) the upper register of the Baroque **trumpet**.

claro. (Sp.) clear, distinct, a commonly used descriptive. (Fr. *clair, claire*; Ger. *klar, deutlich*; It. *chiaro*.)

classical conducting style. This conducting style puts all the beats on the same **horizontal plane** and requires clear separation or **beat placement** between each beat. The emphasis here is on horizontal motion, creating a nice smooth **legato** flow and reserving the **vertical motion** for the **gesture** of **preparation** to the **downbeat** of each coming **bar**.

4/4 pattern in classical style with right hand indicating forte. *Courtesy Derek Brennan.*

Classical Music **magazine.** Published in the United Kingdom, it is issued every two weeks and covers news from the current classical music scene, primarily in Britain. Publication began in 1976. It maintains an active website. See **music magazines**.

classical music radio stations. These stations have been a primary delivery service of classical music since the beginning of radio broadcasting. Before the establishment of **public radio**, there were very few classical music stations; now there are many across the entire United States. Many stations create their own programming. In addition, there are many classical music stations that broadcast on the Internet and can be found by searching the web. Some of the most well-known stations are WBUR, 90.9 FM, Boston; WCLV-FM, Cleveland, Ohio; WCPE-FM, Raleigh, North Carolina: WETA-FM, 90.9, Washington, DC; WFMT, 98.7 FM, Chicago; WGBH-FM, Boston; WGUC-FM, 90.9, Cincinnati, Ohio; WKSU-FM, Kent, Ohio; WQXR-FM,

105.9, New York; WXXI-FM, Rochester, New York; King-FM, 98.1, Seattle; KBPS-FM, Portland, Oregon; KCNV, 89.7 FM, Las Vegas; KMFA-FM, Austin, Texas; KDFC-FM, San Francisco; KUHF, 88.7 FM, Houston; and many others. International stations can also be heard on the Internet either without cost or by subscription. Just a few international online streaming stations are BBC Radio 3, Britain; ABC Classic FM, Australia; the Canadian Broadcasting Corporation; and Deutschland Radio.

Networks that produce their own programming include American Public Radio (APR), the national production and distribution division of Minnesota Public Radio (MPR); Beethoven.com; Interlochen Public Radio (IPR); National Public Radio (NPR); Public Radio International (PRI); and many more. Many orchestras across the country broadcast their concerts on their local public radio station either by tape delay or live.

A few broadcasters have been particularly important in serving classical music in the United States. They include Karl Haas, a German musicologist, who after immigrating to Detroit started the daily program *Adventures in Good Music* on WJR (1959). It was eventually syndicated through WCLV-FM, Cleveland and became the most-listened-to classical music program worldwide. The award-winning show ran until 2007, two years after Haas's death. More recently, American conductor **Bill McGlaughlin** began the program *St. Paul Sunday*, a weekly show with well-known musicians in conversation and performing live on Minnesota Public Radio. In 2002, WFMT Chicago approached McGlaughlin about a daily show that would implicitly take over from Haas's program and one year later, *Exploring Music* debuted.

Classical Recordings Quarterly. A British magazine that is devoted to vintage recordings of classical music. Publication began in 1995. It has a network of reviewers from Britain, Germany, America, and Japan. See also **music magazines**.

Classical Symphony. The name given to Sergei Prokofiev's Symphony No. 1 in D major. It is said to have been written in the **neoclassical style**.

clave. (Sp.) **clef** (lit. "key"). (Fr. *clé, clef*; Ger. *Schlüssel*; It. *chiave*.) See also **C clefs**.

clavecin. (Fr.) harpsichord. (Ger. *Cembalo*, It. *cembalo*, Sp. *clavicémbalo, clavicordio*.)

claves. Two cylindrical, hard pieces of wood that produce tone when struck together. See also **appendix 4: "Percussion Instruments and Their Translations."**

clavicembalo. (It., Sp. *clavicémbalo*) alternative word for harpsichord. *Cembalo* is used most often in Italian.

clavicordio. (Sp.) harpsichord. Also ***clavicémbalo.*** (Fr. *clavecin*; Ger. *Cembalo*; It. *cembalo, clavicembalo*.)

clavier. (Fr.) keyboard or **piano**. (Ger. *Klaviatur*, It. *tastiera*, Sp. *teclado*.) (Ger. *Hammerklavier, Klavier*; It. *piano*; Sp. *piano*.)

clavija. (Sp.) tuning peg on a string instrument. (Fr. *cheville*; Ger. *Wirbel*; It. *bischero, pirolo*.)

clé. (Fr.) **clef** (lit. "key"). Also *clef*. (Ger. *Schlüssel*, It. *chiave*, Sp. *clave*.) See also **C clefs**, **treble clef**, **bass clef**.

clef. Lit. "key." A figure of notation placed on a specific line of the music stave to indicate the name and pitch of the notes standing on that line and hence of those on the other lines and spaces. (Fr. *clé, clef*; Ger. *Schlüssel*; It. *chiave*; Sp. *claves*.) Examples are **treble clef**, **bass clef**, and the **C clefs**.

Cleveland Institute of Music. Founded in 1920 with composer Ernest Bloch as director. The institute has a very close relationship with the **Cleveland Symphony Orchestra**, with more than half of its faculty serving as members of the orchestra. Students at the institute have full access to both academics and the facilities of Case Western Reserve University. The Cleveland Institute maintains an active preparatory division for pre-college-age music students.

Cleveland Orchestra Youth Orchestra (COYO). Established in 1986 in Cleveland, Ohio, by conductor **Jahja Ling**. The COYO is an award-winning orchestra of about one hundred young musicians from Ohio and Pennsylvania who rehearse every week during the academic year, are coached by members of the **Cleveland Symphony Orchestra** (CSO), and are conducted by the CSO's associate or assistant conductors.

Cleveland Symphony Orchestra (CSO). Founded in 1918 with Nikolai Sokoloff as its main conductor. Its music directors have been Artur Rodzinsky (1933–1943), **Erich Leinsdorf** (1943–1944), **George Szell** (1946–1970), **Lorin Maazel** (1972–1982), **Christoph von Dohnányi** (1984–2002), and **Franz Welser-Möst** (appointed in 2002). The impact of **George Szell**'s long tenure on the orchestra was significant. He raised its profile to an international level, creating an orchestral sound modeled on the European tradition. The orchestra is now commonly included in the "big five" top American orchestras. It has made numerous recordings and has its home in Severance Hall, built for the orchestra in 1931. The site of its summer series is the Blossom Festival at the Blossom Music Center in Cuyahoga Falls, Ohio. The orchestra sponsors the **Cleveland Orchestra Youth Orchestra**.

click track. An audible soundtrack consisting of regularly paced clicks, usually heard through an earpiece, that allows a conductor or other performer to coordinate the music being played with a film or recording of computer-generated or other sounds.

clockwise release gesture. A conducting gesture, such as a **cutoff gesture**, given with either the left or right hand in the direction of the hands of a clock. See also **release gestures** for image.

clos. (Fr.) closed, as opposed to *ouvert*, open. A term used to request a specific type of playing in a variety of situations. Also *fermé.* (Ger. *geschlossen*, It. *chiuso*, Sp. *cubierto*.)

Cluytens, André. (1905–1967.) Belgian-born French conductor of opera and symphonic repertoire. Cluytens conducted at the Opéra-Comique in Paris (1947–1953) and was the first Frenchman to conduct at Bayreuth in a performance of **Richard Wagner**'s opera *Tannhäuser* (1955). He succeeded **Charles Munch** as the principal conductor of the Paris Conservatoire Orchestra (1942–1960). He made many recordings with Pathé-Marconi, the French division of **EMI**. He can also be seen on a film made of him conducting works of Maurice Ravel and Pyotr Tchaikovsky, issued on DVD.

C moll. (Ger.) C minor, a minor key, as opposed to a major key such as C major. See *moll* and *dur*.

coda. (It., Sp.) end, a concluding passage of a piece (lit. "tail"). Most commonly used in this, its Italian form. (Fr. *partie finale*; Ger. *Anhang*, *Schlusstiel*.)

col. (It.) with, with the. Also *coll'*, *colla*, *colle*. Commonly heard in a wide variety of phrases. Example: *col arco*, with the bow, a designation often seen after a passage of *pizzicato*. See also *col legno*.

colisa. (Sp.) the wings of a stage, backdrop, scene, side scene, moveable scene. (Fr. *coulisses*, Ger. *Kulisse*, It. *quinte*.)

collé. (Fr.) a bowing technique consisting of a series of short down-bow or up-bow strokes played close to the frog, executed with a small, circular motion in the wrist. See also **bowing terms**.

College Band Directors National Association (CBDNA). Commonly called the CBDNA, it is the main organization for band directors in America. It began as a committee of the **Music Educators National Conference** (MENC). In 1938, **William Revelli** lead a meeting of the group in Chicago. In 1941, they formed the independent University and College Band Conductors Conference, changing their name to its current one in 1947. The organization holds division and national meetings annually and is dedicated to the promotion of college-level bands for the teaching, performance, and cultivation of music.

College-Conservatory of Music (CCM), University of Cincinnati. The conservatory began as part of a girls' finishing school (founded in 1867) that merged with the College of Music of Cincinnati in 1955, creating the College-Conservatory of Music. It became the performing arts college of the University of Cincinnati in 1962. CCM underwent a $93 million renovation in 1999, creating the CCM Village. The conservatory offers a full range of undergraduate and graduate courses, including performance, music education, musicology, music theater, commercial music, arts administration, and more.

College Orchestra Directors Association (CODA). An organization dedicated to serving the needs of college orchestra directors. A national organization divided into five regions, the association has both regional and national conferences.

col legno. (It.) with the wood; play with the wood of the bow, not the hair. Generally composers use *col legno* to get a percussive effect, but occasionally players are asked to use the wood instead of the hair of the bow, drawing an extremely quiet and weak, if not watery, sound from the instrument. (Fr. *avec le bois*; Ger. *mit Holtz*, *mit den Bogen*; Sp. *con la vara*.)

Colonne, Édouard. (1838–1910.) French conductor and violinist. Colonne studied violin and composition with Ambroise Thomas at the Paris Conservatory. Upon graduation, he became a first violin at the Paris Opera. As a conductor, he was a proponent of the music of many important nineteenth-century composers, including **Hector Berlioz**, **Georges Bizet**, César Franck, Camille Saint-Saëns, and **Richard Wagner**. Colonne met Peter Tchaikovsky in Paris in 1878 and later traveled to Russia in order to conduct. He founded the Concerts Colonne, a concert organization that sponsored a regular concert series. He toured Europe, conducting in England, Spain, Portugal, and Germany, where his concerts were well received. Colonne had a reputation as an excellent musician with a flair for romantic music.

Colorado Symphony Orchestra. Founded in 1989 after the dissolution of the Denver Symphony Orchestra, the orchestra offers a Masterworks Classics series, pops, family, and holiday concerts, as well as the Inside the Score and Symphony on the Rocks series. Its current music director is Andrew Litton. Previous music directors include **Marin Alsop** (1993–2005) and Jeffrey Kahane (2005–2010).

color, orchestral color. Defined by the color of each instrument in the orchestra and how its sound combines with other instruments. The study of orchestral color is both the study of orchestration and the cultivation of certain qualities of sound in playing. Also referred to as timbre.

color organ. An electronic device that takes audio signals and translates them into visual color displays, individual or multiple colors, or patterns or colors. It has been used in rare performances of Alexander Scriabin's *La Poème de l'extase*.

colpo d'arco. (It.) the bow stroke itself. Also *arcata*. (Fr. *coup d'archet*; Ger. *Bogenführung, Bogenstrich, Strichart*; Sp. *golpe de arco*.)

colpo di lingua. (It.) tonguing, the technique of attacking at the beginning of a note with the tongue to start the airflow on wind and brass instruments. (Fr. *coup de langue*; Ger. *Zungenstoß, Zungenschlag*; Sp. *golpo de lengua, articulación*.)

Columbia-Princeton Electronic Music Center. Now called the **Computer Music Center (CMC)**, it is the oldest center for electronic and computer music study in the United States. It was founded in the 1950s by Columbia University professors Vladimir Ussachevsky and Otto Leunig and Princeton University professors **Milton Babbitt** and Roger Sessions. After receiving a large grant from the Rockefeller Foundation in order to finance the purchase of the RCA Mark II Sound Synthesizer, the center was the site of the creation and composition of much early electronic music. **Columbia Records** issued an album of music produced on the RCA synthesizer in 1961 under the title *Columbia-Princeton Electronic Music Center*. The advent of digital computer technology brought about the decline of the center and the establishment of the **Computer Music Center** at **Columbia University**. Princeton University pursued a relationship with **Bell Labs** and created a computer music studio known as the Princeton Sound Lab under Godfrey Winham and Paul Lansky.

Columbia Records. Currently under the ownership of **Sony Music Entertainment**, it is part of the Columbia Music Group and one of Sony Music's three record labels, along with Epic Records and RCA Records. Founded in 1888, its origins were in the American Graphophone Company and the Volta Graphophone Company. It is the oldest brand name in prerecorded sound, taking its name from the District of Columbia, where it was originally located. In its early days, the company competed with the Edison Phonograph Company and the Victor Talking Machine Company. From 1903, it worked with a number of **Metropolitan Opera** singers to make recordings with mixed results. Competition and rapid technological developments led to constant changes in the company's structure, ownership, and success. In the 1920s, the company built its catalogue of jazz, blues, and popular artists, including Louis Armstrong, Bessie Smith, and Paul Whiteman and his band. It also founded CBS, the Columbia Broadcasting System, in 1927 as a partnership but got out of it soon after, leaving only the name. CBS later revived the company as the Columbia Record Company (CRC).

The advent of the 78 rpm records on which Columbia issued a performance of Nathan Milstein in the Mendelssohn *Violin Concerto* (1947) and then the 33 rpm record technologies gave Columbia a step-up over one of its main competitors, **RCA Red Seal**. In 1948, they introduced the long-playing (LP) format that was particularly well suited to classical music's longer pieces. LP remained the industry standard for nearly fifty years. Stereo sound was introduced in 1956, with LPs beginning to appear in the format in 1958, enhancing classical orchestral and ensemble recordings in particular. In the 1970s, the company began recording in quadrophonic sound and later, just prior to the CD, in digital sound. It issued an album of music produced on the RCA synthesizer in 1961 under the title *Columbia-Princeton Electronic Music Center*.

Pop musicians such as Bob Dylan; Barbara Streisand; Simon and Garfunkel; Peter, Paul, and Mary; Michael Jackson; and others led the company to great financial success. Conductors such as **Leonard Bernstein**, leading the **New York Philharmonic**, were among its top selling classical artists. See also the **bibliography**.

Columbia Symphony Orchestra. An orchestra established by Columbia Records in the early 1950s for the single purpose of making recordings. **Bruno Walter**, **Sir Thomas Beecham**, **Leonard Bernstein**, and **Igor Stravinsky** are the principal conductors who recorded with the orchestra, which was made up of musicians who were hired on an as-needed, per-service basis from the New York or Los Angeles areas, depending on where the recordings were being made.

Columbia University, Music Department. Founded in 1896, it offers a full range of undergraduate and graduate classes in composition, ethnomusicology, historical musicology, music theory, and music performance, including jazz and computer music.

Columbia University's Alice M. Ditson Award. See **Ditson Conductor's Award**.

combination tone. A tone produced when two loud tones are sounded simultaneously, resulting in a third tone. (Fr. *son combiné*, Ger. *Kombinationston*, It. *suono di combinazione*, Sp. *sonido de combinación*.) Also referred to as "nonlinear systems," such as resonating groups of musical instruments, certain electric circuits in receivers and transmitters, or the cochlea of the human ear, where combination tones are produced and perceived, these acoustical systems create the distortion that produces the third tone. The most prominent are called the "simple" difference tones with the frequency f2–f1 Hz and the "cubic" difference tone with the same frequency, but f1 is the lower, not the higher, frequency. The so-called difference or combination tones, sometimes called the Tartini tone, are heard easily in music-making settings and have been described as early as the eighteenth century by Giuseppe Tartini in his *Trattato di musica seconda la vera scienza dell'armonica* (1754; published in facsimile by Broude Brothers, 1966). See **resultant tone**.

combinatoriality. A characteristic of a specific set of pitches that makes up the first six notes, called a **hexachord**, of the main or prime version of a **twelve-tone row** that, when combined with the first six notes of one or more of its transposed versions, does not produce any duplications of pitch. The term was devised by composer **Milton Babbitt** to describe one of the principle techniques of composition with **twelve-tone rows** as used by **Arnold Schoenberg** and others.

There are three ways of creating combinatoriality: (1) The relationship between the prime version of the **row** and its inversion with the second **hexachord** being an inversion of the first. (2) The prime version and a retrograde inversion with each hexachord being its own inversion. (3) The two transpositions with the second hexachord being a transposition of the first. Example of a combinatorial row: Schoenberg's String Quartet No. 4. See also **all-combinatorial set**, **semi-combinatorial set**, **bibliography**.

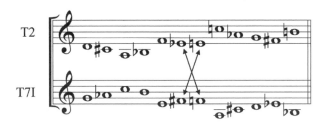

Combinatoriality. *Courtesy Andrew Martin Smith.*

come. (It.) how, like, as, in the manner of. Examples: *come primo*, as at first or as at the beginning; *come sopra*, as above; *come scritto*, as written. (Fr. *comme*, Ger. *wie*, Sp. *como*.)

come está. (Sp.) as it is. (It. *come stà*.) Also *como está escrito*, as written. (Fr. *comme ecrit*, It. *come scritto*.)

come scritto. 1. (It.) as written. (Fr. *comme ecrit, tel quel*; Ger. *wie geschrieben, wie notiert*; Sp. *como está escrito*.) See also ***come stà***.

2. A principle of performance and conducting whereby the performer approaches a piece of music "as written" and without additional interpretation.

come stà. (It.) as it is, as written. (Fr. *comme ecrit, tel quel*; Ger. *wie geschrieben, wie notiert*; Sp. *como está, como está escrito*.)

Comet, Catherine. (b. 1944.) French-born Amercian conductor. Comet served as the music director of the Grand Rapids Symphony Orchestra (1986–1997) and the **American Symphony Orchestra** (1989–199) and as the associate conductor of the **Baltimore Symphony Orchestra** (1984–1986) and the **St. Louis Symphony Orchestra** (1981–1984). She received the **Seaver/National Endowment for the Arts Conductors Award** in 1988. Comet conducted many of North America's leading orchestras, including the **Boston Symphony Orchestra**, **Chicago Symphony Orchestra**, **Cincinnati Symphony Orchestra**, **Detroit Symphony Orchestra**, **Milwaukee Symphony Orchestra**, **New Jersey Symphony Orchestra**, **Philadelphia Orchestra**, **San Francisco Symphony**, **Toronto Symphony Orchestra**, and more.

Catherine Comet.

cómico. (Sp.) droll, funny, a character word. (Fr. *comique*, *drôle*; Ger. *komisch, ulkig*; It. *comico, buffo*.)

comique. (Fr.) comical, funny, a character word. Also *drôle*. (Ger. *komisch, ulkig*; It. *comico, buffo*; Sp. *cómico*.)

Comissiona, Sergiu. (1928–2005.) Romanian-born Israeli and American conductor with a reputation for a colorful personality and flair in his conducting. Comissiona fled the Communist regime in Romania in 1959 and immigrated to Israel. There he founded the Ramat Gan Chamber Orchestra. He directed the Haifa Symphony Orchestra from 1959 to 1966. He was the music director of the **Baltimore Symphony Orchestra** (1969–1984), the **Houston Symphony** (1978–1987), in Helsinki (1990–1995), and many others.

comme ecrit. (Fr.) as written. May be used as the opposite of "as sounding" for a transposing instrument.

commençant. (Fr.) beginning. Example: *en commençant par*, beginning with.

commencez. (Fr.) begin, commence. Example: *Commencez à animer peu à peu*, begin to get faster little by little, from "*Le matin d'un jour de fête*" from "*Ibéria*" of *Images* by Claude Debussy.

commodément. (Fr.) comfortable, easy, a manner of playing. (Ger. *bequem*; It. *comodamente*; Sp. *cómodo, cómodamente.*)

commodo. (It.) comfortable, unhurried, in regards to tempo. Also *comodo*. Used as part of the title of movement two of Symphony No. 3 by **Gustav Mahler**. (Fr. *à l'aise*, Ger. *bequem.*)

common time. A work in 4/4 meter generally using the **C** symbol as opposed to the cut-time sign.

Common time. *Courtesy Andrew Martin Smith.*

como. (Sp.) how, like, as, in the manner of. Often heard in a variety of descriptive phrases. (Fr. *comme*, Ger. *wie*, It. *come*.) See also *como danza.*

comodamente. (It.) comfortable, easy, a manner of playing. (Fr. *commodément*; Ger. *bequem*; Sp. *cómodo, cómodamente.*)

como danza. (Sp.) a character word used to evoke a dance-like style of playing. Also *character danzante* or *carácter de danza*. (Fr. *dansant*, Ger. *tanzend*, It. *danzante.*)

cómodo. (Sp.) comfortable, easy, a manner of playing. Also *cómodamente*. (Fr. *commodément*, Ger. *bequem*, It. *comodamente.*)

como escrito. (Sp.) a directive used after a passage of change or transposition to indicate sounding as written. (Fr. *à sa place*; Ger. *an seinem Platz*; It. *al luogo, loco.*)

compás. (Sp.) bar, measure. (Fr. *mesure*, Ger. *Takt*, It. *misura.*)

compás alla breve. (Sp.) In two beats per measure, also called *alla breve* in English usage. (Fr. *à la blanche*, Ger. *in halben Noten*, It. *alla breve*.) See also **cut time**.

competitions for conductors. See **conducting competitions**.

complementary sonorities. A term coined by composer Howard Hanson to describe harmonic and melodic structures that, while using notes of the chromatic scale, generate a complementary sonority made up of the remaining notes. For example, the whole tone scale C D E F-sharp G-sharp A-sharp yields the additional complementary whole tone scale of D-flat E-flat F G A B. Hanson promotes this theoretical relationship as crucial to the composer in order to expand tonal relationships within a consistent structure.

completamente. (Sp.) full, loud. Also *pleno*. (Fr. *plein, pleine*; Ger. *voll, mit vollem Ton*; It. *pieno.*)

Composers Recordings, Inc. (CRI). Founded by **Otto Luening**, Douglas Moore, and Oliver Daniel in 1954 in order to record and distribute music by contemporary American composers. The company went out of business in 2006, having released over six hundred LPs, cassettes, and CDs. The list of composers whose works are included is a virtual history exhibition of American music of the second half of the twentieth century.

compound beat patterns. See the associated figures for patterns for compound meters 6/8, 9/8, and 12/8.

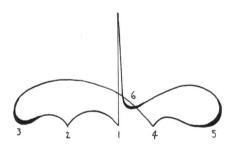

Compound beat pattern, 6/8. *Courtesy Derek Brennan.*

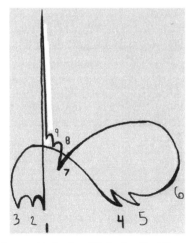

Compound beat pattern, 9/8. *Courtesy Derek Brennan.*

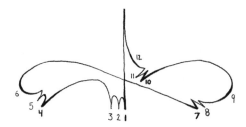

Compound beat pattern, 12/8. *Courtesy Derek Brennan.*

compound meter. Any meter that includes a triple sub-division, such as 6/8 or 12/8, as opposed to any duple subdivision, such as 4/4 or 2/4. See also **compound beat patterns**.

compter. (Fr.) to count. Counting is a basic and vital part of every rehearsal, for example, counting bars of rest before an entrance, counting rhythms, and more. When guest conducting an orchestra in a foreign country, most conductors learn how to count in the language of the orchestra in order to help facilitate rehearsals. (Ger. *zählen*, It. *contare*, Sp. *contar*.) See **subdivide**, **numbers, basic**.

computer music. Music that is created or synthesized from information fed into and then processed by a computer.

Computer Music Center. Organized at Columbia University under the leadership of Brad Garton in 1995 to take over from the **Columbia-Princeton Electronic Music Center**.

con. (It., Sp.) with. (Fr. *avec*, Ger. *mit*.) Commonly used in scores and parts and heard in rehearsal in a wide variety of phrases. Examples: (Sp.) *Tocar con fuerza*, play with force; *Tocar con gran sonido*, play with a big sound.

con alegría. (Sp.) happily, willingly, with pleasure. (Fr. *volontiers*, Ger. *gerne*, It. *volentieri*.)

con brio. 1. (It.) with fire, energy.
2. A commonly used Italian expression often seen as a modifier to tempo markings such as *allegro*, for example, *allegro con brio*.

concept. Conductors must have an overall concept of how a piece should be performed. See also **methods of score study**, **interpretation**.

concertant. (Fr.) a work for a chamber ensemble or orchestra that requires one or more players to take on the role of soloist within the group. Examples include the *Sinfonia concertante in E-flat*, K. 364, for violin, viola, and orchestra by Wolfgang Amadeus Mozart and the *Sinfonia concertante in B-flat* for violin, cello, oboe, bassoon, and orchestra by Joseph Haydn.

concertante. (It.) See *concertant*.

concert band. See **band**.

concert ending. An ending often added in the case of a concert performance of a work such as an opera overture that when performed as part of the whole continues directly into the first scene. Also any other excerpt that needs "finishing," usually in the form of a satisfying harmonic progression or coda leading to a close. Examples: Christoph Willibald Gluck's opera *Iphigenie en Aulide* for which composer **Richard Wagner** wrote a concert ending and Mozart's overture to the opera *Don Giovanni*, which has nine measures added in order to create harmonic completion.

Concertgebouw Orchestra, Royal. See **Royal Concertgebouw Orchestra**.

concertino. (It.) the group of solo players in a standard **concerto grosso**. These solo parts sometimes alternate with the rest of the ensemble, called the *ripieno*, and sometimes join them for *tutti* passages.

concertino. (Sp.) concertmaster, the first-chair first violin. (Fr. *premier violon solo*, Ger. *Kozertmeister/Konzertmeisterin*, It. *primo violon solo*.)

concertmaster. The first-chair first violinist in an orchestra. Often considered the most important member of the orchestra in the hierarchical structure, followed by the first-chair oboist, the first horn, and the timpanist. (Fr. *premier violon solo*, Ger. *Kozertmeister/Konzertmeisterin*, It. *primo violon solo*, Sp. *concertino*.)

concerto. A work for a soloist and orchestra.

concerto for orchestra. A work for an orchestra that puts individual players or groups of players in the ensemble in the more virtuosic role of a soloist. The most famous is by Béla Bartók, but many others have been written by such composers as Witold Lutosławki, Paul Hindemith, Walter Piston, Michael Tippett, and many more.

concerto grosso. A Baroque formal structure also used as a title for works that feature principal players as soloists with the remainder of the ensemble playing the "accompaniment," usually written for string orchestra. George Frideric Handel and Arcangelo Corelli wrote the most famous sets of concerti grossi.

concerto ripieno. In a concerto grosso, the part of the ensemble that plays the "orchestral" or "accompaniment," as opposed to the concertato, which play the solo parts.

concert pitch. For transposing instruments, this is the pitch as it sounds, the so-called sounding or concert pitch, not the written pitch. For instance, when a **clarinet** in B-flat has a written **middle C**, it sounds as the B-flat below. When a **horn** in F has a written middle C, it sounds as the F below. See also **transposition** and **transposing instruments**.

con cierta licencia. 1. (Sp.) with some freedom. (Fr. *avec quelques licences*, Ger. *mit einiger Freiheit*, It. *con qualche licenza*.)
2. A directive seen in parts and heard in rehearsal.

concitato. (It.) excited, agitated, a character word. (Fr. *agité*, Ger. *erregt*, Sp. *agitado*.)

concluir. (Sp.) to end, conclude. (Fr. *terminer*, Ger. *beendigen*, It. *concludire*.)

conclusion. (Fr.) conclusion, end. (Ger. *Abschluss*, It. *conclusione*, Sp. *conclusion*.)

conclusione. (It.) conclusion, end. (Fr. *conclusion*, Ger. *Abschluss*, Sp. *conclusion*.)

conducting. Leading, artistically transporting in musical terms from one place to another, doing everything a conductor is now expected to do. The word *conducting* acquired its present meaning during the nineteenth century, when the practice of conducting, in opera and in concert, evolved to its modern form. (Fr. *direction d'orchestre*, Ger. *Dirigiren*, It. *direzzione d'orchestra*.) See: **conduct, to**; **conducting technique**; **leadership**; **morale**; **motivation in rehearsal**; **principles of conducting**; **psychology of the conductor-orchestra relationship**.

conducting area. See **conducting frame**.

conducting as dialogue. The process of conducting is a give and take, a dialogue based on the music between the **conductor** on the podium and the members of the ensemble. The conductor uses **gestures**, **facial expressions**, and **body language** in order to communicate what is happening or what is desired, and the ensemble interprets what they see. In the case of a good conductor who has a strong **concept** of a piece, a clear technique, and an appealing or somehow effective personality, the dialogue works well. See also **principles of conducting**, **psychology of the conductor-orchestra relationship**.

conducting beat patterns. See **basic conducting patterns for musical styles**, **conducting compound beat patterns**, **conducting pattern styles**, **subdivided beat patterns**.

Conducting beat pattern, in one. *Courtesy Derek Brennan.*

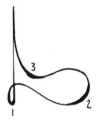

Two pattern in legato style. *Courtesy Derek Brennan.*

Three pattern in legato style. *Courtesy Derek Brennan.*

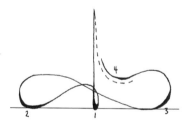

Four pattern in legato style. *Courtesy Derek Brennan.*

conducting careers. Conductors have made careers with orchestras at all levels: community, state, regional, national, and international; professional and amateur; and in the teaching field from elementary, junior high, and high school to colleges, universities, and conservatories and schools of music. Some conductors work in opera or the film world or conduct at summer festivals, and many start their own orchestras, chamber or full-sized. Through various phases of a career, conductors write books, teach, or coach privately.

conducting changing meters. There are two kinds of changing meters: (1) the length of the beat or pulse stays the same but the number of beats within each bar changes and (2) the length of the beat and number of subdivisions within each beat and the number of beats in each bar change. In the first type, the **conductor** changes the basic beat pattern to match the music, and in the second type, the conductor changes the length of each beat according to the number of subdivisions within each beat and uses the pattern appropriate to each bar. When switching between beats that are, for instance, the length of a quarter note versus the length of a dotted quarter note within the same measure or series of measures, the physical height of the beat and possibly also the speed of the gesture will be modified accordingly in order to maintain the constancy of the subdivision of the pulse. See also **conducting technique**.

conducting competitions. Competitions can sometimes help start the careers of young **conductors**. Among the existing competitions are the Eduardo Mata International Conducting Competition in Mexico City, the Tokyo International Music Competition for Conducting, the International Gustav Mahler Conducting Competition (hosted by the Bamberg Symphony in Germany), the Donatella Flick Conducting Competition (sponsored by the London Symphony), the "Arturo Toscanini" International Conducting Competition—Giuseppe Sinopoli Award (Italy), the Jorma Panula Conducting Competition (Finland), the International Besançon Competition for Young Conductors (France), the International Competition of Young Conductors Lovro von Matacic (Coratia), the López-Cobos International Opera Conductors Competition (Spain), and the Malko Competition (hosted by the Danish Radio Symphony in Denmark).

conducting compound patterns. See **compound patterns**.

conducting contrasting dynamics simultaneously. Many orchestral pieces have passages with more than one contrasting dynamic at the same time. The brass may have a quiet marking while the winds and strings are playing with a full *forte*. In such a case, the **conductor** will usually use one hand for the dynamic ruling the majority of players—probably the right hand—and then use the left to indicate a quieter dynamic for the remainder. See also **conducting technique**.

conducting dynamic changes. Dynamic changes appear in two basic ways: gradually changing and suddenly changing. When conducting gradual dynamic changes the size of the beat gradually gets bigger during a *crescendo* and gradually declines in size for a *diminuendo*.

In the case of sudden dynamic changes, the **conductor** runs the risk of drawing a change from the ensemble in advance of where it is printed in the music. In order to show a sudden dynamic change from loud to soft, the conductor has a few options, one being to conduct the loud dynamic at a low beat plane and then switch to a higher beat plane, drawing the line of the louder dynamic

without hinting at or "giving away" the change until the instant the change occurs. Switching from soft back to loud with the same principle involves an almost instantaneous fall from the higher plane back to the lower one. In order to make the dynamic changes all the more effective, the conductor will back them up with added force or lightness as necessary. The trick comes in the nature of **conducting** as a matter of preparation. In sudden dynamic changes, the size of the gesture alternates exactly as it is in the music. See also **beat size**, **beat style**, **conducting technique**, **ready position**.

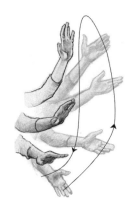

Crescendo-diminuendo gesture. *Courtesy Derek Brennan.*

conducting dynamics. Conducted using a combination of size and force or energy of the beat. Generally, louder dynamics are conducted with larger beats and quieter ones with smaller beats. It should be noted that the force or concentrated energy of a smaller beat can also communicate a loud, powerful dynamic, and a light, flowing large beat is perfectly capable of communicating a soft dynamic. See also **conducting dynamic changes**, **conducting sound**, **conducting technique**, **ready position**. See image under **classical conducting style** for left hand forte gesture.

conducting entrances on incomplete beats. See **fractional beat preparations or entrances on incomplete beats**, **"guillotine downbeat."**

conducting fermatas. See **fermata**.

conducting fractional beat preparations. See **fractional beat preparations or entrances on incomplete beats**.

conducting frame. The space or area in front of the **conductor** in which the beats are given. Often described as being like a window frame, the conductor attempts to keep the beat generally inside the imaginary shape of a window, only going outside that boundary for exceptional musical moments. The conducting frame helps create concise, clear gestures and is especially effective in music with multiple **meter changes** or similar difficulties. It can be used as a pedagogical tool to help develop good beat placement, clarity, and discipline for the young conductor. Sometimes called the "conducting field." See also **conducting technique**.

Courtesy Derek Brennan.

conducting from memory. Some conductors absorb music so quickly that conducting from memory is natural, especially if they have a photographic memory. Others find the process of memorizing so strenuous and their memory so unsure that they may jeopardize a performance by an inadvertent mistake. Leading a performance from memory is a status symbol of sorts to an audience, but it does not necessarily significantly improve the performance except to create opportunities for greater eye contact. It can even create a certain sense of insecurity among the musicians if the **conductor** spends too much time wondering what the next event is or exactly where the orchestra is in the music. **Hans von Bülow** conducted from memory often, popularizing the practice and laying down the challenge for those to follow. **Richard Wagner** was also known to conduct from memory, as were **Arturo Toscanini**, **Dimitri Mitropoulos**, and **Lorin Maazel**. **Max Rudolf** cautions conductors who struggle with memory not to sacrifice security for some pretense of showmanship, suggesting that their time could be better used by delving more deeply into the score. Others who know their scores by heart use the score nonetheless as either a tribute to the composer or just for the extra security. Some conductors have been known to tear a few pages of a particularly tricky spot out of the score, leaving the rest backstage. See also **memorizing the score**.

conducting gestures for musical styles, basic. See **basic conducting patterns for musical styles**.

conducting history. See **history of conducting**.

conducting in four. The four pattern is shaped metrically by a strong downbeat, a weaker second beat, a middle-weight third beat, and a pickup or anacrusis. This accounts for the normal weight and balance within the musical grouping as commonly written. The style of the pattern can be varied endlessly depending on the requirements of the music, from a light staccato executed with the wrist to a broad legato conducted with the arm. See also **center point conducting style**, **beat patterns**, **conducting pattern styles**, **compound beat patterns**, **subdivided patterns**,

Conducting in four. *Courtesy Derek Brennan.*

conducting in one. The one pattern is the most variable. It can have a subdivision of two or three eighth notes. It can be a simple up-and-down motion without a stop at the top, which would create a second pulse and make it a two pattern (see **conducting in two**). It can also be endlessly varied to allow for nuances of weight within the subdivision of the bar. It is only rarely a real circle, but a circle with a pulse at the bottom to secure the ensemble. See also **conducting beat patterns**.

conducting in the pit. When the **conductor** enters the opera pit, a whole new set of challenges ensues. Often judged on how well the singers are heard over the orchestra, the sound the opera conductor hears in the pit is highly distorted, often unrelated to the experience of the audience. The conductor then has to rely on assistant conductors who can either cover in the pit, allowing the conductor to hear the combined sound from the audience's perspective, or take notes during the course of rehearsal. No matter how one chooses to seat the opera orchestra, problems will exist. Usually brass and percussion and sometimes the high sounds of a piccolo will seem uncontrollable, while others, often the strings, will seem to disappear.

These balance problems also affect the singers. When an aria begins with an introduction of pizzicato strings, for instance, even if they play *forte*, they may be inaudible to the stage. This may be solved by on-stage speakers. Other practical considerations include lighting and the height of the podium. The conductor needs to be lit in order to be visible to everyone. Often referred to as a "God light," it usually hangs with the stage lights but is placed right above the conductor. Stand lights are required for the members of the orchestra and the conductor's music stand. The height of the podium has to be high enough so that the conductor can see the entire stage and easily give cues to the singers wherever they are, but it must also be low enough so that the orchestra has good eye contact.

Perhaps the greatest challenge for the opera conductor is the dual role of being both an accompanist and a leader. The conductor must never lose awareness of what is happening on the stage. Opera conducting requires constant minute adjustments both to the stage action and to the music. The opera conductor leads the singers—that is, soloists, ensembles, and choruses, whether standing still, walking, or dancing—carefully, sensitive to their needs. But the conductor must also constantly be attentive to the orchestra and their need for clarity and assurance. It is no wonder that the opera house remains a training ground for conductors in Europe. See also **conducting opera**, **opera in English**, **opera in the original language**, **performance practice and tradition in opera**, **preparing the opera score**, **rehearsing opera**, and **opera pit seating**.

conducting in three. The three pattern is made up of a strong downbeat, a weaker second beat, and an anacrusis, also called an upbeat or pickup. The common form of the pattern allows for great flexibility and nuance of accentuation, phrasing, and more. See also **conducting beat patterns**.

conducting in two. Generally, the two pattern consists of a strong downbeat and a light upbeat. Sometimes it is conducted with the simplest up-and-down motion, the downbeat at the bottom and the second beat at the top. This involves a slight stop at both points, sometimes known as stop-start conducting and is often used to lead a march or dance in two. The legato form of the pattern is much more common and flexible. The shape allows for clarity and all nuances of phrasing, accentuation, and more. See also **conducting beat patterns**.

conducting in uneven meters. A **conductor** uses uneven beat patterns for bars in 5/8 or 7/8, when the division of eighth notes in a measure clearly requires it. For 5/8, the conductor will use a modified two pattern: one beat that is two eighth notes long and the other that is three. The division into three and two eighth notes often alternates between beats one and two, requiring the conductor to switch back and forth between 2 + 3, and 3 + 2 as needed. Another uneven pattern is 7/8. For this, the conductor uses the standard three pattern, adding an extra eighth note to one beat as notated in the score. The division into twos and threes is usually made clear by the composer, but in certain cases, it may not be the same in all instruments. In this case, the conductor decides which is division best serves the music. Contemporary composers may also divide a 4/4 bar into uneven divisions of eighth notes, for example, 3 + 2 + 3. In such a case, the conductor will use a three pattern with eighth-note groupings to match.

Conducting patterns for uneven meters such as 5/4 or 7/4, where the eighth-note subdivision remains the same (duple), is built on the next lowest even pattern with a beat added in the bar where it makes the most sense according to the music. For instance, for a bar of five beats, start with a 4/4 bar and add the fifth beat according to the shaping of the music. Use the same principal for a 7/4 bar, using the divided three or six pattern that most closely resembles the shape and metric accentuation of the music, adding the seventh beat where most appropriate. See **conducting in one**, **fractional meters**, **polymeter**, and **appendix 1: "Six Pieces That Changed Conducting."**

conducting musical character. The **conductor** shows musical character through a combination of details of articulation, energy, speed of motion between the beats, and other elements of body language in order to make each **gesture** reflect the music. See also **conducting technique**.

conducting off-beat accents. The **conductor** gives a strong beat with a good energetic ictus on the beat before the accent, allowing the ensemble to react with confidence. All modifications are made in order to adapt to the actual dynamic and style of the accent. See also **conducting technique**.

conducting opera. In Europe, opera conducting remains the training ground of the young **conductor**. And it is no wonder. Conducting opera involves great clarity and flexibility, an excellent ear, and sensitivity to the needs of both the singers on the stage and the orchestra in the pit. The opera conductor is both an accompanist and a leader, the one who can get a singer out of a tight situation in a live performance like no other. The opera conductor keeps together a chorus that has dance steps to execute while singing and the orchestra in the pit and balances the whole so that the audience can hear the words. The opera conductor has a beat that is visible to everyone whenever needed and is capable of dealing with the working conditions that exist in many opera houses around the world.

Only a few **gestures** are virtually unique to the opera setting. In sequence, they are the left hand discreetly held up to, for example, warn off a singer who seems to be ready to enter early, gently implying "stop"; followed by an extended index finger implying "wait"; then the "**invitational cue**," a gentle turning of the hand; followed by an encouraging breath when the time has come, all done with the left hand. See also **conducting in the pit, opera in English, opera in the original language, rehearsing opera, performance practice and tradition in opera, preparing the opera score**.

conducting patterns. See **basic conducting patterns for musical styles**.

conducting pattern styles. See **center point style, classical conducting style**, and **focal plane style**.

conducting plane. An imaginary **horizontal plane** just above the waist and in front of the **conductor** that may act as a "shelf" on which to place beats for the purpose of consistency, beat separation, and clarity. The plane can help the conductor place the beats equidistant while keeping them at a uniform height. Some conductors refer to this as the **conducting field** or field of beating.

conducting posture/stance. A confident stance and good posture are essential to the **conductor** for two basic reasons: (1) to make it possible to stand for long rehearsals without tiring and (2) to exude a relaxed confidence. Generally, conductors should stand with their feet some inches apart with the toes pointing just slightly out for stability and good balance. Knees should be straight but not locked with weight evenly distributed on both feet. In order to maintain balance, it is also important not to have all your weight on either the balls of the feet or the heels. Shoulders should be back and the chest should be open. The head should be held erect and the neck relaxed. The conductor should strive for a lack of tension. See also **conducting technique, preparatory position**.

conducting preparatory beats with rests before entrances. The **conductor** must account for any rest printed in advance of an entrance. This is due to the fact that most instrumental parts are printed individually and, with the exception of the occasional printed cue for another instrument, the instrumentalist can see only his or her own music. Until the instrumentalist has completely learned the piece, the conductor will help clarify the way through the piece by showing every beat, often in a neutral manner.

When there is more than one rest prior to the entrance, the conductor uses the neutral beat (smaller and without energy) to mark the rests and then the active, slightly larger preparatory beat with a simultaneous breath to facilitate the entrance. When there is only one rest and it is an incomplete beat, the conductor prepares as if the first sound were on the beat.

A special case is when a piece begins with a rest on the downbeat. For this, see **"guillotine" downbeat, conducting technique, marking the beat, fractional beat preparations**.

conducting principles. See **principles of conducting**.

conducting ready position. The position momentarily held by the **conductor** before giving the preparatory beat in order to signal to the ensemble a readiness to begin. This position reflects the dynamic, mood, and energy of the piece to be played. See **ready position**.

conducting recitative. Recitative conducting, when the recitative is accompanied by the orchestra, involves a special set of skills. Knowing the text is paramount. It is also necessary to understand the way the voice moves, breaths, and supports. The **conductor** lets the singer "conduct," and the words, the breath, and the singer's tone guide the conductor. The singer will render his or her part in a tempo close to "speaking tempo," that is, in the speed that the words would be spoken in order to best communicate the emotion behind them.

When conducting recitative, the conductor leads the orchestra, not the singer. Account for every bar using a **neutral** or **dead beat** in order to mark each **downbeat** even if, perhaps especially if, it is empty. (It is also possible to mark the parts accordingly in advance.) When the singer is alone, the baton follows the pattern through the bar, somewhat ahead of the singer, and waits on the beat before the orchestra and singer "meet." That beat is usually the last note for the singer and the beat before the orchestra plays. Move from that beat with a **preparatory gesture** in order to bring in the orchestra at the correct tempo, dynamic, articulation, and style.

Typical operatic recitative moves the drama forward, often involving consideration of the central conflict of the story, and usually includes the use of two basic contrasting tempos, each reflecting a certain mood. Clarity of tempo—which bars are slow and which are fast—is vital to an effective interpretation.

Other considerations are the length and, more specifically, the character of the chords with which the orchestra punctuates the text. Short and loud or longer and soft create significantly different results. See **"guillotine" downbeat, appendix 8: "Conducting Recitative."**

conducting release gestures. See **release gestures**.

conducting skills. The most essential musical skills a **conductor** must have are a good ear and a mind for analyzing what the orchestra is playing in order to determine any and all kinds of mistakes that might happen—mistakes of pitch, rhythm, intonation, balance between the instruments, bowings—and all elements of style in order to correct mistakes or style when necessary. Other skills include (1) good leadership skills, (2) good interpersonal relationship skills, (3) a good memory, (4) a quick mind for learning music, (5) the ability to speak extemporaneously to an audience, (6) the ability to express the music with emotion and understanding through the conducting, and (7) good organizational skills and a drive to get things done successfully. The ability to play the piano or any instrument in the orchestra is an advantage for any conductor but not a requirement. See **conducting as dialogue, conducting technique, leadership, morale, motivation in rehearsal and performance, psychology of the conductor-orchestra relationship**.

conducting sound. The concept of relating to the sound of music as a visceral element of conducting. The **conductor** who feels the texture of a sound while conducting, who feels the quality of a sound as a physical reality, weighty or light, thick or thin, bright or dark, molds his or her gestures in order to reflect that sense. See also **conducting technique**.

conducting style. Conductors are often described as having a certain style. This can refer to the physical nature of their conducting, be it fluid or stiff; their approach to the experience of music making with the orchestra; and certain personal qualities or characteristics that seem to define them. See also **conducting technique, wrist motion, flexibility**.

conducting subdivided patterns. See **subdivided patterns**.

conducting syncopations. The **conductor** gives a strong, steady beat without subdivisions for the ensemble to play off. In some cases, a quick rebound adds energy to the passage without disrupting the ensemble; however, all nuances of dynamic and style must be accounted for. Clarity and a good ictus create security. See also **conducting technique**.

conducting technique. The technique of using the hands, arms, face, and body in order to describe the music in gestures. To demonstrate or show how to play the music through conducting gestures. See also **accent, ambidextrous conducting, attention getting gesture, basic conducting patterns for musical styles, baton hold or grip, beat, beat conformation, beat inevitability, beat patterns, beat placement, beat size, beat style, body language, centerpoint conducting style, changing the number of beats in a bar, circle conducting, conducting accompaniments, conducting changing meters, conducting dynamics, conducting dynamic** changes, **conducting contrasting dynamics simultaneously, conducting frame, conducting musical character, conducting off-beat accents, conducting patterns, conducting pattern styles, conducting plane, conducting posture/stance, conducting preparatory beat with rests before entrances, conducting sound, conducting super-metric patterns, conducting syncopation, conducting tempo changes, conducting in uneven meters, conducting works for orchestra and tape, dead beat, downbeat, expressive conducting, expressive conducting gestures, eye contact, facial expression, fractional beat preparations or entrances on incomplete beats, "guillotine" downbeat, heavy staccato, ictus, impulse of will, independence of hands, left hand conducting technique, legato style, light staccato, marcato style, marking the beat, mirror conducting, mirror gestures, preparatory beat, gesture or motion, pizzicato gesture, preparatory position, psychological conducting, rebound gesture, release gesture, staccato style, tenuto style, wrist motion and flexibility, conducting technique, left hand, left-hand conducting technique, conducting in the pit, conducting opera, leadership, morale, motivation in rehearsal and performance, psychology of the conductor-orchestra relationship**.

conducting tempo changes. There are two basic types of tempo change: (1) gradual changes, that is, either getting faster (**accelerando**) or slower (**ritardando**) over the course of time, and (2) sudden changes that can happen without any preparation. The size of the beat is modified in order to accommodate these tempo differences and changes. A fast tempo is conducted with a smaller beat, while a slower tempo may be led with a larger beat. To gradually get faster, the **conductor** may start with a slightly larger beat and gradually, proportionally, get both faster and smaller until having reached the new tempo. To become gradually slower, start with the smaller, slower beat and gradually, within the number of beats allotted in the music, get slower and larger.

Sudden tempo changes are similar to **sudden dynamic changes** in that the size of the beat changes at the same instant as the tempo. With these abrupt changes, it is important to know that the tempo change is unprepared. Consequently, the ensemble can only discern the new tempo when the second beat of that tempo is reached. This is the same principle as the one that governs comprehension of the length of any line or object. One must see both ends of it. The moment of tempo change requires great clarity and focus on the part of the conductor. See also **changing the number of beats in a bar, conducting technique**.

conducting the preparatory beat. See **preparatory gesture or motion**.

conducting the rebound. See **rebound**.

conducting works for chorus and orchestra. In the situation of conducting works for chorus and orchestra, the orchestra **conductor**'s perspective must be flexible. Many choruses are not used to a conductor who uses a baton and will have to adapt. Choruses often achieve good ensemble entrances through the way they breathe rather than with a good attack. While wind and brass players create attacks through tonguing, string players through the bowing style or pizzicato, and percussion with mallets, choruses create attacks mostly through the clear enunciation of consonants. Their sound comes from a supported breath. Often this leads to a slightly modified conducting style. Orchestras need the precision of a clear ictus, while choruses may find it intrusive. A sensitivity to the voice and vocal production is required, as with opera.

Orchestral conductors conducting works for chorus and orchestra meet well in advance with the choral director in order to discuss the edition that will be used; tempos; any issues from the text, such as what form of Latin when doing a Mass; and the size of the chorus versus the size of the orchestra. When planning for a joint rehearsal or performance, arrangements must be made to accommodate a choral warm-up. See also **conducting technique**.

conducting works for orchestra and tape. The major challenge of such works is the coordination required between recorded sound and the live orchestra. Depending on the demands of the piece, the **conductor** will either use a click track with an earpiece or a stopwatch, coordinating with printed timings in the score. Often sections of recorded sound combined with a live orchestra are alternated with passages where the orchestra plays alone. In other situations, there is a distinct interplay, a "polyphony," between the music of one and that of the other. In some situations, the recorded music will be at a significantly different tempo from the live music, creating special coordination challenges. Every piece for orchestra, or any live ensemble and recorded sound, requires a lot of rehearsal with the technical person, who will need to know the score well and the response time of the equipment in order to avoid any delays when the timings must be precise.

One of the first pieces to use tape, though it's just a brief passage, was Ottorino Respighi's *Pines of Rome* (1924). When rented, the musical materials come with a tape or CD of the specific nightingale song Respighi wanted for movement 3, "The Pine Trees of the Janiculum." Another early example of electro-acoustic music, *A Poem in Cycles and Bells* (1954) for tape and orchestra, was written by Vladimir Ussachevsky, who was one of the most important composers of electronic music. It was based on earlier works for tape alone, one of them by Ussachevsky's colleague Otto Luening. Another important work is Mario Davidovsky's *Synchronisms No. 7* (1974). For this work, Davidovsky notates the music of the tape as if it were another instrument of the ensemble, that is, it is written in the same meter as the other parts except when it is alone, and then it is also in a discernible meter. More recent examples are *Bright Kingdoms* by Ingram Marshall and *Poetry of the Piedmont* (2006) and *Cíthara Mea* (Evocations) (2008) by Stephen Jaffe. Jaffe's work was written as a collaboration with the Nasher Museum of Art's exhibition *El Greco to Velasquez* and uses recorded sound, projections of paintings, and offstage instruments. *The Light Within* by John Luther Adams and *Abstracts* for orchestra and tape (1998) by Jonty Harrison are two other compelling works.

conducting works for soloist and orchestra. A successful performance of a work for a soloist and orchestra hangs upon a good working relationship. The primary duty of the **conductor** is to lead the orchestra in an accompaniment that will make the soloist feel at ease and capable of performing at his or her best. If possible, the conductor meets with the soloist in advance in order to talk about tempos, style, and other aspects of **interpretation**.

When working with singers, it is important to agree on phrasing and breaths. Conducting a piano solo work is facilitated by being able to clearly hear the bass line of the instrument and having good sightlines with the soloist, which allows for the occasional nod in order to coordinate the end of a phrase or a change of tempo. With the piano at center stage in front of the orchestra and the lid open outward in order to project the sound to the audience, the conductor, standing behind the piano, is at a slight disadvantage acoustically. Conductors solve this problem by maintaining close attention to the pianist's touch and a sense of anticipation at all times. Since the pianist doesn't offer the signals that the breath of a singer does or the hints given by the bowing of a string soloist, it is sometimes necessary to give beats just slightly ahead of the pianist in order to have a solid ensemble.

In any accompaniment, the conductor's gestures are reserved for the orchestra, except in the case of coordinating soloist entrances or in the event of an emergency when a soloist needs a bit of help. Usually it is the excellent ears and flexibility of the orchestra that save the day. See also **conducting technique**, **marking the beat**.

conductor. A person who conducts. Most dictionaries give the first definition of "conductor" as something that conveys heat or electricity, a lofty goal for musical conductors. See also **conductor as conduit**.

conductor as conduit. Based on a related dictionary definition of the word *conductor*, a musical conductor is sometimes seen as a conduit for the music, one who transfers the energy of the music to the orchestra and the audience. See also **principles of conducting**.

conductor's baton. See **baton, baton hold or grip, baton, history of the, baton makers, baton technique, conducting technique**.

Conductors Guild, Inc. An international organization of choral, band, opera, and orchestral **conductors** founded by **Harold Farberman** in 1975 at the San Diego Conference of the **American Symphony Orchestra League** (ASOL). At the New York **ASOL** Conference in 1985 the guild became independent of the league. Since then, it has continued its expansion and growth, maintaining a significant role in the training of conductors with its frequent **Conductor Training Workshops** around the country and abroad.

Since 1988, the guild has recognized and supported conductors in the field by presenting awards of national and international significance. The **Theodore Thomas Award** is given biennially to a conductor for outstanding achievement and service to one's colleagues. The **Max Rudolf Award** is presented biennially for outstanding achievement as a conductor and pedagogue and the **Thelma A. Robinson Award**, sponsored by the **National Federation of Music Clubs**, is presented biennially to an outstanding participant in a guild conductor-training workshop.

The guild publishes *Podium Notes*, an online newsletter that carries short articles of interest to conductors; the *Conductor Opportunities Bulletin*, a monthly publication of career opportunities; the *Journal of the Conductors Guild*, published periodically with articles of interest to conductors; and a searchable *Membership Directory*.

Conductor's Institute of South Carolina. A two-week summer conductor-training program run by **Donald Portnoy** and hosted by the School of Music at the University of South Carolina. Participant **conductors** receive daily podium time with comments from instructors and members of the orchestra.

conductor's podium. See **podium, conductor's**.

Conductors Retreat at Medomak. A summer workshop in Maine founded by **Kenneth Kiesler**, director of orchestras and professor of conducting at the University of Michigan.

conductor's score. A full score with all the individual instrument parts. (Fr. *partition de direction*; Ger. *Dirigierpartitur*; It. *partitura per il direttore*; Sp. *partitura de orquesta, partitura de director*.)

conductor's stand. The **conductor**'s music stand. (Fr. *lutin, pupitre*; Ger. *Notenpult, Notenständer*; It. *leggio*; Sp. *artril*.) It is often bigger than the music stand of the players in the ensemble in order to handle the weight of multiple scores or a particularly heavy symphony or opera score. It may also have a lower shelf for any extra scores needed in the course of a concert. The height of the stand is important. It must be low enough so that the conductor's gestures can be easily seen by the ensemble but not so low that the conductor has to lean over to turn the pages.

conductor training. See also **education of the modern conductor**.

conduct, to. The art of communicating musical ideas through gesture and psychological and physical energy; to keep time for a musical ensemble; to make interpretive decisions for the music; to rehearse the ensemble analytically so as to correct points of intonation, articulation, dynamics, style, and other aspects in order to attain a successful, convincing performance. Today's professional conductor is a multifaceted musician with many additional responsibilities, including programming and personnel decisions, leading fund-raising efforts or working in tandem with a board of directors and the organization's management to do so, creating outreach projects (initiatives), and being an arbiter of musical taste within a community. (Fr. *direction*; Ger. *dirigieren, taktschlagen*; It. *direzione, concertazione*; Sp. *dirigir*.) See also **leadership, morale, motivation in rehearsal, principles of conducting, programming, psychology of the conductor-orchestra relationship**.

con el alma. (Sp.) with feeling. (Fr. *avec l'âme*, Ger. *gemütvoll*, It. *con l'anima*.) Also *con sentimento*, with sentiment.

con eleganza. (It.) with elegance. (Fr. *avec élégance*, Ger. *mit Eleganz*, Sp. *con elegancia*.)

con el pulgar. (Sp.) with the thumb. An indication specifically used to describe a particular manner of playing the tambourine. (Fr. *avec les pouce*, Ger. *mit dem Daumen*, It. *con il pollice*.)

con esp. (It.) An abbreviation for the commonly used phrase *con l'espressione*, with expression. Also *con espr.*

con fuerza. (Sp.) with strength, force. (Fr. *force*; Ger. *Kraft*; It. *forza, vigore*.)

conga drum. A Latin American drum usually about thirty inches high and with a single head. It is most often played with the hands, but composers often specify specific mallets. It can be found in different sizes. See **appendix 4: "Percussion Instruments and Their Translations."**

con il pollice. (It.) with the thumb. An indication specifically used to describe a particular manner of playing the tambourine. (Fr. *avec les pouce*, Ger. *mit dem Daumen*, Sp. *con el pulgar*.)

con impulso. (Sp.) with panache, energy, style. (Ger. *mit Schwung*, It. *con slancio*, Fr. *avec élan*.) Most often used in its German form, **mit Schwung**. Example: *Por favor, tocar la frase con mucho impulso*, please play the phrase with a lot of forward energy. The German form, *Schwung*, is understood in many countires.

con l'anima. (It.) with feeling, sentiment. (Fr. *avec l'âme*; Ger. *gemütvoll*; Sp. *con sentimiento, con el alma*.)

con la expression. (Sp.) a commonly used phrase in rehearsal meaning "with expression." (Fr. *avec l'expression*, Ger. *mit Ausdruck*, It. *con l'espressione*.)

con la punta del arco. (Sp.) a bowing term indicating to play with the point of the bow. Also *en la punta del arco*, at the point of the bow. (Fr. *avec la pointe de l'archet, à la pointe*; Ger. *mit der Bogenspitze, an der Bogensptize, an der Spitze*; It. *con la punta d'arco, alla punta d'arco*.)

con la punta d'arco. (It.) a bowing term that indicates to play with the point of the bow. Also *alla punta d'arco*. (Fr. *avec la pointe de l'archet, à la pointe*; Ger. *mit der Bogenspitze, an der Bogenspitze, an der Spitze*; Sp. *con la punta del arco, en la punta del arco*.)

con la vara. (Sp.) an indication to play with the wood of the bow. (Fr. *avec le bois,* Ger. *mit dem Holz,* It. *col legno*)

con l'espressione. (It.) a commonly used phrase in rehearsal meaning "with expression." (Fr. *avec l'expression*, Ger. *mit Ausdruck*, Sp. *con la expresión*.)

con moto. (It.) With motion, a commonly used term seen in scores and parts of many types. (Fr. *avec movement*; Ger. *mit bewegung, bewegt*; Sp. *con movimiento*.)

con movimiento. (Sp.) with motion. (Fr. *avec movement*; Ger. *mit bewegung, bewegt*; It. *con moto*.)

con qualche licenza. (It.) with some freedom. A directive seen in parts and heard in rehearsal and used to evoke a free style of playing, particularly in a passage for solo instrument or voice. (Fr. *avec quelques licences*, Ger. *mit einiger Freiheit*, Sp. *con cierta licencia*.)

con sentimento. (Sp.) with feeling, soul, a character word used to evoke a particular quality of playing. (Fr. *avec l'âme*, Ger. *gemütvoll*, It. *con l'anima*.)

conservatory. 1. A music school.

2. An institution with the goal of preserving the teachings, traditions, and techniques of the past through education. The early roots of the music conservatory were to house young women who were seen to need protection, thus the use of the word *conserve*.

con slancio. (It.) with panache, energy, style. (Fr. *avec élan*, Ger. *mit Schwung*, Sp. *con impulso*.)

consonante. (It., Sp.) consonant, the opposite of dissonant. (Fr. *consonne*, Ger. *Konsonant*.)

consonne. (Fr.) consonant, the opposite of dissonant. (Ger. *Konsonant*, It. *consonante*, Sp. *consonante*.)

con sordino. (It.) A string term that indicates playing with the mute. (Fr. *avec sourdine*, Ger. *mit Dämpfer*, Sp. *con sordina*.)

contact point. The point or exact spot at which the bow touches the string in relationship to the bridge in order to get the best tone. The point changes depending on the amount of bow speed and pressure used. Referred to as the *sounding point* by Ivan Galamian.

contar. (Sp.) to count. Counting is a basic and vital part of every rehearsal, for example, counting the bars of rest before an entrance, counting rhythms, and more. When guest conducting an orchestra in a foreign country, most **conductors** learn how to count in the language of the orchestra in order to help facilitate rehearsals. (Fr. *compter*, Ger. *zählen*, It. *contare*.) See also **subdivide**, **numbers**, **basic**.

contare. (It.) to count. (Fr. *compter*, Ger. *zählen*, Sp. *contar*.) See also *contar*.

Contemporary Youth Orchestra. Founded in 1995, the orchestra rehearses and performs at Cleveland State University in Ohio. Its founding music director, Liza Grossman, created the ensemble for young people with a focus on the music of our time. The orchestra has given over one hundred world premieres in the presence of the composers. It is known for collaboration with rock artists and their series Music and Its Industry, which exposes young people to different career tracks in the filed of music. The orchestra's concerts can be heard on **iTunes** and seen on **DVD** and **Blu-ray**.

con tenerezza. (It.) with tenderness, a character word used to evoke a certain manner of playing. (Fr. *avec tendresse*, Ger. *mit zärtlichkeit*, Sp. *con ternura*.)

con ternura. (Sp.) with tenderness, a character word used to evoke a certain manner of playing. (Fr. *avec tendresse*, Ger. *mit zärtlichkeit*, It. *con tenerezza*.)

continuo. (It.) the collective bass part(s) to a Baroque work. It may consist of harpsichord only or include cello, bass, bassoon, organ, or other instruments used to sustain and support the harmonic structure, especially in Baroque recitative (e.g., therobo, lute, etc.). Sometimes also called *basso continuo*.

con toda fuerza. (Sp.) with all force. (Fr. *de toutes ces forces*, Ger. *mit voller Kraft*, It. *con tutta la forza*.)

contrabass. Another name for the **bass** or **double bass**. (Fr. *contrebasse*, Ger. *Kontrabass*, It. *contrabasso*, Sp. *contrabajo*.) See also **appendix 3: "Instrument Names and Their Translations"**; **double bass** (for range).

contrabass clarinet. With a range an octave lower than the **bass clarinet** and sometimes referred to as **double bass clarinet**, it is a transposing, single-reed instrument in either B-flat or E-flat. When written in B-flat, its range is from a low D3 up to D6, sounding C1 to C4. When written in E-flat, the range is from low E-flat3 up to D6, sounding low G-flat up to F4. (Fr. *clarinette contrebasse*, Ger. *Kontrabassklarinette*, It. *clarinetto contrabasso*, Sp. *clarinete contrabajo*.) See **clarinet**, **clarinet in E-flat or D**, **alto clarinet**, **bass Clarinet**, and **basset horn**.

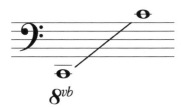

Contrabass clarinet B-flat range as it sounds. *Courtesy Andrew Martin Smith.*

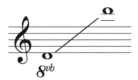

Contrabass clarinet B-flat range as written. *Courtesy Andrew Martin Smith.*

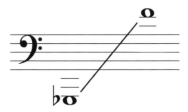

Contrabass clarinet E-flat range as it sounds. *Courtesy Andrew Martin Smith.*

contrabassoon. Extending the range of the bassoon down by an octave, the "contra" is a transposing instrument in that it sounds an octave lower than written. Its written range begins on a low B-flat1 and goes up to a high B-flat4. (Fr. *contrebassoon*, Ger. *Kontrafagott*, It. *contrafagotto*, Sp. *contrafagotto*.) See also **appendix 3: "Instrument Names and Their Translations."**

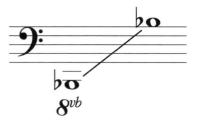

Contrabassoon range as it sounds. *Courtesy Andrew Martin Smith.*

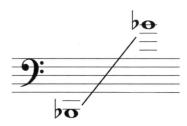

Contrabassoon range as written. *Courtesy Andrew Martin Smith.*

contralto. The lowest of the female voice classifications. See also **voice classifications**.

contratiempo. (Sp.) weak beat. See also ***tempo débil***.

contrattempo. (It.) to play off the beat, to play against the beat, syncopation. Also *sincope*. (Fr. *contre-temps*, *syncope*; Ger. *Synkope*; Sp. *syncopación*.)

contrebasse à pistons. (Fr.) the French equivalent of **bass tuba**. See also **appendix 3: "Instrument Names and Their Translations."**

contre-temps. (Fr.) to play off the beat, to play against the beat, syncopation. Also *syncope*. (Ger. *Synkope*; It. *contrattempo*, *sincope*; Sp. *syncopación*.)

con tutta la forza. (It.) with all force. A directive heard in rehearsal and sometimes seen in music. (Fr. *de toutes ces forces*, Ger. *mit voller Kraft*, Sp. *con toda fuerza*.)

convertirse. (Sp.) to become, a commonly used word in a wide variety of phrases. Also *hacerse*. (Fr. *devenir*, Ger. *werden*, It. *diventare*.)

coperto. (It.) covered, muted, dampened. Often used in timpani parts to indicate the manner of playing in order to create a covered or muffled sound. Also *velato.* (Fr. *couvert, sourd*; Ger. *bedeckt*; Sp. *cubierto, topado.*)

Copland, Aaron. (1900–1990.) Renowned American composer. He composed **Appalachian Spring (1944)**, a ballet with music, commissioned by the Elizabeth Sprague Coolidge Foundation for the American dancer Martha Graham. See under **appendix 1: "Six Pieces That Changed Conducting."**

Copland chord. From the ballet **Appalachian Spring** by **Aaron Copland**, this chord has become representative of an American sound. See also **iconic chords.**

Copland chord. *Courtesy Andrew Martin Smith.*

copyright law. Generally, the right to copy. The laws were established in Europe at the end of the nineteenth century and slightly later in the United States. Copyright laws were instituted in order to protect the rights of composers and other creative artists, treating their work as intellectual property (see also **Gatt Treaty**). The U.S. Copyright Act of 1976 includes the doctrine of "fair use" and adopts the concept of a single term based on the date of the composer's or author's death rather than the previous fixed initial and then renewable terms.

Individual countries legislate copyright that extends either fifty or seventy-five years after the death of the creator. For example, Canadian law establishes a fifty-year term, with the exception that a piece first published after a composer's death is copyrighted for fifty years from the date of first publication. The United States has a seventy-five-year term with no exceptions, and the European Union has a seventy-year term, with the exception that a work first published more than seventy years after a composer's death is copyrighted for twenty-five years from the date of first publication. Copyright laws covering **Urtext editions** vary by country. See **IMSLP.**

cor. (Fr.) **horn**, sometimes called the **French horn**. Also *corne.* See also *cor anglais*; **appendix 3: "Instrument Names and Their Translations."** (It. *corno.*)

cor anglais. (Fr.) **English horn**. The name came from *cor anglé*, meaning "angled horn" and referring to the angled

bocle. In English usage, *anglé* was rendered as *anglais*, meaning "English," and became the standard usage. The instrument is in the **oboe** family and is pitched a fifth lower than the oboe, allowing the range of the "family" to accommodate the desires of composers who wanted to cover a wider range with the same basic instrumental color. (Ger. *Englishhorn*, It. *corno inglese*, Sp. *corno inglés.*) See also **appendix 3: "Instrument Names and Their Translations."** See **English horn** for range.

corchea. (Sp.) eighth note. See also **appendix 7: "Rhythmic Terms and Their Translations."**

corda. 1. (It.) string of a violin, cello, or other instrument with strings. (Fr. *corde*, Ger. *Saite*, Sp. *cuerda.*) See also *corda vuota*; *corde à vide.*
   2. The snare of a snare drum.
   3. Used in the phrase *una corda*—a pedal on the piano that cuts the sound down to one string, making it very quiet.

corda vuota. (It.) open string. Sometimes seen in scores and parts and heard as a directive in rehearsal for string players to use an open or unstopped or unfingered string. (Fr. *corde à vide*, Ger. *leere Saite*, Sp. *cuerda al aire.*)

corde. (Fr.) string of a violin, cello, or other instrument with strings. (Ger. *Saite*, It. *corda*, Sp. *cuerda.*) See also **bowing terms.**

corde à vide. (Fr.) open string. Sometimes seen in scores and parts and heard as a directive in rehearsal for string players to use an open or unstopped or unfingered string. (It. *corda vuota*, Ger. *leere Saite*, Sp. *cuerda al aire.*)

cor de basset. (Fr.) **basset horn.** (Ger. *Bassetthorn*, It. *corno di bassetto*, Sp. *corno di bassetto.*)

cordes. (Fr.) the string section, string players. (Ger. *Streicher*, It. *archi*, Sp. *sección de cuerdo.*)

Corigliano, John. (b. 1938.) Renowned American composer. See **Symphony No. 1 (1990)** in **appendix 1: "Six Pieces That Changed Conducting."**

cornet. A brass instrument in the trumpet family. The cornet was invented in the early nineteenth century and was often used by composers such **Hector Berlioz**, Emmanuel Chabrier, and Pyotr Tchaikovsky. It came into use as a valved instrument before the valved trumpet, allowing access to more pitches than its contemporary trumpet. Its standard size is the cornet in B-flat. (Fr. *cornet*; Ger. *Kornett*; It. *cornetta, cornetto*; Sp. *corneta.*) See also **trumpet, natural trumpet, trumpet transpositions.**

corneta. (Sp.) **cornet** (Fr. *cornet à bouqin*, Ger. *Zink*, It. *cornetto*.)

cornet à bouqin. (Fr.) **cornet**. (Ger. *Zink*, It. *cornetto*, Sp. *corneta*.)

cornet à pistons. (Fr.) valve **cornet**.

cornetto. (It.) **cornet**. (Fr. *cornet à bouqin*, Ger. *Zink*, Sp. *corneta*.)

corno. (It.) **horn**, also known as the **French horn**. See **appendix 3: "Instrument Names and Their Translations."** (Fr. *cor, corne*.)

corno di bassetto. (It., Sp.) **basset horn**. (Fr. *cor de basset*, Ger. *Bassetthorn*.)

corno inglés. (Sp.) **English horn**, a double-reed member of the **oboe** family. (Fr. *cor anglais*, Ger. *Englischhorn*, It. *corno inglese*.) See also **appendix 3: "Instrument Names and Their Translations."**

corno inglese. (It.) **English horn**, a double-reed member of the **oboe** family. (Fr. *cor anglais*, Ger. *Englischhorn*, Sp. *corno inglés*.) See also **appendix 3: "Instrument Names and Their Translations."**

coro, chorus, choir. (It., Sp., Fr. *choeur*, Ger. *Chor*.)

coro maschile. (It.) men's chorus. (Fr. *chœur d'hommes*, Ger. *Männerchor*, Sp. *coro masculino*.)

coro masculino. (Sp.) men's chorus. (Fr. *chœur d'hommes*, Ger. *Männerchor*, It. *coro maschile*.)

corona. (It.) pause, **fermata**. Also *lunga corona*, long pause (fermata). (Fr. *point d'arrêt*; Ger. *Haltung, Fermate*; Sp. *corona, calderón*.)

corona. (Sp.) pause, **fermata**. Also *calderón*. (Fr. *point d'arrêt*; Ger. *Haltung, Fermate*; It. *fermata, corona*.)

correctamente. (Sp.) precisely, justly, exactly. (Fr. *justement*, Ger. *mit Recht*, It. *giustamente*.)

corta, corto. (It., Sp.) short. A commonly heard directive. (Fr. *bref, brève, court*; Ger. *kurz*.)

Costa, Sir Michael. (1808–1884.) British conductor and composer of Italian birth who settled in London. Costa was very influential in a period of great flux when the nature of conducting was changing throughout Europe. As a violinist/leader, he attached a length of leather to a small stick and tied it to his wrist. When his ensemble needed help staying together, he would drop his bow and lift the stick—which was always at the ready—to show the pulse. When he became "maestro al piano" at the King's Theatre in London, he made his mark quickly. In less than two years he abolished the system of dual leadership where the conductor shared leadership responsibility with the concertmaster or pianist, establishing himself as the director with a baton as the tool of authority. By reputation he had a dominant personality and was a strict disciplinarian in rehearsal. **George Bernard Shaw** wrote that Costa was an "autocrat rather than an artist" but had the respect of his musicians because of his excellent conducting technique and the ability to build a great orchestra. Costa also served as the founding conductor of the Royal Italian Opera, beginning in London in 1846, and in the same year he accepted the position of conductor of the **Philharmonic Society of London**, one of the most influential positions in all of Europe at the time. He was featured in an "I Spy" caricature in London's *Vanity Fair* (July 1872).

Sir Michael Costa.
Courtesy Vanity Fair, *1872.*

coulisse. (Fr.) slide, as used with a trombone. (Ger. *Zug*, It. *pompa movile a coulisse*, Sp. *bomba de afinación*.)

coulisses. (Fr.) wings of a stage. (Ger. *Kulisse*, It. *quinte*, Sp. *colisa*.)

counterclockwise release gesture. A conducting gesture given in a counterclockwise direction, most often a release gesture or cutoff of a chord or note. See **release gestures**.

counterpoint. Polyphonic composition or a combination with two or more independent lines sounding simultaneously. (Ger. *Kontrapunkt*, It. *contrappunto*, Sp. *contrapunto*.)

countertenor. A male singer who sings in falsetto. See also **vocal classifications**.

coup. (Fr.) the bow stroke. Also *coup d'archet.* (Ger. *streich, strich*; It. *colpo,* Sp. *golpe de arco.*)

coup d'archet. (Fr.) a bow stroke, bowing. Historically it referred to a loud chord involving a dramatic bow that was used to catch the attention of the audience. (Ger. *Bogenführung, Bogenstrich, Strichart*; It. *colpo d'arco, arcata*; Sp. *golpe de arco.*)

coup de langue. (Fr.) tonguing, the technique of attacking at the beginning of a note with the tongue to start the airflow on wind and brass instruments. (Ger. *Zugenstoß, Zungenschlag*; It. *colpo di lingua*; Sp. *golpe de lengua, articulación.*)

coup sur coup. (Fr.) gradually, step by step. Also *graduel.* (Ger. *allmählich*; It. *gradamente*; Sp. *graduado, poco a poco.*)

courant, en courant. 1. (Fr.) running, rapid. A descriptive term used to evoke a style of playing. (It. *corrente.*)
    2. A type of Baroque dance.

court. (Fr.) short, brief. Also *bref, brève.* (Ger. *kurz*; It. *breve, corto*; Sp. *corto.*)

couvert. (Fr.) covered, dampened, as is done on timpani. Also *sourd.* (Ger. *bedeckt*; It. *coperto, velato*; Sp. *cubierto.*)

couvert(e). (Fr.) covered, as in covering a drum to mute the sound. (Ger. *bedeckt,* It. *coperto,* Sp. *cubierto.*)

Covent Garden, The Royal Opera House. Because of devastating fires, it was the third opera house built on the site of Covent Garden. This building was opened in 1858 with a performance of Giacomo Meyerbeer's opera *Les Huguenots.* In the 1990s, it underwent a massive expansion and reconstruction, reopening in 1999. Commonly referred to simply as Covent Garden, it is the current home of the **Royal Opera**, Royal Ballet, and the orchestra of the Royal Opera House. The original hall was built in 1732, financed by the proceeds from a run of *The Beggar's Opera* by John Gay. Until the nineteenth century it served as a performance space for theater.

cover conductor. A **conductor** who is either on the staff of an orchestra or hired especially to "cover" the music director or guest conductor during a week of rehearsals and concerts. The cover conductor is present at all rehearsals and performances in case of illness or other circumstances that would prevent the main conductor from appearing. In addition, the cover conductor may have other responsibilities, including commenting on balances during the course of rehearsals from the perspective of the concert hall, and may even be asked to lead the orchestra in passages so that the main conductor can listen.

cowbell. In Europe, the actual cowbell is often used. In America, such bells are manufactured in varying sizes. (Fr. *sonnailles*; Ger. *Kuhglocken, Herdenglocken*; It. *cencerro*; Sp. *cenerro.*) Example: Symphony No. 6 by Gustav Mahler. See also **appendix 4: "Percussion Instruments and Their Translations."**

Cracow Philharmonic Orchestra. See **Kraków Philharmonic Orchestra.**

Craft, Robert. (b. 1923.) American **conductor**, writer, and friend to **Igor Stravinsky**. Craft's interests as a conductor were significant in that he brought forth both early music, especially that of Don Carlo Gesualdo, Claudio Monteverdi, and Heinrich Schütz, and contemporary music with the **Second Viennese School** composers **Karlheinz Stockhausen**, **Edgard Varèse**, and **Pierre Boulez** to his public. In 1948, he became associated with Stravinsky, conducting premieres of such works as *Requiem Canticles.* He worked with Stravinsky on many collaborative book projects but also wrote and published much on his own. His works include two volumes of music criticism, *Prejudices in Disguise* (1974) and *Current Convictions* (1977). He also published *Stravinsky: Chronicle of a Friendship* (1972). See the **bibliography**.

crash cymbals. Cymbals played in pairs by crashing them together. They can produce a wide variety of tone depending on the strength of the crash. See also **appendix 4: "Percussion Instruments and Their Translations"**; **cymbals**.

crescendo. (It.) a common dynamic indication meaning to become gradually louder. Abbreviated as *cresc.* or *cres.*

CRI. See **Composers Recordings, Inc.**

criticism, music. See **music criticism**.

croche. (Fr.) eighth note. See **appendix 5: "Rhythmic Terms and Their Translations."**

croisant, en. (Fr.) An indication to play a *glissando* with the hands crossing. Example: *glissando (en croisant),* glissando with the hands crossing, from the harp part of "Jeux de vagues," mvt. 2 of *La Mer* by Claude Debussy.

croma. (It.) eighth note. See **appendix 7: "Rhythmic Terms and Their Translations."**

crook. (Fr. *corps de rechange*; Ger. *Aufsatzbogen, Stimmbogen*; It. *ritorta*; Sp. *tonillo, cuerpo de recambio.*)

cross accents. As defined by **Elizabeth Green** in her text *The Modern Conductor* (see **bibliography**), cross accents are regularly recurring accents that sound in one meter but are written in another. In a score with multiple parts, each part may have accents written so as to create their own dominant metric feel that is not that of the printed meter, while the actual written meter is the same for all of those parts. This technique creates a rhythmic counterpoint between the parts.

cross meter. See **polymeter**.

cross rhythm. When more than one rhythmic pattern occurs simultaneously within a bar. An example would be a pattern of two at the same time as three. The resulting rhythmic effect is a cross rhythm.

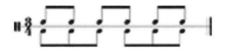

Cross rhythm. *Courtesy Andrew Martin Smith.*

crotales. Also called **antique cymbals**, they are a set of small metal disks of various sizes that are either struck together or hit with a metal beater to produce their tone. Notable use in *Prelude to an Afternoon of a Faun* by Claude Debussy. See **appendix 7: "Rhythmic Terms and Their Translations."**

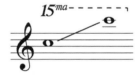

Crotales, high range as it sounds. *Courtesy Andrew Martin Smith.*

Crotales, high range as written. *Courtesy Andrew Martin Smith.*

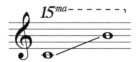

Crotales, low range as it sounds. *Courtesy Andrew Martin Smith.*

Crotales, low range as written. *Courtesy Andrew Martin Smith.*

crotchet. A quarter note in the English rhythmic system. See **appendix 7: "Rhythmic Terms and Their Translations."**

Cruz, Ivo. (1901–1985.) Columbian-born Portuguese composer and **conductor**. Cruz founded the Lisbon Philharmonic in 1937 and the Pro Arte Society, an organization that promoted Portuguese musicians. He became the director of the Lisbon Conservatory in 1938.

crystal glasses. A set of crystal glasses of various sizes tuned to specific pitches by filling them with water. The tone is produced by gently rubbing a moistened finger around the rim. Example: *Aftertones of Infinity* by Joseph Schwanter. See **appendix 7: "Rhythmic Terms and Their Translations."**

C score. A musical score where all parts are represented as they will sound, nontransposed and referred to as being "in C." See also **transposed score**.

cuanto. (Sp.) how much. A word heard in a wide variety of phrases, always in the form of a question. (Fr. *autant que,* Ger. *so viel wie,* It. *quanto.*) Example: *Cuanto tiempo de ensayo tenemos?* How much time do we still have to rehearse?

cuarteto. (Sp.) quartet, as in a group of four musicians such as a string quartet. (Fr. *quatuor,* Ger. *Quartett,* It. *quartetto.*)

cuatrillo. (Sp.) quadruplet, a rhythmic unit such as a group of four sixteenth notes. (Fr. *quartolet,* Ger. *quartole,* It. *quartina.*)

cubierto. (Sp.) covered, dampened, as is done on timpani. (Fr. *couvert, sourd;* Ger. *bedeckt;* It. *coperto, velato.*)

cubierto. (Sp.) **Stopped.** Also *tapado.* (Fr. *bouché, étouffé;* Ger. *gestopft, gedeckt;* It. *chiuso, tappato.*)

cue gesture. A gesture given by a **conductor** to indicate an entrance of a particular instrument, voice, or section. Cues can be given in three separate or combined ways: (1) the **right-hand cue**, in which the gesture from the beat before the entrance to the entrance itself is slightly enlarged, often combined with a breath simultaneous to that of the player; (2) the **left-hand cue**, given in the same manner as the right-hand cue, though often as a **mirror gesture**; (3) eye cue, the conductor establishes eye contact with the player or section some beats in advance of the entrance, this is most often combined with either a right- or left-hand cue gesture or even a nod of the head. In the case of a large section entrance, a conductor may use both hands. All manner and style of gesture are used dependent on the dynamic and dramatic nature of the music moment. See also **invitational cue gesture**, **conducting opera**.

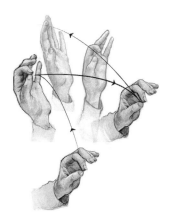

Cue gesture. *Courtesy Derek Brennan.*

cuerda. (Sp.) string of a violin or cello or other instrument with strings. (Fr. *corde*, It. *corda*, Ger. *Saite*.)

cuerda al aire. (Sp.) open string. Sometimes seen in scores and parts and heard as a directive in rehearsal for string players to use an open or unstopped or unfingered string. (Fr. *corde à vide*, Ger. *leere Saite*, It. *corda vuota*.)

cuíca. A Brazilian single-headed, wooden friction drum of varying sizes that has a thin stick mounted on the inside of the drum in the center of the head. Also called a **puita** or **quica**. Used in works of Heitor Villa-Lobos, *The Infernal Machine* by Christopher Rouse, and *Drala* by Peter Lieberson. See **appendix 7: "Rhythmic Terms and Their Translations."**

cuivre. (Fr.) a brassy sound, most often called for by the composer in the horn section. Example: *cuivrez légèrement*, slightly brassy, from "Le matin d'un jour de fête" from *Ibéria* of *Images* by Claude Debussy.

cuivres, les. (Fr.) the instruments made out of brass; the section of the **orchestra** or **band** made up of brass instruments. (Ger. *Blechinstrumente*; It. *gli ottoni, instrumenti a fiato di ottone*; Sp. *instrumentos de metal, metales*.)

cup mute. See **brass mutes**.

cupo. (It.) gloomy, dark, with a dark tone. A character word similar to *buio*. (Fr. *sombre*, Ger. *dunkel*, Sp. *tenebroso*.)

Curtis Institute of Music. Located in central Philadelphia, the institute was founded in 1924 by Mary Louise Curtis Bok, the daughter of Louisa Knapp and Cyrus Curtis of the Curtis Publishing Company. In 1928, the institute became tuition-free for all students, a policy that is maintained today. The institute offers a diploma in performance, a bachelor of music, master of music in opera, and a professional sudies certificate in opera. With a student body that ranges from only 150 to 170, it is among the most selective college-level institutions in America.

cutoff gesture. A gesture used by a **conductor** to indicate a clean end of a chord or note.

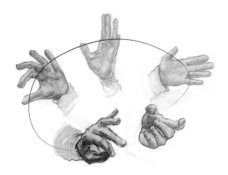

Cutoff gesture. *Courtesy Derek Brennan.*

cut time. In two beats per measure, conducted in two beats per measure. (Fr. *à la blanche*, Ger. *in halben Noten*, It. *alla breve*, Sp. *compás alla breve*.) See **alla breve**.

cycle. One complete vibration or oscillation, described in units of either time or **hertz**. Example. 440 hertz or cycles per second is the pitch **A**, customarily used as a **tuning note** by orchestras.

cycle. (Fr.) **cycle**. (Ger. *Zyklus*, It. *ciclo*, Sp. *ciclo*.)

cycle de quintes. (Fr.) **circle of fifths**. Often used as a teaching or memory device, a circular arrangement of the twelve pitches, their major and relative minor key signatures, and key names. When reading clockwise, they are a fifth apart. (Ger. *Quintenzirkel*, It. *circolo delle quinte*, Sp. *círculo de quintas*.)

cyclic transposition. The transposition of a **twelve-tone row** according to a numerical sequence chosen by the composer. For example, a transposition beginning on the second note of the row that is down a half step, then on the third note down two half steps, on the fourth note down three half steps, and so forth. Also called cyclic permutation.

cylindre. (Fr.) a **valve** on the trumpet or horn. (Ger. *Ventil, Pumpventil*; It. *piston*; Sp. *pistón*.)

cymbal. A curved metal plate available in varying sizes. Cymbals may be suspended and struck individually by various devices, including a wooden drumstick, a triangle beater, a wire brush, or a marimba mallet. They may also be played as **crash cymbals**, where two cymbals are held in the hands with a leather strap and can be played in any number of ways to generate a wide variety of sounds. (Fr. *cymbals*, Ger. *Becken*, It. *piatti*, Sp. *platos*.) See **appendix 7: "Rhythmic Terms and Their Translations."**

cymbalom. (Hung.) **cimbalom.** See **appendix 7: "Rhythmic Terms and Their Translations."**

cymbals. (Fr.) **cymbals.** (Ger. *Becken*; It. *piatti, cinelle*; Sp. *platillos, platos*.) See **appendix 7: "Rhythmic Terms and Their Translations."**

cymbalum. (Fr.) **cimbalom.** (Ger. *Zimbal, Zimbalon*; It. *cimbalom*; Sp. *zimbalón*.)

Czech Philharmonic Orchestra. Founded in 1896 as the orchestra of the Prague National Opera. At its opening concert Antonin Dvořák conducted his own works. The orchestra became an independent ensemble in 1901 and is based at the Rudolfinum concert hall in Prague. **Conductor Václav Talich** built the ensemble into an internationally acclaimed orchestra during his two periods as music director from 1919 to 1931 and from 1933 to 1941. He conducted the orchestra's first recording in 1929 with Bedřich Smetana's *My Country*. **Václav Neumann** was the longest serving chief conductor (1968–1990). Other important conductors include **Rafael Kubelik, Karel Ancerl, Jiří Bělohlávek, Vladimir Ashkenazy,** and **Zdeněk Mácal. Gustav Mahler** conducted the premiere of his Symphony No. 7 with the Czech Philharmonic in 1908.

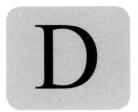

D. 1. A pitch name, the second note in the C major scale.

2. The name of a piece or the main scale of a piece, for example, Symphony in D or Sonata in D major.

d'abord. (Fr.) at first. (Ger. *zuerst*; It. *dapprimo*, *prima*; Sp. *primero*.)

da capo. (It.) back to the beginning (lit. "to the head"). Abbreviated D.C.

Dalcroze eurythmics. Also simply called eurhythmics, it was developed in the early twentieth century by the Swiss musician Émile Jaques-Dalcroze (1865–1950) to enhance the teaching of music education. Dalcroze's overall concept of teaching music contained three basic elements: eurhythmics, the teaching of rhythm, structure, and musical expression through movement; **solfège**, to develop an understanding of pitch, scale, and tonality; and improvisation, to develop an understanding of form and meaning through movement, voice, and instruments. Movement is pursued in order to convey information and understanding back to the student and not to an audience. Students gain musical awareness and confidence by a system that uses all of the senses but in particular the kinesthetic.

Dallas Symphony Orchestra. Founded in 1900 as the Dallas Symphony Club, the symphony has grown along with its city into a major American orchestra. Its founding music director was the German-born Hans Kreissig, who also helped finance the fledgling ensemble. Other music directors have included Walter J. Fried, Carl Nenth, Paul Van Katwiik, and Jacques Singer. After World War II, the symphony grew significantly under the leadership of **Antol Dorati**, followed by Walter Hendl, **Paul Kletski**, **Sir Georg Solti**, Donald Johanos, **Anshel Brusilow**, **Max Rudolf**, and **Louis Lane**. Mexican-born **Eduardo Mata** brought much success to the orchestra from his appointment in 1977 to his retirement in 1993. American Andrew Litton served from 1992 to and was succeeded by **Jaap van Zweden** in 2007. The orchestra performs in the Morton H. Meyerson Symphony Center, designed by architect I. M. Pei and acoustician Russell Johnson. It opened in 1989. The Dallas Symphony has a wide range of educational programs for all age groups, including HeartStrings, a program that distributes tickets thoughout north Texas.

dal segno. (It.) Abbreviationan indication to jump back to "the sign" and play from there on (lit. "to the sign"). Abbreviated D.S.

Dal segno. *Courtesy Andrew Martin Smith.*

damp, dampen. To cause the head of a drum or the strings of a violin, for instance, to cease vibrating.

dämpfen. (Ger.) to dampen, mute. For example, the sound of the timpani is often muted or dampened after a stroke; string instruments have mutes that are placed on the top of the bridge to create a muffled, quiet sound; and brass instruments have a variety of mutes. See also **brass mutes**; ***Dämpfer.***

Dämpfer. (Ger.) mute. (Fr. *sourdine*, It. *sordino*, Sp. *sordina*.) A variety of mutes are used with string and brass instruments. The piano has a damper pedal that dampens the sound. Examples: (Ger.) *Dämpfer ab*, mute off; (Ger.) *Dämpfer auf*, mute on; (Ger.) *Immer mit Dämpfer*, always with the mute; (Ger.) *ohne Dämpfer*, without mute (It. *senza sordino*, Fr. *sans sourdine*, Sp. *sin sordina*.);

(Ger.) *mit Dämpfer*, with mute (It. *con sordino*, Fr. *avec sourdine*, Sp. *con sordina*.) See also *dämpfen*.

Damrosch, Leopold. (1832–1885.) **Conductor**, violinist, and composer. Damrosch received a medical degree in 1854 in Berlin and was appointed violinist/leader of the court orchestra in Weimar by **Franz Liszt**. He moved to America in 1871, where he became conductor of a men's chorus called the Männergesangvrien Arion, founded the Oratorio Society in New York in 1873. He formed his own orchestra and gave the American premiere of Johannes Brahms's Symphony No. 1. His orchestra was reorganized as the **New York Symphony Society**, one of the predecessors of the **New York Philharmonic**, in 1878.

Damrosch, Walter. (1862–1950.) German-born American **conductor** and composer and the son of **Leopold Damrosch** and brother of Frank, also a conductor and music teacher. Damrosch came to America with his family in 1871 and served as the music director of the New York Symphony from 1903 until the orchestra merged with the New York Philharmonic Society in 1928. He is known for having conducted the American premieres of **Richard Wagner**'s opera *Parsifal* and the fourth and sixth symphonies of Pyotr Tchaikovsky. He commissioned George Gershwin's *Piano Concerto* and conducted the premiere of *An American in Paris*. He was the first to conduct an orchestral concert broadcast on radio across the United States, and from 1928 to 1942 he hosted a radio show called the *Music Appreciation Hour*, which became a popular series on classical music. The program was broadcast during the schoolday, and teachers were provided with books and worksheets to enhance the educational experience.

Damrosch was notorious for making up wildly popular, if simple lyrics to go along with the tune of a work in order to help young people and adult music lovers build their music appreciation and knowledge. One well-known example of the day was for Franz Schubert's Symphony No. 8, the "Unfinished" Symphony. Sung to the melody of the first movement, the words were *This is the symphony that Schubert wrote and never finished.*

Daniels, David. (b. 1933.) American **conductor** and author of *Orchestra Music*, a widely used reference tool. See the **bibliography**.

Danish National Radio Symphony Orchestra (DNSO) (DR SymfoniOrkestret). Founded in 1925, it is the flagship orchestra of the Danish Broadcasting Corporation and resident in the Copenhagen Concert Hall. Begun as an ensemble of only eleven players, by 1948 it had grown to ninety-two. Today the ensemble has ninety-nine musicians. Its first conductor was Launy Grøndahl. In 1930, **Nikolai Malko** served as a **conductor**, though

in these early years none of its conductors had a title. German conductor Fritz Busch moved to Denmark to escape the Nazi regime and worked alongside Malko. **Herbert Blomstedt** was given the title of principal conductor during his tenure (1967–1977). Blomstedt made several distinguished recordings with the orchestra. Of particular note were the works of the Danish composer Carl Nielsen. Other conductors have included Lamberto Gardelli (1986–1988), Gerd Albrecht (200–2004), Thomas Dausgaard (2001–2011), and in 2011 **Rafael Frübeck de Burgos** was appointed as the principal conductor. See also **radio symphony orchestras**.

Danish National Symphony Orchestra. See Danish National Radio Symphony Orchestra (DNSO).

Danish Royal Orchestra. See Royal Danish Orchestra.

dann. (Ger.) then. A common word used in a wide variety of phrases. (Fr. *ensuite, puis*; It. *allora, poi*; Sp. *entonces*.)

dansant. (Fr.) dance-like. A character word used to evoke a dance-like style of playing. (Ger. *tanzend*, It. *danzante*, Sp. *como danza*.)

danse. (Fr.) dance. (Ger. *Tanz*, It. *danza*, Sp. *danza*.) See also *dansant*.

dans le temps. (Fr.) in tempo. (Ger. *im Zeitmaß*, It. *in tempo*, Sp. *en el tempo*.)

danza, como. (Sp.) dance-like. A character word used to evoke a dance-like style of playing. Also *character danzante* or *carácter de danza*. (Fr. *dansant*, Ger. *tanzend*, It. *danzante*.)

dapprimo. (It.) at first. Also *prima*. (Ger. *zuerst*, Fr. *d'abord*, Sp. *primero*.)

Darmstadt, Germany. The site of International Summer Courses for New Music (Internationale Ferienkurse für Neue Musik, Darmstadt), which was sponsored by the U.S. State Department beginning in 1946. The focus was **avant-garde** music to the exclusion of past composers whose music was characterized in particular by folk or nationalistic elements. Composers who worked there included **Milton Babbitt**, Luciano Berio, **Pierre Boulez**, **John Cage**, Morton Feldman, Ernst Krenek, René Leibowitz, György Ligeti, Bruno Maderna, **Olivier Messiaen**, **Luigi Nono**, **Karlheinz Stockhausen**, Iannis Xenakis, and many more.

Darmstadt School. The term "Darmstadt School" was coined in 1957 by Italian composer Luigi Nono to refer to serial music being written at the time, as well as the group of composers who promoted it: Luigi Nono, Bruno Maderna, **Karlheinz Stockhausen**, and **Pierre Boulez**. The principles guiding this serial music covered not only pitch but became fundamental to the organization of tempos, durations, register, dynamics, and articulations. Having set their identity at the extremes of musical modernism, these composers, referred to by some as the "dodecaphonic police," began to turn on each other, leading to the decline of any collegiality by the early 1960s. By that time, with the advent of **aleatory** and electronic music, championed by composers such as John Cage, the term had taken on a pejorative meaning that implied music that was based on nothing more than mathematical formulae.

dasselbe. (Ger.) the same. Also *dieselbe, derselbe.* A commonly used word in a wide variety of phrases. (Fr. *même*; It. *stesso, istesso, medesimo*; Sp. *mismo.*)

dasselbe Zeitmaß. (Ger.) the same tempo. Also *im gleichen Tempo.* (Fr. *le même mouvement*; It. *lo stesso tempo, l'istesso tempo*; Sp. *al mismo tempo.*)

Dauer. (Ger.) duration, length of play of piece of music, for instance. Also *Spieldauer.* (Fr. *durée*, It. *durata*, Sp. *duración.*)

Daumen. (Ger.) thumb. (Fr. *pouce*, It. *pollice*, Sp. *pulgar.*) Specifically used to describe a particular manner of playing the tambourine. See also *mit dem Daumen.*

Davidson, Archibald T. (1883–1961.) American choral conductor known as "Doc" Davidson and author of several books including *Choral Conducting* (1940). Davidson graduated from Harvard University and became the director of the Harvard Glee Club (1919–1933). Under Davidson, the glee club and the Radcliffe Choral Society became the choruses of the **Boston Symphony Orchestra** and frequently recorded with them. See the **bibliography**.

Davies Symphony Hall. Also known as the Louie M. Davies Symphony Hall, it is the home of the **San Francisco Symphony**. Completed in 1980, it seats 2,743 and was designed by Skidmore, Owings & Merrill and Pietro Bellushi, with acousticians Bolt, Beranek, and Newman. Kirkegaard Associates made acoustical renovations in 1992.

Davis, Sir Andrew. (b. 1944.) English conductor. Davis studied at the **Royal College of Music** and **King's College, Cambridge**. His first professional position was as the associate conductor for the **BBC Scottish Symphony Orchestra** (1970–1972). He served as the principal guest conductor of the **Royal Liverpool Philharmonic Orchestra** (1974–1977), music director of the **Toronto Symphony Orchestra** (1975–1988), chief conductor of the **BBC Symphony Orchestra** (1988–2000), music director of **Glyndebourne Opera** (1989–2000), and music director of **Chicago Lyric** (2000–present.) He made his conducting debut at the **Metropolitan Opera** in 1996. He is known for having a broad repertory in orchestra, opera, and oratorio that ranges from Wolfgang Amadeus Mozart to the contemporary. Davis particularly promotes British composers, such as **Sir Benjamin Britten**, Frederick Delius, Edward Elgar, Ralph Vaughan Williams, Sir Michael Tippett, and Anthony Payne, having recorded works of all. Davis has been described as achieving good results through a particularly clear conducting technique, a thorough knowledge of the score, an excellent ear, and a respectful manner. His sense of sound favors the strings, and he has a strong affinity to **John Barbirolli**, **Wilhelm Furtwängler**, Ludwig van Beethoven, and **Otto Klemperer**.

Davis, Sir Colin. (1927–2013.) English conductor. Davis studied clarinet at the **Royal College of Music**, where he was not allowed in the conducting class because he didn't play the piano. Instead, he and a group of students formed their own orchestra, the Kalmar Orchestra, and he conducted. The Chelsea Opera Group, which he also led, developed out of the Kalmar. He was appointed the assistant conductor of the **BBC Scottish Orchestra** in 1957 and made his debut at **Sadler's Wells Opera** in 1958. He took over from an ailing **Otto Klemperer** in a concert performance of Wolfgang Amadeus Mozart's *Don Giovanni* in 1959 and one year later did the same for **Sir Thomas Beecham** in *Die Zauberflöte.* He was appointed chief conductor at Sadler's Wells Opera (later the **English National Opera**) in 1959 and later music director (1961–1965). During his time at Sadler's Wells Opera, he conducted **Igor Stravinsky**'s *The Rake's Progress* and *Oedipus rex,* Ludwig van Beethoven's *Fidelio,* and more. He served as the principal conductor for the **BBC Symphony Orchestra** (1967–1971) and debuted at the **Metropolitan Opera** with **Sir Benjamin Britten**'s *Peter Grimes,* later returning to conduct Alban Berg's *Wozzeck* and Claude Debussy's *Pelléas et Mélisande.* Davis succeeded **Sir Georg Solti** as the music director of the **Royal Opera House, Convent Garden**, in 1971, serving until 1986 conducting over thirty operas. From 1983 to 1992 he served as the music director of the **Bavarian Radio Symphony Orchestra**, honorary conductor of the **Dresden Staatskapelle**, and principal conductor of the **London Symphony Orchestra** (1995–present). Davis is known for a legacy of excellent recordings of Jean Sibelius; **Hector Berlioz**, including the operas *Benvenuto Cellini, Romeo et Juliettet,* and *Les Troyens*; several Mozart operas; and his promotion of the work of fellow Englishmen Sir Michael Tippett and Britten. Known as impulsive and passionate as a young man, Davis has been called a visionary and inspirational conductor who knew how to ask for what he wanted from an orchestra without insulting their intelligence. He took the view that the score was a mere two-dimensional view of a piece that needed to be brought to life, leaving a great deal of leeway for interpretation. Davis was knighted in 1980.

Colin Davis. *Courtesy Photofest.*

Dayton Philharmonic Orchestra (DPO). Formed in 1933 in Dayton, Ohio, the orchestra performs classics, chamber orchestra, young people's, family, and pops concerts in addition to performing for the Dayton Opera and running the Dayton Philharmonic Youth Orchestra. The orchestra has received the **ASCAP Award for Adventurous Programming** seven times. The current music director is Neal Gittleman (appointed in 1994). Past music directors include **Isaiah Jackson** (1987–1994), Charles Wendelken-Wilson (1975–1987), Marjorie Kline (1941–1968), and Paul Katz (1933–1941).

db. Abbreviation for **decibel**.

D.C. Abbreviation Abbreviationfor *da capo*.

de. (Fr.) of. (Ger. *von*, It. *di*, Sp. *de*.)

dead beat. A **neutral gesture** that serves to notify the ensemble to where they are in a given measure or phrase. It is called neutral specifically because it is not meant to initiate any sound, only to serve as a "placemarker," and should be conducted without a breath, a preparation, or in any particular tempo. Dead or **neutral beats** can mark any beat in a bar but most often mark **downbeats** (beat one). In this case, the gesture begins at the top of the **conducting pattern** and falls easily to the bottom of the **conducting plane**. The gesture is most commonly used when conducting recitative passages in opera, concerto, or aria accompaniments or in **aleatoric** or "free" passages in contemporary music. When used to show several measures in a concerto or solo work when the orchestra doesn't play, only the **downbeat** of each bar is given. Some pedagogues refer to this as a **dead gesture**. See also **conducting technique**.

dead gesture. See **dead beat**.

débil. (Sp.) plaintive, weak, mournful. A character word used to evoke a manner of playing. Seen in its German translation in scores and parts of **Gustav Mahler**. See also *tiempo débil*. (Fr. *faible*; Ger. *schwach*; It. *flebile*, *fiacco*.)

debilitándose. (Sp.) becoming weaker and softer. A descriptive word used to evoke a certain change in the music. (Fr. *affaiblissez, affaibli*; Ger. *schwachen*; It. *indebolire*.)

de bonne heure. (Fr.) early, soon. Also *tôt*. (Ger. *früh*; It. *presto*; Sp. *temprano, pronto*.)

Debussy, Claude. (1862–1918.) Renowned French composer. See *Prelude to the Afternoon of a Faun* **(1894)** in **appendix 1: "Six Pieces That Changed Conducting."**

début. (Fr.) beginning.

Decca Records. Beginning in Britain as the Decca Gramophone Co. Ltd., it patented and produced a portable gramophone. In 1929, the company was sold to a former stockbroker, Edward Lewis, becoming Decca Records, Ltd. The first British company to introduce the LP, they pursued many technological developments, especially in the 1940s. Its American label was established in 1934, becoming a major firm by signing a long list of popular artists and selling its products at low prices. American Decca became independent in 1939, remaining so until they bought British Decca's parent company in 1998.

In 1942, Decca released the first recording of Irving Berlin's *White Christmas* as sung by Bing Crosby. It remains the best-selling single of all time. In the 1950s, Decca and EMI Records were the top two recording companies in Britain.

Decca Classical, which was released in the United States under the name **London Records**, was successful due to the advent of LP records, stereo sound, and Decca's FFRR (full frequency range recording) technology, a kind of high-fidelity sound that worked best on the new LP. Significant classical releases included those led by **Ernest Ansermet** and **L'Orchestre de la Suisse Romande**. John Culsaw, senior producer of classical recordings, sought to revolutionize the recording of opera, producing **Sir Georg Solti**'s hugely popular complete

Ring Cycle. As a result, the company successfully signed such artists as **Herbert van Karajan**, Joan Sutherland, and others. In 1961, U.S. Decca was purchased by the MCA Corporation, which then lost the rights to use the Decca name.

Popular musicians, rock 'n' roll, blues, country, and original cast albums of Broadway musicals were the main source of the company's financial success throughout its history. However, the vagaries of the market and lost opportunities led to its decline, and eventually both the British and American units became part of the Universal Music Group (UMG). UMG recently made a donation of two hundred thousand of the masters from the 1920s to the 1940s to the Library of Congress.

déchiffrer. (Fr.) play at sight, sight read. Also *jouer à vue.* (Ger. *vom Blatt spielen,* It. *suonare a prima vista,* Sp. *tocar a primera vista.*)

dechiffrer. (Fr.) to play at sight, sight read. Also *jouer à vue.* (Ger. *vom Blatt spielen;* It. *suonare a prima vista, a libro aperto;* Sp. *tocar a primera vista.*)

decibel. A unit of measure for the loudness or intensity of a sound, standing for a tenth of a "bel" and named after scientist Alexander Graham Bell. It is abbreviated as "db." A single decibel is approximately the smallest unit recognizable by the human ear. A bel is a division of a logarithmic scale used to express the ratio of the intensities of two sounds. An increase of ten decibels creates a tenfold increase in sound intensity; twenty equals a hundredfold increase and thirty, a thousandfold increase. The magnitude of the decibel approximates these sounds: very soft violin, 5–10 dbs; a busy street, 50–90 dbs; a full orchestra, 80–90 dbs; and a rock band, 130–40 dbs. The difference between the threshold of human hearing and that of pain is about 120 decibels. See also **noise levels in the workplace.**

décidé. (Fr.) to decide, authoritative, resolute, a character word. (Ger. *entschieden, entschlossen,* It. *deciso, risoluto,* Sp. *decidico, resuelto.*)

decidico. (Sp.) To decide, authoritative, resolute, a character word. Also *resuelto.* (Fr. *décidé;* Ger. *entschieden, entschlossen;* It. *deciso, risoluto.*)

decidio. (Sp.) decisive, decisively, a character word. Also *determinadamente.* (Fr. *determine,* Ger. *bestimmt,* It. *determinato.*)

deciso. (It.) to decide, authoritative, resolute, a character word. Also *risoluto.* (Fr. *décidé;* Ger. *entschieden, entschlossen;* Sp. *decidico, resuelto.*)

decrescendo. (It.) in dynamics, to get gradually softer. Abbreviated as *decresc., decr.*

de façon burlesque. (Fr.) jesting, light. A character word used to describe a mood or manner of playing. (It. *burlesco;* Ger. *scherzhaft;* Sp. *burlón, en broma, chistoso.*)

défaillant, en. (Fr.) dying away, getting softer, fading. (Ger. *hinsterbend, entschwinden;* It. *mancando;* Sp. *desapareciendo.*)

Defauw, Désiré. (1885–1960.) Belgian conductor and violinist. A leading Belgian conductor, Defauw served as the conductor of the **Chicago Symphony Orchestra** from 1943 to 1947. He made a number of recordings with the **Brussels Conservatory Orchestra** and the **Chicago Symphony Orchestra**, including on of the first recordings of Sergei Prokofiev's *Scythian Suite.*

dégagé. (Fr.) bold. A character word used in music. Also *alerte.* (Ger. *keck;* It. *spigliato;* Sp. *audaz, atrevido.*)

degenerate set. A **twelve-tone row** or set that because of its individual characteristics cannot be transformed into the standard forty-eight distinct forms by inversion, retrograde, retrograde inversion, or transposition. One example would be when the row is the same in both its original and retrograde inversion forms.

degno. (It.) dignified, a character word. (Fr. *digne;* Ger. *würdig,* würdevoll; Sp. *digno.*)

degré. (Fr.) a degree or note of a scale. (Ger. *Stufe,* It. *grado,* Sp. *grado.*) Example: *conjoint,* stepwise, by step. (Ger. *stufenweise;* It. *congiunto;* Sp. *por grados, conjunto.*)

dehnen. (Ger.) to broaden, prolong, stretching, the tempo, a phrase, for instance. Also *dehnend.* (Fr. *en s'étendant,* It. *stirando.*)

dehors, en. (Fr.) bring out, bring out of the orchestral texture. Also *en évidence.* (Ger. *hervortretend,* It. *in fuori,* Sp. *destacar.*) Example: *un peu en dehors,* play out a little, from "Jeux de vagues," mvt. 2 of *La Mer* by Claude Debussy.

dejar que vibre. (Sp.) let ring, as in cymbals, triangle, or tam-tam, for instance. Also *dejar que resuene.* (Fr. *laissez vibrer,* Ger. *klingen lassen,* It. *lasciar vibrare.*)

Delaware Symphony Orchestra. Founded in 1929 with the merger of the Wilmington Symphony Orchestra and the Wilmington Music School. By 1940, the orchestra had ninety members. In 1971, it became the Delaware Symphony Orchestra. It is now fully professional. The orchestra performs a classics series, chamber music, educational concerts, and outreach programs. The current music director is David Amado (appointed in 2003). Past music directors include Stephen Guzenhauser (1979–2003), Harry Stausebach (1929–1955), and Van Lier (1956–1978).

deliberamente. (It.) deliberately, a character word. (Fr. *délibérément.*)

délibérément. (Fr.) deliberately, a character word. (It. *deliberamente.*)

delicado. (Sp.) smoothly, delicately, a descriptive word heard in rehearsal to evoke a quality of playing. Also *grácil.* (Fr. *délicat, délicatement*; Ger. *zart, delikat*; It. *delicato, delicatemente.*)

délicat. (Fr.) smoothly, delicate, a descriptive word heard in rehearsal to evoke a quality of playing. Also *délicatement.* (Ger. *zart, delikat*; It. *delicate, delicatemente*; Sp. *delicado, grácil.*)

delicatemente. (It.) smoothly, delicately, a descriptive word heard in rehearsal to evoke a quality of playing. Also ***delicatemente.*** (Fr. *délicat, délicatement*; Ger. *zart, delikat*; Sp. *delicado, grácil.*) Used in the phrase *con delicatezza,* with delicacy.

delicato. (It.) smoothly, delicate, a descriptive word heard in rehearsal to evoke a quality of playing. (Fr. *délicat, délicatement*; Ger. *zart, delikat*; Sp. *delicado, grácil.*)

delikat. (Ger.) smoothly, delicate, a descriptive word heard in rehearsal to evoke a quality of playing. Also *zart.* (Fr. *délicat, délicatement*; It. *delicato, delicatemente*; Sp. *delicado, grácil.*)

Del Mar, Jonathan. (b. 1951.) English conductor and editor of the **Bärenreiter** *New Edition* (*Neue Ausgabe*) of the Ludwig van Beethoven symphonies. Numerous conductors have chosen to use this new edition, including **Claudio Abbado**, **Bernard Haitink**, **Sir Simon Rattle**, **Osmo Vänskä**, **David Zinman**, and others. With his father, **Norman Del Mar**, he is the author of *Conducting Favourite Concert Pieces* (1999) and *Conducting Elgar* (1999). See the **bibliography**.

Del Mar, Norman. (1919–1994.) British conductor, pedagogue, and author. Del Mar played horn in **Sir Thomas Beecham**'s **Royal Philharmonic Orchestra**. He became the assistant conductor of the Royal Philharmonic in 1947 and founded the Chelsea Symphony Orchestra in 1944. He served as the principal conductor of the EOG (1948–1956); the conductor of the Yorkshire Symphony

Orchestra (1954–1955), the **BBC Scottish Symphony Orchestra** (1960–1965), and the **Gothenburg Symphony Orchestra** (1969–1973); and the artistic director of the Aarhus Symphony Orchestra (1985–1988). Del Mar taught at the **Royal College of Music** and the **Guildhall School of Music**, both in London, for many years. Del Mar's books include *The Anatomy of the Orchestra* (1981); *Conducting Beethoven*, vol. 1 (1982) and vol. 2 (1993); *Conducting Brahms* (1993); *Mahler's Sixth Symphony: A Study* (1980); *Orchestral Variations: Confusion and Error in the Orchestral Repertoire* (1981); and *A Companion to the Orchestra* (1987). See the **bibliography**.

demi-pause. (Fr.) half note rest. See also **appendix 7: "Rhythmic Terms and Their Translations."**

demisemiquaver. The equivalent of a thirty-second note in the English rhythmic system. See also **appendix 7: "Rhythmic Terms and Their Translations."**

demi-soupir. (Fr.) Eighth note rest. (Ger. *Achtelpause*, It. *pausa di croma*, Sp. *silencio de corchea*) See **appendix 7: "Rhythmic Terms and Their Translations."**

demi-ton. (Fr.) half step, semitone. (Ger. *Halbton*, It. *semitono*, Sp. *semitono.*) See also **appendix 6: "Basic Interval Names and Their Translations."**

demi-voix, à. (Fr.) half-voice, quietly. Also *à mi-voix.* (It. *mezza voce*, Ger. *mit halber Stimme*, Sp. *a media voz.*)

density. A term used to describe the relative complexity of multiple layers of music sounding simultaneously. This characteristic often pertains to late **Romantic** and twentieth-century instrumental and choral music, such as compositions by **Richard Wagner**, **Richard Strauss**, **Alexander Scriabin**, **Gustav Mahler**, **Arnold Schoenberg**, **Olivier Messiaen**, **Pierre Boulez**, **Karlheinz Stockhausen**, and many others.

Denver Symphony Orchestra. See **Colorado Symphony**.

dépêcher, se. (Fr.) to hurry. (Ger. *zu beeilen*, It. *affrettare*, Sp. *prisa.*)

de plus en plus. (Fr.) more and more, gradually more. An expression heard in rehearsal and seen often in scores and parts. (Ger. *allmählich mehr*; It. *poco a poco più*; Sp. *poco a poco, cada vez más.*)

de plus en plus. (Fr.) little by little. An expression used to evoke a gradual process, such as a crescendo. (Ger. *allmählich mehr*, It. *poco a poco più.*)

DePriest, James Anderson. (1936–2013.) African American conductor. DePriest served as the assistant conductor of the **New York Philharmonic** (1965–1966); principal guest conductor of the Symphony of the New World (1968–1970); associate conductor (1971–1975) and principal guest conductor (1975–1976) of the **National Symphony Orchestra**; and music director of the Quebec Symphony Orchestra (1976–1983), the Oregon Symphony (1980–2003), where he built the orchestra into one of international reputation, and the Malmo (Sweden) Symphony Orchestra (1991–1994). DePriest was made laureate music director of the Oregon Symphony upon his retirement in 2003. He also served as the director of conducting and orchestral studies at the **Juilliard School**. In 2005, he received the National Medal of Arts. DePriest made over fifty recordings and appeared around the globe as a guest conductor with such orchestras as the **Los Angeles Philharmonic, Boston Symphony Orchestra, Chicago Symphony Orchestra, Cleveland Symphony Orchestra, Denver Symphony Orchestra, Detroit Symphony Orchestra, Houston Symphony Orchestra, Indianapolis Symphony Orchestra, Minnesota Symphony Orchestra, Philadelphia Symphony Orchestra, Pittsburgh Symphony Orchestra**, Syracuse Symphony Orchestra (New York), **Toronto Symphony Orchestra**, and many more. DePriest was the nephew of the legendary soprano Marian Anderson. In 1962, on a State Department tour in Thailand, he contracted polio and conducted sitting down for the rest of his career. Later the same year, he won the Dimitri Mitropoulos International Conducting Competition.

James DePriest. *Courtesy Photofest.*

derivation technique. The creation of a **twelve-tone row** or set through the transformation of three-, four-, or six-note pitch groups. Also called a *derivation row* or *derivation set*. An example is a three-note original (prime) combined in any order with its retrograde, its retrograde in-

version, and its inversion to form a **row**. Example: Anton Webern's *Concerto for Nine Instruments*.

dernière. (Fr.) last, ultimate. A term heard in rehearsal. (Ger. *letzter, letzte*; It. *ultima, ultimo*; Sp. *último, final*.) See also *dernière fois*.

dernière fois. (Fr.) last time. (Fr. *derniére fois*, Ger. *letztes Mal*, It. *ultima volta*, Sp. *último tempo*.) Example: *pour la dernière fois*, for the last time.

derrière. (Fr.) behind, behind the stage. Example: *loin derrière la scène*, far offstage. Seen in many French scores, including the ballet *Daphnis et Chloé* by Maurice Ravel.

Des. (Ger.) D-flat. See also **appendix 5: "Pitch Names and Their Translations."**

désaccordé. (Fr.) out of tune. (Ger. *verstimmt*; It. *scordato, stonato*; Sp. *desafinado*.)

desafinado. (Sp.) out of tune. (Fr. *désaccordé*; Ger. *verstimmt*; It. *scordato, stonato*.)

desapareciendo. (Sp.) getting softer, fading, dying away until the end. Also *suavizando*. (Fr. *en défaillant*; Ger. *entschwindend, hinsterbend*; It. *mancando*.)

desarrollo. (Sp.) the development section of a piece. (Fr. *développement*; Ger. *Durchführung*; It. *sviluppo, svolgimento*.)

Des Moines Metro Opera (DMMO). Established in 1973 in Indianola, Iowa, the company presents a three-opera summer season. Since 1975, over one thousand young singers have taken part in its apprentice program. The company presents a combination of standard and rarely heard operatic masterpieces. It also runs the award-winning Opera Iowa Educational Touring Troupe and other outreach initiatives.

Des Moines Symphony. Founded in 1937 in Des Moines, Iowa, its current music director, Joseph Giunta, was appointed in 1989. Under Giunta, the Des Moines Symphony has grown to be a leading regional orchestra. The orchestra performs a five-concert "Masterworks" classics series (all are broadcast on Iowa Public Radio), pops, family, and education concerts. In 2003, the orchestra established the Des Moines Symphony Academy, which offers music classes and lessons. The academy now has over four hundred students.

dessous. (Fr.) under, below. Also *sous*. (Ger. *unter*, It. *sotto*, Sp. *bajo*.)

destacar. (Sp.) bring out, bring forward. A directive heard in rehearsal when adjusting the **balance** between the instruments or parts. (Fr. *en dehors, en évidence*; Ger. *hervortretend*; It. *in fuori*.)

destra. (It.) right, right hand. Also *la destra*, the right. (Fr. *main droite*, Ger. *rechte Hand*, Sp. *mano derecha*.)

desvanesiéndose. (Sp.) dying out, disappear, expire. A descriptive term used to evoke a kind of playing. Also *extinguiéndose, perdiéndose*. (Fr. *éteindre, en se perdant, expirer*; Ger. *erlöschen, sich verlierend*; It. *espirare, extinguere, perdendosi*.)

détaché. (Fr.) the most basic stroke of the bow, alternating down- and up-bows, staying on the string, and generally executed in the middle of the bow. It does not mean detached, as the bowing style is usually smooth.

détendu. (Fr.) getting slower, relaxed. A descriptive term. (Ger. *entspannt*, It. *rilassato*, Sp. *soltar el tempo*.)

determinato. (It.) decisive, decisively, a character word used to evoke a particular style of playing. (Fr. *determine*; Ger. *bestimmt*; Sp. *decidido, determinadamente*.)

determine. (Fr.) decisive, decisively, a character word used to evoke a particular style of playing. (Ger. *bestimmt*; It. *determinato*; Sp. *decidido, determinadamente*.)

de toutes ces forces. (Fr.) with all force. A directive heard in rehearsal and sometimes seen in music. (Ger. *mit voller Kraft*, It. *con tutta la forza*, Sp. *con toda fuerza*.)

Detroit Symphony Orchestra (DSO). Founded 1914, the orchestra is resident in its own Orchestra Hall, built in 1919 in four months and twenty-four days at the insistence of Russian conductor **Ossip Gabrilowitsch** as a condition of him becoming the music director. Gabrilowitsch served from 1918 to 1935, bringing the orchestra to national fame. From 1934 to 1942 (with a hiatus during the war years, 1942–1945), the symphony performed for millions of Americans as the official orchestra of the national radio show the **Ford Symphony Hour**. Through these broadcasts, the Orchestra Hall became known as having one of the finest acoustics of any concert hall in the country.

Following Gabrilowitsch's early death, conductor Viktor Kolar (1940–1942), a series of guest conductors, and then Karl Krueger (1944–1949) led the orchestra. Hit by economic difficulties, the orchestra disbanded temporarily from 1949 to 1951, reorganizing under the leadership of conductor Paul Parray. He served as the music director from 1951 to 1963 and was followed by **Sixten Ehrling** (1963–1973); Aldo Ceccato (1973–1976); **Antol**

Dorati (1977–1981), who led the first European tour in 1979; **Gary Bertini** (1981–1983); **Günther Herbig** (1984–1990); **Neeme Järvi** (1990–2005); and **Lenard Slatkin** (2008–present.) In 1946, the orchestra moved to the Wilson Theater (renamed Music Hall) and then in 1956 to Ford Auditorium, where it remained until 1989 when, following a twenty-year effort, it returned to Orchestra Hall. Renovations to the hall, a $60 million addition known as the Max M. Fisher Music Center and the addition in 2004 of a fine arts high school, the Detroit School of the Arts, have significantly improved the area surrounding Orchestra Hall. The Detroit Symphony Youth Orchestra was founded in 1970 under conductor Paul Freeman. A labor dispute led to a musician's strike that lasted from October 2010 to April 2011 and resulted in a 30 percent pay cut, with some members of the symphony taking positions in other orchestras. In April 2011, the DSO launched Live from Orchestra Hall, the first free webcast by any orchestra. Concerts are streamed live to a worldwide audience.

Deutsch catalogue. A thematic catalogue of the works of Franz Schubert created by Otto Erich Deutsch in the 1950s. See **thematic catalogue**.

Deutsche Grammophon (DG). Founded in 1989 in Hanover, Germany, by Emile Berliner, a gramophone player and the inventor of the record "plate." Patents were registered in Berlin and Washington, DC. Hydraulic presses were imported from the United States to manufacture shellac discs from zinc masters that had been imported from the **Grammophone Company** in London. Initially, DG manufactured their gramophone players with American-made components. By 1900, **Deutsche Grammophon Gesellschaft (DGG)** was a joint stock company located in Berlin with the parent company, the London Grammophone Company. By 1907, DG made the first twelve-inch records with two playing sides, releasing a complete *Die Fledermaus*, followed by *Faust* and *Carmen* in 1908, and annual production had exceeded six millions discs. In 1908, the famous trademark of the dog Nipper listening to "His Master's Voice" (*Die Stimme seines Herrn*) was registered. In 1913, the first recording of a complete symphony was made with **Arthur Nikisch** conducting Ludwig van Beethoven's Symphony No. 5 with the **Berlin Philharmonic Orchestra**. It needed four double-sided discs. During World War I, the two companies, British and German, were separated, and DG's assets were sold to Polyphon Musikwerke. After the war, the new company replenished its roster of artists with some of the most distinguished German conductors and performers of the day on the Polydor label, including **Richard Strauss**, pianist Wilhelm Kempff, soprano Elisabeth Schumann, and many more. By 1925, all nine Beethoven symphonies had appeared, along with Anton

Bruckner's Symphony No. 7 and **Gustav Mahler**'s Symphony No. 2.

In 1927, the one hundreth anniversary of Beethoven's death was marked by the issue of several Beethoven symphonies and the acquisition of the American recording firm, Brunswick. The years 1926–1933 saw the release of **Richard Strauss** conducting his own tone poems, **Bruno Walter** conducting Pyotr Tchaikovsky's Symphony No. 6, **Erich Kleiber** with the *Fledermaus Overture*, and **Hans Knappertsbusch** conducting Joseph Haydn.

By 1929, the company employed over five hundred at its Hanover factory and had annual release figures of ten million. With the turmoil of the international economic downturn in the 1930s and World War II, the company shrank considerably. In 1949, the trademark His Master's Voice was sold. In 1950, the "78," based on DG's variable groove technology, came into existence, and within a year it was updated by the 33 1/3 long-playing (LP) disc. The 1950s and 1960s saw the issue of numerous historically important performances, marked by the signing of conductors **Herbert van Karajan**, who made over 330 recordings for the company; **Karl Böhm**, who was particularly famous for his Wolfgang Amadeus Mozart symphony and opera recordings; **Rafael Kubelik**, who championed the Czech repertoire and led a complete Mahler cycle; and Americans **Lorin Maazel** and later **Leonard Bernstein**, as well as artists such as baritone Dietrich Fischer-Dieskau, who recorded the complete Franz Schubert lieder for male voice and piano.

DG's early music division is **Archiv Produktion**. Recordings included the work of violinist and leader **Reinhard Goebel** with **Musica Antiqua Köln**, Trevor Pinnock with the **English Concert**, **John Elliott Gardiner** and the **English Baroque Soloists**, and many more. The last decades of the twentieth century have seen the rise of many young artists who have continued the DG tradition. In 1998, on its one hundreth anniversary, the company had survived the tumult of history and remained one of the world's largest classical recording companies. DG's list of conductors and artists amounts to a panoply of the best of the best, an invaluable legacy.

Deutsche Grammophon Gesellschaft (DGG). See **Deutsche Grammophon (DG)**.

Deutsche Oper Berlin. See **German Opera Berlin**.

Deutches Symphonie-Orchester Berlin (DSO). See **German Symphony Orchestra Berlin**.

deutlich. (Ger.) clear, distinct. A descriptive term used in rehearsal when a clear articulation is required, for instance. (Fr. *distinct*, It. *distinto*, Sp. *distinto*.)

deux. (Fr.) two. (Ger. *zwei*, It. *due*, Sp. *dos*.) Example: *À deux*, for two, an indication for two players to play the same part. See also **numbers, basic**.

deux fois. (Fr.) an indication that calls for playing something twice, one after another, not doubled or simultaneously. (Ger. *zweimal*, It. *due volte*, Sp. *dos veces*.)

developing an orchestral sound. Conductors and the orchestras and ensembles they work with develop the sound of the orchestra through a wide variety of means, all of which depend on the basic level of the orchestra. At the professional level, the job is generally one of refinement of elements, while at any other level it is often one of establishing basic playing techniques for the individual instruments and for the ensemble as a whole. The elements of a good sound include the following points and much more:

1. Good tone-production techniques on all instruments, including well-developed breathing techniques and support (especially for woodwinds and brass) and relaxed arm weight (especially in the use of the bow), good posture, and adequate strength in the upper body.
2. Knowledge and understanding of one's own instrument with all its strengths and weaknesses.
3. A well-developed ear for intonation in all its settings, including the knowledge and understanding of how to adjust depending on what note of a chord one plays, the harmonic style of the piece, and the tuning tendencies of the other instruments.
4. A good sense of balance within each section of the ensemble and across the orchestra combined with the understanding of the role of the part played, that is, is it a solo, accompanimental, and so forth.
5. A strong understanding of the various styles of music in different historic periods and the differences of playing in each.
6. High-quality instruments that are themselves capable of producing the desired tone. Often wind and brass sections in a given orchestra will seek to unify sound by using instruments from the same maker, or at least of the same type.
7. A rehearsal and concert hall that have good acoustics that enhance the sound of the orchestra.
8. A positive, energetic attitude and a good psychological outlook on the part of the conductor and the players.
9. Adaptability and flexibility.

développement. (Fr.) the development section of a piece. (Ger. *Durchführung*; It. *sviluppo*, *svolgimento*; Sp. *desarrollo*.)

devenir. (Fr.) to become. (Ger. *werden*, It. *diventare*.) A term heard in a wide variety of phrases, such as *Il doit être héritier calme*, it must get soft here.

devolver. (Sp.) to give back, as in tempo in the case of the **rubato** style. (Fr. *render*, Ger. *zurückgeben*, It. *rendere*.) See also **rubato**.

diapason. (It.) tuning fork. (Fr. *diapason*, Ger. *stimmgabel*, Sp. *diapasón*.)

diapasón. (Sp.) tuning fork. (Fr. *diapason*, Ger. *stimmgabel*, It. *diapason*.)

Diapason **(magazine).** First published in 1956, it is a monthly French magazine issued by the Italian media group Mondadori. The magazine prints CD reviews and is responsible for awarding the prestigious **Diapason d'Or** prize every year. See also **music magazines**.

diapason à bouche. (Fr.) **pitch pipe**, a small wind device that when blown through sounds any of several pitches in order to give a choir a starting pitch when no accompaniment precedes the entrance. Also *flûte d'accord*. (Ger. *Stimmpfeife*, It. *diapason a fiato*, Sp. *diapasón de boca*.)

diapason a fiato. (It.) **pitch pipe**. (Fr. *flûte d'accord, diapason à bouche*; Ger. *Stimmpfeife*; Sp. *diapasón de boca*.)

diapasón de boca. (Sp.) **pitch pipe** (Fr. *flûte d'accord, diapason à bouche*; Ger. *Stimmpfeife*, It. *diapason a fiato*.)

Diapason d'Or. A distinguished prize for best recording awarded by the French *Diapason* music magazine.

diatonic. Melody or harmony that mostly uses the pitches of a **diatonic scale**. See also **pandiatonicism**.

diatonic scale. Any major, minor, or modal scale made up of whole and half steps. See **church modes**.

di colpo. (It.) abrupt, sudden, suddenly. Also *repente*. A descriptive term seen in scores and parts and heard in rehearsal. (Fr. *tout á coup, immédiatement, subitement*; Sp. *immediatamente, súbito*.)

Die Musik in Geschichte und Gegenwart **(MGG, Music in History and the Present).** The largest and most comprehensive German music encyclopedia available today. The first edition is seventeen volumes is dated from 1949 to 1968, with a two-volume supplement from 1973 to 1986. The second edition dated from 1994 to 2007, with a supplement from 2008, and consists of a ten-volume subject encyclopedia and a separate seventeen-volume biographical encyclopedia. The current edition contains entries by more than 3,500 scholars from 55 countries and includes more than 20,000 articles on all areas of music, as well as more than 4,000 illustrations. It is published by **Barenreiter**, and a **CD-Rom** version is available in a limited number of libraries.

Die Musik in Geschichte und Gegenwart **(Music in History and the Present).** See *Musik in Geschichte und Gegenwart*.

Die Reihe. (Ger.) In English, "The Row" or "The Series." A German-language music journal edited by Herbert Eimert and **Karlheinz Stockhausen** that was published from 1955 to 1962. An English version of it was issued from 1957 to 1968, published in America by the **Theodore Presser Company** in association with **Universal Edition**. The journal covered subjects such as **serialism**, **electronic music**, and young composers. While it was an important source of information about the field, it was often controversial; differences between the German and English versions, which apparently included some factual errors, caused a stir among American composers and theorists.

dièse. 1. (Fr.) the sharp sign, ♯. (Ger. *Kreuz, Erhöhungszeichen*; It. *dieses*; Sp. *sostenido*.) See also **accidental**.
    2. (Fr.) to sharpen, to raise the pitch. (Ger. *erhöhen, Kreuz, Erhöhungszeichen*; It. *dieses*; Sp. *sostenido*.)

dieser/diese/dieses. (Ger.) this, in its various grammatical forms. Heard and seen in a wide variety of phrases.

diesis. 1. (It.) the sharp sign, ♯. (Fr. *dièse*; Ger. *Kreuz, Erhöhungszeichen*; Sp. *sostenido*.) See also **accidental**.
    2. (It.) to sharpen, to raise the pitch.(Fr. *dièse*; Ger. *erhöhen, Kreuz, Erhöhungszeichen*; Sp. *sostenido*.)

difference tone or **differential tone.** See **combination tone**.

difficile. (Fr.) difficult. A commonly heard descriptive. (Ger. *schwer, schwierig*; It. *difficile*; Sp. *dificil*.)

difficile. (It.) difficult. A commonly heard descriptive. (Fr. *difficile*; Ger. *schwer, schwierig*; Sp. *dificil*.)

dificil. (Sp.) difficult. A commonly heard descriptive. (Fr. *difficile*; Ger. *schwer, schwierig*; It. *difficile*.)

digitación. (Sp.) a term referring to the fingering choices an instrumentalist uses in playing his or her instrument. (Fr. *doigté*, Ger. *Fingersatz*, It. *diteggiatura*.)

Digital Media Association (DiMA). A trade association that works on behalf of its members with the stated goals of encouraging consumers' adoption of legal digital media choices, defending its members against legal and legislative initiatives, and representing its members during industry negotiations and rate-setting proceedings.

digital signal. An electronic signal that consists of magnetic pulses used to represent numbers, symbols, or other information expressed in digits.

digne. (Fr.) dignified. A character word. (Ger. *würdig, würdevoll*; It. *degno*; Sp. *digno*.)

digno. (Sp.) dignified. A character word (Fr. *digne*; Ger. *würdig, würdevoll*; It. *degno*.)

diminuant, en. (Fr.) becoming gradually softer. A descriptive term seen both in scores and parts and heard in rehearsal.

diminuendo. (It.) in dynamics, becoming softer. A descriptive term seen both in scores and parts and heard in rehearsal. Abbreviated *dim., dimin.*

diminution. A technique used in writing music whereby the rhythmic values of a group of notes are decreased by the same proportion. See **rhythmic diminutions, augmentation, rhythmic augmentation**.

di molto. (It.) very. Also *molto, assai.* (Fr. *très*, Ger. *sehr*, Sp. *muy*.) Often seen in music and heard in rehearsal as a part of various phrases. Example: *allegro di molto*, very fast.

dinamica or *dinamico.* 1. (It.) dynamic, as in the various levels of volume in music commonly referred to by their Italian names: *pianissimo, piano, mezzo piano, mezzo forte, forte, fortissimo*, and more. (Fr. *dynamique*; Ger. *dynamisch*; Sp. *dinámica, dinámico*.)
2. (It.) energetic, lively, dynamic. (Fr. *dynamique*; Ger. *dynamisch*; Sp. *dinámica, dinámico*.)

dinámica or *dinámico.* 1. (Sp.) dynamic, as in the various levels of volume in music commonly referred to by their Italian names: *pianissimo, piano, mezzo piano, mezzo forte, forte, fortissimo*, and more. (Fr. *dynamique*, Ger. *dynamisch*, It. *dinamico*.)
2. (Sp.) energetic, lively, dynamic. (Fr. *dynamique*, Ger. *dynamisch*, It. *dinamico*.)

Dirigent. (Ger.) a male **conductor**. (Fr. *chef d'orchestre*, It. *direttore d'orchestra*, Sp. *director de orquesta*.)

Dirigentin. (Ger.) a female **conductor**. (Fr. *chef d'orchestre*, It. *direttora d'orchestra*, Sp. *directora de orquesta*.)

dirigieren. (Ger.) to conduct. (Fr. *diriger*, It. *dirigere*, Sp. *dirigir*.)

Dis. (Ger.) D-sharp. See also **appendix 5: "Pitch Names and Their Translations"**; **accidental**.

di scherzo. (It.) joking. A descriptive word. (Fr. *badin*, Ger. *scherzend*, Sp. *jocoso*.)

disminyuendo. (Sp.) in dynamics, getting gradually softer. The Italian form, *diminuendo*, is a commonly used alternative.

disminyuendo la velocidad. (Sp.) a slowing of the tempo. Also *disminuendo el tempo*.

dissonance. A combination of two or more pitches that require resolution. (Fr. *dissonance*, Ger. *Dissonanz*, It. *dissonanza*, Sp. *disonancia*.) According to established common practice in tonal harmony, all seconds, sevenths, and diminished and augmented intervals are dissonant. However, practices have changed over time and so has the perception of dissonance. During the nineteenth century, harmonic language became more chromatic, taking on an essential, nontransitory aspect in music, while functional triadic harmonies occurred less. In the twentieth century, **Arnold Schoenberg** rejected any absolute distinction between dissonance and **consonance**. Within his system, all intervals were equal.

dissonant. An interval is said to be dissonant when it requires resolution. See also **consonant**.

distance. (Fr.) distance. A descriptive term seen in scores and parts and heard in rehearsal. (Ger. *Entfernung*, It. *distanza*, Sp. *distancia*.)

distancia. (Sp.) distance. A descriptive term seen in scores and parts and heard in rehearsal. (Fr. *distance*, Ger. *Entfernugn*, It. *distanza*.)

distanza. (It.) distance. A descriptive term seen in scores and parts and heard in rehearsal. (Fr. *distance*, Ger. *Entfernung*, Sp. *distancia*.)

distinct. (Fr.) clear, clearly, distinctly. A descriptive term used in rehearsal when a clear articulation is required, for instance. Also *distinctement*. (Ger. *deutlich*, It. *distinto*, Sp. *distinto*.)

distinto. (It., Sp.) clear, distinct. A descriptive term used in rehearsal when a clear articulation is required, for instance. (Fr. *distinct, distinctement*; Ger. *deutlich*.)

diteggiatura. (It.) a term referring to the fingering choices an instrumentalist uses in playing their instrument. (Fr. *doigté*, Ger. *Fingersatz*, Sp. *digitación*.)

Ditson Conductor's Award. Established in 1945 to honor conductors with a commitment to the performance of American music. It is endowed by the Alice M. Ditson Fund at Columbia University. The list of winners is a panoply of highly regarded conductors that begins in 1945 with American composer and conductor **Howard Hanson**.

div. (It.) Abbreviation for *divisi*, meaning divided, as in divided string parts. For instance, when a composer writes more than two or three parts for a string section and asks that it be played divided among the members of that section.

diventare. (It.) to become. (Fr. *devenir*, Ger. *werden*.) An often-heard term used in a wide variety of phrases. Example: *Deve essere morbido qui*, it has to be soft here.

dividanse por atriles. (Sp.) **divide by stand**. (Fr. *par pupitres*; Ger. *pultweise*, *pult*; It. *da leggii*.)

divide by stand. An indication in string parts to play multiple lines on a part with each stand, not each player, playing a single part. Having two players sitting next to each other playing the same music can give more strength to a complicated texture. (Fr. *par pupitres*; Ger. *pultweise*, *pult*; It. *da leggii*; Sp. *dividanse por atriles*.)

divisi. (It.) divided. (Fr. *divisés*; Ger. *geteilt*; Sp. *divididos*, *divisi*.) An indication used to show where string parts are divided into separate lines of music for different players in a section. Abbreviated ***div.***

Dixon, Dean (Charles). (1915–1976.) American **conductor**. Dixon studied at **Columbia University** (1936–1939) and simultaneously studied conducting at the **Juilliard School** with Albert Stoessel. He made his debut in 1937 with the chamber orchestra of the League of Music Lovers and founded the New York Chamber Orchestra (1938) and the American Youth Orchestra (1944). Dixon was the first African American to lead the **New York Philharmonic** (1941), the **NBC Symphony**, and the **Philadelphia Orchestra** (1943). In 1948, he received Columbia University's **Alice M. Ditson Award** for

Dean Dixon. *Courtesy Library of Congress, Carl Van Vechten.*

outstanding contributions to modern American music. This was followed by appearances with the **Israel Philharmonic** (1950–1951) and in the 1970s, the symphonies of Detroit, Milwaukee, Pittsburgh, St. Louis, and San Francisco. Dixon served as the principal conductor of the **Göteberg Symphony** (1953–1960); the **Hesse Radio Symphony Orchestra, Frankfurt** (1961–1970); and the **Sydney Symphony** (1964–1967). He maintained a lifelong affinity for American music and led many first performances in both Europe and Australia. Dixon was quoted as recounting three phases to his career: the first, when he was referred to as "the black American conductor"; the second as "the American conductor Dean Dixon"; and finally, "the conductor Dean Dixon."

Dixon, James. (1929–2007.) American **conductor** and pedagogue. Educated at the University of Iowa, Dixon served in the U.S. Army as the conductor of the Seventh Army Symphony in Germany. He studied conducting with **Dimitri Mitropoulos**, who made Dixon his heir. He conducted the orchestra at the **New England Conservatory** during the years 1959 to 1961, became the assistant conductor of the **Minnesota Orchestra**, and returned to the University of Iowa as a faculty member in 1962. He remained at Iowa until his retirement in 1997. The period of his leadership of the university's orchestra and orchestral conducting program was a distinguished one. Dixon was awarded the **Gustav Mahler Medal** (1963), the Laurel Leaf Award (1978), **Columbia University**'s **Alice M. Ditson Conductor's Award** (1980), and honorary doctorates at Augustana College and St. Ambrose University. Dixon also served as the music director of the **Quad City Symphony** from 1965 to 1994, building the orchestra into "an ensemble of distinction." Always dedicated to new music, Dixon brought the **International Society for Contemporary Music** to America for the first time in 1976, and during his career he led the premieres of many new works.

do bémolle. (It.) C-flat. See also **appendix 5: "Pitch Names and Their Translations," accidental**.

doble. (Sp.) twofold, twice at the same time, double. (Fr. *double*, Ger. *doppelt*, It. *doppio*.) See also ***dos veces***.

doble barra. (Sp.) double bar. As opposed to a single bar line, the double bar is used at the end of a movement or piece. (Fr. *double barre*, Ger. *Doppelstrich*, It. *doppia stranghetta*.)

doble bemol. (Sp.) double flat. A notation sign that indicates the player should lower a pitch by two half steps. (Fr. *double bémol*, Ger. *Doppel-B*, It. *doppio bemolle*.) See also **accidental**.

doble caña. (Sp.) the **double reed** as used by the double reed instruments in the oboe and bassoon families. (Fr. *anche double*, Ger. *Doppelrohrblatt*, It. *ancia doppia*.)

doble sostenido. (Sp.) double sharp. (Fr. *double dièse*, Ger. *Doppelkreuz*, It. *doppio dieses*.) See also **accidental**.

doctor of musical arts degree (DMA). An academic doctoral degree that generally combines advanced study in music performance, composition, or conducting with the study of music history and theory. The degree often takes three to four years to complete after the bachelor's and master's degrees. It prepares students for work as professional performers, conductors, and composers and qualifies the recipient to work in university, college, and conservatory teaching positions. The **Eastman School of Music** at the University of Rochester had an approved DMA degree in 1953. **Howard Hanson**, director of the school, awarded the first DMA in 1955. The **Boston University** School of Music also awarded an early DMA in the same year.

dodecaphonic. See **twelve-tone technique**.

do doppio bemolle. (It.) C double flat. See also **appendix 5: "Pitch Names and Their Translations."**

do doppio dieses. (It.) C double sharp. See also **appendix 5: "Pitch Names and Their Translations," accidental**.

Dohnányi, Christoph von. (b. 1929.) German **conductor** and grandson of composer Ernö Dohnányi. He is also related to the psychiatrist Karl Bonhoeffer and the Protestant theologian Dietrich Bonhoeffer, who was murdered by the Nazis. Born in Berlin, he studied law at the University of Munich (1946–1948) when he enrolled in the **Munich Conservatory**. He won the **Richard Strauss** Prize for conducting in 1951, after which he went to Florida State University in order to study with his grandfather (1951–1952) and with **Leonard Bernstein** at **Tanglewood Music Center**. Dohnányi returned to Germany in order to become assistant conductor to **Georg Solti** at the Frankfurt Opera (1952–1956). He served as the general music director at the opera houses in Lübeck (1957–1963), Kassel (1963–1966), Frankfurt (1968–1977), and Hamburg (1977–1984). His orchestra positions included chief conductor at the **West German Radio Symphony Orchestra** (1964–1970), **Cleveland Orchestra** (1984–2002), and **London Philharmonia** (1997–2008). His debut at the **Salzburg Festival** was in 1962 and with the **Metropolitan Opera** in 1972. He led the premieres of Hans Werner Henze's opera *Der junge Lord* (recorded for **Deutsche Grammophon**) in Berlin in 1965 and *The Bassarids* in Salzburg (1966). He also conducted a complete Ring cycle in Vienna in the 1992–1993 season. Dohnányi has been a guest conductor for numerous orchestras worldwide. His legacy of recordings is distinguished by twentieth-century operas, including Alban Berg's *Wozzeck* and *Lulu*. His conducting style has been described as somewhat reserved and antithetical to any podium display. He is said to demand from himself complete comprehension of the score at hand and a meticulous sense of detail from the orchestra but also adds a warm personality to match the sound he seeks.

doigté. (Fr.) a term referring to the fingering choices an instrumentalist uses in playing his or her instrument. (Ger. *Fingersatz*, It. *diteggiatura*, Sp. *digitación*.)

Dolby, Ray. (1933–2013.) American inventor and engineer. Dolby was responsible for the technology known as the Dolby Sound System, a noise reduction system also referred to as Dolby NR, that significantly advanced analog sound. Dolby worked at Ampex, where he helped develop the videotape recorder. He founded Dolby Laboratories in London in 1965. The patent for Dolby NR was registered in America in 1969 and first used by **Decca Records**. He received many honors during his life, including an OBE (Most Excellent Order of the British Empire) awarded by Queen Elizabeth in 1986.

dolce. (It.) sweet, soft. A commonly used character word that evokes a particular playing quality. Also *dolcemente*, *dolcissimo*. (Fr. *doux*; Ger. *süss*, *weich*; Sp. *dulce*.)

dolcement. (It.) sweetly, gently. A commonly used character word that evokes a particular playing quality. (Fr. *doucement*, Ger. *in sanfter Weise*, Sp. *suavemente*.)

dolent. (Fr.) sad, mournful, plaintive. A commonly used character word that evokes a particular playing quality. (Ger. *schmerzend*, *schmerzhaft*; It. *dolente*; Sp. *triste*.)

dolente. (It.) sad, mournful, plaintive. A commonly used character word that evokes a particular playing quality. (Fr. *dolent*; Ger. *schmerzend*, *schmerzhaft*; Sp. *triste*.)

doloroso. (It., Sp.) painful, sorrowful. A character word that evokes a certain emotion in the playing. Also *con dolore*, with a sad or mournful feeling.

donaire. (Sp.) graceful, elegant. A descriptive term used in rehearsal to evoke a certain quality in the playing. Also *donairoso*, *donairosamente*.

Donaueschingen Music Festival. Founded in 1921 in Germany, the world's oldest festival of new music. The festival grew out of a meeting of several distinguished musicians, including Ferruccio Busoni, Joseph Haas, **Hans Pfitzner**, **Arthur Nikisch**, and **Richard Strauss**, who were looking for a way to present young artists. The first concert presented chamber music by Alois Hába, **Paul Hindemith**, and Ernst Krenek. The festival grew, and in 1927, it moved to Baden-Baden but was mostly abandoned during the war years. After World War II it was reestablished and taken over by **Olivier Messiaen** and his student at the time, **Pierre Boulez**. The **Southwest Germany Radio** in Baden-Baden and its orchestra provided a significant stimulus and promotion for the festival.

do or doh. The **solmization** name for the note C used as an alternative to the French *ut*, the first note or key-note of a C-major scale or triad.

Doppel-B. (Ger.) double flat. A notation sign that indicates the player should lower a pitch by two half steps. (Fr. *double bémol*, It. *doppio bemolle*, Sp. *doble bemol*.) See also **accidental**.

Doppelgriff. (Ger.) double stop. (Fr. *double corde*, It. *doppia corda*, Sp. *tocar con dobles cuerdas*.) Abbreviated ***Dopplgr.*** Example: *Der Doppelgriff (oder Akkord) mit bezeichnet ist stets unison, nicht geteilt auszuführen*, The double stop (or chord) should not be divided, such as in *Das Lied von der Erde*, at fig [8] in mvt. 4 by **Gustav Mahler**.

Doppelkreuz. (Ger.) double sharp. (Fr. *double dièse*, It. *doppio dieses*, Sp. *doble sostenido*.) See also **accidental**.

Doppelrohrblatt. (Ger.) the double reed, as used by the double reed instruments in the oboe and bassoon families. (Fr. *anche double*, It. *ancia doppia*, Sp. *doble caña*.)

Doppelstrich. (Ger.) double bar. As opposed to a single bar line, the double bar is used at the end of a movement or piece. (Fr. *double barre*, It. *doppia stranghetta*, Sp. *doble barra*.)

doppelt. (Ger.) twice. (Fr. *double*; It. *doppio*; Sp. *doble*, *dos veces*.) Example: *doppelt so schnell*, twice as fast.

Doppelzunge. (Ger.) double tonguing. (Fr. *double articulation*, It. *doppio colpo di linqua*, Sp. *articulación doble*.) A technique used by wind and brass players for articulating faster passages. The player uses the two consonants *t-k*, *t-k* repeatedly. See also **tonguing, triple tonguing, flutter tonguing**.

doppio. (It.) double, twice. (Fr. *double*; Ger. *doppelt*; Sp. *doble*, *dos veces*.) Examples: ***doppio bemolle***, double flat; ***doppio colpo di lingua***, double tonguing; *doppio movemento*, twice as fast; ***doppio corda***, double stop.

doppio bemolle. (It.) double flat. A notation sign that indicates the player should lower a pitch by two half steps. (Fr. *double bémol*, Ger. *Doppel-B*, Sp. *doble bemol*.) See also **accidental**.

doppio colpo di lingua. (It.) double tonguing. (Fr. *double articulation*, Ger. *Doppelzunge*, Sp. *articulación doble*.) A technique used by wind and brass players for articulating faster passages. The player uses the two consonants *t-k*, *t-k* repeatedly. See also **tonguing, triple tonguing, flutter tonguing**.

doppia corda. (It.) double stop. Two notes played at the same time on a string instrument, generally using two fingers of the left hand. (Fr. *double corde*, Ger. *Doppelgriff*, Sp. *tocar con dobles cuerdas*.)

doppio stranghetta. (It.) double bar. As opposed to a single bar line, the double bar is used at the end of a movement or piece. (Fr. *double barre*, Ger. *Doppelstrich*, Sp. *doble barra*.)

doppler effect. The frequency change of a sound wave or pitch caused by a change in the distance between the source of the sound or performer and the audience. A common example is in Ludwig van Beethoven's *Leonore Overtures*, in which the offstage trumpet call will sound flat to the audience in the concert hall unless modified. An everyday example of the effect is when one hears the passing of an ambulance siren. The decrease in pitch is made by the gradual increase in distance as the ambulance moves away.

Doráti, Antal. (1906–1988.) Hungarian-born **conductor** and composer. Doráti studied at the **Liszt Academy** in Budapest and with composer Zoltán Kodály (1920–1924). He served at the **Budapest Royal Opera** (1924–1928) and then in Dresden (1928–1929) and Münster (1929–1932). From 1935 to 1945, he conducted ballet at the Ballet Russe de Monte Carlo and others. He moved to the United States in 1940 and was the principal conductor of the **Dallas Symphony Orchestra** (1945–1949) and the **Minneapolis Symphony Orchestra**, with whom he recorded the complete ballets of Pyotr Tchaikovsky for **Mercury Records** (1949–1960). He was also the principal conductor for the **BBC Symphony Orchestra** (1962–1966); **Stockholm Philharmonic Orchestra** (1966–1970); **National Symphony**, Washington, DC (1970–1976); **Rochester Philharmonic Orchestra** (1975–1978); the **Royal Philharmonic Orchestra** (1975–1979); and the **Detroit Symphony Orchestra**, with whom he recorded **Igor Stravinsky's** *The Rite of Spring*, a disk that won the French **Grand Prix de Disque** (1977–1981). He led recordings of the complete Joseph Haydn symphonies and several operas for with the **Philharmonia Hungarica**;

recorded several works of both **Béla Bartók** and Stravinsky, as well as the complete symphonies of Tchaikovsky with the **London Symphony Orchestra**; and was made an honorary KBE by Queen Elizabeth in 1983. Doráti's biography, *Notes of Seven Decades*, was published in 1979. See the **bibliography**.

dorian mode. See **church modes**.

dos. (Fr.) back, as in the back or wood of the bow. (Ger. *zurück*, It. *indietro*, Sp. *atrás*.) Example: *avec le dos de l'archet*, from *Rapsodie Espagnole* by Maurice Ravel.

dos. (Sp.) two. (Fr. *deux*, Ger. *zwei*, It. *due*.) See also **numbers, basic**.

dos veces. (Sp.) an indication that calls for playing something twice, one after another, not doubled or simultaneously. (Fr. *deux fois*, Ger. *zweimal*, It. *due volte*.)

double. (Fr.) twofold, twice, double. (Ger. *doppelt*, It. *doppio*, Sp. *doble*.) Example: *Le double plus lent*, twice as slow, from *Ronde de Printemps* by Claude Debussy.

double articulation. (Fr.) double tonguing. (Ger. *Doppelzunge*, It. *doppio colpo di linqua*, Sp. *articulación doble*.) A technique used by wind and brass players for articulating faster passages. The player uses the two consonants *t-k, t-k* repeatedly. See also **tonguing, triple tonguing, flutter tonguing**.

double barre. (Fr.) double bar. As opposed to a single bar line, the double bar is used at the end of a movement or piece. (Ger. *Doppelstrich*, It. *doppia stranghetta*, Sp. *doble barra*.)

double bass. The lowest pitched and largest of the orchestra's standard string instruments, it is also called simply the **bass**. Generally played standing up or sitting on a high stool, it usually has four strings: E1, A1, D2, and G2, from the bottom string up. Some basses have an additional lower string that extends the range down to a C1. Others have a mechanical extension of the E string that can lower or lengthen it down to a C1. This allows the bass to double the cello part at the lower octave. (Fr. *contrebasse*, Ger. *Kontrabass*, It. *contrabasso*, Sp. *contrabajo*.) See also **extensions, appendix 3: "Instrument Names and Their Translations."**

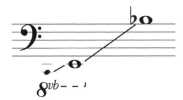

Double bass range as it sounds. *Courtesy Andrew Martin Smith.*

double bass clarinet. See **contrabass clarinet**.

double bémol. (Fr.) double flat. A notation sign that indicates the player should lower the pitch by two half steps. (Ger. *Doppel-B*, It. *doppio bemolle*, Sp. *doble bemol*.) See also **accidental**.

double corde. (Fr.) double stop. Two notes played at the same time on a string instrument, generally using two fingers of the left hand. (Ger. *Doppelgriff*, It. *doppia corda*, Sp. *tocar con dobles cuerdas*.)

double croche. (Fr.) sixteenth note. See also **appendix 7: "Rhythmic Terms and Their Translations."**

double dièse. (Fr.) double sharp. (Ger. *Doppelkreuz*, It. *doppio dieses*, Sp. *doble sostenido*.) See also **accidental**.

double dot. A rhythmic indication. When a dotted rhythm such as a dotted eighth note is given a double dot, increasing its value, it is called double dotted. Also "double dotted." See also **appendix 7: "Rhythmic Terms and Their Translations."**

double flat. A notation sign that indicates lowering a pitch by two half steps. (Fr. *double bémol*, Ger. *Doppel-B*, It. *doppio bemolle*, Sp. *doble bemol*.) See also **accidental**.

double reed. The reed used by the double reed instruments in the oboe and bassoon families. (Fr. *anche double*, Ger. *Doppelrohrblatt*, It. *ancia doppia*, Sp. *doble caña*.)

double sharp. A notation sign that indicates raising a pitch by two half steps. (Fr. *double dièse*, Ger. *Doppelkreuz*, It. *doppio dieses*, Sp. *doble sostenido*.) See also **accidental**.

double stop. Two notes played at the same time on a string instrument, generally using two fingers of the left hand. (Fr. *double corde*, Ger. *Doppelgriff*, It. *doppia corda*, Sp. *tocar con dobles cuerdas*.)

double tonguing. A technique used by wind and brass players for articulating faster passages. The player uses the two consonants *t-k, t-k* repeatedly. (Fr. *double articulation*; Ger. *Doppelzunge*; It. *doppio colpo di linqua*; Sp. *doble/triple stacato, articulación doble/triple*.) See also **tonguing, triple tonguing, flutter tonguing**.

double whole note (American usage). A rhythmic notation or note that is used to last for a whole bar, especially when the bar is longer than four beats. It was first used in medieval music. An excellent example of contemporary use is Samuel Barber's *Adagio for Strings*. See also **breve, appendix 7: "Rhythmic Terms and Their Translations."**

doubling the parts. In certain situations in orchestras with large string sections, it is not uncommon to double wind and brass parts. While the rise of smaller performance practice orchestras has led to plenty of concerts and recordings of the Baroque, Classical, and even some Romantic repertoire played with smaller string sections, larger orchestras still perform such pieces as Ludwig van Beethoven's Symphonies No. 5 and 9 with such large string sections that some doubling in the winds and brass is necessary if they are to be heard. Generally this will be limited to *tutti* passages, with solo lines played singly. See also **reorchestrating the parts**, **preparing the parts**, **Felix Weingartner**.

doucement. (Fr.) sweetly, gently. A character word often seen in French music. (Ger. *in sanfter Weise*, It. *dolcement*, Sp. *suavemente*.) Example: *expressif et doucement soutenu*, expressive and sweetly sustained, from "Les parfums de la nuit" from "Ibéria" of *Images* by Claude Debussy.

douloureux. (Fr.) sorrowful, painful. A descriptive term sometimes heard in rehearsal to evoke a particular emotion or mood. Also *douloureusement.* (Ger. *schmerzlich*, It. *doloroso*, Sp. *doloroso*.)

doux. (Fr.) sweet, soft. A commonly used character word. (Ger. *süss*, *weich*; It. *dolce*; Sp. *dulce*.) Examples: *doux et mélancolique*, sweet and melancholy, from "Gigues"; *doux et léger*, sweet and light, from "Les parfums de la nuit" of "Ibéria," both movements from *Images* by Claude Debussy.

Dover Publications. Located in Mineola, New York, Dover Publications is an American publisher founded in 1941 by Hayward Cirker and his wife, Blanche. They specialize mainly in reissues of books, sheet music, and music scores that are often out of print and in the public domain, making them available at significantly reduced cost, a boon to the young conductor and music lover. They are known for the quality of their paperbacks and paperback scores that were printed on high-quality, non-yellowing paper with the pages sewn in, as with the best hardbound books. For a period Dover began releasing many of their music scores with glued covers, but recently the sewn style has returned.

downbeat. Usually the first beat of the bar as indicated by the **conductor** with a downward gesture and an ictus on the pulse. There are examples of pieces where a composer suggests the feeling of a downbeat on a beat other than one. In these cases, it is up to the conductor to decide if a downbeat gesture will generate the effect intended. (Fr. *temps fort*, Ger. *Abtakt*, It. *in battere*, Sp. *tiempo fuerte*.) Example: Symphony No. 4, beginning of mvt. 1, by Robert Schumann. See also **conducting technique**.

down-bow. The direction of the bow when it is moving from the **frog** to the tip. (Fr. *tiré*, Ger. *Abstrich*, It. *arcata in giù*, Sp. *arco abajo*.) The French down-bow sign is the same sign, only upside down. The French down-bow is still seen in scores of Debussy and other French composers. In the hidden down-bow change sign, the parentheses indicate hiding the bow changes. Sometimes the "hidden" up- and down-bow symbols will be seen in sequence in a score to indicate changing the bow at will and not at the same time another player changes, creating a smoother, more cohesive sound.

Down-bow.
Courtesy Andrew Martin Smith.

Down-bow sign.
Courtesy Andrew Martin Smith.

French down-bow sign.
Courtesy Andrew Martin Smith.

Hidden down-bow change.
Courtesy Andrew Martin Smith.

dramático. (Sp.) dramatic, somewhat exaggerated. A character word that is sometimes used in rehearsal to evoke a particular manner of playing. (Fr. *dramatique*, Ger. *dramatisch*, It. *drammatico*.)

dramatique. (Fr.) dramatic, somewhat exaggerated. A character word that is sometimes used in rehearsal to evoke a particular manner of playing. (Ger. *dramatisch*, It. *drammatico*.)

dramatisch. (Ger.) dramtic, somewhat exaggerated. A character word that is sometimes used in rehearsal to evoke a particular manner of playing. (Fr. *dramatique*, It. *drammatico*.)

drammatico. (It.) dramatic, somewhat exaggerated. A character word that is sometimes used in rehearsal to evoke a particular manner of playing. Also *drammaticamenes, con dramma*, drastically, with drama. (Fr. *dramatique*, Ger. *dramatisch*, Sp. *dramático*.)

drängend. (Ger.) pushing forward, pressing the tempo forward. Often seen in the scores of **Gustav Mahler**. (Fr. *appuyant*, It. *incalzante*, Sp. *empujar*.)

Dr. Beat. An electronic device that can be used for tuning and rhythmic coaching. It has an advanced metronome, playback, multiple sounds, and drum patterns.

drei. (Ger.) three. (Fr. *trois*, It. *tre*, Sp. *tres*.)

dreifach. 1. (Ger., lit. "ternary," "threefold," "three part.") a term that indicates a triple stop, that is, a chord of three notes played simultaneously on a string instrument.
2. An indication that three notes are to be played as a chord.

Dreiklang. (Ger.) triad, a chord of three pitches. (Fr. *triade*, It. *triade*, Sp. *tríada*.)

dreitaktig. (Ger.) in three, three beats in a measure. (Fr. *en trois*, It. *in tre*, Sp. *en tres*.)

Dresden Staatskapelle (*Sächsische Staatskapelle Dresden*). Established in 1548, the orchestra is now resident with the **Saxon State Opera** (*Sächsische Staatsoper*). The composer Heinrich Schütz (1586–1672), who lived in Dresden for part of his life, was one of its early progenitors, serving as **Hofkapellmeister** from 1615 to 1672. In the nineteenth century, both **Carl Maria von Weber** (Hofkapellmeister from 1816 to 1826) and **Richard Wagner** (Hofkapellmeister from 1843 to 1848) were among its principal conductors. Chief conductors in the twentieth century include **Fritz Reiner** (1914–1932), Fritz Busch (1922–1933), **Karl Böhm** (1934–1943), **Herbert Blomstedt** (1975–1985), Hans Vonk (1985–1990), **Giuseppe Sinopoli** (1992–2001), **Bernard Haitink** (2002–1004), **Fabio Luisi** (2007–2010), and **Christian Thielemann** (appointed in 2012). Other conductors associated with the orchestra include **Richard Strauss**, **Colin Davis**, and **Myung-Whun Chung**, who was appointed principal guest conductor in 2012.

dringend. (Ger.) urgent. A character word suggesting a particular style of playing. (Fr. *urgent*; It. *urgente*; Sp. *urgente*, *urgir*.)

drohend. (Ger.) menacing, threatening. A character word that evokes a certain manner of playing.

Druck. (Ger.) pressure, strain. Also *drucken*, to push, to print. Examples: *mehr Druck*, more pressure; *mehr Bogendruck*, more bow pressure; *weniger Bogendruck*, less bow pressure.

drum major. The leader of a marching band or drum and bugle corps whose responsibility it is to coordinate the ensemble by providing commands and keeping the tempo. The drum major's responsibilities may also include other organizational elements.

D.S. Abbreviation for *dal segno*.

Dudamel, Gustavo. (b. 1981.) Venezuelan **conductor** and violinist. Dudamel serves as the principal conductor of the **Gothenburg Symphony Orchestra** in Sweden and as the music director of the **Los Angeles Philharmonic**. One of the most distinguished graduates of **El Sistema**, the program for youth in Venezuela, he is also the artistic director of the **Orquesta Sinfónica Simón Bolívar** in Caracas, Venezuela. He has guest conducted orchestras worldwide, including the **Berlin Philharmonic**, **Israel Philharmonic**, **San Francisco Symphony**, and **Vienna Philharmonic**, and he made his debut at **La Scala, Milan**, leading Wolfgang Amadeus Mozart's *Don Giovanni* in 2006. He signed an exclusive recording contract with **Deutsche Grammophon** in 2005 and was made *Gramophone Artist of the Year* in 2011. Dudamel began recording in 2006 and has already released a large number of CDs and DVDs.

Dudarova, Veronika. (1916–2009.) Russian **conductor**. Born in Baku, Azerbaijan, she studied piano at the **Leningrad Conservatory** (1933–1937) and conducting at the **Moscow Conservatory** (1939–1947). She was an assistant conductor at the **Moscow State Symphony Orchestra** (1947–1960), becoming the principal conductor in 1960, and she continued to lead the orchestra until 2007. Dudarova founded and led the Symphony Orchestra of Russia from 1991 to 2003. She was named a People's Artist of the Russian Republic and attained great fame in her homeland. She was featured leading a performance of Wolfgang Amadeus Mozart's *Requiem* in the 1987 documentary *A Woman Is a Risky Bet: Six Orchestra Conductors*, directed by Christina Olofson. Her repertoire reached beyond the classics of Ludwig van Beethoven, Johannes Brahms, and many well-known Russian composers to the less well-known Nikolai Myaskovsky, Vasily Kalinnikov, Nikolai Rakov, and Vissarion Shebalin. She conducted the premiere of Elena Firsova's *Cello Concerto* and championed the music of Sofia Gubaidulina, Alfred Schnittke, Igor Frolov, and Zara Levine. The asteroid 9737 Dudarova was named after her in 1986.

due. (It.) two. (Fr. *deux*, Ger. *zwei*, Sp. *dos*.) See also **numbers, basic**.

due, in. (It.) in two, felt in two beats to a bar, or an indication to conduct in two. (Fr. *en deux*; Ger. *in zwei, in zwei Schlage*; It. *in due, in due battute*; Sp. *en dos, a dos*.)

dueto. (Sp.) duet, a piece for two musicians. Also *dúo*. (Fr. *duo*, Ger. *Duett*, It. *duetto*.)

Duett. (Ger.) duet, a piece for two musicians. (Fr. *duo*; It. *duetto*; Sp. *dúo, dueto*.)

duetto. (It.) duet, a piece for two musicians. (Fr. *duo*; Ger. *Duett*; Sp. *dúo, dueto*.)

due volte. (It.) an indication that calls for playing something twice, one after another, not doubled or simultaneously. (Ger. *zweimal*, Fr. *deux fois*, Sp. *dos veces*.)

Duffie, Bruce. Interviewer of famous **conductors** and composers, including Riccardo Chailly, **Charles Dutoit**, Jane Glover, Henryk Górecki, **Bernard Haitink, Margaret Hillis**, Neeme Järvi, **Erich Leinsdorf**, Raymond Leppard, Eduardo Mata, Jorge Mester, **Krzysztof Penderecki**, John Pritchard, **Max Rudolf, Gunther Schuller, Gerard Schwarz, Leonard Slatkin, Sir Georg Solti**, Joan Tower, and Gunther Wand. These interviews were mostly made for Chicago's classical music station, **WNIB**, 97.1 FM (also known as **Classical 97**) and featured musicians who were in town for concerts and opera performances.

Duffie created two programs for WNIB, *Who's in Town* and *Chicago Music Dateline*, which won the **ASCAP/Deems Taylor Award** in 1991. Many of the interviews have been transcribed and published or videotaped. Some of those videos are available online.

duftig. (Ger.) delicate (lit. "fragrant"). A descriptive term.

dulce. (Sp.) sweet, soft. A commonly used character word. (Fr. *doux*; Ger. *süss, weich*; It. *dolce*.)

dunkel. (Ger.) dark, gloomy, with a dark tone. A character word that evokes a particular tone or sound. (Fr. *sombre*; It. *buio, cupo*; Sp. *tenebroso*.)

Dunn, Thomas. (b. 1925.) American choral and orchestral **conductor**. Dunn studied at the **Peabody Institute** of John Hopkins University, Harvard University, and the Amsterdam Conservatory. His organ teachers included E. Power Biggs and Ernest White and his conducting teachers included **Robert Shaw** and Anthon van der Horst. In 1963, he conducted four performances of Geroge Frideric Handel's *Messiah*, each one using a different edition.

He served as the music director of the Handel and Haydn Society, Boston (1967–1986), transforming the ensemble into a more progressive organization. He was known for transparent and rhythmic performances of a broad repertoire ranging from Heinrich Schütz to Luigi Dallapiccola and **Igor Stravinsky**. He taught at many American music schools and universities, including the **Indiana University School of Music**.

duo. (Fr.) duet, a piece for two musicians. (Ger. *Duett*; It. *duetto*; Sp. *dúo, dueto*.)

dúo. (Sp.) duet, a piece for two musicians. Also *dueto*. (Fr. *duo*, Ger. *Duett*, It. *duetto*.)

Duole. (Ger.) duplet, a rhythmic figure of two notes. (Fr. *duolet*.)

duple meter. Any bar or measure that has two beats, such as 2/4, 2/2, and 6/8 when fast enough to be felt in two.

Dur. (Ger.) major, as in a major key as opposed to a minor key. (Fr. *majeur*, It. *maggiore*, Sp. *mayor*.)

dur. (Fr.) hard. A descriptive word that may be heard in a wide variety of phrases and uses. (Ger. *hart*, It. *duro*, Sp. *duro*.) See, for instance, hard timpani sticks, (Fr.) **baguettes en bois**, (Ger.) **Holzschlegeln**, (It.) **bacchette di legno**, (Sp.) **baqueta de madera**.

Durand, (Marie) Auguste. (1830–1909.) French organist, publisher, and composer. Durand studied at the Paris Conservatory with Cesar Franck and Camille Saint-Saëns. He founded Durand-Schönewerk & Cie with partner Louis Schönewerk in 1869, quickly acquiring the catalogue of music publisher Gustave-Alexandre Flaxland, which included the rights for early editions of the operas of **Richard Wagner**. Following business disputes, the company was dissolved and reformed with Durand's son Jacques as **A. Durand & Son** (1891). During the twentieth century the company became known as the first publisher of French composers, including Maurice Ravel, Claude Debussy, Albert Roussel, Paul Dukas, Eduoard Lalo, Jules Massenet, and many more. In 2000, the company was bought by **BMG** and merged with **Salabert** to become Durand-Salabert-Eschig. Rentals are currently handled in the United States by **Boosey & Hawkes** with scores on sale by **Hal Leonard**.

Durand music publisher. See **Durand, Auguste (Maire)**.

durant. (Fr.) throughout, during. (Ger. *während*, It. *durante*, Sp. *durante*.)

durante. (It., Sp.) throughout, during. (Fr. *durant*, Ger. *während*.)

durch. (Ger.) through, by, by means of. Also *durchaus*, completely, throughout, by all means; *durchdringend*, piercing, shrill; *durchkomponiert*, through composed. Example: *Durchaus ppp*, *PPP* throughout, from mvt. 4 of Symphony No. 3 by **Gustav Mahler**.

Durchführung. (Ger.) the development section of a piece. (Fr. *développement*; It. *sviluppo, svolgimento*; Sp. *desarrollo*.)

durchlaufend bewegt. (Ger.) perpetual motion. (It. *moto perpetuo, perputuum mobile*; Fr. *movement perpétuel*.)

dureté. (Fr.) hardness. A descriptive term that can be used to describe a particular articulation or sound. (Ger. *Härte*, It. *durezza*, Sp. *dureza*.) Example: *vibrant sans dureté*, vibrating without hardness, from "Fêtes," mvt. 2 of *Nocturnes* by Claude Debussy.

dureza. (Sp.) hardness. A descriptive term that can be used to describe a particular articulation or sound. (Fr. *dureté*, Ger. *Härte*, It. *durezza*.)

durezza. (It.) hardness. A descriptive term that can be used to describe a particular articulation or sound. (Fr. *dureté*, Ger. *Härte*, Sp. *dureza*.)

duro. (It., Sp.) hard. A descriptive word that may be heard in a wide variety of phrases and uses. (Fr. *dur*, Ger. *hart*.) See, for instance, hard timpani sticks, (Fr.) *baguettes en bois*, (Ger.) *Holzschlegeln*, (It.) *bacchette di legno*, (Sp.) *baqueta de madera*.

Dutoit, Charles. (b. 1936.) Swiss **conductor**. Dutoit studied violin and conducting at the conservatory in Lausanne, Switzerland, and then in Geneva. He became the second conductor of the Berne Symphony in 1964 and later was appointed the principal conductor (1967–1978), succeeding **Paul Kletzki**. He conducted the Zürich Radio Orchestra (1964–1967) and the **Zürich Tonhalle Orchestra** (1966–1971) and served as the music director of the National Symphony Orchestra of Mexico (1973–1975), the **Gothenburg Orchestra** (1976–1979). Dutoit was the music director of the **Montreal Symphony Orchestra** from 1977 to 2002. During his tenure the orchestra rose to new heights of international acclaim, much of it due to numerous international tours and the release of over seventy-five recordings, many of them award winning, on the **Decca label**. Dutoit also held positions with the French National Orchestra (1990–2001), and **NHK Symphony Orchestra in Tokyo** (1998–1998 as principal conductor and 1998–2003 as music director) and currently serves as the director of the Philadelphia and Sarasota Spring summer festivals. He has been a guest conductor of the orchestras of **New York**, **Boston**, **Philadelphia**, **Berlin**, **Cleveland**, **Chicago**, **Minnesota**,

Munich, **Pittsburg**, **Los Angeles**, **San Francisco**, and more. He debuted at the **Royal Opera House, Covent Garden**, in 1983 and the **Metropolitan Opera** in 1987 and is known as a particularly inspired conductor of French and Russian repertoire.

DVD. Originally called "digital video disk," an optical disc storage format with significantly more storage capacity than the compact disc (CD) but exactly the same size. It was invented by Philips, **Sony**, Toshiba, and Panasonic in 1995. It is also known as a DVD-ROM. Blank, recordable DVD discs (DVD-R and DVD+R) can be used for recording once, using a DVD recorder. They then function as a DVD-ROM.

Dvořák, Antonin. (1841–1904.) Czech composer who had an important influence on the musical life of America in the later nineteenth century. Dvořák was brought to America by Jeannette Thurber, a wealthy and philanthropic socialite, in order to become the director of the **National Conservatory of Music** in New York (1892–1895). His salary was the astronomical fee of $15,000. While he lived in the United States, he wrote his Symphony No. 9, *"From the New World,"* and the *String Quartet in F major "American."* He spent his American summers residing in the Czech community of Spillville, Iowa. He wrote his *Cello Concerto in B minor* upon hearing the premiere performance of the cello concerto of **Victor Herbert** in New York.

dyad. An interval consisting of two different pitches sounding simultaneously.

dynamic mark or dynamic sign. Notation devices used to indicate loud and soft dynamics and those in between. Examples in their commonly used abbreviations: *FFF*, *FF*, *F*, *mf*, *mp*, *P*, *PP*, *PPP*. These marks are often put in the parts by the composer or an editor but can also be added by players in response to circumstances that occur in rehearsal. One of the most unusual markings is Pyotr Tchaikovsky's use of six *PPPPPP*s on the **contrabassoon** part at the end of the introduction and just before the fast section of the first movement of the Symphony No. 6. (Fr. *signe dynamique*, Ger. *dynamisches Zeichen*, It. *segno dinamico*, Sp. *signos dinámicos*.)

Dynamic mark *mezzo forte*. Courtesy Andrew Martin Smith.

Dynamic mark *forte*. Courtesy Andrew Martin Smith.

ff

Dynamic mark *fortissimo. Courtesy Andrew Martin Smith.*

fff

Dynamic mark *fortississimo. Courtesy Andrew Martin Smith.*

ffff

Dynamic mark *extremely loud. Courtesy Andrew Martin Smith.*

mp

Dynamic mark *mezzo piano. Courtesy Andrew Martin Smith.*

p

Dynamic mark *piano. Courtesy Andrew Martin Smith.*

pp

Dynamic mark *pianissimo. Courtesy Andrew Martin Smith.*

ppp

Dynamic mark *pianississimo. Courtesy Andrew Martin Smith.*

pppp

Dynamic mark even quieter. *Courtesy Andrew Martin Smith.*

pppppp

Dynamic mark extremely quiet. *Courtesy Andrew Martin Smith.*

dynamics. The various levels of volume in music commonly referred to by their Italian names: *pianissimo, piano, mezzo piano, mezzo forte, forte, fortissimo,* and more. (Fr. *dynamique,* Ger. *Dynamik,* It. *dinamica,* Sp. *dinámica.*)

Dynamik. (Ger.) dynamic, as in the various levels of volume in music commonly referred to by their Italian names: *pianissimo, piano, mezzo piano, mezzo forte, forte, fortissimo,* and more. (Fr. *dynamique,* It. *dinamica,* Sp. *dinámico.*)

dynamique. 1. (Fr.) dynamic, as in the various levels of volume in music commonly referred to by their Italian names: *pianissimo, piano, mezzo piano, mezzo forte, forte, fortissimo,* and more. (Ger. *Dynamik,* It. *dinamica,* Sp. *dinámico.*)

2. Energetic, dynamic. A character word sometimes used in rehearsal to evoke a particular kind of playing. (Ger. *dynamisch,* It. *dinamico,* Sp. *dinámico*)

dynamisch. (Ger.) energetic, dynamic. A character word sometimes used in rehearsal to evoke a particular kind of playing. (Fr. *dynamique,* It. *dinamico,* Sp. *dinámico.*)

dynamisches Zeichen. (Ger.) **dynamic mark** or **dynamic sign**. (Fr. *signe dynamique,* It. *segno dinamico,* Sp. *signos dinámicos.*)

E. In music, a pitch or note name. The third note in a C major scale; the name of a scale that begins on E; also part of a title of a piece that is said to be "in E," as in Johann Sebastian Bach's *Partita No. 3 for Violin in E major*.

e. (It.) and. (Fr. *et*, Ger. *und*, Sp. *y*.)

early music ensembles. These ensembles specialize in period performance practices and sometimes performing on period instruments. Since the rise of interest in the field, such ensembles have developed throughout Europe, North America, and elsewhere. A short list of some of them includes the **Academy for Old Music, Berlin** (*Akademie für Alte Musik Berlin*); Apollo's Fire based in Cleveland, Ohio, and led by **Sorrell, Jeannette**; Les Arts Florissants, a French ensemble led by William Christie; Boston Baroque, led by Martin Pearlman; the Boston Early Music Festival, led by Paul O'Dette; the Brandenburg Consort, a British ensemble led by Roy Goodman; Concerto Köln from Germany; the English Baroque Soloists, led by **John Elliott Gardiner**; the Freiburg Baroque Orchestra, led by Gottfried von der Goltz; Musica Antiqua Köln, formerly led by Reinhard Goebel; the **Orchestra of the Age of Enlightenment**; Orchestra of the Eighteenth Century, led by Frans Brüggen; and many more. Many of these ensembles and orchestras have issued fine recordings. Many conservatories and music schools around the country also have exceptionally fine early music training programs.

ear training. The study of musical perception as exemplified in the ability to recognize by ear intervals, melodies, rhythms, and multiple meters and sing them at sight or take them down by dictation. See **sight singing**, **solfège**, **solmization**.

Eastman-Rochester Philharmonic. Founded in 1939 by American composer **Howard Hanson**, director of the **Eastman School of Music**. Its primary function was to record new music by American composers, but it also participated in the American Composers' Concerts and the Symposia of Student Works for Orchestra, both at Eastman. The personnel consisted of the principal players of the **Rochester Philharmonic** and select **Eastman School** students. Hanson led the orchestra in numerous commercial recordings on **Mercury Records**, including works of his own and other American composers such as George Whitefield Chadwick, Charles Tomlinson Griffes, Walter Piston, Bernard Rogers, Roger Sessions, William Grant Still, and more. After Hanson's retirement in 1964 the orchestra stopped making recordings but continued to perform, most likely as a student ensemble, for concerto concerts at the school until 1974.

Eastman School of Music. Founded in 1919 and opened in 1921 by George Eastman, the inventor of the Kodak photographic process. The first of its kind, the school is a college of the University of Rochester and thus, in addition to a comprehensive range of undergraduate-, master's-, and doctoral-level music performance, theory, musicology, and composition classes, it offers students access to classes at the university. The Eastman campus includes the renovated Eastman Theater; **Sibley Music Library**, one of the largest music libraries in the world; and the Student Living Center. Its first director was the American composer **Howard Hanson**, who founded the **Institute for American Music** and the **Eastman-Rochester Philharmonic**.

eccetera. (It.) and so on, et cetera. Abbreviated *etc.* (Fr. *et ainsi de suite*, Ger. *und so weiter*, Sp. *etcétera*.)

échelette. (Fr.) xylophone. See also **appendix 4: "Percussion Instruments and Their Translations."**

échelle. (Fr.) scale. Also *gamme.* (Ger. *Tonleiter*, It *scala*, Sp. *escala*.)

écho. (Fr.) echo. (Ger. *Echo*, It. *eco*, Sp. *eco*.) Example: *son d'écho*, sound of an echo, as seen in the horn parts at the opening of the ballet *Jeux* by Claude Debussy.

Echo. (Ger.) echo. (Fr. *écho*, It. *eco*, Sp. *eco*.)

Echoton. (Ger.) echo tone. (Fr. *son écho*, It. *suono eco*, Sp. *sonido eco*.)

éclat. (Fr.) with a sudden burst, brilliantly. Also *avec.* (Ger. *brillant, hell*; It. *brillante, brillantemente*; Sp. *brillante*.)

éclatant. (Fr.) brilliant, piercing, bright. (Ger. *hell*, It. *luminoso*, Sp. *brillante*.)

eco. (It., Sp.) echo or echo effect. (Fr. *écho*, Ger. *Echo*, Sp. *eco*.)

ed. (It.) and. (Fr. *et*, Ger. *und*, Sp. *y*.)

Eddins, William. (b. 1964.) American **conductor** and pianist. Eddins has been the music director of the Edmonton Symphony Orchestra, Canada, since 2005. He has been the associate conductor of the **Minnesota Orchestra**; assistant (1995–1998), associate (1998–1999), and resident conductor (1999–2004) of the **Chicago Symphony Orchestra**; and principal guest conductor of the RTÉ National Symphony Orchestra, Ireland. He started his own podcast, *Classical Connections*, in order to bring classical music to a wider audience.

edición. (Sp.) edition, as in an edition of a piece of music. (Fr. *edition*, Ger. *Aufgage*, It. *edizione*.)

Edinburgh International Festival (EIF). Established by Rudolf Bing, then general manager of the **Glyndebourne Opera**, and others in 1947 as a post–World War II effort to "provide a platform for the flowering of the human spirit." The festival presents opera, music, dance, theater, visual arts, talks, and workshops. The same year, a group of theater companies established their own Edinburgh Festival Fringe (EFF) as an officially independent, "counterculture" event happening simultaneously. Other festivals have grown up alongside it, including the Edinburgh International Film Festival, the Edinburgh Military Tattoo, a jazz and blues festival, the International Book Festival, Interactive Festival, an art festival, and many more.

edition. (Fr.) edition, as in an edition of a piece of music. (Ger. *Aufgage*, It. *edizione*, Sp. *edición*.)

Éditions Alphonse Leduc Music. Founded in 1842 by Alphonse Leduc and passed down from generation to generation, the company remains in the hands of the Leduc family, currently representing the fifth generation with François Leduc; a nephew, Basile Crichton; and their sons, Jean Leduc and Michel Crichton. The firm initially established its reputation with the publication of instrumental and vocal method books. As with many music publishing houses, they grew by acquiring other smaller companies. The firm was not known for any major composers until 1934 when they began putting out the music of **Olivier Messiaen**, becoming his exclusive publisher in 1961. Since then, they have become a major publisher of contemporary music. In 1980, Leduc bought the company **Heugel** and most recently, the American brass publisher **King Music.** Leduc also functions as the French agent for several foreign music publishing companies. In the United States, they are represented by **G Schirmer.**

Editions Durand. See **Durand, Auguste (Maire).**

Éditions Salabert. A French music-publishing company founded in Paris in 1894 by **Edouard Salabert**. In the beginning, the company focused on popular music. **Francis Salabert** built a catalogue of music from film, music halls, and recordings. In addition to original works, he wrote many arrangements of light music from Europe, Latin America, and the United States. By 1945 there were shops not only in Paris but in New York, Milan, Brussels, and Geneva. The catalogue had grown to over 800 works for **orchestra**, 350 **operettas**, and 80,000 songs. From 1927 to 1938 Éditions Salabert issued their own seventy-eight recordings. They also opened a studio for film dubbing. In 1930, they began handling serious concert music for the first time, purchasing the catalogues of more than fifty other publishers. Following the death of Francis, his widow, Mica Salabert, continued to develop the company as a leader in publishing contemporary music. By 1968 they had developed a special catalogue of pieces by young composers.

edizione. (It.) edition, as in an edition of a piece of music. (Fr. *edition*, Ger. *Aufgage*, Sp. *edición*.)

education of the modern conductor. There is no single educational path for the modern **conductor**. The skills required of the conductor make a long and complex list that includes a discerning ear for pitch, harmony, texture, and balance; an excellent sense of rhythm; basic skills on the piano, a string instrument, and any other instrument of the orchestra (basic is good, but excellence is always better); a knowledge of languages, music history, theory, musical styles, performance practice issues, and public speaking; the ability to speak about music in a manner that appeals to both musicians and nonmusicians; good baton technique that is clear and communicative; and much more. Then there are the intangibles: the ability to lead a group of musicians, many of whom are better at their job than you are at yours; the art and balance of musical interpretation; the ability to inspire an orchestra; and perhaps the most important, musical and personal honesty.

Most American university and conservatory undergraduate programs only offer one or two semesters of conducting classes. As a consequence, most undergraduates leave school without the necessary prerequisites for a master's program. The young conductor needs to take advantage of private instruction, summer programs, and whatever else exists in the community while concentrating on the skills listed above that provide a strong foundation for further development. In the United States, summer programs and conducting workshops provide opportunities for students to be instructed, to gain experience, and to be seen by influential professionals.

European music schools and universities usually begin by training the beginning conductor at the piano. In the European system, the young conductor often begins as a vocal coach in a small opera house, biding his or her time until a chance comes to conduct a full opera and hoping that it leads to further performances. If that happens, European conductors often work up through the ranks of opera houses, gradually building a career. But even that is not the only road to becoming a conductor. More and more, conductors are either opera conductors or symphony conductors. See also **conducting techniques**, **bibliography**.

Edwards, Sian. (b. 1959.) English **conductor**. Edwards studied at the **Royal Northern College of Music** and the **Leningrad Conservatory** (1983–1985) with Professor A. I. Music. She won the **Leeds Conductors' Competition** in 1984, subsequently working with several major orchestras such as the **Berlin Symphony**, **Cleveland Orchestra**, **Los Angeles Philharmonic**, **Orchestre de Paris**, **St. Petersburg Philharmonic**, **Vienna Symphony Orchestra**, and more. Edwards made her operatic debut in 1986 with the Scottish Opera, conducting Kurt Weill's *Mahagonny* and with the **Royal Opera House, Covent Garden**, in 1988, conducting Sir Michael Tippet's *The Knot Garden*. She served as the music director of the **English National Opera** (1993–1995). Her discography includes Judith Weir's opera *Blond Eckbert* with the **English National Opera**.

Effron, David. (b. 1938.) American **conductor** and educator. Effron taught conducting and conducted orchestra and opera at the **Curtis Institute of Music** (1970–1977), the **Eastman School of Music** (1977–1998), and the **University of Indiana Jacob School of Music** (1998–present). He also conducted at the **New York City Opera** and at other opera houses and with orchestras in Germany, the United States, and Asia. He led the **Brevard Music Center** from 1997 to 2007. Effron's recording of Aaron Copland's *Lincoln Portrait* with narrator William

Warfield and the Eastman Philharmonia won a **Grammy Award** for best spoken-word recording.

égal. (Fr.) equal. Also *égaux.* (Ger. *gleich*, *gleichmäßig*; It. *uguale*; Sp. *igual.*) A descriptive term heard in rehearsal. Example: *les triolets éqaux*, equal triplets.

également. (Fr.) equally. (Ger. *gleichmäßig*; It. *ugualmente*, *eqaumente*; Sp. *igualmente.*)

eguale. (It.) even, smoothly. Also *egualmente*. A descriptive term heard in rehearsal. (Fr. *égal*, Ger. *gleich*, Sp. *igual.*)

Ehrling, Sixten. (1918–2005.) Swedish **conductor**. Ehrling studied at the **Swedish Royal Academy of Music** and was coached at the **Swedish Royal Opera** in Stockholm, making his debut there in 1940. He was assistant conductor to **Karl Böhm** at the **Dresden State Opera** (1941). Appointed to lead the Stockholm Concert Society in 1943, he was the music director of the **Swedish Royal Opera** (1953–1960) and served as the music director of the **Detroit Symphony** (1963–1973), leading over twenty-four premieres. His **Metropolitan Opera** debut was in 1973 with **Sir Benjamin Britten**'s *Peter Grimes*. He also led a complete **Ring cycle** with Birgit Nilsson and the Metropolitan Opera's first performance of Béla Bartók's *Bluebeard's Castle*. Ehrling led the conducting programs at the **Juilliard** and **Manhattan** schools of music. His conducting students including **JoAnn Falletta**, **Andrew Litton**, **Myung-Whun Chung**, and **Andreas Delfs**. His recordings include a noted performance of Karl Nielsen's Symphony No. 3 and a set of Franz Berwald symphonies on the **BIS label**. A champion of contemporary composers throughout his career, he was often described as a conductor of integrity, craftsmanship, and consistency.

Eight O'Clock Pops. A concert series started by **Erich Kunzel** with the **Cincinnati Pops Orchestra** in 1965.

eilen (nicht). (Ger.) rush (do not). (Fr. *précipiter*; It. *affrettarsi*, *precipitarsi*; Sp. *correr*, *prisa*, *precipitarse.*) Examples: *eilend*, hurrying; *eilte*, hurried; *mit Eile*, with haste; *eilig*, rushing.

einfach. (Ger.) simple, plain. A descriptive word sometimes heard in rehearsal to evoke a particular manner of playing. (Fr. *simple*; It. *semplice*; Sp. *simple*, *sencillo.*)

Eingang. 1. (Ger.) entrance, of an instrument in the course of a piece.
2. (Ger.) introduction.
3. (Ger.) a short, cadenza-like passage for the soloist in a classical concerto that leads into a solo section. (Fr. *entrée*, It. *entrata*, Sp. *entrada.*)

Einklang. (Ger.) unison. (Fr. *unisson*, It. *unisono*, Sp. *unísono*.) Though still occasionally seen and heard, this use is out of date. ***Unisono*** is preferred.

Einleitung. (Ger.) introduction, a musical introduction. (Fr. *introduction*, It. *introduzione*, Sp. *introducción*.)

einmal. (Ger.) once, one time. (Fr. *une fois*, It. *una volta*, Sp. *una vez*.)

eins. (Ger.) one. See also **numbers, basic**.

Einsatz. (Ger.) cue, entrance of an instrument or voice. (Fr. *entrée*, It. *entrata*, Sp. *entrada*.)

ein wenig. (Ger.) a little. (Fr. *un peu*, It. *un poco*, Sp. *un poco*.) An expression heard in a wide variety of phrases. Example: *Ein wenig schneller*, a little faster.

Eis. (Ger.) E-sharp. See also **accidental**, **appendix 4: "Pitch Names and Their Translations."**

ejecutar. (Sp.) to perform, to execute. (Fr. *exécuter*, Ger. *vortragen*, It. *esequire*.)

élan. (Fr.) with panache, energy, style. A character expression heard in rehearsal to evoke a particular quality in the playing. Also *avec*. (Ger. *mit Schwung*, It. *con slancio*, Sp. *con el impulso*.)

élargir. (Fr.) to broaden or slow down the tempo. An expression used to describe an interpretation of the pacing of a passage. To amplify, broaden, expand. Also *en agrandissant*. (Ger. *erweitern*; It. *allargare, ampliando, espander*; Sp. *alargar, ampliar, expandir*.)

elargissant. (Fr.) *allargando*, a slowing or broadening of the tempo. Example: *En élargissant*, broadening, from *Pavane for a Dead Princess* by Maurice Ravel.

élargissant, en. (Fr.) a broadening of the tempo or pacing. The process of becoming slower or more drawn out. (Ger. *breiter werden*, It. *allargando*, Sp. *allargando*.)

Elder, Sir Mark Philip. (b. 1947.) English **conductor**. Elder studied at Cambridge University (1966–1969) and was a vocal coach, chorus master, and assistant conductor at **Glyndebourne** (1970–1972). A protégé of **Sir Edward Downes**, he made his professional debut with the **Royal Liverpool Orchestra** in 1971 and conducted opera in Australia for the 1972–1974 seasons. He moved to London, where he served on the staff of the **English National Opera (ENO)**. He conducted at the **Royal Opera House, Covent Garden**, in 1976 with Giuseppe Verdi's *Falstaff*. He served as the principal guest conductor of the **London Mozart Players** (1980–1983) and the music director at the ENO (1979–1993), where he led over thirty new productions, including David Blake's *Toussaint* (1977) and the British premiere of Ferruccio Busoni's *Doktor Faust* (1986).

Elder served as the principal conductor of the **BBC Symphony Orchestra** (1982–1985), principal guest conductor of the **City of Birmingham Symphony Orchestra** (1992–1995), and music director of the **Rochester Philharmonic Orchestra** (1989–1994) and the **Hallé Orchestra** (1999–present.) He was made a commander of the Order of the British Empire (CBE) by Queen Elizabeth in 1989 and was knighted in 2008. Elder has written about music for the *Guardian* newspaper and promoted English music with recordings of Nicholas Maw's opera *Odyssey* (1987) and works by Jonathan Harvey, David Matthews, and the premiere recordings of Colin Mathews's *Pluto*, written as a final movement to Gustav Holst's *The Planets*.

electronic music. Music that is partially or completely created with electronically generated processed or reproduced sounds. It is made possible with the onset of the tape recorder and eventually the synthesizer and the computer. The history of electronic music may be described through various electronic studios, the first being at Radio Cologne in Germany, established and run by Herbert Eimert in 1951. Composers who worked there included Eimert, Robert Beyer, and **Karlheinz Stockhausen**. Composers Luciano Berio and Bruno Maderna established a studio at the Italian radio in Milan, and Americans **Otto Luenig** and Vladimir Ussachevsky did early pioneering work, becoming directors of the **Columbia-Princeton Electronic Music Center** in the 1950s. Early examples of electronic music include **musique concrète**.

electronic musical instruments. An instrument that uses electronic means to produce musical sounds. Inventor Theodore Cahill conducted experiments in the development of electronic instruments in the late nineteenth century. Russian Leon Theremin, who was most active in the 1920s and 1930s, invented a number of instruments, including various so-called **theremins** made famous in Alfred Hitchcock's movie *Psycho*. Active at about the same time, Germans Jörg Mager and Friedrich Trautwein invented a variety of instruments, including the trautonium. Frenchman Maurice Martenot invented the **ondes martenot** used by composer Olivier Messiaen in his *Turangalila Symphonie* and often performed by the inventor's sister, Ginette Martenot. Other composers who used the instrument were **Pierre Boulez**, Arthur Honegger, Darius Milhaud, and Edgar Varèse. Invented by Americans Laurens Hammond and John M. Hanert in the 1930s, the **Hammond organ** may be one of the most commonly used electronic instruments, especially in churches.

electronic tuner. An electronic device used to detect the tuning of an individual note. Tuners have a small, built-in microphone that detects whether a pitch being played right in front of it is flat, sharp, or in tune. The tuner uses an LCD display of a needle that will stabilize at a center point when a played note is adjusted to the correct tuning. Tuners can also sound the tuning note for an individual player or an ensemble.

elegancia, con. (Sp.) with elegance. A descriptive phrase. (Fr. *avec élégance*, Ger. *mit Eleganz*, It. *con eleganza*.)

élégant. (Fr.) elegant, graceful. A character term that can be heard in rehearsal in order to evoke a certain quality in the playing. (Ger. *elegant*, It. *eleganza*, Sp. *elegante*.)

elegant. (Ger.) Elegant, graceful. (Fr. *élégant*, It. *elegante*, Sp. *elegante*.)

elegante. (It., Sp.) elegant. Also *con eleganza*, with elegance. (Fr. *élégance*, Ger. *elegant*, Sp. *elegante*.)

Elephant Task Force (ETF). See **Andrew W. Mellon Foundation**.

éloignant. (Fr.) distant. Example: *et tourjours en s'éloignant davantage*, always becoming more distant, from "Fêtes," *Nocturnes* by Claude Debussy.

El Sistema. A publically funded foundation in Venezuela designed to provide musical experiences for young children from impoverished communities. Founded in 1975 by economist and musician **José Antonio Abreu**, the program is now known as the Fundación Musical Simón Bolívar. The foundation now reaches between 310,000 to 370,000 children in various instrumental ensembles, including 31 symphony orchestras. All children participate voluntarily. The **Simon Bolivar Orchestra** is its most prominent ensemble. **Gustavo Dudamel**, the music director of the **Los Angeles Philharmonic Orchestra**, is one of the program's most distinguished graduates. See Tunstall, Tricia. *Changing Lives: Gustavo Dudamel, El Sistema, and the Transformative Power of Music*. New York: W. W. Norton & Co., 2012. See also **bibliography**.

embocadura. (Sp.) mouthpiece, as on brass and wind instruments. (Fr. *embouchure*; Ger. *Mundstück*; It. *bocchino*, *imboccatura*.)

embouchure. (Fr.) mouthpiece, as used by brass and wind instruments. (Ger. *Mundstück*; It. *bocchino*, *imboccatura*; Sp. *embocadura*.) See also **embouchure**.

embouchure. The muscles of the face and lips as used with the mouthpiece of any woodwind or brass instrument in order to produce the best possible sound on the instrument across its entire full range. (Fr. *embouchure*, Ger. *Embouchure*, It. *imboccatura*, Sp. *embocadura*.)

EMI Records (Electrical & Musical Industries, Ltd.) Formed in 1931 as a result of the merger of the European **Columbia Gramophone Company** and the **Gramophone Company**, with **RCA** as a major stockholder. In the same year, they opened their studios at Abbey Road, where the Beatles would record thirty years later. The worldwide depression hit the industry hard. A dizzying number of mergers and takeovers during this period led to licensing issues so complex that various "parts" of any given recording company—a trademark, an artist—were moved around like a board game with made-up rules. Suffice it to say that in the 1930s and 1940s, **Arturo Toscanini**, **Sir Edward Elgar**, and **Otto Klemperer** were among their most renowned classical artists. EMI was often reticent to try new technologies, not switching to the forty-five single until five years after it was available; however, they remain known for their pioneering engineer **Alan Blumlein**, who invented stereo sound. In 2000, EMI merged with the **Warner Music Group**, but it was an unsuccessful relationship, and by 2007 the company had been taken over by a private equity firm and most of their leading musicians had left the label. Vestiges of EMI, such as EMI Classics, still exist as a part of the **Universal Music Group**.

Empfindsamkeit. (Ger.) sensitivity. A quality of playing that is often sought. (Fr. *sensibilité*, It. *sensibilità*, Sp. *sensibilidad*.)

Empfindsam Stil. (Ger.) a style of composition that developed in eighteenth-century Germany. It was intended to reflect natural human feelings and featured sudden mood changes. Composers Wihelm Friedemann Bach and C. P. E. Bach were among its proponents.

Empfindung. (Ger.) feeling, perception, sensation. Also *mit Emfindung*, with feeling; *empfinden*, to feel, to sense. (Fr. *sensation*, It. *sensazione*, Sp. *sentimiento*.)

empflindlich. (Ger.) sensitively. A character word sometimes heard in describing music, passages of music, or a manner of playing. (Fr. *sensiblement*, It. *sensibilmente*, Sp. *sensibilmente*.)

empfunden. (Ger.) heartfelt. A character word used in the title of movement 6 of Symphony No. 3 by **Gustav Mahler**.

empujar. (Sp.) driving, pushing ahead. A character term that indicates pressing the tempo forward. (Fr. *appuyant*, Ger. *drängend*, It. *incalzante*.)

en agrandissant. (Fr.) to broaden or slow down the tempo. An expression used to describe an interpretation of the pacing of a passage; to amplify, broaden, expand. Also *élargir.* (Ger. *erweitern*; It. *allargare, ampliando, espandere*; Sp. *alargar, ampliar, expandir.*)

en arriére. (Fr.) back. (Ger. *zurück*, It. *indietro*, Sp. *de Nuevo.*) Examples of "Back, please" (in order to repeat a passage): (Fr.) *En arrière, s'il vous plaît*; (Ger.) *Zurück, bitte*; (It.) *Di nuovo, per favore*; Sp. *De nuevo, por favor.*

encantado. (Sp.) enchanted, delighted, bewitched. A character word. (Fr. *enchaînez*, Ger. *verzauberten*, It. *incantato.*)

enchaînez. (Fr.) connnect, link together. Also *enchaîner.* Seen in French music by composers such as Claude Debussy. (Ger. *Verkettung*; It. *concatenamento*; Sp. *encadenar, enlazar.*)

enchanté. (Fr.) enchanted, delighted, bewitched. Also *enchaînez.* A character word. (Ger. *verzaubert*, It. *incantato*, Sp. *encantado.*)

encore. (Fr.) again. Also *de nouveau.* (Ger. *wieder*; It. *di nuove, ancora*; Sp. *nuevamente, de nuevo.*)

encore! (Fr.) Again! Once more! An expression of approval cried out by the audience (mostly in Europe) when they want a performer to play an **encore**. (It. *bis*, Ger. *nochmal! noch einmal! Zugabe!* Sp. *bis.*) Also used in rehearsal in order to ask for the repetition of a passage. Example: *encore plus vite*, again faster. Also (Sp.) *otra vez más rapido*, again but faster; (Sp.) *una vez más, pero ahora más rapido*, one more time, but this time faster (more polite). See also **ancora**.

en croissant. (Fr.) an indication to play glissandos with the hands crossing each other. Examples: **glissando** *(en croissant)*, glissando with the hands crossing each other, from the harp part in "Jeux de vagues," mvt. 2 of *La Mer* by Claude Debussy.

Endangered Instruments Program. A program started by the **Seattle Youth Symphony Orchestra** and local schools in order to encourage young people to take up less popular instruments such as the **oboe**, **bassoon**, **viola**, **double bass**, and **horn**. The program has been emulated in other North American cities.

en défaillant. (Fr.) getting softer, fading, dying away. (It. *mancando*; Ger. *entschwindend, ausklingen lassend*; Sp. *desapareciend, muriendo.*)

en dehors. (Fr.) Bring out, bring forward. Also *en évidence.* (Ger. *außerhalb, hervortretend*; It. *in fuori*; Sp. *destacar.*)

Example: *un peu en dehors*, play out a little, from "Jeux de vagues," mvt. 2 of *La Mer* by Claude Debussy. Example from Spanish: *Que el oboe quede en eividencia*, let the oboe be in evidence (literal).

en dehors. (Fr.) bring out, to play a part so that it can be heard above others. Also *en évidence.* (Ger. *hervortretend*, It. *in fuori*, Sp. *destacar.*) Example: *un peu en dehors*, play out a little, from "Jeux de vagues," mvt. 2 of *La Mer* by Claude Debussy.

en deux. (Fr.) in two, as in two beats to a bar. (Ger. *in zwei, in zwei Schlage*; It. *in due, in due battute*; Sp. *en dos, a dos.*)

en dos. (Sp.) in two. Also *a dos.* (Fr. *à deux*; Ger. *in zwei, in zwei Schlage*; It. *in due, in due battute.*) Examples: *Voy a dirigir este pasaje en dos*, I will conduct this passage in two; *este compás se va a marcar a dos*, this bar will be conducted in two.

en élargissant. (Fr.) slowing down, broadening. (It. *slargando, allargando*; Ger. *breiter werdend*; Sp. *moderar el tiempo.*)

en el diapasón. (Sp.) on the fingerboard, an indication seen in string parts to play with the bow above the fingerboard. (It. *sul tasto, sulla tastiera*; Fr. *Sur la touche*; Ger. *am Griffbrett.*)

en el punta. (Sp.) a bowing term indicating to play at the point of the bow. (Ger. *mit der Bogenspitze*, It. *con la punta d'arco.*) En el punta del arco is more specific.

en el tempo. (Sp.) in tempo. (Fr. *dans le tempo*, Ger. *im Zeitmaß*, It. *in tempo.*)

energético. (Sp.) vigorous, powerful, energetic. A character word used to evoke a particular style of playing. (Fr. *énergique*, Ger. *energisch*, It. *energico.*)

energico. (It.) vigorous, powerful, energetic. A character word used to evoke a particular style of playing. (Fr. *énergique*, Ger. *energisch*, Sp. *energético.*) Also *con energia*, with energy.

énergique. (Fr.) vigorous, powerful, energetic. A character word used to evoke a particular style of playing. (Ger. *energisch*, It. *energico*, Sp. *energético.*)

energisch. (Ger.) vigorous, powerful, energetic. A character word used to evoke a particular style of playing. (Fr. *énergique*, It. *energico*, Sp. *energético.*)

Englisches horn. (Ger.) **English horn.** (Fr. *cor anglais*, It. *corno inglese*, Sp. *corno inglés.*) See also **appendix 3: "Instrument Names and Their Translations."**

English horn. A double-reed member of the **oboe** family that extends the range downward. The English horn is a transposing instrument that sounds a perfect fifth lower than written. Its written range is B3 to G6, sounding E3 to C6. (Fr. *cor anglais*, Ger. *Englisches horn*, It. *corno inglese*, Sp. *corno inglés*.) See also **appendix 3: "Instrument Names and Their Translations."**

English horn range as it sounds. *Courtesy Andrew Martin Smith.*

English horn range as written. *Courtesy Andrew Martin Smith.*

English National Opera (ENO). An opera company in London that produces its operas in English and maintains, as part of its mission, reasonably priced tickets. The company originated as the **Sadler's Wells Opera** when it was founded by Lilian Baylis in a theater of the same name. Salder's Wells was closed during World War II, but the company returned in 1945 for the premiere of **Sir Benjamin Britten**'s opera *Peter Grimes*. In 1968, the company moved to the London Coliseum, retaining the name Sadler's Wells Opera until the mid-1970s, when it was changed to the English National Opera. The colesium underwent a significant renovation between 2000 and 2004 and is known for its innovative productions with high musical standards. In 2009, Giacomo Puccini's *La bohème* was broadcast live in a worldwide first on Sky Arts 2 and Sky Arts HD, while live streamed on Sky Arts 1. In 2010, ENO's first site-specific opera was staged at the Great Eastern Quay, Newham, with composer Stephen Oliver's *The Duchess of Malfi* produced in an award-winning collaboration with the theater company Punchdrunk. In 2011, the ENO created the world's first opera live in 3–D broadcast, collaborating with BSkyB in a performance of Gaetano Donizetti's *Lucrezia Borgia*. **Conductors** and music directors of the ENO include **Sir Charles Mackerras**, **Sir Mark Elder**, **Sian Edwards**, and others. The ENO offers its Motley Theater Design course to help train future designers. In addition, ENO Baylis, founded in 1985, is an education department that focuses on building new audiences. The company has issued several recordings on **EMI** and **Chandos** throughout its history.

English rhythmic names. Crotchet, quaver, semiquaver, demisemiquaver, hemidemisemiquaver, minim, breve, semibreve. See also **Appendix 7: "Rhythmic Terms and Their Translations."**

enharmonic. When the same pitch is spelled differently, it is said to be enharmonic. (Fr. *enharmonique*, Ger. *enharmonisch*, It. *enarmonico*, Sp. *enarmónico*.)

Enharmonic. *Courtesy Andrew Martin Smith.*

enigmatic scale. A scale first used by Giuseppe Verdi in his *Ave Maria* for a cappella choir from the *Four Sacred Songs* in 1898. It consists of seven notes spelled from low to high, beginning on C, then D-flat, E-natural, F-sharp, G-sharp, A-sharp, and B.

en la punta del arco. (Sp.) an indication for string players to play at the point or tip of the bow. Also *con la punta del arco*. (Fr. *à la pointe*, *avec la pointe de l'archet*; Ger. *an der Bogenspitze*, *an der Spitze*, *mit der Bogenspitze*; It. *alla punta d'arco*, *con la punta d'arco*.)

enlever. (Fr.) remove, remove the mute. Also *enlever la sourdine*. (Ger. *Dämpfer ab*, *Dämpfer weg*; It. *togliere*, *togliere il sordino*; Sp. *quitar la sordina*.)

en meme temps. (Fr.) simultaneously, at the same time. (Ger. *gleichzeitig*, It. *contempraneamente*, Sp. *al mismo tiempo*.)

enragé. (Fr.) raging, furious. A character word used to evoke a particular style of playing. Also *rageur*. (Ger. *wütend*; It. *arrabbiato*, *rabbioso*; Sp. *furioso*.)

en revenant au movement. (Fr.) returning to tempo. (Ger. *zum Zeitmaß zurückkehrend*, It. *tornando al tempo*, Sp. *volviendo al tempo*.)

ensayar. (Sp.) to rehearse.

ensayo. (Sp.) rehearsal. (Fr. *répétizione*; Ger. *Probe*, *proben*; It. *prova*, *ripetizione*.)

ensayo general. (Sp.) **General rehearsal** or final rehearsal. (Fr. *la répétition générale*; Ger. *Generalprobe*; It. *la ripetizione generale*, *la prova generale*.)

ensemble. (Fr.) together. A commonly heard directive. (Ger. *zusammen*, It. *insieme*, Sp. *juntos*.) Examples: *Nous ne sommes pas ensemble*, **We are not together**; *Ce doit être ensemble*, **This must be together**.

Ensemble InterContemporain, (EIC). Founded by **Pierre Boulez** in 1976, in Paris, as a group of soloists who could play any literature, orchestral, chamber, or solo, but would specialize in the presentation of contemporary music mostly in the European modernist tradition with a large number of premieres each year. Originally part of **IRCAM**, the ensemble needed a larger performing space so it moved to the **Cité de la Musique**, where it presents a full season of concerts. EIC has a specialty in **spectral music**, particularly music by Gérard Grisey, Tristan Murail, Hugues, and others. Its current music director is Matthias Pintscher (appointed in 2013). Past music directors include **David Robertson** (1992–2000), Jonathan Nott (2000–2003), and **Susanna Mälkki** (2006–2012). EIC has recorded numerous CDs and received many awards, including a **Gramophone Award** and the **Diapason d'Or**.

en se perdant. (Fr.) disappearing, dying away to nothing, describing a manner of playing. Also *éteindre*, *expirer*. (Ger. *erlöschen*, *sich verlierend*; It. *espirare*, *extinguere*, *perdendosi*; Sp. *desvanesiéndose*, *extinguiéndose*, *perdiéndose*.)

en s'éteignant. (Fr.) dying away, extinguishing. An expression used to describe a manner of playing. (It. *estinguendo*, Ger. *verlöschend*, Sp. *extinción*.)

ensuite. (Fr.) then, after. Also *puis*. (Ger. *dann*; It. *allora*, *poi*, *dopo*; Sp. *después*, *entonces*.)

entendre. (Fr.) to hear. (Ger. *hören*, It. *udire*, Sp. *oír*.) Also *entendu*, heard.

Entfernung. (Ger.) distance. (Fr. *distance*, It. *distanza*, Sp. *distancia*.)

entonación. (Sp.) **pitch**, a sound perceived as a tone, pitch, or musical note, technically the function of a fundamental frequency or number of oscillations per second as measured in **Hertz**. (Fr. *hauteur*, Ger. *Tonhöhe*, It. *intonazione*.) See also **Tonhöhe**.

entonces. (Sp.) then. Also *después*. (Fr. *puis*, *ensuite*; Ger. *dann*, It. *allora*, *poi*, *dopo*.)

entr'acte. (Fr.) interlude, a musical number often occurring between two scenes or acts of an opera, in practical terms, often to provide time for a scene change on stage. (Ger. *Zwischenspiel*, It. *interludio*, Sp. *intermedio*.)

entrada. (Sp.) cue, entrance of an instrument or voice. (Fr. *entrée*, It. *entrata*, Ger. *Einsatz*.) Examples: *Me dara mi entrada?* Will you give me a cue? *Espere mi entrada*, wait for my cue (commonly heard comments from a member of an ensemble and a conductor, respectively).

entrata. (It.) cue, entrance of an instrument or voice. (Fr. *entrée*, Ger. *Einsatz*, Sp. *entrada*.)

en tre. (It.) in three, an expression that indicates conducting in three beats to a bar. (Fr. *en trois*, Ger. *dreitaktig*, Sp. *en tres*.)

entrée. (Fr.) cue, entrance of an instrument or voice. (Ger. *Einsatz*, It. *entrata*, Sp. *entrada*.)

en tres. (Sp.) in three, an expression that indicates conducting in three beats to a bar. (Fr. *en trois*, Ger. *dreitaktig*, It. *en tre*.)

en trois. (Fr.) in three, an expression that indicates conducting in three beats to a bar. (Ger. *dreitaktig*, It. *en tre*, Sp. *en tres*.)

entschieden. (Ger.) to decide, authoritative, decisive. Also *entschlossen*. (Fr. *décidé*, It. *deciso*, *risoluto*; Sp. *decidico*, *resuelto*.) A character word sometimes used to describe a particular way of playing. Used in the title of movement one of Symphony No. 3 of **Gustav Mahler**.

entschwindend. (Ger.) getting softer, fading, dying away. A directive that describes a particular way of playing. (Fr. *en défaillant*; It. *mancando*; Sp. *desapareciendo*, *suavizando*.)

envelope. In acoustics, the amplitude curve of a sound from its attack to its steady state and then decay.

environmental music. The use of sounds from the environment for artistic purposes, such as composers using birdcalls or other nature sounds to elicit aesthetic effect. It can be ambient or so-called ambient space music that reproduces sounds of nature and is sometimes used for relaxation or meditation. It can also be music conceived for outdoor performance. Examples of works conceived to evoke or be performed outdoors: John Luther Adams, *Become Ocean* (2013); Stephen Jaffe, *Poetry of the Piedmont* (2006); Robert Morris, *Playing Outdoors* (2000); John Cage, *Fifty-Eight* (1991); Salvatore Sciarrino, *La Perfezione di Uno Spirito Sottile* (1985); Kalevi Aho, Symphony No. 12 *"Lusto"* (2003); and more.

en voz baja. (Sp.) quietly, subdued, in an undertone (lit. "under the voice"). Also *susurrar*, *susurrando*. (Fr. *à voix basse*; Ger. *"unter der Stimme," mit leiser Stimme*; It. *sotto voce*.)

eoliphone. See **wind machine**.

épisode. (Fr.) episode, a structural unit within a piece. (Ger. *Zwischensatz*, It. *episodio*, Sp. *episodio*.)

episodio. (It., Sp.) episode, a structural unit within a piece. (Fr. *épisode*, Ger. *Zwischensatz*, Sp. *episodio*.)

éponge, baguette d'. (Fr.) sponge-headed mallet or stick, as in a timpani mallet with a sponge head. (Ger. *Schwammschlägel*, It. *bacchettta di spugna*, Sp. *baqueta de esponja*.)

equal temperament. A tuning system in which the twelve notes of the scale are separated by an equal distance of one hundred **cents**, creating perfect octaves. It is now the most commonly used tuning system in Western music and is used, in particular, to tune a piano.

erhöhen. (Ger.) to sharpen, to raise the pitch. (Fr. *dièse*, It. *dieses*, Sp. *sostenido*.)

Erhöhungzeichen. (Ger.) The sharp sign, ♯. (Fr. *dièse*, It. *dieses*, Sp. *sostenido*.)

Ericson, Eric Gustaf. (b. 1918–2013.) Swedish choral **conductor** and educator. Ericson studied at the **Royal College of Music in Stockholm** and the Schola Cantorum Basilienses, Switzerland. Known for his innovative teaching and wide repertoire, he served as the principal conductor of the Orphei Drängar choir at Uppsala University (1951–1991) and as the founding conductor and choirmaster of the **Swedish Radio Choir** (1951–1982). Ericson taught at his alma mater, the Stockholm Royal College of Music, beginning in 1951. He also founded and led the Eric Ericson Chamber Choir. Ericson won many awards in his lifetime, and through his many performances and a legacy of recordings was a promoter of contemporary Swedish choral music.

erlöschen. (Ger.) dying out, disappear, expire. (Fr. *éteindre, expirer*; It. *espirare, extinguere*; Sp. *desvanesiéndose, perdiéndose*.)

erlöscht. (Ger.) barely audible, extinguished. Also *audgelöscht*. (Fr. *éteint*; It. *estinto, spento*; Sp. *extinto*.)

ermüdet. (Ger.) weary, exhausted. As used in *Das Lied von der Erde*, mvt. 2, by **Gustav Mahler**.

erniedrigen. (Ger.) a term used to call for a lowering of the pitch or tuning. Also *herunterstimmen*. (Fr. *baisser l'accord, baisser l'intonation*; It. *abbassare l'intonature, abbassare l'accordatura*; Sp. *bajar la afinación, bemolar*.) See also **scordatura**.

erregt. (Ger.) excited, agitated. (Fr. *agité*, It. *agitato*, Sp. *agitado*.)

Ersatz. (Ger.) substitute. (Fr. *substitut*, It. *sostituto*, Sp. *sostituto*.)

ersterben. (Ger.) to die away, die down. A descriptive term heard on occasion in rehearsal. (Fr. *mourir, dépérissement*; It. *morire lontano*; Sp. *alejándose, muriendo, desvaneciéndose, perdiéndose*.)

erste Sängerin. (Ger.) the leading lady in an opera. (Fr. *premiere chanteuse*, It. *prima donna*, Sp. *prima donna*.)

erstes Mal. 1. (Ger.) the first and second endings of sections of a piece that are repeated.
2. (Ger.) when followed by additional instructions, how to play a section of a piece the first time and then the second time. (Fr. *premiere fois*; It. *prima volta, seconda volta*; Sp. *primer tiempo*.)

erweitern. (Ger.) an expression used to describe an interpretation of the pacing of a passage; to expand, amplify, expanding; to broaden the tempo or style of playing. (Fr. *élargir, en agrandissant*; It. *allargar, ampliando, espandere*; Sp. *alargar, ampliar, expandir*.)

Erzähler. (Ger.) narrator. (Fr. *narrateur*, It. *narratore*, Sp. *narrador*.)

Es. (Ger.) E-flat. See also **accidental**; **appendix 5: "Pitch Names and Their Translations."**

esatto. (It.) strictly, exactly. A descriptive term heard in rehearsal. Also *giusto*. (Fr. *exact, juste*; Ger. *genau, richtig*; Sp. *exactamente, preciso*.)

escala. (Sp.) scale. Also *gama*. (Fr. *gamme*; Ger. *Skala, Tonleiter*; It. *scala*.) See also **alternative scales**.

escena. (Sp.) the stage, of an opera house, for instance. Also *etapa*. (Fr. *scène, planches*; It. *scena, palcoscenico*; Ger. *Bühne, Szene*.)

Eschenbach, Christoph. (b. 1940.) German **conductor** and pianist. Eschenbach is the current music director of the **National Symphony Orchestra (NSO)** and the **John F. Kennedy Center for the Performing Arts**, both in Washington, DC. Orphaned as a child—his mother died giving birth to him and his father died as a protester against the Nazis—Eschenbach lost the ability to speak for over a year, only regaining it when his caretaker, a cousin, Wallydore Eschenbach, asked him if he wanted to play music. She adopted him in 1946 and became his piano teacher. He was greatly influenced by hearing an orchestra performance led by **Wilhelm Furtwängler** in 1951 and four years later entered the Cologne Conservatory of Music (*Musikhochschule*) to study piano and conducting. Eschenbach also studied conducting with **George Szell** and **Herbert van Karajan**. In 1986, having established himself as a top performer, he was the soloist for the premiere of Heinz Werner Henze's Piano Concerto No. 2.

Eschenbach was the music director of the Rheinland-Pflaz State Philharmonic Orchestra from 1981 to 1982 and became the principal guest conductor of the **Tonhalle Orchestra Zurich** in 1981, serving as the chief conductor from 1982 to 1986. He was the music director of the **Houston Symphony** (1988–1999); coartistic director of the Pacific Music Festival (1992–2005); chief conductor of the **NDR Symphony Orchestra, Hamburg** (1998–2004); music director of the **Ravinia Festival**, summer home of the **Chicago Symphony Orchestra** (1994–2005); artistic director of the **Schleswig-Holstein Music Festival, Germany** (1999–2003); music director of the **Orchestre de Paris** (2000–2010); and music director of the **Philadelphia Orchestra** (2003–2008). Eschenbach has made many recordings as a pianist and conductor, as well as leading from the piano. The period of his tenure at the **Houston Symphony Orchestra** was particularly successful as he was credited with having raised the orchestra's profile to an international level and garnered the respect of both the orchestra players and the community. His tenure with the **Philadelphia Orchestra** drew controversy that played out in the local and nation media.

esequire. (It.) to perform, execute. (Fr. *exécuter*, Ger. *vortragen*, Sp. *ejecutar*.)

esercizio. (It.) exercise, **etude**. (Fr. *étude*, Ger. *Etüde*, Sp. *estudio*.)

es folgt. (Ger.) continue without pause. (Fr. *ça suit*, It. *segue*, Sp. *sigue*.)

espandere. (It.) an expression used to describe an interpretation of the pacing of a passage, to expand, amplify, expanding. Also *ampliando*. (Fr. *en agrandissant*; Ger. *erweitern*; Sp. *alargar, ampliar*.)

esperar, por favor. (Sp.) wait, please; one moment, please. A directive often heard in rehearsal. (Fr. *Attendez s'il vous plait*; Ger. *Warten, bitte*; It. *Attendere, prego*.)

espirare. (It.) dying out, disappear, expire. Also *extinguere*. (Fr. *éteindre, expirer*; Ger. *erlöschen*; Sp. *desvanesiéndose, perdiéndose*.)

esponja, baqueta de. (Sp.) Sponge-headed mallet or stick, as in a timpani mallet with a sponge head. (Fr. *baguette d'éponge*, Ger. *Schwammschlägel*, It. *bacchetta di spugna*.)

espressivo. (It.) expressive, a manner of playing. Abbrevated *esp., espr., express.* (Fr. *espressif*, Ger. *ausdrucksvoll*, Sp. *expresivo*.)

estilo. (Sp.) style, as in playing in the correct style. (Ger. *stil*, Fr. *style*, It. *stile*.)

estinguendo. (It.) dying away, extinguishing. (Fr. *en s'éteignant*; Ger. *verlöschend*; Sp. *extinction, extinguiéndose*.)

estinguendo. (It.) dying away, extinguishing. A manner of playing. (Fr. *en s'éteignant*, Ger. *verlöschend*, Sp. *extinctión*.)

estinto. (It.) barely audible, extinguished. Also *spento*. (Fr. *éteint*; Ger. *erlöscht, audgelöscht*; Sp. *extinto, apenas audible, perdido*.)

Estonian National Symphony Orchestra (Eesti Riiklik Sümfooniaorkester, ERSO). Founded in 1926 in Tallin as a radio orchestra, the ERSO is the longest continually functioning professional orchestra in Estonia. **Neemi Järvi** was made the principal conductor and artistic director in 2010. Paavo Järvi served as the artistic advisor from 2002. Past principal conductors include Olav Roots (1939–1944), Paul Karp (1944–1950), Roman Matsov (1950–1963), Neeme Järvi (1963–1979), Peeter Lije (1980–1990), Leo Krämer (1991–1993), Arvo Volmer (1993–2001), and Nikolai Alexeev (2001–2010). The orchestra won a Grammy for its 2004 recording of Jean Sibelius cantatas on the Virgin Classics label and has made several recordings of contemporary Estonian music, including music by Arvo Pärt. The ERSO has toured Europe, Russia, and the United States, giving a performance in the Great Hall of the **St. Petersburg Philharmonic** in 2012.

estrade. (Fr.) conductor's podium. Also *podium*. (Ger. *Podium, Podest*; It. *podio, pedana*; Sp. *podium*.) See **podium, conductor's**.

estreno. (Sp.) first performance, first night, or opening night of a series of performances of an opera or musical. (Fr. *premiére*; Ger. *Premiere, erste Vorstellung*; It. *prima*.)

estreno mundial. (Sp.) the first performance of a piece of music, world premiere. (Fr. *première execution mondiale*; Ger. *Uraufführung*; It. *prima esecuczione mondiale, creazione*.)

estudio. (Sp.) exercise, a short piece used to practice and develop instrumental technics. (Fr. *étude*, Ger. *Etüde*, It. *esercizio*.)

et. (Fr.) and. (Ger. *und*, It. *e*, Sp. *y.*)

et ainsi de suite. (Fr.) and so on, et cetera. (Ger. *und so weiter*, It. *eccetera*, Sp. *etcétera*.)

etapa. (Sp.) the stage, of an opera house, for instance. Also *escena.* (Fr. *scène, planches*; Ger. *Bühne, Szene*; It. *scena, palcoscenico*.)

etcétera. (Sp.) and so on, et cetera. (Fr. *et ainsi de suite*, Ger. *und so weiter*, It. *eccetera*.)

éteindre. (Fr.) dying out, disappear, expire. Also *expirer.* (Ger. *erlöschen*; It. *espirare, extinguere*; Sp. *desvanesiéndose, perdiéndose*.)

éteint. (Fr.) barely audible, extinguished. A character word used to evoke a particularly delicate manner of playing. (Ger. *erlöscht, audgelöscht*; It. *estinto, spento*; Sp. *extinto*.)

ètendue. (Fr.) compass, range, of an instrument, for instance. (Ger. *Umfang, Raum, Ausdehnung*; It. *gamma*; Sp. *rango*.)

étouffé. (Fr.) damped, muted. Sometimes used to mean **stopped**. (Ger. *gestopft, gedeckt*; It. *chiuso, tappato*; Sp. *cubierto, tapado*.) See also **bouché**.

etude. An exercise written for a solo instrument for practicing technique, also sometimes used for displaying technical mastery, as in a showpiece. (Fr. *étude*, Ger. *Etüde*, It. *studio*, Sp. *estudio*.)

étude. (Fr.) exercise, **etude**, a short piece used to practice and develop instrumental technics. (Ger. *Etüde*, It. *esercizio*, Sp. *estudio*.)

Etüde. (Ger.) exercise, **etude**, a short piece used to practice and develop instrumental technics. (Fr. *étude*, It. *esercizio*, Sp. *estudio*.)

etwas bewegter. (Ger.) somewhat moving, *piu mosso*. An expression seen in scores and parts and heard in rehearsal.

etwas zurückhaltend. (Ger.) somewhat held back. An expression seen in scores and parts and heard in rehearsal.

Eugene Symphony. A professional orchestra in Eugene, Oregon, that offers classics, pops, and education concerts in addition to outreach programs in local schools; opportunities for adult amateurs to receive coaching from symphony musicians, culminating with a public performance at the end of the concert season; and a young artist's competition. The Eugene Symphony also has its own Symphony Chorus. The current music director is Danail Rachev. Past music directors include founding conductor Lawrence Maves (1966–1981), William McGlaughlin (1981–1985), Adrian Gnam (1985–1989), Marin Alsop (1989–1996), Miguel Harth-Bedoya (1996–2002), and Giancarlo Guerrero (2002–2009).

euphonium. The euphonium has the same range as the bass trombone and is a nontransposing instrument. In the United States, it has generally replaced Richard Wagner's tenor tuba. However, as the Wagner tenor tuba was written in B double-flat (BB-flat), when playing such a part on the euphonium, it is necessary to transpose down a major nineth. (Fr. *euphonium*, Ger. *Baritonhorn*, It. *bombardino*, Sp. *bombardino*.) See also **bass trombone**.

euphonium. (Fr.) **euphonium**. (Ger. *Baritonhorn*, It. *bombardino*, Sp. *bombardino*.) See also **appendix 3: "Instrument Names and Their Translations."**

eurhythmics. See **Dalcroze Eurhythmics**.

exact. (Fr.) strictly, as in strictly in tempo. Also *juste.* (Ger. *genau, richtig*; It. *esatto, giusto*; Sp. *exactamente, preciso*.)

exactamente. (Sp.) strictly, as in strictly in tempo. Also *preciso.* (Fr. *exact, juste*; Ger. *genau, richtig*; It. *esatto, giusto*.)

exécuter. (Fr.) to perform, to execute. (Ger. *vortragen*, It. *esequire*, Sp. *ejecutar*.)

exercises for independence of hands. (1) Conduct a smooth circle with the right hand while conducting the left hand in a vertical motion, palm up as the hand goes up and palm down as the hand goes down. Keep the motion smooth. Switch the hands. (2) Conduct a four pattern in the right hand while lifting the left hand, palm upward, from the bottom to the top of the conducting area, reversing the palm for the downward motion. Vary the left hand so that it isn't always a straight line up and down, allowing it to move out and up, away from the body, and then down and in, back to the starting point. (3) Conduct a four pattern with the right hand while practicing giving cue gestures on every beat of the bar with the left. Vary the location of the instrument you are cuing. (4) Conduct one pattern in one hand and another in the other. Switch hands.

exoticism. The use of foreign musical elements in composition. Composers often look to other cultures for musical materials and inspiration. While numerous examples exist going back to the Classical period and before, interesting contemporary works include Benjamin Britten's ballet *The Prince of the Pagodas*, which re-creates the sounds of a Balinese gamelan; John Cage's Far East–influenced *Music of Changes*; Charles Tomlinson Griffes's *The Pleasure Dome of Kubla Kahn*, based on a poem of Samuel Taylor Coleridge; along with several compositions by both Alan Hovhaness and Lou Harrison and Frenchman Darius Milhaud's *La Creation du Monde*, in which he draws on an African creation myth for inspiration.

expandir. (Sp.) to broaden or slow down the tempo. An expression used to describe an interpretation of the pacing of a passage; to amplify, broaden, expand. Also *en expansion, ampliar.* (Fr. *élargir, en agrandissant*; Ger. *erweitern*; It. *allargare, ampliando, espandere.*)

expresivo. (Sp.) expressive, expression, musical feeling. (Fr. *expressif*, Ger. *ausdrucksvoll*, It. *espressivo.*)

expressif. (Fr.) expressive, expression, musical feeling. (Ger. *ausdrucksvoll*, It. *espressivo*, Sp. *expresivo.*) Example: *expressif un peu marqué*, expressive and a little marked, from "Gigues" of *Images* by Claude Debussy.

expression. (Fr.) expression. Example: *En animant avec une grande intensité dans l'expression*, animating with great intensity in the expression, from "Les parfums de la nuit" from "Iberia" of *Images* by Claude Debussy.

expressionism. First developed in the visual arts as a movement that featured the outward portrayal of inward consciousness, the irrational, primitive, savage, and mysterious aspects of humankind. Champions of expressionism in music were **Richard Strauss**, as exhibited mainly in his two operas *Elektra* and *Salome*; **Arnold Schoenberg** in *Pierrot Lunaire*, using a half sung, half spoken **Sprechstimme** technique; and Alban Berg in his opera *Wozzeck*. Musical elements of expressionism include distortions of melody with extreme leaps, rhythms, registers, new instrumental textures, and an expansion of the harmonic language.

expression marks. Symbols, words, and phrases used in music in order to suggest a certain manner of playing. (Fr. *signe d'expression*, Ger. *Ausdrucksbezeichnung*, It. *segno d'espressione*, Sp. *signo de expresión.*)

expressive conducting. Conducting in a manner that shows some aspect of musical expression, a gentle turn of a phrase, the power of a climax, the tender transparency of sound in a French masterpiece to the excitement of an overlapping brass stretto in the Bartók *Concerto for Orchestra*. Often thought of as based in emotion, musical expression is at its root about itself, not in a limited sense, but in the all-consuming sense that is the power of music. See also **conducting technique**.

expressive conducting gestures. Any conducting gesture given in a way that expresses something musical, in particular gestures that show phrasing, musical line, rhythmic excitement, dramatic tension and resolution, and much more. See also **conducting technique**.

extended instrumental techniques. In the twentieth century, new playing techniques have been added to almost all orchestral instruments. String players may be required to bow behind the bridge on the tailpiece, on the bridge (***ponticello***), on the fingerboard (***sul tasto***), or on the fingerboard behind the fingers, which are holding down pitches one at a time (see George Crumb, *Black Angles*). Woodwinds may be asked to use **multiphonics** (the simultaneous sounding of more than one pitch), to blow air through the instrument or the mouthpiece without making a pitch, to use key clicks, to play on the reed or mouthpiece in order to create noises, and to use slap tonguing. Brass players may have to blow air through the mouthpiece or the instrument without pitches, use key clicking (on the trumpet and horn), or sing while playing. Percussionists are now often asked to combine two or more instruments, such as placing cymbals on the heads of timpani, playing the timpani with maracas (see Leonard Bernstein, Symphony No. 1 *"Jeremiah"*), bowing crotales, vibraphone, xylophone, and marimba. See also ***Threnody to the Victims of Hiroshima* (1960)** in **appendix 1: "Six Pieces That Changed Conducting,"** for list of musical symbols for extended techniques.

extensions, instrument. Several instruments of the orchestra have had their ranges extended during the twentieth century, most often because composers have asked for it.

1. The modern **bassoon** and **contrabassoon** have a new mechanical key that extends the range down from B-flat one half step lower to A. This A was first called for in the *Woodwind Quintet* by Carl Nielsen. At first, bassoonists would put a piece of rolled cardboard in the top of the instrument to give it the length required to get the pitch.
2. The modern **bass clarinet** has an extension that lowers its range to C, B, and B-flat (in concert pitch). **Igor Stravinsky**'s ballet *Petrouchka*, with its low C (concert pitch), is perhaps the first solo use of the extended bass clarinet. Dmitri Shostakovich's Symphony No. 7 uses the low C-sharp (concert [sounding] B-natural). See **bass clarinet** for range.
3. The **double bass** has two options for a lower extension. One is an added fifth string, a C string, one-third lower than the standard E string. The other is a device attached to the scroll that extends the actual length of the E string so that it becomes a C string. Various kinds of extensions exist, some allowing the string to be converted back to the E—that is, shortened—at

the will of the performer. Many European orchestras mandate the five-string bass.

4. The **trombone** extension is a **trigger mechanism** that facilitates the playing of additional pitches by producing other **overtone series**. The most common configuration is the F trigger on the tenor trombone. The traditional **bass trombone** includes two triggers, usually pitched in F and G-flat or G, allowing easy access to the low B-natural above the lowest regular B-flat on the instrument.

extinción. (Sp.) dying away, extinguishing. A manner of playing. (Fr. *en s'éteignant*, Ger. *verlöschend*, It. *estinguendo*.)

extinguiéndose. (Sp.) disappearing, dying away to nothing, describing a manner of playing. Also *desvanesiéndose*, *perdiéndose*. (Fr. *éteindre*, *expirer*; Ger. *erlöschen*; It. *espirare*, *extinguere*.)

extinto. (Sp.) barely audible, extinguished. A manner of playing. (Fr. *éteint*; Ger. *erlöscht*, *audgelöscht*; It. *estinto*, *spento*.)

eye contact. Eye contact between the **conductor** and the members of the ensemble establishes communication of all musical elements. It also establishes a sense of trust and shows the ensemble that the conductor knows the score and is in command of all its details. Eye contact is particularly used as a part of **cue gestures**. It acts to reassure a player or section of the ensemble of a coming entrance. Combined with **facial expressions**, eye contact can also communicate the **character** of a given passage of music. See also **conducting technique**.

eye music. Contemporary music scores that use visual patterns, graphic symbols, or other unusual notation devices designed to attract the eye. Examples: George Crumb, *Echoes of Time and the River*; Luciano Berio, *Circles*; and Heitor Villa-Lobos, *New York Skyline*. It can be associated with word painting, such the use of ascending and descending scales when paired words of similar implication. The term is sometimes used as a pejorative for music that looks appealing on the page but may sound less successful to the ear. See also *Augenmusik*.

F

F. A musical pitch or note name. Also the name of a scale that begins on the note F. The key of a composition, as in Beethoven's *Sonata in F minor* for piano solo. Also, when italicized, the Abbreviation for *forte*.

fa. 1. In solmization, the fourth note of the scale, F-natural. 2. The name given by Guido d'Arezzo to the fourth note in his hexachords. See also **solmization**, **solfège**.

fa bémol. (Fr.) F-flat. See also **accidental**; **appendix 5: "Pitch Names and Their Translations."**

fa bémolle. (It.) F-flat. See also **accidental**; **appendix 5: "Pitch Names and Their Translations."**

Fach. (Ger.) categories of vocal types, subject, profession. See also **voice types**.

facial expression. Expressions used by the conductor to communicate some element of the music, either character or energy. Facial expressions show the life and the urgency of the moment in music making and are important for effective communication. See also **conducting technique**.

facile. (Fr.) easily, as in a style of playing. Also floating, flowing, running. Seen in in its German translation in scores by **Gustav Mahler**. Also *facilement*. (Ger. *leicht, einfach, fließend*; It. *facile, facilmente*; Sp. *fácil, fácilmente*.)

facilmente. (It.) easily. A descriptive term for a particular manner of playing. Also *facile*. (Fr. *facile, facilement*; Ger. *leicht, einfach, fließend*; Sp. *fácil, fácilmente*.)

fa dièse. (Fr.) F-sharp. See also **accidental**; **appendix 5: "Pitch Names and Their Translations."**

fa diesis. (It.) F-sharp. See also **accidental**; **appendix 5: "Pitch Names and Their Translations."**

fagot. (Sp.) **bassoon**. See also **appendix 3: "Instrument Names and Their Translations."**

Fagott. (Ger.) **bassoon**. See also **appendix 3: "Instrument Names and Their Translations."**

fagotto. (It.) **bassoon**. See also **appendix 3: "Instrument Names and Their Translations."**

faible. (Fr.) plaintive, weak, mournful. A character word used to evoke a manner of playing. Seen in its German translation in the scores and parts of **Gustav Mahler**. (Ger. *schwach*; It. *flebile, fiacco*; Sp. *débil*.)

fair use. See **copyright law**.

Falletta, JoAnn. (b. 1954.) American **conductor**. Falletta graduated from the **Juilliard School of Music** with a doctorate in conducting in 1989 and was the associate conductor of the **Milwaukee Symphony Orchestra** (1985–1988) and the music director of the Queens Philharmonic Orchestra (1978–1988), the Denver Chamber Orchestra (1983–1992), the **Bay Area Women's Philharmonic** (1986–1996), the Long Beach Symphony Orchestra (1989), and the **Virginia Symphony Orchestra** (1991–present.) Falletta is also the music director of the **Buffalo Philharmonic** (1998–present). In 2011, she was appointed as the principle conductor of the Ulster Orchestra, Belfast, Northern Ireland, and serves as the artistic director for the **Hawaii Symphony**. An advocate of women and American composers, Falletta has won numerous **ASCAP awards** for adventurous programming and has made recordings with the English Chamber Orchestra, the **London Symphony Orchestra**, the Bay

Area Women's Philharmonic, and the Virginia Symphony Orchestra. She has received many awards, including **Columbia University**'s **Alice M. Ditson Award**, the **Seaver/National Endowment for the Arts Conductors Award**, the Bruno Walter Award, the Toscanini Award, and others. She has led the Buffalo Philharmonic in recordings on the **Naxos label**. These recordings have earned two **Grammy Awards**.

JoAnn Falletta.

falsetto. A specific method of singing that extends the range of the voice upward. Falsetto is produced by vibrating the edges of the vocal folds. It sounds much lighter than the normal voice. Some tenors slip into falsetto when they cannot or do not want to use their full voice or when desired for comic effect. (Fr. *fausset*; It. *fausset*; Ger. *Falsett, Fisterstimme*; Sp. *falsete*.)

family concerts. Concert programs designed for families and adults with children. They are outreach initiatives organized by orchestras as part of their overall programming. See also **programming**.

***Fanfare* (magazine).** An American magazine founded in 1977, it is published every two months. It reviews recorded music in all formats, primarily classical but now also jazz. In addition to reviews, it prints interviews and feature articles. Digital subscribers have access to an archive of past issues. See also **music magazines**.

Fantasia. An animated film made in 1940 by Walt Disney Productions that featured a classical repertoire performed by **Leopold Stokowski** with the **Philadelphia Orchestra**. The music included *Toccata and Fugue in D minor* (Johann Sebastian Bach), *The Nutcracker Suite* (Pyotr Tchaikovsky), *The Sorcerer's Apprentice* (Paul Dukas), ***The Rite of Spring* (Igor Stravinsky)**, *Pastoral Symphony* (Ludwig van Beethoven), *Dance of the Hours* (Amilcare Ponchielli), *Night on Bald Mountain* (Modest Mussorgsky), and *Ave Maria* (Franz Schubert). Featuring Mickey Mouse as a magician and **Deems Taylor** as narrator, it was the first commercial film recorded and shown in stereo sound. Initially it failed to generate the income and positive reaction hoped for, but over the long haul, it has become the twenty-second highest earning film in the United States.

Farberman, Harold. (b. 1929.) **Conductor**, composer, and percussionist. Faberman studied at the **Juilliard School** and the **New England Conservatory of Music**. He was a percussionist and timpanist with the **Boston Symphony Orchestra (BSO)** from 1951 to 1963. He was the founder and first president of the **Conductors Guild** (1975) and established its summer **Conductor's Institute** at the University of West Virginia in 1981. He served as a professor of conducting at the **Hartt School of Music** (1990–), conducted the Oakland Symphony Orchestra (1971–1979), and made guest conducting appearances throughout his career, including with the **BBC Symphony Orchestra**, Bournemouth Symphony, **Royal Philharmonic**, **Swedish Radio Symphony**, Mozarteum Orchestra, and many more. Farberman is currently on the faculty of Bard University. His recordings include the symphonies of **Gustav Mahler** with the **London Symphony Orchestra**. His compositions include the opera *The Losers*, commissioned by the **American Opera Center of the Juilliard School** on its move to **Lincoln Center** (1971). He is the author of *The Art of Conducting Technique*. See **bibliography**.

Fargo-Moorhead Symphony Orchestra (FMSO). A fully professional orchestra in Fargo, North Dakota, its current music director, Christopher Zimmerman, was appointed in 2013. The orchestra was officially chartered in 1931 as the Fargo Civic Orchestra with Harry Rudd conducting. Other music directors were Sigvald Thompson (1937–1974), J. Robert Hanson (1974–1990), Joel Revzen (1990–2002), and Bernard Rubenstein (2003–2012). The orchestra offers a five-concert classics series, pops, family, and educational concerts, as well as a chamber music series.

farouche. (Fr.) wild, fierce. A character word seen in its German translation in scores and parts. (Ger. *wild*, It. *selvaggio*, Sp. *feroz*.)

Fassung. (Ger.) version, as in a version of a piece or composition. (Fr. *version*, It. *versione*, Sp. *versión*.)

feierlich. (Ger.) solemn, ceremonial. Seen in scores and parts as a character word. Also *festlich*. (Fr. *solennellement*, It. *solennemente*, Sp. *solennemente*.)

Felder, Harvey. (b. 1955.) African American **conductor**. Among his positions, he has served as the **Affiliate Artists/National Endowment for the Arts Conductor** with the **Milwaukee Symphony Orchestra** (1988–1991), assistant conductor of the **Milwaukee Symphony Orchestra** (1991–1994), resident conductor of the **St. Louis Symphony Orchestra** (1994–1995), and music director of the **Tacoma Symphony Orchestra** (1994–2014), of which he is now conductor laureate. Felder is now an associate professor of music and the director of orchestral studies at the University of Connecticut (appointed in 2013).

Harvey Felder. *Courtesy Harvey Felder.*

Felsenstein, Walter. (1901–1975.) Austrian theater and opera director. He began his career at the Burgtheater in Vienna and from 1923 to 1932 was an actor in the theaters of Lübeck and Mannheim, Germany, and Bytom, Poland. He worked as an opera director in Cologne (1932–1934), Frankfurt (1934–1936), Zurich (1938–1940), and the Berlin Schillertheater (1940–1944). He produced *The Marriage of Figaro* under the baton of **Clemens Kraus** at the Salzburg Mozart festival in 1942. He created the **Komische Oper** in what was East Berlin in 1947 and worked there as a director until his death, developing his concept of "realistic" opera. Felsenstein attempted to create opera that would be an authentic and indispensable means of human expression. His most famous students were **Götz Friedrich** and Harry Kupfer. He was awarded the National Prize of the DDR in 1950, 1951, 1956, 1960, and 1970. He toured the USSR with his own productions from the Komische Oper more than once. He translated numerous French and Italian operas into German, including Georges Bizet's *Carmen* and Giuseppi Verdi's *La traviata*. Among his most renowned productions were *The Magic Flute* (1954), *The Tales of Hoffman* (1958), and Leoš Janáček's *The Cunning Little Vixen* (1956).

Fennell, Frederick. (1914–2004.) American **wind ensemble conductor** and pedagogue. He received his bach-

elor's and master's degrees from the **Eastman School of Music**, and on his graduation he was appointed to be an ensemble conductor (1939–1962). He founded the **Eastman Wind Ensemble** in 1952 and spent many decades developing a repertoire for his ensemble of wind soloists. Fennell wrote to four hundred composers worldwide asking for new compositions for his new ensemble and the first to respond were Percy Grainger, Vincent Persichetti, and Ralph Vaughan Williams. He also conducted twenty-two recordings for the **Mercury label**, which established the reputation of the new wind ensemble and led to the founding of over twenty thousand similar ensembles around the world in the years that followed, mostly in American schools and universities. Fennell was conductor-in-residence at the University of Miami (1965–1980) and was the conductor of the Kosei Wind Orchestra in Tokyo (1985–1995), becoming the conductor laureate on his retirement. He was a guest conductor with several major orchestras, including the **Cleveland Orchestra**, **Minneapolis Symphony Orchestra**, **London Symphony Orchestra**, and the **Boston Pops**. He was also the principal guest conductor at the **Interlochen Arts Academy**. He edited innumerable works for **band** and wind ensemble, and his writings include *Time and the Winds*, *The Drummer's Heritage*, *The Wind Ensemble*, and a series of articles that appeared in the *Instrumentalist*. Fennell was married to Elizabeth Ludwig, who ran **Ludwig Music Publishing Co.** His fellow band conductor **Jerry Junkin** was quoted in Fennell's *New York Times* obituary, saying that Fennell "was arguably the most famous band conductor since John Philip Sousa." Fennell received **Columbia University**'s **Alice M. Ditson Conductor's Award**, was presented a Star of the Order from the John Philip Sousa Memorial Foundation (1985) and an honorary doctorate from **Eastman** (1988), and was inducted into the **National Band Association**'s Hall of Fame of Distinguished Band Conductors (1990). Only five feet, one inch tall, he nonetheless cut a commanding presence on the podium and suffered fools lightly. A great believer in the dignity of the band musician, he brought a seriousness of intent to music making that inspired the ensembles he led. He was known for an animated, energetic conducting style tempered by an insistence on the correctness of detail. See also **bibliography**.

fermata. The Italian term is commonly used among musicians internationally. Literally, it means to stop, while in music it can also mean to pause. There are three important aspects to consider in handling each fermata. The approach, the duration, and the exit.

Fermata. *Courtesy Andrew Martin Smith.*

The approach is either in tempo or modified with a **ritardando** or **accelerando** as established in the music.

The duration is determined by a few things: (1) the actual rhythmic value of the note under the fermata sign, (2) whether a sense of counting continues and the fermata fills out a phrase within the structure of the passage in which it appears, and (3) all sense of counting is suspended, in which case the length of the fermata is determined by dramatic elements such as how a crescendo or diminuendo is needed before going on. During the fermata itself the conductor always beats to the last point of attack under the fermata.

The exit is generally handled in one of three ways: (1) Go on in tempo without a cutoff (the least amount of separation, though a choir will be able to fit in a breath, if necessary), (2) cut off and go on in tempo (allowing for a short separation or break in time), or (3) cut off with a full stop giving a new preparation. The third option is usually used at structural points when a certain definite separation or pause is needed.

For clarity, fermatas are generally given with the baton or conducting hand stopping or pausing on the necessary beat within the pattern being conducted. Sometimes it is helpful to show a sustained sound during the fermata by a horizontal or linear motion. Breathing simultaneously with the gesture to go ahead is always vital (See **preparatory gesture**).

Fermatas in Johann Sebastian Bach's *Chorales* are an exception to the custom of duration. They are used to signify cadential points and require only a breath while going on. The left hand can easily be used to show **cutoff gestures**, while the baton hand remains still for fermata exits numbers 2 and 3.

Conduct until the last point of attack under the fermata. *Courtesy Derek Brennan.*

fermata. (It.) a pause, or stop indicated by the sign, **fermata**. Also *corona*. (Fr. *point d'arrêt*, *point d'orgue*; Ger. *Fermate*; Sp. *calderón*, *corona*.)

Fermate-Zeichen. (Ger.) **fermata** sign.

fermé or **fermées.** (Fr.) closed. Heard in various phrases, such as in "humming" with the mouth closed, and others. Also *fermez*, *fermer*. (Ger. *geschlossen*, It. *chiuso*, Sp. *cerrado*.)

fern. (Ger.) distant, far away, soft. Seen in scores and parts as a directive to play as if from a distance. (Fr. *lointain*, It. *lontan*, Sp. *lejano*.) See also **Ferne**.

Ferne. (Ger.) distance. Abbreviated *fern*. Examples: *in der Ferne*, offstage or in the distance, from Gustav Mahler's Symphony No. 1, mvt. 1; *in weiter Entfernung*, as if further in the distance; *in sehr weiter Entferrung aufgestellt*, placed very far offstage; *wie aus der Ferne*, as if in the distance.

feroce. (It.).) fierce, harsh. A descriptive term sometimes seen in scores and parts. (Fr. *féroce*, *sauvage*; Ger. *heftig*, *wild*; Sp. *feroz*.)

féroce. (Fr.) fierce, harsh. A descriptive term sometimes seen in scores and parts. Also *sauvage*. (Ger. *heftig*, *wild*; It. *feroce*; Sp. *feroz*.)

feroz. (Sp.) fierce, harsh. A descriptive term sometimes seen in scores and parts. (Fr. *féroce*, *sauvage*; Ger. *heftig*, *wild*; It. *feroce*.)

Ferrara, Franco. (1911–1985.) Italian **conductor** and pedagogue. Ferrara taught at the **Accademia Musicale Chigiana, Siena**, Italy, and the **Accademia di Santa Cecilia, Rome**. He made his debut in Florence in 1938. While he began to build his reputation as one of the great talents of his generation, he developed a nervous disease that cut short his career, and he spent most of his life cultivating the talents of others. His students included many of the most important conductors of the twentieth century, including **Riccardo Chailly**, **Myung-whun Chung**, **Jesus Lopez-Cobos**, **Sir Andrew Davis**, **Eliahu Inbal**, **Jorma Panula**, Hans Vonk, and many others. In 1976, he was invited by Seiji Ozawa to teach conducting at the **Toho School** in honor of **Hideo Saito**, Ozawa's teacher. Ferrara periodically taught conducting at the **Curtis Institute of Music**, the **Juilliard School**, and the **Berkshire Music Center at Tanglewood**.

Fes. (Ger.) F-flat. See also **accidental**; **appendix 5: "Pitch Names and Their Translations."**

fest. (Ger.) steady, strict. (Fr. *fixé*, It. *fisso*, Sp. *fijo*.) Example: *festes Zeitmaß*, steady tempo.

festeggiante. (It.) rejoicing, celebrating. Also *allegramente*. (Fr. *joyeusement*, *allègrement*; Ger. *vergnügt*, *feiernd*; Sp. *alegremente*.)

festlich. (Ger.) festive, solemn. A descriptive term seen in scores and parts. Also *feierlich*. (Fr. *de fête*, *solennel*; It. *festivo*, *solenne*; Sp. *festive*, *solenne*.)

Feuer. (Ger.) fire. A character word used to evoke a particular energy and intensity in the playing. (Fr. *feu*, It. *fuoco*, Sp. *fuego*.)

feurig. (Ger.) fervent, fervently, fiery. Example: *sehr feurig*, very fiery or fervent, from *The Prelude to Die Meistersinger von Nürenberg* by **Richard Wagner**.

FF. (It.) Abbreviation for *fortissimo*. Also *fff*. See also **dymanics**.

F-hole. The holes on the front of a string instrument through which the sound waves travel. Called F-holes because the shape resembles a cursive letter *f*.

fiacco. (It.) weak, languishing. A character word that evokes a certain manner of playing. Also *flebile*. Seen in its German translation in the scores and parts of **Gustav Mahler**. (Fr. *faible*, Ger. *schwach*, Sp. *débil*.)

fiato. (It.) a breath. (Fr. *soufflé*, Ger. *Atem*, Sp. *aliento*.) See also **breathe, to**.

Fibonacci sequence. A sequence of numbers generated by an additive process in which one number is added to the next. For example, 1, 1, 2, 3, 5, 8, 13, 21, 34, 55, 89, and so on. Discovered and described by the Italian mathematician Leonardo Fibinacci (1170–1240), it has been recognized as a structural element in the music of several composers but particularly that of Béla Bartók. Music theorist **Ernö Lendavi** notes the use of the sequence in Bartók's *Music for Strings, Percussion and Celeste*, observing that the eighty-nine-bar-long first movement is divided into sections of fifty-five and thirty-four bars and further divided into groups of thirty-four plus twelve and thirteen plus twenty-one. It is sometimes called the Fibonacci series.

Fiedler, Arthur. (1894–1979.) American **conductor** and violinist. He studied with his father, Emanuel Fiedler, who was a member of the **Boston Symphony Orchestra (BSO)**, and the renowned Kneisel String Quartet. Fiedler went to Berlin as a youngster to study violin, piano, and conducting at the Conservatory for Music (Hochschule für Musik). He returned to the United States on the outbreak of World War I and joined the BSO as a violist, playing under such conductors as **Karl Muck**, **Pierre Monteux**, and **Serge Koussevitzky**. In 1924, he formed the Boston Sinfonietta with twenty-five fellow BSO musicians, and they toured Massachusetts and other nearby states. In 1929, he organized and conducted the successful **Esplanade Concerts** in Boston. Due to the huge success of these concerts, Fiedler was appointed the conductor of the **Boston Pop Orchestras** (1930). The Boston Pops, which consisted of many members of the BSO, was so successful that it became the model for many other such orchestras around the United States, and Fiedler was often asked to guest conduct these ensembles as they grew. He led the **San Francisco Pops Orchestra** in a summer pops season (1949–1978), created a separate Pops Tour Orchestra in 1953, and made many international guest appearances. His forceful and convincing personality in tandem with a flair for choosing appealing repertoire and presenting it in flashy orchestral arrangements led to a lifelong success in the field. He has been noted as the "founding father" of the pops orchestra phenomenon in the United States. His commercial success was substantial, and there were innumerable television, radio, and recording projects that helped establish his enormous reputation and legacy.

field of beating. See **conducting plane**, **conducting frame**.

filarmonica. (It.) The Italian equivalent of **philharmonic**, a name taken by certain musical organizations, especially orchestras, one of the oldest being the **Vienna Philharmonic Orchestra**. The Oxford English Dictionary defines it as one who loves harmony or is fond of or devoted to music. (Fr. *philharmonique*, Ger. *Philharmoniker*, Sp. *filarmónico*.)

filarmónico. (Sp.) **Philharmonic**. (Fr. *philharmonique*, Ger. *Philharmoniker*, It. *filarmonica*.)

Filz. (Ger.) Felt, as in a felt-covered timpani stick. (Fr. *feutre*, It. *fletro*, Sp. *fieltro*.)

fin. (Fr.) The end. (Ger. *Ende*; It. *fine*; Sp. *final, conclusión*.)

final. (Sp.) The end. Also *conclusión*. (Fr. *fin*, Ger. *Ende*, It. *fine*.)

finale. 1. The final movement of a symphony, sonata, or other related form. The Italian term is commonly used (*finale*).

2. The last portion of an act of an opera, where a sequence of scenes are tied together through all the elements of music—harmony, rhythm, tempo, and so on—and the plot or narrative in order to achieve a formal structure that either completes the act or sets up the next act. Examples: finales to acts 2 and 4 of Wolfgang Amadeus Mozart's *The Marriage of Figaro* and acts 1 and 2 of *Don Giovanni*, in which Mozart uses small onstage ensembles that perform simultaneously with the orchestra in the pit.

fin' al segno. (It.) An instruction to the performers to play a piece up to the sign. See *dal segno*.

fine. (It.) The end. (Fr. *fin*; Ger. *Ende*; Sp. *final, conclusión*.)

fingerboard. The piece of hardwood on a string instrument, usually made of ebony, fixed to the neck of the instrument over which the strings are stretched and then stopped by the fingers of the player in order to produce the various pitches. (Fr. *touche*; Ger. *Griffbrett*; It. *tastiera*; Sp. *diapason, batidor*.) See also **bowing terms**.

finger cymbal. A pair of small metal plates approximately two inches in diameter held by attached leather strips. They are struck together to produce their tone. (Fr. *cymbals digitales*, Ger. *Fingerzimblen*, It. *cimbalini*, Sp. *platos de dedo*.) See also **appendix 4: "Percussion Instruments and Their Translations."**

fingered tremolo. A string term for when two notes are alternated by the fingers of the left hand in rapid succession under one bow.

Fingered tremolo. *Courtesy Andrew Martin Smith.*

Fingersatz. (Ger.) Fingering. (Fr. *doigté*, It. *diteggiatura*, Sp. *digitación*.)

Finnish Radio Symphony Orchestra (FRSO). Founded in 1927 in Helsinki with only ten musicians, it is the official orchestra of the Finnish Broadcasting Company. It has grown into a full-size symphony orchestra presenting a comprehensive concert season each year. The current music director is Hannu Lintu (appointed in 2013). He was preceded by Sakari Oramo (2003–2012), **Jukka-Pekka Saraste** (1987–2001), Leif Segestam (1977–1987), Okko Kamu (1971–1977), **Paavo Berglund** (1962–1971), Nils-Eric Fougstedt (1950–1961), and Toivo Haapanen (1929–1950). The broadcasting company is committed to creating new music through its commissioning program, which began in 1977, with the orchestra giving over five hundred premieres.

Fires of London. A **new music ensemble** founded in 1965 and active until 1987. Originally known as the Pierrot Players, from 1967 it was jointly run by the composers Harrison Birtwistle and **Peter Maxwell Davies**. Formed in order to perform **Arnold Schoenberg**'s revolutionary work *Pierrot Lunaire*, it had the same instrumentation—flute, clarinet, violin/ viola, cello, piano, and reciter—with the occasional addition of a percussionist. Birtwistle left the group in 1970, and as sole director, Davies changed the name to the Fires of London. During the next twenty years the ensemble gave numerous

premieres, often of works of Davies, including *Eight Songs for a Mad King* and *The Maryrdom of St. Magnus*. Other premieres included Elliott Carter's *Triple Duo* and works of Morton Feldman, **Oliver Knussen**, and Hans Werner Henze.

First Viennese School (Wiener Schule). While some historians maintain that the so-called First Viennese School is exemplified by Franz Joseph Haydn, Wolfgang Amadeus Mozart, Franz Schubert, and Ludwig van Beethoven, composers who perfected the classical style, others believe that its existence as a true entity, in the sense of the **Second Viennese School**, is debatable.

Fis. (Ger.) F-sharp. See **accidental**; **appendix 5: "Pitch Names and Their Translations."**

fischietto. (It.) Fife, whistle. (Fr. *sifflet*, Ger. *Pfeife*, Sp. *pito*.)

Fisher, Carl. (1849–1923.) Music publisher. He founded **Carl Fisher Music** in 1872. See also **Fisher Music Publisher, Carl**.

Fisher Music Publisher. Founded in 1872 in New York City. In 2004, the company joined together with the **Theodore Presser Company** under common ownership, with Presser handling performance promotion, the rental library, and music distribution.

Flageolett. (Ger.) **Harmonics**. Abbreviated *flag*. Also *Flageolettöne*. (Fr. *sons harmoniques, flageolet*; It. *suoni armonici, zufolo*; Sp. *armónicos, octavín*.) See also **artificial harmonics**, **harmonic series**, **string harmonics**.

flat. (Fr. *bémol*. Ger. *Be*, It. *bemolle*, Sp. *bemol*.) 1. The notation symbol used to lower the pitch of a note by one half step, ♭. See also **accidental**.
2. A term used to describe out-of-tune playing when the sound is under the pitch.

Accidental flat. *Courtesy Andrew Martin Smith.*

Flatterzunge. (Ger.) Flutter tongue technique on a wind or brass instrument. (Fr. *trémolo dental*, It. *frullato*, Sp. *trémolo dental*.)

flautando. 1. (It.) A flute-like sound, a light sound.
2. (It.) In bowing, the light, airy sound created by playing with the bow above the fingerboard with relative speed. See also **fingerboard, bowing terms**.

flautín. (Sp.) **Piccolo.** See also **appendix 3: "Instrument Names and Their Translations."**

flautino. (It.) **Piccolo.** See also **appendix 3: "Instrument Names and Their Translations."**

flauto. (It.) **Flute.** See also **appendix 3: "Instrument Names and Their Translations."**

flauto bajo. (Sp.) **Bass flute.** (Fr. *flûte bass*, Ger. *Bassflöte*, It. *flauto basso*.) See also **appendix 3: "Instrument Names and Their Translations."**

flauto basso. (It.) **Bass flute.** (Fr. *flûte bass*, Ger. *Bassflöte*, Sp. *flauto bajo*.) See also **appendix 3: "Instrument Names and Their Translations."**

flebile. (It.) Plaintive, weak, mournful. A character word used to evoke a manner of playing. Also *fiacco.* Seen most often in its German translation in the scores and parts of **Gustav Mahler.** (Fr. *faible*, Ger. *schwach*, Sp. *débil.*)

flehend. (Ger.) Imploring, beseeching, entreating. A character word seen in scores and parts used to evoke a certain style of playing. (Fr. *suppliant*, It. *supplichevole*, Sp. *suplicando.*)

Fleischmann, Ernest. (1924–2010.) German-born American impresario and administrator. Born in Frankfurt, he and his family escaped the rise of the Nazis and immigrated to South Africa. There he studied music, especially conducting, receiving degrees in both music and accounting. He served as the general manager of the **London Symphony Orchestra** (1959–1967) and worked for a short time as the European director of **CBS Masterworks.** His most important position was as the executive director of the **Los Angeles Philharmonic** (1969–1997), becoming the executive vice president and managing director in 1988. During his time with the orchestra, he was able to double the salary of the musicians and add a summer season at the **Hollywood Bowl.** He successfully brought **Carlo Maria Giulini** to the orchestra as the music director from 1978 to 1985 and hired the young **Esa-Pekka Salonen** and the very young **Gustavo Dudamel.** During his tenure the orchestra acquired a $50 million donation from Lillian Disney to build a new concert hall, the **Walt Disney Concert Hall,** as designed by architect Frank Gehry. A controversial figure in the business, he was described by a coworker in his *New York Times Magazine* obituary as an "egocentric, completely unprincipled and yet incredibly brilliant monomaniac in music."

flessibile. (It.) Agile, flexible. A descriptive term often used to evoke a particular manner of playing. (Fr. *flexible*, Ger. *flexible*, Sp. *flexible.*)

flexatone. A metal instrument of the percussion family. It has a vibrating or tremolo sound that is particularly effective in executing *glissandi* and is characterized by a high-pitched sound. Examples of use: Dmitri Shostakovich in his opera *The Nose* (1928) and **Arnold Schoenberg** in *Variations for Orchestra* (1928). See also **appendix 4: "Percussion Instruments and Their Translations."**

flicorno. (It., Sp.) **Flugelhorn.** (Fr. *bugle à pistons*; Ger. *Bügelhorn*, *Flügelhorn.*)

fließend. (Ger.) Flowing, floating, running. Also *fließender*, more flowing. Seen in scores and parts, in particular those of **Gustav Mahler.** (Fr. *facile*; It. *fluente*; Sp. *fluente*, *fluido.*)

Florida Orchestra. Established in 1968 in St. Petersburg as the Florida Gulf Coast Symphony when the St. Petersburg Symphony Orchestra and the Tampa Philharmonic merged. The name was changed in 1984. The first music director was Irwin Hoffman (1968–1987), followed by Jahja Ling (1988–2002) and Stefan Sanderling (2003–2012). In 2015, Michael Francis assumed this position. Stuart Molina was named as the principal guest conductor in 2012. **Jeff Tyzik** serves as the principal pops conductor. The orchestra performs in Tamps, Clearwater, and St. Petersburg, Florida, and presents a full range of Masterworks, pops, morning coffee concerts, as well as their classic rock series, which combines classic rock music with the symphonic orchestra.

Flöte. (Ger.) **Flute.** (Fr. *flûte*, It. *flauto*, Sp. *flauta.*) See also **appendix 3: "Instrument Names and Their Translations."**

flottant. (Fr.) Floating. Example: *doux et flottant*, sweet and floating, from *Rondes de Printemps* by Claude Debussy.

flotter. (Ger.) Faster, brisk. Example: *noch etwas flotter*, even somewhat faster, from *Das Lied von der Erde* by **Gustav Mahler.**

fluente. (It., Sp.) Flowing, floating, running. Seen in in its German translation in the scores of **Gustav Mahler.** (Fr. *facile*, It. *fluente*, Sp. *fluido.*)

Flügel. (Ger.) The grand piano, so-called because of the shape (lit. "wing").

flugelhorn. Related to the bugle and cornet. As a subset of the trumpet family, the flugelhorn, with its mellow tone, is only rarely seen in orchestra writing but appears more often in compositions in the jazz genre and for **wind ensemble** or wind symphony. Today the most common flugelhorn is the instrument in B-flat with a range of F-sharp3 to C6, sounding a major second lower, E3 to B-flat5. The instrument is used in **Igor Stravinsky**'s *Threni*, Vaughan Williams's Symphony No. 9, and Sir Michael Tippett's Symphony No. 3. (Ger. *Flügelhorn*.)

fluido. (Sp.) Flowing, floating, running. Seen in in its German translation in the scores of **Gustav Mahler**. Also *fluente*. (Fr. *facile*, Ger. *fließsend*, It. *fluente*.)

Flummerfelt, Joseph. (b. 1937.) American choral **conductor** and educator. He earned his academic degrees from DePauw University (bachelor of music, 1958), the Philadelphia Conservatory of Music (master of music, 1962), and the University of Illinois (doctor of musical arts, 1971). He studied with **Julius Herford**, **Elaine Brown**, and **Nadia Boulanger**. He taught at the University of Illinois (1963–1964), DePauw University (1964–1968), and Florida State University (196–1971). From 1971 to 2004 he was the artistic director and choral master at **Westminster Choir College** in Princeton, New Jersey. Flummerfelt was also the chorus master for the Festival of Two Worlds (Il Festival dei Due Mondi) in Spoleto, Italy, from 1971 to 1993 and the artistic director of choral activities at the Spoleto Festival USA in Charleston, South Carolina. He founded the New York Choral Artists in 1979 and became the principal choral director for the **New York Philharmonic Orchestra** in the same year. With these ensembles he had led more than forty-five recordings, receiving multiple **Grammy awards**. He has appeared as a guest conductor with many orchestras, including the **New Jersey Symphony Orchestra**, the **Orchestra of St. Luke's**, the **Juilliard** Symphony Orchestra, and others. He was named **Musical America**'s 2004 Conductor of the Year.

Flüstern. (Ger.) Whisper, murmur. Also *bisbigliando*. (Fr. *chuchoter*, It. *susurrare*, Sp. *susurrar*.)

flute. The only nonreed instrument in the woodwind section, the flute is particularly agile in what it can play. It has a range from C4 up to C7, although the modern flute can play up to C-sharp7 or D7. Historically, the flute range began with D (above middle C) as its lowest note. It was extended to the low C in the nineteenth century. In the twentieth century, a low B foot was added to extend the range to a B3. Therefore, when Wolfgang Amadeus Mozart transcribed the *Oboe Concerto in C* for the flute, he had to transpose it to D major. (Fr. *flûte*, Ger. *Flöte*, It. *flauto*, Sp. *flauta*.) See also **alto flute**; **appendix 3: "Instrument Names and Their Translations"**; **bass flute**; **piccolo**.

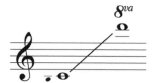

Flute range. *Courtesy Andrew Martin Smith.*

flûte. (Fr.) **Flute**. (Ger. *Flöte*, It. *flauto*, Sp. *flauta*.) See also **appendix 3: "Instrument Names and Their Translations."**

flûte bass. (Fr.) **Bass flute**. (Ger. *Bassflöte*, It. *Flauto basso*, Sp. *flauto bajo*.)

flûte d'accord. (Fr.) **Pitch pipe**, a small wind device that when blown through sounds any of several pitches in order to give a **choir** a starting pitch when no accompaniment precedes the entrance. Also *diapason à bouche*. (Ger. *Stimmpfeife*, It. *diapason a fiato*, Sp. *diapasón de boca*.)

flutter tongue technique. A type of articulation used by some woodwind and brass instruments in which the performer rolls his tongue using a *"drrr"* sound, which results in a tremolo effect on a single pitch. **Richard Strauss** used it in the **tone poem** *Don Quixote* in 1898, and it has remained in common use since. (Fr. *trémolo dental*, Ger. *Flatterzunge*, It. *frullato*, Sp. *trémolo dental*.)

flying spiccato. A bowing term that indicates a series of *spiccato* strokes played in one direction, usually up-bow, with the bow leaving the string between each note. Also called **staccato volante**.

focal plane style. This conducting style places each beat on the same **vertical plane**, each one slightly higher until the preparation of the next **downbeat**. Also referred to as the **"Christmas tree pattern."** The figure illustrates this most common occurrence of this style.

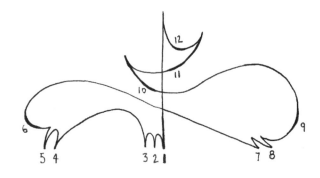

12/8 pattern with focal-plane style. *Courtesy Derek Brennan.*

focoso. (It.) Fiery. A character word sometimes seen in scores and parts. (Fr. *ardent*, Ger. *feurig*, Sp. *ardiente*.) See also *fuoco, con*.

fois. (Fr.) Time. (Ger. *Zeit*, It. *tempo*, Sp. *tiempo*.) Examples: *deux fois*, two times; *dernière fois*, last time.

folgen. (Ger.) To follow quickly, as in *attacca*, or to follow a soloist. (Fr. *suivez*, It. *seguite*, Sp. *seguir*.)

folgend. (Ger.) Subsequent, following, as in the next section or movement of a work. (Fr. *suivant*, It. *successivo*, Sp. *siguiente*.) Example: *Der nächste Satz folgt so fort*, the next movement is *attacca*.

force. (Fr.) With strength, force. Example: *avec force*, forcefully. See *Kraft, mit*. (Ger. *Kraft*; It. *forza*, *vigore*; Sp. *fuerza*.)

Ford Foundation. A private foundation started by Henry Ford and his son, Edsel, in 1936 with a gift of $25,000; it now has an endowment of $10.9 billion. On the death of the two founders, the foundation owned 90 percent of the nonvoting shares of the Ford Motor Company. From 1955 to 1974 its holdings were sold, leaving the foundation no role in the car company. In 1958, the foundation committed $25 million to build and operate **Lincoln Center**, renewing that commitment in 2006 with a $15 million gift renovation. In 1965, the foundation gave $85 million to orchestras nationwide. The gift brought about the National Arts Stabilization Fund. In 2000, the foundation launched New Directions/New Donors in order to build donor support for all of America's cultural organizations. Its current goals focus on reducing poverty and injustice, promoting democratic values, and advancing human achievement.

Ford Symphony Hour. An hour-long concert radio show in Detroit from 1934 to 1942 (with a hiatus during World War II, 1942–1945), it featured the **Detroit Symphony Orchestra** as its official orchestra. **Conductors** who were featured include **Sir John Barbirolli**, Victor Kolar, Wilfred Pelletier, and **Fritz Reiner**. Featured soloists include singers Kirsten Flagstad, Richard Tauber, John Charles Thomas, and Lawrence Tibbett.

foreground. A term used by **Heinrich Schenker** to describe those musical elements most easily discernable to the listener. In his analysis, this includes themes, texture, motives, and the main structural units. See also **background**; **middleground**; **Schenkerian analysis**; **Urlinie**; **Ursatz**.

formalism. A term used by government officials in 1940s Russia in order to denigrate the music of Dmitri Shostakovich, Sergei Prokofiev, and Nikolai Miaskovsky. The official government view was that their music was characterized by a lack of substance, content, and emotional values that did not and could not appeal to the masses.

fort. (Fr.) Loud, strong in dynamic. The opposite of the dynamic *piano*. (It. *forte*.) See also **dynamics**.

forte. (It.) Loud, strong in dynamic. The opposite of the dynamic *piano*. (Fr. *fort*.) See also **dynamics**.

fortepiano. (It.) A dynamic marking that calls for a loud beginning to a note that becomes suddenly soft or *piano*. Abbreviated *fp*. See also **dynamics**.

fortissimo. (It.) Very loud, louder than *forte*. Abbreviation-Abbreviated *FF*. See also **dynamics**.

Fort Wayne Philharmonic Orchestra. Founded in 1944 in Fort Wayne, Indiana, the fully professional orchestra offers a Masterworks series, pops concerts, a chamber orchestra series called Signature Series, and the Freimann chamber music series in addition to outreach and education programs. The orchestra's current music director is Andrew Constantine (appointed in 2009). Past music directors include Edvard Tchivzhel (1993–2008), Ronald Ondrejka (1978–1993), Thomas Briccetti (1970–1977), James Sample (1967–1970), Igor Buketoff (1948–1966), and Hans Schwieger (1944–1948). The Fort Wayne Philharmonic has won five **ASCAP Awards for Adventurous Programming** since 1980. The Philharmonic Chorus participates in several concerts each season.

forza, con. (It.) With strength, a descriptive seen in scores and parts and heard in rehearsal in order to evoke a certain manner of playing. Examples: "With all your strength": (It.) *con tutte le forze*, (Fr.) *de toutes ses forces*, (Ger.) *mit aller Kraft*, (Sp.) *con todas sus fuerza*.

forzando or *forzato.* (It.) A sharp, strong accent. Abbreviation-Abbreviated *fz*.

Forzando. *Courtesy Andrew Martin Smith.*

fp. Abbreviation for the dynamic indication *fortepiano*.

fractional beat preparations or **entrances on incomplete beats.** The preparatory gesture that is used when a piece starts with a note or chord that has rhythmic value equal to one half or less of a beat. The **conductor** decides between a **one-count preparation** or a **two-count preparation**, depending on the speed, style, or context of the music.

The one-count preparation is similar to the regular preparatory beat in that it incorporates the fractional rhythm into the preparatory beat. The conductor must not attempt to beat the fraction or divide the beat but must allow the players to sit it into the allotted space dictated by the tempo. In other words, these entrances are usually conducted as if they were on the beat. This kind of fractional beat preparation works best when the tempo isn't too fast.

The two-count preparation is effective for passages where the ensemble may need the extra gesture in order to be precise in execution. It is vital that the conductor use a **neutral gesture** on the first count, even if it is in tempo, so as not to signal to anyone that they should start after that first count. The second count or **beat** is contrastingly active, signaling the sound and attack to come. A special case is when a piece begins with a rest on the downbeat. See **conducting technique.**; **"guillotine" downbeat**.

fractional meter. A meter, such as 4-and-one-half /8, that equals 4/8 plus 1/16. Such meters are usually used when the rhythmic pattern begins or ends with a half beat. Examples may be found in much twentieth-century music, including **Pierre Boulez**'s *Le marteux sans maître* and Edgard Varèse's *Integrales* and *Octandre*. See **conducting uneven meters**.

Fractional meter. *Courtesy Andrew Martin Smith.*

fragile. (Fr., It.) Weak, soft. A character word sometimes used to evoke a particular sound. (Ger. *empfindlich, zerbrechlich*; Sp. *frágil*.)

frame notation. A means of notation used in **aleatoric music** that allows the performer to choose certain modes of operation within a specific framework established by the composer. Examples: **Pierre Boulez**'s *Piano Sonata No. 2* and **Witold Lutosławksi**'s *String Quartet No. 2*. See **boxes**; **graphic notation**.

Frankfurt Opera. One of Germany's major opera houses, the current music director is Sebastian Weigle (appointed in 2008). He was preceeded by Paolo Carignani (1999–2008), **Sylvain Cambreling** (1993–1997), **Gary Bertini** (1987–1991), **Michael Gielen** (1977–1987),

Christoph von Dohnáanyi (1967–1977), Lovro von Matačić (1961–1966), and **Sir Georg Solti** (1952–1961). Earlier music directors include Clemens Krauss (1924–1929). Opera has been performed in Frankfurt since around 1700. Wolfgang Amadeus Mozart's opera *The Abduction from the Seraglio* was performed in 1783, with *Don Giovanni* and *The Marriage of Figaro* performed in 1788. In 1880, a new opera house was opened and was the site of performances led by **Richard Wagner**, **Richard Strauss**, and other luminaries of the day. Destroyed during World War II, a new house was completed in 1963. The new company has an enormous season of operas, including many premieres, and offers special programs for youth in addition to training programs for young professionals.

frappé. (Fr.) A term that is used to designate the physical downbeat gesture given by a **conductor**. (It. *battuta in terra*; Ger. *Abtakt*; Sp. *primer tiempo, tiempo fuerte*.)

frapper. (Fr.) To strike, to hit, as in a drum. (Ger. *schlagen*, It. *colpire*, Sp. *golpear*.)

frase. (It., Sp.) A musical phrase, a short sequence of pitches forming a generally cohesive unit within a period, movement, or piece. The phrase is often understood in linguistic terms as closely linked to the rise and fall of a song text. In musical terms, it is a combination of melody, harmony, and rhythm that creates an organized unit with a beginning, middle, and end. In the Baroque and Classical periods, when balance was of primary importance, a phrase usually consisted of an antecedent and consequent supported by melodic, harmonic, and rhythmic elements in the sense of a statement and response. In the Romantic Era and beyond, there have been many changes to this fundamental structure in all musical aspects. (Fr. *phrase*, Ger. *Phrase*.)

fraseggio. (It.) Phrasing. A descriptive word that appears in a wide variety of forms and is often heard in rehearsal. (Fr. *phrase*, Ger. *Phraierung*, Sp. *fraseo*.)

fraseo. (Sp.) Phrasing. (Fr. *phrasé*, Ger. *Phrasierung*, It. *fraseggio*.) See *fraseggio*.

Frauenchor. (Ger.) Women's chorus. (Fr. *Choeur de femmes*; It. *Coro delle donne*; Sp. *coro de voces femeninas, coro femenino*.)

freddo. (It.) Cold, without emotion. A character word used to evoke a particular quality of sound. (Fr. *froid*, Ger. *kalt*, Sp. *frío*.)

Frederic Chopin University of Music. Now known as the Frederic Chopin University of Music (*Uniwersytet*

Muzyczny Fryderyka Chopina). Founded in Warsaw, Poland, as a music school for singers and actors in 1810, it was reorganized to include a wider curriculum in 1820. It became known as the Warsaw Conservatory in 1918 and took its current name in 2008 as part of the European Union's reorganization of institutes of higher education. It currently offers a comprehensive curriculum of performance, composition, conducting, and music theory and has both a distinguish faculty and alunni.

Frederick the Great (Friedrich II, king of Prussia). (1712–1786.) German king who reigned from 1740 to 1786; also a composer, flutist, and patron of music. He studied with **Johann Joachim Quantz** and established a court orchestra in Berlin (1740) and an opera house there in 1742. He employed **C. P. E. Bach** as a harpsichordist beginning in 1740. Johann Sebastian Bach visited his court in Potsdam in 1747. Subsequently, Bach's *Musical Offering* was composed using one of Frederick the Great's themes. He composed symphonies, opera, marches, arias, and wrote librettos for K. H. Graun. His legacy lasts through the music and musicians he supported.

free atonality. Music written without a tonal center. Arnold Schoenberg used the term in order to describe the transitional phase between tonality and a more strictly ordered system of twelve-tone composition.

Freeman, Paul Douglas. (b. 1936.) African American **conductor**. He was the founding conductor and music director of the Chicago Sinfonietta (1987–2011), associate conductor of the **Dallas Symphony Orchestra** (1968–1970), conductor-in-residence of the **Detroit Symphony Orchestra** (1970–1979), principal guest conductor of the Helsinki Philharmonic Orchestra (1974–1976), and music director of the Victoria (Canada) Symphony Orchestra (1979–1988), where he was appointed director emeritus in 1988. Freeman has been a frequent guest conductor across the globe with the orchestras of **Atlanta**, **Baltimore**, **Buffalo**, **Chicago**, **Cleveland**, **Denver**, **Houston**, **St. Louis**, and **Toledo**, in addition to several orchestras in Canada and Europe. He has been an active proponent of the music of African American composers throughout his career. Freeman received his bachelor's, master's, and doctoral degrees from the **Eastman School of Music** and is widely known for his optimism. He has received broad critical acclaim throughout North America.

Freeman, Robert. (b. 1936.) American music educator and musicologist known for having served as the director of the **Eastman School of Music** (1971–1996) and the **New England Conservatory of Music** (1996–1999) and the dean of performing arts at the **University of Texas, Austin (UT)** (1999–2006). After stepping down as dean at UT, Freeman remains on the faculty as a professor of musicology. He received a bachelor's of music at **Harvard University**, a diploma in piano at the **Longy School of Music**, and a master's and doctorate in musicology from **Princeton University**. He received a **Fulbright** scholarship to study in Vienna (1960–1962) and a **Martha Baird Rockefeller Foundation Award** (1962). He taught at Princeton University (1963–1968) and at the **Massachusetts Institute of Technology** (1968–1972) before moving to the Eastman School. A distinguished leader in the field of music education, Freeman succeeded in building the strongest programs wherever he served, raising funds for building projects, resident string quartets and other ensembles, scholarship funds, and much more. A man of the highest standards and lofty goals, his publications have spurred a renewed interest in the field of music education. See Freeman, Robert. *The Crisis of Classical Music in America: Lessons from a Life in the Education of a Musician.* Lanham, MD: Rowman & Littlefield, 2014. See also the **bibliography**.

free preparation gesture. A preparatory gesture that has no tempo, only preparing dynamic, the quality of the attack, sound, and expression. See **attention-getting gesture**.

frei. (Ger.) Free, ad libitum. Often seen in scores and parts to suggest a freedom of tempo and expression in the playing. (Fr. *libre*; It. *libero*, *leberamente*; Sp. *libre*.)

freihängend. (Ger.) Suspended, free hanging, as with a suspended cymbal. (Fr. *suspension libre*, It. *impiccagione libero*, Sp. *libre suspensión*.)

French horn. See **horn**.

French National Orchestra (Orchestre national de France). Run by **Radio France**, it has also been known as the **Orchestre national de la Radiodiffusion française** (French National Radio Broadcasting Orchestra) and **Orchestre national de l'Office de Radiodiffusion Télévision Française (ORTF)**. The current music director is **Daniel Gatti**. The list of past music directors includes one distinguished conductor after another: **Kurt Mazur** (2002–2008), **Charles Dutoit** (1991–2001), **Lorin Maazel** (1977–1991), **Sergiu Celibidache** (1973–1975), **Jean Martinon** (1968–1973), **Charles Munch** (1962–1968), Maurice Le Roux (1960–1967), **André Cluytens** (1951–1960), Roger Désormière (1947–1951), Manuel Rosenthal (1944–1947), and Désiré-Emile Inghelbrecht (1934–1944). The orchestra performs in the Théâtre des Champs-Élysées, Paris. See also **radio orchestras**.

frenetico. (It.) Wild, frantic, frenzied. A descriptive term used to evoke a certain manner of playing. (Fr. *frénétique*, Ger. *hektisch*, Sp. *frenetico*.)

fretta. (It.) Haste, hurry. (Fr. *précipitation*, *hâte*; Ger. *Hast*; Sp. *prisa*.)

frettando. (It.) Hastening, hurrying. Used mainly in its German translation. (Fr. *en pressant*, Ger. *eilend*, Sp. *apresurándo*.)

Freude, Freudig. (Ger.) Joy, joyful, happiness, delight. An evocative term that can be heard in rehearsal. (Fr. *joie*, It. *gioia*, Sp. *alegría*)

Fricsay, Ferenc (1914–1963). Hungarian **conductor**. He served as the principal conductor of the Budapest State Opera (1945–1948) and the **RIAS Symphony Orchestra** and as the music director of the **German Opera Berlin** (Deutsche Oper Berlin; 1949–1952) and the **Bavarian State Opera Munich** (1956–1959). He guest conducted throughout Europe and in the United States and was made the music director of the **Houston Symphony Orchestra**, a position in which he survived only a single season, apparently because of U.S. tax laws. Fricsay made highly acclaimed recordings of the music of Béla Bartók and Zoltán Kodály, two of his early teachers, as well as the music of Wolfgang Amadeus Mozart and Ludwig van Beethoven, many of them on the **Deutsche Grammophon** label. He wrote the book *On Mozart and Bartók* (**Über Mozart and Bartók**) in 1962. See the **bibliography**.

friedlich or ruhig. (Ger.) Tranquil, calm, placid. A descriptive word used to evoke a certain manner of playing. (Fr. *placide*, It. *placido*, Sp. *placido*.)

Friedrich, Götz. (1930–2000.) German opera and theater director. He studied with **Walter Felselstein** at the **Komische Oper** in what was East Berlin. Friedrich was the principal director at the **Hamburg Opera** (1972–1981); director of productions at the **Royal Opera House, Covent Garden** (1977–1981); and general director of the **Deutsche Oper** in what was **West Berlin** (1981–2000). In 1972, he defected to the West during work on a production of Leoš Janáček's *Jenufa* at the Stockholm Opera. In the same year, he became known for a "controversial" production of **Richard Wagner**'s *Tannhäuser* in **Bayreuth**. Known for his productions of Wagner, his first **Ring cycle** was at Covent Garden during the years 1973–1976 under the baton of **Colin Davis**. In the 1980s, he directed a new Ring cycle at the **Deutsche Oper** that was later taken to Covent Garden and was also staged in Japan and Seattle, Washington. A number of his productions are available on DVD, including a 1974 *Salome* and a 1981 *Elektra*, both conducted by **Karl Böhm**; a 1992 *Die Frau ohne Schatten* conducted by **Georg Solti**; and his infamous 1972 *Tannhäuser*.

Frisch. (Ger.) Fresh, lively. Also *etwas frischer*, somewhat fresher, livelier. A descriptive term seen in scores and parts. (Fr. *frais*, It. *fresco*, Sp. *fresco*.)

frissonnant. (Fr.) Fluttering, trembling, thrilling. A character word seen in music. (Ger. *begeistert*, It. *entusiasta*, Sp. *emocionado*.)

frog. Also heel in British usage. The end of the bow, where the string player holds the bow. (Fr. *talon*, *hausse*; Ger. *Frosch*; It. *tallone*, Sp. *nuez*.) Example: *at the frog*, an indication to play at the frog of the bow. (Fr. *au talon*, Ger. *am Frosch*, It. *al tallone*, Sp. *con el talón*.)

frölich or lustig. (Ger.) Cheerful, happy. A character word seen in scores and parts and used in rehearsal. (Fr. *gai*, *gaiement*; It. *gaio*, *giocoso*; Sp. *alegre*.)

From the top, please. An expression used when asking an ensemble to begin at the beginning of a piece. (Fr. *Du début, s'il vous plaît*; Ger. *Vom Anfang, bitte*; Sp. *Desde el principio*.)

Frosch. (Ger.) The **frog** or heel of the bow. (Fr. *talon*, *hausse*; It. *tallone*; Sp. *talón*.) Also *am Frosch*, an indication to play at the frog of the bow. See also **bowing terms**.

früh. (Ger.) Early, soon. (Fr. *de bonne heure*, *tôt*; It. *presto*; Sp. *temprano*, *pronto*.) Example: *Nicht früh!* Not early! Also *früher*, earlier, formerly, previous, prior; *früheres Tempo* or *früheres Zeitmaß*, earlier tempo.

frullato. (It.) **Flutter tonguing**, humming, buzzing. (Fr. *tremolo dental*, Ger. *Flatterzunge*, Sp. *trémolo dental*.)

fuerte. (Sp.) Loud, strong. (Fr. *fort*, Ger. *stark*, It. *forte*.)

fuerza, con. (Sp.) With strength, force. (Fr. *force*, Ger. *Kraft*, It. *forza*.) See also *con forza*.

Fuge. (Ger.) Fugue, a musical form or structural unit. (Fr. *fugue*, It. *fuga*, Sp. *fuga*.)

führen. (Ger.) To lead. Example: *Die Oboe führt in dieser Phrase*, the oboe leads in this phrase.

führend. (Ger.) Leading. Example: *eine führende Stimme*, a leading voice.

Fulbright Program. Founded in 1946 by U.S. snator J. William Fulbright in order to provide highly competitive grants for study and research abroad. Many conductors with foreign language skills have taken advantage of the program and spent a year or more studying abroad.

***Fünfliniesystem Liniensystem* or *System*.** 1. (Ger.) Staff, stave, system. The five-line system on which music is written. (Fr. *portée*; It. *pentagramma, sistema*; Sp. *pentagramma, pauto*.)

2. (Ger.) In a score, two or more staves connected by a "brace" or bar line.

Fun Zone. An Internet resource on the website of the **Baltimore Symphony Orchestra** including links to coloring pages, online games, and other online resources for young people interested in classical music.

***fuoco, con*.** (It.) With fire, energy. An evocative term used in rehearsal. (Fr. *avec le feu*, Ger. *mit Feuer*, Sp. *con fuego*.)

***fuori, di*.** 1. (It.) From backstage, outside. A term used for an offstage part, such as the trumpet solo in the *Overture to Leonore* No. 3 by Ludwig van Beethoven. (Fr. *en dehors*; Ger. *außerhalb, draußen*; Sp. *fuera*.)

2. (It.) Play out, bring forward. (Fr. *en dehors, en évidence*; Ger. *hervortretend*; Sp. *destacar*.)

furioso or ***furiosamente*.** (It., Sp.) Furious, passionate. A descriptive word seen in scores and parts and heard in rehearsal. (Fr. *frieux*; Ger. *wild, wütend*.)

***furioso*.** (Sp.) Raging, furious. A descriptive word seen in scores and parts and heard in rehearsal. (Fr. *enragé, rageur*; Ger. *wütend*; It. *arrabbiato, rabbioso*.)

Furtwängler, Wilhelm. (1886–1954.) German **conductor** and composer. Furtwängler studied in Munich and began as a vocal coach at the Breslau opera (1905–1906), followed by a position at the Zurich opera (1906–1907), the Munich court opera assisting **Felix Mottl** (1907–1909), and as third assistant conductor to Hans Pfitzner in Strasbourg (1910–1911). He was the director of the Lübeck Opera and the conductor of the Lübeck Symphony Orchestra (1911–1915), the Mannheim Opera (1915–1920), the Tonkünstler Orchestra in Vienna (1919–1924), the **Leipzig Gewandhaus Orchestra** (1922–1928), and the **Berlin Philharmonic Orchestra** (1922–1954). He conducted the **Vienna Philharmonic** in 1944 and was their principal conductor from 1927 to 1928 and from 1933 until 1954. His debut at **Bayreuth** was in 1931, and he returned there several times. He debuted in London in 1924; New York in 1925; the **Royal Opera House, Convent Garden**, in 1935; and from 1937 on, he conducted regularly at the **Salzburg Festival**. Furtwängler was a proponent of the music of **Arnold Schoenberg, Igor Stravinsky, Paul Hindemith**, Béla Bartók and **Richard Strauss**, leading many premieres of their music. After World War II there was controversy about his activities and attitude toward the Nazi regime, and in 1945, he fled to Switzerland. One year later he was cleared of pro-Nazi activities and was able to resume his international career. Considered legendary even during his lifetime, Furtwängler was known as a conductor who had a free, if not improvisatory approach to music making. His beat was described as indecisive, his technique as uncertain, if not insecure. He was also known for frequent changes of tempo within movements. But others felt that these very qualities led to depths of insight that few could approach.

***fusa*.** (Sp.) Thirty-second note, demisemiquaver (British usage). (Fr. *triple croche*, Ger. *Zweiunddreißigstel*, It. *biscroma*.) See also **appendix 7: "Rhythmic Terms and Their Translations."**

futurism. An art movement founded in early twentieth-century Italy by the writer Filippo Tommaso Marinetti that sought to stress the machine age and the energetic character of the time. Followers of the movement advocated an "art of noises" that regarded all sounds as music. Composer Luigi Russolo invented noisemaking devices and wrote music for them. (It. *futurismo*.)

fz*.** (It.) Abbreviation for ***forzando, forzato.

G. 1. A musical note or note name.

2. The fifth note of the C major scale.

3. The key of a composition said to be "in G," such as Ludwig van Beethoven's *Piano Concerto No. 4 in G*, opus 58.

Gabrilowitsch, Ossip. (1878–1936.) **Conductor** and concert pianist. Born in St. Petersburg, he was the founding conductor of the **Detroit Symphony Orchestra** and demanded that a new hall be built as a stipulation of his acceptance of the position of music director. It was completed in four months and twenty-four days in 1919. He married Mark Twain's daughter Clara Clemens, a singer.

gai or gaiement. (Fr.) Gay, cheerful, happy. (Ger. *fröhlich, lustig*; It. *gaio, giocoso*; Sp. *alegre*.) Example: *gai et fantasque*, cheerful and whimsical, from "Le matin d'un jour de fête," from "Ibéria" of *Images* by Claude Debussy.

gaimme. (Fr.) Scale. (Ger. *Skala, Tonleiter*; It. *scala*; Sp. *gama, escala*.) See also **alternative scales**.

gaio. (It.) Gay, cheerful, happy. (Fr. *gai, gaiement*; Ger. *fröloch, lustig*; Sp. *alegre*.)

Gaisberg, Fred William. (1873–1951.) American musician, recording engineer, and an early producer of gramophone recordings of classical repertoire. In 1898, he went to work for the new **Gramophone Company** in London to market Emile Berliner's gramophone player. Gaisberg was in charge of searching out talent for recordings for the new gramophone. He traveled Europe and Asia, making wax discs of local musicians. In 1902, he made the sensational recordings of tenor Enrico Caruso for the Victor "Red Seal" label. He also recorded artists such as Feodor Chaliapin, Nellie Melba, John McCormack, and Frits Kreisler. He made the only recording of a castrato singer, Alesssandro Moreschi, and the first recordings in India and Japan (1902 and 1903). He made several trips to Russia just before the revolution that spurred one of the business' largest early markets. Without trying to influence how artists performed, he operated more in the manner of an anthropologist; he simply tried to make as many recordings, or so-called recording photographs, as possible. In 1921, he became the director of the artists' wing of **HMV (His Master's Voice)** and remained in the position as the firm and **Columbia** merged to create **EMI (Electric and Musical Industries)** in 1931. During the next decade his projects included recordings of Edward Elgar's symphonies and other major works. Gaisberg continued to be influential after retiring in 1939. He remained an advocate for new technologies, including long-play (LP) records, which were introduced by Columba Records in 1948, and the development of stereo sound. He was also influential in the building of the Abby Road Studios in London. One of his protégés was **Walter Legge** of **EMI**.

gama or escala. (Sp.) Scale. (Fr. *gamme*; Ger. *Skala, Tonleiter*; It. *scala*.) See also **alternative scales**.

gamba. (It.) Short for *viola da gamba*, a bowed instrument most prominent in sixteenth- and seventeenth-century Italy. It is often used today in Baroque ensembles as part of the **continuo**.

gambe. (Fr.) The French equivalent of *gamba*, as in the instrument that is often used today in Baroque ensembles as part of the **continuo**.

gambo. (It.) Stem of a note. (Fr. *queue de la note, hampe*; Ger. *Notenhals*; Sp. *plica*.)

gamma. (It.) Compass, range, of an instrument, for instance. (Fr. *ètendue*; Ger. *Umfang, Raum, Ausdehnung*; Sp. *rango*.)

Ganze. (Ger.) Whole note. See **appendix 7: "Rhythmic Terms and Their Translations."**

ganze Pause. (Ger.) Whole note rest. See **appendix 7: "Rhythmic Terms and Their Translations."**

garder le mesure. (Fr.) To keep or to hold the tempo. (Ger. *Takt halten*, It. *tenere il tempo*, Sp. *mantener el mismo compás*.)

Gardiner, Sir John Eliot. (b. 1943.) English **conductor**. He studied at Cambridge University; with Thurston Dart at King's College, London; and with **Nadia Boulanger** in Paris (in her will she left him her scores of Claudio Monteverdi, Giacomo Carissimi, Jean-Philippe Rameau, Marc-Antoine Charpentier, and others). He also studied conducting with **George Hurst** with the BBC Northern Symphony and with **Antol Dorati**. He founded the Monteverdi Choir, making his debut with them in 1966 and in 1968 with the Monteverdi Orchestra. In 1977, the orchestra switched to using period instruments, and to signal the significance of that move, they changed their name to the English Baroque Soloists. A proponent of performance practices, Gardiner established those principles at the center of his interpretations as he served as a guest conductor at the **English National Opera** in Wolfgang Amadeus Mozart's *Magic Flute* (1969) and Christoph Willibald Gluck's *Iphigénie en Tauride* at the **Royal Opera House, Covent Garden** (1973). His own ensemble performed at the 1977 Innsbruck Festival of Early Music with George Frideric Handel's *Acis and Galatea*. In 1979, he made his U.S. debut with the **Dallas Symphony Orchestra**. Gardiner served as the principal conductor of the CBC Vancouver Orchestra (1980–1983), as the music director of the Opéra National de Lyon (1983–1988), and as the artistic director of the Göttingen Handel Festival (1981–1990). In 1990, he formed a new period-instrument orchestra, the **Orchestre Révolutionnaire et Romantique**, with the aim of bringing the same focus on performance practice style to nineteenth-century music. He was also the principal conductor of the **North German Radio Symphony Orchestra** (1991–1995).

The focus of Gardiner's music making was not of building a conducting career in the traditional way but of championing major musical projects. His projects included a European tour with Hector Berlioz's rediscovered *Messe solennelle* with the **Orchestre Révolutionnaire et Romantique**; his Bach Cantata Pilgrimage, during fifty-two weeks he perform all of Johann Sebastian Bach's sacred cantatas in churches of Europe and the United States; a tour of France and Spain during which he led the Monteverdi Choir in works of the *Codex Compostelanus* along the Camino de Santiago, where much of it had been written; and innumerable recordings, over 250, many of them extraordinary, on

Deutsche Grammophon, **Philips Classics**, and the Soli Deo Gloria labels. He has not limited his repertoire to early music, guest conducting the **Berlin Philharmonic**; the symphony orchestras of Boston, Chicago, Cleveland, and London; the **Philharmonia Orchestra**; the **Royal Concertgebouw Orchestra**; and the **Vienna Philharmonic**. In 2013, he published the book *Bach: Music in the Castle of Heaven*. See the **bibliography**.

GATT Treaty 1994 (General Agreement on Tariffs and Trade). A set of rules governing international trade originally signed in 1947 and lasting until 1994 when it was replaced by the World Trade Organization (WTO 1995). The WTO expanded the scope of the GATT to include intellectual property rights, putting back into copyright the works of many twentieth-century Russian composers such as Sergei Prokofiev and Dmitri Shostakovich. Although the GATT was replaced by the WTO, the WTO maintained much of the GATT text in its documents. It is still often referred to at the GATT Treaty. The 1994 documents were the first to codify intellectual property and copyright laws. See also **Agreement on Trade-Related Aspects of Intellectual Property Rights (TRIPS)**.

gauche. (Fr.) Left. (Ger. *links*, It. *sinistra*, Sp *izquierdo*.) Example: *main gauche*, left hand. (Ger. *Linke*, It. *mano sinistra*, Sp. *mano izquierdo*.)

Gebrauchsmusik. (Ger.) Music created for practical use, such as in a home or school setting, as opposed to music written for the concert hall (lit. "music for use"). The term first came into use in the 1920s and is often associated with German composer **Paul Hindemith**. This music is normally more direct in nature and less difficult to perform.

gebrochen. (Ger.) Broken. Also *nicht gebrochen*, not broken or arpeggiated, as in the chords of a harp part.

gebunden. (Ger.) Slurred, smooth, legato. Example: *nicht gebunden, aber sehr gehalten*, not slurred, but very connected, from *The Prelude to Die Meistersinger von Nürenberg* by **Richard Wagner**.

gedämpft. (Ger.) Dampened, muted, as in timpani. Can be an indication to release the snares off of the snare drum.

gedeckt. (Ger.) **Stopped**. Abbreviation Also *gestopft*. Abbreviated *gest.* (Fr. *bouché, étouffé*; It. *chiuso, tappato*; Sp. *cubierto, tapado*.)

geflüstert. (Ger.) Whispered. Example: *tonlos geflüstert*, unpitched whisper, from *Pierrot Lunaire* by Arnold Schoenberg.

gefühlvoll. (Ger.) Full of feeling, a descriptive word. Also *mit Gefühl*, with feeling.

gegen. (Ger) Against, versus, contrary to. Example: *gegen dis 2. Violinen zart hervortretend*, from *Das Lied von der Erde*, mvt. 1, by **Gustav Mahler**.

gehalten. (Ger.) Connected, sustained. Example: *sehr gehalten*, very connected, molto tenuto, from the prelude to *Die Meistersinger von Nürenberg* by **Richard Wagner**.

geheimnisvoll. (Ger.) Mysterious. (Fr. *mystérieux*, It. *misterioso*, Sp. *misterioso*.)

gehen. (Ger.) To go, to walk, to proceed. Also *gehend* or *gehende*, moving, walking, moderately, a similar tempo to **andante**. (Fr. *aller*, It. *andare*, Sp. *ir*.)

Gehör spielen, nach. (Ger.) See *nach Gehör spielen*.

gehüpft. (Ger.) A short, light, fast bow stroke that makes the bow bounce off of the string. (Fr. *sautillé*; It. *saltellato*, *balzellato*.)

Geige. (Ger.) **Violin**. (Fr. *violin*, It. *violino*, Sp. *violín*.) See also **appendix 3: "Instrument Names and Their Translations."**

gemächlich. (Ger.) Leisurely, unhurried. Example: *Im Anfang sehr gemächlich*, in the beginning, very leisurely, from Symphony No. 1, mvt 1, by **Gustav Mahler**.

Gemeinschaftsmusik. (Ger.) A term used in Germany in the 1930s to describe music that was intended to be sung or played but not necessarily listened to by an audience (lit. "music for society"). Often written to create a "community" experience of music. Paul Hindemith's *Das Neue Werk* from 1927 consisted of this kind of music and was meant to be "performed" or "put on" by those who came to the "concert."

gemessen. (Ger.) Measured, in time, steady. (It. *misurato*, Fr. *mesuré*, Sp. *mensurada*.)

gemütvoll. (Ger.) With feeling, sentiment. A descriptive term heard in rehearsal. (Fr. *avec l'âme*, It. *con l'anima*, Sp. *con sentimiento*.)

genau. (Ger.) Strictly, in strict tempo. Also *richtig*. (Fr. *exact*, *juste*; Sp. *exactamente*, *preciso*; It. *esatto*, *giusto*.)

Generalmusikdirektor. (Ger.) A term used mainly in Germany. The equivalent of the American term **music director**.

Generalpause. (Ger.) **Grand pause** or general pause. Abbreviation **G.P.** Also *Schweigezeichen*. (Fr. *pause générale*, It. *pausa generale*, *vuoto*; Sp. *pausa general*, *silencio general*.)

Generalprobe, die. (Ger.) **General rehearsal** or final rehearsal. (Fr. *la répétition générale*, It. *la ripetizione generale*, Sp. *ensayo general*.)

general rehearsal. A term often used in Europe and other places to signify the final dress rehearsal with the concert program being read mostly without stopping and often in concert order. (Fr. *la répétition générale*, Ger. *die Generalprobe*, It. *la ripetizione generale*, Sp. *ensayo general*.)

gentiment. (Fr.) Gently, daintily. A character word used in rehearsal. (Ger. *sanft, in sanfter Weise*; It. *delicatimente*, *dolcement*; Sp. *suavemente*.)

George Enescu Philharmonic Orchestra (Filarmonica George Enescu). Founded in 1886 in Bucharest under the auspices of the Romanian Philharmonic Society and **conductor** Eduard Wachman, who led the ensemble until 1907. Other past conductors include Dimitrie Dinicu (1907–1920) followed by **George Georgescu**, a student of both George Enescu and **Arthur Nikisch**. Georgescu led the orchestra for over four decades. Since 1889, when the Romanian Athenaeum was opened, all concerts have been presented there. The orchestra was renamed after the Romanian composer Enescu in 1955. Current conductors include Horia Andreescu, Christian Badea, and Camil Marinescu. The artistic director is pianist Nicolae Licaret.

George, Vance. (b. 1933.) American choral **conductor**. Vance served as the director of the San Francisco Symphony Chorus (1983–2006), preparing the ensemble for performances of such significant works as **Gustav Mahler**'s Symphonies No. 2 and 3, Johannes Brahms's *German Requiem*, and more. Under his leadership the chorus won four **Grammy Awards** and an Emmy for the 2001 concert performance of Stephen Sondheim's *Sweeney Todd*. Vance has appeared as a guest conductor with the orchestras of Akron, Indianapolis, Minneapolis, Spokane, Sydney, and Australia, as well as at the Berkshire Choral Festival in Massachusetts and the Ventura Bach Festival in California. He received a Lifetime Achievement Award from **Chorus America** in 1999.

Gergiev, Valery Abisalovich. (b. 1953.) Russian **conductor**. Gergiev is currently the general director and artistic director of the **Mariinsky Theater**, the principal conductor of the **London Symphony Orchestra**, and the artistic director of the **White Nights Festival** in St. Petersburg, Russia. He studied conducting with **Ilya Musin**, one of the most important Russian conducting pedagogues, at the Leningrad Conservatory (1972–1977). Gergiev was the assistant conductor at the **Kirov Opera** (now the Mariinsky Opera) under **Yuri Temirkanov**, making his debut leading Sergei Prokofiev's *War and Peace*. He was the chief conductor of the Armenian Philharmonic Orchestra (1981–1985). Gergiev made his European operatic debut conducting Modest Mussorgsky's *Boris Godunov* at the **Bavarian State Opera** and his American debut with *War and Peace* at the San Francisco Opera, all in 1991. He was the principal conductor of the Rotterdam Philharmonic Orchestra (1995–2008) and the **Metropolitan Opera**, New York (1997–2008). Gergiev was directly involved in raising funds for the Mariinsky Hall. He is scheduled to take over as the music director of the **Munich Philharmonic** in 2015. Gergiev is well known for conducting either with a mere toothpick or with no baton at all. A highly honored conductor, he is often described as passionate and driven, at his best in dramatic, exciting works. He often becomes involved in social and political issues. Widely recorded, his repertoire is predominantly Russian but includes all of the symphonies of **Gustav Mahler**.

Valery Gergiev. *Courtesy Photofest.*

German Opera Berlin (Deutsche Oper Berlin). The company was founded in 1911 when the German Opera house was built. The building was destroyed during World War II (1943), and during that time performances were held at a nearby theater. A new modern opera house designed by German architect Fritz Bornemann was opened in 1961. The current music director is **Donald Runnicles** (appointed in 2009). Past music directors include Ignatz Waghalter (1912–1923); **Bruno Walter** (1925–1929); Kurt Adler (as resident conductor, 1932–1933); Artur Rother (1935–1943 and 1953–1958); Karl Manner (1937–1943); **Ferenc Fricsay** (1949–1952); Richard Kraus (1954–1961); Heinrich Hollreiser (as chief conductor, 1961–1964); **Lorin Maazel** (1965–1971); Gerd Albrecht (as resident conductor, 1972–1974); **Jesús**

López-Cobos (1981–1990); **Giuseppe Sinopoli**, who died on the podium during a performance of Giuseppe Verdi's opera *Aida* (1990); **Rafael Frühbeck de Burgos** (1992–1997); **Christian Thielemann** (1997–2004); and Renato Palumbo (2006–2008). The company has a distinguished recoding history that continues today. The opera presents performances for youth, has family days for specific performances, and much more.

German Symphony Orchestra Berlin (Deutsches Symphonie-Orchester Berlin, DSO). Founded in 1946 by American occupying forces as the RIAS Symphony Orchestra (RIAS-Symphonie-Orchester). RIAS is the abbreviation for Radio in the American Sector (*Rundfunk im amerikanischen Sektor*). The orchestra was renamed the **Berlin Radio Symphony Orchestra** in 1956 and took its present name in 1995. The orchestra's current principal conductor is **Tugan Sokhiev** (appointed in 2012). Past principal conductors include **Ferenc Fricsay** (1948–1954 and 1959–1963), **Lorin Maazel** (1964–1975), **Riccardo Chailly** (1982–1989), **Vladimir Ashkenazy** (1989–1999), **Kent Nagano** (2000–2006), and Ingo Metzmacher (2007–2010). The orchestra has issued several notable recordings.

gerne. (Ger.) Happily, willingly, with pleasure. A commonly used expression. (Fr. *volontiers*, It. *volentieri*, Sp. *con alegría*.)

Ges. (Ger.) G-flat. See **appendix 5**.

Gesang. (Ger.) Song. Also ***Lied***. (Fr. *chanson*; It. *canto*, *canzone*; Sp. *canción*, *canto*.)

gesangvoll. (Ger.) Cantabile, lyrical. Example: *sehr gesangvoll*, very lyrical, from Symphony No. 1, mvt. 3, by **Gustav Mahler**.

Geschmack, mit. (Ger.) With relish, with style, with taste. (Fr. *avec goût*, It. *con gusto*, Sp. *con gusto*.)

geschwindig. (Ger.) Quick, nimble, speedy. (It. *svelto*, Fr. *rapide*, Sp. *rápido*.)

Gesellschaft. (Ger.) A musical society that promotes the work and knowledge of a particular composer and more. For example, the **Bach-Gesellschaft**, formed in 1850 to oversee the publication of the complete works of Johann Sebastian Bach.

gestimmt. (Ger.) Tuned, true, tempered. (Fr. *accordé*, It. *accordato*, Sp. *afinado*.) Example: *NB. Der I. Solo-geiger hat sich mit 2 Instrumenten zu versehen, won denen das eine um einen Ganzton höher, das andere normal gestimmt ist*, The concertmaster has to have two instruments on hand, one of which is to be tuned a whole tone higher and the other in regular tuning, from Symphony No. 4, mvt. 2, by **Gustav Mahler**. Common practice is to tune the extra violin a quarter-tone higher, not a whole tone, and that that produces the particular "fiddle-like" quality Mahler sought.

gestochen. 1. (Ger.) A short, quickly released note, like staccato. 2. (Ger.) In bowing, short detached notes produced without changing the direction of the bow. (Fr. *piqué*; It. *piccato, picchiettato*; Sp. *picado*.)

gestopft. (Ger.) **Stopped**. Also *gedeckt*. Abbreviated *gest*. (Fr. *bouché, étouffé*; It. *chiuso, tappato*; Sp. *cubierto, tapado*.)

gestrichen. (Ger.) Bowed or struck. Example: *col legno gestrichen*, struck with the wood of the bow, from ***Pierrot Lunaire*** by Arnold Schoenberg.

gesture of syncopation. A conducting gesture that, most importantly, gives clarity and security to players entering on or playing syncopations for an extended passage. The gesture does not give the syncopation itself but sets it up with a clear ictus on the beat and may be followed by a relatively brisk, energetic rebound.

getheilt. (Ger.) Divided, *divisi*. Abbreviated *geth*.

getragen. (Ger.) A bow stroke where the bow pulses slightly between notes; generally written under a slur, moving in one direction. It is the same as *louré*. (Fr. *porté*, It. *portato*, Sp. *portato*.)

getrennt. (Ger.) Separated. Usually used as a directive to play in a separated manner. (Fr. *détaché*, It. *staccato*.) Examples: *Die Noten getrennt spielen, bitte*, Please separate the notes; *Getrennt spielen, bitte*, Separated, please.

Gewandhaus, Leipzig. See **Leipzig Gewandhaus**.

gewichtig. (Ger.) Weighty. Example: *sehr gewichtig*, very weighty or heavy, from the prelude to *Die Meistersinger von Nürenberg* by **Richard Wagner**; *sehr voll und gewichtig*, very full and heavy, from *Pierrot Lunaire* by **Arnold Schoenberg**.

gewirbelt. (Ger.) Rolled; for instance, a timpani roll.

gewöhnlich. (Ger.) Customary, ordinary, to play in the ordinary manner, such as after a passage of *sul ponticello* for strings. (Fr. *ordinaire*, It. *ordinario*, Sp. *ordinario*.) Example: *wieder gewöhnlich*, return to the usual way of playing, from *Pierrot Lunaire* by **Arnold Schoenberg**.

gezupft. (Ger.) Plucked, **pizzicato**. Pizzicato is internationally understood as a string term for plucking the string.

Gibault, Claire. (b. 1945.) French **conductor**, politician, and member of the European Parliament for the southeast of France. Gibault sits on the Committee on Culture and Education and the Committee on Women's Rights and Gender Equity and the European Parliament's Women's Rights Committee. She was a prize-winning violin student at Le Mans Conservatory. She also attended the Paris Higher National Conservatory of Music and received first prizes for orchestra conducting and theory. She was the music director of the Chamber Orchestra of Chambéry (1976–1983) and Orchestra of the Opéra Notional de Lyon and assistant to **John Eliot Gardiner** (1983–1989). She conducted the orchestra of **La Scala** (1995) and musicians of the **Berlin Philharmonic** in the opera *Jacob Lenz* by Wolgang Rihm. From 1991 to 1998 Gilbaut was in charge of the Lyrical and Choral Workshop at the Lyon Opera and also served as the music director for many productions, including *Pelleas et Mélisande, The Barber of Seville, The Abduction from the Seraglio*, Hector Berlioz's *Romeo and Juliet*, and more. She was the music director of Music for Rome (Musica per Roma), leading performances of Hans Werner Henze's *Pollicino*, Engelbert Humperdinck's *Hansel and Gretel*, Leonard Bernstein's *West Side Story*, and Wolfgang Amadeus Mozart's operas. Gilbault has served as a guest conductor at Glyndebourne; the **Royal Opera House, Covent Garden**; the Edinburg Festival; many French opera houses; and with several orchestras, such as the Hallé, Royal Scottish, RTÉ National Symphony Orchestra, RAI National Symphony, Belgium National Orchestra, Liège Philharmonic Orchestra, and the Copenhagen Philharmonic, and she has recorded with the Royal Philharmonic. She is the recipient of the Officier des Palmes Académiques and Chevalier of the National Order of Merit (France) and the French Legion of Honor.

Gibson, Sir Alexander. (1926–1995.) Scottish **conductor**. Gibson served as the assistant conductor of the **BBC Scottish Symphony Orchestra** (1952–1954) and was appointed the music director of **Sadler's Wells Opera** in London, now known as the **English National Opera**, in 1957, serving a two-year stint. In 1959, he became the first Scottish-born principal conductor and artistic director of the Scottish National Orchestra, remaining in the position until 1984. With the orchestra, he cultivated an international reputation for high-quality performances and recordings. Gibson founded the Scottish Opera in 1962 and was the music director until 1986. In 1967, he was made a commander of the Order of the British Empire (CBE), and in 1977, he was knighted. In 1998, the Alexander Gibson School of Opera, named in his honor, was opened. Gibson was known particularly for his affinity for the music of Jean Sibelius and Carl Nielsen. He also maintained a commitment to contemporary music, founding the Musica Viva new music festival in Glasgow in 1961.

Gielen, Michael. (b. 1927.) Austrian **conductor**, composer, and pianist. Gielen was a noted champion of contemporary European music, in particular the works of the **Second Viennese School**. His family immigrated to Argentina in 1939. He studied piano there and in 1947 became a *répéteur* at the **Teatro Colón** in Buenos Aires. In 1949, he gave a recital of the complete piano works of **Arnold Schoenberg**. In 1950, he returned to study in Vienna and became a coach and conductor at the Vienna State Opera (1952–1960). He conducted at the Swedish Royal Opera (1960–1965) and Cologne (1965–1968), leading the premiere of Bernd Alois Zimmermann's opera *Die Soldaten*. Gielen served as the music director at the Belgian National Orchestra, Brussels (1969–1972); chief conductor at the Netherlands Opera (1973–1975); music director and chief conductor at the Frankfurt Opera (1977–1987); principal guest conductor of the **BBC Symphony Orchestra** (1980–1986); music director at the **Cincinnati Symphony Orchestra** (190–1986); and conductor of the **Southwest German Radio Orchestra** (1986–1999). He was a professor of conducting at the **Salzburg Mozarteum** (1987–1995). Beginning in the 1990s, he conducted regularly at the **Berlin State Opera** and with the **Berlin Symphony Orchestra**. In 1995, he made his Salzburg Festival debut, conducting Alban Berg's *Lulu*. Gielen has made a major contribution to music of the twentieth century through his many premiere performances and recordings, including the first commercial stereo recording of **Arnold Schoenberg**'s *Moses and Aron* (1974). His performances are noted for their great clarity and intellect paired with commitment, force, and energy.

gigelira. (It.) Xylophone. Also *xilofono*. (Fr. *xylophone*, Ger. *Xylophon*, Sp. *xilófono*.) See also **appendix 4**.

Gilbert, Alan. (b. 1967.) Music director of the **New York Philharmonic** 2009–2017, Gilbert has served as the music director of the **Stockholm Philharmonic Orchestra** (2000–2008) and the **Santa Fe Opera** (2003–2006) and as the principal guest conductor of the **North German Radio Symphony Orchestra**, Hamburg (since 2004). He appeared at the **Metropolitan Opera**, New York, conducting American composer John Adams's opera *Doctor Atomic*. The DVD of the performance won a **Grammy Award**. Gilbert also serves as the director of conducting and orchestral studies at the **Juilliard School**. In 2011, he was awarded **Columbia University**'s **Ditson Award for Conductors**.

giocoso. (It.) Playful. A character word most often heard in its Italian form. (Fr. *badin*, Ger. *spielerisch*.)

Girard, Narcisse. Violinist and **conductor**. Girard conducted the premiere of Hector Berlioz's *Harold in Italy*, and he conducted orchestras at the Hotel de Ville. From 1830 to 1832 he was the conductor of the Opéra Italien. He served as the chief conductor at the Paris Opéra-Comique from 1837 to 1846 and then moved to the Paris Opéra. He succeeded **François Habeneck** as the conductor of the *Societe des Concerts du Conservatoire* (the orchestra founded by Habeneck in 1828), conducting over one hundred concerts from 1848 to 1860.

Gis. (Ger.) G-sharp. See also **appendix 5**.

Gitarre. (Ger.) Guitar. (Fr. *Guitar*, Sp. *Guitarra*, It. *chitarra*.)

giustamente. (It.) Precisely, justly, exactly. (Fr. *justement*, Ger. *mit Recht*, Sp. *correctamente*.)

giusto. (It.) Strict, precise. Also *esatto*. (Fr. *exact, juste*; Ger. *genau, richtig*; Sp. *exactamente, preciso*.) Example: *tempo giusto*, in a strict tempo.

gleich. 1. (Ger.) Equal, alike, even, smoothly. Also *gleichmäßig*. (Fr. *égal*, It. *eguale*, Sp. *igual*.) Examples: *immer gleichmäßig leicht*, everything very light, from the prelude to *Die Meistersinger von Nürenberg* by Richard Wagner; *gleich sein*, to be equal; *gleichen*, to equal something; *sehr ruhig und gleichmäßig*, very calm and even, from *Pierrot Lunaire* by **Arnold Schoenberg**.
2. (Ger.) Similar. (Fr. *semblable, pareil*; It. *simile*; Sp. *similar*.)

gleichmäßig. (Ger.) Equal. (Fr. *égal*, It. *uguale*, Sp. *igual*.) Also equally. (Fr. *également*; It. *ugualmente, equamente*; Sp. *igualmente*.)

gleichzeitig. (Ger.) Simultaneously, at the same time. (Fr. *en meme temps*, It. *contemporaneamente*, Sp. *al mismo tiempo*.)

gli. (It.) The. Example: *gli altri*, the others, used in string writing when one or more players play their own part(s) and "the others" play something else.

Glimmerglass Festival. Established in 1975 as the Glimmerglass Opera, the company presents a summer opera season of four operas near Cooperstown, New York. Currently all operas are performed in their original language with projected translations. The company founded its Young American Artists Program in 1988 to provide opportunities for professional development.

glissando. (It., pl. *glissandi*) AbbIn string playing, a sliding of a finger of the left hand from one note to another in order to create a specific effect. It slso appears in harp and piano parts. Some glissandos are notated with a straight line between the beginning and ending notes of the glissando, while others have all the chromatic pitches written, accompanied by the indication *glissando*, or *gliss.* Abbreviated **gliss.** Examples: *glissando (en croisant)*, glissando with hands crossing, from the harp part in "Jeux de vagues," mvt. 2 of *La Mer* by Claude Debussy.

Glissando. *Courtesy Andrew Martin Smith.*

glissez. (Fr.) Slide, as in **glissando**. Example: *Glissez en effleurant la corde du côté du chevalet*, slide the finger lightly over the string near the bridge, from "Feria" of *Rapsodie Espagnole* by Maurice Ravel.

Glocke. (Ger.) Bell, chime. See also **appendix 4**.

Glockenspiel. (Ger.) Orchestra bells, also called glockenspiel in English. Abbreviated **Gsp.** See also **appendix 4**.

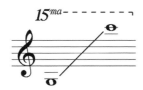

Glockenspiel range as it sounds. *Courtesy Andrew Martin Smith.*

Glockenspiel range as written. *Courtesy Andrew Martin Smith.*

Glover, Jane. (b. 1949.) English **conductor** and musicologist. Glover studied at Oxford University, leading the university's Opera Group in a performance of *The Marriage of Figaro* (1971). She has served as the artistic director of the **London Mozart Players** (1984) and joined the staff of the **Glyndebourne Opera** in 1979, serving as the chorus director (1980–1984) and leading the touring opera from 1981 to 1985. She was the conductor of the Hud-

dersfield Choral Society (1989–1996). An active opera conductor, she has led productions at Glyndebourne and made her debut with the **Royal Opera House, Covent Garden** (1988) and the **English National Opera** (1989). In 2000, she led Claudio Monteverdi's *Orfeo* at the **Lyric Opera of Chicago** and *Hippolyte and Aricie* in St. Louis, Missouri, in 2001. Glover has also been a lecturer in music at St. Hugh's College, Oxford (1976–1984); St. Anne's College (1976–1980); and Pembroke College (1979–1989). She has conducted several contemporary operas, including works of **Sir Benjamin Britten**, and premieres by Judith Bingham, David Matthews, Salle Beamish, Roger Steptoe, and others. Glover continues to lead opera and symphony performances all over the United States, Europe, and beyond. Recently she made her **Metropolitan Opera** debut in *The Magic Flute*. She has recorded works of Joseph Haydn, Wolfgang Amadeus Mozart, Franz Schubert, and others. She is also the author of *Mozart's Women* (2006). In 2003, she was made a commander of the Order of the British Empire (CBE) by Queen Elizabeth II. See the **bibliography**.

glühend. (Ger.) Glowing fervently. As used in *Das Lied von der Erde*, mvt. 1, **Gustav Mahler**.

Glyndebourne Festival Opera. An English opera festival held in East Sussex, England, since 1934, with the exception of 1941–1945 and 1993, when the theater was being rebuilt. Founded by John Christie on his country estate, the festival is renowned for its performances of the operas of Wolfgang Amadeus Mozart. Recent years have seen the repertoire expanded to include George Gershwin's *Porgy and Bess* and works of Leoš Janáček and George Frideric Handel. The **London Philharmonic** serves as the resident orchestra, while Gardiner's **Orchestra of the Age of Enlightenment** also often performs. Music directors have included Fritz Busch (1934–1951), Vittorio Gui (1952–1963), John Pritchard (1964–1977), and **Bernard Haitink** (1978–1988).

Goldovsky, Boris. (1908–2001.) Russian-born American **conductor** and producer. Goldovsky studied at the Moscow Conservatory, then moved to Germany and studied in Berlin and Budapest. He immigrated to the United States in 1930 and studied with **Fritz Reiner** at the **Curtis Institute of Music**. An enthusiastic proponent of opera in America, he served as the head of the opera department (1942–1962) at the **New England Conservatory of Music** and director of the opera workshop at the **Berkshire Music Center, Tanglewood** (1946–1962), where he led the American premieres of **Sir Benjamin Britten**'s *Peter Grimes* and *Albert Herring*. He was also an intermission commentator at the Metropolitan Opera for over forty years. His books include *Accents on Opera* (1953), *Bringing Opera to Life* (1968), and *My Road to Opera* (1979). See the **bibliography**.

golpe de aire. (Sp.) **Preparatory gesture**.

golpe de arco. (Sp.) A bow stroke, bowing. Historically it referred to a loud chord involving a dramatic bow that was used to catch the attention of the audience. (Fr. *coup d'archet*; Ger. *Bogenstrich, Strichart, Bogenführung*; It. *arcata, colpo d'arco*.)

golpe de aro. (Sp.) Rim shot. A percussion term that describes a sharp hit by a snare drumstick on the rim of the drum.

Gong. (Ger.) Gongs are metal plates that come in a wide variety of sizes and thicknesses, each with its own tone. The **Tam-tam** is usually the largest and deepest in tone. See also **appendix 4**.

Google Play Books. An e-book, or electronic book, provider formerly known as Google eBooks and Google Editions. Books purchased at the site are stored online and linked to the customer's Google account. They may be read online or downloaded in different ways for offline reading.

Gothenburg Symphony Orchestra (Göteborgs Symfoniker, GSO). Founded in 1905, the orchestra achieved the national honor of being name a Swedish National Orchestra in 1997. It performs in the Gothenburg Concert Hall, which was built in 1935 and has been praised for its superior acoustics. **Gustavo Dudamel** served as the music director from 2007 to 2012. He was preceded by the Swiss conductor Mario Venzago (2004–2007) and **Neeme Järvi** (1982–2004). Earlier conductors include **Sergiu Comissiona** (1967–1972) and American **Dean Dixon** (1953–1960).

goût, avec. (Fr.) With relish, style, taste. A commonly heard character expression. (Ger. *mit Geschmack*, It. *con gusto*, Sp. *con gusto*.)

G.P. Abbreviation for **grand pause**.

G.P. Abbreviation for **grand pause**, an indication that everyone in the orchestra rests for the duration of the bar together.

gracia, con. (Sp.) With grace. An evocative expression heard in rehearsal. Also *gracioso*, graceful; *graciosamente*, gracefully. (Fr. *gracieux*, Ger. *graziös*, It. *grazioso*.)

gracieux or *gracieuse.* (Fr.) Graceful. A character word used to evoke a particular manner of playing. Also *gracieusement, avec grâce*.

grácil. (Sp.) Delicate. See also *delicado*.

gradamente. (It.) Gradually, step by step. (Fr. *graduel, coup sur coup*; Ger. *allmählich*; Sp. *graduado, poco a poco*.)

gradazione, con. (It.) With gradation, by degrees.

gradevole. (It.) Pleasant, agreeable. (Fr. *agréable*, Ger. *angenehm*, Sp. *agradable*.)

grado. (It.) A degree or note of a scale. (Fr. *degré*, Ger. *Stufe*, Sp. *grado*.) Example: *congiunto*, stepwise, by step. (Ger. *stufenweise*; Fr. *conjoint*; Sp. *por grados, conjunto*.)

grado. (Sp.) A degree or note of a scale. (Fr. *degré*, Ger. *Stufe*, It. *grado*.) Example: *por grados* or *conjunto*, stepwise, by step. (Fr. *conjoint*, Ger. *stufenweise*, It. *congiunto*.)

grado a grado la corda. (It.) Scale step by step on the string. A direction for string players to change gradually, one step at a time, to playing on the string.

graduado. (Sp.) Gradually. Also *poco a poco*, step by step. (Fr. *graduel, coup sur coup*; Ger. *allmählich*; It. *gradamente*.)

graduel. (Fr.) Gradually. Also *coup sur coup*, step by step. (It. *gradamente*; Ger. *allmählich*; Sp. *graduado, poco a poco*.)

Grammy Awards. See **National Academy of Recording Arts and Sciences**.

Gramophone **(magazine).** A monthly publication issued in London that was founded in 1923. Each issue features reviews of and recommendations for recent recordings. *Gramophone* currently maintains an archive service whereby subscribers to the digital edition can access reviews going back to the original publication date. The magazine also presents the distinguished **Gramophone Awards** every year. See also **music magazines**.

Gramophone Awards. Celebrated award given annually for best recording by *Gramophone* magazine.

gran cassa. (It.) **Bass drum**. Also *gran tamburo*. (Fr. *grosse caisse*, Ger. *Grosse Trommel*, Sp. *bombo*.) See also **appendix 4**.

grand détaché. (Fr.) In bowing, alternating up-bows and down-bows with broad strokes, sometimes also called *sostenuto*.

grandiosità, con la. (It.) With grandeur. A phrase sometimes used in rehearsal to evoke a particular manner of playing. (Fr. *avec grandeur*, Ger. *mit Herrlichkeit*, Sp. *con grandeza*.)

grand pause. A bar or measure where everyone in the ensemble is silent. Abbreviated **G.P.**

Grand Prix du Disque. The most important French award for musical recordings. Established in 1948 by the Charles Cros Academy (Académie Charles Cros), it presents awards in numerous musical categories that vary from year to year, including ancient music, blues, choral music, French song, instrumental and symphonic music, jazz, modern music, and world music. Its top prize is awarded annually and is the Grand Prix du Disque.

Grand Rapids Symphony. Founded in 1930 in Grand Rapids, Michigan, the orchestra offers classics and pops series, in addition to its SymphonicBoom, MusicNOW, Rising Stars, Coffee Classics, Lollipop concerts, and more. The orchestra also runs a youth orchestra program. Its current music director is David Lockington. Past music directors include Karl Wecker (1930–1940), **Thor Johnson** (1940–1942), **Nicolai Malko** (1942–1946), Rudolph Ganz (1946–1948), Jose Enchaniz (1948–1954), Désiré Defauw (1954–1958), Robert Zeller (1959–1964), Carl Karapetian (1964–1968), Gregory Millar (1968–1973), Theo Alcantara (1973–1979), **Semyon Bychkov** (1980–1985), and **Catherine Comet** (1986–1997). The symphony has made several recordings.

gran tamburo. (It.) **Bass drum**. Also *gran cassa*. See also **appendix 4**.

graphic notation. A system of musical notation used in **aleatoric music** in which directions for the performer are given on graph paper. This notation sometimes uses boxes or squares containing information about time elements and durations. Since the 1950s, nontraditional visual notation symbols have been used to suggest, guide, and sometimes inspire the choices of performers in **aleatoric** music. Sometimes these notational devices will illustrate phrase shapes, dynamics, pitch contours, and rhythmic patterns as geometric designs. The composers who used and developed this notation are Morton Feldman, Earle Brown, Karlheinz Stockhausen, and Cornelius Cardew. See also **boxes, frame notation**.

grave. 1. (It., Fr.) Grave, solemn, slow, considered to be as slow as **adagio**. Also *gravemente, con gravità*.
2. (It., Fr.) Flat, as in low pitched.

Grawemeyer Awards. Given annually by the University of Louisville (Kentucky), prize categories include the fields of education, improving world order, music composition, religion, and psychology. The first award was for music composition and was presented in 1985. Funded by H. Charles Grawemeyer (1912–1993), industrialist and philanthropist, he created the awards in 1984 with an initial endowment of $9 million.

grazio, con. (It.) With grace, elegance. A commonly used descriptive expression.

graziös. (Ger.) Graceful. A commonly used character word. (Fr. *gracieux*, It. *grazioso*, Sp. *gracioso*.)

grazioso. (It.) Graceful. A commonly used character word. (Fr. *gracieux*, Ger. *graziös*, Sp. *gracioso*.)

Green, Elizabeth A. H. (1906–1995.) Best known for her conducting text, ***The Modern Conductor*** (1961), it appeared in its seventh edition in 2004 and was based on the principles of the Russian American conductor **Nikolai Malko**, with whom Green studied. She also completed and published Malko's unfinished companion volume to his 1950 book, titled *The Conductor and His Score* (1975, reissued in 1985 as *The Conductor's Score*), with coauthor credits for Green and Malko. Other publications include *Orchestral Bowings and Routines* (1949, 1957) and *The Dynamic Orchestra* (1987).

Green graduated from Wheaton College (1928) with a B.S. in philosophy and a minor in physics, having fulfilled the musical requirements before she finished high school. She became a strings teacher in Waterloo, Iowa; organized and played in the Waterloo Symphony; and completed a master's of music at Northwestern University (1939). She became the director of the orchestra at the Ann Arbor Michigan Public Schools (1942) and built the group from just nine players to a full, sixty-piece symphony orchestra. Later, Green was hired to teach at the University of Michigan (1945–1974). She spent many summers working with Ivan Galamian and taught his violin techniques and principles. See the **bibliography**.

greifen. (Ger.) To play, to touch. Also *spielen*. (Fr. *jouer, toucher*; It. *suonare, tocare*; Sp. *tocar*.)

grezzo. (It.) Harsh, rough, rude. A character word sometimes heard in rehearsal. Used by Maurice Ravel in the score to his ballet *Daphnis et Chloé*. (Fr. *rude*, Ger. *rau*, Sp. *áspero*.)

Griffbrett. (Ger.) **Fingerboard**. The term refers to playing with the bow above the fingerboard on a string instrument. In German the expression is "*am* [on the] *Griffbrett.*"

gross, grosse, grosser. (Ger.) Big, great, large, ample. (Fr. *grand*; It. *gran, grande*; Sp. *gran*.)

grosse caisse. (Fr.) **Bass drum**. (Ger. *Grosse Trommel*; It. *gran cassa, gran tamburo*; Sp. *bombo*.) See also **appendix 4**.

Grosse Trommel. (Ger.) **Bass drum**. Abbreviated **G. Tr.** (Fr. *grosse caisse*; Sp. *bombo*; It. *gran cassa, gran tamburo*.) See also **appendix 4**.

G. Tr. (Ger.) Abbreviation for *Grosse Trommel*, **bass drum**.

Grove, George. (1820–1900.) Founding editor of *Grove's Dictionary of Music and Musicians*, now known as *The New Grove Dictionary of Music and Musicians*, an encyclopedic dictionary. Next to *Die Musik in Geschichte und Gegenwart*, it is the largest reference work on Western music. It is now available as the Internet resource *Grove Music Online*, an important part of **Oxford Music Online**.

Grove Music Online. An Internet resource available to subscribers, such as universities, online. It contains the complete text of *The New Grove Dictionary of Music and Musicians* with updates when they become available.

Grove's Dictionary of Music and Musicians. A music dictionary of encyclopedic scope. Along with the German-language *Die Musik in Geschichte und Gegenwart*, it is one of the largest reference works on Western music. Originally published as *A Dictionary of Music and Musicians*, it became *Grove's Dictionary of Music and Musicians* and is now known as *Grove Music Online*. First published in 1878 and edited by George Grove, *The New Grove Dictionary of Music and Musicians* was released in 1980 with senior editor Stanley Sadie. Supplemental dictionaries include *The New Grove Dictionary of Opera*, *The Grove Dictionary of American Music*, and *The New Grove Dictionary of Musical Instruments*.

ground bass. A Baroque term for figured bass, a bass line written with chord numbers below. Usually to be improvised by the performer. (Fr. *basse continue*, It. *basso continuo*.)

Grundbrechung. (Ger.) A term used by **Heinrich Schenker** to describe the use of a fundamental triad horizontally projected over the duration of a work in the bass line. According to **Schenkerian analysis**, the *Grundbrechung* and the **Urlinie** combined to make the **Ursatz** or fundamental harmonic structure of a piece. See also **Schenkerian Analysis**.

Grundgestallt. (Ger., lit. "basic shape.") Term coined by **Arnold Schoenberg** to describe the underlying conception of a work, including all of its aspects, not just the **twelve-tone row**.

Grundreihe. (Ger.) The basic or prime form of a **twelve-tone row** without putting it through any transposition or transformation.

Gsp. (Ger.) Abbreviation for *Glockenspiel*.

Guggenheim, John Simon Memorial Foundation. See **John Simon Guggenheim Memorial Foundation Fellowships**.

Guildhall School of Music and Drama. Located next to the **Barbican Centre** in the City of London since 1977, the school offers both undergraduate and graduate programs in music, opera, drama, and technical theater arts, as well as a college preparatory program called Junior Guildhall. Founded in 1880, the school has grown to nine hundred students. In 2008, work began on the renovation of the Milton Court complex, providing new performance and rehearsal spaces, offices, teaching studios, a TV studio, and a costume department.

"guillotine" downbeat. This technique is used when a piece begins with a rest on the downbeat. The **conductor** holds the baton at the top of the beat in the ready position and allows the baton to drop to the beat plane, defining the downbeat with an ictus that the ensemble responds to. It is often used when conducting orchestral recitative. See also **appendix 8: "Conducting Recitative."**

Guillotine downbeat. *Courtesy Derek Brennan.*

Guinand, María. (b. 1953.) Venezuelan choral **conductor**. Guinand studied at the University of Bristol, England. She has been the dean at the Jose Angel Lamas Music School and a professor of music at the Simón Bolívar University in Caracas. She leads several **choirs** in Venezuela and has served on the executive committee of the International Music Council of UNESCO. Guinand is known for her work with Osvaldo Golijov's *St. Mark Passion*, commissioned by **Helmuth Rilling** and premiered at the 2000 European Music Festival, having performed it around the world. She wan a **Grammy** nomination for her recording of the work in 2001. In 2006, she served as chorus master for the premiere of John Adams's opera *A Flowering Tree* in Vienna and the subsequent recording with the **London Symphony Orchestra** on **Nonesuch Records**.

guiro. A large gourd, thin at the ends and large in the middle with a serrated side that is scraped with a wooden stick. See also **appendix 4**.

guitar. A widely popular instrument that exists in many different types; most broadly, it divides into acoustic and electric. Usually having six strings that are plucked or strummed, it belongs to the instrument family of chordophones and is made of wood with nylon or steel strings. The acoustic guitar is a quiet instrument, and when used in the orchestra or as a solo instrument, it requires amplification. (Fr. *guitare*, Ger. *Gitarre*, It. *chitarra*, Sp. *guitarra*.)

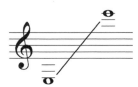

Guitar range as it sounds. *Courtesy Andrew Martin Smith.*

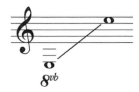

Guitar range as written. *Courtesy Andrew Martin Smith.*

guitar. (Fr.) **Guitar**. (Ger. *Gitarre*, It. *chitarra*, Sp. *guitarra*.) Example: *Quasi Guitara le Violon sous le bras*, a directive to play the chords in the music like a guitar, with the violin beneath the arm, from "Le matin d'un jour de fête" from "Ibéria" of *Images* by Claude Debussy.

guitarra. (Sp.) **Guitar**. (Fr. *guitar*, Ger. *Gitarre*, It. *chitarra*.)

Gulbenkian Orchestra. Founded in 1962 in Lisbon, Portugal, as the Gulbenkian Chamber Orchestra, it has grown to an ensemble of sixty-six permanent musicians. The orchestra has recorded for Teldec and Virgin Classics. The current principal conductor is Paul McCreesh. Past conductors include Lawrence Foster (2002–2013), Muhai Tang (1988–2001), Claudio Scimone (1979–1986), Juan Pablo Izquierdo (1976–1979), and Michael Tabachnik (1973–1976). **Susanna Mälkki** became the principal guest conductor in 2013.

Gustav Mahler Conducting Prize. A conducting competition for young **conductors** thirty-five years and younger in Bamberg, Germany. It was founded by the Bamberg Symphony Orchestra with the goal of helping young conductors at the beginning of their careers. In 2013, the winner was Israeli conductor Lahav Shani.

gusto, al. (Sp.) At the pleasure of the performer, a directive that suggests freedom of tempo and expression on the part of the performer. (Fr. *librement*, Ger. *nach Belieben*, It. *a piacere*.)

gusto, con. (It., Sp.) With relish, with style, with taste. A descriptive expression that may be heard in rehearsal. (Fr. *avec goût*, Ger. *mit Geschmack*.)

***gut* or *gut gemacht*.** (Ger.) Good, well done. Often heard in rehearsal. (Fr. *bien*; It. *ben, bene*; Sp. *bueno*.)

H

H. (Ger.) B natural.

Habeneck, François-Antoine. (1781–1849.) French violinist, **conductor**, and composer. Having studied violin at the **Paris Conservatory**, he joined the orchestra at the Opera Comique in 1804, but after a very short tenure he moved to the **Paris Opéra**. In 1817, he became the principal violinist, a position that at that time was similar to being the assistant conductor in that he was considered the leader of the strings. Habeneck was the director of the Paris Opéra (1821–1824), shared the position of *premier chef* with conductor **Henri Valentino** (1824–1831), and when Valentino became the conductor at the Opéra-Comique, he served again on his own (1831–1846). During those years, he went from being a leader on the violin to a conductor who lead with a baton, making the transition from one of many leaders in the pit to the sole leader. As a conductor, he was known for raising the standard of playing to an unprecedented level and became known as one of the leading conductors of his day. Habeneck conducted numerous operatic premieres, including Gioacchino Rossini's *Guillaime Tell*, Giacomo Meyerbeer's *Robert le diable* and *Les Huguenotes*, Fromental Halévy's *La Juive*, and **Hector Berlioz**'s *Benvenuto Cellini*. He also conducted the premiere of Berlioz's *Symphonie fantastique* in 1830.

His most notable and perhaps most enduring legacy was introducing symphonies of Ludwig van Beethoven to the French audiences. Habeneck led the student orchestra at the Paris Conservatory from 1896 to 1915 in what were called *exercices publics*. Under Habeneck's leadership the student ensemble gave the Paris premiere of Beethoven's Symphony No. 1 in 1807 quickly followed by the Symphony No. 2. Some mention was made of a performance of the Symphony No. 3 "Eroica" in 1811 with the same ensemble. In 1818, Habeneck took over the *concerts spirituels* at the opera, a forum he used to introduce overtures and the "Allegretto" of Beethoven's Symphony No. 7. In 1826, he conducted the third symphony again with a group of invited musicians and two

years later in 1828, the ensemble now officially a professional orchestra under the name **Orchestre de la Société des Concerts du Conservatoire**. In March of the same year, they performed the Symphony No. 3 yet again. Under Habeneck's leadership, they were an orchestra of eighty-six musicians when the standard complement was closer to sixty. Shortly after the "Eroica" they performed Symphony No. 5 and in 1831 Symphony No. 9. Habeneck remained with the orchestra until his death, conducting 184 concerts, and he successfully maintained a reputation for the highest standards of performance, drawing public acclaim from both Felix Mendelssohn and **Richard Wagner**. He taught violin at the Paris Conservatory twice, once from 1808 to 1816 and again from 1825 to 1848. His violin method book appeared sometime around 1835. It is understood that Habeneck conducted from the violin part with instrumental cues written in while using a bow, early on in his career playing along with his section in the traditional manner. Only later did he begin to use a baton and take on the role of the sole leader or conductor. See D. K. Holoman. "The Emergence of the Orchestral Conductor in Paris in the 1830s." In *Music in Paris in the Eighteenth-Thirties*, edited by Peter Bloom. Stuyvesant, NY: Pendragon Press, 1987.

François-Antoine Habeneck.

hacerse. (Sp.) To become. Also **convertirse**. (Fr. *devenir*, Ger. *werden*, It. *diventare*.) Used frequently in phrases such as "becoming louder." Example: *Debe hacerse más fuerte*, it has to become louder.

Haïm, Emmanuelle. (b. 1967.) French harpsichordist and **conductor**. Haïm was a founding member and the artistic director of the orchestra and chorus of Le Concert d'Astrée. The ensemble has been in residence at the Lille Opéra since 2004 and has toured widely in Europe and the United States. Since 2011, they have had an exclusive recording contract with **Virgin Classics**. Haïm studied harpsichord with Kenneth Gilbert and Christophe Rousset and conducting at the Centre de Musique Baroque de Versailles and the **Paris Conservatory**. She conducted Geroge Frideric Handel's *Rodelina and Theodora* for the Glyndebourne Touring Opera, followed by Handel's *Giulio Cesare* (2006) and Claudio Monteverdi's *L'Incoronazione di Poppea* (2008) at the main **Glyndebourne Festival**. She has served as a guest conductor with the **City of Birmingham Symphony Orchestra**, the **Scottish Chamber Orchestra**, the Deutsche Sinfonie-Orchester Berlin, the Frankfurt Radio Symphony Orchestra, and the **Berlin Philharmonic Orchestra**.

Haitink, Bernard. (b. 1929.) Dutch **conductor**. Haitink studied violin and conducting at the Amsterdam Conservatory, joined the **Netherlands Radio Philharmonic Orchestra** as a violinist, participated in two annual conductors' courses run by the Netherlands Radio Union (1954–1955), and was guided early on by conductor Ferdinand Leitner. In 1955, he was appointed as the second conductor at the Radio Union, working with four orchestras. In 1956, he was a successful last-minute replacement for a performance of Luigi Cherubini's *Requiem* with the **Royal Concertgebouw Orchestra**; the next year he became the principal conductor of the Netherlands Radio Philharmonic Orchestra. In 1961, he became the youngest principal conductor of the Royal Concertgebouw Orchestra (1961–1988). Initially, it was in a joint appointment with **Eugen Jochum**, but he became the sole conductor in 1964. Haitink guest conducted the **London Philharmonic Orchestra** in 1964 and became its principal conductor and artistic adviser in 1967 and then artistic director in 1970, remaining until 1979. He served as the music director of the **Glyndebourne Festival** from 1977 to 1988. Among his performances there, many of which were released as live recordings, were Wolfgang Amadeus Mozart's *Così fan tutte*, *Don Giovanni*, and *Le nozze di Figaro*; Ludwig van Beethoven's *Fidelio*; **Richard Strauss**'s *Arabella*; Sergei Prokofiev's *The Love for Three Oranges*; and **Sir Benjamin Britten**'s *A Midsummer Night's Dream*. Haitink made his **Metropolitan Opera** debut in 1982,

conducting *Fidelio*, and guest conducted several times at the **Royal Opera House, Covent Garden**, becoming its music director in 1987. Among his most acclaimed Covent Garden performances were **Richard Wagner**'s *Tristan und Isolde*, *Die Meistersinger*, and a **Ring cycle**; Pyotr Tchaikovsky's *The Queen of Spades* (alternatively known as *Pique Dame*); Giuseppe Verdi's *Don Carlos* and *Falstaff*; Alexander Borodin's *Prince Igor*; and Britten's *Peter Grimes*. He was known for introducing purely orchestral concerts with the Covent Garden Orchestra. Haitink was the principal guest conductor of the **Boston Symphony Orchestra** (1995–2004), chief conductor of the **Dresden Staatskapelle** (2002–2004). Following a guest conducting engagement with the **Chicago Symphony Orchestra** in 2006, Haitink accepted the orchestra's position of principal conductor, working with them until 2010. He has recorded principally for Phillips, **Decca**, **EMI** Classics, LSO Live (London Symphony), KCO Live, and CSO Resound (Chicago Symphony), including the complete symphonies of Beethoven, Johannes Brahms, Robert Schumann, Tchaikovsky, Anton Bruckner, **Gustav Mahler**, Dmitri Shostakovich, and Ralph Vaughan Williams; the late operas of Mozart; the Ring cycle of Wagner; and much more. His recording of Leoš Janáček's *Jenůfa* with the Royal Opera House, Covent Garden, received a **Grammy Award** for best opera recording in 2004. He has received many awards and honors, including an honorary knight commander of the Order of the British Empire (1977) and the Order of the House of Orange in the Netherlands (2000). He was named **Musical America**'s Musician of the Year in 2007.

Haitink is known as a man of few words, often leading an entire rehearsal virtually without speaking, except perhaps to correct a wrong note in a part. He has been called unassuming but confident, shy but approachable. In interviews, he reveals a preference for being a conductor who fits into a collaborative musical organization, not one that simply dictates. He calls the experience of concert performance instinctual but also feels that he never has enough time to finish his score study. For Haitink, words don't help if the conductor doesn't have the ability to communicate with the orchestra through manual dexterity, a musical personality, and genuine love of the music. His interpretations demonstrate a strong sense of the architecture of a piece, his deep understanding creating a sense of satisfaction for his audience.

Halbe. (Ger.) Half note. Also *halb*, half. (Fr. *blanche*; It. *metà*, *minima*; Sp. *blanca*.) Example: *schlagen in halben Noten*, conducted in half notes. See also **appendix 7**.

Halbe Pause. (Ger.) Half note rest. (Fr. *demi-pause*, It. *pausa di minima*, Sp. *silencio de blanca*.) See also **appendix 7**.

Halbton. (Ger.) Half tone, semitone. (Fr. *demi-ton*, It. *semitono*, Sp. *semitono*.) See also **appendix 6**.

Hälfte. (Ger.) Half the section in a divided string passage, usually the outside players on each stand. This indication only appears in string parts. (Fr. *la moitié*, It. *la metà*, Sp. *mitad*.)

Hallé, Charles. (1819–1895.) German **conductor** who moved to Manchester, England, from Paris after the Revolution of 1848 and turned what was an occasional orchestra into a permanent one with an ongoing season. See also **Hallé Orchestra**.

Hallé Orchestra. Now known as "the Hallé," the orchestra was founded in 1857 by German **conductor Charles Hallé**. It is the oldest extant orchestra in the United Kingdom. **Hans Richter** served as the conductor from 1899 to 1911, giving the premiere of Sir Edward Elgar's Symphony No. 1. During the years of World War II, the orchestra suffered financially, but from 1943 to 1970, while serving as the principal conductor, **Sir John Barbirolli** gradually restored the orchestra to prominence. Under his direction, they made several first recordings of works such as Ralph Vaughan Williams's Symphony No. 8. Other distinguished conductors include **Sir Thomas Beecham** (musical advisor 1915–1920), Sir Hamilton Harty (1920–1934), **Sir Malcolm Sargent** (1939–1942), James Loughran (1972–1983), Stanisław Skrowaczewski (1983–1992), **Kent Nagano** (1992–1999), and Mark Elder (2000–present.)

hall tours. An outreach program offered in many communities where interested people are invited to go on a tour of a concert or opera hall, usually including the backstage area, a part of the hall generally not seen by the public.

Hals. (Ger.) The neck of a string instrument. (Fr. *manche*; It. *manico*; Sp. *mango*, *mástil*.)

Hals und Beinbruch! (Ger.) An expression meaning "Good Luck!" or "Break a leg!" used before a concert or performance. Also *"Toi, toi, toi."* (Fr. *trois fois merde*, It. *in bocca al lupo*, Sp. *buena suerte*.)

Halt. (Ger.) Stop, hold. Also *halten*, to stop, to hold; *aushalten*, to hold out, to sustain. (Fr. *tenir*, It. *tenere*) See also *tenuto*, *fermata*.

Haltebogen. (Ger.) Tie, as in to tie or slur two or more notes together. (Fr. *signe de tenue*; It. *legatura di valore*; Sp. *ligar*, *ligadura de prolungación*.)

Haltung. (Ger.) **Fermata**, pause. Also *Fermate*. (Fr. *point d'arrêt*; It. *fermata*, *corona*; Sp. *calderòn*, *corona*.)

Hamburg Philharmonic State Orchestra (Philharmoniker Hamburg). The orchestra of the **Hamburg State Opera**, it was founded in 1828 as the Philharmonic Society. In 1934, it merged with the orchestra of the State Theater. Its current music director is Australian **Simone Young**. Past music directors have included **Karl Muck**, Eugen Jochum, Wolfgang Sawallisch, Horst Stein, Aldo Ceccato, Hans Zender, Gerd Albrecht, and Ingo Metzmacher.

Hamburg State Opera (Hamburgische Staatsoper). Founded in 1678 to bring secular music to Germany in the form of opera, making it available to the people. The first opera house in Hamburg was erected in 1677. Some of the great composers of the time worked in Hamburg, including George Frideric Handel, Johann Mattheson, and Georg Philipp Telemann, to name just a few. Handel worked as a violinist and harpsichordist with the opera. Through the vicissitudes of history, funding problems, religious controversy, and world wars, opera has continued in Hamburg. Today Hamburg remains an important European opera capital. The host to significant premieres, innovative productions, world famous conductors and soloists, the opera is also the home of the **Hamburg Philharmonic State Orchestra (Philharmoniker Hamburg)**. Its current principal music director is Australian **Simone Young**.

Hamlisch, Marvin Frederick. (1944–2012.) American composer and **conductor**. Hamlisch is one of only eleven to have won an Emmy, **Grammy**, Oscar, and Tony (abbreviated as EGOT). A successful composer of film music (including *The Way We Were* and *The Sting*), Broadway musicals (including *A Chorus Line*), and popular songs, Hamlisch was the prinicpal pops conductor of the Baltimore, Buffalo, Dallas, Milwaukee, Pittsburgh, San Diego, and Seattle symphonies, the **National Symphony**, and Pasadena Symphony Pops.

hammered. A bowing term indicating a hard, heavily articulated stroke with one bow per stroke. Also called *martellato* and *martelé*.

hampe. (Fr.) Stem of a note. Also *queue de la note*. (Ger. *Notenhals*, It. *gambo*, Sp. *plica*.)

Hand. (Ger.) Hand. (Fr. *main*, It. *mano*, Sp. *mano*.) Examples: *die linke Hand*, the left hand; *die rechte Hand*, the right hand.

Handel and Haydn Society (H&H). Founded in 1815 in Boston, it is the oldest oratorio society in the United States. The society has presented American premieres of numerous major European works, and under its current music director, Harry Christopher, it is now recognized for its performance practice style with a period instrument orchestra and fully professional choir. H&H is widely known through its tours and performances broadcast on **WGBH/99.5 Classical**, **NPR**, and **American Public Media**.

Hanson, Howard. (1896–1981.) American composer, **conductor**, and pedagogue. He was the first American composer to win the **Prix de Rome**, spending three years there studying with Ottorino Respighi (1921–1923). On his return, he was appointed as the director of the **Eastman School of Music** in Rochester, New York, serving from 1924 to 1964. He built the school, which was founded in 1921, into one of American's most important music schools by appointing an outstanding faculty, expanding the curriculum, and building the orchestra program. He led them on a worldwide tour in the 1961–1962 season. In 1964, he founded the **Institute of American Music** at the Eastman School. The organization is devoted to the promotion of the publication and study of American music. A champion of American music, Hanson also founded the American Composers Concerts, an annual festival, where he led over 1,500 new works during his tenure at Eastman.

Hanson served on the boards of many national music organizations, including the **National Association of Schools of Music** (NASM), the **Music Teachers National Association** (MTNA), and the **Music Educators National Conference** (MENC), now the **National Association for Music Education** (NAfME), organizations that remain among American's important leadership organizations in the music field today. His list of compositions includes two operas—*Merry Mount* was presented at the **Metropolitan Opera**, New York, in 1934; seven symphonies, No. *2 "Romantic"* being the most famous (its main theme is played at the end of every concert at the **Interlochen Center for the Arts** and is known as the *Interlochen Theme*); several large choral works, including the *Song of Democracy* with a text by Walt Whitman; chamber music; and much more.

He was also an active conductor, making his début with the **New York Symphony Orchestra** (1924) at the invitation of **Walter Damrosch**. Hanson founded and conducted the **Eastman-Rochester Philharmonic**, an orchestra that consisted of the principal players of the **Rochester Philharmonic** and selected students from the Eastman School. It became a vehicle for recording not only his own music but also that of many other American composers. Recorded mostly on Mercury Records, they have been reissued on CD.

In addition to many articles and music criticism, Hanson wrote *The Harmonic Materials of Modern Music* (1960), an important text for the study of twentieth-century music. See the **bibliography**.

happening. A musical, theatrical, or multimedia event or performance, often involving improvisation and of a relatively informal and sometimes random nature. Such an event could have an overall theme or guiding principle and might include poetry readings, photographic projections, musical pieces, the playing of recordings, dance, and paintings. Historically they began in the 1950s and continued into the 1970s.

Harfe. (Ger.) **Harp**. (Fr. *harpe*, It. *arpa*, Sp. *arpa*.) See also **appendix 3**.

harmonic analysis. The study of a score according to its harmonic elements. See also **score study**.

harmonic cluster. A **tone cluster** performed on a piano by silently pressing down a group of adjacent keys and thus creating sympathetic vibrations.

harmonic motion. See **harmonic rhythm**.

harmonic planes. A term used to describe harmonic materials within a piece of music that are separated by key, as in **bitonality** or a **bichordal** structure, or by register, rhythmic contrast, or orchestration. Example: *Three-Score Set* by William Schumann (1943).

harmonic rhythm. The speed at which changes of harmony occur. In tonal music, harmonic rhythm feels stronger when the chords occur in root position and weaker when they are in first or second inversion. Similarly, harmonic rhythmic is stronger when chord changes happen on the strong beats of a measure rather than on weak ones. Harmonic rhythm can be either regular or irregular. It does not depend on tempo as the chord shifts that create it may occur any number of times during a measure, a phrase, or even a whole passage. In nontonal music, harmonic rhythm can be felt in similar ways depending on the harmonic system established in the piece by the composer. For instance, in minimal music, harmonic rhythm is created by changes of pattern.

harmonics. Also known as harmonic partials, harmonics are notes that occur naturally on string instruments, including the harp. So-called natural harmonics occur at the points or nodes of the overtone series on the string. Harmonics can also be produced on woodwind instruments by overblowing notes of the **harmonic series**. The most commonly used harmonic is at the interval of the octave. (Fr. *harmoniques*; Ger. *Flageoletttöne*, *Flageolett*; It. *suoni armonici*, *zufolo*; Sp. *armónico*.) See also **artificial harmonics**, **harmonic series**, **string harmonics**.

harmonic series. A composite of the natural **harmonics** that vibrate along with the fundamental pitch, as on a string, wind, brass, and some percussion instruments. The series or partials rising above the fundamental pitch C are: c, g, c′, e′, g′, b♭, c″, d″, e″, f♯″, g″, a″, b♭″, b♮, c‴.

Harmonic series. *Courtesy Andrew Martin Smith.*

harmonics, string. See **string harmonics**.

harmonie. (Fr.) Harmony, chords. (Ger. *Harmonie*, It. *armonia*, Sp. *armonía*.)

Harmonie. (Ger.) Harmony, chords. (Fr. *harmonie*, It. *armonia*, Sp. *armonía*.)

harmonique. (Fr.) Harmonic. (Ger. *Flageolett*; It. *armonico*, *zufolo*; Sp. *armónico*.) See **artificial harmonics, harmonics, harmonic series, string harmonics**.

harmoniques. (Fr.) **Harmonics**. (Ger. *Flageoletttöne*; It. *suoni armonici*; Sp. *armónico*.) See also **artificial harmonics, harmonic series, string harmonics**.

Harmon mute. See **brass mutes**.

harmony. The simultaneous sounding of pitches. Basic harmony is the formation of chords underlying a melody. Western harmony originated with counterpoint, the simultaneous sounding of independent lines. For detailed discussions of the study of harmony, see "Analytical and Theoretical Books" in the **bibliography**. See also **axis system, pandiatonicism, parallelism**.

Harnoncourt, Nicholas. (b. 1929.) Austrian **conductor**. A renowned early music specialist, Harnoncourt began as a cellist in the **Vienna Symphony** (1952–1969). He founded the period-instrument ensemble Concentus Musicus Wien with his wife, Alice Hoffelner, in 1953. Harnoncourt made his operatic debut at **La Scala, Milan**, in 1970, leading a performance of Claudio Monteverdi's *Il ritorno d'Ulisse in patria*. Having left his position in the Vienna Symphony, he has dedicated the rest of his life to conducting. One of his first major projects was a near twenty-year-long collaboration with conductor **Gustav Leonhardt** to record all of the Bach Cantatas (**Teldec**) in their originally intended form using an all-male choir and soloists, except in Nos. 51 and 199, which specify female voice. In recent years, his repertoire has expanded to include the music of the nineteenth and twentieth centuries. He recorded Anton Bruckner's Symphony No. 9 and George Gershwin's *Porgy and Bess*. Other significant

recording projects include a Beethoven symphony cycle with the **Chamber Orchestra of Europe** and the Johann Sebastian Bach's *St. Mathew Passion*.

harp. The modern orchestral harp is a chromatic string instrument that changes pitch by means of a pedal. It has seven pedals from left to right. When all of the pedals are up, it produces D-flat, C-flat, B-flat, E-flat, and on the right, F-flat, G-flat, A-flat. When the pedals are depressed one notch, the strings yield the above pitches as all naturals, and when they are depressed to the lowest or third notch, the strings will sound with all pitches sharp. (Fr. *harpe*, Ger. *Harfe*, It. *arpa*, Sp. *arpa*.) See also **appendix 3**.

Harp range. *Courtesy Andrew Martin Smith.*

harpe. (Fr.) **Harp**. (Ger. *Harfe*, It. *arpa*, Sp. *arpa*.) See also **appendix 3**.

harpsichord. A keyboard instrument with a mechanism that plucks the strings, unlike the piano, which uses hammers. Used especially in the Baroque era both to realize figured bass and as a solo instrument. A revival of the instrument and its repertoire occurred in the twentieth century led by Wanda Landowska and encouraged contemporary composers to compose for the instrument once again. (Fr. *clavecin*, Ger. *Cembalo*, It. *cembalo*, Sp. *clavicordio*.)

Harris, Margaret. First black woman to lead a major symphony orchestra. Harris led the **Chicago Symphony Orchestra** in 1971. In the early 1970s, she conducted two Broadway hits, *Hair* and *Two Gentlemen of Verona*.

Harry Fox Agency. Founded in 1927 by the **American Music Publishers Association**, it is an agency that collects and distributes mechanical-recording license fees on behalf of American music publishers.

hart. (Ger.) Hard. A descriptive term used to evoke a particular tone, especially from percussionists. (Fr. *dur*, It. *duro*, Sp. *duro*.)

Hartfilz. (Ger.) A hard, felt-headed stick for timpani.

Harth-Bedoya, Miguel. (b. 1968.) Peruvian **conductor** who helped to establish the Orquesta Filarmonica de

Lima and the Compañía Contemporánea de Opera. Harth-Bedoya served as the music director of the **New York Youth Symphony** from 1993 to 1997, music director of the **Eugene Symphony** from 1996 to 2002, and became the music director of the **Fort Worth Symphony Orchestra** in 2000. In 2007, he founded the multimedia project **Caminos del Inka** in order to promote South American music, and in 2012, he was made the principal conductor of the Norwegian Radio Orchestra (KORK).

Hartt School. Founded in 1920 by Julius Hartt, the school has been a part of the University of Hartford since 1957. It offers undergraduate and graduate degrees in music, dance, and theater. It is the performing arts conservatory of the university.

The Harvard Biographical Dictionary of Music. Companion biographical dictionary to ***The Harvard Dictionary of Music***. See the **bibliography**.

The Harvard Dictionary of Music. A standard reference tool for music, first published in 1944. The first and second editions (1969) were edited by Willi Apel. The third edition appeared with the new title *The New Harvard Dictionary of Music* in 1986. It was edited by Don Michael Randel and was expanded to include additional entries on the twentieth century and world music. The fourth edition (2003) changed back to the original title. The dictionary does not include biographical entries but has a companion, ***The Harvard Biographical Dictionary of Music***.

Harvey, Raymond Curtis. (b. 1950.) African American **conductor**. Harvey served as the music director of the Texas Opera Theater (1978–1980), associate conductor of the **Des Moines Metro Opera, Exxon/Affiliate Artists/Arts Endowment Conductor** with the Indianapolis Symphony (1980–1983), music director of the Marion (Indiana) Philharmonic Orchestra (1982–1983), Springfield (Massachusetts) Symphony Orchestra (1986–1994), Fresno Philharmonic (1993–2000), El Paso Opera (1995–2007); associate conductor of the **Buffalo Philharmonic Orchestra** (1983–1986); and as artistic director of the El Paso Opera (2007–2009). He was appointed the music director of the Kalamazoo Symphony in 1999. Harvey has appeared as a guest conductor with the orchestras of Cleveland, Denver, Detroit, Los Angeles, Louisville, Minnesota, New York, Rochester, San Antonio, St. Louis, Tucson, Virginia, as well as the **Boston Pops Orchestra**, the **Houston Grand Opera**, the Indianapolis Opera, and the Berkshire Choral Institute, in addition to conducting the Radio City Music Hall production of George Gershwin's *Porgy and Bess*. Harvey received a DMA from the **Yale University School of Music** in 1984.

Hast. (Ger.) Haste, hurry. (Fr. *hâte*, *précipitation*; It. *fretta*; Sp. *prisa*.) Example: *ohne Hast*, without rushing, from Symphony No. 3, mvt. 3, by **Gustav Mahler**.

hasta. (Sp.) Until. (Fr. *jusque*; Ger. *zu bis*; It. *sin*, *sino*.) Example: *hasta el final*, to the end. (Fr. *à la fin*. Ger. *bis zum End*, *bis zum Schluss*; It. *al fine*.) See also **hasta el fin**.

hasta el fin. (Sp.) To the end. A directive sometimes used in pieces with multiple repeated sections in order to indicate the section that finishes the piece. (Fr. *à la fin*; Ger. *bis zum Ende*, *bis zum Schluss*; It. *alla fine*.)

hastig. (Ger.) Hurried, hasty. A descriptive word sometimes used in rehearsal. (Fr. *hâtif*, *pressé*; It. *affrettato*; Sp. *apresurado*.)

hâte. (Fr.) Haste, hurry. Also **précipitation**. (Ger. *Hast*, It. *fretta*, Sp. *prisa*.) Also *sans hâte*, without haste, leisurely. Example: *ne hâtez pas*, don't rush.

hâtif. (Fr.) Hurried hasty. A descriptive sometimes used in rehearsal. Also **pressé**. (Ger. *hastig*, It. *affrettato*, Sp. *apresurado*.)

Haupt. (Ger.) Head, principal, main. (Fr. *principal*, It. *principale*, Sp. *principal*.) See also **Haptrhythmus, Hauptstimme, Hauptthema, Hauptzeitmaß**.

Hauptrhythmus. (Ger.) Main rhythm. May refer to a particularly significant rhythmic figure or pattern in a composition. Most commonly used to describe elements of twelve-tone music.

Hauptrhythmus. Courtesy Andrew Martin Smith.

Hauptstimme. (Ger.) A notational device indicating the main voice or theme. A symbol often used by **Arnold Schoenberg**, Alban Berg, Anton Webern, and many composers thereafter to aid the conductor and performer in analyzing a complex composition. See also **Nebenstimme**.

Hauptstimme. Courtesy Andrew Martin Smith.

Hauptthema. (Ger.) The main theme or first theme. (Fr. *thème principal*; It. *primo tema, tema principale*; Sp. *tema principal*.)

Hauptzeitmaß. (Ger.) Main tempo. Example: *mäßig im Haput-zeitmaß*, moderately in the main tempo, from *The Prelude to Die Meistersingers von Nürnberg* by **Richard Wagner**.

Hausmusik. (Ger.) Music written to be played in the home. Generally, not technically difficult and often written for instruments with piano, such as the recorder or violin. See also ***Gebrauchtsmusik***.

hausse. (Fr.) **Frog** or heel (British usage) of the bow. Also ***talon***. Example: *à la hausse*, at the frog.

haut or ***haute.*** (Fr.) High in pitch or tuning. (Ger. *hoch*, It. *alto*, Sp. *alto*.)

hautbois. (Fr.) **Oboe**, also hoitboy (obsolete spelling). See also **appendix 3**.

hautbois d'amour. (Fr.) See *oboe d'amore*.

hauteur. (Fr.) **Pitch**. (Ger. *Tonhöhe*, It. *intonazione*, Sp. *entonación*.)

Hawaii Symphony Orchestra. Formerly known as the Honolulu Symphony Orchestra, the symphony was founded in 1900, making it the oldest orchestra in the western United States. The symphony has survived difficult financial times. In 2010, it was disbanded under bankruptcy laws but reformed as the Hawaii Symphony. The new orchestra is currently offering classics concerts, and **JoAnn Falletta** is its artistic director. Previous music directors include Samuel Wong (1996–2004), Fritz Hart (1937–1949), and Donald Johanos (1979–1994).

Hb. (Fr.) Abbreviation for ***hautbois***. See also **oboe**.

heavy staccato. Often conducted with either a heavy wrist flick on its own or combined with a motion in the elbow. The exact style of the gesture corresponds to the music.

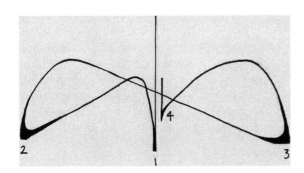

Conducting style, heavy staccato. *Courtesy Derek Brennan.*

Conducting style, heavy staccato in one. *Courtesy Derek Brennan.*

heckelphone. Named after its inventor, Wihlem Heckel, the heckelphone is a kind of bass **oboe**; it adds a half step to the low end of its range. It is written from A3 up to E6 but sounds an octave lower. (Fr. *heckelphone*, Ger. *Heckelphon*, It. *heckelphon*, Sp. *heckelfono*.)

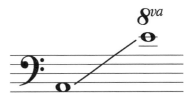

Heckelphone range as it sounds. *Courtesy Andrew Martin Smith.*

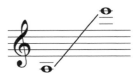

Heckelphone range as written. *Courtesy Andrew Martin Smith.*

heiter. (Ger.) Cheerful, happy, lively. Also ***fröhlich***. (Fr. *joyeuse, allègre*; It. *allegro*; Sp. *alegre*.)

hell. (Ger.) Brilliant, piercing, bright. (Fr. *éclatant*, It. *luminoso*, Sp. *brillante*.)

Helmholtz, Hermann. (1821–1894.) German scientist and founding director of the National Institute for Science and Technology (Physikalisch-Technische Bundesanstalt) in Berlin. The results of his studies are preserved in *On the Sensations of Tone* (*Die Lehre von den Tonempfindungen als physiologische Grundlage für die Theorie der Musik*, 1863, translated by A. J. Ellis and published in 1875) in which he makes connections between the natural sciences and music theory for the first time. Known for having studied the role of **harmonics**, explaining it in relation to timbre, explaining the nature of combination tones, and in particular discovering the higher combination or resultant tones. His work changed our understanding of music and set the stage for many developments in the twentieth century. See the **bibliography**.

Helsinki Philharmonic Orchestra. Founded in 1882, it is the first professional symphony orchestra founded in the Nordic countries. It has grown from an ensemble of 36 to 102 regular members. IT merged with the Helsinki Symphony Orchestra in 1914 and served as the orchestra for the Finnish National Opera until 1962. The inaugural chief conductor was Robert Kajanus (1892–1923). Other music directors have included **Paavo Berglund** (1975–1979) and Leif Segerstam (1995–2007). Segerstam led recordings of the complete Jean Sibelius symphonies, including the "original" Kullervo Symphony on the Ondine label. The orchestra won the French **Diapason d'Or Award** in 2008. Other recordings have included works of Einojuhani Rautavaara and Americans **John Corigliano** and Christopher Rouse. The current music director is John Storgards (appointed in 2008).

hemidemisemiquaver. A sixty-fourth note in English terminology. See also **rhythmic terms**.

hemiola. Based on the ratio of 3:2, a common compositional devise, the rhythmic hemiola is when three notes are written in the time of two. **Conductors** must decide whether to adjust the beat they give to the hemiola rhythm or stay with the underlying rhythm of two. A pitch hemiola, also determined by the 3:2 ratio, refers to the length of two strings that, when sounded together, produce a perfect fifth. Examples: the opening of the first movement of Symphony No. 3 by Johannes Brahms, and the final "Allejulah" section in the third movement of *Mathis der Maler* by Paul Hindemith.

Henry Wood's Promenade Concerts. See **BBC Proms**.

heptachord. A collection of seven pitches, in particular, the **diatonic scale**.

heptatonic scale. A scale of seven pitches. For example, the **diatonic scale**.

Herabstimmen. (Ger.) To tune down, of a string, for example. See also **scordatura**.

Heraufstimmen. (Ger.) To tune up or raise the pitch, of a string, for example.

Herbert, Victor. (1859–1924.) American composer, cellist, and **conductor**. Herbert was the cofounder, with John Philip Sousa, Irving Berlin, and others, of the **American Society of Composers, Authors and Publishers** (ASCAP), an agency that helped establish copyright benefits. He served as vice president for many years. As a cellist, he performed his own second cello concerto with the **New York Philharmonic Society** (1894), which is said to have inspired **Antonin Dvořák** to write his own. He was on the faculty of the **National Conservatory of Music**, teaching both cello and composition. Herbert served as the conductor of the **Pittsburgh Symphony** (1898–1904) and founded the Victor Herbert Orchestra, leading concerts of mostly light concert music and many recordings for **Edison Records** (1909–1911) and the **Victor Talking Machine Company** (1911–1923). He wrote over forty operettas, including *Babes in Toyland* (1903) and *Naughty Marietta* (1910), in addition to some of the first through-composed film scores, for example, *The Fall of a Nation* (1916) and *Indian Summer* (1919). His music has been widely performed and recorded.

Herbig, Günther. (b. 1931.) Czech-born conductor. Herbig studied conducting with **Hermann Scherchen**, Arvids Jansons (father of **Mariss Jansons**), and **Herbert von Karajan**. He made his debut at the Erfurt opera (1957); was appointed as the conductor to the German National Theather, Weimar (1957–1962); and was the director of the Hans-Otto Theater, Potsdam (1962–1966) and assistant conductor of the **Berlin Symphony Orchestra**, where **Kurt Sanderling** was the chief (1966–1972). In 1972, he became the music director of the Dresden Philharmonic Orchestra (1972–1977), taking it on tour throughout Europe, Japan, and the USSR. He returned to the Berlin Symphony as its chief conductor (1977–1983) and then began receiving invitations to conduct outside of East Germany, serving as the principal guest conductor with the **Dallas Symphony Orchestra** (1979–1981) and the BBC Northern Symphony Orchestra, Manchester (1981–1984). In 1984, he became the music director of the **Detroit Symphony Orchestra**, serving until 1990 and taking up residence in the United States. He guest conducted such orchestras as the Chicago and Boston symphonies, the New York and Los Angeles philharmonics, and the **Philadelphia Orchestra**. He held the same position with the **Toronto Symphony Orchestra** from 1988 to 1994. He continued to guest conduct into East Germany and received a national arts prize there in 1973. Herbig was the chief conductor of the German Radio Philharmonic, Saarbrücken Kaiserlautern, and was the principal guest conductor and music advisor (2003–2006 and 2009–present) of the Columbus Symphony Orchestra. He was also the artistic adviser and principal guest conductor of the Taiwan National Symphony Orchestra (2008–2010). Herbig has made several recordings with his orchestras in Berlin (Johannes Brahms's four symphonies and **Gustav Mahler**'s Symphony No. 5), Dresden (Joseph Haydn's Symphonies Nos. 93 to 104 on the East German Eterna label), Manchester, and Toronto, in addition to his recordings with the **Royal Philharmonic** and **Philharmonia** in London. He has been a proponent of composers in East Germany, leading premieres of works by Hans Eisler, Siegfried Matthus, Siegfried Thiele, Manfred Schubert, and Ruth Zechlin.

Herford, Julius. (1901–1981.) German-born American choral **conductor**, author, and pedagogue. His given name was Julius Goldstein. He studied at the Stern Conservatory in Berlin (1917–1923) and toured and worked as a pianist. In 1939, he accepted a position at the Teacher's College of Columbia University (1939–1941), changing his name to Herford on his arrival in New York. He also taught at the **Juilliard School, Berkshire Music Center**, Union Theological Seminary, **Manhattan School of Music**, and **Westminster Choir College** before moving to the **Indiana University School of Music**, where he remained for the rest of his career (1964–1980). He served as the director of graduate studies for the Department of Choral Conducting and was one of the most influential choral conductors and teachers in America. His students included **Robert Shaw, Margaret Hillis, Roger Wagner**, and **Elaine Brown**. He was a lifelong student of the repertoire, publishing numerous articles in a wide variety of professional journals.

hertz. A term derived from the name of the nineteenth-century German scientist **Heinrich Hertz** to stand for cycles per second. One hertz equals one cycle per second. See also **kilohertz**.

Hertz, Heinrich Rudolf. (1857–1894.) German scientist who first described, created, and measured electromagnetic waves of sound. See also **hertz**.

herunterstimmen. (Ger.) A term used to call for a lowering of the pitch or tuning. Also ***erniedrigen, tiefer stimmen***. (Fr. *baisser l'accord, baisser l'intonation*; It. *abbassare l'intonazione, abbassare l'accordatura*; Sp. *bajar la afinación*.) Examples of short directives concerning intonation: *Es ist zu hoch*, It is too high (in pitch); *Es ist ein bischen zu tief*, It is a little to low. See also ***scordatura***.

hervortretend. (Ger.) Indicates a main or prominent voice, theme, or motive that should be brought out. (Fr. *en dehors, en évidence*; It. *in fuori*; Sp. *destacar*.)

heterophony. The simultaneous presentation of two or more different versions of essentially the same melody. Often in the form of a melody presented with an ornamented version of itself, presented by a singer and then an instrumentalist. Appears in improvised music.

Heugel Music Publishing Company. Dating back to 1839 when Jacques Léopold Heugel worked in the company known as Jean-Antoine Meissonnier. He took over sole ownership in 1842. The firm was passed on to his son, Henri, stayed in the family until 1970, and was sold to Alphonse Leduc in 1980. Known in the nineteenth century for publishing opera and operetta, including the works of Jules Massenet, Jacques Offenbach, Ambroise Thomas, and others, in the twentieth century their collection was dominated by contemporary music of such composers as **Pierre Boulez**, Henri Dutilleux, Betsy Jolas, and **Gilbert Amy**.

hexachord. A series of six ascending stepwise pitches usually following the pattern of a whole step, whole step, half step, whole step, whole step, as occurs with the first six pitches of the C major scale, C–D–E–F–G–A, that are referred to as *ut–re–mi–fa–sol–la* in the **solmization** system. In this system, it is used as a memory tool along with the eight-note **diatonic scale**. In the twentieth century, the hexachord became known in **twelve-note music** used to describe the first or second six notes of the **row**. See Rochberg, George. *The Hexachord and Its Relation to the Twelve-Tone Row*. Bryn Mawr, PA: Presser, 1955.

hexatonic scale. Any scale using a sequence of six notes within an octave. The **whole-tone scale** is such a scale.

Hexatonic scale. *Courtesy Andrew Martin Smith.*

hier. (Ger.) Here, in place. Example: *von heir bis . . .* , from here until . . .

hierarchy in the orchestra. In a professional orchestra, the concertmaster ranks first, followed by the principal oboist, the principal horn, and then the timpanist. All other section principals outrank their section members. Access to the chief conductor can be based on this hierarchy.

High Fidelity. A music magazine published in America from 1951 to 1989 and a great source of information about developing technology, audio equipment, recordings, and articles about music history, as well as brief biographies. See also ***Ultra High Fidelity***.

hi-hat cymbal. A pair of cymbals about thirteen to fifteen inches in diameter operated by a foot pedal, usually part of a drum set and sometimes called a foot or "sock" cymbal. See also **appendix 4**.

Hilfslinien. (Ger.) Ledger lines, lines added above and below the **staff** in order to accommodate higher and lower pitches. (Fr. *ligne supplément*; It. *taglio addizionale, linea adicional, linea suplementaria*.)

Hillis, Margaret. (1921–1998.) American **conductor**. Hillis taught choral conducting at the **Juilliard School** (1951–1953) and the Union Theological Seminary (1950–1960). She formed the American Choral Foundation (now **Chorus America**) in 1954 and through it promoted higher standards of performance among choral ensembles. Hillis was invited by **Fritz Reiner** to become the founding conductor of the Chicago Symphony Choir. The first woman to conduct the **Chicago Symphony Orchestra**, Hillis was hailed when she substituted on short notice for an ailing **Sir Georg Solti** in a performance of **Gustav Maher**'s Symphony No. 8 (known as the "Symphony of a Thousand" because of its extremely large choral forces) in **Carnegie Hall**. She also served as the choral conductor at the **Cleveland Orchestra** (1969–1971) and the **San Francisco Symphony Orchestra** (1982–1983). She was the director of choral activities at Northwestern University (1970–1977). She was known among the members of her choirs as a conscientious leader who achieved excellent results through a detail-oriented rehearsal technique. She created a pamphlet called *At Rehearsals* that was used at the Chicago Symphony Choir throughout her tenure.

Hillis's guest conducting included the Baltimore, Columbus, Indianapolis, Milwaukee, Minnesota, National, Oregon, Saint Paul, San Antonio, San Francisco, and Spokane symphony orchestras; the New York Choral Society; the Los Angeles Master Chorale; the Gloria Dei Cantores; and the **Santa Fe Opera**.

himno. (Sp.) Hymn. (Fr. *hymne*, It. *inno*, Ger. *Hymne*.)

Hindemith, Paul. (1895–1963.) Prolific German composer, violinist, violist, **conductor**, and teacher. As a conductor, Hindemith led distinguished and important recordings of his own music, mainly with the **Berlin Philharmonic Orchestra** on **Deutsche Grammophone**, the **Philharmonia Orchestra** of London on **EMI**, and the **London Symphony**. He conducted his Requiem, *When Lilacs Last in the Dooryard Bloom'd*, with the **New York Philharmonic** on **Columbia Records** and appeared on television with the **Chicago Symphony** in the series Music from Chicago.

hinsterbend.(Ger.) Dying away, getting softer, fading. Also *entschwinden*. (Fr. *en défaillant*, It. *mancando*, Sp. *desapareciendo*.)

Hintergrund. (Ger.) Background. A term from **Schenkerian analysis** that describes background textures or harmonies.

His. (Ger.) B-sharp. See also **accidental**, **appendix 5**.

history of conducting. See **appendix 2**.

history of the baton. Precedents of the modern baton have been illustrated in artworks of the seventeenth to the nineteenth centuries. They often show a full-length staff used to audibly pound the beat on the floor; a shorter staff, approximately two to three feet long, held at the middle and raised up and down to show the beat (this can still be seen today in the marching band as led by the drum major); a white handkerchief held; a single roll of paper held in the middle that is used to beat silently; or even two roles of paper, one in each hand! Another precursor to the baton was the violin bow, used by the orchestra's concertmaster to show the pulse. The baton used today came into use in the nineteenth century by such conductors as **Hector Berlioz**, **Sir Michael Costa**, **Felix Mendelssohn**, and **Louis Spohr**. See also **baton**, **appendix 2**.

hoch. (Ger.) High. Also *höchst*, extreme, greatly; *höchster*, most extreme, highest, maximum. (Fr. *haut*, It. *alto*, Sp. *alto*.)

Hofkapelle. (Ger.) The court chapel. While it began as an institution for sacred music, in the seventeenth century the range of music expanded to include secular repertoire and even opera. During the nineteenth century the primary association with sacred music disappeared completely, and the term was used for any orchestra or other ensemble. See also *Hofkapellmeister*, *Kapellmeister*.

Hofkapellmeister. (Ger.) The main conductor at the *Hofkapelle*. The musical leader of a chapel. See also *Kapellemeister*.

Hofmannstahl, Hugo von. (1874–1929.) Austrian novelist, librettist, and poet. Hofmannstahl met composer **Richard Strauss** in 1900 and wrote the libretti for several of his operas, including *Elektra* (1909), *Der Rosenkavalier* (1911), *Ariadne auf Naxos* (1912, rev. in 1916), *Die Frau ohne Schatten* (1919), *Die ägyptische Helena* (1927), and *Arabella* (1933).

Hogg, Ima. (1882–1975.) American philanthropist. Hogg funded the first incarnation of the **Houston Symphony**, an ensemble of thirty-five musicians, beginning in 1913. She was a noted art collector who owned works of Pablo Picasso, Paul Klee, and Henri Matisse and donated hundreds of artworks to Houston's Museum of Fine Arts. She attended the University of Texas at Austin (1899–1902) studying music and moved to New York to study piano and music theory and after her father's death in 1906. She later traveled to Europe and studied music in Vienna.

Her family's wealth came in the form of oil discovered on their property and as such she felt that since it had been earned through luck, not through work, that most of the income should go to the people of Texas. Among her many charitable projects, she founded the Houston Child Guidance Center. She never married, and the beneficiary of the bulk of her will was the Ima Hogg Foundation, which she founded in 1964. The foundation carries on philanthropic work to this day. Contrary to popular belief, she never had a sister named Ura, only brothers. She donated property near **Round Top**, Texas, to the University of Texas at Austin that is now used for the Round Top Music Festival and museum.

Hogwood, Christopher (1941–2014.) English **conductor**, musicologist, and harpsichordist. Hogwood studied at Pembroke College, Cambridge, and Charles University, Prague. His early influences were the musicologist Thurston Dart, conductor **Raymond Leppard**, and his harpsichord teachers, Rafael Puyana and Gustav Leonhardt. He was a founding member with **David Munrow** of the influential **Early Music Consort** (1967–1976). In 1973, he and Peter Wooldand, a producer for **Decca Records**, established the **Academy of Ancient Music** with the purpose of recording the orchestral music of Thomas Arne. Its success on the **L'Oiseau Lyre** label led to many more such projects, beginning with Baroque music, Antonio Vivaldi, Johann Sebastian Bach and his sons, and soon expanding to cover the classics, with recordings of the complete symphonies of Wolfgang Amadeus Mozart and Ludwig van Beethoven, several Joseph Haydn symphonies, and the five Beethoven piano concertos with **Robert Levin** as soloist. Other collaborators were musicologist Neal Zaslaw and concertmaster Jaap Schroder. In 2006, he gave up the leadership position, becoming director emeritus. Under his leadership, the academy released over two hundred recordings on the **Decca** label, including several oratorios and Mozart's *Requiem* in a new edition by Richard Maunder, omitting all of Franz Xaver Sussmayr's posthumous additions. Hogwood has also led numerous performances and recordings of operas by such composers as Georg Frideric Handel, Henry Purcell, Mozart, Haydn, and **Igor Stravinsky** (*The Rake's Progress*). He has published several articles of relevance to the early music field and produced numerous music editions, among them music of John Dowland, the new complete works of C. P. E. Bach, Francesco Geminiani, Felix Mendelssohn, and the complete works of Bohuslav Martinů. His published books include a biography of Handel. Hogwood was the artistic director of the **Handel and Haydn Society**, Boston (1986–2001), and the Mostly Mozart Festival, London (1983–1985), and the conductor and early music specialist with the **St. Paul Chamber Orchestra** (1987),

becoming the principal guest conductor in 1991. More recently, his repertoire has expanded into the nineteenth and twentieth century, with a focus on composers such as Martinů, Stravinsky, **Sir Benjamin Britten, Aaron Copland**, Michael Tippet, and Arthur Honegger. Hogwood has appeared as a guest conductor with several American orchestras, including the Boston, Chicago, Detroit, and St. Louis symphonies. In addition to holding positions at several academic institutions in Britain and the United States, he is the recipient of many honors and awards. In 1989, he was made a CBE (commander of the British Empire, an honorary title) and in 1998 granted the ISM (Incorporated Society of Musicians, UK) Distinguished Music Award. See the **bibliography** for several books by Hogwood.

Hohe. (Ger.) High. Also *höher,* higher, superior; *noch höher*, still higher.

Höhe. (Ger.) Height, elevation. Example: *in die Höhe*, elevated, in the air, as in raising the bell of a wind or brass instrument. Seen often in symphonies of **Gustav Mahler** and others.

Höhepunkt. (Ger.) Climax, high point, as in a movement or piece. (Fr. *point culminant*, It. *punto culminante*.)

hold. Another term for *fermata*.

Hollywood Bowl. An outdoor amphitheater in Los Angeles, California, used since 1922 mostly for music performances. The summer home of the **Los Angeles Philharmonic**, it is renowned for its fine acoustics.

Holst, Imogen. (1907–1984.) English composer and conductor, daughter of Gustav Holst, and author of books about her father and a number of music text books, including *An ABC of Music, Conducting a Choir, Tune* (a study of the invention of melody and anthology of folksongs), and others. She was **Sir Benjamin Britten**'s assistant at the **Aldeburgh Festival** and served as its artistic director (1956–1977). She was made a commander of the Order of the British Empire (CBE) in 1975 and received several honorary degrees during her lifetime. See the **bibliography** for books by Imogen Holst.

Holz. 1. (Ger.) Wood. Example: *Holzschlägen*, wooden mallets.
   2. The woodwind section of an **orchestra** or **band**. (Fr. *instruments à vent, les bois*; Ger. *Blasinstrumente*; It. *strumenti a fiato, i legni*; Sp. *instrumentos de viento*.)

Holzbläser. (Ger.) Woodwind instruments. Also *Holz*. (Fr. *bois*; It. *legni, strumentini*; Sp. *instrumentos de madera*.)

Holzschlegeln. 1. (Ger.) Hard, wooden sticks. (Fr. *baguettes en bois*, Ger. It. *bacchette di legno*, Sp. *baqueta de madera*.)

2. An indication for the timpanist to play with wooden sticks.

Hong Kong Philharmonic. Originally established in 1895 as the amateur Sino-British Orchestra, it was renamed in 1957 and became entirely professional in 1974. The orchestra attracts players, **conductors**, and soloists from around the world and gives a full range of classics, educational, and outreach programs with over 150 concerts each year. The orchestra toured China in 1986 and North America in 1995. In 2003, it toured Europe, performing in London, Ireland, and Paris. The current music director, **Jaap van Zweden** (also music director of the **Dallas Symphony**), was appointed in 2012. Past music directors include Kek-tjiang Lim (1974–1975), Hans-Gunther Mommer (1977–1978), Ling Tung (1979–1981), Kenneth Schermerhorn (1984–1989), David Atherton (1989–2000), Samuel Wong (2000–2003), and **Edo de Waart** (artistic director and chief conductor, 2004–2012).

hooked bow. A term that describes a technique used by string players. Two separated **down-bows** in a row followed by two similarly separated **up-bows**, commonly used with dotted rhythms such as dotted eighth notes followed by sixteenth notes. This technique makes passages of repeated dotted rhythms flow easily, while bowing them as a down-bow followed each time by an up-bow creates more separation and is better in slower tempos with a heavier feel.

hörbar. (Ger.) Audible. Also *unhörbar*, inaudible. Example: *aber deutlich hörbar*, but clearly audible, from *Pierrot Lunaire* by **Arnold Schoenberg**.

hören. (Ger.) To hear, heard. (Fr. *entendre, entendu*; It. *udire*; Sp. *oír*.)

Horenstein, Jascha. (1899–1973.) Ukrainian-born **conductor**. As a young conductor, Horenstein was **Wilhelm Furtwängler**'s assistant and made his debut with the **Vienna Symphony Orchestra** in 1923. He became the music director of the **Berlin Symphony Orchestra** in 1925 and the chief conductor and later music director at the Düsseldorf Opera in 1928. There he conducted Alban Berg's opera *Wozzeck* under the composer's supervision. Banished by the Nazis in 1933, he traveled throughout the world, conducting orchestras in France, Belgium, Poland, the USSR, Australia, New Zealand, Scandanavia, and Palestine before moving to the United States in 1940, where he conducted the **New York Philharmonic**, the American Opera Society in a concert performance of Ferruccio Busoni's *Doktor Faust*, and the **American Symphony Orchestra** (1969). After the war years, he returned to Europe to conduct the **Deutsche Oper**, Berlin, and also at the **Royal Opera House, Covent Garden**. Horenstein made several superb recordings of **Gustav Mahler**'s and Anton Bruckner's symphonies, establishing a reputation for clarity of intent and sticking to the content of the score. His recordings also included works of **Paul Hindemith**, **Richard Strauss**, and Carl Nielsen's opera *Saul and David*.

horizontal motion. In conducting, this describes directional motions often used to indicate smoothness or legato style.

horn. Sometimes called the **French horn**, it is a transposing instrument that, in the orchestra, sometimes functions as a member of the woodwind section and sometimes as a member of the brass section. During the Classical period, it was commonly paired with the timpani, serving almost as a member of the percussion. The modern horn transposes down a fifth. It is standard practice to divide the modern horn section of four players into two of each, high and low. The normal range for the lower player is written C3 (with possible lower notes G2 and C1) and up to G5, sounding a fifth lower. The high pair generally play in a range written from C4 up to C6, sounding down a fifth. This division of labor allows players to concentrate on the techniques particular to the two ranges, which can be significantly different. (Fr. *cor*, Ger. *Horn*, It. *corno*) See also **appendix 3, natural horn**.

Horn F range as it sounds. *Courtesy Andrew Martin Smith.*

Horn F range as written. *Courtesy Andrew Martin Smith.*

Hörner. (Ger.) Plural of **horn**.

horn transpositions. Refer to the following table.

Horn written in:	Sounds:
C alto	as written
B-flat alto	major second lower
A	minor third lower
A-flat	major third loser
G	perfect fourth lower
F	perfect fifth lower
E	minor sixth lower
E-flat	major sixth lower
D	minor seventh lower
C basso	octave lower
B-flat basso	major ninth lower
A basso	octave and a major third lower

house parts. An expression referring to a set of parts to musical works that are owned by the library of an orchestra. Orchestras maintain these sets so that they can use them for repeated performances without having to remark bowing, articulation, and phrasing markings. Some orchestras will retire sets of parts that were marked in the hand of a particularly noted conductor or composer and keep them in an archive. For example, the **Cleveland Symphony Orchestra** Archive maintains many sets of parts and scores that conductor **George Szell** marked.

Houston Grand Opera (HGO). Founded in 1955, the HGO has presented more than forty-three world and six American premieres in the past forty years. Under the tenure of artistic and musical director Patrick Summers, the company grew significantly. The company maintains an impressive young artists' development program called the Houston Grand Opera Studio that was founded in 1977 by American composer Carlisle Floyd. The HGO is also active in outreach and educational programming. It runs teacher workshops, programs for students, presents Opera on the Go! portable performances to local schools, and has summer camps for young students interested in singing, composing, designing, and otherwise doing opera. The company also runs the Nexus Initiative to make sure that low-priced tickets are available to groups in the community who might not otherwise be able to afford them. The HGO has released many of its performances on recording on labels such as **Deutsche Grammophon**, **RCA**, and **Albany**.

Houston Symphony. As with most American orchestras, the Houston Symphony's history is somewhat erratic. The first performance by an ensemble that was eventually to become the Houston Symphony was in 1913 and sponsored by philanthropist **Ima Hogg**. The group had thirty-five part-time members at that time. They gave concerts until the beginning of World War I, disbanding in 1918. The orchestra formed again in 1930 as a semipro group, and in 1936, they officially became the Houston Symphony Society. By 1971, the orchestra had achieved its first fifty-two-week contract. Past music directors include Ernst Hoffman (1936–1947), **Leopold Stokowski** (1955–1961), **John Barbirolli** (1961–1967), **André Previn** (1967–1969), Lawrence Foster (1971–1979), **Sergiu Comissiona** (1980–1988), **Christoph Eschenbach** (1988–1999), and Hans Graf (2001–2013). The current music director is **Andrés Otozco-Estrada**.

Hsu, Apo (Apo Ching-Hsin Hsu). (b. 1956.) Chinese **conductor**. Hsu is the music director of the National Taiwan Normal University Symphony Orchestra and the Springfield Symphony Orchestra (Missouri.) She was also the artistic director of the **Women's Philharmonic** (San Francisco). She has guest conducted numerous orchestras, including the **National Symphony Orchestra**, the **San Francisco Symphony Orchestra**, the **Minnesota Orchestra**, the **Saint Louis Symphony Orchestra**, and others.

huitiéme de soupir. (Fr.) Thirty-second-note rest. See **appendix 7.**

Humor, mit. (Ger.) With humor. An expression sometimes used to evoke a particular character in music. Also *humorvoll.*

Hungarian National Philharmonic (Nemzeti Filharmonikus Zenekar). Founded in 1923 in Budapest as the Metropolitan Orchestra, the Hungarian National Philharmonic is one of the most distinguished in Hungary. The current music director is Zoltán Kocsis (appointed in 1997). Past conductors include Ken-Ichiro Kobayashi (1987–1997), János Ferencsik (1952–1984), László Somogyi and **Ferenc Fricsay** (1945–1952), Béla Csilléry (1939–1945), and Dezsö Bor (1923–1939). The orchestra was renamed the Hungarian Philharmonic in 1998. In 2003, a recording of the music of Claude Debussy and Maurice Ravel was released under the direction of Zoltán Kocsis and won Record of the Year from the Hungarian *Gramophone* magazine. Kocsis has also undertaken a recording project of the complete works of composer Béla Bartók on the Hungaroton label. In 2005, the orchestra, the National Choir, and the National Music Library moved into the Palace of Arts. The orchestra has expanded its concert series to include young people's concerts, a five o'clock concert series, and a series of open rehearsals of chamber music.

Hungarian scale. A seven-note scale used in Hungarian folk music that occurs in two forms.

Hungarian Scale

Hungarian scale 1. *Courtesy Andrew Martin Smith.*

Hungarian Scale

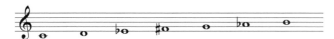

Hungarian scale 2. *Courtesy Andrew Martin Smith.*

Hungarian State Opera (Magyar Állami Operaház). Hungary's main opera company, located in Budapest, it maintains numerous operas in its repertoire, ranging from the standards to contemporary. Musicians from the state opera make up the **Budapest Philharmonic Orchestra**.

Hunsberger, Donald. (b. 1932.) Well-known wind ensemble **conductor**, pedagogue, and author (with Roy Ernst) of a conducting text, ***The Art of Conducting***. He served as the conductor of the **Eastman Wind Ensemble** from 1965 until his retirement in 2001. The ensemble made several recordings under his direction, including one with trumpeter Wynton Marsalis (CBS Masterworks). Hunsberger is also known for rescoring and conducting music for silent films and performance with major American orchestras. He has also made numerous transcriptions of orchestra works for **band**. He is a proponent of the **wind ensemble** concert with its fixed instrumentation based on the orchestral woodwinds, brass, and percussion, with one player on a part.

hüpfend. (Ger.) Frisky. Seen in the score for ***Pierrot Lunaire*** by **Arnold Schoenberg**.

hurtig. (Ger.) Quickly, fleet. (Fr. *vite,* It. *tosto,* Sp. *rápido.*)

Hymne. (Ger.) Hymn. (Fr. *hymne,* It. *inno,* Sp. *himno.*) See also **Lobgesang**.

hymne. (Fr.) Hymn. (Ger. *Hymne,* It. *inno,* Sp. *himno.*)

Hz. Abbreviation for **hertz**. See also **Hertz, Heinrich**.

I. The designation for the inversion of a **twelve-tone row**.

I°. (It.) First. Abbreviation for *primo, prima*.

ICE (International Contemporary Ensemble). A group of thirty-three players, singers, and composers that performs in various combinations, from solo and duo to large ensembles, in a range of venues, from concert halls to bars and clubs. Founded in 2001, ICE has premiered over five hundred works and issued recordings on the **Naxos**, Bridge, Tzadik, and New Focus labels. ICE's goals to build new audiences for contemporary music include the **Listening Room**, an educational initiative that uses team-based composition and **graphic notation** while interacting with students in a creative and experimental setting. See also **new music ensembles**.

Iceland Symphony Orchestra (ISO, Sinfóníuhljómsveit Íslands). Founded in 1950 in Reykkjavik with **conductor** Olav Kielland, the orchestra has ninety full-time musicians giving sixty concerts annually, including symphonic, family, and school concerts. It also tours internationally and has made several notable recordings on the BIS, Chandos, and Naxos labels, including a Sibelius symphony cycle, and the complete orchestral music of Icelandic composer Jón Leifs. The current music director is Ilan Volkov (appointed in 2011), who started a new contemporary music festival, "Tectonics."

I Ching. Commonly referred to in English as the *Book of Changes*, a Chinese manual dating from before 1000 BC and relating to the interpretation of sixty-four hexagrams formed by the manipulation of stalks. Used by John Cage in his **aleatoric** or **chance music** to generate and work with musical materials in a random way. Numerous English translations and commentaries are available.

iconic chords. Chords that through time have acquired a figurative or cultural meaning through association with a specific piece. See also **Copland chord**, **Petrouchka chord**, **Prometheus chord (mystic chord)**, **Schwantner chord**, **Tristan chord**.

Iconic chords. *Courtesy Andrew Martin Smith.*

ictus. From the Latin *icere*, to strike. A recurring stress or beat in a rhythmic or metric series of sounds. In conducting, an ictus is an incisive stroke that can occur on any beat of the bar, adding definition and clarity to the beat. See also **conducting technique**.

idée fixe. (Fr.) Leading motive or theme. Coined by **Hector Berlioz**, a recurring theme or motive that connects the movements of a symphonic work. (Ger. *Leitmotiv*; It. *motivo conduttore, motivo ricorrente*; Sp. *motivo conductor*.) See also ***Symphony Fantastique***.

igual. (Sp.) Equal, even. (Fr. *égal*, Ger. *gleich*, It. *equale*.) Example: *tresillos iguales*, equal triplets.

igualmente. (Sp.) Equally. (Fr. *également*; Ger. *gleichmäßig*; It. *ugualmente, equamente*)

im gleichen Tempo. (Ger.) The same tempo. Also ***dasselbe Zeitmaß***. (Fr. *le même mouvement*; It. *lo stesso tempo, l'istesso tempo*; Sp. *al mismo tempo*.)

imitieren. (Ger.) To imitate. Seen in scores and parts. Example: *Klarinette imitiert genau den Vortrag der Bratsche*, Clarinet imitate exactly the execution (playing) of the viola, from *Pierrot Lunaire* by **Arnold Schoenberg**.

immediatamente. (Sp.) At once, immediately, abrupt, sudden, suddenly. A descriptive word seen in scores and parts and heard in rehearsal. Also *súbito*. (Fr. *immédiatment, tout de suite*; Ger. *sofort, sogleich, unmittelbar*; It. *immediatamente, subito*.)

immediatamente. (It.) At once, immediately, abrupt, sudden, suddenly. A descriptive word seen in scores and parts and heard in rehearsal. Also *subito*. (Fr. *immédiatment, tout de suite*; Ger. *sofort, sogleich, unmittelbar*; Sp. *immediatamente, súbito*.)

immédiatement. (Fr.) Immediately, right away, abrupt, sudden, suddenly. A descriptive word seen in scores and parts and heard in rehearsal. Also **subitement, tout de suite, tout á coup**. (Ger. *sofort, sogleich, unmittelbar*; It. *immediatamente, subito*; Sp. *immediatamente, súbito*.)

immer. (Ger.) Always. Examples: *immer gleichmäßig leicht*, always consistently light; *immer bewegter im Vortrage*, always played with forward motion (lit. "always moving in its presentation"), from *The Prelude to Die Meistersinger von Nürenberg* by **Richard Wagner**; *immer schnell*, always fast; *immer forte*, always loud.

immer geteilt. (Ger.) Always divided. A directive that tells players to divide the music throughout a piece or passage or until notified. Most often seen in string parts as orchestral music is often divided between players within a string section.

immer mit Dämpfer. (Ger.) Always muted.

immer schwacher und schwacher. (Ger.) Always getting softer and softer.

immobile. (It.) Immobile, motionless.

imperceptible. (Fr., Sp.) Imperceptible, indiscernible, imperceptibly, as referring to an extreme dynamic. (Ger. *unmerklich, unvernehmlich*; It. *impercettibile*.)

impercettibile. (It.) Imperceptible, indiscernible, imperceptibly, as referring to an extreme dynamic. (Fr. *imperceptible*; Ger. *unmerklich, unvernehmlich*; Sp. *imperceptible*.)

impiccagione libero. (It.) Suspended, free hanging, as with a suspended cymbal. (Fr. *suspension libre*, Ger. *freihängend*, Sp. *libre suspensión*.)

impressionism. A movement that began in the visual arts in the late nineteenth century with painters such as Paul Cézanne, Claude Monet, Camille Pissaro, Pierre-Auguste Renoir, Alfred Sisley, and others who created images generally set outdoors using diffuse light, often more suggestive than specific. In music, impressionism is chiefly associated with Erik Satie, Claude Debussy, and Maurice Ravel, beginning with Satie's elusive piano pieces, *Gymnopédies*, and then with most of the works of Ravel and Debussy, whose compositions are often characterized by an avoidance of strong cadences, the use of whole tone scales, parallel harmonies, and finely conceived orchestral colors. The only American impressionist composer was Charles Griffes, who studied in Paris. In the twentieth century, some composers, such as Toru Takemittsu, took up the impressionist mantle.

impulse of will. The ability of a **conductor** to use will power to convincingly communicate intent to the orchestra. See also **active gestures, conducting technique**.

im Takt. (Ger.) In time, steady. A directive used often in rehearsal. Also *taktmässig*. See also **Takt, Taktart, Takt halten, Taktmesser, Takt schlagen, taktieren, Taktstrich, Taktzahl, Taktzeichen**.

Inbal, Eliahu. (b. 1936.) Israeli **conductor**. Inbal studied violin and composition with Paul Ben-Haim at the **Jerusalem Academy of Music**, making his first appearance as a conductor with the Youth Symphony Orchestra of Israel in 1956. During his compulsory military service, he was assigned to lead the Army Symphony Orchestra. In 1958, he went to Europe to study with **Franco Ferrara** in Holland; **Sergiu Celibidache** in Hilversum, the Netherlands; and then with Max Fourestier at the **Paris Conservatoire** (1960–1963). He won the 1963 Guido Cantelli conducting prize in Novara, Italy. He made his Salzburg Festival debut with the Vienna Philharmonic in 1969 and had his British debut with the **London Philharmonic Orchestra** in 1965, leading to invitations to conduct other orchestras in Britain. He had several early successes with opera, conducting **Richard Strauss**'s *Elektra* in Bologna, Italy; Giuseppe Verdi's *Don Carlos* in Verona, Italy; and the first performance of Luigi Cherubini's opera-ballet *Anacréon, or L'amour fugitif* since its premiere in 1803/1804. Inbal held the position of chief conductor of the **Frankfurt Radio Symphony Orchestra** from 1974 to 1990 and was made conductor laureate in 1996. Inbal was the honorary conductor of the Orchestra Nazionale della RAI, Turin, Italy, from 1995 to 2001. He served as the artistic director at the **Teatro La Fenice** in Venice from 1986 to 1989 and again from 2007 to 2011. He also conducted the **Berlin Symphony Orchestra**, now known as the **Konzerthaus Orchester Berlin**, from 2001 to 2006.

Inbal's legacy of recordings includes orchestral works of Hector Berlioz, Maurice Ravel, Alexander Scriabin, Robert Schumann, **Igor Stravinsky**, **Strauss**, and the **Second Viennese School** composers and symphonies of Anton Bruckner, **Gustav Mahler** (complete), and Dmitri Shostakovich with such orchestras as the **RSO Frankfurt**, the **Philharmonia Orchestra**, **London Symphony Orchestra**, the **Orchestre National de France**, the **Vienna Symphony**, the Tokyo Metropolitan Symphony Orchestra, and the **Royal Concertgebouw Orchestra**, mostly on the Philips and Telefunken labels. His recordings of Bruckner's Symphonies Nos. 3, 4, and 8 are of the rarely recorded original versions.

in battere. (It.) **Downbeat**. Usually the first beat of the bar as indicated by the **conductor** with a downward gesture and an **ictus** on the pulse. (Fr. *temps fort*; Ger. *Abtakt*; Sp. *primer tiempo, tiempo fuerte*.) See also **conducting technique**.

in bocca al lupo. (It.) Good luck, break a leg. (Fr. *trois fois merde*; Ger. *Hals und Beinbruch, toi, toi, toi*; Sp. *buena suerte*.)

incalzando. (It.) A term that indicates pressing the tempo forward. (Fr. *appuyant*, Ger. *drängend*, Sp. *empujar*.)

incantando. (It.) Enchanted, delighted, bewitched. A character word. (Fr. *enchaînez, enchanté*; Ger. *verzaubert*, Sp. *encantado*.)

indebolire. (It.) Becoming weaker and softer. A descriptive term often used in rehearsal. (Fr. *affaibli, affaiblissez*; Ger. *schwächen*; Sp. *debilitándose*.)

independence of the hands. The ability to conduct different things at the same time in both hands. For example, using the left hand to cue the first violin section while simultaneously showing a decrescendo to the low brass. A good independence of hands is important to the **conductor** and can be developed. See also **ambidextrous conducting**, **conducting technique**, **exercises for independence of hands**.

in der Ferne. (Ger.) As if in the distance, to be played offstage. Examples: *in weiter Entfernung*, further in the distance, *in sehr weiter Entferung aufgestellt*, from Symphony No. 1, mvt. 1, by **Gustav Mahler**.

in der Oktave. (Ger.) A direction in music to play a passage up an octave. (Fr. *à l'octave*, It. *all'ottava*, Sp. *a la octava*.)

indeterminacy. As described by American composer John Cage, a new concept of music largely created outside of the intellectual control of the composer and removed from any strictures or boundaries previously conceived as guides for writing music. It is closely associated with **aleatoric music** in the sense that most choices are left up to the performer. An example of such a piece would be one in which a composer drips ink on a page of manuscript paper and asks the performer to interpret the resulting pitches, rhythms, and all other musical elements from the marks on the page. Another example is a piece where a sheet of music paper is displayed on an overhead projector, a jar of ants is emptied onto it, and the performer creates music according to the motion of the ants as they walk across the paper. See also **aleatory**, **chance music**.

Indianapolis Symphony Orchestra (ISO). Founded in 1930 by **conductor** and violinist Ferdinand Schaefer (music director 1930–1937). At the beginning it was made up of amateur musicians. It became a professional ensemble in 1937 and has grown into a fully constituted orchestra. Past music directors include Fabien Sevitsky (1937–1955), Izler Solomon (1956–1975), John Nelson (1976–1987), **Raymond Leppard** (1987–2001), and Mario Venzago (2002–2009). The current music director is Krzysztof Urbanski (appointed in 2011). Pops conductors have been **Erich Kunzel** (1982–2002) and Jack Everly (2002–present.)

Indiana University Jacobs School of Music. A music department was established in 1910 at the university in Bloomington and officially became the Jacobs School of Music in 1921, subsequently growing into one of the largest schools of music in the world. It has a comprehensive curriculum at the undergraduate and graduate levels. Wilfred C. Bain served as the dean from 1947 to 1973 and was responsible for changing the emphasis to performance and the development of performers, with performances of full operas and orchestral concerts. He built a distinguished faculty, increased the size of the student body to 1,700, and oversaw the building of the Musical Arts Center (completed in 1972). In 1973, Charles Webb, who had served as the assistant dean beginning in 1964, was appointed as the dean, serving until 1997. Under his leadership, the school continued to grow, adding an Early Music Program and performing opera in the original language. Webb saw to it that operas were performed by students, even if graduates. In addition, both the opera and orchestras toured nationally and internationally. Gwyn Richards was appointed as the dean in 2001.

India Symphony Orchestra. See **Symphony Orchestra of India (Mumbai)**.

in due or *in due battute.* (It.) In two, in two beats. (Fr. *à deux*; Ger. *in zwei, in zwei Schläge*; Sp. *a dos, en dos*.)

in fuori. (It.) Play out, bring forward, to play a part so that it can be heard above others. (Fr. *en dehors, en évidence*; Ger. *hervortretend*; Sp. *destacar*.)

in halben Noten. (Ger.) In two beats per measure, conducted in two beats per measure. (Fr. à *la blanche*, It. *alla breve*, Sp. *compás alla breve*.) See also **alla breve**.

in levare. (It.) **Upbeat**, one or more notes that occur before the first measure of a work or phrase; anacrusis; pickup. (Fr. *levée*, Ger. *Auftakt*, Sp. *alzada*.)

inner, innere, inneres. (Ger.) Inner, interior.

innerlich. (Ger.) Intimate, inward. A character word used to evoke a particular quality in the playing. (Fr. *interior, intime*, It. *interno, intimo*; Sp. *íntimo*.)

innig. (Ger.) Expressive, heartfelt, intimate. Examples: *sehr innig*, very expressive; *innig, sehr zart und weich*, expressive, very tender and delicate, from **Pierrot Lunaire** by **Arnold Schoenberg**.

inno. (It.) Hymn. (Fr. *hymne*, Ger. *Hymne*, Sp. *himno*.)

inquiétant. (Fr.) Eerie, sinister, weird, weirdly, uncanny. (Ger. *unheimlich*; It. *inquietante, misterioso, sinistro*; Sp. *extraño, inquietante, misterioso, siniestro*.)

inquietante. (It.) Eerie, sinister, weird, weirdly, uncanny. Also *misterioso, sinistro*. (Fr. *inquiétant*; Ger. *unheimlich*; Sp. *extraño, inquietante, misterioso, siniestro*.)

inquietante. (Sp.) Eerie, sinister, weird, weirdly, uncanny. Also *extraño, misterioso, siniestro*. (Fr. *inquiétant*; Ger. *unheimlich*; It. *inquietante, misterioso, sinistro*.)

in sanfter Weise. (Ger.) Sweetly, gently. (Fr. *doucement*, It. *dolcemente*, Sp. *suavemente*.)

insieme. (It.) Together. A commonly used word in rehearsal. (Fr. *ensemble*, Ger. *zusammen*, Sp. *juntos*.) Examples: *Non siamo insieme*, **We are not together**; *Questo deve essere insieme*, **This must be together**.

Institute of American Music. Founded by **Howard Hanson** at the **Eastman School of Music** in 1964 for the promotion of American composers and their music through commissions, recordings, performances, study, and preservation. Now called the Hanson Institute for American Music, the program also provides support for scholarly publications by the University of Rochester Press and Eastman composition student projects.

Instrumentalist (**magazine**). An American monthly magazine for music educators. First published in 1946, it sponsors the John Phillip Sousa Musical Talent Award for leadership, cooperation, and musical talent. See also **music magazines**.

instrumente a fiato di ottone. (It.) Brass instruments. (Fr. *les cuivres*, Ger. *Blechinstrumente*, Sp. *instrumentos de metal*.)

instrument extensions. See **extensions, instrument**.

instrumentos de madera. (Sp.) Woodwind instruments. (Ger. *Holz, Holzbläser*; It. *legni, strumentini*; Fr. *bois*.)

instrumentos de metal. (Sp.) The instruments made out of brass; the section of the **orchestra** or **band** made up of brass instruments. Also *metales*. (Fr. *cuivres*, Ger. *Blechinstrumente*, It. *ottoni*.)

instrumentos de viento. (Sp.) The woodwind instruments of the **orchestra** or **band**. Also *instrumentos de madera*. (Fr. *instruments à vents, les bois*; Ger. *Blasinstrumente*; It. *i legni, strumenti a fiato*.)

instruments à vents. (Fr.) The woodwind instruments of the **orchestra** or **band**. Also *les bois*. (Ger. *Blasinstrumente*; It. *i legni, strumenti a fiato*; Sp. *instrumentos de madera, instrumentos de viento*.) See also **appendix 3**.

in tempo. (It.) In tempo, in time. (Fr. *dans le tempo*, Ger. *im Zeitmaß*, Sp. *en el tempo*.)

intendant. The title generally used in Europe for the administrative position of general director of an opera house. The intendant may be a public employee with managerial authority over all aspects of the company. (Fr. *intendant*, Ger. *Intendant*, It. *intendente*, Sp. *intendente*.)

intenso. (It.) Intense, violent. Also, *con intensità, intensamente, intensito*.

interchangeability. A kind of **aleatoric procedure** in which musical lines, sections, or even whole movements can be performed in any order as selected by the performer. Examples: **Pierre Boulez**'s Piano Sonata No. 3, Witold Lutosławski's String Quartet No. 2.

Interlochen Arts Camp. See **Interlochen Center for the Arts**.

Interlochen Center for the Arts. Founded by **Joseph E. Maddy** in 1928, the center houses the Interlochen Arts Academy, the **Interlochen Arts Camp** (formerly the National Music Camp), Adult Arts Programs, its own public radio station, and a concert series. The academy is a high school level boarding school specializing in arts education and a college preparatory academic curriculum. Major areas are music, theater, comparative arts, creative writing, motion picture arts, dance, and visual arts. The arts camp has programs that are one, two, three, four, and six weeks long, with most running between the third week of June and the first week of August. It is divided by age into high school (grades 9–12), intermediates (grades 6–9), and juniors (grades 3–6). The curriculum of the camp covers the same topic areas as the academy, except for the college preparatory curriculum. The camp has ensembles of all types but is especially known for its **World Youth Orchestra**. It draws a distinguished faculty who teach for periods of one week to the whole six-week term. Adult programs cover a variety of music areas, creative writing, and media and visual arts. Interlochen Public Radio is at the call number 88.7 in Interlochen, Michigan, and can also be heard on the Internet. During the school year, the concert series features Interlochen student ensembles and guest artists. During the summer, the list is expanded to include popular musicians. The Interlochen Center for the Arts has several performance facilities, including Corson Auditorium, Dendrinos Chapel and Recital Hall, the Phoenix Theater, and the Harvey Theater. In the summer, two outdoor amphitheaters host concerts, Kresge Auditorium and The Bowl.

interlude. (Fr.) Interlude. Also *entr'acte.* (Ger. *Zwischenspiel*; It. *interludio, intermedio, intermezzo*; Sp. *interludio*.)

interludio. (It., Sp.) Interlude. Also (It.) *intermedio*, (It.) *intermezzo*. (Fr. *entr'acte, interlude*; Ger. *Zwischenspiel*.)

intermedio. (It.) Interlude. Also *interludio, intermezzo*. (Fr. *entr'acte, interlude*; Ger. *Zwischenspiel*; Sp. *interludio*.)

intermezzo. (It.) Interlude. Also *interludio, intermedio*. (Fr. *entr'acte, interlude*; Ger. *Zwischenspiel*; Sp. *interludio*.)

International Association of Music Information Centres (IAMIC). Founded in 1958, the IAMIC is a worldwide network of national organizations that promote new music. In 1962, it became an offshoot of the **International Association of Music Libraries, Archives and Documentation Centres (IAML)**, lasting until 1991 when the IAMIC became independent. Each music information center has as their mandate the documentation and promotion of their national music, usually emphasizing contemporary art music and often collecting scores, parts, recordings, books and articles, and press materials. These organizations are located in Europe, North and South America, the Middle and Far East, Russia, and beyond.

International Association of Music Libraries, Archives and Documentation Centres (IAML). Founded in

Paris in 1951 to promote international cooperation and the standardization and exchange of materials between music libraries. IAML has a quarterly journal, *Fontes artis musicae (FAM)*. IAML has been responsible for the initiation of the **Répertoire International des Sources Musicales (RISM)**, an inventory of musical sources in print and manuscript before 1800, and **Répertoire international de littérature musicale (RILM)**, an Internet service that provides abstracts and bibliographies of scholarly writings on music. In addition, the **Répertoire International d'Iconographie Musicale (RIdIM)** documents visual materials relating to music, and the **Répertoire International de la Presse Musicale (RIPM)** creates abstracts and an index of the contents of certain periodicals focused on the music of the eighteenth to the twentieth centuries.

International Besançon Competition for Young Conductors. Established in 1951 in Besançon, France, as part of the Besançon International Music Festival. The list of first prize winners includes several who have attained international careers, including **Seiji Ozawa**, **Jesús López-Cobos**, **Sylvain Cambreling**, Yoel Levi, and **Zdenek Mácal**.

International Conference of Symphony and Opera Musicians (ICSOM). Founded in 1962 to promote the livelihood of the skilled orchestral performer and to enrich the cultural life of society. ICSOM represents over four thousand musicians in fifty-one major orchestras and is a Players' Conference of the **American Federation of Musicians (AFM)**. Its stated mission is to facilitate communication between member orchestras and the greater musical community and to offer support and assistance. ICSOM's newsletter is *Senza Sordino*.

International Federation for Choral Music (IFCM). Founded in 1982 in Altea, Spain, the IFCM publishes the *International Choral Bulletin* and sponsors the triennial World Symposium on Choral Music.

International Music Score Library Project (IMSLP). Also known as the **Petrucci Music Library**, an Internet-based project that has created an electronic library of public-domain music scores and parts. Established in 2006, over 260,000 scores and 27,000 recordings for over 61,000 works by over 7,500 composers have been uploaded. IMSLP states that its goal is to comply with Canadian copyright laws. The site provides information about copyright in Canada, the United States, and the European Union. See also **copyright law**.

International Record Review. Founded in 2000, it is an independent British monthly classical music magazine.

The review prides itself on publishing longer and more detailed reviews than its main British competitors. See also **music magazines**.

International Society for Contemporary Music (ISCM). Founded in 1922, ISCM is an organization that promotes the advancement, dissemination, and interchange of new music around the world. The annual ISCM World New Music Days Festival is the organization's main focus. The *World New Music Magazine* is published in connection with the annual festival. ISCM also awards an annual prize to a composer under the age of thirty-five whose work is then performed at the festival and who receives a monetary prize and commission for a new piece. Regional meetings and concerts also occur around the world.

Internet radio. Also known as streaming radio. An audio broadcast, often associated with a traditional broadcast radio service but provided over the Internet, generally without the capability of pausing or being replayed. Some major networks, such as CBS Radio and Chrysalis, both in the United States, limit listening to their individual country in order to avoid licensing conflicts. See also **satellite radio**.

Internet Radio Fairness Act. See **Digital Media Association (DiMA)**.

Internet orchestra. See **YouTube orchestra**.

intero. (It.) Whole note. See also **appendix 5**.

interpretation. The **conductor**'s interpretation is based on the creative tension between knowledge of the score in all its elements and a unique personal insight that brings the piece to life. It is a combination of hard work over years of study and a kind of magic that grows through experience, allowing a piece to speak for itself, and the freedom that comes from thorough knowledge.

The urge to discover the composer's intent through an understanding of the musical language; the musical style; performance practice considerations, which can change and develop; and the correct execution of all orchestral techniques and the handling of the structurally based dramatic narrative are all part of the conductor's private endeavor that is realized and made public through rehearsal and performance. See also **aesthetics**.

interval class. A term coined by **Milton Babbitt** that denotes intervals defined as equivalent in **twelve-tone music**. An example would be all forms of a major third, including that third, a major tenth, a minor sixth, and a minor thirteenth.

Intervall. (Ger.) Interval, the distance between two pitches. (Fr. *intervalle*, It. *intervallo*, Sp. *intérvalo*.) See also **appendix 6**.

intervalle. (Fr.) Interval, the distance between two pitches (Ger. *Intervall*, It. *intervallo*, Sp. *intérvalo*.) See also **appendix 6**.

intervallo. (It.) Interval, the distance between two pitches. (Fr. *intervalle*, Ger. *Intervall*, Sp. *intervalo*.) See also **appendix 6**.

intervalo. (Sp.) Interval, the distance between two pitches. (Fr. *intervalle*, Ger. *Intervall*, It. *intervallo*.) See also **appendix 6**.

interval of transposition. The interval of **pitch**, either up or down, between the notes being read and the notes being heard when one plays a transposed part on the piano or other instrument.

interval terms and translations. See **appendix 6**.

intime. (Fr.) Intimate, inward. A character word used to evoke a particular quality in the playing. Also *interior*. (Ger. *innerlich*, It. *intimo*, Sp. *íntimo*.)

intimo. (It.) Intimate, inward. A character word used to evoke a particular quality in the playing. (Fr. *interior*, *intime*; Ger. *innerlich*; Sp. *íntimo*.)

íntimo. (Sp.) Intimate, inward. A character word used to evoke a particular quality in the playing. (Fr. *interior*, *intime*; Ger. *innerlich*; It. *intimo*.)

intonare. (It.) To pitch or to tune. (Fr. *entonner*, Ger. *anstimmen*, Sp. *afinar*.)

intonation. 1. The ability to play or sing in tune. See also **tuning systems**.
2. The act of intoning, as in chanting.
3. The manner or way of speaking, as in the rise and fall of pitch in the speaking voice.

intonazione. (It.) **Pitch**, a sound perceived as a tone or musical note, technically the function of a fundamental frequency or number of oscillations per second as measured in **hertz**. (Fr. *hauteur*, Ger. *Tonhöhe*, Sp. *entonación*.) See also *Tonhöhe*.

invariant. A musical element that does not change within a given structure or piece. In **twelve-tone technique**, invariant properties of a **tone row** are those that do not change when the row is transformed by **inversion**, **retrograde**, or **transposition**. In the case of inversion, the most common invariant procedure, the pitches are different but the sequence of intervals remains the same.

inversion. The alteration of a group of pitches or a chord by changing each ascending interval to a descending one and vice versa. Used in **twelve-tone music**, fugues, and many fugal procedures.

in zwei. (Ger.) In two. Also *in zwei Schläge.* (Fr. à *deux*; It. *in due, in due battute*; Sp. *a dos, en dos*.) Example: *Dieser Takt wirdin zwei geschlagen*, this bar will be conducted in two.

Ionian mode. See **church modes**.

Ioannides, Sarah. (b. 1972.) Australian **conductor** and violinist. Ioannides studied at Oxford University; the **Guildhall School of Music**, London; the **Curtis Institute** on a **Fulbright Scholarship**; and the **Juilliard School** with **Otto-Werner Mueller**. Music director of the Spartanburg Philharmonic Orchestra since 2005, Ioannides has appeared as a guest conductor with such orchestras as the Rochester and Buffalo philharmonic orchestras; the Louisville, Charleston, North Carolina, and Chautauqua symphonies; the Orchestra Nationale de Lyon; the Flemish Radio Orchestra; the Gothenburg and **BBC** symphony orchestras; the **London Sinfonietta**; and others. She has recorded with the RIAS Kammerchor, SWR Vokalensemble, the Bachakademie, Stuttgart, and the Royal Philharmonic, London. From 2005 to 2011 she served as the music director of the El Paso Symphony Orchestra and from 2002 to 2004 as the assistant conductor of the **Cincinnati Symphony Orchestra**. She was appointed as the music director of the **Tacoma Symphony** in 2013. A strong supporter of living composers, she has worked with **John Corigliano**, Tan Dun, Jennifer Higdon, and others.

ir. (Sp.) To go, to walk, to proceed. (Fr. *aller, allez*; Ger. *gehen*; It. *andare*.) See also ***andante***.

isorhythm. A compositional technique dating back to the fourteenth-century isorhythmic motet of Guillaume de Machaut; it is still used in various ways by contemporary composers. Isorhythm is the repetition of a rhythmic or melodic pattern within a piece of music, often occurring over a long structural period. An isorhythmic section of a work normally contains two patterns that are repeated several times, a rhythmic pattern called *talea* and a melodic pattern called *color*. The two patterns need not be the same length.

Israel Philharmonic Orchestra (IPO). This Tel Aviv orchestra traces its beginnings to the **Palestine Symphony Orchestra**, founded in 1936 by the violinist Bronislaw Huberman, who brought Jewish musicians from Central Europe in order to escape the rising Nazi regime. Its first concert—December 1936—was under the baton of **Arturo Toscanini**. Past conductors have included Leo Kestenberg (1939–1945), William Steinberg (1936–1938), **Leonard Bernstein** (1947–1949 and laureate conductor 1988–1990), Paul Paray (1949–1951), Bernardino Molinari (no date available), and Jean Martinon (1957–1959). **Zubin Mehta** was appointed in 1968 and served as the music advisor until 1977, when he was appointed as the music director for life. The IPO has made numerous recordings with both Mehta and Bernstein for the **Decca label**.

iTunes Pass. The **New York Philharmonic** and other orchestras sell a "pass" that, with the use of a password, allows an interested person access to select audio files via iTunes. Access to this program is available through the orchestra's website.

Ives, Charles. (1874–1954.) An American iconoclast, Ives was a composer of innovative works, including *The Unanswered Question, Universe Symphony*, and Symphony No. 4, all of which require more than one **conductor**. Much of his orchestral music is available in new critical performing editions. See also **multiple conductor works**.

invitational cue gesture. Most often used in opera conducting, this gesture is one given by the left hand in a gentle, rounded fashion, usually reaching slightly toward the person entering in such a way as to give them a relaxed confidence. See also **conducting opera, cue gesture**.

IRCAM (Institut et Recherche et Coordination Acoustique/Musique). A French research institute for the study of the scientific properties of music, sound, and electro-acoustical art music. Located in Paris at the Pompidou Center, it was founded in the early 1970s by **Pierre Boulez**, with Boulez serving as the first director. The institute sponsors an annual International Computer Music Conference. It is responsible for the development of several software programs, including OpenMusic, AudioSculpt, OMax, Orchidée, and others. Other composers associated with the institute include Luciano Berio, George Benjamin, Harrison Birtwhistle, Unsuk Chin, Gérard Grisey, Jonathn Harvey, Magnus Lindberg, Frank Zappa, **Iannis Xenakis**, and many more.

Ireland National Symphony Orchestra (RTÉ National Symphony Orchestra). The ensemble is the concert orchestra of the official Ireland Radio Television Broadcasting Organization (Raidió Teilifís Éireann, RTÉ). The orchestra was founded in 1947 in Dublin as the broadcasting authority began to expand, requiring a full-size ensemble. Since Ireland had been neutral during World War II and spared much damage, it was easy to attract musicians from around Europe. The orchestra presents a full season of concerts and outreach events with many of them broadcast on RTÉ Lyric FM. The current music director is Alan Buribayev (appointed in 2010). The orchestra has a commissioning and resident composer program.

ironique. (Fr.) Ironic. Example: *ironique et léger*, ironic and light, from the ballet *Jeux* by Claude Debussy.

"It is a little sharp"/"It is a little flat." A phrase often heard in rehearsal. (Fr.) *C'est un peu trop aigu/C'est un peu grave.* (Ger.) *Ein bischen zu hoch*/Ein *zu tief.* Also (Ger.) *Ein bischen höher, bitte/Ein bischen tiefer, bitte*, a little higher, please/a little lower, please; (Sp.) *Un poco muy alto, por favor/Un poco muy bajo, por favor*, a little high, please/a little lower, please.

izquierdo. (Sp.) Left. (Fr. *gauche*, Ger. *links*, It. *sinistra*.) Example: *mano izquierdo*, left hand. (Fr. *main gauche*, Ger. *Linke*, It. *mano sinistra*.) See also **right hand**.

J

Jackson, Isaiah. (b. 1945.) African American **conductor** who broke several color barriers during his career. Jackson studied Russian history and literature at Harvard University, graduating cum laude in 1966; he received a master of music at Stanford University (1969) and a doctorate from the **Juilliard School** (1973). He also attended the Aspen, Tanglewood, and Fontainbleau summer music institutes, studying with **Nadia Boulanger** at Fontainbleau. He served as the assistant or associate conductor with the American Symphony Orchestra (1970–1971), the **Baltimore Symphony Orchestra** (1971–1973), and the **Rochester Philharmonic Orchestra** (1973–1987) He was also the music director of the Flint Symphony Orchestra, Michigan, and the Dayton Philharmonic Orchestra (1987–1994) and the principal conductor of the Royal Ballet, Covent Garden (1986), serving as its music director from 1987 to 1990. Jackson has guest conducted many of America's great orchestras, including the **New York Philharmonic**, **Cleveland Orchestra**, **San Francisco Symphony Orchestra**, **Houston Symphony**, **Dallas Symphony Orchestra**, **Detroit Symphony Orchestra**, Indianapolis Symphony, Louisville Orchestra, **Toronto Symphony Orchestra**, Youngstown Symphony

Isaiah Jackson. *Courtesy Mike Spencer Photography.*

Orchestra, and the **Boston Pops**. In Europe, he has guest conducted the **Orchestre de la Suisse Romande**, BBC Concert Orchestra, **Vienna Symphony**, **Berlin Symphony Orchestra**, Royal Liverpool Philharmonic, and others. He served as the music director of the **Pro Arte Chamber Orchestra**, Boston (2000–2007), and is now conductor emeritus. He made recordings with the Berlin Symphony of music by film composers Bernard Herrmann, Miklós Rózsa, and Franz Waxman for **Koch International Classics (KIC)**; of the music of William Grant Still, also for KIC; of a New Year's Eve concert with the **Berlin Symphony**; and others. Jackson has also published several articles on music and culture.

Jacobs, René. (b. 1943.) Belgian **conductor** and countertenor who specializes in Baroque and early opera and oratorio. He has made impressive recordings of Wolfgang Amadeus Mozart's *The Marriage of Figaro*, which won several awards when it was issued in 2004; George Frideric Handel's *Rinaldo*; Joseph Haydn's *The Seasons*; Johann Sebastian Bach's *B minor Mass*; Roberto Cavalli's *Xerxes*; and many more. He is known for his work with Concerto Köln, the **Orchestra of the Age of Enlightenment**, the **Academy for Old Music Berlin**, the Freiburg Baroque Orchestra, the Netherlands Chamber Choir, and the **RIAS Chamber choir**. Jacobs served as the artistic director of the Innsbruck Festival of Old Music from 1991 to 2009.

Janissary music. Turkish military music used by the personal guard of Turkish sultans from the fourteenth century until they were disbanded in 1826. Janissary instruments such as the bass drum, triangle, and cymbals became popular in Europe in the seventeenth and eighteenth centuries and particularly in Austria following the defeat of the Turks in 1683. They began to be used in the music of the Classical period soon after appearing in Wolfgang Amadeus Mozart's opera *Abduction from the*

Seraglio (*Die Entführing aus dem Serial*), set in Turkey; Joseph Haydn's Symphony No. 100, "Military"; and Ludwig van Beethoven's Symphony No. 9, "Finale," in the "*alla marcia*" section. Mozart also used the marking "*Alla Turca*" in the Piano Sonata No. 11, K. 331, to suggest a particular character or style. (Fr. *bande turque*, Ger. *Janitscharenmusik*, It. *banda turca*.)

Janowski, Marek. (b. 1941.) Polish **conductor**. Janowski was born in Warsaw but was brought to Germany with his family and educated there. He studied mathematics first, switching to music in Cologne, where his conducting teacher was **Wolfgang Sawallisch**. Janowski served as the assistant conductor for the opera houses of Aachen, Cologne, and Düsseldorf and guest conducted in Hamburg, Munich, Paris, and Berlin. He has served as the music director for the Freiburg (1973–1975) and Dortmund operas (1975–1979) and as the conductor of the French Radio Nouvel Orchestre Philharmonique, now known as the Orchestre Philharmonique de Radio France (1984–2000); the Royal Liverpool Philharmonic (1983–1987); and the Gürzenich Orchestra in Cologne (1986–1991). From 2000 to 2006, he was the music director of the Orchestre Philharmonique de Monte Carlo, and 2002–2016, he led the **Berlin Radio Symphony Orchestra (Rundfunk-Sinfonieorchester Berlin)**. From 2004 to 2012, he served as the chief conductor of the **Orchestra de la Suisse Romande** in Geneva. From 2005 to 2008, he was one of three conductors who served with the **Pittsburgh Symphony Orchestra** in the absence of a single music director. Janowski has conducted most of the world's major opera companies, including the **Metropolitan Opera** of New York and many others. He led the first digital recording of **Richard Wagner**'s **Ring cycle** with the **Dresden Staatskapelle** for RCA, **Krysztof Penderecki**'s opera *The Devils of Loudon* with the **Hamburg State Opera** just after he had conducted the premiere in 1969, Carl Maria von Weber's *Euryanthe* in 1974 for Philips, and **Richard Strauss**'s *Die scheigsame Frau*, also in Dresden, for EMI in 1976. He also recorded the four symphonies of Johannes Brahms with the **Pittsburgh Symphony Orchestra**.

Jansons, Mariss. (b. 1943.) Latvian **conductor**. Jansons studied violin and conducting at the Leningrad Conservatory (now the **St. Petersburg Conservatory**) and later with **Hans Swarosky** in Vienna, **Herbert von Karajan** in Salzburg, and **Yevgeny Mravinsky** in Leningrad (St. Petersburg). After winning second prize at the Herbert con Karajan Conducting Competition in 1971, he conducted in the Soviet Union, Europe, and the United States. In 1973, he was appointed the associate conductor of the **Leningrad Philharmonic Orchestra**, later becoming the associate principal conductor (1985–1997). He was the principal conductor of the **Oslo Philhar-**

monia Orchestra (1979–2000), music director of the **Pittsburgh Symphony Orchestra** (1997–2002) and the **Bavarian Radio Symphony Orchestra** (2003–present), and chief conductor of the **Royal Concertgebouw Orchestra** (2004–present). He has also been a guest conductor for most of the world's great orchestras, including the **New York Philharmonic**, **Chicago Symphony Orchestra**, and the **Cleveland Symphony Orchestra** in the United States. He has recorded the complete Tchaikovsky symphonies; works of Antonin Dvořák, Edvard Grieg, Jean Sibelius, and Arthur Honegger in Oslo; and the complete orchestral works of Sergei Rachmaninoff in St. Petersburg, as well as Dmitri Shostakovich's complete symphonies with the **Bavarian Radio Symphony Orchestra**. Additionally, he has recorded the works of Hector Berlioz, **Gustav Mahler**, Maurice Ravel, and Richard Wagner. He was made a professor of conducting at the **St. Petersburg Conservatory** in 1995.

Japan Philharmonic Orchestra. Founded in 1956 in Tokyo under the Nippon Cultural Broadcasting Association. It became part of Fuji Television in 1959. Its first conductor was Akeo Watanabe, who led recordings of the complete symphonies of Jean Sibelius in the early 1960s. The orchestra toured the United States and Canada in 1963 and has since visited Europe four times. In 1972, the orchestra lost the support of the Nippon Broadcasting and Fuji Television companies. About one-third of the players stayed together and formed the New Japan Philharmonic, led by **Seiji Ozawa**, the same year. Only one year later, the name reverted to the original. The orchestra has had many distinguished guest conductors, including **Valery Gergiev**, **Neeme Järvi**, Jiří Bělohlávek, and others.

Järvi, Neeme. (b. 1937.) American **conductor** of Estonian birth. Järvi has made over four hundred CDs on labels such as **Deutsche Grammophon**, **Chandos**, and **BIS**, making him one of the most recorded conductors ever. This enormous legacy of recordings is evidence of an unsurpassed appetite for a wide variety of music and a passion for introducing his audience to the unfamiliar. He has been a proponent of his countrymen Eduard Tubin anad Arvo Pärt and released recordings of many complete works for the first time, such as the incidental music for Edvard Grieg's *Peer Gynt* and Pyotr Tchaikovsky's incidental music for *The Snow Maiden*. Included on his list of recordings are many rarely heard American works, such as the *Gaelic Symphony* of Amy Beech. In this way, Järvi has been said to have a positive impact on concert programming by orchestras in the United States.

Järvi's early professional positions include music director of the Estonian Radio and Television Orchestra and the Estonian Opera from 1964 to 1977. In 1980, he and his family immigrated to the United States. He was also the principal conductor of the **Gothenburg Symphony Orchestra** (1982–2004), the CGSO (1981–1984), and the Scottish National Orchestra (1984–1988); music director of the **Detroit Symphony Orchestra** (1990–2005) and the **New Jersey Symphony Orchestra** (2005–2009); chief conductor of the **Residentie Orchestra of The Hague** (2004–present); and artistic and music director of the **Orchestre de la Suisse Romande** (2012–present). Järvi has guest conducted virtually all of the major orchestras of the world and made his **Metropolitan Opera** debut in 1979, conducting Tchaikovsky's opera *Eugene Onegin*. He has said that he prefers recording to concerts because he and the orchestra don't have to wear uncomfortable evening dress, making them more relaxed and free. He believes in spontaneity in music making; no two performances should be exactly the same—that would be boring and uninteresting.

Järvi, Paavo. (b. 1962.) Estonian American **conductor** and son of conductor **Neeme Järvi**. Järvi studied at the **Curtis Institute of Music** and has served as the music director of the **Cincinnati Symphony Orchestra** (2001–2011); the **Frankfurt Radio Symphony Orchestra** from 2006, becoming conductor laureate in 2013; and the **Orchestre de Paris** (2009–present) He is also the artistic director of the Deutsche Kammerphilharmonie Bremen (2004–present). He was appointed the chief conductor of the **NHK Symphony Orchestra** in 2015. He has been a guest conductor with the **Berlin Philharmonic**, Philharlmonia Orchestra, **Deutsches Symphonie-Orchester Berlin**, **Mariinsky Theater Orchestra** at the **Stars of the White Nights Festival**, **Gewandhaus Orchestrer Leipzig**, **Munich Philharmonic**, **Russian National Orchestra**, **Vienna Philharmonic**, and the **Staatskapelle Dresden**.

Järvi has recorded with his orchestras in Cincinnati, Frankfurt, the Deutsche Kammerphilharmonie Bremen, and others. His repertoire includes Anton Bruckner (complete symphonies), **Gustav Mahler**, Carl Nielsen, Ludwig van Beethoven (complete symphonies), Maurice Ravel, Robert Schumann, Gabriel Fauré, Arvo Pärt, Antonín Dvořák, Bohuslav Martinů, **Igor Stravinsky** (*The Rite of Spring*, *Petrouchka*, and the *Firebird Suite*), and many others on the **Telarc**, **Virgin Classics**, and **RCA Red Seal** labels. Järvi is a proponent of his Estonian countrymen, including composers Arvo Pärt, Erkki-Sven Tüür, Lepo Sumera, and Eduard Tubin. He has given conducting master classes at the Järvi Academy. In 2013, he was awarded the Order of the White Star by the president of Estonia for contributions to Estonian culture.

jawbone. See **vibraslap**.

jazz chords. Chords and chord symbols that are commonly found in jazz music and harmony. Each chord is described as a series of intervals above the root (bottom) note of the chord. See the **bibliography** for books on jazz chords.

Jazz chords. *Courtesy Andrew Martin Smith.*

Jean, Kenneth. (b. 1952.) American **conductor**. Jean served as the assistant conductor of the **Cleveland Orchestra**, resident conductor of the **Detroit Symphony Orchestra** (1979–1985), principal guest conductor of the **Hong Kong Philharmonic** (1984–1993), music director of the Florida Philharmonic Orchestra (1986–1992), associate conductor of the **Chicago Symphony Orchestra** (1986–1993), and music director of the **Tulsa Philharmonic Orchestra** (1997–2002). In 1990, he was awarded the **Seaver/National Endowment for the Arts Conductors Award**. Jean is a proponent of contemporary classical music and in particular that of Chinese composers. Among others, he has led recordings for **Naxos**.

jede, jeder, jedes. (Ger.) Each, every, any. (Fr. *chaque*; It. *chiascuno, ogni, tutto/a*; Sp. *cada, todo/a*.)

jedesmal. (Ger.) Every time. A directive often heard in rehearsal. (Fr. *à chaque fois que, toutes les fois*; It. *ogni volta*; Sp. *cada vez*.)

Jerusalem Academy of Music and Dance. Founded in 1933 by violinist Emil Hauser, who also served as its first director, as the Jerusalem Conservatory of Music. Also formerly known as the Rubin Academy of Music. The Academy is located on the Givat Ram campus of the Hebrew University of Jerusalem and offers a bachelor of music and bachelor of education in addition to a bachelor of dance and a master of arts in music in conjunction with the Hebrew University.

Jerusalem Symphony Orchestra. The orchestra of the Israel Broadcasting Authority, it was originally the Palestine Broadcasting Service Orchestra, giving weekly concerts at the Jerusalem YMCA. In 1948, it was named the Kol Israel Orchestra for the Israeli Broadcasting Association, and in 1973, it became the Jerusalem Symphony Orchestra. The orchestra played an important role in the developing culture of the newly formed state of Israel and performs works of contemporary Israeli and foreign composers. The current music director is Fréréric Chaslin (appointed in 2012). Former music directors include Leon Botstein (2003–2013), David Shallon

(1992–2000), Lawrence Foster (1988–1992), **Gary Bertini** (1978–1987), Lukas Foss (1972–1976), and Mendi Rodin (1963–1972). Recent premieres include **Krzystof Penderecki**'s *The Seven Gates of Jerusalem* under **Lorin Maazel**.

jeté. (Fr.) A bowing term indicating a thrown bow. Also known as **ricochet** or **flying staccato**.

jeu de timbres. (Fr.) Alternative name for **glockenspiel**. See also **appendix 4**.

Jeune France. A group of young French composers who came together in 1936 with the goal of being free from past strictures and to promote the music of both young and less well-known French composers. They included Olivier Messiaen, André Jolivet, Yves Baudrier, and Daniel Lesur.

jeu ord. (Fr.) Abbreviation for ***jeu ordinaire***.

jeu ordinaire. (Fr.) An indication to play in the normal or ordinary way. Also ***ordinario***. Abbreviated as *jeu ord.*, *j. ord.*, *j. o.*

Jinbo, Michael. (b. 1956.) American **conductor** and pedagogue. Jinbo is a student of **Pierre Monteux** and the director of the **Monteux School**, Hancock, Maine, since 1995, when he succeeded **Charles Bruch**. He served as the assistant conductor of the North Carolina Symphony for four years and has been the music director of the Nittany Valley Symphony since 1989. He was educated at the University of Chicago (B.A.) and has a master of music in conducting from Northwestern University, Chicago. He has guest conducted in Europe and North and South America. Jinbo was born in Honolulu, Hawaii.

Jochum, Eugen. (1902–1987.) German **conductor**. Jochum studied at the **Munich Academy of Music** (1922–1924) and had his conducting debut with the **Munich Philharmonic Orchestra** in 1926, conducting Ludwig van Beethoven's overture *Leonore No. 3* and Anton Bruckner's Symphony No. 7. Following that success came a series of appointments, first at the Kiel Opera (1926–1929), where he conducted seventeen operas in his first season, including Giacomo Puccini's *Turandot*, **Richard Wagner**'s *The Flying Dutchman*, and **Richard Strauss**'s *Der Rosenkavalier*; then at the Mannheim Opera (1929); in Duisberg (1930); and with the **Berlin Radio Symphony Orchestra** (1931–1933) while simultaneously appearing with the **Berlin Philharmonic** and the **Berlin State Opera**. Upon the rise of the National Socialists he left Berlin and became the head of the **Hamburg Opera** and **Philharmonic Orchestra**, succeeding **Karl Muck** and **Karl Böhm**, respectively, and remaining there until 1949. He

succeeded in not joining the Nazi Party and avoided the direct attention of the powerful in Berlin, even though he performed music by composer **Paul Hindemith**, who had been officially banned as "degenerate." Following the war, he moved to Munich and founded the **Bavarian Radio Symphony Orchestra** (1949), serving as the principal conductor until 1974, by which time it had become one of the most important orchestras in Germany. In 1953, he made his first appearance at **Bayreuth**, conducting Wagner's *Tristan and Isolde* and returning in 1971, 1972, and 1973. A frequent opera conductor, from 1962 he appeared regularly at the **German Opera Berlin**. He was appointed co-conductor of the **Royal Concertgebouw Orchestra** along with **Bernard Haitink**, with Haitink appointed as the music director in 1964 but Jochum remaining a frequent guest. Jochum toured widely, visiting the United States first in 1958 and Japan twice, in 1961 and 1968. In 1975, he was appointed conductor laureate of the **London Symphony Orchestra**. He was also the principal conductor of the Bamberg Symphony from 1969 to 1973.

While known primarily for his interpretations of the romantic school of Austro-German composers, Jochum himself claimed that he felt closest to Johann Sebastian Bach, Wolfgang Amadeus Mozart, and Ludwig van Beethoven. His recordings of the *B minor Mass* and the *St. Matthew* and *St. John* passions, which came later in his career, are recognized not for their attention to performance practice as understood even at his time but for their great feeling and the powerful impact of their dramatic sense according to the text. Jochum was firmly grounded in the interpretive tradition of such conductors as **Wilhelm Furtwängler**, standing in opposition to those on the side of Arturo Toscanini with his dedication to the pursuit of the composer's will. He shaped his performances of Beethoven, Johannes Brahms, and Bruckner with frequent internal tempo changes and was always in search of the drama, character, and spirituality within. Given that was his way, he left a legacy of heartfelt renditions of whatever he recorded, even if some have been described as mannered and lacking in architectural sense. His range of conducting gestures has been described as small and focused, yet powerful.

Jochum recorded the late Mozart symphonies with the **Royal Concertgebouw Orchestra** (except for No. 41, which was with the Bavarian Radio Orchestra) and Joseph Haydn's Symphonies Nos. 95 to 104 with the **London Philharmonic Orchestra** and Nos. 93–95 and 98 with the **Dresden Staatskapelle**. He issued three sets of Brahms symphonies with the Berlin Philharmonic, Royal Concertgebouw, and the London Symphony. All nine Bruckner symphonies were issued on **Deutsche Grammophon** with the Berlin Philharmonic and Bavarian Radio Orchestra, and **EMI** issued a second set with the Dresden Staatskapelle.

jocoso. (Sp.) Happy, cheerful, lively, gay. Also *alegre.* (Fr. *gai, gaiement*; Ger. *frölich, lustig*; It. *gaio, giocoso.*)

Johannesburg Philharmonic Orchestra (JPO). Founded in 2000 after the dissolution of the National Symphony Orchestra. In 2007, the orchestra became a full-time professional ensemble. It also sponsors an academy for the training of young musicians. During its ten-year history, the JPO has presented regular concerts of symphonic music and performed for Opera Africa. In 2009, it was allotted funding for three years from the National Lottery Distribution Trust Fund and performed for the inauguration of President Jacob Zuma. In 2009 and 2010, the orchestra made the recordings for the ceremonies of the FIFA Confederation Cup. The JPO uses guest conductors.

John F. Kennedy Center for the Performing Arts. See **Kennedy Center**.

John S. and James L. Knight Foundation. A private American nonprofit foundation established in 1950 as the Knight Foundation and reincorporated under its current name in 1993. It is known primarily for grants that support journalism, media, and fostering the arts in communities. Over a three-year period, they funded more than one thousand **"Random Acts of Culture pop-up" performances** to "bring artists out of concert halls and into peoples' everyday lives" (www.knightfoundation.org).

John Simon Guggenheim Memorial Foundation Fellowships. The fellowships are intended as midcareer awards for those who have already demonstrated exceptional capacity for scholarship or creativity in the arts. Fellowships are awarded twice each year, once for citizens and permanent residents of the United States and Canada and once for citizens and permanent residents of Latin America and the Caribbean. While between 3,500 and 4,000 applications are filed each year, only 2,000 fellowships are awarded.

Jones, Julia. (b. 1961.) English **conductor**. Jones studied at the Chetham School of Music, the University of Bristol, and the **Guildhall School of Music**, London. She became a **repetiteur** at the Cologne Opera and the Stuttgart State Opera, was "*kapellmeisterin*" and assistant to the general music director Alicja Monk at the Ulm Municipal theater, conducted at the Darmstadt State Theater (1995–1997), was the principal conductor at the Basel Opera (1998–2002), and became the principal conductor of the Orquestra Sinfóninca Portuguesa at the San Carlo Opera House in Lisbon. Jones has conducted Wolfgang Amadeus Mozart's *Così fan Tutte* with the **Vienna Philharmonic**, worked with the **State Opera Berlin** and the Vienna Volksoper, and made her debut at the **Royal Opera House, Covent Garden**, London, in 2010.

jouer. (Fr.) To play, to touch. Also *toucher.* (Ger. *greifen, spielen*; It. *suonare, tocare*; Sp. *tocar.*)

jouer à vue. (Fr.) To read at sight, to sight read. Also *déchiffrer.* (Ger. *vom Blatt spielen*, It. *suonare a libro aperto, suonare a prima vista*; Sp. *tocar a primera vista.*)

jouer d'oreille. (Fr.) To play by ear. (Ger. *nach Gehör spielen*, It. *suonare a orecchio*, Sp. *tocar de oído.*)

jouer par coeur. (Fr.) To play by heart. (Ger. *auswendig spielen*, It. *suonare a memoria*, Sp. *tocar de memoria.*)

joyeuse, joyeux. (Fr.) Happy, cheerful, joyful. (Ger. *fröhlich, heiter*; It. *allegro*; Sp. *alegre.*) Example: *joyeux et rythmé*, joyful and rhythmic, from "Le matin d'un jour de fête" from "Ibéria" of *Images* by Claude Debussy.

joyeusement. (Fr.) Merrily, rejoicing. Also *allègrement.* (Ger. *feiernd, vergnügt*; It. *allegramente, festeggiante*; Sp. *alegremente.*)

JSTOR. An Internet resource for academic journal articles, it is available by subscription to students at many American colleges and universities. The music section has articles from over five hundred sources.

Juilliard School, New York. Founded as the Institute of Musical Art by Frank Damrosch and J. Loeb in 1905. In 1920, Augustus D. Juilliard, a New York resident and cotton merchant, left $20 million for the creation of the Juilliard Music Foundation. The trustees of the foundation created the Juilliard Graduate School in 1924 to help music students complete their education. In 1926, the Institute of Musical Art and the graduate school merged to become the Juilliard School of Music under a single president, Columbia University professor John Erskine. He was followed by concert pianist and composer Ernest Hutcheson, who served until 1945. American composer William Schuman was president from 1945 to 1962, composer Peter Mennin served from 1962 to 1983, and from 1984 to the present, Juilliard's president has been **Joseph W. Polisi**. The school moved to its current location at Broadway between 65th and 66th Streets on the north part of **Lincoln Center for the Performing Arts**. It officially became the Juilliard School instead of the Juilliard School of Music with the 1952 addition of the dance department. In 1968, the drama division was added. The opening of the Juilliard Theater in 1970 was celebrated with the first production of the Juilliard Opera Center, **Igor Stravinsky**'s *The Rake's Progress*. In 1990, the Meredith Wilson Residence Hall was opened as a dormitory. Several important additions to the curriculum have been made during the **Polisi** administration, including new programs in jazz studies, early music, an expansion of educational and community outreach programs, and the school's liberal arts programs. In the fall of 2009, a major renovation and expansion of the building was completed.

Jullien, Louis Antoine. (1812–1860.) French **conductor** and composer. Jullien studied at the Paris Conservatory in the early 1830s. He left in 1836, it is said because he preferred dance music to studying counterpoint. He established "entertainments" in the Parisian *Jardin Turc* that soon gained wide popularity. Following more than one duel, he left for England in 1838. Jullien spent the rest of his musical life pursuing the goal of entertaining his audience while gently educating them with more sophisticated examples of the classics, often sandwiching them in between the most popular quadrille of the day.

During his years in England, 1838 to 1850, some say that he created the "promenade concert" concept that many years later led to **Sir Henry Woods Promenade Concerts**, which are still held today as the **BBC Proms**. Others believe that the model already existed and that he simply enhanced and promoted it.

Jullien led a series of summer concerts (*concerts d'ete*) at the Drury Theater in 1840, so-called Monster Concerts at the Surrey Zoological Gardens, a season of grand opera, tours of provincial England each year, and private publicity-seeking tours to the European continent. Finally broken by a series brazenly conceived projects that went bankrupt, he returned to Paris and following personal instability, spent the final month of his life in an asylum.

Jullien was known as what might now be called a "publicity hound." He was a pioneer of the relatively new conducting baton, using it as a means to attract even greater attention. He would conduct Beethoven with a jewel-covered baton that would be presented to him at the podium on a silver platter, lending a particularly precious atmosphere to the performance of a piece by the master. He became a household name who, with the frequent publications of caricatures and appearances in *Punch* magazine, began to rival the most notable politicians of the day. He toured the United States at the invitation of P. T. Barnum in 1853–1854, giving more than 214 concerts in less than a year. His concerts consisted mainly of popular music such as waltzes, quadrilles, and other dance numbers but also symphonies of Ludwig van Beethoven and **Felix Mendelssohn**. Known as a showman with a great talent for publicity, Jullien succeeded in bringing a broad-based public to the experience of classical music. See the **bibliography**.

Juneau Symphony. Founded in 1962 in Juneau, Alaska, the orchestra is made up of professional and amateur musicians. Kyle Wiley Pickett served as music director, 1999–2014, and Troy Quinn was appointed in 2015. The symphony now has over eighty musicians, a full-time administrator, and runs a youth orchestra program. The ensemble performs a combination of classics, pops, and educational programs.

juntos. (Sp.) Together. A commonly heard directive. (Fr. *ensemble*, Ger. *zusammen*, It. *insieme*.) Examples: *No estamos juntos*, **We are not together**; *Esto debe estar juntos*, **This must be together**.

jusqu'à, jusqu'au. (Fr.) Up to. Examples: *jusq'à la fin*, up to the end; *Animez progressivement jusqu'au très moderé*, progressively get faster (more animated) up to the very moderate tempo marking, from *Daphnis et Chloé* by Maurice Ravel.

jusque. (Fr.) To, in, until. (Ger. *zu*; It. *sin*, *sino*; Sp. *hasta*.) Examples: *à la fin*, to the end. (Ger. *bis zum End*, *bis zum Schluss*; It. *al fine*; Sp. *hasta el final*.) See also *bis zu*.

juste. (Fr.) Strict. precise. Also *exact*. (Ger. *genau*, *richtig*; It. *esatto*, *giusto*; Sp. *exactamente*, *preciso*.) Example: *tempo giusto*, in a strict tempo.

justement. (Fr.) Precisely, justly, exactly. (Ger. *mit Recht*, It. *giustamente*, Sp. *correctamente*.)

just intonation. See **tuning systems**.

K

K., KV. Abbreviation for **Köchel-Verzeichnis**, the thematic catalogue of Wolfgang Amadeus Mozart's compositions written by **Ludwig Ritter von Köchel**.

Kadenz. (Ger.) A cadenza, as in a concerto, a harmonic cadence. (Fr. *cadence*, It. *cadenza*, Sp. *cadencia*.)

kadenzierend. (Ger.) Cadential. (Fr. *candentiel*; It. *cadenzale, cadenzante*; Sp. *cadencial*.) Example: *quasi kadenzierend*, almost like a cadenz, from ***Pierrot Lunaire*** by **Arnold Schoenberg**.

Kalmus, Edwin F. (1893–1989.) American music publisher who founded the **Kalmus Music** publishing house in 1926. He worked with his son-in-law, Lawrence Gallison, who became vice president and general manager in 1961.

Kalmus Music Publisher. Founded by **Edwin F. Kalmus** in New York in 1926. Lawrence Gallison, Edwin Kalmus's son-in-law, became vice president and manager in 1961 and later chairman of the board. Under Gallison's leadership, Kalmus began to print its own music. They concentrated on releasing works that were in the public domain and available for reprints at low cost. In 1976, publisher Belwin-Mills purchased everything in the Kalmus catalogue, except for the orchestral department. Located in Boca Raton, Florida, since 1971, they concentrate on selling and renting orchestral music.

Kamensek, Karen. (b. 1970.) American **conductor** who studied at the University of Indiana and now works mainly in Germany. Kamensek has served as first **Kapellmeister** at the Vienna Volksoper (2000–2003), general music director at the Freiburg Stadttheater (2003–2006), chief conductor of the Slowenian National Theater in Maribor (2007–2008), assistant music director at the Hamburg Staatsoper (2008–2011), and music director at the Hannover Staatsoper (2011–present). She has been a guest conductor at the Frankfurt opera; Deutsche Oper and Komische Oper in Berlin; Opera Australia in Melbourne; Royal Opera, Copenhagen; Hannover Staatsorchester; Hamburg Philharmonic; Linz Bruckner Orchester; and others. She is also known for having conducted the premiere of Philip Glass's opera *Les Enfants Terribles* (1996) and Mervyn Burtch's *The Raven King* (1999).

Kappelle. (Ger.) Chapel. See also ***Hofkapelle.***

Kapellmeister. (Ger.) A title designating the person in charge of music, at a chapel, for instance (lit. "Chapel master"). The title has evolved to designate the musician in charge of music making for a monarch. For example, Joseph Haydn held such a role for the Austrian Eszterházy family and George Frideric Handel was Kapellmeister for the Elector of Hanover, who became King George I of England. The term has fallen out of favor in modern use, except in places such as the **Leipzig Gewandhaus**, where tradition calls for the title *Gewandhauskapellmeister*. In other German opera houses, the Kapellmeister title is subordinate to the *Generalmusikdirector* (general music director), who, for all intents and purposes, is the chief or principal conductor. Also ***Capellmeister.*** (Fr. *maître de chapelle*, It. *maestro de capelle*, Sp. *maestro di capilla*.)

Kaprálová, Vítezslava (1915–1940). Czech composer and **conductor**. **Kaprálová** studied at the Brno Conservatory. She studied composition with Vilem Petrzelka and conducting with Zdenek Chalabala, later continuing her studies in Prague with composer Vitezslav Novak and conductor **Vaclav Talich**. From 1937 to 1940, she studied in Paris with Bohuslav Martinů, **Charles Munch**, and **Nadia Boulanger**. During that period, she conducted the Czech Philharmonic and the **BBC Symphony Orchestra** in her own compositions. Despite her early death, she left a substantial opus of music that has been performed by many distinguished concert artists. Her works have been published by a variety of companies, including Barenreiter Verlag, Editio Praga, La Siréne Editions Musicales, Editio Supraphone, and others.

kapriziös. (Ger.) Capricious, fanciful. A word sometimes heard in rehearsal to evoke a certain character. (Fr. *capricieux*, It. *capriccioso*, Sp. *capricho*.)

Karajan, Herbert von. (1908–1989.) Austrian **conductor**. While mostly known for his long tenure with the **Berlin Philharmonic** (1954–1989), Karajan was a dominating figure in Europe for most of the second half of the twentieth century. He held positions with the **Vienna State Opera** (music director, 1956–1964) and the **Salzburg Festival** (artistic director, 1956–1960 and 1964–1988), where he founded the **Salzburg Easter Festival** in 1967. He served as the music director of the **Berlin State Opera** from 1939 to 1945 and conducted the **Philharmonia Orchestra** in London from 1948 to 1960. He also served with the **Vienna Symphony Orchestra** (1948–1958), the **Orchestre de Paris** (1969–1971), and at **La Scala Opera** in Milan (1948–1989). Karajan's American debut came in 1955 with the **Berlin Philharmonic Orchestra**, and his **Metropolitan Opera** debut was in 1967 in a production of **Richard Wagner**'s *Die Walküre*.

Karajan was born in Salzburg, where he studied at the **Mozarteum** as a schoolboy. He soon moved on to the **Vienna Music Academy** and began his conducting studies. He made his conducting debut at the early age of nineteen, conducting Ludwig van Beethoven's *Fidelio* at the Salzburg Landestheater (1927). Soon after, he was appointed principal conductor at the Ulm Opera (1929–1934), where a performance of Mozart's *Marriage of Figaro* drew critical acclaim, followed by a similar position in Aachen (1934–1942). A performance of *Tristan und Isolde* at the **Berlin State Opera** in 1937 was a defining moment in his early career, so successful that critics began to refer to him as "Das Wunder Karajan."

His activities during the time of World War II dogged him for years afterward, and in certain circles he remained controversial until the end of his life. While he did not deny his membership in the Nazi Party, he always claimed that it was necessary for his career. Banned from conducting public performances, he spent the last six months of the war in Italy, followed by two years petitioning for "de-Nazification." It was granted just in time for performances with London's **Philharmonia Orchestra** and the **Vienna Symphony Orchestra**. A year later he returned to the Salzburg Festival.

The 1950s were years of great success that established Karajan as the so-called *Generalmusikdirektor* of Europe. He conducted Wagner's Ring and *Die Meistersinger* at **Bayreuth** (1951), toured Europe with London's

Philharmonia, and succeeded **Wilhelm Furtwängler** at the Berlin Philharmonic and **Karl Böm** at the **Vienna State Opera**. He also began what was to be one of the most significant recording careers ever documented, working with English record producer **Walter Legge** under contract with **Columbia, EMI, and Deutsche Grammophon**, as well as Polydor and **Decca**. By the end of his career, he had issued four Beethoven symphony sets, as well as complete collections of Anton Bruckner, **Gustav Mahler**, Johannes Brahms, and Pyotr Tchaikovsky and works from Johann Sebastian Bach, including the Brandenburg Concertos and *B minor Mass*, to those of the **Second Viennese School**, **Arnold Schoenberg**, Anton Webern, and Alban Berg, Claude Debussy's *Pelléas et Mélisande*, and **Igor Stravinsky**'s *Rite of Spring*, and much more. He also issued numerous operas, including those of Richard Wagner, **Richard Strauss**, and Wolfgang Amadeus Mozart. He had an operatic repertoire of over fifty works. Not a champion of either unfamiliar or new music, Hans Werner Henze was the only living composer whose music he chose to perform. In 1965, he founded a company, **Cosmotel**, to produce films of operas that he not only conducted but also produced and directed. Karajan would not tolerate any performance that was not up to his standards and sought total control over every element. He began to believe in the supremacy of recorded performances over live ones; it was there that he could completely control the outcome. Karajan, more than any other conductor, succeeded in using his recordings to solidify his celebrity and stature as the dominant European conductor of his day.

In Berlin, he oversaw the design and building of the new **Philharmonie**, the concert hall of the **Berlin Philharmonic**, which opened in 1963. In 1967, he was named the philharmonic's conductor for life. He founded the Karajan Foundation, which, among other projects, created the Philharmonic Academy, an international program for postgraduate instrumental students who come to Berlin in order to train with members of the philharmonic. This program has now been imitated all over the world.

To this day there is discussion about the particular sound he inherited from Furtwängler and which he then cultivated. Karajan was known by many as having all of the elements of a musical genius. His legacy is preserved by the many excellent recordings he made throughout his career.

kaum. (Ger.) Barely, hardly, scarcely, scant. (Fr. *à peine*, It. *appena*, Sp. *apenas*.) Often used in phrases such as *kaum crescendo*, almost no crescendo.

keck. (Ger.) Bold. (Fr. *alerte*, *dégagé*; It. *spigliato*; Sp. *atrevido*, *audaz*.) Examples: *Keck, aber nicht zu schnell*, bold, but not too fast, from *Das Lied von der Erde* by

Gustav Mahler; *Lustig im Tempo und keck im Ausdruck*, cheerful in tempo and bold in expression, from the title of mvt. 5 of Symphony No. 3 by Mahler.

Keene, Christopher. (1946–1995.) American conductor with a well-established reputation as an advocate of new music and especially of American composers. During the height of his career he served as music director of the New York City Opera (1982–1986) and its general director (1989–1995). He left a legacy of over three hundred performances of more than fifty operas. Composers who particularly interested him were Gian Carlo Menotti, Carlisle Floyd, John Corigliano, David Diamond, Philip Glass, Hans Werner Henze, Paul Hindemith, Toshiro Mayuzumi, Thomas Pasatieri, Aribert Reimann, and Roger Sessions.

In 1966, he served as the assistant conductor with the San Francisco Opera and the next year with the San Diego Opera. He conducted *The Saint of Bleecker Street* at composer Menotti's invitation at Spoleto Festival in 1968, and in 1969, he received the first Julius Rudel Award. He worked in various positions at Spoleto from 1971 to 1980, became the music director of the Syracuse Symphony (1975–1984), and founded the Long Island Philharmonic Orchestra, conducting it from 1979 to 1990. He appeared as a guest conductor throughout Europe and America, including with the Metropolitan Opera, New York; Deutsche Opera, Berlin; Lyric Opera of Chicago; and Vienna Volksoper, as well as with the Chicago Symphony Orchestra and the New York Philharmonic. His discography includes the first recording of Philip Glass's *Satyagraha* on CBS/Sony (1984) and the score to the film *Altered States* (1980), featuring the music of John Corigliano, and Giuseppe Verdi's *Il Trovatore* with the Utrechts Symfonieorkes.

Keeping Score. An educational television series hosted by Michael Tilson Thomas. The nine-part, one-hour documentary series, paired with live concert performances, explores the music and lives of Gustav Mahler, Dmitri Shostakovich, Charles Ives, Hector Berlioz, Aaron Copland, Igor Stravinsky, Peter Ilyich Tchaikovsky, and Ludwig van Beethoven.

keine, kein, keiner. (Ger.) No, not, none. (Fr. *aucun*; It. *niente*; Sp. *nada, ningún, ninguna*.) Often used in phrases such as *kein crescendo heir*, no crescendo here.

Kempe, Rudolf. (1910–1976.) German conductor known especially for his performances of Richard Wagner. Between 1955 and 1957, he led *Tannhäuser*, *Die Meistersinger*, and *Tristan und Isolde* at the Metropolitan Opera in New York and the first American performances of Richard Strauss's *Arabella*. He served with the Tonhalle Orchester Zürich (1965–1972), and in the last

months of his life, he was the chief conductor of the BBC Symphony Orchestra. At the time of his death, he was scheduled to conduct Ludwig van Beethoven's *Missa Solemnis* at the opening concert of the 1976 BBC Proms. Instead, the concert became a memorial to him.

Born in Dresden, he studied at the Saxon State Opera School in Dresden. In 1929, he was appointed first oboe in the Dortmund opera orchestra, moving shortly to the same position in the Leipzig Gewandhaus Orchestra. Some of the conductors he worked with were Wilhelm Furtwängler, Richard Strauss, Sir Thomas Beecham, Bruno Walter, Otto Klemperer, and Erich Kleiber. He became a vocal coach at the Leipzig Opera in 1933, and during World War II, he was the principal conductor of the Chemnitz opera house. He was music director of the Dresden State Opera and Staatskapelle (1949–1953), succeeded Georg Solti as chief conductor of the Bavarian State Opera in Munich (1952–1954), and did much guest conducting, including performances at the Royal Opera House, Covent Garden, where he was offered but declined the position of music director. He had a long association with Beecham's Royal Philharmonic Orchestra in London, serving first as the associate conductor and then on Beecham's death as he principal conductor. From 1963 to 1975, he was the orchestra's artistic director.

While considered a Wagnerite, the opera he conducted most often was Georges Bizet's *Carmen*; and though he had great success with *The Ring*, his musical taste encompassed everything from Wolfgang Amadeus Mozart to Hans Pfitzner, whose opera *Palestrina* he led at the Salzburg Festival in 1955. Regarded by orchestra members as having a baton technique that clearly communicated his musical wishes, he was relaxed in rehearsal, giving few comments. In performances, his personality became passionate and energetic, often inspiring the musicians to great heights. His catalogue of recordings is a legacy of standards—symphonies of Ludwig van Beethoven, Johannes Brahms, and Anton Bruckner and several operas—but also such works as Erich Wolfgang Korngold's *Symphony in F sharp* and Leoš Janáček's *Glagolithic Mass*.

Kennan, Kent. (1913–2003.) American composer, teacher, and author of an orchestration book, *The Technique of Orchestration* (1952; 3rd ed., 1983; 5th ed., 1997), and the theory book *Counterpoint: Based on Eighteenth-Century Practice* (1959; 4th ed., 1998). Kennan studied composition with Howard Hanson at the Eastman School of Music (bachelor of music 1934, master of music 1936). He won the Rome Prize and spent three years there, studying for a short period with the Italian composer Ildebrando Pizzetti. His first teaching position was at Kent State University, followed by the University of Texas, Austin; service as an army bandmaster; a position at Ohio State University; and then his return to the University of Texas. See the bibliography.

Kennedy Center. Known formally as the John F. Kennedy Center for the Performing Arts and located in Washington, DC, the Kennedy Center is home to the **National Symphony Orchestra**, the Washington National Opera, and the Suzanne Ferrell Ballet. Opened in 1971, it remains a living memorial to President Kennedy. The center has a tradition of educational programs, commissioning, producing, and presenting arts events for students and programs to engage adults with master classes, open rehearsals, workshops, and more. The National Symphony Orchestra, the main tenant of the center, has its own educational events, including an "Instrument Petting Zoo" and concerts designed specifically to introduce young audiences to classical music in a fun atmosphere. The center sponsors Explore the Arts Online, with an on-demand archive of arts videos, interactive arts exploration sites, and live broadcasts.

Kennedy Center Friedheim Award. An annual award for instrumental composition by an American composer given by the **John F. Kennedy Center for the Performing Arts** from 1978 to 1995. Established by Eric Friedheim (1910–2002) to honor his father, the pianist Arthur Friedheim (1859–1932), who had been a student of **Franz Liszt**. Prizes were awarded to seventy composers.

Kertész, István. (1929–1973.) Hungarian-born **conductor** of Jewish heritage. During his relatively short career, Kertész conducted many of the world's top orchestras, including the **Berlin Philharmonic**, **Royal Concertgebouw Orchestra**, **Israel Philharmonic**, **London Symphony**, Vienna Philharmonic, and many American orchestras, including Chicago, Cleveland, Los Angeles, Minnesota, New York, Philadelphia, Pittsburgh, and San Francisco. He made his U.S. debut with the **Detroit Symphony** in the 1961–1962 concert season. In spite of the family going into hiding during the Holocaust, his mother saw to it that he received a musical education. He studied the violin from the age of six and entered the Royal Academy of Music, now the **Franz Liszt Academy**, studying composition with Zoltán Kodály and conducting with **János Ferencsik** and **László Somogyi**. After graduation, he became the chief conductor of the Philharmonic Orchestra in Győr (1953–1955) and led the **Budapest Opera Orchestra** (1955–1957). He moved to Rome in 1956 in order to continue his studies and conducted the Santa Cecilia Orchestra, at the same time as guest conducting at several opera houses in Germany. Kertész accepted a guest position in Hamburg, conducting Ludwig van Beethoven's *Fidelio* and Giacomo Puccini's *La Bohème* to particular acclaim. He developed a reputation for his performances of Wolfgang Amadeus Mozart in addition to works of **Richard Strauss** and Giuseppe Verdi in his position as music director at the Augsburg Opera in Germany. He began to guest conduct frequently at this time, appearing at the **Salzburg Festival**, the **Deutsche Oper** in Berlin, and many others. One of his most notable performances was of Sergei Prokofiev's *The Flaming Angel* at the **Festival of Two Worlds** in Spoleto, Italy. In 1964, he became the music director of the Cologne Opera, introducing **Sir Benjamin Britten**'s opera *Billy Budd* to the German audience. He served as the principal conductor of the **London Symphony** from 1965 to 1968 and of the **Ravinia Festival**, the summer home of the **Chicago Symphony**, from 1970 to 1972. The members of the **Cleveland Orchestra** voted for Kertész as their choice to replace George Szell, although that position ultimately went to **Lorin Maazel**. He was known for an almost relaxed manner in rehearsal but for electrifying performances that won him much public adulation.

Kertész had an exclusive contract with **Decca/London** and in a short period created an impressive collection. It includes the first complete recording of Mozart's *La clemenza di Tito* and several symphonies and other works of Mozart; the complete symphonies of Johannes Brahms, Antonin Dvořák (still considered classics), and Franz Schubert; Béla Bartók's *Bluebeard's Castle* and Piano Concerto No. 3; Kodály's complete *Háry János*, *Dances of Galanta*, *Psalmus Hungaricus*, and the *Peacock Variations*; and several works of Franz Liszt. Kertész died in a drowning accident off the coast of Israel at the age of forty-three.

kettledrum. Outmoded term for timpani.

key. The principal tonality of a musical composition such as *Symphony in C* or *Sonata in f minor*. (Fr. *tonalité*, Ger. *Tonart, Tonalität*, It. *tonalità*, Sp. *tonalidad*)

keyboard score reading. The ability to read a score, with all its multiple parts, transposing and otherwise, at the keyboard. Works for solo and orchestra, such as concertos, normally come with a **piano reduction** prepared in order to facilitate the preparation or accompaniment of a work when an orchestra is unavailable.

key click. Used primarily on woodwind instruments, a sound made when a player strikes a key with enough force to make a hard, metallic "click." Usually indicated by the sign +.

key signature. A notational devise indicating the predominant key of a musical composition. In much twentieth-century music, the key signature has been discarded, especially in nontonal music where extensive chromaticism makes a signature confusing. (Fr. *armature, armure de la clé*; Ger. *Tonartvorzeichnung*; It. *armature di chiave*; Sp. *armadura*.)

kHz. Abbreviation for **kilohertz**.

Kidzone! Part of the **New York Philharmonic**'s website designed for young people. It includes games, activities, and information that facilitate a child's experience when they attend a philharmonic concert.

Kiesler, Kenneth. (b. 1953.) Well-known conductor and pedagogue. Kiesler serves as the director of university orchestras and professor of conducting at the University of Michigan (1995–present). He has led the **National Symphony Orchestra**, the **Chicago Symphony**, and orchestras of Utah, Detroit, New Jersey, Florida, Indianapolis, Menphis, San Diego, Albany, Virginia, Jerusalem, Daejeon and Pusan in Korea, Hang Zhou in China, and others. He served as the music director of the Illinois Symphony from 1980 to 2000 and as its music advisor from 2010 to 2012. He has been awarded the 1988 Helen M. Thompson Award given by the **League of American Orchestras** (formerly the ASOL) and the Silver Medal at the 1986 Stokowski competition in Salt Lake City. Kiesler is a proponent of contemporary composers in both programming and recording. His students have won major competitions and hold positions with major orchestras, opera companies, and several music schools. He has been the director of the Conductors Programme of Canada's National Arts Center since 2006 and every summer leads the **Conductors Retreat** at Medomak, Maine.

kilohertz. A unit of frequency equivalent to one thousand cycles per second or **hertz**. Abbreviated **kHz**. See also **Hertz, Heinrich**.

Kimmel Center for the Performing Arts, Philadelphia. Opened in 2001, the Kimmel Center is home to Verizon Hall, a 2,500-seat concert hall that is home to the **Philadelphia Orchestra** and Peter Nero and the Philly Pops; the Perelman Theater, a 650-seat recital hall that is home to PHILADANCO, the Chamber Orchestra of Philadelphia, the Philadelphia Chamber Music Society, and American Theater Arts for Youth; and the Innovation Studio, a black box theater. The center also operates the **Academy of Music**, owned by the Philadelphia Orchestra and the orchestra's original home, currently home to Opera Philadelphia and the Pennsylvania Ballet, and the Merriman Theater, owned by the University of the Arts and home to student events ten weeks each season.

Kinect technology. See **philharmonia orchestra**.

King's College, Cambridge. Founded in 1441 by King Henry VI, it is one of thirty-one colleges at the University of Cambridge and is world famous for its chapel and choir. Its Festival of Nine Lessons and Carols is broadcast around the world. Undergraduate music study covers harmony, counterpoint, analysis, history, and more. Distinguished alumni include conductors **Sir John Elliott Gardiner** and **Sir Andrew Davis** and composers Judith Weir and George Benjamin.

Kirchhoff, Craig. (b. 1949.) American **band conductor**. Kirchhoff is a professor of conducting and the director of bands at the University of Minnesota. He is the director the **wind ensemble** and coordinates the graduate program in wind ensemble/band conducting. Past president of the **College Band Directors National Association (CBDNA)**, and a member of the **American Bandmasters Association**, among others, he was a founding editor of the *CBDNA Journal*. Professor Kirchoff has garnered praise from many contemporary American composers for his work promoting and encouraging new music for band. He is a frequent guest conductor of the **Tokyo Kosei Wind Orchestra** and other ensembles around the world.

Kl. (Ger.) Abbreviation for ***Klarinette***. See **clarinet**.

Klage. (Ger.) A lament, elegy, threnody. Also ***Klagelied***. (Fr. *lamentation, plaint*, It. *lamento*, Sp. *lamento*.)

Klagend. (Ger.) Plaintive, mournful. A character word used to evoke a particular playing style. (Fr. *plaintif*, It. *lamentoso*, Sp. *lamentable*.)

Klang. (Ger.) Sound, tone, ring. Also ***Schall***. (Fr. *son*, It. *suono*, Sp. *sonido*.) Example: *Die drei instrumente in vollständige gleicher Klangstärke, alle ohne jeden Ausdruck*, The three instruments at completely the same dynamic, all without any expression, from ***Pierrot Lunaire*** by **Arnold Schoenberg**.

Klangfarbe. (Ger.) Tone color, timbre. (Fr. *couleur, timbre*; It. *colore, timbre*; Sp. *color de tono, timbre*.)

Klangfarbenmelodie. (Ger.) Tone-color melody or a succession of pitches, each played by a different instrument, creating a "melodie" of instrumental colors not only, or as an alternative to, a melody of pitches. **Arnold Schoenberg** wrote about the idea in his 1911 book, *Harmonielehre*. A *Klangfarbernmelodie* based on a single pitch can be found in Elliott Carter's *Eight Studies and a Fantasy for Woodwind Quartet*. A single G (g′) is employed, leaving the creation of musical expression solely to the elements of timbre and dynamics.

Other examples include **Arnold Schoenberg**, *Five Pieces for Orchestra*, movement three, titled "Farben." Also heard in Anton Webern's *Six Bagatelles for String Quartet*, opus 9, and in the final movement of the *Lyric Suite* by Alban Berg, where the opening theme of **Richard Wagner**'s prelude to *Tristan and Isolde* is presented in different string colors.

Klarinette. (Ger.) **Clarinet**. (Fr. *clarinette*, It. *clarinetto*, Sp. *clarineto*.) See also **appendix 3**.

Klavier. (Ger.) **Piano** (the instrument). (Fr. *clavier, piano*; It. *piano*; Sp. *piano*.) See also **appendix 4**.

Klavierauszug. (Ger.) A piano reduction of an orchestral or other large score. (Fr. *partition pour piano*, It. *riduzione per piano*, Sp. *reducción para piano*.)

Kleiber, Carlos. (1930–2004.) Austrian **conductor** of German birth. The son of conductor **Erich Kleiber**, he was born in Berlin and given the name Karl. When the family immigrated to Buenos Aires and became Argentinian citizens, his name was changed to Carlos. According to Charles Barber, who had a lengthy correspondence with Kleiber, after returning to Europe he refused to turn his back on his South American upbringing, melding elements of the vitality and spirit of Latin dance with his rigorous Germanic discipline and drive to understand the form and analysis into a cultural "biochemistry."

Educated at residential schools in Argentina and Chile, Kleiber had only sporadic musical training. His parents were not eager for him to become a musician; he taught himself to play the **piano** and sought his own musical education. At school in Zürich, he studied chemistry. However, at the age of twenty, he volunteered as a vocal coach at the Gärtnerplatztheater in Munich, and four year later (1954), he conducted his first performance in Potsdam under the pseudonym Karl Keller. It wasn't until 1958 that he made his formal debut under his given name. During his lifetime he held only a few full-time positions, such as at the Zürich Opera (1964–1966) and the Württembergisches Staatstheater in Stuttgart (1966–1968). For ten years he served as a contracted long-term guest conductor for the Staatsoper in Munich, but thereafter only accepted engagements as a guest. While he had a commanding knowledge of a vast repertoire of works, from the 1970s forward he limited himself to conducting a rather small number of works, and over the course of his career he led fewer than 90 concerts and about 620 opera performances. He was known for cancelling at the last minute and told **Herbert von Karajan** that he conducted only when he was hungry. Some said he was temperamental, while others saw this as his way of "reaching for the highest standards of musicianship."

Kleiber conducted Alban Berg's *Wozzeck* at the Edinburgh Festival in 1966, *Tristan und Isolde* at the **Vienna Staatsoper** (1973) and the next year in **Bayreuth**, and **Richard Strauss**'s *Der Rosenkavalier* at both the **Royal Opera House, Covent Garden**, and **La Scala, Milan**, in 1974. Some of the orchestras he conducted include the **Chicago Symphony Orchestra** (1979), **London Symphony Orchestra** (1981), and **Berlin Philharmonic** (1981). In 1982, he conducted *La Bohème* at the

Metropolitan Opera in New York, returning for performances of *Otello* and *Der Rosenkavalier*. As his reputation grew, he was able to demand and receive many more rehearsals than normally allotted, with thirty-four for his Munich *Wozzeck* and seventeen for *La Bohème* at Covent Garden. He often wrote little notes to members of the orchestra, placing them on their music stands before rehearsal, which became known as "Kleibergrams." The first choice of the Berlin Philharmonic to replace Karajan, he refused the position.

His discography is equally small but highly acclaimed and includes Ludwig van Beethoven's Symphonies Nos. 4, 5, 6, and 7; Franz Schubert's Symphonies Nos. 3 and 8; Johannes Brahms's Symphony No. 4; Richard Strauss's *Elektra* and *Der Rosenkavalier*; Carl Maria von Weber's *Der Freischutz*; Giueseppe Verdi's *La Traviata*; **Richard Wagner**'s *Tristan und Isolde*; and two New Year's concerts with the **Vienna Philharmonic** from 1989 and 1992. In 2010, **Deutsche Grammophon** released a twelve-CD set of his complete recordings. He can also be seen on several DVDs that document both opera and concert performances and in two documentaries, *Carlos Kleiber: I am Lost to the World* (2010) and *Carlos Kleiber: Traces to Nowhere* (2011). Referred to as a genius by conductor **Bernard Haitink**, Kleiber is generally regarded as one of the greatest conductors of the twentieth century. See the **bibliography**.

Kleiber, Erich. (1890–1956.) Austrian **conductor** and composer. Kleiber served as the principal conductor of the Darmstadt Opera (1912–1919), where he debuted with Jacques Offenbach's *Le Belle Hélène* and also conducted **Arnold Schoenberg**'s *Pierrot Lunaire*, **Gustav Mahler**'s *Das Lied von der Erde*, and the Verdi *Requiem*. He moved from there to various German opera houses, ending up at the **Berlin State Opera** (1923–1934). He led acclaimed performances of Alban Berg's *Wozzeck*, Leoš Janáček's *Jenufa*, and Darius Milhaud's *Christophe Colomb* and performed many new works with the **Berlin Philharmonic** by such composers as Ferruccio Busoni, Schoenberg, **Richard Strauss**, Alban Berg, and Béla Bartók. He left Germany in 1934 as a matter of protest when the Nazi's rose to power, guest conducting frequently, and in 1939, he became a resident, and later a citizen, of Buenos Aires, Argentina.

From 1943 to 1948 Kleiber served as the conductor of the Havana Philharmonic Orchestra. He returned to Europe in 1952 and was appointed to the position of principal conductor of the **Berlin State Opera** in East Berlin. His tenure there was relatively short as he resigned in 1955 because of dissatisfaction with the conditions. He remained in demand as a guest conductor to the end of his life.

Kleiber had a reputation as a perfectionist but without forsaking musicality and feeling. He said, "When I conduct, I leave it to my heart, and my feelings, and my respect for what the composer wrote, to tell me what to do. Everything else comes second to me—if it comes at all!" During his tenure in Berlin, he was reputed to call rehearsals on the day of performance with the sole purpose of delivering notes on mistakes from the previous day's dress rehearsal that he claimed had been brought to his attention by the composer himself. In these instances, no playing occurred. By the time the concert arrived, he would used only minimal gestures, allowing the orchestra to do what they needed to do without putting on a show for the audience. Kleiber fought against laziness in orchestra playing, saying, "There are two enemies to good performance: one is routine and the other is improvisation."

Kleiber's list of recordings is impressive and long. His best were made under contract with Decca in the last decade of his life. They include Ludwig van Beethoven's Symphonies 3, 5, 6, and 7 with the **Amsterdam Concertgebouw Orchestra** No. 9 with the **Vienna Philharmonic**, and *Der Rosenkavalier* and *The Marriage of Figaro* at the Vienna State Opera; Peter Ilyich Tchaikovsky's **Symphonies Nos. 4 and 6** with the **Paris Conservatory Orchestra**; and Wolfgang Amadeus Mozart's Symphony No. 40 with the **London Philharmonic Orchestra**. It has been argued that his recording of Beethoven's Symphony No. 5 may be the greatest ever made, at least until that of his son, Carlos, which appeared in 1975. His recording of Mozart's *Figaro* has been described as a miracle of style and ensemble. See the **bibliography**.

klein. (Ger.) Little, small. Also *wenig*. (Fr. *petit, peu*; It. *piccolo, poco*; Sp. *pequeño/a*.)

kleine Flöte. (Ger.) **Piccolo**. See also **appendix 3**.

kleine Trommel. (Ger.) **Snare drum**. See also **appendix 4**.

Klemperer, Otto. (1885–1973.) German **conductor** and composer. Klemperer studied at the Hoch Conservatory in Frankfurt and the Klindworth-Schwarwenka and Stern Conservatories in Berlin where he was a composition and conducting student of Hans Pfitzner. He had an early opportunity to work with **Gustav Mahler**, conducting the offstage orchestra in a performance of his Symphony No. 2, "*Resurrection*," under the baton of Oskar Fried with the composer in attendance. In 1906, he replaced Fried, who had had a difference of opinion with director **Max Reinhardt**, and conducted his production of *Orpheus in the Underworld* about fifty times at the Neues Theater in Berlin. Klemperer met Mahler again in Vienna, where he played his own piano transcription of the Scherzo movement of the Symphony No. 2 for him from memory. Mahler gave him a recommendation written on the back

of a business card that turned out to be influential in helping Klemperer at the beginning of his career. In 1907, he was appointed to the Neues Deutsches Theater in Prague and then Hamburg (1910–1912). He moved on to Bremen (1913–1914), Strasbourg (1914–1917), Cologne (1917–1924), and Wiesbaden (1924–1927). Klemperer was appointed music director to the third opera house in Berlin, the Kroll Opera, when **Erich Kleiber** was at the State Opera and **Bruno Walter** was at the Charlottenburg Opera. He served there from 1927 until it was forced to close because of political pressures in 1931. At the beginning, he found the artistic environment to his liking and was able to program several significant contemporary operas, including **Arnold Schoenberg**'s *Erwartung* and *Die glückliche Hand*, **Igor Stravinsky**'s *Oedipus Rex* and *Mavra*, Paul Hindemith's *Cardillac*, and *Neues vom Tage*, Leoš Janáček's *From the House of the Dead*, Kurt Weill's *Der Jasager*, in addition to many orchestral works. But they also mounted newly conceived, experimental productions of such operas as Wagner's *Der fliegende Holländer*, Ludwig van Beethoven's *Fidelio*, and Wolfgang Amadeus Mozart's *Don Giovanni* that had an enormous influence on the course of opera productions even after the war. After the closure of the Kroll Opera, Klemperer conducted at the State Opera, where in 1933 he led performances of *Tannhäuser* on the fiftieth anniversary of Wagner's death. Coming from a Jewish family, he was forced to leave Germany upon the rise of the Nazi's even though Hitler himself had presented Klemperer with a Goethe Medal for outstanding contributions to German culture. After Austria and then Switzerland, he ended up as conductor of the **Los Angeles Philharmonic Orchestra**, remaining in California from 1935 to 1939. While there he took advantage of the presence of composer Arnold Schoenberg and studied composition with him. His output includes several operas, nine string quartets, and six symphonies. During these years, Klemperer also guest conducted the **New York Philharmonic-Symphony** and the **Philadelphia Orchestra** and was brought in to reorganize the **Pittsburg Symphony**. In 1939, in America, he underwent an operation for a brain tumor that left him partially paralyzed. He was no longer able to use a baton. His recovery was lengthy and for quite a while he did not conduct. He also suffered from a disease that caused extremes mood swings, most likely he was bipolar. He became an American citizen in 1940 but eventually returned to Europe when opportunities arose there. His next permanent engagement came at the **Hungarian State Opera** in Budapest (1947–1954). An accident resulting in a back injury in the Montreal Airport in 1951 forced him to sit when he conducted. In 1954, he settled in Zürich, Switzerland, though most of his professional activities for the remainder of his life were in London. In 1959, he was appointed principal conductor of **Walter Legge**'s **Philharmonia Orchestra**.

When in 1964 Legge sought to disband the orchestra, the members reformed as the **New Philharmonia**, inviting Klemperer to be not only their conductor but also their president. He also conducted often at the **Royal Opera House, Covent Garden**, including *Fidelio* (1961), *Die Zauberflöte* (1962), and *Lohengrin* (1963).

In contrast to his early years, where he established his reputation with the newest repertoire, in his later years he was primarily known for performances of Beethoven, Mahler, and Anton Bruckner. His cycles of the Beethoven symphonies in London are remembered as major events, and he became known as one of the greatest conductors of the century. His association with Legge led to a contract with the recording company EMI, which had an enormously positive impact on his lasting reputation. Known early as a towering figure—he was even taller than **Wilhelm Furtwängler**—his health problems led to an affect of heroism. Active at the same time as **Arturo Toscanini**, in many aspects they were opposites; Toscanini grew to favor brisk tempos, Klemperer sought to let the music unfold in a more leisurely manner. While the reasons for this cannot be definitively established, they both claimed the score as their only authority, passing on to future generations of conductors the principal of intense score study and dedication to the intentions of the composer as essential to conducting. Klemperer's writings include *Minor Recollections* (1964) and *Klemperer on Music* (ed. M. Andersen, 1986). See the **bibliography**.

Otto Klemperer. *Courtesy Photofest.*

Kl. Fl. (Ger.) Abbreviation for ***kleine Flöte***. See also **appendix 3, piccolo**.

klingen. (Ger.) To sound, to ring. Also *klingen lassen,* let it ring, as in cymbals, triangle, or tam-tam, for instance. (Fr. *laissez vibrer*, Ger. *klingen lassen*, It. *lasciar vibrare*, Sp. *dejar que vibre*.) Examples: *klingt*, sounds, rings.

klingen wie geschrieben, klingen wie notiert. (Ger.) Sounding as written or as notated. (Fr. *comme ecrit*, Sp. *como escrita*.)

Kl. Tr. (Ger.) Abbreviation for ***kleine Trommel***. See also **appendix 3, snare drum**.

Kletzki, Paul. (1900–1973.) Polish-born Swiss **conductor** and composer. He studied at the **Warsaw Conservatory** and the **Hochschule für Musik**, Berlin. Both **Arturo Toscanini** and **Wilhelm Furtwängler** conducted his compositions in the 1920s with the **Berlin Philharmonic Orchestra** (1925), the Berlin Radio Symphony, and orchestras of Bremen, Dresden, Essen Dortmund Heidelberg, Gothenburg, Sweden, and others. But because he was Jewish, he left Nazi Germany in 1933, and moved first to Italy, where he taught composition in Milan. In 1939, he settled in Switzerland. After World War II he gave up composition, commenting, "The shock of all that Hitlerism . . . destroyed also in me the spirit and will to compose." Some say that at that point he acted as if his own music had ceased to exist. Kletzki became known as a conductor who used an excellent technique to evoke lively and spirited music making. He had a broad repertoire that ranged from Ludwig van Beethoven to **Gustav Mahler** and his countrymen Karol Szymanowski and **Witold Lutosławski**. Keltzki made his British debut in 1947 with the **Philharmonia Orchestra**, was the principal conductor of the **Liverpool Philharmonic Orchestra** (1954–1955), toured Central and South America, and conducted the **Philadelphia Orchestra** (1959). He then served as the music director of the **Dallas Symphony Orchestra** (1960–1963), the Berne Symphony Orchestra, Switzerland (1964–1968), and after **Ernest Ansermet**'s retirement, **the Orchestra de la Suisse Romande**, Geneva (1967–1970). The **Naxos** Classical Archives catalogue lists recordings that Kletzki conducted of Felix Mendelssohn's Symphony No. 3, "Scottish," and a *Midsummer Night's Dream*, and on the CD Accord list, Franz Schubert's Symphony No. 9, also known as the *"Great" C major*.

Knappertsbusch, Hans. (1888–1965.) German **conductor**. At the urging of his parents, he studied philosophy at university but then attended the Cologne Conservatory in order to study conducting. He made his debut with the orchestra in Mülheim, Germany, and was subsequently appointed as principal conductor (1910–1912). At the same time, he worked as an assistant to Siegfried Wagner and **Hans Richter** in **Bayreuth**, the site of his greatest triumph, the 1951 *Parsifal*, known as the greatest performance of **Richard Wagner**'s final opera in the twentieth century. Grounded in the conducting traditions that preceded him, it was in the opera house that Knappertsbusch excelled, bringing an impeccable sense of dramatic tension to bear, especially in the slow tempi he preferred. Because he didn't like to travel, his reputation as a superb conductor has always been somewhat localized to Germany and Austria.

From 1913 to 1918 he was the principal conductor at the opera in Bochum/Eberfeld, Germany, moving to Leipzig for the 1918–1919 season and then Dessau (1919–1922). In 1922, he became the conductor at the **Bavarian State Opera**, Munich, succeeding Bruno Walter. While there, he led the premieres of Albert Coates's *Samuel Pepys* (1929) and Hans Pfitzner's *Das Herz* (1931). He remained until 1936 when Hitler personally gave the order that he be fired because of his refusal to join the Nazi Party. He was almost immediately invited to Vienna, where he conducted at the **Vienna State Opera** and the **Vienna Philharmonic Orchestra** until the Nazis annexed Austria. In 1936, he had conducted at the **Royal Opera House**, **Covent Garden**, but also lost his permit to travel outside Germany. Once World War II was over, Knappertsbusch reemerged as a conductor of the Germanic repertoire, particularly of Ludwig van Beethoven, Johannes Brahms, Wagner, Anton Bruckner, and **Richard Strauss**, serving as a regular guest conductor of the **Vienna Philharmonic**. In 1951, he established himself at Bayreuth, conducting there until 1964. He returned to the **Bavarian State Opera** in Munich in 1954, though he delayed that return by a full season to protest the slow reconstruction of the opera house.

Knappertsbusch is often described as essentially conservative both as a musician and as a person. But he was mostly a man of principle, who had no qualms making his opinions known, even if the result would have a negative impact on his career. Nor did he give much credence to his admirers or the press. He often left a concert by the back door before the applause was even over. Orchestra members loved him because he didn't see the need to rehearse works that he and the orchestra had already performed, preferring a spontaneous approach to music making. This meant that he was not really well disposed to the discipline of recording. As a consequence, his legacy of recordings is relatively sparse. A recording of his triumphant Bayreuth *Parsifal* issued by **Decca** was actually put together from rehearsals and performances. After the war, he did record Wagner's *Die Meistersinger* with the Vienna Philharmonic Orchestra. It was issued act by act, with act 2 being one of the first long-playing (LP) records in the **Decca** catalogue. Other LPs include Bruckner's Symphonies Nos. 3, 4, 5, and 7 with the Vienna Philharmonic and No. 8 with Munich.

Knarre. (Ger.) **Ratchet, rattle**. See also **appendix 4**.

Knight Foundation, John S. and James L. See **John S. and James L. Knight Foundation**.

Knussen, Oliver. (b. 1952.) British composer and **conductor**. Knussen made his conducting debut at the age of fifteen when he led the premiere of his *First Symphony* after István Kertész became ill. A distinguished composer of numerous orchestral works and two fantasy operas, *Where the Wild Things Are* and *Higglety Pigglety Pop!* both based on stories by Maurice Sendak, Knussen studied composition with John Lambert and then with **Gunther Schuller** at **Tanglewood**. He has maintained a close relationship with Tanglewood for many years, serving as the dead of contemporary music activities from 1986 to 1993. From 1983 to 1998 he was the artistic director of the **Aldeburg Festival** in England and became the music director of the **London Sinfonietta** in 1998. In 2002, he became the sinfonietta's conductor laureate. He was the chief conductor of the Residentie-Orkest in The Hague (1992–1996) and has conducted many of America's top orchestras. His performances of contemporary music are known for clarity; he is said to have the ability to make the most complex work coherent. Since 1995, he has had a recording contract with **Deutsche Grammophon**, a relationship that has produced award-winning results.

Köchel, Ludwig Ritter von. (1800–1877.) Austrian musicologist, writer, composer, botanist, and publisher. Köchel is best known for creating and publishing the **Köchel-Verzeichnis**, a catalogue of Wolfgang Amadeus Mozart's complete works, and having originated the "Köchel" or "K" numbering system, by which the works are known.

Köchel-Verzeichnis. The chronological thematic catalogue for the works of Wolfgang Amadeus Mozart created by **Ludwig Ritter von Köchel** and first published in 1862. Revisions were published in 1937 by musicologist Alfred Einstein, with a sixth edition appearing in 1964. It is abbreviated as **KV**. See also **thematic catalogue**.

Komische Oper Berlin. This German company began in the late nineteenth century as a presenter of operetta and musicals and now offers a full range of opera, operetta, musicals, symphony concerts, and special productions for young people. The acclaimed director Walter Felsenstein founded the new Komische Oper in 1947, leading it until his death in 1975. Felsenstein was assisted by the esteemed director Götz Friedrich. A resident company, it won the Opera House of the Year award from the German magazine *Opernwelt* in 2007 and again in 2013. The current *Intendant* (director) is Barrie Kosky, who was appointed in the 2012–2013 season. General music directors have included Rolf Reuter (1981–1993), Yakov Kreizberg (1994–2002), Kirill Petrenko (2002–2007), Carl St. Clair (2008–2010), Patrick Lange (2010–2011) and Henrik Nánási (2012–).

Kondrashin, Kirill Petrovich. (1914–1981.) Russian **conductor**. He became well known in the United States after conducting at the Tchaikovsky Competition for the American winner Van Cliburn (1958). He and Cliburn toured the United States, performing and recording Sergei Rachmaninov's Piano Concerto No. 3 and Peter Ilyich Tchaikovsky's first piano concerto. The Tchaikovsky concerto, issued by RCA, was the first long-playing (LP) recording in history to go platinum.

Kondrashin studied both piano and conducting at the **Moscow Conservatory**. His early appointments were in opera; he was the assistant conductor at the Nemirovich-Danchenko Musical Theater (1934–1937); conductor at the Maly Theater, Leningrad (1938–1942); and permanent conductor at the **Bolshoi Theater**, Moscow (1943–1956). He became the conductor of the **USSR State Symphony Orchestra** (1956–1960) and began to focus on symphonic repertoire. He served as the music director at the **Moscow Philharmonic** (1960–1976), teaching briefly at the **Moscow Conservatory** (1977–1978). In that position, he premiered both Symphony No. 4 and No. 13 by Dmitri Shostakovich. He also expanded the repertoire to include works of **Sir Benjamin Britten**, Anton Bruckner, **Gustav Mahler**, and Paul Hindemith. He was a highly honored conductor in his homeland, receiving the Stalin Prize in both 1948 and 1949 and the State Prize of the Russian Soviet Federative Socialist Republic in 1969, and he was named the People's Artist of the USSR in 1972. Nonetheless, he felt restricted by the heavy hand of the Soviet regime, and in 1978, while on tour in Amsterdam, he went into hiding and sought and received political asylum. The same year he was named the permanent guest conductor of the **Amsterdam Concertgebouw Orchestra** and also became a regular guest conductor at the **Vienna Philharmonic**.

Kondrashin was known as a dazzling master of the Russian repertoire. His recordings of Shostakovich are particularly successful examples, full of style and power. Kondrashin wrote several books on conducting that have not yet been translated into English.

Konsonant. (Ger.) Consonant, the opposite of dissonant. (Fr. *consonne*, It. *consonante*, Sp. *consonante*.)

Kontrabass. (Ger.) **Double bass**. See also **appendix 3**.

Kontrafagott. (Ger.) **Contrabassoon**. See **appendix 3**.

Konzertmeister, Konzertmeisterin. (Ger.) Concertmaster. (Fr. *premier violon solo*; It. *primo violin, spalla*; Sp. *concertino/concertina*.)

Konzertstück. (Ger.) Concert piece, often referring to a work for solo instrument and orchestra other than a concerto.

Kopfstimme. (Ger.) Head voice. (Fr. *voix de tête*, It. *voce di testa*, Sp. *voz de cabeza*.)

Kornett. (Ger.) **Cornet**.

Kostelanetz, André. (1901–1980.) Russian-born American **conductor**. Kostelanetz immigrated to the United States in 1922. Known mainly for his efforts in popularizing classical music, he commissioned Aaron Copland's *Lincoln Portrait*, William Schuman's *New England Triptych*, Paul Creston's *Frontiers*, Ferde Grofe's *Hudson River Suite*, Alan Hovhaness's *Floating World*, and works of other living composers. He conducted the premiere and recording of William Walton's *Capriccio burlesco*, a work that was dedicated to him, with the **New York Philharmonic** in 1968. He also served as the principal conductor of the philharmonic's Promenade Concerts (1963–1979), conducting the orchestra for a total of twenty-seven years. Throughout his career, he made many arrangements of lighter music for orchestral pops concerts and worked often in radio and film. Kostelanetz's many recordings on the **Columbia Records Masterworks** series remain excellent representatives of advances in recorded sound that he pioneered. His most popular LP, *Meet André Kostelanetz*, issued in 1955, rose to the top of the charts. His last public performance was *A Night in Old Vienna* with the **San Francisco Symphony Orchestra** in 1979. He was married to Lily Pons from 1938 to 1958, and they performed together often, including entertaining troops abroad during World War II. See the **bibliography**.

Koussevitzky Music Foundation. Founded in 1943 after the death of conductor Serge Koussevitzky's second wife, Natalie, in her honor. The foundation is now located in the Library of Congress in Washington, DC, and accepts applications from performing organizations for musical commissions every year. The list of composers who have been commissioned includes virtually all of the important American composers and also many from Europe and, more recently, Asia.

Koussevitzky, Serge Alexandrovich. (1874–1951.) Russian-born **conductor**, composer, and double bassist. He served as the music director of the **Boston Symphony Orchestra** from 1924 to 1949, conducting many first performances of works by both American and European composers. A champion of contemporary music, these works include Béla Bartók's *Concerto for Orchestra*; the American premiere of Sergei Prokofiev's Symphony No. 5; **Leonard Bernstein**'s Symphony No. 3, *"Kaddish"*; **Aaron Copland**'s *Appalachian Spring* **(Suite)**; Maurice Ravel's orchestration of Modest Mussorgsky's *Pictures at an Exhibition*; and more. He founded the **Berkshire Music Center at Tanglewood**, Massachusetts, and began to teach there in 1940. In 1943, he founded the **Koussevitzky Music Foundation** in memory of his second wife, using the foundation to commission many works, including Bartók's *Concerto for Orchestra* and **Sir Benjamin Britten**'s opera *Peter Grimes*. Koussevitzky left a significant legacy of recordings, mostly on the RCA Victor label and including Maurice Ravel's *Bolero*; an orchestral suite of **Igor Stravinsky**'s *Petrouchka*; Prokofiev's *Romeo and Juliet* and Symphony No. 1, "Classical"; and much more. Early in his career, Koussevitzky was an active double bassist and member of the Bolshoi orchestra. He composed a concerto and other works for the **double bass** that are still performed.

Serge Koussevitsky. *Courtesy Photofest.*

Kraft. (Ger.) Power, strength; also *kräftig* (adv.), *kraftvoll* (adj.), powerful, forceful. Examples: *mit Kraft*, with force; *mit aller Kraft*, with all your strength; *sehr kräftig*, very strong, all from *The Prelude to Die Meistersinger von Nürenberg* by **Richard Wagner**. Also *mit voller Kraft*, with full strength, from *Das Lied von der Erde* by **Gustav Mahler**.

Kräftig bewegt. (Ger.) Powerful motion. Seen in Symphony No. 1 in D major, mvt. 1, by **Gustav Mahler**.

Kraków Philharmonic Orchestra. Also known as the Symphony Orchestra of the Karol Szymanoski Philharmonic (Orkiestra Symfoniczna Filharmonii im. Karola Szymanowskiego). Although its roots can be traced back to the eighteenth century, the modern Kraków orchestra was founded in 1945 as the first active professional symphony in postwar Poland. Its first **conductor** was Zygmunt Latoszewski, a survivor of the Warsaw Uprising. The orchestra was named after Polish composer Karol Szymanowski in 1962. The composer **Krzysztof Penderecki** served as the artistic director of the symphony from 1988 to 1990. The Kraków Philharmonic is widely recorded and has toured extensively in Europe, as well as

in Japan, Canada, South Korea, Lebanon, Turkey, Iran, and the United States.

Kramer, Jonathan. (1942–2004.) American composer, theorist, teacher, and author. Kramer taught music at Columbia University (1988–2004); the University of California, Berkeley (1969–1970); **Oberlin Conservatory** (1970–1971); Yale University (1971–1978); and the **University of Cincinnati**'s **College-Conservatory of Music** (1978–1990). A distinguished American composer, Kramer studied with **Pierre Boulez**, Leon Kirchner, and Billy Jim Layton. He did postgraduate work with **Karlheinz Stockhausen**, Andrew W. Imbrie, Roger Sessions, and others. Kramer served as the program annotator for the **Cincinnati Symphony Orchestra** (1984–1992), the **San Francisco Symphony** (1967–1970), and the **National Symphony Orchestra** (1989–1992). His many stimulating program notes were collected and published in *Listen to the Music* (1988). He is the author of over twenty-five books and fifty articles, among them his important book *The Time of Music* in which he analyzes how the left and right sides of the brain process music. See the **bibliography**.

Kranik, Ardis. (1929–1997.) American mezzo-soprano and the general director of the **Lyric Opera of Chicago** from 1982 to 1997. After graduating from college, she became a secretary at the Lyric Opera while also singing as a secondary mezzo-soprano. In 1965, she became the artistic administrator under general director Carol Fox. During her tenure, the Lyric Opera was able to put its finances in order. In 1996, the Lyric's theater was renamed the Ardis Kranik Theatre in her honor. She was also awarded the Chicago History Museum's Making History Award for distinction in the performing arts.

Kremerata Baltica. A chamber orchestra founded in 1997 by the Latvian violinist Gidon Kremer. Its members come from Estonia, Latvia, and Lithuania. They tour often and usually perform without a **conductor**. They have recorded more than twenty remarkable CDs, many on the Nonesuch label. The disk *After Mozart* won a **Grammy Award** for best small ensemble performance when it was released in 2002. Many of their recordings feature contemporary music.

Kreuz. (Ger.) The sharp sign. Also ***Erhöhungszeichen***. (Fr. *dièse*, It. *dieses*, Sp. *sostenido*.) See also **accidental**.

Kreutzer, Rudolphe. (1766–1831.) French violinist, teacher, composer, and **conductor**. He was the dedicatee of Ludwig van Beethoven's *Violin Sonata No. 9 in A major* and the leader from the violin and later the conductor of the orchestra at the **Paris Opera**. A person of influence in the musical world of Paris, Kreutzer was not a friend to the young **Hector Berlioz**, having rejected the score of *Scène héroïque* for a possible premiere without even looking at it. The wife of Berlioz's teacher at the **Paris Conservatory**, Jean-François Le Sueur, approached Kreutzer and asked him "what he thought would become of young composers if they were denied a chance" to get their music known. Kreutzer's reply was, "What would become of us if we pushed them forward like that?" See Cairns, David. *Berlioz.* vol. 1, *The Making of an Artist, 1803–1832* and *Berlioz.* Vol. 2, *Servitude and Greatness, 1832–1869.* Berkeley: University of California Press, 1999–2000. See the **bibliography**.

Krips, Josef. (1902–1974.) Austrian **conductor**. Krips studied with **Felix Weingartner** at the **Vienna Academy of Music** and then served as his assistant at the Vienna Volksoper (1921–1924). He then went to the Dortmund (1925–1926) and Karlsruhe operas (1926–1933) as music director. His next step was to be resident conductor at the **Vienna Staatsoper** and simultaneously a professor at the **Vienna Academy**. When Nazi Germany annexed Austria in 1938, he lost both positions due to his Jewish heritage. After one year as the conductor of the Belgrade opera and orchestra, he secretly made a living as an opera coach while working openly as a storekeeper in a food-processing factory. Beginning with the armistice in 1945, Krips was put in charge of reorganizing virtually the entire musical life of Vienna. He conducted performances at the Vienna Staatsoper, at the Volksoper, and at the **Theater an der Wien**, including Ludwig van Beethoven's *Fidelio* only two weeks after the conclusion of the war. In addition to the **Vienna Philharmonic Orchestra**, he was the principal conductor of the Hofmusikkapelle, both of which performed at the **Musikverein**. In 1946, he led the reopening of the **Salzburg Festival** with Wolfgang Amadeus Mozart's *Don Giovanni*, making repeat appearances often. From 1947 to 1950, he toured Europe with the Vienna Philharmonic, giving performances of Mozart's *Le nozze di Figaro*, *Don Giovanni*, and *Cosi fan Tutte* at the **Royal Opera House, Covent Garden**, to remarkable acclaim. Krips served as the principal conductor of the **London Symphony Orchestra** from 1950 to 1954. On his first trip to conduct in America, he was turned back at the port of New York for unknown reasons, perhaps because he had conducted in Russia in 1947. He never made his destination of the Chicago Symphony but did guest conduct the **Buffalo Philharmonic Orchestra** in 1953, followed almost immediately by his appointment as its music director one year later (1953–1963). He guest conducted many of America's greatest musical institutions, including the **Metropolitan Opera**, New York (debut 1966), and the **New York Philharmonic** and was the conductor of the **San Francisco Symphony** (1963–1970).

His repertoire list was always broad-based; even in his early years at Karlsruhe he conducted not only German but also French and Italian opera. While he was a distinguished conductor of Joseph Haydn, Wolfgang Amadeus Mozart, **Beethoven**, Franz Schubert, Johannes Brahms, Anton Bruckner, **Gustav Mahler**, **Richard Strauss**, and Johann Strauss, he also performed works of Béla Bartók, Paul **Hindemith**, and **Igor Stravinsky**. He also demonstrated great commitment to contemporary music by leading several local premieres of music by such composers as Leoš Janáček, **Sir Benjamin Britten**, Boris Blacher, and Dmitri Shostakovich. As a conductor, he sought to achieve abundant nuance and lyricism, to make the instruments breath and sing like the operatic voice he loved. Krips held Mozart up as a pinnacle of music and looked to his music as an example for how to conduct everything else, saying, "Every opera is by Mozart; even Wagner, even Richard Strauss, has to sound clear, transparent and spirited, or we have a bad performance" (Holmes, 1988). He believed in the necessity of long experience in building good conductors and claimed that he studied Mozart's *G minor Symphony* for twenty-five years before he had the courage to conduct it, saying, "Mozart is, of all composers, the most difficult to conduct. And I can tell you why: two bars and you are suddenly transported to heaven. It is hard to keep your bearings when you are there" www.naxos.com.

Krips made many recordings on 78s and on LPs for **EMI**, **Decca**, and others. Perhaps the most notable are his recordings of Mozart's late symphonies, recorded for **Philips** with the **Royal Concertgebouw Orchestra**; Mozart's *The Abduction from the Seraglio* and *Don Giovanni*; Schubert's Symphony No. 9 (also with the Concertgebouw); and Beethoven's piano concertos with Arthur Rubenstein as soloist. See the **bibliography**.

Josef Krips. *Courtesy Photofest.*

Kubelik, Rafael. (1914–1996.) Swiss **conductor** and composer of Czech birth. Kubelik began studying at the Prague Conservatory at the age of fourteen. Proficient in violin and piano, he also learned composition and conducting. He made his conducting debut with the **Czech Philharmonic Orchestra** and was appointed as the conductor when he was twenty-one. From 1939 to 1941, when the Nazi regime closed the theater, he was the music director of the **Brno Opera**, giving the Czech premiere of **Hector Berlioz**'s mammoth opera *Les Troyens*. He then returned to Prague and was invited to become the principal conductor of the **Czech Philharmonic Orchestra** (1941–1948). With the onset of the Communist era, Kubelik defected to the West. He became the music director of the **Chicago Symphony Orchestra** (1950–1953), resigning after only three years due to claims that he programmed too many new works, demanded too many rehearsals, and engaged too many black artists. Kubelik became the music director at the **Royal Opera House, Covent Garden**, in 1955, but when **Sir Thomas Beecham** criticized the house for hiring foreign conductors, he resigned and began to concentrate on symphonic repertoire. He was the principal conductor of the **Bavarian Radio Symphony Orchestra** in Munich from 1961 to 1978. In 1967, he became a Swiss citizen and then became the music director of the **Metropolitan Opera, New York**. His time with the Metropolitan Opera lasted less than a year due to the death of Göran Gentele, the general manager who hired him.

Kuckuck. (Ger.) Cuckoo. (Fr. *coucou*, It. *cuculo*, Sp. *cuco*.) Examples: *Der Ruf eines Kukuks nachzuahmen*, imitate the sound of a cuckoo, from **Gustav Mahler**'s Symphony No. 1, mvt. 1; **clarinet**, spelled *Kukuk*, from Ludwig van Beethoven's Symphony No. 6, at the end of mvt. 2.

Kulisse. (Ger.) Wings of a stage, backdrop, scene, side-scene, moveable scene. (Fr. *coulisses*, It. *quinte*, Sp. *colisa*.)

Kunzel, Erich. (1935–2009.) American orchestra **conductor**. Known primarily as a pops conductor, Kunzel was the music director of the Rhode Island Philharmonic (1960–1965), resident conductor of the **Cincinnati Symphony Orchestra** (1965–1977), conductor of the **Cincinnati Pops Orchestra** (CPO) for thirty-two years, and principal pops conductor of the **Indianapolis Symphony** (1982–2002). He conducted more than one hundred concerts with the **Boston Pops Orchestra** when **Arthur Fiedler** was its chief conductor, toured in Japan, was the first American pops conductor to perform in China, and conducted concerts on the U.S. Capitol lawn every Memorial Day and Fourth of July from 1991 to 2009. His large discography is an impressive legacy of lighter classical music. Many of his CDs have thematic headings such as *A Disney Spectacular, Amen!—a Gospel Celebration, American Jubilee*, and several were award winners. He was presented with a National Medal of Arts by President George W. Bush in 2006, and in 2009, he was inducted into the **American Classical Music Hall of Fame**.

kurz. (Ger.) Short. (Fr. *bref, court*; It. *breve, corto*; Sp. *breve, corto*.) Examples: *sehr kurz*, very short; *sehr kurz gestoßen*, bowed (played) very short, from the prelude to *Die Meistersinger von Nürenberg* by **Richard Wagner**.

La. 1. The solmization name for the pitch A; in the fixed do system, the note A; and in the moveable do system, the sixth note of the C scale.

2. The note name given by Guido d'Arezzo to the sixth note in his hexachords, sometimes used in French and Italian as the name of the note A.

Laban/Bartenieff Institute of Movement Studies (LIMS). Founded in 1978 in New York by Irmgard Bartenieff, student and collaborator of Rudolf Laban. It provides educational programs and workshops in the study of Laban principles and publishes a journal.

Laban Movement Analysis (LMA) and Bartenieff Fundamentals. A study of body movement originating with the work of Rudolf Laban used by dancers, actors, musicians, athletes, and others. Laban's fundamental principles were further developed by his student and collaborator, Irmgard Bartenieff, and are useful in describing and teaching the general movements of the **conductor**. They are organized into four sections: body, effort, shape, and space. More specifically they are the *core*, or center of gravity; *posture*, consistent active flow of movement throughout the whole body; *connectivity* of movement between the upper and lower body; *shaping* of movement within an ever-changing three-dimensional space produced by a combination of rotation, extension, and abduction of the torso, limbs, and head; *kinesphere*, the area around the body and the use of that space without changing place; the outer extreme of the kinesphere, called the *distal* space; three pathways of shaping and movement, *central*, *peripheral*, and *transversal*, the areas of spatial shaping of gestures; and *tensions and countertensions*, the balances necessary to keep motions from collapsing at the completion of a gesture.

Laban's category *effort* can be used to describe the physicality of conductors' gestures. It has four categories, referred to here as "effort factors," each with two opposites, fighting and indulging. See the following chart (adapted from *Wikipedia*):

Effort Factors	Effort element *Fighting*	Effort element *Indulging*
Space	Direct	Indirect (flexible)
Weight	Strong	Light
Time	Sudden (quick)	Sustained
Flow	Bound	Free

Laban combined the first three categories (space, weight, and time) under the name "effort actions." They are further described in eight subcategories used for organizing conducting gestures: float, punch (or thrust), glide, slash, dab, wring, flick, and press. The fourth category, flow, is present in all of them and described in two types, bound and free.

For further reading, see Bartenieff, Irmgard, and Dori Lewis. *Body Movement: Coping with the Environment.* New York: Gordon and Breach, 1980. Laban, Rudolf. *The Mastery of Movement.* 4th ed. Revised and extended by L. Ullmann. London: MacDonald and Evans, 1980. See also **Alexander Technique** and the **bibliography**.

labbra. (It.) Lip. (Fr. *lèvre*, Ger. *Lippe*, Sp. *labio*.) See also *embouchure*.

la bémol. (Fr.) A-flat. See **accidental**, **appendix 5**.

Labuta, Joseph. Professor emeritus of music, former associate director of the music department, and director of music education at Wayne State University in Detroit. Labuta is the author of the text *Basic Conducting Techniques* (6th ed., 2009) and *Teaching Musicianship in the High School Band* (1972). See the **bibliography**.

lacrimoso. 1. (It.) Mournful, tearful. A character word used to evoke a particular manner of playing. Also *lagrimoso*. (Fr. *larmoyant*; Ger. *tränenvoll*; Sp. *lloroso, fúnebre*.) 2. (It.) A movement from a Mass.

la dièse. (Fr.) A-sharp. (It. *la diesis*.) See **accidental, appendix 5**.

la diesis. (It.) A-sharp. (Fr. *la dièse*.) See **accidental, appendix 5**.

Lage. (Ger.) Position, as in the position of the left hand on a string instrument or on a trombone.

Lahti Symphony Orchestra (Sinfonia Lahti). Founded in 1910, in Finland, under the auspices of the Lahti municipal government in 1949, the orchestra is conducted by Okko Kamu (appointed in 2011). He was preceeded by **Osmo Vänskä** (1988–2008), Ulf Söderblom (1985–1988), Jouko Saari (1978–1984), Urpo Pesonen (1959–1978), and Martti Similä (1951–1957). Under the leadership of Osmo Vänskä, the orchestra achieved an unprecedented level of international acclaim, especially through recordings led by Vänska of the music of Jean Sibelius, Einojuhane Rautavaara, and Robert Kajanus on the Swedish **BIS label**, as well as through many international tours that included the United States and Japan. The orchestra maintains an active educational program, especially through its Hey, Let's Compose! Program, which involves school visits.

laisser. (Fr.) To let, to allow, as in to let the cymbals ring, for instance. (Ger. *lassen*, It. *lasciare*, Sp. *dejar*.) See also *laissez vibrer*.

laissez vibrer. (Fr.) To let or to allow to vibrate or sound, do not dampen, as in cymbals or triangle, for instance. (Ger. *klingen lassen*; It. *lasciar, lasciar suonare, lasciar vibrare*; Sp. *dejar que vibre*.)

lament. A poem or song of mourning that originated in the Middle Ages. Seventeenth-century French composers took on the term *tombeau* for instrumental pieces written in tribute to celebrated musicians, establishing a tradition that has continued into the twentieth century with Maurice Ravel's work *Le tombeau de Couperin*. (Fr. *lamentation, plaint*; Ger. *Klage*; It. *lamento*; Sp. *elegia, lamento*.)

lamentable. (Sp.) Plaintive, mournful. A character word used to describe a certain manner of playing. (Fr. *plaintif*, Ger. *Klagend*, It. *lamentoso*.)

lamentoso. (It.) Plaintive, mournful. A character word used to describe a certain manner of playing. (Fr. *plaintif*, Ger. *Klagend*, Sp. *lamentable*.)

Landini cadence. A double-leading tone cadence combined with motion to the sixth note of the scale in the top part. It is used frequently in the music of the fourteenth-century Italian composer **Francesco Landini**.

Landini cadence.
Courtesy Andrew Martin Smith.

Landini, Francesco. (ca. 1325–1397.) Italian composer and organist. Landini became known for a style of cadence often heard in his music and known as the **Landini cadence**.

Ländler. (Ger.) An Austrian and South German slow, waltz-type dance in 3/4.

Landon, H. C. Robbins. (1926–2009.) American musicologist who specialized in the study of Franz Joseph Haydn. A highly prolific author and editor, Landon founded the Haydn Society in 1949 and at the same time began publishing critical editions of Haydn's work, including scores of symphonies, operas, and oratorios. He was editor of the *Haydn Yearbook* from its beginning in 1962. He is also the author of numerous books, including *The Symphonies of Joseph Haydn* (1955); the five-volume work *Haydn: Chronicle and Works* (1976–1980); *1791: Mozart's Last Year* (1988); *Mozart: the Golden Years 1781–1791* (1989); *Vivaldi: Voice of the Baroque* (1993); and *Essays on Viennese Classical Style: Gluck, Haydn, Mozart, Beethoven* (1970), many journal articles, and more. Landon held positions at many universities, was the recipient of at least four honorary doctorates, and was presented the Siemens Prize (1991) and the Medal of Honor of the Handel and Haydn Society in 1993. See the **bibliography**.

Lane, Louis. (b. 1923.) American **conductor**. His longest association with any orchestra was with the **Cleveland Orchestra**, where he served as the assistant conductor (1955–1960), associate conductor (1960–1970), and resident conductor (1970–1973). While working in Cleveland, Lane was awarded both the **Mahler Medal** and **Ditson Conductor's Award**. He served as the music director of the **Akron Symphony Orchestra** (1959–1983) and the Lake Erie Opera Theatre (1964–1972), principal guest conductor of the **Dallas Symphony Orchestra**

(1973–1978), co-conductor of the **Atlanta Symphony Orchestra** (1977–1983), and principal guest conductor (1982–1983) and principal conductor (1984–1985) of the National Symphony Orchestra of the South African Broadcasting Corporation. Lane was also adjunct professor at the University of Akron (1969–1983) and served as an artistic advisor and conductor at the **Cleveland Institute of Music** (1982–2004) and director of orchestra studies at the **Oberlin Conservatory of Music** (1995–1998)

lang. (Ger.) Long. (Fr. *long, longue*; It. *lungo/a*; Sp. *luengo/a.*) Example: *lang gestrichen*, long or full bows, from *Das Lied von der Erde* by **Gustav Mahler**.

lange Bogen or lang gezogen. (Ger.) A bowing term indicating long or full bows. Similar to the French *grand détaché*. (Fr. *arche long*, It. *archi lunghi*, Sp. *arqueada longa.*)

lang gestrichen. (Ger.) Play with long bows. As seen in Symphony No. 1, mvt. 1, by **Gustav Mahler**.

langhallenden. (Ger.) Long resounding, let ring or vibrate. Also *hallend*, reverberant. See also *klingen lassen, lasciar suonare, lasiar vibrare.*

langsam. (Ger.) Slow, slowly. Also *langsamer*, slower. Similar to the Spanish *lento* and the French and Italian *lentamente.* (Fr. *lent, lentement*; Sp. *lento.*) Example: *sehr langsam*, very slow, from Symphony No. 3, mvt. 4, by **Gustav Mahler**.

langsamer werden. (Ger.) To become slower. (Fr. *en retardant*; It. *ritardando*; Sp. *disminyuendo el tempo, disminyuendo la velocidad.*)

langue. (Fr.) Tongue, as used to articulate by wind and brass players. (Ger. *Zunge*, It. *linguetta*, Sp. *lengua.*)

Lansch, Enrique Sánchez. (b. 1963.) Prize-winning Spanish German film director and screenwriter. His work includes ***Rhythm Is It!*** codirected with Thomas Grube, a film about a dance project initiated by **Sir Simon Rattle** and the **Berlin Philharmonic** incorporating schoolchildren in a performance of **Igor Stravinsky**'s ***The Rite of Spring***; *Sing for Your Life!* about participants in the International Singing Competition Neue Stimmen (New Voices); *Das Reich Orchester*, a documentary about the Berlin Philharmonic between 1933 and 1945; *The Promise of Music*, a documentary about the young **Gustavo Dudamel**, the Sinfónia de la Juventud Venezolana Simon Bolívar; and *Piano Encounters*, a film exploring piano playing with young children and pianists Emanuel Ax, Katia and Marielle Labéque, Gabriela Montero, and the Duo Tal & Groethuysen.

largamente. (It.) Broadly, sometimes used as a movement title. (Fr. *largement*; Ger. *breit*; Sp. *amplio/a.*)

largando. (It.) Becoming slower, broadening. Also *allargando.*

large. (Fr.) Broad, fairly slow. A tempo indication; also a style of playing. (Ger. *breit*, It. *largo*, Sp. *amplio.*)

larghetto. (It.) A little less slow, a little quicker than *largo*. Diminutive form of *largo*, sometimes used as a movement title.

largo. (It., Sp.) A broad, very slow tempo, sometimes used as a movement title. (Fr. *large*, Ger. *breit*, Sp. *amplio/a.*)

La Scala. An Italian opera house and company officially known as Teatro alla Scala, in Milan. Established in 1778, the theater is home to the opera, ballet, chorus, orchestra, and the La Scala Theatre Academy, which provides training in associated opera fields. Throughout its history, La Scala has premiered many operas, including Giuseppi Verdi's *Otello* and *Falstaff*, Giacomo Puccini's *Madama Butterfly*, Francis Poulenc's *Dialogues of the Carmelites*, three operas by **Karlheinz Stockhausen**, and many more. The house underwent a major renovation between 2002 and 2004. Its current music director is **Daniel Barenboim**, and **Riccardo Chailly** has been appointed to a term beginning in 2015. Previous conductors include Franco Faccio (1871–1889), **Arturo Toscanini** (1898–1908, 1921–1929), Tulio Serafin (1909–1914, 1917–1920), Victor de Sabata (1930–1953), Carlo Maria Giulini (15553–1956), Guido Cantelli (1956), Giandandrea Gavazzeni (1966–1968), **Claudio Abbado** (1968–1986), and **Riccardo Muti** (1986–2005).

lasciare. (It.) To let, to allow, as in to let the cymbals ring. (Fr. *laisser*, Ger. *lassen*, Sp. *dejar.*)

lasciare vibrare. (It.) Let it ring or vibrate. (Fr. *laisser résonner, laisser vibrer*; Ger. *klingen lassen*; Sp. *dejar que vibre.*)

lasciar suonare. (It.) Let sound, to let ring. (Fr. *laisser résonner, laisser vibrer*; Ger. *klingen lassen*; Sp. *dejar que vibre.*)

lasciar suonare or lasciar vibrare. (It.) To let ring or to let vibrate. Often heard in context with the length of notes played by percussion instruments but also by strings if a concert hall has a long echo or reverberation. (Ger. *klingen lassen*, Sp. *dejar que vibre.*)

lassen. (Ger.) To let, to allow. (Fr. *laisser*, It. *lasciare*, Sp. *dejar.*)

Latvian National Symphony Orchestra (LNSO, Latvijas Nacionālais simfoniskais orķestris). Founded in 1926 in Riga under the **conductor** Arvids Parups, the entirely professional orchestra gives a full series of symphony concerts and records and makes broadcasts. It performs in the Great Guild Concert Hall of Riga. The current chief conductor and artistic director is Karel Mark Chichon. Past conductors have included **Andris Nelsons**, Andris Vecumnieks, Yuri Simonos, and Alexander Vilumanis.

laúd. (Sp.) The lute. (Fr. *luth*, Ger. *Laute*, It. *liuto*.)

laut. (Ger.) Loud. Also *lauter*, louder. (Fr. *fort*, It. *forte*.)

Laute. (Ger.) The lute. (Fr. *luth*, It. *liuto*, Sp. *laúd*.)

layering. A commonly used contemporary compositional technique, building musical textures through the stratification of different rhythmic patterns or contrasting and combining melodic ideas one over the other in order to produce a unified texture.

leadership. The modern **conductor** knows that leadership is something given to them based on their skills and musicianship, trust, and honesty in both their personal manner and music making. See also **morale, motivation in rehearsal and performance, psychology of the conductor-orchestra relationship**.

League of American Orchestras (LAO). Formerly known as the American Symphony Orchestra League (ASOL). Founded in 1942 and chartered by Congress in 1962, the league is an organization of American and Canadian orchestras. With over eight hundred orchestras of all types, it is a diverse network of instrumentalists, conductors, managers, board members, volunteers, staff members, and business partners. The league sponsors an annual conference; publishes the quarterly journal *Symphony Magazine* and its online version, *Symphony*Online; and is responsible for bestowing the Gold Baton award. Its mission includes the dissemination of information and providing educational and leadership opportunities, advocacy, innovation, and service.

League of Composers. Formed in 1923 as an offshoot of the International Composers Guild. Both the league and the guild were instrumental in the formation of many contemporary music ensembles in the 1960s and 1970s, sponsoring concerts around the world. Some composers who were associated with the league were **Aaron Copland**, Roger Sessions, Ernest Bloch, Arthur Honegger, Darius Milhaud, and Egon Wellesz.

lebhaft. (Ger.) Lively, vivacious. A character word seen in scores and parts of German composers. (Fr. *vif, vivant*; It. *vivo*; Sp. *vivo*.)

lebhafter or *lebhafter werden.* (Ger.) Becoming livelier, animated. Seen in Symphony No. 1, mvt. 1, by **Gustav Mahler**. (Fr. *en animant*, It. *animando*, Sp. *animando*.)

Ledger, Phillip Sir. (b. 1937.) English organist, pianist, and choral **conductor**. Ledger studied at King's College, Cambridge, and the Royal College of Music, London. He served as master of the music at Chelmsford Cathedral (1961–1965); director of music at the University of East Anglia, Norwich (1965–1973); artistic director of the **Aldeburgh Festival** (beginning in 1968); director of music and organist of King's College, Cambridge (1974–1982); and principal (a position similar to director) of the **Royal Scottish Academy of Music and Drama** (1982–2002). He edited the music of William Byrd, *The Oxford Book of English Madrigals* (London, 1978), two volumes of *Anthems for Choirs*, and a performing edition of Henry Purcell's opera *King Arthur*, which he also conducted. He was knighted in 1999.

Leduc, Alphonse. (1804–1868.) Parisian composer and music publisher who founded Éditions **Alphonse Leduc Music** in 1842. He was a student of Anton Reicha and a prolific composer of perhaps 1,300 works. Leduc was succeeded at the firm by his son, Alphonse-Charles, whose widow took over and ran Leduc from 1891 to 1902, when it was passed on to their son, Emile (also known as Alphonse-Henri), and his partner Paul Bertrand.

leer. (Ger.) Empty, open. (Fr. *vide*, It. *vuoto*.) See also *leere Saite*.

leere Saite. (Ger.) Open string. Sometimes seen in scores and parts and heard as a directive in rehearsal for string players to use an open, unstopped, or unfingered string. (Fr. *corde à vide*, It. *corda vuota*, Sp. *cuerda al aire*.)

left-hand conducting technique. Left-hand technique is often limited to the expressive in conducting. Dynamic and dynamic changes, phrase shaping, force, and delicacy can all be shown by the left hand in order to enhance the musicality of the conducting. However, when well developed, the right hand can be equally expressive and the left hand an equally important time beater. It is important for the **conductor** to develop **independence of the hands** so that, when necessary, the left hand can indicate one thing and the right something different. See also **conducting sound, expressive conducting**.

left-hand pizzicato. A string term referring to pizzicato when the string is plucked with the fingers of the left hand instead of the right hand, as usual.

Left-hand pizzicato. *Courtesy Andrew Martin Smith.*

légal. (Fr.) Strict. Also *exact, juste.* (Ger. *genau, richtig*; It. *esatto, giusto.*) Example: *mouvement legal*, strict tempo.

legare. (It.) To tie or slur any two or more consecutive notes. (Fr. *lier*, Ger. *binden*, Sp. *ligado.*)

legato. (It.) Indicates smooth, connected playing. Can be a bowing term that calls for a smooth stroke during which the bow stays on the string, consisting of a **down-bow** followed by an **up-bow**.

legato style. Shown by the conductor with smooth, flowing gestures in the wrist and forearm, often eschewing the vertical in favor the horizontal. This is said to mimic the motion of the bow and to draw a particularly empathetic response from the string players but must also emulate the breath of both the brass and wind players, building a sense of supporting the breath. Legato style means to move the baton physically from beat to beat in a consistent speed without any abrupt fluctuations of tempo or direction, connecting one note to the next without accentuation of any kind. It is best achieved by lessening the strength or intensity of the ictus, or beat, creating pulse points with nothing but a smooth change of direction.

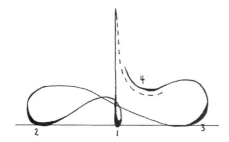

Conducting style, legato. *Courtesy Derek Brennan.*

legatura. (It.) Slur, a music notation sign that connects two or more notes. (Fr. *liaison*, Ger. *Bindebogen*, Sp. *ligar.*) See also **slur.**

legatura di valore. (It.) Tie. (Fr. *signe de tenue*; Ger. *Halte-bogen*; Sp. *ligadura de prolungación, ligar.*)

legen. (Ger.) To put. Also *setzen, stellen.* (Fr. *mettez*, It. *mettere*, Sp. *poner.*)

léger. (Fr.) Light. (Ger. *leicht*, It. *leggiero, leggero*, Sp. *ligero.*) Example: *léger et précis*, light and precise, from "Le matin d'un jor de fête" from "Ibéria" of *Images* by Claude Debussy.

leger line. Lines added above and below the **staff** in order to accommodate higher and lower **pitches**. (Fr. *ligne supplément*; Ger. *Hilfslinien*; It. *taglio addizionale*; Sp. *linea adicional, linea suplementaria.*)

légèrment. (Fr.) Lightly. A character word heard often in rehearsal to describe a particular manner of playing. (Ger. *leicht*, It. *leggermente*, Sp. *ligeramente.*)

leggermente. (It.) Lightly. A character word heard often in rehearsal to describe a particular manner of playing. (Fr. *légèrement*, Ger. *leicht*, Sp. *ligeramente.*)

leggero **or** *leggiero.* (It.) Light, quick. Character words heard often in rehearsal to describe a particular manner of playing. (Fr. *léger*, Ger. *leicht*, Sp. *ligero.*)

leggio. (It.) Music stand, desk of a musician in an ensemble. String players sit in pairs (bass players sometimes prefer to have their own stand in order to see the music better); woodwind and brass players sit on their own; percussion players often have multiple stands in order to accommodate multiple instruments. (Fr. *pupitre*; Ger. *Notenpult, pult*; Sp. *atril.*)

Leginska, Ethel. (1886–1970.) English-born pianist, composer, and **conductor** born Ethel Liggins. She was a pioneer for women performers and conductors. Leginska studied at the conservatories of Frankfurt, Vienna, and Berlin; made her solo piano debut in London at sixteen; and toured Europe at that time. In 1913, she moved to the United States and began studying composition. She studied with Ernest Bloch in 1918 and wrote songs, chamber music, symphonic poems, and two operas. She studied conducting and led several orchestras in Europe and America, including the **New York Symphony Orchestra** (1925), the **Boston Women's Symphony** (1926–1930), and the **Women's Symphony of Chicago** (1927–1929). In 1926, she founded the Boston Philharmonic. She moved to Los Angeles in 1940, where she continued to teach piano.

Ethel Leginska.

legni, i. (It.) The woodwind instruments of the **orchestra** or **band**. Also *strumenti a fiato.* (Fr. *instruments à vent, les bois*; Ger. *Blasinstrumente*; Sp. *instrumentos de viento.*)

legni, strumenti di. (It.) See *strumenti di legni.*

legno, col. (It.) An indication to play a string instrument with the wood of the bow.

legno frullante. (It.) **Bull-roarer.** Also *tavoletta sibilante.* (Fr. *planchette ronflante*, Ger. *Schwirrholz*, Sp. *roncador.*) See **appendix 4.**

legno, legni. (It.) Wood, as in *stromenti di legno*, woodwind instruments. Example: *col legno*, with the wood of the bow.

Leibowitz, René. (1913–1972.) Polish-born French musicologist, composer, and **conductor**. Leibowitz studied composition with Anton Webern and **Arnold Schoenberg**, orchestration with Maurice Ravel, and conducting with **Pierre Monteux**. He moved to France in 1945 and built a reputation as a conductor of the music of the **Second Viennese School** composers— Schoenberg, Alban Berg, and Webern. Leibowitz wrote influential books such as *Schoenberg and His school* (1947), *Introduction á la musique de douze sons* (1949), and *Thinking for Orchestra* with J. Maguire (1961). He gave private classes to students in Paris, including **Pierre Boulez** and Hans Werner Henze, and taught at the **Darmstadt** summer program. As a conductor, he insisted on following the score in detail and was analytical in his approach to the music he performed. He conducted a complete cycle of Beethoven symphonies for **RCA** with the **Royal Philharmonic Orchestra** (1962) that was reissued on **CD** in 1992.

leicht. (Ger.) Light, easy, simple. A character word heard often in rehearsal to describe a particular manner of playing. (Fr. *léger*, It. *legero*, Sp. *ligero*.) Example: *sehr leicht*, very light.

Leidenschaft. (Ger.) Passion, fervor. Example: *trotz zarter Tongebung stets mit leidenschaftlichstem Ausdruck*, in spite of a sweet tone, always with a fervent expression, from *Das Lied von der Erde*, mvt. 1, by **Gustav Mahler**. See also *leidenschaftlich.*

leidenschaftlich. (Ger.) Impassioned. Example: *Leidenschaftlich aber zart*, passionate but tender, as seen in Symphony No. 2, mvt. 4, by **Gustav Mahler**. (Fr. *passionné*, It. *appassionata*, Sp. *apasionado*.)

Leinsdorf, Erich. (1912–1993.) Austrian-born American **conductor**. Leinsdorf moved to the United States in 1937 as an assistant conductor to **Artur Bodansky** at the **Metropolitan Opera, New York**, making his debut one year later with **Richard Wagner**'s *Die Walküre* followed by **Richard Strauss**'s *Elektra* and *Parsifal*. He was appointed music director for the **Cleveland Orchestra** in 1943, but having become an American citizen one year earlier, he was subject to military service and during his absence, the orchestra hired someone else. While he conducted the orchestra again, it was only as a guest. Leinsdorf was the music director with the **Rochester Philharmonic** (1947–1956) and the **New York City Opera** (1956). He then returned to the Metropolitan Opera in 1957 and in 1962, succeeded **Charles Münch** as the music director of the **Boston Symphony**. He was said to have been the polar opposite of Münch, both musically and personally, and while he expanded the repertory and restored precision and technical finesse, his demanding, if not rigid, personality and way of making music was not a good fit, and he left in 1969. Leinsdorf was at his best in large-scale, complex operas and symphonic works. His recordings include impressive renditions of *Die Walküre*, *Turandot*, *Ariadne auf Naxos*, and the complete *Lohengrin*, the largest operatic recording venture in America at the time.

Leinsdorf is the author of *The Composer's Advocate: A Radical Orthodoxy for Musicians* (1981); an autobiography, *Cadenza: A Musical Career* (1976); and a collection of essays under the title *Erich Leinsdorf on Music* (1991). See the **bibliography**.

Leipzig Conservatory. See **University of Music and Theater "Felix Mendelssohn Bartholdy," Leipzig**.

Leipzig Gewandhaus Orchestra. While the earliest roots of the city orchestra can be seen in the 1479 appointment of a small number of city musicians, it was the founding of a concert organization, Große Concerte (Grand Concerts), in 1743 that laid the groundwork for the future hall, the Gewandhaus, that the current city orchestra is named after. The first Gewandhaus concert took place in 1781 with a thirty-two-piece orchestra. In 1786, the musicians and the city signed an agreement establishing organizational, disciplinary, and artistic matters and a pension fund for the musicians. Seen as a solidarity contract, it attempted to ensure the reputation of the orchestra with an "all for one, one for all" pledge. In 1879, Wolfgang Amadeus Mozart gave a concert in the Gewandhaus. In 1811, Ludwig van Beethoven's Fifth Piano Concerto was premiered there, and in the 1825–1826 concert season the first complete cycle of his symphonies followed. Felix Mendelssohn was the conductor and music director of the orchestra from 1835 to 1843 and again from 1845 to 1847. During his tenure, **Felix Mendelssohn** conducted the premieres of his Symphony No. 3, the "Scottish," and the *Concerto for Violin in E minor*, as well as works of Robert Schumann and Franz Schubert.

A new concert hall (Neues Gewandhaus) was opened in 1884, at which **Arthur Nikisch**, **Wilhelm Furt-wängler**, **Bruno Walter**, and others served as music director and composers Johannes Brahms, Peter Ilyich Tchaikovsky, Edvard Grieg, and Richard Strauss visited in order to conduct their own works. The building and the city's opera house were both destroyed in World War II. A new opera house opened in 1960, but a new Gewandhaus not not open until 1981. It was the only hall dedicated exclusively to concerts in the former Communist East Germany. Music director **Kurt Mazur** receives much of the credit for the realization of the project. A fascinating early image of the orchestra rehearsing standing up can be seen in *The New Grove Dictionary of Music and Musicians*. See the **bibliography**.

Leipziger Allgemeine musikalische Zeitung (AmZ of Leipzig). See **Allgemeine musikalische Zeitung**.

leise. (Ger.) Quiet, gentle, hushed, soft. A character word used to describe a particularly delicate manner of playing. (Fr. *doux*, It. *piano*, Sp. *piano*.)

Leitmotiv. (Ger.) Leading motive or theme. Coined by **Hector Berlioz**, a recurring theme or motive that connects the movements of a symphonic work. (Ger. *Leitmotiv*; It. *motivo conduttore, motivo ricorrente*; Sp. *motivo conductor*.) See also Berlioz's *Symphony Fantastique*.

Leitton. (Ger.) Leading tone, also heartfelt, sensitive. (Fr. *sensible*, It. *sensibile*, Sp. *sensible*.)

lejano. (Sp.) Distant, far away, soft. (Fr. *lointain*, Ger. *Fern*, It. *lontano*.)

Le Maire, Jean. (1581–1650.) French mathematician, engineer, and inventor. Le Maire created an equal-tempered scale of eight degrees, added a seventh syllable to the hexachordal solmization system, built a new kind of lute, and invented a musical notation system called *musique almérique* that didn't survive the controversy it generated. He lived in Toulouse and Paris and was active in architecture, language, mnemotechnics, and typography. See also **tuning systems**.

le même mouvement. (Fr.) The same tempo. (Ger. *im gleichen Tempo, dasselbe Zeitmaßs*; It. *l'istesso tempo, lo stesso tempo*; Sp. *al mismo tempo*.)

lengua. (Sp.) Tongue, as used to articulate by wind and brass players. (Ger. *Zunge*, Fr. *langue*, It. *linguetta*.)

Leningrad Conservatory. See **Saint Petersburg Conservatory**.

lenteur. (Fr.) Slowness. Example: *Modéré, sans lenteur*, moderate, without slowness, from "De l'aube á midi sur la mer," mvt. 1 of *La Mer* by Claude Debussy.

lent, lentement. (Fr.) Slow, slowly. (Ger. *langsam*; It. *lento, lentamente*; Sp. *lento*.)

lento. (Sp.) Slow, slowly. (Fr. *lent, lentement*; Ger. *langsam*; It. *lento, lentamente*.)

lento, lentamente. (It.) Slow, slowly. (Fr. *lent, lentement*; Ger. *langsam*; Sp. *lento*.)

Leonhardt, Gustav. (1928–2012.) Dutch keyboard player, **conductor**, musicologist, teacher, and editor. A leading figure in the performance practice and period instrument movement, Leonhardt founded the Leonhardt Consort in 1955. Between 1971 and 1990 he and **Nikolaus Harnoncourt** undertook the project of recording all of the Johann Sebastian Bach cantatas on period instruments with their various ensembles. Leonhardt recorded the *St. Matthew Passion*, *Mass in B minor*, and the *Magnificat*. He also recorded widely as a harpsichordist. Among the many honors and awards he received was the Order of Arts and Letters in France (2007) and the Commander of the Order of the Crown in Belgium (2008).

Leppard, Raymond. (b. 1927.) English **conductor**, harpsichordist, and scholar. Leppard established a reputation as a conductor of early music, most notable with performances of his own edition of Claudio Monteverdi's opera *L'incoronazione di Poppea* in the **Glyndebourne Festival** in 1962. His performing editions of other operas, such as Monteverdi's *Orfeo* and *Il ritorno d'Ulisse* and Francesco Cavalli's *L'Ormindo* and *La Calisto*, among others, have been important in bringing this repertoire before a wider public; however, they have been seen by some as too free in their adaptation of the original materials. Leppard has conducted at the **Royal Opera House, Covent Garden**; the **English National Opera**; and the English Chamber Orchestra. He conducted **Sir Benjamin Britten**'s opera *Billy Budd* at New York's **Metropolitan Opera** in 1978 and served as the principal guest conductor of the **St. Louis Symphony Orchestra** (1984–1990). He was the principal conductor of the BBC Northern Symphony Orchestra, Manchester (1973–1980), and the **Indianapolis Symphony Orchestra** (1987–2001). He guest conducted many of America's major orchestras, including the **New York Philharmonic**, **Chicago Symphony Orchestra**, and the **Detroit Symphony**. From 2004 to 2006 he was the music advisor to the **Louisville Orchestra**. He made several recordings, two for **Decca**, a CD of twentieth-century American music and a Mozart disc. With the Indianapolis Symphony he recorded works of Robert Schumann, Ralph Vaughan Williams, Peter

Ilyich Tchaikovsky, and Ludwig van Beethoven on Koss Classics. He was made a Commander of the Order of the British Empire (CBE) in 1983.

Les Six. (Fr.) The name given in 1920 to composers, Louis Durey, Arthur Honegger, Darius Milhaud, Germaine Tailleferre, Georges Auric, and Francis Poulenc by music critic Henri Collet, who saw them as analogous to the **Russian Five** (Mily Balakirev, Alexander Borodin, César Cui, Modest Mussorgsky, and Nikolai Rimsky-Korsakov). They were united by the principles of Erik Satie and Jean Cocteau: that music should be straightforward, appealing, witty, and take its inspiration from the everyday. It was reactionary in the sense that it was deliberately a movement away from the influence of **Richard Wagner**, **Richard Strauss**, **Igor Stravinsky**, and **Arnold Schoenberg**. A short-lived phenomenon, within about five years the members of the group had mostly moved on. Only Poulenc retained the group's affect, and Auric continued to collaborate with Cocteau in filmmaking.

letzten, letztes. (Ger.) Last, previous. (Fr. *derniére fois*, It. *ultima volta*, Sp. *último tempo*.) For an example, see *letztes Mal*.

letztes Mal. (Ger.) Last time. (Fr. *derniére fois*, It. *ultima volta*, Sp. *último tempo*.)

leuchtend. (Ger.) Luminous, luminescent, shiny, bright. (Fr. *lumineux*; It. *lucente, luminoso*; Sp. *luminoso*.)

levare. (Sp.) Upbeat, pickup, the **conductor**'s upbeat. (Fr. *levée*, Ger. *Auftakt*, It. *battuta in aria*.)

levata, in levare. (It.) Upbeat, one or more notes that occur before the first measure of a work or phrase, anacrusis, pickup. (Fr. *levée*; Ger. *Auftakt*; Sp. *alzada, anacrusa*.)

levée. (Fr.) Upbeat, one or more notes that occur before the first measure of a work or phrase, anacrusis, pick-up. (Ger. *Auftakt*; It. *in levare, levata*; Sp. *alzada, anacrusa*.)

levee. (Fr.) Upbeat, pickup, the **conductor**'s upbeat. (It. *battuta in aria*, Ger. *Auftakt*, Sp. *levare*.)

Levi, Hermann. (1839–1900.) German **conductor**. Descended from a family of distinguished rabbis, Levi became devoted to the music of **Richard Wagner**. Even though Wagner was unsuccessful in his attempts to persuade Levi to convert to Christianity, Wagner thought enough of him as a musician to allow Levi to conduct the premiere of his most Christian opera, *Parsifal*, which he did to great acclaim in 1882. Levi was court *Kapellmeister* in Karlsruhe from 1864 to 1872 and then *Kapellmeister* (1872) and later *Generalmusikdirektor* (1894–1896) in Munich (see **history of conducting**). He was a friend of Johannes Brahms, though his association with Wagner damaged the relationship.

During his tenure in Munich, Levi conducted the German premieres of operas by Charles Gounod, Léo Delibes, Emmanuel Chabrier, and **Hector Berlioz**; made German translations of Wolfgang Amadeus Mozart's three Italian operas, which remained in the repertoire into the 1930s; and was an important proponent of the music of Anton Bruckner and **Richard Strauss**, establishing himself as one of the most important German conductors of his time. He was known as a conductor of great spirituality and for an economy of gesture and masterful technique that had a great impact on those who came after him, including **Felix Weingartner**.

Levine, James. (b. 1943.) American **conductor** and pianist born in Cincinnati, Ohio. Levine became the first principal conductor of the **Metropolitan Opera** (the Met), New York, in 1973 and was made was the music director in 1975. In 1986, he was made the artistic director, the first time a conductor was elevated to this position. Levine studied conducting with **Jean Morel** and piano with Rosina Lhévinne at the **Juilliard School** and was one of **Geroge Szell**'s assistant conductors at the **Cleveland Orchestra** from 1964 to 1970. In 1971, he conducted the **Chicago Symphony Orchestra** in a performance of **Gustav Mahler**'s Symphony No. 2, becoming the director of their summer Ravinia Festival in 1973 and serving in that position for twenty years. He conducted at the **Royal Opera House, Covent Garden**, for the first time in 1974, leading Strauss's *Der Rosenkavalier*, and at the **Salzburg Festival** in 1975 with the **London Symphony Orchestra**. He also appeared at the **Bayreuth Festival** between 1982 and 1985 and again in 1988. Levine served as the chief conductor of the **Munich Philharmonic** from 1999 to 2004 and was a regular guest conductor of the **Berlin** and **Vienna** philharmonic orchestras, the **Philharmonia** in London, the **Dresden Staatskapelle**, and others. Known for having built the orchestra of the Metropolitan Opera into one of the great ensembles of the world, he insisted that the orchestra also perform on the stage, giving concerts of symphonic repertoire and chamber music. Levine has also been a supporter and promoter of young talent in the opera field, initiating the Lindeman Young Artists Development Program at the Met and serving as the conductor of the Verbier Festival Orchestra, the all-student resident orchestra at the summer music festival in Verbier, Switzerland (2000–2006).

Levine was appointed music director of the **Boston Symphony Orchestra** in 2004 with the unusual stipulation that there would be greater flexibility in scheduling rehearsals of more challenging works. For instance, when preparing for a premiere of a lengthy new work by composer **Milton Babbitt**, an initial rehearsal to familiarize the musicians with the challenges of the piece was held some months in advance. The orchestra also established a special Artistic Initiative Fund of some $40 million in order to support these more expensive endeavors. With the onset of health problems and more than one health-related sabbatical, Levine resigned the position with the Boston Symphony, many say prematurely, in 2011.

Levine's legacy of recordings is no less impressive. Known to prefer long or even complete **takes** that establish and maintain the momentum of a live performance, he made his first recording in 1973 for **EMI** of Giuseppe Verdi's little known opera *Giovanni d'Arco*. A virtual legion of opera and symphonic recordings includes operas of Verdi, **Richard Wagner**, and Wolfgang Amadeus Mozart; and symphonies of Johannes Brahms, Mahler, Robert Schumann; the late symphonies of Mozart; and Ludwig van Beethoven's piano concertos with pianist Alfred Brendel. Most appeared on the **RCA** label.

Levine has been quoted saying, "For the modern conductor with a modern orchestra the hardest styles are Mozart-Haydn-Schubert on the one side, and Verdi-Puccini-Mascagni-Giordano on the other." For both it is because the technical difficulties are relatively few, but the style inherently difficult. While he strives for precision and technical excellence, Levine is primarily interested in being faithful to the score. "You can read the words of composers from Bach to Stravinsky, and what you find them screaming into the night about is not the technical execution but the conception, the balance, the spirit, the purpose, what was supposed to be conveyed." See Holms, John L. *Conductors: A Record Collectors Guide*. London: Gollancz, 1988. See the **bibliography**.

Lewis, Daniel. (b. 1924.) American **conductor**, violinist, and pedagogue. Conductor emeritus at the **Thorton School of Music** at the **University of Southern California**, Lewis studied at the Hochschule für Musik in Munich and was a member of the **Bavarian Radio Symphony Orchestra**. He was the music director of the Pasadena Symphony from 1971 to 1982. He was a guest conductor with many American and European Orchestras but may have had his most significant impact as a teacher of orchestral musicians and young conductors.

Lewis, Henry. (1932–1996.) African American **conductor**. Lewis was known as a brilliant musician whose professional life was one of many "firsts." He was the first black to become a member of a major orchestra when, at the age of sixteen, he joined the **double bass** section of the **Los Angeles Philharmonic**. Lewis was the first black conductor to become the music director of a major orchestra, serving the **New Jersey Symphony Orchestra** from 1968 to 1976. He built the orchestra into one with a fine international reputation and a one-hundred-plus concert season, reaching out to the inner city and other audiences around the state. In 1972, he was the first black conductor to conduct at the **Metropolitan Opera**.

Among the other major positions he held are music director of the **Seventh Army Symphony Orchestra** (1956); founding music director of the String Society of Los Angeles, now the Los Angeles Chamber Orchestra (1959–1963); associate conductor of the **Los Angeles Philharmonic** (1962–1965); and chief conductor of the Dutch Radio Symphony Orchestra (1989–1991). He appeared as a guest conductor with the Baltimore, Boston, Buffalo, Chicago, Cleveland, Detroit, Philadelphia, Rochester, and San Francisco symphonies in addition to the **New York Philharmonic**; **New York City Opera**; **Royal Opera House, Covent Garden**; **Welsh National Opera**; **Netherlands Opera**; **La Scala, Milan**; all the major London orchestras; several in Italy; and many more. His legacy of recordings includes several operas. A recording for RCA with Leontyne Price won a **Grammy Award**. Lewis was married to soprano Marilyn Horne from 1960 to 1979.

James Levine. *Courtesy Photofest.*

Henry Lewis. *Courtesy Photofest.*

L. H. (Eng., Ger.) Abbreviation for left hand (Ger., *linke Hand*) and also for **lower half**.

L. H. Abbreviation for **left hand**.

liaison. (Fr.) **Slur**, a music notation sign that connects two or more notes. (Ger. *Bindebogen*, It. *legatura*, Sp. *ligar*.)

libero. (It.) Free, a directive suggesting freedom in the tempo and expression. Also *liberamente*. (Fr. *libre*, Ger. *frei*, Sp. *libre*.)

libre. (Fr.) Free, a directive to play freely. Example: *librement expressif*, freely expressive, from "Gigues" of *Images* by Claude Debussy; *trés libre (suivez les solos)*, very free (follow the solos), from Maurice Ravel's ballet score *Daphnis et Chloé*. See also **librement**.

librement. 1. (Fr.) Freely, a directive to play freely.
2. (Fr.) At the pleasure of the performer, a directive suggesting freedom in the tempo and expression. (It. *a piacere*, Ger. *nach Belieben*, Sp. *al gusto*.)

libre suspensión. (Sp.) Suspended, free hanging, as with a suspended cymbal. (Fr. *suspension libre*, Ger. *freihängend*, It. *impiccagione libero*.)

libreto. (Sp.) **Libretto**, the text of an opera. (Fr. *livret d'opera*, Ger. *Operntextbuch*, It. *libretto*.)

libretto. (Eng., It.) The text of an opera. For the purposes of study many are available separately. (Fr. *livret d'opera*, Ger. *Operntextbuch*, Sp. *libretto*.) The author is called the librettist.

libro aperto, a. (It.) At sight, **sight reading**. Also *sounare a prima vista*. (Fr. *déchiffrer, jouer à vue*; Ger. *vom Blatt spielen*, Sp. *tocar a primera vista*.)

lieblich. (Ger.) Sweet, gentle, soft, mild, suave. (It. *soave*, Fr. *suave*, Sp. *suave*.)

Lied. (Ger., pl. *Lieder*.) Song. (Fr. *chanson*; It. *canto, canzone*; Sp. *canción, canto*.)

lier. (Fr.) To tie, to **slur**. (Ger. *binden*, It. *legare*, Sp. *ligado*.)

ligado. (Sp.) To tie, to **slur**. (Fr. *lier*, It. *legare*, Ger. *binden*.)

ligadura de prolungación. (Sp.) Tie, **slur**. (Fr. *signe de tenue*, Ger. *Haltebogen*, It. *legatura di valore*.) See also *ligar*.

ligar. (Sp.) **Slur**, a music notation sign that connects two or more notes. (Fr. *liaison*, Ger. *Bindebogen*, It. *legatura*.)

ligero. (Sp.) Light, airy. (Fr. *léger*, Ger. *leicht*, It. *leggero*.) Example: *a la ligera*, lightly.

light staccato. Often conducted with a quick wrist motion, a flick. The exact speed of the gesture must correspond to the music.

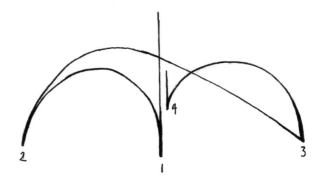

Conducting style, light staccato. *Courtesy Derek Brennan.*

ligne. (Fr.) Staff, musical staff, line. (It. *linea, rigo*; Ger. *Linie*; Sp. *linea*.)

ligne supplément. (Fr.) **Ledger lines**. (Ger. *Hilfslinien*; It. *taglio addizionale*; Sp. *linea adicional, linea suplementaria*.)

Limelight. Founded in 1976 with the name *ABC Radio 24 Hours* as the magazine of the Australian Broadcasting Corporation, it was relaunched as *Limelight* in 2003. It is a monthly Australian magazine that covers the current arts and music scene. The magazine holds its own annual *Limelight* Awards, where the public is invited to vote. See also **music magazines**.

Lincoln Center for the Performing Arts, Inc. A 16.3-acre complex of buildings constructed mostly in the 1960s in New York. The center was designed to be a focal point for presentation of the arts for America and the world. Performance facilities include **Alice Tully Hall**; **Avery Fisher Hall**; the Metropolitan Opera House; the David H. Koch Theater, originally known as the New York State Theater; the Vivian Beaumont Theater; the Mitzi E. Newhouse Theater; the Walter Reade Theater; the Elinor Bunin Munroe Film Center; the Bruno Walter Auditorium at the New York Public Library for the Performing Arts; the David Rubenstein Atrium; the Clark Studio Theater; Damrosch Park; the Daniel and Joanna Rose Rehearsal Studio; the Josie Robertson Plaza; the **Juilliard School**, which houses Morse Recital Hall, Paul Recital Hall, the Juilliard Drama Theater, and Peter J. Sharp Theater; the Stanley H. Kaplan Penthouse in the Rose Building; and Jazz at Lincoln Center, housed in the Time Warner Building at Columbus Circle.

The project began in the 1950s when the city's Slum Clearance Committee was given permission to designate the area for urban renewal. In 1956, Lincoln Center for the Performing Arts, Inc., was officially established, with John D. Rockefeller III as president. In the next few years, the **New York Philharmonic**, the Juilliard School, and the **Metropolitan Opera** all decided to become resident institutions. Over the course of several years, other institutions joined. Philharmonic Hall opened in 1962, and in 1973, its name was officially changed to Avery Fisher Hall in recognition of a major donor. The New York State Theater opened in 1964, the Vivian Beaumont Theater in 1965, the Metropolitan Opera in 1966, and the Juilliard School in 1969. In 1976, **PBS** broadcast the first *Live from Lincoln Center*. In 1987, the School of American Ballet also became resident in the center. The Samuel B. and David Rose Building opened in 1990. It houses several offices and, on the upper floors, the dormitory for the Juilliard School and the School for American Ballet. In 1991, the Walter Reade Theater opened. In 2004, Jazz at Lincoln Center opened the Frederick P. Rose Hall. In 2012, the expansion of the Juilliard School, the Film Society's new Elinor Bunin Munroe Film Center, Alice Tully Hall, the School for American Ballet, and the President's Bridge connecting the two sides of 65th street were complete.

linea. (Sp.) Staff, musical staff, line. (Fr. *ligne*, Ger. *Linie*, It. *linea*, *rigo*.)

linea adicional, linea suplementaria. (Sp.) **Ledger lines**. (Fr. *ligne supplément*, Ger. *Hilfslinien*, It. *taglio addizionale*.)

Ling, Jahja. (b. 1951.) Chinese American **conductor** and pianist. Ling studied conducting at the **Juilliard School** with **Otto-Werner Mueller**, received the **Seaver/National Endowment for the Arts Conductor's Award**, a career development grant, and the Bernstein Conducting Fellowship at the **Tanglewood Institute**. He has guest conducted worldwide, served as the artistic director of the Taiwan National Symphony (1998–2001), and has maintained a long-term relationship with the **Cleveland Orchestra**, serving as associate conductor (1984–1985), resident conductor (1985–2002), and as director of the orchestra's Blossom Music Festival (2000–2005). He became the music director of the **San Diego Symphony** in 2004, where he has led several premieres and released recordings on the **Telarc** and **Naxos** labels. Under his artistic leadership, the San Diego Symphony has been designated a Tier One major orchestra by the **League of American Orchestras**.

linguetta. (It.) Tongue, as used to articulate by wind and brass players. (Ger. *Zunge*, Fr. *langue*, Sp. *lengua*.)

linie. (Ger.) Staff, musical staff, line. (Fr. *ligne*; It. *linea*, *rigo*; Sp. *linea*.)

Liniensystem. (Ger.) Staff, stave, system. The five-line system on which music is written. In a score, two or more staves connected by a "brace" or bar line in a score. Also *System*, *Fünfliniesystem*. (Fr. *portée*; It. *pentagramma*, *sistema*; Sp. *pauto*, *pentagramma*.)

Linke, die. (Ger.) Left hand. (Fr. *main gauche*, It. *mano sinistro*, Sp. *mano izquierdo*.)

links. (Ger.) Left. (Fr. *gauche*, It. *sinistra*, Sp. *izquierdo*.) Examples: *die Linke*, the left hand. (Fr. *main gauche*, It. *mano sinistra*, Sp. *mano izquierdo*.)

lion's roar. A friction drum and member of the membranophone percussion family. It is cylinder shaped with the bottom end open and a membrane on top with a hole in the center through which a cord is threaded and attached. The cord is extended relatively tightly above the upside-down instrument by one hand, while the other rubs the chord with a damp cloth, drawing the roar from the echo chamber below. Varying the tension of the cord varies the **pitch**. Early versions of the instrument were made of washtubs, while newer ones have a tall stick that holds the cord taught above the head of the instrument. See also **appendix 4**.

Listening Room. An educational initiative designed by the **International Contemporary Ensemble (ICE)** to engage public school music students whose programs have been cut in a collaborative setting using team-based composition and **graphic notation** in order to nurture musical creativity and experimentation.

Listen: Life with Classical Music. A **music magazine** published in the United States since 2002 by ArchivMusic. The magazine contains interviews with active performing musicians; recommendations for recordings, books, and film; articles about destinations of interest to classical music lovers; and more.

l'istesso tempo, lo stesso tempo. (It.) The same tempo. (Fr. *le même mouvement*; Ger. *dasselbe Zeitmaß, im gleichen Tempo*; Sp. *al mismo tempo*.)

Liszt, Franz. (1811–1886.) Important and influential Hungarian composer and pianist. A musical leader of the Romantic era, Liszt also had a significant impact on the development and history of conducting. His activities as a **conductor** were relatively short-lived; he conducted his first orchestral concert in Pest in 1840 and stopped sometime after 1859, when he left his position as conductor of the Weimar orchestra. He was known to have used dramatic and widely contrasting gestures to evoke dynamic extremes, kneeling down over the podium for quiet passages and leaping up for louder ones.

Though he was greatly influenced by **Hector Berlioz**'s conducting style, Liszt abandoned his square-shaped conducting patterns for rounder ones that more effectively illustrated longer phrase shapes. He often set down his baton, using his hands in order to show the musical line.

Liszt, who had a personality of extreme energy and emotion, used this strength to forge the role of conductor as "musician-in-chief." No longer a "staid, old-fashioned" *Kapellmeister*, the conductor now held the task of inspiring the orchestra to new levels of performance. Facial expressions were used to reflect all musical emotions and to draw the musicians together into one interpretation. Liszt is also known to have introduced and promoted the rubato style or "*tempo rubato*" in orchestra playing as he had done in his piano performances. The next generation of conductors, such as **Felix Weingartner**, **Hans von Bülow**, and **Hans Richter**, who were disciples of Liszt, inherited these innovations and then passed them on to twentieth-century conductors such as **Wilhelm Furtwängler**, among others. Liszt left an enormous library of piano transcriptions and paraphrases of both orchestral and operatic works by such composers as Ludwig van Beethoven, Robert Schumann, Vincenzo Bellini, **Richard Wagner**, and others.

Franz Liszt.

Litton, Andrew. (b. 1959.) American **conductor**. Litton has been the principal conductor of the **Bournemouth Symphony Orchestra** (1988–1994), music director of the Dallas Symphony Orchestra (1994–2006), and music director and principal conductor of the Bergen Philharmonic Orchestra, Norway (2003–present). In 2012, he became the artistic adviser to the **Colorado Symphony Orchestra**, and in 2013, he was named music director. As a young conductor, Litton was a participant in the **Affiliate Artists' Exxon/Arts Endowment Conductors Program**. He has led several recordings, including a **Grammy**-winning performance of William Walton's *Belshazzar's Feast* with the Bournemouth Symphony.

Litton, James. American choral **conductor**. Litton was the music director of the **American Boychoir** in Princeton, Jew Jersey, from 1985 to 2001. He was made music director emeritus and then served a two-year term as choirmaster of the Washington National Cathedral. Litton continues as the conductor of the **American Boychoir** Alumni Chorus.

liuto. (It.) The lute. (Fr. *luth*, Ger. *Laute*, Sp. *laúd*.)

live electronic music. A form of music in which certain electronic aspects are created and/or modified live at a performance.

Live from Lincoln Center. An Emmy and **Grammy Award**–winning series of live televised broadcasts produced in conjunction with Thirteen/WNET, New York City, the PBS affiliate, and Lincoln Center. It began in 1976 with a concert featuring **André Previn** and pianist Van Cliburn. Since then, ballet, theater, recitals, jazz, and opera have all been included. Part of its mission is to make up for the disappearance of classical performances on commercial stations.

Liverpool Philharmonic Orchestra. See **Royal Liverpool Philharmonic Orchestra**.

livret d'opera. (Fr.) **Libretto**. (Ger. *Operntextbuch*, It. *libretto*, Sp. *libreto*.)

llorando. (Sp.) Plaintive, crying. (Fr. *en pleurs*; Ger. *weinend*; It. *lacrimando*, *piangendo*.)

Lobgesang. (Ger.) Hymn of praise, as in **Felix Mendelssohn**'s Symphony No. 2, *"Lobgesang."*

Lockhart, Keith. (b. 1959.) American **conductor**. Lockhart is the current music director and principal conductor of the **Boston Pops Orchestra** and the principal conductor of the BBC Concert Orchestra. From 1998 to 2009 he served as the music director of the **Utah Symphony**. Lockhart has led numerous recordings on the **RCA** label, mostly with the Boston Pops. He is also the artistic advisor and principal conductor of the Brevard Music Center summer institute and festival.

loco. (It.) An indication seen in parts for a player to switch to playing in the normal position or register after playing an octave higher or lower.

Loebel, David. (b. 1950.) American **conductor**. Loebel served as the music director of the Memphis Symphony, associate and associate principal conductor of the Saint Louis Symphony, and associate conductor of the Cincinnati Symphony Orchestra. He was awarded the **Seaver/National Endowment for the Arts Conductors Award**. Loebel has appeared as a guest conductor with many of America's major orchestras, including the symphonies of Baltimore, Buffalo, Chicago, Kansas City, New Jersey, Philadelphia, Rochester, Saint Paul, Seattle, and many more. He has conducted internationally in Japan, Taiwan, Australia, and South America. In 2010, he joined the faculty of the **New England Conservatory of Music** as the associate director of orchestras.

log drum. See **appendix 4**, **slit drum**.

lointain. (Fr.) Distant, far away. Also *loin.* (Ger. *Fern*, It. *lontano*, Sp. *lejano*.) Example: *loitain et expressif*, distant and expxressive, from "Les parfums de la nuit" from "Ibéria" of *Images* by Claude Debussy.

London Classical Players (LCP). Active from 1978 to 1997 and founded by **Roger Norrington**, the orchestra specialized in historically informed orchestral performance practices and played on period instruments. An influential member of the ensemble was its **concertmaster**, violinist John Holloway. Through its many recordings on the **EMI Classics label**, the legacy of the ensemble represents a significant step forward in the understanding and promulgation of historically informed performance practice among musicians worldwide. Their recordings include the complete symphonies and piano concertos of Ludwig van Beethoven, Symphonies Nos. 38–41 of Wolfgang Amadeus Mozart, Symphonies Nos. 4–6 of Franz Schubert, and more radically, extending Norrington's ideas of performance practice significantly farther into the Romantic era than had been done before, **Hector Berlioz**'s *Symphonie fantastique*, Anton Bruckner's Symphony No. 3, Robert Schumann's Symphonies No. 3 and 4, even a **Wagner** disk.

London Philharmonic Orchestra (LPO). Founded by Sir Thomas Beecham in 1932, the LPO has been the resident orchestra at the **Glynbourne Festival Opera** since 1964. It has been performing at the Royal Festival Hall on London's Southbank Centre since 1951 and became the hall's resident orchestra in 1992. The LPO has broken out of the mold of only giving classical concerts, recording soundtracks for well-known films such as *Lawrence of Arabia* and the Oscar-winning score

to The Lord of the Rings trilogy and *The Hobbitt: An Unexpected Journey.* Music directors have included **Sir Thomas Beecham** (1932–1939), **Eduard van Beinum** (1947–1950), **Sir Adrian Boult** (1950–1957), William Steinberg (1958–1960), Sir John Pritchard (1962–1966), **Bernard Haitink** (1967–1979), **Sir Georg Solti** (1979–1983), **Klaus Tennstedt** (1983–1987), **Franz Welser-Möst** (1990–1996), **Kurt Mazur** (2000–2007), and Vladimir Jurowski (2007– present).

London Records. See **Decca Records**.

London Sinfonietta. Established in 1968, it is one of the resident ensembles of the Southbank Centre. Since its inception, the sinfonietta has commissioned over three hundred works and given the premieres of hundreds more. With a core ensemble of eighteen principal players, the sinfonietta supports young performers through its Emerging Artists Programme, where young players are selected to work and perform with members of the ensemble. The sinfonietta's first music director was David Atherton (1968–1973). Michael Vyner was the artistic director (1972–1989), Paul Corssley (1988–1994), Markus Stenz was the music director (1994–1998), and Olivier Knussen (1998–2002). The ensemble has an extensive collection of recordings that have been issued on numerous labels, including their own, the London Sinfonietta label.

London Symphony Orchestra (LSO). The LSO gave its first concert in 1904 under the direction of **Hans Richter** at the Queen's Hall. It was Britain's first independent, self-governing orchestra, the players serving as shareholders and the profits divided among them at the end of each season. The LSO was formed by members of other London orchestras who were dissatisfied with the proposed imposition of a "no substitute" rule at a time when no full-time positions existed and orchestral musicians struggled to make a living playing in music halls, theaters, opera, orchestras, whatever was available, accepting the best paying job on short notice even if they already had another commitment. The practice of sending substitutes was eventually abandoned as the orchestra became more successful and able to provide its members with adequate income and full-time positions. After Richter, **conductors** who appeared with the LSO in the early years included **Arthur Nikisch** and **Wilhelm Mengelberg**, among others. Nikisch led the orchestra on a tour of the United States in 1912. Scheduled to travel on the *Titanic*, they were delayed and ended up making a successful crossing on the *RMS Baltic*.

During World War I, at a time of financial difficulty, **Sir Thomas Beecham** provided significant financial support to the orchestra, as he also did for the **Hallé Orchestra** and the **Royal Philharmonic Society**. Yet in

1917, concerts were suspended. At the end of the war, the orchestra reformed and rebuilt with such conductors as Sir Edward Elgar, Beecham, **Otto Klemperer**, **Bruno Walter**, **Wilhelm Furtwängler**, and **Serge Koussevitsky**, with outstanding soloists such as Yehudi Menuhin making his debut at the age of twelve. After World War II, financial constraints were such that the orchestra found it necessary to abandon their profit-sharing scheme in favor of state funding.

To date, the LSO continues the practice of engaging a series of guest conductors rather than one chief conductor. Conductors who have served as principals are **Hans Richter** (1904–1911), Sir Edward Elgar (1911–1912), **Arthur Nikisch** (1912–1914), Albert Coates (1919–1922), Sir Hamilton Hardy (1932–1935), **Josef Krips** (1950–1954), **Pierre Monteux** (1961–1964), **István Kertész** (1965–1968), **Andre Previn** (1968–1979), **Claudio Abbado** (1979–1988), **Michael Tilson Thomas** (1988–1995), **Sir Colin Davis** (1995–2006), and **Valery Gergiev** (2006–present). Beecham (1915–1916) and **Wilhelm Mengelberg** (1930–1931) conducted often but were not given an official title. Sir William Walton, Sir Arthur Bliss, **Karl Böhm**, **Leonard Bernstein**, and Sir Colin Davis all served as president of the orchestra, an honorary position.

At times in its history, competition from other London orchestras, such as the new **BBC Symphony** (1929) under **Sir Adrian Boult**; Beecham's **London Philharmonic Orchestra**, formed in 1932 and then in 1946; and his **Royal Philharmonic**, drew prominent members of the LSO away, initially affecting the quality of the ensemble. However, in the end, the LSO took advantage of many talented young conservatory graduates and reemerged successfully. Since the 1960s, the LSO has kept the reputation as one of the two best orchestras in England's capital city. In 1966, the orchestra founded the LSO Chorus with John Aldis as director. During the Previn years, the orchestra reached a new level of popularity. BBC television created *André Previn's Music Night*, a program that helped attract a younger audience.

The LSO began its long history of recording in 1913, making one of the first gramophone recordings ever under the direction of Nikisch and with pioneering engineer and producer **Fred Gaisberg**. Since then, recordings have documented periods of great artistic success. The LSO began recording for film scores as early as the 1920s and reached a peak of success in the late 1970s when it received a **Grammy Award** for its performance of John Williams's music for *Star Wars*.

In 2000, **LSO Live** was launched as the first orchestra-owned record label, much to the distress of many executives in the field. However, the precedent was set, and orchestras around the world have quickly followed suit. LSO Live has released over ninety titles available on CD and for Internet downloading. Resident in the city's

Barbican Center since 1982, the LSO has long had successful educational programs, including LSO Discovery, which according to the orchestra's website, reaches over sixty thousand people each year. It also publishes an Internet journal titled *Inspire* that provides information about concerts and events, as well as connections to other arts organizations around the world.

Longy, Georges. (1868–1930.) Oboist, educator, and **conductor**. Longy was the founder and director of the **Longy School of Music** in Cambridge, Massachusetts (1911). First oboist of the **Boston Symphony Orchestra** (1898–1925), Longy served as the conductor of the Boston Orchestral Club (1899–1913), the MacDowell Club (1915–1925), and the Cecilia Society Chorus. He resigned from the Boston Symphony in 1925 and returned to France.

Longy School of Music. Founded by **Georges Longy** in 1915 to provide training in musicianship on the **Paris Conservatory** model, it is now a degree-granting conservatory in Cambridge, Massachusetts. Longy was succeeded as the director by his daughter, Renée Longy-Miquelle, who brought many of her father's **Boston Symphony Orchestra** colleagues to the faculty of the school and added **Dalcroze eurhythmics** to the curriculum. The school moved from Boston to Cambridge in 1930. It had a distinguished faculty, including Walter Piston, E. Power Biggs, and **Sarah Caldwell**. **Nadia Boulanger** taught at the school from 1938 to 1945. In 1970, the Edward M. Pickman Concert Hall was added. The faculty was enlarged under director Roman Totenberg (1978–1985), who also established the Young Performers Program. In 1992, the Bakalar Music Library was opened. In 2012, the Longy School merged with **Bard College** (Annadale-on-Hudson, New York) and is now known as the Longy School of Bard College. In March 2013, the Longy School announced that it would discontinue its preparatory and continuing studies programs.

lontano. (It.) Distant, far away. (Fr. *lointain*, Ger. *Fern*, Sp. *lejano*.)

López Cobos, Jesús. (b. 1940.) Spanish **conductor** who studied in Madrid, graduating with a degree in philosophy. López Cobos studied conducting with **Franco Ferrara** in Italy and later **Han Swarowsky** at the **University of Music and Performing Arts** in Vienna. He was the general music director of the Deutsche Opera Berlin (1981–1990), music director of the Orquestra Nacional de España (1984–1988), music director of the **Cincinnati Symphony Orchestra** (1986–2000), principal conductor of the Orchestre de Chambre de Lausanne (1990–2000), and music director of the Teatro Real in Madrid (2003–2010). He has also served as the principal guest conductor of the **London Philharmonic** (1981–1986). With the Cincinnati Symphony he released many CDs on the **Telarc** label, including works of his compatriots Isaac Albéniz and Manuel de Falla. López Cobos is also the permanent conductor of the Orchestre Français des Jeunes, a summer training orchestra in Paris.

L'Orchestre de Paris. Founded in 1967 after the **Orchestra de la Société des Concerts du Conservatoire** was disbanded. **Charles Munch** was the founding conductor and **Herbert von Karajan** was the interim music advisor (1969–1971). The orchestra's music directors have been **Sir Geog Solti** (1972–1975), **Daniel Barenboim** (1975–1989), **Semyon Bychkov** (1989–1998), **Christoph Eschenbach** (2000–2010), and **Paavo Järvi** (appointed in 2010). **Christoph von Dohnányi** served as the artistic advisor from 1998 to 2000. An orchestra of nearly 120 musicians, Barenboim founded Le Choeur de l'Orchestre de Paris during his tenure.

Los Angeles Philharmonic Orchestra. Founded in 1919 by businessman and amateur musician William Andrews Clark Jr., who hired Walter Henry Rothwell as its first music director when Sergei Rachmaninoff refused the position. Rothwell served until his death in 1927 and was followed by Georg Schnéevoigt (1927–1929), **Artur Rodzinski** (1929–1933), **Otto Klemperer** (1933–1939), Alfred Wallenstein (1943–1956), **Eduard van Beinem** (1956–1959), **Zubin Mehta** (1962–1978), **Carlo Maria Giulini** (1978–1984), **André Previn** (1985–1989), **Esa-Pekka Salonen** (1992–2004), and **Gustavo Dudamel** (2009–present).

When Clark died in 1927 without leaving an endowment, the Southern California Symphony Association was formed in order to help achieve the necessary funding. Its president, Harvey Mudd, stepped up to guarantee music director Otto Klemperer's salary. Another great philanthropist was the heiress Dorothy Buffum Chandler, who helped raise the funds, nearly $19 million, for the Dorothy Chandler Pavilion, the orchestra's home from 1964 until 2003. In 1969, **Ernest Fleischmann** became executive vice president and general manager, initiating several new ideas, the Los Angeles Philharmonic Chamber Music Society, the Los Angeles Philharmonic New Music Group, and its **"Green Umbrella"** new music concert series, all using members of the orchestra as performers. Under Salonen, the philharmonic had a residency at the **Salzburg Festival** in Austria, the first American orchestra to do so. They also performed at the Lucerne Festival, the **BBC Proms** in London, and at the Théâtre du Chatelet in Paris. In 2000, Deborah Borda, who had been the executive director of the **New York Philharmonic**, began her tenure in Los Angeles as president and chief executive officer. She succeeded in bringing the orchestra to a stable financial condition and managed its move in 2004 to the Walt Disney Concert Hall, designed by architect Frank Gehry. Gustavo Dudamel, the most successful graduate of the **El Sistema** Program in Venezuela, has used that program as a model in establishing the Youth Orchestra LA (known as YOLA). It provides free instruments, intensive music training, and academic support to youth from underserved areas of Los Angeles. He also established a conductor fellowship program, inviting four young conductors to participate in consecutive four to six week residencies. The philharmonic is known for its **Composer-in-Residence** program with William Kraft (1981–1985), John Harbison (1985–1988), Rand Steiger (1987–1989), Steven Stucky (1988–2009), and **John Adams** (2009–present); its education and community outreach programs; and its unusual program of jazz chairs, John Clayton (1998–2001), Dianne Reeves (2002–2005), Christian McBride (2006–2010), and Herbie Hancock (2010–present). The orchestra has issued acclaimed classical and film recordings on a variety of labels and recently branched out into a new genre, that of recording music for video games. It recorded the music for *Bioshock 2* from composer Garry Schyman. The philharmonic also gave the American premiere of the Final Fantasy franchise game music: *Dear Friends: Music from Final Fantasy* composed by Nobuo Uematsu.

lo stesso. (It.) The same. (Fr. *pareil, semblade*; Ger. *gleich*; Sp. *mismo.*) Example: *lo stesso tempo*, the same tempo.

lo stesso tempo. (It.) The same tempo. Also *l'istesso tempo.* (Fr. *le même mouvement*; Ger. *dasselbe Zeitmaß, im gleichen Tempo*; Sp. *al mismo tempo.*)

"Louder, please." A rehearsal directive. (Fr. *beaucoup plus fort, plus fort, s'il vous plaît, un peu plus fort*; Ger. *bitte, etwas mehr* (somewhat more), *viel mehr, bitte* (a lot more); Sp. *más fuerte, por favor.*)

lourd. (Fr.) Heavy, weighty. Also *pesant.* (Ger. *schwer*, It. *pesante*, Sp. *pesado.*)

louré. (Fr.) A bow stroke used by string players where the bow pulses slightly between notes, generally written under a **slur**, moving in one direction.

LSO Live. Established in 2000, the recording label of the London Symphony Orchestra (LSO). LSO Live works in collaboration with the Mariinsky label of the **Mariinsky Theater Orchestra**, making their recordings available as well.

lucente, luminoso. (It.) Luminous, luminescent. (Fr. *lumineux*, Ger. *leuchtend*, Sp. *luminoso.*)

Lucerne Festival Orchestra. Founded in 2003 by conductor **Claudio Abbado** and executive director Michael Haefliger and modeled after **Arturo Toscanini**'s 1938 ensemble of virtuosi at the same festival. The orchestra consists of principal players, chamber musicians, and music teachers who join together by invitation and under the leadership of Abbado. The core of the orchestra is drawn from the forty-five members of the **Mahler Chamber Orchestra**, also founded by Abbado. Many of the orchestra's performances have been recorded and released on CD and DVD, including a live recording of **Gustav Mahler**'s Symphony No. 9, which won the **BBC Music Magazine** Award, the International Classical Music Award, and the Diapason d'Or Prize in 2012. In addition to performances at the summer Lucerne Festival, the orchestra tours and has performed in Japan, the United States, and throughout Europe.

Luck's Music Library. An American music distributor in Madison Heights, Wisconsin, with a wide circulation, Luck's began in the home of Arthur Luck, former member and librarian of the **Detroit Symphony** and **Philadelphia Orchestra**. Primarily a resource for orchestras, Luck's has symphonic, pops, holiday, and educational materials.

luengo, luenga. (Sp.) Long. (Fr. *long, longue*; Ger. *lang, lange*; It. *lungo/a*.)

Luening, Otto. (1900–1996.) Born in Milwaukee, Wisconsin, an American composer, **conductor**, and teacher who began piano lessons with his father at the age of six. Luening is known primarily for his innovative experiments using tape-recorded sound in composition. The Leuning family moved to Munich in 1912, where he studied at the Conservatory for Music (Staatliche Hochschule für Musik), and then to Zürich in 1917, where he studied at both the conservatory and university. His teachers there included the composer and pianist Ferruccio Busoni. Luening played flute in both the **Tonhalle Orchestra** and Municipal Opera Orchestras, and he conducted both operetta and concert repertoire. His early compositions were premiered at the conservatory. Luening and his family moved back to the United States in 1920, where his first position was as the conductor at the American Grand Opera Company in Chicago. He held positions at the **Eastman School of Music** (head of the opera department 1925–1928), University of Arizona, Bennington College, and Barnard College (1944–1964). His most recognized association was with **Columbia University**, where he taught from 1944 to 1970. At Columbia he collaborated with **Vladimir Ussachevsky**, presenting the first concert of music for synthesized sound. Thereafter, they collaborated on several pieces that combined recorded sound and orchestra, including

Rhapsodic Variations for Tape Recorder and Orchestra (1953). In 1959, they founded the **Columbia-Princeton Electronic Music Center**, which attracted many composers interested in new technologies, including **Milton Babbitt**. Luening cofounded the **American Composers Alliance** (1938), the **American Music Center** (1939), and **Composers Recordings, Inc.** (1954). In addition to his own opera, *Evangeline*, he led the premieres of Virgil Thomson's opera *The Mother of Us All* and Gian Carlo Menotti's *The Medium*. During his lifetime, he wrote over 350 compositions in a wide variety of styles. Luening's autobiography is *The Odyssey of an American Composer* (1980). See the **bibliography**.

Luftpause. (Ger.) A short, often sudden pause, sometimes indicated with a **breath mark**.

lugubre. (Fr., It.) Lugubrious, mournful, gloomy. (Gr. *schwermütig*, Sp. *lúgubre*.)

lúgubre. (Sp.) Lugubrious, mournful, gloomy. (Fr. *lugubre*, It. *lugubre*, Ger. *schwermütig*.)

Luis-Bassa, Natalia. (b. 1966.) Venezuelan-born **conductor** living in England. Luis-Bassa is the music director of the Haffner Orchestra in Lancaster, the Hallam Sinfonia in Sheffield, and a member of the conducting faculty of the **Royal College of Music**, London. She also serves as the music director of the Orquesta Sinfónica de Falcón (Venezuela). She won the second prize of the **Maazel-Vilar Conductor's Competition** in New York (2002) and has guest conducted several orchestras in Britain and South America.

Luisi, Fabio. (b. 1959.) Italian **conductor**. Luisi has served as the principal conductor of the **Metropolitan Opera**, New York, since 2011, and the general music director of of the Zurich Opera, Switzerland, since 2012. He worked at the Graz Opera, Austria; was artistic director and chief conductor of the **Tonkünstlerorchester**, Vienna (1995–2000); principal conductor of the **Orchestre de la Suisse Romande**, Switzerland (1997–2002); chief conductor of the **Staatskapelle** and **Semperoper**, Dresden (2007–2012); and chief conductor of the **Vienna Symphony** (2005–2013). Luisi won a **Grammy Award** for recordings of **Richard Wagner**'s *Siegfried* and *Götterdämmerung* on **Deutsche Grammophon**.

Lully, Jean-Baptiste. (1632–1687.) Italian-born French composer, **conductor**, and dancer who had some music instruction as a child. Lully was taken to France on the death of his mother in order to serve in the household of a cousin of Louis IX. Recognized for his talent as a violinist and dancer, he became the composer of instrumental music for the court, writing music for ballets and then dancing in them.

Jean-Baptiste Lully.

Because of his skill as a violinist, Lully was made a member of the famous Vingt-Quatre Violons du Roi, but finding them undisciplined, he requested and received permission to begin the slightly smaller sixteen-member Petits Violons, which he conducted from the violin and trained to his own standards. They were part of the king's entourage, performing at his dinners and traveling with him on demand. Lully became a French citizen in 1661, and with such close contact to the king, he was promoted to the position of master of music to the royal family. He collaborated with the playwrite Molière on a series of "comedy-ballets" that were forerunners to French opera, culminating with *Le Bourgeois gentilhomme* (1670) and worked closely with the librettist and poet Philippe Quinault.

As opera became more popular with the Parisian public, Lully made use of his influence in order to gain a royal privilege that amounted to a form of professional protection. For the rest of his life, he dominated the Paris music scene, almost single-handedly establishing an operatic style that would survive for more than a century. Among his musical innovations were the "French overture" and replacing the Italian style of **dry recitative** with recitative accompanied by instruments. At the height of his career, Lully wielded tremendous influence over the Paris music scene and was known to have been unscrupulous in his quest for power.

Lully was following the common practice of conducting a performance of his *Te Deum* while audibly beating time on the floor with a long staff when he famously struck his foot. The wound became gangrenous, but even so, Lully refused medical assistance. With the infection spreading throughout his system, it eventually caused his death.

lumineux. (Fr.) Luminous, luminescent. (Ger. *leutchtend*, It. *lucente, luminoso*; Sp. *luminoso*.)

luminoso. (It., Sp.) Luminous, luminescent. (Fr. *lumineux*, Ger. *leutchtend*, It. *lucente*.)

luminoso. (It.) Brilliant, piercing, bright. (Ger. *hell*, Fr. *éclatant*, Sp. *brillante*.)

lungo, lunga. (It.) Long. (Fr. *long, longue*; Ger. *lang, lange*; Sp. *luengo/a*.) Example: *pausa lunga*, a long pause.

lustig. (Ger.) Playful. Also ***frölich***. (Fr. *gai, gaiement*; It. *gaio, giocoso*; Sp. *alegre*.)

luth. (Fr.) The lute. (Ger. *Laute*, It. *liuto*, Sp. *laúd*.)

Lydian mode. See **church modes**.

Lyric Opera of Chicago. Following a tradition of opera in Chicago that dates back to 1850, the Lyric Opera, one of America's major companies, was founded in 1954. With its own orchestra of seventy-five and a chorus of forty-eight members with a supplemental group of twelve, the company established a tradition of outstanding performances in its first season when soprano Maria Callas made her American debut in the title role of Vincenzo Bellini's *Norma*. Under the guidance of manager Carol Fox, and subsequently under **Ardis Kranik**, the company has continually attracted world-famous artists to its stage. **Conductors** who have appeared at the Lyric include **Sir Georg Solti**, **Christoph von Dohnányi**, and **Zubin Mehta**. **Sir Andrew Davis** has been the music director since 2000. The Ryan Opera Center was established in 1974 to support the professional development of young singers. In 2005, the Lyric celebrated its fiftieth anniversary with performances of **Richard Wagner**'s complete **Ring cycle**.

lyrique. (Fr.) Lyric, lyrical. (Ger. *Lyrik, lyrisch*; It. *lirico*; Sp. *lírico*.)

M

M. Abbreviation for *main*, *mano*, **metronome**, *mezzo* (as in *mezzoforte*), and also for **middle of the bow**.

Maazel, Lorin. (1930–2014.) American **conductor**, composer, and violinist. Maazel was the music director of the symphony orchestras of Cleveland (1972–1982) and Pittsburgh (1988–1996) and the French National Orchestra (1977–1982). He was the first American to serve as the artistic and general director of the **Vienna Staatsoper** (1982–1984), where he was appointed with a four-year contract, but left after two years due to political disputes. He also served as the artistic director of the Deutsche Opera and music director of the Radio Symphony Orchestra, both of Berlin (1965–1971), and as the music director of the **Bavarian Radio Symphony Orchestra**, Munich (1993–2002), and the **New York Philharmonic** (2002–2009). Maazel was also the music director of the Orquestra de la Comunitat Valenciana (2006–2011), where he conducted his own opera, *1984*. He was the chief conductor of the **Munich Philharmonic** from 2011 until 2014. Also a prodigious conductor of opera, Maazel has made over three hundred recordings. He began the summer **Castleton Festival** at his Virginia estate in 1997 to nurture young musicians. Maazel was known as having an excellent memory and baton technique.

Lorin Maazel. *Courtesy Photofest.*

Maazel-Villar Conductors Competition. A competition that took place over a period of months in 2001 and 2002, led by **Lorin Maazel** and financed by philanthropist Alberto Vilar. The initial rounds took place around the world in six locations. The finals were at **Carnegie Hall** in New York. Begun with the vision of aiding aspiring conductors, it does not look as if the competition will repeat, as Vilar was convicted of money laundering and fraud and sentenced to nine years in prison in 2010.

Mácal, Zdeněk. (b. 1936.) Czech **conductor**. Mácal studied at the Brno Conservatory and the Janáček Academy of Music and Performing Arts. He became the principal conductor of the **Prague Symphony Orchestra** and won the 1965 International Conducting Competition in Besançon, France, and the 1966 **Dimitri Mitropoulos** Competition in New York. Mácal left Czechoslovakia after the Soviet-led invasion of Prague in 1968. He made his American debut conducting the **Chicago Symphony Orchestra** in 1972. Mácal served as the music director of the **Milwaukee Symphony Orchestra** (1986–1995) and the **New Jersey Symphony Orchestra** (1993–2002) and was appointed chief conductor of the **Czech Philharmonic** in 2003. He resigned the position in 2007.

mächtig. (Ger.) Powerful, heavy, mighty. Examples: *mächtig bewegt*, powerfully moving. *Anmerkung f. d. Dirigenten: Das* cresc. *dauert bis zum Eintritt der Streicher und Holzbläser und muss sehr mächtig sein*, Note for the conductor: The crescendo lasts until the entrance of the strings and woodwinds and must be very powerful, from Symphony No. 2, mvt. 5, by **Gustav Mahler**.

Mackerras, Sir Charles. (1925–2010.) Australian **conductor** with vast experience in both operatic and orchestral repertoire. Mackerras made his greatest contribution with the operas of Leoš Janáček and as a specialist in period performance practices in music of the Baroque and

Classical eras at a time when doing standard repertory in this manner was in its infancy. One of his most noteworthy contributions was a performance of Wolfgang Amadeus Mozart's *The Marriage of Figaro* with the addition of ornamentation and period-appropriate appoggiaturas.

His performances were governed by careful concern for stylistic accuracy, attention to the score, and scrupulous preparation of the orchestra parts. Mackerras left a legacy of recordings issued by many of the most important recording companies that spanned the eras of 78s to CDs. Among them were the first recording of *Lucia di Lammermoor* with period instruments; a 1967 recording of *Messiah* that incorporated ornamentations and appoggiaturas, bowings, and phrasing in what was thought to be "Handelian" style; George Frideric Handel's *Saul* and *Israel in Egypt*; the first issue of Christoph Willibald Gluck's O*rfeo* in Italian; all of the symphonies of **Gustav Mahler**, Ludwig van Beethoven, and Johannes Brahms; and works of W. S. Gilbert and Arthur Sullivan. His 1959 recording of Handel's *Music for the Royal Fireworks* won critical acclaim for its attempt to re-create the sound and style of the original performance. His Vienna Philharmonic cycle on the **Decca** label became legendary.

Mackerras's passion for the operas of Leoš Janáček began during his student days in Prague and led to many performances: *Kát'a Kabanová* (1951), *The Makropoulos Affair* (1964), *From the House of the Dead* (1965), *The Cunning Little Vixen* (1970), *The Excursions of Mr. Broucek* (1970), and *Jenufa* (9174). Though he conducted worldwide, perhaps his most important association was with the **English National Opera** (originally **Sadler's Wells Theater**).

macrotonal scale. Any scale that is made up of intervals larger than whole tones.

Madrid Symphony Orchestra (Orquesta Sinfónica de Madrid, OSM). Founded in 1903, it is the oldest existing orchestra in Spain not linked to an opera house—it was founded on the principal of operating independently. In its first season, the orchestra gave the Spanish premieres of Peter Ilyich Tchaikovsky's Symphony No. 4 and Johannes Brahms's Symphony No. 1. The orchestra's activities were interrupted by the Spanish Civil War, and during the Franco regime and World War II, it was very difficult to get musicians, especially string players. After the death of Franco in 1975, the orchestra reorganized and took on the responsibility of serving as the orchestra of the Teatro de la Zarzuela for opera and ballet. In 1997, it moved to the Teatro Real, where it presents a full season of opera, ballet, and chamber and symphonic concerts, along with a great deal of contemporary music, including new opera. Now an orchestra of one hundred members, it also runs an active youth orchestra. Past **conductors** have included **Jesús**

López-Cobos (2002–2010), Luis Antonio Garcia Navarro (1999–2001), Vicente Spiteri (1958–1977), José María Franco Bordons (1951–1958), Conrado del Campo (1946–1950), Enrique Jordá (1940–1945), and Enrique Fernández Arbós (1905–1939). The founding conductor was Alonso Cordelás (1903–1904).

Maelzel (Mälzel), Johann Nepomuk. (1772–1838.) German inventor of musical devises, including the **metronome**. Maelzel was the son of an organ builder. When he was twenty, he moved to Vienna, where he made a living developing various mechanical devices and teaching music. One of his early accomplishments was an improved version of a musical **chronometer** used to regulate and dictate tempi. A precursor to the metronome, it was built like a large wall clock, with a pendulum, audible hammers, and bells. Ludwig van Beethoven was one of those who used it.

The inventor's other creations included various "automatons," automatic instruments constructed of organ pipes based on the sounds of a **Janissary band** that played the music of Franz Joseph Haydn and Wolfgang Amadeus Mozart; a so-called panharmonicon that with the addition of string instruments resembled a chamber orchestra; and an automatic trumpeter that could play marches and signal calls.

Having attained the position of court "mechanician" in Vienna in 1808, he took his gadgets on tour, displaying and selling them whenever possible. Having befriended Beethoven, he convinced him to write his *Battle Symphony* for the panharmonicon for tours that promoted both Beethoven's music and Maelzel's inventions. It was on one of those tours in Amsterdam in 1814 that Maelzel met **Dietrich Nikolaus Winkel** and appropriated his design for what was to become the metronome. Maelzel perfected the mechanics by adding numerical tempo divisions indicating the number of beats per minute. He patented the new creation in 1815 and saw to it that it was manufactured and promoted all over Europe.

Maelzel understood the importance of endorsements to the success of his product, and though it took some time, he convinced Beethoven to switch from the old chronometer to the new metronome. In 1817, when Beethoven wrote an article for the **Leipzig** *Allgemeine Musik-Zeitung* with a list of metronome markings for his first eight symphonies, it signaled a major coup for Maelzel.

Maelzel is also known for having created an ear trumpet that, Beethoven used as his hearing faded, according to biographer **A. W. Thayer**. In 1826, Maelzel sailed to the United States, where he spent ten years traveling extensively and exhibiting and selling his various inventions. He died in 1838 aboard an American ship returning from a financially disastrous journey to Venezuela, the West Indies, and Cuba. It is believed that he was buried at sea. See Thayer, A. W. *Thayer's Life of Beethoven*. Revised and edited by Elliot Forbes. Princeton, NJ: Princeton University Press, 1967. See the **bibliography**.

maestoso. (It.) Majestic. A character word used to evoke a particular manner of playing. (Fr. *majestueux*, Ger. *majestätisch*, Sp. *majestuoso*.)

maestro de capilla. (Sp.) Chapel master, the leader of a musical chapel or choir. (Fr. *maître de chapelle*, Ger. *Kapellmeister*, It. *maestro di capilla*.)

maestro di capilla. (It.) Chapel master, the leader of a musical chapel or choir. (Fr. *maître de chapelle*, Ger. *Kapellmeister*, Sp. *maestro de capilla*.)

maestro, maestra. (It., Sp.) Master, teacher. Often used to address an orchestra conductor.

maggiore. (It.) Major, as in major mode, major scale, major third, or other interval. (Fr. *majeur*, Ger. *Dur*, Sp. *mayor*.)

Mahler Chamber Orchestra (MCO). Founded in 1997 by former members of the **Mahler Youth Orchestra** with the support of that orchestra's founding music director, **Claudio Abbado**. The orchestra's management office is in Berlin, but its forty-five core members come from twenty different countries and live all over Europe. The MCO does not receive state funding but makes up its income from concert revenues and private donations. It maintains a flexible structure, allowing it to perform works of a wide variety and makes decisions by consensus. The ensemble established itself as a top ensemble when it appeared under Abbado's baton in a production of Wolfgang Amadeus Mozart's *Don Giovanni* at the Aix-en-Provence festival in 1998. **Daniel Harding** was named the principal guest **conductor** in 1998 at the age of twenty-two, music director in 2003, and conductor laureate in 2011. The orchestra partners with leading soloists and conductors, including **Esa-Pekka Salonen**, **Pierre Boulez**, Leif Ove Andsnes, **Sir John Elliot Gardiner**, and many others. They have released twenty-five CDs, including a CD of composer George Benjamin's opera *Written on Skin*, which they premiered in 2012. The orchestra has initiated an outreach program for hearing-impaired children throughout Europe called Feel the Music.

Mahler Conducting Prize. See **Gustav Mahler Conducting Prize**.

Mahler, Gustav. (1860–1911.) Austrian composer and **conductor**. Known as one of the great composers of the late nineteenth and early twentieth centuries, Mahler spent much of his life making his living as a conductor. Hav-

ing started out conducting operetta, he worked his way up to become the director of the **Vienna Opera House** (1897–1907), where he conducted highly acclaimed performances of **Richard Wagner**'s **Ring cycle** and operas of Wolfgang Amadeus Mozart.

Subsequently, Mahler became the conductor of the **Metropolitan Opera** in New York, conducting *Tristan und Isolde* for his debut. The next season, opera management brought in **Arturo Toscanini** to share the podium. Mahler conducted the **New York Philharmonic** and resigned from the opera in order to become the music director there. During his years in New York, he would return to Austria for the summers in order to concentrate on composing. The wear and tear of intense work and travel affected his health. He conducted his final concert in February 1911, sick with heart disease. Cutting short the season, he returned to Vienna, where he died in May of the same year.

While he was effective in insisting on the highest performance standards, Mahler as a conductor was also very temperamental. His conducting and leadership style was considered histrionic and dictatorial, often resented by those in the orchestra and the staff. It may be said that Mahler divided his time fairly equally between composition and conducting and had much of his greatest influence introducing his own works. Mahler is known for having written copious notes for conductors and musicians throughout his scores.

Gustav Mahler. *Courtesy Library of Congress.*

Mahler Youth Orchestra (Gustav Mahler Jugendorchester, GMJO). Founded in Vienna in 1986 by its music director, **Claudio Abbado**, with Thomas Angyan and Hans Landesmann in an effort to create opportunities for young musicians from both Eastern and Western Europe and Russia to perform together. While it does not receive state funding, it is under the patronage of the Council of Europe. The orchestra has performed in many of the great concert halls of Europe and with many top **conductors** and soloists. Open to musicians up to the age of twenty-six, its alumni can be found in top orchestra across the European continent.

mailloche. (Fr.) Mallet, as in the sticks used to play timpani. (Ger. *Schlägel*; It. *mazza, mazzuolo*; Sp. *maza*.)

main. (Fr.) Hand. (Ger. *Hand*, It. *mano*, Sp. *mano*.) Example: *main gauche*, left hand; *main droite*, right hand; *main dans le pavillon*, hand in the bell (as used with a **horn**, for instance).

main droite. (Fr.) Right hand. (Ger. *rechte Hand*, It. *destra*, Sp. *mano derecha*.)

maître de chapelle. (Fr.) Chapel master, the leader of a musical chapel or choir. (Ger. *Kapellmeister*, It. *maestro de capella*, Sp. *maestro de capilla*.)

majestätisch. (Ger.) Majestic. A character word used to evoke a particular manner of playing. (Fr. *majestueux*, It. *maestoso*, Sp. *majestuoso*.)

majesteux. (Fr.) Majestic. A character word used to evoke a particular manner of playing. (Ger. *majestätisch*, It. *maestoso*, Sp. *majestuoso*.)

majestuoso. (Sp.) Majestic. A character word used to evoke a particular manner of playing. (Fr. *majestueux*, Ger. *majestätisch*, It. *maestoso*.)

majeur. (Fr.) **Major**. (Ger. *Dur*, It. *maggiore*, Sp. *mayor*.)

major. As in major mode, major scale, major third, or other interval (Fr. *Majeur*, Ger. *Dur*, It. *Maggiore*, Sp. *mayor*.)

Major Orchestra Library Association (MOLA). Founded in 1983, MOLA has over 270 performance organizations with more than 450 librarians from around the world. Through MOLA, these librarians share information and resources as they do the job of acquiring, preparing, cataloguing, and maintaining music for each institution. MOLA works to facilitate communication between librarians, to educate and assist them in the services that they provide, and to work with publishers in order to achieve the highest standards in the music performance materials that they provide. See also **Nieweg, Clint.**

Mälkki, Susanna. (b. 1969.) Finnish **conductor** and cellist. **Mälkki** studied at the **Sibelius Academy** with conductor **Jorma Panula.** Having also trained and performed as a cellist, she was the music director of the Stavanger Symphony Orchestra (2002–2005) and the **Ensemble Intercontemporain** (EIC) (2006–2–13) and was appointed principal guest conductor of the **Gulbenkian Orchestra**, Portugal (2013). A proponent of contemporary music, Mälkki led premieres of operatic and orchestral literature, including the first performance in Finland of Thomas Ades's *Powder Her Face* (1999). She has guest conducted many of Europe and America's best orchestras, including the **Royal Concertgebouw Orchestra**; **Berlin Philharmonic**; London's **Philharmonia Orchestra**; the **Los Angeles Philharmonic**; the **Chicago, San Francisco, Detroit, Pittsburgh**, and **Gothenburg Symphony Orchestras**; among others. Also an opera conductor, Mälkki appeared at **La Scala, Milan** in 2011.

Malko, Nikolai. (1883–1961.) Ukranian-born **conductor** and influential teacher of conducting who studied with Nikolai Rimsky-Korsakov, Alexander Glazunov, and Anatoly Lyadov at the **St. Petersburg Conservatory** and with **Felix Mottl** in Munich. He was the chief conductor at the **Mariinsky Theater** and taught at the **Moscow** and **Leningrad Conservatories**. Malko served as the conductor of the **Leningrad Philharmonic**, where he premiered Symphony No. 1 by his student Dmitri Shostakovich and Nikolai Myaskovsky's Symphony No. 5. He was succeeded at the philharmonic by his student **Yevgeny Mravinsky.** Malko left the Soviet Union in 1929 with invitations to conduct in Europe, where he helped found the Danish Radio Orchestra and became a permanent guest conductor there. In 1920, he moved to the United States and taught at Mills College and wrote his influential *The Conductor and His Baton* (1950). The work was turned into a conducting text by American educator Elizabeth A. H. Green; available as *The Modern Conductor*, it is based on Malko's principles. He recorded for **EMI** in Copenhagen and London, was the principal conductor of the Yorkshire Symphony (1954), and moved to Australia as the chief conductor of the Sydney Symphony Orchestra (1956), remaining there until his death. See the **bibliography.**

mancando. (It.) Getting softer, fading, dying away. (Fr. *en défaillant*; Ger. *entschwindend, hinsterben*; Sp. *desapareciendo, sauvizando*.)

manche. (Fr.) The neck of a string instrument such as the violin or cello. (Ger. *Hals*; It. *manico*; Sp. *mango, mástil*.)

mango. (Sp.) The neck of a string instrument such as the violin or cello. Also *mástil*. (Fr. *manche*, Ger. *Hals*, It. *manico*.)

Manhattan School of Music (MSM). Founded as a community music school in 1917 by pianist and philanthropist Janet D. Schenek, it is a music conservatory that now offers degrees at the bachelor's, master's, and doctoral levels in a wide variety of program areas, including jazz. It also has a precollege division that services at least five hundred students annually. Its ensembles include three orchestras, a **wind ensemble**, a contemporary music ensemble, and a jazz philharmonic consisting of a full big band and orchestra, in addition to multiple other jazz ensembles.

It was originally called the Neighborhood Music School with a mission to provide musical training to the immigrant communities of the city. In 1938, the name was changed to its current Manhattan School of Music, and by 1943, a bachelor's degree was offered. The school moved to its current location on the Upper West Side of Manhattan in 1969. An opera program was added in the 1970s under the leadership of George Schick, who served as the president of the school from 1969 to 1976. Marta Casals Istomin served as president from 1992 to 2005, and during her tenure, the Anderson Residence Hall opened. Robert Sirota was president from 2005 to 2013, overseeing a Contemporary Performance Program, a Center for Music Entrepreneurship, and a new recital hall. The school has grown to over eight hundred students from over forty countries and has a distinguished faculty. Its alumni list includes many important musicians.

manico. (It.) The neck of a string instrument such as the violin or cello. (Fr. *manche*; Ger. *Hals*; Sp. *mango, mástil*.)

Männerchor. (Ger.) Men's chorus. (Fr. *chœur d'hommes*, It. *coro maschile*, Sp. *coro masculino*.)

Mannes School of Music. Founded in 1916 by David Mannes, concertmaster of the **New York Philharmonic** and Carla Damrosch, sister of **Walter Damrosch**, the **conductor** of the philharmonic. In 1989 the school merged with the New School to become the Mannes College the New School for Music, it functions as the conservatory of the New School, offering programs in three divisions, college (295 students), preparatory (490), and an extension division for adults (350). In 1985, the school moved to its current location on West 85th Street. Under the leadership of Dean Joel Lester (1996–2011), the faculty and the opera program were both expanded. Current dean Richard Kessler continues to develop the curriculum with the goal of addressing the relationship between the musician and society. Mannes maintains a distinguished faculty, and its alumni number among America's most acclaimed musicians.

Manns, August. (1825–1907.) German conductor who went to England at the invitation of George Grove to conduct the resident wind band at the Crystal Palace. He reorganized it into a symphony orchestra and started a series of Saturday concerts. These concerts were widely popular and inspired the Henry Wood's Promenade Concerts that developed into the **BBC Proms**, one of the longest music festivals in the world, held every summer at the Royal Albert Hall, London. Manns had a reputation for the seriousness with which he approached the music he conducted; he performed it the way the composer wrote it.

mano. (It., Sp.) Hand. (Fr. *main*, Ger. *Hand*.) Examples: (It.) *mano destra*, right hand; (It.) *mano sinistra*, left hand; (Sp.) *mano derecha*, right hand; (Sp.) *mano izquierdo*, left hand.

mano derecha. (Sp.) Right hand. (Fr. *main droite*, Ger. *rechte Hand*, It. *mano destra*.)

Manson, Anne. American **conductor**. Music director of the Manitoba Chamber Orchestra (appointed in 2008). Manson was the first woman to conduct at the **Salzburg Festival** in Austria when she stepped in to replace an ailing **Claudio Abbado**, appearing with the **Vienna Philharmonic Orchestra** in a performance of Modest Mussorgsky's opera *Boris Godunov* in 1994. Particularly well regarded as an opera conductor, Manson has led performances at the Washington National Opera; the Grand Theatre de Genève, Switzerland; the Royal Opera Stockholm; the opera program at the **Juilliard School**; the **San Francisco Opera**; Canadian Opera; Spoleto Festival USA; and more. She held the position of music director of the Kansas City Symphony from 1999 to 2003. A graduate of Harvard University, Manson has also guest conducted the **Los Angeles** and **London Philharmonic** orchestras and the **St. Paul Chamber Orchestra**.

mantener el mismo compás. (Sp). To keep or hold the tempo, to conduct, a commonly heard directive in rehearsal. (Fr. *garder le mesure*, Ger. *Takt halten*, It. *tenere il tempo*.)

maracas. A Latin American instrument that comes in pairs. It is made of a gourd or similarly shaped wooden shell that contains pellets or seeds and is shaken. **Leonard Bernstein** used it in an innovative way in his Symphony No. 1, "Jeremiah," where he instructs the timpanist to use maracas to hit the drumheads. See also **appendix 4**.

maravilloso. (Sp.) Wonderful, marvelous. A character word sometimes used to give praise. (Fr. *merveilleux*; Ger. *erstaunlich, wunderbar*; It. *meravigliosoo, stupendo*.)

marcado. (Sp.) Marked, a form of articulation. (Fr. *marqué*, Ger. *markiert*, It. *marcato*.) See also *marcato*.

marcar. (Sp.) To mark. (Fr. *marquer*, Ger. *markieren*, It. *marcare*.) Examples: *marcar el compás*, to beat time;

marcar el ritmo, the rhythm; *Este compass se va a marcar a dos*, This bar will be conducted in two; *Voy a dirigir este pasaje a cuatro*, I will conduct this passage in four.

marcare. (It.) To mark. (Fr. *marquer*, Ger. *markieren*, Sp. *marcar*.)

marcar el compás. (Sp.) To beat the time, as in conducting. Also *llevar el compás*. (Fr. *batter la mesure*, Ger. *Takt schlagen*, It. *battere il tempo*.)

marcato. (It.) Accented, marked, emphasized. When used for string players, it indicates an accented, marked bowing with the strokes separated. Also *marcando*. Abbreviated *marc*. (Fr. *marqué*, Ger. *markiert*, Sp. *marcado*.)

marcato style. Most often conducted by a hammer-like gesture in the elbow of the baton arm. The precise nature of the gesture should correspond to the music.

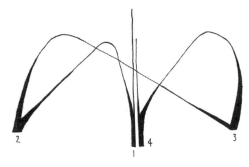

Conducting style, marcato. *Courtesy Derek Brennan.*

marcha. (Sp.) March, a type of piece, a style. (Fr. *marche*, Ger. *Marsch*, It. *Marcia*.)

marcha fúnebre. (Sp.) Funeral march, a type of piece, a style. (Fr. *marche funèbre*, Ger. *Trauermarsch*, It. *Marcia funebre*.)

marche. (Fr.) March, a type of piece, a style. (Ger. *Marsch*, It. *Marcia*, Sp. *marcha*.) Example: *Dans un rythme de Marche lointaíne, alerte et joyuese*, in the rhythm of a distant march, alert and joyous, from "Le matin d'un jour de fête," from "Ibéria" of *Images* by Claude Debussy.

marche funèbre. (Fr.) Funeral march, a type of piece, a style. (Ger. *Trauermarsch*, It. *marcia funebre*, Sp. *marcha fúnebre*.)

marcia. (It.) March, a type of piece, a style. (Fr. *marche*, Ger. *Marsch*, Sp. *marcha*.) Examples: *all marcia*, in march time, in the manner of a march, march-like; *marcia funebre*, funeral march.

marcia funebre. (It.) Funeral march, a type of piece, a style. (Fr. *marche funèbre*, Ger. *Trauermarsch*, Sp. *marcha fúnebre*.)

marcial. (Sp.) Martial. A character word sometimes used to evoke a certain character in playing. (Fr. *martial*, Ger. *kriegerisch*, It. *marziale*.)

Mariinsky Theater Orchestra. Founded in 1783 in Saint Petersburg during the reign of Catherine the Great and known as the Russian Imperial Opera Orchestra until after the revolution, it is one of the oldest musical institutions in Russia. In 1935, Joseph Stalin named the orchestra and ballet the Kirov, after Sergei Kirov, the first secretary of the Communist Party. In 1992, after the collapse of the Soviet Union, the named reverted to the Mariinsky. The current artistic and general director of the theater and the orchestra is **Valery Gergiev.** Under his leadership, the orchestra has become internationally acclaimed. Since 2009, the orchestra records on its own Mariinsky label, presenting opera, ballet, and symphonic repertoire. Downloads are available on iTunes, Amazon, Google Music, and eMusic. The Mariinsky label works in collaboration with **LSO Live**, the label of the **London Symphony Orchestra.**

marimba. Similar to the **xylophone** but with wooden bars that create a mellow tone and are arranged in same way as the **piano**. (*Fr. marimba*, Ger. *Marimbaphon*, It. *marimba*, Sp. *marimba*.) See also **appendix 4**.

Markevitch, Igor. (1912–1983.) Ukranian-born French **conductor** and composer. Markevitch left Kiev at age two and moved first to Paris and then Switzerland. He distinguished himself early as a composer and studied with **Nadia Boulanger** and Alfred Cortot. Markevitch wrote many notable works, including a piano concerto, cantata, and concerto grosso. Later compositions, such as *L'envoi d'Icarem*, *Le paradis perdu*, *Cantique d'amour*, and *Psaume*, to name just a few, were written under an exclusive contract with the German publisher **Schott** and widely performed.

Due to financial hardship during and after World War II, Markevitch began a "second life" as a conductor, having previously studied with **Pierre Monteux**. He moved to Italy and became part of the resistance and traveled widely. He conducted the **Boston Symphony** (1955), became the resident principal in both Stockholm (1952–1955) and **Montreal** (1956–1960), and gave master classes at the **Salzburg Mozarteum** (1948–1956), **Mexico City Philharmonic Orchestra** (1957–1958), the **Moscow Conservatory** (1963), Madrid (1965–1969), and Monte Carlo (1969). As a conductor, he was guided by high regard for details in the score and known for his acute hearing and the practice of using the right hand as a neutral time beater while using the left to give gestures of expression. He conducted phrasing and expression gestures distinctly in advance of the orchestra (see **conducting principles**). Markevitch wrote a well-known article, *The Problems of the Education of Today's Conductors* (see **education of conductors**), that was published in *The Conductor's Art* (1965). See the **bibliography**.

markieren. (Ger.) To mark, as in articulate. (Fr. *marquer*, Sp. *marcar*, It. *marcare*.) See also *markiert*.

markiert. (Ger.) Marcato, accented, an articulation term. (Fr. *marqué*, It. *marcato*, Sp. *marcado*.) Example: *Immer sehr markiert*, Always very marked or always very marcato, from *The Prelude to Die Meistersinger von Nürenberg* by **Richard Wagner**.

marking a score. Conductors often mark scores in order to remind themselves of certain key events that will facilitate conducting it. That includes phrase shapes, especially in the case of uneven or irregular ones, cues, and even dynamics. For some conductors, marking the score is part of the learning process and helps them absorb all of the details. It may also facilitate the memory process. For others, they find that marking the score in any way distracts from the music and the details on the page. Some conductors go as far as to color code their dynamics, using red for loud and blue for soft.

marking parts. The process of marking in bowings for string players or putting in editorial marks, including dynamics, articulations, and changes of music when necessary, such as when a revision is made or a mistake discovered.

marking the beat. Similar to a **dead** or **neutral beat**, marking the beat is done during accompanimental passages of a concerto or opera recitative when the orchestra doesn't play. It allows the **conductor** to indicate the passing of each bar and the ensemble player to know where he or she is when counting the empty measures. Marking the beat is a principal aspect of orchestral or band conducting. In instrumental music, the players only have their own parts, with the exception of the occasional printed cue of another instrument in their music. Choral singers usually have all of the vocal parts on one page and so can see, and hear, where everyone is during the course of the piece. See also **conducting accompaniments, conducting patterns, conducting technique**.

marqué. (Fr.) Marcato, accented, an articulation term. Also *marquee*. (Ger. *markiert*, It. *marcato*, Sp. *marcado*.)

marquer. (Fr.) To mark, as in articulation. (Ger. *markieren*, It. *marcare*, Sp. *marcar*)

Marriner, Neville Sir (b. 1924). English **conductor** and violinist, founder of the **Academy of St. Martins in the Fields** (chamber orchestra) in 1959. Marriner was the first music director of the Los Angeles Chamber Orchestra (1969–1978), music director of the **Minnesota Orchestra** (1979–1986), and principal conductor of the Stuttgart Radio Symphony Orchestra (1986–1989). He studied conducting in Hancock, Maine, with **Pierre Monteux** and made many recordings, mostly with the **Academy of St. Martins in the Fields** under the Argo, L'Oiseau Lyre, Philips, and **EMI** Classics labels.

Marsch. (Ger.) March, a type of piece, a style. (Fr. *march*, It. *marcia*, Sp. *marcha*.)

martelé. (Fr.) A bowing term calling for a very short bow with a very strong, if not forceful, release on each note. Can be played in every section of the bow; however, when played at the **frog**, the effect will be generally heavier and rougher. Also called **hammered** and *martellato*.

martellato. (It.) Same as *martelé*. Sometimes also called **hammered**.

Martenot, Maurice. (1898–1980.) French musician and inventor of the **Ondes Martenot**. Patented in 1922 but not produced until 1928, the Ondes Martenot was one of the early electronic instruments and followed quickly on the footsteps of the **Theremin**. Composer Olivier Messiaen used it in his *Turangalîla Symphony* and Arthur Honegger used it in *Jeanne d'Arc au Bûcher*. See also **Moog synthesizer**.

martial. (Fr.) Martial. A character word sometimes used to evoke a certain character in playing. (Ger. *kriegerisch*, It. *marziale*, Sp. *marcial*.)

Martinez, Odaline de la. (b. 1949.) Cuban American composer and **conductor** who immigrated to the United States in 1961. She studied at Tulane University and then moved to England in order to attend the **Royal Academy of Music**, London (1972–1976), and the University of Surrey. She founded the contemporary ensemble Lontano, based in London, and has made several recordings with them on their own label, LORELT (Lontano Records, Ltd.). In 1984, she became the first woman to conduct a full concert at the **BBC Proms**. In 1990, she organized the European Women's Orchestra for the Chard Festival of Women in Music in Britain (1990–2003). She has appeared as a guest conductor with several orchestras in Britain, including all of the **BBC** orchestras, the **New Zealand Symphony Orchestra**, and others. In 2006, she founded the biennial London Festival of American Music with the Lontano ensemble. Her recordings include collections of music by British women, including her own, and works by Eleanor Alberga, Lindsay Cooper, Nicola LeFanu, Elizabeth Maconchy, Melinda Maxwell, Hilary Tann, Errollyn Wallen, and Judith Weir.

Martinon, Jean. (1910–1976.) French **conductor** and composer. Martinon studied first at the Lyon Conservatory and then the **Paris Conservatory** with composers Vincent d'Indy and Albert Roussel and then at the Sorbonne, where he studied with conductors Roger Désormière and **Charles Munch**. During World War II, he spent two years in a prisoner of war camp where he was able to pursue composition, creating several works, including a symphony and works for chorus and orchestra. Munch conducted the first performance of Martinon's *Chant des Captifs* in 1942 when Paris was still under occupation, and on his release, he was invited to conduct the premiere of the symphony written under internment with the Pasdeloup Orchestra. After the war, he was the assistant to Munch with the Paris Conservatory (1944–1946) and the principal conductor of the Bordeaux Philharmonic Orchestra (1943–1945). Martinon was made the associate conductor of the **London Philharmonic Orchestra** under **Sir Adrian Boult** (1947–1949), conductor of the Radio Eireann Orchestra (1948–1950), and music director of the Lamoureux Orchestra (1951–1958). He conducted the **Boston Symphony Orchestra** in 1957 and served as music director of the **Israel Philharmonic** (1958–1960); the Düsseldorf Symphony (1960–1969); the **Chicago Symphony** (1963–1969); the **French Radio Orchestra**, also known as the **ORTF** (1968–1975); and The Hague Philharmonic Orchestra, now known as The Hague Residentie Orchestra (1975–1976). His list of compositions includes four symphonies, opera, oratorio, two violin concertos, a cello concerto, two string quartets, and more. He was known as an elegant and stylish conductor with an unexpected preference for German classics. In Chicago, he led fresh but sometimes controversial interpretations known for their emphasis on clarity over power of the music of Franz Joseph Haydn, Wolfgang Amadeus Mozart, Ludwig van Beethoven, Franz Schubert, Robert Schumann, **Felix Mendelssohn**, **Richard Wagner**, and Johannes Brahms. His list of recordings includes a cycle of the symphonies of Sergei Prokofiev but is topped off by excellent performances of Claude Debussy and Maurice Ravel.

marziale. (It.) Martial. A character word sometimes used to evoke a certain character in playing. (Fr. *martial*, Ger. *kriegerisch*, Sp. *marcial*.)

más. (Sp.) More. (Fr. *plus*; Ger. *mehr*; It. *più, di più*.) Example: *Más fuerte!* Louder! *Más acento!* More accent!

mäßig (also *mässig, mässige*). (Ger.) Moderate, moderately (often used together with *Tempo* or *Zeitmaß*), similar to *moderato* in Italian. (Fr. *modérément*, It. *moderatamente*, Sp. *moderamente*.) Examples: *sehr mäßig bewegt*, very moderately moving, from the prelude to *Die Meistersinger von Nürenberg* by **Richard Wagner**; *mässig rasch*, moderately quick, and *mässig langsam*, moderately slow, from *Pierrot Lunaire* by **Arnold Schoenberg**. Also *sehr mäßig*, very moderately, seen often in the symphonies of **Gustav Mahler**, such as the title of the second movement of the Symphony No. 3.

master classes. A class with a "master" teacher, usually someone of great renown, given in front of a group of fellow students, but sometimes in front of the public, in a manner similar to a performance. One performer at a time will play or sing a piece and take comments from the teacher. Master classes can also be an outreach program that some professional orchestras, schools, or community centers offer for adult amateur musicians where the amateur is allowed to perform in front of other amateurs and receive comments from a professional.

master of music (degree). The academic degree received after the bachelor's and before the doctorate. The degree implies an added level of expertise above and beyond the basic level of the bachelor's degree.

Mata, Eduardo. (1942–1995.) Mexico's most important **conductor**. Mata studied composition with one of Mexico's most important composers, Carlos Chávez, and became the director of the music department of the University of Mexico when he was twenty-three. He founded the orchestra there the next year. He conducted the Symphony Orchestras of Guadalajara (1965–1966), **Phoenix** (1975–1978), and **Dallas** (1977–1993) and was a guest conductor worldwide throughout his life. Mata made over seventy recordings with many orchestras; was known as a conductor of twentieth-century music, including that of his native Mexico; and was frequently praised for a conducting style of clarity, precision, and transparency. He died in a plane crash at the age of fifty-three.

matrix. Containing all possible forty-eight permutations and transpositions of a **twelve-tone row** and sometimes called a "twelve-by-twelve square," it is often used by serial composers to organize parameters other than pitch, such as rhythm, duration, dynamics, and so on. It is also known as a **Babbitt** square. See George Perle's *Twelve Tone Tonality* and Joseph Straus's *Introduction to Post-Tonal Theory*. See also **twelve-tone matrix**.

Masur, Kurt. (b. 1927.) German **conductor**. Masur served as the conductor of the Dresden Philharmonic Orchestra (1955–1958, 1967–1972) and chief conductor of the **Komische Oper** in Berlin, where he collaborated with distinguished director **Walter Felsenstein** on several acclaimed productions He was appointed music director of the **Leipzig Gewandhaus Orchestra** (1970–1996), and under his direction, a new concert hall was opened in 1981. Masur became the principal guest conductor of the **Dallas Symphony Orchestra** (1976) and the **London Philharmonic** (1988). He gave a daring public speech calling for calm negotiation as the East German government threatened military action in October 1988. The speech was critical in the downfall of Communist rule and elevated Masur to the level of a national hero. He served as the music director of the **New York Philharmonic** (1991–2002), principal conductor of the **London Philharmonic** (2000–2007), and music director of the **French National Orchestra** (2001–2008).

mayor. (Sp.) **Major.** (Fr. *majeur*, Ger. *Dur*, It. *maggiore*.) Example: *tono mayor*, major key.

maza. (Sp.) Mallet, as in the sticks used to play timpani. (Fr. *mailloche*; Ger. *Schlägel*; It. *mazza, mazzuolo*.)

mazza del tambur maggiore. (It.) Drum major's baton. (Fr. *canne de tambour major*; Ger. *Tambourstab*; Sp. *bastòn de mando, maza de tambor mayor*.)

mazza, mazzuolo. (It.) Mallet, as in the sticks used to play timpani. (Fr. *mailloche*, Ger. *Schlägel*, Sp. *maza*.) Example: *con la mazza*, with the mallet, as in striking a suspended symbol with a mallet.

M. B. Abbreviation for middle of the bow, an indication to bow in the middle of the bow as opposed to the tip or **frog**, for instance.

M. D. Abbreviation for *main droite* (Fr.). Example: *mano destra* (It.), right hand.

mean-tone temperament. See **tuning systems**.

measure. A notational device used to group notes into a unit of musical time with a set number of note values dependent on the **meter**, that is, delineated by two bar lines, one on each side. Also called a **bar**. (Fr. *mesure*, Ger. *Takt*, It. *misura*, Sp. *compás*.)

measure number. Numbers inserted in scores and parts to facilitate rehearsal. Also **bar number**. (Fr. *nombre de mesures*, Ger. *Taktzahl*, It. *numero di battutue*, Sp. *número del compás*.)

media voz. (Sp.) Half-voice, softly. The Italian form, *a mezza voce*, is commonly used internationally. The German form is archaic. (Fr. *à mi-voix*, Ger. *mit halber Stimme*, It. *a mezza voce*.)

medley. A collection of well-known melodies put together for performance purposes; often a collection of popular songs. Overtures to light operas or musicals can be medleys of the melodies in the work. A good example is the *Overture to Die Fledermaus* of Johann Strauss II. Orchestral arrangements of medleys from popular musicals or movies are often made for performance at pops concerts.

Meet the Composer. See **New Music USA**.

megahertz. AbbreviationA unit of frequency equal to one million cycles per second, or one million **hertz**. Abbreviated **mHz**.

mehr. (Ger.) More. Used in a number of phrases. (Fr. *plus*; It. *piú, di più*; Sp. *más*.)

mehrfach. (Ger.) Multiple, a bunch of times, manifold. (Fr. *multiple*, It. *multiplo*, Sp. *multiple*.) Also *mehrfach besetzt*, several to a part (**besetzt** meaning occupied or engaged).

mehrstimmig. (Ger.) Polyphonic. (Fr. *polyphonique*, It. *polifonico*, Sp. *polifónico*.)

Mehrstimmigkeit, Polyphonie. (Ger.) **Polyphony**. (Fr. *polyphonie*, It. *polifonia*, Sp. *polifonía*.)

Mehta, Zubin. (b. 1936.) Born in Bombay (now Mumbai), he is the son of Meli Mehta, a violinist and **conductor**, and the founder of both the Bombay Symphony Orchestra and the Bombay String Quartet. His younger brother is Zarin Mehta, who studied accounting and business, became an orchestra manager, and eventually became the president and executive director of the **New York Philharmonic Orchestra**. After early experience conducting his father's orchestra, Zubin went to the **Vienna Academy** to study with **Hans Swarowsky**, organizing and giving concerts with his own student orchestras. He also studied for two summers with Carlo Zecchi at the Siena, Italy, **Accademia Musicale Chigiana**. Mehta won the main prize at the first international **Royal Liverpool Philharmonic Orchestra** conducting competition in 1958 and was awarded a one-year position as the assistant conductor. That was followed by appearances with the Vienna, Berlin, and Los Angeles philharmonic orchestras and the **Montreal Symphony**, where he was soon appointed music director (1961–1967).

What might be called a "mishandling of circumstances" led to Mehta also becoming the music director in Los Angeles. Management made him the associate conductor in 1961 without consulting recently appointed music director **Sir George Solti**, who resigned in protest. Mehta replaced him, serving from 1962 until his subsequent appointment with the **New York Philharmonic**, where he was the longest serving music director (1978–1991). He also conducted the **Israel Philharmonic Orchestra** in 1962 and toured with them in 1966. He went to Israel during the Arab-Israel War in 1967 in order to lead special concerts and was made the music adviser in 1968, music director in 1977, and music director for life in 1981. He conducted at **La Scala, Milan**, in 1962 and the **Metropolitan Opera**, New York, in 1965. Mehta has been the chief conductor of the Teatro del Maggio Musicale Fiorentino, Florence; music director of the **Bavarian State Opera**, Munich (1998–2006); honorary conductor of the **Munich Philharmonic**; and conductor, along with **Lorin Maazel**, at the new opera house, the **Palau de les Arts Reina Sofia** (Queen Sofia Palace of the Arts) in Valencia, Spain (2005). Renowned as an energetic and perhaps flamboyant conductor, Mehta has named **Wilhelm Furtwängler** as his most admired predecessor. For him, the forward-moving line of a work is the most important. His early experiences in Vienna gave him a lifelong compulsion for seeking a beautiful orchestral sound, a warm tone, and a relaxed, lyrical style of playing. While some hear a superficial quality to his performances, others praise his integrity, charm, and respectful manner toward both the music and the musicians. His list of recordings (CDs and some DVDs) reveals a preference for late nineteenth-century works—both symphonic and operatic—and includes performances with the Vienna, Israel, Los Angeles, and New York philharmonic orchestras. Of special note are several specially compiled tribute collections and remastered CDs.

Meier, Gustav. (b. 1929.) Renowned Swiss-born American **conductor** and pedagogue. Meier serves as the director of the Orchestra Conducting Program at the **Peabody Institute** and has been the music director of the Greater Bridgeport Symphony Orchestra since 1971. He is the author of ***The Score, the Orchestra, and the Conductor*** (2009). Meier has guest conducted worldwide and taught at **Yale University, School of Music** (1960–1973); **Eastman School of Music** (1973–1976); the **University of Michigan** (1976–1995); and **Tanglewood Music Center** (1980–1996). He is one of the most distinguished conducting pedagogues of our time and has students placed in countless positions across the globe, including **Marin Alsop** (**Baltimore Symphony**), Yakov Kreisberg (Netherlands Philharmonic and **Vienna Symphony**), Jun Märkl (Mannheim National Theater, Lyon National Symphony), Rico Saccani (Budapest Philharmonic), **Carl St. Clair** (**Komische Oper, Berlin**, and Pacific Symphony) Antonio Pappano (**Royal Opera, Covent Garden)**, Mark Gibson (**Cincinnati Conservatory**), and Bobby McFerrin (frequent guest conductor). See the **bibliography**.

Melbourne Symphony Orchestra (MSO). Founded in 1906 with one hundred permanent members, it is the oldest professional orchestra in Australia. It is supported by the Victoria state government, the Australian federal government through the Australia Council, private donors and corporations, and Symphony Services International. The founding **conductor** was Alberto Zelman. In 1934, it became one of the Australian Broadcasting Commission's orchestras. In 1949, it took the name Victorian Symphony Orchestra, and in 1965, reverted back to the Melbourne Symphony. The current chief conductor is **Sir Andrew Davis** (appointed in 2013). Past conductors have included Taddaki Otaka (2009–2012, principal guest conductor); Oleg Caetani (2005–2009); Markus Stenz (1998–2002); Hiroyuki Iwaki (1974–1997), the orchestra's longest serving chief conductor; and others. In 2008, the orchestra won the Outstanding Contribution Award to Australian Music in Education for its ArtPlay ensemble touring program and music theater project *Hunger*. The orchestra has performed in Carnegie Hall and in Russia, Japan, Korea, and Europe. It has made several crossover appearances with rock musicians such as Elton John, KISS, and others. It offers a series of pops concerts, recently featuring Disney classics, and has recorded several times on its own label, MSO Live.

Mellon Foundation, Andrew W. See **Andrew W. Mellon Foundation**.

melodia. (It.) Tune, melody, air, theme. (Fr. *mélodie*, Ger. *Melodie*, Sp. *melodía*.)

melodía. (Sp.) Tune, melody, air, theme. (Fr. *mélodie*, Ger. *Melodie*, It. *melodia*.)

Melodie. (Ger.) Tune, air, melody, theme. (Fr. *mélodie*, It. *melodia*, Sp. *melodía*.)

mélodie. (Fr.) Tune, air, melody, theme. (Ger. *Melodie*, It. *melodia*, Sp. *melodía*.)

Melodiya. A Russian record label. Established in 1964 as the All-Union Gramophone Record Firm of the USSR Ministry of Culture Melodiya, by the 1970s the company had sales of close to two hundred million records with exports to more than seventy countries of mostly classical music. In the United States, their recordings were released under the label Monitor Records and later on Melodiya/Angel. State owned until 1989, Melodiya recordings are now available over the Internet.

méme. (Fr.) Same. Used as part of numerous phrases.

méme corde. (Fr.) The same string. Example: *sur la méme corde*, on the same string. A directive in the music for string players to all of the notes of a passage on the same string, creating a particular tone.

même mouvt. (Fr.) Same tempo, with *mouvement* in its abbreviated form. Example: *Même mouvt. (plus exactement rythmé)*, the same tempo, more exactly rhythmic, from "Gigues" of *Images* by Claude Debussy.

même tempo, le. (Fr.) The same tempo. (Ger. *das gleiche Tempo*, It. *l'istesso tempo*, Sp. *el mismo tiempo*.)

meme temps, en. (Fr.) Simultaneously, at the same time. (Ger. *gleichzeitig*, It. *contemporaneamente*, Sp. *al mismo tiempo*.)

memorizing the score. **Conductors** memorize music in a variety of ways but most often as a result of extensive study. Conductors with a photographic memory hold a mental image of the pages of the score. Photographic memory sometimes occurs together with perfect pitch, helping the conductor remember where they are within a **harmonic** or **pitch** structure. For others, perfect pitch on its own acts as a memory aid by prompting the conductor to remember sequences of events on hearing a certain pitch played by a particular instrument, thus combining pitch and timbre memory.

The main difference between memorizing a score for conducting as opposed to singing or playing is that there is no real physical or tactile memory of how "it feels" to perform it; conductors must rely on their visual and aural memory. To compensate, memory tools have been developed based on musical knowledge and experience with the process. They include the understanding of musical forms and using them like a map to be followed during the course of the piece. An image of the orchestra, or other ensemble, in front of you can facilitate the memory of cue sequences by associating either the instrument or the face of the person playing the instrument. Some conductors make charts of scores, reducing them to important elements. Exercises based on these methods are then used to test memory in advance of the first rehearsal. See **conducting from memory**.

MENC. See **Music Educators National Conference**.

Mendelssohn, Felix. (1809–1847.) German composer, **conductor**, pianist, and watercolorist. Mendelssohn was the grandson of renowned Jewish philosopher Moses Mendelssohn. He was a child prodigy and wrote in his mature style by the age of sixteen (*Octet for Strings in E-flat*). His first conducting experiences came when he led the first performance of the *St. Matthew Passion* since Johann Sebastian Bach's death (1750).

Mendelssohn made his London debut in 1829, notably using a baton, returning to conduct many times. His first paid conducting position was in Düsseldorf in 1833, where he performed George Frideric Handel's oratorio *Israel in Egypt* and his first opera, Wolfgang Amadeus Mozart's *Don Giovanni*. In 1835, he was appointed conductor of the **Leipzig Gewandhaus Orchestra**, leading a subscription series of twenty concerts each season. He was the first conductor at Leipzig to use a baton, and he presented works of his own and many contemporaries, including the young **Richard Wagner**, and incorporated concert performances of opera into the repertoire. In 1839, he began a series of "historical" concerts where celebrated composers of the past were performed. In 1939, He premiered Franz Schubert's Symphony No. 9 after Robert Schumann brought him the manuscript he had discovered. He also premiered Schumann's Symphony No. 1 (1841). Mendelssohn was known as a meticulous and elegant conductor who succeeded in raising standards of performance to great critical acclaim. In 1843, Mendelssohn founded the **Leipzig Conservatory**, now the **Hochschüle für Musik und Theater "Felix Mendelssohn Bartholdy,"** and persuaded his teacher **Ignaz Moscheles** and friend Schumann to join him. Other faculty included violinist/composer Ferdinand David and violinist Joseph Joachim. The first school of music in Germany, it was part of a trend toward professionalism in the music field. While Mendelssohn believed in it mightily, he did not teach much, taking only a few students of composition and ensemble playing. In the same year, **Hector Berlioz** visited Mendelssohn, and at his request, they exchanged batons. Mendelssohn had a reputation of conducting from memory and keeping the musicians of his orchestra completely focused through his own "electricity."

Mengelberg, Wilhelm. (1871–1051.) Mengelberg was the music director of the **Concertgebouw Orchestra** for an astonishing fifty years (1895–1945), creating one of the most accomplished orchestras in history. Dutch-born, he studied at the Cologne Conservatory, winning awards in conducting, piano, and composition. Dedicated to the music of **Gustav Mahler**, **Richard Strauss**, **Arnold Schoenberg**, and Max Reger, he developed close personal relationships with all four. In pursuit of authoritative performances, he corresponded at length with each composer regarding interpretive details. His Mahler scores are packed with notes and contain retouching by the composer. Mengelberg led the first cycle of Mahler's major works with the Concertgebouw in 1925. Strauss dedicated *Ein Heldenleben* to him. He was a conductor who did not hesitate to make changes in a score if he thought it would benefit. He saw this not only as artistic license but as his duty. His performances of the Beethoven symphonies, some of which can be heard in recording, are filled with sudden changes of tempo, *rubato*, and even string *portamento*, a style of playing that was no longer deemed appropriate for works from the Classical period. He conducted concerts in New York, Britain, and Salzburg and from 1945 was banned from conducting in the Netherlands because of alleged collusion with the Nazis. He retired to Switzerland and died just months before the prohibition ran out.

meno. (It.) Less, slower. (Fr. *moins*, Ger. *weniger*, Sp. *menos*.) Example: *meno mosso*, less motion.

menor. (Sp.) Minor, as in a minor key, C minor, as opposed to C major. (Fr. *mineur*, Ger. *Moll*, It. *minore*.) Example: *tono menor*, minor key.

menos. (Sp.) Less. (Fr. *moins*, Ger. *weniger*, It. *meno*.)

menuetto, tempo di. (It.) In the tempo of a minuet, a type of dance. Seen, for example, in the title of the second movement of the Symphony No. 3 by **Gustav Mahler**.

mensurada. (Sp.) Measured, in time. (Fr. *mesuré*, Ger. *gemessen*, It. *misurato*.)

Mensurstrich. (Ger.) Bar line. (Fr. *barre de mesure*, It. *barra*, Sp. *barra de compás*.)

meravigliosoo. (It.) Wonderful, marvelous. Also ***stupendo***. A character word sometimes used to give praise. (Fr. *merveilleux*; Ger. *erstaunlich, wunderbar*; Sp. *maravilloso*.)

Mercury Records. Founded in 1945, an American record company that is now owned by Universal Music Group. It is known for having made the first high-fidelity recordings that led to the Mercury Living Presence series of recordings. Particularly renowned for recordings of the **Chicago** and **Minneapolis orchestras**, Paul Paray and the **Detroit Symphony**, and numerous releases conducted by American composer **Howard Hanson** with the **Eastman Rochester Orchestra**.

merklich. (Ger.) Measurably, appreciable, noticeably, perceptible. (Fr. *nettement*, It. *marcatamente*, Sp. *marcadamente*.) See also ***unmerklich***.

merveilleux. (Fr.) Wonderful, marvelous. A descriptive word sometimes used to give praise. (Ger. *erstaunlich, wunderbar*; It. *meravigliosoo, stupendo*; Sp. *maravilloso*.)

Mester, Jorge. (b. 1935.) Mexican **conductor** of Hungarian parents. Mester studied at the **Juilliard School** with Jean Morel and worked with **Leonard Bernstein** at the **Berkshire Music Center**. He has served as the music director of the **Louisville Orchestra** (1967–1979), Pasadena Symphony Orchestra (1984–2010), and Naples Philharmonic Orchestra, Florida (2004–present), and again as

the music director of the **Louisville Orchestra** (2006–present). Mester was the music director of the **Aspen Music Festival** from 1970 to 1990, founding the Aspen Chamber Symphony. He was appointed music director of the **Mexico City Philharmonic Orchestra** in 1998. During his initial tenure with the **Louisville Orchestra**, Mester led over seventy recordings of contemporary composers such as Henry Cowell, George Crumb, Luigi Dallapiccola, Alberto Ginastera, Enrique Granados, **Krzysztof Penderecki**, Goffredo Petrassi, **Gunther Schuller**, and many others. An acclaimed teacher of conducting, he was on the faculty of the Juilliard School between 1958 and 1988. His impressive list of recordings includes many on the **Naxos** and **First Edition** labels.

mesure. (Fr.) **Bar**, measure. (Ger. *Takt*, It. *misura*, Sp. *compás*.)

mesure. (Fr.) **Meter**, measure. Example: *à la mesure, en mesure*, in time or *a tempo*.

mesuré. (Fr.) Measured, in strict tempo. (It. *misurato*, Ger. *gemessen*, Sp. *mensurada*.)

metà, la. (It.) Half of a string group or section. (Fr. *la moitié*, Ger. *die Hälfte*, Sp. *mitad*.)

metá, minima. (It.) **Half note** or minum (British usage). (Fr. *blanche*, Ger. *Halbe*, Sp. *blanca*.) See also **appendix 7**.

meter. The pattern in which regular, successive musical rhythm is organized with one complete group being a **measure** or **bar** defined on each side by a bar line, creating a measure or bar. In Western music, each meter is given a numerical sign that indicates the basic division of the bar, such as 4/4, 3/4, 2/4, 5/8, 6/8, 7/8, 9/8, 12/8, and many more. In contemporary music, meter is often characterized by a lack of regularity, with frequent metric shifts from bar to bar. See **Igor Stravinsky**'s ***The Rite of Spring*** and **Aaron Copland**'s ***Appalachian Spring***, both in **appendix 1**. (Fr. *mesure*; Ger. *Takt, Taktart*; It. *misura, tempo*; Sp. *compás, tiempo*.)

Meter 4/4. *Courtesy Andrew Martin Smith.*

Meter 2/4. *Courtesy Andrew Martin Smith.*

Meter 3/4. *Courtesy Andrew Martin Smith.*

Meter 1/4. *Courtesy Andrew Martin Smith.*

Meter 5/8. *Courtesy Andrew Martin Smith.*

Meter 6/8. *Courtesy Andrew Martin Smith.*

Meter 8/8. *Courtesy Andrew Martin Smith.*

Meter 9/8. *Courtesy Andrew Martin Smith.*

Meter 12/8. *Courtesy Andrew Martin Smith.*

methods of score study. Begin with the basics: the title of the piece and the name of the composer. Look at the first page of the score for the movement title, tempo indication (if any), orchestration and score layout, basic meter, and key signature. If it is a concerto or other work with a soloist, notice where the solo part lies in the score. Read through the score to identify overall elements of style. Going from larger to smaller features, look for and identify large-scale formal structures, harmonic language, and phrases, while also noting rhythmic and motivic details. Make note of the **harmonic rhythm**.

Investigate the composer's orchestral language, and in contemporary pieces, be aware of any nontraditional ways of playing the instruments. Always note when string players are required to use mutes, making sure you know when they go on and off. Do the same for the brass, noticing the type of mute required, if stated. Identify potential problems that may come up in rehearsal and how to solve them. When you have an understanding of the phrases, do the bowings. If you are not a string player, meet with one who you trust to do this. Then put the work in a historic and social context. Find out as much as possible about the composer and the motivation for the work. Once this is accomplished, the **conductor** will be able to begin the development of a convincing concept of the piece. See also **charts**, **score study**, **Seven Trips Through the Score**.

metric modulation. A transition from one meter or tempo to another through a common rhythmic unit, such as note values or tempo proportions. A compositional device used to handle such transitions, especially in contemporary music. See also **metric relations**.

metric relations. Refers to the practice of using a subdivision of the pulse as a common denominator between sections of a piece of music when the tempo changes. In the Baroque and Classical periods, when the first movement of a suite or symphony begins with a slow introduction followed by a quick section, it is very common to make a two-to-one relationship between the two tempos, that is, the fast section is twice as fast as the slow one. Other relationships, such as four to one and two to three, are also often used by **conductors** between movements of dance suites or symphonies in order to create a sense of architectural continuity. In the twentieth century, composers often specify metric connections. See the original and revised versions of **Igor Stavinsky**'s *Octet for Winds* for an interesting look at how the composer handled and revised the metric connections. Also consult **John Corigliano**'s **Symphony No. 1**, as described in **appendix 1, "Six Pieces That Changed Conducting."** Other examples include Elliott Cater's *Variations for Orchestra* (1952). The most common metric connection is eighth note = eighth note.

Metric relation, eighth note remains constant.
Courtesy Andrew Martin Smith.

mètre de Maelzel. (Fr.) The speed or tempo of the beats as specified on **Johann Maelzel**'s **metronome**.

metronome. A device that produces regular series of clicks, beats, or visible but silent flashes that are used to determine tempi. Modern metronomes exist in the form of downloadable applications (**aps**) available on computers or smartphones. They are also available as battery-operated digital machines that have the capacity to produce not only tempos but also complex rhythmic patterns, including cross rhythms. Some can also store more than one tempo and allow the operator to switch quickly back and forth, facilitating learning quick tempo changes. One of these is the commonly used modern digital device called **Dr. Beat**. It allows the musician to practice various difficult rhythmic passages, provides tuning notes, and has **MIDI** input. Some contemporary composers have actually used the classic metronome as an "instrument" in their works. For example, **György Ligeti**'s *Poème symphonique* (1962) for one hundred metronomes, and the English composer Gordon Crosse used them in his *Play Ground* (1977). Even Ludiwg van Beethoven, an early promoter of **Johann Maelzel**'s metronome, imitated it in the second movement of his Symphony No. 2.

The first commonly used metronome was a relatively simple one developed, if not invented, by the Dutchman **Dietrich Nikolaus Winkel** (c. 1776–1826) but copied, modified, and patented by the more business savvy Johann Nepomuk Maelzel. Winkel's design was a double-weighted pendulum device built into a case. The top weight, which was visible on the pendulum, slides up and down according to the desired speed, slower at the top and faster at the bottom. The bottom weight balances the pendulum and sits hidden in the case. This metronome also has an internal spring that when wound up and then released, would power the pendulum to swing back and forth, producing audible clicks at a specified rate per minute. Maelzel's contributions included determining what the most common tempi were and adding slots to the pendulum that accurately indicated tempo markings. Thus the top weight would slip into the specific slot and the metronome would generate the desired tempo. The final list, which took Maelzel a few years to complete, remains in common usage and includes the following, from fast to slow: 208, 200, 192, 184, 176, 168, 160, 152, 144, 140, 136, 132, 128, 124, 120, 116, 112, 108, 104, 100, 98, 95, 88, 84, 80, 76, 72, 69, 66, 63, 60, 58, 56, 52, 48, 46, 44, 42, and 40. Maelzel patented the device with his name "metronome" in both Paris and London on December 5, 1815, and in a few short years **Maelzel Metronome (MM)** numbers became commonly used.

See Harding, Rosamond E. M. *The Metronome and Its Precursors*. Henley-on-Thames, UK: Gresham Books, 1983. (Originally published 1938.) See the **bibliography**.

metrónomo. (Sp.) **Metronome.** (Fr. *metronome*; Ger. *Zeitmesser, metronom*; It. *metronome*.)

Metropolitan Opera. Founded in 1880 in New York and often called the "Met," it is the largest opera company in North America, offering at least twenty-seven opera productions each season in a combination of standards, less well-known, and new operas from the Baroque to contemporary with many of the worlds' best singers, conductors, and stage directors. The company had adapted new technologies throughout its history as they became available: radio broadcasts since 1931, television since 1977, and most recently live satellite radio, Internet broadcasts, and high-definition video transmissions of performances in designated movie theaters across North America. The Metropolitan Opera channel is available on **Sirius XM Radio**. In first years of the twentieth century, recordings were made on Mapleson Cylinders, preserving the sounds of singers, chorus, and orchestras of the day. From 1898 to 1986 the Met went on tours of America, appearing in communities around the country that had no opera companies locally. In 1995, the company developed a system called "Met Titles," where translations are displayed on a small screen on the back of every seat in the house.

The current music director is **James Levine** and the general manager is Peter Gelb. Gelb was preceded by Joseph Volpe (1990–2006), Rudolf Bing (1950–1972), Edward Johnson (1935–1950), Giulio Gatti-Casazza (1908–1935), and Heinrich Conried (1903–1908). Past **conductors** have included Anton Seidl (1885–1897), **Walter Damrosch** (1884–1902), Alfred Hertz (1902–1925, as principal conductor of German repertory), **Gustav Mahler** (1908–1910), **Arturo Toscanini** (1908–1915), **Artur Bodandanzky** (1915–1939, as principal conductor of German repertory), Tulio Serafin (1924–1934), Fausto Cleva (1931–1971), **Erich Leinsdorf** (1938–1942, as principal conductor of German repertory), **George Szell** (1942–1946), Cesare Sodero (1942–1947), Fritz Busch (1945–1949), **Fritz Reiner** (1949–1953), **Dimitri Mitropoulos** (1954–1960), **Erich Leinsdorf** (1957–1962), Kurt Adler (1943–1973, chorus master and conductor), **Rafael Kubelik** (1973–1974, music director), **James Levine**, (1973–present, became music director in 1976), **Valery Gergiev** (1997–2008 as principal guest conductor), and **Fabio Luisi** (principal guest conductor 2010–2011, principal conductor 2011–present). The "Met" is supported by members of the Opera Guild, who receive the ***Opera News Magazine*** and other benefits. The company also provides numerous outreach and education program for youth and adults.

mettere. (It.) To attach, to put on. Example: *mettere la sordina*, put on the mute. (Fr. *mettre*, Ger. *setzen, legen, stellen*, Sp. *poner*) See also ***togliere***, take off.

mettez. (Fr.) Attach, put on. Examples: *mettez les sourdines*, put on the mutes; *ôtez*, take off. Seen in many French works of the twentieth century. (Ger. *setzen, legen, stellen*; It. *mettere*; Sp. *poner*.)

Mexico City Philharmonic Orchestra (MCPO). Founded in 1978 by the government of Mexico at the initiative the former president's wife, Mrs. Carmen Romano de López Potillo. The orchestra has been a major proponent of music by Mexican composers through its many recordings, some of them on the **Naxos label**. The philharmonic supports young Mexican performers with competitions for young performers and commissions from young composers. Music directors have included founder Fernando Lozano (1978–1984), Enrique Bátiz, Luis Herrera de la Fuente, and **Jorge Mester** (1998–present).

mezza voce, a. (It.) Half-voice, softly. This, the Italian form, is preferred. The German form is archaic. (Fr. à *mi-voix*; Ger. *mit halber Stimme*; Sp. *media voz*.)

mezzo, mezza. (It.) Half, medium, middle. Examples: *mezzo forte*, moderately loud; *mezzo piano*, half or moderately piano; *mezza voce*, half voice. (Fr. *á mi-voix*, Ger. *halber Stimme*, Sp. *media voz*.)

mezzo soprano. A female voice classification that lies below the soprano and above the alto. See **voice classifications**.

mf. (It.) Abbreviation for *mezzo forte*.

M. G. (Fr.) Abbreviation for *main gauche*, left hand.

M. G. G. (Ger.) Abbreviation for *Die Musik in Geschichte und Gegenwart* (Music in History and Present), a comprehensive music encyclopedia.

mHz. Abbreviation for **megahertz**.

mi. The **solmization** name for the note E, the third note of the major scale beginning on do (*Ut* in French, or C); in the **moveable *do* system**, the third note of the major scale and the fifth note of the minor scale. In some solmization practice, the flattening of the third note of the scale is indicated by the use of *ma* instead of *mi*. See **solfège**, **solmization**.

mi bémol. (Fr.) E-flat. See **accidental**; **appendix 5**.

mi bémolle. (It.) E-flat. See **accidental**; **appendix 5**.

Michigan Opera Theatre (MOT). Established in Detroit by founding general director David DiChiera as Overture to Opera (OTO), an opera outreach and education program in 1963. It presented its first full-length opera in 1970 and became MOT in 1971. In 1989, the company purchased its current home, the Detroit Opera House, raising the money for an extensive renovation, the additional purchase of the remaining buildings on the block,

and the construction of a large stage house. Luciano Pavarotti got behind the project, helping to raise money and promising to sing at the opening gala that took place in 1996. MOT has built a reputation through presenting premieres and performances of rarely heard operas such as Karol Szymanowski's *King Roger*, in addition to opera standards. It performs four opera productions and hosts visiting dance companies. Operas are presented in the original language with English supertitles. The company runs community outreach programs, including a Young Artist Apprentice Program, and has been awarded the Success in Education Award by **Opera America**.

microtone. An interval that is less than a half step, such as a quartertone or a sixteenth tone. More common in non-Western music and electronic or computer music.

microtonalism. Music that is based on intervals of less than a half step. The most common microtonal interval is the quartertone. While not traditional in Western music, some examples exist in the music of such composers as Harry Partch, who created a scale dividing the octave into forty-three equal steps, and Alois Hába, known for using both quartertone and sixth-tone relationships. Both Haba and **Krzysztof Penderecki** have developed successful microtone notation systems. The flexibility inherent in electronic and computer music has led to increased interest in microtonal composition.

mi dièse. (Fr.) E0sharp. See **accidental**; **appendix 5**.

mi dieses. (It.) E-sharp. See **accidental**; **appendix 5**.

middle C. The C in the middle range of the piano.

Middle C. *Courtesy Andrew Martin Smith.*

middle ground. A term used in **Schenkerian analysis** to describe the second and most complex level consisting of linear relationships between the pitches of structurally important harmonies perceived more long-term both within and between phrases. The middle ground also consists of fundamental harmonies perceived as defining sections of the work. (Ger. *Mittelgrund*.)

Milwaukee Symphony Orchestra (MSO). Established in 1959, the orchestra presents a full range of classics, pops, and family concerts, as well as their Classical Connections series. The MSO is the orchestra for Florentine Opera (Milwaukee) productions and tours the state widely. The MSO has performed twelve times in New York's Carnegie Hall and traveled to Europe, Japan, the Dominican Republic, and Cuba (1999). The orchestra has performed more than one hundred world and American premieres of contemporary composers. MSO concerts are broadcast nationally through the **WFMT radio network** (New York). The MSO was the first orchestra in the United States to offer live recordings for download through online music stores such as **iTunes**. Its current music director is Edo de Waart (appointed in 2009). Past music directors include Harry John Brown (1959–1968), Kenneth Schermerhorn (1968–1980), Lukas Foss (1981–1986), **Zdeněk Mácal** (1986–1995), and Andreas Delfs (1997–2009).

mineur. (Fr.) Minor, as in a minor key, C minor, as opposed to C major. (Ger. *Moll*, It. *minore*, Sp. *menor*.)

minim. The equivalent of the half note in the British rhythmic system. (Fr. *blanche*, Ger. *Halbe*, It. *minima*, Sp. *blanca*.) See **appendix 7**.

minima. (It.) Half note. (Fr. *blanche*, Ger. *Halbe*, Sp. *blanca*.) See **appendix 7**.

minimalism. First developing during the 1960s and 1970s, a style of the visual arts and music that strives for expression through simplified means. Making a radical break with past trends toward complexity, the music can be characterized by repetition with gradual chordal and rhythmic manipulation over long passages, sometimes referred to as "process music." Prominent composers include La Monte Young, Terry Riley, Steve Reich, Phillip Glass, and John Adams.

Minneapolis Symphony. Founded in 1903 and since 1968 known as the **Minnesota Orchestra**.

Minnesota Opera. Established in 1963 by the Walker Art Center in Minneapolis. While the company also performs many standard operas, it is most well known for its many premieres, including *Where the Wild Things* are by Oliver Knussen and most recently the Pulitzer Prize–winning opera *Silent Night* by American composer Kevin Puts and librettist Mark Campbell. The company offers summer camps and other program for young singers and others interested in opera, special services for teachers and students, and many other outreach initiatives for adults and community members.

Minnesota Orchestra. Founded in 1903 by Emil Oberhoffer and originally known as the **Minneapolis Symphony**. Its list of conductors after Oberhoffer, who led the ensemble until 1922, includes Henri Verbrugghen (1923–1931), **Eugene Ormandy** (1931–1936), **Dimitri Mitropoulos** (1937–1949), **Antal Doráti** (1949–1960), **Stanislaw Skrowaczewski** (1960–1979), **Sir Neville Marriner** (1979–1986), **Edo de Waart** (1986–1995), **Eiji Oue** (1995–2002), and **Osmo Vänskä** (2005–present). The Minnesota Orchestra has had a long-standing summer festival that started as the Viennese Sommerfest under the direction of **Leonard Slatkin**. It's name was changed to MusicFest in 2001. The orchestra suffered a long lockout that lasted from October 1, 2012, to January 14, 2014. During the strike, several of the orchestra's musicians accepted positions with other professional orchestras, and Vänskä resigned, saying he would not return as long as Executive Director Michael Henson remained. Ultimately, Henson left and Vänskä returned. The orchestra has issued numerous recordings, including one of the first electrically recorded versions of **Gustav Mahler**'s Symphony No. 2, "Resurrection," with Eugene Ormandy conducting. When he was music director, Dimitri Mitropoulos had an exclusive contract with **Columbia Records** and led the premiere recording of Mahler's Symphony No. 1. Former music director Stanislaw Skrowaczewski led several recordings on **Vox Records**, and Osmo Vänskä has conducted a Beethoven and Sibelius symphony cycle for the **BIS label**.

minor. A minor key, as in C minor, as opposed to C major. (Fr. *mineur*, Ger. *Moll*, It. *minore*, Sp. *menor*.)

minore. (It.) **Minor**. (Fr. *mineur*, Ger. *Moll*, Sp. *menor*.)

mirror conducting. When a **conductor** uses the same gesture in both hands so that they are the mirror image of each other. These **mirror gestures** can be used effectively to draw attention to important or difficult moments in the music. However, if a conductor uses mirror conducting over long periods, it becomes dull, if not counterproductive. See also **conducting technique**.

mirror gestures. Gestures given with both hands that are the mirror image of each other. See also **conducting technique**, **mirror conducting**.

mirror technique. A compositional technique in which a motive, a group of notes such as a chord, is inverted with the exact interval structure but progressing in the opposite vertical direction, as though one saw the notes in a mirror.

Mirror Technique

Mirror technique. *Courtesy Andrew Martin Smith.*

mismo. (Sp.) Same. Examples: *lo mismo* (or *la misma* [fem.]), the same; *lo mismo que*, the same as; *el mismo acento*, the same accent; *ahora mismo*, right now.

mismo tiempo, al. (Sp.) At the same tempo. (Fr. *le même tempo*, Ger. *das gleiche Tempo*, It. *l'istesso tempo*.)

misterioso. (It., Sp.) Mysterious, a commonly used character word, heard especially with younger orchestras. Used in the title of the fourth movement of Symphony No. 3 by **Gustav Mahler**. (Fr. *mystérieux*, Ger. *geheimnisvoll*.)

misura. (It.) Meter, measure, beat. Examples: *alla misura*, in strict meter; *senza misura*, freely. (Fr. *mesure*, Ger. *Takt*, Sp. *compás*.)

misurato. (It.) Measured, in time. (Fr. *mesuré*, Ger. *gemessen*, Sp. *mensurada*.)

mit. (Ger.) With. Examples: *mit schmerzlichem Ausdruck*, with heartfelt grief, from **Pierrot Lunaire** by **Arnold Schoenberg**. (Fr. *avec*, It, *con*, Sp. *con*.)

mitad. (Sp.) Half of a string group or section. (Fr. *la moitié*, It. *la metà*, Ger. *die Hälfte*.)

mit Ausdruck. (Ger.) With expression, a commonly used phrase. (Fr. *avec l'expression*, It. *con l'espressione*, Sp. *con la expresión*.)

mit bewegung. (Ger.) With motion. Seen regularly in German scores, especially those of **Gustav Mahler**. Also *bewegt*, motion. (Fr. *avec movement*, It. *con moto*, Sp. *con movimiento*.)

mit Bogenspitze. (Ger.) With the point of the bow, an indication for string players to play at the point or tip of the bow. Also *mit der Bogenspitze*, *an der Bogenspitze*, *an der Spitze*. (Fr. *à la pointe*, *avec la pointe de l'archet*; It. *alla punta d'arco*, *con la punta d'arco*; Sp. *con la punta del arco*, *en la punta del arco*.)

mit Dämpfer. (Ger.) Muted, with the mute. Seen often in **horn** parts as *gedämpft*. (Fr. *Avec sourdine*, It. *con sordino*, Sp. *con sordina*.)

mit dem Bogen, mit dem Bogen geschlagen. (Ger.) A bowing term indicating hitting the string of the instrument with the wood of the bow. Same as *col legno*.

mit dem Daumen. (Ger.) With the thumb. An indication used with the tambourine, a particular way to play the tambourine. (Fr. *avec les pouce*, It. *con il pollice*, Sp. *con el pulgar*.)

mit dem Holtz des Bogens. (Ger.) With the wood of the bow, a bowing term directing the player to use of the wood of the bow instead of the hair. The Italian *col legno* is commonly used internationally. (Fr. *avec le bois*, It. *col legno*, Sp. *con la vara*.)

mit der Bogenspitze. (Ger.) With the point of the bow, an indication for string players to play at the point or tip of the bow. Also *mit Bogenspitze*, *an der Bogenspitze*, *an der Spitze*. (Fr. *à la pointe*, *avec la pointe de l'archet*; It. *alla punta d'arco*, *con la punta d'arco*; Sp. *con la punta del arco*, *en la punta del arco*.)

mit der Bogenstange. (Ger.) An indication to play with the wood of the bow, the Italian *col legno* is commonly used internationally. (Fr. *avec le bois*, It. *col legno*, Sp. *col la vara*.)

mit einiger Freiheit. (Ger.) With some freedom. A directive seen in parts and heard in rehearsal. (Fr. *avec quelques licences*, It. *con qualche licenza*, Sp. *con cierta licencia*.)

mit Eleganz. (Ger.) With elegance. An expression of character. (Fr. *avec élégance*, Ger. *mit Eleganz*, It. *con eleganza*, Sp. *con elegancia*.)

mit grossem Ton. (Ger.) With a big tone. Used in **Gustav Mahler**'s Symphony No. 1, mvt. 4.

mit grosser Wildheit. (Ger.) With enormous wildness. Used in **Gustav Mahler's** Symphony No. 1, mvt. 4.

mit halber Stimme. (Ger.) Half-voice, softly. Archaic usage; the Italian form is preferred. (Fr. *à mi-voix*, It. *a mezza voce*, Sp. *media voz*.)

Mitropoulos, Dimitri. (1896–1960.) Greek-born American **conductor**, pianist, and composer. Mitropoulos served as the music director of the **New York Philharmonic** from 1949 to 1958. After studies in Brussels and Berlin with Ferruccio Busoni and **Erich Kleiber**, he established himself as a brilliant concert pianist in 1930 when he performed the Prokofiev Piano Concerto No. 3 with the **Berlin Philharmonic** while conducting from the keyboard. Mitropoulos served as the music director of the then **Minneapolis Symphony Orchestra** (now the **Minnesota Orchestra**) from 1937 to 1949. With a phenomenal memory and mastery of detail, he always conducted without a score and eschewed a baton for most of his career. He conducted the premiere of Samuel Barber's *Vanessa* at the **Metropolitan Opera** and made many recordings, including Ralph Vaughan Williams's *Fourth Symphony*, Dmitri Shostakovitch's Symphony No. 10, and the first ever of **Gustav Mahler**'s Symphony No. 1.

mit Schwung. (Ger.) With panache, with energy, with style. A commonly used expression of character and style. Used most often in German. (Fr. *avec élan*, It. *con slancio*.)

Mitte. (Ger.) Middle, as in the middle of a drumhead or the middle of the bow. (Fr. *mileu, du mileu*; It. *mezzo, di mezzo*; Sp. *medio*.)

Mittelgrund. (Ger.) **Middleground**. See also **Schenkerian analysis**.

mi-voix, à. (Fr.) Half-voice, softly. The Italian form is commonly used internationally. The German form is archaic. (Ger. *mit halber Stimme*, It. *a mezza voce*, Sp. *media voz*.)

mit vollem Ton. (Ger.) Full, loud. A descriptive phrase often used for dynamics or sound. (Fr. *plein, pleine*; It. *pieno*; Sp. *pleno*.)

mit voller Kraft. (Ger.) With all force. A expression of character. (Fr. *de toutes ces forces*, It. *con tutta la forza*, Sp. *con toda fuerza*.)

mixed media, multimedia. The use of several different artistic media from different art forms into a single expressive entity. Such combinations may include sculpture, film, and music either recorded or live and may be seen in museums or other public spaces. They are sometimes called "installations." Opera, which combines music and text with staging, is perhaps one of the oldest forms of mixed media that is generally not referred to as such. An early twentieth-century example is the color organ created by Alexander Scriabin, which combined colored light and music and the use of film in an operatic production. The rise of electronic music has contributed to many mixed-media projects that combine the visual with computer-generated music. Examples of these include Mario Davidovsky's series of Synchronisms Nos. 1–8, in which he combines live instrumentalists with recorded sound.

mixed meters. The use of several alternating meters in a single piece. See **Igor Stravinsky**'s ***The Rite of Spring*** and **Aaron Copland**'s ***Appalachian Spring*** in **appendix 1: "Six Pieces That Changed Conducting."** See also **conducting uneven meters**.

mixolydian mode. See **church modes**.

M.M. Abbreviation for **Johann Maelzel**'s **metronome** marks. See **Maelzel, Johann**; **metronome**.

mobile. (It.) Changeable, moveable. (Fr. *mobile*, Ger. *beweglich*, Sp. *móvil*.)

mobile applications. These applications, or "apps," are sometimes available on orchestra websites to be downloaded so that interested people can listed to weekly radio broadcasts or podcasts with a mobile phone, smartphone, or other mobile device. They are a tool for promoting interest in the individual orchestras, guest artists, and the music being performed.

modality. The use of the **church modes** as scale and harmonic resources for composition.

modal modulation. The modulation of a given mode from one tonal center to another. An example is moving from E Dorian to B Dorian.

mode. Major or **minor**. See **church modes**.

moderado. (Sp.) Moderate, a moderate tempo, same as *moderato*. (Fr. *modéré*, Ger. *mäßig*, It. *moderato*.)

moderamente. (Sp.) Moderate, moderately, usually referring to tempo. (Fr. *modérément*, Ger. *mäßig*, It. *moderatamente*.)

moderar el tiempo. (Sp.) Slowing down, broadening. (Fr. *en élargissant*; Ger. *breiter werdend*; It. *slargando, allargando*.)

moderatamente. (It.) Moderate, moderately, usually referring to tempo. (Fr. *modérément*, Ger. *mäßig*, Sp. *moderamente*.)

moderato. (It.) Moderate, a moderate tempo. (Fr. *modéré*, Ger. *mäßig*, Sp. *moderado*.)

modéré. (Fr.) Moderate, a moderate tempo, moderato. Examples: *Modéré mais toujours trés rythme*, moderate tempo but always very rhythmic, from *Fêtes*, movement two of *Nocturnes* by Claude Debussy; *Modéré* ♩= 100 *pour le 1re mesure*, ♩= 72 *pour le 2me, et ainsi durant toute le danse*, moderate ♩= 100 for the first measure, ♩= 72 for the second, and thus throughout the whole danse, from *Daphnis et Chloé* by Maurice Ravel. (Ger. *mäßig*, It. *moderato*, Sp. *moderado*.)

modérément. (Fr.) Moderate, moderately, usually referring to tempo. (Ger. *mäßig*, It. *moderatamente*, Sp. *moderamente*.)

The Modern Conductor. A conducting text by **Elizabeth Green**, now in its seventh edition. The book covers the basics of conducting, score study, clefs, and transpositions. It includes chapters on the "mechanics" of choral, band, and orchestral scores; interpretation; memorization; and useful appendixes with seating charts, orchestral bowing terms, musical forms, terminology for the **conductor**, physical exercises, and an excellent bibliography. In the book, Green introduced the concept of **psychological conducting** as a form of technical mastery. Once baton technique is developed, Green suggests that psychology takes over and that musicians will respond to "the messages they receive from the conductor's hands and baton alone," implying "a transfer of ideas from the conductor's mind to the performer's mind through the medium of correct and precise conductorial technique without the use of verbal directions or written notation." See the **bibliography**.

modo ordinario. (It.) In the normal way, in the ordinary way, after *sul ponticello* or *sul tasto*. (Fr. *mode ordinaire,* Ger. *gewöhnlich,* Sp. *arco normal.*)

möglich. (Ger.) Possible, feasible. Examples: *möglichst,* as fast as possible; *so bald wie möglich,* as soon as possible; *Es ist nicht möglich,* It is not possible. (Fr. *possible,* It. *possibile,* Sp. *posible*).

moins. (Fr.) Less. Example: *Moins vif,* slower (lit. "less fast"), from *Daphnis et Chloé* by Maurice Ravel. (Ger. *weniger,* It. *meno,* Sp. *menos.*)

moitié, la. (Fr.) Half of a string group or section. (Ger. *die Hälfte,* It. *la metà,* Sp. *mitad.*)

Moll. (Ger.) **Minor**. (Fr. *mineur,* It. *minore,* Sp. *menor.*)

molle. (It.) Soft. An expression sometimes used in rehearsal to evoke a particular quality or character. Also *mollemente.*

mollezza, con. (It.) With delicacy. An expression of character or style of playing sometimes used in rehearsal.

molto, di molto, assai. (It.) Very, many, much. Often seen in music and heard in rehearsal as a part of various phrases. Example: *molto allegro,* very fast. (Fr. *très, beaucoup;* Ger. *sehr, viel, viele;* Sp. *muy, mucho.*)

Mongolian Symphony Orchestra. Founded in 1957 in Ulan Bator by decree of the ministry of culture. Ts. Namsraijav was the first **conductor**. In 2012, there was a gala concert celebrating the fifty-fifth anniversary of the orchestra and Ts. Namsraijav's eighty-fifth birthday in the State Academic Theater of Opera and Ballet.

monodrama. A dramatic stage work for a single actor or in the case of opera, only one singer. **Arnold Schoenberg**'s *Erwartung* (1909) is a prime example from the early twentieth century, as is the final work of **Sir Benjamin Britten,** *Phaedra,* for soprano and chamber orchestra.

monter l'intonation. (Fr.) Raise the pitch, retune. (Ger. *höher stimmen,* It. *alzare l'intonatura, alzare l'intonazione,* Sp. *subir la afinación.*)

Monteux, Pierre. (1875–1964.) American **conductor** and pedagogue of French birth. Monteux began as a ballet conductor and took over rehearsals for the premiere of **Igor Stravinsky**'s *Petrouchka.* When the original conductor returned, Stravinsky insisted that Monteux stay, as no one could know the score as well as he. Monteux was made conductor of the Ballets Russes in Paris, conducting the premieres of *Petrouchka* (1911), Maurice Ravel's *Daphnis et Chloe* (1912), Stravinsky's ***The Rite of Spring*** (1911), Claude Debussy's *Jeux* (1913), and Stravinsky's *Le Rossignol* (1914). He was appointed conductor of the **Boston Symphony** (a primarily French orchestra at the time) in 1919. He served as the music director of the **San Francisco Symphony** (1935–1952) and was given a twenty-five-year contract to become the principal conductor of the **London Symphony** in 1961. He also held positions with the **Metropolitan Opera,** the Amsterdam **Concertgebouw,** and was the founding conductor of the **Orchestre Symphonique de Paris**.

Monteux made numerous recordings with the Paris Symphony and the **San Francisco Symphony,** both as 78s and on LP. They were technologically important as they were among the first to be made on magnetic tape. He became an American citizen and settled in Hancock, Maine, where he founded the **Pierre Monteux School for Conductors and Orchestra Musicians**. Well-known alumni of the school include **Sir Neville Marriner, Lorin Maazel, David Zinman,** Erich Kunzel, **José Serebrier,** Harry Ellis Dickson, George Cleve, Michael Stern, and **Hugh Wolff**. Monteux left an enormous legacy as a conductor, leading an astounding number of premieres, and as a teacher as well. See **Monteux's "Rules for Young Conductors."**

Monteux's "Rules for Young Conductors." As they appeared in *Pierre Monteux, Maitre* by John Canarina (see the **bibliography**):

Eight "musts":
1. Stand straight, even if you are tall.
2. Never bend, even for a *pianissimo.*
3. Be always dignified from the time you come on stage.
4. Always conduct with a baton, so the players far from you can see your beat.
5. Know your score perfectly.
6. Never conduct for the audience.
7. Always mark the first beat of each measure very neatly, so the players who are counting and not playing know where you are.
8. Always in a two-beat measure, beat the second beat higher than the first. For a four-beat bar, beat the fourth higher.

Twelve "don'ts":

1. Don't over conduct; don't make unnecessary movements or gestures.
2. Don't fail to make music; don't allow music to stagnate. Don't neglect any phrase or overlook its integral part in the complete work.
3. Don't adhere pedantically to metronome time—vary the tempo according to the subject or phrase and give its own character.
4. Don't permit the orchestra to play always a boresome *mezzo-forte.*
5. Don't conduct without a baton; don't bend over while conducting.
6. Don't conduct solo instruments in solo passages; don't worry or annoy sections or players by looking intently at them in "ticklish" passages.
7. Don't forget to cue players or sections that have long rests, even though the part is seemingly an unimportant inner voice.
8. Don't come before the orchestra if you have not mastered your score; don't practice or learn the score "on the orchestra."
9. Don't stop the orchestra if you have nothing to say; don't speak too softly to the orchestra, or only to the first stands.
10. Don't stop for obviously accidental wrong notes.
11. Don't sacrifice ensemble in an effort for meticulous beating—don't hold sections back in technical passages where the urge comes to go forward.
12. Don't be disrespectful to your players (no swearing); don't forget individual's rights as persons; don't undervalue the members of the orchestra simply because they are "cogs" in the "wheels."

Montreal Symphony Orchestra (Orchestre symphonique de Montréal, OSM). The OSM traces its beginnings to a concert given in 1935 by an ensemble called Les Concerts Symphoniques and conducted by Rosario Bourdin. It took its current name in 1954. Past **conductors** include Wilfried Pelletier (1935–1940), Désiré Defauw (1941–1952), **Otto Klemperer** (1950–1953 as artistic advisor), **Igor Markevitch** (1957–1961), **Zubin Mehta** (1961–1967), Franc-Paul Decker (1967–1975), **Rafael Frübeck de Burgos** (1975–1976), **Charles Dutoit** (1977–2002), Jacques Lacombe (2002–2006 as principal guest conductor), and **Kent Nagano** (2006–present). The orchestra made its way onto the international stage under the direction of Charles Dutoit, who led the orchestra in numerous highly successful recordings on the **London/Decca label** in the 1980s and 1990s. During the same period, they toured widely to Europe, Asia, and both North and South America. After some years of financial difficulties, Kent Nagano has begun making recordings with the ensemble that are receiving favorable notice.

Moog, Robert A. (1934–2005.) Known chiefly for developing the **Moog synthesizer**, Moog worked both with classical and popular musicians, inventing and developing a wide range of electrical devices that facilitated instruments, tape recorders, and amplifiers and would equip complete electronic music studios, including one for **Wendy Carlos**. The technology developed very quickly beginning in 1964 when his company sold the first commercial modular synthesizer, causing him to seek out collaborators. Over the years, Moog's companies went through several manifestations. In the 1980s, Moog began a new company, Big Briar, that further developed versions of touch-sensitive keyboards and Theremin-type electronics with MIDI technology. In the 1990s, Big Briar produced new versions of the **Theremin.**

Moog synthesizer. The electronic voltage-controlled synthesizer developed by **Robert A. Moog** in collaboration with composer Herbert Deutsch. It was first demonstrated in 1964 and soon after manufactured as the first commercial synthesizer. Used in **Wendy Carlos**'s famous recording *Switched-On Bach*, which appeared in 1968 and sold over one million copies. The name Moog was used early on to refer to any type of synthesizer.

Moral, Carmen. (b. 1943.) Peruvian **conductor**. Moral studied at the **Manhattan School of Music**, Columbia University, and the Sorbonne, Paris. The first woman to win a permanent position with a major Latin American orchestra, Moral served as the music director of Peru's National Symphony Orchestra. She has also served as the music director of the Bogotá Philharmonic Orchestra (Columbia), the Symphony Orchestra of Mimar Sinan University (Istanbul), and was the principal conductor of the Istanbul State Opera. She has served as a guest conductor with numerous orchestras, including the George Enescu Philharmonic (Bucharest), the Symphony Orchestra of Russia (Moscow), the Tonkunstlerorchester (Vienna), the Buenos Aires Philharmonic, the National Symphony of Mexico, and many others. She currently teaches at the **Berklee School of Music** in Boston.

morale. Positive morale is vital in achieving a high level of performance. Most **conductors** today use a proactive, constructive approach in their dealings with the orchestra, management, and the board of directors in order to establish and maintain positive morale based on shared, realistic goals. See also **leadership**, **motivation**, **psychology of the conductor-orchestra relationship.**

morbido. (It.) Silky, tender, soft. A character word. (Fr. *tendre, soyeux*, Ger. *zart*, Sp. *suave, sedoso.*)

mordace, mordent. (It.) Biting. A descriptive word used most often for articulation. (Fr. *mordant*, Ger. *bissig, spitzig*, Sp. *mordaz.*)

mordant. (Fr.) Biting. A descriptive word used most often for articulation. (Ger. *bessig, spitzig*; It. *mordace, mordent*; Sp. *mordaz*.)

mordaz. (Sp.) Biting. A descriptive word used most often for articulation. (Fr. *mordant*; Ger. *bissig, spitzig*; It. *mordace, mordent*.)

mordent superior. (It., Sp.) An inverted mordent or mordant with the note above. (Fr. *mordant supérieur*; Ger. *Pralltriller, Schneller, Praller*; Sp. *mordent superior*.)

Morel, Jean. (1903–1975.) **Conductor** and teacher at the **Juilliard School** (1949–1971), where he influenced a generation of American conductors, including **James Levine, Jorge Mester**, and **Leonard Slatkin**. French-born, Morel had taught at the **American Conservatory in Fontainebleau** from 1921 to 1936. He conducted opera at the **New York City Center Opera, Metropolitan Opera**, and in Rio de Janeiro and Mexico.

morendo. (It.) Dying away, fading. A common expression of character. (Fr. *en mourant*, Ger. *sterbend, ersterbend*, Sp. *muriendo*.)

moribundo. (Sp.) Dying away, fading. A common expression of character. (Ger. *sterbend*, It. *morendo*, Sp. *desvanecerse*.)

morire lontano. (It.) To die away, to die down. A common expression of character. (Fr. *mourir, dépérissement*, Ger. *ersterben*, Sp. *muriendo, desvaneciéndose, perdiéndose*.)

mormorò. (It.) Whispered, murmured. A character word used to evoke a particular sound or dynamic. (Fr. *murmuré*, Ger. *murmelte*, Sp. *murmurado*.)

Moscheles, Ignaz. (1794–1870.) Bohemian composer, piano virtuoso, and occasional **conductor**. Moscheles learned Ludwig van Beethoven's *Pathétique* Sonata as a student at the Prague Conservatory. In 1808, he moved to Vienna in order to be close to the great composer and meanwhile became one of the favored pianists of the musical city. Between 1815 and 1825 he toured Germany as a recitalist, also stopping in London, Paris, and Prague. In 1824, he met the young **Felix Mendelssohn** and gave him a few lessons. They became lifelong friends, and in 1846, Mendelssohn hired him as professor of piano at his newly formed **Leipzig Conservatory**. Moscheles would hold this position until his death. From 1825 to the time he moved to Germany he lived in London, was codirector of the **Philharmonic Society** (1832–1841), and conducted London premieres of Beethoven's *Missa solemnis* (1832), as well as multiple performances of Beethoven's Symphony No. 9 (1837 and 1838). Known as a classicist in his interpretive approach, Moscheles also looked backward for his repertoire, performing works of Franz Joseph Haydn, Wolfgang Amadeus Mozart, George Frideric Handel, Muzio Clementi, and Domenico Scarlatti. Though he composed and performed a great deal of his own music to great acclaim, it is mostly through his piano etudes that today's musicians know him.

Moscow Conservatory. The second oldest conservatory in Russia after the **St. Petersburg Conservatory**. It was founded in 1866 and is named after Peter Ilyich Tchaikovsky, who taught there from its opening to 1878. The list of alumni and faculty is a panorama of internationally known artists, and the curriculum is that of a distinguished conservatory. **Gennady Rozhdestvensky** is the head of the opera and symphony conducting division. Other conducting faculty include Anatoly Levin, Valery Polyansky, and Vladimir Pon'kin.

Moscow State Symphony Orchestra (MSSO). Founded in 1943 by the Kremlin with its first chief conductor, Lev Steinberg. Following Steinberg's death, he was succeeded by Nikolai Anosov (1945–1950), Leo Ginzburg (1950–1954), Mikhail Terian (1954–1960), and **Veronica Dudarova** (1960–1989). The current music director is Pavel Kogan (appointed in 1989). The orchestra has toured widely, including appearances in the United States, Europe, China, and South Korea. It has also made numerous live and studio recordings and performed on both radio and television.

mosso. (It.) With movement. Examples: *piu mosso*, faster; *meno mosso*, slower. (Fr. *mouvement*, Ger. *bewegt*, Sp. *movimiento*.)

motivation in rehearsal and performance. An essential aspect of good **conducting**. Most **conductors** today use motivation as a positive force. Aspects of motivation include setting high but realistic standards for the ensemble based on an empathy for the musicians; understanding of the instruments and the circumstances of the rehearsal and performance, that is, the quality of the acoustics and comfort of the space; but especially a conviction and deep understanding of the music being performed. The most effective form of motivation is based on honesty and shared goals and outcomes. The modern **music director** in America also uses these skills in dealings with volunteers, colleagues, staff, and a board of directors. See also **leadership, morale, psychology of the conductor-orchestra relationship**.

motivo conductor. (Sp.) Leading motive or theme. Coined by **Hector Berlioz** as *idée fixe*, a recurring theme or motive that connects the movements of a symphonic work. (Fr. *idée fixe*, Ger. *Leitmotiv*, It. *motivo conduttore, motivo ricorrente*.)

motivo conduttore, motivo ricorrente. (It.) Leading motive or theme. Coined by **Hector Berlioz** as *idée fixe*, a recurring theme or motive that connects the movements of a symphonic work. (Fr. *idée fixe*, Ger. *Leitmotiv*, Sp. *motivo conductor*.)

moto. (It.) Motion, tempo. (Fr. *mouvement*, Ger. *Bewegung*, Sp. *movimiento*.) Example: *con moto*, with motion.

moto, con. (It.) With motion; a moving, flowing tempo; not too slow. (Fr. *avec movement*, Ger. *mit Bewegung*, Sp. *con movimiento*.)

moto, movimento. (It.) Movement, motion. A common descriptive word. (Fr. *mouvement*, Ger. *Bewegung*, Sp. *movimiento*.)

moto perpetuo, perputuum mobile. (It.) Perpetual motion. The title of a piece or movement, can also be a style of music. (Fr. *movement perpétuel*, Ger. *durchlaufend bewegt*.)

Mottl, Felix. (1856–1911.) Austrian **conductor**, arranger, and composer who left a legacy of exceptional performances of the music of his time and was known for raising the performance standards of the orchestras he worked with. Renowned as one of the first great **Wagner** conductors after the life of the composer, Mottl attended the **Vienna Conservatory**, studying **music theory** and **conducting**. He conducted the **Bayreuth** premieres of *Tristan und Isolde*, *Tannhäuser*, *Lohengrin*, and *Der fliegende Holländer*, in addition to *Parsifal*, *Die Meistersinger von Nürenberg*, and the *Ring*. He introduced many French composers to German audiences with performances of such works as **Hector Berlioz**'s *Beatrice et Bénédict*, the first-ever complete production of *Les Troyens*, Emmanuel Chabrier's *Gwendoline* and *Le roi malgrè lui*, André Grétry's *Raoul Barbe-bleue*, and others. Mottl traveled to London to conduct, where **George Bernard Shaw** described him a conductor of the very first rank, with immense physical energy and influence. He also served as the music director of the Munich Opera from 1903 until his death.

mourant, en. (Fr.) Dying away. A common expression of character. (Ger. *sterbend*, It. *morendo, morente*, Sp. *muribundo, desvanecerse*.)

mourir, dépérissement. (Fr.) To die away, to die down. An expression used to evoke a particular manner of playing. (Ger. *ersterben*, It. *morire lontano*, Sp. *muriendo, desvaneciéndose, perdiéndose*.)

mouthpiece. The part of a woodwind or brass instrument closest to the lips. For the flute, it is part of the head joint; for the reed wind instruments, it holds the reed. (Fr. *embouchure*, Ger. *Mundstück*, It. *bocchino*, Sp. *embocadura*.)

mouvement. (Fr.) A movement of a symphony or any multimovement work. (Ger. *Satz*, It. *movimento*, Sp. *movimiento*.) Can also refer to **tempo**, as in speed, or **motion** within a passage. (Ger. *Bewegung*, It. *moto, movimento*, Sp. *movimiento*.) Examples: *Mouvt. initial*, tempo I, from the score to the ballet *Jeux* by Claude Debussy, using the abbreviated form of movement; *mouvement du début*, tempo of the beginning, from *Rapsodie Espagnole* by Maurice Ravel. Also *avec mouvement*, with motion. (Ger. *mit Bewegung*, It. *con moto*, Sp. *con movimiento*.)

moveable do(h). A **solmization** system common in the United States in which the syllable *do(h)* represents the first scale degree of a major scale, regardless of which scale it is, and is consequently "moveable" to any pitch. (Sp. *método de la tónica, do* móvil.) See also **solfège**, **solmization**.

movement. A term used to refer to a part of a symphony or sonata. Usually each movement has a different tempo and character, sometimes they are in a different but related key. (Fr. *mouvement*, Ger. *Satz*, It. *movimento*, Sp. *movimiento*.) Can also refer to **tempo** or motion. Example: With motion, (Fr.) *avec mouvement*, (Ger.) *mit Bewegung*, (It.) *con moto*, (Sp.) *con movimiento*.

movement, en. (Fr.) Moving along. (Ger. *bewegend*, It. *movendo*, Sp. *movimiento*.)

movement, mouvementé. (Fr.) Tempo, motion. Examples: *au mouvement*, in tempo; *movement du début*, tempo I or *tempo primo*; *Un peu plus mouvementé*, a little faster, from *De l'aube à midi sur la mer*, mvt. 1 of *La Mer* by Claude Debussy. Also *avec mouvement*, with motion. See also **Bewegung**, **moto**.

movement perpétuel. (Fr.) Perpetual motion. The title of a piece or movement, can also be a style of music. (Ger. *durchlaufend bewegt*, It. *moto perpetuo, perputuum mobile*.)

movendo. (It.) Moving along. (Fr, *en movement*, Ger. *bewegend*, Sp. *movimiento*.)

movimento, moto. (It.) A movement of a symphony or any multimovement work. (Fr. *movement*, Ger. *Satz*, Sp. *movimiento*.) Can also refer to **tempo** or motion. (*Bewegung*, It. *moto*.) Example: With motion, (It.) *con moto*, (Fr.) *avec mouvement*, (Ger.) *mit Bewegung*, (Sp.) *con movimiento*.

movimiento. (Sp.) Moving along. (Fr, *en movement,* Ger. *bewegend,* It. *movendo.*)

movimiento. (Sp.) Movement, motion. (Fr. *mouvement,* Ger. *Bewegung,* It. *moto, movimento.*) Example: *con movimiento,* with motion. (Fr. *avec mouvement,* Ger. *mit Bewegung,* It. *con moto.*)

Moyse, Blanche Honegger. (1909–2011.) Swiss-born American **conductor** and violinist. Moyse studied with the German violinist Adolf Busch and debuted with the **L'Orchestre de la Suisse Romande** in Ludwig van Beethoven's violin concerto at age sixteen. She married the pianist Louis Moyse and moved to Vermont in 1949, where they were part of the founding of the **Marlboro Music Festival.** Moyse founded the Brattleboro Music Center in 1951 and served as its artistic director. In the late 1960s, she began studying and conducting the music of Johann Sebastiann Bach and made her **Carnegie Hall** debut at the age of seventy-eight, conducting the **Orchestra of St. Luke's** in Bach's *Christmas Oratorio.* An influential teacher worldwide, Moyse left her greatest legacy to the people of Vermont.

Mozarteum Orchestra Salzburg. Founded in 1841 with the assistance of Wolfgang Amadeus Mozart's sons, Franz Xaver and Karl Thomas, and his widow, Constanze. The orchestra has become one of Austria's leading ensembles and performs regularly at the **Salzburg Festival.** The current principal **conductor** is Ivan Bolton, with Trevor Pinnock as the principal guest conductor. Former conductors include Hans Graf (1984–1994) and Hubert Soudant (1994–2004).

Mozarteum, Salzburg. See **Salzburg Mozarteum.**

mp. (It.) Abbreviation for *mezzo piano.* See **dynamics** for musical symbol.

Mravinsky, Yevgeny. (1903–1988.) Legendary Russian **conductor** and teacher and champion of Soviet composers. Mravinsky conducted premieres of many works of Sergei Prokofiev and Dmitri Shostakovitch but also of Paul Hindemith, Béla Bartók, Jean Sibelius, Arthur Honegger, Claude Debussy, and **Igor Stravinsky.** Renowned for thrilling performances, he had a great influence on nearly all Soviet conductors since **Nikolai Malko,** including **Valery Gergiev,** Mariss Jansons, Yuri Temirkanov, and **Kurt Sanderling.** He was the principal conductor of the **Leningrad Philharmonic Orchestra** from 1938 to 1988 and made many studio recordings between 1938 and 1961. Other recordings were taken from live performances. Known to thrive on spontaneity in performance, he often conducted without a baton.

M.S. (It.) Abbreviation for *mano sinistra,* left hand.

Muck, Karl. (1859–1940.) German **conductor.** Muck began as a pianist and taught himself **conducting.** He was hired in 1886 as the music director at the Landstheater in Prague. In 1892, he moved to the **Berlin State Opera** and served as the music director of the **Boston Symphony Orchestra** from 1912 to 1917. From 1901 to 1930, Muck conducted often at **Bayreuth.** Anti-German sentiments in America during World War I lead to his arrest and internment from March 1918 to August 1919 for suspected pro-German activities. On his release, he and his wife returned to Europe, where he resumed his conducting career with positions as the principal conductor of the **Hamburg Philharmonic Orchestra** and concerts with the **Royal Concertgebouw Orchestra** in Munich and again at the **Bayreuth Festival.** One of his conducting students was the Dutch-born American conductor **Antonia Brico.**

mudo. (Sp.) Mute, silent. (Fr. *muet,* Ger. *stumm,* It. *muto.*)

Mueller, Otto-Werner. (b. 1926.) Important **conducting** pedagogue. Mueller immigrated to Canada from Germany in 1951. He is emeritus faculty at the **Juilliard School.** Mueller also taught at the **Yale University School of Music** and the University of Wisconsin–Madison. His former students include **Alan Gilbert,** music director of the **New York Philharmonic; Paavo Järvi,** music director of the **Cincinnati Symphony Orchestra** (2001–2011); and **Miguel Harth-Bedoya,** music director of the **Fort Worth Symphony Orchestra.** Other former students have been **conductors** of the San Diego, Pittsburgh, and Fort Worth symphonies and associate or assistant conductor of the **Philadelphia, Cleveland, Boston, St. Louis, Los Angeles,** and **Munich** symphonies.

muet, muette. (Fr.) Silent, mute. (Ger. *still, stumm,* It. *silenzioso, muto,* Sp. *silencioso, mudo.*)

muffled. A descriptive used often with timpani or other percussion instrument. (Fr. *étouffé,* Ger. *gedämpft,* It. *smorzato,* Sp. *sordo.*)

multimedia art. A musical genre that employs two or more art forms in addition to music, such as film, dance, video, or lighting effects. Examples include *The Maze* by Larry Austin, which involves the audience, lighting effects, and musical performers who are also actors and *Third Planet from the Sun* by Ramon Zupko, which includes electronic sounds; recorded voices; actors who pantomime; a chorus that speaks, sings, and acts; plus film and special lighting effects.

multiphonics. A term coined by Bruno Bartolozzi and used to describe multiple sounds produced simultaneously on a woodwind instrument. Multiphonics are created by the predominance of certain **harmonic** partials produced by specific fingerings, especially if an open key corresponds to the node of a fundamental. The resulting sound is modified when certain partials are emphasized and others are lessened. Lip pressure, the mouthpiece, and other characteristics of individual instruments and players determine the success or lack thereof of multiphonic sounds. A similar technique is used by brass instruments, involving humming and playing simultaneously, but it only creates two concurrent pitches. See Bartolozzi, Bruno. *New Sounds for Woodwind*. 2nd ed. Translated and edited by Reginald Smith Brindle. London: Oxford University Press, 1982.

multiple conductor works. Works that require more than one **conductor**. Examples: Charles Ives's *The Unanswered Question*, Symphony No. 4, and unfinished *Universe Symphony* conceived of at least two, if not more orchestras; **Karlheinz Stockhausen**'s *Grüppen* for three orchestras, each requiring their own conductor; and **Hector Berlioz**'s *Requiem Mass*. See also **multiple orchestra works**.

multiple orchestra works. Works written for more than one orchestra and consequently usually more than one **conductor**. Examples include Johann Christian Bach's *Sinfonia No. 1 in E-flat, opus 18 for Double Orchestra*; Louis Spohr's *Symphony No. 7, opus 121*; Karlheinz Stockhausen's *Grüppen* for three orchestras (1955–1957); and Elliott Carter's *Symphony of Three Orchestras* (1976).

Münch, Charles. (1891–1968.) Alsatian **conductor** who made his greatest impact with premieres of works by such composers as Arthur Honegger, Jacques Ibert, Bohuslav Martinů, Francis Poulenc, Albert Roussel, Heitor Villa-Lobos, Samuel Barber, **Aaron Copland**, Lukas Foss, Walter Piston, Robert Schumann, Roger Sessions, and others. Münch toured widely and led the **Leipzig Gewandhaus Orchestra** from 1926 to 1933. He made his American debut in 1946 with the **Boston Symphony** and succeeded **Serge Koussevitsky** as its chief conductor in 1949. He founded the **Orchestre de Paris** in 1967. Münch made many recordings, including influential versions of **Hector Berlioz**'s *Grande messe des morts* and Maurice Ravel's *Daphnis et Chloé*. He was renowned for his sensitive but impulsive and spontaneous performances.

Mund. (Ger.) Mouth. (Fr. *bouche,* It. *bocca,* Sp. *boca*.)

Mundstück. (Ger.) Mouthpiece, as on brass and wind instruments. (Fr. *embouchure,* It. *bocchino,* Sp. *embocadura*.)

Munich Conservatory. See **University of Music and Performing Arts**.

Munich Philharmonic Orchestra (Münchner Philharmoniker). Founded in 1983 as the Kaim Orchestra. **Felix Weingartner** conducted it from 1898 to 1905. Between 1901 and 1910 **Gustav Mahler** conducted the premiere performances of his *Symphonies No. 4 and 8*. In 1911, just six months after the composer's death, **Bruno Walter** led the premiere of Mahler's *Das Lied von der Erde*. The orchestra's name was officially changed in 1924. **Conductors** have included Siegmund von Hausegger (1920–1938), Oswald Kabasta (1938–1945), Hans Robaud (1945–1948), Fritz Rieger (1949–1966), **Rudolf Kempe** (1967–1976), **Sergiu Celibidache** (1979–1996), **James Levine** (1999–2004), **Christian Thielemann** (2005–2011), and **Lorin Maazel** (2012–2014). In recent years, the orchestra has developed programs for younger listeners.

Munrow, David. (1942–1976.) English musician and early music specialist. Munrow was the founder of the Early Music Consort (1967) and renowned as one of the finest recorder players of his day. He studied at Cambridge University (1961–1964), was a lecturer in early music history at Leicester University (1967–1976), and professor of recorder at the **Royal Academy of Music**, London (1968–1976). Munrow was a champion of medieval and Renaissance music. He appeared frequently on the radio and his own series, *Pied Piper* (1971–1976), was especially successful. Performances by the Early Music Consort under his direction have been described as thrilling and were effective in bringing the repertoire to a wider public. Munrow also arranged and composed music that they would perform for television and film. He is the author of *Instruments of the Middle Ages and Renaissance* (1976).

munter. (Ger.) Cheerful, alert, animated, perky. A character word. (Fr. *allègrement,* It. *allegramente,* Sp. *alegremente*.)

muriendo. (Sp.) Dying away, fading. A common expression of character. (Fr. *en mourant,* Ger. *sterbend, ersterbend*. It. *morendo*.)

muriendo, desvaneciéndose, perdiéndose. (Sp.) To die away, to die down. A common expression of character. (Fr. *mourir, dépérissement,* Ger. *ersterben,* It. *morire lontano*.)

murmelte. (Ger.) Whispered, murmured. A character word used to evoke a particular sound or dynamic. (Fr. *murmuré,* It. *mormorò,* Sp. *murmurado*.)

murmullo. (Sp.) Murmuring. (Fr. *murmuré,* Ger. *murmeln, gemurmel,* It. *mormorio.*)

murmurado. (Sp.) Whispered, murmured. A character word used to evoke a particular sound or dynamic. (Fr. *murmuré,* Ger. *murmelte,* It. *mormorò.*)

mumurando. (Fr.) Murmuring. Seen in a passage of divided strings in the score to the ballet *Jeux* by Claude Debussy.

murmuré. (Fr.) Whispered, murmured. A character word used to evoke a particular sound or dynamic. (Ger. *murmelte,* It. *mormorò,* Sp. *murmurado.*)

musica a programma. (It.) **Program music.** Music that intentionally strives to depict nonmusical concepts, stories, or scenes without including any sung words. Franz Liszt introduced the term and specified that the program be supplied to the audience so that they would not draw false conclusions about the piece they were hearing. Many composers feel the opposite: the program should be self-evident, and if the audience doesn't understand it, a printed description does no good. Program music, in contrast to **absolute music,** seeks to dramatize human experience or thought in music. While earlier composers had used various forms of tone painting, Liszt devised the **symphonic poem** or **tone poem** as a musical form for the purpose of developing program music. (Fr. *musique á programme,* Ger. *Programmusik,* Sp. *música programática.*)

música cingara. (Sp.) Gypsy music. (Fr. *musique tzigane,* Ger. *Ziegeunermusik,* It. *musica gitana.*)

musica contemporanea. (It.) Contemporary music. (Fr. *musique contemporaine,* Ger. *Zeitgenössiche Musik, neue Musik,* Sp. *música contemporánea.*)

música contemporánea. (Sp.) Contemporary music. (Fr. *musique contemporaine,* Ger. *Zeitgenössiche Musik, neue Musik,* It. *music contemporanea.*)

música de escena. (Sp.) Incidental music or stage music for a play or music played on stage in an opera. (Fr. *musique de scène,* Ger. *Bühnenmusik,* It. *musica di scena.*)

musica di scena. (It.) Incidental music or stage music for a play or music played on stage in an opera. (Fr. *musique de scène,* Ger. *Bühnenmusik,* Sp. *música de escena.*)

musica gitana. (It.) Gypsy music. (Fr. *musique tzigane,* Ger. *Ziegeunermusik,* Sp. *música cingara.*)

Musical America. An American music magazine founded as a weekly in 1989. The magazine had an unstable history, having been owned by numerous individuals and organizations during its long history. Since 1998, it exists as a website, MusicalAmerica.com, posting news stories that relate to the classical music field each week. The complete contents are only available to subscribers. Some of its distinguished editors include its founder, John Christian Freund, Milton Weil, **Deems Taylor,** A. Walter Kramer, and Shirley Fleming. Some American libraries maintain digitized copies of early issues that are of historical interest. The magazine recognizes musicians in various categories, such as Conductor of the Year, on an annual basis.

musical saw. A metal instrument manufactured without teeth to be used in performance and played by holding it between the knees, with one hand holding the top while bending the saw and the other drawing a violin bow along the side of the saw, producing its unusual sound. (Fr. *lame musicale,* Ger. *Singende Säge,* It. *sega cantante,* Sp. *serrucho.*) See **appendix 4.**

Musical Times. Established in Britain in 1844 and still in production today, it is the oldest music magazine in continuous existence. Originally released as a monthly under the title *The Musical Times and Singing Class Circular* (1844–1903), it is now a quarterly journal of academic standards, concentrating on classical music. It can be accessed by subscription through the online resource site **JSTOR.**

música programática. (Sp.) **Program music.** (Fr. *musique á programme,* Ger. *Programmusik,* It. *musica a programma.*) See *musica a programma.*

Music Critics Association of North America (MCANA). Established in 1956, the MCANA sponsors conferences together with summer music festivals, professional conferences, and educational seminars to promote high standards of music criticism.

music desk. See **music stand.**

music director. A title used by many symphony orchestras to designate the main or principal **conductor** and artistic leader of an orchestra. The title, which became common in the middle of the twentieth century, is used primarily in the United States; in Europe the most common title is principal conductor or chief conductor. The difference is that a music director has the added responsibilities of overseeing *everything* that the orchestra does, all concerts, not only the **subscription or classics series** but all **educational programming, pops concerts,** orchestra player auditions, any other outreach initiatives, and fundraising efforts. The principal or chief conductor would be the one who conducts the majority of concerts in a season but would have no overall oversight or fund-raising responsibilities. Without the state funding that is common in Europe, the American music director's position includes a major time commitment to community relations and fund-raising. Since the 1990s, shared responsibility between the conductor and members of the orchestra and the administration have become much more common. Some orchestras have gone so far as to give up the music director designation in favor of the title principal conductor with great success.

The title music director is also used for the person in charge of music at a radio station, the main bandmaster of a military band, the head organist or choirmaster of a church, and the musician in charge of the overall musical performance in music theater and opera. See also **assistant conductor**, **associate conductor**, **resident conductor**.

Music Educators National Conference (MENC). Now called the **National Association for Music Education (NAfME)**.

music magazines. See *American Record Guide*, *ARCHI magazine*, *BBC Music Magazine*, *Classical Music Magazine*, *Classical Recordings Quarterly*, *Diapason*, *Fanfare*, *Gramophone*, *International Record Review*, *Limelight*, *Music Scene* (Fr. *La Scene musicale*), *Musical America*, *Opera News*, *Opernwelt* (*Opera World*), *Pizzicato Magazine*, *The Strad*.

Music Publishers Association of the United States. Established in 1895, it is the oldest music trade organization in the United States. A nonprofit association, it seeks to serve as a forum for music publishers, advance compliance with copyright law, advocate protection of intellectual property rights on the legal and legislative fronts, and facilitate communication among publishers, dealers, music educators, and performers.

music publishers, selected. See **Bärenreiter Verlag**, **Boosey & Hawkes**, **Breitkoph & Härtel**, **Dover Publishers**, **Ernest Eulenburg**, **European American**, **Faber Music**, **Carl Fischer Music**, **Henle Verlag**, **International Music Publishers**, **Hal Leonard Corporation**, **Kalmus Music Publisher**, **Éditions Alfonse Leduc**, **Luck's Music**, **Music Sales Group**, **Novello & Co.**, **Edition Peters**, **Theodore Presser Company**, **Oxford**, **Ricordi**, **Éditions Salabert**, **G. Schirmer Music Publishers**, **Schott Music**, **Simrock Verlag**, **Universal Edition**.

Music Scene (*La Scene musicale*) A quarterly bilingual Canadian magazine to promote classical music. Every issue has a concert calendar; reviews of CDs, DVDs, and books of interest; interviews with musicians; and feature articles. It is a free magazine that is distributed nationally.

music stand. A wooden, metal, or sometimes plastic stand used to hold the music at a height that makes it easy to read. Generally, music stands are flexible enough that they can be raised for musicians who need to stand and lowered for those who sit. **Conductors'** stands may be more substantial so that they can support the size and weight of conductors' scores. Referred to as a music desk in British usage. (Fr. *Le pupitre á musique*, Ger. *das Pult*, It. *Il leggio*, Sp. *atril*.)

Music Teachers National Association (MTNA). Founded in 1876 by music publisher Theodore Presser and a group of sixty-two colleagues with the purpose of advancing the study of music and music making in America and supporting the careers and professionalism of music teachers. Today MTNA has over twenty thousand members in all fifty states with more than five hundred state affiliates.

music theory. The study and analysis of musical elements such as form, melody, rhythm, harmony, and counterpoint. See the **bibliography** for books of interest.

music therapy. A health profession that consists of a trained music therapist using music and all of its facets—physical, emotional, mental, social, aesthetic, and spiritual—to help patients improve their health, especially in the areas of cognitive function, motor skills, and emotional development. The first undergraduate degree program in the United States began at Michigan State University in 1944. The American Music Therapy Association (AMTA) was founded in 1998 when two other related organizations merged. In order to become certified, one must have a completed music therapy degree from a board-certified institution, complete an internship, and pass a board-certification exam.

Musiker. (Ger.) Musician. Also *Musikerin*, female musician. (Fr. *musicien*, It. *musicisto, musicista*, Sp. *músico, música*.)

Musikverein, Vienna (Wiener Musikverein). A concert hall in Vienna, Austria and home to the **Vienna Philharmonic**. Opened in 1870, its main performance space is commonly called the Goldener Sall (Golden Hall) because of the gold leaf that adorns many of the interior surfaces. It is most well known for its annual New Year's Day concert with the **Vienna Philharmonic**, which is broadcast around the world.

Musin, Ilya. (1904–1999.) Russian **conductor** and one of the most important Russian **conducting** pedagogues. Musin's career was shortened because he never joined the Soviet Communist Party. Beginning in 1932, he taught at the **St. Petersburg Conservatory**, then known as the Leningrad Conservatory, where he developed a theoretical system to allow the conductor to communicate with the orchestra only through gesture without speaking. He wrote *The Technique of Conducting* in 1967, but it is only available in Russian and Bulgarian. His list of conducting students is extensive and includes Rudolf Barshai, **Semyon Bychkov**, Oleg Caetani, **Sian Edwards**, Ennio Nicotra, **Yuri Temirkanov**, **Valery Gergiev**, and **Tugan Sokhiev**. See the **bibliography** for a textbook by Ennio Nicotra.

musique á programme. (Fr.) **Program music**. (Ger. *Programmusik*, It. *musica a programma*, Sp. *música programática*.)

musique concrète. (Fr.) One of the earliest forms of electronic music in which almost any sound that could be heard was thought to be viable material for a composition, including man-made and natural sounds, sounds of city life, the speaking voice, and animal sounds. All of the sounds were tape-recorded and then manipulated by speeding up or slowing down the tape, changing the direction of the tape, adding reverberation, and multiple kinds of editing processes used to create compositions. The technique was developed by Pierre Schaeffer in 1948 at the French National Radio in Paris. Examples of compositions include Edgard Varèse's *Déserts* (1954) and his *Poème électronique*, written for the Brussels Worlds Fair in 1958 for a pavilion designed by **Iannis Xenakis** when he was working for architect Le Courbusier; Karlheinz Stockhausen's *Gesang der Jünglinge*; and Henri Pousseur's *The Streets of Liege*. All are considered masterpieces of the genre.

musique contemporaine. (Fr.) Contemporary music. (Ger. *Zeitgenössiche Musik, neue Musik*, It. *musica contemporanea*, Sp. *música contemporánea*.)

musique de scène. (Fr.) Incidental music or stage music for a play or music played on stage in an opera. (Ger. *Bühnenmusik*, It. *musica di scena*, Sp. *música de escena*.)

musique tzigane. (Fr.) Gypsy music. (Ger. *Ziegeunermusik*, It. *musica gitana*, Sp. *música cíngara*.)

muta. (It.) An indication used in timpani parts when a **pitch** is required. Also used in wind instruments when a change from one instrument to another is necessary. Example: *muta in piccolo*, Change from flute to piccolo. (Fr. *changez en petite flute*, Ger. *Piccolo nehmen*, Sp. *cambiar a flautín*.)

mute. A device used with several instruments in order to muffle the sound. String mutes exist in two basic styles, the concert mute and the practice mute. The practice mute muffles the sound so that it cannot be heard through a wall, producing a very restricted sound. **Brass mutes** come in a wide variety of styles, each creating a specific sound. (Fr. *sourdine*, Ger. *Dämpfer*, It. *sordino*, Sp. *sordina*.)

Muti, Riccardo. (b. 1941.) Italian **conductor** and music director of the Chicago Symphony Orchestra beginning in the 2010/2011 concert season. Muti studied at the Conservatory in Milan and with **Franco Ferrara** in Venice. He won the Guido Cantelli Conducting Competition, followed by much conducting in Italy. Muti made his U.S. debut with the **Philadelphia Orchestra** in 1972, serving as the music director there from 1980 to 1990. He championed fund-raising that brought about the building of a new concert hall to replace the long-term home of the orchestra, the **Academy of Music** the new hall is the **Kimmel Center for the Performing Arts**. He was the principal conductor of the Philharmonia in London from 1973 to 1982 and the music director of **La Scala, Milan**, from 1986 to 2005. Muti conducted at Salzburg; the **Royal Opera House, Covent Garden**; and the **Vienna Philharmonic Orchestra**, including the celebrated New Year's concerts in 1993, 1997, 2000, and 2004. He is an eminent interpreter of the Romantic repertory, specifically opera, and has also performed works of contemporary composers such as Luciano Berio, Mario Davidovsky, Shulamit Ran, and Christopher Rouse. He is known as a demanding conductor with a great intellect and an excellent **baton technique**.

Riccardo Muti. *Courtesy Photofest.*

muto. (It.) Mute, silent. (Fr. *muet*, Ger. *stumm*, Sp. *mudo*.)

muy. (Sp.) Very. Often seen in music and heard in rehearsal in numerous phrases. (Ger. *sehr*, It. *molto, di molto, assai*)

Muy bien! Genial! Excelente! (Sp.) Very good! Excellent! (Fr. *Trés bien!*, Ger. *Sehr gut!* It. *bravissimo!*)

M.V. (It.) Abbreviation for *mezza voce*.

mystérieux. (Fr.) Mysterious. A commonly used character word, heard especially with younger orchestras. (Ger. *geheimnisvoll*, It. *misterioso*, Sp. *misterioso*.)

mystic chord. A six-note **chord** created by the Russian composer Alexander Scriabin along with its resulting scale or group of **pitches**, as used in many of his compositions but most notably in the work *Prometheus, Poem of Fire* (Symphony No. 5). The pitches are, from bottom to top, C, F-sharp, B-flat, E, A, and D but may be spelled in many different ways while maintaining the intervallic distribution. Also referred to as the **Prometheus chord**. See also **iconic chords**.

Mystic chord. *Courtesy Andrew Martin Smith.*

nach. (Ger.) After, behind. Examples: *nach und nach*, little by little; *nachgeben*, broaden, easing, accommodating; *nachhorchend*, listening; *nachlassen*, to slacken, to relax; *nachzuahmen*, to imitate, to copy. (Fr. *après, ensuite*, It. *dopo, poi*, Sp. *después*.)

nach Belieben. (Ger.) At the pleasure of the performer, suggesting freedom of tempo and expression. (Fr. *librement*, It. *a piacere*, Sp. *al gusto*.)

nach, dann, anschlidßend. (Ger). After, afterwards, then. Example: *poi la coda*, "and then play the coda." (Fr. *après, ensuite*, It. *poi*, Sp. *después*.)

nach Gehör spielen. (Ger.) To play by ear. (Fr. *jouer d'oreille*, It. *suonare a orecchio*, Sp. *tocar de oído*.)

Nachschlag. (Ger.) Afterbeat. Any ornamental note or notes that either end a trill or are added to a note, taking their rhythmic value from the note they follow, hence the name afterbeat or stroke. May be abbreviated *Nachschlg.* (Fr. *gruppetto final, terminasion*, It. *chiusa del trillo*, Sp. *resolución, terminación del trino*.)

Nachspiel. (Ger.) Postlude, sequel. (Fr. *postlude*, It. *postludio*, Sp. *postludio*.)

nächste. (Ger.) Next. (Fr. *prochain*, It. *prossimo*, Sp. *próximo*.) See also **nächstes Mal**.

nächstes Mal. (Ger.) Next time. (Fr. *prochaine fois*, It. *prossimo volta*, Sp. *próximo vez*.)

Nachtmusik. (Ger.) A serenade, as in *Eine kleine Nachtmusik* (*A Little Night Music*) by Wolfgang Amadeus Mozart.

nada, ningún, ninguna. (Sp.) Nothing, not, none. Example: *a la nada*, to nothing. The Italian form, *a niente*, is commonly used internationally. (Fr. *aucun*, It. *niente*, Ger. *keine, kein, keiner*.)

Nagano, Kent. (b. 1951.) American **conductor** of Japanese descent. Nagano was appointed music director of the Hamburg State Opera and Philharmonic Orchestra (2015). He is the music director of the Bayerische Staatsoper Munich and the **Orchestre symphonique de Montréal** (both 2006) and the principal guest conductor of Sweden's **Gothenburg Symphony** (2013). Nagano served as the artistic director and chief conductor of the **Deutsches Symphonie-Orchester Berlin** (2000–2006). He is known for his performances of late nineteenth- and twentieth-century music and for performances of living composers such as Unsuk Chin, Wolfgang Rihm, Kaija Saariaho, Peter Eötvös, George Benjamin, Jörg Widmann, and **John Adams**. He has long been committed to the music of Olivier Messiaen, conducting the composer's only opera, *Saint François d'Assise*, on several occasions. He has a long-term relationship with **Sony Classical** but has also recorded on Erato, Teldec, Pentatone, **Deutsche Grammophon**, and Harmonia Mundi. He is known for conducting without a baton.

nahe. (Ger.) Near, close. Example: *sich Nähernd*, to draw near, to approach, to advance. (Fr. *prés*; It. *vicino, presso*; Sp. *cerca, próximo, vecino*.)

nana. (Sp.) Lullaby, cradlesong. Also *canción de cuna*. (Ger. *Wiegenlied*, It. *ninna nanna*.)

narrador. (Sp.) Narrator. Examples of piece that have a narrator include Sergei Prokofiev's *Peter and the Wolf*, Joseph Schwantner's *New Morning for the World*, and Aaron Copland's *Lincoln Portrait*. (Fr. *narrateur*, Ger. *Erzähler*, It. *narratore*.)

narrateur. (Fr.) Narrator. (Ger. *Erzähler,* It. *narratore,* Sp. *narrador.*) See **narrador.**

narrator. (It.) Narrator. (Fr. *narrateur,* Ger. *Erzähler,* Sp. *narrador.*) See **narrador.**

National Academy of Recording Arts and Sciences (NARAS). Also known as the Recording Academy, it is an American organization dedicated to "honoring artistic achievement in the recording arts and supporting the music community" (www.grammy.org/recording-academy). Founded in 1957, its most well-known activity is the sponsorship of the **Grammy Awards**. The first awards ceremony was held in 1959. In 1997, the Latin Academy for Recording Arts and Sciences, Inc., was established. Members are musicians, producers, engineers, and other music professionals. NARAS has a Producers and Engineers Wing (P&E Wing) that actively supports those involved in the technical side of music production, the Grammy University Network (Grammy U) for college students, and MusiCares, a charitable organization with the mission of providing assistance to musicians in times of need.

National Assembly of State Arts Agencies (NASAA). An organization that brings together state agencies in order to promote the arts as part of American life. The mission is to strengthen state arts agencies by facilitating the transfer of knowledge and ideas, building community, and providing national representation.

National Association for Music Education (NAfME). Formerly known as the **Music Educators National Conference (MENC)**. A professional advocacy organization founded in 1907 and dedicated to the advancement and support of music education in the United States. With over 130,000 members, NAfME has state affiliates across the country. It sponsors Music in Our Schools Month (MIOSM); two annual conferences, the NAfME National In-Service Conference and the Music Research and Teacher Education National Conference; the Give a Note Foundation; the National Anthem Project; public relations activities; websites; and several publications. NAfME developed the National Standards for Music Education for grades K–12 in the 1990s with a grant from the U.S. Department of Education.

National Broadcasting Corporation (NBC). Sponsored the **NBC Symphony** for **Arturo Toscanini**, who conducted it from 1937 to 1954, and then the **Symphony of the Air** with **Leopold Stokowski** as the **conductor** from 1954 to 1963.

National Conservatory of Music. Founded in 1885 in New York by **Jeannette Thurber** on the model of the **Paris Conservatory**, where Thurber had studied. In the early 1890s, she persuaded Antonin Dvořák to come to New York as the head of the school. He served in that position from 1892 to 1895. At the beginning, the school had only about eighty students, but by 1900, there were close to three thousand. The school was mostly free of charge and dependent upon private donations for support. It remained active until the 1920s, when increased competition from other, newer institutions began to bring about its decline. In 1904, the Institute of Musical Art of the City of New York was founded. It became the **Juilliard School** of Music in 1924.

National Council on the Arts. The committee of advisors to the chairman of the **National Endowment of the Arts**. The council considers and advises on issues such as applications for federal grants, guidelines for funding categories, leadership initiatives and partnerships with other agencies, budget levels, allocations and priorities, and policy directions, in addition to recommending individuals and organizations for the National Medal of the Arts, a presidential award.

National Endowment for the Arts (NEA). Founded in 1965, an independent agency of the U.S. federal government that provides financial support for the arts. The NEA works in tandem with state arts organizations, with a significant portion of its funding going directly to them. Funding for the NEA is granted by Congress and has risen and fallen as a result of political pressures. The organization is governed by a chairman who is appointed by the president and confirmed by Congress and is advised by its **National Council on the Arts**.

National Music Publishers Association (NMPA). Founded in 1917, the NMPA is the largest music publishing trade association in the United States. The association seeks to protect its member's intellectual property rights in the legislative, legal, and regulatory arenas. In 1927, the NMPA established the **Harry Fox Agency** to serve as a mechanical rights (recording rights) collecting agent. The NMPA advised in the writing of the Copyright Act of 1976 and works together with the Music Publisher's Association (MPA) to enforce **copyright laws** and the rights of composers.

National Orchestra and Chorus of Spain (Orquesta y Coro Nacionales de España). This Madrid orchestra presents a full schedule of symphonic concerts and outreach and educational programming, including the Satélites concerts, with a wide variety of repertoire and flexible ensembles. The current principal **conductor** is David Afkham (appointed in 2014). One of its most influential artistic leaders was **Rafael Frühbeck de Burgos** (1962–1978), who is now conductor emeritus.

Other past conductors include Josep Pons (2003–2013), Aldo Ceccato (1991–1994), **Jesús López-Cobos** (1984–1989), Antoni Ros-Marbà (1978–1981), Araúlfo Argenta (1947–1958), and Bartolomé Pérez Casas (1942–1947).

National Orchestral Association (NOA). Founded by **Leon Barzin** in 1930, it was the longest running training orchestra for young professional musicians in America. Alumni of the association became members of professional orchestras across the United States.

National Public Radio (NPR). A nonprofit, membership-supported media organization founded in 1970 that serves over 950 public radio stations in the United States through syndication. Funded both privately and publically, it is primarily a news and information organization. However, member station programming has long included many genres of music, such as classical, jazz, and world music, that are neglected by commercial media. Member stations may also opt to broadcast programming from other sources, such as the **Metropolitan Opera**, **Lyric Opera of Chicago**, and many major American orchestras. NPR maintains several digital platforms from its website, NPR.org, including NPR Music, launched in 2007 as a free online service. See also **classical music radio stations**.

National Superior Conservatory of Paris for Music and Dance (Conservatoire National Supérior de Musique et de Danse de Paris, CNSMDP). Also known as the **Paris Conservatory**, it was founded in 1795. In 1946, it was divided into two schools, one for acting, theater, and drama, the Conservatoire national superior d'art dramatique (CNSAD), and the other for music and dance. Continuing from its earliest days, the school has maintained a faculty of some of the most well-known performers and composers of the day, including composer Luigi Cherubini; violinist Rudolphe Kreutzer in the early nineteenth century; violinist and **conductor François Habeneck**; composers Anton Reicha, Fromental Halévy, Adolphe Adam, Ambroise Thomas, and later César Frank, Charles-Marie Widor, Gabriel Fauré; and many more. The alumni list may be said to be even more impressive, including Claude Debussy, Maurice Ravel, and Olivier Messaien, to name just a few.

National Symphony Orchestra of Ukraine (NSOU). Established in 1918 in Kiev with **conductor** Oleksandr Horily as the Lysenko State Symphonic Orchestra. (Mykola Lysenko was a well-known composer.) In 1923, the name was changed to the Kyiv (Kiev) State Philiharmonic and to its current name in 1994. Many internationally renowned conductors and soloists have appeared with the orchestra during its history. The orchestra has toured Europe, Australia, Hong Kong, Kazakhstan, the United Arab Emirates, and in 1994, won an Australian Broadcasting Award for best CD of the year in performances of Boris Lyatoshynsky's Symphonies Nos. 2 and 3. Several other recordings, including works of Sergei Prokofiev, Dmitri Shostakovich, Rodion Shchedrin, Vasily Kalinnikov, and many more, have been issued on the **Naxos label**. The current conductor, Volodymyr Sirenko (appointed in 1999), has led many recordings. Past conductors include Mykhailo Kannerstein (appointed in 1929); Herman Adler (1935–1937); Natan Rakhlin (1938–1962); Evhenia Shabaltina, the first female conductor to work with the orchestra (1946); Stephan Truchak (beginning in the early 1960s); Volodymyr Kozhukhar (1968–1973); Fedir Hluschenko (appointed in 1978); Ihor Blazhkov (appointed in 1988); and American Theodore Kuchar (appointed in 1992).

natural. (Sp.) The **natural sign**. (Fr. *bécarre*, Ger. *Auflösungszeichen*, It. *bequadro*.) See also **accidental**.

natural harmonics. See **harmonics**.

natural horn. Constructed from brass tubing, the basic natural horn used an eight-foot tube that had a fundamental pitch of C. The range of pitches was then generated by the overtone series, the fundamental, and a few others not being playable, going up to about the twelfth partial. Some pitches in the series were achieved by stopping the note with the hand. Stopped notes sounded significantly different from open notes, and even in the music of composers as late as Johannes Brahms, they were sometimes preferred. To play in all keys, different lengths of tubing were used, each with its own fundamental and harmonic series. It is from this practice that the horn has so many different transpositions, each is associated with a different tube length. See also **horn transpositions**.

natural sign. A notational device used to cancel a sharp or flat or to caution the performer against the unintended use of either. In the latter case, it is referred to as a "cautionary" mark. (Fr. *bécarre*, Ger. *Auflösungszeichen,* It. *bequadro,* Sp. *becuadro*.) See **accidentals** for the musical symbol.

natural trumpet. Similar in some ways to the **natural horn**, the natural trumpet also has a fundamental pitch based on the length of its tubing and consequent size. Instead of various sizes of tube that could be inserted into the instrument, several sizes of instruments were built. The range of the natural trumpet depended on the harmonic series above the fundamental and was generally playable up to the sixteenth partial in the Baroque period and the twelfth partial in the nineteenth century.

The early Baroque trumpet was known for its **clarino**, or high register, and difficult soloistic playing. These parts were typically written for the smaller trumpets, either the **piccolo trumpet** or **trumpet in D**. In the nineteenth century, that style disappeared in favor of a sound that fit in to the developing orchestra. The use of the larger **C** and **B-flat trumpets** that played in a slightly lower register became more common. See also **trumpet, trumpet transpositions**.

Naturhorn. (Ger.) The **natural horn**.

Naturlaut, Wie ein. (Ger.) The expression "Like sounds of nature." Used in the opening bars of **Gustav Mahler**'s Symphony No. 1, "Titan."

natürlich. (Ger.) Natural, naturally. (Fr. *naturel,* It. *naturale,* Sp. *natural*.)

Naturtrompete. (Ger.) The **natural trumpet**.

Naxos Recording Company. Founded in 1987 by Klaus Heymann, a German-born entrepreneur and music enthusiast living in Hong Kong, with the goal of selling CDs at an affordable price, Naxos has become the world's leading classical music label. By focusing on the music instead of the artists, profits are invested in recordings of new or unusual music rather than recordings that already exist in several versions.

The Naxos catalogue includes the **American Classics series**, a comprehensive recording project of American concert music; the **Naxos Historical series**, a restoration project that focuses on classical, jazz, and pop music from the first half of the twentieth century; **Naxos World**, including music of different cultures and genres; **Naxos AudioBooks**, which combines music recordings with readings of literary classics; and **Naxos.com**, an Internet service that streams classical music recordings. See also **The Story of Naxos** by Nicolas Soames (2012) in the **bibliography**.

NBC Symphony Orchestra. A **radio orchestra** established in 1937 for the **conductor Arturo Toscanini**. Founded by **David Sarnoff**, president of RCA, the organization that owned both **RCA Victor** and the **National Broadcasting Company (NBC)**, it was modeled on the European **radio orchestra** that still exists today. Sarnoff gave Toscanini a free hand in recruiting musicians. Consequently, the orchestra immediately became one of the best in the country. The orchestra gave its first performance on Christmas Night 1937 and performed under the name NBC Symphony Orchestra until 1954 as the house orchestra for the network. At that time, a new orchestra was formed, called the **Symphony of the Air**, performing under the leadership of **Leopold Stokowski** and others from 1954 to 1963. Among its notable roster of musicians, many went on to perform with major

American orchestras (such as the **Chicago Symphony**) after 1954, while some remained in the reconstituted orchestra until it disbanded in 1963.

The symphony made numerous recordings on **RCA Victor** as early as 1938 and the Columbia, United Artists, and Vanguard labels, as well as radio and television opera broadcasts. One of its most famous was the 1963 telecast of Gian Carlo Menotti's opera written specifically for the occasion, *Amahl and the Night Visitors*. The orchestra sometimes recorded as the **RCA Victor Symphony**, including a well-known recording of Richard Rodgers's *Victory at Sea*.

Other conductors who appeared with either manifestation of the ensemble include **Leonard Bernstein, Walter Hendl**, Thor Johnson, **Pierre Monteux, Fritz Reiner, Artur Rodziski, Bruno Walter, Sir Thomas Beecham**, Alfred Wallenstein, and **Josef Krips**.

Nebennote. (Ger.) Nonharmonic tone, auxiliary note. (Fr. *note secondaire,* It. *nota ausiliare,* Sp. *nota auxiliar*.)

Nebensatz, Nebenthema. (Ger.) A secondary theme, as in sonata form.

Nebenstimme. (Ger.) A secondary melody, part, or voice. A symbol often used by **Arnold Schoenberg**, Alban Berg, Anton Webern, and many composers thereafter, to aid the **conductor** and performer in analyzing a complex composition. See also *Hauptstimme*.

Nebenstimme symbol. *Courtesy Andrew Martin Smith.*

negra. (Sp.) Quarter note or crotchet in British usgae. (Fr. *noire,* Ger. *Viertel,* It. *quarto,* Sp. *negra*.) See also **appendix 7**.

nehmen. (Ger.) To take or to change to, as in to switch to a different clarinet in the course of a piece or movement. (Fr. *prendre,* It. *prendere,* Sp. *tomar*.) Example: *Die 3 Tromp. Nehmen ihren Platz im Orchestrer ein*, The third trumpet should take his place in the orchestra again, from Symphony No. 1, mvt. 1, by **Gustav Mahler**.

Nelson, John Wilton. (b. 1941.) American orchestral and choral **conductor**. Nelson served as the music director of the **Indianapolis Symphony Orchestra** (1976–1987), music director of the **Opera Theater of Saint Louis** (1985–1988) and its principal conductor (1988–1991), and music director of the Caramoor Festival (1983–1990). He has performed works of the contemporary composers Toru Takemitsu, Henryk Górecki, and Paul Schoenfield and is praised for his recording of **Hector Berlioz**'s *Béatrice et Bénédict*. He conducted the American premiere of **Sir Benjamin Britten**'s opera *Qwen Wingrave* in Santa Fe, New Mexico, in 1973.

Nelsons, Andris. (b. 1978.) Latvian **conductor**. Nelsons is currently the music director of the **City of Birmingham Symphony Orchestra** (2008–2015) and is the music director of the **Boston Symphony Orchestra** for the 2013–2015 concert season. He has also served as the principal conductor of the Latvian National Opera (2003–2007) and chief conductor of the Northwest German Philharmonic of Herford (2006–2009). **Mariss Jansons** is his mentor.

neoclassicism. A style trend that developed in the 1920s as a reaction against the large-scale romantic works of the late nineteenth and early twentieth centuries. It is known for qualities of expressive restraint, lean harmony, emphasis on counterpoint, clarity of form, and a variety of ensembles, including a smaller orchestra. Sergei Prokofiev's *Classical Symphony* (1917) may be one of the first neoclassical works. But it was composer **Igor Stravinsky** who defined the style with such works as the ballets *Pulcinella* (1919) and *Le baiser de la fée* (1928). They were also "newly classical' not only in style but because they used music from other, earlier composers. *Pulcinella* uses music not by Giovanni Pergolesi, as originally thought, but by several other eighteenth-century Italian composers and *Le baiser* uses melodies by Peter Ilyich Tchaikovsky. Other neoclassical works by Stravinsky include his *Symphony in C* and the *Piano Concerto with Winds*. In Germany, both Paul Hindemith and **Richard Strauss** added compositions to the genre, as did Manuel de Falla in Spain and **Aaron Copland** in the United States.

neomodality. The use of modal scales and harmonies in contemporary music. Examples: Béla Bartók (multiple works); Jean Sibelius, Symphony No. 4; Aaron Copland, Violin Sonata; Modeste Mussorgsky, *Pictures at an Exhibition*; Roy Harris, Symphony No. 3, *American Ballads*; Randall Thompson, *String Quartet No. 1*; Ralph Vaughan Williams, especially in his sacred works; and many more. Other composers delved into modal materials to expand harmonic and melodic possibilities beyond diatonic major and minor scales, using folk materials that are by-and-large modally based.

neoromanticism. A term for a movement in the arts, including music, that occurred in the 1920s and into the 1940s as a reaction against highly complex styles and neoclassicism. Harkening back to concepts of humanism and sentiment, it manifested itself through a resurgence of melody and sometimes programmatic music in the works of Samuel Barber, Carl Orff, **Howard Hanson**, Virgil Thomson, William Walton, and others.

nervioso. (Sp.) Nervous, nervously. (Fr. *nerveusement,* Ger. *nervös,* It. *nervosamente.*)

Netherlands Radio Philharmonic Orchestra (Radio Filharmonisch Orkest, RFO). It was established in 1945 and serves as the orchestra for Dutch public broadcasting, giving concerts and performing as the orchestra for the Netherlands Opera. In 2010, the Dutch government planned to remove funding for the Broadcasting Music Center, the umbrella organization of the orchestra, but following public protests and advocacy by such high-profile **conductors** as **Bernard Haitink**, partial funding was restored. The current conductor is Markus Stenz (appointed in 2012). Past conductors include founder Albert van Raalte (1945–1949), Paul van Kempen (1949–1955), **Bernard Haitink** (1957–1961), Jean Fournet (1961–1978), Hans Vonk (1978–1979), **Sergiu Comissiona** (1982–1989), **Edo de Waart** (1989–2004), and **Jaap van Zweden** (2005–2012).

netto, chiaro. (It.) Clean, clear, distinct. A quality of playing that is often sought. (Fr. *clair, claire*; Ger. *klar, deutlich*; Sp. *claro, neto.*)

neu belebend. (Ger.) Becoming livelier in tempo and or feeling. (Fr. *en ranimant,* It *avvivando,* Sp. *avivando.*)

Neue Musik. (Ger.) New music. A general term that refers to various forms of music written in the twentieth and twenty-first centuries. Atonality, serialism, aleatory, and electronic music are among them. See **new Music Ensemble**.

Neuen, Donald. (b. 1933.) American choral **conductor** and pedagogue. Neuen has been Distinguished Professor of Conducting and director of choral activities at the University of California, Los Angeles, since 1993. He is the former choral conductor at the Eastman School of Music. Neuen has released *Choral Concepts: A Text for Conductors* and a series of videos, some are intended for the development of the choral singer and some for the choral conductor. Refer to Donald Neuen's *Artistic Musical Conducting 1 and 2,* a video made available by The Choral Excellence Press (2001).

Neue Zeitschrift für Musik. A journal founded in 1834 by Robert Schumann, it was organized in a similar manner to the *Allgemeine musikalische Zeitung* but with a different perspective. Schumann's goal was to establish a new literary standard-bearer for the romantic era in music, to restore poetry to art, and to create a forum for the creative artist, not the general reader. He oversaw the journal, publishing many of his own essays, until it began to take too much of his time and sold it in 1844.

neutral gesture, neutral beat. A gesture given without any sense of intent, except to clearly mark an empty beat or bar. It is solely for purposes of keeping the orchestra together. See also **dead beat**.

new complexity. A term dating from the 1980s and exemplified by such composers as the Englishmen Brian Ferneyhough and Michael Finnissy. It is music characterized by the use of highly complex notation and often extensive use of irregular, multilayered rhythms; extended instrumental techniques; microtonality; disjunct melodic shapes; and abrupt changes in texture.

New England Conservatory of Music. Founded in 1867 in Boston by Eben Tourjée (1834–1891). In its early years, it was the largest music school in the United States. Its directors have included composers George W. Chadwick (1897–1931) and **Gunther Schuller** (1966–1977). Chadwick created the NEC Symphony Orchestra, now led by **conductor Hugh Wolff**. The conservatory has a Department of Entrepreneurial Musicianship that strives to give students the skills needed in the music world today. Several members of the **Boston Symphony Orchestra** serve on the faculty.

The New Grove Dictionary of Music and Musicians. The second edition of a multivolume resource encyclopedic dictionary released in 1980. See also ***Grove's Dictionary of Music and Musicians***,**Grove Music Online**.

New Haven Symphony. This New Haven, Connecticut, orchestra is the fourth oldest in the United States, having given its first concert in 1895. With over seventy members, the orchestra presents classics, pops, and family series, in addition to young people's concerts, a Young Composer Project, and other outreach projects. The current music director is William Boughton (appointed in 2007).

New Jersey Symphony Orchestra (NJSO). Founded in 1922 in Newark, the orchestra performs in multiple venues throughout the state. Its current music director is Jacques Lacombe (appointed in 2010). Past music directors include Kenneth Schermerhorn (1962–1968), **Henry Lewis** (1968–1976), Tomans Michalak (1977–1983), Hugh Wolff (1985–1991), **Zdeněk Mácal** (1993–2002), and **Neeme Järvi** (2005–2009). The orchestra made several recordings under Mácal on the Delos label. The NJSO offers classics, pops, family, and neighborhood concerts and has its own youth orchestra program. The orchestra has given numerous premieres of works by many of America's most distinguished composers.

new media. Most new media technologies are digital, such as video games and Internet websites. One of its characteristics is on-demand access at any time and any place, usually through a digital device. Also characteristic is the real-time creation of unregulated content.

New Mexico Philharmonic. Formed in 2011 in Albuquerque soon after the dissolution of the **New Mexico Symphony Orchestra**, the philharmonic is a fully professional orchestra that offers a classics series; pops, neighborhood, and educational concerts; and a chamber music series, in addition to a special series titled Sunday Afternoons at the National Hispanic Cultural Center. The orchestra uses guest **conductors**.

New Mexico Symphony Orchestra. Founded in 1932 as the Albuquerque Civic Symphony, the orchestra operated until April 2011. The founding **conductor** was Grace Thompson Edmister, head of the University of New Mexico music department. She led the orchestra until 1941. Other conductors include William Kunkel (1941–1945), Hans Lange (1950–1958), Maurice Bonney (1958–1968), Yoshimi Takeda (1970–1984), Neal Stulberg (1985–1993), David Lockington (1995–2000), and Guillermo Figueroa, who served from 2000 to 2011 when the orchestra was declared bankrupt. The symphony's notable achievements included the premiere of **Arnold Schoenberg**'s *A Survivor from Warsaw*, a work in memory of the Warsaw Ghetto Uprising in World War II. The **New Mexico Philharmonic** was formed as a new orchestra in May 2011, giving its first concert in December of the same year.

New Music Box. A multimedia website run by **New Music, USA**, that focuses on the music of American composers. The site includes access to **G. Schirmer** and **Associated Music Press**'s library of digital perusal scores, as well as an Internet radio station known as Counterstream.

new music ensemble. An ensemble of varying instrumentation that focuses on the performance of contemporary music. Such ensembles began to appear after the premiere of ***Pierrot Lunaire*** by **Arnold Schoenberg** (1912), **Igor Stravinsky**'s *The Soldier's Tale* (1919), and other pieces written for smaller ensembles during World War I and soon thereafter, when money for commissions was hard to come by. *Pierrot Lunaire* was written for an ensemble of seven members, many of whom played more than one instrument in the work: **flute/piccolo, clarinet/bass clarinet, violin/viola, cello, piano**, percussion, and a singer/narrator who uses ***Sprechstimme***. This contingent has become iconic, even generic; that is, any ensemble of this instrumentation is a *Pierrot* ensemble. *The Soldier's Tale* calls for an ensemble that includes one high and one low instrument of each type: **violin** and **double**

bass, clarinet and bassoon, trumpet and trombone, and also percussion, narrator, actor, and dancer. Both of these works remained significantly influential during the twentieth century. And their very size—relatively small—began to open new horizons for living composers. New music ensembles, generally small but with flexible instrumentation, were formed at universities and conservatories throughout Europe and North America in order to accommodate the enormous repertoire of works that followed. Some of the most renowned independent ensembles include Peter Maxwell Davies's **The Fires of London**; David Stock's **The Pittsburgh New Music Ensemble**; Arthur Weisberg's **Contemporary Chamber Ensemble**; **ICE (International Contemporary Ensemble)**; Bang on a Can, a New York–based ensemble that often puts on giant marathon concerts; Alarm Will Sound, a twenty-piece chamber orchestra; and the San Francisco Contemporary Music Players. And many **conductors** became known for their association with such ensembles and repertoire, including Brad Lubman, conductor of Musica Nova at the **Eastman School**; Jeff Mylarski, artistic director of AXIOM at the **Juilliard School**; and Joel Sachs, conductor of the New Juilliard Ensemble and codirector of Continuum. Other important new music ensembles have grown up at summer festivals, including the Aspen Contemporary Ensemble (ACE) at the Aspen Music Festival and School, conducted by Sydney Hodkinson. The **Tanglewood Music Center** presents the Festival of Contemporary Music every year, though it includes orchestral performances in addition to chamber music.

New Music USA. An organization founded in 2011 with the merger of the **American Music Center** and **Meet the Composer**. New Music USA provides over $1 million annually in grant support for the creation and performance of new music. **New Music Box**, an Internet site, profiles composers as one of their projects, along with **Counterstream Radio**, a site that streams an around-the-clock catalog for new music and an "online home" for composers' own music.

new romanticism. A sequel to neoromanticism earlier in the twentieth century. New romanticism, beginning in the late twentieth century and continuing into the twenty-first, is sometimes also called the "New Beauty." A reaction to a period of great experimentation, it is exemplified by composers such as David Del Tredici, Aaron Kernis, Christopher Theofanidis, Kevin Puts, and Jennifer Higdon.

New World Symphony. America's only full-time ensemble dedicated to the training of young musicians for careers in symphony orchestras. Founded in 1987 in Miami Beach, Florida, under the direction of **conductor** Michael Tilson Thomas with its major funding coming from Ted Arison, founder of the Carnival Cruise Line. The program includes orchestra, chamber music, new music, family concerts, festivals, and recitals between October and May of each season. The symphony has a Fellowship Program for members that encourages the development of entrepreneurial and outreach skills. It also tours worldwide and issues commercial records. There are now hundreds of New World Symphony alumni performing in orchestras across the world. The symphony is currently located in the New World Center Building, designed by architect Frank Gehry.

New York City Opera (NYCO). An opera company active in New York City from 1943 until its dissolution in 2013. Established with the stated purpose of making opera available to a wider audience at reasonable cost, the company sought to present an innovative repertory, in particular operas by American composers, and to develop young rising stars. During its history, American opera and operetta amounted to nearly one-third of its productions and included Douglas Moore's *The Ballad of Baby Doe*, Carlisle Floyd's *Susannah*, **Leonard Bernstein's** *Candide*, Mark Adamo's *Little Women*, and many more. Among the conductors who led the company were **Julius Rudel** (1957–1979), Christopher Keene (1982–1986 as music director, 1989–1995 as general director), and George Manahan (1996–2011).

New York Philharmonic Orchestra (NYPO). Officially the **Philharmonic-Symphony Society of New York, Inc.**, reflecting its history as the result of the merger of the New York Symphony and Philharmonic orchestras, among others. In 1842, the American **conductor** and violinist Ureli Corelli Hill joined forces with other interested musicians to found the **Philharmonic Society of New York**. It is the oldest continuously functioning orchestra in America. For the first ten years, the orchestra had between fifty-five and sixty-seven players and several conductors, who often came from the ranks of the orchestra. The opening concert had three conductors, Hill, H. C. Timm, and Denis-Germain Etienne, and several soloists. The program, which was several hours long, included Ludwig van Beethoven's Symphony No. 5 led by Hill; works by Carl Maria von Weber, Jan Kalliwoda, and Johann Nepomuk Hummel; and arias by Beethoven, Wolfgang Amadeus Mozart, and Gioacchino Rossini. For the rest of the nineteenth century, the philharmonic competed with the **New York Symphony**, especially when it was under the leadership of **Leopold Damrosch** and later his son **Walter Damrosch**. The philharmonic concentrated on Germanic repertoire, giving the first American performance of Beethoven's Symphonies No. 3 and No. 9. The orchestra's conductors included Carl Bergmann (1855–76), **Theodore Thomas** (1877–1891), and **Anton Seidl** (1891–1891). By 1867, it had grown to one hundred members. **Gustav Mahler** served as the music director from 1909 to 1911, followed by Josef Stransky from 1911 to 1922). In the 1920s, the philharmonic merged with several New York orchestras, essentially absorbing them. In 1921, it merged with the New National Symphony Orchestra, the City Symphony, the American National Orchestra, and the State Symphony Orchestra. In 1928, it merged with its long-time competitor, the **New York Symphony Orchestra**, becoming the **Philharmonic-Symphony Society of New York**. That year, **Arturo Toscanini** became its principal conductor, remaining until 1936. The orchestra's list of music directors is nothing short of stellar, including **John Barbirolli** (1936–1943), **Artur Rodzinski** (1943–1947), **Bruno Walter** (music advisor, 1947–1949), **Dimitri Mitropoulos** (1949–1957), **Leonard Bernstein** (1958–1969), and **Pierre Boulez** (1971–1978), followed by **Zubin Mehta** (1978–1991), **Kurt Mazur** (1991–2002), **Lorin Maazel** (2002–2009), and currently **Alan Gilbert**.

The orchestra began broadcasting concerts on the radio in 1922, and in 1924, a series of children's concerts was launched that continues to this day. During his tenure as music director, Leonard Bernstein developed a series of **young people's concerts** for CBS television. Under the leadership of **Pierre Boulez**, the philharmonic began a series of **"Rug Concerts"** with a more casual atmosphere in the hope of appealing to a younger audience. Boulez also initiated a series called Prospective Encounters that brought living composers together with the orchestra in concerts that took place in alternative venues. At the same time, the *Live from Lincoln Center* television broadcasts were launched.

Under **Alan Gilbert**, the philharmonic has started a series of contemporary music concerts called Contact! Gilbert has announced a new joint initiative, a New York Philharmonic Biennial, similar to the Venice Biennale but for music, partnering with the Museum of Modern Art, the **Juilliard School**, and others. In addition, Gilbert keeps up the tradition of outdoor summer concerts in the New York City area. The philharmonic's website has comprehensive historical collections, an extensive archive, and online exhibits.

New York Philharmonic Society. See **New York Philharmonic**.

New York Symphony Orchestra. Founded in 1878 by **Leopold Damrosch** and sponsored by the New York Symphony Society. Damrosch conducted until his death in 1885 when his son **Walter Damrosch** took over. The orchestra, competing with the **New York Philharmonic**, concentrated on presenting works by French and Russian composers while the philharmonic concentrated on Germanic repertoire. Both orchestras presented enormous

music festivals to large audiences. In 1881, Leopold Damrosch led 1,500 musicians in **Hector Berlioz's** *Grande messe des morts* before an audience that was reported to be 10,000 strong. **Walter Damrosch** led the opening concert at **Carnegie Hall** in 1891. The performance included Peter Ilyich Tchaikovsky conducting his own *Marche solennelle*. In 1898, Walter's brother **Frank Damrosch** founded the **Young People's Symphony Concerts of New York**. In 1903, the orchestra made its first recording under the name the Damrosch Orchestra on **Columbia Records**. In 1920, the symphony was the first American orchestra to tour Europe, and in 1923, it began broadcasting its concerts on the radio.

Though it presented many innovative concerts and had excellent **conductors**, the orchestra's history in the first decades of the twentieth century was tenuous. It lapsed several times and finally merged with the **New York Philharmonic** in 1928, becoming the **Philharmonic-Symphony Society of New York**.

New Zealand Symphony Orchestra (NZSO). Founded in 1946 in Wellington as the national orchestra, it is owned by the government and until 1989 was run by Radio New Zealand. Known for performing across the country, the NZSO has also appeared at the **BBC Proms** in London, the **Concertgebouw** in Amsterdam, and the World Expo in Japan. For many years, the orchestra relied on guest **conductors**. The first to hold the title of music director was James Judd (1999–2007). Pietari Inkinen became the orchestra's second music director in 2008. Paul Decker was its chief conductor from 1991 to 1996. The orchestra has made several LPs and CDs on the **Koch** and **Naxos** labels, including music of Jean Sibelius and Einojuhani Rautavaara. Many of its concerts are broadcast in real time on Radio New Zealand. The NZSO has recorded for film and made an enhanced e-book version with the music of Salman Rushdie's short story "In the South." The orchestra also runs the National Youth Orchestra of New Zealand and the New Zealand Chamber Orchestra.

NHK Symphony Orchestra. Located in Tokyo, Japan, the orchestra began as the New Symphony Orchestra in 1926, Japan's first professional orchestra. It changed its name to the Japan Symphony Orchestra, and on receiving funding from the NHK (the Japanese Broadcasting Corporation) in 1951, it took the name it has today and became an orchestra in the tradition of European **radio orchestras**. The orchestra's **conductors** have included Vladimir Ashkenazy (2004–2007), now conductor laureate; **Charles Dutoit** (1998–2003), now music director emeritus; and **Andre Previn** (2009–2012), now honorary guest conductor. The orchestra's website lists Yuzo Toyama and Tadaako Otaka as among its permanent conductors and **Herbert Blomstedt** as an honorary conductor. The symphony performs about 150 concerts every year, many of them broadcast throughout Japan on both television and radio.

nicht. (Ger.) Not. (Fr. *ne . . . pas*, It. *non*, Sp. *no*.) Used in various phrases. Examples: *Nicht eilen*, don't rush; *nicht schleppen*, don't drag; *nicht schnell*, not fast.

nicht viel. (Ger.) Not much. Seen in music often as part of a phrase. (Fr. *pas beaucoup*, It. *non molto*, Sp. *no mucho*.)

nicht zu schnell. (Ger.) Not too fast. (Fr. *pas trop vite*, It. *non troppo rapido*, Sp. *no demasiado rápido*.)

nicht zuviel. (Ger.) Not too much. Often used as a directive meaning "not too loud." (Fr. *pas trop*, It. *non troppo*, Sp. *no demasiado*.)

niederdrücken. 1. (Ger.) To depress, as in the keys of a piano. An example from *Pierrot Lunaire* by Arnold Schoenberg: *tonlos niederdrücken*, keys of the piano are depressed without sound so that only the resonance of the piano strings is heard.
　2. (Ger.) To lower the pitch or tuning. (Fr. *baisser l'accord, baisser l'intonation*; Ger. *herunterstimmen*; It. *abbassare l'intonazione, abbassare l'accordatura*; Sp. *bajar la afinación, bemolar*.)

niente. (It.) Nothing. Often seen indicating the degree of a diminuendo: *a niente*, to nothing. (Fr. *rien*, Ger. *nichts*, Sp. *nada*.)

Nieweg, Clint. Former librarian of the **Philadelphia Orchestra** and founder of the **Major Orchestra Librarians' Association (MOLA)**. He has overseen the issue of over fifty-six corrected editions in the *Nieweg Performance Editions* published by **Edwin F. Kalmus & Co.**, including Claude Debussy's *La Mer*; Gustav Holst's *The Planets*; Maurice Ravel's *Alborado del Gracioso, Daphnis et Chloé*, and *La Valse*; and many more.

nimmt. (Ger.) Take or "change to," as in to switch to a different **clarinet** in the course of a piece or **movement**. (Fr. *prend*, It. *prende*, Sp. *tomar*.) Examples: *Nimmt grosse Flöte*, Take the **flute** (appears after the performer has been playing the **piccolo**); *nimmt wieder Piccolo*, take the **piccolo** again, both from *Pierrot Lunaire* by **Arnold Schoenberg**.

ninna nanna. (It.) Lullaby, cradlesong. (Fr. *berceuse*, Ger. *Wiegenlied*, Sp. *canción de cuna*.)

Nishimoto, Tomomi. (b. 1970.) Japanese pianist and **conductor**. She studied at the Osaka College of Music and then went to the **St. Petersburg Conservatory of Music**. She made her debut in Japan in 1998 with the Kyoto Symphony Orchestra. She served as the principal guest conductor of the St. Petersburg Mussorgsky State Academic Opera and Ballet Theater (2004–2006) and is currently the artistic director and principal conductor of the IlluminArt Philharmonic Orchestra.

noch einmal! Zugabe! (Ger.) An expression of approval cried out by the audience (mostly in Europe) when they want a performer to play an **encore**. (Fr. *encore!* It. *bis!* Sp. *bis!*)

noch, wieder. (Ger.) Still, also, again, as well. (Fr. *encore*, It. *ancora*, Sp. *otra vez*.) Examples: *noch lauter*, still louder; *noch stärker*, still stronger; *noch mal*, again or once more; *noch bewegter*, still more agitated.

no demasiado. (Sp.) Not too much. Often meaning not too loud. (Fr. *pas trop*, Ger. *nicht zuviel*, It. *non troppo*.)

no demasiado rápido. (Sp.) Not too fast. (Fr. *pas trop vite*, Ger. *nicht zu schnell*, It. *non troppo rapido*.)

noire. (Fr.) Quarter note. For translations, see **rhythmic terms**.

noise levels in the workplace. In the United States, the Occupational Safety and Health Administration (OSHA) states that noise levels should not exceed 85 dB for an averaged eight-hour time period and that "exposure to impulsive or impact noise should not exceed 140 dB peak sound pressure level" (www.osha.gov). The European Union also regulates decibel levels in the workplace, specifying daily or weekly averages of no more than 85 dB. Beyond that level, employers must provide hearing protection. Musicians who perform regularly in an opera pit are at increased risk because of the enclosed space and close quarters. In American orchestras, it has become common to use acoustic shields, especially for performers who sit directly in front of brass players. Some musicians wear earplugs in particularly loud settings. See also **decibel**.

nombre de mesures. (Fr.) Measure number, bar number. Numbers inserted in scores and parts to facilitate rehearsal. Often appearing every three bars or positioned within a piece at structurally important places. (Ger. *Taktzahl*, It. *numero di battutue*, Sp. *número del compás*.)

no mucho. (Sp.) Not much. Often seen as part of a longer phrase. (Fr. *pas beaucoup*, Ger. *nicht viel*, It. *non molto*.)

noncombinatoriality. A **twelve-tone row** or **set** that does not have the properties of **combinatoriality**.

non div. (Fr.) Not divided, with the abbreviated form of *divisi*. A directive seen in many French works.

Nonesuch Records. An American record label established in 1964 by Jac Holzman in order to produce affordable LPs. Now owned by **Warner Music Group** and distributed by Warner Bros. Records, the label issued many important recordings of contemporary music such as George Crumb's *Ancient Voices of Children*, which sold seventy thousand copies; Steve Reich's *Desert Music* (1985); John Adams's *Harmonielehre* (1986); Philip Glass's *Mishima* (1985); and much more.

non molto. (It.) Not much. Often seen as part of a longer phrase. (Fr. *pas beaucoup*, Ger. *nicth viel*, Sp. *no mucho*.)

nontertian harmony. Chords built out of intervals other than thirds.

nontriadic tonality. Tonality, as the characteristic of centeredness around a given **pitch**, in which a sense of gravitational pull toward that pitch is created without the use of traditional, so-called common practice, harmonic means. See also **polarity**.

non troppo rapido. (It.) Not too fast. (Fr. *pas trop vite*, Ger. *nicht zu schnell*, Sp. *no demasiado rápido*.)

normale. (It.) An indication to return to the normal way of playing, tuning, and so on, after a passage of playing on the fingerboard, an octave higher, an so forth.

Norrington, Sir Roger. (b. 1934.) A noted and influential **conductor** who has built his career as a specialist in the area of period performance practices. He founded his own orchestra, the **London Classical Players** (LCP), in 1978 with the purpose of exploring all aspects of period performance, how the works of composers from the classical through the romantic eras would have been played in their own time, including playing styles, size of the ensemble, and various seating possibilities. He has led highly celebrated recordings of Franz Joseph Haydn, Wolfgnag Amadeus Mozart, and a complete cycle of Beethoven symphonies, which represented his detailed study of available manuscripts and early editions of scores and parts. The LCP was disbanded in 1997 but replaced by the **Orchestra of the Age of Enlightenment**. Norrington is a frequent guest conductor worldwide.

North Carolina Symphony. Founded in 1932 in Raleigh, the symphony became the first state-supported orchestra in the United States. As such, it is known for giving concerts throughout the state, in cities and town of all sizes. The symphony sponsors the Triangle Youth Philharmonic, gives over forty-five free concerts a year annually for school children throughout the state, and has a **youth concerto competition**. It can be heard on radio broadcast

and has released several CDs. Its current music director is Grant Llewellyn.

North German Radio Symphony (Sinfonieorchester des Norddeutschen Rundfunks). The symphony orchestra of the North German Radio was founded in Hamburg after World War II by British occupying forces. Assembled during the initial months after armistice, the symphony gave its first concert in 1945. It functions as a traditional radio orchestra in that it often performs and records for broadcast. The symphony has recorded on the **Deutsche Grammophon**, **RCA Victor Red Seal**, and **EMI** labels, many conducted by Gunther Wand, music director from 1982 to 1990. In addition to comprehensive programming that includes new music and concerts that focus on Baroque and early music, the orchestra has an academy for the training of young orchestra players. The city of Hamburg is building a new performance facility called the **Elbphilharmonie** (the Elb is the river and "philharmonie" is the building) that will house both the symphony and the city's opera. One of the most exciting if not extravagant performance halls to being built in the world today, its opening has been delayed and its cost has risen to more than double original projections. Other **conductors** have included **Herbert Blomstedt**, **Christoph Eschenbach**, **Christoph Dohnányi**, and Thomas Hendelbrock. Its current principal guest conductor is American **Alan Gilbert**.

nota. (It. Sp.) **Note**, as in a musical note. (Fr. *note*, Ger. *Note*, It. *nota*.)

nota pedal. (Sp.) **Pedal note**, **pedal point**, a **pitch** held, usually in the bass, for a period while **dissonant** chords are sounded in the voices above. Originating with works for organ, a pedal-point passage generally begins and ends with a chord consonant to the bass. Although a pedal point can occur with any scale degree, it is most common for it to be either the dominant, as a return of the tonic is prepared, or at the end of a piece, using the tonic to reinforce the final key center. (Fr. *pédale*, Ger. *Orgepunkt*, It. *pedale*, Sp. *bajo de órgano*.)

notation. The techniques used to write down music in all of its varieties. (Fr. *notation*, Ger. *Notation*, It. *notazione*, Sp. *notación*.)

note. A notation symbol used to represent a **pitch**. Notes exist in a variety of forms that indicate length and are placed on a music stave that represents pitch. (Fr. *note*, Ger. *Note*, It. *nota*, Sp. *nota*.)

note blanche. (Fr.) Half note. See also **appendix 7**.

note class. See **pitch class**.

note complex. Any combination of pitches that sound simultaneously. The term is used in contemporary music to describe nontriadic chordal structures. Sometimes alternatively called a "simultaneity" or "vertical structure," also as an alternative to the traditional chord with its association with triadic harmony.

Notenhals. (Ger.) Stem of a **note**, such as the quarter note or half note. (Fr. *queue de la note, hampe*; It. *gambo*; Sp. *plica*.)

note noir. (Fr.) Quarter note. See also **appendix 7.**

Notenpult, pult. (Ger.) **Music stand**. (Fr. *pupitre*, It, *leggio*, Sp. *atril*.)

note qualities. A synonym for **pitch classes**, as devised by composer **György Ligeti** and others.

Notfall. (Ger.) Necessity, emergency, contingency. Example: *nur im Notfall zur*, only if necessary for.

notturno. (It.) Nocturne, a title of a piece or **movement**. (Fr. *nocturne*, Ger. *Notturno, Nachtstück*, Sp. *nocturno*.)

nouveau, de. (Fr.) Again, afresh. A directive often heard in rehearsal. (Fr. *encore*, Ger. *wieder*, It. *di nuove, ancora*, Sp. *nuevamente, de nuevo*.)

nouve, di, ancora. (It.) Again, afresh. A directive often heard in rehearsal. (Fr. *encore*, Ger. *wieder*, Sp. *nuevamente, de nuevo*.)

Novello, Alfred (1810–1896). English musician, singer, and publisher. Son of **Vincent Novello**, he began publishing at the age of nineteen. Referred to as "Alfred's shop" by the family, it developed into the publishing house **Novello & Co.** His business savvy and hard work added much to his father's initial efforts. In 1837, he acquired the copyright to Felix Mendelssohn's oratorio *St. Paul*. He founded two music journals, the *Musical World* and the *Musical Times*.

Novello & Co. A music publishing house begun in London by **Vincent Novello** in 1811. Through its publications, the firm had an enormous impact on the growth of choral singing in nineteenth-century England. One of its first publications was a two-volume *Collection of Sacred Music*; followed by *Twelve Easy Masses*, some of which Novello wrote himself; and later masses of Franz Joseph Haydn and Wolfgang Amadeus Mozart, which were unknown in England at the time. These editions included first-time printings of Novello's piano reductions of the full orchestra scores in the form of **vocal scores** or **octavo parts**. Key to their success was their playability. In 1825,

he published the famous five-volume set of seventeenth-century church music under the title *The Fitzwilliam Music*, and between 1826 and 1829, he published five volumes of Henry Purcell's sacred music. In 1829, Vincent's son **Alfred Novello**, age nineteen, began to work in the firm, setting up the first store. One of Alfred's most successful ventures was the first publication of individual pieces in the form of sheet music at very low cost, instead of the customary publication by subscription.

Novello, Vincent (1781–1861). English organist, **conductor**, composer, and publisher of Italian roots. In 1811, he began publishing music at his own expense and out of his home in order to make it available to a wider audience but also to his own choir. He organized performances of the choral music of Franz Joseph Haydn and Wolfgang Amadeus Mozart at a time when they were unfamiliar in England. Novello was a founding member of the Philharmonic Society of London (1813), frequently serving as one of their conductors, leading from the keyboard. He was also the conductor and accompanist for the Angelica Catalani opera company of the King's Theater. He married Mary Sabilla Hehl, and their home became a gathering place for the artists and musicians of day. The young Felix Mendelssohn and poets Percy Shelley and John Keats were among their visitors.

NS. Abbreviation for note series, as used in **twelve-tone practice**. Alternatively called "**original**" or "**prime**."

N. Simrock Verlag. A music publisher founded in 1793 by **Nikolaus Simrock**. Simrock Verlag issued many works of Wolfgang Amadeus Mozart, Ludwig van Beethoven, and Franz Joseph Haydn. The business was continued by Nikolaus's son, Peter Joseph, and grandson Fritz, who moved the firm to Berlin in 1870. They oversaw the publication of pieces by Johannes Brahms, Robert Schumann (*Symphony No. 3*), Max Bruch (*Violin Concerto No. 1*), Felix Mendelssohn (the oratorios *Elias* and *Paulus*), and Antonín Dvořák.

nuage. (Fr.) Cloud, also *nuages*, clouds, as seen in *Nuages*, the title of the first movement of Claude Debussy's *Nocturnes*. (Ger. *Wolke*, It. *nuvola*, Sp. *nube*.)

nuevamente, de nuevo. (Sp.) Again, afresh. A directive often used in rehearsal. (Fr. *encore, de nouveau*; Ger. *wieder*; It. *di nuove, ancora*.)

numbers, basic. It is extremely helpful to know numbers in the language of the orchestra or ensemble you are conducting. Following are some representative numbers in a selection of languages:

English: One, two, three, four, five, six, seven, eight, nine, ten, eleven, twelve, thirteen, fourteen, fifteen, sixteen, seventeen, eighteen, nineteen, twenty, twenty-one, thirty, forty, fifty, sixty, seventy, seventy-one, eighty, eighty-one, ninety, ninety-one, one hundred, one hundred one, two hundred, three hundred one.

French: un, deux, trois, quatre, cinq, six, sept, huit, neuf, dix, onze, douze, treize, quatorze, quinze, seize, dix-sept, six-huit, dix-neuf, vingt, vingt-et-un, trente, quarante, cinquante, soixante, soixante-dix, soixante et onze, quatre-vingts, quatre-vingt-un, quatre-vingt-dix, quatre-vingt-onze, cent, cent un, deux cent, trois cent un.

German: eins, zwei, drei vier, fünf, sechs, sieben acht, neun, zehn, elf, zwölf, dreizehn, vierzehn, fünfzehn, sechzehn, siebzehn, achtzehn, neunzehn, zwanzig, einundzwanzig, dreißig, vierzig, fünfzig, sechzig, siebzig, einundsiebzig, achtzig, einundachtzig, neunzig, einundneunzig, hundert (einhundert), hunderteins, zweihundert, dreihunderteins.

Italian: uno, due, tre, quattro, cinque, sei, sette, otto, nove, dieci, undici, dodici, tredici, quattordici, quindici, sedici, diciasette, diciotto, diciannove, venti, ventuno, trenta, quaranta, cinquanta, sessanta, settanta, settantuno, ottanta, ottantuno, novanta, novantuno, cento, centouno, duecento, trecentouna.

Spanish: uno, dos, tres, cuatro, cinco, seis, siete, ocho, nueve, diez, once, doce, trece, catorce, quince, dieciséis, diecisiete, dieciocho, diecinueve, veinte, viente uno, treinta, cuarenta, cincuenta, sesanta, setenta, setenta y uno, ochenta, ochenta y uno, noventa, noventa y uno, cien, ciento uno, doscientos, trescientos y uno.

número del compás. (Sp.) Measure number or bar number. Numbers inserted in scores and parts to facilitate rehearsal. (Fr. *nombre de mesures,* Ger. *Taktzahl,* It. *numero di battutue.*)

numero di battute. (It.) Measure number or bar number. Numbers inserted in scores and parts to facilitate rehearsal. (Fr. *nombre de mesures,* Ger. *Taktzahl,* Sp. *número de compás.*)

nuovo. (It.) New. (Fr. *neuf,* Ger. *neu,* Sp. *nuevo.*) Example: *nuova versione,* new version. (Fr. *nouvelle version,* Ger. *Neufassung,* Sp. *nueva versión.*)

nur. (Ger.) Only. (Fr. *seulement,* It. *soltanto,* Sp. *solo.*) Examples: *Nur ein kürzer Halt,* only a short stop; *Nur ein kurzes Anhalten,* just a short fermata.

nut. The devise at the bottom of the bow that is used to adjust the tension of the bow hair.

o. (It., Sp.) Or. (Fr. *ou,* Ger. *oder.*)

obbligato. (It.) From the word for "obligatory" in Italian. An essential but subordinate instrumental part. In the late eighteenth century, it became even more important.

Oberlin Conservatory of Music. Founded in 1865 in Oberlin, Ohio, it is the oldest continuously operating conservatory in the United States. The conservatory functions as part of Oberlin College, and its students have the opportunity to received dual degrees in both music and liberal arts. Primarily an undergraduate school, the conservatory was the recipient of the 2009 National Medal of the Arts. Its Technology in Music and Related Arts program (TIMARA) was the first conservatory program in electronic music, beginning in 1967.

oboe. A basically lyric double-reed instrument. Its range is from B-flat3 to G6. (Fr. *hautbois,* Ger. *Oboe,* It. *oboe,* Sp. *oboe.*) See also **appendix 3**, **bass oboe**, **oboe d'amore**, **heckelphone**.

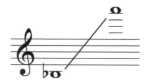

Oboe. *Courtesy Andrew Martin Smith.*

oboe d'amore. The mezzo soprano member of the **oboe** family, the oboe d'amore is a transposing instrument that sounds a minor third lower than written. Its written range is from B3 up to E6, sounding G-sharp3 to C-sharp6. (Fr. *hautbois d'amour,* Ger. *Oboe d'amore, Liebesoboe,* It. *oboe d'amore,* Sp. *oboe de amor.*)

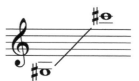

Oboe d'amore range as it sounds. *Courtesy Andrew Martin Smith.*

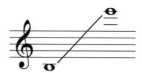

Oboe d'amore range as written. *Courtesy Andrew Martin Smith.*

octatonic scale. An eighth-note scale that alternates intervals of whole and half steps. Example: Joseph Schwantner's *Aftertones of Infinity.*

Octatonic Scale (HW)

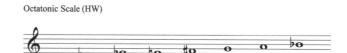

Octatonic scale 1. *Courtesy Andrew Martin Smith.*

Octatonic Scale (WH)

Octatonic scale 2. *Courtesy Andrew Martin Smith.*

octava. (Sp.) **Octave**. (Fr. *octave,* Ger. *Oktave,* It. *ottava.*) Examples: *octava baja,* octave lower; *octava superior,* octave higher. See also **appendix 6**.

octave. The interval made up of twelve half steps. Abbreviated 8va, 8a, 8.

octave. (Fr.) **Octave**. (Ger. *Oktave,* It. *ottava,* Sp. *octava.*) Examples: *octave supérieure,* octave higher; *octave inférieure,* octave lower. See also **appendix 6**.

octave equivalence. In tonal music, the principle that **notes** at the interval of an octave have the same harmonic function. In **twelve-tone music**, the concept that **pitches** an octave apart occupy the same position in the **twelve-tone row** or **set**.

octavin. (Fr.) **Piccolo**. See also **appendix 3**.

octavín, armónicos. (Sp.) **Harmonics**. Abbreviation *flag.* (Fr. *sons harmoniques, flageolet,* It. *suoni armonici, zufolo.*) See also **artificial harmonics, harmonic series, string harmonics**.

oeuvre. (Fr.) Work, similar to **opus**.

offen. (Ger.) **Open**, not muted, unstopped. (Fr. *ouvert,* It. *aperto, sfogato,* Sp. *abierto.*)

ogni, ciascuno. (It.) Each, every, any. (Fr. *chaque,* Ger. *jede, jeder, jeder,* Sp. *todo, cada.*) See also *ogni volta*.

ogni volta. (It.) Every time. A directive heard in rehearsal. (Fr. *toutes les fois, chaque fois que,* Ger. *jedesmal,* Sp. *cada vez.*)

ohne. (Ger.) Without. (Fr. *sans,* It. *senza,* Sp. *sin.*) Examples: *ohne Nachschlag,* without a turn (at the end of a trill, for instance); *ohne zu wechseln,* without changing; *ohne Wiederholung,* without repeating (Fr. *sans changer, sans reprise,* It. *senza cambiare, senza replica,* Sp. *sin repetición.*)

ohne Dämpfer. (Ger.) Without the mute. (It. *senza sordino,* Fr. *sans sourdine,* Sp. *sin sordina.*)

oîdo absolute. (Sp.) **Absolute pitch, perfect pitch**. The ability to recall any **pitch** without reference to any instrument or tuning device. (Fr. *oreille absolue,* Ger. *absolutes Gehör,* It. *orecchio assoluto.*)

oír. (Sp.) To hear, heard. (Ger. *hören,* It. *udire,* Fr. *entendre, entendu.*) See also **play by ear, to**.

Oktave. (Ger.) **Octave**. (Fr. *octave,* It. *ottava,* Sp. *octava.*) Examples: *Oktave höher,* octave higher; *Oktave tiefer,* octave lower. See also **appendix 6**.

Oktavflöte. (Ger.) Archaic name for the **piccolo**. See also **appendix 3**.

ombre, dans l'. (Fr., It.) As in the shadow, background. (Ger. *Im Schatten.*)

"On Conducting; Theory of the Art of Conducting." An essay written by **Hector Berlioz** at a time when the technique of **conducting** was beginning to develop standards. Berlioz lays out in diagram form conducting patterns for each meter and solutions to numerous problems that might present themselves in the known repertoire. He acknowledges the difficulty of mastering the totality of **conducting techniques**, including the ability to read a score, to hear and to see, to understand the nature and range of the instruments, to be resourceful and energetic, and additional "almost indefinable gifts, without which the invisible contact between" **conductor** and "performers cannot be established. Lacking these, he cannot transmit his feelings to the players and has no dominating power or guiding influence. He is no longer a director and leader, but simply a time-beater, provided he is able to beat and divide time regularly."

He also vividly described the damage the conductor can carry out on a perfectly good piece of contemporary music. Lamenting that "when new works are performed for the first time, the public and even listeners endowed with the highest musical intelligence are unable to recognize the ravages perpetrated by the stupidities, blunders and other offenses of the conductor."

In his essay on the orchestra, he describes a rather extravagant ideal ensemble, one that he feels he could put together in Paris, as numbering 465 instrumentalists! That includes 120 **violins**, 37 **bass** players of various kinds, 12 **bassoons**, 3 ophicleides, multiple saxophones, 30 **harps**, 30 pianofortes, and masses of percussionists! The sheer numbers would demand at least one conductor, if not more than one. He also suggested improvements in rehearsal methods for both choirs and orchestras, for the first time coming up with the idea of sectionals as a better way to initially learn difficult pieces. See the **bibliography**.

ondeggiando. (It.) Undulating. (Fr. *ondulé, ondoyant,* Ger. *wogend,* Sp. *ondulante.*) See *ondulé*.

ondes Martenot. An electronic instrument invented by **Maurice Martenot** (1898–1980). Several versions of the instrument were made during the twentieth century, changing according to the technical developments that facilitated its function. Its sound is characterized by wide glissandos and expressive **portamentos** that are vocal in nature. Of the many composers who used it, Olivier Messiaen may have been the most influential, incorporating it into in his *Trois petites liturgies de la presence divine* (1943–1944), in addition to *Turangalîlq Symphony* (1946–1948). Other composers who used the instrument are Edgar Varèse, Tristan Murail, Maurice Jarre, and **Pierre Boulez**. See also **electronic instruments, Moog synthesizer, Theremin**.

ondulante. (Sp.) Undulating. (Fr. *ondulé, ondoyant,* Ger. *wogend,* It. *ondeggiando.*) See *ondulé.*

ondulé. (Fr. lit. "undulating.") A bow stroke in which the bow alternates between two adjacent strings in the same direction. There can be as few as two notes alternating or several, and it can be done between two different "versions" of the same **pitch**, say an open string and a stopped, or a fingered "version" of the same **note**, thus creating a specific coloring effect. (Ger. *wogend,* It. *ondeggiando,* Sp. *ondulante.*)

one-count preparation. See **entrances on incomplete beats, fractional beat preparations**.

one-interval set. A **twelve-tone row** devised by repeatedly using the same interval. An example is the use of successive fifths or fourths, C–G, D–A, E–B, and so on.

op. Abbreviation for **opus**.

open. An indication that is seen in brass parts after the notation "closed," when the player mutes the sound by inserting the hand partway into the bell of the instrument or using by a mute. When stopping the horn with the hand, the pitch rises by a half step and the player must adjust. When using the mute, the pitches don't change. (Fr. *ouvert,* Ger. *offen,* It. *aperto, sfogato,* Sp. *abierto.*) See also **brass mutes, stopped**.

open chord. A term used in contemporary music to describe the "open sound" of chords built on fourths and fifths. Examples include Aaron Copland's *Appalachian Spring* and Samuel Adler's String Quartet No. 10.

open forms. An aleatoric compositional technique by which the order of events is left up to the **conductor** or performers. Examples include Lucas Foss's *Baroque Variations,* Earle Brown's *Twenty-five Pages* for multiple pianos, and Witold Lutosławski's String Quartet No. 2.

open rehearsals. Orchestra rehearsals that, in contrast to most, are made open to an audience. They are often used as perks for supporters of an orchestra, a special event in addition to a purchased subscription to a concert series or a donation. Most often the open rehearsal will be the final **dress rehearsal** before a concert, when most details of interpretation have been established. Those in attendance will, as a consequence, usually hear a complete run-through of each work.

open strings. A string played without any fingers holding down a **pitch**. The open string has a particular openness and resonance because the entire length of the string is vibrating. Some composers specify the use of open strings because of this sound. (Fr. *corde à vide,* Ger. *leere Saite,* It. *corda vuota,* Sp. *cuerda al aire.*)

Oper. (Ger.) **Opera.** (Fr. *opera,* It. *opera,* Sp. *ópera.*)

opera. (It.) **Opera.** (Fr. *opera,* Ger. *Oper,* Sp. *ópera.*)

opera. A drama set to music with singers, orchestra, and sometimes ballet. Early opera forms included the **opera seria** and **opera buffa**, both of which had accompanied **recitative**, as well as the *Singspiel,* which used spoken dialogue. In the nineteenth century, developments included **grand opera** and **opéra comique**, both with ballet. Opéra comique often had spoken dialogue, while grand opera had accompanied recitative. One of the most influential opera composers of the nineteenth century, **Richard Wagner**, created the *Gesamtkunstwerk* (lit. "total work of art"), now commonly referred to as the **music drama**, where instrumental music took on a greater role in presenting the dramatic situation. In this form, the recitative was replaced with through-composed music. The twentieth century has seen a great expansion of forms, including the **monodrama**, an opera with one singer, such as *Erwartung* by **Arnold Schoenberg**, and the growth of the short, one-act opera; TV operas; and chamber operas. (Fr. *opera,* Ger. *Oper,* It. *opera,* Sp. *ópera.*)

ópera. (Sp.) **Opera.** (Fr. *opera,* Ger. *Oper,* It. *opera.*)

Opera America. A national service organization for **opera** in America, it was established in 1970 to support the "creation, presentation and enjoyment of opera" (www.operaamerica.org). Its membership includes nearly 150 professional companies, 300 associate and business members, and 2,000 individual members. It has over sixteen thousand subscribers to its electronic news service and has an annual conference, regional workshops, and other resources for its members.

Opera Australia (OA). The main **opera** company in Australia, it has an eight-month season at the **Sydney Opera House** and spends the rest of the year at the Arts Centre Melbourne. The company has had a long association with the great Australian soprano Dame Joan Sutherland and her husband, **conductor** Richard Bonynge, who served as the opera's music director from 1976 to 1987. Both Sutherland and Bonynge helped bring about the construction of the Sydney Opera House (opened in 1973) and the growth of the company itself. Other important periods of growth included the tenure of Edward Downes, who served a music director from 1972 to 1976. Downes led the first Australian performances of **Richard Strauss**'s *Der Rosenkavalier* and Sergei Prokofiev's *War and Peace*, in addition to many others. OA has had many innovative programming initiatives, including The National Opera Workshop, which presented operas of select Australian composers in a workshop format. They are also very active in presenting opera for youth across all of Australia. From 2011, OA has begun to bring high-definition recorded performances to broadcast in cinemas and has promoted **DVDs**, **Blu-ray**, and **CDs** released on its own label.

opera buffa. A term used for a genre of comic **opera** that developed in Italy in the eighteenth century. The form developed along side **opera seria**, fulfilling the public's desire for a comic outlet. As the form developed, it took on a wider variety of subjects; sometimes serious topics were presented in a comic setting. Wolfgang Amadeus Mozart's opera buffa *Don Giovanini*, which he called a "*Dramma giocoso*," is such an example.

Opera Carolina. Established in 1948 as the Charlotte Opera Association, it was renamed after a merger with North Carolina Opera in 1986. The general director and principal **conductor** is James Meena. The company presents a three-**opera** season of opera standards with the Charlotte Symphony Orchestra. Operas are performed in the original language with projected translations.

opéra comique. Specifically a French operatic form of the eighteenth, nineteenth, and twentieth centuries. Opéra comique was written with spoken dialogue and always had ballet. It began as a sort of antidote to **grand opera**, having its own public appeal, and over time took on more serious topics. Georges Bizet's *Carmen* was premiered at the Opéra-Comique in Paris in 1874 but only achieved success when it was performed with accompanied **recitative** in Vienna in 1875, three months after the composer's death.

Opera Company of Philadelphia. Now called **Opera Philadelphia**, the company merged with the Philadelphia Lyric Opera Company in 1975.

opera conducting. See **conducting in the pit**, **conducting opera**, **conducting technique**, **preparing the opera score**, **performance practice and tradition in opera**, **rehearsing opera**.

Opera House of the Year Award. An award given every year since 1994 for a distinguished **opera** house in Austria, Germany, or German-speaking Switzerland. In 2011, for the first time the prize went to La Monnaire, a house in Brussels.

opera in English. Sung in English, **opera** becomes more accessible to an audience that isn't multilingual. However, clear diction, even in English, can be an insurmountable issue, especially in a large house. No matter what, an overhead projection of text is valuable. See **conducting opera**, **conducting in the pit**, **opera in the original language**, **rehearing opera**, **performance practice and tradition in opera**, **preparing the opera score**.

opera in the original language. Setting the words to enhance the meaning is one of the principal goals of the **opera** composer. Expression in opera is an intricately bound combination of melodic shape and line, harmony, and rhythm with the meaning and sound of the words as sung. This is often the justification for doing opera in the original language. Another reason is the simple lack of a good translation. Some opera companies accommodate their English-speaking audiences by providing an overhead projection of an English translation. Others provide a synopsis of the plot in a program. See **conducting opera**, **conducting in the pit**, **opera in English**, **rehearing opera**, **performance practice and tradition in opera**, **preparing the opera score**.

Opera News. Published since 1936 by the **Metropolitan Opera**, it is a monthly magazine that focuses on **opera**. It provides information of interest to listeners of Met Opera radio broadcasts but also includes articles about the American and international opera scene. In addition, it includes artist and production profiles, performance reviews, and CD and DVD reviews. The magazine annually gives five **Opera News Awards** for distinguished achievement.

Opera News Awards. Five prizes given every year for distinguished achievement by *Opera News* magazine.

Opera Philadelphia. As of 2013, the name for the Philadelphia Opera Company. The company stages five productions each season, three in the **Academy of the Arts** and two chamber operas in the **Kimmel Center**'s Perelman Theatre. The company participates in the **Random Acts of Culture** initiative of the **John S. and James L. Knight Foundation**. In 2010, their "**pop-up**" **performance** of the *Brindisi* chorus from Giuseppi Verdi's *La Traviata* received over 3.4 million hits on YouTube, and more recently, a similar performance of the *Hallelujah* chorus from George Frideric Handel's *Messiah* at City Center Philadelphia attracted over 8 million. The company programs opera by contemporary composers such as Osvaldo Golijov and American Ricky Ian Gordon.

opera pit seating. Seating of an orchestra in an **opera** pit is organized in order to create the best acoustic result for the audience and particularly in a manner that will allow the singers to be heard easily. While each pit is different according to size and depth (how far under the stage it goes), the strings and winds are generally in the front, open area, with the brass and percussion further back. Horns are placed carefully so that their bells are not directly in front of a wall that will reflect their sound too quickly, making a louder and sometimes brittle sound.

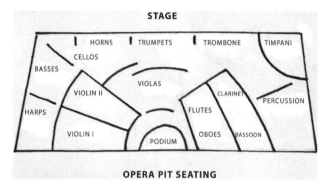

Opera pit orchestra seating. *Courtesy Derek Brennan.*

opera recitative. See **recitative, conducting recitative, appendix 8.**

opera seria. A term used to describe a form of Italian **opera** of the eighteenth and nineteenth century that was based on a serious or heroic tale. One of the great proponents of opera seria was the librettist Pietro Metastasio. He established a broad new stylistic basis for the structure of opera, principally, eliminating stories of a comic nature altogether. He changed the standard number of acts from five to three, shortened **recitatives**, and used arias that either revealed the singer's state of mind or somehow addressed the situation at hand. He made sure that all major roles had the same number of arias and never repeated the same type of aria twice in a row. There were three basic types of arias, virtually all da capo in structure. The bravura, display aria; the lyric cantabile; and the parlante, which was more speech-like in style. Two of the main composers in the style were Johann Adolf Hasse in Germany and later Venice and Niccolò Jommelli in Italy. Christoph Willibald Gluck (1714–1787), who had composed within the Metastasian framework, attempted to revitalize it by getting rid of its staid, overly formal nature in his operas *Orfeo ed Euridice* (1762), *Alceste* (1767), and others. Wolfgang Amadeus Mozart, who was greatly influenced by Gluck and his reforms, wrote

several opera serias, *Idomeneo* (1781) and *La Clemenza di Tito* (1791) being the two most famous.

operation. A term used in **twelve-tone music** to describe the permutation techniques, such as retrograde, inversion, and retrograde-inversion.

operetta. Light **opera**. Generally more popular and lighter in affect, operetta uses spoken dialogue, songs, and dance. The form was at its apex in the late nineteenth and early twentieth centuries and evolved into the musical and musical comedy. W. S. Gilbert and Arthur Sullivan in England, Johann Strauss and Franz Lehar in Austria, and Jacques Offenbach in Paris are among its greatest exemplars. In America, operetta began with Sigmund Romberg and Victor Herbert, developing into the musical with such composers as George Gershwin, Jerome Kern, Cole Porter, and Richard Rogers.

Operntextbuch. (Ger.) **Libretto**. (Fr. *livret d'opera*, It. *libretto*, Sp. *libreto*.)

***Opernwelt* (Opera World).** A monthly magazine for **opera**, **operetta**, and ballet in Germany. It includes articles and interviews with composers and performers; reviews of CDs, DVDs, and books; calendars of performances; and articles about opera houses and other performance spaces. Since 1994, it has selected an opera house in Austria, Germany, or German-speaking Switzerland for an **Opera House of the Year Award**. In 2011, for the first time the prize went to La Monnaire, a house in Brussels.

ophicleide. An instrument that was in use mainly in the first half of the nineteenth century. **Hector Berlioz, Felix Mendelssohn**, Robert Schumann, and others wrote for it. It has been completely replaced by the **tuba**, except for the occasional performance of Berlioz's ***Symphonie Fantastique*** or other such work in a place where the original instruments are available. The ophicleide looks somewhat like a metal **bassoon**. (Fr. *ophicléide*, Ger. *Ophikleide*, It. *oficleide*, Sp. *oficleide*.)

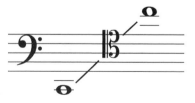

Ophicleide. *Courtesy Andrew Martin Smith.*

oppure. (It.) Or else. Indicates a possible alternative passage. Seen in Giuseppi Verdi, *oppure* is less commonly used than ***ossia***. Abbreviated *opp.*

opus. (Lat.) Work. Abbreviated *op.* (Fr. *oeuvre,* Ger. *Werk,* Sp. *obra.*)

Opus **(magazine).** An American music magazine that featured reviews of classical music recordings. It was published every other month from November 1984 to March 1988. James R. Oestreich was the editor.

Orchester. (Ger.) **Orchestra.** (Fr. *orchestre,* It. *orchestra,* Sp. *orquesta.*)

orchestra. An ensemble of strings, woodwinds, brass, and percussion instruments, with the possible addition of piano, other keyboards, and even electronic instruments. The modern orchestra is a flexible ensemble of various sizes that performs a wide variety of concert works such as symphonies; tone poems; works for orchestra and recorded sound; as an accompaniment to **opera,** oratorio, ballet, and compositions with a soloist, including concertos; and innumerable other forms of composition. The name "orchestra" may also apply to other types of ensembles, dance orchestras, jazz orchestras, and wind orchestras. (Fr. *orchestra,* Ger. *Orchester,* It. *orchestra,* Sp. *orquesta.*) See the **bibliography.**

orchestra balance. Refers to the relationship between the instruments of the **orchestra** in a performance. Good balance suggests that all of the instruments can be heard at any given moment.

orchestra bells. Alternative name for **glockenspiel.** Alternative foreign names are *carillon* (Fr.) and *campanette* (It.). See also **appendix 4.**

orchestral color. A visual reference used to describe various combinations of orchestral instruments. The idea of color in orchestral music developed as the variety of instruments and their capabilities grew, culminating in the music of the late nineteenth and twentieth centuries with the music of **Richard Strauss,** Maurice Ravel, **Claude Debussy,** and many others who followed.

orchestral hierarchy. See **hierarchy in the orchestra.**

Orchestra of the Age of Enlightenment (OAE). Established in 1986 as a self-governing ensemble of period instrument specialists, the OAE remains without a regular **conductor** but works with some of today's most distinguished conductors, including **Marin Alsop,** Harry Bicket, Christopher Hogwood, **René Jacobs,** Gustav Leonhardt, **Roger Norrington, Simon Rattle,** and others. The award-winning OAE is a resident ensemble of the Southbank Centre in London. In 2007, they began a young conductor program, inviting one conductor each season to work with the ensemble. The orchestra also has an apprenticeship program for young musicians interested in pursuing period instrument performance.

Orchestra of the Maggio Musicale Florence (Orchestra del Maggio Musicale Fiorentina). Founded in 1928, the orchestra became the official orchestra of the Florence Maggio Musicale Festival five years later (1933). Past **conductors** include **Riccardo Muti** (1969–1981) and **Zubin Mehta** (since 1985). The orchestra performs symphonic, **opera,** and ballet programming and has toured widely across the globe.

Orchestra of the National Academy of Santa Cecilia (Orchestra dell'Accademia Nazionale di Santa Cecilia). Founded in 1908 in Rome, the orchestra's current music director is Antonio Pappano (2005–present). Past music directors have included **Myung-Whun Chung** (1997–2005); Daniele Gatti (1992–1997); Uto Ughi (1987–1992); Guiseppe Sinopoli (1983–1987); Thomas Schippers, who died before being able to take the position (1976); Igor Markevitch (19973–1975); Fernando Previtali (1953–1973); **Franco Ferrara** (1944–1945); and Bernardino Molinari (1912–1944). The orchestra offers a full season of symphonic concerts and a wide variety of outreach programs directed toward families and youth, including Tutti a Santa Cecilia (Everyone at Santa Cecilia), a series for families; Mettiamoci all prova! (Let's Give It a Try!), where children get to sit on the stage alongside **orchestra** musicians; the JuniOrchestra (Youth Orchestra); Voci Bianche and Cantoria (Children's Choruses); the "Do, Re, Mi Fa . . . bene!" ("Do, Re, Mi . . . Is Good for Me!") series of concerts in hospitals; and Musica in-attesa (Music for Moms-to-Be).

orchestra score. The printed music that has all of the instruments and the music that they play represented on a single page. From top to bottom, the order begins with the woodwinds: **flute, oboes, clarinets, bassoons;** then the brass: **horns, trumpets, trombones, tubas;** timpani, followed by percussion; **harp,** keyboards; and strings: **violin** I, violin II, **violas, cellos,** and **basses.** The horn remains in the middle, even though its **pitch** is generally lower than the trumpet, because throughout history composers have used it either as a member of the woodwind section or the brass section. The trumpet and timpani are adjacent because in the classical era they were nearly always used as a unit. See also **Score in C, transposed score.**

orchestra seating charts. The history of the arrangement of the **orchestra** on the stage is fascinating and full of creative solutions to acoustic problems. Currently, there are two common seating charts, as seen in these figures. For further information, see Adam Carse, *The Orchestra from Beethoven to Berlioz* and *The Orchestra in the 18th century* (see the **bibliography**).

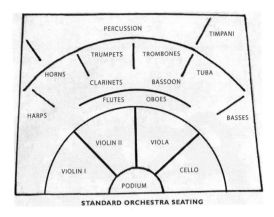

STANDARD ORCHESTRA SEATING

Courtesy Derek Brennan.

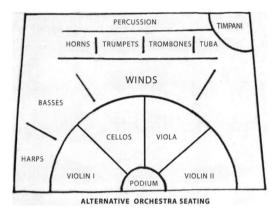

ALTERNATIVE ORCHESTRA SEATING

Alternative orchestra seating chart. *Courtesy Derek Brennan.*

orchestration. The art of combining the instruments of the **orchestra** to create sounds, colors, and textures. The term is sometimes used interchangeably with the more specific "instrumentation" in that it can apply to scoring for band or other ensemble. Orchestration has clearly grown along the development of the instruments of the ensemble, from the earliest Baroque orchestra to the largest works of **Richard Strauss**, **Arnold Schoenberg**, and **Igor Stravinsky**. (Fr. *orchestration*, Ger. *Orchestration*, It. *orchestrazione*, Sp. *orquestación*.) For further information and reference material, see the **bibliography**.

orchestre. (Fr.) **Orchestra**. (Ger. *Orchestrer*, It. *orchestra*, Sp. *orquesta*.)

Orchestre de la Société des Concerts du Conservatoire. Founded in 1828 in Paris by **François-Antoine Habeneck** (chief conductor, 1828–1848) with an opening concert featuring the music of contemporaries Ludwig van Beethoven, Gioacchino Rossini, Luigi Cherubini, and more. The **orchestra** was at the center of Parisian, if not European, musical life throughout its history. Run by the **Paris Conservatoire**, its first **conductor**, Habeneck led the premiere of **Hector Berlioz**'s *Symphonie fantastique*

and introduced the symphonies of Beethoven to the Parisian public. Other chief conductors include **Narcisse Girard** (1848–1860), Philippe Gaubert (1919–1938), **Charles Munch** (1938–1946), and **André Cluytens** (1946–1960). See also Holoman, D. Kern. *The Société des Concerts du Conservatoire (1828–1967)*. University of California Press, 2004. (See the **bibliography**.)

Orchestre de la Suisse Romande (OSR). Founded by **conductor Ernest Ansermet** in 1918 in Switzerland. He served as the artistic and music director, guiding the **orchestra** through its development into an internationally important ensemble until 1967. Ansermet made over three hundred recordings with the Suisse Romande. The current music director is **Neeme Järve** (2012–2015). Previous conductors include **Paul Kletzi** (1967–1970), **Wolfgang Sawallisch** (1970–1980), Horst Stein (1980–1985), Armin Jordan (1985–1997), **Fabio Luisi** (1997–2002), Pinchas Steinberg (2002–2005), and **Marek Janowski** (2005–2012).

Orchestre de Paris. Founded by **Charles Munch** in 1967 after the dissolution of the **Orchestra de la Société des Concerts du Conservatoire**. After Munch died in 1968, **Herbert von Karajan** served as the musical advisor until 1971. The **orchestra** has had a series of internationally renowned music directors, including **Sir Georg Solti** (1972–1975); **Daniel Barenboim** (1975–1989), who formed a partner chorus, the Chorus of the Orchestre de Paris (Coeur de l'Orchestre de Paris) in 1976; Semyon Bychkov (1989–1998); **Christoph von Dohnányi** (1998–2000, artistic advisor); and **Christoph Eschenbach** (2000–2010). The current music director is Paavo Järvi (2010–present). The orchestra offers many advantages to younger audience members and students through discounted tickets, attendance at open rehearsals, and more.

Orchestre symphonique de Montréal. See **Montreal Symphony Orchestra**.

OrchKids. A program for kids run by the **Baltimore Symphony Orchestra**. This is an after-school program with the goal of "effecting social change and nurturing promising futures" (BSOmusic.org). Children from inner-city schools in Baltimore commit to participating for a school year and learn how to play an instrument while also taking music skills classes and participating in ensemble experiences.

ordered pitch classes. A group of three or more pitches in a **twelve-tone** work, each from a different **pitch class** and having a specific order. An example being E, B-flat, and F, appearing in that order at different places in the composition. See also **unordered pitch classes**.

ordinaire. (Fr.) Normal, ordinary, to play in the ordinary manner, such as after a passage of ***sul ponticello*** for strings. (Ger. *gewöhnlich,* It. *ordinario,* Sp. *ordinario.*)

ordinario. (It., Sp.) Customary, normal, ordinary, to play in the ordinary manner, such as after a passage of ***sul ponticello*** for strings. Also ***modo ordinario.*** (Fr. *ordinaire,* Ger. *gewöhnlich.*)

oreille absolue. (Fr.) **Absolute pitch**, **perfect pitch**. The ability to recall any **pitch** without reference to any instrument or tuning device. (Ger. *absolutes Gehör,* It. *orecchio assoluto,* Sp. *oído absolute.*)

organ. A wind instrument with pipes and one or more keyboards. Its sound is produced by pressurized air driven through the pipes by valves that are controlled by a keyboard. In some organs, the air is gathered by a bellows, while many others have an air reservoir. The simplest organ has one pipe for each key, while more complicated ones use stops to control ranks of pipes that are capable of creating a wide variety of colors. An ancient instrument, its invention is attributed to Ctesibius of Alexandria in approximately 300 BC. (Fr. *orgue,* Ger. *Orgel,* It. *organo,* Sp. *órgano.*)

organized sound. A term coined by composer **Edgar Varèse** in order to define the concept of timbres, rhythms, and dynamics—elements of music other than melody or **pitch**—as music in themselves. The various aspects of organization would make a specific collection of sounds pleasing to the listener. Varèse's most notable work in this style is *Ionization* for thirteen percussionists.

Orgelpunkt. (Ger.) **Pedal note**, **pedal point**. (Fr. *point d'orgue,* It. *pedale,* Sp. *nota pedal.*)

orlo. (It.) Rim. Example: *all'orlo,* rim shot, an indication to play at the rim or edge of a drum. (Fr. *bord,* Ger. *Rand,* Sp. *aro.*)

Ormandy, Eugene. (1899–1985.) American **conductor** of Hungarian birth. A child prodigy violinist, Ormandy served as the music director of the **Philadelphia Orchestra** for forty-two years, from 1938 to 1980. He followed **Leopold Stokowski** and though less flamboyant, he emulated Stokowski's manner of conducting without a baton and often from memory. Ormandy built on the lush sound that Stokowski had established with repertoire from the late nineteenth and early twentieth century but also premiered a great deal of new music, including Sergei Rachmaninov's *Symphonic Dances* and Béla Bartók's Piano Concerto No. 3, in addition to works of **Sir Benjamin Britten**, Paul Hindemith, Bohuslav Martinů, Darius Milhaud, Vincent Persichetti, Anton Webern, and much American music by composers such as Samuel Barber,

Paul Creston, David Diamond, **Howard Hanson**, Walter Piston, Ned Rorem, William Schuman, Roger Sessions, and Virgil Thompson.

Orpheus Chamber Orchestra. A **conductor**-less chamber **orchestra** founded in 1972 in New York with the idea of exploring a variety of leadership styles. Without a conductor, the orchestra assigns members to take leadership roles in the interpretation and execution of individual pieces. To share these responsibilities, section principals rotate and rehearsals are organized so that members have the opportunity to express their opinions and ideas at set times. The **Grammy Award**–winning orchestra has released over seventy CDs, including works of all historical periods, and have been heard with many of today's outstanding solo artists. The leadership model they espouse, now called the Orpheus process, has attracted the attention of many both in and out of the music profession.

orquesta. (Sp.) **Orchestra.** (Fr. *orchestre,* Ger. *Orchester,* It. *orchestra.*)

Orquesta Sinfónica Simón Bolívar. See **Simón Bolívar Symphony Orchestra.**

Orquestra y Coro Nacionales de España. See **National Orchestra and Chorus of Spain.**

Oslo Philharmonic Orchestra (Filharmonien Oslo). Founded in 1919, the **orchestra** saw its greatest development during the long tenure of **Mariss Jansons** (1979–2002). Former chief **conductors** have included **Herbert Blomstedt** (1962–1968), **André Previn** (2002–2006), and **Jukka-Pekka Sarasate** (2006–2013). The current conductor is Vasily Petrenko (appointed in 2013). The orchestra presents a full season of symphonic, chamber music, family, and educational concerts.

ossia, oppure, ovvero. (It.) Otherwise, or, else. An indication to play an alternative (usually easier) version of a passage.

ostinato. (It., Sp.) A compositional technique involving the constant repetition of a musical phrase or motive, as in a passacaglia (lit, "obstinate," "persistent"). See ***basso ostinato.***

ôte, ôtez, ôtent. (Fr.) Remove, take away. Examples: ôtez la sourdine, remove the mute; *les 4 Cors ôtent la sourdine,* the four horns take out the mutes, from *De l'aube à midi sur la mer,* movement one from *La Mer* by Claude Debussy; ôtez vite les Sourdines, quickly remove the mutes, from *Gigues* of *Images* by Debussy. (Fr. *enlever la sourdine,* Ger. *Dämpfer ab, Dämpfer weg,* It. *togliere, togliere il sordino,* Sp. *quitar la sordina.*)

otra vez más rapido. (Sp.) Again, but faster. A phrase often used in rehearsal. Also *una vez más, pero ahora más* *rapido,* one more time, but this time faster (more polite). See also *encore, ancora.*

ottava. (It.) **Octave.** (Fr. *octave,* Ger. *Oktave,* Sp. *octava.*) See **appendix 6.**

ottavino, flauto piccolo. (It.) **Piccolo.** (Fr. *petite flûte, flûte piccolo,* Ger. *Pikkoloflöte, kleine Flöte,* Sp. *flautín.*) See **appendix 3.**

ottetto. (It.) Octet, an ensemble of eight performers. (Fr. *octuor,* Ger. *Oktett.*)

ottoni, stromenti d'ottoni. (It.) The instruments made out of brass; the section of the orchestra or band made up of those instruments. (Fr. *les cuivres,* Ger. *Blechblasinstrumente, Blechinstrumente,* It. *strumenti a fiato di ottone, gli ottoni,* Sp. *instrumentos de metal, metales.*)

outreach concerts. Concerts designed with the purpose of reaching nontraditional audiences. To achieve the goal, orchestras will often travel to perform in churches and community centers and include more popular repertoire, sometimes designed for an ethnically specific audience, and soloists who have audience-specific appeal.

outreach programs. Programs and concerts designed by orchestras to reach nontraditional audiences. This includes educational projects for young people and adults, concerts scheduled in unusual venues and at unusual times, concerts with unusual programs and guest artists, and much more. See entries for individual orchestras.

ouvert. (Fr.) **Open.** (Ger. *offen,* It. *aperto, sfogato,* Sp. *abierto.*)

overblowing. The technique used by certain wind players to sound a harmonic pitch higher than the fundamental. For instance, the **flute** is capable of sounding the second harmonic, an **octave** above the fundamental, when overblown. The **clarinet,** which sounds the odd-numbered harmonics, can be overblown at the twelfth, the third harmonic. For some instruments, a change in the **embouchure** combined with adjusted airflow can be used to produce higher harmonic tones. See also **harmonics, harmonic series.**

overtime. When any ensemble but particularly an **orchestra** rehearsal goes beyond the agreed upon time, it is considered overtime. Orchestral contracts cover overtime, generally specifying the amount of additional payment orchestra members will receive. (Fr. *Les heures supplémentaires,* Ger. *Überstunden,* It. *Ore supplementary.*)

overtone scale. A synthetic scale consisting of the eighth through the fourteenth partials of the **harmonic series.**

overtones, overtone series. See **harmonics, harmonic series.**

overture. A composition for **orchestra** written to introduce an **opera** or dramatic or vocal work, such as an oratorio. In the nineteenth to the twentieth century and beyond, the form of the independent concert overture has become common. Often opera overtures are extracted and performed on their own, occasionally needing the composition or arrangement of a **concert ending.** (Fr. *ouverture,* Ger. *Ouvertüre,* It. *ouverture, sinfonia,* Sp. *obertura.*)

The Oxford Companion to Music. A single-volume dictionary in the series of Oxford Companions published by Oxford University Press. The original was written by Percy Scholes and published in 1938. The next two versions were done by Denis Arnold (1983, two volumes) and Alison Latham (2002, single volume). The 2002 version is accessible on the Internet through **Oxford Music Online.**

Oxford Music Online. An Internet resource and portal for ***The Oxford Companion of Music,*** *The Oxford Dictionary of Music,* and ***The New Grove Dictionary of Music and Musicians.*** It is updated on an ongoing basis and is available by subscription to individuals and to libraries worldwide.

Ozawa, Seiji. (b. 1935.) American **conductor** of Japanese descent. Ozawa began studying at the **Toho School of Music** in Tokyo at age sixteen, switching from piano to **conducting** and composition after breaking two fingers playing rugby. His main conducting teacher was **Hideo Saito.** He conducted the **NHK Symphony Orchestra** in 1954 and the Japan Philharmonic Orchestra in 1958. Ozawa served as the music director of the **Toronto Symphony Orchestra** (1965–1969), the **San Francisco Symphony Orchestra** (1970–1976), and the **Boston Symphony Orchestra** (1973–2002). He founded the **Saito Kinen Orchestra** (Japan) in 1984. Ozawa credits his teacher Saito with his renowned technique and graceful style on the podium. He has a reputation for detailed and intense rehearsals and an excellent knowledge of the score. His most celebrated recordings are his **Mahler** symphony cycle with the Boston Symphony and a world premiere recording of Olivier Messiaen's *St. François d'Assise.*

Seiji Ozawa. *Courtesy Photofest.*

P. 1. Abbreviation for the dynamic *piano*.

2. The designation for the **prime version** of a **twelve-tone row**.

pabellón. (Sp.) Bell, of a **horn**, for instance. (Fr. *pavillon*, Ger. *Schalltrichter*, It. *padiglione*.) Example: *pabellón en alto*, bells up. (Fr. *pavillon en l'air*, Ger. *Schalltrichter auf*, It. *padiglioni in alto*.)

padiglioni. (It.) Bell of a **horn**. (Fr. *pavillon*, Ger. *Schalltrichter*, Sp. *pabellón*.) Example: *padiglioni in alto*, bells up. (Fr. *pavillon en l'air*, Ger. *Schalltrichter auf*, Sp. *pabellón arriba*.)

page, feuille. (Fr.) A sheet, leaf, or page of music. (Ger. *Blatt, Seite*, It. *pagina, foglia*, Sp. *página, folio*.)

Page, Robert. (b. 1927.) Choral/**orchestra conductor**. Page is music director emeritus of the Mendelssohn Choir of Pittsburgh and director of choral studies and the Paul Mellon Professor of Music at Carnegie Mellon University. He served as assistant conductor and director of choruses at the **Cleveland Orchestra** (1971–1989), conducting national radio and television broadcasts. Page is a founding member of **Chorus America**, a national service organization.

pagina, foglia. (It.) A sheet, leaf. or page of music. (Fr. *page, feuille*, Ger. *Blatt, Seite*, Sp. *página, folio*)

página, folio. (Sp.) A sheet, leaf. or page of music. (Fr. *page, feuille*, Ger. *Blatt, Seite*, It. *pagina, foglia*.)

Pak, Jung-Ho. (b. 1962.) American **conductor**. Pak served as the artistic director of the **San Diego Symphony** from 1989 to 2002 and of the **New Haven Symphony Orchestra** from 1999 to 2007. He is currently the music director

of the **World Youth Symphony Orchestra** and director of orchestras at the **Interlochen Center for the Arts** and the Cape Cod Symphony Orchestra.

palabra. (Sp.) Word. (Fr. *parole*, Ger. *Wort*, It. *parola*.)

palcoscenico, scena. (It.) Stage, of an opera house, for example. (Fr. *scène, planches*, Ger. *Bühne, Szene*, Sp. *escena, etapa*.)

palindrome. Anything that reads the same way forward and backward. Melodies, rhythmic patterns, chord progressions, and even **operas**, have been written with this technique. Retrograde canons are palindromes. Composer Paul Hindemith used the technique in various ways, his Fugue in F from *Ludus Tonalis*, uses a musical palindrome and in his opera *Hin und zurück*, both the music and plot are written as palindromes.

panchromatic chord. A group of notes sounded simultaneously that uses most or all twelve pitches of the **chromatic scale**. See also **tone cluster**.

panchromaticism. The free use of all twelve pitches of the **chromatic scale**.

pandereta. (Sp.) Tambourine. (Fr. *tambour de basque, tambourin basque*, Ger. *Schellentrommel, Tamburin*, It. *tamburello basco*.) See also **appendix 4**.

pandiatonicism. A compositional technique that freely uses all of the pitches of a given **diatonic scale**. Often in the form of a cluster melody or harmonic, it functions outside the rules of common practice tonality. Used by such composers as **Aaron Copland**, Roy Harris, Henry Cowell, William Schuman, and others, the term was coined by American musicologist **Nicholas Slonimsky**.

panno. (It.) A piece of cloth used to **muffle** a drum. See also *couvert, sourd, coperto, velato, bedeckt, cubierto, tapado*.

pantonality. A term **Arnold Schoenberg** preferred above **atonality** in order to describe his **twelve-tone** practices. He regarded it as a synthesis of tonalities as opposed to a combination of all tonalities. Now used interchangeably with "atonality."

Panula, Jorma. (b. 1930.) Finnish **conductor** and pedagogue at the Sibelius Academy of Music in Helsinki, Finland; the **Royal College of Music in Stockholm**, Sweden; and the Royal Danish Academy of Music. Panula served as the artistic director and chief conductor of the Turku Philharmonic (1963–1965), the **Helsinki Philharmonic Orchestra** (1965–1972), and the Arhus Symphony Orchestra (1973–1976). His many successful students include **Esa-Pekka Salonen, Jukka-Pekka Saraste, Osmo Vänskä**, and others.

par. (Fr.) By. Example: *par pupitre*, by stand or one stand at a time.

parallele Tonarten. (Ger.) The relative minor to a major key or visa versa. Example: A minor is the relative minor key of C major, and B minor the relative of D major. (Fr. *relative majeur, relative mineur*, It. *tonalità relativa*, Sp. *tonalidad relativa* or *tonalidad paralela*.)

parallel harmony. The motion of chords, mostly in stepwise fashion, up or down, in which the structure of the chords, that is, the pitch relationships, are maintained. Frequently used in **impressionistic music** to cloud the traditional harmonic functions of individual chords and create a coloristic effect. Examples include Claude Debussy's *Nuages* from Nocturnes or his work for piano solo, *The Sunken Cathedral*, but also **Igor Stravinsky's** *Petrouchka* and the trumpet passage at the opening of the second act of Giacomo Puccini's *La boheme*.

parallelism. A term originating in Gregorian chant and parallel organum where a melody is doubled throughout in parallel fifths. In the late nineteenth and twentieth centuries it appears as the simultaneous movement of two or more musical lines at the same interval. Examples are the second movement of *Game of Pairs* (*Giuoco delle Coppie*) from the *Concerto for Orchestra* by Béla Bartók and Claude Debussy's *Nuages* from the Nocturnes.

parameter. A term adopted from mathematics in the twentieth century to describe the various functions in music. For example, pitch, rhythm, harmony, orchestration, texture, and form.

Paris, L'orchestre de. See **L'orchestre de Paris**.

Paris Conservatory (Conservatoire de Paris). See **National Superior Conservatory of Paris for Music and Dance (Conservatoire National Supérior de Musique et de Danse de Paris, CNSMDP)**.

Paris National Opera (Opéra de Paris). Founded in 1669, **Jean-Baptiste Lully** was the director from 1672 to until his death in 1687. The opera has two main venues, the Opéra Bastille, opened in 1989, and the older Palais Garnier. There is also a smaller hall beneath the Bastille. The company produced **opera** and ballet, running over 380 performances each season. Throughout its history, the Paris Opera has given numerous important operatic premieres.

Paris National Superior Conservatory for Music and Dance. See **National Superior Conservatory of Paris for Music and Dance (Conservatoire National Supérior de Musique et de Danse de Paris, CNSMDP)**.

Parker, Harlan. Well-known wind ensemble **conductor** and pedagogue. Parker has been the conductor of the Peabody Wind Ensemble since 1990 and the Peabody Youth Orchestra since 2007. He has given over thirty premieres with the wind ensemble and many successful recordings on the **Naxos** label. Parker is a well-known specialist in the **Laban movement technique**, having studied at the **Laban/Bartenieff Institute of Movement Studies** in New York.

parlando, parlante. (It.) Speech-like, singing in a speech-like manner, can be said to be in between aria and **recitative** style. (Fr. *en parlant, en disant*, Ger. *sprechend, redent*.) Related to *parlare, dire* (It.), to speak. (Fr. *parler, dire*, Ger. *sprechen, sagen*.)

parlato. (It.) Spoken, as opposed to sung, for example. The dialogue in an **operetta** such as *The Merry Widow* by Franz Lehár and *The Magic Flute* by Wolfgang Amadeus Mozart.

parola. (It.) Word. (Fr. *parole*, Ger. *Wort*, Sp. *palabra*.)

parole. (Fr.) Word. (Ger. *Wort*, It. *parola*, Sp. *palabra*.)

Parra, Alondra de la. (b. 1980.) Mexican **conductor** and founding conductor of the New York–based Philharmonic Orchestra of the Americas. Parra has also served as the artistic director of the Jalisco Philharmonic Orchestra. She studied **piano** and **conducting** at the **Manhattan School of Music** with **Kenneth Kiesler**.

parte. (It.) Part, role. Example: *colla parte*, with the part, meaning play with or accompany the solo part. (Fr. *partie, role*, Ger. *Partie, Rolle*, Sp. *parte*.)

partials. See harmonic series.

particella. (It.) A detailed sketch of a work in a few staves, sometimes more than two but not as many as in a full score. The particella is a version of a piece similar to a **short score** with much of the musical material is worked out but the orchestration is only suggested by instrument names or abbreviations.

partie. (Fr.) Part. Example: *Div. en 3 parties*, divided into three parts, from *Jeux du vagues*, movement two of *La Mer* by Claude Debussy. (Ger. *Partie*, It. *parte*, Sp. *parte*.)

partie finale. (Fr.) End, the concluding passage of a piece. (Ger. *Anhang, Schlusstiel*, It. *coda*, Sp. *coda*.)

partition. (Fr.) Full score. (Ger. *Partitur*, It. *partitura*, Sp. *partitura*.)

partition pour piano. (Fr.) Reduction for piano. (Ger. *Klavierquszug*, It. *riduzione per piano*, Sp. *reducción para piano*.)

Partitur. (Ger.) Full score. (Fr. *partition*, Ger. *Partitur*, It., Sp. *partitura*.)

partitura. (It., Sp.) Full score. (Fr. *partition*, Ger. *Partitur*.)

pas beaucoup. (Fr.) Not much, not enough. (Ger. *nicht viel*, It. *poco*, Sp. *no mucho*.)

pasión, con. (Sp.) With passion. An expression heard in rehearsal in order to evoke a particular character in the playing. (Fr. *avec passion*, Ger. *mit Passion*, It. *con passione*.)

passaggio. (It). A transition or modulation. Also passage work.

Pass auf! (Ger.) Attention! A valuable expression in rehearsal when a difficult moment approaches. (Fr. *Gare à toi!*, It. *Attenta!*, Sp. *¡Ten cuidado!*)

passion, avec. (Fr.) With passion. An expression heard in rehearsal in order to evoke a particular character in the playing. (Ger. *mit Passion*, It. *con passion*, Sp. *con passion*.)

Passion, mit. (Ger.) With passion. An expression heard in rehearsal in order to evoke a particular character

in the playing. (Fr. *avec passion*, It. *con passion*, Sp. *con passion*.)

passionné. (Fr.) Impassioned. A descriptive character word. (Ger. *leidenschaftlich*, It. *appassionata*.)

passionnément. (Fr.) Passionately. Seen in the score to the ballet *Jeux* by Claude Debussy.

passive gesture. A **conducting** gesture that does not motivate anyone to play. A gesture that marks a downbeat or series of downbeats. See also **dead beat**, **neutral gesture**.

pas trop. (Fr.) Not too much. (Ger. *nicht zuviel*, It. *non troppo*, Sp. *no demasiado*.)

pas trop vite. (Fr.) Not too fast. Seen in many French scores. (Ger. *nicht zu schnell*, It. *non troppo rapido*, Sp. *no demasiado rápido*.)

patterns, conducting. See **conducting beat patterns**, **conducting compound beat patterns**, **conducting dynamic changes**, **conducting in four**, **conducting pattern styles**, **subdivided beat patterns**, **conducting technique**.

Pauke, Pauken. (Ger.) **Timpani**, kettledrums. (Fr. *timbales*, It. *timpani*, Sp. *timbales*.) See also **appendix 4**.

pauroso. (It.) Fearful, timid. (Fr. *effroi*, Ger. *angstvoll*, Sp. *de miedo*.)

pausa. (It., Sp.) Rest. Example: *pause di blanca*, half rest. See **appendix 7** for translations.

pausa di biscroma. (It.) Thirty-second-note rest. See also **appendix 7**.

pausa di croma. (It.) Eighth-note rest. See also **appendix 7**.

pausa di minima. (It.) Half-note rest. See also **appendix 7**.

pausa di semibiscroma. (It.) Sixty-fourth-note rest. See also **appendix 7**.

pausa di semibreve. (It.) Whole-note rest. See also **appendix 7**.

pausa di semiminima. (It.) Quarter-note rest. See also **appendix 7**.

pausa general, silencio general. (Sp.) **Grand pause**, general pause (Fr. *pause générale*, Ger. *Generalpause, Schweigezeichen*, It. *pausa generale, vuoto*.)

pausa generale, vuoto. (It.) *General pause*, general pause. (Fr. *pause generale,* Ger. *Generalpause, Schweigezeichen,* Sp. *silencio general, pausa general.*)

pause. (Fr.) Rest. See **appendix 7** for translations.

Pause. (Ger.) Break, intermission, pause, rest, **fermata**. Examples: *halbe Pause,* half rest; *viertel Pause,* quarter rest. See **appendix 7** for translations.

pause generale. (Fr.) **Grand pause**, general pause (Ger. *Schweigezeichen,* It. *pausa generale, vuoto,* Sp. *pausa general, silencio general.*)

pauto, pentagramma. (Sp.) Staff, stave. The five-line system on which music is written. In a score, two or more staves connected by a "brace" or bar line. (Fr. *portée,* Ger. *Liniensystem, System, Fünfliniesystem,* It. *sistema, rigo.*)

pavillon. (Fr.) Bell of a wind instrument. (Ger. *Schalltrichter,* It. *padigiloni,* Sp. *pabellón.*) Example: *pavillon en l'air,* bells up. (Ger. *Schalltrichter auf,* It. *padiglioni in alto,* Sp. *pabellón arriba.*)

Peabody Institute. Founded in 1857 in Baltimore, Maryland, by philanthropist George Peabody, it is the second oldest music school in the United States after the **Oberlin Conservatory** in Ohio. Since 1985, it has been the Music School of **Johns Hopkins University**. The institute maintains a comprehensive curriculum of music studies, including a doctorate of musical arts in performance, **conducting**, and composition. The orchestral conducting program is directed by **Gustav Meier**. Markan Thakar is also on its faculty. Students work with a designated conductor's **orchestra** every week.

pedale. (It.) **Pedal point**, pedal note. (Fr. *point d'orgue,* Ger. *Orgelpunkt,* Sp. *nota pedal.*)

pedal glissando. On the timpani, a glissando made by depressing or loosening the pedal to glissando from one **pitch** to another pitch, up or down. Pedal glissando can also be accomplished on the harp by plucking a string and immediately depressing or loosening the pedal affecting that string either by a half or whole step.

pedal note. See **pedal point**.

pedal point. A note in the bass line that is sustained while the harmony in the upper parts changes. Although a pedal point can occur with any scale degree, it is most common for it to be either the dominant, as a return of the tonic is prepared or at the end of a piece, using the tonic to reinforce the final key center. It originated with works for the **organ**. (Fr. *point d'orgue,* Ger. *Orgelpunkt,* It. *pedale,* Sp. *nota pedal.*)

Penderecki, Krysztof. (b. 1933.) Polish composer and **conductor**. Penderecki is known especially for his compositions that use extended performance techniques and **graphic notation**, such as *Threnody for the Victims of Hiroshima, The St. Luke Passion,* his opera *The Devils of Loudon,* and many others that created significant new challenges for the conductor. Penderecki became a conductor, primarily of his own works, partly because it was helpful to have him present in order to clarify unfamiliar procedures and notations. In 1998, he led the premiere of his *Credo* for soloists, chorus, and **orchestra** at the Oregon Bach Festival. Penderecki has also conducted recordings of many of his orchestral works on **EMI**. In the past twenty or so years, there has been a marked change in Penderecki's compositional style and in his symphonies, viola concertos, cello concertos, and others; the style is much more traditionally twentieth century. See also *Threnody for the Victims of Hiroshima* (1960) in **appendix 1; aleatoric music, graphic notation**. See the **bibliography**.

pensieroso, pensoso. (It.) Thoughtful, pensive. A descriptive word. (Fr. *pensif,* Ger. *gedankenvoll,* Sp. *pensativo.*)

pensif. (Fr.) Thoughtful, pensive. A descriptive word. (Ger. *gedankenvoll,* It. *pensieroso, pensoso,* Sp. *pensativo.*)

pentagramma. (It.) **Staff, stave**, system. (Fr. *portée,* Ger. *Liniensystem, Fünfliniensystem,* Sp. *sistema de pentagramas.*)

pentagramma, pauto. (Sp.) **Staff, stave**, system. (Fr. *portée,* Ger. *Liniensystem, System, Fünfliniensystem,* It. *sistema.*)

pentatonic scale. A scale consisting of five **pitches** to the **octave**, easily remembered as the five black keys on the piano keyboard, starting on C-sharp. It can be transposed to begin on any pitch as long as that interval relationship is maintained. It is most commonly found in music of the Far East and Africa and composers such as Giacomo Puccini (*Madame Butterfly, Turandot*) Béla Bartók, Claude Debussy, Lou Harrison, and Henry Cowell. (Fr. *pentatonique,* Ger. *pentatonisch,* It. *péntatonico,* Sp. *escala pentáronica.*)

pequeño, pequeña. (Sp.) Little, small. Example: *pausa pequeña,* short rest. (Fr. *peu, petit,* Ger. *klein, wenig,* It. *poco, piccolo.*)

percussion. The section of the **orchestra** or **band** that includes all percussion instruments. The percussion is the most varied of all orchestra sections. To systematize this collection of instruments, this section is commonly divided into two large categories: instruments of definite pitch and instruments of indefinite pitch. In each category are idiophones, that is, instruments that produce sound through the vibration of the entire body, and membranophones, which produce sound by the vibration of a skin or membrane stretched over a resonating cavity. See also **appendix 4**.

percussione, strumenti a. (It.) Percussion instruments. (Fr. *instruments á percussion,* Ger. *Schlaginstrumente,* Sp. *instrumentos de percusión.*) See also **appendix 4**.

perdant, en se. (Fr.) Disappearing, dying away to nothing. Describing a manner of playing. (Ger. *sich verlierend, verebbend,* It. *perdendosi,* Sp. *desvaneciéndose, perdiéndose.*)

perdendosi. (It.) Disappearing, dying away to nothing. Describing a manner of playing. (Fr. *en se perdant,* Ger. *sich verlierend, verebbend,* Sp. *desvaneciéndose, perdiéndose.*)

perdiéndose, extinguiéndose, desvanesiéndose. (Sp.) Disappearing, dying away to nothing. Describing a manner of playing. (Fr. *en se perdant,* Ger. *sich verlierend, verebbend,* It. *perdendosi.*)

perfect pitch. The ability to sing any **pitch** without reference to any pitched instrument or device. Also **absolute pitch**. (Fr. *oreille absolue,* Ger. *absolutes Gehör,* It. *orecchio assoluto,* Sp. *oído absoluto.*) See also **relative pitch**.

"perfect" tempo. The ability to recall any tempo on demand without reference to a **metronome** or other such devise. Many **conductors** develop this ability by associating certain works with certain tempos. The metronome mark of quarter note = 120 is commonly associated with John Phillip Sousa's march *The Stars and Stripes.* With that tempo secure in his or her mind, the conductor can easily find other tempos through proportional relationships.

per finire. (It.) To the end, in order to finish. (Fr. *pour finir,* Ger. *zum Schluss,* Sp. *por último, para terminar.*)

performance. Fr. *exécution,* Ger. *Ausführung,* It. *esecuzione,* Sp. *representación, concierto.*

performance marks. Words, abbreviations, and symbols beyond those of **pitch** and rhythm that indicate the way in which the music should be played. The presence of such markings has increased as music has become more complex, but over time, composers have added marks and even instructional comments to facilitate the performance of a piece when they cannot be present.

performance practice. Trying to simulate the performance style of earlier musical periods based on scholarship. (Fr. *pratique de l'exécution,* Ger. *Aufführungspraxis,* It. *prassi d'esecuzione, pratica d'esecuzione,* Sp. *práctica de la interpretación, práctica de la ejecución.*) See also **performance practice and tradition in opera**.

performance practice and tradition in opera. While good critical editions of **opera** scores are only slowly coming into existence, opera **conductors** have the benefit of traditional recordings led by conductors such as **Arturo Toscanini**, who knew and worked with Giuseppi Verdi. Other conductors, such as **Rene Jacobs**, have made the study and application of performance-practice style to opera their focus, **conducting** exciting and inspiring recordings of repertoire ranging from George Frideric Handel to Wolfgang Amadeus Mozart and others. These recordings are an invaluable resource, especially as they document a growing knowledge of style and past practice.

One of the main issues opera conductors have to address is making cuts. While these decisions have to be made in consultation with the stage director, it should be noted that so-called traditional cuts were often based on difficulties in a specific opera house and never intended by the composer to be permanent. Composer **Gustav Mahler**, who, though not a composer of opera, did rise to become the music director of the **Vienna State Opera** and the early **Metropolitan Opera** in New York, commented that *tradition ist schlamperei,* that is, tradition is slothfulness. Investigation of cuts is up to good opera conductors and good editors.

Other common issues are adding notes, particularly high notes, and changing the key of an aria in order to accommodate a voice. Singers often want to add high notes to draw applause and conductors who object can be labeled "purists," if not "fuddy-duddies." The job of the conductor is to study each composer and ascertain a predilection to added notes. Mozart apparently encouraged the embellishment of arias. In his concert aria *Non so, d'onde viene* (K. 294), he wrote them in, not only on the repeat but at the beginning as well. Early works of Verdi show the use of cadenzas, but he dropped them altogether in his late operas. In *Un ballo in maschera,* Verdi incorporated cadenzas into the concluding bars of an aria. But his last operas are written out in every detail. Regarding the changing of keys, doing this was not unusual in a certain style of opera, especially **operetta**, where the arias were primarily a vehicle for the singer. It is also common to change the key of an aria when it is done on its own in an opera gala. However, the opera conductor must be very hesitant to change the key of an aria in any opera where it would negatively affect the overall harmonic sequence. See also **conducting opera, conducting in the pit, opera in English,**

opera in the original language, **preparing the opera score**, **rehearsing opera**. See also Pier Francesco Tosi, *Observations in the Florid Songs* (1743), and Johann Adam Hiller, *Treatise on Vocal Performance and Ornamentation* (1780, reissued in translation 2001). See the **bibliography**.

performance rights. These rights are issued by publishers until the music comes into public domain. (Fr. *droits d'execution*, Ger. *Aufführungsrecht*, It. *diritti d'esecuzione*, Sp. *derecho de interpretación*.) See **copyright law**, **ASCAP**, **BMI**, **publishers**.

Performing Arts Alliance (USA). The Performing Arts Alliance is a national network of more than thirty-three thousand organizational and individual members, making up the professional, nonprofit performing arts and presenting fields. For more than thirty years, the Performing Arts Alliance has been the premiere advocate for America's professional nonprofit arts organizations, artists, and their publics before the U.S. Congress and key policymakers. Through legislative and grassroots action, the Performing Arts Alliance advocates for national policies that recognize, enhance, and foster the contributions the performing arts make to America.

performing edition. An edition of a piece that was prepared with the needs of the performer in mind, containing editorial marks that make it easy to play without questions and debate.

performing the score. The concept of performing a piece exactly as it is printed.

period. In formal structure, a unit that combines the antecedent and consequent units of a phrase.

peripheral vision. The kind of vision that is often used by members of an ensemble when their primary focus has to be the music or **notes** on the page in order to keep track of the **conductor**'s gestures and indications.

per l'ultima volta. (It.) For the last time. (Fr. *pour la dernière fois*, Ger. *zum letzten Mal*, Sp. *por última vez*.)

permanecer. (Sp.) To stay, to remain. Example: *Permanezca fuerte todo el compás*, Stay loud the whole bar. (Fr. *rester*, Ger. *bleiben*, It. *restare, rimanere*.)

permutation. A term used to describe a change to the ordering of **pitches** in a **twelve-tone row**, including **inversion**, **retrograde**, and **retrograde inversion** of the row or a version of the row that begins on a pitch other than the first pitch of the original form of the row.

perpetual variation. A compositional technique using continuous transformation of musical material and avoiding exact repetition.

per tutta la durata. (It.) For the whole length, as in the whole note value. An expression used in rehearsal. (Fr. *Toute da durée, s'il vous plaît*, Ger. *Die ganze Länge, bitte*, Sp. *para toda la duración, por favor*.)

pesado. (Sp.) Heavy, weighted, weighty. A useful character word heard most often in the Italian form. (Fr. *pesant, lourd*, Ger. *schwer, schwerfällig*, It. *pesante, ponderato*)

pesante, ponderato. (It.) Heavy, weighted, weighty. A useful character word heard most often in the Italian form. (Fr. *pesant, lourd*, Ger. *schwer, schwerfällig*, Sp. *pesado*.)

pesant, lourd. (Fr.) Heavily, weighted, weighty. A useful character word heard most often in the Italian form. (Ger. *schwer, schwerfällig*, It. *pesante, ponderato* Sp. *pesado*.)

Peters, Carl Friedrich. (1779–1827.) Music publisher. Peters built his company through the purchase of two other firms and published first complete editions of the works of Johann Sebastian Bach and Franz Joseph Haydn. On his death in 1827, **Peters Music Publishing** was continued by several notable directors. Max Abraham (1831–1900) added works of Johannes Brahms, Edvard Grieg, Max Bruch, and **Richard Wagner** and started the "Peters edition" of inexpensive scores and the Peters Library, which was open to the public. His nephew, Henri Hinrichsen (1868–1942), took over in 1900, adding works of **Gustav Mahler**, **Richard Strauss**, Hugo Wolf, Max Reger, and Hans Pfitzner. In the early 1930s, Hinrichsen's three sons joined him in the business. Max Hinrichsen (1901–1965) moved to London in 1937, where he opened Hinrichson Edition. Its name was changed to Peters Edition in 1975. Max's brother Walter Hinrichsen settled in the United States, establishing C. F. Peters Corp. in 1948 and releasing the music of several American composers. The third son, Hans-Joachim Hinrichsen, died in a concentration camp during World War II. Though the business left the Hinrichsen family in 1939, after the war it was returned and is now divided into three equal parts in London, New York, and Frankfurt.

Peters Music Publishing. See **Peters, Carl Friedrich**.

Petrenko, Kirill. (b. 1972.) Russian **conductor**. Petrenko studied at the Vienna Academy and served as Kapellmeister at the Vienna Volksoper (1997–1999); music director of the Meiningen, Germany, **opera** (1999–2002), where he conducted the entire **Ring cycle** of **Richard Wagner**; and music director of the **Komische oper Berlin** (2002–2007). He was appointed music director of the **Bavarian State Opera** in 2013. Petrenko has been a guest conductor at the **Metropolitan Opera, New York**; the **Royal Opera House, Covent Garden**; and the **Vienna State Opera**. He has appeared as a guest conductor with the **Berlin Philharmonic**, the **Israel Philharmonic**, the **Gulbenkian Orchestra**, the **Cleveland Orchestra**, and many more.

Petrouchka chord. From the ballet *Petrouchka* by **Igor Stravinsky**. See also **iconic chords**.

Petrushka Chord

Petrouchka chord. Courtesy Andrew Martin Smith.

Petrucci Music Library. See **International Music Score Library Project (IMSLP)**.

peu á peu. (Fr.) Little by little. Example: *Animez peu à peu jusqu'à l'entrée du 6/8*, getting faster little by little up to the 6/8, from *De l'aube à midi sur la mer*, movement one of *La Mer* by Claude Debussy.

peu, petit. (Fr.) Little, small. Examples: *un peu*, a little; *un peu animé*, a little faster; *un petit peu*, a little bit. (Ger, *klein, wenig*, It. *poco, piccolo*, Sp. *pequeño, pequeña*.)

pezzo, brano. (It.) Piece, composition. Seems to be used for a work that is relatively small when compared to a symphony, for example, the *Pezzo Capriccioso* by Peter Ilyich Tchaikovsky, a piece for cello and orchestra. (Fr. *piece, morceau*, Ger. *Stück*, Sp. *pieza*.)

Pf. Abbreviation for pianoforte, the instrument, or the dynamic *poco forte*, which occurs rarely except in the works of Johannes Brahms.

Pfeife. (Ger.) Fife, whistle. (Fr. *sifflet*, It. *fischietto*, Sp. *pito*.)

phase, phasing. A compositional technique in which two or more instrumentalists or singers perform the same music at different rates of speed, going in and out of phase. Often beginning together and then using varying increases and/or decreases of speed in order to create the effect, coming back together at the end of a section or piece. It was first used in electronic music by composers such as **Karlheinz Stockhausen** and then adopted by Steve Reich and other minimalists.

Philadelphia Lyric Opera Company. Active between 1958 and 1974. It merged with the Philadelphia Grand Opera Company in 1975 to form the Opera Company of Philadelphia.

Philadelphia, Opera Company of. See **Opera Company of Philadelphia**.

Philadelphia Orchestra. Founded in 1900. Its music directors include Fritz Scheel (1900–1907), Karl Pohlig (1908–1912), **Leopold Stokowski** (1912–1938), **Eugene Ormandy** (1936–1980), **Riccardo Muti** (1980–1992), **Wolfgang Sawallisch** (1993–2003), **Christoph Eschenbach** (2003–2008), **Charles Dutoit** (2008–present, chief conductor 2008–2012), and **Yannick Nézrt-Séguin** (chief conductor 2013–present). The orchestra performed at the **Academy of Music** from its founding until 2001 when it moved into the **Kimmel Center**. Notable events in the history of the orchestra include composer **Richard Strauss** conducting a concert of his own music in 1904, a 1906 performance at the White House, and a tour to the then People's Republic of China under the direction of Ormandy in 1973. In 1925, it was the first orchestra to make electronic recordings; in 1929, it became the first orchestra to make a radio broadcast; in 1948, it made the first television broadcast; in 1997, it was the first major orchestra to give a live cybercast of a concert on the Internet; and in 2006, it was the first orchestra to offer downloads from its own website. It also simulcasts concerts into theaters, schools, and other performing arts centers through the company Specticast. Stokowski conducted the American premiere of **Gustav Mahler**'s *Symphony No. 8, Symphony of a Thousand* in 1916, and Ormandy conducted the premiere of Sergei Rachmaninoff's *Symphonic Dances* in 1941. The Philadephia Orchestra has recorded for several labels during its history, including **RCA Victor**, **Columbia**, and more recently the Finnish company Ondine. The orchestra has a tradition of outreach to the community with children's concerts dating back to 1921 under Stokowski. The orchestra maintains family concerts specifically for children ages six to twelve and their elders, the Sound All Around series for children ages three to five, eZseatU, and a membership program for full-time college students.

Philadelphia Singers. Founded in 1972 by Michael Korn, the choir is the resident choir of the **Philadelphia Orchestra**. It is known for American premieres of works by **Krysztof Penderecki**, James MacMillian, Luciano Berio, August Read Thomas, Daniel Kellogg, and Jennifer Higdon. David Hayes is the current music director.

Philharmonia Orchestra. Founded in 1945 in London by Walter Legge with many members just returning from war service. **Herbert von Karajan** and **Otto Klemperer**

were among its early influential **conductors**. One of the most recorded orchestras in the world, the Philharmonia has released over one thousand LPS and CDs and made soundtracks for several films, going back to the 1944 classic version of William Shakespeare's *Henry the Fifth* with Laurence Olivier. The orchestra has commissioned over one hundred new works and has an active profile on new media, including video **podcasts**, many of which appear on **YouTube**. **Riccardo Muti** was the principal conductor from 1973 to 1982, followed by Giuseppe Sinopoli (1984–1994) and **Christoph von Dohnányi** (1997–2008). Its current principal conductor is **Esa-Pekka Salonen** (2008–present), who together with the orchestra developed two innovative digital installation projects, *Universe of Sound* and *RE-RITE*. Filmed with multiple cameras (*RE-RITE* with twenty-nine and *Universe* thirty-seven), the projects use high-definition video and audio to transform a space into a virtual orchestra. Both projects allow the public to experience what it is like to be a member of the ensemble, a conductor, or even a composer. *Universe of Sound* uses the **Kinect technology** from **Xbox**, with conducting "pods" allowing visitors to try their hand at conducting the **orchestra**.

philharmonic. A name taken by certain musical organizations, especially orchestras, one of the oldest being the **Vienna Philharmonic Orchestra**. *The Oxford English Dictionary* defines it as one who loves harmony or is fond of or devoted to music. (Fr. *philharmonique*, Ger. *Philharmoniker*, It. *filarmonica*, Sp. *filarmónico*.)

philharmonic, philharmonia. Commonly used terms, along with **symphony** and **orchestra**, in the names of orchestral ensembles. Examples: **New York Philharmonic**, **London Philharmonia**, **Berliner Philharmoniker**, and so on.

Philharmonic Society (London). See **Royal Philharmonic Society**.

Philharmonic-Symphony Society of New York, Inc. The official name of the **New York Philharmonic** when it merged with the **New York Symphony Society** in 1928.

Philharmoniker. (Ger.) **Philharmonic.** (Fr. *philharmonique*, It. *filarmonica*, Sp. *filarmónico*.)

philharmonique. (Fr.) **Philharmonic.** (Ger. *Philharmoniker*, It. *filarmonica*, Sp. *filarmónico*.)

Phoenix Symphony (Arizona). Founded in 1947 to allow local musicians the opportunity to perform together, the orchestra has grown to become a fully professional full-time orchestra, giving over 275 concerts annually. The symphony presents classics and pops concerts and educational and chamber music programs in both Phoenix and the central Arizona area. Its most recent music director, Michael Christie (2005–2013), was made **conductor** laureate. Previous music directors include Hermann Michael (1997–2004), James Sedares (1989–1995), Theo Alcantara (1978–1988), **Eduardo Mata** (1972–1978), and others.

phonograph. The name used by Thomas Edison for his record player. The name is commonly used in the United States while "**gramophone**" is preferred in Britain.

photo galleries. Often seen on the Internet websites of **orchestras**. They usually feature photographs of orchestra members, the music director or **conductor** and other musical staff, soloists, guest artists, events of particular interest, tour concerts, and festivals where the orchestra performed. A photo gallery is a promotional tool that enables individuals to "get to know" or "stay in touch" with an orchestra that they are interested in.

photographic memory. The ability to remember music, among other things, at sight.

phrase. (Fr.) **Phrase.**

Phrase. (Ger.) **Phrase.**

phrase. A short sequence of **pitches** forming a generally cohesive unit within a period, **movement**, or piece. The phrase is often understood in linguistic terms to be closely linked to the rise and fall of a song text. In musical terms, it is a combination of melody, harmony, and rhythm that creates an organized unit with a beginning, middle, and end. In the Baroque and Classical periods, when balance was of primary importance, a phrase usually consisted of an antecedent and consequent supported by melodic, harmonic, and rhythmic elements in the sense of a statement and response. In the romantic era and beyond, there have been many changes to this fundamental structure in all musical aspects. (Fr. *phrase*, Ger. *Phrase*, It. *frase*, Sp. *frase*.)

phrasé. (Fr.) **Phrasing.** (Ger. *Phrasierung*, It. *fraseggio*, Sp. *fraseo*.)

Phrasierung. (Ger.) **Phrasing.** (Fr. *phrase*, It. *fraseggio*, Sp. *fraseo*.)

phrasing. The way a performer uses all possible techniques, such as dynamic, intensity, rhythm, and articulation, in order to realize the shape and character of the **phrase**.

Phrygian mode. See **church modes**.

piacere, a. (It.) At the pleasure of the performer, suggesting freedom of tempo and expression. Also *liberamente.* (Fr. *librement,* Ger. *nach Belieben,* Sp. *al gusto.*)

piacevole, gradevole. (It.) Pleasing, pleasant, agreeable. (Fr. *plaisant, agréable,* Ger. *angenehm,* Sp. *agradable, amable.*)

piangendo, lacrimando. (It.) Plaintive, crying. A character word. (Fr. *en pleurs,* Ger. *weinend,* Sp. *llanto.*)

pianissimo. (It.) Very soft, a dynamic indication commonly used in its Italian form. Abbreviated *PP.* See **dynamics** for musical symbols.

piano **(dynamic).** (It.) Quiet, a dynamic indication commonly used in its Italian form. Abbreviated *P.* See **dynamics** for musical symbols.

piano (instrument). A large stringed-keyboard instrument. Its strings are struck by hammers instead of being plucked, as in the case of the earlier **harpsichord.** Modern pianos come in two shapes, the grand piano, which has the strings lying horizontally, and the upright, with the strings vertical. The performer uses a keyboard that operates a system of felt-covered hammers that strike the strings, creating the tone. It should be noted that some models of the Bösendorfer piano have ninety-seven instead of the standard eighty-eight keys, giving the instrument eight **octaves.** (Fr. *clavier, piano,* Ger. *Klavier,* It. *piano,* Sp. *piano.*)

Piano range. *Courtesy Andrew Martin Smith.*

piano **(instrument).** (It., Sp.) **Piano (instrument).** (Fr. *clavier, piano,* Ger. *Klavier, Hammerklavier.*)

piano arrangement. A version of a work transcribed for **piano** that was originally for a different medium.

piano-conductor score. Used most often in musicals and **operettas,** it is a reduced version of the **full orchestra score.** The individual instrumental parts are represented on two or possibly three staves, with the vocal lines above. Occasionally it will include indications in the form of abbreviations of what instruments play which **notes** or lines. The advantage for the **conductor** is the ease of reading fewer staves; the disadvantage is not always knowing who in the **orchestra** plays which part.

pianoforte. See **piano (instrument).**

piano reduction. A version of an orchestral piece arranged or transcribed for the **piano.** It was most popular in the eighteenth and nineteenth centuries before the advent of radio and records, when the only way one could hear the music was at a concert or at home, as played on the piano. Piano reductions now exist primarily for concertos, **operas,** and musicals where a pianist is needed for rehearsal.

piano score. An arrangement or adaptation of an instrumental piece for **piano** alone.

piano-vocal score (PVO). A version of a score of a musical, **opera,** song, or other work for voice and accompaniment in a version for the voice(s) and **piano** alone.

piatti, cinelli. (It.) **Cymbals.** (Fr. *cymbals,* Ger. *Becken,* Sp. *platos.*) See **appendix 4.**

picado. 1. (Sp.) **Tonguing.** (Fr. *coup de langue,* Ger. *Zungenstoß, Zungenschlag,* It. *colpo di lingua.*)

    2. (Sp.) A short, quickly released note, like staccato.

    3. (Sp.) In bowing, short, detached notes produced without changing the direction of the bow. (Fr. *piqué,* Ger. *gestochen,* It. *piccato, picchiettato.*)

Picardy third. A practice begun around 1500 in the Picardie district of France in which the raised or major third of the tonic triad is used as the final chord in a piece that is otherwise predominantly the minor mode. (Fr. *tierce de Picarde,* Ger. *picardische Terz,* It. *terza picarda,* Sp. *tercera de Picardía.*) See also **tuning systems.**

piccato, picchiettato. 1. (It.) A short, quickly released note, like staccato.

    2. In bowing, short, detached notes produced without changing the direction of the bow. (Fr. *piqué,* Ger. *gestochen,* Sp. *picado.*)

picchettato. (It.) In string playing, to play with the wood of the bow. Most often heard in the Italian form **col legno.** (Fr. *avec le bois,* Ger. *mit der Bogenstrange.*)

piccolo. Extending the range of the **flute** family up an **octave,** the piccolo is a transposing instrument in that it sounds one octave higher than written. This range is written from D1 up to C7. The instrument has a powerful sound and can usually be heard above almost anything else in the orchestra. (Fr. *Petite flûte,* Ger. *Kleine Flöte,* It. *Flauto piccolo,* Sp. *flautín, octavin.*) See also **alto flute, appendix 3, bass flute.**

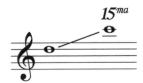

Piccolo range as it sounds. *Courtesy Andrew Martin Smith.*

Piccolo range as written. *Courtesy Andrew Martin Smith.*

piccolo, poco, scarso. (It.) Small. (Fr. *peu, petit,* Ger. *klein, wenig, knapp,* Sp. *pequeño, pequeña.*)

piccolo trumpet. A **trumpet** in D or E-flat, it appeared prominently in Baroque, twentieth-century, and twenty-first-century music. Examples: Johann Sebastian Bach's *Magnificat, Mass in B minor,* and Brandenburg Concerto No. 2; **Igor Stravinsky**'s *The Rite of Spring* and *Petrouchka;* **John Corigliano**'s *Circus Maximus* and *Symphony No. 3 for Large Wind Ensemble;* and many others.

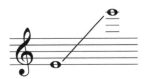

Piccolo trumpet range as it sounds. *Courtesy Andrew Martin Smith.*

Piccolo trumpet range as written. *Courtesy Andrew Martin Smith.*

pickup, upbeat gesture. As in a pickup gesture that happens just before a downbeat, anacrusis. (Fr. *levée, anacrouse,* Ger. *Auftakt, Anakrusis,* It. *in levare, levata, anacrusis.*) See also **preparatory gesture.**

piece. A musical work or composition, a piece of music. (Fr. *piece, morceau,* Ger. *Stück,* It. *pezzo,* Sp. *pieza.*)

pièce. (Fr.) **Piece.** (Ger. *Stück,* It. *pezzo,* Sp. *pieza.*)

piece, morceau. (Fr.) **Piece,** composition. (Ger. *Stück,* Sp. *pieza,* It. *pezzo, brano.*)

pieghevole. (It.) Flexible, accommodating, supple. A character word used to describe a particular manner of playing.

pieno. (It.) Full, loud. A descriptive term often used for dynamics or sound. (Fr. *plein, pleine,* Ger. *voll, mit vollem Ton,* Sp. *pleno.*)

Pierre Monteux School for Conductors and Orchestral Musicians. The summer school is an intensive training ground for **conductors** and **orchestra** musicians, annually covering a long list of both standard and less well-known orchestral works. Founded by **Pierre Monteux** in 1943 in Hancock, Maine, the school has had input from members of the Monteux family until recently. **Charles Bruck,** a French conductor and former student of Monteux, was the director from the mid-1960s until his death in 1995 and has been followed by conductor Michael Jinbo.

Pierrot Ensemble. A **new music ensemble** based on the instrumentation of **Arnold Schoenberg**'s work *Pierrot Lunaire.* With the seven performers, some doubling instruments, it has **flute/piccolo, clarinet/bass clarinet, violin/viola, cello, piano,** and a singer/narrator who uses *Sprechstimme.* See also **new music ensemble.**

Pierrot Lunaire. Composed by **Arnold Schoenberg** and premiered in 1912. An expressionist and atonal, though not twelve-tone, work for narrator and instruments, it uses twenty-one poems from Albert Giraud's poetic cycle of the same name as translated into German by Otto Eric Hartleben. A pivotal work in twentieth-century music, the narrator uses *Sprechstimme;* a combination of speaking and singing, it is often called a "melodrama." One of its distinguishing traits is the nature of its title character Pierrot as both hero and fool. *Pierrot* also signals the beginning of the era of the **new music ensemble,** the creation of smaller ensembles based on its instrumentation: **flute/piccolo, clarinet/bass clarinet, violin/viola, cello,** and **piano,** with a soprano serving as the narrator. It is sometimes performed with a **conductor.**

pieza. (It., Sp.) **Piece,** composition. (Fr. *pièce,* Ger. *Stück.*)

pincé. (Fr.) 1. Pizzicato, plucked.
    2. In the late seventeenth and eighteenth centuries, mordent. Also pinched. (Ger. *gezupft, Mordent,* It. *pizzicato, mordente,* Sp. *pizzicato.*)

piqué. (Fr.) 1. A short, quickly released note, like **staccato.**
    2. In bowing, short, detached notes produced without changing the direction of the bow. (Ger. *gestochen,* It. *piccato, picchiettato,* Sp. *picado.*)

piston. A **valve.** (Fr. *piston, cylinder,* Ger. *Ventil, Pumpventil,* It. *piston,* Sp. *pistón.*)

piston. (It.) A **valve.** (Fr. *piston, cylinder,* Ger. *Ventil, Pumpventil,* Sp. *pistón.*)

pistón. (Sp.) A **valve.** (Fr. *piston, cylinder,* Ger. *Ventil, Pumpventil,* It. *piston.*)

piston, cylinder. (Fr.) A **valve.** (Ger. *Ventil, Pumpventil,* It. *piston,* Sp. *pistón.*)

Piston, Walter. (1894–1976.) American composer, teacher, and author. A distinguished figure in American music, Piston wrote important books, including *Principles of Harmonic Analysis* (1933), *Harmony* (1941), *Counterpoint* (1947), and perhaps the most famous, *Orchestration* (1955). Piston wrote eight symphonies (Nos. 3 and 7 won the Pulitzer Prize), five string quartets, and several concertos. His *Symphony No. 2,* the *Viola Concerto,* and the *Fifth String Quartet* all won the New Music Critics' Circle Award. He taught at Harvard University from 1926 to his retirement in 1960. See also *trattenuto.*

pitch. A sound perceived as a tone or musical **note,** technically the function of a fundamental frequency or number of oscillations per second as measured in **Hertz.** As the number of frequencies increase, the pitch raises, and as they decrease, the pitch lowers. On the gamut of pitched sound, any point can be a pitch or tone; the fixed standard-given frequency is associated with a given pitch or tone, as in A440 for the normal tuning note of an **orchestra** in the United States (the norm being higher in many European countries). (Fr. *hauteur,* Ger. *Tonhöhe,* It. *intonazione,* Sp. *entonación.*)

pitch class. A **pitch,** such as C, without reference to which **octave** it is, such as c′. Consequently all Cs, no matter what octave, are the same pitch class. In Western music, each pitch class is represented once in each octave so that there are twelve pitch classes in the standard scale. **Milton Babbitt** coined the term in relation to **twelve-tone** or serial music in particular, but it is now used more broadly in the analysis of twentieth-century music.

pitch names. The pitch names or **note** names follow the order of the Western alphabet: A, B, C, D, E, F, and G. As they lie on the piano keyboard, they are all the white keys. To achieve names for the black keys, sharps and flats are used, as in A-sharp, B-sharp . . . A-flat, B-flat, and so on. To accommodate the more chromatic writing of composers, A-double-sharp and similarly B-double-flat have been added.

pitch names and their translations. See **appendix 5.**

pitch number. Originally meaning the number given to a **pitch** in a **twelve-tone row** that is based on an ascending **chromatic scale,** beginning with the first **note** of the prime or original version of the **row.** Current use assigns the integers 0 to 11 to the pitches of the chromatic scale, beginning on C. 0 = C, 1 = C-sharp, 2 = D, and so on.

pitch pipe. A small device that when blown through sounds any of several **pitches** in order to give a choir a starting pitch when no accompaniment precedes the entrance. (Fr. *choriste, flûte d'accord, diapason á bouche,* Ger. *Stimmpfeife,* It. *corista, diapason a fiato,* Sp. *diapasón de boca.*)

pito. (Sp.) Whistle, fife. (Fr. *sifflet,* Ger. *Pfeife,* It. *fischietto.*)

Pittsburgh Symphony Orchestra. Founded 1895, with **Victor Herbert** as its **conductor,** the **symphony**'s history, like many, was not continuous. Due to financial problems and a dispute between the local musicians and conductor Emil Paul, who wanted to bring in European players, the orchestra was dissolved in 1910. It was reestablish primarily through local initiative in 1926. **Fritz Reiner** served as the music director from 1938 to 1948. **William Steinberg** was the music director from 1952 to 1976, followed by **Andre Previn** (1976–1984), **Lorin Maazel** (1984–1996), and **Mariss Jansons** (1996–2004). For a few years, the **orchestra** worked with a team of conductors, **Sir Andrew Davis,** Yan Pascal Tortelier, and **Marek Janowski.** In 2008, Manfred Honeck was appointed music director, and **Leonard Slatkin** was appointed principal guest conductor.

più, di piu. (It.) More. Examples: *più allegro,* faster; or *piu forte,* louder; *più tosto,* more quickly. (Fr. *plus,* Ger. *mehr,* Sp. *más.*)

pizzicato. (It.) 1. Plucked. Widely understood in its Italian form. (Abbreviated pizz.)

2. Plucking the strings of a string instrument, most often with the fingers of the bow hand. Example: *pizz à vide,* pizzicato, open string, from *Jeux de vagues,* movement two from *La Mer* by Claude Debussy. See also **Bartók pizzicato.**

pizzicato gesture. A term for the gesture that is used when the strings are playing a pizzicato at the same time. While there are numerous ways of giving the gesture, it is characterized by a clarity that evokes unity of placement. Some **conductors** use a **preparatory beat** that begins and ends with an **ictus,** the first drawing the attention of the players and the second being simultaneous with the actual **pizzicato.** Others only give the second ictus, but preceded by a clear, smooth lift and followthrough. This kind of ictus is mostly in the wrist and is particularly swift off the pulse.

Pizzicato **magazine.** Founded in 1991, a monthly magazine published in Luxembourg that is devoted to classical music. It includes articles about the classical music scene and CD and DVD reviews.

placide. (Fr.) Tranquil, calm, placid. A character word often used to evoke a particular manner of playing. (Fr. *placide,* Ger. *friedlich, ruhig,*It., Sp. *placido.*)

placido. (It., Sp.) Tranquil, calm, placid. A character word often used to evoke a particular manner of playing. (Fr. *placide,* Ger. *friedlich, ruhig.*)

plaining. See **parallelism.**

plaintif. (Fr.) Plaintive, mournful. A character word often used to evoke a particular manner of playing. (Ger. *Klagend,* It. *lamentoso,* Sp. *lamentable.*)

plaisant, agréable. (Fr.) Pleasing, pleasant, agreeable. (Ger. *angenehm,* It. *piacevole, gradevole,* Sp. *agradable, amable.*)

planches, scène. (Fr.) Stage, of an opera house. for example. (Ger. *Bühne, Szene,* It. *scena, palcoscenico,* Sp. *escena, etapa.*)

planchette ronflante. (Fr.) **Bull-roarer.** (Ger. *Schwirrholz,* It. *legno frullante, tavoletta sibilante,* Sp. *roncador.*) See also **appendix 4.**

plaqué. (Fr.) An indication that the notes of a chord are to played together, not arpeggiated.

platillos. (Sp.) **Cymbals.** See also *piatti.* (Fr. *cymbals,* Ger. *Becken,* It. *piatti.*) See **appendix 4.**

please. A useful term. (Fr. *si'l vous plait,* Ger. *Bitte,* It. *per favore,* Sp. *por favor.*)

plectrum. (Fr.) A piece of hard plastic shaped as a rounded triangle used to pluck the strings of a guitar or other such instrument. A set of string players are required to play their instruments with the plectrum in **John Corigliano**'s *Symphony No. 1.*

plein, pleine. (Fr.) Full, loud. A descriptive term often used in describing dynamics or sound. Example: *avec en pleine sonorité,* with a full sound. (Ger. *voll, mit vollem Ton,* It. *pieno,* Sp. *pleno.*)

pleurs, en. (Fr.) Plaintive, crying. (Ger. *weinend,* It. *piangendo, lacrimando,* Sp. *llorando.*)

plica. (Sp.) **Note** stem, as on a quarter note or half note. (Fr. *hampe, queue de la note,* Ger. *Notenhals,* It. *gambo.*)

plötzlich. (Ger.) Abrupt, sudden, suddenly. A descriptive word seen in scores and parts and heard in rehearsal. Example: *plötzlich viel langsamer,* suddenly much slower, from *Pierrot Lunaire* by **Arnold Schoenberg.** (Fr. *tout á coup,* It. *di colpo, repente,* Sp. *subito.*)

plus. (Fr.) More. Examples: *le plus,* the most; *le plus vite possible,* as fast as possible; *plus encore,* still more; *plus encore vif,* still livelier; *de plus en plus,* more and more; *comme plus haut,* as above or as before. (Ger. *mehr,* It. *piú, di piú,* Sp. *más.*)

plus lent que. (Fr.) Slower than. . . . Example: *Un peu plus lent que le prelude,* a little slower than the prelude, from *Rapsodie Espagnole* by Maurice Ravel.

poco a poco cada vez más. (Sp.) An indication that indicates moving forward or increasing little by little, as in an **accelerando.** (Fr. *de plus en plus,* Ger. *allmählich mehr,* It. *poco a poco più.*)

poco a poco, graduado. (Sp.) Gradually, little by little, as in a gradual **crescendo** or **diminuendo.** (Fr. *graduel, coup sur coup,* Ger. *allmählich,* It. *gradamente.*)

poco a poco più. (It.) An indication that indicates moving forward or increasing little by little. (Fr. *de plus en plus,* Ger. *allmählich mehr,* Sp. *poco a poco cada vez más.*)

poco forte. A dynamic indication often used by Johannes Brahms. Abbreviated *PF.*

poco, piccolo. (It., Sp.) A little. Examples: *poco a poco,* little by little; *poco meno,* a little less; *poco più,* a little more. (Fr. *peu, petit,* Ger, *klein, wenig,* Sp. *pequeño, pequeña.*)

podcasts. A technology of making audio files available online via an automatic feed on a website. One can listen to podcasts on demand, whenever you want. Offered by many **orchestras** on their websites. Orchestras such as the **New York Philharmonic** produce audio podcasts with a known host preceding concerts as a way of promoting interest in upcoming events. Often orchestras maintain a library or archive of podcasts that can be accessed via the Internet. Podcasts are often created in subscription series.

podest, podium. (Ger.) Conductor's podium. (Fr. *podium, estrade,* It. *podio, pedana,* Sp. *pódium.*) See **podium, conductor's.**

podio, pedana. (It.) Conductor's podium. (Fr. *podium, estrade,* Ger. *Podium, Podest,* Sp. *pódium.*) See **podium, conductor's.**

pódium. (Sp.) Conductor's podium. (Fr. *podium, estrade,* Ger. *Podium, Podest,* It. *podio, pedana.*) See **podium, conductor's**.

podium, conductor's. A box, usually made out of wood, that **conductors** use so that they are elevated above the members of the ensemble and thus more visible to those who sit further away. Sometimes podiums have a metal bar across the back to provide a barrier between the conductor and the audience. It can be reassuring to the conductor in the case of a steep drop at the edge of the stage. Podiums can be carpeted on top to muffle the sound of the conductor's feet. (Fr. *podium, estrade,* Ger. *Podium, Podest,* It. *podio, pedana,* Sp. *pódium.*)

poetico. (It.) Poetic, lyrical. (Fr. *poétique,* Ger. *dichterisch,* Sp. *poético.*)

poético. (Sp.) Poetic, lyrical. (Fr. *poétique,* Ger. *dichterisch,* It. *poetico.*)

poétique. (Fr.) Poetic, lyrical. (It. *poetico,* Ger. *dichterisch,* Sp. *poético.*)

poi. (It.) After, afterward, then. Example: *poi la coda,* then play the coda. (Fr. *ensuite, puis,* Ger. *dann,* Sp. entonces.)

point. Also called the **tip**. A bowing term that indicates playing at the tip or point of the bow. (Fr. *pointe de l'archet,* Ger. *Bogenspitze,* It. *punta d'arco,* Sp. *con la punta.*) See **at the point**.

point d'arrêt. (Fr.) **Fermata**, pause. (Ger. *Haltung, Fermate,* It. *fermata, corona,* Sp. *calderòn, corona.*)

point d'orgue. (Fr.) **Pedal note**, pedal point. (Ger. *Orgelpunkt,* It. *pedale,* Sp. *nota pedal.*)

pointe, à la. (Fr.) 1. An indication to play at the **point** or **tip** of the bow. Example: *avec la pointe de l'archet,* with the point of the bow, from *Sirénes,* movement three of *Nocturnes* by Claude Debussy.
2. Point of the bow of a string instrument. Examples: *a la punta d'arco,* point or tip of the bow, *a punta,* at the tip of the bow. (Ger. *an der Sptize,* It. *punta,* Sp. *en el punta.*)

polarity. The attraction of a **pitch**, interval, or group of pitches toward a central point or pitch as described by **Igor Stravinsky** in *Poetics of Music* (1948). The term is used most often to apply to music composed outside of common harmonic practices.

polifonía. (Sp.) **Polyphony**. (Fr. *polyphonie,* Ger. *Mehrstimmigkeit, Polyphonie,* It. *polifonia.*)

polifonico. (It.) Polyphonic, many-voiced,. (Fr. *polyphonique,* Ger. *mehrstimmig, Vielstimmig,* Sp. *polifónico.*)

polifónico. (Sp.) Polyphonic, many-voiced. (Fr. *polyphonique,* Ger. *mehrstimmig, Vielstimmig,* It. *polifonico.*)

Polisi, Joseph. (b. 1947.) President of the **Juilliard School** since 1984. During his tenure, the Juilliard Residence Hall was built and the building underwent a major overhaul with the addition of a second orchestral rehearsal hall and many classrooms and studios. In partnership with Juilliard board president Bruce Kovner, the school has added an Early Music Program and has gained a collection of significant music manuscripts. Polisi is the author of *The Artist as Citizen* (2005) and *American Muse: The Life and Times of William Schuman* (2008).

pollice. (It.) Thumb. Specifically used to describe a particular manner of playing the tambourine. (Fr. *pouce,* Ger. *Daumen,* Sp. *pulgar.*) See also ***pollice, con il***.

pollice, con il. (It.) With the thumb. An indication specifically used to describe a particular manner of playing the tambourine. (Fr. *avec les pouce,* Ger. *mit dem Daumen,* Sp. *con pulgar.*)

polychord, polyharmony. A chord that consists of two or more identifiable tonal structures, such as the dominant and tonic of the tonality sounding simultaneously. For example, in **Aaron Copland**'s *Appalachian Spring* the opening material positions an A major chord in first inversion against an E major chord in second inversion. In other words, the I and V chord sounding simultaneously.

polymeter. The simultaneous use of two or more metric structures, generally producing cross accents. Used in **Igor Stravinsky**'s *The Soldier's Tale,* Charles Ives's *Three Places in New England,* and many more.

Polymeter: *The Soldier's Tale,* Igor Stravinsky, excerpt. *Courtesy Andrew Martin Smith.*

polyphonie. (Fr.) **Polyphony**. (Ger. *Mehrstimmigkeit, Polyphonie,* It. *polifonia,* Sp. *polifonía.*)

polyphonique. (Fr.) Polyphonic, many-voiced. (Ger. *mehrstimmig, Vielstimmig,* It. *polifonico,* Sp. *polifónico.*) See **polyphony**.

polyphony. Compositions that combine multiple distinct voices simultaneously, as opposed to monophony, which has only one. (Fr. *polyphonie,* Ger. *Mehrstimmigkeit,* It. *polifonia,* Sp. *polifonia.*)

polyrhythm. The simultaneous use of multiple rhythmic patterns within the same meter. For example, 3/4 simultaneously used with 6/8.

Polyrhythm: *Prelude to an Afternoon of a Faun,* Claude Debussy, excerpt. *Courtesy Andrew Martin Smith.*

polytonality, bitonality. The juxtaposition of two or more tonalities in which the scales and keys retain their identity. When only two are in use, the term **bitonality** is appropriate. Used by composers such as **Igor Stravinsky,** Béla Bartók, Darius Milhaud, and others.

pompa. (It., Sp.) Pomp. A character word sometimes used to describe a particular style of playing. Example: *con pompa,* with pomp. (Fr. *pompeux,* Ger. *prunkvoll,* It. *pomposo.*)

pompa movile a coulisse. (It.) Slide, a tuning device, as used with a trombone, for instance. (Fr. *coulisse,* Ger. *Zug,* Sp. *bomba de afinación.*)

pompeux. (Fr.) Stately, pompous. A character word. (Ger. *prunkvoll,* It. *pomposo,* Sp. *pomposo.*)

pomposo. (It., Sp.) Stately, pompous. A character word. (Fr. *pompeux,* Ger. *prunkvoll.*)

poner. (Sp.) To put. Examples: *poner la sordina,* put on the mutes; *poner la sordina gradualmente,* put on the mutes gradually. (Fr. *mettez,* Ger. *setzen, legen, stellen,* It. *mettere.*)

ponticello. (It.) The bridge of a string instrument. Also *sul ponticello,* on the bridge. A term used by string players to indicate playing with the bow very close to the bridge, creating a metallic quality of sound and an eerie, exotic effect. (Fr. *chevalet,* Ger. *steg,* It. *ponticello.* Sp. *puente.*)

"pop-up" performance. Unannounced performances usually held in places where the public gathers, such as malls, train stations, and so on. Used as an outreach technique by many performing organizations. See also

John S. and James L. Knight Foundation, Opera Philadelphia.

por fin. (Sp.) Finally, lastly. An indication seen in scores and parts that directs the performers to a closing section of a piece, such as a Vienese waltz. (Fr. *à la fin,* Ger. *zuletzt,* It. *alla fine.*)

portamento. (It., Sp.) Carrying the voice. In string playing, it refers to the glissando-like continuous movement of the finger between two **pitches** that creates a connected, sliding pitched sound. For singers it is similar, referring to the style of vocalizing the interval between two **notes** for expressive purposes. The Italian term is widely used.

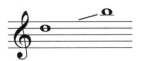

Portamento. *Courtesy Andrew Martin Smith.*

portato. (It. Sp.) A bow stroke where the bow pulses slightly between **notes,** generally written under a **slur,** moving in one direction. (Fr. *porté,* Ger. *getragen.*)

porté. (Fr.) (It. *protato,* Ger. *getragen,* Sp. *portato*) See ***portato.*** Same as ***louré.***

portée. (Fr.) **Staff,** stave, system. (Ger. *Liniensystem, Fünfliniensystem,* It. *pentagramma, sistema, rigo,* Sp. *sistema de pentagramas.*)

Portland Symphony Orchestra. This Portland, Maine, **orchestra**'s origins can be traced to 1923, when a group of area musicians recognized the need for an ensemble that they could play in. In 1924, the so-called Amateur Strand Symphony Orchestra, performing in the Strand Theatre, had seventy-five members. In 1939, the orchestra established Young People's Concert, the Portland Pops, and the Women's Auxiliary, which later became the Friends of the PSO, all of which continue to this day. In 1969, the orchestra changed its name to the current Portland Symphony Orchestra. In 1974, a commissioning program was launched, and works by composers Walter Piston and Elliott Schwartz were premiered. During the tenure of Bruce Hangen, the Portland Symphony Chamber Orchestra was founded, KinderKonzerts for very young children began, and the Portland Youth Wind Ensemble and Young People's String Consort were added. In 1980, the Magic of Christmas program was inaugurated. In 1984, Ned Rorem was commissioned to write an organ concerto and new summer concerts were added. Now a fully professional orchestra, it offers a wide variety of programming and outreach events. All classics concerts are broadcast on Maine Public Radio. Previous music directors include Richard Burgin, who at the time was also concertmaster and associate conductor of the **Boston Symphony Orchestra** (1952–1956); Rouben Gregorian (1958–1961); Arthur Bennett Lipkin (1962–1967); Paul Vermel (1967–1975); Bruce Hangen (1976–1986); and Toshiyuki Shimada (1986–2006). Its current music director is Robert Moody.

Portland Youth Philharmonic. Founded in 1924 as the Portland Junior Symphony. In 1910, music teacher Mary V. Dodge, who lived in Burns, Oregon, purchased instruments for children and organized an orchestra that became known as the Sagebrush Symphony Orchestra. The orchestra disbanded when Dodge moved to Portland, but that move created new opportunities. Hoping to create a permanent orchestra, Dodge convinced Jacques Gershkovitch to become the music director of the Portland Junior Symphony. On his death in 1953, **Jacob Avshalomov** took over the leadership position, serving for fifty-four years.

Portnoy, Donald. American **conductor** and pedagogue. Portnoy was the music director of the Augusta Symphony Orchestra from 1990 to 2009. He is professor of conducting and violin at the University of South Carolina and the director of the **Conductors Institute**, a summer program.

por última vez. (Sp.) For the last time. (Fr. *pour la derniére fois,* Ger. *zum letzten Mal,* It. *per l'ultima volta.*)

por último, para terminar. (Sp.) To the end, in order to finish. (Fr. *pour finir,* Ger. *zum Schluss,* It. *per finire.*)

Pos. 1. Abbreviation for *Posaune* (Ger.).
2. Abbreviation for left-hand positions on a string instrument.

Posaune. (Ger.) Trombone. See **appendix 3**.

posible. (Sp.) Possible, feasible. (Fr. *possible,* Ger. *möglich,* It. *possibile.*)

position ordinaire. (Fr.) In the normal or ordinary position. An indication in the music to change back to ordinary playing after a passage of playing in a special manner.

pos. nat. 1. (Fr.) An indication to play in the ordinary manner.
2. Abbreviation for *position natural.*

possibile. (It.) Possible, feasible. Example: *presto possibile,* as fast as possible. (Fr. *possible,* Ger. *möglich,* Sp. *posible.*)

possible. (Fr.) Possible, feasible. (Ger. *möglich,* It. *possibile,* Sp. *posible.*)

postlude. (Fr.) Postlude, sequel. (Ger. *Nachspiel,* It., Sp. *postludio.*)

postludio. (It., Sp.) Postlude, sequel. (Fr. *postlude,* Ger. *Nachspiel.*)

postmodernism. Music written in rebellion against the rigidity of modernism, manifested in a freedom of expression with widely eclectic styles. The term refers to compositions created in recent years that have moved back to a more traditional concept of tonality, melody, harmony, and form but not necessarily rejecting all the advances by the **avant garde** of the twentieth century. Examples of composers include **Krzysztopf Penderecki**, György Ligeti, Henryk Górecki, John Adams, Steve Reich, Philip Glass, Lou Harrison, John Zorn, and many others.

Potpourri. (Ger.) Potpourri, medley (lit. "rotten pot"). (Fr. *pot-pourri,* It. *pot-pourri,* Sp. *popurrí.*)

pouce. (Fr.) Thumb. (Sp. *pulgar,* Ger. *Daumen,* It. *pollice.*) See also *pouce, avec la.*

pouce, avec la. (Fr.) With the **thumb**. An indication specifically used to describe a particular manner of playing the tambourine. (Ger. *mit dem Daumen,* It. *con il pollice,* Sp. *con pulgar.*)

pour finir. (Fr.) To the end, in order to finish. (Ger. *zum Schluss,* It. *per finire,* Sp. *por último, por fin, para terminar.*)

pour la derniére fois. (Fr.) For the last time. (Ger. *zum letzten Mal,* It. *per l'ultima volta,* Sp. *por última vez.*)

poussé. (Fr.) A bowing term indicating to play up-bow, that is, in the direction going from the tip or point of the bow to the **frog** or heel (British usage). (Ger. *Aufstrich, Anstrich,* It. *arcata in su,* Sp. *arco arriba.*)

PP. Abbreviation for the dynamic *pianissimo,* meaning very soft.

Prague Conservatory. Founded in 1808 the school provides education in performance, composition, conducting, and acting. It has its own ensembles, all offering public performances, and a theater company. The list of alumni includes many distinguished musicians.

Prague Philharmonic Orchestra, City of. See **City of Prague Philharmonic Orchestra**.

Prague Symphony Orchestra. Founded in 1934 as an **orchestra** that would record for Czech film and radio and perform both **opera** and concerts. From the beginning, it had the acronym F-O-K (Film-Opera-Koncert), and it was this very diversity that guaranteed its existence and continued growth. The orchestra has recorded mostly for the **Supraphon** label.

Pralltriller, Schneller, Praller. (Ger.) An inverted mordent or mordent with the **note** above. (Fr. *mordant supérieur,* It. *mordent superior,* Sp. *mordent superior.*)

Prausnitz, Frederik. (1920–2004.) German-born American **conductor**. Prausnitz was the director of the **orchestra** at the **Peabody Institute** from to 1976 to 1980 and director of the orchestral **conducting** program from then until 1998. He is the author of *Score and Podium: A Complete Guide to Conducting* (1983) and "Roger Sessions: How a 'Difficult' Composer Got That Way" (2002). Prausnitz was an advocate for contemporary music throughout his career.

präzis. (Ger.) Exact, precise. A practical directive often used in rehearsal. (Fr. *précis,* It. *preciso,* Sp. *preciso.*)

précédent. (Fr.) Former, preceding. (Ger. *vorergehend, im Vorigen,* It. *precedente, anteriore,* Sp. *anterior.*)

precedente, anteriore. (It.) Former, preceding. (Fr. *précédent,* Ger. *vorergehend, im Vorigen,* Sp. *anterior.*)

precipitado. (Sp.) Rushed, hurried. (Fr. *précipité, bousculé,* Ger. *überstürtz, überhetzt,* It. *precipitato, precipitoso.*)

precipitarse, correr, prisa. (Sp.) To rush or to run ahead. Often heard as part of a negative directive, such as *No precipitarse!* Don't rush! Examples: *No precipitarse al final de la frase,* don't rush at the end of the phrase; *sin prisa,* without rushing. (Fr. *précipiter,* Ger. *eilen, drängend,* It. *precipitare.*)

précipitation, hâte. (Fr.) Haste, hurry. A descriptive often heard in the negative. Example: *sans précipitation,* without hurrying; *sans hâte,* without haste. (Ger. *Hast,* It. *fretta,* Sp. *prisa.*)

précipité, pressé, bousculé. (Fr.) Rushed, hurried. (Ger. *eilend, drängend,* It. *precipitoso, affrettando,* Sp. *apresurado.*)

précipiter. (Fr.) To rush or to run ahead. (Ger. *eilen, drängen,* It. *affretttarsi,* Sp. *correr, prisa, precipitarse.*)

precipitoso, affrettando. (It.) Hasty, rushing. Example: *non precipitoso,* not hasty. (Fr. *précipité, bousculé,* Ger. *eilend, drängend, Hastig,* Sp. *precipitado.*)

précis. (Fr.) Exact, precise. A very practical directive term. (Ger. *präzis,* It. *preciso,* Sp. *preciso.*) Example: *Assez animé (dans un rythme alerte mais précis).* Very animated (in an alert but precise rhythm), from *Gigues* of *Images* by Claude Debussy.

preciso. (It., Sp.) Exact, precise. A practical directive term. (Fr. *précis,* Ger. *präzis*)

prélude. (Fr.) Prelude, similar to an overture. (Ger. *Vorspiel,* It., Sp. *preludio.*)

Prelude to the Afternoon of a Faun (Prélude à L'apres mide d'un faune, 1894). A work by **Claude Debussy**. See **appendix 1**.

preludio. (It., Sp.) Prelude, similar to an overture. (Fr. *prélude,* Ger. *Vorspiel.*)

première. (Fr.) First performance, first night or opening night of a series of performances of an **opera** or musical. (Ger. *Premiere, erste Vorstellung,* It. *prima,* Sp. *estreno.*)

première chanteuse. (Fr.) The leading lady in an **opera**. (It. *prima donna,* Sp. *prima donna.*)

Premiere, erste Vorstellung. (Ger.) First performance, first night or opening night of a series of performances of an **opera** or musical. (Fr. *première,* It. *prima,* Sp. *estreno.*)

première execution mondiale. (Fr.) World premiere performance. (Ger. *Uraufführung,* It. *prima esecuczione mondiale,* Sp. *estreno mundial.*)

première execution mondiale, création. (Fr.) The first performance of a piece of music, the world première. (Ger. *Uraufführung,* It. *prima esecuczione mondiale, creazione,* Sp. *estreno mundial.*)

premiere fois. (Fr.) First time. The first and second endings of sections of a piece that are repeated or, followed by additional instructions, how to play a section of a piece the first time and then the second time. (Ger. *erstes Mal,* It. *prima volta, seconda volta,* Sp. *primer tiempo.*)

première représentation. (Fr.) First performance of a piece of music. (Ger. *Uraufführung,* It. *prima esecuzione,* Sp. *primera representación.*)

premier violon solo. (Fr.) Concertmaster, the first-chair player of the first violin section of the orchestra. (Ger. *Konzertmeister,* It. *primo violin, concertino/concertina,* Sp. *concertino.*)

prendere. (It.) To take up, to prepare to play a certain instrument. Example: *prendere il flauto,* take up the **flute**. (Fr.

prendre la flûte, Ger. *nehmen die Flüte,* Sp. *cambia el piccolo, cambia a la flauta.*)

prendre. (Fr.) Take. See ***prendere.***

preparation. See **score study**.

preparatory beat. See **preparatory gesture**.

preparatory beats with rests before entrances, conducting. See **conducting preparatory beats with rests before entrances**.

preparatory gesture. The motion given by the **conductor** in advance of the first sound that, creating inevitability through a simultaneous breath and smooth motion in the tempo, dynamic, and style of the music to come, prepares the ensemble for a precise entrance. Preparatory gestures can be given on any **beat** of the bar, depending on the composer's requirements. See also **conducting technique, fractional beat preparations, entrances on incomplete beats, conducting preparatory beats with rests before entrances, preparatory beat**.

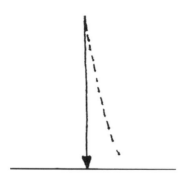

Preparatory gesture. *Courtesy Derek Brennan.*

preparatory motion. See **preparatory gesture**.

preparatory position. See **ready position**.

prepared piano. A **piano** in which the sounds of individual **notes** have been altered by placement of various objects, such as bolts, screws, pieces of felt, or rubber erasers, onto or woven into the strings. It originated with Henry Cowell and used by John Cage, George Crumb, and others.

preparing the opera score. The primary difference between preparing an orchestral work and an **opera** is the **libretto**. Opera **conductors** begin their work learning text of the libretto. If the opera is in a language they don't know, the conductor must learn it using a literal translation and perhaps enhancing it with a good poetic one. The meaning, expression, and proper execution of the text are vitally important. The conductor may meet with the vocal coach, whose job it will be to train the singers in correct diction and inflection. The next steps involve learning the vocal lines and the orchestral parts with equal effort and special attention to how they work together. Since good critical editions of opera scores are only slowly coming into existence, preparing an opera score based on "tradition" is a difficult matter. See Nico Castel's literal translations of opera librettos published by Leyerle Publications Mt. Morris, New York in the **bibliography**. See also **conducting in the pit, conducting opera, opera in English, opera in the original language, performance practice and tradition in opera, rehearsing opera, score study**.

preparing the parts. Conductors prepare the parts in order to save time in rehearsal. While time consuming, it is far worse to suffer the frustration of the ensemble under time pressure. Many issues can be avoided if the parts have been checked for accuracy. The fortunate conductor has a librarian to help with this process. Most important is the simple legibility of the music. However, often there isn't much that can be done, except finding a different edition or a printed rather than of handwritten set of parts. Other problems to look for are difficult page turns; checking for all *arco* and *pizzicato* markings; checking for all mute markings, that is, when they go on and when they come off; accuracy of clef changes; and consistency of articulation and bowings.

In the case of page-turn problems, **orchestra** players should be provided with extra copies of a page so that they can set it up on the music stand in order to keep reading the music until a convenient spot. Most important may be marking the bowings. Many professional concertmasters mark bowings as a matter of course, but this is not always true, so conductors need to verify that the parts on hand are already marked. While some conductors want their own bowings and will bring their own parts, some orchestras have a tradition of **"house parts"** that are already marked, and they will only play from them. See also **doubling parts, reorchestrating the parts**.

près. (Fr.) Near, close. (Ger. *nahe,* It. *vicino, presso.*) Example: *près de la table,* on the harp, near to the sounding board of the instrument, in order to achieve a more resonant sound. See also ***prés du chevalet***.

prés du chevalet. (Fr.) Close to the bridge. An indication to play with the bow on or near the bridge of a string instrument. This generates a more strained sound. (Ger. *am Steg,* It. *sul ponticello,* Sp. *sobre el puente.*)

presque. (Fr.) Almost, nearly, as if. (Ger. *beinahe, fast, als, ob,* It. *quasi,* Sp. *casi, cercano a, como, parecido a.*)

pressant. (Fr.) Pressing, pushing the tempo forward. Example: *au Mouvt et en pressant*, a tempo and pressing forward, from *Daphnis et Chloé* by Maurice Ravel.

Presser Company, Theodore. See **Theodore Presser Company**.

presser, pressé. (Fr.) Hurrying, hurried. (Ger. *eilen, eilte*, It. *affretando, affrettato*, Sp. *apresurándose, apresurando*.)

Presser, Theodore. (1848–1925.) American music publisher born in Pittsburgh, Pennsylvania. Presser founded the **Music Teachers National Association** and *The Etude*, a music magazine. Due to the success of the new magazine, he moved his publication facility to Philadelphia. It was just the beginning of the music-publishing establishment that continued and grew significantly after his death. See also **Theodore Presser Company**.

prestissimo. (It.) As fast as possible, extremely fast. (Fr. *trés vite*, Ger. *sehr schnell*, Sp. *rapidamente*.)

presto. 1. (It.) A very quick tempo, faster than **allegro**. (Fr. *vite*, Ger. *schnell*, Sp. *rápido*.)
2. (It.) Early, soon. (Fr. *de bonne heure, tôt*, Ger. *früh*, Sp. *temprano, pronto*.)

Previn, André. (b. 1929.) German-born American pianist, **conductor**, and composer. A versatile musician, Previn served as the music director of the **Houston Symphony** (1967–1969), the **London Symphony Orchestra** (1968–1979), the **Pittsburgh Symphony** (1976–1984), and the **Los Angeles Philharmonic** (1985–1989). He was also the principal conductor of the **Royal Philharmonic Orchestra**, London, from 1985 to 1988. Previn's compositions include many film scores (four received Academy Awards), two **operas**, and numerous works in both the classical and jazz genres. His recorded performances as a piano soloist in George Gershwin's *Rhapsody in Blue* and the *Concerto in F* remain unsurpassed classics. After his family left Berlin, Germany, he grew up in Los Angeles, California, where he worked in Hollywood and later toured as a jazz pianist.

prima. 1. (It.) First, before. Commonly heard in rehearsal when telling the ensemble where to being playing. (Fr. *avant*, Ger. *vor*, It. *prim*, Sp. *antes*.) Example: *Quatre avant D*, Four before D. Fr. *Quatre avant D*, Ger. *Vier vor Buchstabe D*, It. *Quattro prima D*, Sp. *Cuatro antes D*.)
2. The declarative, *Prima!* Great!

prima donna. (It., Sp.) The leading lady in an **opera**. Used most often in its Italian form. (Fr. *premiere chanteuse*.)

prima esecuzione mondiale. (It.) World premiere performance. (Fr. *première execution mondiale*, Ger. *Uraufführung*, Sp. *estreno mundial*.)

prima rappresentazione, prima. (It.) First, first performance, first night or opening night of a series of performances of an **opera** or musical. (Fr. *premiére*, Ger. *Premiere, erste Vorstellung*, Sp. *estreno*.)

prima vista, cantare a. (It.) Sight singing. (Fr. *chanter á vue*, Ger. *vom Blatt singen*, Sp. *cantar a primera vista*.)

prima vista, suonare a. (It.) Play at sight, sight read. (Fr. *jouer à vue, déchiffrer*, It. *suonare a prima vista, a libro aperto*, Sp. *tocar a primera vista*.)

prima volta, seconda volta. (It.) The first and second endings of sections of a piece that are repeated or, followed by additional instructions, how to play a section of a piece the first time and then the second time. (Fr. *premiere fois*, Ger. *erstes Mal*, Sp. *primer tiempo*.)

prime. The original, basic form of a **twelve-tone row**. Twelve-tone compositional techniques include transforming the original **row** through **inversion**, **transposition**, and creating a **retrograde** or **retrograde-inversion** form of the row, generating a variety of **pitch** materials for the composer.

primer tiempo. 1. (Sp.) **Downbeat**. (Fr. *temps fort*, Ger. *Abtakt*, It. *in battere*.) See also *tiempo fuerte*.
2. (Sp.) The first and second endings of sections of a piece that are repeated or, followed by additional instructions, how to play a section of a piece the first time and then the second time. (Fr. *premiere fois*, Ger. *erstes Mal*, It. *prima volta, seconda volta*.)

primero. (Sp.) At first, first. (Fr. *d'abord*, Ger. *zuerst*, It. *dapprimo, prima*.)

primo, secondo. (It.) In a duet, a piano reduction, or original piece for **piano** for four hands or two pianos, the first and second parts for the players.

primo tema, tema principale. (It.) The main theme or first theme. (Fr. *thème principal*, Ger. *Hauptthema*, Sp. *tema principal*.)

primo violon solo. (It.) Concertmaster, the first-chair player of the first violin section of the orchestra. (Fr. *premier violon solo*, Ger. *Konzertmeister/Konzertmeisterin*, Sp. *concertino*.)

principal player. The first or leading player of a section within the **orchestra**. The first-chair player of the first violins has the title concertmaster and ranks at the top in the hierarchy of the orchestra. In European orchestras, first-chair players are often referred to as the "solo" or "first solo" player. In German orchestras, if a member of the orchestra has a teaching position at a conservatory, they are often listed in the concert program as "professor."

principal. 1. (Fr., Sp.) Head; principal; main, as in the main theme or tempo of a piece or **movement** of a piece.

2. The principal or main player of a section of an **orchestra**. (Ger. *Haupt,* It. *principale.*)

principale. 1. (It.) Principal, main, as in the main theme or tempo of a piece or **movement** of a piece.

2. The principal player of a section of an **orchestra**. (Fr. *principal,* Ger. *Haupt,* Sp. *principal.*)

principio. (It.) Beginning. Examples: *dal principio al fine,* from the beginning to the end; *come in principio,* as at the beginning.

principles of conducting. 1. The **conductor** must know the score in all of its aspects, including elements of style, performance traditions, and practices and the historic and sociological context, and have a fully developed concept of the appropriate sound, the balance of all parts within the whole, the structure, and its musical narrative.

2. The conductor must be able to realize the score as close to the composer's intention as possible.

3. And through technique, strength of concept, personal will, and imagination, without verbal explanation, the conductor must be able to effectively communicate the essence of the music to the **orchestra**. Many conductors have left us with other important priorities. For example, according to his obituary in the *New York Times,* the Viennese conductor **Josef Krips** said, "without love there is no music." And the German **Erich Leinsdorf** wrote a book titled *The Composer's Advocate,* espousing the concept of fidelity to the composer.

principles of Schenker theory. See **Schenker theory, principles**.

prisa. (Sp.) To hurry. Example: *Sin prisas,* without hurrying. (Fr. *se dépêcher,* Ger. *zu beeilen,* It. *affrettare.*)

Prix de Rome. A prize given out annually by the French Académie des Beaux-Arts to artists and composers. Funded by the French government, the competition was held annually, from 1803—except for the years of World War I and World War II—until 1968, when it was abolished during the student uprisings. Its purpose was to foster French culture and art. The U.S. congress established an American Rome Prize in 1894, and there is also a Belgian Prix de Rome. See also **Rome Prize**.

Probe. (Ger.) Rehearsal. (Fr. *répétizione,* It. *prova, ripetizione,* Sp. *ensayo, ensayar.*)

proben. (Ger.) To rehearse. (Fr. *répéter,* It. *provare,* Sp. *ensayar.*)

prochain. (Fr.) Next. (Ger. *nächste,* It. *prossimo,* Sp. *próximo.*)

prochaine fois. (Fr.) Next time. (Ger. *nächstes Mal,* It. *prossimo volta,* Sp. *próximo vez.*)

programming, concert. Choosing the repertoire that an ensemble will perform in its concerts. A standard orchestral concert program is made up of an overture, concerto, and following intermission, a **symphony**. However, for many years the model has not been adequate to satisfy the imagination of **conductors**, managers, or the audience. **Orchestras** all over the world are seeking new and innovative ways to program, with the hope of bringing in new audiences. Interactive aspects, such as Twitter Zones in the concert hall, are being explored, in addition to many other programming innovations.

program music. Music that intentionally strives to depict nonmusical concepts, stories, or scenes without including any sung words. Franz Liszt introduced the term and specified that the program be supplied to the audience so that they would not draw false conclusions about the piece they were hearing. Many composers feel the opposite: the program should be self-evident, and if the audience doesn't understand it, a printed description does no good. Program music, in contrast to **absolute music**, seeks to dramatize human experience or thought in music. While earlier composers had used various forms of tone painting, Liszt devised the **symphonic poem** or **tone poem** as a musical form for the purpose of developing program music. (Fr. *musique á programme,* Ger. *Programmusik,* It. *musica a programma,* Sp. *música programática.*)

Programmusik. (Ger.) **Program music.** (Fr. *musique á programme,* It. *musica a programma,* Sp. *música programática.*)

program symphony. An orchestral work in the form of a **symphony** that has a descriptive title or program linked to it, similar to a **symphonic poem**. The importance of the program may vary significantly from a mere association to a dramatic narrative or "story." Examples: **Hector Berlioz**'s *Symphonie fantastique,* **Franz Liszt**'s *Faust Symphony,* Peter Ilyich Tchaikovsky's *Manfred Symphony,* and Olivier Messiaen's *Turangalîla Symphony.* See also **program music**.

Promenade Concerts. Also know as the Proms or the BBC Proms but originally called the **Henry Wood** Proms, they consist of an eight-week summer music festival held every year at the Royal Albert Hall in West London. One of the most exciting festivals in the world, performers and ensembles travel widely to participate. Unique to the Proms is that the floor in front of the stage has all of the chairs removed, creating a space for members of the audience who pay a minimal amount for a ticket to sit or stand, depending on the space available. Called "promenaders" or "prommers," audience members who want these standing-room tickets often line up for hours before a concert. It has become traditional for members of this section of the audience to make group cheers and sometimes short shout-outs to performers on the stage. For instance, when a concertmaster plays a tuning A on a **piano** before a piano concerto is performed, he will receive a standing ovation, and when the stagehands lift the lid of that piano into place, the audience will rhythmically call out "heave-ho!" The spirit of the Proms culminates in the *Last Night at the Proms*, a widely broadcast concert of traditional and often patriotic music that garners enormous enthusiasm.

Prometheus chord. Also known as the **mystic chord**, a six-note chord and its resulting scale of a group of **pitches** created and used by the Russian composer Alexander Scriabin. The pitches are, from bottom to top, C, F-sharp, B-flat, E, A, and D but may be spelled in many different ways while maintaining the intervallic distribution. See also **iconic chords**.

Prometheus scale. A six-note scale based on the so-called **mystic chord** of Alexander Scriabin in his work *Prometheus, Poem of Fire* (Symphony No. 5). Starting with **middle C**, the scale is C, D, E, F-sharp, A, B-flat. See also **iconic chords**.

Proms. See **Promenade Concerts**.

pronto. 1. (It. Sp.) Promptly, right away, suddenly. (Fr. *promptement, subitement,* Ger. *prompt, sofort, sogleich,* It. *subito, presto.*)
   2. (Sp.) Early, soon. (Fr. *de bonne heure, tôt,* Ger. *früh,* It. *presto.*)

prossimo. (It.) Next. (Fr. *prochain,* Ger. *nächste,* Sp. *próximo.*)

prossimo volta. (It.) Next time. (Fr. *prochaine fois,* Ger. *nächstes Mal,* Sp. *próximo vez.*)

prova generale, ripetizione generale. (It.) **General rehearsal**. (Fr. *La répétition générale,* Ger. *Generalprobe,* Sp. *ensayo general.*)

prova, ripetizione. (It.) Rehearsal. (Fr. *répétition,* Ger. *Probe, Korrepetition,* Sp. *ensayo.*)

próximo. (Sp.) Next. (Fr. *prochain,* Ger. *nächste,* It. *prossimo.*)

próximo vez. (Sp.) Next time. (Fr. *prochaine fois,* Ger. *nächstes Mal,* It. *prossimo volta.*)

prunkvoll. (Ger.) Pomp. A character word sometimes used to describe a particular style of playing. (Fr. *pompeux,* Ger. *prunkvoll,* It. *pomposo, pompa,* Sp. *pompa.*)

Ps. 1. (Ger.) Abbreviation for *Posaune* (trombone).
   2. Abbreviation for psalm.

psychoacoustics. The field of knowledge concerning how people perceive and process musical sounds. The German scientist **Hermann Helmholtz** wrote *On the Sensations of Tone* in 1863, making the connection between the natural sciences and music theory for the first time. In the twentieth century, the field has had great importance as composers explore new sound sources in both **electronic music** and experimental instrumental and vocal techniques.

psychological conducting. A term used by **Elizabeth Green** in her conducting text *The Modern Conductor* (also see the **bibliography**) to describe **conducting** that has reached a high level of virtuosity, the point at which a **conductor** can use readability of gesture, **impulse of will**, and mental alertness in order to influence a group of singers or instrumentalists to respond. See also **conducting technique**.

psychology of the conductor-orchestra relationship. The psychology of the **conductor-orchestra** relationship is based on mutual respect. To garner that respect, the conductor must possess excellent music skills; intelligence; a thorough knowledge of the score; a confidence in front of the ensemble; an efficient and effective rehearsal technique; a convincing, if not inspiring concept of the piece at hand; enthusiasm for that piece and the process; sensitivity to time; a good humor; honesty, especially in music making; the ability to cooperate; and a good stick technique. Honesty is key; the conductor must not make a mistake and then blame it on someone else. Conductors must be aware that the ensemble is a group of individuals, players who must have skill, discipline, artistry, love of music, and a drive to succeed to even get into the ensemble. The conductor's goal is to create a situation where the orchestra will play its best and be secure in its performance of the score. See also **morale**, **motivation**, **leadership**.

Pt. Abbreviation for the point of the bow, an indication to play at the point of the bow.

Public Broadcasting System (PBS). A nonprofit television network founded in 1970 by Hartford N. Gunn Jr. of WGBH-TV in Boston, Massachusetts, as the Corporation for Public Broadcasting. Much of the funding for PBS comes from third-party sources. Some is raised through pledge drives. Unlike **National Public Radio (NPR)**, PBS is not organized around a central production department; all programming is created by member stations such as WGBH, WETA-TV (Washington, DC), WNET (New York), WPBT (Miami), and others. PBS is one of the few television networks that broadcasts fine arts programming and is known for the series *Great Performances*.

publishers, music. See **music publishers**.

publishing music. The field of music publishing has changed radically with the advent of the Internet and the rising cost of producing and distributing parts and scores. Most music publishers now require composers to submit camera-ready scores and parts that will be printed out only on-demand. Many composers resort to self-publishing, using social media to promote their music.

puente. (Sp.) Bridge of a string instrument. (Fr. *chevalet,* Ger. *Steg,* It. *ponticello.*)

Puerto Rico Symphony Orchestra (PRSO) (Orquestra Sinfónica de Puerto Rico). Created during the first Casals Festival in 1957 by an act of the state legislature, its first concert was in 1958. The **orchestra** is one of the premiere cultural organizations of Puerto Rico and has over eighty musicians. It has a forty-eight-week season and also presents special programs, according to the dream of its first music director, Pablo Casals, in order to foster classical music in Puerto Rico. These programs include the Orchestra in the Projects (La Sinfónica en los Residenciales), the Orchestra in Your Town (La Sinfónica en tu Pueblo), and Know Your Orchestra (Conoce tu Orquestra). The first Puerto Rican–born music director was **Guillermo Figueroa**, and its current music director is Maximiliano Valdés.

puis, ensuite. (Fr.) Then. (Ger. *dann,* It. *poi,* Sp. *entonces.*)

puita. See *cuíca,* also see **appendix 4**.

pulgar. (Sp.) Thumb. (Fr. *pouce,* Ger. *Daumen,* It. *pollice.*) See also *pulgar, con el*.

pulgar, con el. (Sp.) With the thumb. An indication specifically used to describe a particular manner of playing the tambourine. (Fr. *avec les pouce,* Ger. *mit dem Daumen,* It. *con il pollice.*)

pulso, tempo. (Sp.) Beat, pulse. Example: *en el segundo tempo,* on the second beat (as in, it is on the second beat of the bar). (Fr. *batter, frapper,* Ger. *Schlag, schlagen,* It. *battere, percuotere.*)

Pult. (Ger., pl. *Pulte.*) **Music stand, conductor's stand.** (Fr. *pupitre,* It. *leggio,* Sp. *atril.*)

Pultweise geteilt. (Ger.) Divided by or at the stand, generally used for string players.

Pumpventil, Ventil. (Ger.) **Valve** on a **trumpet** or **horn**. (Fr. *piston, cylindre,* It. *piston,* Sp. *pistón.*)

punta. (It. Sp.) A term for the point or tip of the bow of a string instrument. Examples: *a la punta d'arco,* at the point of the bow; *a la punta,* at the tip of the bow. (Fr. *à la pointe,* Ger. *an der Sptize, Bogenspitze,* Sp. *en el punta.*) See also **at the point**.

punta, en el. (Sp.) A bowing term that directs the player to play at the point or tip of the bow. "*En el punta del arco*" is more specific. (Fr. *à la pointe,* Ger. *an der Sptize,* It. *punta.*)

pupitre. (Fr.) **Music stand** or desk, **conductor's stand**. Example: *div. par pupitre,* divided by stand, from *Gigues* of *Images* by Claude Debussy. (Ger. *Pult, Notenpult,* It. *leggio,* Sp. *atril.*)

Quad City Symphony (QCSO). Founded in 1916 in Davenport, Iowa, the ninety-six-member QCSO offers a masterworks and pops series, chamber music concerts, outreach events in the region, and runs a youth orchestra program. Originally the **Tri-City Symphony Orchestra**, it changed its name in the 1980s in order to better reflect the region. The current music director is Mark Russell Smith (appointed in 2008). Past music directors include Ludwig Becker (1916–1933), Frank Kendrie (1933–1936), Frank Laird Waller (1936–1937), Oscar Anderson (1938–1949), Harry John Brown (1949–1954), Piero Bellugi (1954–1956), Charles Gigante (1956–1965), **James Dixon** (1965–1994), Kim Allen Kluge (1995–1997), and **Donald Schleicher** (1999–2007). Soloists who have appeared with the orchestra include Mario Lanza, Richard Tucker, Itzhak Perlman, Jascha Heifetz, Midori, and many more.

quadruple-croche. (Fr.) Sixty-fourth note in British use. See **appendix 7**.

quadruple meter. Meter consisting of repeated groups of four, 4/4, for example.

quadruplet. A group of four notes of equal value, such as four sixteenth notes or four eighth notes barred together.

quanto. (It.) As much as, how much. (Fr. *autant que*, Ger. *so viel wie*, Sp. *cuanto*.)

Quantz, Johann Joachim. (1697–1773.) Flutist and composer. Quantz is the author of the important treatise *Versuch einer Anweisung die Flöte traversiere zu spielen* (1792), a great resource for those interested in performance-practice issues of the classical period. He also taught **Frederick the Great**.

quartal harmony. Chordal structures based on the interval of the fourth. Paul Hindemith and Béla Bartók are both known for their use of quartal harmony.

quart de soupir. (Fr.) Sixteenth rest. See **appendix 7**.

quarter note. See **appendix 7**.

quarter tone. One half of a semitone. The **octave** divides into twenty-four quarter tones. (Fr. *musique en quarts de ton, musique microtonale,* Ger. *Vierteltonmusik,* It. *musica a quarti di tono,* Sp. *quarto de tono.*) The interval is difficult to achieve on instruments with keys; however, **pianos** have been specially manufactured with quarter-tone tunings. Charles Ives, **Pierre Boulez**, Karlheinz Stockhausen, and Béla Bartók have used quarter-tone **pitches** to achieve a variety of effects. Although there is no universal agreement on how to designate quarter tones, one common notational devise is shown in these figures.

Quarter-tone flat. *Courtesy Andrew Martin Smith.*

Quarter-tone sharp. *Courtesy Andrew Martin Smith.*

quartet. A group of four musicians or a piece written for such a group. The **string quartet** is one of the most commons groups, another being a vocal quartet.

quarteto de cuerdo. 1. (Sp.) **String quartet**. Also the title of a piece for this ensemble. (Fr. *quartour, quartour á cordes,* Ger. *Streichquartett,* It. *quartetto d'archi.*)

Quartett. (Ger.) **Quartet.** (Fr. *quatuor,* It. *quartetto,* Sp. *cuarteto.*)

quartetto. (It.) **Quartet.** (Fr. *quatuor,* Ger. *Quartett,* Sp. *cuarteto.*)

quartetto d'archi. (It.) **String quartet.** (Fr. *quartuor á cordes,* Ger. *Streichquartett,* Sp. *cuarteto de cuerda*)

quartetto d'archi. (It.) **String quartet.** Also the title of a piece for this ensemble. (Fr. *quartour, quartour á cordes,* Ger. *Streichquartett,* Sp. *quarteto de cuerdo.*)

quartina. (It.) **Quadruplet.** (Fr. *quartolet,* Ger. *quartole,* Sp. *cuatrillo.*)

Quartole. (Ger.) **Quadruplet.** (Fr. *quartolet,* It. *quartina,* Sp. *cuatrillo.*)

quartolet. (It.) **Quadruplet.** (Ger. *quartole,* It. *quartina,* Sp. *cuatrillo.*)

quartour. (Fr.) **Quartet.** (Ger. *Quartett,* It. *quartetto,* Sp. *cuarteto.*)

quartour á cordes. (Fr.) **String quartet.** Also the title of a piece for this ensemble. (Ger. *Streichquartett,* It. *quartetto d'archi,* Sp. *quartet de cuerdo.*)

quasi. (Fr., It.) Almost, as if, nearly. Example: *quasi cadenza,* like a **cadenza**. Seen in orchestral parts to indicate free playing in the manner of a cadenza. In French, also *presque.* (Ger. *fast, beinahe, wie, als ob,* Sp. *casi.*)

quasi niente. (It.) Almost nothing. (Fr. *presque rien,* Ger. *fast nichts,* Sp. *casi nada.*)

quattro. (It.) Four. Example: *à Quattro mani,* for four hands. (Fr. *quatre,* Ger. *Vier,* Sp. *cuatro.*)

quatuor á cordes. (Fr.) **String quartet.** (Ger. *Streichquartett,* It. *quartetto d'archi,* Sp. *quarteto de cuerdo.*)

quaver. The rhythmic value of an eighth note in the English system. See **appendix 7**.

Queen's Hall. Opened in 1893 in London as a concert venue and destroyed in a German air raid in 1941. It was the original home of the **Promenade Concerts** founded by **Sir Henry Wood.** Known for its superb acoustics, in the 1930s it became the residence of both the **BBC Symphony Orchestra** and the **London Philharmonic Orchestra**. After World War II it was replace by the Royal Festival Hall (opened in 1952) on the South Bank and the **Royal Albert Hall** (opened in 1871) in South Kensington.

Queler, Eve. (b. 1931.) American **conductor** and founder (1971) and emerita conductor of the Opera Orchestra of New York (OONY), an organization dedicated to presenting concert performances of rarely heard **operas**. Queler has conducted over ninety concerts with the OONY on stage in Carnegie Hall. Perhaps that greatest successes were **Richard Wagner**'s *Rienzi,* **Hector Berlioz**'s *Benvenuto Cellini,* Bedřich Smetana's *Dalibor,* and **Richard Strauss**'s *Die Liebe der Danae.* Many successful singers gave early performances with the ensemble.

queue de la note, hampe. (Fr.) Tail or stem of a **note**. (Ger. *Notenhals,* It. *gambo,* Sp. *plica.*)

quieto, calmo. (It.) Quiet, hushed, calm. (Fr. *calme, calmement,* Ger. *ruhig,* Sp. *calmo.*)

quintal chord. A chord based on intervals of fifths.

quintal harmony. Harmony based on intervals of fifths.

quitar la sordina. (Sp.) Take off the mute. While this is accurate, the Spanish use the Italian **senza sordino,** meaning "without mute." (Fr. *enlever la sourdine,* Ger. *Dämpfer ab, Dämpfer weg,* It. *togliere la sordina.*)

quinte. (It.) The wings of a stage, backdrop, scene, side-scene, moveable scene. (Fr. *coulisses,* Ger. *Kulisse,* Sp. *colisa.*)

Quintenzirkel. (Ger.) **Circle of fifths.** (Fr. *cycle des quintes,* It. *circolo delle quinte,* Sp. *círculo de quintas.*)

quintet. A composition or piece for a group of five musicians, such as a woodwind or string quintet. (Fr. *quintette,* Ger. *Quintett,* It. *quintetto,* Sp. *quintet.*)

Quintole. (Ger.) **Quintuplet.** (Fr. *quintolet,* It. *quintina,* Sp. *quintillo, cinquillo.*)

Quintolet. (Fr.) **Quintuplet.**

Quintsaite. (Ger.) The E-string (the highest string) on the **violin**.

quintette. (Fr.) **Quintet.** (Ger. *Quintett,* It. *quintetto,* Sp. *quinteto.*)

quintette á vent. (Fr.) Woodwind **quintet**. (Ger. *Bläserquintett,* It. *quintetto per (di) fiato,* Sp. *quintet de viento.*)

quintuplet. Any rhythmic unit of five equal notes, such as five equal eighth notes. (Fr. *quintolet,* Ger. *Quintole,* It. *quintina,* Sp. *quintillo, cinquillo.*)

R

R. The designation of the **retrograde version** of a **twelve-tone row**.

rabbia, con. (It.) With rage, furious. An alternative is *furioso*, which is widely used. (Fr. *avec rage*, Ger. *mit Wut*, Sp. *con rabia, con enojo*.)

raccontando. (It.) See *raccontare*.

raccontare. (It.) To tell, to narrate. (Fr. *raconter*, Ger. *erzählen*, Sp. *narrar*.) Also *raccontando*, narrated or told. (Sp. *narrarado*.)

Rachleff, Larry. American **conductor** and pedagogue. Rachleff is professor of music and the music director of the Shepherd School Symphony and Chamber Orchestra at **Rice University**, Texas. He is also the music director of the Rhode Island Philharmonic and Chicago's Symphony II. He has appeared as a guest conductor with several American and European orchestras and is widely known as a teacher of **conducting**, as well as an advocate for contemporary music, having worked with **Samuel Adler**, Luciano Berio, George Crumb, John Harbison, and others.

radio. Still one of the most important vehicles through which **orchestras** are heard. Radio broadcasts and **podcasts** are often promoted on the websites of individual orchestras. Relationships between orchestras and community radio stations are often cultivated for mutual benefit. See also **WQXR, New York Philharmonic**.

Radio Cologne. The site of the first major electronic music studio. Established in 1951 by Herbert Eimert, **Karlheinz Stockhausen** and Robert Beyer also worked there.

radio orchestras. Also known as broadcast orchestras, **orchestras** that provide programming for **radio** and sometimes television, while also occasionally providing **incidental music** and themes for various shows and sometimes light music. Radio orchestras are often funded by the state and associated with specific broadcasting companies. In the United States, the most famous broadcast orchestra was the **NBC Symphony Orchestra** (1937–1954), conducted by **Arturo Toscanini**. The last broadcasting orchestra in North America was the **CBC Radio Orchestra** of Canada, which existed from 1938 to 2008. Germany has the most of such orchestras, known mostly for their peformances and recordings of classical and contemporary orchestral music, while Britain is known for its **BBC** symphony orchestras. (Fr. *orchestra de la radio,* Ger. *Rundfunkorchester,* It. *orchestra della radio,* Sp. *orquesta de la radio.*)

Radio Symphony Orchestra Berlin (Rundfunk-Sinfonieorchester Berlin, RSB). An orchestra of 103 musicians, it was established in 1923 by the German Radio (Deutschlandradio) as the resident orchestra with its partner choir, the Rundfunkchor. They are two of the four radio music ensembles in Berlin, alongside the **RIAS Chamber Choir** (RIAS Kammerchor) and the **German Symphony Orchestra Berlin** (Deutsches Symphonie-Orchester Berlin, DSO). They have issued many acclaimed recordings. Past **conductors** include **Sergiu Celibidache**, **Eugen Jochem**, Hermann Abendnroth, Rolf Kleinert, Heinz Rögner, and **Rafael Frühbeck de Burgos**. **Marek Janowski**, appointed in 2002, will step down after the 2015/16 season.

ralentir. (Fr.) To slow down. (Ger. *verlangsamen*, It. *rallentare*, Sp. *ralentir*.)

rallentando, lentando. (It.) Slowing down, getting slower. Abbreviated *rall*. (Fr. *en ralentissant*, Ger. *langsamer werdend*.)

rallentato. (It.) Slower. (Fr. *ralenti*, Ger. *verlangsamt*.)

"Random Acts of Culture." See **John S. and James L. Knight Foundation**, **"pop-up" performance**.

random music. See **aleatoric music**, **chance music**, **indeterminacy**.

ranges of the instruments. See individual instrument entries.

rango. (Sp.) Compass, range. (Fr. *ètendue*, It. *gamma*, Ger. *Umfang, Raum, Ausdehnung.*)

raniment, en. (Fr.) Becoming livelier in tempo and/or feeling. (Ger. *neu belebend*, It. *avvivando*, Sp. *avivando.*)

rapide, rapidement. (Fr.) Fast, quick, quickly, a very quick tempo, faster than **allegro**. (Ger. *rasch, schnell*, It. *rapido, rapidamente*, Sp. *rápido, rápidamente.*) Also *vite*, fast; *très vite*, very fast.

rapido, rapidamente. (It.) Rapid, fast, quickly, a very quick tempo, faster than **allegro**. (Fr. *rapide*, Ger. *schnell, rasch*, Sp. *rápido, rápidamente.* Also *veloce, velocemente, prestissimo.*

rápido, rápidamente. (Sp.) Rapid, fast, quickly, a very quick tempo, faster than **allegro**. (Fr. *rapide, vite*, Ger. *schnell, rasch*, It. *rapido, rapidamente.*) Also *veloz.*

rapproché. (Fr.) Near. Example: *un peu rapproché*, a little closer, from *Fêtes*, movement two of *Nocturnes* by Claude Debussy. (Ger. *in der Nähe von*, It. *vicino*, Sp. *cerca.*)

rasch, rascher. (Ger.) Fast, faster, swift. Example: *rascher werdend*, quickening, from **Pierrot Lunaire** by **Arnold Schoenberg**. (Fr. *rapide, rapidement*, It. *rapido rapidamente*, Sp. *rápido, rápidamente.*) Also *schnell*, fast; *sehr schnell*, very fast.

ratchet. Also known as the cog rattle, it is made of a wooden, grooved cylinder and a hard board mounted on a rotating handle. When spun it produces a loud clacking sound. (Fr. *crécelle*, Ger. *Ratsche*, It. *raganella*, Sp. *carraca.*) See **appendix 4**.

Ratsche, Knarre, Schnarre. (Ger.) **Ratchet**, rattle. (Fr. *crécelle*, It. *raganella*, Sp. *carraca.*) See **appendix 4**.

Rattle, Sir Simon. (b. 1955.) English **conductor**. Knighted in 1994, Rattle held the position of principal **conductor** of the **City of Birmingham Symphony Orchestra (CBSO)** in 1979 and was made the music director in 1990, serving until 1998. During his tenure, he raised the profile of the **orchestra** significantly, partnering with the city to build a new concert hall and releasing several significant recordings. He became the principal conductor of the **Berlin Philharmonic** in 2002. As a condition of signing his contract, Rattle insisted that the orchestra become independent from city government and that members of the orchestra not only be paid fairly but participate in the running of the orchestra. Rattle has overseen several collaborative outreach programs, especially in music education, and concerts in nontraditional venues, such as in a hangar of the former Tempelhof airport. Suggestions of a turbulent relationship with the Berlin Philharmonic seem to be refuted by the extension of his contract to 2018. Rattle has led nearly all major American orchestras and the **Metropolitan Opera** in New York.

At one time, when Rattle had already made many recordings, he acknowledged the difficulty of recording with the necessity of bringing a sense of a cohesive performance into the exacting, detail-oriented process of recording. Rattle has released over seventy recordings with both the CBSO and the Berlin Philharmonic under an exclusive contract with **EMI**. They include **Sir Benjamin Britten**'s *War Requiem*, Anton Bruckner's *Symphonies*, **Gustav Mahler**'s *Symphonies No. 2, 9*, and *10* (Deryk Cooke version) and *Das klagende Lied*, Leoš Janáček's *Galgolithic Mass*, and Johannes Brahms's *Requiem*, among others. In Berlin, he has also released DVDs, including ***Rhythm Is It!*** a video project of **Igor Stravinsky**'s ***Rite of Spring*** with students dancing. Nicholas Kenyon wrote *Simon Rattle: The Making of a Conductor* (1987; see the **bibliography**).

Sir Simon Rattle. *Courtesy Mat Hennek.*

rau. (Ger.) Harsh, rough, rude. A character word sometimes heard in rehearsal. Used by Maurice Ravel in the score to his ballet *Daphnis et Chloé*. (Fr. *rude*, It. *grezzo*, Sp. *áspero.*)

Raum, Umfang, Ausdehnung. (Ger.) Compass or range, of an instrument, for instance. (Fr. *ètendue*, It. *gamma*, Sp. *rango.*)

ravvivando. (It.) Animating, reviving, rekindling, getting faster. A descriptive word. (Fr. *en ravivant*, Ger. *wieder-belebend*, Sp. *reavivando, reviviendo, animando*.)

ravvivato. (It.) Revived. A descriptive word. (Fr. *ravivé*, Ger. *wieder belebt*, Sp. *revivido*.)

RCA Records. Now one of the principal recording labels of **Sony Music Entertainment (SME)** and the second oldest recording company in the United States. RCA (Radio Corporation of American, renamed RCA Corporation) has three divisions, RCA Records for pop, rock, and so on; RCA Victor for blues and world music, jazz, and musicals; and RCA Red Seal (formerly RCA Victor Red Seal) for classical music. The company became RCA-Victor when, in 1929, it purchased the Victor Talking Machine Company, which manufactured phonograph players. Throughout its history the company had a distinguished classical music catalogue and was responsible for many technological innovations, including the introduction of the first 33 1/3 rpm record (1931) and the first quadraphonic four-channel eight-track tape cartridge (1970).

RCA-Victor. See **RCA Records**.

RCA Victor Symphony. The **NBC Symphony Orchestra**, sometimes recorded as the RCA Victor Symphony during the years of its existence (1937–1954).

re. The **solmization** name for the note D in the fixed-do system; the note D; and in the moveable do system, the second note of the scale.

ready position. The position of the **conductor**'s arms that bring an ensemble to attention in advance of the **preparatory gesture**. The ready position may also signal the dynamic and style of the music to come through **posture**, **facial expression**, and other elements of **body language**. Usually the arms are held slightly in front of the torso, elbows at the positions of five and seven on a clock face,

Ready position indicating strength. *Courtesy Derek Brennan.*

with the hands slightly lifted. The **left hand** is often used in the preparatory position to indicate the coming dynamic. See also **conducting technique**, **posture/stance**.

Ready position indicating quiet. *Courtesy Derek Brennan.*

re bémol. (Fr.) D-flat. See **appendix 5**.

re bémolle. (It.) D-flat. See **appendix 5**.

rebound gesture. The motion of the **baton** or hand after the **ictus** or attack of the **pulse**. The rebound occurs in the style of the music at that specific moment in time and can reflect the energy of the **attack**. It immediately becomes the **preparation** of the next **beat**. See also **conducting technique**, **pizzicato gesture**.

rebound of the beat. See **rebound gesture**.

Recht. (Ger.) 1. (n.) Law, authorization, privilege.
2. (adv.) Quite, right, justly, well. Example: *mit Recht*, strictly or precisely.

rechte Hand. (Ger.) The right hand. Abbreviated R.H. (Fr. *main droite*, It. *destra*, Sp. *mano derecha*.)

récit. (Fr.) **Recitative**. Example: *en récit. très libre de mesure*, like a recitative, in very free time, from *Rapsodie Espagnole* by Maurice Ravel. Also *récitatif*.

recitative. (Fr. *récitatif*, Ger. *Rezitativ*, It. *recitativo*, Sp. *recitativo*.) See **conducting recitative**, **appendix 8**.

recitative, accompanied. (Fr. *récitatif accompagné*, Ger. *begleitetes Rezitativ*, It. *recitativo accompagnato*.) See **conducting recitative**, **appendix 8**.

recitative conducting technique. See **conducting recitative**, **appendix 8**.

recitative, dry. Recitative accompanied only by **harpsichord**. (Fr. *récitatif seulement avec continuo, "sec"*;

Ger. *Rezitativ nur mit Cembalo, "trocken"*; It. *recitativo secco*, Sp. *recitativo seco*.) See also **conducting recitative, appendix 8**.

recitativo. (It.) **Recitative**. Abbreviated *recit*. (Fr. *récitatif*, Ger. *Rezitativ*, It. *recitativo*, Sp. *recitativo*.) See also **conducting recitative, appendix 8**.

reco-reco. A Brazilian metal instrument with one, two, or three springs strung lengthwise on a hollow base with a horn-shaped bell that acts to enhance tone production. The springs are commonly scraped with a beater similar to a triangle beater. It comes in various sizes. Used in Heitor Villa-Lobos's *Concerto for Violin and Orchestra*. See also **appendix 4**.

recording. Fr. *enregistrement*, Ger. *Aufzeichnung, Aufnahme*, It. *registrazione*. Sp. *grabación*.

recording, history of. The history of recording classical music may be dividing according to the following phases of technological development:

1. The era of acoustical recording where the sound was recorded directly onto the recording medium. The phonograph, which used wax cylinders that were very difficult to reproduce was invented by Thomas Edison in 1878. The gramophone machine, which used flat discs that could be mass produced on a stamping machine, was invented and patented by Emil Berliner in 1887. Both technologies involved the musician(s) standing near the horn or bell of the recording machine and responding to the air pressure of the sound, a stylus would correspondingly etch the surface of the cylinder or disc, creating a groove. Playback involved a needle tracing that surface and mechanical amplification of the sounds. After some time, the 78 rpm became standard.

2. The era of electronic recording began in 1925, making it possible to use electronic microphones and improving the quality of the sound significantly, although performances were still recorded directly to the disc; no editing was possible. It was possible, however, to record one part or voice and rerecord that and one more onto a second disc, creating a multitrack effect. The development of the long-playing (LP) disc that ran at 33 1/3 rpm made it possible to have more music on a single disc.

3. The era of magnetic tape; the reel-to-reel tape recorder; and a bit later, stereo tape recorders and the cassette began in earnest in the 1930s and led to significant improvements in sound quality. Companies that created and refined the new technologies included AEG (the German General Electricity Company), IG Farben, the Brush Development Company, and the 3M Company in Minnesota.

4. The era of the multitrack recording and the rise of stereo and then quadrophonic sound, which was invented in the 1940s and first used with magnetic tape technology involving the simultaneous use of multiple microphones. At this time, even though it was mostly 33 1/3 rpm and 45 rpm vinyl records that were being sold to the mass market, recordings were made on tape and then transferred.

5. The rapid rise of digital recording technology, first on tape through various formats and the subsequent creation of the digital **compact disc (CD)** as both a hard recording disc similar to tape but with much greater capacity and as an audio storage device, mass-produced for sale, has led quickly to its own near demise. Sound—music—can now be accessed through any computer medium. Thanks to digital technology, the consumer no longer needs to purchase an actual physical disc. Anyone who owns a computer, smartphone, or other such devise can download music and listen to it at will. See also the **bibliography, BIS Records, Columbia Records, Decca Records, Deutsche Grammophon, EMI Records, Mercury Records, Naxos Recording Company, RCA Records, Sony Music Entertainment, Universal Music Group (UMG), Warner Music Group**.

re dièse. (Fr.) D-sharp. See **appendix 5**.

re dieses. (It.) D-sharp. See **appendix 5**.

redoblante. (Sp.) Tenor drum. See **appendix 4**.

redonda. (Sp.) Whole note. See **appendix 7**.

reducción. (Sp.) **Reduction**.

reduction. A reduction of a full score to one the size of a piano score, sometimes called a short score or piano score. (Fr. *réduction*, Ger. *Reduktion*, It. *riduzione*.)

réduction. (Fr.) **Reduction**. (Ger. *Reduktion*, It. *riduzione*, Sp. *reducción*.)

Reduktion. (Ger.) **Reduction**. (Fr. *réduction*, It. *riduzione*, Sp. *reducción*.)

reforzar. (Sp.) To strengthen, to reinforce. Mostly used in its Italian form, ***rinforzando***. (Fr. *renforcer*, Ger. *verstärken*, It. *rinforzare*.)

regelmässig. (Ger.) Regular, uniform, even. Often used when referring to tempo. (Fr. *régulier*, It. *regolare*, Sp. *regular*.)

regie. (Ger.) Stage direction. (Fr. *régie*, It. *regia*, Sp. *acotación*.) See also ***Regisseur***.

régisseur. (Fr.) General manager, stage manager, director, or theatrical director. The person in charge of staging. A term sometimes used in opera houses, it is from the French *régir*, to manage.

Regisseur. (Ger.) Stage director or manager. A term used widely in Europe. See also *régisseur*.

régulièrement. (Fr.) Uniformly, equally. (It. *ugualmente, uniformemente*, Ger. *gleichmäßig*, Sp. *igualmente, uniformemente*.)

rehearsal. A gathering of musicians in order to practice the music for a concert performance. (Fr. *La répétition*, Ger. *Die Probe*, It. *La prova*, Sp. *ensayo*.)

rehearsal. A gathering of musicians in order to practice the music for a concert performance. (Fr. *répétition*, Ger. *Probe*, It. *prova*, Sp. *ensayo*)

rehearsal directives in English with their translations. See **Articulate more, please; From the top, please; Good afternoon; Good evening; Good morning; It is a little sharp/it is a little flat; It's not together; Long, please; Louder, please; Please; Short, please; Softer, please; Thank you; Thank you very much; Watch, please; We are not together; With me.**

rehearsal letters. Letters inserted periodically in a full score and matching parts to be used in order to facilitate **rehearsals**. The distance between these letters may be dictated by a regular number of bars or it may relate to structural events in the music, such as the beginning of the development section in a symphony. Introduced by **Louis Spohr.**

rehearsal numbers. Numbers inserted periodically into a full score and the matching parts in order to facilitate **rehearsals**. These numbers may correlate to the actual bar numbers of a piece or they may be independent numbers inserted regularly, perhaps ten bars apart or more.

rehearsal plan. There are two rehearsal plans for every **rehearsal**: one for the musicians so that they know how to prepare and exactly when to be present and a second for the **conductor** that establishes goals for the allotted time. The musician's plan or schedule is posted well in advance and must include the schedule of **movements** of longer works so that players who only participate in certain movements know when to be present. The conductor's plan is usually kept private, sometimes not even written down, but always made. It will identify any problems from a previous rehearsal and set all goals in order to reach a successful performance in the time allotted.

A rehearsal plan for an **opera** may be a comprehensive plan that covers a long series of rehearsals over a period of some weeks, from working with singers to staging and orchestral rehearsals, to the final dress rehearsal. If working with a college or conservatory **orchestra**, the plan may cover a series of rehearsals over some weeks and include time for drilling and repetition of the most difficult passages and attention over several rehearsals to intonation, sound quality, and simply making sure that all of the musicians know their parts and how they fit together with everything else.

rehearsal strategies. First and foremost, a good **conductor** always arrives at the first **rehearsal** knowing the score. This is the only way a conductor gains authority with an **orchestra**. A good conductor speaks clearly, concisely, and not very much. Never repeat any passage without saying why. Keep a positive but demanding attitude and never waste time. Stick to the clock. Never be late to begin and never go overtime. Listen actively to make sure that you hear mistakes, but never correct a mistake when it is obvious that the player or players know that they made a mistake already. Trust the musicians.

The English conductor **Sir Thomas Beecham** promoted the strategy of playing through the piece and then doing it again, claiming that the musicians would take care of most of the mistakes. The Romanian conductor **Sergiu Celibidache** was known as an extremely detailed rehearsal conductor, demanding up to thirty rehearsals per concert program, while the Russian **Yevgeny Svetlanov** was known to have dismissed the **London Symphony Orchestra** before a performance of Peter Ilyich Tchaikovsky's *Romeo and Juliet* with the succinct comment "Tonight, watch very carefully."

rehearsal technique. The techniques, methods, or strategies that the **conductor** uses to lead the ensemble through a **rehearsal** with optimum results. A widely held basic technique falls into three parts: 1. play through the music while listening, evaluating, and analyzing; 2. Make corrections, establish elements of style and interpretation, give any necessary explanations, rehearse any trouble spots; and 3. play through again. Conductors often develop a **rehearsal plan** that lays out specific goals in advance.

rehearsal warm-ups. Exercises used by both instrumental and choral ensembles to help prepare the musicians for the **rehearsal** itself. In a choral ensemble, the warm-up prepares the voice and the ear for the music to come, while the instrumental warm-up prepares the instrument and the ear. Instrumental warm-ups may include playing through a chorale and/or a B-flat scale for good tone development, intonation, and balance and blend across the ensemble. Choral warm-ups may include singing pitched vowel exercises, often a series of five descending scale **notes**, going up by half steps. Focusing on vowels develops tone and the ear. Choral **conductors** will often select a specific passage from a piece to be rehearsed as a warm-up for diction and clarity. Many conductors develop their own warm-up exercise sequences.

rehearsing opera. Involves multiple stages: 1. Meet with the stage director. 2. Make sure everyone has the appropriate **libretto** and score, including any cuts. 3. Singers learn their parts. 4. Choral **rehearsals**. 5. Attend as many staging **rehearsals** as possible. 6. Prepare the orchestral parts and lead the **orchestra** rehearsals. 7. A **"sitz probe,"** that is, a rehearsal with the singers sitting on the stage with the orchestra in the pit so that both can get used to hearing the other. 8. Technical rehearsals. 9. **Piano** dress rehearsals. 10. Dress rehearsals with the orchestra in the pit, running the **opera** without stopping. In the final stages, when the opera is done without pause, note giving is done at the end. Dress rehearsals are often done at the same time as performances to facilitate building the stamina of all of the performers. See also **conducting opera**, **conducting in the pit**, **opera in English**, **opera in the original language**, **performance practice and tradition in opera**, **preparing the opera score**.

Reihenkomposition. (Ger.) Composition with tone rows. (Fr. *série dodecaphonisme*, It. *serie dodecafonia*, Sp. *serie dodecafónica*.)

rein. (Ger.) In the tuning of intervals, acoustically pure. Example: *reine Stimmung*, just intonation or regarding types of intervals, perfect (lit. "clean").

Reiner, Fritz. (1888–1963.) Hungarian-born American **conductor**. Reiner moved to the United States to accept the position of music director of the **Cincinnati Symphony Orchestra** (1922–1931). At that time, he became professor of **conducting** at the **Curtis Institute of Music** in Philadelphia (1931–1941), where his students included **Leonard Bernstein** and **Lukas Foss**, among others. From 1935 to 1938 he appeared as a guest conductor with several ensembles, including the **Covent Garden Opera** in London and the **San Francisco Opera**. In 1938, he was appointed music director and conductor of the **Pittsburgh Symphony Orchestra**, serving there until 1948. He was a conductor at the **Metropolitan Opera** from 1948 to 1953. The culmination of his career was his time as the music director of the **Chicago Symphony Orchestra** (1953–1962).

Reiner was a conductor at a time when it was not only accepted but expected that one would essentially be a strongman, if not a dictator on the podium. His reputation as a ruthless taskmaster and disciplinarian was notorious. Among musicians, his baton technique remains a legend.

Having modeled himself after **Arthur Nikisch**, Reiner cultivated an intense stare bordering on the hypnotic. It has been said that he confined his conducting gestures to those he made with the tip of the baton and that would fit on a postage stamp. He believed in a style of conducting based on maximum results for minimum effort. Not liked by the members of his orchestra, he was widely respected for his comprehensive knowledge of the music and the success he achieved, especially building the Chicago Symphony into one of "the most precise and flexible in the world" (Holmes, 1988). Reiner's repertoire ranged from the baroque to Franz Joseph Haydn and Wolfgang Amadeus Mozart, **Richard Strauss**, Paul Hindemith, **Igor Stravinsky**, and Béla Bartók. His many recordings demonstrate the high level of playing achieved in Chicago and include Ludwig van Beethoven, Franz Schubert, **Gustav Mahler**'s *Symphony No. 4* and *Das Lied von der Erde*, Bartók's *Concerto for Orchestra* of, Ottorino Resphigi's *Fountains of Rome* and *Pines of Rome*, and Strauss's tone poems.

relative majeur, relative mineur. (Fr.) The relative minor to a major key or visa versa. Example: A minor is the relative minor key of C major, and B minor the relative of D major. (Ger. *parallele Tonarten*, It. *tonalità relativa*, Sp. *tonalidad relativa, tonalidad paralela*.)

relative pitch. The ability to read and sing a sequence of **pitches** or intervals without reference to any pitched instrument or device. See also **perfect pitch**.

release gesture. A term for the gesture that shows how and when to stop the sound. Given in a manner that evokes the style of the musical moment, it can be slow and drawn out, quick and concise, or somewhere in between. It is given either by the right hand in a counterclockwise gesture or the left hand in a clockwise gesture. The end of the sound comes when the gesture closes the circle. Release gestures can happen on any beat of the bar. See also **conducting technique**, **clockwise release gesture**, **counterclockwise release gesture**, **cutoff gesture**.

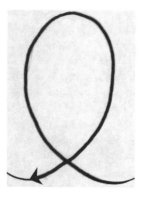

Clockwise release. *Courtesy Derek Brennan.*

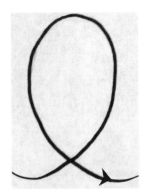

Counterclockwise release. *Courtesy Derek Brennan.*

render. (Fr.) To give back. Used in reference to **rubato** style. (Ger. *zurückgeben,* It. *rendere,* Sp. *devolver.*)

rendere. (It.) To give back. Used in reference to **rubato** style. (Ger. *zurückgeben,* Fr. *render,* Sp. *devolver.*)

renforcer. (Fr.) To strengthen, to reinforce. (Ger. *verstärken,* It. *rinforzare,* Sp. *reforzar.*)

reorchestrating the parts. Through history, **conductors** have changed orchestration details, particularly as the instruments changed and developed. This has been true in particular with the symphonies of **Ludwig van Beethoven** and Robert Schumann. **Felix Weingartner** wrote essays about the reorchestration of Beethoven, but at the end of his career he changed his mind and decided that they should be performed in their original state. Schumann was thought of as being a poor orchestrator, leading to generations of conductors thinning out his scores. It is now much more commonplace to use his originals.

There are a few notable spots worth mentioning. (1) Peter Ilyich Tchaikovsky's *Symphony No. 6* "Pathetique." In movement one, just before the *Allegro vivo,* the **bassoon,** continuing a descending line in the **clarinet,** is marked with an extraordinary *pppppp* on four notes in its low register, where it is virtually impossible to play quietly in a good tone. Today the part is often taken over by the **bass clarinet,** in spite of the fact that it will be the only notes the player has in the whole piece. (2) Beethoven's Symphony No. 5, first movement. The second theme is forcefully first introduced by the **horns,** and when the passage returns at bars 303–5, it is scored in the **bassoons** (the needed pitches couldn't be produced on the E-flat horn). But sounding quite a bit thinner, it is now common practice now to either change to horns or at least add horns to the bassoons. Conductors have also modified writing perceived as awkward for the brass in some works of Beethoven. Generally speaking, performance-practice research combined with the ability of today's musicians have led us back to the original orchestration for its own sake. See also **doubling the parts, preparing the parts.**

repeat sign. Fr. *signe de repetition,* Ger. *Wiederholungzeichen,* It. *segno di ripetizione, segno di ritornello,* Sp. *signo de repetición.*

Repeat sign. *Courtesy Andrew Martin Smith.*

repente, di colpo, subito. (It.) Abrupt, sudden, suddenly. A descriptive term seen in scores and parts and heard in rehearsal. (Fr. *tout á coup, immédiatement, subitement,* Sp. *immediatamente, súbito.*)

Répertoire International de la Litérature Musicale (RILM, International Repertory of Music Literature). Jointly sponsored by the International Musicological Society and the International Association of Music Libraries, RILM is a vast bibliography of writings on music. According to its website, RILM includes over 730,00 records in 214 languages from 1,151 countries. It is housed at the CUNY Graduate Center in New York City. See also **International Association of Music Information Centres (IAMIC).**

Répertoire International des Sources Musicales (RISM; International Inventory of Musical Sources; Ger., Internationales Quellenlexikon der Musik). An international nonprofit organization that, according to their website, aims to locate and document primary music sources, including manuscripts, printed music, libretti, and writings on music worldwide. Founded in Paris in 1952, RISM records what exists and where it can be found in a comprehensive inventory that is available to those interested in the field of music. See also **International Association of Music Information Centres (IAMIC).**

Répertoire International d'Iconographie Musicale (RIdIM). An international organization that specializes in documenting visual materials relating to music. See also **International Association of Music Information Centres (IAMIC).**

Répertoire International de la Presse Musicale (RIPM). An international organization that creates abstracts and an index of the contents of particular periodicals focused on the music of the eighteenth to the twentieth centuries. See also **International Association of Music Information Centres (IAMIC).**

répéter. (Fr.) To repeat, to rehearse. To repeat a passage as marked in the parts with a repeat sign or to repeat for purposes of rehearsal. (Ger. *proben, wiederholen,* It. *ripetere,* Sp. *repetir, ensayar.*) Example: *Répétez!* Repeat!

repetición. (Sp.) Repeat, repetition. To repeat a passage as marked in the parts with a repeat sign or to repeat for purposes of rehearsal. (Fr. *répétition, reprise,* Ger. *wiederholen, wiederholung,* It. *ripetizione, ripresa.*)

répétiteur. (Fr.) Vocal coach, one who rehearses the singers for an **opera** production or concert. Also private teacher, assistant teacher, or coach. (Ger. *Korrepetitor,* It. *ripetitore, maestro sostituto,* Sp. *repetidor.*)

répétition générale. (Fr.) Final rehearsal or **general rehearsal**. (It. *prova generale,* Ger. *Generalprobe,* Sp. *ensayo general.*)

répétition générale, la. (Fr.) **General rehearsal**. (Ger. *Die Generalprobe,* It. *La ripetizione generale, prova generale,* Sp. *ensayo general.*)

répétition, reprise. (Fr.) Repetition, repeat, reprise. Can also mean **rehearsal**. (Ger. *Wiederholung,* It. *ripetizione, ripresa,* Sp. *repetición.*)

répétizione. (Fr.) **Rehearsal**, to rehearse. (Ger. *Probe, proben,* It. *prova, ripetizione,* Sp. *ensayo, ensayar.*)

replica. (It.) Repeat performance, repeat, repetition. Example: *senza replica,* without repeat. (Fr. *reprise, réplique,* Ger. *Wiederholung.*)

repos. (Fr.) Rest, repose. Sometimes heard in rehearsal to encourage players to rest between longer, difficult passages. (Ger. *ruhe,* It. *riposo,* Sp. *resto.*)

reprendre, reprenez. (Fr.) To take back, to retake, to resume. Examples: *Reprenez peu á peu le Mouvt.,* little by little go back to the tempo, from *Dialogue du vent et de la mer,* movement three of *La Mer* by Claude Debussy; *reprenez la Mailloche,* retake the (in this case, **bass drum**) mallet, from *Rapsodie Espagnole* by Maurice Ravel; *reprenez le mouvement,* resume tempo. (Ger. *wieder anfangen, wieder aufnehmen,* It. *riprendere.*)

representación. (Sp.) Performance. Also *interpretación.* (Fr. *représentation, concert,* Ger. *Aufführung, Konzert,* It. *Rappresentazione, concerto.*)

reprise, réexposition. (Fr.) Repeat, recapitulation. (Ger. *Reprise, Wiederverkehr,* It. *ripresa, riesposizione,* Sp. *repetición, reexposición.*)

RE-RITE. A digital instillation project of the **Philharmonia Orchestra** in London. Filmed with multiple, cameras it uses high-definition video and audio to transform a space into a virtual **orchestra**.

resident conductor. A title used most often by **orchestras** that have a music director who is often out of town. The resident **conductor** then takes over many of the responsibilities of the senior conductor, often overseeing programming of outreach concerts and initiatives, educational concerts, pops concerts, and more. Orchestras that have resident conductors often also have an associate or assistant conductor who leads the associated youth orchestra and other concerts, in addition to serving as a **cover conductor**.

résolu, résolue. (Fr.) Resolute, determined, bold. A character word used to evoke a particular character in the playing.

résonné. (Fr.) Resonant, a full sound, resounding. A character word used to evoke a particularly full sound. Also *résonner.*

respecter le doigté. (Fr.) Follow the fingering. Used to specify uniformity in the fingering of a specific passage in order to achieve a certain sound.

respiración. (Sp.) Breath. Example: *Marque una repiración aqui,* mark a breath here. (Fr. *soufflé,* Ger. *Atmen,* It. *respiro.*) Also *la respiración,* breathing. (Fr. *la respiration,* Ger. *die Atmung,* It. *la respirazione.*)

respirar. (Sp.) To breath. Example: *Respire en ritmo!* Breath in rhythm! (Fr. *respirer,* Ger. *atmen,* It. *respirare.*)

respirare. (It.) To breath. Example: *Respira con me!* Breathe with me! (Fr. *respirer,* Ger. *atmen,* Sp. *respirar.*)

respiration, la. (Fr.) Breathing. (Ger. *die Atmung,* It. *la respirazione,* Sp. *la respiración.*)

respirazione, la. (It.) Breathing. (Fr. *la respiration,* Ger. *die Atmung,* Sp. *la respiración.*)

respiro. (It.) A breath. Example: *Segnare un respire qui,* mark a breath here. (Fr. *souffle,* Ger. *Atem,* Sp. *aliento.*)

rest. An interval of silence of a specific duration. Also the sign used to denote such a pause. See **rhythmic terms** for translations.

restare, rimanere. (It.) To stay, to remain. Used in rehearsal to direct string players to stay in a certain hand position on a certain string, for instance. (Fr. *rester,* Ger. *bleiben,* Sp. *permanecer.*)

rester, restez. (Fr.) To stay, to remain. (Ger. *bleiben,* It. *restare, rimanere,* Sp. *permanecer*) See also *restare, rimanere.*

resto. (Sp.) Rest, peace. Sometimes heard in rehearsal to encourage players to rest between longer, difficult passages. (Fr. *repos,* Ger. *Ruhe,* It. *riposo.*)

resuelto. (Sp.) Resolute, determined. (Fr. *résolu,* Ger. *entschlossen,* It. *risoluto.*)

resultant tone. The tone produced when two loud, independent tones sound simultaneously at frequencies that produce a third tone, the result of the difference between the frequencies of the two tones. When the resultant tone is low in pitch it is called a "difference tone," when high and usually faint it is called a "summation tone." See also **combination tone.**

retardant, en. (Fr.) Slowing down.

retardar. (Sp.) To slow down, to delay. (Fr. *retarder,* Ger. *verzögern,* It. *ritardare.*)

retarder. (Fr.) To hold back, to delay. (Ger. *verzögern,* It. *ritardare.*)

retener el tempo. (Sp.) To hold back the tempo. Also *frenar.* (Ger. *zurückhalten,* Fr. *retenir,* It. *ritenere.*)

retenir, retenant. (Fr.) To hold back. Example: *En retenant peu à peu,* getting slower little by little, from movement one of *La Mer* by Claude Debussy. (Ger. *zurückhalten,* It. *ritenere.*)

retenir. (Fr.) To hold back. It can be used to express holding back the sound, volume, or the tempo. (Ger. *zurückhalten,* It. *ritenere,* Sp. *retener.*)

retenu, retenez. (Fr.) Held back, slower. (Ger. *zurückhalten,* It. *ritenut,* Sp. *retener el tempo.*)

retourner. (Fr.) To return. (Ger. *zurückkehren,* It. *ritornare,* Sp. *volver.*) Also *retournez,* return.

retrograde. A backward version of a group of **pitches,** beginning with the last pitch and proceeding to the first. A compositional technique commonly used in fugue writing and twelve-tone music.

retrograde-inversion. A backward statement of the inversion of a motive, theme, or **twelve-tone row.**

rêve. (Fr.) Dream. Example: *Après un rêve,* a work for voice and piano by Gabriel Fauré.

Revelli, William. (1902–1994.) American **band conductor.** Revelli was director of bands at the **University of Michigan** from 1935 to 1971. Under his direction, the Michigan Marching Band was the first to synchronize music and movement on the field, the first to score original music to their shows, and the first to use an announcer. A strict disciplinarian, Revelli strived to instill self-respect and pride in a job well done, believing that it would last a lifetime. He was a founder of the **College Band Directors National Association (CBDNA)** in 1941 and a president of the Band Association and the American Bandmasters Association.

revenir. (Fr.) To return. Also *revenez,* return. Examples: *revenez au mouvement,* return to tempo; *revenir progressivement au I° tempo,* return gradually to tempo I. (Ger. *zurückkehren,* It. *ritornare,* Sp. *volver.*)

rêveur. (Fr.) Dreamy, dreamer. Example: *Lent et rêveur,* slow and dreamy, from *Les parfums de la nuit* of *Iberia* by Claude Debussy.

rezitativ. (Ger.) **Recitative.** Also *Recitatif.*

Rf., Rfz. Abbreviation for *rinforzando.*

R.H. Abbreviation for right hand, used most often in keyboard music.

Reinhardt, Max. (1873–1943.) Austrian-born American stage and film director. He established the **Salzburg Festival** in collaboration with **Richard Strauss** and Hugo von Hofmannsthal, Strauss's librettist. Reinhardt was influential in developing new staging techniques in the early twentieth century.

rhythm. From the Latin *Rhythmus.* (Fr. *rhythme,* Ger. *Rhythmus,* It. *ritmo,* Sp. *ritmo.*) The measured flow of patterns of musical sounds forming countable units organized according to duration (short and long) and periodic stress. The pattern of movement in time.

rhythmic. Fr. *rythmique, rythmé,* Ger. *Rhythmisch,* It. *ritmico.* Sp. *ritmico.*

rhythmic augmentation. A compositional technique in which the durations of a given set of **notes** are increased proportionally, such as twice the value or half again the value.

Rhythmic Augmentation

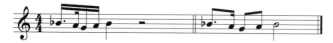

Rhythmic augmentation. *Courtesy Andrew Martin Smith.*

rhythmic diminution. A technique used in writing music whereby the **rhythmic** values of a group of notes are decreased by the same proportion.

Rhythmic Diminution

Rhythmic diminution. *Courtesy Andrew Martin Smith.*

rhythmic displacement. The placement of a motive or musical segment in a different position than would be expected in the metrical context. See in **appendix 1** *Appalachain Spring* by **Aaron Copland** and the last movement of Johannes Brahms's *Symphony No. 1* after rehearsal letter [M].

rhythmic terms. See **appendix 7**.

Rhythm Is It! A documentary video put together by the **Berlin Philharmonic** under the baton of music director **Simon Rattle**. Directed by **Enrique Sánchez Lansch** and Thomas Grube and choreographed by Royston Maldoom, the project covered the staging of a performance of **Igor Stravinsky**'s ***The Rite of Spring*** with over 250 Berlin schoolchildren in an effort to bring classical music to a wider, younger audience. The video won numerous prizes and has been widely sold.

Rhythmus. (Ger.) Rhythm. (Fr. *rythme*, It. *ritmo*, Sp. *ritmo*.)

rhytmisch. (Ger.) **Rhythmic**, measured, in a precise rhythm. Example: *Anmerkung für den Dirigenten: Celli und Bässe "rhytmisch," nicht Triolen spielen*, Note for the **conductor**: **Cellos** and **basses** must be rhythmic, don't play triplets, from *Symphony No. 2, mvt. 1* by **Gustav Mahler**. (Fr. *rythmique, rythmé*, It. *ritmico*, Sp. *rítmico*.)

RI. The designation for the **retrograde inversion** of a **twelve-tone row**.

RIAS Chamber Choir (RIAS Kammerchor). A professional choir in Berlin, the choir was established in 1948 by the American occupying forces. RIAS is the abbreviation for "Radio in the American Sector" (Rundfunk im amerikanischen Sektor). The choir quickly developed an international reputation for fine performances of Baroque to contemporary repertoire. They have collaborated often with the **Berlin Philharmonic**, the **Academy for Old Music Berlin** (Akademie für Alte Musik Berlin), and the **Berlin Radio Symphony Orchestra**, one of its partner organizations under the umbrella of the Berlin Radio Organization. The current **conductor** is Hans-Christoph Rademann. The choir has made many distinguished recordings, including the first issue of Avo Pärt's *Stabat mater* for choir and string **orchestra**. Guest conductors who have worked with the ensemble include **René Jacobs**, **Nikolaus Harnoncourt**, **John Elliot Gardiner**, and many more.

RIAS Symphony Orchestra. See **Berlin Radio Symphony Orchestra**.

Rice University Shepherd School of Music. Founded in Houston, Texas, in 1974, the school offers a comprehensive curriculum at the undergradute and master's levels and a DMA in composition and theory. Ensembles include **orchestras**, **opera**, collegium musicum, brass choir, a **string quartet** residency, percussion ensemble, and the Rice Chorale.

Richter, Hans. (1843–1916.) Known as a devotee and promoter of the music of **Richard Wagner**, Richter succeeded **Charles Hallé** as **conductor** of the **Hallé Orchestra** in 1897 and stayed in the position until 1911. During those years, he had an enormous impact on musical life in England, leading the British premieres of many works by composers such as Johannes Brahms, Antonin Dvořák, Peter Ilyich Tchaikovsky, and English composers Sir Edward Elgar, Sir Hubert Parry, and Charles Villiers Stanford. In 1876, he conducted the first complete performance of Wagner's Ring cycle at **Bayreuth** and the next year made his debut in England, assisting the ailing Wagner, who was conducting a series of concerts in London. In 1908, he helped put on the first English-language production of the Ring cycle at **Covent Garden**. He maintained an active conducting schedule in Vienna and at Bayreuth, conducting the premieres of many works, and was particularly notable for bridging the divide between the music of Wagner and Brahms by conducting the music of both at a time when they appeared to be at polar opposites.

Richter, Karl. (1926–1981.) German organist and **conductor** who formed the Munich Bach Choir and Orchestra, performing, touring, and recording with them for many years. Richter, who was one of Germany's distinguished harpsichordists, organists, and conductors, released over one hundred recordings for **Deutsche Grammophon (DGG)**, including all of Johann Sebastian Bach's major oratorios and many of his cantatas and instrumental pieces and works of George Frideric Handel, Wolfgang

Amadeus Mozart, and Ludwig van Beethoven. Known for meticulous preparation of each piece, his recordings reflect his deep understanding and mastery of the style. His first appearance in the United States was in 1965 when he brought the Munich ensemble to **Carnegie Hall**, and his last appearance was only one year before his death in 1980. D. K. McIntire wrote a biographical essay "Karl Richter (1926–1981)" in *Le Grand Baton* (March 1981) (See the **bibliography**).

richtig, genau, präziser. (Ger.) Strict, precise. Example: *Tempo giusto*, in a strict tempo. (Fr. *exact, juste*, It. *giusto, esatto*, Sp. *exactamente, preciso*.)

ricochet. (Fr.) A bowing term for the technique where the bow is thrown in a controlled manner so that it bounces off the string. Ricochet is done with two or three down-bows followed by a single up-bow. It works best is the upper-middle part of the bow.

Ricordi, Casa. A music publishing house founded in Milan, Italy, in 1808 as G. Ricordi & Co. by the violinist **Giovanni Ricordi**. As with many publishing companies, Ricordi grew through the purchase of other smaller firms. Ricordi purchased the entire collection of the **La Scala** opera house in 1825, and in 1839, the copyright to Giuseppe Verdi's music. Within ten years they had become the largest music-publishing firm in southern Europe, expanding beyond Milan in the 1860s to the 1880s. Several generations of the family ran the company until 1919 when they began to use outside management. Giovanni's son Tito Ricordi started the *Musical Gazette* of Milan in 1842, and Tito's son, Giulio, worked closely with Giacomo Puccini, establishing a virtual partnership in the creation of **opera**. He also began the popular commissioning of graphic art posters with operatic themes. G. Ricordi & Co. was purchased by the BMG division (Bertelsmann Music Group) in 1994 and are now owned by **University Music Publishing Group**. It remains Italy's largest music publisher.

Ricordi, Giovanni. (1785–1853.) Italian music publisher in Milan, Italy, who started his business in 1808 copying and printing music. Ricordi published the first catalogue of editions in 1814 and took on the responsibility of copying all the **opera** scores and parts for **La Scala**. He paid his composers fixed shares of the profits and with this helped establish the foundation for the copyright laws of the future. See also **Casa Ricordi**.

riducción para piano. (Sp.) **Piano reduction.** (Fr. *partition pour piano*, Ger. *Klavierauszug*, It. *riduzione per piano*.)

riduzione. (It.) Reduction, as in a **piano reduction** of a score. (Fr. *réduction*, Ger. *Reduktion*, Sp. *reducción*.)

riduzione per piano. (It.) **Piano reduction.** (Fr. *partition pour piano*, Ger. *Klavierauszug*, Sp. *reducción para piano*.)

right hand. Fr. *main droite*, Ger. *rechte Hand*, It. *destra*, Sp. *mano derecha*.

rigo, linea. (It.) Staff, musical staff, line. (Fr. *ligne*, Ger. *Linie*, Sp. *linea*.)

rigoroso. (It.) Rigorous, in strict tempo. (Fr. *rigoureux*, Ger. *streng*, Sp. *riguroso*.)

rigoureux. (Fr.) Strict, rigorous. Examples: *en la rigeur*, strictly (as written); *sans riguer*, freely. (Ger. *streng*, It. *rigoroso*, Sp. *riguroso*.)

rigueur. (Fr.) Rigor, strictness. Example: *sans rigueur*, without rigor, from *Les parfums de la nuit* of *Ibéria* by Claude Debussy.

Rilling, Helmut. (b. 1933.) German **conductor** who founded the Gächinger Kontorei, the Stuttgart Bach-Collegium orchestra, and joined them together to record all the major works of Johann Sebastian Bach. Rilling does not advocate using period instruments or performances practices except in such a way so as to guide a style of playing. In 1970, he founded the Oregon Bach Festival and conducted there until 2013. He commissioned **Krzyztof Penderecki**'s *Credo* for the Oregon festival in 2003.

RILM. See **Répertoire International de la Litérature Musicale**.

rimshot. A percussion sound made when the rim of a snare drum is hit instead of the head of the drum.

Rimsky-Korsakov, Nicolai. (1844–1908.) Russian composer, member of the group the **Russian Five** (Mily Balakirev, César Cui, Modest Mussorgsky, and Alexander Borodin), and author of *Foundations of Orchestration*, which was completed by his son-in-law Maximilian Steinberg in 1913 (see the **bibliography**).

Rimsky-Korsakov Saint Petersburg State Conservatory. Sometimes called simply the St. Petersburg Conservatory, its official name is the N. A. Rimsky-Korsakov Saint Petersburg State Conservatory. Founded in 1862 by the Russian pianist and composer Anton Rubenstein, the school offers a comprehensive curriculum in performance, composition, and **conducting**. Notable alumni include Peter Ilyich Tchaikovsky, Sergei Prokofiev, Dmitri Shostakovich, Jascha Heifetz, **Valery Gergiev**, **Mariss Jansons**, **Yuri Temirkanov**, and many others.

rinforzando. (It.) Stronger, louder, strengthen. (Fr. *en renforçant,* Ger. *verstärkend,* Sp.) Abbreviated *r., rf., rfz.,* or *rinf.* Also *rinforzare,* to reinforce, to strentghen.

Ring cycle. The set of operas by **Richard Wagner** based on Norse sagas. Its full name is *The Ring of the Niebelung* (*Der Ring des Nibelungen*).

ringtones. Brief musical excerpts suitable to serve as the ring on a mobile phone, often made available via an orchestra's website for personal downloading.

ripetizione generale, la, prova generale. (It.) **General rehearsal.** (Fr. *La repétition générale,* Ger. *Die Generalprobe,* Sp. *ensayo general.*)

ripetizione, prova. (It.) **Rehearsal**, a repeat. (Fr. *répétition,* Ger. *Probe,* Sp. *ensayo.*)

ripieno. (It.) In a concerto grosso, the part of the ensemble that plays the "orchestral" or "accompaniment" as opposed to the *concertato,* which play the solo parts.

riposo. (It.) Rest, peace. Sometimes heard in **rehearsal** to encourage players to rest between longer, difficult passages. (Fr. *repos,* Ger. *Ruhe,* Sp. *resto.*)

riprendere. (It.) To retake, to resume, an original tempo, for example. (Fr. *reprendre,* Ger. *wieder anfangen, wieder aufnehmen.*)

ripresa. (It.) Repeat. (Fr. *reprise,* Ger. *Wiederholung,* Sp. *repetición.*)

RISM. See **Répertoire International des Sources Musicales**.

risoluto, deciso. (It.) Resolute, decided. (Fr. *décidé,* Ger. *entschlossen, entschieden,* Sp. *resuelto.*)

ritardando. (It.) To slow down gradually. Abbreviated *rit.* or *ritard.* (Fr. *en retardant,* Ger. *verzörgernd,* Sp. *disminyuendo la velocidad, disminyuendo el tempo.*)

ritardare. (It.) To delay. (Fr. *retarder,* Ger. *verzögern,* Sp. *retardar.*)

ritenere. (It.) To hold back, the tempo or a **crescendo,** for instance. (Ger. *zurückhalten,* Fr. *retenir,* Sp. *retener.*)

ritenuto, tratenuto. (It.) Held back, the tempo, for instance. (Fr. *retenu,* Ger. *zurückgehalten.*)

Rite of Spring, The. (1913.) A work by **Igor Stravinsky**. See **appendix 1**.

ritmico. (It., Sp.) Rhythmic. A commonly used directive in rehearsal. (Fr. *rythmique, rythmé,* Ger. *rhytmisch,* Sp. *rítmico.*)

ritmo. (It., Sp.) Rhythm. (Fr. *rythme,* Ger. *Rhythmus.*)

ritmo di quattro battute. An indication in the Scherzo of Ludwig van Beethoven's Symphony No. 9 that indicates a grouping of 3/4 measures fast enough to be conducted in one beat to a bar in groups of four bars. See also **appendix 1**, *ritmo di tre battute*.

ritmo di tre battute. Appearing in the Scherzo of Ludwig van Beethoven's Symphony No. 9 to indicate a change from four-bar to three-bar groupings. Since the movement has a meter of 3/4 and a fast tempo marking, it would be conducted in one. A **conductor** might choose to use a **supermetric pattern** of three in this passage. A few phrases later, Beethoven switches back to *ritmo di quattro battute*. See also **appendix 1**.

ritornello. (It.) A return or a repeat of a passage, the name of a structural unit in a piece. (Fr. *ritournelle,* Ger. *Ritornell.*)

ritournelle. (Fr.) See *ritornello*.

rivelatore. (It.) A pickup gesture or beat, anacrusis. (Ger. *Tonabnehmer,* Sp. *anacrusa.*)

Roberts, Kay George. (b. 1950.) African American **conductor**. Roberts serves as professor of music and **conductor** of the University Orchestra at the University of Massachusetts at Lowell (1978–present). He was the music director of the New Hampshire Philharmonic Orchestra (1982–1987), Cape Ann Symphony Orchestra (1986–1988), and founding conductor of the Ensemble Americana in Stuttgart, Germany (1989). As a guest conductor, Roberts has appeared with the symphony orchestras of Bangkok, Chattanooga, Cleveland, Dallas, Dayton, Detroit, Nashville, and others. He received a DMA from the **Yale University School of Music**.

Robertson, David. (b. 1958.) American **conductor**. Robertson is the music director of the **Saint Louis Symphony Orchestra** (appointed in 2005) and the Sydney Symphony Orchestra, Australia (appointed in 2014). From 1992 to 2000 he served as the music director of the **Ensemble Intercontmporain (EIC)**, Paris, and the Orchestre National de Lyon, France (2000–2004). Robertson served as the principal guest conductor of the **BBC Symphony Orchestra** beginning in 2005. He has conducted at the **Metropolitan Opera, New York**, and recorded for Sony Classical, EMI/Virgin Classics, Naxos, Nonesuch, and other labels. In 1997, he was awarded the **Seaver/National Endowment for the Arts Conductors Award**, and in 2006 he received **Columbia University**'s **Ditson Conductor's Award**.

Rochester Philharmonic Orchestra (RPO). Founded in 1922 by George Eastman. The RPO presents over two hundred conducts annually and has an important music education outreach program, having named Michael Butterman the principal conductor for education and outreach. The first such position in the United States, it is funded by the Louise and Henry Epstein Family Chair. The **orchestra** has received the ASCAP Award for Adventurous Programming in 2005, 2006, and 2012. The orchestra's list of music directors includes Eugéne Goossens (1923–1931), José Iturbi (1936–1944), **Erich Leinsdorf** (1947–1955), Walter Hendl (1968–1970), Samuel Jones (1970–1971), **David Zinman** (1974–1985), Jerzy Semkow (1985–1988), Mark Elder (1989–1994), Robert Bernhardt (1994–1998), Christopher Seaman (1998–2011), and Arild Remmereit (2011–2013). Its pops conductor is **Jeff Tyzik**. RPO concerts are rebroadcast on WXXI 91.5 FM. The orchestra has made numerous recordings under the direction of **Howard Hanson, David Zinman, Jeff Tyzik**, Christopher Seaman, and others.

Rodzinski, Artur. (1892–1958.) In 1925, **Leopold Stowkowski** appointed the Polish-born **conductor** Rodzinski as guest conductor of his **Philadelphia Orchestra**, promoting him to assistant conductor one year later. Rodzinski became the conductor of the **Los Angeles Philharmonic** in 1929 and served as the music director of the **Cleveland Orchestra** from 1933 to 1943, where he introduced the unusual idea of performing complete **operas** in concert, conducting the American premiere of Dmitri Shostakovich's opera *Lady Macbeth of Mitzensk* in 1935. He became the conductor and music director of the **New York Philharmonic** in 1943, but due to his demanding nature and extravagant artistic ideas, he had problems with the management and left amid controversy after only a few years. Almost immediately, he was appointed to the same position with the **Chicago Symphony**, but he suffered from similar circumstances and lasted only one season (1947–1948). With the recurrence of such a difficult state of affairs, he returned to Europe, remaining active as a guest conductor for several years. One of the great accomplishments of this period of his career was leading the European premiere of Sergei Prokofiev's mammoth opera *War and Peace*. In 1958, he was invited to conduct at the **Lyric Opera of Chicago**, but failing health forced him to cancel, and he died in a hospital in Boston. Donald Brook wrote about him in *International Gallery of Conductors* (1951) and his widow, Halina Rodzinski, published a biography, *Our Two Lives*, in 1976 (see the **bibliography**).

Rohrblatt. (Ger.) Reed. (Fr. *anche, épiglotte,* It. *ancia,* Sp. *caña.*) Example: *Rohrblattinstrumente,* reed instruments. See also *Doppelrohrblatt.*

Röhrenglocken. (Ger.) Tubular bells. (Fr. *cloches tubulaires,* It. *campane tubolari,* Sp. *campana tubular.*) See **appendix 4**.

roll. As on a drum. For example, a snare drum roll. (Sp. *redoble.*)

Rolltrommel, Tenortrommel, Rührtrommel, Wirbeltrommel. (Ger.) Tenor drum. (Fr. *caisse roulant,* It. *cassa rulante, cassa chiara,* Sp. *redoblante.*) See **appendix 4**.

romantic period. An artistic movement that originated in German literature in the late eighteenth-century. Commonly described as beginning around the death of Ludwig van Beethoven in 1827 and spanning the nineteenth century to **impressionism** in France and the early works of **Arnold Schoenberg**.

Rome Prize. Established in 1894, a prize given annually by the American Academy in Rome for young artists in architecture, design, historic preservation and conservation, literature, musical composition, and visual arts and scholars in the areas of ancient, medieval, Renaissance, and early modern or modern Italian studies. Recipients spend a year living at the academy in Rome. Many of America's most active composers are on its list of winners.

roncador. (Sp.) **Bull-roarer.** (Fr. *planchette ronflante,* Ger. *Schwirrholz,* It. *legno frullante, tavoletta sibilante.*) See **appendix 4**.

ronde. (Fr.) Whole note. See **appendix 7**.

Rosbaud, Hans (1895–1962). Austrian **conductor** with a gift for contemporary music. Rosbaud served as the music director of the Frankfurt Radio (1928–1937), where he conducted the premieres of **Arnold Schoenberg**'s Four Songs with orchestra and Béla Bartok's *Concerto for Piano No. 2* with the composer as the soloist. He was the music director in Münster (1937–1941) and Strasbourg (1941–1944), with the **Munich Philharmonic Orchestra** (1945–1948), and with the **Southwest German Radio Orchestra** (1948–1962). He was awarded the Schoenberg Medal by the **International Society for Contemporary Music** (ISCM) in 1952 and conducted the premiere of Schoenberg's *Moses und Aron* in 1954. Known for a self-effacing intellect and restrained style, he had a great influence on many younger conductors, including **Pierre Boulez**.

rosin. Used by string players to lightly cover the bow, allowing it to grip the string a bit more in order to get a stronger tone.

Rostropovich, Mstislav. (1927–2007.) Celebrated Russian cellist and **conductor**, both his father and grandfather were cellists. Rostropovich studied at the **Moscow Conservatory**, joining the faculty upon graduation in 1948. Among his teachers was composer Dmitri Shostakovich, who became a close friend and later wrote many works for him. Having become one of the greatest cellists of his day and a champion of new music, many composers wrote specifically for him, including Shostakovich but also Sergei Prokofiev, Luciano Berio, **Sir Benjamin Britten**, Henri Dutilleux, Witold Lutosławski, Olivier Messiaen, **Krzysztof Penderecki**, Alfred Schnittke, and others. In total, there are over one hundred works dedicated to Rostropovich. As a conductor, he was virtually self-taught, claiming that he learned nearly everything he knew from watching those conductors he played concertos with, observing the effectiveness of their **rehearsal techniques** and what worked and what didn't. He also believed that as a string player he was a natural leader for an **orchestra**, knowing exactly what he could ask for and what he couldn't. Rostropovich was an example of a conductor who believed in the power and effectiveness of the individual conductor/interpreter. He claimed the mantle of such conductors as **Arturo Toscanini**, **Wilhelm Furtwängler**, **Bruno Walter**, and **Otto Klemperer** as examples of those who allowed their musical feeling to lead the way with great success. He did not particularly like the **metronome** or its markings in scores. **Seiji Ozawa** said of him, "Slava doesn't interpret, he feels." Rostropovich served as the music director of the **National Symphony Orchestra** from 1977 to 1994. He recorded all of the symphonies of Peter Ilyich Tchaikovsky and Shostokovich's opera *Lady Macbeth of Mtsensk* with the **London Philharmonic Orchestra**. He was married to the soprano Galina Vishnevskaya.

roto-tom. A relatively recent addition to the **orchestra** percussion section and developed to extend the range of the timpani. The roto-tom comes in seven sizes, is tuned by stretching the head, and can play specific **pitches**. See also **appendix 4**.

Round Top Festival Institute. The music festival was founded in 1971 in Round Top, Texas, by the pianist James Dick in order to provide young pianists an opportunity to focus on music. Run by the James Dick Foundation for the Performing Arts, the Festival Institute has a season of thirty concerts in June and July, in addition to programs of education and performance year round.

Royal Academy of Music. Founded in London in 1822, it is England's first degree-granting music school. The academy offers a broad-based curriculum with the LRAM diploma and the BMus and other degrees, including the PhD, offered in partnership with the University of London. In addition, its Junior Academy provides training for younger students. Although most students are classical performers, the academy also offers classes in musical theater performance and jazz. Drawing students from over fifty countries, the academy has relationships with conservatories worldwide, participating in the European Commissions SOCRATES international faculty and student exchange program. The academy's list of alumni includes many of the most well-known musicians of the twentieth century.

Royal Albert Hall. The concert hall was opened in London, in 1871, by Queen Victoria to honor her late husband and consort, Prince Albert. Perhaps most famous for the **BBC Proms**, a music festival that lasts throughout the summer, the Royal Albert Hall has also been the scene of major sporting events, auto shows, and political events. In 1873, the shah of Persia was present at a demonstration of the first use of electricity at the hall, and in 1891, the German emperor visited. In 1908, a meeting of the Women's Liberal Federation, a group that supported women's right to vote, took place in the hall. In 1914, Sergei Rachmaninov performed his Piano Concerto No. 2 there, and in 1920, the **New York Symphony Orchestra** appeared there with conductor Walter Damrosch and violin soloist Jascha Heifetz. More recently, the hall has been the site of rock and pop music concerts.

Royal College of Music (RCM). Founded in London in 1882, its first director was Sir George Grove. At first, the school was located in what is now the Royal College of Organists, a building that was too small for the ambitions of the RCM's founders. A new, significantly larger structure was built nearby and opened in 1894. It remains the site of the school today. Grove was succeeded by Sir Hubert Parry, who died in 1918, and Sir Hugh Allen (1919–1937). Other directors have included Sir Keith Falkner (1960–1974), Sir David Willcocks (1974–1984), Michael Gough Mathews (1985–1993), Dame Janet Ritterman (1993–2005), and Colin Lawson (appointed in 2005). The curriculum of the RCM covers Western art music from the undergraduate to the doctoral levels. The college also has a preparatory department, with youth from ages eight to eighteen attending on Saturdays. The college is widely known for its Museum of Instruments dating back to 1480. The list of alumni includes many of the most distinguished musicians of the twentieth and twenty-first centuries.

Royal College of Music. Established in 1771 in Stockhom as the conservatory of the Royal Swedish Academy of Music, it was made independent in 1971.

Royal Concertgebouw Orchestra. Founded in Amsterdam just after the opening of the Concertgebouw (Concert

Hall), the **orchestra** gave its first concert in 1888 with **conductor** Willem Kes. The orchestra has had several renowned conductors, including **Willem Mengelberg** (1895–1945), who built the orchestra over the stunningly long tenure of fifty years to one of international acclaim, capable of championing the then contemporary music of **Richard Strauss** and **Gustav Mahler**. The orchestra maintains a relationship with the music of Mahler today. Other conductors who worked with the orchestra during Mengelberg's tenure included **Karl Muck** (1921–1925), **Pierre Monteux** (1924–1934), **Bruno Walter** (1934–1939), and **Eugen Jochum** (1941–1943). From 1945 to 1959 the principal conductor was **Eduard van Beinum**, who was renowned for his interpretation of the symphonies of Anton Bruckner. From 1961 to 1963 Jochum and **Bernard Haitink** shared the position of conductor of the orchestra. Haitink served as the principal conductor from 1963 to 1988. Under his leadership the orchestra made numerous recordings on the **Philips Records**, **EMI**, and **Columbia labels**. Riccardo Chailly served as the first non-Dutch chief conductor from 1988 to 2004 and was followed by Latvian **Mariss Jansons** (appointed in 2002). *Concertgebouw* means "concert building" in Dutch. The **Royal Concertgebouw Orchestra** is the orchestra resident in the main concert hall of Amsterdam and is the most important orchestra in Holland.

Royal Conservatoire of Scotland. Formerly **Royal Scottish Academy of Music and Drama**, it was established in 1845. In 1993, it became the first British conservatory to have its own degree-granting priviledges. The name was changed in 2011, and in recent years, £8.5 million were invested in facilities, including performance spaces, dance studios, practice rooms, recording studios, theatrical spaces, and much more.

Royal Conservatory of Brussels. Founded in 1832; in 1967, it was split into two separate conservatories, the French-speaking Conservatoire Royal de Bruxelles and the Flemish-speaking Koninklijk Conservatorium Brussel. The Royal Conservatory has been part of the reorganization of higher education programs throughout Europe taking place since about 1999, according to the **Bologna accords**. It is now an official conservatory of higher education as part of the Free University of Brussels. It offers courses of study in music and theater and the performing arts. It has an extensive library with collections dating back to Carl Philipp Emanuel Bach and Georg Philipp Telemann.

Royal Danish Academy of Music (Det Kongelige Danske Musikkconservatorium). First founded in 1825. Following a cessation, it was brought back in 1967 in Copenhagen by composer Niels Gade. It is the oldest professional music education institute in Denmark. Among its well-known alumni are composer Carl Nielsen.

Royal Danish Orchestra (Det Kongelige Kapel). The **orchestra**'s Danish name signals its 1448 origins, when it provided music, mostly in the form of a **trumpet** corps, for the royal court of King Christian I. By the eighteenth century, the orchestra had become resident in the Royal Danish Theatre, where one of its leaders was Christoph Willibald Gluck. The orchestra continued to grow in size, and during the tenure of **conductor** Johan Svendsen (1883–1908), symphonic concerts became an established tradition. Composer Carl Nielsen worked with the orchestra as both a conductor and as a member of the second **violin** section. Many famous twentieth-century conductors have appeared on the podium, including **Leonard Bernstein**, **Daniel Barenboim**, **Sergiu Celibedache**, **Otto Klemperer**, **Georg Solti**, **Richard Strauss**, and **Igor Stravinsky**. Currently a fully professional ensemble of 130 musicians, the orchestra performs primarily at the Pritzker Architecture Prize–wining Copenhagen Concert Hall (opened in 2009) of the Danish Radio and is the pit orchestra for the Royal Danish Opera. The chief conductor and artistic advisor is Michael Boder. Past principal conductors include Michael Schøonwandt (2000–2011), **Paavo Berglund** (1993–1998), John Frandsen (1936–1980), and others.

Royal Flemish Philharmonic (Koninklijke Filharmonie van Vlaanderen). Known in Flemish simply as deFilharmonie, the **orchestra** was founded in 1956 and performs in multiple venues in Antwerp, Brussels, Bruges, and Ghent. The current chief **conductor** is Edo de Waart (appointed in 2011). Past conductors include Jaap van Zaeden (2008–2011), Daniele Callegari (2002–2008), Philippe Herreweghe (1998–2002), Grant Llewellyn (1995–1998), Muhai Tang (1991–1995), Günter Neubold (1986–1991), and others. The orchestra gives a full season of symphonic, chamber, family, and educational concerts, in addition to tours and recordings. Many of its concerts can be seen on WebTV.

Royal Liverpool Philharmonic Orchestra. Founded in 1840 and administered by the Royal Liverpool Philharmonic Orchestra Society, it is England's longest surviving professional orchestra; it also maintains a philharmonic choir and youth orchestra. The orchestra offers classics concerts, a series of family concerts, and founded the 10/10 Ensemble for the performance of contemporary music in 1997. It tours throughout the United Kingdom and abroad. The current principal **conductor** is Vasily Petrenko (appointed in 2006). Past conductors include Jakob Zeugheer (1843–1865), Alfred Mellon (1865–1867), Julius Benedict (1867–1880), Max Bruch (1880–1883), **Charles Hallé** (1883–1895), Frederick Cowen (1896–1913), **Henry J. Wood** and Louis Cohen (1930s), **Malcolm Sargent** (1942–1948), Hugo Rignold (1948–1954), **Paul Kletzki** (1954–1955), Efrem

Kurtz (1955–1957), John Pritchard (1957–1963), Charles Groves (1963–1977), Walter Weller (1977–1980), David Atherton (1980–1983), **Marek Janowski** (1983–1987), Libor Pešek (1987–1997), Petr Altrichter (1997–2001), and **Gerard Schwarz** (2001–2006).

Royal Opera House, London. See **Covent Garden, Royal Opera House at**.

Royal Philharmonic Orchestra (RPO). Formed in 1946 by **Sir Thomas Beecham**, who secured playing commitments at the **Glyndebourne Opera Festival** and the **Royal Philharmonic Society**. After Beecham's death in 1961, the **orchestra** suffered financially until the British Arts Council recommended that it receive a government subsidy. Financial difficulties have recurred, but the orchestra has managed to succeed. In the 1980s, the orchestra secured its finances, at least temporarily, by recording the extremely successful **Hooked on Classics** series, a rock version of various popular classics that was used worldwide for aerobic exercise classes. In 2004, the RPO got its first permanent hall, Cadogan Hall, in the Chelsea section of London.

Royal Philharmonic Society. Founded in 1813 as the Philharmonic Society of London when there was no full-time orchestra giving concerts. The society's aim was to encourage and support such performances. Supported by members of the aristocracy, it was run by professional musicians, giving eight concerts per season until 1897. No permanent **conductor** was appointed until 1845. Performances were led by the principal violinist and from the keyboard. **Louis Spohr**, who appeared as a guest conductor in 1820, claimed that he introduced the baton to the London audience at that time. The society supported both British and European performers and composers. They awarded a gold medal to distinguished performers and composers and were responsible for the commissioning of many important works, including **Felix Mendelssohn**'s *Symphony No. 4, the "Italian"* and Ludwig van Beethoven's *Symphony No. 9*. In 1912, on its one hundreth anniversary, the name was changed to the **Royal Philharmonic Society**.

Royal Scottish Academy of Music and Drama. See **Royal Conservatoire of Scotland**.

Royal Stockholm Philharmonic Orchestra (RSPO). The original ensemble was created in 1902 as the Stockholm Concert Society; it became permanent in 1914. In 1937, it became the orchestra of Swedish Radio. The **orchestra** performs every year at the Nobel Prize ceremony and at the Polar Music Prize award ceremony. The first principal **conductor** was Georg Schnéevoigt (1915–1924). He was followed by **Václav Talich** (1926–1936), Fritz Busch (1937–1940), Carl Garaguly (1942–1953), Hans Schmidt-Issersredr (1955–1964), Antal Doráti (1966–1974), **Gennady Rozhdestvensky** (1974–1977, 1991–1995), Yuri Ahronovitch (1982–1987), **Baavo Berglund** (1987–1990), **Andrew Davis** and **Paavo Järvi** (1995–1998), and **Alan Gilbert** (2000–2008). The current conductor is Sakaro Oramo. The orchestra has made numerous recording on the Swedish **BIS label**, including music by American composer Christopher Rouse. The orchestra has several outreach programs including a club, the Piccolaklubben, for young people between the ages of six and ten.

Rozhdestvensky, Gennady Nikolayevich. (b. 1931.) A Russian **conductor** known for championing the music of Russian composers, especially Sergei Prokofiev, Dmitri Shostakovich, **Igor Stravinsky**, and Alfred Schnittke and the Europeans Alban Berg, Darius Milhaud, **Arnold Schoenberg**, Arthur Honegger, and Francis Poulenc. After studying conducting with his father, Nikolai Anosov, at the **Moscow Conservatory**, he became the assistant conductor of the Bolshoi Theater (1951–1961) and the music director and conductor of the Symphony Orchestra of All-Union Radio and Television (1961–1974). He returned to the Bolshoi Theater as the principal conductor (1964–1970) and was the principal conductor of the Stockholm Philharmonic Orchestra (1974–1977), chief guest conductor of the **BBC Symphony Orchestra** (1978–1981), chief conductor of the **Vienna Symphony** (1980–1982), and principal conductor of the USSR State Symphony Orchestra (1981–1992) and the **Royal Stockholm Philharmonic** (1992–1995). He was also a frequent guest conductor with virtually all of the world's great **orchestras**. Among the many premieres he conducted were the original version of Sergei Prokofiev's *The Gambler*, the Russian premiere of **Sir Benjamin Britten**'s opera *A Midsummer Night's Dream*, the Western premiere of Dmitri Shostakovich's *Symphony No. 4*, Sofia Gubaidulina's *Stimmen . . . Verstummen . . .*, and several works of Alfred Schnittke, including the *Symphonies Nos. 1, 8, and 9*. Schnittke considered Rozhdestvensky a close colleague and friend. A versatile conductor with a supple technique and noted sense of the dramatic, Rozhdestvensky made numerous recordings on the **Melodiya** label, including lauded performances of Prokofiev's symphonies and several of his operas; all of the symphonies of Shostakovich, Alexander Glazunov, and Peter Ilyich Tchaikovsky; Tchaikovsky's ballets *The Nutcracker*, *Swan Lake*, and *The Maid of Orleans*; the symphonies of Jean Sibelius; a suite from Leoš Janáček's opera *The Cunning Little Vixen*; and many other works. He was married to the pianist Viktoriya Postnikova. In 1974, he published *Technique of Conducting* (Leningrad, and in 1975 in Moscow) and *Thoughts about Conducting*, a collection of essays (see the **bibliography**).

rubato. (It., lit. "robbed.") The practice of playing flexibly, that is, stretching the tempo at the beginning of a phrase, for instance, and then giving it back at the end by moving forward. Example: *tempo rubato*, in rubato style (lit. "stolen time").

Rücksicht. (Ger.) Consideration, regard. Examples: *ohne Rücksicht*, without regard; *ohne Rücksicht auf*, irrespective of; *Clar. ohne Rücksicht auf das Tempo I*, Clarinet, without consideration of the first tempo, all from *Symphony No. 1*, first movement by **Gustav Mahler**.

rude. (Fr.) Rough. A character word sometimes heard in rehearsal to evoke a particular style of playing. Example: *animé et très rude*, lively and very rough, from *Daphnis et Chloé* by Maurice Ravel. (Ger. *rau*, It. *grezzo*, Sp. áspero.)

Rudel, Julius. (b. 1921–2014.) Austrian-born American **opera** and **orchestra conductor**, known for championing operatic works of American composers. Rudel made his debut at the **New York City Opera (NYCO)** in 1944 and served as its music director from 1957 to 1979, commissioning twelve American operas. During his tenure the company's reputation grew substantially. In three seasons, 1959–1960, the company presented exclusively American opera, including Hugo Weisgall's *Six Characters in Search of an Author* (after the book by Luigi Pirandello). In 1966, the company moved into the **New York State Theater** at **Lincoln Center**. Rudel left the New York City Opera in order to become the music director of the **Buffalo Philharmonic**, serving from 1979 to 1985. He also often conducted the **Philadelphia Lyric Opera Company** and other ensembles around the world. He left an extensive list of opera recordings and DVDs.

Rudolf, Max. (1902–1995.) German-born American **conductor** and leading pedagogue. Rudolf moved to the United States in 1940, conducted at the **Metropolitan Opera** in New York from 1945 to 1958, and was the music director of the **Cincinnati Symphony Orchestra** from 1958 to 1970. He taught at the **Cleveland Institute of Music** (1970–1973) and at the **Curtis Institute of Music** in Philadelphia (1970–1973, 1983–1989). Rudolf may have had his greatest influence as a teacher of **conducting**; many of today's leading conductors studied with him at Curtis. He is the author of *The Grammar of Conducting* (1950); the third edition was released in 1995 (see the **bibliography**).

Ruf. (Ger.) Cry, call. Example: *Der Ruf eines Kukuks nachzuahmen*, imitating the call of a cuckoo, from *Symphony No. 1*, first movement by **Gustav Mahler**.

Rug Concerts. A series of casual concerts given by the **New York Philharmonic** in the 1970s under the direction of then music director **Pierre Boulez**.

Ruhe. (Ger.) Rest, peace. Sometimes heard in **rehearsal** to encourage players to rest between longer, difficult passages. (Fr. *repos*, It. *riposo*, Sp. *resto*.)

Ruhe! (Ger.) Quiet! Rarely heard but sometimes used in **rehearsal**. (Fr. *Taissez-vous! Silence!* It. *Silenzio!* Sp. *Silencio!*)

Ruhevoll. (Ger.) Peaceful. A character word used in the title of movement six of the Symphony No. 3 by **Gustav Mahler**.

ruhig, ruhiger. (Ger.) Tranquil, peaceful, quiet. Example: *sehr ruhig, ohne Ausdruck*, very calm, without expression, from *Pierrot Lunaire* by **Arnold Schoenberg**. Also *ruhelos*, restless or uneasy; *ruhevoll*, peaceful. (Fr. *tranquille*, It. *tranquillo*, Sp. *tranquilo*.)

Rührtrommel. (Ger.) Tenor drum. See also **appendix 4**, **Rolltrommel**.

Rundfunk-Sinfonieorchester Berlin. See **Berlin Radio Symphony Orchestra**.

Russian Five. A group of Russian composers also known as the Mighty Handful, the Balakirev Circle, or simply as the Five, who aligned themselves during the years 1856–1879 to produce a specifically Russian style of art music at a time when European music was dominant. They were Mily Balakirev, César Cui, Modest Mussorgsky, and Alexander Borodin.

Russian State Symphony Orchestra. See **State Academic Symphony Orchestra of the Russian Federation**.

rustico, rusticano. (It.) Rustic, plain. A descriptive word used to evoke a particular style of playing. (Fr. *rustique*, Ger. *ländlich*, Sp. *caracter rústico*.)

Rusty Musicians Program. An outreach program at the **Baltimore Symphony Orchestra (BSO)** for adult amateur musicians who come together periodically in order to receive coaching and then play alongside musicians of the BSO. The program has been duplicated throughout the United States. At the **Toledo Symphony Orchestra**, a similar program is called the Pro-Am Project.

Rute. (Ger.) A birch brush used in playing various percussion instruments. In the twentieth century, it has been replaced by a wire brush.

rythme. (Fr.) Rhythm. (Ger. *Rhythmus*, It. *ritmo*, Sp. *ritmo*.)

rythmique, rythmé. (Fr.) Rhythmic, measured, in a precise rhythm. (Ger. *rhytmisch*, It. *ritmico*, Sp. *ritmico*.)

S

S. Abbreviation for *segno*. See *dal segno*.

Sacher, Paul. (b. 1906–1999.) Swiss **conductor** and patron. Sacher studied with **Felix Weingartner** and formed the Basel Chamber Orchestra (1926), an ensemble that specialized in "historical performance." He commissioned works from Béla Bartók, Paul Hindemith, Arthur Honegger, Frank Martin, Bohuslav Martinů, **Igor Stravinsky**, and others. He established the Sacher Foundation, which houses all of the commissioned works, other important manuscripts, and additional source material for the music field.

Sadler's Wells Opera, London. See **English National Opera**.

Saint Paul Chamber Orchestra (SPCO). Founded in 1959 in Saint Paul, Minnesota, the SPCO is American's only full-time professional **chamber orchestra**. In the 2004–2005 concert season, the orchestra decided to eliminate the position of music director and since then has worked with a group of five artistic partners. Current partners are the Italian **conductor** Roberto Abbado, violinist Patricia Kopatchinskaja, Dutch conductor **Edo de Waart**, German pianist Christian Zacharias, and Austrian violinist Thomas Zehetmair. The SPCO won a **Grammy Award** for its recording of Aaron Copland's *Appalachian Spring* (see **appendix 1**), one of the first digital audio recordings made.

Saint Petersburg Conservatory. See **Rimsky-Korsakov Saint Petersburg State Conservatory**.

Saint Petersburg Philharmonic. Established in 1882, it is Russia's oldest **orchestra**. In its early years, it performed privately for the court of Alexander III. After 1900 it began to give public concerts. One of its earliest guest **conductors** was **Richard Strauss** in 1912. After the revolution it became known as the State Philharmonic Orchestra of Petrograd. Guest conductors during the 1920s included **Bruno Walter**, **Ernest Ansermet**, and **Hans Knappertsbusch**. When Vladimir Lenin died and the city of Petrograd was renamed, so was the orchestra, becoming the Leningrad Philharmonic Orchestra. It was during the long tenure of **Yevgeny Mvravinsky** (1938–1988) that the orchestra came to international acclaim. During that time, the orchestra made a total of fifty-four recordings. When Mvravinsky stopped recording, concerts were taped and later released. One of Mvravinsky's long-time, distinguished associates was **Kurt Sanderling**, who also conducted the orchestra from 1941 to 1960. In 1991, the city changed its name once again, with the orchestra following its lead and becoming the Saint Petersburg Philharmonic. The current music director is **Yuri Temirkanov** (appointed in 1988).

Saite. (Ger.) String of a **violin** or **cello** or other string instrument. Also *Saiteninstrument*, stringed instrument; *leere Saite*, open string. Example: *auf der G-Saite*, on the G string. (Fr. *corde*, It. *corda*, Sp. *cuerda*.)

Saito, Hideo. (1902–1974.) Japanese cellist and **conductor**. Saito studied in Germany at the Leipzig Conservatory and later at the Berlin Hochschule für Musik (now the **Hans Eisler Hochschule für Musik**). He returned to Japan to become the principle cellist of the **NHK Symphony Orchestra**. In 1948, he founded the **Toho Gauken School of Music**. Among his students were **Seiji Ozawa** and **Kazuyoski Akiyama**. Saito toured the USSR and United States with the Toho Chamber Orchestra.

Saito Kinen Orchestra. Founded by **Seiji Ozawa** and **Kazuyoshi Akiyama** in 1984 in a series of concerts to honor teacher and founder of the **Toho Gakuen School of Music**, Hideo Saito. The ensemble consisted of over one hundred musicians who were his former students. Now the resident ensemble of the Saito Kinen Festival, the **orchestra** has toured internationally to great acclaim.

Salabert, Edouard. (1838–1903.) Founder of the music publisher **Éditions Salabert**.

Salabert, Francis. (1884–1946.) Music publisher. He took over the business from his father, **Edouard Salabert**. See Éditions **Salabert**.

Salonen, Esa-Pekka. (b. 1958.) Finnish **conductor** and composer. Salonen is currently the principal conductor and artistic advisor for the **Philharmonia Orchestra, London**, and conductor laureate of the **Los Angeles Philharmonic**. He studied **horn** and composition at the **Sibelius Academy** and **conducting** with **Jorma Panula**. He made his conducting debut in 1979 with the **Finnish Radio Symphony Orchestra** and in 1983 he conducted **Gustav Mahler**'s *Symphony No. 3* as a short-notice replacement for **Michael Tilson Thomas** with the **London Philharmonia**. From 1985 to 1994 he was the principal conductor of the London Philharmonia and also of the Swedish Radio Symphony Orchestra (1984–1995). Salonen made his debut with the Los Angeles Philharmonic in 1984 and served as its music director from 1992 until 2009, raising the profile of the orchestra. During his tenure in Los Angeles, he made an enormous contribution to contemporary music, commissioning over 54 new works and giving the American premieres of over 120. On his departure, the orchestra created the Esa-Pekka Salonen Commissions Fund to both honor his work and continue it in the future. Salonen also oversaw the construction of the new Walt Disney Concert Hall, where the orchestra is in residence. Salonen has also led numerous notable recordings, including his **Grammy** and Gramophone Award–winning recording of Witold Lutosławski's, *Symphony No. 3*, a Grammy Award–winning recording of Béla Bartók's Piano Concertos No. 1, 2, and 3 with pianist Yefim Bronfman, and many more. Salonen is also a successful composer in his own right.

saltando, saltato. (It.) A short, fast stroke played in the middle or just above the middle of the bow so that the bow bounces slightly off the string. Similar to **spiccato** but not as strong or controlled and not dropped, it starts from the string.

saltellato, saltato. (It.) A bowing term that calls for a short, light, fast bow stroke that makes the bow bounce off of the string when used in fast tempos. Similar to **spiccato** but not as controlled or strong. (Fr. *sautillé*.)

saltillo. (Sp.) There are several variations for this term: *salto* (It., Sp) is a leap, skip, the opposite of by step; a melody that moves in leaps instead of by step (Fr. *saut*, Ger. *Sprung*); *saut* (Fr.) is a leap, skip, the opposite of by step—a melody that moves in leaps instead of by step (Ger. *Sprung*, It. *salto*, Sp. *salto*); and *sautillé* (Fr.) is an alternative term for *saltando* or *saltato* (Ger. *gehüpft*, It. *saltellato, balzellato*).

Salzburg Festival. One of the most famous festivals in the world, it was revived in Austria after World War I by the poet and librettist Hugo von Hofmannsthal; composer **Richard Strauss**, who often collaborated with Hofmannsthal; scenic designer Alfred Roller; and stage director Max Reinhardt with a performance of Hofmannsthal's play *Jedermann*. The first **opera** produced there was Wolfgang Amadeus Mozart's *Don Giovanni*, conducted by Strauss, a known Mozart expert, in 1922. Recovering from closure during World War II, the festival has continued to grow, add performance spaces, and put on highly reputable operatic, orchestral, and chamber performances that attract artists and audiences from around the world.

Salzburg Mozarteum. Named after Salzburg's most famous resident, Wolfgang Amadeus Mozart, it has been known as the **Universität Mozarteum Salzburg** since 1998. The school offers courses in the performing and visual arts, including study in all instruments, composition, conducting, acting, stage direction and design, music education, and music theater. The Mozarteum has a distinguished faculty and alumni list, including some of the most reputable musicians of the twentieth century. Founded in 1841 through the efforts of Mozart's widow, Constanze Weber Mozart, as the Cathedral Music Association and Mozarteum.

Salzburg Mozarteum Orchestra. Founded as part of the first music school in Salzburg, the Cathedral Music Association (see **Salzburg Mozarteum**), in Salzburg in 1841. It is a fully professional orchestra with a long-term association with the **Salzburg Festival**. The orchestra specializes in music of the classical period.

Samuel, Gerhard. (1924–2008.) German-born American **conductor**, composer, and pedagogue. Samuel was the director of orchestral studies at the Cincinnati College—Conservatory of Music (1976–1997). He was also the music director of the Oakland Symphony and the San Francisco Ballet, the founder of the San Francisco Chamber Orchestra, and the first conductor of the **Cabrillo Music Festival**.

sand blocks. Also sometimes called sandpaper blocks, they are two blocks wrapped with sandpaper and rubbed together to produce the tone. See **appendix 4**.

San Diego Symphony Orchestra. Formed as the San Diego Civic Orchestra in 1910, the orchestra has become a fully professional ensemble offering classics, pops, educational, and other concerts. The orchestra has struggled with periodic financial difficulties, reorganizing most recently in

1998 under the leadership of local philanthropist Larry Robinson with **Jung-Ho Pak** serving as the artistic director (1989–2002). In 2004, the orchestra received the single largest gift ever announced, $120 million from Joan and Irwin Jacobs, which led to increased salaries and a forty-one-week season. The current **conductor** is **Jahja Ling**. Previous conductors include B. Roscoe Schryock (1912–1920), Nino Mrcelli (1936–1937), Nikolai Sokoloff (1939–1941), Fabien Sevitzky (1949–1951), Robert Shaw (1953–1958), Ear Bernard Murray (1959–1966), Soltán Rozsnyai (1967–1971), Peter Erôs (1972–1979), **David Atherton** (1980–1987), and Yoav Talmi (1989–1996). The orchestra's archivist, Melvin G. Goldzband, has published a history of the orchestra titled *San Diego Symphony from Overture to Encore*.

San Francisco Conservatory of Music. Incorporated under its current name in 1923, Isaac Stern and Yehudi Menuhin were among its early students, and composer Ernest Bloch was one of its early directors. The conservatory offers a bachelor of music degree, an artist certificate in chamber music, a master of music degree, a postgraduate diploma in vocal performance, and a professional studies diploma in instrumental performance. The school has a close connection with the **San Francisco Symphony**, with many of its members on the faculty.

San Francisco Opera. Established in 1923 by **conductor** Gaetano Merola who served as the general director from 1923 to 1953. Merola was followed by Kurt Herbert Adler, who served as the general director from 1953 to 1981. Adler expanded the season, founded the Merola Opera Program to foster young singers, and began the Opera in the Park series. Terence McEwen served in the top administrative position from 1982 to 1988 followed by Lotfi Mansouri from 1988 to 2001. Pamela Rosenburg served from 2001 to 2005, and was followed by David Gockley, 2006 to the present. Gockley brought many of the world's best-known singers to the San Francisco stage, began a **Ring cycle** in 2008, and brought about several technological innovations such as live simulcasts (from 2006) and using screens in the opera house to project close-up images from the stage. Music directors have included John Pritchard (1986–1989), Donald Runnicles (1992–2009), and Nicola Luisotti (appointed in 2009). The company presents both operatic standards and new work, including Philip Glass's **opera** *Appomattox*, Christopher Theofanidis's *Heart of a Soldier*, Mark Adamo's *The Gospel of Mary Magdalene*, and Tobias Picker's *Dolores Claiborne*.

San Francisco Symphony (SFS). Gave its first concerts in 1911. Among its music directors were **Pierre Monteux**, **Josef Krips**, **Seiji Ozawa**, **Edo de Waart**, and **Herbert Blomstedt**. Since 1995 **Michael Tilson Thomas** has served as the music director. The symphony engages in many educational and outreach programs, including its series **Adventures in Music** (begun in 1988), offering music to all public schoolchildren in grades 1 through 5. According to the symphony's website, the program reaches more than twenty-three thousand students. Its Instrumental Training and Support program puts professionals into the public schools to coach students, and in 2002, the online program sfskids.org was launched as a music education resource. The orchestra has been offering **young people's concerts**, now called **Concerts for Kids**, since 1919. A program for adult amateurs, **Community of Music Makers**, offers workshops and events. In 2006, Michael Tilson Thomas began a multimedia program called *Keeping Score*. It is available online and on DVD and Blu-ray. They perform in Louise M. Davies Symphony Hall.

sanfter Weise, in. (Ger.) Gently, softly, daintily. (Fr. *doucement, gentiment*, It. *delicatimente, dolcement*, Sp. *suavemente*.)

sanft, weich. (Ger.) Gentle, soft, gently, daintily, sweetly. (Fr. *doux, gentiment*, It. *dolce, delicatimente, dolcement,* Sp. *dulce, suavemente*.) Examples: *mit Sanftheit* or *mit Sanftmut*, with softness. (Fr. *avec douceur*, It. *con dolcezza*.) Also *sehr sanft*, very soft. (Fr. *trés douce*, It. *dolcissimo*, Sp. *muy dulce*.)

sans. (Fr.) Without. (Ger. *ohne*, It. *senza*, Sp. *sin*.) Examples: *sans courir*, without hurrying. (Ger. *ohne davonzurennen*, It, *senza correre*, Sp. *sin correr*.) See also ***sans changer, sans durété, sans reprise, sans sourdine***.

sans changer. (Fr.) Without changing. (Ger. *ohne zu wechseln*, It. *senza cambiare*, Sp. *sin cambiar*.)

sans durété. (Fr.) Without hardness. Seen in *Sirèns*, movement three of *Nocturnes* by Claude Debussy.

sans reprise. (Fr.) Without repetition. (Ger. *ohne Wiederholen,* It. *senza replica*, Sp. *sin repetición*.)

sans sourdine. (Fr.) Without the mute. (It. *senza sordino*, Ger. *Ohne Dämpfer*, Sp. *sin sordina*.)

Santa Fe Opera (SFO). Launched in 1957 by founding director and unofficial principal **conductor** John Crosby, who served until 2000. The SFO is widely known for its annual combination of operatic standards and premieres, having presented forty-four works by American composers and eleven international premieres and having made ten commissions. Having established an apprenticeship program for young singers early on in its history, the SFO provides important training and experience on the stage, in the chorus, and understudying major roles, and many alumni have gone on to major careers.

Sarasota Orchestra. Formerly known as the Florida West Coast Symphony, the eighty-member, fully professional Sarasota Orchestra presents a complete range of classics, pops, and family concerts and sponsors a fifty-year-old youth orchestra program. It was established in 1949 when interested community members pooled their musical and financial resources. The current music director is Estonian conductor **Anu Tali**. Past music directors include Lyman Wiltse (1950), Alexander Bloch (1951–1960), Paul Wolfe (1961–1996), and Lief Bjaland (1997–2012).

Saraste, Jukka-Pekka. (b. 1956.) Finnish **conductor** and violinist. Saraste studied at the **Sibelius Academy** with **Jorma Panula**. He and **Esa-Pekka Salonen** cofounded the Avanti! Chamber Orchestra to present predominantly contemporary music. Saraste served as the chief conductor of the **Finnish Radio Symphony Orchestra** (1987–2001) and the principal conductor of the **Scottish Chamber Orchestra** (1987–1991). He became the music director of the Toronto Symphony Orchestra in 1994, serving until 2001. He was the principal guest conductor of the **BBC Symphony Orchestra** (2002–2005), music director of the Oslo Philharmonic (2006–2013), artistic advisor of the Lahti Symphony Orchestra (2008–2011), and was made the principal conductor of the WDR Symphony Orchestra, Cologne, in 2010. As a guest conductor, he has worked with many orchestras throughout Europe and the United States. Saraste has recorded the complete symphonies of Jean Sibelius and Carl Nielsen and has made respected recordings of Henri Dutilleux's *Symphony No. 2*, **Arnold Schoenberg**'s *Pelleas and Melisande*, and others.

Sargent, Sir Malcolm. (1895–1967.) English **conductor**, organist, and composer. Sargent served as the chief conductor of the **BBC Proms**, London's internationally famous summer festival, from 1948 to 1967. He took over the festival from its founder, **Sir Henry Wood**. He was regarded as a particularly fine choral conductor and by many as an excellent concerto accompanist. Sargent led many performances of works by W. S. Gilbert and Arthur Sullivan and was a proponent of many English and other contemporary composers. After the death of **Sir Thomas Beecham**, Sargent played a major role in saving the **Royal Philharmonic Orchestra**.

Satellite Digital Audio Radio Service (SDARS). A service operated by **Sirius XM Radio**.

satellite radio. A radio service broadcast by satellite reaching a much wider geographical area than traditional radio stations. Mostly servicing automobiles, it is available by subscription, remains primarily commercial free, and provides a far larger number of stations. See also **Sirius XM Radio**.

Satz. (Ger.) A **movement** of a **symphony** or any multi-movement work. (Fr. *mouvement*, It. *movimento*, Sp. *movimiento*.)

sauté de la pointe. (Fr.) A specialized bowing technique in which the player bounces the tip of the bow against the strings.

sauvage. (Fr.) Wild, unrestrained. Sometimes seen as a descriptive term in scores and parts. (Fr. *féroce*, It. *feroce, furiosamente*, Sp. *feroz, indomable*.)

Sawallisch, Wolfgang. (1923–2013.) German **conductor** and pianist. Sawallisch was the youngest conductor to ever appear at the **Bayreuth Festival** when he conducted **Richard Wagner**'s *Tristan and Isolde* in 1957. He served as the music director or principal conductor for many orchestras, including the **Vienna Symphony** (1960–1970), the Hamburg Symphony, the **Orchestre de la Suisse Romande**, the **Bavarian State Opera**, and the **Philadelphia Orchestra** (1993–2003). His recording legacy includes primarily German works of the nineteenth century.

Sax, Adolphe. (1814–1894.) Belgian music instrument maker and inventor of the **saxophone**. Sax was also responsible for many improvements and developments of instruments such as the **bass clarinet**; bugles; the so-called saxhorn, which over time developed into the **flugelhorn**; and the now nonexistent saxotromba. His most famous instrument, the saxophone, was patented in 1846 and designed for use in both the **band** and **orchestra**. Sax designed a full-range family of instruments from sopranino to subcontrabass.

Saxon State Opera (Sächsische Staatsoper). See **Dresden Staaskapelle**.

saxophone. A brass wind instrument invented by **Adolphe Sax** and patented by him in 1846. Commonly used in the winds and band. While not often used in the **orchestra**, important examples exist, such as Modest Mussorgsky's *Pictures at an Exhibition*, Maurice Ravel's *Bolero*, and Sergei Rachmaninov's *Symphonic Dances*. (Fr. *saxophon*, It. *sassofono*, Ger. *Saxophon*, Sp. *saxófono*.)

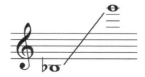

Saxophone range. *Courtesy Andrew Martin Smith.*

Saxophone B-flat soprano range as it sounds. *Courtesy Andrew Martin Smith.*

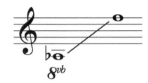

Saxophone B-flat tenor range as it sounds. *Courtesy Andrew Martin Smith.*

Saxophone E-flat alto range as it sounds. *Courtesy Andrew Martin Smith.*

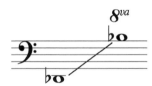

Saxophone E-flat baritone range as it sounds. *Courtesy Andrew Martin Smith.*

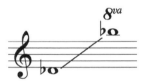

Saxophone E-flat soprano range as it sounds. *Courtesy Andrew Martin Smith.*

scala. (It.) **Scale**. (Fr. *gamme*, Ger. *Tonleiter*, Sp. *escala*). See also **alternative scales**.

scale. An ordered set of **pitches** that can be ascending, descending, or both. The most common scales, including the major, minor, and all modal scales, have a set order of whole and half steps. See also **alternative scales**.

scena, palcoscencio. (It.) Stage, of an opera house, for example. (Fr. *scène, planches*, Ger. *Bühne, Szene*, Sp. *escena, etapa*.)

scenario. An outline or summary of an **opera libretto**. (Fr. *scénario*, Ger. *Szenario,* It. *scenario*.)

scène, planches. (Fr.) Stage, of an opera house, for example. (Ger. *Bühne, Szene,* It. *scena, palcoscenico,* Sp. *escena, etapa*.)

schalkhaft. (Ger.) Roguish, waggish. Also *Schlau*, cunning, clever, artful. (Fr. *avec fourberie, rusé, malin,* It. *furbescamente, furbo,* Sp. *astuto*.)

Schall, Klang. (Ger.) Sound, ring, bang. (Fr. *son, sonneire* It. *suono, squillo* Sp. *sonido*.)

Schallplatte. (Ger.) Phonograph record. (Fr. *disque,* It. *disco,* Sp. *disco, disco gramóonico*.)

Schalltrichter auf! (Ger.) Bells up. (Fr. *pavillon en l'air,* It. *padiglioni in alto,* Sp. *pabellón arriba*.) A directive used for woodwind and **horn** players to lift the bells of the instruments up. This happens most often in the music of **Gustav Mahler**. Also *Schalltrichter in die Höhe!* Bells lifted! Abbreviated *Schalltr.*

Schalltrichter, Schallbecher. (Ger.) Bell of an instrument, such as the **horn** or **trumpet**. (Fr. *pavillon,* It. *padiglione,* Sp. *pabellon*.) See also *Schalltrichter auf!*

scharf. (Ger.) Sharp, shrill. Sometimes used as a descriptive term. (Fr. *aigu,* It. *acuto*.)

Schelle. (Ger., pl. *Schellen*.) Sleigh bells. (Fr. *sonnailles,* It. *sonagliera,* Sp. *cascabeles*.) Used, for example, in **Gustav Mahler**'s *Symphony No. 4*, first movement.

Schellenbaum. (Ger.) Bell tree. (Fr. *pavillon, chapeau chinois,* It. *mezza luna, cappello cinese,* Sp. *chinesco*.) See **appendix 4**.

Schellentrommel, Tamburin. (Ger.) Tambourine. (Fr. *tambour de basque,* It. *tamburello basco,* Sp. *tambourin*.) See **appendix 4**.

Schenker, Heinrich. (1868–1935.) Austrian theorist, writer, and pianist. He studied composition at the **Vienna Conservatory** with Anton Bruckner and law at the university. He was a private piano and theory teacher, music critic, editor, and performer. His students included **Wilhelm Furtwängler**. Schenker's theoretical writings were very influential and his techniques and principles continue to be taught in music schools today. His main work was published in *Neue musikalische Theorien und Phantasien*, divided into *Harmonielehre* (1906), *Kontrapunkt* (1922), and *Der freie Satz* (1935). Other important publications include *Beethovens Neunte Sinfonie* (1912),

Beethovens Fünfte Sinfonie (1925), *Der Tonwille* (ten issues published between 1921 and 1924), his three-volume *Das Meisterwerk in der Musik* (1925–1930), and *Fünf Urlinie-Tafeln* (1932). Most of his publications have been translated into English by Felix Salzer. Several texts about Schenker's theoretical principles have been published in the United States. Schenker had a great influence on many American theorists, resulting in *Structural Hearing* by Felix Salzer (1952) and books by Edward Cone, Allen Forte, Carl Schacter, and others (see the **bibliography**).

Schenkerian analysis, principles of. **Heinrich Schenker** based his analysis on the idea that the structure of any well-composed tonal piece could be described in multiple layers of complexity that he called *Schichten*. Schenker called the most apparent level of composition the foreground, or *Vordergrund*. It included all of the work's most evident, surface activity. The second level is the complex middle ground, or *Mittelgrund*, consisting of linear relationships between the **pitches** of structurally important harmonies perceived more long-term, both within and between phrases. The middle ground also consists of fundamental harmonies perceived as defining sections of the work.

The deepest, most fundamental level of a piece, the *Ursatz*, or background, includes an overall melodic stepwise descent to the tonic, referred to as the *Urlinie*, supported by a bass progression of I-V-I arpeggiated and projected over the course of the work, called the *Baßbrechung*. Additional melodic and harmonic elements would be considered subordinate and a result of what he referred to as the *Auskomponierung*, meaning to complete the composition. Schenker and his followers developed a graph system that uses both standard notation and specific symbols to designate the important elements of a work as he saw them. Such graphs can be seen in *Fünf Urlinie-Tafeln* (1932), published with an English translation and edited by Felix Salzer in 1969. The American theorist Edward Cone wrote, "The greatest ideas of Schenker stem from the fact that his system reveals how a piece of music should be heard, in that it shows how basic patterns and cells unfold into a complete composition" (see Boretz and Cone in the **bibliography**).

Scherchen, Hermann. (1891–1966.) German **conductor**. Author of three books on **conducting**, including *Treatise on Conducting* (*Lehrbuch des Dirigierens*; see the **bibliography**). Scherchen began his conducting career assisting **Arnold Schoenberg** for the premiere of *Pierrot Lunaire* (1912). He was considered an ideal **conductor** for the music of the **Second Viennese School**, Luigi Dallapiccola, Paul Hindemith, Sergei Prokofiev, and **Igor Stravinsky**.

scherzando, scherzoso. (It., lit. "jesting.") A character word that refers to the tempo and style of a **scherzo**, a fast dance in 3/4. Used in the title of movement three of **Gustav Mahler**'s Symphony No. 3 (Fr. *en badinant, en plaisantant,* Ger. *scherzend, neckisch,* Sp. *jocoso.*)

scherzend. (Ger.) Jokingly, playfully, joking. Sometimes associated with a musical character. (Fr. *plaisantant,* It. *scherzoso, giocoso,* Sp. *jocoso.*)

scherzhaft. (Ger.) Jesting, light. (Fr. *de façon burlesque,* It. *burlesco,* Sp. *burlón, en broma, chistoso.*)

scherzo. (It., lit. "joke.") A common movement in a **symphony** from Ludwig van Beethoven forward.

scherzoso. (It.) Jokingly. See also *Scherzhaft*.

Schirmer, Gustav. (1829–1893.) German born. Schirmer immigrated to America in 1837. He was the son and grandson of instrument makers, and he took a position with the music publisher Scharfenberg & Luis. Schirmer became the manager of the music publishing house Breusing's. He joined forces with the company Beer, working as Beer & Schirmer until 1866 when he established G. Schirmer Music Publishers, Importers and Dealers in New York. Hoping to recoup his failing health, he traveled to Germany, dying there in 1893. See also **Schirmer Music Publishers**.

Schirmer, Gustave. (1864–1907.) American music publisher and son of **Gustav Schirmer**.

Schirmer Music Publishers. Established in 1866 by **Gustav Schirmer**, the company established its reputation with the collection Schirmer's Library of Musical Classics, which is still in use to this day. In the early 1900s, the company introduced the music of Gabriel Fauré and at the same time published the music of American composers Edward MacDowell and Horatio Parker. Schirmer began publishing *Musical Quarterly* in 1915 with editor Oscar Sonneck, who had been the first chief of the **Music Division of the Library of Congress**. In the next decades, the company focused on building a catalogue of music by American composers. In 1964, they purchased Associated Music Publishers, solidifying their status as one of the major publishers in America. Currently owned by the **Music Sales Corporation**, they have continued to develop their extensive catalogue through the purchase and promotion of smaller publishers. They also serve as the American agent for many European music publishers.

Schirmer, Rudolph Edward. (1859–1907.) Son of **Gustav Schirmer**, who founded **Schirmer Music Publishers**. He pursued the development of music education in

America and participated in the planning and establishment of the Institute of Musical Art (1904), which became part of the **Juilliard School**.

Schlag. (Ger.) Beat, pulse. (Fr. *batter, frapper,* It. *battere, percuotere,* Sp. *pulso, tempo.*) Example: *von einem geschlagen,* played by one person, from the Symphony No. 5, movement one, by **Gustav Mahler**. See also *schlagen, Schlaginstrumente, Schlagwerk, Schlagzeug,* **percussion instruments**.

Schlagen. (Ger.) To beat, to strike, as in to beat the time, to conduct. (Fr. *battre,* It. *battere.*)

Schlagzeug. (Ger.) The percussion section of the **orchestra**, can also be a drum roll. (Fr. *batterie,* It. *batteria,* Sp. *batería.*)

schleichend. (Ger.) Creeping, sneaking. Example: *etwas schleichend,* somewhat creeping, from *Das Lied von der Erde* by **Gustav Mahler**.

Schleicher, Donald. (b. 1954.) American **conductor**. Schleicher has been professor of **conducting** and the director of orchestral studies at the University of Illinois since 1995. He was the music director of the Quad City Symphony Orchestra from 1999 to 2007, and he has guest conducted orchestras in China, Ukraine, South Korea, Mexico, and more. He has given many **conducting** master classes at educational institutions, including the Eastman School of Music, Oberlin Conservatory, Ohio State University, the Shepherd School of Music at Rice University, and more.

schleppen. (Ger.) To drag. Examples: *Nicht schleppen,* don't drag; *ohne zu schleppen,* without dragging; *Schleppend,* dragging, from *Symphony No. 1,* and others by **Gustav Mahler**.

Schluss. (Ger.) Close, end. (Fr. *fin,* It. *fine,* Sp. *final.*) Example: *zum Schluss,* to the end.

Schlüssel. (Ger.) Clef. (Fr. *clé, clef,* It. *chiave,* Sp. *clave.*) See also **C clefs**.

Schmerz. (Ger.) Pain, sorrow. Also *schmerzvoll,* painful, sorrowful. A charcter word sometimes heard in connection with mood of feeling. (Fr. *douleur,* It. *dolore,* Sp. *dolor.*)

schmerzlich. (Ger.) Sorrowful, painful. (Fr. *douloureux,* It. *doloroso,* Sp. *doloroso.*)

schmetternd. (Ger.) An indication for **horn** players that asks for a "brassy" sound. It is achieved by putting the hand into the bell and using more air.

schnell, schneller. (Ger.) Fast, faster. Similar to ***presto*** in Italian. (Fr. *vite,* It. *presto,* Sp. *rápido.*) Examples: *Schnell bis zum Schluss,* fast until the end; *schneller werdend,* becoming faster; *sehr schnell,* very fast.

Schoenberg, Arnold. (1874–1951.) Austrian composer known primarily for developing the twelve-tone compositional technique. See also the **bibliography**, *Pierrot Lunaire*, **Second Viennese School**, **twelve-tone technique**, **twelve-tone row**, **twelve-tone chord**, **matrix**.

Schott, Bernhard. (1748–1809.) Music publisher. Schott founded the firm that became known as B. Schotts Söhne (1770). It was continued by his sons, Johann Andreas (1781–1840) and Johann Joseph (1782–1855). They published some of the late works of Ludwig van Beethoven (*Missa solemnis,* Symphony No. 9, and the late string quartets) and late operas of **Richard Wagner**, including the **Ring Cycle**, *Die Meistersinger*, and *Parsifal*.

Schritt, Schrittmässig. (Ger.) Degree, stepwise. (Fr. *degré,* It. *grado,* Sp. *por grados, de grado.*)

Schuller, Gunther. (1925–2015.) American composer, **conductor**, author, and **horn** player. Schuller is the author of *The Compleat Conductor* (see the **bibliography**). He played horn with many professional ensembles early in his career, including the **Cincinnati Symphony Orchestra** (1943–1945) and the **Metropolitan Opera** (1945–1950). He founded the Modern Jazz Society with pianist John Lewis. While teaching at Brandies University in the late 1950s, he coined the term "third-stream" to describe music that combined components of jazz and classical music. He went on to compose many works that were a manifestation of this style. He collaborated with many jazz artists, including Ornette Coleman, Bill Evans, and others.

He was the president of the **New England Conservatory** from 1967 to 1977. While there, he founded the New England Ragtime Ensemble, which toured widely. He was the artistic director of the **Tanglewood Music Center** (1970–1984) and established Margun Music in 1975 and Gunmar Music in 1979, publishing many contemporary composers and jazz/third-stream music. He later sold them to **G. Schirmer**. He won the **Pulitzer Prize** for his composition *Of Reminiscences and Reflections* and won a **MacArthur Foundation Award** in 1991 and a **Ditson Conductor's Award** in 1970. The first volume of his autobiography, *Gunther Schuller: A Life in Pursuit of Music and Beauty*, was published in 2011 (see the **bibliography**).

Schuman, William. (1910–1992.) Prolific American composer, innovative educator, and administrator. As president of the **Juilliard School** (1946–1962), he oversaw a period of extensive growth in the curriculum, including the addition of the dance division and the beginnings of the drama division. He brought a number of distinguished American composers to the faculty who not only taught composition but also assisted in the development of the school's literature and martials of music curriculum. Further, he added major **conductors** to strengthen the teaching of **conducting**. They included **Jean Morel**, **Sixten Ehrling**, and **Otto Werner Mueller**.

From 1962 to 1968 he served as the president of **Lincoln Center**, bringing the **New York City Opera**, New York City Ballet, and the Juilliard School all into residence at the center. While there, he supported young American composers by commissioning and performing their music, started the Chamber Music Society of Lincoln Center, the Film Society, and a summer music series that later grew into the **Mostly Mozart Festival**.

Among his most widely performed compositions, the *New England Triptych*, which exists in versions for orchestra and band, uses tunes by **William Billings**, one of the first American-born composers (1746–1800). His **opera** *The Mighty Casey* may be the first baseball opera. Current Juilliard School president **Joseph Polisi** wrote the latest biography, *American Muse: The Life and Times of William Schuman* (2008; see the **bibliography**).

schütteln. (Ger.) To shake. A direction used in percussion parts. Also ***Schütteln***, agitation orvibration. (Fr. *secouer*, It. *scuotere*, Sp. *sacudir*.)

schwach, schwacher. (Ger.) Weak, weaker, faint, fainter. (Fr. *faible*, It. *debile, debole, fievole*, Sp. *débil*.) Example: *Immer schwacher und schwacher*, always fainter and fainter, from Symphony No. 1, movement one, by **Gustav Mahler**.

schwachen. (Ger.) Becoming softer and weaker. A directive. (Fr. *affaiblissez, affaibli*, It. *indebolire*, Sp. *debilitándose*.)

schwacher Taktteil. (Ger.) Weak beat, offbeat (Fr. *temps faible*, It. *tempo debole*, Sp. *tiempo débil*.)

Schwammschlägel. (Ger.) Sponge-headed mallet or stick, as in a timpani mallet with a sponge head. (Fr. *baguette d'*éponge, It. *bacchettta di spugna*, Sp. *baqueta de esponja*.)

Schwann Catalogue. A record magazine established in 1949 by William Schwann. At the beginning, the catalogue focused on listings and reviews of classical records. In the 1970s, it appeared in two volumes, one for classical music and one for pop. It went bankrupt in 2002.

Schwantner chord. Has become iconic through its influence on other composers. See also **iconic chords**.

Typical
Schwantner Chord

Schwantner chord. *Courtesy Andrew Martin Smith.*

Schwarz, Gerard. (b. 1947.) American **conductor** and trumpeter. Schwarz was the music director of the **Seattle Symphony** from 1985 to 2011. Under Schwarz's musical direction, the **Seattle Symphony** made over 125 commercial recordings under a unique agreement with the musicians' union. These recordings included works of many American composers such as David Diamond, Alan Hovhaness, and others. Schwarz served as the music director of the Los Angeles Chamber Orchestra in the 1970s, the **Lincoln Center**'s **Mostly Mozart Festival** (1982–2001), and the **Royal Liverpool Philharmonic Orchestra (RLPO)** from 2001 to 2006. His recordings list includes performances with the **Czech Philharmonic**, **Berlin Radio Symphony Orchestra**, **French National Orchestra**, **Philadelphia Orchestra**, and others. Schwarz won **Columbia University**'s **Ditson Award** for conductors in 1989 and was **Musical America**'s Conductor of the Year in 1994.

schweige. (Ger.) Silent. (Fr. *silencieux*, It. *silenzioso*, Sp. *silencioso*.)

Schweigezeichen. (Ger.) **Grand pause** (Fr. *pause generale*, It. *pausa generale, vuoto*, Sp. *pausa general, silencio general*.)

schwer, schwerfällig. (Ger.) Difficult, heavy, weighted, weighty. (Fr. *pesant, lourd*, It. *pesante, ponderato*, Sp. *pesado*.) See also ***schwierig***.

schwermütig. (Ger.) Lugubrious, mournful, gloomy. (Fr., It. *lugubre*, Sp. *lúgubre*.)

schwierig, schwer. (Ger.) Difficult. A commonly heard descriptive. (Fr. *difficile*, It. *difficile*, Sp. *dificil*.)

Schwirrholz. (Ger.) **Bull-roarer.** (Fr. *planchette ronflante*, It. *legno frullante, tavoletta sibilante*, Sp. *roncador*.) See also **appendix 4**.

Schwung. (Ger.) Drive, energy, swing. (Fr. *enlevé*, It. *brio*, Sp. *brío*.) Examples*: mit Schwung*, with verve. Also ***Lebhaftigkeit***, liveliness.

schwungvoll. (Ger.) Full of energy, excitement, spirited. (Fr. *avec verve, enlevé*, It. *brio, con brio*, Sp. *brío*.)

sciolto. (It.) Free, unconstrained. A charcter word used to evoke a certain syle in the playing. (Fr. *délié,* Ger. *ungebunden,* Sp. *suelto.*)

scordato, stonato. (It.) Out of tune. (Fr. *désaccordé,* Ger. *verstimmt,* Sp. *desafinado.*)

scordato, stonato. (It.) Out of tune, off pitch. (Fr. *désaccordé,* Ger. *verstimmt,* Sp. *desafinado.*)

scordatura. (It.) to tune one or more strings to a different **pitch**, from *scordare,* to mistune. (Fr. *scordatura,* Ger. *Skordatur,* Sp. *scordatura.*) Examples of scordatura occur in the *Sinfonia Concertante* of Wolfgang Amadeus Mozart, where the solo **violist** is asked to tune its upper strings to A-flat, E-flat, and B-flat, a practice that is generally no longer followed, and the Symphony No. 4 of **Gustav Mahler**, in which the concertmaster must have a second **violin** on hand to perform the solo part in movement two. Mahler requested that it be tuned to A, E, B, and F-sharp, bottom to top, but current practice is to tune the strings up a 1/4 tone. In Camille Saint-Säens's *Danse Macabre,* the violin solo requires the top string, E, to be tuned down to an E-flat, creating tritones with the A string. For the last chord of the **cello** part of *The Rite of Spring,* **Igor Stravinsky** asks cellists to lower the A string to a G-sharp so that the chord can be play nonarpeggiato (without spreading the chord). The seventeenth-century Bohemian composer Heinrich Biber was known for having made extensive use of scordatura tuning in his violin and string music.

score. The printed music that includes all of the parts of the **orchestra, band, choir,** or other ensemble in the form of horizontal staves, each with a different part on a single page. also See **score order, orchestra score.** (Fr. *partition,* Ger. *Partitur, die,* It. Sp. *partitura.*)

score in C. A **score** that is created with all transposing instruments, such as the **clarinets, horns,** and so forth, appearing at sounding pitch or so-called **concert pitch.** This kind of score became much more common in the twentieth century, likely beginning with the scores of Sergei Prokofiev.

score layout. Orchestral **scores** exist in a wide variety of layouts depending on the tradition at the time, as well as the composer's wishes. In the twentieth century, **aleatoric music** often requires different designs (see **box notation, frame notation, graphic notation**). Generally, scores are laid out according to a standard **score order.** However, on occasion that order is different. A few examples include Franz von Suppé's *Light Cavalry Overture,* which has the **violins** and **violas** at the top, followed by the **flute, piccolo, oboes, clarinets, horns,** trumpets, and then **bassoons, trombones, percussion,** and finally the **cellos** and **basses.** Another example is found in the cutout scores of **Igor Stravinsky,** in particular *Movements for Piano and Orchestra.* In works such as this, Stravinsky drew his own staves, leaving blank white space on the page when an instrument wasn't playing. In some editions, the trumpets will be placed above the horns, perhaps an indication that the register of the instruments is a priority over the dual role of the horns as both members of the woodwind and brass sections. It is tradition in most band scores to place the trumpets above the horns.

score order. The order in which the instruments appear, from top to bottom, in the **conductor**'s **score.** For a standard orchestral score, the order begins at the top with wind instruments: **piccolo, flutes, oboes, English horn, clarinets, bass clarinet, bassoons, contrabassoon.** This is followed by the brass: **horns, trumpets, trombones, tuba.** Next are the instruments of the percussion section: **timpani** first, followed by the remaining percussion instruments. Next are harp and any keyboard instrument, such as **celeste** or **piano.** Finally the strings: **violin** I, violin II, **viola, cello, bass.** Earlier scores did not have an established order and sometimes the order varied depending on where it was written or published.

In standard score order, horns usually appear above the trumpets even though they generally sound in a **tessitura** below them. The reason is that in the classical period horns were considered part of the woodwind section, while the trumpets performed regularly as a unit with the timpani. This practice has continued to our day. The score order for today's **wind ensemble** or **band** puts the trumpets above the horns.

score reading. The ability to read a **score,** with all its parts, transposing and otherwise, and hear the entirety without reference to a musical instrument or recording.

score reading, keyboard. 1. The ability to play an orchestral **score** with all its parts, in transposition and those in C, on the keyboard.
2. A class for the study of the skill of score reading.

score study. The study of the **score** by the **conductor** preparing for **rehearsal** and performance or by one who seeks a deeper knowledge of the piece. Some conductors possess photographic memory, making the process much easier. Others spend whatever time it takes to discover the inner logic of the work, the connections that tie it together, that make it possible to know the piece so well that one can sing through it without hesitation. See also **charts, harmonic rhythm, methods of score study,** *Seven Trips through the Score.*

score, transposed. A **score** that is created with the transposing instruments printed with the same **pitches** that the players see in their individual parts (see **transposition**). Opinion is divided over which type of score is most useful to the **conductor**, the transposed, where the conductor sees the same part as the player, or the **score in C**, where the conductor sees the parts at sounding pitch. Either way, the conductor must know how to transpose so that clear direction can be given from the podium.

Scottish Chamber Orchestra (SCO). Established in 1974, it is Scotland's national chamber **orchestra**, performing throughout the country. Based in Edinburgh, it regularly performs at the London **Proms** and the **Aldeburgh Festival**. The first **conductor** was Roderick Brydon (1974–1983), followed by **Jukka-Pekka Saraste** (1987–1991), Ivor Bolton (1994–1996), and Joseph Swensen (1996–2005). The current conductor is Robin Ticciati. The orchestra is known for its performances of contemporary music by such composers as Gordon Crosse, Peter Maxwell Davies, and Einojuhani Rautavaara. Having commissioned over one hundred new works, they have also made numerous recodings. **Sir Charles Mackerras** recorded several Mozart symphonies with the ensemble for Linn Records.

scucito. (It.) Detached. (Fr. *détache*, Ger. *abtrennt*, Sp. *separado*.)

scuro, tenebroso, oscuro. (It.) Dark, gloomy. A charcter word. (Fr. *ténébreux*, *obscur*, Ger. *finster*, *dunkel*, Sp. *oscuro*.)

seating charts. See **orchestra seating charts**.

Seattle Opera. Established in 1963, the Seattle Opera season runs from August to May. Speight Jenkins has been the general director since 1983 and has overseen years of significant development and artistic accomplishment. The company is known for its Wagner **Ring cycles** given between 1975 and 1983 and again in 2001, 2005, and 2009. The Seattle Opera maintains many outreach programs for youth and adults, including the BRAVO! Club for young people between the ages of twenty-one and thirty-nine. One of the largest such clubs of its kind in the United States, it provides discounted tickets and social events.

Seattle Symphony Orchestra. Founded in 1903. Its music directors have included **Sir Thomas Beecham** (1941–1944) and Milton Katims (1954–1976). **Gerard Schwarz** became the music advisor of the **orchestra** in 1983 and was named music director in 1985, serving until 2011. Under his direction, the orchestra performed and recorded the works of many neglected American composers such as Howard Hanson and David Diamond. Over 125 recordings were released on the Delos and Naxos labels, twelve receiving **Grammy** nominations. This was made possible by a unique accommodation achieved between the musicians' union and the orchestra. Since 1998 the orchestra has performed in Benaroya Hall. The current music director is Ludovic Morlot.

Seattle Youth Symphony Orchestra (SYSO). One of the most distinguished **youth orchestras** in the United States, it was founded in 1942 and has grown to the point that is has four full-sized **orchestras**, serving over 1,500 youth annually. Its **conductor** from 1960 to1988, **Vilem Sokol**, led the orchestra through a long period of growth. The SYSO has many innovative programs, including the **Endangered Instruments Program**, which encourages young people to take up less popular instruments such as the **oboe**, **bassoon**, **viola**, **double bass**, and **horn**. The orchestra's current music director is Stephen Rogers Radcliffe.

Seaver/National Endowment for the Arts Conductors Award. Established in 1985 as the **Affiliate Artists' Conducting Award**, it was given out every two or three years until 2002 when **JoAnn Falletta** and **Miguel Harth-Bedoya** received it. Earlier winners were **Hugh Wolff** and **Kent Nagano** (1985); **Catherine Comet**, **Jahja Ling**, **Neal Stulberg** (1988); **Kenneth Jean** and **Carl St. Clair** (1990); **David Loebel** and **Christopher Wilkins** (1992); **Robert Spano** (1994); **Alan Gilbert** and **David Robertson** (1997); and **Williams Eddins** (2000).

se bisogna. (It.) If necessary. (Fr. *si nécessaire*, Ger. *wenn nötig*, Sp. *si pueda*.)

sec, sèche. (Fr.) Dry. A directive to play a note short and dry, seen often in French music. (Ger. *trocken*, It. *secco*, Sp. *seco*.)

sección de cuerdo. (Sp.) The string section, string players. (Ger. *Streicher*, Fr. *cordes*, It. *archi*.)

Second Viennese School (Zweite Wiener Schule). A group of composers including **Arnold Schoenberg** (1874–1951) and his two students Alban Berg (1885–1935) and Anton Webern (1883–1945) who lived and taught off and on between about 1903 and 1925. They were the first major composers of the **twelve-tone music**. See also **First Viennese School (Wiener Schule)**.

secco recitative. (It.) An operatic **recitative** that only uses a **harpsichord** and no other instrument, such as a **cello** and/or **bassoon**.

Sechzehntel. (Ger.) Sixteenth note. Also *Sechzehntelnote.* See also **appendix 7**.

Sechzehntelpause. (Ger.) Sixteenth-note rest. See also **appendix 7**.

seconda volta. (It.) Second time, as in a repeat. See also *prima volta* (first time).

secuencia. (Sp.) A repetition of a phrase or gesture, often at a different tonal level. (It. *sequenza,* Fr. *sequence,* Ger. *Sequenz.*)

sedicesimo. (It.) Sixteenth note. See also **appendix 7**.

seelenvoll. (Ger.) Soulful.

segno. (It.) Sign, a musical sign such as a sharp or flat, or the **dal segno**. (Sp. *signo,* Fr. *signe,* Ger. *Zeichen.*) Examples: *al segno* or *dal segno,* to the sign; *fin' al segno,* end at the sign; *sin' al segno,* until the sign.

segno d'espressione. (It.) Symbols, words, and phrases used in music to suggest a certain manner of playing. (Fr. *signe d'expression,* Ger. *Ausdrucksbezeichnung,* En. expression marks, Sp. *signo de expresión.*)

segno dinamico. (It.) **Dynamic sign**. (Fr. *signe dynamique,* Ger. *dynamisches Zeichen,* Sp. *signos dinámicos.*)

segue. (It.) Continue without a pause, it follows. (Fr. *ça suit,* Ger. *es folgt,* Sp. *sigue.*)

seguir. (Sp.) To follow quickly as in *attacca,* follow a soloist. (Fr. *suivez,* Ger. *folgen,* It. *seguite.*)

seguire il canto. (It.) Follow the singer. Also *col canto,* with the singer.

seguite. (It.) To follow quickly as in *attacca,* follow a soloist. (Fr. *suivez,* Ger. *folgen,* Sp. *seguir.*)

Sehnsucht. (Ger.) Longing. A character word. Also *Sehnsuchtvoll,* filled with longing.

Sehr gut! (Ger.) Very good! Excellent! (Fr. *Trés bien!,* It. *bravissimo!* Sp. *Muy bien!, Genial!, Execelente!*)

sehr schnell. (Ger.) As fast as possible, extremely fast. (Fr. *trés vite,* It. *prestissimo,* Sp. *rapidamente.*)

sehr, viel. (Ger). Very, much, plenty. (Fr. *beaucoup, très,* It. *molto, di molto, assai,* Sp. *muy.*) Examples: *Sehr gesangvoll,* in a singing style; *sehr rhythmisch,* very rhythmic. *sehr schnell,* very fast; *sehr frei vorzutragen,*

played very freely, from *Pierrot Lunaire* by **Arnold Schoenberg**.

Seidl, Anton. (1850–1898.) Hungarian **conductor**. Seidl attended the **Leipzig Conservatory**. In 1872, he went to **Bayreuth**, where he assisted in making the first fair copy of the **score** to the **Ring cycle**. On **Richard Wagner**'s recommendation, he was appointed to the **Leipzig State Opera**. In 1885, he was appointed music director of the **Metropolitan Opera** in New York, followed in 1891 by a similar appointment to the **New York Philharmonic**. He conducted the premiere of Antonin Dvořák's Symphony No 9, *"From the New World."*

Seite, Blatt. (Ger.) A sheet, leaf, or page of music. (Fr. *page, feuille,* It. *pagina, foglia,* Sp. *página, folio.*)

seizième de soupir. (Fr.) Sixty-fourth note. See **appendix 7**.

selbe, selben. (Ger.) Same. Example: *das selbe Zeitmass,* the same tempo.

semblable, pareil. (Fr.) Similar. (It. *simile,* Ger. *gleich,* Sp. *similar.*)

semibiscroma. (It.) Sixty-fourth note. See **appendix 7**.

semibreve. (It.) A whole note in the English system. (Fr. *ronde,* Ger. *Ganze note,* Sp. *semibreve.*) See **appendix 7**.

semicombinatorial set. A **twelve-tone row** created in such a way that the first six notes, or **hexachord**, of any of its versions, excluding retrograde, do not duplicate any of the first six **pitches** of the original. See **combinatoriality**, **all-combinatorial set**, **twelve-tone technique**.

semicorchea. (Sp.) Sixteenth note. See **appendix 7**.

semicroma. (It.) Sixteenth note. (Fr. *double croche,* Ger. *Sechzehntel note,* Sp. *semicorchea.*) See **appendix 7**.

semifusa. (It.) Sixty-fourth note. See **appendix 7**.

semiminima. (It.) Quarter note. (Fr. *noire,* Ger. *viertelnote,* Sp. *negra, seminima.*) See **appendix 7**.

semiquaver. The rhythmic value of a sixteenth note in the English system. See **appendix 7**.

semitone. A half step in English terminology. (Fr. *demi-ton,* Ger. *Halbton,* It., Sp. *semitono.*) See **appendix 7**.

semitono. (It., Sp.) Half step, **semitone**. (Fr. *demi-ton,* Ger. *Halbton.*) See **appendix 7**.

Semperoper. The opera house of the **Dresden Staatkapelle**.

semplice. (It.) Simple, plain. (Fr. *simple*, Ger. *einfach*, Sp. *simple*.)

semplicemente. (It.) Simply. (Fr. *simplement*, Ger. *in einfacher Weise*.) Also *con semplicità*, with simplicity. (Fr. *avec simplicité*, Ger. *mit Einfachheit*, Sp. *con sencillez*.)

sempre, constantemente. (It.) Always, constantly. (Fr. *toujours, constamment*, Ger. *immer, stets, ständing*, Sp. *siempre*.) Also *sempre lo stesso*, always the same. (Ger. *stets das Gleiche*, Fr. *toujours le (la) meme*, Sp. *siempre la misma*.)

sensación. (Sp.) Feeling, perception, sensation. (Fr. *sensation*, Ger. *Empfindung*, It. *sensazione*.)

sensation. (Fr.) Feeling, perception, sensation. (Ger. *Empfindung*, It. *sensazione*, Sp. *sensación*.)

sensazione. (It.) Feeling, perception, sensation. (Fr. *sensation*, Ger. *Empfindung*, Sp. *sensazione*.)

sensibilmente. (It., Sp.) Sensitively. (Fr. *sensiblement*, Ger. *empfindlich*.)

sensibilidad. (Sp.) Sensitivity. A directive heard in rehearsal. (Fr. *sensibilité*, Ger. *Empfindsamkeit*, It. *sensibilità*.)

sensibilità. (It.) Sensitivity. (Fr. *sensibilité*, Ger. *Empfindsamkeit*, Sp. *sensibilidad*.)

sensibilité. (Fr.) Sensitivity. (Ger. *Empfindsamkeit*, It. *sensibilità*, Sp. *sensibilidad*.)

sensible. (Fr.) Leading tone, also sensitive. Appears in French music by such composers as Claude Debussy. (Ger. *Leitton*, It. *sensibile*, Sp. *sensible*.)

sensible. (Sp.) Leading tone, also heartfelt, deep, sensitive. See *sensibile*.

sensiblement. (Fr.) Sensitively. (Ger. *empfindlich*, It. *sensibilmente*, Sp. *sensibilmente*.)

sentimiento, con. (Sp.) With feeling, sentiment. (Fr. *avec âme*, Ger. *mit Empfindung*, *gemütvoll*, It. *con l'anima*.)

sentito. (It.) Heartfelt. Example: *con sentito*. (Fr. *avec sentiment*, Ger. *mit Empfindung*, *mit Gefühl*, Sp. *con sensibilidad*.)

senza. (It.) Without. (Fr. *sans*, Ger. *ohne*, Sp. *sin*.) Examples: *sans courir*, without hurrying. (Ger. *ohne davonzurennen*, It, *senza correre*, Sp. *sin correr*.) See also *senza sordino*, *senza cambiare*, *senza replica*.

senza cambiare. (It.) Without changing. (Fr. *sans changer*, Ger. *ohne zu wechseln*, Sp. *sin cambiar*.)

senza replica. (It.) Without repetition. (Fr. *sans reprise*, Ger. *ohne Wiederholen*, Sp. *sin repetición*.)

Senza sordino. (It.) Without the mute. (Fr. *sans sourdine*, Ger. *Ohne Dämpfer*, Sp. *sin sordina*.)

Seoul Philharmonic Orchestra (SPO). Founded in 1948, the SPO is the oldest and premiere **orchestra** in South Korea. It has toured through Southeast Asia, including Japan and Beijing, and visited the United States several times. Its current music director is Myung-Whun Chung. Past **conductors** include Seung Kwak (2003), Mark Ermler (200–2002), Eun-Seong Park (1990–1991), Jae-Dong Jeong (1974–1990), Man-Bok Kim (1961–1969), and Saeng-Ryeo Kim (1948–1961). The orchestra signed with **Deutsche Grammophon** in 2011 and has gone on to make several recordings led by its current music director, Myung-Whun Chung, including **Gustav Mahler**'s Symphonies Nos. 1 and 2 and Ludwig van Beethoven's Symphony No. 9. The orchestra recently established a composer-in-residence program with Korean composer Unsuk Chin, who lives in Germany. She also founded and directs the series Ars Nova, presenting over one hundred Korean premieres.

septet. A chamber ensemble made up of seven performers. (Fr. *Septour*, Ger. *Septett*, It. *settimino*, Sp. *septeto*, *septimino*.)

septuplet. A rhythmic grouping of seven rhythmic units. (Fr. *septolet*, Ger. *Septole*, It. *settimina*, Sp. *septillo*.)

sequence. A repetition of a phrase or gesture, often at a different tonal level. (Fr. *sequence*, Ger. *Sequenz*, It. *sequenza*, Sp. *secuencia*.)

sequence. (Fr.) **Sequence**. (Ger. *Sequenz*, It. *sequenza*, Sp. *secuencia*.)

Sequenz. (Ger.) **Sequence**. (Fr. *sequence*, It. *sequenza*, Sp. *secuencia*.)

sequenza. (It.) **Sequence**. (Fr. *sequence*, Ger. *Sequenz*, Sp. *secuencia*.)

serial music. Music composed according to the permutations or transformations of a group of elements used in a specified order or series. These elements include **pitch**, rhythm or duration, dynamic, tone color or instrument, register, or any other musical parameter. Serial music includes **twelve-tone technique** but now suggests primarily music that extends those techniques beyond pitch to other elements. Such music is sometimes termed "total" serialism. French composer **Olivier Messiaen** wrote works as early as 1948 that explored serialism of musical elements other than pitch without being strict. Proponents of serialism who developed the techniques further include **Karlheinz Stockhausen** (*Gruppen for Three Orchestras*, 1957), **Pierre Boulez**, Luciano Berio, Luigi Nono, and Henri Pousseur in Europe and **Milton Babbitt**, George Rochberg, and Charles Wuorinen in the United States. See Reginald Smith Brindle's *Serial Composition* (1972) and George Perle's *Serial Composition and Atonality* (1966) (see the **bibliography**).

series, row. The classic **row** technique used in twelve-tone composition that organizes the twelve **pitches** of the scale into a system of independent pitches, each being unrelated to any other in the series. (Fr. *série*, Ger. *Reihe, Tonreihe*, It. *serie*, Sp. *serie*.)

serioso, serio, grave. (It.) Serious, grave. A word heard to describe a particular character in music. (Fr. *sérieux, grave*, Ger. *Ernst, würdevoll*, Sp. *serio, grave*.)

serrant, en. (Fr.) Getting faster. (Ger. *zusammendrängend, almählich schneller werdend*, It. *stringendo, serrando*.) Examples: *De plus en plus sonore et en serrant le movement*, with more and more sound and speeding up the tempo, from *Fêtes*, movement two of *Nocturnes* by Claude Debussy.

serré. (Fr.) Tight, fast. Example: *trem. serré*, as seen in the score to the ballet *Jeux* by Claude Debussy, using the abbreviated form of **tremolo**.

serrez. (Fr.) To speed up, get faster. See *serré*.

sessantaquattresimo. (It.) Sixty-fourth note. See **appendix 7**.

sestetto. (It.) Sextet. (Fr. *sextour*, Ger. *Sextett*, Sp. *sexteto*.)

set. A specified group of **pitches** used in twelve-tone or serial music compositional procedures. A term introduced by **Milton Babbitt** in his 1946 article, "The Function of Set Structure in the Twelve-Tone System." While the term originated as a moniker for **twelve-tone row**, it now also refers to groups of pitches of less than twelve and also to specific groups of pitches that do not derive from twelve-tone techniques but are also used as source materials for composition.

set complex. The forty-eight different forms of a **twelve-tone row** that are created by various transformation techniques, inversion retrograde, and retrograde-inversion to all twelve pitch levels of the **chromatic scale**. See also **matrix**.

set theory. A method of study and analysis of music that uses half-step intervals as an organizing principle, generally stemming from **twelve-tone techniques**. See Robert Morris's *Composition with Pitch-Classes: A Theory of Compositional Design* (1988).

setzen, legen, stellen. (Ger.) To put, as in to put on the mute. (Fr. *mettez*, It. *mettere*, Sp. *poner*.)

seule, seulement. (Fr.) Only, alone. (Ger. *nur*, It. *solo, soltanto*, Sp. *solo*.)

Seventh Army Symphony Orchestra. (1952–1962.) The only **orchestra** ever to exist under the auspices of the U.S. Army, the Seventh Army Symphony Orchestra was founded in 1952 in Germany by American composer and **conductor Samuel Adler**, who was a corporal in the Second Armoured Division. Its purpose was to demonstrate the shared cultural heritage of Europe and America. The orchestra gave concerts throughout Europe and the Middle East during its history and was decommissioned when the military draft came to an end in 1962. Conductors included Edward Alley (1958–1960), **John Canarina** (1959–1960), **James Dixon** (1953–1954), John Ferritto (1959–1960), Henry Lewis (1955–1956), Ronald Ondrejka (1954–1956), Kenneth Schermerhorn (1953–1955), and Ling Tung (1956–1958). Conductor **John Canarina** documented the life of the orchestra in the book *Uncle Sam's Symphony* (see the **bibliography**).

Seven Trips through the Score. Developed by the **conducting** class at the Belgium National Conservatory of Music as a guide for approaching **score study**. (1) Instrumentation, including clefs and transpositions. (2) Major transitions and tempos. (3) Form. (4) Harmonic structure and analysis. (5) Phrasal analysis. (6) Melodic analysis and cues. (7) Dynamics. See also **score study**.

sextet. A group of six chamber musicians, such as a string sextet, or a piece written for such an ensemble. (Fr. *sextette, sextour*, Ger. *Sextett*, It. *sestetto*, Sp. *sexteto*.)

sf. Abbreviation for *sforzando, sforzato*.

Sf. Courtesy Andrew Martin Smith.

sfogato. (It.) An open, unrestrained level of expression. From the Italian verb *sfogare*, meaning to vent or pour forth. See also **soprano acuto sfogato**, **voice classifications**.

sforzando, sforzato. (It.) Forceful, a strong accent. Abbreviation *sf.*, *sfz.*

sfp. Abbreviation for *sforzando piano.*

Sfp. Courtesy Andrew Martin Smith.

sfz. Abbreviation for **sforzato**, can also be **sforzando**.

Sfz. Courtesy Andrew Martin Smith.

Shanghai Philharmonic Orchestra (SPO). This Chinese **orchestra** is the result of more than one merger of earlier orchestras, beginning the merger in 1996 of the Shanghai Broadcasting Orchestra (founded in 1950) and the Shanghai Film Orchestra (founded in 1954). The combined ensemble was called the Shanghai Broadcasting Symphony Orchestra, and their first music director was Yongyan Hu. In 2004, the name was changed once again to its current title, and Zuohuang Chen was appointed music director. Muhai Tang was appointed music director in 2009 with the goal of basing the orchestra's operations and performances on Chinese cultural values. As part of the mission, the orchestra promotes young Chinese soloists and composers and often performs concerts related to government cultural events. The orchestra has made numerous recordings for the **Naxos** label.

Shara, Inma. (b. 1972.) Spanish **conductor**. Shara has conducted the **London Philharmonic**, **Israel Philharmonic**, **Royal Philharmonic**, **Russian National Symphony**, **Czech National Symphony**, **Rome Symphony**, and the **Latvian National Symphony**, among others. Since 2007, she has been sponsored by the Swiss manufacturer of watches, Vacheron Constantin. In 2008, she led a concert at the Vatican celebrating the sixtieth anniversary of the Universal Declaration of Human Rights in the presence of Pope Benedict XVI.

sharp. The notation sign that indicates raising a pitch by a half step. (Fr. *dièse*, Ger. *Kreuz*, *(Diesis)*, It. *diesis*, Sp, *sostenido*.) Also a term used for out-of-tune playing when the sound is above the pitch. See also **accidental**.

Shaw, George Bernard. (1856–1950.) Irish playwright. He was influential as a cultural critic, earning much of his income writing for various London newspapers and journals. His music criticism was published in the three-volume collection *Shaw's Music: The Complete Musical Criticism of Bernard Shaw*. In the journal known as *London Music*, he published under the byline Corno de Bassetto. He also wrote *The Perfect Wagnerite* (1898) now available in a publication by **Dover Press** (see the **bibliography**).

Shaw, Robert. (1916–1999.) American **conductor** who achieved his greatest fame through his gift with choirs. He founded the Robert Shaw Chorale, an ensemble of about forty professionals, in 1945 and toured with them until 1965 when they disbanded. He commissioned Paul Hindemith's large work *When Lilacs Last in the Dooryard Bloom'd* in 1946. For his chorale he commissioned works from Béla Bartók, Darius Milhaud, **Sir Benjamin Britten**, and **Aaron Copland**. He served as the assistant conductor to **George Szell** with the **Cleveland Orchestra** (1956–1967) and became the music director of the **Atlanta Symphony Orchestra** (1967–1988). An innovative and effective choral conductor, he would often seat a chorus in quartets made up of single **soprano**, **alto**, **tenor**, and **bass**. His **choirs** were capable of achieving the loudest and softest dynamics and performed works as widely contrasting as the Bach *Mass in B minor* and GiuseppiVerdi's *Requiem*.

shift, shifting. As in string playing and moving the hand from one position on the **fingerboard** to another. **Conductors** often request unity in the shifting and fingering of a piece or passage of a piece in order to create a unified sound.

short score. A version of a **score** in which the music appears in relatively few **staves**. In the process of writing a piece, many composers will create a three-staved so-called short score that has most if not all of the music but not necessarily the instrumentation. (Fr. *La partition réduite*, Ger. *Die kleine Partitur*, It. *La partitura ridotta*.) See also *particella*.

Si. (Ger.) B-natural. See **accidental**, **appendix 7**.

Sibelius Academy. Founded in 1882 as the Helsinki Music Institute, it is now part of the University of the Arts, Helsinki. The only university-level music school in

Finland, it has a student body of nearly 1,700. In 1939, it was renamed the **Sibelius Academy** to honor one of its most famous alumni and Finland's great composer. The academy offers both the bachelor's and master's degrees in music but also has a doctoral degree and other postgraduate degrees. It is where the most famous Finnish conducting pedagogue, **Jorma Panula**, taught from 1973 to1994.

Si bémol. (Ger.) B-flat. See **accidental**, **appendix 7**.

si bémolle. (It.) B-flat. See **accidental**, **appendix 7**.

sicher. (Ger.) Certain, definite. A character word. (Fr. *assuré, certain,* Sp. *cierta, cierto,* It. *certo.*)

sich verlierend, verebbend. (Ger.) Disappearing, dying away to nothing. (Fr. *en se perdant,* Ii. *perdendosi,* Sp. *desvaneciéndose, perdiéndose.*)

side-by-side concerts. Concerts where a professional, community, or regional **orchestra** invites amateur adult or student musicians to sit "side-by-side" with them in order to rehearse and present outreach concerts.

Si dièse. (Ger.) B-sharp. See **accidental**, **appendix 7**.

si dieses. (It.) B-sharp. See **accidental**, **appendix 7**.

siempre. (Sp.) Ever, always. (Ger. *stets,* Fr. *toujours, constamment,* It. *sempre, constantemente.*) Also: *siempre la misma,* always the same. (Fr. *toujours le (la) meme,* Ger. *stets das Gleiche,* It. *sempre lo stesso.*)

sifflet. (Fr.) Fife, whistle. (Ger. *Pfeife,* It. *fischietto,* Sp. *pito.*)

sight lines. Established between the **conductor** and members of an ensemble in order to bring the **conducting** gesture into greater focus. Especially useful when conducting a small group of musicians within the **orchestra** but also effective with whole sections.

sight-read. 1. Reading music at sight without having heard it before. This skill is facilitated by having **perfect pitch**, but it can also be learned through the study of **solfège** and **ear training**. (Fr. *déchiffrer,* Ger. *Blattspiel,* It *suonare a prima vista, a libro aperto,* Sp. *lectura a primera vista.*) 2. To sing at sight. (Fr. *chanter á vue, déchiffrer,* Ger. *vom Blatt singen,* It. *Cantare a prima vista,* Sp. *cantar a primera vista.*)

signe. (Fr.) Sign, a musical sign such as a sharp or flat. (Ger. *Zeichen,* It. *segno,* Sp. *signo.*) See also ***dal segno.***

signe d'expression. (Fr.) Symbols, words, and phrases used in music to suggest a certain manner of playing. (Ger. *Ausdrucksbezeichnung,* It. *segno d'espressione,* Sp. *signo de expresión.*) See also **accidental**.

signe de répétition. (Fr.) **Repeat sign**, a notation device to signal a repeat of a passage. (Ger. *Wiederholungszeichen,* It. *segno di ripetizione,* Sp. *signo de repetición.*)

signe de tenue. (Fr.) Tie, a notation devise that connects two or more notes together. (Ger. *Haltebogen,* It. *legatura di valore,* Sp. *ligar, ligadura de prolungación.*) See also **slur**.

signe dynamique. (Fr.) **Dynamic sign** (Ger. *dynamisches Zeichen,* It. *segno dinamico,* Sp. *signos dinámicos.*)

signo. (Sp.) Sign, a musical sign such as a sharp or flat. (Fr. *signe,* Ger. *Zeichen,* It. *segno.*) See also ***dal segno.***

signo de expresión. (Sp.) Symbols, words, and phrases used in music to suggest a certain manner of playing. (Fr. *signe d'expression,* Ger. *Ausdrucksbezeichnung,* It. *segno d'espressione,* En. *Expression marks.*)

signo de repetición. (Sp.) **Repeat sign**, a notation device to signals a repeat of a passage. (Fr. *signe de répétition,* Ger. *Wiederholungszeichen,* It. *segno di ripetizione.*)

signos dinámicos. (Sp.) **Dynamic sign**. (Fr. *signe dynamique,* Ger. *dynamisches Zeichen,* It. *segno dinamico.*)

sigue. (Sp.) Continue without a pause. (Fr. ça suit, Ger. *es folgt,* It. *segue.*)

silence. (Fr.) A rest or **grand pause**. See **appendix 7**.

silencio de corchea. (Sp.) Eighth-note rest. (Fr. *demi-soupir,* Ger. *Achtelpause,* It. *pausa di croma.*) See **appendix 7**.

silencio, silencioso. (Sp.) A musical rest or silence. Example: *silencio de negra,* a quarter rest. See **appendix 7**.

Silk Road Project and Ensemble. A project launched by cellist Yo-Yo Ma to promote artistic collaboration and multicultural exchange among artists and institutions along the former Silk Road trade route. Meant to encourage a "passion-driven learning" (www.silkroadproject.org) in the arts, it has exposed many to crossover music from Azerbaijan and other Eurasian countries. The ensemble has a flexible contingent of performers, composers, arrangers, and visual artists.

similar. (Sp.) Similar. Abbreviated *sim.* (It. *simile,* Fr. *semblable, pareil,* Ger. *gleich.*)

simile. (It.) Similar. Abbreviated *sim.* (Fr. *semblable, pareil,* Ger. *gleich,* Sp. *similar.*)

Simmpfeife. (Ger.) **Pitch pipe.** (Fr. *flûte d'accord, diapason á bouche,* It. *diapason a fiato,* Sp. *diapasón de boca.*)

Simón Bolívar Symphony Orchestra (Orquesta Sinfónica Simón Bolívar). Founded in 1975 in Caracas, Venezuala, by **José Antonio Abreu** as a part of his **El sistema** project, the average age of the **orchestra** has risen so that it is no longer a **youth orchestra** but an orchestra of young professionals. The orchestra tours internationally, having performed in many musical capitals. The current **conductor** is **Gustavo Dudamel** (also current music director of the **Los Angeles Philharmonic Orchestra**), who has led three recordings with the orchestra on the **Deutsche Grammophon** label, including one of Latin American music (see the **bibliography**).

simple. (Fr.) Simple, plain. Also, *simplement.* (Ger. *einfach,* It. *semplice,* Sp. *simple, sencillo.*)

simple. (Sp.) Simple, plain. Also *sencillo.* (Ger. *einfach,* It. *semplice,* Fr. *simple, simplement.*)

Simrock, Nikolaus. (1751–1832.) German music publisher. He played the **horn** in the Bonn, Germany, court **orchestra** with Ludwig van Beethoven, who was also his friend. He founded the **N. Simrock Verlag** publishing house in Bonn in 1793.

Simrock Verlag. See **N. Simrock Verlag.**

simultaneity. Any two or more **pitches** sounding at the same time.

sin. (Sp.) Without. (Fr. *sans,* Ger. *ohne,* It. *senza.*) Example: *sin correr,* without hurrying. (Fr. *sans courir,* Ger. *ohne davonzurennen,* It, *senza correre.*)

sin cambiar. (Sp.) Without changing. (Fr. *sans changer,* Ger. *ohne zu wechseln,* It. *senza cambiare.*)

sinfonia. (It.) **Symphony.** (Fr. *symphonie,* Ger. *Sinfonie,* Sp. *sinfonía.*)

sinfonía. (Sp.) **Symphony,** as in a symphony orchestra or a piece of music. (Fr. *symphonie,* Ger. *Sinfonie,* It. *sinfonia.*)

Sinfonie. (Ger.) **Symphony,** as in a symphony orchestra or a piece of music. (Fr. *symphonie,* It. *sinfonia,* Sp. *sinfonía.*)

singend, singen. (Ger.) Singing, to sing. Often used to address instrumentalists in order to evoke a particular manner of playing. (Fr. *chantant, chanter,* It., *cantando, cantare,* Sp. *cantando.*) Example: *sehr weich gesungen,* sung very tenderly.

siniestro, inquietante. (Sp.) Eerie, sinister, weird, weirdly, uncanny. (Fr. *inquiétant,* Ger. *unheimlich,* It. *inquietante, sinistro.*)

sinistra. (It.) Left. (Fr. *gauche,* Ger. *links,* Sp. *izquierdo.*) Example: *mano sinistra,* left hand. (Fr. *main gauche,* Ger. *Linke,* Sp. *mano izquierdo.*)

sinistro, inquietante. (It.) Eerie, sinister, weird, weirdly, uncanny. (Fr. *inquiétant,* Ger. *unheimlich,* Sp. *inquietante, siniestro.*)

Sinopoli, Giuseppe. (1946–2001.) Italian **conductor** and composer. Sinopoli studied at the **Vienna Academy of Music** with **Hans Swarowsky.** He served as the music director of the **Orchestra dell'Accademia Nazionale di Santa Cecilia** (1983–1987) and the principal conductor of the **Philharmonia** in London (1984–1994) and the **Dresden Staatskapelle** (1992–2001). Sinopoli died of a heart attack while conducting Giuseppi Verdi's *Aida* at the **Deutsche Oper,** Berlin. He made several recordings with the Philharmonia and other orchestras, including his last recordings, **Richard Strauss**'s *Ariadne auf Naxos* and Antonin Dvořák's *Stabat Mater.*

sin repetición. (Sp.) Without repetition. (Fr. *sans reprise,* Ger. *ohne Wiederholen,* It. *senza replica.*)

sin, sino. (It.) Up to, until. (Fr. *jusque,* Ger. *bis, zu,* Sp. *hasta.*) Also *sino al,* up to, to the, until; *fino al segno,* up to the sign.

sin, sino. (It.) To, in, until. (Ger. *zu,* Fr. *jusque, depuis,* Sp. *hasta.*)

sin sordina. (Sp.) Without the mute. (It. *senza sordino,* Fr. *sans sourdine,* Ger. *Ohne Dämpfer.*)

sintetizador. (Sp.) **Synthesizer.** (En. *synthesizer,* Fr. *synthétiseur,* Ger. *Synthesizer,* It. *sintetizzatore.*)

sintetizzatore. (It.) **Synthesizer.** (En. *synthesizer,* Fr. *synthétiseur,* Ger. *Synthesizer,* Sp. *sintetizador.*)

Sirius XM Radio. Launched in 2002 to provide access to multiple satellite channels of music and sports, news, and entertainment to listeners on a pay-for-service model. Offering predominantly rock and pop music, they provide access to a few classical channels, including Met Opera Radio and Symphony Hall.

sistema. (It.) Staff, stave, system. (Fr. *portée,* Ger. *Liniensystem, System, Fünfliniesystem,* Sp. *pentagramma, pauto.*)

sistema de pentagramas. (Sp.) Staff, **stave**, system. (Fr. *portée,* Ger. *Liniensystem, Fünfliniensystem,* It. *pentagramma.*)

Sitzprobe. (Ger., lit. "a sitting rehearsal.") A **rehearsal** in **opera** where the **orchestra** is in the pit and the cast sits in a straight line across the front of the stage. When time allows, the **conductor** will lead the ensemble of singers and orchestra through the entire opera so that they can hear each other in the performance setting for the first time.

sizzle cymbal. Suspended on a stand and with added rivets, small chains, or other rattles through holes drilled in the surface of the cymbal to produce its unique sound.

Skala, Tonleiter. (Ger.) **Scale**. (Fr. *gamme,* It. *scala,* Sp. *escala, gama*) See also **alternative scales**.

sketch. Compositional notes for a work written in a composer's handwriting. Ludwig van Beethoven and other composers kept books of sketches of musical ideas. Many of them exist in historic library collections maintaining limited access.

slapstick. Also known as the **whip**, it is made of two pieces of wood attached at the bottom and clapped together to produce the tone. (Fr. *fouet,* Ger. *Peitsche,* It. *frusta,* Sp. *látigo.*) See also **appendix 4**.

slap-tongue technique. An effect created when the performer strikes the tongue against the mouthpiece.

slargando, allargando. (It.) Slowing down, broadening. A descriptive word seen in scores and parts. (Fr. *en élargissant,* Ger. *breiter werdend,* Sp. *moderar el tiempo.*)

Slatkin, Leonard. (b. 1944.) American **conductor**. Slatkin is currently the music director of the **Detroit Symphony Orchestra** and the Orchestre National de Lyon, France. He is also the principal guest conductor of the **Pittsburgh Symphony Orchestra**. In 2012, his book, *Conducting Business*, was published by Amadeus Press. Slatkin began his career as the music director of the **St. Louis Symphony Orchestra**, followed by the **National Symphony Orchestra** in Washington, DC. He has been the principal guest conductor of both the **Philharmonia Orchestra** and the **Royal Philharmonic** and the chief conductor of the **BBC Symphony Orchestra**, all in London. He has conducted virtually all of the great **orchestras** and **opera** houses in the world. He has made over one hundred recordings and won seven **Grammys** with sixty-four nominations. He founded and ran the National Conducting Institute while in Washington, DC; founded the St. Louis Symphony Youth Orchestra; and has won many national and international awards. He is a proponent of American composers, and he maintains his own blog (see the **bibliography**).

Leonard Slatkin. *Courtesy Donald Dietz.*

sleigh bells. Small bells mounted on a wooden handle and shaken up and down to produce the sound. (Fr. *grelots,* Ger. *Schellen,* It. *sonagli,* Sp. *cascabeles.*) See also **appendix 4**.

slentando, allentando. (It.) Loosening of the tempo. Mainly used in its Italian form.

slit drum. Also known as the **log drum**, a hollow log closed at each end with an opening cut across the top that is divided down the middle by a small piece of wood. Various **pitch** levels can be obtained depending on where the drum is struck. See also **appendix 4**.

Slonimsky, Nicolas. (1894–1995.) Born Nikolai Leonidovich Slonimskiy in Saint Petersburg, Russia. His family was Jewish, but on the birth of his older brother, they converted to the Russian Orthodox Church. In 1923, he was brought to Rochester, New York, where he worked as an accompanist at the newly opened **Eastman School of Music**. After two years, he moved to Boston in order to work for **Serge Koussevitsky**. At this time, he also began writing music articles for various newspapers and journals, and it was in this area that he made his mark. In 1958, he took over *Baker's Biographical Dictionary of Musicians,* remaining as head editor until his death in 1995. He wrote an autobiography under the title *Perfect Pitch: A Life Story* (1988; see the **bibliography**).

Slovak Philharmonic (Slovenská filharmónia). Recognized for its many recordings on the **Naxos label**, the **orchestra** was founded in 1949 and has been in residence at the Reduta Bratislava Concert Hall, built in 1773, since the 1950s. The orchestra has toured Europe, Japan, and the United States. The current principal **conductor** is Emmanuel Villaume.

slur. A music notation sign that connects two or more notes. (Fr. *liaison*, Ger. *Bindebogen*, It. *legatura*, Sp. *ligar*.)

Slur. *Courtesy Andrew Martin Smith.*

slurred. A musical line where the notes are run into one an-tother as opposed to being separate. In bowing technique, two or more notes played in one bow, that is, without changing the direction of the bow stroke and smoothly, without any separation.

smorzando. (It.) Dying away, subsiding. A descriptive word most often seen in its Italian form. (Fr. *en amortissant*, Ger. *dämpfend, abd*, Sp. *desvanecerse*.)

snap pizz. A **pizzicato**, or plucked note, where the string snaps against the **fingerboard** of the instrument when released, creating a percussive sound. The same as **Bartók pizzicato**.

snare drum. A two-headed drum with one head on the top and one on the bottom that has the snares. The drum has a lever on the side so that the snares can be switched off. The drum is played with wooden sticks and has a fully developed, intricate technique. See also **appendix 4**.

so. (Ger.) As, thus, so. Examples: *so viel*, so much; *so laut wie möglich*, as loud as possible; *so schell als . . .* , as fast as . . . ; *so viel wie möglich*, as much as possible.

soave. (It.) Sweet, gentle, soft, mild, suave. (Fr. *suave*, Ger. *lieblich*, Sp. *suave*.)

sobre. (Sp.) On, on the, above. (It. *sopra*, Fr. *sur, sur le, sur la*, Ger. *auf, auf der, auf die auf das*.)

sobre el batidor. (Sp.) In string playing, it indicates using the bow above or on the **fingerboard**. (Fr. *Sur la touché*, Ger. *nahe am Griffbrett*, It. *sulla tastiera, flautando*.)

sobre el peunte. (Sp.) An indication to play with the bow on or near the bridge of a string instrument. (Fr. *prés du chevalet*, Ger. *am Steg*, It *sul ponticello*.)

sobre el peuntecillo, sobre el puente. (Sp.) On the bridge. (Fr. *prés du chevalet*, Ger. *am Steg*, It *sul ponticello*.)

Society of Composers, Inc. Founded in 1966 as the American Society of University Composers to promote the performance, recording, publication, and understanding of new American music. Its membership ranges from the independent professional to the student and composer-professors.

sociology of music. The study of music in its sociological or social context. Many American universities offer courses in the subject, and there are numerous publications on the topic. See Steven Cornelius and Mary Natvig's *Music: A Social Experience* (2012).

Sofia Philharmonic Orchestra. Founded in 1928 by Alexander Popov, who served as chief **conductor** until 1956. This Bulgarian organization currently has a symphony **orchestra** of 120 musicians, a chamber orchestra, a choir, and several chamber ensembles. The current chief conductor is Martin Panteleev. Other conductors include Ljubka Biadjioni and Ilia Mihaylov.

sofort, sogleich, plötzlich. (Ger.) Abrupt, sudden, suddenly. A descriptive word seen in **scores** and parts and heard in **rehearsal**. (Fr. *tout á coup, immédiatement, subitement*, It. *di colpo, repente, subito*, Sp. *immediatamente, súbito*.)

Sokhiev, Tugan. (b. 1977.) Russian **conductor**. Sokhiev is the current chief conductor of the **Deutches Symphonie-Orchester, Berlin** (appointed in 2012), music director of the **Bolshoi Theater**, and principal conductor of the **Bolshoi Orchestra**, Moscow (appointed in 2014). He was the music director of the Welsh National Opera (WNO) from 2003 to 2004 and the principal guest conductor and music advisor of the Orchestre National du Capitole de Toulouse (2005), becoming music director in 2008. He has conducted both the **Vienna** and **Berlin philharmonic orchestras** to critical acclaim and has been a regular guest conductor at the **Mariinsky Theater** in St. Petersburg, as well as with the **London Philharmonia Orchestra**. He gave his **Metropolitan Opera, New York**, debut in 2003, **conducting** Peter Ilyich Tchaikovsky's *Eugene Onegin* and has also appeared at the **Houston Grand Opera**, **Vienna State Opera**, and many others, particularly with **operas** presenting Russian literature. One of the last conductors to study with the reknowned Russian teacher **Ilya Musin** in St. Petersburg, Sokhiev was born in Vladikavkas, North Ossetia.

Sokol, Vilem. (1915–2011.) Czech-American **conductor**, violist, and music educator. Sokol taught at the University of Washington (1948–1985) and led the **Seattle Youth Symphony Orchestra** from 1950 to 1988. Under his direction, the **orchestra** performed and recorded **Gustav Mahler**'s *Symphony No. 10*, the first **youth orchestra** to do so.

sol bémol. (Fr.) G-flat. See **appendix 5**.

sol bémolle. (It.) G-flat. See **appendix 5**.

sol dièse. (Fr.) G-sharp. See **appendix 5**.

sol dieses. (It.) G-sharp. See **appendix 5**.

solenne. (It.) Solemn. (Fr. *solennel*, Ger. *feierlich*, Sp. *solemne*.) Example: *con solennitá*, with solemnity.

solfège. (Fr.) A system of learning scales, intervals, and melodic exercises to **solmization** syllables. Widely developed and used in France, this system is used throughout the United States as a way of learning **sight-singing** and can be based on either a fixed do, where do is always the note C, or on moveable do, where do is the tonic note of whatever **scale** is in use in a given piece, for example, if a piece is in the key of D major, do is the first note of the scale, that is, the note D. See also **solmization**.

solfeggio. (It.) See *solfège*.

solmization. The designation of syllables in place of letter names for **pitches** in order to facility the learning or memorizing of music. The syllables, commonly used in Europe, North and South America, and many other countries, are known as the **solfège** syllables and are: do, re, mi, fa, sol, la, ti (or si). This system of syllables is based on the work of Guido d'Arezzo, who lived and worked in the eleventh century. (Fr. *solmization*, Ger. *Solmisation*, It. *solmisazione*.)

solo. (It.) A work for a single instrument. (Fr. *seul*, Ger. *Solo*.)

Solo. (Ger.) A work for a single instrument. (Fr. *seul*, It. *solo*, Sp. *solo*.)

sólo. (Sp.) A work for a single instrument. (Fr. *seul*, Ger. *Solo*, It. *solo*.)

sólo. (Sp.) Only. (Fr. *seule, seulement*, Ger. *nur*, It. *solo, soltanto*.)

solo, soltanto. (It.) Only. (Fr. *seule, seulement*, Ger. *nur*, Sp. *sólo*.)

Solti, Sir Georg. (1912–1997.) Hungarian **conductor**. Solti was a vocal coach at the **Hungarian State Opera** in the 1930s and assisted **Arturo Toscanini** at the **Salzburg Festival** (1936 and 1937). He fled Hungary during the rise of the Nazis, spending the war years in Switzerland working as a pianist. He was appointed music director of the **Bavarian State Opera** (Munich) in 1946, and in 1952, he moved to Frankfurt, where he held the same position. He became a (West) German citizen in 1953 at a time when he was virtually "stateless." He moved to London to take over the musical leadership of the **Royal Opera House, Covent Garden**, in 1961, becoming a British subject in 1972. In 1969, he was appointed music director of the **Chicago Symphony Orchestra (CSO)**, staying there until 1981. Solti expanded the repertoire of the CSO, commissioning Witold Lutosławski's Symphony No. 3 and Sir Michael Tippet's Symphony No. 4. He also presented works by such American composers as **Elliott Carter** and **Charles Ives**.

Solti served as the music director of the **London Philharmonic Orchestra** (1979–1983) and the **Orchestre de Paris** (1992–1975). He collaborated with the actor Dudley Moore on a television series designed to introduce novice audiences to the **orchestra**; directed the Solti Orchestral Project at **Carnegie Hall**, which trained young musicians; and founded the World Orchestra for Peace for the fiftieth anniversary of the United Nations. He left an enormous legacy of recordings (over 250 with 32 **Grammys**, all on the **Decca label**), including a complete set of **Richard Wagner**'s *Der Ring des Nibelungen* (see **Ring cycle**), made with the Chicago Symphony. Solti was one of the first conductors to use stereo recording techniques in order to enhance to sound of **opera**, in particular. He was known for the great energy and physicality of his **conducting**.

sombre. (Fr.) Gloomy, dark, with a dark tone. (Ger. *dunkel*, It. *buio, cupo*, Sp. *tenebroso, sombrio*.)

sombrio. (Sp.) Dark, gloomy, with a dark tone. Also *tenebroso*. (Fr. *sombre*, Ger. *dunkel*, It. *buio, cupo*.)

Somogi, Judith. (1941–1988.) American **conductor** and pianist. Somogi studied at the **Juilliard School** and at **Tanglewood**. Early in her career, she was the pianist for several organizations, including the Oratorio Society of Queens. She became a staff pianist at the **New York City Opera** beginning in 1966. Somogi was the first woman to conduct at the New York City Opera when, in 1974, she made her debut, leading both W. S. Gilbert and Arthur Sullivan's *The Mikado* and Giuseppi Verdi's *La Traviata*. She served as the music director of the Utica Symphony from 1977 to 1980, and in 1977, she made her debut with the **New York Philharmonic**.

She served as first **Kapellmeister** under **Michael Gielen** at the Frankfurt Opera (1981–1987), debuting with Giacomo Puccini's *Madama Butterfly*. Among other **operas** she conducted were Gioacchino Rossini's *Il*

Turco in Italia, Verdi's *Un Ballo in Maschera*, and Jacques Offenbach's *Tales of Hoffmann*. Somogi also served as a guest conductor in Europe and North America. She died from cancer at the age of forty-seven. Her last performance was **conducting Richard Wagner**'s *Das Rheingold*. Known as a dynamic conductor, Somogi received praise for her clarity and dramatic flair. She was featured in the television program *Onstage with Judith Somogi*.

son. (Fr.) Sound. (Ger. *Klang, Schall,* Sp. *sonido.*) Examples: *son fundamental,* fundamental tone (Ger. *Grundton, Tonika,* It. *suono fundamentale*); *sons harmoniques,* harmonics (Ger. *FlageotettTöne,* Sp. *armónicos*); *sons ouverts* or *sons naturels,* natural notes or tones; *sons partiels,* partials (Ger. *Teiltöne,* It. *suoni parziali,* Sp. *parcialels, armónicos*); *sons réel,* real sound, from *Rapsodie Espagnole, Habanera,* by Maurice Ravel.

son écho. (Fr.) Echo tone. (Ger. *Echoton,* It. *suono eco,* Sp. *sonido eco.*)

sonido. (Sp.) Sound, tone. (Fr. *son;* Ger. *Klang, Schall.*)

sonido eco. (Sp.) Echo tone. (Fr. *son écho,* It. *suono eco,* Ger. *Echoton.*)

sonido tapado. (Sp.) Stopped tone. Used for brass players. (Fr. *ton bouché,* Ger. *gestopfter Ton,* It. *tono chiuso.*)

sonore, sonorité. (Fr.) Sonorous. Seen in the **horn** parts in the ballet *Jeux* by Claude Debussy. (Ger. *klangvoll,* It. *sonoro, sonoramente,* Sp. *sonoro.*)

sonority. The tonal quality, resonance, fullness of sound of a performer. In the twentieth century, it may refer to a simultaneity or vertical sonority, also a sound that is a particular combination of timbres or registers.

sons harmoniques. (Fr.) Harmonics. Also *flageolet.* (Ger. *Flageolett,* It. *suoni armonici, zufolo,* Sp. *armónicos, octavîn.*) See also **harmonic series, string harmonics**.

Sony Corporation. A Japanese multinational corporation that focuses mainly on entertainment through electronics, games, film, music, and recordings. Sony introduced the portable **Walkman** (1979) and developed the compact disc (CD), PlayStation, and many other products. **Sony Music Entertainment** is the second largest music recording company and is run by Sony Corporation of America. It purchased the CBS Record Group in 1987 and has the Beatles, Michael Jackson, Usher, Eminem, and many other pop artist catalogues.

Sony Music Entertainment (SME). Sometimes known simply as Sony Music, it is an American company owned and run by Sony Corporation of America, a subsidiary of **Sony Corporation**, Japan. Its origins go back to the 1929 founding of the American Record Corporation, which became part of **Columbia Records** in 1938. In 2004, Sony Music Entertainment and Bertelsmann Music Group (BMG) merged, but in 2008, Sony purchased BMG's part of the company and the name reverted to SME, becoming the second largest of the world's three principal record companies, between **Universal Music Group** and **Warner Music Group**.

Sony Walkman. See **Walkman, Sony**.

sopra. (It.) On, on the, above. (Fr. *sur, sur le, sur la,* Ger. *auf, auf der, auf die auf das,* Sp. *sobre.*) Example: *come sopra,* as above.

soprano. The highest female voice classification. See also **voice classifications**.

soprano acuto sfogato. A **soprano** that sings with ease in the very high register, above F‴. See also **voice classifications**.

soprano clef. One of the so-called **C clefs**. (Fr. *clé d'ut premiére ligne,* Ger. *Sopranschlüssel,* It. *chiave di soprano,* Sp. *clave de do en primera línea.*)

sordina. (Sp.) **Mute**. (Fr. *sourdine,* Ger. *Dämpfer,* It. *sordino.*) Examples: *sin sordina,* without mute; *con sordina,* with mute.

sordino. (It.) **Mute**. (Fr. *sourdine,* Ger. *Dämpfer,* Sp. *sordina.*) Examples: *senza sordino,* without mute; *con sordino,* with mute.

Sorrell, Jeannette. (b. 1965.) American musician and founder and leader of Apollo's Fire (1992), the Cleveland-based early music ensemble. An accomplished harpsichordist, Sorrell studied **conducting** at the Aspen and **Tanglewood** music festivals and holds an artist diploma from the **Oberlin Conservatory of Music** and an honorary doctorate from Case Western University. She has led the ensemble Apollo's Fire in over twenty commercial CDs to great acclaim. See also **early music ensembles**.

sospirando. (It.) Sighing. A descriptive term sometimes used to evoke a particular shape or quality in playing. (Fr. *en soupirant,* Ger. *seufzend,* Sp. *suspirando.*)

sostenido. (Sp.) The sharp sign. (Fr. *diése,* Ger. *Kreuz, Erhöhungszeichen,* It. *diesis.*) See also **accidental**.

sostenido. 1. (Sp.) To sharpen, to raise the pitch. (Fr. *diése,* Ger. *erhöhen,* It. *diesis.*)

2. (Sp.) The sharp sign. (Fr. *diése*, Ger. *Kreuz, Erhöhungszeichen*; It. *diesis*.)

sostenido. (Sp.) Sustained. A common descriptive word most often seen in its Italian and French forms. (Fr. *soutenu*, It. *sostenuto*.)

sostenuto, sostenendo. (It.) Sustained. Abbreviated *sost.* (Fr. *soutenu*, Ger. *verhalten, getragen*, Sp. *sostenido*.)

sostituto. (It.) Substitute. (Fr. *substitut*, Ger. *Ersatz*, Sp. *sustituto*.)

sotto. (It.) Under, below. (Fr. *dessous, sous*, Ger. *unter*, Sp. *bajo*.) See also **sotto voce**.

sotto voce. (It., lit. "under the voice.") Quietly, subdued, in an undertone. (Fr. *á voix basse*, Ger. "*unter der Stimme*," *mit leiser Stimme*, Sp. *en voz baja*.)

souffle. (Fr.) A breath. (Ger. *Atem*, It. *respire*, Sp. *respiración*.) Example: *Marquer un souffle ici*, Mark a breath here; *Souffle dans le temps*, Breath in time.

sound, developing an orchestral. See **developing an orchestral sound**.

soundscape. A term first coined by composer R. Murray Schafer to denote environmental sounds, such as the sounds of the city, industry, conversations, and more, but now also used to denote the natural environment, all of which can be part of a composer's source material.

soupir. (Fr.) A quarter rest. (Ger. *Viertelpause*, It. *pausa disemiminima*, Sp. *pausa de seminima*.) See also **appendix 7**.

soupirant, en. (Fr.) Sighing. A descriptive term often used to evoke a shaping of notes. (Ger. *seufzend*, It. *sospirando*, Sp. *suspirando*.)

souple. (Fr.) Flexible, supple. Also *souplement, avec souplesse*, with flexibility. Example: *Dans un rythme très souple*, in a very supple rhythm, from *De l'aube à midi sur la mer*, movement one from *La Mer*, by Claude Debussy.

sourd. (Fr.) Muffled, muted. (Ger. *bedeckt*, It. *coperto, velato*, Sp. *cubierto*.)

sourdement. (Fr.) Secretly. Example: *sourdement agité*, secretly agitated, a modifier to the tempo of *assez animé* (very animated) at the beginning of the second movement of *Le Martyre de Saint Sébastien* by Claude Debussy.

sourdine. (Fr.) **Mute**. (Ger. *Dämpfer*, It. *sordino*, Sp. *sordina*.) Example: *sans sourdine*, without mute; *avec sourdine*, with mute; *Sourdines aux 1er 2e et 3e Trombones*, **Trombones** 1, 2, 3 with mutes, from *De l'aube à midi sur la mer*, movement one from *La Mer*, by Claude Debussy.

Sousa, John Phillip. (1854–1932.) American composer and bandmaster. Sousa is the composer of the official march of the United States, *The Stars and Stripes Forever*, and is known as the "March King"; he was regarded as virtually a national institution. Sousa was appointed as the fourteenth conductor of the U.S. Marine Band in 1880, remaining with them for twelve years and raising their standards and profile. He left the military and formed his own **band**, called Sousa's Band, and toured with them nationally and internationally for several years. He was well known as a composer and orchestrator of **operettas**. During the years of the Great Depression, when it became more difficult to travel, the band began to broadcast concerts on radio. In the last years of his life, he became more interested in music education and the promotion of music through band festivals and contests.

sous, dessous. (Fr.) Under, below. (Ger. *unter*, It. *sotto*, Sp. *bajo*.)

soutenu. (Fr.) Sustained. (Ger. *verhalten, getragen*, It. *sostenuto*, Sp. *sostenido*.) Example: *soutenu et trés expressif*, sustained and very expressive, from *Gigues* of *Images* by Claude Debussy.

South Dakota Symphony Orchestra (SDSO). Founded in 2000 in Sioux Falls, the **orchestra** is a combination of semiprofessional and professional musicians. The current music director, Delta David Gier, was appointed in 2004. The orchestra runs a four-orchestra **youth orchestra** program; the Lakota Music Project to build bridges with the Native American Lakota community; a Music as Medicine program in collaboration with the University Health Center and the Avera McKennan Hospital to make music part of the healing process; a program of chamber music for the very young, called Pied Piper; and chamber music for retirees, alongside its classics, pops, and educational concerts. The SDSO has also sponsored residencies of composers Paul Moravec and Steven Stuckey.

Southwest German Radio Orchestra (Sudwestrunkfunk Orchester or Sinfonieorchester des Südwestrundfunks). Also known as the SWR Symphony Orchestra or the SWR Baden-Baden Freiburg Symphony Orchestra. **Hans Rosbaud**, known as a proponent of contemporary music, was the first **conductor**, and ever since, the **orchestra** has been known for its performances of new music. **Michael Gielen** was the chief conductor from 1986 to 1999. He was followed by **Sylvain Cambreling**

(1999–2011) and François-Xavier Roth (appointed in 2011). In 2012, the SWR Radio Council voted to merge the orchestra with its Stuttgart counterpart, the **Stuttgart Radio Symphony Orchestra**, in 2016. The orchestra has been closely tied to the **Donaueschingen Music Festival** for many years and has released numerous recordings of a wide variety of repertoire.

so viel wie. (Ger.) As much as. Usually referring to dynamics. Example: *so viel wie möglich,* as much as possible. (Fr. *autant que,* It. *quanto,* Sp. *cuanto.*)

Spanish National Orchestra. See National Orchestra and Chorus of Spain.

Spano, Robert. (b. 1961.) American **conductor**. Spano is the music director of the **Atlanta Symphony Orchestra** (appointed in 2001) and the Aspen Music Festival (beginning in 2012), where he also teaches **conducting** and oversees Aspen's American Academy of Conducting. He often programs works of American composers, such as Christopher Theofanidis, Jennifer Higdon, and Michael Gandolfi.

spectral music. A term coined by Hugues Dufourt in 1979 that refers to a highly technical compositional style that emerged as a reaction to integral serialism (Fr. *musique spectrale*). It is based on the study of the psychoacoustic properties of the spectrum of sound, tone color, and the harmonic overtones. One specific resulting technique uses the spectrum of a single **note** played by a specific instrument, such as the **trombone**, as analyzed by a sonogram for elements of timbre that are then re-created in the **pitches** played by other instruments. Such techniques have been developed through research carried out at **IRCAM** in Paris and involve the use of acoustic properties of harmonies as a means of generating pitch collections and the combination of spectral characteristics of electronic sounds re-created by an instrumental ensemble and sometimes for instruments in combination with computer-generated sounds. Composed mainly in Europe since the 1970s, composers associated with spectral music are Gérard Grisey (1946–1998) and Tristan Murail, in addition to other members of the French Groupe de l'Itinéraire and the German Feedback group. Other composers who have been influenced by the self-titled spectralists are Magnus Lindberg and Unsuk Chin. Murail has described his music as being about the sensation of the sound, with Unsuk Chin adding that her music is a reflection of her dreams, where she sees "the play of light and color through the room and at the same time forming a fluid sound sculpture" (see Auner, 2013, in the **bibliography**).

speech melody. See *Sprechstimme*.

speech song. See *Sprechstimme*.

Sphinx Organization. Located in Detroit, Michigan, and founded by violinist Aaron Dworkin in 1996, Sphinx is dedicated to building diversity in classical music through its annual competition, the Sphinx Chamber Orchestra and Symphony, and the Harlem and Catalyst String Quartets. The organization also has several outreach programs for youth, including the Sphinx Preparatory Institute, Performance Academy, and the School Dayz and Musical Encounters programs. Founding president Dworkin and Sphinx have won many awards, including the Michigan Governors Award for Arts and Culture, the MacArthur Fellow Program, the *Newsweek* Giving Back Award, and the MLK Spirit Award.

spianato. (It.) Smooth, even. A charcter word. (Fr. *aplani,* Ger. *geebnet, ungekünstelt,* Sp. *liso.*)

spiccato. (It.) A bowing term indicating a bouncing bow, whereby the bow is dropped to the string and bounces back and forth, down-bow alternating with up-bow, creating space between each **note**. Best used in fast tempos.

spielen. (Ger.) To play, to touch. (Fr. *jouer, toucher,* It. *suonare, tocare,* Sp. *tocar.*)

spielen. (Ger.) To play, as in, to play an instrument. Examples: *spielenrein,* play in tune; *spielunrein,* play out of tune; *spielen zu hoch,* play sharp; *spielen zu tief,* play flat. Also *Spieler,* player.

spielerisch. (Ger.) Playful. A character word. (Fr. *badin,* It. *giocoso.*)

spigliato. (It.) Bold. (Fr. *alerte, dégagé,* Ger. *keck,* Sp. *audaz, atrevido.*)

spiritoso, spirito. (It.) Spirited, spirit. (Fr. *esprit, spiritual,* Ger. *geistreich, geistvoll, witzig.*) Example: *con spirito,* with spirit.

Spitze, an der. (Ger.) Point of the bow of a string instrument. (Fr. *à la pointe,* It. *punta,* Sp. *en el punta.*)

spitzig. (Ger.) Pointed, spiky (spikey), biting. A descriptive word used for articulation.

Spohr, Louis. (1784–1859.) German composer, violinist, and **conductor**. Spohr was a composer of many **operas**, symphonies, and chamber music. He also wrote the important *School of Violin Playing* (1831), which is still used as a resource for the study of **performance-practice** style. In 1820, he traveled to London to be the director of the **London Philharmonic Society**. He wrote his second

symphony and an overture for the occasion, **conducting** them in **rehearsal** in the then novel way, with a baton. At the performance, he reverted to his normal practice of leading from the **violin** with the bow. Spohr was known for disciplined rehearsals and greatly improving the performance standards of the ensembles he led. He became the **concertmaster** at the Theater an der Wien in 1812, writing his opera *Faust* and his well-known *Nonet* and *Octet* while there. He became the **Kappellmeister** in Kassel, Germany (1822), composing his opera *Jessonda*, his oratorio *Die letzten Dinge*, and the first two of his *Double String Quartets*. In Kassel, he conducted **Richard Wagner**'s *Der fliegende Holländer* (1843) and *Tannhäuser* (1853). During this period, he was recognized in Germany and England as a leading composer and musician of his time, the heir to the classical tradition.

Spohr played a significant role in the development of conducting. His life and influence spanned and exemplified a period of the transition from that of the instrumental leader, such as a violinist or harpsichordist, to the disciplined conductor who leads silently with a baton. Spohr is also known for having introduced **rehearsal letters** to orchestral **scores** and parts as a convenience during rehearsals. He wrote *Louis Spohr's Autobiography* (1865, reprinted 1969; see the **bibliography**). See also **appendix 2**.

Spokane Symphony. Founded in 1945 in Spokane, Washington, the **orchestra** presents a ten-concert classics series, a pops series, and a chamber series. Each summer the orchestra is featured at the Sandpoint Festival in Idaho. All classics concerts are broadcast on Spokane Public Radio, 91.1 KPBX-FM. Selected classics concerts are made available over Internet2 through Pacific Northwest Gigapop and sponsored by the University of Washington. The current music director is Eckart Preu (appointed in 2004). Past music directors include Fabio Mechetti (1993–2004), Vakhtang Jordania (1991–1993), Bruce Ferden (1985–1991), **Gunther Schuller** (1984–1985), **Donald Thulean** (1962–1984), and Harold Paul Whelan (1945–1961).

Spontini, Gaspare. (1774–1851.) Italian composer and **conductor**. After studying in Naples, Italy, he went to Paris in 1803, eventually becoming a major figure in its musical life. His **opera** *Fernand Cortez* was an enormous success and was performed often in Paris. In 1814, he became the **Kapellmeister** in Berlin, where he composed less but conducted more, building a distinguished reputation in his day, one that, in spite of his influence on such composers as **Richard Wagner** and **Hector Berlioz**, has not survived him.

Spotify. Established in 2006, a Swedish music-streaming company that commercially provides content from the Sony, EMI, Warner Music Group, and Universal record labels. Content is available on numerous digital systems.

Sprechgesang. (Ger.) Literally, speech song. Generally used interchangeably with **Sprechstimme**, but sometimes intended to make a distinction between the manner of performance (*Sprechgesang*) and the printed vocal part (*Sprechstimme*).

Sprechstimme. (Ger.) Literally, speech part. May refer to the actual printed page of a piece of music written in **Sprechgesang** style. Often used interchangeably with *Sprechgesang*, meaning "spoken song" or "speech singing." This is a technique of half singing and half speaking in which singers approximate indicated **pitches** in rhythm. Composers usually choose to designate these approximate pitches by an *x* with a stem. The most widely known piece using the technique is in **Arnold Schoenberg**'s *Pierrot Lunaire*. Other examples include Alban Berg's **operas** *Wozzeck* and *Lulu* and Luciano Berio's *Circles*.

Springbogen. (Ger.) **Spiccato**.

spring bow arpeggio. A slightly bounced stroke where the bow plays single **notes** on three to four strings in one direction before switching to the opposite direction. Violinists and violists normally start on a down-bow, while due the to principles of weight and balance, cellists begin on a up-bow. **Bass** players select the bowing direction depending on whether they use a **French** or **German bow**.

springend. (Ger.) A style of bowing, a directive to string players to bounce the bow off the string.

Spring for Music Festival (S4M). Founded in 2008 by David V. Foster, the president of the management firm Opus 3 Artists, providing administration of the festival; Thomas W. Morris, a consultant and the artistic director of the Ojai Festival (CA), serving as artistic director; and Mary Lou Falcone, a public-relations consultant, overseeing publicity and marketing. The first festival was in 2011. Founding sponsors were the **Andrew W. Mellon Foundation**, Marguerite and Gerry Lenfest, and Jan and Daniel R. Lewis. The festival provides a vehicle for **orchestras**, both regional and national, to showcase their artistic creativity in a concentrated and highly competitive format in the world's most renowned concert venue. The media partner is **WQXR** New York. The 2011 orchestras were the Oregon, **Albany**, **Toledo**, and **Dallas** symphonies, the **Orpheus** and **Saint Paul** chamber orchestras, and the **Orchestre symphonique de Montréal**. The 2012 orchestras were the **Houston**, Edmonton, New Jersey, Alabama, Milwaukee, and

Nashville symphonies. The 2013 orchestras were the **Detroit**, **Albany**, **Baltimore**, and **National** symphonies and the **Buffalo Philharmonic**. The 2014 orchestras were the **Seattle**, Winnipeg, and **Pittsburgh** symphonies; the **New York Philharmonic**; the **Rochester Philharmonic**; and the **Cincinnati Symphony** and **May Festival Chorus**.

Sprung. (Ger.) A leap, skip; the opposite of by step; a melody that moves in leaps instead of by step. (Fr. *saut*, It., Sp. *salto*.)

spugna, di bacchetta. (It.) Sponge-headed mallet or stick, as in a timpani mallet with a sponge head. (Ger. *Schwammschlägel*, Fr. *baguette d'éponge*, Sp. *baqueta de esponja*.)

Staatskapelle Berlin. The **orchestra** of the **Berlin State Opera** (Berliner Staatsoper Unter den Linden). The ensemble traces its history back to 1570, when the Elector of Brandenburg established an orchestra at court. The first affiliation with an **opera** house was in 1742, when **Frederick the Great** established the Royal Court Opera. Since 1842, the ensemble has given both concert and opera performances under a music director known as the **Kapellmeister**. Currently the title is **Staatskapellmeister**, the designation for the music director of both the orchestra and the opera. Currently **Daniel Barenboim** holds this position. Past music directors have included Otmar Suitner (1964–1990), Franz Konwitschny (1955–1962), **Erich Kleiber** (1954–1955), Joseph Keilberth (1948–1951), **Herbert von Karajan** (1941–1945), **Clemens Kraus** (1923–1934), **Erich Kleiber** (1923–1934), Leo Blech (1913–1920), **Richard Strauss** (1899–1913), and others. The orchestra has given numerous significant operatic premieres and made many important recordings.

Staatskapelle Dresden. See **Dresden Staateskapelle**.

staccato. (It.) An articulation term indicating short, separated **notes**. In bowing, a short stroke where the bow stops between each change of direction, down-bow and up-bow.

staccato style. Shown by the conductor with quick gestures in the wrist and sometimes the forearm, they can be used for either a **light** or a **heavy staccato**.

staccato volant, bondi. (Fr.) A bowing term that calls for a series of **spiccato** strokes played in one direction, usually up-bow, with the bow leaving the string between each **note**. Also known as flying **staccato**. (It. *balzato, balzando,* Ger. *Springbogen, fliegendes Staccato*, Sp. *staccato volante*.)

staccato volante. (Sp.) A bowing term that calls for a series of **spiccato** strokes played in one direction, usually up-bow, with the bow leaving the string between each **note**. Also known as flying **staccato**. (It. *balzato, balzando,* Fr. *bondi, staccato volant,* Ger. *Springbogen, fliegendes Staccato*.)

staff, stave. The five-line **system** on which music is written. (Fr. *portée*, Ger. *Liniensystem, System*, It. *sistema, rigo*, Sp. *pentagrama, pauto*.)

stand, conductor's. See **conductor's stand**.

Stange. (Ger.) Stick, usually wood, sometimes used to refer to the bow of a string player. It can also be used to indicate *col legno*.

stark. (Ger.) Strong. (Fr. *fort*, It. *forte*, Sp. *fuerte*.) Also *stärker*, stronger. Example: *starker besetzt*, more players on a part.

State Academic Symphony Orchestra of the Russian Federation. Also known as the Svetlanov Symphony Orchestra and founded in 1936 as the USSR State Symphony Orchestra under the baton of Alexander Gauk, who led the ensemble from 1936 to 1941. The current music director is Vladimir Jurowski, who was appointed in 2011. Other past **conductors** include Natan Rakhlin (1941–1945), Konstantin Ivanov (1946–1965), **Evgeny Svetlanov** (1965–2000), Vassily Sinaisky (2000–2002), and Mark Gorenstein (2002–2011).

St. Clair, Carl. (b. 1952.) American **conductor**. St. Clair has been the music director of the Pacific Symphony since 1990, leading the **orchestra** in a period of significant growth. He has served as the music director for the **Komische Oper Berlin**, the German National Theater, and Staatskapelle Weimer (Germany) and as guest conductor for many orchestras and festivals in the United States and abroad. He conducted the premiere and recordings of Richard Danielpour's *American Requiem* and Elliot Goldenthal's *Fire Water Paper: A Vietnam Oratorio*.

Steg. (Ger.) Bridge of a string instrument. (Fr. *chevalet*, Sp. *puente*, It. *ponticello*.) See also *Steg, am*.

Steg, am. (Ger.) An indication for string players to play near or at the bridge. (Fr. *prés du chevalet*, It. *sul ponticello*, Sp. *cerca del puente*.)

steigern. (Ger.) To increase, to augment, to heighten, similar to **crescendo**. (Fr. *augmenter*, It. *augmentare*, Sp. *aumentar*.) Example: *steigernd, beschleunigend*, getting louder and faster. Also *Steigerung*, augmentation, climax.

Steinberg, William. (1899–1978.) German-born American **conductor**. Steinberg became the music director of the Frankfurt Opera in 1929, conducting the premieres of **operas** by **Arnold Schoenberg**, George Antheil, and an early performance of Kurt Weill's *Mahagonny*. At the time, he also conducted at the **Berlin Staatsoper**. During the rise of Adolf Hitler, he left Germany for Israel, where he was cofounder and later conductor of the great violinist Bronislaw Hubermann's **Palestine Orchestra** (later the **Israel Philharmonic Orchestra**). He went to the United States as **Arturo Toscanini**'s associate with the **NBC Orchestra** in 1938, became the music director of the **Buffalo Philharmonic Orchestra** (1945–1953), and then held the same position with the **Pittsburgh Symphony** (1952–1976). He held many other positions, including music director of the **Boston Symphony Orchestra** from 1969 to 1972, and was known as a conductor of exceptionally clear baton technique.

stellen, setzen, legen. (Ger.) To put, as in to put on the **mute**. (Fr. *mettez*, Sp. *poner*, It. *mettere*.)

sterbend. (Ger.) Dying away. A descriptive word used to evoke a particular quality in the playing. Also *ersterbend*. (Fr. *en mourant*, It. *morendo*, Sp. *desvaneciéndose*.)

Stereophile. Founded in 1962 by J. Gordon Holt as a monthly music magazine that focuses on high-end audio equipment. It continues to be published and has an active website.

stereophonic sound. The technology that allows sound to be recorded and played back using two or more independent audio channels, thereby creating a more realistic effect of live sound. In 1881, Clément Ader exhibited the first two-channel telephonic audio system in Paris. Listeners could listen to a transmission of a performance at the Paris Opera with two receivers, one for each ear. In the 1930s, **Alan Blumlein** developed stereophonic recording methods and the stereo disc and patented stereo records, stereo film, and also surround sound while working at **EMI**. This included the technology of producing an LP, where the two "walls" of the groove each carried a channel of sound. **Leopold Stokowski** led the **Philadelphia Orchestra** in the first stereo recording in the **Academy of Music** in 1932.

stesso. (It.) Same. Also *medesimo, istesso*. (Fr. *meme*, Ger. *derselbe, dieselbe, dasselbe*, Sp. *mismo*.) Example: *l'istesso tempo*, the same tempo. (Fr. *le même tempo*, Ger. *das gleiche Tempo*, Sp. *el mismo tiempo*.)

stetig. (Ger.) Steady, stable. (Fr. *constant, stable*, It. *costante, stabile*, Sp. *estable*.)

stets. (Ger.) Ever, always. Also *immer, ständig*. (Fr. *toujours, constamment*, It. *sempre, constantemente*, Sp. *siempre*.) Example: *stets das Gleiche*, always the same. (Fr. *toujours le (la) meme*, It. *sempre lo stesso*, Sp. *siempre la misma*.)

Stil. (Ger.) Style. (Fr. *style*, It. *stile*, Sp. *estilo*.)

stile. (It.) Style. (Ger. *stil*, Fr. *style*, Sp. *estilo*.)

Stimme. 1. (Ger.) Voice. (Fr. *voix*, It. *voce*, Sp. *voz*.)
    2. A part, such as first **violins** or **sopranos** or the physical parts, that is, the music itself.

stimmen. (Ger.) To tune. Also *einstimmen*. (Fr. *accorder*, It. *accordare*, Sp. *afinar*.)

Stimmgabel. (Ger.) Tuning fork. (Fr. *diapason*, It. *corista*, Sp. *diapason*.)

Stimmstock. (Ger.) Soundpost of a string instrument. (Fr. âme, It. *anima*, Sp. *alma*.)

Stimmung. 1. (Ger.) Intonation, **pitch**. Also *Intonation, Tongebung*. (Fr. *intonation*, It. *intonazione*, Sp. *entonación, afinación*.)
    2. (Ger.) mood, atmosphere. (Fr. *climat, atmosphere*, It. *stato d'animo, atmosfera*, Sp. *atmósfera*.) Example: *reine Stimmung*, in tune.

St. Louis Symphony. Founded in 1890, the symphony performs in Powell Hall. The **orchestra** saw a period of major growth under music director Leonard Slatkin (1979–1996), particularly through many recordings on Angel, **EMI**, Columbia, RCA Victor, Red Seal, Telarc, and Vox/Turnabout. The symphony now has its own recording company, Arch Media. Slatkin founded the St. Louis Youth Symphony in 1970. The current music director is David Robertson. The orchestra has many community outreach and education programs, including IN UNISON, a partnership with several African American churches.

Stock, Frederick. (1872–1942.) **Conductor** of the **Chicago Symphony Orchestra (CSO)** for thirty-seven years (1905–1942). The CSO's music director **Theodore Thomas** brought Stock from Germany to be in the **viola** section. He was appointed assistant conductor in 1899, and when Thomas died in 1905, Stock became Thomas's successor. Stock held the position until his death. He was an active promoter of the music of his own time, programming works of Claude Debussy, Maurice Ravel, **Gustav Mahler**, Alexander Scriabin, **Arnold Schoenberg**, and Paul Hindemith. Sergei Prokofiev performed the premiere of his *Piano Concerto No. 3* as the pianist with

Stock **conducting**. Stock also introduced **young people's concerts** and started the **Chicago Civic Orchestra** as a training ensemble sponsored by the **symphony**.

Stockhausen, Karlheinz. (1928–2007.) German composer who sought to develop serial techniques to include musical parameters other than **pitch**, using hierarchies of rhythmic values and dynamic levels. Stockhausen explored acoustic and spatial possibilities in his work for three **orchestras** (and three **conductors**), *Grüppen* (1955–1957), and created a union of music and language in his tape piece, *Gesang der Jünglinge* (1955–1956). Between 1977 and 2003 he worked on a massive **opera** cycle, *Licht*: *Die sieben Tage der Woche* (*Light: The Seven Days of the Week*). It uses forces that go beyond any other opera. Besides singers, dancers, instrumentalists, and electronics, in the third scene of *Mittwoch aus Licht* (*Wednesday from Licht*), titled "Helikopter-Streichquartett" (Helicopter–String Quartet), Stockhausen calls for the four members of the **quartet** to perform in four separate helicopters, flying over the concert hall. While synchronized by a click track, the sounds they play are combined with the sounds of the helicopters through electronic means and are heard by the audience. In addition, video transmission of each performer is projected in the hall. The work has had several performances in Germany and been recorded by the Arditti Quartet. No conductor is required. Coordination is handled electronically.

Stockholm Philharmonic Orchestra, Royal (RSPO). See: **Royal Stockholm Philharmonic Orchestra**.

Stokowski, Leopold. (1882–1977.) English-born, self-taught orchestral **conductor**. Stokowski was the music director of the **Philadelphia Orchestra** (1912–1936). Although not always recognized for it, he had an enormous impact on the contemporary music of the day. In addition to several hundred world premieres, including Sergei Rachmaninoff's *Symphony No. 3*, *Rhapsody on a Theme of Paganini*, and **Arnold Schoenberg**'s *Violin Concerto*, he conducted the American premieres of **Gustav Mahler**'s *Symphony No. 8*, Schoenberg's *Gurrelieder*, and **Igor Stravinsky**'s *The Rite of Spring*.

Stokowski believed that interpretation was an art form in itself. He dedicated his life to the broad popularization of classical music through an artistically liberal approach to the music and the newest technical means available. He sought drama in performance whenever possible, abandoning the baton for the sake of sweeping gestures that helped create or illustrate the lush sound he cultivated in the **orchestra**. His idea of "free bowing" and the doubling wind players made it possible to have a continuity of sound without gaps, for example, no audible breaths, thus the famous "Philadelphia sound."

Stokowski not only strove to achieve the most exciting sound possible by editing the **scores** of works he performed, adding instruments, for instance, but he also orchestrated several works of Johann Sebastian Bach, including the Toccata and Fugue in D minor. In 1940, he collaborated with Walt Disney in the creation of the cartoon movie *Fantasia*, which used classical works as accompaniment. He was one of the very first conductors to take advantage of stereophonic sound, leading the **Philadelphia Orchestra** in the first stereo recording in the **Academy of Music** in 1932.

Leopold Stokowski. *Courtesy Photofest.*

stopped. 1. To put the hand in the bell of a **horn** in order to create a muffled sound. When the hand is inserted into the horn, it raises the **pitch** one half step and the player adjusts accordingly. While certain terms may be used to signify either stopped or muted, it should be noted that only the horn is stopped; other brass instrument can be muted but not stopped. (Fr. *bouché*, étouffé; Ger. *gestopft*, *gedeckt*; It. *chiuso*, *tappato*; Sp. *cubierto*, *tapado*.)

2. Stopped tones. (Fr. *ton bouché*, Ger. *gestopfter Ton*, It. *tono chiuso*, Sp. *sonidos tapados*.)

3. When a timpanist stops the sound of the drum.

stopping. When a player stops the sound of the instrument so abruptly that it doesn't ring, as on a string, percussion instrument, or the **piano**.

Strad, The. Founded in 1889, a British monthly classical music magazine that focuses on string instruments. It publishes articles and photographs about instruments, concerts, profiles of leading performers, master classes, **orchestras** and music schools, and the craft of instrument making.

straff. (Ger.) Strict, tense, tight. A character word sometime used to emphasize strictness and steadiness of playing.

straight mute. See **brass mutes**.

strappare. (It.) A way of playing a note; to break, break off, to sever, to tear off. Seen in its German form in the symphonies of **Gustav Mahler**. (Fr. *arracher*, Ger. *abreissen*.)

strascicando. (It.) Dragging. A descriptive word used often in its German form in the symphonies of **Gustav Mahler**. (Fr. *en traînant*, Ger. *schleppend, verschleppend*.)

Strauss, Richard. (1864–1949.) German composer and conductor. A prolific and influential composer of **tone poems**, **operas**, concerti, many works for solo and **orchestra**, and much more, Strauss achieved the peak of his gift in his mastery of the nineteenth-century orchestra. He made his **conducting** debut at an early age in his own Suite in E-flat for Winds (1884) and went on to become an accomplished conductor not only of his own music but especially that of Wolfgang Amadeus Mozart. Strauss was one of the first conductors to leave a legacy of recordings of his own works as a vital resource for interpretive choices for future generations. Another contribution to future conductors was his *Ten Golden Rules for a Young Conductor* (as translated by Willi Schuh, see the **bibliography**):

1. Bear in mind that you are not making music for your own pleasure, but for the pleasure of your audience.
2. You must not perspire while conducting; only the public must get warm.
3. Direct *Salome* and *Elektra* as if they had been written by Mendelssohn: Elfin music.
4. Never encourage the brass, except with a curt glance, in order to give an important entrance cue.
5. On the contrary, never let the horns and woodwinds out of your sight; if you can hear them at all, they are too loud.
6. If you think that the brass is not blowing loud enough, mute it by a couple of degrees.
7. It is not enough that you yourself understand the singer's every work, which you know from memory; the public must be able to follow without effort. If the audience does not understand the text, it falls asleep.
8. Always accompany the singer so that he can sing without strain.
9. When you think that you have reached the most extreme *prestissimo*, take the tempo again as fast.
10. If you bear all this cheerfully, you, with your beautiful talent and great knowledge, will ever be the untroubled delight of your listeners.

Stravinsky, Igor. (1882–1971.) Renowned Russian composer. See *The Rite of Spring* **(1913)** in **appendix 1**.

straziante. (It.) Agonizing, heartrending.

streichen. (Ger.). To stroke, as in bowing; to bow. Example: *breit streichen*, bowed broadly.

Streicher. (Ger.) The string section, string players. (Fr. *cordes*, It. *archi*, Sp. *sección de cuerdo*.)

Streichquartett. (Ger.) **String quartet**. Also the title of a piece for this ensemble.

streich, strich. (Ger.) The bow stroke. Also *Schlag, Stoß*. (Fr. *coup*, or *coup d'archet*, It. *colpo*, Sp. *golpe de arco*.) Examples: *Strich für Strich*, one bow per **note**; *strich bis*, cut to.

streng. (Ger.) Strict, rigorous. A directive used in various contexts to emphasize steadiness of tempo or some other aspect of playing in an ensemble. (Fr. *rigoureux*, It. *rigoroso*, Sp. *estricto*.) Example: *Streng im Takt*, strict in tempo (Fr. *rigoureux*, It. *rigoroso*, Sp. *estrictamente de tempo, estricto, tiempo justo*); *mit Strenge*, with severity (Fr. *avec sévérité*, It. *con severitá*, Sp. *con severidad*).

stretta, stretto. (It.) Accelerated, faster, a concluding passage of a work in a faster tempo. (Fr. *strette*, Ger. *schneller Schlussteil* [specifically the faster ending passage of a piece], Sp. *stretta*.) Examples: *alla stretta* (lit. narrow), faster stretta, a stretto passage. In a fugue, "stretto" means narrowing the distance between the entrances of the voices. (Ger. *Engführung*.)

stringendo. (It.) Getting gradually faster. (Fr. *en serrant*, Ger. *almählich schneller werdend*.)

string bowings. A term that refers to the choice of the direction (up- or down-bow) and style of the bowing in the playing of string instruments.

string harmonics. **Harmonics**, also known as harmonic partials, on string instruments are achieved in two ways, naturally occurring harmonics achieved by lightly touching one of several vibrating nodes on any string or by creating a so-called **artificial harmonic** by holding down a string with one finger (usually of the left hand) and lightly touching the created node above it with another finger. When one lightly touches the node, an interval of one-forth above the lower held **note**, the harmonic created will be two **octaves** higher than the solidly held note. This is sometimes called a "touch 4 harmonic." When one lightly touches the node an interval of a fifth above the held note (this is a "touch 5 harmonic"), one achieves a harmonic an octave above the node (the lightly held note).

Cellists and **bass** players also have the possibility of so-called **touch 3 harmonics**, that is, when you touch the node a major third above an open string, say the

C string on the **cello**, you will get the pitch two octaves and a major third above the open string (the fundamental), an e'. If you touch the node a minor third above an open string, say the D string (either cello or bass), you will get the pitch two octaves and a minor third above the open string, an f''. These are **natural harmonics**, but touch 3 harmonics can also be produced in the same way that all artificial harmonics are: solidly holding down a note (creating fundamental) and lightly touching the node one third (major or minor) above will generate the pitch two octaves and a major or minor third above the fundamental, depending on the node. Another way of producing the resulting harmonic two octaves and a major third above the open string is to touch the node a major sixth above the open string. Natural harmonics from the halfway point up on the string are the same as those from the halfway point going down in pitch.

The notation of both natural and artificial harmonics has created great confusion because of the question of whether to write the pitch as it will sound or as the player will play it in order to get the desired pitch. The best solution, which many composers use, is to include both with the resultant pitch written in parenthesis. The following brief excerpt by Maurice Ravel shows the notation of both the desired sounding pitch at the top and the way of achieving it through various artificial harmonics.

String harmonics: *Piano Concerto in G*, Maurice Ravel, mvt. 1, excerpt. *Courtesy Andrew Martin Smith.*

string quartet. 1. A chamber ensemble consisting of two **violins** (first and second), a **viola**, and a **cello**.

2. The music performed by a string quartet. Franz Joseph Haydn was commonly called the father of the string quartet because he wrote so many of them and had an enormous influence on the development of the style.

strings. Refers to the common string instruments of the **orchestra**, generally, **violin** sections one and two, **violas**, **cellos**, and **double basses**, in descending order of range. **Harp** and **piano** are not usually included in the list of orchestral string instruments but as separate entities unto themselves.

strisciando, strisciante. (It.) Touching the string lightly and making a glissando over the **natural harmonics**.

strumenti di legni. (It.) Woodwind instruments. (Fr. *bois, instruments à vent*; Ger. *Holz, Holzbläser, Holzblasinstrumente*; Sp. *instrumentos de madera, instrumentos de viento.*)

Stück. (Ger.) A piece of music, composition, musical work. In its Italian form, *pezzo*, it is generally used for a smaller work. (Fr. *pièce, morceau*, It. *pezzo, brano*, Sp. *pieza.*)

Stufe. (Ger.) A degree or **note** of a **scale**. (Fr. *degré*, It. *grado*, Sp. *grado*.) Example: *stufenweise*, stepwise, by step. (Fr. *conjoint*, It. *congiunto*, Sp. *por grados, conjunto*.)

Stulberg, Neal. (b. 1954.) Current professor and director of orchestral studies at the University of California Los Angeles. Stulberg has conducted the **symphony orchestras** of Atlanta, Houston, Indianapolis, New Jersey, Philadelphia, Saint Louis, San Francisco, and many others. He is also a frequent guest conductor in Europe, Asia, and Russia. In 1988, he received the **Seaver/National Endowment for the Arts Conductors Award**.

stumm. (Ger.) Mute, silent. (Fr. *muet*, It. *muto*, Sp. *mudo*.) Example: *stumm niederdrücken*, [the piano keys] silently depressed, from ***Pierrot Lunaire*** by **Arnold Schornberg**.

stürmisch. (Ger.) Stormy, rushing, raging. A character word sometimes seen in works to describe a certain kind of intensity in the playing of a passage. (Fr. *tempétueux*, It. *tempestoso*, Sp. *tempestuoso*.) Example: *Stürmisch bewegt*, *in a stormy motion*, the subtitle to the fourth movement of Symphony No. 1 by **Gustav Mahler**.

Stuttgart Radio Symphony Orchestra (Radio-Sinfonieorchester Stuttgart des SWR). Established in 1945 by American occupying forces as the **orchestra** of Radio Stuttgart. The orchestra has a broad-based reputation for the performance of contemporary music, but each **conductor** brings his or her own expertise, such as **Roger Norrington** with his knowledge and perspective of performance-practice style. In 2012, the Southwest Radio Broadcast Council voted to merge the Stuttgart Orchestra with the **Southwest German Radio Symphony Orchestra** in Baden-Baden. The merger will take place in 2016. The current principal conductor is Stéphane Denève (appointed in 2011). Past principal conductors include Hans Müller-Kray (1948–1969), **Sergiu Celibidache** (1971–1977), **Neville Marriner** (1983–1989), Gianluigi Gelmetti (1989–1998), and Roger Norrington (1998–2011). The orchestra has released numerous recordings.

style. (Fr.) Style. (Ger. *stil,* It. *stile,* Sp. *estilo.*)

su, sul, sulla. (It.) On, on the. (Fr. *sur, sur le, sur la,* Ger. *auf, auf der, auf die, auf das,* Sp. *en sobre.*) Examples: *sul G,* on the G string; *sul tasto,* on the fingerboard (Ger. *am Griffbrett,* Fr. *sur la touche,* Sp. *sobre el batidor*).

suave. (Sp.) Sweet, gentle, soft, mild, suave. (Fr. *suave,* Ger. *lieblich,* It. *soave.*)

suavemente. (Sp.) Sweetly, gently, daintily. (Fr. *doucement, gentiment,* Ger. *sanft, in sanfter Weise,* It. *dolcement, delicatimente.*)

suavemente. (Sp.) Sweetly, gently, daintily. (Fr. Ger. *sanft, in sanfter Weise,* It. *dolcement, delicatimente.*)

suave, sedoso. (Sp.) Silky, tender, soft. (It. *morbido,* Fr. *tendre, soyeux,* Ger. *zart.*)

suavizando. (Sp.) Getting softer, fading away. (Ger. *entschwindend,* Fr. *en défaillant,* It. *mancando.*)

subdivided beat patterns. Used in slower tempos, each main beat is subdivided into a division of duple eighth notes. For 5/8, 6/8, 9/8, and 12/9 see **compound beat patterns**. See also **conducting in uneven meters, conducting pattern styles, conducting technique**.

Subdivided two pattern. *Courtesy Derek Brennan.*

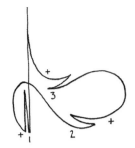

Subdivided three pattern. *Courtesy Derek Brennan.*

Subdivided four pattern. *Courtesy Derek Brennan.*

subdivision. The division of the beat or pulse into smaller increments either counting out loud, silently or while **conducting**. See also **beat patterns**.

subit. (Fr.) Sudden. Example: *PPP subit,* sudden *PPP,* as seen in Maurice Ravel's ballet *Daphnis et Chloé.* Often seen in its Italian form, *subito.*

subitement. (Fr.) Suddenly. (Ger. *sofort, sogleich,* It. *subito,* Sp. *pronto.*) Example: *Subitement moins animé,* suddenly less animated, from *Rapsodie Espagnole* by Maurice Ravel.

súbito. (Sp.) Abrupt, sudden, suddenly. A descriptive term seen in scores and parts and heard in rehearsal. (Fr. *tout á coup, immédiatement, subitement,* Ger. *plötzlich, sofort, sogleich,* It. *di colpo, repente, subito.*)

subito, immediatamente. (It.) Suddenly, at once, immediately. A commonly used term often asking for a sudden dynamic change. (Fr. *subitement, immédiatement, tout di suite,* Ger. *sofort, sogleich,* Sp. *súbito.*)

substitut. (Fr.) Substitute. (Ger. *Ersatz,* It. *sostituto,* Sp. *sustituto.*)

Sudwestrunkfunk Orchester. See **Southwest German Radio Orchestra.**

suivez. (Fr.) To follow quickly, as in *attacca.* (Ger. *folgen*, It. *seguite*, Sp. *seguir.*) Example: *Suivez le Solo*, follow the solo, from *Rapsodie Espagnole* by Maurice Ravel.

Suisse Romande Orchestra (Orchestre de la Suisse Romande, OSR). Founded in 1918 by **conductor Ernest Ansermet**, the **orchestra** plays both symphonic concerts and serves as the **opera** orchestra for the Grand Théâtre de Genève. The current music director is **Neeme Järvi** (2012–2015). Past conductors include Marek Janowski (2005–2012), Pinchas Steinberg (2002–2005), Fabio Luisi (1997–2002), Armin Jordan (1985–1997), Horst Stein (1980–1985), Wolfgang Sawallisch (1970–1980), Paul Kletzki (1967–1970), and its founding conductor, Ernset Ansermet (1918–1967). The Suisse Romande has made over three hundred recordings for the **Decca** label, beginning under Ansermet with Claude Debussy's *La Mer* in 1947. The orchestra has also recorded works of the Swiss composers Arthur Honegger and Frank Martin. The orchestra maintains outreach programs in order to develop younger audiences, and many of its concerts are broadcast live on Espace 2, radio or Internet.

sul ponticello. (It.) A bowing term that calls for playing with the bow on or close to the bridge. (Fr. *prés au chevalet*, Ger. *am Steg*, Sp. *sobre el puente.*)

sul tasto, sulla tastiera. (It.) A bowing term that indicates playing with the bow on or above the **fingerboard**. (Fr. *sur la touche*, Ger. *am Griffbrett*, Sp. *en el diapasón.*)

summen, summend. (Ger.) Humming, buzzing with the mouth closed. (Fr. *á bouche fermée*, It, *a bocca chiuso*, Sp. *boca cerrado.*)

suonare. (It.) To play, to touch, to sound. (Fr. *jouer, toucher*, Ger. *spielen, greifen*, Sp. *tocar.*) Example: *lasciar suonare*, let it sound, ring.

suonare a memoria. (It.) To play by heart. (Fr. *jouer par coeur*, Ger. *auswendig spielen*, Sp. *tocar de memoria.*)

suonare a orecchio. (It.) To play by ear. The ability to hear a piece and play it back without music. (Fr. *jouer d'oreille*, Ger. *nach Gehör spielen*, Sp. *tocar de oído.*)

suonare a prima vista. (It.) To play at sight, to sight-read. (Fr. *déchiffrer, jouer à vue*, Ger. *vom Blatt spielen*, Sp. *tocar a primera vista.*) Also *a libro aperto.*

suoni armonici, zufolo. (It.) **Harmonics.** (Fr. *sons harmoniques, flageolet*, Ger. *Flageolettöne, Flageolett*, Sp. *armónico, octavín.*) See also **artificial harmonics, harmonic series, string harmonics**.

suoni parziali. (It.) Partials. (Fr. *sons partiels*, Ger. *Teiltöne*, Sp. *parcialels*) See also **harmonics, string harmonics**.

suono eco. (It.) Echo tone. (Fr. *son écho*, Ger. *Echoton*, Sp. *sonido eco.*)

supermetric conducting patterns. Some **conductors** organize passages that are in a series of 3/4 or 3/8 bars and conducted in one to a bar into groups of four bars by superimposing a four pattern. Some conductors will use three, five, six or other patterns to organize bars, **conducting** in one into larger groups. These so-called supermetric patterns can bring emphasis to the phrase groups.

suplicando. (Sp.) Imploring, beseeching, entreating. A character word most often seen in its German translation. (Fr. *suppliant*, Ger. *flehend*, It. *supplichevole.*)

suppliant. (Fr.) Imploring, beseeching, entreating. A character word most often seen in its German translation. (Ger. *flehend*, It. *supplichevole*, Sp. *suplicando.*)

supplichevole. (It.) Imploring, beseeching, entreating. A character word most often seen in its German translation. (Fr. *suppliant*, Ger. *flehend*, Sp. *suplicando.*)

Supraphon Record label. A Czech recording company that specializes in the music of Czech and Slovak composers. In 1932, the company also had one of the first electric record players. The catalogue includes many recordings with the **Prague Philharmonic Orchestra**, conducted by **conductors** such as **Václav Talich, Karel Ančerl**, Václav Neumann, **Jiří Bělohlávek**, and **Sir Charles Mackerras**. In 2012, Supraphon became the Czech distributor of **Warner Music Group**.

sur. (Fr.) On, over. Also *sur le, sur la.* (Ger. *auf, auf der, auf die, auf das*, It. *su, sul, sulla*, Sp. *en, sobre.*) Example: *sur le chevalet*, on (over) the bridge on a stringed instrument; *sur la touche*, on the fingerboard. (Ger. *nahe am Griffbrett*, It. *sulla tastiera, flautando*, Sp. *sobre el batidor*).

surdo. A Brazilian double-headed bass drum that comes in three sizes. It is usually suspended from the drummer's neck and played with a beater in one hand while the other muffles the playing head as needed. It is used in Peter Lieberson's *Neruda Songs*. Also called tambor surdo. See also **appendix 4**.

sur la touche. (Fr.) An indication to play with the bow on or above the **fingerboard**. (It. *sul tasto*, Ger. *am Griffbrett*, Sp. *sobre el diapasón.*)

sur le chevalet. (Fr.) On the bridge. See also *au chevalet*.

sur le temps. (Fr.) On the beat. Example: *la petite note sur le temps*, play the little note on the beat, from *Rapsodie Espagnole* by Maurice Ravel.

surround sound. A sound system made up of additional audio channels from speakers placed around the listener in an optimum 360-degree radius, enhancing the audio experience.

suspended cymbal. A **cymbal** that is suspended on a stand and struck with a beater, sometimes a soft timpani stick or a hard wooden stick. See also **appendix 4**.

suspension libre. (Fr.) Suspended, free hanging, as with a **suspended cymbal**. (Ger. *freihängend*, It, *impiccagione libero*, Sp. *libre suspensión*.)

süss. (Ger.) Sweet, soft. A character word used to describe a particular approach to playing a passage. Also, *sanft, weich.* (Fr. *doux,* It. *dolce,* Sp. *dulce.*)

sussurrare. (It.) Whisper, whispered. (Fr. *chuchoter, chuchoté,* Ger. *flüstern,* Sp. *susurrar.*)

susurrar, susurrando. (Sp.) Whisper, whispered, in an undertone. (Fr. *chuchoter, chuchoté,* Ger. *flüstern,* It. *sussurrare.*)

sustituto. (Sp.) Substitute. (Fr. *substitut,* It. *sostituto,* Ger. *Ersatz.*)

svelto. (It.) Quick, nimble, speedy. A character word to describe a certain approach or motion in a passage. (Fr. *rapide,* Ger. *geschwindig,* Sp. *rápido.*)

Svetlanov Symphony Orchestra. Founded as the USSR State Symphony Orchestra and now known as the **State Academic Symphony Orchestra of Russia. Yevgeny Svetlanov** conducted the orchestra from 1965 to 2000, when he was dismissed by the minister of culture for spending too much time **conducting** outside of Russia. Soon after Svetlanov's death, the orchestra took his name as an additional, honorary title.

Svetlanov, Yevgeny. (1928–2002.) Russian **conductor** and composer. Born in Moscow, Svetlanov studied at the Moscow Conservatory. He was the assistant conductor at the **Bolshoi Theater** from 1955 to 1965, when he was appointed as music director. He served as the principal conductor of the USSR State Symphony Orchestra (currently the **State Academic Symphony Orchestra of Russia**) from 1965 to 1995. It was known as "his" orchestra, representing the pinnacle of the "Russian sound." He was appointed principal guest conductor of the **London Symphony Orchestra** (1979) and was the

music director of The Hague Philharmonic (1992–2000) and the **Swedish Radio Symphony** (1997–1999). He was fired from his position with the **Russian State Symphony Orchestra** because "he was spending too much time conducting abroad, and not enough at home." He was renowned for his interpretations of Russian music—he recorded much of it—and was one of the few Russian conductors to perform all of **Gustav Mahler**'s symphonies.

Yevgeny Svetlanov. *Courtesy Photofest.*

sviluppo, svolgimento. (It.) The development section of a piece, also development of material within a piece. (Fr. *développement,* Ger. *Durchführung,* Sp. *desarrollo.*)

Swarovsky, Hans. (1899–1975.) Born in Hungary, a **conductor** and teacher of **conducting**. Swarovsky studied with **Felix Weingartner** and **Richard Strauss**. He became the conductor of the Vienna State Opera at the invitation of **Herbert van Karajan**. In addition to the standard repertoire, he performed works of **Sir Benjamin Britten**, Gottfried von Einem, Paul Hindemith, Hans Pfitzner, and **Igor Stravinsky**. Among the recording labels he had a relationship with were **Nonesuch, Vanguard, Vox,** and Weltbild. Beginning in 1946, he was professor of conducting at the **Vienna Music Academy**, where his students included **Claudio Abbado,** Iván Fischer, **Jesús López Cobos, Zubin Mehta, Gustav Meier, Giuseppe Sinopoli,** and others. His lectures and collected essays were issued in *Wahrung der Gestalt* (Keeping Shape), a resource for performers and conductors.

Swedish Radio Symphony Orchestra. A **radio orchestra** that is based in Stockholm, Sweden, the **orchestra** existed in many forms before achieving its current name and status. Its **conductors** have been **Sergiu Celibidache** (1965–1971), **Herbert Blomstedt** (1977–1982), **Esa-Pekka Salonen** (1984–1995), **Yevgeny Svetlanov** (1997–1999), Manfred Honeck (200–2006), and Daniel

Harding (2007–present). The orchestra performs and premieres much music by Swedish composers.

swing. A style of playing, often associated with jazz, where duple or dotted rhythms are stretched to feel similar to but not exactly triplets. American composer and conductor **Gunther Schuller**, who developed the **third-stream** style of combining jazz and classical idioms, wrote about swing style as propelling forward over a steady regular pulse with an emphasis on weak beats.

SWR Sinfonieorchester Baden-Baden und Freiburg. See **Southwest German Radio Orchestra**.

Sydney Opera House. See **Opera Australia**.

symphonic band. See **band**.

symphonic poem. Sometimes also called a **tone poem**, it is an orchestral piece that is accompanied or inspired by a program, poem, or other text, which is often included in the concert program so that it can be read by the audience in advance. The text can be specific, even suggesting a narrative, or quite vague, perhaps only suggestive in nature. The term was devised by **Franz Liszt** as a subtitle for his work *Tasso* (1854), and following its success, he created a repertoire of similar works in the same genre. The openness of the formal structure was appealing to composers of the late nineteenth century and has been used and further developed in a wide variety of ways up to today. A few examples include Bedřich Smetana's *Má Vlast*, part of the nationalism movement; **Richard Strauss**'s *Don Juan*, *Till Eulenspiegel*, and *Also sprach Zarathustra*; **Arnold Schoenberg**'s *Verkärlte Nacht*, originally for string **sextet**, sometimes played by a full string orchestra; Ernest Bloch's *Schelomo* for **cello** and orchestra; George Gershwin's *American in Paris*; David Del Tredici's Alice series; Aaron Kernis's *Musica Celestis*; Jenifer Higdon's *blue cathedral*; and many more. While some are not titled symphonic poems, they retain the effect. (Fr. *poéme symphonique*, Ger. *symphonische Dichtung*, It. *poema sinfonico*.)

symphonie. (Fr.) **Symphony**. (En. *symphony*, Ger. *Sinfonie*, It. *sinfonia*, Sp. *sinfonía*.)

symphony. A symphony **orchestra** or a piece of music in the form of a symphony. From the Greek and Latin *symphonia*, sounding together. The terms "symphony," "orchestra," and "**philharmonic**" are virtually interchangeable as the name of an orchestral ensemble. (Fr. *symphonie*, Ger. *Sinfonie*, It. *sinfonia*, Sp. *sinfonía*.)

Symphony No. 1, John Corigliano. (1990.) Written for the **Chicago Symphony Orchestra** and premiered under the baton of **Daniel Barenboim**, the Symphony No. 1 is often referred to as the "AIDS symphony." Written at the height of the epidemic, it commemorates and memorializes friends of the composer who had lost their battle with the disease. See also **appendix 1**.

Symphony No. 9 in D minor, Ludwig van Beethoven. (1824.) See **appendix 1**.

Symphony of the Air. The resident orchestra of the **National Broadcasting Corporation** (NBC) from 1954 to 1963. Led by **Leopold Stokowski**.

Symphony Orchestra of India (SOI). Founded in 2006 in Mumbai by the National Centre for the Performing Arts as India's first fully professional **symphony orchestra**, presenting two seasons of concerts in September and February each year. Members of the orchestra are international, with a core serving as the resident musicians at the National Centre year round. Several principal players also serve as teachers, and the orchestra's mission emphasizes developing musical talent within India. The orchestra performed at the Festival of World's Symphony Orchestras in Moscow, Russia. The first and current music director is Marat Bisengaliev.

Symphony Orchestra of the Karol Szymanoski Philharmonic (Orkiestra Symfoniczna Filharmonii im. Karola Szymanowskiego). See **Kraków Philharmonic Orchestra**.

Symphony Orchestra of the Karol Szymanoski Philharmonic. See **Kraków Philharmonic Orchestra**.

syncopación. (Sp.) **Syncopation**. (Fr. *contre-temps*, *syncope*, Ger. *Synkope*, It. *contrattempo*, *sincope*.)

syncopation. To play off the beat, to play against the beat, to emphasize the weak beat. (Fr. *contre-temps*, *syncope*, Ger. *Synkope*, It. *contrattempo*, *sincope*, Sp. *syncopación*.) See also **conducting syncopations**, **gesture of syncopation**.

synesthesia. A neurological condition in which the experience of one sensation stimulates an involuntary, automatic experience in another. Sometimes called cross-sensory perception, cases are known of musicians who experience colors when they hear music, also called chromesthesia. Other forms include color-word, color-taste, and color-odor synesthesia. Russian composer Alexander Scriabin claimed to have had synesthesia, but some now say it was contrived. **Olivier Messiaen** created a method of composition that was said to have translated his experience of sound-color synesthesia. American composer Amy Beach, who had **perfect pitch**, was said to perceive musical keys as having specific colors. Other musicians who are known to be synesthetes include **Leonard Bernstein**, **György Ligeti**, **Franz Liszt**, Itzhak Perlman, Nicolai Rimsky-Korsakov, Michael Torke, and Jean Sibelius.

synthesizer. An electronic instrument sometimes used to duplicate the sounds of musical instruments and to create new sounds for electronic music compositions. Often used to substitute for an **organ** or **celeste** when none is available. (Fr. *synthétiseur,* Ger. *Synthesizer,* It. *sintetizzatore,* Sp. *sintetizador.*)

Synthesizer. (Ger.) **Synthesizer**. (Fr. *synthétiseur,* Ger. *Synthesizer,* It. *sintetizzatore,* Sp. *sintetizador.*)

synthetic scale. A term used to describe **scales** that are based on the major and minor scales and the traditional **church modes** but include some kind of alteration thereof, usually raising or lowering one or more **pitches** by a half step. A well-known example is Alexander Scriabin's **Prometheus scale**. It is derived from a whole tone scale, in itself a synthetic scale, with one altered pitch. Others are the enigmatic scale, quarter-tone scale, pentatonic scale, overtone scale, and others. See Nicholas Slonimsky, *Thesaurus of Scales and Melodic Patterns* (1947; see the **bibliography**).

synthétiseur. (Fr.) **Synthesizer**. (Ger. *Synthesizer,* It. *sintetizzatore,* Sp. *sintetizador.*)

system. In a **score**, two or more **staves** connected by a "brace" or bar line. (Fr. *portée,* Ger. *Liniensystem,* *Fünfliniensystem,* It. *pentagramma, sistema,* Sp. *sistema de pentagramas.*)

System, Fünfliniesystem Liniensystem. (Ger.) **Staff, stave, system**. (Fr. *portée,* It. *pentagramma, sistema,* Sp. *pentagramma, pauto.*)

Szell, George. (1897–1970.) Hungarian-born American **conductor** and pianist. Szell was a self-taught conductor and made his debut with the **Vienna Symphony Orchestra** in 1913. As a young conductor, he was mentored by **Richard Strauss**. Under Strauss, he cultivated a pursuit of detail and discipline in **rehearsal** that he kept his entire life. He moved to the United States in 1939, and from 1942 to 1946 had an association with New York's **Metropolitan Opera**, simultaneously teaching at the **Mannes School of Music**. He was the music director of the **Cleveland Symphony Orchestra** from 1946 until his death in 1970, building the ensemble into an indisputably world class **orchestra**. Among his assistant conductors were **James Levin** and **Michael Charry**. Szell made numerous recordings with the Cleveland Orchestra, mostly for **Columbia** Masterworks. They include complete Beethoven, Brahms, and Schuman symphonies, late symphonies of Franz Joseph Haydn, Wolfgang Amadeus Mozart, Franz Schubert, Antonin Dvořák, and many more. DVDs of Szell **conducting** in rehearsal are also available. See the videos *The Art of Conducting* and *Great Conductors of the Past* (see the **bibliography**).

Szene. (Ger.) Stage. Also *Bühne*. (Fr. *scène, planches,* It. *scena, palcoscenico,* Sp. *escena.*)

T

tace. (It.) Tacet (Lat.), literally, "Be silent." Tacet is used in music to let a player know that they don't play for a whole section or **movement** of a piece or **opera**.

Tacoma Symphony Orchestra. Established in 1946 in Tacoma, Washington, the **orchestra** has been fully professional since 1993. The eighty-member ensemble offers a classics series, pops, a new Mini Maestros series for children from ages two to eight, and its Simply Symphonic education program. **Harvey Felder** served as music director 1994–2014. His tenure has seen significant growth in the standards and reach of the orchestra. **Sarah Ioannides** was appointed music director in 2013.

tactus. A unit of time, a beat, a bar. In the fifteenth and sixteenth centuries it referred to a unit of time as measured by a movement of the hand (by the **conductor** or leader), a **downbeat** and an upbeat of equal length, consequently, a bar or measure. In triple time, the downward motion, the downbeat, was twice as long as the upbeat.

taglio addizionale. (It.) **Ledger lines**. (Fr. *ligne supplément,* Ger. *Hilfslinien,* Sp. *linea adicional, linea suplementaria.*)

take. Commonly refers to an excerpt of a piece, either long or short, as recorded or "taken" during a recording session. When recording a work, many takes will be made so that they can be reviewed in the editing process, the best being selected for the finished product.

Taki Concordia Conducting Fellowship. Founded by conductor **Marin Alsop** in 2002 in order to create opportunities for women who are studying to become orchestral **conductors**. The fellowship is awarded on a biannual basis.

Takt. (Ger.) Pulse, beat, bar, measure. (Fr. *mesure,* It. *battuta,* Sp. *compás* [specifically, the bar or measure].) Also

im Takt, *taktmässig,* in strict tempo. Example: *Ganze Takte, nicht schnell,* all the measures, not too fast, from *Das Lied von der Erde* by **Gustav Mahler**.

Takt halten. (Ger.) To keep or hold the tempo. (Fr. *garder le mesure,* It. *tenere il tempo,* Sp. *mantener el mismo compás.*)

Taktart. (Ger.) Time signature. (Fr. *indication de la mesure,* It. *tempo,* Sp. *quebrado del compás.*)

taktieren. (Ger.) To beat, to conduct, to show with a regular gesture the beats of the music so as to keep the musicians together. (Fr. *batter la mesure,* It. *battere la misure,* Sp. *batir el compás.*)

Taktmesser. (Ger.) **Metronome.** (Fr. *métronome,* It. *metronomo,* Sp. *metrónomo.*)

Taktschlag. (Ger.) Beat, bar. (Fr. *mesure,* It. *battuta,* Sp. *compás.*)

Takt schlagen. (Ger.) To beat the time. (Fr. *battre la mesure,* It. *battere il tempo,* Sp. *marcar el compás.*) Example*: Dieser Takt wird geschlagen in zwei.* This bar will be conducted in two.

Taktstock. (Ger.) **Conductor's baton**. (Fr. *bâton,* It. *bacchetta,* Sp. *batuta.*)

Taktstrich. (Ger.) Bar, bar line. (Fr. barre *de mesure,* It. barra, Sp. *barra de compás.*)

Taktwechsel. (Ger.) Change of time or meter. (Fr. *changement de mesure, changement de temps,* It. *cambiamente ce tempo, cambio di misura,* Sp. *cambio de ritmo.*)

Taktwechsel. (Ger.) Change of time or meter. (Fr. *changement de mesure, changement de temps,* It. *cambiamente ce tempo, cambio di misura,* Sp. *cambio de compás.*)

Taktzahl. (Ger.) Bar number, measure number. (Fr. *nombre de mesures*, It. *numero di battute*, Sp. *número del compás*.)

Taktzeichen, Taktvorzeichnung. (Ger.) Time signature. (Fr. *indication de la mesure*, It. *tempo*, Sp. *quebrado del compás*.)

Tali, Enu. (b. 1972.) Estonian **conductor**. Tali was appointed music director of the **Sarasota Orchestra** in June 2013.

Talich, Václav. (1883–1961.) **Conductor**, violinist, and pedagogue. Talich was the chief conductor of the **Czech Philharmonic Orchestra** (1919–1941). He toured widely and recorded for **EMI**. He rebuilt the Czech Philharmonic into a newworld ranking and was known for having initiated sectional **rehearsals** to the **orchestra**'s normal routine. In 1924, he organized a Prague Festival of Contemporary Music. Talich was also the chief conductor for the Scottish National Orchestra (1926–1927) and the Stockholm Konsertföreningen Orchestra (1926–1936), now the **Royal Stockholm Philharmonic Orchestra**. He also served as leader of the National Theater in Prague from 1935 to 1944, when the theater was closed by the Nazi regime. After World War II, in spite of open dissent, he was accused of collaboration with the Germans and imprisoned without charge for six months. In 1946, he was part of the effort to begin the **Prague Spring Festival**. As a teacher at the **Prague Conservatory**, he founded the Czech Chamber Orchestra, a vehicle for training young professionals. He conducted the orchestra until the minister of culture insisted that its members choose a different conductor or face dissolution. They chose to dissolve.

Talich was known for his advancement of Czech composers, especially Leoš Janáček, having conducted many of his **operas** and the premiere of his Sinfonietta. His conducting students included **Karel Ancerl** and **Charles Mackerras**.

tallone. (It.) **Frog** or **heel** (British usage) of a bow. (Fr. *talon, hausse*, Ger. *Frosch*, Sp. *talone*.) Example: *al tallone*, at the frog.

talon. (Fr.) **Frog** or **heel** (British usage) of a bow. See also *au talon*.

Tamarkin, Kate. (b. 1955.) American **conductor** and pedagogue. Tamarkin served as the associate conductor of the **Dallas Symphony Orchestra** (1989–1994), music director of the **Vermont Symphony Orchestra** (1991–1999), and music director of the Monterey Symphony (1999–2004). She is currently the music director of the Charlottesville and University Symphony at the University of Virginia.

tambales. One-headed drums that come in pairs and are mounted on metal stands. (Fr. *timbales cubaines*, Ger. *Kuba-Pauken*, It. *timpanetti*, Sp. *pailas*, or *timbales cubanos*.) See also **appendix 4**.

tambor. (Sp.) Drum. See also **appendix 4**.

tambour. (Fr.) Drum. Examples: *tambour de Basque*, **tambourine**; *tambour militaire*, **snare drum**. See also **appendix 4**.

tambour de Basque. (Fr.) **Tambourine**. See also **appendix 4**.

tambourine. A single-headed instrument with a skin or membrane stretched across its wooden frame. On the sides are open slates with pairs of metal disks that jingle when shaken. In **Igor Stavinsky**'s *Petrouchka*, the composer represents Petrouchka's death with the direction to the player to drop a tambourine on the floor from a close distance, creating a hollow sound with only a slight jingle. (Fr. *tambour de basque*, Ger. *Schellentrommel*, It. *Tamburo basco* Sp. *pandereta*.) See also **appendix 4**.

tamburo. (It.) Drum. Examples: *tamburo grande* or *tamburo grosso*, bass drum; *tamburo rullante*, tenor drum; *tamburo militare*, **snare drum**. See also **appendix 4**.

tam-tam. The largest of the **gongs**. See also **appendix 4**.

Tanglewood Music Center (TMC). In 1940, three years after the **Boston Symphony Orchestra** established Tanglewood as its summer home, music director **Serge Koussevitsky** founded the music center as an academy for advanced musical study. It was his known as his "pride and joy" for the rest of his life. Known as one of America's primary summer music institutes for young musicians and composers, it attracts students from around the world. Some of its most prominent teachers have included **Aaron Copland, Leonard Bernstein**, and **Seiji Ozawa**. Since the early 1960s, the festival has hosted the renowned Festival of Contemporary Music. It was lead for many years by American composer **Gunther Schuller** and financially supported by the contemporary music patron **Paul Fromm** and the **Fromm Foundation**. Its Fellowship Program allows students to attend with significant financial support. Many of America's most renowned performers and composers list Tanglewood on their resumes.

tanto. (It.) So much, too much. Examples. *allegro ma non tanto*, allegro, but not too much; *allegro non tanto*, allegro, not too much.

Tanz. (Ger.) Dance. (Fr. *danse*, It. *danza, ballo*, Sp. *danza*.)

tapado. (Sp.) **Stopped**. Also *cubierto*. Abbreviated *gest.* (Fr. *bouché, étouffé,* It. *chiuso, tappato.*) Also stopped tones. (Fr. *ton bouché,* Ger. *gestopfter Ton,* It. *tono chiuso,* Sp. *sonidos tapados.*)

tape music. Music that uses the manipulation of magnetic tape as a compositional process, including reversing the direction of the tape, altering the speed of the tape, splicing to create fragments, making loops where fragments are repeated constantly, and the superimposition of sounds from one recording to another. With the rise of digital recording, the technique has virtually disappeared, while methods of manipulating recorded sound have advanced through various computer programs.

tape recorder. An out-of-date electronic devise that converts sound to electric energy for storage on magnetic tape and reconverts the electronic energy into sound. Used to create recorded sound for purposes of commercial recordings and electronic music composition up to the advent of digital technology. (Fr. *magnétphone,* Ger. *Magnetbandgerät, Tonbandgerät,* It. *registratore,* Sp. *magnetófono, grabadora.*)

tappato. (It.) **Stopped**. Also *chiuso.* (Fr. *bouché, étouffé*; It. *chiuso, tappato*; Sp. *cubierto, tapado.*) Also stopped tones. (Fr. *ton bouché,* Ger. *gestopfter Ton,* It. *tono chiuso,* Sp. *sonidos tapados.*)

tardo, tardamente. (It.) Slow, slowly. Also *tardando,* slowing. Similar to *lento.* (Fr. *lent,* Ger. *langsam,* Sp. *lento.*)

tartaruga. A Brazilian instrument made from a giant tortoise shell. "*Tartaruga*" means "turtle" in Portuguese. It is a friction instrument that is treated with oil and rubbed with the hands. See also **appendix 4**.

Taste. (Ger.) Key of a keyboard instrument. (Fr. *touche,* It. *tasto,* Sp. *tecla.*)

Tasteninstrument. (Ger.) Keyboard instrument. (Fr. *instruments à clavier,* It. *strumento a tastiera,* Sp. *instrumento de teclado.*) See also *Tastenmusik.*

Tastenmusik. (Ger.) Keyboard music.

tastiera. 1. (It.) **Fingerboard** on a string instrument. (Fr. *touche,* Ger. *Griffbrett,* Sp. *diapason, batidor.*) Example: *sulla tastiera,* indication to bow over the fingerboard.
   2. (It.) Keyboard. (Fr. *clavier,* Ger. *Klaviatur,* Sp. *teclado.*)

tasto, sul. (It.) An indication for string players to bow over the **fingerboard**.

Taylor, Deems. (1885–1966.) American composer, music critic, and promoter of classical music. Taylor served as a music critic for the *New York World* from 1921 and was the editor of **Musical America** from 1927 to 1929. He was a commentator for broadcasts of the **New York Philharmonic** and appeared in the film **Fantasia** as master of ceremonies but also had a say in what musical excerpts were used. The first president of **ASCAP**, he was honored for his work there by the establishment of the **ASCAP Deems Taylor Awards**. He was associated with the Algonquin Round Table and briefly dated one of its members, Dorothy Parker.

tbn. Abbreviation for **trombone**. See also **appendix 4**.

Teatro alla Scala. See **La Scala**.

Teatro Colón. Translated into English as the Columbus Theatre, it is the main **opera** house in Buenos Aires, Argentina. It is thought by many to be one of the best performing halls in the world. The hall was significantly renovated to the tune of $100 million and reopened in 2011 with a performance of Giuseppi Verdi's *Aida*.

Teatro Real (Royal Theater). The Royal Theater opened as an **opera** house in Madrid, Spain, in 1850. Originally named for Queen Isabel II, the hall was inaugurated with a performance of Gaetano Donizetti's opera *La Favorita*. The early years saw visits by Giuseppe Verdi for a performance of his *La Forza del Destino* and by Sergei Diaghilev's **Ballets Russe**, with the great dancer Vaslav Nijinsky and composer **Igor Stravinsky** on hand. The theater was closed in 1925 when structural damage caused by the construction of the Madrid Metro was discovered. It was reopened in 1966 and served as a concert theater until its remodeling as a formal opera house in 1997. It now presents a full season of opera, ballet, and symphonic programs. The resident orchestra is the **Madrid Symphony Orchestra**.

teclado. (Sp.) Key, keyboard, keyboard instrument. (Fr. *clavier,* Ger. *Klaviatur,* It. *tastiera.*)

Teil. (Ger.) Part, section. (Fr. *part, partie,* It. *parte,* Sp. *parte.*) See also *Theil.*

Teiltöne. (Ger.) Partials or the **harmonic series**. (Fr. *sons partiels,* It. *suoni parziali,* Sp. *armónico.*)

Telarc Records. Officially known as the Telarc International Corporation, it was founded in 1977 in Cleveland, Ohio, by Jack Renner and Robert Woods. Telarc has long had a close association with the orchestras of Cleveland, Cincinnati, Atlanta, and St. Louis. Purchased by Concord Records in 2005 and currently run under the Concord

Music Group, Telarc is known for the high-quality sound of its releases, having received forty **Grammy Awards**.

television broadcasting. See **Public Broadcasting System (PBS)**.

Teller. (Ger., pl. *Tellern*.) Crash **cymbal** plate(s). Example: *mit Tellern*, with crash cymbals. See also **appendix 4**.

tel quel. (Fr.) As it is, as written. (Ger. *wie geschrieben, wie notiert,* It. *come stà,* Sp. *como está, como está escrito*.)

tema. (It.) Theme, subject. (Fr. *theme,* Ger. *Thema,* Sp. *tema*.)

tema principal. (Sp.) The main theme, or first theme. (Fr. *thème principal,* It. *primo tema, tema principale,* Ger. *Hauptthema*.)

tema principale. (It.) The main theme, or first theme. Also *primo tema*. (Fr. *thème principal,* Ger. *Hauptthema,* Sp. *tema principal*.)

tem. I. Abbreviation for *tempo I* or **tempo primo**.

Temirkanov, Yuri Khatuevich. (b. 1938.) Russian **conductor**. Temirkanov has been the music director and chief conductor of the **St. Petersburg Philharmonic** since 1988. He studied **conducting** with **Ilya Musin** at the **Leningrad Conservatory**, one of the most important Russian conducting pedagogues. He served as the principal conductor of the **Royal Philharmonic Orchestra** (1992–1998), music director of the **Baltimore Symphony Orchestra** (2000–2006), and principal guest conductor of the **Danish National Symphony Orchestra**.

temperament. The slight modification of an acoustically pure or just interval. (Fr. *temperament,* Ger. *Temperatur,* It. *temperamento, sistema participatio,* Sp. *temperamento*.) See also **tuning systems**.

Temperatur. (Ger.) **Temperament**. Example: *gleichschwebende Temperatur, ungleichschwebende Temperatur,* equal or unequal temperament. See also **tuning systems**.

tempestoso, tempestosamente. (It.) Tempestuous, stormy. A character word. (Fr. *tempétueux,* Ger. *stürmisch,* Sp. *tempestuoso*.)

tempestuoso. (Sp.) Tempestuous, stormy. A character word. (Fr. *tempétueux,* Ger. *stürmisch,* It. *tempestoso, tempestosamente*.)

temple blocks. Similar to **wood blocks**, a graduated series of five rounded wooden blocks mounted on a stand, producing their tone when struck by drumsticks. See also **appendix 4**.

tempo. (It. Sp.) Pace, speed, time. *Tempo,* as referring to speed, is most common in its Italian form. (Fr. *temps,* Ger. *Zeitmaß*.) Examples: (It.) *tempo di menuetto,* tempo (speed) of a minuet.

tempo changes, conducting. See **conducting tempo changes**.

tempo, dans le. (Fr.) In tempo. (Ger. *im Zeitmaß,* It. *in tempo,* Sp. *en el tempo*.)

tempo debole. (It.) Weak beat. (Fr. *temps faible,* Ger. *schwacher Takteil,* Sp. *tiempo débil*.)

tempo giusto. (It.) Steady or strict tempo. Heard most often in the Italian form. (Fr. *exact, juste,* Sp. *exactamente, preciso*.) See also **giusto**.

tempo, en el. (Sp.) In tempo. (Ger. *im Zeitmaß,* Fr. *dans le tempo,* It. *in tempo*.)

tempo, in. (It.) In tempo. (Ger. *im Zeitmaß,* Fr. *dans le tempo,* Sp. *en el tempo*.)

tempo modulation. The process of moving from one tempo or speed to another using a common denominator. A common example is seen in first movements of classical symphonies where the introduction, marked Adagio, will move to a connected Allegro using a two-to-one relationship. In the twentieth century, **Igor Stravinsky** made much use of such connections, many of them more complicated than two to one, in many of his works. For examples, see his *Petrouchka,* the Octet for Winds, and much more.

tempo ordinario. (It.) Common time, 4/4; a tempo that is neither very fast or slow.

tempo primo. (It.) Original tempo or an indication to return to the first tempo after a change of tempo has occurred. Also, *tempo I*. (Fr. *temps premier,* Ger. *erstes Zeitmaß,* Sp. *primero tempo*.)

tempo rubato. (It.) **Rubato**.

temprano, pronto. (Sp.) Early, soon. (Fr. *de bonne heure, tôt,* Ger. *früh,* It. *presto*.) Example: *Fue muy pronto,* It was too soon (as in for an entrance of an instrument).

temps. (Fr.) Tempo, speed, pace. (Ger. *Zeitmaß,* It. *tempo,* Sp. *tempo*.)

temps, en meme. (Fr.) In the same tempo. See also *l'istesso tempo*.

temps faible. (Fr.) **Upbeat**, pickup, anacrusis, weak beat. Also *levée*. (Ger. *Auftakt*, It. *in levare*, Sp. *alzada*.)

temps fort. (Fr.) **Downbeat**. (Fr. *temps fort*, Ger. *Abtakt*, It. *in battere*, Sp. *tiempo fuerto*.) See also **conducting technique**.

ten. Abbreviation for *tenuto*.

tendre. (Fr.) Tender, silky, soft. Also *soyeux*. (It. *morbido*, Ger. *zart*, Sp. *suave, sedoso*.)

tendre, tendrement. (Fr.) Tender, delicate, tenderly. (Fr. *délicat*, Ger. *zart, zärtlich*, It. *tenero, delicate, teneramente*, Sp. *tierno, tiernamente*.)

tendresse, avec. (Fr.) With tenderness. (Ger. *mit zärtlichkeit*, It. *con tenerezza*, Sp. *con ternura*.)

tenebroso. (Sp.) Gloomy dark, with a dark tone. Similar to the Italian *buio*. (Fr. *sombre*, Ger. *dunkel*, It. *cupo*.)

tenebroso. (Sp.) Dark, with a dark tone. (Fr. *sombre*, Ger. *dunkel*, It. *buio*.)

tenere. (It.) To hold, to hold on to a note for its full value. (Fr. *tenir*, Ger. *aushalten*.)

tenerezza, con. (It.) With tenderness. (Ger. *mit zärtlichkeit*, Fr. *avec tendresse*, Sp. *con ternura*.)

tenere il tempo. (It.) To keep or hold the tempo. (Fr. *garder le mesure*, Ger. *Takt halten*, Sp. *mantener el mismo compás*.)

tenero, teneramente. (It.) Tender, tenderly. (Fr. *tendre, tendrement*, Ger. *zart, zärtlich*, Sp. *tierno, tiernamente*)

Ten Golden Rules for a Young Conductor. See **Strauss, Richard**.

Tennstedt, Klaus. (1926–1998.) German **conductor**. Tennstedt was the music director of the **Dresden Staatsoper** (1958–1962) and Mecklenburg Staatstheater, Schwerin, Germany (1962–1971). He defected from East Germany to Sweden during a guest engagement in 1971 and was the music director at the Kiel Opera from 1972 to 1976. He became widely known in Europe and North America through his charismatic and commanding performances of **Gustav Mahler** and Anton Bruckner. Tennstedt served as the principal guest conductor of the Minnesota (1979–1983) and London Philharmonic (1980–1983) Orchestras and conducted Ludwig van Beethoven's **opera** *Fidelio* at New York's **Metropolitan Opera** in 1983. His recording legacy culminated in a cycle of the Mahler symphonies with the **London Philharmonic Orchestra**.

tenor. The highest male **voice classification**, resting above the **baritone** and the **bass**.

tenor drum. Slightly bigger and with a deeper tone, it is similar to the **snare drum** but without snares. (Fr. *Caisse roulante*, Ger. *Wirbeltrommel* or Rührtrommel, It. *Cassa rullante*, Sp. *tambor tenor*.) See also **appendix 4**.

tenuto. (It.) Held, an instruction to hold on to a **note**, to sustain it slightly. From *tenere*, to hold.

tenuto style. A true tenuto style is sometimes illusive. To some it means to extend the value of a note, to others it means to stress the note, almost to press it with the gesture. For our purposes, it means to differentiate between the sequence of tenuto markings, where one will stress or press each note with a slight separation between each that suggests a heightened expressiveness and the individual note in a line or melody where the tenuto marking suggests actual stretching of the value of the note. In any event, conducting tenuto requires an extra emphasis, an added weight that is usually accomplished with the wrist with occasional support of the forearm. See **tenere, conducting technique**.

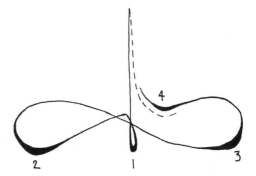

Conducting style, tenuto. *Courtesy Derek Brennan.*

tenuto style. See **basic conducting patterns for musical styles**, **conducting technique**.

ternura, con. (Sp.) With tenderness. (Ger. *mit zärtlichkeit*, Fr. *avec tendresse*, It. *con tenerezza*.)

tertian harmony. Any chord based on a series of thirds, such as a triad, seventh, ninth, and eleventh chord. Example: C, E, G, B (or B-flat), D, F, A.

tetrachord. Four adjacent pitches of a **twelve-tone set**.

Terzett. (Ger.) A trio, a work for three instruments. (Fr. *trio*, Sp. *trío*.)

terzetto. (It.) A trio, a work for three instruments. (Fr. *trio*, Sp. *trío*.)

terzina. (It.) Triplet, a rhythmic group of three equal notes. (Fr. *triolet*, Ger. *Triole*, Sp. *tresillo*.)

tessitura. (It.) Range, the normal range of a specific singer or instrument. Also refers to the general range of a specific piece or part thereof. (Fr. *tesiture, registetre*, Ger. *Stimmumgang*, It. *tessitura, estensione vocale*, Sp. *tesitura, rango*.)

texture. See **orchestration**.

Thank you. A commonly used and vital expression. (Fr. *merci, merci beaucoup* [many thanks], Ger. *Danke, vielen danke* [many thanks], It. *grazie* [thanks], *molte grazie* [many thanks], *grazie mille* [a thousand thanks], *grazie tante* [thanks a lot], Sp. *gracias* [thanks], *muchas gracias* [many thanks].)

Thayer, Alexander Wheelock. (1817–1897.) Early biographer of Ludwig van Beethoven. See *Thayer's Life of Beethoven* (1967; see the **bibliography**).

Theater an der Wien. A theater in Vienna where Ludwig van Beethoven's *Fidelio* (1805); Symphony No. 2 (1803); No. 3 (1805); Symphonies 5 and 6, *Choral Fantasy* and Piano Concerto No. 4 (1808); and *Violin Concerto* (1806) were all premiered. From 1945 to 1954 it served as the temporary home of **Vienna State Opera**, which was being reconstructed after World War II. Currently, the theater specializes in contemporary and Baroque **opera** and the operas of Wolfgang Amadeus Mozart.

Theil. (Ger.) Out-of-date spelling of *Teil*. Example: *Contrabässe zu drei gleichen Theilen*, **double basses** divided in three equal parts, from Symphony No. 1, first movement, by **Gustav Mahler**.

thematic catalogue. A catalogue of themes of a composer's works collected into an index. Alternatively, it may be a list of the holdings of an individual library or other collection or it may be a list of the known complete works, not just the themes, of an individual composer. Some composers, such as Wolfgang Amadeus Mozart, made their own themes list, and others were done by music historians. After Mozart's death **Ludwig von Köchel** catalogued his works, giving each a designated **K** or **KV** number, with the *Requiem* in D minor receiving the last number, K 626. The so-called **Köchel-Verzeichnis** catalogue has been updated in

subsequent years. In 1951, Otto Erich Deutsch created a catalogue of the works of Franz Schubert according to the date of composition. Each work is given a D number from 1 to 998. The **Bach Werk Verzeichenis (BWV)**, or Bach Works Catalogue, is a thematic, not chronological, catalogue of works that was created in the mid-twentieth century by Wolfgang Schmieder. It has also been updated over time.

thème principal. (Fr.) The main theme or first theme. (Ger. *Hauptthema*, It. *primo tema, tema principale*, Sp. *tema principal*.)

Theodore Presser Company. The company grew with the purchase of other, smaller music-publishing firms, such as the John Church Company (1930), the Oliver Ditson Company (1931), and Elkan-Vogel (1972). In addition to a significant catalogue of contemporary composers, Presser also represents and distributes music for more than seventy foreign and domestic music firms, such as **Éditions Alphonse Leduc** and **Bärenreiter-Verlag**.

Theodore Thomas Orchestra. During the years 1906 to 1912 the **Chicago Symphony Orchestra** was renamed by its trustees for its founding conductor, Theodore Thomas, as a gesture of respect. In 1913, during the tenure of **Frederick Stock** (music director, 1905–1942), it was changed back to the Chicago Symphony Orchestra and has remained so to the present.

therapy, music. See **music therapy**.

theremin. An electronic instrument invented in the 1920s by the Russian Lev Sergeyevich Termen, also known as Léon Theremin. It preceded the **ondes Martenot** as one of the first successful electronic instruments. First demonstrated in 1920, Termen traveled to the United States in 1927 to give concerts. Beginning in 1929, **RCA** manufactured the instrument. As the technology improved, different versions of the instrument became available, and as late as the 1990s, Robert A. Moog, known for the invention of the **Moog synthesizer**, and several other manufacturers developed more than fifteen new models with the latest technology. The theremin has been used in many film scores and in over one hundred concert works. Composer Edgar Varese used two theremins in his work *Ecuatorial*, though he later replaced them with the ondes Martenot, and at one time conductor **Eugene Ormandy** used the theremin to reinforce the sound of the **double basses** of the **Philadelphia Orchestra**. Video of the modern theremin can be seen on **YouTube**.

Thessaloniki State Symphony Orchestra (TSSO). Founded in 1959 by the composer Solon Michaelides, it became an official state **orchestra** of Greence ten years later. Today it is an orchestra of one hundred musicians, and the current artistic director is Alexandre Myrat, who also founded the Athens Camerata (La Kamerata). He has promoted Greek musical culture with the TSSO through recordings of well-known Greek composers on **Naxos**, **EMI** Classics, **RCA** red label, and others. The orchestra performs throughout Greece and has toured Europe.

Thielemann, Christian. (b. 1959.) German **conductor**. An assistant to **Herbert von Karajan** early in his career, Thielemann has served as the music director of the **Munich Philharmonic Orchestra** (2001–2011) and was appointed chief conductor of the **Dresden Staatskapelle** in 2012. In 2000, he conducted Hans Pfitzner's *Palestrina* at the **Royal Opera House, Covent Garden**; made his **Bayreuth** debut with **Richard Wagner**'s *Die Meistersinger*; and recorded Carl Orff's *Carminia Burana* and **Richard Strauss**'s *Ein Heldenleben*. A live recording of Wagner's *Tristan und Isolde* with the **Vienna Staatsoper** was released in 2004. He has been a guest conductor at the **Metropolitan Opera, New York**; the **San Francisco Opera**; the **Vienna State Opera**; and the **Bayreuth** and **Salzburg** festivals.

third stream. Music that combines elements of jazz and twentieth-century art music. Composer **Gunther Schuller** coined the term in the 1950s and worked with composer John Lewis to create a repertoire of complex music that sought to maintain the energy characteristic of jazz improvisation. Early examples of such musical crossovers include Claude Debussy's *Golliwog's Cakewalk*, **Igor Stravinsky**'s *Ragtime*, Darius Milhaud's *The Creation of the World*, Milton Babbitt's *All Set* (1957), and Dave Brubeck's *The Light in the Wilderness* (1968). Alban Berg's **opera** *Lulu* and Kurt Weill's *Three Penny Opera* also contain jazz elements.

thirteenth tone. A term coined by composer John Cage to refer to silence.

"This must be together!" A commonly heard directive. (Fr.) *Ce doit être ensemble*, (Ger.) *Dies muss zusammen sein*, (It.) *Questo deve essere insieme*, (Sp.) *Esto debe estar juntos*.

Thomas, Theodore. (1835–1905.) German-born American **conductor** and violinist. Thomas's family moved to New York in 1845. As a young man, he made a living playing in many **orchestras** and **opera** houses. He was also a well-known, busy soloist and chamber musician. While not formally educated, he was influenced by the musicians around him, including conductors **Karl Eckert** and **Louis Jullien**. He built his reputation as a conductor through programming a mixture of popular light and more serious repertoire whenever he got the chance. He joined the **violin** section of the part-time **New York Philharmonic Society** in 1954 and was made its conductor twenty-three years later, serving from1877 to 1891. He conducted the American premiere of *Der Fliegende Holländer* (*The Flying Dutchman*).

In 1864, he started the series Symphonic Soirés, in which he began to perform more serious concert programs, including music of Ludwig van Beethoven, Franz Liszt, Robert Schumann, and **Richard Wagner**. The New York Philharmonic Society performed and toured frequently, playing in Boston and Chicago, until both cities established their own resident orchestras. Thomas was the founding music director of the **Cincinnati May Festival** (1873–1904).

His ambition to have a full-time permanent orchestra of his own was realized in 1891 when he was approached by a group of businessmen in Chicago with a proposal to start an orchestra there. The position, which put him in the history books of American orchestras, also drained him physically. His struggles to get an adequate concert hall were only realized in 1904, when Orchestra Hall was opened just a few weeks before his death. He dedicated his life's work to the development of concert music in America. Many of his efforts were hugely successful, leaving an influence that is still felt today.

Thompson, Helen M. (1908–1974.) American orchestra manager. Thompson was the head of the then **American Symphony Orchestra League** (now the **League of American Orchestras [LAO]**) from 1950 to 1970 and manager of the **New York Philharmonic** from 1970 to 1973. She began her work with the LAO when the organization was in its infancy and built it into perhaps the most important performing arts advocacy organization in the United States. On her retirement, she was presented with the **Gold Baton Award**. She was also instrumental in organizing the **Association of California Symphony Orchestras**, the **Music Critics Association**, and the **Associated Councils of the Arts**. She studied music and later psychology and wrote an important guide to the building of community **orchestras**.

Thompson, Mallory. (b. 1957.) American **band conductor**. Thompson is the coordinator of conducting and ensembles and director of bands at the Bienen School of Music at Northwestern University, Illinois. She conducts the Northwestern Symphonic Wind Ensemble, teaches graduate and undergraduate conducting, and has appeared as a guest conductor with the U.S. Army Band, the U.S. Army Field Band, the U.S. Air Force Band, the West Point Band, the U.S. Navy Band, and the Dallas Wind Symphony. Thompson has recorded with the Northwestern Symphonic Wind Ensemble on the Summit recording label.

Thorton School of Music at the University of Southern California. See **University of Southern California Thorton School of Music**.

threnody. Lament, from the Greek *threnos* and the Latin (pl) *threni.* (Fr. *lamentation, plaint,* Ger. *Klage,* It. *lamento,* Sp. *elegia, lamento.*)

Threnody to the Victims of Hiroshima. By **Krzysztof Penderecki** (1960). See **appendix 1**.

thumb. (Fr.) *pouce,* (Ger.) *Daumen,* (It.) *pollice,* (Sp.) *pulgar.*

thunder sheet. A large sheet of metal hung from a stand that may be shaken by hand or struck with a beater. Used in Christopher Rouse's *Bump* and *Gorgon* and **Richard Strauss**'s *Alpensinfonie.* See also **appendix 4**.

tie. A notation device formed by a curved line connecting two **notes** of the same **pitch**, indicating that the instrumentalist or singer does not rearticulate the second note but sustains the two notes so that they sound as one. (Fr. *signe de tenue,* Ger. *Haltebogen,* It. *legatura di valore,* Sp. *ligar.*)

tief, tiefgründig. (Ger.) Deep or low in **pitch**. Also *tiefer,* lower. (Fr. *profond,* It. *profondo,* Sp. *grave, bajo.*)

tiefer stimmen. (Ger.) A term used to call for a lowering of the **pitch** or tuning. Also ***herunterstimmen.*** (Fr. *baisser l'accord,* It. *abbassare l'intonature, abbassare l'accordatura,* Sp. *bajar la afinación.*) See also ***scordatura.***

tiempo. (Sp.) Tempo, rate of speed. Most often used in its Italian form.

tiempo débil. (Sp.) Weak beat. Also *contratiempo.* (Fr. *temps faible,* Ger. *schwacher Takteil,* It. *tempo debole.*) Example: *No accentuar el tiempo débil,* Don't accent the weak beat.

tiempo fuerte. (Sp.) **Downbeat**. (Fr. *temps fort,* Ger. *Abtakt,* It. *in battere.*) See also **conducting technique**.

tierno, tiernamente. (Sp.) Tender, tenderly. A character word. (Fr. *tendre, délicat, tendrement,* Ger. *zart, zärtlich,* It. *tenero, delicate, teneramente.*)

tierno, tiernamente. (Sp.) Tender, tenderly. (Fr. *tendre, délicat, tendrement,* Ger. *zart, zärtlich,* It. *tenero, delicate, teneramente.*)

Tilson Thomas, Michael. (b. 1944.) American **conductor**, pianist, and composer. Tilson Thomas is the music director of the **San Francisco Symphony Orchestra** and founding artistic director of the **New World Symphony Orchestra**, a training institute for young professional musicians in Miami Beach, Florida. He conducted **young people's concerts** for the **New York Philharmonic** from 1971 to 1977, served as the music director of the **Buffalo Philharmonic** (1971–1979), and was the principal guest conductor of the **Los Angeles Philharmonic Orchestra** (1981–1984) and of the **London Symphony Orchestra** (1988–1995). Tilson Thomas started the educational television series ***Keeping Score***, exploring the music of **Gustav Mahler**, Charles Ives, Aaron Copland, and others. He is a major proponent of American music, programming such repertoire often in San Francisco. In 2000, the orchestra presented a twelve-concert festival called American Mavericks. Recordings made with the San Francisco Symphony have been released on the high-resolution Super Audio CD format on the orchestra's own label. In 2009, he collaborated with **YouTube** to create the **YouTube Symphony Orchestra**. Over three thousand video applications were submitted from thirty countries, resulting in an orchestra "summit" in New York at the **Juilliard School** and a final concert at **Carnegie Hall**. In 2011, he conducted the YouTube Symphony Orchestra 2 (YTSO2) in Sydney, Australia.

timbal. (Sp., pl. *timbales*) **Timpani**. See also **appendix 4**.

timbales. (Fr.) **Timpani**. See also **appendix 4**.

tiempo fuerte. (Sp.) **Downbeat**. Also ***primer tiempo.*** (Fr. *temps fort,* Ger. *Abtakt,* It. *in battere.*)

tierno, tiernamente. (Sp.) Tender, tenderly. (Fr. *tendre, délicat, tendrement,* Ger. *zart, zUartlich,* It. *tenero, delicato, teneramente.*)

timballo. (It.) **Timpani**. See also **appendix 4**.

timbre. (Fr., Sp.) Tone color, **timbre**. Used to refer to the color of the instruments of the orchestra on their own and in combination. (Ger. *Klangfarbe, Tonfarbe,* It. *colore, timbre,* Sp. *color de tono.*)

time-beating gestures. See **conducting gestures**.

time signature. (Fr.) *indication de la mesure,* (Ger.) *Taktart,* (It.) *tempo,* (Sp.) *quebrado del compass.* See **meter**.

" . . . times." (Fr.) *. . . fois,* (Ger.) *. . . fach, . . . mal,* (It.) *. . . volta,* (Sp.) *. . . veces.* Examples: two times, (Fr.) *deux fois,* (Ger.) *zwei mal,* (It.) *due volte,* (Sp.) *dos veces.* Commonly used in **rehearsal**.

timpani. The oldest percussion instrument of the **orchestra**, its sound is produced when the calfskin or synthetic membrane stretched over the head of the drum is struck. Timpani now come is five interlocking sizes. See also **appendix 4**.

21"

Twenty-one-inch timpani range. *Courtesy Andrew Martin Smith.*

23"

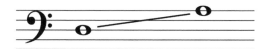

Twenty-three-inch timpani range. *Courtesy Andrew Martin Smith.*

25"

Twenty-five-inch timpani range. *Courtesy Andrew Martin Smith.*

28"

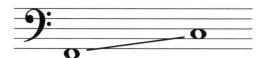

Twenty-eight-inch timpani range. *Courtesy Andrew Martin Smith.*

32"

Thirty-two-inch timpani range. *Courtesy Andrew Martin Smith.*

tip. An indication seen in string parts indicating to play at the highest part of the bow, also known as the **point**.

Tipton, Chelsea. (b. 1964.) American **conductor**. Tipton has been the music director of the Symphony of Southeast Texas since 2008. He as appointed principal pops conductor of the New Haven Symphony (2014–2015) and has conducted such orchestras as the Cleveland, Chicago, Detroit, Houston, New Jersey, Nashville, and San Antonio symphonies, as well as the Brooklyn, Louisiana, and Rochester philharmonic orchestras. Tipton has been featured as the conductor of the Sphinx Competition Showcase. From 2003 to 2010 he served as the resident conductor of the **Toledo Symphony Orchestra** (1993–2003) and as the associate conductor of the Savannah Symphony Orchestra. See also **Sphinx Organization**.

tirare. (It., lit. "to draw.") Down-bow.

tiré, tirer, tirez. (Fr., lit. "to draw.") **Down-bow**.

tocar. (Sp.) To play, to touch. (Fr. *jouer, toucher;* Ger. *spielen, greifen,* It. *suonare, tocare.*)

tocar a primera vista. (Sp.) To Sight-read, to play at sight. (Fr. *déchiffrer, jouer à vue,* Ger. *vom Blatt spielen,* It. *suonare a prima vista, a libro aperto.*)

tocar de memoria. (Sp.) To play by heart, to play by memory. (Fr. *jouer par coeur,* Ger. *auswendig spielen,* It. *suonare a memoria.*)

tocar de oído. (Sp.) To play by ear. The ability to hear a piece and play it back without music. (Fr. *jouer d'oreille,* Ger. *nach Gehör spielen,* It. *suonare a orecchio.*)

tocare. (It.) To play, to touch. Also *suonare*. (Fr. *jouer, toucher;* Ger. *spielen, greifen,* Sp. *tocar.*)

toda, todo. (Sp.) All, everything. Used most often in its Italian form, *tutto*. (Fr. *tout,* Ger. *alle,* It. *tutto, tutta.*)

todo el mondo. (Sp.) Everyone. A directive sometimes heard in **rehearsal**. For example, to tell everyone in a section to play after a period where only single instruments played. Seen most often in its Italian form, *tutti*. (Fr. *tout le monde,* Ger. *alle,* It. *tutti.*)

togliere. (It.) Remove. (Fr. *enlever la sourdine,* Ger. *Dämpfer ab, Dämpfer weg,* Sp. *quitar la sordina.*) Example: *togliere il sordino,* remove the **mute**.

Toho Gakuen School of Music. Founded in 1948 by **Hideo Saito** as a school for children. Two years later it became a high school, and it is now a music university. In 1995, the Toho Orchestra Academy was established, and in 1999, a graduate school was added. Many distinguished **conductors** are among it alumni, including **Seiji Ozawa,**

Kzuyoshi Akiyama, Tadaaki Otaka, and Eiji Oue. The founding members of the Tokyo String Quartet were also graduates.

Toi, toi, toi. (Ger.) Expression meaning "good luck" or "break a leg." Also ***Hals und Beinbruch!*** (Fr. *trois fois merde*, It, *in bocca al lupo*, Sp. *buena suerte*.)

Tokyo Kosei Wind Orchestra (TKWO). Established in 1960, it is a professional touring and recording ensemble, releasing numerous recordings throughout its history. It was conducted by **Frederick Fennell** from 1984 to 1996 and is currently conducted by Douglas Bostock. The TKWO is a proponent of contemporary music for wind **orchestra**, performing works of many Japanese composers, as well as those by other contemporary composers. Its membership includes many of the most reputable wind players in Japan.

Toledo Symphony Orchestra. Founded in 1943 in Toledo, Ohio, as the Friends of Music and incorporated as the Toledo Orchestral Association in 1951, the **symphony** has grown from a core of twenty-two part-time musicians to a regional **orchestra** of nearly eighty musicians. In 2000, the **Andrew W. Melton Foundation** (New York) invited the orchestra to submit proposals to participate in its Orchestra Forum project. Successful participation has brought over $2 million in support for innovative programming and other musical activities. The current principal **conductor** is Stefan Sanderling (appointed in 2003). Past music directors include Andrew Massey (1991–2002), Ole Schmidt (interim, 1989–1991), Yuval Zaliouk (1980–1989), Joseph Silverstein (interim, 1979–1980), Serge Fournier (1964–1979), and Joseph Hawthorne (1955–1963). See also **Rusty Musicians Program.**

tombeau. (Fr.) The title of a musical work that originated in the poetry of the Middle Ages as a lament written in tribute on the death of famous musicians. In the twentieth century, Maurice Ravel continued the tradition when he wrote *Le tombeau de Couperin*, first for **piano** and then for **orchestra**. (Fr. *lamentation, plaint*, Ger. *Klage,* It. *lamento*, Sp. *elegia, lamento*.)

tom-toms. Often tuned to approximate **pitches** and used in groups of four, notated on a single **stave** in the four spaces to show the pitch range. They come in pairs, each pair mounted on a metal stand. See also **appendix 4.**

Ton. (Ger.) **Pitch**, tone. (Fr. *ton*, It. *tono, tuono*, Sp. *tono*.) Also *tonlos*, toneless, monotonous; *Tonhöhe*, pitch, pitch level (Fr. *hauteur du son,* It. *altezza del suono*, Sp. *altura*); *Tonvoll*, full of tone or sound. Example: *trotz zarter Tongebung stets mit leidenschaftlichstem Ausdruck*, despite a soft rendering of the tone, with a most

passionate expression, from *Das Lied von der Erde* by **Gustav Mahler**.

ton, tonalité. (Fr.) **Pitch**, tone, key. (Ger. *Ton, Tonart*, It. *tono*, Sp. *tonalidad, tono*.)

Tonabnehmer. (Ger.) As in a pickup gesture or beat, anacrusis. (It. *rivelatore*, Sp. *anacrusa*.)

Tonabstand. (Ger., lit. "gap between the tones.") Interval. Also *Intervall.* (Fr. *intervalle*, It. *intervallo*, Sp. *intervalo*.)

tonada. (Sp.) Melody, tune. Also *melodia.* (Fr. *mélodie*, Ger. *Melodie,* It. *melodia*.)

tonalidad relativa, tonalidad paralela. (Sp.) The relative minor to a major key or vice versa. For example, A minor is the relative minor key of C major, and B minor the relative of D major. (Fr. *tonalité relative*, Ger. *Parallele Tonarten*, It. *tonalità relativa*.)

tonalità relativa. (It.) The relative minor to a major key or vise versa. For example, A minor is the relative minor key of C major, and B minor the relative of D major. (Fr. *tonalité relative*, Ger. *Parallele Tonarten*, Sp. *tonalidad relativa, tonalidad paralela*.)

tonalité relative. (Fr.) The relative minor to a major key or vise versa. For example, A minor is the relative minor key of C major, and B minor the relative of D major. (Ger. *Parallele Tonarten*, It. *tonalità relativa*, Sp. *tonalidad relativa, tonalidad paralela*.)

tonality. A characteristic of music written with a strong tonal center, sometimes synonymous with **key**.

tonal music. Music that uses the principles of tonic-dominant tonality as opposed to **modality** or other systems of organizing **pitches**, such as the **twelve-tone system**.

Tonart. (Ger.) **Key**. (Fr. *tonalité,* It. Sp. *tonalidad*.)

Tonartvorzeichnung. (Ger.) Key signature. Also *Vorzeichen.* (Fr. *armure de la clé, armature*, It. *armatua di chiave*, Sp. *armadura*.)

Tondichtung. (Ger.) **Tone poem, symphonic poem.**

tone. Pitched sound. Since the early twentieth century, the definition of tone has been expanded to include extramusical noises. (Fr. *ton*, Ger, *Ton*, It. *tono*, Sp. *tono*.)

tone cluster. A term coined by composer Henry Cowell to describe a group of closely spaced **pitches** sounded simultaneously, resulting in dissonance. Often played on a **piano** or other keyboard instrument by using the fist, flattened hand, or forearm, depending on the size of the cluster. There are generally two ways to notate the tone cluster: when the number of pitches is small, all of them are written out; when a larger cluster is desired, the outer limits are specified with a line drawn between them. Examples can be seen in works of Henry Cowell, **Charles Ives**, Béla Bartók, and many others. (Fr. *groupe de sons, groupe de notes,* Ger. *Tontraube, Tonballung,* It. *gruppo di suoni, gruppo di note,* Sp. *cluster.*) See the **bibliography**.

tone color. Literally, the color of the **tone**. The term has various meanings depending on its usage in electronic music, where tone color can be manipulated electronically, and in instrumental and vocal music, where the color of a tone depends on the characteristic of the individual instrument or voice but can also be manipulated to various extents by the performer.

tone poem. See **symphonic poem**.

tone row. An ordering of **pitches** in a specific sequence that becomes the basis for the melodic and or harmonic structure of a piece. This compositional technique is most commonly used in but not limited to **twelve-tone music**.

Tonfall. (Ger.) Inflection. (Fr., Sp. *inflexion,* It. *inflessione.*)

Tonfarbe. (Ger.) **Tone color**. Also *Klangfarbe.* (Fr. *timbre,* It. *colore, timbre,* Sp. *color de tono, timbre.*)

Tongeschlecht. (Ger.) Mode, either major or minor.

tonguing. The use of the tongue to articulate in playing wind and brass instruments. Single tonguing uses the consonant *t* to stop the airflow for an instant and separate the **notes** played. Repeated use of the *t* is called single tonguing. Different consonants can be used to create different styles of attack. Each instrument has a slightly different way of articulating. Brass instruments can use a *th* to achieve a softer attack or have the tongue touching the roof of the mouth, further back. See also **double tonguing, triple tonguing**.

Tonhalle Orchestra of Zürich (Tonhalle Orchester Zürich). Founded in 1868, the Tonhalle has a long and distinguished history. The most recent principal **conductor** was American **David Zinman** (1995–2014). Past principal conductors include Claus Peter Flor (permanent guest conductor, 1991–1995), Hiroshi Wakasugi (1987–1991), **Christoph Eschenbach** (1982–1986), Gerd Albrecht (1975–1980), **Charles Dutoit** (1967–1971), **Rudolf Kempe** (1965–1972), **Hans Rosbaud** (1957–1962),

Erich Schmid (1949–1957), Volkmar Andreae (1906–1949), and Friedrich Hegar (1868–1906). With over one hundred musicians, the **orchestra** is widely recorded under many conductors, including David Zinman, who has led cycles of Beethoven and Schumann symphonies. Also under Zinman's leadership, the orchestra has experimented with reaching new, especially younger audiences, starting a Tonhalle Late series of concerts. Throughout its history, the orchestra has been led by some of the greatest conductor-composers of its time, including Johannes Brahms, **Richard Wagner**, **Richard Strauss**, and Paul Hindemith. Other renowned guest conductors are **Wilhelm Furtwängler**, **Otto Klemperer**, **Georg Solti**, **Bernard Haitink**, **Mariss Jansons**, and many more.

Tonhöhe. (Ger.) **Pitch**. (Fr. *hauteur,* It. *intonazione,* Sp. *entonación.*) Also, register of a pitch. (Fr. *hauteur du son,* It. *altezza del suono,* Sp. *altura del tono.*)

tonic sol-fa. A system of teaching music, particularly vocal music, based on the **solmization** or **solfeggio** syllables. Introduced by Rev. John Curwen in about 1850, single letters, *d, r, m,* and so on, were used instead.

tonic sol-faist. One who advocates or uses the **tonic sol-fa** system.

Tonkunst. (Ger.) Music, musical art.

Tonkünstler. (Ger.) Musician. (Fr. *musicien,* It. *musicista,* Sp. *músico.*)

Tonkünstler Orchestra (*Tonkünstler-Orchesters Niederösterreich*). This Austrian **orchestra** gave its first concert in 1907 and premiered **Arnold Schoenberg**'s enormous work *Gurrelieder* in 1913. It continued to perform during the Nazi regime under different names, and in 2002, was restructured and given its current name. The current **conductor** is Yutaka Sado (beginning in 2015). Past conductors have included Andrés Orozco-Estrada (2009–2014), Kristjan Järvi (2004–2008), Carlos Kalmar (2000–2003), **Fabio Luisi** (1994–2000), and others.

Tonkünstlerorchester. See **Tonkünstler Orchestra**.

Tonleiter. (Ger.) **Scale**. (Fr. *gamme,* It. *scala,* Sp. *escala.*) See also **alternative scales**.

tonlos. (Ger.) Unpitched, toneless. May refer to breathing through the mouthpiece of a brass instrument or the instrument itself without any **pitch**, just the sound of air. Also when strings are asked to bow silently, just for the visual effect. (Fr. *atone,* It. *atono.*) Example: *tonlos geflüstert,* unpitched whisper.

tonlos niederdrücken. (Ger.) A term that describes the technique of pressing and holding down keys of the **piano** without a sound and then playing other **notes** so that the resonance of depressed strings can be heard. **Arnold Schoenberg** uses the technique in ***Pierrot Lunaire***, and it was later used by **many** other composers of the twentieth century.

Pierrot lunaire - Arnold Schoenberg
15. Heimweh

Tonlos niederdrücken. Courtesy Andrew Martin Smith.

Tonmeister. (Ger.) Recording engineer. (Fr. *ingénieur du son*, It. *tecnico di suono*, Sp. *ingeniería de sonido*.)

tono. (It., Sp.) **Tone**, **pitch**, key. (Fr. *tonalité*, Ger. *Tonart, Ton*, Sp. *tonalidad*.)

Tonreihe. (Ger.) **Tone row**, series. Also *Reihe*. (Fr. *série*, It. *serie*, Sp. *serie*.)

Tonschrift. (Ger.) Notation. (Fr. *notation*, It. *notazione*, Sp. *notazción*.)

Tonstück. (Ger.) Composition, piece. Also *Stücke*. (Fr. *morceau, pièce*, It. *brano, pezzo*, Sp. *pieza*.)

Topilow, Carl. (b. 1947.) American **conductor** and pedagogue. Topilow is the director of the orchestral program and teacher of **conducting** at the Cleveland Institute of Music and themusic director of the Cleveland Pops Orchestra and the National Repertory Orchestra, a summer music festival in Breckenridge, Colorado. Has served as the principal pops conductor for the **Toledo** and Southwest Florida symphonies.

to play by ear. The ability to hear a piece and play it back without music. (Fr. *jouer d'oreille*, Ger. *nach Gehör spielen*, It. *suonare a orecchio*, Sp. *tocar de oído*.)

tornado al tempo. (It.) Returning to tempo. (Ger. *zum Zeitmaß zurückkehrend*, Fr. *en revenant au movement*, Sp. *volviendo al tempo*.)

Toronto Symphony Orchestra (TSO). Founded in 1922, the current music director is Peter Oundjian (2004– present). Past music directors include **Jukka-Pekka Saraste** (1994–2001), **Günther Herbig** (1988–1994), **Sir Andrew Davies** (1975–1988), Victor Feldbrill (1973–1978), **Karel Ancerl** (1969–1973), **Seiji Ozawa** (1965–1969), Walter Susskind (1956–1965), Sir Ernest MacMillan (1931–1956), and Kuigi von Kunits (1922–1931). Under the leadership of Oundjian, the **orchestra** has established the annual New Creations Festival, where new and commissioned works are presented. Another TSO outreach initiatives is **TSOUNDCHECK**, designed to connect young people to classical music through reduced-price tickets made available to those ages fifteen to thirty-five. The **Adopt-a-Player** program connects elementary schools to individual musicians in the TSO, who will visit classes over a period of weeks to teach and interact with students.

Toscanini, Arturo. (1867–1957.) Italian **conductor** and cellist. Toscanini was the music director of **La Scala, Milan**, (1898–1903, 1906–1908, 1921–1929), where he conducted still-famous performances of Giuseppi Verdi's *Falstaff*, Ludwig van Beethoven's *Fidelio*, **Richard Wagner**'s *Die Meistersinger*, and Claude Debussy's *Pelléas et Mélisande*. He was also the music director of the **New York Philharmonic Orchestra** (1929–1936) and the **NBC Symphony Orchestra**, with which he made most of his recordings (1937–1954). His guest conducting engagements included **Bayreuth** (1930, 1931), the **Vienna Philharmonic Orchestra** (1933), **Salzburg** (1934–1937), and the **BBC Symphony Orchestra** (1935, 1937–1939). He led the first performances of the **Palestine Symphony Orchestra**, now the **Israel Philharmonic Orchestra**, in 1936. He had an openly contentious relationship with the National Socialists, refusing to conduct in Germany, Austria, and Italy during the Nazi and Fascist regimes.

Toscanini conducted numerous operatic premieres, including *I Pagliacci* (1892), *La Boheme* (1896), the Italian premieres of *Götterdämmerung* (1895) and *Siegfried* (1899), Verdi's *La fanciulla del West* (*The Girl of the Golden West*) in 1910, the American premiere of Modest Mussogsky's *Boris Gudonov* (1913), *Turandot* in 1926, and more. From the beginning, he demonstrated a formidable musical talent with an unusual memory and ear. When he was nineteen and second-chair cellist of a touring **opera** company, without any experience or training in **conducting**, he substituted for a performance of Verdi's *Aida*. Conducting from memory on short notice, he launched his career as a conductor. He became known as a demanding and exacting conductor and spent his career battling poor, if not just lazy performance traditions. He rehearsed the singers and **orchestra** in minute detail, sometimes bar by bar, in order to achieve his goals, attaining what is still known as a "Golden Age" at La Scala, Milan.

But he was not only an operatic conductor by any means. Toscanini's relationship with the NBC Symphony, an orchestra created for him, left an incredible legacy of recordings. Dating from 1937 to 1954, a short list of the repertoire they recorded includes symphonies of Ludwig van Beethoven, Johannes Brahms, Franz Schubert, **Felix Mendelssohn**, and Wolfgang Amadeus Mozart and works of Ottorino Respighi, Debussy, Maurice Ravel, **Richard Strauss**, Wagner, Verdi, George Gershwin, Ferde Grofé, John Philip Sousa, and Samuel Barber. Most of the recordings were issued on **RCA** Victor, and many have been digitally remastered and reissued on **CD**.

Contrary to the prevailing view of the conductor as ultimate interpreter whose "duty" it was to manipulate the music at will, Toscanini believed that the composer's intentions as set down in the **score** were right and that the conductor should follow them absolutely. With his intense drive for perfection focused on the will of the composer, he overturned years of performing traditions and left an enormous legacy for the next generations of conductors.

Arturo Toscanini.

tosto. (It.) Quickly, fleet. (Fr. *vite*, Ger. *hurtig*, Sp. *rápido*.) Example: *piu tosto*, quicker.

tôt, de bonne heure. (Fr.) Early, soon. (Ger. *früh*, It. *presto*, Sp. *temprano*, *pronto*.)

touche. 1. (Fr.) A key of a keyboard instrument.
   2. (Fr.) The **fingerboard** of a string instrument. Example: *sur la touche*, play with the bow above or on the fingerboard.

toucher, jouer. (Fr.) To play, to touch. (Ger. *spielen*, *greifen*, It. *suonare*, *tocare*, Sp. *tocar*.)

toujours. (Fr.) Always. (Ger. *immer*, It. *sempre*, Sp. *siempre*.) Example: *et toujours en s'éloignant advantage*, always becoming more distant, from *Nocturnes, Fêtes*, by Claude Debussy; *toujours le (la) meme*, always the same (Ger. *immer das Gleiche*, It. *sempre lo stesso*, Sp. *siempre la misma*).

tous, tout, toute. (Fr.) All, everyone. An indication used to tell everyone in a section to play after a period where only single instruments played. (Fr. *tous*, Ger. *alle*, It. *tutti*, Sp. *todos*.)

tout à coup, tout de suite, immédiatment, subitement. (Fr.) Abrupt, sudden, suddenly. A descriptive term seen in scores and parts and heard in **rehearsal**. (Ger. *plötzlich*, *sofort*, *sogleich*, It. *di colpo*, *subito*, Sp. *subito*.)

tout l'archet. (Fr.) An indication to play with the whole bow.

tout le monde. (Fr.) See **tous, tout, toute**.

tout le temps. (Fr.) Everytime. (Ger. *jedesmal*, It. *ogni volta*, Sp. *cada vez*.)

Tovey, Sir Donald Francis. (1875–1940.) British pianist, composer, **conductor**, and author. In 1914 Tovey, was appointed to the Reid Chair of Music at Edinburg University. Three years later, he formed and subsequently conducted the Reid Orchestra and its concert series. His legacy is the extensive program notes that he wrote for that series. They were collected in ***Essays in Musical Analysis*** and set a new standard for English writing about music. Volumes 1 and 2 cover standard symphonies and volume 3 covers concertos (see the **bibliography**).

tpt. or **tp.** Abbreviation for **trumpet**.

tr. Abbreviation for trill.

tranquille. (Fr.) Peaceful, tranquil, quietly. (Ger. *ruhig*, It. *tranquillo*, Sp. *trqnquilo*.)

tranquillo. (It.) Peaceful, tranquil, quietly. (Fr. *tranquille*, Ger. *ruhig*, Sp. *tranquilo*.)

tranquilo. (Sp.) Peaceful, tranquil, quietly. (Fr. *tranquille*, Ger. *ruhig*, It. *tranquillo*.)

transcription. The adaptation of a work for a medium other than its original one, making possible the performance of the work by different ensembles. Many orchestral works, for example, are transcribed for symphonic **band**. Often works originally written for **piano** solo are transcribed for **orchestra**. That process is often referred to as **orchestration**. Maurice Ravel wrote many works for piano and then created even more famous versions for orchestra. Examples include *Tombeau de Couperin* and *Pavane for a Dead Princess*. Samuel Barber's *Adagio for Strings* began as the slow movement of his String Quartet, opus 11, and became a work for string orchestra, which was then transcribed for choir under the title *Agnus Dei.*

transposed score. A full **score** where all the music of all of the instruments is notated in its transposed form, appearing the same as it does for the players. The nontransposed score is called the **score in C.** It is notated with all parts at their sounding pitch, with the exception of all **octave transpositions**. For example, the **double bass** sounds an octave lower than written and the **piccolo** an octave higher. See individual instrument entries.

transposing instruments. Instruments such as the **clarinet** in B-flat and the **horn** in F, whose written music is at a different **pitch** than it sounds. The interval of **transposition** is determined by the intervallic difference between **concert pitch**, called C, and the key of the instrument. For instance, the interval of transposition for the clarinet in B-flat is down a major second (C down to B-flat). For the horn in F, the interval of transposition is down a perfect fifth, from C down to F. See the individual instrument entries.

transposition. The rewriting or performance of music in a key other than the original one, a process that entails changing each **pitch** by the same interval. Often used to lower or raise the key of a song to make it suitable for a given singer. Transposition is also used when a player of a **transposing instrument** must play from a part written in a key other than that of their instrument. For example, when a clarinetist only has a B-flat **clarinet** and has to play from a part written for clarinet in A, every note of the part has to be transposed down a half step so that it sounds at the correct pitch level.

transposition intervals. See **intervals of transposition**.

traps. A drum set or trap set; a collection of drums and other **percussion** instruments assembled to be played by a single player. The set usually includes a **snare drum**, pedal bass drum, **hi-hat cymbal**, **tom-tom** drums, and other **suspended cymbals**. Often used in jazz bands. See also **appendix 4**.

trascinare, trascinando. (It.) To drag, dragging. Example: *senza trascinare*, without dragging.

trattenuto. (It.) Held back or ritardando. A term used by **Walter Piston** is his symphonies. (Fr. *retenu*, Ger. *zurückgehalten*, Sp. *cohibirse*.)

tratto. (It.) Drawn out. See also *trattenuto*.

Trauermarsch. (Ger.) **Funeral march**. (Fr. *marche funèbre*, It. *Marcia funebre*, Sp. *marcha fúnebre*.)

Trauermusik. (Ger.) Funeral music. (Fr. *musique funèbre*, It. *musica funebre*, Sp. *música Funeral*.)

Traurig, Trauernd. (Ger.) Sad, mournful. (Fr. *triste*, It. *abbacchiato*, Sp. *triste*.)

tre. (It.) Three. Example: *a tre voce*, for three voices. (Fr. *trois*, Ger. *drei*, Sp. *tres*.)

treble clef. A figure of notation placed on second line up of the music **stave** to indicate the **pitch** name G and hence of those on the other lines and spaces. See also **clef, C clefs, bass clef**.

Treble clef. *Courtesy Andrew Martin Smith.*

tremolo, tremolando. (It.) A technique that involves a fast, nonrhythmic repetition of one or more **notes**. In string playing, it is executed as very fast, alternating down- and up-bows in the upper-half to middle of the bow. Used most often in orchestral playing for its acoustic, shimmering, or energetic effect. It appears in much contemporary solo music. Most commonly used in its Italian form. (Fr. *trémolo*, Sp. *trémolo*, Ger. *Tremolo*.)

Tremolo sign. *Courtesy Andrew Martin Smith.*

Tremolo. (Ger.) **Tremolo**. (Fr. *trémolo*, It. *tremolo*, Sp. *trémolo*.) See also *tremolo, tremolando*.

trémolo. (Fr., Sp.) **Tremolo**. (Ger. *Tremolo*, It. *tremolo*.) See also *tremolo, tremolando*.

tremolo dental. (Fr.) Flutter tonguing. (Ger. *Flatterzunge,* It. *frullato,* Sp. *trémolo dental.*)

trémolo dental. (Sp.) Flutter tonguing. (Fr. *tremolo dental,* Ger. *Flatterzunge,* It. *frullato.*)

tremolo (Harfe). (Ger.) In harp playing, a light, rapid back-and-forth motion of the fingers, creating a **tremolo** out of the notes of a chord; whispering. (Fr. *trémolo (harpe),* It. *bisbigliando,* Sp. *bisbigliando.*)

trémolo (harpe). (Fr.) In harp playing, a light, rapid back-and-forth motion of the fingers, creating a **tremolo** out of the notes of a chord; whispering. (It. *bisbigliando,* Ger. *tremolo (Harfe),* Sp. *bisbigliando.*)

trémolo très serré. (Fr.) Very fast **tremolo**. Seen in French scores and parts.

trenaduesimo. (It.) Thirty-second note. See also **appendix 7**.

tres. (Sp.) Three. (Fr. *trois,* Ger. *drei,* It. *tre.*)

très. (Fr.) Very. Often seen in music and heard in **rehearsal** as a part of various phrases. (Ger. *sehr,* It. *molto, di molto, assai,* Sp. *muy.*) Examples: *trés vif,* very lively, fast; *très rapide presque en accord,* very fast, almost as a chord, from *Rapsodie Espagnole, Feria,* by Maurice Ravel. See also *tr.*

Très bien! (Fr.) Very good! Excellent! An expression often used in **rehesarsal**. (It. *bravissimo!* Ger. *Sehr gut!* Sp. *Muy bien! Genial! Execelente!*)

tresillo. (Sp.) Triplet. (Fr. *triolet,* Ger. *Triole,* It. *terzina.*)

tresillo. (Sp.) Triplet. (Fr. *triolet,* Ger. *Triole,* It. *terzina.*)

très vite. (Fr.) As fast as possible, extremely fast. (It. *prestissimo,* Ger. *sehr schnell,* Sp. *rapidamente.*)

triad. An aggregate of three **pitches** stacked in the following manner: major triad, major plus a minor third; minor triad, minor third plus a major third; diminished triad, minor third plus a minor third; augmented triad, major third plus a major third.

tríada. (Sp.) Triad. (Fr. *triade,* Ger. *Dreiklang,* It. *triade.*)

triade. (Fr., It.) Triad. (Ger. *Dreiklang.*)

Triangelschlägel. (Ger.) **Triangle** beater.

triangle. A triangle-shaped metal instrument of varying sizes that produces sound when struck by a metal beater.

(Fr. *triangle,* Ger. *Triangel,* It. *triangolo,* Sp. *triángulo.*) See also **appendix 4**.

Tri-City Symphony Orchestra. See **Quad City Symphony Orchestra**.

trill. A fast exchange of two neighboring pitches. (Fr. *trille,* Ger. *Triller,* It. *trillo, tremolo, groppo,* Sp. *trino.*)

trille. (Fr.) **Trill**. (Ger. *Triller,* It. *trillo,* Sp. *trino.*)

Triller (Ger.) **Trill**. See above. (Fr. *trille,* It. *trillo,* Sp. *trino*)

trillo. (It.) **Trill**. (Fr. *trille,* Ger. *Triller,* Sp. *trino.*) Example: *quasi trillo,* as seen in the score above a **finger trill** to the ballet *Jeux* by Claude Debussy.

trino. (Sp.) **Triplet**. (Fr. *trille,* Ger. *Triller,* It. *trillo.*)

trio. (It.) **Trio**.

trio. A group of three instruments or voices. Also a work written for a group of three musicians.

Triole, Triolen. (pl.) (Ger.) **Triplet**. (Fr. *triolet,* It. *terzina,* Sp. *tresillo.*) Example: *Diese Triole jedesmal mit spring. Bogen rfz am Steg (in Nachahmung der Mandolinen),* Always play these triplets ricochet *rfz* at the bridge in imitation of a mandolin, from *Das Lied von der Erde, mvt.* 4, by **Gustav Mahler**.

triolet. (Fr.) **Triplet**. (Ger. *Triole,* It. *terzina,* Sp. *tresillo.*)

triple croche. (Fr.) Thirty-second note, demisemiquaver (British usage). (It. *biscroma,* Ger. *Zweiunddreißigstel,* Sp. *fusa.*) See also **appendix 7**.

triple meter. A meter in three, such as 3/4. See **meter** for musical images.

triple tonguing. A technique used on the **flute** and certain brass instruments to articulate. The triple articulation is achieved by using the sequence of consonants, *t-t-k, t-t-k,* repeatedly. While techniques have advanced and players are sometimes able to use the triple tonguing technique, the **trombone** uses it only occasionally and the **tuba** rarely. See also **tonguing, double tonguing, flutter tonguing**.

TRIPS. Abbreviation for the **Agreement on Trade-Related Aspects of Intellectual Property Rights** as part of the **GATT** treaty of 1994.

Tristan chord. The first chord sounded in **Richard Wagner**'s *Tristan und Isolde,* it is also prominent in other places in the **opera**. It was considered revolutionary because the non-chord **tones** resolve up instead of down. However, the same chord and its resolution, which somewhat obscures the tonality, already appeared in the prelude to Franz Joseph Haydn's *Creation* to portray chaos, while in Wagner's *Tristan* it was to represent the height of human sensuality. While the spelling F, B, D-sharp, G-sharp is a half-diminished seventh chord, its analytical function is often disputed. See also **iconic chords**.

Tristan Chord

Tristan chord. *Courtesy Andrew Martin Smith.*

triste. (Fr., Sp.) Sad. An expressive term seen in French scores and parts. Example: *doux et triste*, sweet and sad, from the ballet *Jeux* by Claude Debussy.

trois. (Fr.) Three. (Ger. *drei*, It. *tre*, Sp. *tres*.)

Trois fois merde! (Fr.) An expression used before a concert or performance to mean "good Luck." (Ger. ***Toi, toi, toi! Hals und Beinbruch!*** It. *in bocca al lupo*, Sp. ***Buena suerte!***)

tromba bassa. (It.) **Bass trumpet**.

trombone. A nontransposing brass instrument with great versatility, power, lyricism, and warmth. There are three basic types: the alto, tenor, and bass. The tubing of the trombone is formed in two pieces, one sliding into the other. This mechanism allows **pitch** changes and fine-tuning by the movement of the outer tube, called the **slide**. It is notated in **bass** and **tenor clefs**. It has seven playing positions, each with a fundamental tone generating the pitches of its **harmonic series**. In practical terms, each begins with the second partial of the series, the fundamental only being obtainable in the first three positions. While the lowest pitch is E2 to B4, the highest **notes** depend greatly on the ability of the performer. (Fr. *trombone*, Ger. *Posaune*, It. *trombone*, Sp. *trombón*.) See also **appendix 3**, **tenor trombone**, **bass trombone**, **alto trombone**, **extensions**.

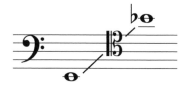

Trombone range. *Courtesy Andrew Martin Smith.*

Trommel. (Ger.) Drum. See also **appendix 4**.

trompa. (Sp.) **French horn**. See also **appendix 4**.

trop. (Fr.) Too much. (Ger. *zu viel*, It. *troppo*, Sp. *demasiado*.)

troppo. (It.) Too much. (Fr. *trop*, Ger. *zu viel*, Sp. *demasiado*.) Example: *Allegro ma non troppo*, allegro, but not too much (too fast).

trumpet. The highest member of the brass family, the trumpet comes in a variety of sizes, from the small **piccolo trumpet** to the large **bass trumpet**. Most are transposing instruments (see **trumpet transpositions**) with the C trumpet the only trumpet written at **pitch**. While the range is still based on the **harmonic series** above the fundamental, the modern trumpet, developed in the nineteenth century, has **valves** that allow the player to perform pitches in the range (see **natural trumpet**). In the late romantic era, the trumpet in F was the instrument of choice by such composers as **Gustav Mahler** and Anton Bruckner. In the twentieth century, the C, B-flat, and D trumpets have become the instruments of choice. The range of the C trumpet is from a low F-sharp3 to the high C6. The B-flat trumpet range is from a written low F-sharp3 to a high D6, sounding E3 to C6. While the low written F-sharp is the standard lowest note, there is a famous example in the **opera** *Carmen* by Georges Bizet that requires an F one half step lower than can be achieved. (Fr. *trompette*, Ger. *Trompete*, It. *tromba*, Sp. *trompeta*.) See also **appendix 3**, **cornet in B-flat**, **flugelhorn in B-flat**, **clarino**.

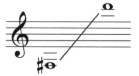

Trumpet range. *Courtesy Andrew Martin Smith.*

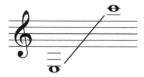

Trumpet B-flat range as it sounds. *Courtesy Andrew Martin Smith.*

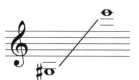

Trumpet D range as it sounds. *Courtesy Andrew Martin Smith.*

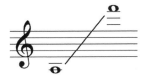

Trumpet E-flat range as it sounds. *Courtesy Andrew Martin Smith.*

trumpet transpositions. These are as follows:

Trumpet written in:	Sounds:
F	up a perfect fourth
E	up a major third
E-flat	up a minor third
D	up a major second
C	as written
B	down a minor second
B-flat	down a major second
A	down a minor third

tuba. Sometimes also called the bass tuba, it exists in several sizes, including the **euphonium** (the smallest or highest), the F tuba, CC tuba, and the largest (also lowest), the BB-flat tuba, sometimes called the **B-double-flat tuba** (also an old Italian name for the **trumpet**). The modern tuba is a nontransposing instrument with a range from low D1 up to G4. The typical performer will own or have access to more than one size instrument. The selection of instrument depends on the piece being played and personal preference. (It. *tuba*, Sp. *tuba*.) See also **appendix 3**, **tenor tuba**, **Wagner tuba**, **baritone**, **ophicleide**.

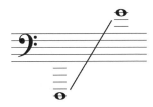

Tuba range. *Courtesy Andrew Martin Smith.*

tubular bells. Alternate name for **chimes**, a group of cylindrical bells of varying lengths that are arranged chromatically on a rack. The sound is produced by striking an individual bell with a mallet. (Fr. *cloches tubulaires*, Ger. *Röhrenglocken, Glocken*, It. *campane tubolari*, Sp. *campanólogo*.) See also **appendix 4**.

Tulsa Philharmonic. See **Tulsa Symphony Orchestra (TSO)**.

Tulsa Symphony Orchestra (TSO). Established in 2005 by musicians from the Tulsa Philharmonic, the **orchestra** is predominantly run by its musicians. They serve as performers and participate as members of the staff, the board of directors, and twelve committees that oversee the organization. The orchestra performs with guest **conductors** and offers a classics series, chamber music concerts, and Symphony in the Park concerts. Each concert is recorded for broadcast on public radio, 88.7 KWYU.

tune. 1. A melody.
2. To adjust the tuning of an instrument.

tuner. An electronic device used to **tune** instruments. Some electronic tuners simply play a variety of **tuning** pitches, others analyze a **pitch** being played and show on a spectrum if it is **sharp** or **flat** according to a predetermined standard. See also **Dr. Beat**.

tuning. The practice of bringing the fundamental **pitch** or pitches of an instrument into agreement with itself and other instruments according to established standards. (Fr. *accord*, It. *accordatura*, Ger. *Stimmung*, Sp. *afinación*.) See also **tuning systems**.

tuning fork. A two-pronged metal device invented in 1711 by the English trumpeter John Shore (1662–1752), who was famous for his performances of Henry Purcell and George Frideric Handel. The tuning fork works by striking the top end of a prong and then touching the bottom end to wood, so that the tips vibrate freely, sounding a clear **pitch**. String players usually strike the top and then create the louder tone by touching the bottom end to the bridge of their instrument. The average tuning fork is said to sound its **tuning** note at two **octaves** and a sixth above its fundamental. (Fr. *diapason*, Ger. *Stimmgabel*, It. *corista*.)

tuning nonpitched instruments. In the case of these instruments, **pitch** exists but is approximated. Such instruments are "tuned" higher or lower to affect the timbre and create contrast within a set of nonpitched instruments, such as woodblocks. A higher tuning creates a brighter timbre, a lower one creates a darker timbre. The timbre of nonpitched drums is altered by the tension of the drumhead itself.

tuning of unpitched percussion instruments. The **tuning** of these **percussion** instruments is not necessarily **pitch** specific, but a matter of relative high, middle, and low sounds. The degree of difference can be changed in the manufacture of the instrument.

tuning practices. Methods of **tuning** by individuals and ensembles. Virtually all musicians **tune** using an accepted reference **pitch**. In an **orchestra**, the tuning **note** is **A=440 Hz**, although some orchestras use a higher A (see **Hertz**). It is sounded by the principal **oboe** or the principal clarinetist if no oboist is present and in a string orchestra, by the **concertmaster**. Some orchestras tune using more than one sounding of the A, starting with winds and brass and ending with strings. In this case, the concertmaster takes the final A alone and then plays it for the all of the strings. **Bands** generally tune to multiple pitches, a B-flat, an A, and an E-flat, played by the principal clarinetist. When performing a work with a soloist playing a fixed-pitch instrument, such as the **piano**, ensembles will tune to that instrument.

The American music industry agreed upon A=440 Hz in 1926. In 1936, A=440 Hz was officially established as the standard tuning note by the American National Standards Institute (ANSI). The International Organization for Standardization set the same standard in 1955 and reaffirmed it in 1975. But current practice has changed. While A=440 Hz is still the standard in North American and the United Kingdom, the tendency in American orchestras is toward tuning to at least A=442 Hz, if not just above. European orchestras commonly cite A=442 Hz as their current standard but often tune to A=444 Hz or even a bit higher. In orchestras, the oboist generally gives the tuning note because it has the most stable pitch. This stability is not automatic and must be developed in the young players.

Many professional orchestras have official **tuning forks**, bells, or **chimes** backstage to establish the tuning pitch. In the period-instrument, performance-practice movement the standard tuning note for a Baroque pitch is A=415 Hz and for classical period music is A=432 Hz.

Orchestras being made up of the string sections, winds, brass, and percussion, and sometimes with piano, have the enormous challenge of attempting to tune a large ensemble of instruments that have differing tendencies and different roles in the harmonic and melodic texture of a piece of music. Generally players "tune down," they listen to the lowest instrument playing to establish a chord. Often called "vertical listening," this is always balanced with horizontal listening, where the notes are coming from and where they are going. To achieve good tuning overall it is better to encourage good breathing and tone quality in an orchestra than to spend too much time focusing on individual chords or notes. The **conductor** achieves this by an affinity with the musicians and how they play their instruments. For instance, while it is not necessary for the conductor to actually breath when giving a cue gesture or entrance, doing so will positively impact the quality of the sound by the way in which it encourages the musicians.

Choirs use a variety of reference notes, depending on the circumstances. When singing **a cappella** (without accompaniment), the choir tunes to a reference pitch appropriate to the piece they are performing using a **pitch pipe**. When singing with a piano or other accompaniment, the chorus gets its pitch from the harmony or pitches of the introduction. There is also a special church

music pitch, called Chorton pitch, where A=466 Hz, essentially A-sharp.

String players tune their instruments to perfect fifths. At a ratio of two to three, the intervals are meant to be "beatless" or pure. When playing a solo, a concertmaster, or first violinist in a **string quartet**, may tune slightly higher, thus making the sound a bit brighter. String players generally tune using the modern **well-temperament system**, which incorporates set intervals and pitches but allows for adjustments to tune individual notes to each other.

Wind instruments. Each instrumental family, **flute**, oboe, **clarinet**, and **bassoon**, has its own tendencies as does each individual instrument, due to the fact that they are handmade, and even each player. Not all models or makes of instruments are the same. Certain models are known for a brighter sound, while others have a darker one. Some are known as being difficult to play in tune while having a particularly sought-after, beautiful tone. While each instrument also has its own general timbre, players may develop a preference for a certain timbre, and that can confuse the ear when attempting to discern the intonation of specific chords or notes. Players may prefer a timbre or sound, even though it is higher in pitch, because it carries or projects. Soloists may even adjust their tuning when playing with an orchestra for that very reason. The flute and the clarinet, for instance, have the opposite tendencies in their high ranges, the flute tending to be low and the clarinet high. Low notes on the bassoon have a tendency to be sharp, and since the second bassoon player generally has the lowest note in any woodwind chord, its accuracy is critically important to good tuning. Another issue is vibrato. To begin with, no one should ever vibrato more than the principal player in the section. In addition, not matching vibrato between flutes and clarinets or within a section can negatively impact tuning.

The intonation problems of the auxiliary instruments, **piccolo**, **English horn**, E-flat clarinet, **bass clarinet**, and **contrabassoon**, are magnified because of their extended ranges. As a consequence, wind players spend their careers modifying and adjusting, using the official tuning note as a starting point but nothing else.

Brass instruments have the same characteristic of wind instruments in that the specific make and design of an instrument can significantly affect the sound or timbre and the tuning tendencies of the instrument. For instance, the shape of the bell of a horn, how much it is tapered, will make a distinct difference in tone. All brass instruments have a "tuning slide" that adjusts the basic pitch of the instrument. When it is lengthened, the pitch is lowered, and when shortened, the pitch is raised.

Pitched percussion. Timpani are now designed to have mechanical tuning-assist devices on the pedals. They are never enough to do the fine tuning, and many professional players don't use them at all. Most timpanists have tuning forks or pitch pipes to help set pitch.

The tuning of xylophones and marimbas is determined by the length of the bars and not normally adjusted.

tuning systems. A variety of tuning methods that set the relationships between the **pitches** according to set ratios. All tuning systems that don't use set, just intervals are called temperaments.

Equal temperament is the system used today to tune a **piano**. It divides the **octave** into twelve equal intervals, each one having a distance of one hundred **cents**. The system produces perfect octaves, each with a ratio of 1:2. While there are other ways to divide an octave, equal temperament is the most commonly used tuning system in Western music.

In **just intonation**, while the frequencies of the pitches are established by simple ratios, not all of the **notes** will be perfect. Small adjustments must be made that modify the ratios as the register climbs. This can be done technically on the computer or other device, but when used by live performers, it requires constant adaptation (see **tuning practice**).

The **Pythagorean tuning** system was of primary importance in the Medieval and Renaissance periods of music history. It uses ratios derived from the 3:2 ratio and is also a kind of just intonation system, where certain intervals must be modified in order that the whole octave of notes sounds well. In Pythagorean tuning, the intervals of the major and minor third end up somewhat impure, heightening their commonly held dissonant aspect. (That is one of the reasons the Picardie third became so common in the Renaissance.)

The **meantone tuning system** averages out ratios occurring in pairs and used for the same interval. Known as the quarter-comma meantone form, major thirds are tuned using two perfect whole steps by slightly flattening the fifths.

Today **well temperament** is an umbrella category that includes all systems in which the ratios between intervals are unequal but close to those used in just intonation. Unlike other tuning systems, in well temperament, the ratios result from tuning individual notes to each other (see **tuning practice**). This system makes it possible to play in all keys.

There are other tuning systems of varying importance, including the natural overtone scale (derived from the **harmonic series**); the forty-three-tone scale, created by the composer **Harry Partch**; the **Bohlen-Pierce scale**; the **alpha**, **beta**, **delta**, and **gamma scales** created by composer **Wendy Carlos**; the **microtonal scales** devised by composer **Easley Blackwood Jr.**; the quarter-tone scale; and others.

tuono, tono. (It.) **Tone**, **pitch**. (Fr. *ton*, Ger. *Ton*, It. *tono*, Sp. *tono*.)

tutta, tutto. (It.) Each, every, any. (Fr. *chaque*, It. *chiascuno*, Sp. *cada, todo, toda*.)

tutti, tutte. (It.) All, everyone. An indication used to tell everyone in a section to play after a period where only single instruments played. (Fr. *tous, tout le monde*, Ger. *alle*, Sp. *todo el mondo*.) Example: *tutta la forza*, play with all the force you have.

twelve-tone chord. A chord using the **pitches** of the **twelve-tone row**. The pitches may be stacked in a variety of intervals, thirds, fourths, seconds, or using other twelve-tone technique principles.

twelve-tone matrix. See **matrix**.

twelve-tone music. See **twelve-tone technique**.

twelve-tone row or series. The sequence or arrangement of the twelve chromatic **pitches** that form the basis of the harmonic and melodic material of a twelve-tone piece.

twelve-tone technique. A system of composition developed by **Arnold Schoenberg**. Principles include: (1) The twelve **notes** of the **chromatic scale** are arranged in a sequence where no pitch is repeated, creating a tone row. (2) Each tone row or series has four basic forms, prime (the original), inversion, retrograde, and retrograde inversion. (3) The intervallic structure of the row or series remains the same throughout the piece, while **octave** equivalence and **transpositions** of its basic forms (see principle 2) are allowed. (4) The pitches of the tone row may be used in chords or melodies. (5) Doubling at the octave should be avoided. See the **bibliography**.

Twitter Zone. An area set aside in a concert hall or **opera** house where audience members who want to may participate in Twitter activities about the performance. The **Cincinnati Orchestra** in one of the first American **orchestras** to have a Twitter Zone at its concerts.

two-count preparation. See **entrances on incomplete beats**, **fractional beat preparations**.

tympani. Outdated spelling of **timpani**.

Tyzik, Jeff. (b. 1951.) American pops **conductor**, trumpeter, and arranger. Tyzik has served as the pops conductor of the **Rochester Philharmonic Orchestra** (1994–present) and additionally with the **Vancouver Symphony Orchestra**, Winnipeg Symphony Orchestra, Oregon Symphony, the **Florida Orchestra**, the **Detroit Symphony Orchestra**, and the **Seattle Symphony**.

tzigane. (Fr.) Literally, gypsy. Also a title for a piece of music written in a "gypsy" style, such as Maurice Ravel's *Tzigane* for **violin** and **piano** or **orchestra**.

üben. (Ger.) To practice. (Fr. *exercer*, It. *exercitare*, Sp. *practicar, ejercer*.)

über. (Ger.) On, upon, above. (Fr. *dessus*, It. *sopra*, Sp. *sobre*.) Also *übergehen*, to give way to something; *über das ganze Orchestrer hinaus*, rising above the whole **orchestra**; *übernimmt*, change to (as in change to another instrument).

Übergang, Durchgang. (Ger.) Transition. (Fr. *transition*, It. *transizione*, Sp. *transición*.)

überraschen. (Ger.) To surprise. Also *Überraschung*, surprise (Fr. *surprise*, It. *sorpresa*, Sp. *sorprender*); *überraschend*, astonishing, surprising.

überstürtz, überhetzt. (Ger.) Rushed, hurried. (Fr. *précipité, bousculé*, It. *precipitato, precipitoso*, Sp. *precipitado*.)

übertönen. (Ger.) To predominate, to drown out. See also **übertönend**.

übertönend. (Ger.) Rising above, dominating. Example: *alles übertönend*, louder than the rest of the **orchestra**.

Übung. (Ger.) **Etude**, exercise. (Fr. *exercice*, It. *exercizio*, Sp. *estudios, ejercicio*.)

udire. (It.) To hear, heard. (Fr. *entendre, entendu*, Ger. *hören*, Sp. *oír*.)

uguale, eguale. (It.) Equal, the same. Often used in **rehearsal** as a directive. (Fr. *égal*, Ger. *gleichmäßig*, Sp. *igual*.)

ugualmente, equamente. (It.) Equally. (Fr. *également*, Ger. *gleichmäßig*, Sp. *igualmente*.)

U.H. Abbreviation for "upper half," a commonly used indication in string parts to play in the upper half of the bow.

Ukraine National Symphony Orchestra. See **National Symphony Orchestra of Ukraine**.

ultima, ultimo. (It.) Last, ultimate. (Fr. *dernier, dernière*, Ger. *letzter, letzte*, Sp. *último, final*.) Example: *ultima volta*, last time (Fr. *derniére fois*, Ger. *letztes Mal,* Sp. *último tempo*).

último. (Sp.) Last. (Fr. *dernier, dernirère*, Ger. *letzter, letzte*, It. *ultima, ultimo*.) Example: *último tempo*, last time (Fr. *derniére fois*, Ger. *letztes Mal*, It. *ultima volta*).

Ultra High Fidelity. A music magazine published in Canada since 1982, it now has a prominent web identity.

Umfang, Raum, Ausdehnung. (Ger.) Compass, range, of an instrument, for instance. (Fr. *ètendue*, It. *gamma*, Sp. *rango*.)

umstimmen. (Ger.) To retune to another **pitch**. (Fr. *réaccorder*, It. *risintonizzare*, Sp. *afinación diferente*.)

un. (Fr.) One. See also **numbers, basic**.

una vez. (Sp.) Once, one time. (Fr. *une fois,* It. *una volta,* Ger. *einmal*.)

Una vez más, pero ahora más rapido. (Sp.) One more time, but this time faster. Also *Otra vez más rapido*, Again, but faster (less polite, more brisk). See also **encore, ancora**.

una volta. (It.) Once. (Fr. *une fois*, Ger. *einmal,* Sp. *una vez*.)

unbetond. (Ger.) Unaccented, unstressed.

und. (Ger.) And. (Fr. *et,* It. *e,* Sp. *y.*)

und so weiter. (Ger.) And so on, et cetera. (Fr. *et ainsi de suite,* It. *eccetera, etc.* Sp. *etcétera.*)

une fois. (Fr.) Once. (Ger. *einmal,* It. *una volta,* Sp. *una vez.*)

ungefähr. (Ger.) About, around, approximate, approximately.

ungerader Takt. (Ger.) Triple or odd-numbered meter.

ungezwungen. (Ger.) At ease, effortlessly. (Fr. *sans effort, avec facilité,* It. *senza sforzo,* Sp. *sin esfuerzo.*)

unheimlich. (Ger.) Eerie, sinister, weird, weirdly, uncanny. (Fr. *inquiétant,* It. *inquietante, sinistro,* Sp. *misterioso, extraño.*)

unis. Abbreviation for **unison** or *unisono.*

unison. 1. The interval made by two soundings of the same **pitch**.

2. A passage played by more than one instrument or instrument group at the same pitch. (Fr. *unisson,* Ger. *unisono,* It. *unisono,* Sp. *unísono.*)

unisono. (It.) **Unison,** in unison. (Fr. *unisson,* Sp. *unísono.*) Example: *unisono all' . . . ,* in unison until . . . (Fr. *á l'unisson jusqu'à . . . ,* Ger. *Unisono bis . . . ,* Sp. *al unisono hasta . . .*). See also **appendix 6**.

unisono. (Ger.) In **unison.** Also *Einklang.* See also **appendix 6**.

unisono. (It.) **Unison.** (Fr. *unisson,* Ger. *Einklang, Unisono,* Sp. *unísono.*) See also **appendix 6**.

unísono. (Sp.) **Unison.** (Fr. *unisson,* Ger. *Unisono,* It. *unisono.*) See also **appendix 6**.

Unisono bis . . . (Ger.) In **unison** until . . . A directive seen in **scores** and parts. (Fr. *à l'unisson jusqu'à . . . ,* It. *unisono all' . . . ,* Sp. *al unísono hasta . . .*)

unísono hasta, al. (Sp.) In **unison** until . . . A directive seen in **scores** and parts. (Fr. *á l'unisson jusqu'à . . . ,* Ger. *Unisono bis . . . ,* It. *unisono all' . . .*)

unisson. (Fr.) **Unison.** (Ger. *Einklang, Unisono,* It. *unisono,* Sp. *unísono.*) See also **appendix 6**.

Universal Music Group (UMG). The largest music corporation in existence, it is an American-based, French-owned corporation that is part of the Paris media firm Vivendi. When UMG bought **EMI** in 2012, it was on the condition of the divestment of several of its catalogues. It currently holds the Island, Polydor, **Decca,** Virgin EMI, and Capitol labels. The other largest music corporations are **Warner Music Group** and **Sony Music Group**.

Universe of Sound. An orchestral outreach program of the **Philharmonia Orchestra** in London.

Universität Mozarteum Salzburg. See **Salzburg Mozarteum**.

University of Cincinnati College-Conservatory of Music. See **Cincinnati College-Conservatory of Music (CCM).**

University of Michigan, School of Music, Theater and Dance. Located in Ann Arbor, Michigan, the school is a public institution with comprehensive programs in both undergraduate and graduate levels. Its fifteen departments include the Department of Performing Arts Technology.

University of Music and Performing Arts (Universität für Musik und darstellende Kunst Wien, MDW). Founded in 1817 in Vienna, it now has a student body of over three thousand, making it one of the largest music conservatories in the world; it has twenty-four institutes. The university was reorganized and renamed in 1970 in order to reflect the unification of multiple programs. Considered a feeder school for many Austrian **orchestras**, it has a close relationship with the **Vienna Philharmonic**. Its list of alumni is a pantheon of famous performers and includes **Herbert von Karajan, Arthur Nikisch, Gustav Mahler**, and **Claudio Abbado**.

University of Music and Performing Arts Munich (Hochschule für Musik und Theater München). Established in 1846 as the Royal Conservatory for Music, it was supported by King Ludwig II, patron of **Richard Wagner**. The school offers courses of study in music performance, music education, and ballet and has a partnership with the Bavarian Theater Academy for **opera**, acting, directing, and lighting design. The university has a very distinguished alumni and faculty list.

University of Music and Theater "Felix Mendelssohn Bartholdy" (Hochschule für Musik und Theater "Felix Mendelssohn Bartholdy"). Founded in 1843 by **Felix Mendelssohn**, who was the music director or the **Leipzig Gewandhaus Orchestra** at the time. Musicians of the **orchestra** were among the faculty, which also included many of Mendelssohn's friends and compatriots, including Robert and Clara Schumann, Ferdinand David, and others. Distinguished alumni have included

Sir Arthur Sullivan, Edvard Grieg, Leoš Janáček, **Felix Weingartner**, **Sir Adrian Boult**, **Karl Richter**, **Kurt Mazur**, and many others.

University of Southern California Thorton School of Music. Founded in 1884, it is named for Flora L. Thorton, who made a donation of $25 million in 1999. The school has a comprehensive curriculum in areas of performance, composition, **conducting**, film scoring, and music industry, with specialized programs in early music. It maintains a distinguished faculty and has an impressive alumni list.

University of Southern California, Thorton School of Music. Located in Los Angeles, California, the school offers a complete array of degrees at both the undergraduate and graduate levels. It also includes undergraduate programs in film scoring, music industry, and early music. Since 2009, it also offers a major in popular music performance and songwriting. The school has a close connection with the **Los Angeles Philharmonic**, with more than 20 percent of the **orchestra** serving on its faculty.

unmerklich, unvernehmlich. (Ger.) Imperceptible, indiscernible, imperceptibly. (Fr. *imperceptible*, It. *impercettibile*, Sp. *imperceptible*.) Example: *Von hier allmählich und unmerklich zu Tempo I zurückkehren*, From here gradually and unnoticeably go back to tempo I, from *Symphony No. 2, mvt. 1*, by **Gustav Mahler**.

unmittelbar, sofort, sogleich. (Ger.) At once, immediately. (Fr. *immédiatment, tout de suite*, It. *subito, immediatamente*, Sp. *immediatamente, súbito*.)

uno. (It., Sp.) One. See also **numbers, basic**.

unordered pitch classes. A group of three or more **notes** in a **twelve-tone** piece, with each note from a different **pitch class**, where the order of the notes is not specified or consistent. See also **ordered pitch classes**.

un peu. (Fr.) A little. (Ger. *ein wenig*, It. *un poco*, Sp. *un poco*.) Example: *Un peu retenu*, a little holding back, from *Fêtes,* movement two, of *Nocturnes*, by Claude Debussy.

un poco. (It., Sp.) A little. A commonly used expression. (Ger. *ein wenig*.) Examples: (It.) *un poco crescendo*, a little crescendo; (It.) *un poco rallentando*, a little rallentando; (It.) *un poco piu forte*, a little louder.

unter. (Ger.) Under, below. Seen most often in its Italian form, ***sotto***. (Fr. *dessous, sous*, It. *sotto*, Sp. *bajo*.) See also ***sotto voce***.

unter der Stimme, mit leiser Stimme. (Ger., lit. "under the voice.") Quietly, subdued, in an undertone. (It. *sotto voce,* Fr. *á voix basse*, Sp. *en voz baja*.)

unterstützung. (Ger.) Reinforcement, support. (Fr. *soutien*, It. *supporto*.)

upbeat. One or more **notes** that occur before the first measure of a work or phrase, anacrusis, pickup. (Fr. *levée, anacrouse*, Ger. *Auftakt, Anakrusis*, It. *in levare, levata, anacrusis,* Sp. *alzada, anacrusa*.)

up-bow. The direction of the bow when it moves from the tip to the **frog**. (Fr. *poussé*, Ger. *Aufstrich, Anstrich*, It. *arcata in su*, Sp. *arco arriba*.) For the hidden up-bow change sign, the parentheses indicate hiding the bow changes.

Up-bow sign. *Courtesy Andrew Martin Smith.*

Hidden up-bow change. *Courtesy Andrew Martin Smith.*

Uraufführung. (Ger.) World premiere performance. (Fr. *première execution mondiale*, It. *prima esecuczione mondiale*, Sp. *estreno mundial*.)

urgent. (Fr.) Urgent. A character word used to evoke a particular manner of playing. (Ger. *dringend*, It. *urgente*, Sp. *urgente, urgir*.)

urgente. (It., Sp.) Urgent. A character word used to evoke a particular manner of playing. Also (Sp.) *urgir*. (Fr. *urgent*, Ger. *dringend*.)

Urlinie. A term used by the Austrian theorist **Heinrich Schenker** in his analytical system to designate the overall melodic structure of a piece. See also **Schenkerian analysis**.

Ursatz. A term used in **Schekenrian analysis** to describe the large-scale structure of a work when the **Urlinie** and the **Grundbrechung** are perceived in combination.

Urtext editions. From the German, meaning "original version." (Fr. *version originale*, It. *versione originale*.)

Many publishers issue editions based on original manuscripts and other source materials, such as individual **orchestra** parts, referring to them as "Urtext" editions. **Copyright laws** covering Urtext editions vary by country. See also **Bärenreiter-Verlag**.

usw. (Ger.) Abbreviation for *und so weiter*, and so forth, et cetera.

ut. (Ger.) C-natural. See also **appendix 5**.

Utah Symphony Orchestra. Became a full-time ensemble under the direction of **Maurice Abravanel**. He served as he music director from 1947 until 1979 and built the symphony from a part-time community **orchestra** into an orchestra of national importance through his many recordings. Subsequent music directors include Joseph Silverstein, former concertmaster of the **Boston Symphony**, and then Keith Lockhart, who was simultaneously the conductor of the **Boston Pops**. Thierry Fischer is the orchestra's current music director. The orchestra serves the entire state of Utah through its outreach concerts. In 2002, it merged with the Utah Opera and maintains a summer home at the Deer Valley Music Festival.

ut bémol. (Ger.) C-flat. See also **appendix 5**.

ut dièse. (Ger.) C-sharp. See also **appendix 5**.

ut double-bémol. (Ger.) C-double-flat. See also **appendix 5**.

ut double-diése. (Ger.) C-double-sharp. See also **appendix 5**.

V

va. (It.) Go, go on. From ***andare***, to go, to walk. (Fr. *aller*, Ger. *gehen*, Sp. *ir*.)

Valentino, Henri. (1785–1865.) French violinist and **conductor**. Valentino became the second conductor of the Paris Opéra in 1820, sharing **conducting** responsibilities with **François Habeneck** from 1824 to 1830. There he led the premieres of Daniel Auber's *La muette de Portici* and Gioacchino Rossini's *Guillaume Tell*, as well as the premiere of **Hector Berlioz**'s Mass in 1825. In 1831, he became the chief conductor of the Opéra-Comique and it was there that he conducted the premiere of Ferdinand Herold's *Zampa*. He directed the Concerts St. Honoré of Paris from 1836. Programs included instrumental works of Franz Joseph Haydn, Wolfgang Amadeus Mozart, Ludwig van Beethoven, and other important contemporary composers of the day, which he would conduct, in addition to popular dances conducted by others. The series became known as the Concerts Valentino, but in spite of a large proportion of popular repertoire, they didn't last. Valentino refused an invitation to succeed Habeneck as the conductor of the Paris **opera** in 1846. During his life, he was known as an excellent and influential conductor who was praised for his ability to inspire musicians and audience alike.

vals. (Sp.) Waltz. (Ger. *Walzer*, It. *valzer*, Fr. *valse*.)

valse. (Fr.) Waltz. (Ger. *Walzer*, It. *valzer*, Sp. *vals*.)

valve. A mechanism of the **trumpet** or **horn** that, when engaged, changes the length of the instrument's tubing and, consequently, the **pitch**. Modern trumpets have three valves, most commonly piston valves, but also, and especially in Europe, rotary valves. Modern horns mostly have rotary valves. The so-called Vienna horn uses double-piston valves. (Fr. *piston, cylinder,* Ger. *Ventil,* It. *pistone, cilindro*, Sp. *pistòn*.)

valzer. (It.) Waltz. (Ger. *Walzer*, Fr. *valse,* Sp. *vals*.)

vamp. A passage of music repeated as necessary to prepare for the entrance of a soloist or to provide continuous chordal background above which a soloist may improvise.

Vancouver Symphony Orchestra (VSO). Founded in 1919, with concerts suspended from 1921 to 1930, it is the third largest **orchestra** in Canada. Current music director Bramwell Tovey assumed the position in 2000. Under his direction, the orchestra won the **Grammy** for best instrumental soloist performance with Canadian violinist James Ehnes in 2008. Past music directors have included **Sergiu Comissiona** (1991–2000) and **Kazuyoshi Akiyama** (1972–1985). In 2011, the VSO opened the VSO School of Music, a community music school with programs for all ages. The VSO recorded *Open Heart Symphony*, live with the **band** Spirit of the West in 1996. The orchestra maintains an active program of Kids' Koncerts, Tiny Tots Concerts, and other educational and outreach programs.

Vänskä, Osmo. (b. 1953.) Finnish **conductor**, clarinetist, and composer. Vänska studied **conducting** with **Jorma Panula** at the **Sibelius Academy**. He became the principal guest conductor of the **Lahti Symphony Orchestra** (1985) and was made chief conductor there in 1988. He recorded a complete cycle of Sibelius symphonies and numerous contemporary Finnish composers with the **orchestra** on the **BIS label**. He served as the chief conductor of the Iceland Symphony Orchestra (1993–1996) and the **BBC Scottish Symphony** (1996–2002), with whom he recorded a cycle of Nielsen symphonies. He became the music director of the **Minnesota Orchestra** in 2003. He is credited with bringing the orchestra to a new level. He resigned this position in 2013 but was reappointed in 2014 with a contract until 2019.

velado. (Sp.) Veiled, filmy. Used to describe a particular sound quality. (Fr. *voilée*, Ger. *verschleierte*, It. *velato*.)

velato. (It.) Veiled, filmy. Used to describe a particular sound quality. (Fr. *voilée*, Ger. *verschleierte*, Sp. *velado*.)

veloce. (It.) Fast, quick, quickly. A character word. (Fr. *rapide, rapidement*, Ger. *rasch*, Sp. *veloz*.)

veloz. (Sp.) Fast, quick, quickly. (Fr. *rapidement, rapide*, Ger. *rasch*, It. *veloce, velocemente*.)

vent. (Fr.) Wind. (Ger. *Wind*, It. *vento*, Sp. *viento*.) Example: *instruments à vent*, **wind instruments**.

Ventil, Pumpventil. (Ger.) **Valve** on a **trumpet** or **horn**. (Fr. *piston, cylindre*, It. *piston*, Sp. *pistón*.)

Ventil, Ventilhorn. (Ger.) **Valve**, valve horn. (Fr. *cylindre, piston*, It. *valvola*, Sp. *pistón, trompa con pistones*.)

vento. (It.) Wind. (Ger. *Wind*, Fr. *vent*, Sp. *viento*.)

verändern. (Ger.) To change, to alter. (Fr. *changer*, It. *cambiare*, Sp. *cambiar*.)

Veränderungen. (Ger.) The variation. (Fr. *variation*, It. *variazione*, Sp. *la variación*.)

Verbrugghe, Henri. Belgian inventor of an "electic **metronome**." **Hector Berlioz** met Verbrugghe on a trip to Belgium and was so convinced by the invention that he brought it to Paris for a concert of "gargantuan" proportions, including excerpts from his *Te Deum*, Carl Maria von Weber's *Der Freischütz* overture, movements from Ludwig van Beethoven's Symphony No. 5, Wolfgang Amadeus Mozart's *Ave verum*—so much music and so many musicians (the **orchestra** had over 1,250 individuals) that it required the participation of five subconductors. Berlioz wrote about Verbrugghe's invention (see the **bibliography**):

The wires are described as going beneath the stage, connecting the conductor's desk with a remote moveable baton attached "by a pivot in front of a board which is placed at any desired distance . . . The desk is furnished with a copper key similar to a piano key, which has at its bottom a small protuberance of about a quarter of an inch. Immediately under this protuberance is a little copper cup filled with quicksilver. When the conductor wants to mark a beat, he presses the copper key with the forefinger of his left hand (his right hand holds the baton, as usual), where by the protuberance makes contact with the quicksilver. The electrical connection thus effected makes the baton at the other end of the wires oscillate. The electrical contact and the movement of the baton take place simultaneously, regardless of the dis-

tance. The musicians behind the scenes watching the electric baton are thus practically under the immediate direction of the conductor, who might, if it were necessary, conduct from the middle of the Opéra orchestra in Paris a performance taking place in Versailles."

verdoppeit, verdoppeln. (Ger.) Doubled, to double. (Fr. *doublé*, It. *duplicato, duplicare*, Sp. *doblado*.) For example, to double an instrument, as in having a passage played by more than one **flute**, for instance.

vergnügt, feiernd. (Ger.) Merrily, rejoicing. (Fr. *joyeusement, allègrement*, It. *allegramente, festeggiante*, Sp. *alegremente*.)

vergrößern. (Ger.) To increase, to magnify. (Fr. *s'agrandir*, It. *accrescersi*, Sp. *ampliarse*.)

verhallen. (Ger.) Die away, become fainter. Also *verhallend*, becoming fainter. (Fr. *se perdu au loin*, It. *perdersi in lontanza*, Sp. *extinguirse, desvaneciéndose*.)

verhalten, getragen. (Ger.) Sustained. (Fr. *soutenu*, It. *sostenuto*, Sp. *sostenido*.)

Verkleinerung. (Ger.) **Diminution**.

verklingen. (Ger.) Die away, fade. Also *verklingend*, dying away. (It. *svanire*, Sp. *extinguirse, desvaneciéndose*.)

verkürzung. (Ger.) The shortening of a note-value, **diminution**.

verlöschend. (Ger.) Dying away, extinguishing. A manner of playing. (Fr. *en s'éteignant*, It. *estinguendo*, Sp. *extinción*.)

Vermont Symphony Orchestra (VS). Founded in Woodstock, Vermont, in 1934, it is one of the few, as well as the oldest state-supported **symphony** orchestras in the United States. As part of its mission, the **orchestra** performs throughout the state and does not have a regular hall. Its current music director is Jaime Laredo (1999–present). Previous music directors include Efraín Guigui Abbo (1974–1989), and its chorus director is Richard De Cormier. The orchestra offers numerous outreach and educational programs, such as its Musicians-in-the-Schools and Orchestra Youth Concerts and SymphonyKids Concerts.

verschleierte. (Ger.) Veiled, flimy. Used to describe a particular sound quality. (Fr. *voilée*, It. *velato*, Sp. *velado*.)

Verschwinden, verschwinden. (Ger.) Disappearance, to disappear, to vanish, to fade away. Example: *Bis zum gänzlichen Verschwinden*, until it completely disappears, from *Symphony No. 1*, first movement, by **Gustav Mahler**.

verstärken. (Ger.) To reinforce, to amplify, to bolster, to enforce.

verstimmt. (Ger.) Out of tune. (It. *scordato, stonato,* Fr. *désaccordé,* Sp. *desafinado*.)

verticalization. The concept that any group of **pitches** that has melodic significance will also present in the chords that accompany it.

verzaubert. (Ger.) Enchanted, delighted, bewitched. A character word. (Fr. *enchanté, enchaînez,* It. *incantato,* Sp. *encantado*.)

Verzierungen. (Ger.) Ornaments, embellishments. (Fr. *ornement,* It. *ornamento,* Sp. *ornamento*.)

vez, á la. (Sp.) Simultaneously, at the same time. Also *juntos.* (Fr. *en même temps,* Ger. *gleichzeitig,* It. *auf einmal,* Sp. *al mismo tiempo*.)

via. (It.) Away. Examples: *via sordini,* remove **mutes** (Fr. *enlevez les sourdines,* Ger. *Dämpfer weg,* Sp. *quitar sordina*). Can also be used as a command: *Via!* Go away!

vibrado. (Sp.) **Vibrato.** The Italian form is universal.

vibrant. (Fr.) Vibrant. (Ger. *dynamisch,* It. *vibrante, tremolante,* Sp. *vibrando*.) Example: *vibrant sans dureté,* vibrant without hardness, from *Fêtes,* movement two of *Nocturnes,* by Claude Debussy.

vibrante. (Sp.) Vibrating. See also **vibrato**.

vibraphone. A keyboard **percussion** instrument played with **mallets**. See also **appendix 4**.

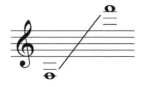

Vibraphone range. *Courtesy Andrew Martin Smith.*

vibrar. (Sp.) To vibrate, as in string **vibrato**.

vibraslap. A modern version of the **jawbone**, a **percussion** instrument made of metal and wood. A single wooden ball on the end of a stiff wire rod bent into a U-type shape that allows it to hit a hollow V-shaped wooden box on the opposite end of the rod, which contains a small metal mechanism made of pins or rivets that rattle when the instrument is shaken, making the ball hit the box. Used in Christopher Rouse's *Concerto for Cello.* See also **appendix 4**.

vibrato. (It., lit. shake, *vibrare,* to shake). In singing, vibrato occurs spontaneously because of a tremor in the larynx or diaphragm. With string instruments, it is a cultivated technique in which the left hand and arm slightly pulse the tip of the finger, varying the **pitch** of the **note** being played. Accepted as expressive, the technique ranges from a hand-only vibrato to one that may include motion of the wrist and arm. Most musicologists agree that performers during the Renaissance, baroque, and even the classical period used less vibrato, if any at all, while in the romantic era and beyond, its use has been consistent.

Wind players usually incorporate vibrato by modifying the airflow through the instrument, using a pulsation of the diaphragm or by varying the tension of the vocal chords in a throat vibrato. In brass playing, the embouchure is quickly varied, creating a repeated bending of the pitch called "lip vibrato." Other methods of brass vibrato exist but are not encouraged in orchestral playing. In contemporary practice, composers have specified a variety of vibratos: a slight vibrato, a wide vibrato, fast or slow vibrato, or no vibrato at all (see **white tone**), using either verbal descriptions or new notation devices such as those used by **Krzysztof Penderecki** in *Threnody to the Victims of Hiroshima* (see **appendix 1**). The Italian term is universal. (Fr. *vibré,* Ger. *vibriet, Bebung,* It. *vibrato,* Sp. *vibrado*.) Example: (It.) *lasciar vibrare,* let the sound vibrate.

vibré. (Fr.) **Vibrato.** Example: *laissez vibrer,* let it ring, seen in many pieces, especially the French repertoire.

VI-DE. (It., lit. "see.") The instruction to make a cut, moving from one spot in a part or **score** to another. It is commonly marked VI- (at the beginning of the cut) -De (at the end of the cut). Most often used in **opera**.

vide. (Fr.) Empty. (It. *vuoto,* Ger. *leer*.) See also *cuerda al aire* (Sp.), open string.

viel, viele. (Ger.) Much, many. Often heard as part of directive phrases in **rehearsals**. (Fr. *beaucoup,* It. *molto,* Sp. *mucho*.)

Vielstimmig. (Ger.) Many voiced, polyphonic. (Fr. *polyphonique,* It. *polifonico,* Sp. *polifónico*.)

Vienna Academy of Music. See **University for Music and the Performing Arts (Universität für Musik and Darstellende Kunst, Wien)**.

Vienna Philharmonia Orchestra (Wiener Philharmoniker). Founded in 1842 and based in the Musikverein. Members of the philharmonic are selected from among the players in the **orchestra** of the **Vienna State Opera**. A minimum three-year stint in the **opera** is a prerequisite for consideration for membership in the philharmonic. From its founding to 1933, the orchestra used a system of "subscription" **conductors**, conductors who were hired for the purpose of leading subscription concerts in the Musikverein. (**Gustav Mahler, Felix Weingartner**, and **Wilhelm Furtwängler** are on this list.) The have never had principal conductors or music directors. In 1933, they shifted to only guest conductors. Among these guests have been many of the most distinguished conductors of their time, including **Arturo Toscanini, Hans Knappertsbusch, Otto Klemperer, Geroge Szell, Carlo Maria Giulini, Erich Kleiber, James Levine, Leonard Bernstein, Lorin Maazel, Valery Gergiev**, and **Franz Welser-Möst**. The history of the orchestra has included some controversy, especially regarding the time of the National Socialists before, during, and after World War II, and recently with the issue of membership of women and people of other ethnicities. They tune to an A=443 Hz, noticeably higher than the A=440 Hz used in the United States. Their website says that there is a waiting list of six years for weekday subscription concerts and thirteen years for weekend subscriptions.

Vienna Staatsoper. See **Vienna State Opera**.

Vienna State Opera (Wiener Staatsoper). Both an opera house and **opera** company, its music directors have included **Gustav Mahler**, Karl Böhm, **Herbert von Karajan, Lorin Maazel**, and **Franz Welser-Möst**. In recent years, the opera has begun to incorporate outreach programs. They constructed a large movie screen outside the opera house, where they broadcast occasional live performances, and have developed a program for teaching opera to children, as well as special productions designed for younger audiences.

Vienna Symphony (Wiener Symphoniker). Founded in 1900 as the Vienna Concert Society (Wiener Concertverein), the ensemble merged with the Tonkünstler Orchestra in 1919, and the current name was taken in 1933. The **orchestra** was temporarily suspended in 1944 but reestablished just a few years later. **Conductor** Josef Krips led the first postwar concert in 1945 with **Gustav Mahler**'s *Symphony No. 3*. The current conductor is Philippe Jordan (appointed in 2014). Previous conductors include the founding conductor, Ferdinand Löwe (1920–1925); **Wilhelm Furtwängler** (1920s and 1930s); Oswald Kabasta (1933–1940s); **Hans Swarowsky** (1945–1947); **Herbert von Karajan** (1948–1960); **Wolfgang Sawallisch** (1960–1970); **Josef Krips** (1970–1973); **Carlo**

Maria Giulini (1973–1976); **Gennady Rozhdestvensky** (1980–1982); George Prêtre (1986–1991); **Rafael Frühbeck de Burgos** (1991–1996); Vladimir Fedoseyev (1997–2005); and **Fabio Luisi** (2005–2013).

Vienna Volksoper. An **opera** house in Vienna that was built in 1989 primarily for plays; its first operatic production was Giuseppe Verdi's *Tosca* in 1907. In the late 1920s, the house began to specialize in light opera, but by the mid-1950s, in addition to **operettas** and musicals, it had become an alternative venue for opera. The Volksoper gives approximately three hundred performances each season, which currently also include ballet and children's programming.

Viennese School, First. See **First Viennese School (Wiener Schule)**.

Viennese School, Second. See **Second Viennese School (Zweite Weiner Schule)**.

viento. (Sp.) Wind. (Ger. *Wind*, It. *vento*, Fr. *vent*.)

vier. (Ger.) Four. Also *Vierteilig*, four-part; *Viertel*, quarter note; *Viertelpause*, quarter-note rest; *Viertelschlag*, conduct in four; *Vierundsechzigstel*, sixty-fourth note; and *Vierundsechzistelpause*, sixty-fourth-note rest. See also **appendix 7**.

vif, vivant. (Fr.) Quick, lively. (Ger. *lebhaft*, It. *vivo, vivace*, Sp. *vivo*.)

viola. The **alto** voice of the orchestral string instruments, its strings are tuned C3, G3, D4, A4, one **octave** above the **cello**. The standard range is from its low open C3 to D7. It is a standard member of the **orchestra** and **string quartet**. (Fr. *alto*, Ger. *Viola, Viole, Bratsche*. It. *viola*, Sp. *viola*.) See also **appendix 3**.

Viola range. *Courtesy Andrew Martin Smith.*

viola. (It., Sp.) **Viola**. (Fr. *alto*, Ger. *Bratsche*.)

violent. (Fr.) Violent, fierce. Seen in the score to the ballet *Jeux* by Claude Debussy.

violin. The highest of the orchestral string instruments, its strings are tuned to G3, D4, A4, E5, from bottom to top.

The normal range is from the low, open G to approximately B7. Standard **orchestras** and **string quartets** have both first and second violin sections, with the "firsts" generally playing higher and "seconds" lower. During the baroque period and earlier, the violin bow was convex. Since the late eighteenth century it has been concave in shape, resulting in increased tension and the capability to produce more sound. (Fr. *violon,* Ger. *Violone, Geige,* It. *violino,* Sp. *violín.*) See also **appendix 3**.

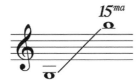

Violin range. *Courtesy Andrew Martin Smith.*

violino. (It.) **Violin.**

violón. (Sp.) **Double bass**. See also **appendix 3**.

violoncello or cello. Early in its history, the cello was the sole **bass** member of the **violin** family and was called the bass violin. During the eighteenth century, the desire for an extended lower range brought about the creation of another bass instrument. Known as the **double bass**, it plays an **octave** lower than the cello. As the two instruments were standardized, the bass was significantly larger in size, and the cello was smaller. In the eighteenth and nineteenth centuries, the technique of playing the cello, as well as the instrument itself, developed significantly. With its increased range and flexibility, it became capable of great virtuosity. Now also a solo instrument, the cello performs a wide variety of music, from **recitative** accompaniment to orchestral melodic lines and solo concertos. The cello is a standard member of the **orchestra** and any **string quartet**. Its strings are C2, G2, D3, A3, from bottom to top. Its standard "orchestral" range is from its low, open C2 up to A6. (Fr. *violoncelle,* Ger. *Violoncello,* It. *violoncello,* Sp. *violoncello.*) See also **appendix 3**.

Violoncello range. *Courtesy Andrew Martin Smith.*

Virginia Symphony Orchestra (VSO). Founded in 1920 as the Norfolk Symphony. In 1979, the **orchestra** reformed through mergers with the Peninsula Symphony Orchestra and the Virginia Beach Pops Symphony, taking on its current name. The orchestra presents a full range of classics, pops, and educational concerts, in addition to its PB&J Family series. Its current music director is **JoAnn Falletta**, appointed in 1991. Past music directors include Henry Cowles Whitehead (1934–1948), Edgar Schenkman (194801966), Russell Stanger (1966–1980), Richard Williams (1980–1986), and Winston Dan Vogel (1986–1990).

virtuoso. An exceptional or brilliant performer. (Fr. *virtuose,* Ger. *Virtuos,* It. *virtuoso,* Sp. *virtuoso.*)

vista. (It.) View, as in sight-reading. Example: *a prima vista* (lit. "at first sight"), sight-reading. See also *vom Blatt spielen, vom Blatt singen.*

vite, vitement. (Fr.) Quickly, fleet. A very quick tempo, faster than **allegro**. (Ger. *schnell* It. *presto,* Sp. *rápido.*) Example: *très vite,* very fast.

vivo. (It., Sp.) Lively, vivace. (Fr. *vif, vivant,* Ger. *lebhaft,* Sp. *vivo.*)

vla. Abbreviation for **viola**. See also **appendix 3**.

vlc., vcl., or vc. Abbreviation for **violoncello**, also known simply as cello. See also **appendix 3**.

vln. Abbreviation for **violin**. See also **appendix 3**.

vocal classifications. Called *Fach* or *Fächer* (pl.), in the German **opera** house system. These classifications are used to identify roles and the singers who sing them. In Germany, singers become known as specialists in a particular vocal classification. The list below is a compilation according to the classifications used in Germany (adapted from the website IPA Source).

Soprano, the highest female voice category is divided into the following types: soubrette (C4–C6), *Koloratursopra/Koloratur Soubrette* or lyric coloratura (C4–F6), dramatic coloratura (C4–F6), *Lyrischer-Sopran* or full lyirc soprano (C4–C6), *Jugenlischer-Dramatischersopran* or spinto soprano (C4–C6), *Charktorsopran* (B3–C6), *Dramarischer Sopran* or dramatic soprano (B4–C6), and *Hochdramatic Sopran* or Wagnerian soprano (G3–C6).

The coloratura category is also subdivided into types. They are lyric coloratura, **soprano leggero**, dramatic coloratura, and soprano acuto **sfogato**.

(Eng. Dramatic soprano, high dramatic soprano, Fr. *soprano dramatique,* Ger. *dramatisher Sopran, hochdramatischer Sopran, Soprano drammatico.*) (Eng. *coloratura soprano,* Fr. *soprano léger,* Ger. *Koloatursopran,* It. *soprano leggero,* Sp.) (Eng. *Lyric soprano,* Fr. *soprano lyrique,* Ger. *lyrischer Sopran,* It. *soprano lirico,* Sp.) (Eng. *Young dramatic soprano,* Fr. *soprano dramatique lyrique d'agilité,* Ger. *judendlich-dramatischer Sopran,* It. *soprano lirico spinto.*)

The mezzo-soprano (Fr. *mezzo-soprano,* Ger. *Mezzosopran,* It. *mezzosoprano*) is the middle female voice with a range from about the A below middle C to the A two **octaves** above. Subtypes include: *Lyrischer Mezzosopran* or lyric mezzo-soprano (g–b″), coloratura mezzo-soprano and *Dramatischer Mezzosopran* or dramatic mezzo-soprano I (g–b″), and *Dramatischer Alt* or dramatic mezzo II (g–b″).

The alto, or in German, the *Tiefer Alt* (f–a″), is the lowest female voice in Germany, lower than the mezzo.

The contralto is a designated vocal category in Italy. In Germany, it would be the alto (Fr. *alto,* Ger. *Alt, Altistin,* It. *contralto*). It is the lowest female voice, with a range from F below middle C to the second F above, and sometimes when a contralto is called for, the role will be sung by a mezzo-soprano.

The tenor is the highest male voice, and its types are classified as *Spieltenor/Tenorbuffo* or buffo tenor (c–b′); the *Lyrischer (Hoher) Tenor* or light lyric tenor (c–c″); *Italienischer Tenor* or; fully lyric tenor (c–c″); *Charaktertenor,* a crossover *Fach* (B–b′); *Jugendlicher heldentenor* or spinto tenor (c′–c″); and *Heldentenor* or dramatic tenor (B–b′)

It should be noted that the tenor voice is mostly notated in **treble clef** and sounds an octave lower than written. If written in **bass clef**, it sounds at **pitch.** (Eng. *heroic tenor,* Fr. *ténordramatique, tenor héroïque,* Ger. *Heldentenor,* It. *tenore draammatico, tenore eroico, tenore di forza,* Sp.) (Eng. *lyrical tenor,* Fr. *tenor lyrique,* Ger. *lyrischer Tenor,* It. *tenore lirico.*)

The baritone (Fr. *baryton,* Ger. *Bariton,* It. *baritone*) is the most common male voice, with a range between that of a tenor and a bass. Subcategories of the voice are *Lyischer (Hoher) Bariton/Spielbariton* or lyric baritone (B–g); Kavalierbariton, this term is used in both English and German (A–g sharp); dramatic baritone, *Chrakter-Bariton,* or Verdi baritone (A–a flat); and *Heldelbariton* or *Heldenbariton* (G–f sharp).

The bass is the lowest male voice, with the following subtypes: the *Speilbaß/Baßbuffo* or buffo-bass (E–f′), Schwerer Spielbaß or heavy buffo (C–f′), the *Carakterbaß/Baßbariton* or bass-baritone (E–f′), and *Seriösbaß/Schwarzerbaß* or basso cantabile (C–f′). (Eng. *basso buffo,* Fr. *basse bouffe,* Ger. *Bass-Buffo,* It. *basso buffo.*)

The male singer can also be a countertenor (Fr. *hautecontre,* Ger. *Kontratenor,* It. *contraltista, falsettista*) using the **falsetto** register to produce the tone. The range of this voice type is usually that of a contralto or mezzo-soprano.

voce. (It.) Voice. Example: *colla voce,* with the voice, used to indicate playing in an accompanimental, flexible manner.

voce di testa. (It.) Head voice. (Fr. *voix de tête,* Ger. *Kopfstimme,* Sp. *voz de cabeza.*)

Vogelstimme. (Ger.) Bird song. (Fr. *chant d'oiseau,* Sp. *canto de un pájaro.*)

voilée. (Fr.) Veiled, filmy. A character word used to describe a particular sound quality. (Ger. *verschleiert,* It. *velato,* Sp. *velado.*)

voix. (Fr.) Voice. (Ger. *Stimme,* It. *voce,* Sp. *voz.*)

voix de tête. (Fr.) Head voice. (Ger. *Kopfstimme,* It. *voce di testa,* Sp. *voz de cabeza.*)

volante. (It.) Flying, rushing. (Fr. *en Volant, Volant,* Ger. *fliegend,* Sp. *volando.*)

volé, dérobé, en dérobant. (Fr.) Robbed, in **rubato** style, to play with some freedom, to play it at an uneven tempo. (Ger. *ein wenig frei,* It. *rubato, rubando,* Sp. *rubato.*)

volentieri. (It.) Happily, willingly. (Ger. *gerne,* Sp. *con alegría, con gusto.*)

voll, mit vollem Ton. (Ger.) Full, loud. A descriptive term often used for dynamics or sound. (Fr. *plein, pleine,* It. *pieno,* Sp. *pleno.*)

volontiers. (Fr.) Happily, willingly. (Ger. *gerne,* It. *volentieri,* Sp. *con alegría.*)

volta. (It.) Time, occasion. Examples: *prima volta,* first time; *seconda volta,* second time (as in a repeated passage); *un'altra volta,* another time; *ultima volta,* the last time.

volta subito. (It.) An expression used to indicate "turn the page quickly," usually seen in string parts. Used most often in its Italian form. Abbreviated **V.S.** (Fr. *tournez aussitôt,* Ger. *sofort umblättern.*)

volteggiando. (It.) Crossing hands, as on a keyboard instrument.

volviendo al tempo. (Sp.) Returning to tempo. (Ger. *zum Zeitmaß zurückkehrend,* Fr. *en revenant au movement,* It. *tornando al tempo.*)

vom Blatt singen. (Ger.) To sing at sight, to sight-read. (Fr. *chanter á vue,* It. *cantare a prima vista,* Sp. *cantar a primera vista.*)

vom Blatt spielen. (Ger.) To play at sight, to sight-read. (Fr. *jouer à vue, déchiffrer,* It. *suonare a prima vista, a libro aperto,* Sp. *tocar a primera vista.*)

von hier. (Ger.) From here. Example: *von hier ab bis zum Zeichen unmerklich aber stetig breiter werden*, "from here to the sign becoming unnoticeably broader," from Symphony No. 1, movement one, by **Gustav Mahler**.

vor. (Ger.) Before. Commonly heard in **rehearsal** when telling the ensemble where to being playing. (Fr. *avant*, Ger. *vor*, It. *prim*, Sp. *antes*.) Example: *Vier vor Buchstabe D*, four before D.

vorergehend. (Ger.) Former, preceding. Also ***im Vorigen.*** (Fr. *précédent*, It. *precedente, anteriore*, Sp. *anterior*.) Example: *Im Vorigen Zeitmaß*, in the previous tempo.

vorher, vorhin. (Ger.) Before, beforehand, previously, earlier. Example: *wie vorhin*, as before, from *Symphony No. 1*, first movement, by **Gustav Mahler**.

Vorschlag. (Ger.) Grace note, appoggiatura. (Fr. *appoggiature*, It. *appoggiatura*, Sp. *apoyatura*.) Examples: *Vorschläge so schnell als möglich*, grace notes as fast as possible, from Symphony No. 5, mvt. 1, by **Gustav Mahler**; *Alle Vorschläge* vor *dem Taktteil und so schnell als möglich*, All grace notes before the beat and as fast as possible, from *Das Lied von der Erde*, by Mahler.

Vorspiel. (Ger.) Prelude, similar to an overture. (Fr. *prélude*, It., Sp. *preludio*.)

Vortrag. (Ger.) Interpretation, performance, but also lecture. Examples: *mit freiem Vortrag,* in a free style; *Immer bewegter im Vortrage*, Always played with forward motion, from *The Prelude to Die Meistersinger von Nürenberg*, by **Richard Wagner**.

vortragen. (Ger.) To perform, to execute. (Fr. *exécuter*, It. *esequire*, Sp. *ejecutar*.) Example: *sehr frei vorzutragen*, played very freely, from ***Pierrot Lunaire***, by **Arnold Schoenberg**.

vorwärts. (Ger.) Forward, moving forward. (Fr. *en avant, en avançant,* It. *avanti*, Sp. *adelante*.) Example: *Vorwärts drängend*, pushing forward, as seen in the symphonies of **Gustav Mahler**.

Vorzeichen. (Ger.) **Accidental** (Fr. *accident*, It. *accidente*, Sp. *accidente*) or key signature (Fr. *armure de la clé, armature*, It. *armature di chiave*, Sp. *armadura*). See also **Tonartvorzeichen.**

voz de cabeza. (Sp). Head voice. (Fr. *voix de tête*, Ger. *Kopfstimme*, It. *voce di testa*.)

V.S. (It.) Abbreviation for **volta subito**.

vuoto. (It.) Empty. (Fr. *vide*, Ger. *leer*.) Example: *corda vuota*, open string. See also **cuerda al aire**.

Waart, Edo de. (b. 1941.) Dutch **conductor**. De Waart is currently the music director of the **Milwaukee Symphony Orchestra** and the **Royal Flemish Philharmonic**, in addition to serving as an artistic partner with the **Saint Paul Chamber Orchestra**. He served as the conductor and then the music director of the Netherlands Wind Ensemble from 1967 to 1979. De Waart served as the music director of the **Minnesota Orchestra** (1986–1995), the **Netherlands Radio Philharmonic** (1989–2004), chief conductor and artistic adviser of the Sydney Symphony Orchestra (1993–1999), and chief conductor of the **Hong Kong Philharmonic Orchestra** (2004–2012). In 2012, he became the chief conductor of the **Royal Flemish Philharmonic**. De Waart has also conducted **opera** around the globe, including productions at the **Royal Opera House, Covent Garden**; **Bayreuth Festspielhaus**; **San Francisco Opera**; **Sante Fe Opera**; Paris' **Bastille Opéra**; the **Salzburg Festival**; and many others.

Wagner, Richard. (1813–1883.) German composer who developed the concept of *Gesamtkunstwerk*, the "total work of art," that combined elements of dance, music, and poetry with architecture, sculpture, and painting. His new ideal form of **opera**, he called them "music dramas," would be created to satisfy social and communal need and simultaneously be the "art of the future," while also bringing a return to classical Greek drama. Wagner was not only one of the great and most influential composers of the nineteenth century but also an active **conductor** and writer about **conducting** (and much more). The composer wrote on conducting in the essay "On Conducting" (*Über das Dirigieren*), published in Leipzig in 1869 and translated into English in 1887 (see the **bibliography**).

Wagner, Roger. (1914–1992.) French-born American choral **conductor**. His family immigrated to Los Angeles in 1921, where his studies included preparing for the priesthood. His father was an organist, and following in those footsteps, he became the organist at St. Ambrose Church in West Hollywood at the age of twelve. In 1931, Wagner returned to France to study with Marcel Dupré, served in the French army (1934–1936), and returned to Los Angeles in 1937 with a position as organist and choirmaster. In the 1940s, he studied conducting with **Bruno Walter** and composition with Lucien Caillet, and in 1946, he founded the Roger Wagner Chorale. The ensemble developed an enviable reputation through its many recordings, radio and television broadcasts, worldwide tours, and even film soundtracks. Wagner was known as a specialist in early music, receiving a PhD from Montreal University and becoming an expert in the music of Josquin des Prez. Wagner formed the Los Angeles Master Chorale as a resident ensemble of the new Los Angeles Music Center, along with the **Los Angeles Philharmonic** in 1964. He elicited great devotion from the many singers he worked with and promoted choral singing as an ideal form of social action, bringing together people of diverse backgrounds with the common purpose of elevating the human experience through ensemble singing. He taught at Marymount College (1951–1966), Pepperdine University, and the University of California (1959–1991). Wagner published numerous choral arrangements, received two honorary doctorates, and for his contributions to sacred music, was given a papal knighthood by Pope Paul VI in 1966.

Wagner tuba. Conceived and used by **Richard Wagner** in his **Ring cycle** operas, the **Wagner tuba** is shaped more like a **horn** and sounds more like it as well. The instrument also exists in different sizes and with different ranges so that a choir of them can play complete chords and chorale-like music. (Fr. *tuba Wagner, tuba tenor*, Ger, *Wagner-Tuba, Waldhorn-Tuba*, It., Sp. *tuba wagneriana*.) See also **appendix 3**.

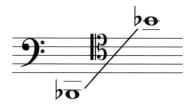

Wagner tuba range. *Courtesy Andrew Martin Smith.*

während. (Ger.) During, throughout. (Fr. *durant,* It. Sp. *durante.*)

Waldhorn, Horn. (Ger.) **French horn, horn.** (Fr. *cor,* It. *corno.*) See also **appendix 3.**

Walkman, Sony. Introduced in 1979, the first portable music player that used a compact cassette tape format and small-size earphones.

Walter, Bruno. (1876–1962.) German-born American **conductor** and composer. Born in Berlin, Walter made his first solo appearance as a pianist with the **Berlin Philharmonic Orchestra** in Ignaz Moscheles's *Piano Concerto in E-flat* at the age of thirteen. A devotee of the music of **Gustav Mahler,** Walter served as his assistant at the Vienna Hofoper from 1901 to 1912. He led a performance of his own Symphony No. 1 there in 1909. After Mahler's death in 1911, Walter conducted the premiere of *Das Lied von der Erde* and the Symphonies No. 8 and No. 9 in 1912, continuing to perform and promote his music throughout his life. He made his debut in London **conducting** Wagner's *Tristan und Isolde* in 1910 and Ethel Smyth's *The Wreckers,* both at the **Royal Opera House, Covent Garden.** Walter was **Felix Mottl**'s successor as the general music director at the **Munich Opera** (1913–1922, conducting Erich Wolfgang Korngold's *Violanta* and *Der Ring des Polykrates* (1916) and Han Pfitzner's *Palestrina* (1917). From 1919 to 1932 he regularly conducted the **Berlin Philharmonic Orchestra,** once sharing the podium with Ethel Smyth in a concert of his music (1928). The last position he held in Germany was as **Kapellmeister** at the **Leipzig Gewandhaus** (1929–1933). On the rise of the Nazis, Walter temporarily moved to Austria Traveling throughout Europe, he served as the artistic director of the **Vienna Staatsoper** from 1936 to 1938, making several highly regarded recordings with the **Vienna Philharmonic.** When Hitler entered Austria, Walter, who was Jewish, first moved to France and then to American, becoming an American citizen in 1946. His **Metropolitan Opera** debut was in 1941 when he led a notable *Fidelio.* He had a long and fruitful relationship with the **New York Philharmonic,** conducting many performances and several outstanding recordings (1941–1953).

Walter was known as a conductor who cared little about technique. It was said that any clarity came not from the stick but from a musicianship and concept that was so strong it simply took over. During his last years, he made several recordings with the **Columbia Symphony Orchestra,** including the late symphonies of Wolfgang Amadeus Mozart and the complete symphonies of both Johannes Brahms and Ludwig van Beethoven. On the occasion of a rehearsal for one of these recordings, the entire session was surreptitiously recorded. While Walter was initially disturbed that anyone would ever have access to such a working session, it was eventually released as *The Birth of a Performance* (see Holmes, below). Walter published an autobiography, *Theme and Variations,* in 1947 and a sequel, *Of Music and Musicians,* in 1957.

See Holmes, John L. *Conductors: A Record Collector's Guide.* Victor Gollancz, Ltd., 1988.

waltz. A dance in 3/4 meter with Austrian origins. (Fr. *valse,* Ger. *Walzer.* It. *valzer* Sp. *vals.*) Also Viennese waltz. (Fr. *valse viennoise,* Ger. *Wienerwaltzer,* It. *valzer viennese,* Sp. *vals vienés.*)

Walzer. (Ger.) **Waltz.** (Fr. *valse,* It. *valzer,* Sp. *vals.*)

Wand, Günther. (1912–2002.) German **conductor** and composer. Wand studied composition and piano at the Cologne conservatory and **conducting** in Munich. He was closely associated with the city of Cologne throughout his life, serving as a conductor at the **opera** from 1939 to 1944, when it was bombed, and returning as the music director after reconstruction in 1945. One year later, he became conductor of the Gurzenich Orchestra, the concert-giving branch of the Cologne Opera Orchestra, remaining in the position until 1974. As a young conductor, Wand was a proponent of the music of Olivier Messiaen, Edgard Varèse, Bernd Alois Zimmerman, György Ligeti, and others. But he is primarily remembered as an important interpreter of the symphonies of Anton Bruckner. Wand was appointed chief conductor of the **North German Radio Symphony Orchestra** in 1982, remaining as honorary conductor for life. In that position, he recorded Bruckner's Symphonies Nos. 3 to 9, cycles of the symphonies of both Ludwig van Beethoven and Johannes Brahms, and much more on the **Nonesuch, EMI** Angel, and **RCA** Red Seal labels. He served as the principal guest conductor of the **BBC Symphony Orchestra** (1980s) and was a regular guest conductor of the **Berlin Philharmonic Orchestra.** He made his American debut at the age of seventy-seven with the **Chicago Symphony Orchestra.** Wand was known for demanding and receiving considerable extra **rehearsal** time. Among his many awards were the **Diapason d'Or,** the German Recording Award, and the German Record Critic's Prize.

Warland, Dale. (b. 1932.) American choral **conductor** and founder and conductor of the Dale Warland Singers, Minneapolis. Warland studied at St. Olaf College, the University of Minnesota, and the University of Southern California. He spent two years in the U.S. Air Force, where he formed a choir of servicemen and was appointed director of choral activities at Macalester College, Saint Paul. He founded the Dale Warland Singers in 1972. An award-wining and widely traveled ensemble with a reputation for fine performances of contemporary choral music, the Dale Warland Singers have made several recordings, including the 1993 CD *Walden Pond*, which received a **Grammy** nomination. The ensemble was disbanded in 2004.

Wärme, mit. (Ger.) With warmth. A character word often heard in rehearsal to describe the tone or sound. (Fr. *avec chaleur*, It. *con calore*, Sp. *con calidez*.)

warm-ups. See **rehearsal warm-ups**.

Warner Music Group (WMG). Established in 1958 as Warner Bros. Records, the company holds three major recording subdivisions: Warner Bros., Parlophone Records, and Atlantic Records. The company also publishes sheet music under the Warner/Chappell name. It is one of the three largest music corporations worldwide along with **Sony Music Entertainment** and **Universal Music Group**.

Warsaw Conservatory. See **Frederic Chopin University of Music**.

Warsaw Philharmonic Orchestra (Orkiestra Filharmonii Narodowej w Warszawie). Established in 1901. Up to the outbreak of World War II, the **orchestra** hosted some of Europe's most distinguished musicians. Since 1927, the orchestra has organized and performed at the Chopin International Piano Competition. During WWII, the ensemble lost nearly half of its members on the battlefield, in addition its concert hall was destroyed in a bombing raid and was not rebuilt until 1955. After the war, **conductor** Witold Rowicki (1950–1955, 1958–1977) led the modernization of the orchestra with performances of living Polish composers such as Henryk Górecki and Witold Lutosławski. The orchestra also performs annually at the Warsaw Autumn International Festival of Contemporary Music and has toured widely across the globe. The current principal conductor is Jacek Kaspszyk (appointed in 2013). Past conductors have included Antoni Wit (2002–2013), Kazimierz Kord (1977–2001), Stanisław Wisłocki (1961–1967), Bohdan Wodiczko (1955–1958), Władysław Raczkowski (1949–1950), Witold Rudziński (1948–1949), Jan Maklakiewicz (1947–1948), Andrzej Panufnik (1946–1947),

Olgierd Straszynski (1945–1946), Józef Oziminski (1938–1939), Roman Chojhacki (1918–1938), and others. The orchestra offers a full season of symphonic and chamber concerts, programming for young people, **open rehearsals**, and other outreach initiatives.

Warten, bitte* or *Warten Sie, bitte. (Ger.) Wait, one moment, please. A directive often heard in **rehearsal**. (Fr. *Attendez s'il vous plait*, It. *Attendere, prego*, Sp. *Esperar, por favor.*)

Waterloo-Cedar Falls Symphony. Founded in 1929 in Waterloo, Iowa, by G. T. Bennett, director of the East Waterloo High School Orchestra, and called the Waterloo Symphony Orchestra. The orchestra performs a wide variety of classics, pops, young people's, and educational concerts, in addition to outreach events, a Young Artist Concerto Competition and a Conducting Fellowship. The current **conductor**, Jason Weinberg was appointed in 2002 and serves as artistic director and CEO. Past music directors include Edward Kurtz (1931–1935), Beorge Dasch (1935–1944), Neanette Sheerer (1944–1947), Otto Jelinek (91947–1955), Matys Abas (1955–1958), Myron Russell (1958–1971), Joseph Guinta (1974–1992), and Elizabeth Schulze (1994–1997).

wa-wa mute. Also known as the Harmon mute. See also **brass mutes**.

W.B. Abbreviation for "whole bow," commonly used as an indication to for string players to use the whole bow.

We are not together! A commonly heard directive. (Fr. *Nous ne sommes pas ensemble*, Ger. *Wir sind nicht zusammen*, It. *Non siamo insieme*, Sp. *No estamos juntos.*)

Weber, Carl Maria von. (1786–1826.) Composer, **conductor**, pianist, and critic. A child prodigy, Weber spent his early years with his father's traveling theater company. While his early first **opera**, *Die Macht de Liebe* (The Power of Love), has been lost, his second, *Das Waldmädchen* (The Forest Maiden), was premiered in 1800. Weber became **Kapellmeister** in Breslau in 1804, where the first opera he conducted was *La clemenza di Tito* of Wolfgang Amadeus Mozart. He already had a reformer's bent, changing the seating of the **orchestra** in the pit and imposing stricter discipline at **rehearsals**. With a lot of resistance to these changes, the position only lasted a few years, and Weber left to spend more time composing and touring. His next position came in 1813 when he was appointed **Kapellmeister** at the Estates Theater in Prague. But he spent the bulk of his career in Dresden, where he created and directed the German-language Royal Opera.

Weber's masterpiece, *Der Freischütz*, was premiered in Berlin in 1821, establishing him as one of the great opera composers of his day. His next opera, *Euryanthe*, was performed for the first time in Vienna in 1823, and in 1826, *Oberon* was premiered in London. Weber conducted the initial performances of all of his operas and those of many other composers of the time, including works of Luigi Cherubini, **Louis Spohr**, Gaspare Spontini, Ludwig van Beethoven, and others. He had an enormous influence on the composers who followed him, drawing admiration all the way to Claude Debussy, who admired his use of orchestral color. As a frequent cultural and musical critic and a great reformer of opera through his own compositions, Weber is recognized as having set the ground rules for nineteenth-century German opera. As a conductor, Weber was known for excellent results and high standards with his orchestras. He was a baton conductor and an early proponent of tempo flexibility that allowed for a greater expression and passion in performance. He regularly battled other opera directors who appropriated his music and staged it under new titles or added it to other operas, setting precedents for the establishment of laws protecting intellectual property that would come later in the century.

Carl Maria von Weber, illustrated conducting at Covent Garden Theatre, 1826.

websites. Created by individual **orchestras** to promote interest. The content varies widely from simply providing information about upcoming concerts to orchestra archives with historical information, photo galleries, and biographical information about the music director and the musicians of the orchestra, a composer-in-residence, artist-in-residence, festivals, staff, board members, and so on. They may contain available podcast subscriptions, publicity for weekly radio broadcasts, video features, and access to Internet shops where souvenirs are sold. Access for donations is often seen. Sites also allow individuals to share material they enjoy with their friends via Twitter, Facebook, YouTube, or other social media.

wechsel, wechselnd. (Ger.) Change, changing. (Fr. *en changeant*, It. *cambiando, cangiando, mutando*, Sp. *cambio*.)

wechseln. (Ger.) To change, as when a player is asked to change an instrument in the course of a piece or **movement**. (Fr. *changer*, It. *cambiare*, Sp. *cambiar*.)

Wechselnote, Wechselton. (Ger.) Changing note. (Fr. *cambiata, note changée*, It. *nota cambiata*, Sp. *cambiano nota*.)

weg. (Ger.) Away, off. Also *wegnehmen*, to take away, to remove. (Fr. *enlever, lever*, ôter, Sp. *quitar*.) Example: *Dämpfer weg*, **mute** off.

wehmütig. (Ger.) Lugubrious, melancholy. (Fr. *nostalgique*, It. *malinconico*, Sp. *melancólico*.)

weich. (Ger.) Soft, tender. (Fr. *doux*, It. *dolce*, Sp. *dulce*.) Example: *sehr weich gesungen*, played, or sung, very softly, from Symphony No. 1, first movement, by **Gustav Mahler**.

weinend. (Ger.) Plaintive, crying. (Fr. *en pleurs*, It. *piangendo, lacrimando*, Sp. *llorando*.)

Weingartner, Felix. (1863–1942.) Austrian **conductor**, composer, pianist, and author. He studied philosophy at Leipzig University and music at Leipzig Conservatory (1881–1883) and was a pupil of **Franz Liszt** in Weimar (1884). Weingartner held several positions as conductor in German **opera** houses, including Hamburg (1887–1889) and again as guest conductor (1912–1914) and Mannheim (1889–1891). He was the court **Kapellmeister** in Berlin (1891–1898), succeeded **Gustav Mahler** at the Vienna Hofoper (1907–1911), was principal conductor at Darmstadt (1914–1919), director of the Vienna Volksoper (1919–1924), and was a guest conductor of the Boston Opera Company (1912–1913). His orchestral positions included Munich (1898–1905); the **Vienna Philharmonic Orchestra**, with whom he toured South America twice (1907–1927); and Basle (1927–1933). He served as the director of the Basle Conservatory from 1927 to 1935 and was the director of the **Vienna Opera** (1935–1936). His **Royal Opera House, Covent Garden**, debut was in 1939, when he led *Parsifal*. Weingartner was a guest conductor with the **New York Philharmonic Society** (1905–1908) and was the composer of seven symphonies, several operas, concertos, choral works, five **string quartets**, and more. A prolific writer and editor, his essays included "On Conducting" and "On the Performance of Beethoven's Symphonies," in which he discusses the benefits of reorchestration. He is known to have retracted the advice later in life. Weingartner was recognized as a conductor of great clarity and economy, with flexibility in his tempos. He is one of the first major conductors to leave a legacy of recordings that provides a fascinating documentation of ideas of interpretation of the time. Made initially between 1910–1914 and 1923–1925, the works included the complete symphonies of Ludwig van Beethoven and Johannes Brahms, a selection of Mozart symphonies, works of Johann Sebastian Bach, George Frideric Handel, **Hector Berlioz**, **Felix Mendelssohn**, Franz Liszt, and **Richard Wagner**. The early recordings were all redone when electronic recording technology was introduced in 1925. In 1932, he also made a film version of a performance of Carl Maria von Weber's overture to *Freischütz*. See the **bibliography**.

Weisberg, Arthur. (1931–2009.) American bassoonist, **conductor**, composer, and author. Born in New York, Weisberg studied **bassoon** at the **Juilliard School** and **conducting** with **Jean Morel**. He was a principal bassoonist with the Houston and Baltimore symphonies and second bassoon with the **Cleveland Symphony Orchestra**. He returned to New York and spent fourteen years as the bassoonist of the New York Woodwind Quintet. As a conductor, he was known as a champion of contemporary music. Weisberg was the founding conductor of the **Contemporary Chamber Ensemble** (1961). The influential ensemble toured the United States and the world, giving over one hundred premieres and making numerous recordings, including works of **Arnold Schoenberg**, Edgard Varèse, Olivier Messiaen, Elliott Carter, Stefan Wolpe, and others, primarily on the **Nonesuch** label. Weisberg also conducted the Orchestra of the 20th Century and Ensemble 21 and appeared with the **Milwaukee Symphony Orchestra** and the **New York Philharmonic**, with whom he recorded George Crumb's *A Haunted Landscape*, in addition to the Sjaelands and Aalborg orchestras in Denmark. Weisberg is the author of *The Art of Wind Playing* and *Performing 20ᵗʰ-Century Music: A Handbook for Conductors and Instrumentalists*. He taught at the **Juilliard School**, the State University of New York at Stony Brook, and Yale University.

Weise. (Ger.) Tune, melody, or in the manner of. (Fr. *á la manière de*, It. *nel modo di*.)

weiter. (Ger.) Far, further, onward. Example: *In sehr weiter Entferung aufgestellt*, placed very much in the distance, meaning that the player should be far offstage when playing the passage, from *Symphony No. 1, movement one*, by **Gustav Mahler**.

welche. (Ger.) Which. (Fr. *qui*, It. *che*, Sp. *que*.)

Welser-Möst, Franz. (b. 1960.) Austrian **conductor** who is the current music director of the **Cleveland Orchestra** and the **Vienna State Opera**. Welser-Möst served as the principal conductor of the Austrian Youth Orchestra (1979–1985). He made his debut at the **Salzburg Festival** in 1985 with the **Mozarteum Orchestra**, his British debut with the **London Philharmonic** in 1986, his opera debut in Vienna in 1987, and his American debut in 1989 with the **St. Louis Symphony Orchestra**. He served as he principal conductor of the **London Philharmonic** (1990–1996), music director of the **Zurich Opera** (1995–2000), and general music director in Zurich in 2005. He stepped down from the position upon his appointment in Vienna. Welser-Möst signed an exclusive recording contract with **EMI** during his tenure with the London Philharmonic, recording Franz Schmidt's Symphony No. 4, a CD that won the **Gramophone Award** for best orchestral conducting. He has also recorded both Anton Bruckner's Mass No. 3 and the *Te Deum* and works of Erich Korngold and has since recorded both with the Zurich Opera and the Cleveland Orchestra. Many performances have also been released on DVD.

wenig, ein. (Ger.) A little, somewhat. (Fr. *un peu*, It. *un poco*, Sp. *un poco*.) Example: *Ein wenig rallent*, a little slowing or ritardando, from the prelude to *Die Meistersinger von Nürenberg* by **Richard Wagner**.

weniger. (Ger.) Less, slower. (It. *meno*, Fr. *moins*, Sp. *menos*.)

werden. (Ger.) To become. (Fr. *devenir*, It. *diventare*.) Used commonly in phrases such as *es muss heir leiser werden*, it has to get softer here.

West-Eastern Divan Orchestra. Founded by **conductor Daniel Barenboim** and Edward Said in 1999 to promote understanding between Israelis and Palestinians. In addition, it brings together young musicians from Israel and several Arab countries, including Egypt, Iran, Jordan, Lebanon, Syria, and others. Currently based in Seville, Spain, and supported by the Andalusian government, it also attracts many young Spanish musicians. The **orchestra** meets annually, studying and rehearsing with Barenboim, and then makes an international concert tour. The orchestra has released several CDs and DVDs with Warner Music. They have performed in venues from Berlin to Istanbul and Paris to Ramallah. They were awarded the Echo Klassik Award in 2006 for the best DVD production of the year. In 2012, Barenboim founded the Barenboim-Said Academy in Berlin. The academy will train young musicians from the Middle East in the study of music and the liberal arts, with a focus on music and intellectual history, for a two-year period. The new academy will have a new concert hall designed by Frank Gehry.

Westminster Choir College. Founded by John Finley Williamson in 1920 at the Westminster Presbyterian Church in Dayton, Ohio, and followed by the founding of the college in 1926. In 1929, they moved to Ithaca College and in 1932 to Princeton, New Jersey, where they remained. The college offers a four-year undergraduate and graduate school music curriculum. The college merged with Rider College in 1992. Notable historic events include a 1934 tour to the former Soviet Union, where they broadcast a concert back to the United States. In 1939, they began their association with the **New York Philharmonic**. In 1957, they made a five-month worldwide tour on behalf of the U.S. State Department. The **choir** has continued to perform and record throughout its history, releasing standard masterpieces and introducing works of some of America's most important composers. American **conductor Joseph Flummerfelt** served as the artistic director and principal conductor for thirty-three years, retiring in 2004.

West Virginia Symphony Orchestra. The **orchestra**'s origins go back to 1939 in Charleson, West Virginia, when an inaugural concert was performed with an orchestra of fifty-five under the baton of conductor William R. Wiant. During its first years, the orchestra already gave a variety of concerts, including children's and pops concerts, **opera**, and ballet. During World War II, the orchestra partnered with local businesses, in particular Union Carbide, to bring musicians to the area. The companies searched for employees who were also musically talented enough to play in the orchestra. The orchestra's first general manager was **Helen Thompson**, who also came to national fame through her work founding the American Symphony Orchestra League (see **League of American Orchestras**). The orchestra's current music director is Grant Cooper. Past music directors include Antonio Modarelli (1942–1954), Geoffrey Hobday (1954–1964), Charles Gabor (1964–1965), Charles Schiff (1965–1977), Ron Dishinger (1977–1979), Sidney Rothstein (1980–1984), and Thomas Conlon (1984–2001).

whip. An instrument in the **percussion** section made of two connected pieces that are clapped together. Also called a slapstick. See also **appendix 4**.

Whispa mute. See **brass mutes**.

whistle. (Fr.) *chalumeau, pipeau,* (Ger.) *Hirtenpfeife,* (It.) *zufolo,* (Sp.) *pito.*

Whitacre, Eric. (b. 1970.) American composer and **conductor**. Whitacre received a BA in music education at the University of Nevada, Las Vegas, and a master's in composition at the **Juilliard School**, where he studied with **John Corigliano** and David Diamond. In 2008, his choral CD *Cloudburst* was recorded with the British

vocal ensemble Polyphony and earned a **Grammy** nomination. Whitacre signed an exclusive contract with **Decca** in 2010, and two years later won a Grammy for his first CD as both composer and conductor, *Light & Gold*. Whitacre has composed for the **London Symphony Orchestra** and Chorus, Chanticleer, Julian Lloyd Weber, the **Philharmonic Orchestra**, Rundfunkchor Berlin, the King's Singers, and others. Among his many projects, Whitacre has been responsible for several virtual choir projects where he brings together individual singers from around the world via the Internet to virtual choirs.

White Nights Festival. An international summer festival in St. Petersburg, Russia. The current music director and artistic director is **Valery Gergiev**.

white noise. A nonpitched, electronic sound somewhat like a hiss or rushing air consisting of a random distribution of all audible frequencies at varying but equal intensities.

white tone. A tone without **vibrato**; a passage or single **pitch** to be played without vibrato. **Aaron Copland** called for it specifically in the **clarinet** part at the opening and closing of *Appalachian Spring* (see **appendix 1**).

whole tone. An interval between two **pitches** that is made up of two half steps. See also **whole tone scale**.

whole tone scale. A perfectly symmetrical **scale** built on a sequence of six whole tones to the **octave**. Without half steps, the scale lacks any association with tonal function. In Western music, it exists in only two versions, C D E F-sharp G-sharp A-sharp and C-sharp D-sharp F G A B, or the enharmonic equivalents. Claude Debussy incorporated the scale in his *Preludes* for piano, as did the Russian Mikhail Glinka in his overture *Ruslan and Ludmilla*, as well as **Franz Liszt**, Eric Satie, and others.

wie. (Ger.) Like, as, in the manner of. (Fr. *comme,* It. *come,* Sp. *como.*) Examples: *wie vorher,* as before; *wie früher,* as earlier; *wie möglich,* as possible; *so schnell wie möglich,* as fast as possible; *wie ein Naturlaut,* like a sound of nature, all from Symphony No. 1, opening of *mvt. 1,* by **Gustav Mahler**.

wieder. (Ger.) Again, afresh. (Fr. *encore, de nouveau,* It. *di nuove, ancora,* Sp. *nuevamente, de nuevo.*) Examples: *wieder langsam,* slowly again (lit. again slowly); *wieder wie am Anfang,* again, like the beginning; *Wieder Halbe schlagen!* Again, beat in 2!; *wieder etwas bewegter* or *wie im Anfang,* again somewhat moving or as in the beginning; *wieder wie früher,* again as before, all from *Verklärte Nacht* by **Arnold Schoenberg**.

wiederholen, wiederholung. (Ger.) To repeat, a repeat, repetition. (Fr. *répétition, reprise,* It. *ripetizione, ripresa,* Sp. *repetición.*)

Wiederholungszeichen. (Ger.) **Repeat sign.** (Fr. *signe de répétition,* It. *segno di ripetizione,* Sp. *signo de repetición.*)

Wiegenlied. (Ger.) Lullaby, cradlesong. (Fr. *berceuse,* It. *ninna nanna,* Sp. *canción de cuna, nana.*)

wie geschrieben, wie notiert. (Ger.) As written, as notated. (Fr. *tel quel,* It. *come scritto, come stá,* Sp. *como esricto.*)

Wienerwaltzer. (Ger.) A Viennese **waltz.** (Fr. *valse viennoise,* It. *valzer viennese,* Sp. *vals vienés.*)

wild, wildheit. (Ger.) Wild, ferocious. (Fr. *féroce, sauvage,* It. *feroce,* Sp. *feroz.*) Example: *Mit grosser Wildheit,* with great ferocity, from *Symphony No. 1, movement four,* by **Gustav Mahler.**

Willcocks, Sir David. (b. 1919.) English choral **conductor,** organist, and composer. He studied as a boy chorister at Westminster Abbey (1929–1934) and then at Clifton College (1934–1938), where he became the organ scholar at King's College, Cambridge. Willcocks served in the British Army in World War II, returning to complete his studies when he was elected a fellow of King's College and made conductor of the Cambridge Philharmonic Society. Several notable positions followed at such distinguished institutions as Salisbury and Worchester Cathedrals, principal conductor of the Three Choirs Festival (1951, 1954, and 1957), and more. From 1957 to 1974 he was director of music at his alma mater, King's College, Cambridge. In that position, he led numerous performances of **Sir Benjamin Britten**'s *War Requiem,* touring widely with his ensemble, the Cambridge University Musical Society. In 1960, he became the musical director of the Bach Choir in London. Willcocks served as director of the **Royal College of Music, London,** from 1974 to 1984.

Wilkins, Christopher. (b. 1957.) American **conductor.** Wilkins has been the music director of the **Akron Symphony Orchestra** since 2006, the Orlando Philharmonic, and the Boston Landmarks Orchestra, a summer orchestra. He has appeared as a guest conductor with the orchestras of Boston, Buffalo, Chicago, Cincinnati, Detroit, Houston, Indianapolis, Los Angeles, Pittsburgh, and San Francisco. In 1992, he was awarded the **Seaver/National Endowment for the Arts Conductors Award.** He has been the associate conductor of the **Utah Symphony** and the assistant conductor of the **Cleveland Symphony Orchestra** and the Oregon Symphony.

Wilson, Antonia Joy. Educated at the St. Louis Conservatory of Music and the University of Southern California,

Wilson received the bachelor's and doctoral degrees at the University of Denver and also studied conducting at Yale University. She is currently the conductor for the Shen Yun Performing Arts Organization International Orchestra. Wilson has led orchestras throughout North and South America, Europe, and the Far East. She was artistic director for the Midland Orchestra (2008–2011); principal guest conductor for the Bulgarian National Radio Orchestra (2001–2003); conductor of the Imperial Symphony Orchestra, Florida (1998–2001); the Jefferson Symphony, Colorado (1994–1999); and the Livingston Symphony, New Jersey (1990–1994). In 1981–1982 she served as **Exxon Affiliate Artist Assistant Conductor** of the **St. Louis Symphony.**

Wilson, Keri-Lynn. (b. 1967.) Canadian **conductor.** Wilson studied at the **Juilliard School** when she graduated with a bachelor's and two master's degrees, one in **flute** and one in **conducting.** She was the associate conductor of the **Dallas Symphony** (1994–1998) and became the chief conductor of the Slovenian Philharmonic Orchestra in 2013. A frequent guest conductor, Wilson has conducted opera throughout Europe, including Stockholm, Zurich, Salerno, Warsaw, the **Vienna State Opera,** the **Bavarian State Opera, Munich,** and many more. She has led orchestras in Paris, Munich, Aachen, Leipzig, Moscow, St. Petersburg, Madrid, Jerusalem, Hong Kong, Los Angeles, Montreal, Toronto, Houston, and more. She released a recording of Latin American music with the **Simon Bolivar Symphony Orchestra** on Dorian Records.

Wind. (Ger.) Wind. (Fr. *vent,* It. *vento,* Sp. *viento.*)

wind chimes. All wind chimes are constructed in the same manner: pieces of wood (often bamboo), glass, or metal are suspended from a small brace. The sound is produced by jangling or stroking the suspended pieces. Each type creates its own sound. See also **appendix 4.**

wind ensemble. An ensemble of wind soloists, that is, one player on a part, based on the model of the woodwind section of an **orchestra.** American **conductor Frederick Fennell** founded the first wind ensemble, the **Eastman Wind Ensemble,** in 1952. He spent the next several decades developing a repertoire for his ensemble, successfully commissioning many of the most distinguished composers of his day. Its great success led to the founding of over twenty thousand such groups across America and the world.

wind machine. An instrument included in the **percussion** section that is constructed to simulate the sound of rushing wind. Used in **Richard Strauss**'s *Don Quixote* and *Alpine Symphony,* Maurice Ravel's *Daphnis et Chloe,* and Ralph Vaughan Williams's *Sinfonia Antartica*, among others. (Fr. *machine á vent*, Ger. *Windmaschine*, It. *eolifono*, Sp. *maquina de viento*.) See also **appendix 4**.

wind symphony. See **band**.

winds. The woodwind instruments of the **orchestra** or **band**. (Fr. *instruments à vent, les bois*, Ger. *Blasinstrumente*, It. *strumenti a fiato, i legni*, Sp. *instrumentos de viento*.) See also **woodwind instruments**.

Winkel, Dietrich Nikolaus. (c. 1776–1826.) Dutch inventor of a **metronome** that had a double-ended pendulum. **Johann Nepomuk Maelzel** apparently appropriated certain aspects of Winkel's metronome and used them for his own.

Wirbel. (Ger.) A tuning peg of a string instrument. (Fr. *cheville*, It. *bischero, pirolo*, Sp. *clavija*.) Also *Wirbelkasten*, pegbox; *Wirbeltrommel*, **snare drum**.

Wittry, Diane. American **conductor**, composer, and author. Wittry is currently the music director of the Allentown Symphony Orchestra (since 1995). She has served as the music director of the Norwalk Symphony and the Symphony of Southeast Texas and as the artistic director of the Ridgewood Symphony. She studied **conducting** with **Daniel Lewis** at the University of Southern California, where she was named "Outstanding Alumnus" in 2013. Wittry received the **League of American Orchestras'** Helen M. Thompson Award for outstanding artistic leadership of a regional orchestra and has served as a national conducting mentor for other music directors of regional orchestras in their first or second year. She published *Beyond the Baton*, a book about artistic leadership for young conductors in 2007 and now leads an annual iInternational conducting workshop based on elements of the book (see the **bibliography**). Wittry has served as a guest conductor throughout North America, Japan, and Europe.

wogend. (Ger., lit. "undulating.") A bow stroke in which the bow alternates between two adjacent strings in the same direction. There can be as few as two **notes** alternating or several, and it can be done between two different "versions" of the same **pitch**, say an open string and a stopped or fingered "version" of the same note, thus creating a specific coloring effect. (Fr. *ondulé*, It. *ondeggiando*, Sp. *ondulante*.)

Wolff, Hugh. (b. 1953.) American **conductor**. Wolff served as the music director of the **New Jersey Symphony Orchestra** (1986–1993) and principal conductor of the **Saint Paul Chamber Orchestra** (1988–1992), as well as its music director (1992–2000). He was the principal conductor of the Grant Park Music Festival (1994–1997) and the chief conductor of the Frankfurt Radio Symphony Orchestra (1997–2006). He received the **Seaver/ National Endowment for the Arts Conductors Award** in 1985. Wolff has guest conducted many of the world's major **orchestras**, including the **symphony** orchestras of Boston, Chicago, Cleveland, New York, Philadelphia, San Francisco, and many more. Currently he is the director of orchestral activities and **conducting** teacher at the **New England Conservatory of Music**, Boston.

women's orchestras in the United States. Founded to satisfy the desires of women to play in **orchestras** at a time they were denied entry into established ensembles, they often, but not always had men as **conductors**. The Fadette Women's Orchestra of Boston, founded in 1888 and conducted by Caroline B. Nichols, provided employment for its all-female members. Others included the Los Angeles Woman's Symphony Orchestra, which ran from 1939 to 1961 and was conducted by Ruth Haroldson; the Long Beach Women's Symphony Orchestra (1925–1948) under the direction of Eva Anderson; the Cleveland Women's Symphony Orchestra, founded in 1935 and still active in 1985; the Woman's Symphony Orchestra of Chicago (1929–1938) with Ebba Sundstrom and Gladys Welge; the Chicago Woman's Symphony Orchestra (1924–1928) under Elena Moneak; the Philadelphia Women's Symphony Orchestra (1921–1952); and many more. Most were short lived.

See Ammer, Christine. *Unsung: A History of Women in American Music*. Greenwood Press, 1980. Bowers, Jane, and Judith Tick, eds. *Women Making Music, The Western Art Tradition, 1150–1950*. Jagow, Shelley M. *Women Orchestral Conductors in America: The Struggle for Acceptance—an Historical View from the Nineteenth Century to the Present*. College Music Symposium, Vol. 38 (1988), pp. 126–145.

Women's Philharmonic. Originally known as the Bay Area Women's Philharmonic, it was founded in San Francisco in 1981 by Elizabeth Seja Min (music director, 1981–1985), Nan Washburn (artistic director and associate conductor, 1981–1990), and Miriam Abrams. Other music directors were **JoAnn Falletta** (1986–1997) and **Apo Hsu** (1997–2003). The repertoire of the **orchestra** was exclusively made up of works by women composers, both historic and contemporary. Known as an important organization in its time, the orchestra made over 130 premiers, 40 commissions, and several recordings. The orchestra disbanded in 2004.

womöglich, wo möglich. (Ger.) If possible, when possible. An expression used in rehearsal in a wide variety of phrases. (Fr. *peut-être meme que*, It. *possibimente*, Sp. *a lo major*.)

wood blocks. A member of the **percussion** section, sometimes called the Chinese block or **temple block**. Noted use in the *Hoe-Down* from *Rodeo* by **Aaron Copland**. (Fr. *templeblock, wood bloc, bloc de bois*, Ger. *Tempelblock, Woodblock, Holzblock*, It. *block cinese, testi di morto, wood block*, Sp. *caja china*.) See also **appendix 4**.

Wood, Sir Henry. (1869–1944.) English **conductor**. Founded the **Promenade Concerts** at the Queen's Hall in 1895 at the behest of the hall's manager, Robert Newman. The Queen's Hall was destroyed in a German air raid in 1941 and the series of concerts moved to the Royal Albert Hall, where it has developed into one of the most extensive summer festivals in the world and remains to this day.

woodwind instruments. (Fr.) *les bois*, (Ger.) *Holzblasinstrumente*, (It.) *strumenti a fiato di legno, i legni*, (Sp.) *instrumentos de madera*. See **winds**.

woodwinds. The section of the **orchestra** including **flutes, oboes, clarinets, bassoons**, and **horns** (although the horns are also referred to as members of the brass section).

Worby, Rachael. (b. 1950.) American **conductor** and former First Lady of West Virginia. Worby studied **conducting** privately with **Otto Werner-Mueller** and **Max Rudolf** and attended Indiana University, Brandeis, and the Crane School of Music at SUNY-Potsdam. She served as the music director of the Symphony Orchestra in Wheeling, West Virginia (1986–2003). Worby is the artistic director and conductor of MUSE/IQUE in Pasadena, California, and the music director of the American Music Festival in Romania. She served as the conductor of the Pasadena Pops (2000–2010), and has guest conducted across North America, Europe, Australia, and Asia. Early in her career she was the **EXXON/Arts Endowment Assistant Conductor** for the Spokane Symphony.

works for multiple conductors. See **multiple conductor works**.

works for multiple orchestras. See **multiple orchestra works**.

World Association of Symphonic Bands and Ensembles (WASBE). Founded in Manchester, England, in 1981. An international organization of symphonic wind orchestras and wind symphonies with more than 1,200 members from over 50 countries. WASBE supports the development of repertoire for their ensembles and has conferences every two years. It also publishes a journal in cooperation with the Institute for Band Research at the University of Music in Graz, Austria.

world premiere. The first performance of a piece of music. (Fr. *première execution mondiale*, Ger. *Uraufführung*, It. *prima esecuzione mondiale*, Sp. *estreno mundial*.)

World Youth Symphony Orchestra (WYSO). The top **orchestra** of the **Interlochen Arts Camp** that runs every summer, attracting talented high school–aged young people from around the globe. Often called WYSO, the orchestra performed at the Summer Olympics in Atlanta, Georgia, in 1996.

Wort. (Ger.) Word. (Fr. *parole*, It. *parola*, Sp. *palabra*.)

WQXR, 105.9 FM. Wqxr.org, "The Radio Station of the **New York Philharmonic**." See also **radio, radio orchestras, classical music radio stations**.

wrist motion and flexibility. The motion in the wrist of the **baton** or **conducting** hand. Flexibility in the wrist helps create nuance in the gesture as amplified in the tip of the baton. For example, a quick flick in the wrist will create a nice light **staccato** gesture, while a smooth wrist motion can facilitate a good **legato**. Any combination of the two may be used to show a combination of **slurs** and staccatos that occur in music. See also **basic conducting patterns for musical styles, conducting technique, legato style**.

wrong note harmonization. The use of chords that deliberately sound wrong in the context of a given piece. Used in order to create a sense of parody or humor. For example, Wolfgang Amadeus Mozart's *The Musical Joke* and Dmitri Shostakovich's *Polka* from *The Golden Age* (1930).

wuchtig, wuchtiger. (Ger.) Powerful, more powerful. As seen in the *Symphony No. 2, movements one and five*, by **Gustav Mahler**. Example: *immer wuchtig*, always powerful; *a tempo subito, aber wuchtiger*, suddenly a tempo, but stronger (or more powerful); *etwas wuchtiger*, somewhat more powerful.

wunderbar. (Ger.) Wonderful, marvelous. (Fr. *magnifique, merveilleux*, It. *meraviglioso*, Sp. *maravilloso*.)

würdig, würdevoll. (Ger.) Dignified. A character word. (Fr. *digne*, It. *degno*, Sp. *digno*.)

wütend. (Ger.) Raging, furious. A character word, seen most often in its German form. (Fr. *enragé, rageur*, It. *arrabiato*, Sp. *furioso*.)

Wyoming Symphony Orchestra. The **orchestra**, based in Casper, Wyoming, gives six concerts annually, including a classics series, a holiday concert, and a gala fundraising concert. The orchestra's current music director is Mathew Savery, appointed in 2008. Savery has introduced an outreach program titled Music on the Move, which serves to bring chamber music to organizations throughout the region without charge.

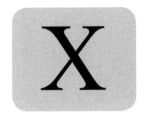

Xbox. See **Philharmonia Orchestra**.

Xenakis, Yannis. (1922–2001.) Romanian-born French **avant garde** composer born to Greek parents. In addition to composition, Xenakis worked as an architect, assisting French architect Le Corbusier in the design of the Philips Pavilion at the 1958 Brussels World's Fair in which **Edgard Varèse**'s purely electronic *Poème électronique*, performed with multiple speakers on the ceiling of the pavilion, was premiered. Zenakis wrote many elector-acoustic works; visited Japan, where he was influenced by Asian music; taught at Indiana University (1967–1972); and was a visiting professor at the Sorbonne (1973–1989).

Xiamen Philharmonic Orchestra. Founded in 1998 under **conductor Zheng Xiaoying**, the **orchestra** is the only non-state-funded orchestra in China. **Zheng**, who continues as its artistic and musical director, leads over eighty concerts each year and has taken the orchestra on tours throughout China; Asia, including Japan and Hong Kong; and Europe. One of the goals of the orchestra is the development of Xiamen Island as a "Musical Island of the Orient." The city was designated a "treaty port" in the nineteenth century, opening it to the west, and in the 1980s it was one of four original "special economic zones" open to international investment.

xilófono. (It., Sp.) **Xylophone**. See also **appendix 4**.

Xilophon. (Ger.) **Xylophone**. See also **appendix 4**.

xucalho. The same as the **chocalho**, it exists in both a wooden and metal form. See also **appendix 4**.

xylomarimba. A large **xylophone** that covers the ranges of both the **marimba** and the xylophone. Found in *Gruppen for Three orchestras* (1959) by **Karlheinz Stockhausen** and *Le marteau sans Maître* (1955) by Pierre Boulez. (Fr. *xylomarimba*, Ger. *Xylomarimba*, Sp. *xilorimba*.) See also **appendix 4**.

xylophone. A keyboard **percussion** instrument played with mallets. (Fr. *xylophone*, Ger. *Xylophon*, It. *xilófono*, Sp. *xilófono*.) See also **appendix 4**.

Xylophone range as it sounds. *Courtesy Andrew Martin Smith.*

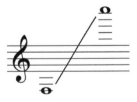

Xylophone range as written. *Courtesy Andrew Martin Smith.*

xylorimba. A combination of the **xylophone** and the **marimba**. Used in *Le Marteau sans Maître* by **Pierre Boulez**.

y. (Sp.) And. (Fr. *et*, Ger. *und*, It. *e*.)

Yale School of Music. See **Yale University, School of Music**.

Yale University, School of Music. Known as the Yale School of Music, the school offers a comprehensive curriculum with both the master's and doctoral degrees and a combined undergraduate/master's degree program. In 1889, Yale University established its department of music, with its first bachelor's degree given in 1894. That same year the department was reorganized into the School of Music. As of 2005, all students at the school attend on full scholarship because of a donation of $100 million from Yale alumnus Stephen Adams. The school is widely known for its musical instrument collection; Sprague Memorial Hall; the Collegium Musicum, which was established by composer **Paul Hindemith** in 1941; its Institue of Sacred Music; and much more. In 1973, **Otto-Werner Mueller** became the resident conductor of the Philharmonia Orchestra of Yale and professor of **conducting**. The school has a distinguished list of faculty.

Yampolsky, Victor. (b. 1942.) Russian-born American **conductor** and violinist. Yampolsky is currently on the faculty of Northwestern University and music director of the Peninsula Music Festival in Door County, Wisconsin. He is the honorary director of the Scotia Festival of Music in Halifax and music director emeritus of the Omaha Symphony Orchestra. He studied **violin** with David Oistrakh at the **Moscow Conservatory** and **conducting** with Nicolai Rabinovich at the Leningrad Conservatory. He immigrated to the United States in 1973 and studied at the **Tanglewood Music Center**. Yampolsky became a member of the **Boston Symphony Orchestra** and served as the music director of the National Symphony Orchestra, Johannesburg; music director of the Atlantic Symphony Orchestra, Halifax (1977–1983); resident conductor of the **Chicago Civic Orchestra**; and has been a frequent guest conductor worldwide. Yampolsky is also a well-regarded conducting pedagogue and director of **orchestras** at Northwestern University's Bienen School of Music.

Yomiuri Nippon Symphony Orchestra. Founded in 1962, a professional **orchestra** resident in Tokyo. The current principal **conductor** is **Sylvain Cambreling**. Past conductors have included Willis Page (1962–1963), Hiroshi Wakasugi (1965–1975), **Rafael Frühbeck de Burgos** (1980–1983), Heinz Rögner (198401990), Tadaaki Otaka (1992–1998), Gerd Albrecht (1998–2007), and Stanisław Skrowaczewski (2007–2010).

young people's concerts. Concerts designed specifically for younger audiences with the intent of introducing classical music to the next generation. **Conductor Theodore Thomas** led so-called family matinees in New York as early as 1885. Frank Damrosch led the Young People's Symphony Concerts of New York beginning in 1898 with the **New York Symphony Orchestra**. Josef Stransky developed the idea under the name Young People's Concerts beginning in 1914. The **New York Philharmonic** began such a series under Ernest Schelling in 1924, and they continue in the same style, talking-explaining, followed by playing, to today. **Leonard Bernstein** brought the Young People's Concerts to a much higher level when, as the conductor of the **New York Philharmonic**, he conducted them himself instead of giving them to an assistant. Over fifty-three such performances were broadcast nationally on CBS television from 1958 to 1972 and are now available on DVD. Nearly every **orchestra** and many chamber ensembles and soloists in the United States give concerts of this type as a matter of outreach and education. Often programmed for specific age ranges, they are called Children's Concerts, Concerts for Kids, Family Concerts, Youth Concerts, and so on.

Many orchestras work with local school districts to bring multiple classes in by school bus to concerts scheduled during the schoolday.

Young, Simone. (b. 1961.) Australian **conductor**. Young studied composition, piano, and **conducting** at the Sydney Conservatory of Music. She worked as a vocal coach at Opera Australia, making her debut at the Sydney Opera House in 1985. She assisted James Conlon at Cologne Opera, and **Daniel Barenboim** at the **Berlin State Opera** and the **Bayreuth Festival**. Young was the first woman to conduct at the **Vienna State Opera** in 1993 and the **Vienna Philharmonic** in 2005. She served as the principal conductor for the Bergen Philharmonic Orchestra (1998–2002) and the chief conductor of Opera Australia (2001–2003). Since 2005 she has been the chief executive of the **Hamburg State Opera** and chief conductor of the **Hamburg Philharmonic**, Germany. Her contract will end in 2015 when she will be replaced by **Kent Nagano**. She has recorded symphonies of Anton Bruckner, a complete **Ring cycle**, and much more.

Simone Young. *Courtesy Reto Klar.*

youth orchestras. Existing the world over to cultivate the skills and talent of young people and expose them to great music. The youth **orchestra** tradition in America is long and impressive. The **Portland Youth Philharmonic** is the oldest, founded in 1924. It was followed by the Young People's Symphony Orchestra, Berkeley in 1935, and the Dayton Philharmonic Youth Orchestra in 1937. The **Seattle Youth Orchestra** Organization, founded in 1942, serves over 1,500 musicians in four full orchestras every year. By 1963, there were about fifteen thousand youth and junior orchestras across the country. **Conductors** for these ensembles include music educators from all levels, in addition to assistant and associate conductors and sometimes music directors of professional orchestras. **Leopold Stokowski** established the All-American Youth Orchestra, auditioning thousands of young musicians who would make up the one-hundred-member ensemble that, due to World War II, lasted only two years (1940–1942). The National Youth Orchestra of the United States of America was founded in 2012 by the Weill Music Institute of Carnegie Hall. In 2013, the orchestra toured America and performed in London, St. Petersburg, and Moscow. See also **all-state orchestras**, **NAfME**, **El sistema**, **José Antonio Abreu**.

YouTube. An Internet site where video is shared. A resource for video and audio of contemporary and historic performances.

YouTube Symphony Orchestra (YTSO). An **orchestra** put together by posting audition videos on **YouTube**. Those selected met in New York in April 2009 for the YouTube Symphony Orchestra summit, playing at **Carnegie Hall** under **Michael Tilson Thomas**. The second formation of the **symphony** took place in 2011 in Sydney, Australia, also under the direction of Tilson Thomas. The live stream of the final concert was the largest YouTube had on record, with 30.7 million computer users and 2.8 million mobile device users connected during the performance.

zählen. (Ger.) To count, as in counting numbers. (Fr. *compter*, It. *contare*, Sp. *contar*.) See also **numbers, basic**.

Zählzeit. (Ger.) The beats in a bar: 1, 2, 3, 4. Example: *in zwei Zählzeiten*, in two beats.

zärtlichkeit, mit. (Ger.) With tenderness. A commonly expressive phrase. (Fr. *avec tendresse*, It. *con tenerezza*, Sp. *con ternura*.)

zart, zärtlich, delikat. (Ger.) Tender, delicate, tenderly. (Fr. *tendre, délicat, tendrement*, It. *tenero, delicato, teneramente*, Sp. *tierno, tiernamente, delicado*.) Examples: *zart bewegt*, tenderly moving; *Sehr zart und ausdrucksvoll*, Very tender and expressive, from *The Prelude to Die Meistersinger von Nürenberg* by **Richard Wagner**; *zart gesungen*, tenderly or sung tenderly.

Zäsur. (Ger.) **Caesura**, slight pause or break. (Fr. *césure*, It. *cesura*, Sp. *cesura*.)

Zeichen. (Ger.) Sign, a musical sign such as a sharp or flat or the *dal segno* sign. (It. *segno*, Sp. *signo*, Fr. *signe*.) Example: *Steigerung bis zum Zeichen*, "build (increase) to the sign," from *Symphony No. 1, mvt. 1*, by **Gustav Mahler**.

Zeit. (Ger.) Time. (Fr. *temps*, It. *tempo*, Sp. *tempo, tiempo*.) Example: *Zeit lassen*, take time.

Zeitgenössische Musik, neue Musik. (Ger.) Contemporary music. (Fr. *musique contemporaine*, It. *musica contemporanea*, Sp. *música contemporánea*.)

Zeitmaß. (Ger.) Tempo. (Fr. *temps*, It., Sp. *tempo*.)

Zeitmaß, im. (Ger.) In tempo. (Fr. *dans le tempo*, It. *in tempo*, Sp. *en el tempo*.)

Zeitmesser, metronom. (Ger.) **Metronome**. (Fr. *metronome*, It. *metronome*, Sp. *metrónomo*.) See also **Maelzel, Johann Nepomuk**.

Zheng, Xiaoying. (b. 1929.) Chinese **conductor**. Zheng studied **piano** as a child. She took part in in the revolution and was in charge of training a sixty-member song and dance troupe and also conducted some Chinese **operas**. After the establishment of the People's Republic in 1948, she entered the **Beijing Central Conservatory of Music**. The Russian choral conductor Nicolai Tumascheve visited the conservatory in the mid-1950s and gave her **conducting** lessons. She was sent to study at the **Moscow Conservatory** for three years, where her teacher was Nikolai Anosov, father of **Gennady Rozhdestvensky**. She made her opera debut leading a performance of Giuseppi Verdi's *Tosca* at the Stanislowski National Theater. She was subsequently invited to become a faculty member of the Beijing Central Conservatory on her return to China. She was the conductor of the Beijing Central Opera and Philharmonic Orchestra, but her work there was disrupted by the onset of the Cultural Revolution. For twelve years, there was no classical music in China. During this time, Zheng conducted a *Concerto for Piano and Orchestra*, sometimes called the *National Hymn* but also commonly known as the *Song of the Communist Party*. After the Cultural Revolution ended, Zheng was assigned to serve again as the chief conductor of the Beijing Central Opera (1979–1991). After years of neglect, she oversaw the lengthy process of rebuilding the company, leading performances of such operas as *La Traviata, Madama Butterfly, The Magic Flute, the Marriage of Figaro, Rigoletto*, and others. In the 1980s, she collaborated with the French conductor Jean Perrison when he visited Beijing to make the first translation of *Carmen* into Chinese. Among her guest conducting opportunities was a performance of **Gustav Mahler**'s *Das Lied von der Erde* (Song of the Earth) with the Shanghai Philharmonic. Zheng was also the founding conductor of the Xiamen Philharmonic Orchestra (1998)—she stepped down in 2013—and the Beijing Women's Philharmonic (1993). In 2011, she received the Golden Melody prize from the Chinese Musicians' Association. She was featured in the film *Symphony of the Century: Fifteen Outstanding Chinese Musicians and Founders of Chinese Symphony Music*.

Xiaoying Zheng. *Courtesy of Zheng Xiaoying.*

Ziegeunermusik. (Ger.) Gypsy music. (Fr. *musique tzigane*, It. *musica gitana*, Sp. *música cíngara*.)

ziemlich. (Ger.) Rather, quite. (Fr. *assez*, It. *assai*, Sp. *muy*.) Example: *ziemlich langsam*, rather slow.

zigzag way. A term coined by the Brazilian **conductor** Eleazar de Carvalho to describe a method of **score** study. Gustav Meier writes about it in his book *The Score, the Orchestra, and the Conductor*. The method is a way of exploring and prioritizing the multiple disparate elements of a score into "points of attention" for the conductor. It accounts for how a conductor must jump from issue to issue, one bar at a time, as the music requires it.

Zimbal, Zimbalon. (Ger.) **Cimbalom**. (Fr. *cymbalum*, It. *cimbalom*, Sp. *cimbalón, zimbalón*.)

zimbalón. (Sp.) **Cimbalom**. (Fr. *cymbalum*; Ger. *Zimbal, Zimbalon*; It. *cimbalom*.)

Zink. (Ger.) **Cornet**. (Fr. *cornet á bouqin*, It. *cornetto*, Sp. *corneta*.)

Zinman, David. (b. 1936.) American **conductor** and violinist. Zinman studied at the **Oberlin Conservatory** and the University of Minnesota and studied **conducting** at **Tanglewood** and with **Pierre Monteux** at his school in Maine (1958–1962). He served as Monteux's assistant from 1961 to 1964. Zinamn was the principal conductor of the Netherlands Chamber Orchestra (1965–1977); music director of the **Rochester Philharmonic** (1974–1985); chief conductor of the Rotterdam Philharmonic (1979–1982), after two years as principal guest conductor, music director of the **Baltimore Symphony Orchestra** (1985–1998), where he led premiere of many new works; and music director of the **Tonhalle Orchestra Zürich** (1995–2014). He was artistic director of the **Aspen Music Festival** (1998–2010), where he founded the **American Academy of Conducting**. Zinman has been a guest conductor worldwide and made numerous recordings, including a cycle of the Schumann symphonies and a great deal of American music with the Baltimore Symphony Orchestra. Zinman has documented his approach to performance-practice ideas with the Tonhalle-Orchestra Zurich through a complete cycle of Beethoven symphonies.

zu. (Ger.) To, in, until. (Fr. *jusque*, It. *sin, sino*, Sp. *hasta*.)

zu 2, 3, or 4. (Ger.) To be played by 2, 3, or 4 members of the same instrument section.

zu artikulieren. (Ger.) To articulate. (Fr. *articular*, It. *articulare*, Sp. *articular*.)

zu beeilen. (Ger.) To hurry (Fr. *se dépêcher*, It. *affrettare*, Sp. *prisa*.)

zuerst. (Ger.) At first. (Fr. *d'abord*, It. *dapprimo, prima*, Sp. *primero*.)

zufolo, suoni armonici. (It.) **Harmonics**. (Ger. *Flageolettöne, Flageolett*, Sp. *armónico*.) See also **artificial harmonics**, **harmonic series**, **string harmonics**.

Zug. 1. (Ger.) A term used in **Schenkerian** analytical graphs that describes fundamental stepwise linear progressions through a specific interval, a third, for instance, is a *Terzzug*.
   2. A slide, as on a **trombone**. (Fr. *coulisse*, It. *pompa movile a coulisse*, Sp. *bomba de afinación*.)

Zugabe! (Ger.) Encore! (Fr., It., Sp. *Bis!*)

Zugposaune. (Ger.) Slide **trombone**. (Fr. *trombone á coulisse*, It. *trombone a tiro*, Sp. *trombón de varas*.)

Zugtrompete. (Ger.) Slide **trumpet**. (Fr. *trompette á coulisse*, It. *tromba a tirarse, tromba a tiro*.)

Zukunftsmusik. (Ger.) Music of the future. (Fr. *musique du futur,* It. *musica dello futuro,* Sp. *música del future.*) Also the title of an essay by **Richard Wagner**.

zuletzt. (Ger.) Finally, lastly. (Fr. *à la fin,* It. *alla fine,* Sp. *por fin.*)

zum Ende. (Ger.) To the end. A directive sometimes used in pieces with multiple repeated sections to indicates the section that finishes the piece. (Fr. *à la fin,* It. *alla fine, Sp. hasta el final.*)

zum letzten Mal. (Ger.) For the last time. (Fr. *pour la derniére fois,* It. *per l'ultima volta,* Sp. *por última vez.*)

zum Schluss. (Ger.) To the end, in order to finish. (Fr. *pour finir,* It. *per finire,* Sp. *por último, para terminar.*)

zum Zeichen. (Ger.) To the sign. (Fr. *au signe,* It. *al segno, dal segno,* Sp. *a la señal*) See also ***Zeichen, dal segno.***

zum Zeitmaß zurückkehrend. (Ger.) Returning to tempo. (Fr. *en revenant au movement,* It. *tornando al tempo,* Sp. *volviendo al tempo.*)

Zunge. (Ger.) Tongue, used to articulate by wind and brass players. (Fr. *langue,* It. *linguetta,* Sp. *lengua.*)

Zungenschlag, Zugenstoß. (Ger.) **Tonguing.** (Fr. *coup di langue,* It. *colpo di lingua,* Sp. *golpe de lengua.*)

zurückgeben. (Ger.) To give back. Used in **rubato**. (Fr. *render,* It. *rendere,* Sp. *devolver.*)

zurückhalten. (Ger.) Hold back. (Fr. *retenir,* It. *ritenere,* Sp. *retener.*) Also *zurückhaltend.* Example: *Etwas zurückhaltend,* somewhat held back; *Immer noch zurückhaltend,* always still holding back; *Sehr zurückhaltend,* very held back, from *Symphony No. 1, movement 1,* by **Gustav Mahler**.

zurückkehren, zurückkommen. (Ger.) Go back to, to return, revert to. (Fr. *revenir,* It. *tornare, ritornare,* Sp. *regresar, volver.*)

zurückziehen. (Ger.) An expression used to emphasize a big pulling back in the dynamic in a musical passage. The opposite is *leichtes zurückziehen,* a small pulling back. Both may be heard in **rehearsal**.

zusammen. Ger.) Together. (Fr. *ensemble,* It. *insieme,* Sp. *juntamente, juntos.*) A commonly heard directive, as in "**We are not together.**" (Fr. *nous ne sommes pas ensemble,* Ger. *wir sind nicht zusammen,* It. *non siamo insieme,* Sp. *no estamos juntos*); This must be together (Fr. *ce doit être ensemble,* Ger. *dies muss zusammen sein,* It. *questo deve essere insieme,* Sp. *esto debe estar juntos*).

zu viel. (Ger.) Too much. (Fr. *trop,* It. *troppo,* Sp. *demasiado.*)

zu zweit. (Ger.) Both, both players play the same thing. (Fr. *à deux,* It. *a due,* Sp. *en dos.*)

Zweden, Jaap van. (b. 1960.) Dutch **conductor** and violinist. Van Zweden is the current music director of the **Dallas Symphony Orchestra** (2008–pres.) He attended the **Juilliard School** at the age of fifteen as a student of Dorothy Delay. He became the youngest **concertmaster** ever of the **Royal Concertgebouw Orchestra** when he was appointed at the age of nineteen, remaining in the position until 1995. Van Zweden was chief conductor of the Netherlands Symphony Orchestra (1996–2000); the **Residentie Orchestra in The Hague** (2000–2005), recording a complete Beethoven symphony cycle; and chief at the **Netherlands Radio Philharmonic**, Hilversum (2005–2012), and also at the **Royal Flemish Philharmonic** (2008–2011). In 2012, he was named Musical America's Conductor of the Year. He also became music director of the **Hong Kong Philharmonic Orchestra**. He has appeared as guest conductor of the **Berlin Philharmonic**, **New York Philharmonic**, the **Tonhalle-Orchestra Zurich**, **Boston Symphony Orchestra**, and many others. His recordings include **Igor Stravinsky**'s *The Rite of Spring*, **Sir Benjamin Britten**'s *War Requiem*, and the complete Beethoven, Brahms, and Bruckner symphonies.

zwei. (Ger.) Two. (Fr. *deux,* It. *due,* Sp. *dos.*) See also **numbers, basic**.

zweimal. (Ger.) An indication that calls for playing something twice, one after another, not doubled or simultaneously. (Fr. *deux fois,* It. *due volte,* Sp. *dos veces.*)

zweiunddreißigstel. (Ger.) Thirty-second note, demisemiquaver (British usage). (Fr. *triple croche,* It. *biscroma,* Sp. *fusa.*) See also **appendix 7**.

zweiunddresigstelpause. (Ger.) Thirty-second-note rest. See also **appendix 7**.

Zwischensatz. (Ger.) Episode. (Fr. *épisode,* It. *episodio,* Sp. *episodio.*)

Zwischenspiel. (Ger.) Interlude. (Fr. *entr'acte, interlude,* It. *interludio, intermezzo, intermedio,* Sp. *interludio.*)

Zyklus. (Ger.) Cycle. (Fr. *cycle,* It., Sp. *ciclo.*)

APPENDIX 1

Six Pieces That Changed Conducting

1. *SYMPHONY NO. 9 IN D MINOR* (1824), LUDWIG VAN BEETHOVEN

When the *Symphony No. 9* was premiered, the idea of a single conductor had not yet developed. While Beethoven stood near the front of the assembled musicians, urging them on with his prodigious energy, consumed by the musical details, sudden changes of dynamic and tempos, nuances of phrasing and articulation, his task was mainly to indicate the tempos of the movements.

According to Thomas Forrest Kelly in his book *First Nights*, Beethoven recruited one of the most reputable violinists of the day, Ignaz Schuppanzigh, to lead the orchestra from the position of first-chair violin and the violinist Michael Umlauf, with whom he had often worked in the same capacity, to stand next to him at the front and serve as the main conductor, generally keeping things together. It is also likely that the pianist Conradin Kreutzer sat at a piano in front of the soloists to keep them on pitch and help with entrances. In the tradition of the *chef d'attaque*, there may also have been lead members in each choral section helping with entrances.

While we know that the performance was significantly under-rehearsed, it was an enormous artistic success for the famous composer. The symphony challenged everyone involved with an unprecedented level of difficulty, especially the strings, many of whom were only used to playing simple accompaniments.

Beginning with his *Symphony No. 5*, Beethoven was building the orchestra. Once again, in No. 9, he required many instruments that were still unusual, three trombones, piccolo plus two flutes, contrabassoon, triangle, cymbals, and bass drum, in addition to the standard timpani, but here the timpani part was suddenly soloistic.

But it is the musical demands that made the prospect of a successful performance so mindboggling. A first movement that requires such precision of ensemble playing, a Scherzo, with its startling timpani solo and unexpected patterns of bars grouped in three (*ritmo di tre battute*), an Adagio so

slow that it unfolds its form in such a complex way that the pacing becomes critical to its understanding. And the Finale, marked *presto*, dotted half note = 66, begins on an offbeat! After a quick seven-bar introduction, the double bass section is given the "vocal part" of an entirely orchestral recitative followed by an unprepared interruption of the introductory material. And back and forth it goes; themes from each movement, each in a different tempo, are briefly presented and abruptly interrupted, as if to say "No! Not that!" by the double basses giving their instrumental commentary. This is only the beginning of a movement, with soloists and chorus and continued tempo changes, that doesn't get any easier.

The entire symphony requires a combination of ensemble playing, virtuosity, and musicianship that was unheard of, all in the service of an intensity of musical expression that brought about a the new romantic age. Here the conductor is forced to be not just a time beater but an interpreter, a single leader, what we now know of as the conductor, who establishes a concept of the whole, the limits to be explored, just as Beethoven did when he put the music down on paper.

2. *PRELUDE TO THE AFTERNOON OF A FAUN* (1894), CLAUDE DEBUSSY

This is often referred to as *the* work that signaled the shift from music of the nineteenth to that of the twentieth century. Debussy's musical language rose out of the world of Richard Wagner and established something unique for the future. The challenges to the conductor exist in mastering the inherent connection between every musical element of the work. William A. Austin wrote in his essay published in the Norton Critical Score of *Prelude to the Afternoon of a Faun*, "Every part of this music clings to every other part so firmly, so naturally, that it is hard to identify parts when we want to talk about them." All elements, melody, harmony, and rhythm are so interrelated, so organically united, that they cannot be separated one from the other.

It is in the conductor's main purview, the maintenance of pulse, that the greatest challenge lies: how to *beat* a piece in which a sense of beat is mostly elusive. The *Prelude* is full of long passages where the sense of pulse is held at bay by a delicate, sinuous, seemingly constant syncopation, but then, thankfully, balanced by passages of underlying harmonic and rhythmic clarity. And even though it is a ballet, it is clearly not a dance in which one feels the regular beat of feet on the floor, but a flexibility, a subtle ebb and flow of tempo, a "smoothness" similar to flowing water instead.

This relates directly to the choice the conductor must make regarding the flute solo in the opening bars. Some conductors believe it is against the nature of the piece to conduct the opening solo, while others assert that it is in these opening bars that the conductor establishes the essential elements that form the foundation of everything that follows.

Prelude to the Afternoon of a Faun, Claude Debussy, opening.
Courtesy Boosey & Hawkes.

Among the conductor's considerations is the importance of not bringing motion to a stop at the end of a passage or phrase before moving on. All transitions of tempo must be smooth and natural so as not to inadvertently create structural divides where they don't exist. An example of this can be observed at the climax of the piece, where the predominant pitch is D-flat, enharmonically the same as the first pitch, C-sharp. Is Debussy suggesting a kind of stasis, a kind of arrival without arriving, or is it simply another hint at the completely organic nature of the work?

The piece also requires the conductor to choose between beating the 12/9 and 9/8 bars in either large beats made up of dotted quarter notes, or the small subdivisions of eighth notes. A very successful technique can be the conducting of the "one+" subdivision of the dotted quarter notes, where the main beat and the first eighth note subdivision only is given. This conducting pattern style allows a bit more control while also creating a sense of forward motion. (Note that Hector Berlioz describes a similar style of beating in his essay "On Conducting" at the back of his orchestration book.) Debussy is so concerned with maintaining the smooth rhythmic flow that he clearly marks eighth note = eighth note when switching from the 12/8 to the 3/4 meter. See **subdivided beat**.

3. *THE RITE OF SPRING* (1913), IGOR STRAVINSKY

Much has been written about the revolutionary nature of Stravinsky's ballet, *The Rite of Spring*, and it is undoubtedly

a work that shook the music world when it was premiered in Paris in 1913. Stravinsky's radical modernism was based on a combination of folk music made primitive, which when realized onstage with the choreography of Vaslav Nijinsky and the costumes and stage designs of artist Nikolai Roerich, an expert in folk art and ritual, created a shocking expression of base humanity that some have said presaged the wars and revolutions just around the corner.

From the point of view of the conductor it is also a pivotal work. Stravinsky took his compositional material and chopped it up into uneven, disjointed, sometimes fitful and breathless rhythmic elements that are difficult to manage even one hundred years later. While the work presents many passages of significant difficulty, it is the section of the piece called the "Sacrificial Dance" (*Danse Sacrale*) that has brought the most attention. In the ballet, this is where a young woman has been selected for sacrifice and proceeds to dance herself to death. The music is characterized by powerful, jagged, unstable rhythms and meters; it is easy to miss any regular pulse.

"Sacrificial Dance" from *The Rite of Spring*, Igor Stravinsky.
Courtesy Boosey & Hawkes.

However, an internal logic is sensed when the conductor groups the bars together and simply learns how each group is different from the one before and the one after. On deep study, one gains a sense of an internal regularity, perhaps hidden on its face, but there nonetheless. The expansion and contraction of the rhythmic units or cells is in itself logical, if not predictable. It is easier when the conductor doesn't conduct a stream of bars in one but actually superimposes a two, three, or four pattern when it fits Stravinsky's groupings. See **conducting uneven meters**.

4. *APPALACHIAN SPRING* (1944), AARON COPLAND

This ballet was commissioned by the Elizabeth Sprague Coolidge Foundation for Martha Graham. The original instrumentation was for thirteen instruments. Copland also made a version for full orchestra, with passages necessary only for the choreography removed. Originally titled "Ballet for Martha," *Appalachian Spring* has become an iconic work in American culture. And while it does not present rhythmic difficulties beyond those of many earlier works, it is the most common work by any American composer to appear regularly in conducting auditions.

Copland's use of mixed meters, quick tempo changes, and rhythmic patterns that overlay bar lines all create challenges. And these are the passages that the young conductor can expect to turn up regularly. The passage at figures [12] to [14] begins with music of a certain dance-like regularity but moves quickly into bars of changing meters with uneven groups of subdivisions. This includes bars in which the weight or accent of the downbeat is temporarily shifted, and the conductor's beat changes to reflect this.

Appalachian Spring, Aaron Copland, figures [13]–[14], mixed meters with uneven subdivisions and shifting emphasis. *Courtesy Boosey & Hawkes.*

Appalachian Spring, Aaron Copland, figures [13]–[14], mixed meters with uneven subdivisions and shifting emphasis. *Courtesy Boosey & Hawkes.*

Appalachian Spring, Aaron Copland, figures [13]–[14], mixed meters with uneven subdivisions and shifting emphasis. *Courtesy Boosey & Hawkes.*

Measures [31] to [32] begin with a four-bar vamp establishing a rhythm that shifts easily between 2/4 and 5/8, followed by the addition of a jaunty dance tune. At [33], *molto moderato*, the conductor must manage a sudden change of tempo and dramatic feeling. Figure [35], a brisk *allegro*, is one of the most difficult passages of mixed meters in the work and is often used at conducting auditions.

Appalachian Spring, Aaron Copland, figures [31]–[32], mixed meters in a dance-like passage. *Courtesy Boosey & Hawkes.*

Appalachian Spring, Aaron Copland, figures [31]–[32], mixed meters in a dance-like passage. *Courtesy Boosey & Hawkes.*

Appalachian Spring, Aaron Copland, figure [33], sudden change of tempo and feeling. *Courtesy Boosey & Hawkes.*

Appalachian Spring, Aaron Copland, figures [35]–[37], mixed meters in a fast tempo. *Courtesy Boosey & Hawkes.*

Appalachian Spring, Aaron Copland, figures [35]–[37], mixed meters in a fast tempo. *Courtesy Boosey & Hawkes.*

Appalachian Spring, Aaron Copland, figures [35]–[37], mixed meters in a fast tempo. *Courtesy Boosey & Hawkes.*

The short, quick accelerando transition into the *presto* at [37] is one of the most challenging passages of the piece to handle smoothly and with a natural feeling. See **conducting uneven meters**, **mixed meters**.

5. *THRENODY TO THE VICTIMS OF HIROSHIMA* (1960), KRZYSZTOF PENDERECKI

Written for a fifty-two-piece string orchestra, it creates a radical new sound world, a world of sonic pitched and non-pitched textures, music that no longer uses the discipline of the regular bar line to guide the flow of rhythm but a new **graph notation** instead. Sometimes called a "polyphony of sound," this "revolutionary" music creates new challenges for the conductor and player alike. For the player there are numerous new techniques to learn in addition to the notation devices that go along with them. For the conductor, the work becomes a series of cues within a measured framework suggested by timings listed at the bottom of each section. Each section is given a number, appearing sequentially at the top of the score, that facilitates staying together both for rehearsal purposes and in performance.

Cues are prioritized according to whether they are for individual players, small groups of players, or for the entire ensemble. They are also divided between the left and right hands, the right hand generally being reserved for more important cues, especially *tutti* cues, and the left for cues involving smaller numbers of players. Two-handed cues, or **double-handed** cues, are saved to indicate major structural units or places where they will simply help keep the entire ensemble together. The "geography of the cues—exactly where the players receiving the cues are sitting in relation to each other"—becomes an essential consideration for the conductor, especially when the cues happen in quick succession. Cue gestures are also effective tools for dynamic changes, changes in the speed of vibrato and glissandos, and handling the expansion and contraction of tone clusters. In one of the most active sections of the work, Penderecki uses dotted bar lines along with timings, not for any metric effect but to organize the complexity of the music and create a visual guide for the passage of time. These are easily cued as a succession of downbeats, perhaps ending with a double-handed downbeat when the textures begin to break up again.

One of the most significant challenges for the conductor is, in the case of an orchestra unacquainted with the style of writing, the need to explain so much. It is essential to circulate both the parts and lists of the notational devices and their meanings well in advance of the first rehearsal. The conductor then has to develop an organized plan for leading the work that will be clear and easy to understand.

The first title for the piece was a completely abstract, probable "tip of the hat" to John Cage, "8′ 37″," the duration of the piece as specified according to the score. Soon after the first performance, Penderecki changed it to *Threnody*, giving it a direct programmatic connection to one of the horrors of World War II.

It should also be noted that Penderecki has said that the timings are not as important as the acoustic effect generated by the sounds; that is, it is up to the conductor to shape the piece. While in the score the composer indicates a length of 8′ 26″, his own recording lasts 9′ 45″.

Composing in this new style, Penderecki used many new notation devices that have been adopted universally. Selected examples of other important works with similar challenges include Witold Lutosławski's *Venetian Games* (1961), *Livres* (1968), and others; Earle Brown's *Available Forms 2* (1965); John Cage's *Concerto for Prepared Piano and Chamber Orchestra* (1951); Jacob Druckman's *Windows* (1972); and other works of Penderecki, such as *Utrenja* (1970) and *De Natura Sonoris* (1971).

	sharpen a quarter-tone
	sharpen three quarter-tones
	flatten a quarter-tone
	flatten three quarter-tones
	highest note of the instrument (no definite pitch)
	play between bridge and tailpiece
	arpeggio on four strings behind the bridge
	play on the tailpiece (arco) by bowing the tailpiece at an angle of ninety degrees to its longer axis
	play on the bridge by bowing the wood of the bridge at a right angle at its right side
	Percussion effect: strike the upper sounding board of the violin with the nut or the finger-tips
	several irregular changes of bow
	molto vibrato
	very slow vibrato with a quarter-tone frequency difference produced by sliding the finger
	very rapid non rhythmisized tremolo
ord.	ordinario
s. p.	sul ponticello
s. t.	sul tasto
c. l.	col legno
l. batt.	legno battuto

6. *SYMPHONY NO. 1* (1990), JOHN CORIGLIANO

Written for the Chicago Symphony Orchestra and premiered under the baton of Daniel Barenboim, John Corigliano's Symphony No. 1, is predominantly grounded in commonly used notation, combined with passages of box notation that are now mostly familiar to the orchestral musician. However, in the first movement of the symphony, Corigliano creates an unusual challenge for the conductor. He uses a technique of metric modulation combined with accelerando in order to create the sense of an enormous, powerful machine building momentum in such a way that we feel it may overwhelm us if it cannot be stopped.

Corigliano does this by establishing a starting tempo in 4/4 at a pulse of quarter = 60, with a motive that contains a written in accelerando based on the speeding up of the subdivisions from eighth notes to multiple sixteenth notes that is passed back and forth between sections of the orchestra. Then two bars before adding the actual accelerando, he has entrances of free box notation figures in the piccolo, first oboe, first clarinet, glockenspiel, crotales, and piano that must be planned for and rehearsed, if not actually individually cued. Immediately following, while maintaining the speed of the beat, he switches to 2/2 (half note = 60) and gives the conductor twelve bars to increase the tempo so that we arrive at the next metric connection, a meter of 2/1, whole note = 96, all the while giving clear, forceful indications of chords both on and off the beat that create a kind of cranking up of an engine, supported by large crescendos in the brass.

From here the tempo continues to speed up for four bars; the chords crash in closer and closer together until we reach 4 / double whole note = 96. Now the conductor has two bars, during which the chords come at a constant pulse of sixteenth notes, to reach 2/2 where the half note = 60 (quarter=120). Here the whole orchestra falls away in a great release of energy leading to a long, sustained melody, marked *P* and *PP*, in the violins. It is in this passage that we first hear the offstage pianist playing Isaac Albéniz's *Tango* in an independent meter from the orchestra.

After a period of slow music, we once again, having started at a low point of 2/2 (half note = 60), begin the giant build-up. Handled with similar metric shifts, we arrive at an enormous *presto* marked *tutti, F possibile*. There are three bars of 2/1 and one bar of 3/1 with the whole note marked at 120.

Finally, with two bars of 2/1, the composer asks for an extended *rallentando*. The rhythmic texture is now remarkably simplified to nothing but quarter notes, passing through several bars ending in a fermata. By the end of the bar, only the strings are playing. The score is marked *tutti, F possibile*. After sustaining the *F* for two fermatas, the score is marked with a gradual diminuendo to *PPP*. Here we begin a completely new quiet and reflective passage. One more recurrence of the dramatic forceful music is short lived, and we are drawn into music of remembrance highlighted by the melodies of the offstage pianist.

It is the handling of these massive accelerandos, the power and force required to perform the music as written while cuing lines in the winds and overseeing growing sequences of chords and also manage a fearsome forward drive without arriving at the new tempo too soon—or too late—the sense of pacing required so that the music passes from one meter to the next without a great jolt that is the great challenge for the conductor. See **multiple conductor works, multiple orchestra works, new music ensemble**.

APPENDIX 2

The History of Conducting

The origins of conducting are found in the simple necessity to keep ensemble musicians together in rehearsal and performance. Gradually, as music became more complex, an individual musician was delegated to the responsibility. This is first seen in fifteenth- and sixteenth-century church choirs. As instrumental ensembles grew larger in the seventeenth and eighteenth centuries, the duty was given to either the first-chair violinist, often known as the "leader," the harpsichordist, or sometimes both. The Italian-born English musician **Sir Michael Costa** was a primary example of such a leader. At that time, the instrumental time-beater often kept the time audibly with some kind of a staff that was pounded on the floor when needed. Even at this time, conducting, or time beating, was only done when necessary to keep the ensemble together; the leader was primarily an instrumentalist. Up to this point, the idea of what a conductor was remained fairly simple, keeping the group together. Beginning in the eighteenth century, dictionaries and other texts about music making describe conducting patterns as up and down gestures, accounting for heavy and light beats within a measure but without any suggestion of expression. As conductors mastered the technical aspects of clear beating, they gradually also began to ask for more. Dynamics came next, and as the music demanded it, and conductors saw the potential benefits, multiple levels of expression, phrasing, and much more followed.

In Germany, there were three leadership levels within the musical organization: (1) At the top was the *Kapellmeister*, a composer and principal supervisor. (2) The *Musikdirektor*, who ran the orchestra under the guidance of the Kapellmeister. (3) The *Concertmeister*, an instrumentalist who kept track of all performance details. In France, they had the *maître de musique*, who was in charge of all musical activities. When works for combined choir and orchestra were done, there was a *chef d'attaque* to keep the choir together and assist with entrances and a so-called *capo de instrumenti*, equivalent of a concertmaster, who was responsible for the orchestra. In the event of a particularly large chorus, each vocal section would have its own chef d'attaque. In England, the organization was run by a **music director**, assisted by a **concertmaster** who, to this day, is commonly called "leader." In what seems to have been an anomaly, at the Paris Opera (**Paris National Opera**), it was the practice to use a time-beater (*betteur de mesure*) who held some kind of baton, probably a stick, to give audible and visual signals to singers, dancers, and the orchestra. This was probably also the practice of **Jean-Baptiste Lully** (1632–1687) at the Académie Royale de Musique, though he most likely made predominantly audible signals. Gradually, as musicians began to perceive the audible beat as intrusive, various other devices came into being, a roll of paper, a white glove, and finally the baton. By the end of the eighteenth century, the French opera was led by a *maître* who stood in the pit with his back to the orchestra, directing or conducting the singers with a baton. He was called *chef d'orchestre*.

Throughout Europe in the nineteenth century, as music continued to become more complex and ensembles, orchestras, and choirs grew, the conductor gradually left his instrument behind and took up the baton, becoming the sole authority over the ensemble. This also coincided with the beginning of a period of the founding of music conservatories for the training of professional instrumentalists and singers. (See *Symphony No. 9 in D minor* **[1824], Ludwig van Beethoven** in **appendix 1**; **Leipzig Gewandhaus, Paris Conservatory**.)

Not only conductors but also audiences were becoming more demanding and less tolerant of orchestras filled with amateurs. Competition between cities and courts for bragging rights to the title "best orchestra" also came into play as transportation became easier and newspapers more prevalent. They wanted better performances, and conductors such as **Louis Spohr, François-Antoine Habeneck, Hector Berlioz, Felix Mendelssohn, Carl Maria von Weber**, and others were there to show how it could be done.

The first document that describes conducting as something more than time-beating is Hector Berlioz's important essay **"On Conducting; Theory of the Art of Conducting,"** published in 1855. Berlioz establishes the great difficulty of being a good conductor by stressing the many skills necessary, describes techniques to handle many tricky situations, addresses the demands of **interpretation**, the importance of good temperament, and the ability to communicate in an indefinable way with the musicians. In combination with his *Memoirs* and the essay "The Orchestra," one can garner significant insight, if from Berlioz's unique perspective, about conducting at that time. Louis Spohr's book *Grand Violin School*, in the version with text and not just the etudes, provides his perspective on certain technical aspects of conducting. His autobiography, which appeared in 1865, falsely claims that he introduced the baton to London audiences in 1820. We now know that he only used it in rehearsal. (See **Spohr, Louis [1784–1859]**.)

Felix Mendelssohn was perhaps the most important conductor of the 1830s and 1840s. He developed a disciplined rehearsal style and was successful at raising the standards of many of the orchestras he worked with in Germany and England. He is not known as having taught conducting, even though he was one of the founding faculty members of the Leipzig Gewandhaus, and there are no known publications where he discusses his views on conducting as a developing art.

Richard Wagner's book *On Conducting* (1869) affirms the rise of the conductor as interpreter, as does Karl Schröder's *Handbook of Conducting* (1889). Elliott Galkin's important history of orchestral conducting (see the **bibliography**) cites many fascinating sources that lay out the long-lasting practice of conducting with the violin bow and the slow rise of the conductor. **Felix Weingartner**'s book *On Conducting*, especially as published in combination with essays on the performance of Ludwig van Beethoven, Wolfgang Amadeus Mozart, Robert Schumann, and Franz Schubert's symphonies, presents the baton conductor as having become master of the orchestra responsible, if not accountable, for all decisions about style and performance. He goes so far as to decry the conductor who doesn't stick to the intent of the composer as represented in the score. He also criticized the new "craze" of conducting without a score as something that distracted from the music itself.

The late nineteenth and early twentieth centuries were a time when the profession of the professional conductor associated with a particular city was on the rise. **Hans von Bülow** was in Hamburg and Berlin, Vienna had **Hans Richter**, Paris had **Édouard Colonne**, **Theodore Thomas** was in New York and Chicago, and a bit later **Henry Wood** was active in London. (See also *Prelude to the Afternoon of a faun* **[1894], Claude Debussy** in **appendix 1**.)

The year 1913 in Paris was a pivotal one for the world of conducting. Igor Stravinsky's ballet *The Rite of Spring* was premiered under the baton of Pierre Monteux, creating whole new challenges for the conductor. (See ***The Rite of Spring* [1913], Igor Stravinsky** in **appendix 1**.)

Arturo Toscanini, who was active in New York City, personified the image of the maestro. Known as a tyrant in rehearsal, he also established a new trend in conducting that was characterized by growing physical restraint, smaller gestures, and detailed attention to the score. At the same time, **Wilhelm Furtwängler** was also a legendary figure but occupied the opposite realm of music making, that of the German romantic whose performances were free and flexible if not improvisatory. In his world, there was no need for precision in the gestures of the baton; it was the antithesis of the experience. His music making had the lofty goal of virtually bringing the audience on a spiritual journey. From then on there have been two paths for the conductor, service to the composer through the score or the conductor who sees it as a duty to interpret and perform the music with a unique artistic identity, or some combination of the two.

The onset of recording in the twentieth century changed everything in the music field. Suddenly performances could be documented, shared, and compared. The rapid development of the technology and improvements made to the quality of the sound also created a new vehicle for experiencing music, conductors, and orchestras in the home. (See **Columbia Records**, **Decca Records**.)

While many major conductors explored contemporary music, including for instance, **Ernest Ansermet** (premiered Stravinsky's *The Soldier's Tale*, the German premiere of *The Rite of Spring*, and much more) and **Pierre Monteux** (premiered Stravinsky's *The Rite of Spring*, Maurice Ravel's *Daphnis et Chloe*, Claude Debussy's *Jeux*, and much more); **Erich Kleiber** (premiered of Alban Berg's opera *Wozzeck* in 1925) and **Leopold Stowkowski** (American premiere of *Wozzeck*); **Serge Koussevitsky** conducted premieres (world and American) of works by Béla Bartók, such as his *Concerto for Orchestra*, Sergei Prokofiev's *Symphony No. 5*, and more; and **Adrian Boult** (English premieres, Berg's *Wozzeck* and the *Symphonic Pieces* from the opera *Lulu*), until the 1960s conducting technique did not change significantly.

It was the advent of new experimental styles of composition, especially that involving **aleatory** and **works for orchestra and tape** that brought about the next major changes in technique. See also ***Threnody to the Victims of Hiroshima* (1960), Krzysztof Penderecki** and ***Symphony No. 1* (1990), John Corigliano** in **appendix 1**, and the **bibliography**.

APPENDIX 3

Orchestral Instrument Names and Their Translations into French, German, Italian, and Spanish

English	French	German	Italian	Spanish
violin	violon	Geige/Violine	violin	violin
viola	alto	Bratsche	viola	viola
violoncello/cello	violoncelle	Violoncello	violoncello	violonchelo/chelo
double bass/bass	contrebasse	Kontrabass	contrabbasso	contrabajo
flute	flûte	Flöte	flauto	flauta
alto flute	flûte en sol	Altflöte	flauto contralto	flauto contralto/flauto
bass flute	flûte bass	Bassflöte	flauto basso	flauto bajo
piccolo	petite flute	kleine Flöte	piccolo pikkolo	ottavino flauto piccolo flautín/octavín
oboe	hautbois	Oboe	oboe	oboe
English horn	cor anglais	Englischhorn	corno inglese	corno inglés
bass oboe/heckelphone	heckelphone	Heckelphon	Heckelphon	heckelfono
oboe d'amore	hautbois d'amour	Oboe d'amore/Liebesoboe	oboe d'amore	oboe de amor
clarinet	clarinette	Klarinette	clarinetto	clarinete
bass clarinet	clarinette basse	Bassklarinette	claarinetto basso	clarinete bajo
e-flat/soprano clarinet	petite clarinette	kleine Klarinette	clarinetto piccolo	clarinete soprano
alto clarinet	clarinette alto	Altklarinette	clarinetto alto	clarinete alto/ clarinet contralto
bassett horn	cor de basset	Bassetthorn	corno di bassetto	corno di bassetto
contrabass clarinet	clarinette contrebasse	Kontrabassklarinette	clarinetto contrabasso	clarinete contrabajo
saxophone	saxophon	Saxophon	sassofono	saxófono
bassoon	basson	Fagott	fagotto	fagot
contrabassoon	contrebassoon	Kontrafagott	contrafagotto	contrabassoon
French horn/horn	cor	Horn/Waldhorn	corno	trompa
trumpet	trompette	Trompete	tromba	trompeta
bass trumpet	trompette basse	Basstrompete	tromba bassa	trompeta bajo
valve trumpet	trompette á pistons	Ventiltrompete	tromba a pistoni	trompeta de pistones
cornet	cornet	Kornett	cornetta/cornetto	corneta
trombone	trombone	Posaune	trombone	trombón
bass trombone	Bass-trombone/ trombone basse	Bass Posaune	trombono basso	trombón bajo
tuba	tuba	Tuba	tuba/cimbasso	tuba
ophicleide	ophicléide	Ophikleide	oficleide	oficleide
euphonium	euphonium	Euphonium	eufonio	eufonium
harp	harpe	Harfe	arpa	arpa
piano	clavier/piano	Klavier	piano	piano
harpsichord	clavecin	Cembalo	cembalo	clavicordio
guitar	guitar	Gitarre	chitarra	guitarra

See also **Appendix 4: Percussion Instruments and Their Translations**.

APPENDIX 4

Percussion Instruments and Their Translations

The section of the orchestra or band that includes all percussion instruments. The percussion is the most varied of all orchestra sections. To systematize this collection of instruments, this section is commonly divided into two large categories, instruments of definite pitch and instruments of indefinite pitch. In each category are idiophones, that is, instruments that produce sound through the vibration of the entire body, and membranophones, instruments that produce sound by the vibration of a skin or membrane stretched over a resonating cavity.

INSTRUMENTS OF DEFINITE PITCH

Idiophones				
English	**French**	**German**	**Italian**	**Spanish**
xylophone	xylophone or claquebois	Xylophon or Holzharmonika	xilofono	xilofón
marimba	marimba	Marimbaphon	marimba	marimba
vibraphone	vibraphone	Vibraphon	vibrafono	vibráfono
glockenspiel or jeu de timbres	glockenspiel or Stahlspiel	Glockenspiel	campanelli	glockenspiel
orchestra bells (alt. name for glockenspiel)	alt Fr. carillon	Glockenspiel	alt. It. campanette	glockenspiel
tubular chimes, tubular bells	jeu des cloches	Röhrenglocken or Glocken	campane or capane tubolari	campanófono
crotales	crotales or cymbales	Zimbeln	crotali	crótalos
musical saw	lame musicale	Singende Säge	sega cantante	serrucho
flexatone	flexatone	Flexaton	flessatono	flexatón

Membranophones				
English	**French**	**German**	**Italian**	**Spanish**
roto tom	roto-tom	Tom-Tom-Speil	roto-tom-tom	rototoms
timpani	timbales	Pauken	timpani	timbales

Chordophones				
English	**French**	**German**	**Italian**	**Spanish**
cimbalom	cymbalum	Zimbal or Zimbalom	cimbalom	cimbálom
piano	piano	Klavier	pianoforte	piano
celesta	céleste	Celesta	celesta, celeste	celesta
harpsichord	clavecin	Cembalo	cemballo	clavecín
harmonium	harmonium	Harmonium	organetto	armonio
organ	orgue	Orgel	organo	organo

(*continued*)

INSTRUMENTS OF INDEFINITE PITCH

Membranophones

English	French	German	Italian	Spanish
snare drum	caisse claire or tambour	Kleine Trommel	tamburo piccolo or tamburo	caja clara
—with snares	avec timbres	mit Schnarrsaite	colle corde	con bordones
—without snares	sans timbres	ohne Schnarrsaite	senza le corde	sin bordones
tenor drum	caisse roulante	Wirbeltrommel or Rührtrommel	cassa rullante	tambor tenor, or redoblante
bass drum	grosse caisse	Grosse Trommel	gran cassa or gran tamburo	bombo
tom-toms	tom-tom	Tom-tom	Tom-tom	tom-toms
timbales	timbales cubaines	Kuba-Pauken	tampanetti	pailas
bongos	bongos	Bongos	bongos or bonghi	bongós
conga drum	conga	Conga-Trommel or Tumba	tumba	conga
tambourine	tambour de basque	Schellentrommel or Tamburin	tamburo basco	Tamburin or pandereta
lion's roar				

Metal Idiophones

English	French	German	Italian	Spanish
crash cymbals	cymbales	Becken or Tellern	piatti or cinelli	platos
suspended cymbal	cymbale suspendue	Hängendes Becken	piatti sospeso	platos suspendidos
sizzle cymbal	cymbale sur tiges	Nietenbecken	piatto chiodat	plato claceteado
finger cymbal	cymbales digitales	Fingerzimbeln	cimbalini	platos de dedo
Chinese cymbals	cymbals chinoises	chinesische Becken	piatti cinesi	platillos chinos
hi-hat cymbal	cymbales hi-hat	Charlestonmaschine	charleston	platillos del hi-hat.
triangle	triangle	Triangle	triangolo or Acciarino	triángulo
anvil	enclume	Amboss	incudine	yunque
cowbell	sonnailles or cloches à vaches	Kuhglocken or Herdenglocken	campanaccio	cencerro
tam-tam	tam-tam	Tamtam	tamtam	tam-tam
gongs	gong	Gong	gong	gong
sleigh bells	grelots	Echellen	sonagli	cascabeles
bell tree	pavillon or chapeau chinois	Schellenbaum	mezza luna or cappello cinese	chinesco(s)
brake drum				
thunder stick	plancette ronflante	Schwirrholz	legno frullante or tavoletta sibilante	bramadera or zumba
thunder sheet or thunder machine	machine pour le tonnerre	Donnermaschine	macchina per il tuono	máquina de truenos
metal wind chimes	baguettes metalliques	Metall-Windglocken	bacchette di matallo sospese	cortina
vibraslap				

(continued)

Wind chimes				
English	**French**	**German**	**Italian**	**Spanish**
wooden wind chimes	baguettes de bois suspendues	Holz-Windglocken	bacchette di legno	cortina de madera
bamboo wind chimes	bambou suspende	Bambusrohre	tubi di bamboo	cortina de bambú
glass wind chimes	baguettes de verre suspendues	Glas-Windglocken	bacchette di vetro sospese	cortina de cristal

Wooden Idiophones				
English	**French**	**German**	**Italian**	**Spanish**
wood blocks	blocs de bois	Holzblöcke	blocci de legno cinese	cajas chinas
temple blocks	temple-blocs	Tempel-Blöcke	blocci de legno cereano	temple-blocks
claves	claves	Claves or Holzstab	claves	claves
castanets	castagnettes	Kastagnetten	castagnette or nacchere	castañuelas
sandpaper blocks	papier de verre	Sandpapier or Sandblöcke	Carta vetrata	Lija
maracas	maracas	Kürbisrassel or Rumbakugeln	maracas	maracas
guiro	guiro	Guiro or Kürbisrassel	guiro	güiro or calabazo.
ratchet	crécelle	Ratsche	raganella	carraca
slapstick, whip	fouet	Peitsche	frusta	látigo
log drum	tambor de tronco			
slit drum	tamour de bois	Schlitztrommel	tamburo di legno a fessura	tambor de hendidura
wood block temple block	bloc de bois temple block	Holzblock	blocco di legno	bloque de madera
wind machine	maschine à vent	Windmaschine	eolifono	máquina de viento

BRAZILIAN PERCUSSION INSTRUMENTS

Composer Hector Villa-Lobos introduced many traditional Brazilian percussion instruments to a wider audience in his series of compositions titled *Choros* (Portuguese for weeping or crying), written between 1920 and 1929. These works are based on music played by street musicians and are a synthesis of African, European, and Brazilian musical styles. *Choros No. 10*, "Rasga o Coração" (It Tears Your Heart), for chorus and orchestra and *Choros No. 11* for piano and orchestra, in particular, make extensive use of the instruments listed below.

Camisão (large and small). A large, single-headed frame drum often played with a leather strap or whip.

Caxambu. A large, single-headed drum.

Caxixi. A woven basket rattle.

Chocalho. A metal or wooden tube shaker filled with pellets. Also called **xucalho**.

Cuíca. A single-headed, wooden friction drum capable of many pitches, it has a thin stick mounted on the inside of the drum in the center of the head. It is played held attached to a strap under the arm. While one hand pulls on the internal stick with a cloth, the other applies pressure to the outside head of the drum near the attachment of that stick, changing the pressure and, consequently, the pitch. Similar to the lion's roar, it has been said to imitate the sound of the animal. Also called a **puita** or quica, it is a member of the membranophone category. Used in works of Villa-Lobos, *The Infernal Machine* by Christopher Rouse, and *Drala* by Peter Lieberson.

Puita. Also called cuíca.

Reco-Reco. A metal instrument with one, two, or three springs strung lengthwise on a hollow base with a horn-shaped bell that acts to enhance tone production. The springs are commonly scraped with a beater similar to a triangle beater. It comes in various sizes.

Surdo or **tambor surdo.** A double-headed bass drum that comes in three sizes. It is usually suspended from the drummer's neck and played with a beater in one hand while the other muffles the playing head as needed.

Tartaruga. Made from a giant tortoise shell ("tataruga" means turtle in Portuguese), a friction instrument that is treated with oil and rubbed with the hands.

Xucalho. The same as **chocalho**.

APPENDIX 5

Pitch Names and Their Translations into French, German, and Italian

English	French	German	Italian
B-sharp	Si dièse	His	Si diesis
B-natural	Si	H	Si
B-flat	Si bémol	B	Si bémolle
A-sharp	La dièse	Ais	La diesis
A-natural	La	A	La
A-flat	La bémol	As	La bémolle
G-sharp	Sol dièse	Gis	Sol diesis
G-natural	Sol	G	Sol
G-flat	Sol bémol	Ges	Sol bémolle
F-sharp	Fa dièse	Fis	Fa diesis
F-natural	Fa	F	Fa
F-flat	Fa bémol	Fes	Fa bémolle
E-sharp	Mi dièse	Eis	Mi diesis
E-natural	Mi	E	Mi
E-flat	Mi bémol	Es	Mi bémolle
D-sharp	Re dièse	Dis	Re diesis
D-natural	Re	D	Re
D-flat	Re bémol	Des	Re bémolle
C-sharp	Ut dièse	Cis	Do diesis
C-natural	Ut	C	Do
C-flat	Ut bémol	Ces	Do bémolle
C-double-sharp	Ut double-diése	Cisis	Do doppio dieses
C-double-flat	Ut double-bémol	Ceses	Do dopio bemolle

SPANISH

Si sostenido   Mi sostenido
Si   Mi
Si bemol   Mi bemol
La sostenido   Re sostenido
La   Re
La al bemol   Re bemol
Sol sostenido   Do sostenido
Sol   Do
Sol bemol   Do bemol
Fa sostenido   Do doble sostenido
Fa   Do doble bemol
Fa bemol

APPENDIX 6

Basic Interval Names and Their Translations

English	French	German	Italian	Spanish
unison (prime)	unisson	Unisono	unisono	primera
minor second	seconde	kleine	seconda	segunda
	mineure	Sekunde	minore	menor
major second	seconde	große	secunda	segunda
	majeure	Sekunde	maggiore	mayor
augmented second	secondes	übermäßige	secunda	segunda
	augmenté	Sekunde	aumentata	aumentada
diminished third	tierce	verminderte	terza	tercera
	diminué	Terz	diminuito	disminuida
minor third	tierce	kleine	terza	tercera
	mineure	Terz	minore	menor
major third	tierce	große	terza	tercera
	majeure	Terz	maggiore	mayor
perfect fourth	quarte	reine	quarta	cuarta
	juste	Quarte	giusti	justa
augmented fourth	quarte	übermäßige	quarte	cuarta
	augmenté	Quarte	aumentate	aumentada
tritone	triton	Tritonus	tritono	tritono
perfect fifth	quinte	reine	quinta	quinta
	juste	Quinte	giusti	justa
augmented fifth	quinte	übermäßige	quinta	quinta
	ausmenté	Quinte	aumentate	aumentada
minor sixth	sixte	kleine	sesta	sexta
	mineure	Sexte	minore	menor
major sixth	sixte	große	sesta	sexta
	majeure	Sexte	maggiore	mayor
minor seventh	septième	kleine	settima	séptima
	mineure	Septime	minore	menor
major seventh	septième	große	settima	séptima
	majeure	Septime	maggiore	mayor
octave	octave	Oktave	ottava	octava justa

APPENDIX 7

Rhythmic Terms and Their Translations

NOTE NAMES AND NAMES OF RESTS

American English	British English	French	German	Italian	Spanish
64th note	hemidemi-semiquaver	quadruple croche	Vierundsechzigstel	sessanta-quattresimo/ semibiscorma	semifusa
32nd note	demisemiquaver	triple croche	Zweiunddreißigstel	biscroma/ trentaduesimo	fusa
16th note	semiquaver	double croche	Sechzehntel	sedicesimo/semicroma	semicorchea
8th note	quaver	croche	Achtel	ottavo/croma	corchea
quarter note	crotchet	noire	Viertel	quarto/semiminima	negra
half note	minimum	blanche	Halbe	metá/minima	blanca
whole note	semibreve	ronde	Ganze	intero/semibreve	redonda
whole note rest	semibreve rest	pause	ganze Pause	pausa di semibreve	silencio de retonda
half note rest	minum rest	demi-pause	halbe Pause	pausa di minima	silencio de blanca
quarter note rest	crochet rest	soupir	Viertel Pause	pausa di semiminia	silencio de negra
eighth note rest	quaver rest	demi-soupir	Achtel Pause	pausa di croma	
16th note rest	semiquaver rest	quart de soupir	Sechzehntelpause	pausa di semicroma	
32nd note rest	demisemiquaver rest	huitiéme de soupir	Zweiunddreißigstel-pause	pausa di biscroma	
64th note rest	hemidemisemi-quaver rest	seiziéme de soupir	Vierundsechzigstel-pause	pausa di semibiscroma	

APPENDIX 8

Conducting Recitative

The recitative in the figure shown in this appendix, which precedes the aria *Come scoglio*, sung by Fiordiligi in Wolfgang Amadeus Mozart's opera *Così fan Tutte*, has just about all of the challenges of any classical orchestral recitative. Beginning at the marked bar, the conductor uses a **"guillotine" downbeat** with the baton at the top in the **ready position**, falling to the empty downbeat with a good **ictus** to start. The quarter note is long and requires a cutoff, either in the right or left hand will work. Following the text, the conductor meets the singer on the next empty downbeat, "*teme ravi*," moving forward in tempo, cutting off the quarter note and going ahead to beat four, ready to meet the singer again on the next downbeat, "*questo loco*," and once again cutting off the long quarter.

Courtesy Derek Brennan.

411

As shown, both the dynamic and tempo change to reflect the text. The preparatory beat for the next bar (bar 4 of the excerpt) is a little slower and gentler and can last the duration of the singer's three-note pickup on the words "*e non pro-fani*." The left hand is often used effectively to signal this change. The conductor moves through to the end of the bar, a bit ahead of the singer in order to be ready for the next bar. In this bar, the conductor gives a clear one and three while being ready to stretch just a bit on beats two and four in case the singer holds back. Often the singer will push forward to the end of the sentence completely in tempo, but one must always be ready. The quarter note in bar 6 needs a cutoff unless specified as short. For bar 7, the conductor takes the tempo from the singer, giving a clear preparatory beat for the cellos and basses. The *fortepiano* (*fp*) requires a quick pulling back of the dynamic right after the downbeat so that the text can be understood. The conductor moves to the end of the bar to be ready to mark the next bar with a **"dead"** or **neutral beat**, immediately moving forward to give the chord change on beat three "*cerca*."

Following the singer through the bar and cutting off after beat one, "*nostro alme*," is easily accomplished. In this bar, bar 10 of the excerpt, it is not unusual to ignore the quarter note rest and go right on. Bar 11 requires a preparatory gesture for the downbeat and a good, strong *forte* dynamic. There is a tradition of subdividing the last quarter note of the bar within a ritardando and adding a slight ***Luftpause*** before the sudden *piano* (*p*) on the downbeat of bar 12. Although sometimes bar 11 is done in tempo, with or without the Luftpause, depending on the desired effect. The choice here *will* change the dramatic impact. In the next bars, 12–14, the conductor keeps a clear beat but follows the singer, generally in a moderately slow tempo. After the cutoff gesture in bar 16, the conductor follows the singer's lead to give the preparatory gestures for the downbeat of bar 17, moving through it to the cutoff after one in the next bar. Here no more beats are required, the conductor waits at beat 4, takes the lead from the singer, and gives a strong preparatory gesture for the empty downbeat, meeting the singer on "*serbar*."

Bar 20 takes a neutral or "dead" beat to make sure that the orchestra always knows where they are. Bar 21 requires a good prep in tempo for the strong downbeat. The conductor beats through to the cutoff after one of bar 22, moves through the bar and waits for a moment, then following the singer's lead, giving beats one and two of bar 23 with the singer and preparing beat three for the orchestra. The next downbeat takes a cutoff gesture. Beats one and two of the last bar are given with neutral beats, beat three is prepped for the orchestra in the tempo of the aria that follows **attacca**, right over the bar line.

Recitative conducting, when the recitative is accompanied by the orchestra, involves a special set of skills. Knowing the text is paramount. Next is understanding the way the voice moves, breaths, and supports. The conductor lets the singer "conduct" them. The words, the breath, and the singer's tone guide the conductor. The singer will render their part in a tempo close to "speaking tempo," that it, in the speed that the words would be spoken in order to best communicate the emotion behind them.

The conductor leads the orchestra, not the singer. Account for every bar using a neutral or dead beat to mark each downbeat, even if, perhaps especially if, it is empty. (It is also possible to mark the parts accordingly in advance.) When the singer is alone, the baton follows the pattern through the bar, somewhat ahead of your singer, and wait on the beat before you "meet." That is usually the last note for the singer and the beat before the orchestra plays. Move from that beat with a preparatory gesture to bring in the orchestra in the correct tempo, dynamic, articulation, and style.

Typical operatic recitative moves the drama forward, often involving consideration of the central conflict of the story. That often includes the use of two basic contrasting tempos, each reflecting a certain mood. Clarity of tempo, which bars are slow and which are fast, is vital to an effective interpretation.

Other considerations are the length and, more specifically, the character of the chords with which the orchestra punctuates the text. Short and loud or longer and soft create significantly different results.

Selected Bibliography

CONDUCTING TEXTS

Berlioz, Hector. *The Conductor: The Theory of His Art.* Excerpt from the *Grand traité d'instrumentation et d'orchestration modernes.* Translation and commentary by Hugh Macdonald. Cambridge and New York: Cambridge University Press, 2002.

Boult, Adrian C. *A Handbook of Conducting.* Oxford: Hall the Printer, 1936.

Davidson, Archibald T. *Choral Conducting.* Cambridge, MA: Harvard University Press, 1959. Olin Downes wrote in the *New York Times*: "A book containing more information, taste, and common sense on the subject tan any we have seen. . . . It should be worth its weight in gold to choral singers and choral conductors."

Farberman, Harold. *The Art of Conducting Technique: A New Perspective.* Miami, FL: Warner Bros., 1997.

Green, Elizabeth A. H. *The Modern Conductor.* Fourth Edition. Englewood Cliffs, NJ: Prentice-Hall, Inc., 1987. Includes an appendix titled "100 Terms That the Young Conductor Should Know." Organized into "terms of a general nature," "terms affecting the tempo and time-beating," "terms affecting the handling of the instruments themselves," and "some specialized percussion terms." Includes a valuable appendix titled "Classification of Bowing."

Hunsberger, Donald, and Roy E. Ernst. *The Art of Conducting.* 2nd ed. New York: McGraw-Hill, Inc., 1992. Contains examples for classroom use of scores and individuals parts for transposing and nontransposing instruments.

Labuta, Jospeh A. *Basic Conducting Techniques.* 6th ed. Upper Saddle River, NJ: Prentice Hall, 2010. Available with a resource DVD that contains examples of scores for classroom use.

McElheran, Brock. *Conducting Technique: For Beginners and Professionals.* New York and Oxford: Oxford University Press, 1989.

Meier, Gustav. *The Score, the Orchestra, and the Conductor.* New York: Oxford University Press, 2009. A comprehensive book that deals with issues from the basics through many nuances of the conductor's art. Meier introduces the ZigZag Way, a method of organizing score study.

Nicotra, Ennio. *Introduzione alla Technica della Direzione d'Orchestra: Secondo il sistema di Ilya Musin.* Milan, Italy: Edizioni Curci, 2010. Based on the techniques of the famous Russian conducting pedagogue Ilya Musin. Although the book is published in Italy, all chapters appear in English, German, Italian, and Spanish. It comes with a DVD.

Prausnitz, Frederik. *Score and Podium: A Complete Guide to Conducting.* New York: Alpha Books, 1983. A comprehensive book with an interesting chapter on memorization.

Rudolf, Max. *The Grammar of Conducting: A Comprehensive Guide to Baton Technique and Orchestral Interpretation.* 1st ed. New York: Schirmer Books, 1980 (3rd ed., 1994).

Scherchen, Hermann. *Handbook of Conducting [Lehrbuch des Dirigierens].* Translated by M. D. Calvocoressi. Oxford: Oxford University Press, 1989.

Wagner, Richard. *Wagner on Conducting.* Translated by William Reeves. New York: Dover, 1989.

SELECTED CONDUCTOR RESOURCES

Ammer Christine. *Musician's Handbook of Foreign Terms.* New York: Schirmer Books, 1971.

Ammer, Christine. *Unsung: A History of Women in American Music.* Greenwood Press, 1980.

Auner, Joseph. *Music in the Twentieth and Twenty-First Centuries.* New York: W. W. Norton and Co., 2013.

Baker, Theodore, ed. *Pocket Manual of Musical Terms.* 5th ed. New York: Schirmer Books, 1985.

BBC Music Guides. Published mostly in the 1960s and 1970s by the University of Washington Press, Seattle. There are at least thirty-three volumes covering composers from Johann Sebastian Bach to Arnold Schoenberg.

Bowen, José Antonio, ed. *The Cambridge Companion to Conducting.* Cambridge Companions to Music. Cambridge: Cambridge University Press, 2003.

Bowers, Jane and Judith Tick. *Women Making Music: The Western Art Tradition, 1150–1950.* Urbana and Chicago: University of Illinois Press, 1987. Includes essays on women musicians in history, women composers, and women's orchestras in the United States from 1925 to 1945.

Braccini, Roberto. *Wörterbuch der Musik* [Dictionary of music: Practical vocabulary of music]. Mainz, Germany: Schott Music

GmbH and Co., 1912. Terms appear in English, French, German, and Italian.

Casado, Pedro González. *Términos Musicales* [Musical terms]. Madrid: Ediciones Akal, S. A., 2000. Terms are translated from Spanish into English and vice versa.

Castel, Nico. *Italian, French Belcanto Opera Libretti.* 3 vols. Geneseo, NY: Leyerle Publications Mt. Morris. Contains International Phonetic Alphabet transcriptions and word-for-word literal translations of opera librettos, with a foreword by Dame Joan Sutherland.

Bowen, José Antonio, ed. *The Cambridge Companion to Conducting.* Cambridge: Cambridge University Press, 2003. A collection of essays on the practice and history in addition to contemporary issues in the field.

Cambridge Music Handbooks is a valuable series of smaller books, each of which concentrates on either a single work or shorter related works by the same composer. Titles include: Stravinsky: *The Rite of Spring,* by Peter Hill (2000); Mahler: *Das Lied von der Erde* (The Song of the Earth), by Stephen E. Hefling (2000); Tchaikovsky: *Symphony no. 6* (Pathétique), by Timothy L. Jackson (1999); Beethoven: *Symphony No. 9,* by Nicholas Cook (1993); Berg: *Violin Concerto,* by Anthony Pope (1991); Haydn: *The "Paris" Symphonies,* by Bernard Harrison (1998); Handel: *Water Music and Music for the Royal Fireworks,* by Christopher Hogwood (2005); and more.

Cirone, Anthony J. *The Great American Symphony Orchestra.* Galesville, MD: Meredith Music Publications, 2011.

Cooper, Barry, ed. *The Beethoven Compendium: A Guide to Beethoven's Life and Music.* London: Thames and Hudson, Ltd., 1991.

Daniels, David. *Orchestra Music.* 4th ed. Lanham, MD: Scarecrow Press, 2005.

Fink, Robert, and Robert Ricci. *Twentieth Century Music: A Dictionary of Terms.* New York: Macmillan, 1975.

Frisch, Walter. *Music in the Nineteenth Century.* New York: W. W. Norton and Co., 2013.

Galkin, Elliott W. *A History of Orchestral Conducting in Theory and Practice.* New York: Pendragon Press, 1988.

Green, Elizabeth A. H. *The Dynamic Orchestra: Principles of Orchestral Performance for Instrumentalists, Conductors and Audiences.* Englewood Cliffs, NJ: Prentice-Hall, 1987.

Griffiths, Paul. *Modern Music and After.* Oxford and New York: Oxford University Press, 1995.

Harding, Rosamond E. M. *The Metronome and Its Precursors.* Henley-on-Thames, England: Gresham Books, 1983. (Orig. 1938.) This small book has a long bibliography of articles of interest in French, German, and English that cover the early development of various musical "time keepers" and is packed with information about early inventions that preceded the modern tool.

Jagow, Shelley M. "Women Orchestral Conductors in America: The Struggle for Acceptance—An Historical View from the Nineteenth Century to the Present." *College Music Symposium* 38 (1988): 126–45.

Larsen, Jens Peter. *Handel's Messiah.* 2nd ed. New York: W. W. Norton and Co., 1972.

Leinsdorf, Erich. *The Composer's Advocate.* New Haven, CT: Yale University Press, 1981.

Lucas, John. *Thomas Beecham: An Obsession with Music.* Suffolk, UK: Boydell & Brewster, Ltd., 2008.

Neuls-Bates, Carol. *Women in Music: An Anthology of Source Readings from the Middle Ages to the Present.* New York: Harper and Row, 1982. Includes essays on women's symphony orchestras, conductor Antonia Brico, and several women composers.

Norton Critical Scores, published by W. W. Norton and Co., New York. Each includes a score and numerous essays about the work. The series includes: Bach, *Cantata No. 4,* ed. by Gerhard Herz; Bach, *Cantata No. 140,* ed. by Gerhard Herz; Beethoven, *Symphony No. 5 in C minor,* ed. by Elliot Forbes; Berlioz, *Fantastic Symphony,* ed. by Edward T. Cone; Debussy, *Prelude to "The Afternoon of a Faun,"* ed. by William W. Austin; Haydn, *Symphony No. 103 in E-flat major* ("Drum Roll"); Mozart, *Symphony in G minor, K. 550,* ed. by Nathan Broder; Schubert, *Symphony in B minor* ("Unfinished") ed. by Martin Chusid; Stravinsky, *Petrushka,* ed. by Charles Hamm; Wagner, *Prelude and Transfiguration from Tristan and Isolde,* edited by Robert Bailey; and more.

Rice, John. *Music in the Eighteenth Century.* New York: W. W. Norton and Co., 2013.

Schwartz, Elliott, Godfrey, Daniel. *Music since 1945: Issues, Materials and Literature.* New York: Schirmer Books, 1993.

Slonimsky, Nicholas. *Baker's Biographical Dictionary of Musicians.* New York: Schirmer Books, 2001.

Weingartner, Felix. *On Music & Conducting.* New York: Dover Publications, Inc., 1969. Includes: "On Conducting," "On the Performance of Beethoven's Symphonies," "The Symphony since Beethoven."

Weisberg, Arthur. *Performing Twentieth-Century Music: A Handbook for Conductor and Instrumentalists.* New Haven, CT: Yale University Press, 1993.

Zaslow, Neal. *Mozart's Symphonies: Context, Performance Practice, Reception.* Oxford: Clarendon Press, 1989.

ABOUT CONDUCTORS

Barber, Charles. *Corresponding with Carlos: A Biography of Carlos Kleiber.* New York: Scarecrow Press, 2011.

Berlioz, Hector, *Memoirs of Hector Berlioz.* Annotated and translated by Ernest Newman. New York: Alfred A. Knopf, Inc., 1932.

Blankenburg, Elke Mascha. *Dirigentinnen im 20: Jahrhundert, Porträts von Marin Alsop bis Simone Young.* Hamburg: Europäische Verlagsanstalt, 2003. Included, although it is in German, because of the rarity of any publications on women conductors. Includes essays about numerous European and American women.

Brook, Donald. *International Gallery of Conductors.* Westport, CT: Greenwood Press, 1973.

Brown, Clive, *Louis Spohr: A Critical Biography.* New York: Cambridge University Press, 1984.

Cairns, David. *Berlioz: The Making of an Artist, 1803–1832* Berkeley, CA: University of California Press, 1999–2000.

———. *Berlioz: Servitude and Greatness, 1832–1869.* Berkeley, CA: University of California Press, 1999–2000.

Carse, Adam. *The Life of Jullien.* Cambridge: W. Heffer and Sons, Ltd, 1951.

Gradenwitz, Peter. *Leonard Bernstein: The Infinite Variety of a Musician.* New York: St. Martin's Press, 1987.

Grogan, Christopher, ed. *Imogen Holst: A Life in Music*. Rochester, NY: Boydell Press, 2007.

Ewen, David. *Dictators of the Baton*. Chicago and New York: Ziff-Davis Publishing Company, 1948.

Handy, D. Antoinette. *Black Conductors*. Lanham, MD: Scarecrow Press, 1995.

Heyworth, Peter. *Otto Klemperer: His Life and Times*. Cambridge: Cambridge University Press, 1996.

Holden, Raymond. *The Virtuoso Conductors*, New Haven, CT: Yale University Press, 2005. Essays about Hans von Bülow, Arthur Nikisch, Gustav Mahler, Felix Weingartner, Richard Strauss, Bruno Walter, Otto Klemperer, Wilhelm Furtwängler, and Herbert von Karajan.

———. *Richard Strauss, a Musical Life*. New Haven, CT: Yale University Press, 2011. This volume focuses on Strauss the conductor.

Holmes, John L. *Conductors: A Record Collector's Guide*. London: Victor Gollancs, Ltd., 1988. Although this book is limited by a cutoff date of 1977, it includes a vast list of conductors with biographies for each.

Holoman, D. Kern. *Charles Munch*. Oxford: Oxford University Press, 2012.

Jacobson, Bernard. *Conductors on Conducting*. Frenchtown, NJ: Columbia Publishing Co., 1979. Essays include: James Levine on Verdi and Mozart, Harnoncourt on Bach, Mackerras on Handel, Colin Davis on Berlioz, Haitink on Mahler, Serebrier on Ives, Boult on Elgar, and Giullini on Brahms.

Kenyon, Nicholas. *Simon Rattle: The Making of a Conductor*. London: Faber and Faber, 1987.

Kessler, Daniel. *Sarah Caldwell: The First Woman of Opera*. Lanham, MD: Scarecrow Press, 2008.

Lebrecht, Norman. *The Maestro Myth: Great Conductors in Pursuit of Power*. New York: Carol Publishing Group, 1991.

Leichtentritt, Hugo. *Serge Koussevitzky: The Boston Symphony Orchestra and the New American Music*. Cambridge, MA: Harvard University Press, 1946.

Marsh, Robert Charles. *Toscanini and the Art of Conducting*. New York: Collier Books, 1962.

Matheopoulos, Helena. *Maestro, Encounters with Conductors of Today*. New York: Harper and Row, Publishers, 1982.

Nally, Donald. *Conversations with Joseph Flummerfelt: Thoughts on Conducting, Music and Musicians*. Lanham, MD: Scarecrow Press, 2010.

Robinson, Ray, ed. *Studies in Penderecki*. Vol. 1. Princeton, NJ: Prestige Publications, 1998.

Schonberg, Harold C. *The Great Conductors*. New York: Simon and Schuster, 1967.

Shore, Bernard. *The Orchestra Speaks*. London: Longmans, Green and Co., 1938. A series of essays by conductors of the day written by the principal violist of the BBC Symphony Orchestra.

Stern, Michael. *Max Rudolf: A Musical Life, Writings and Letters*. Hillsdale, NY: Pendragon Press, 2001.

Stoddard, Hope. *Symphony Conductors of the U.S.A.* New York: Thomas Y. Crowell Co., 1957. Includes essays about many of the renowned conductors in America at the time and a series of "thumbnail sketches" of more than four hundred conductors working in amateur, semiprofessional, and professional orchestras and opera houses in America.

Vermeil, Jean. *Conversations with Boulez—Thoughts on Conducting*. Translated by Camille Naish. Portland, OR: Amadeus Press, 1996.

Wagar, Jeannine, ed. *Conductors in Conversation, Fifteen Contemporary Conductors Discuss Their Lives and Profession*. Boston: G. K. Hall and Co., 1991.

BY CONDUCTORS

Bamberger, Carl. *The Conductor's Art*. New York: Columbia University Press, 1965. Essays include: Berlioz, "On Conducting"; Robert Schumann, "About Conducting"; Liszt, "A Letter on Conducting"; Bruno Walter, "The Conductor"; Gustav Mahler, Stokowski, "Conducting"; Furtwängler, "About the Handicraft of the Conductor"; Boult, "Arthur Nikisch"; Hindemith, "Conductors"; Barbirolli, "The Art of Conducting"; Ormandy, "Art of Conducting"; and more.

Beecham, Thomas. *A Mingled Chime—Leaves from an Autobiography*. New York: G. P. Putnam, 1943.

Bernstein, Leonard. *The Infinite Variety of Music*. New York: Anchor Books, 1966.

———. *The Joy of Music*. Pompton Plains, NJ: Amadeus Press, 1959.

———. *Young People's Concerts*. Milwaukee, WI, and Cambridge: Amadeus Press, 1962.

———. *The Unanswered Question: Six Talks at Harvard*. Cambridge, MA: Harvard University Press, 1976.

Boult, Adrian. *A Handbook on the Technique of Conducting*. 7th ed. Oxford: Hall, 1951.

———. *My Own Trumpet*. London: Hamish Hamilton, 1973.

———. *Thoughts on Conducting*. London: Phoenix House, 1963.

Boult, Adrian. *Boult on Music: Words from a Lifetime's Communication*. London: Toccata Press, 1983. Contains essays on conductors, conducting, musicians, composers, and music in general.

Caldwell, Sarah, with Rebecca Matlock. *Challenges: A Memoir of My Life in Opera*. Middletown, CT: Wesleyan University Press, 2008.

Canarina, John. *Pierre Monteux, Maître*. Pompton Plains, NJ: Amadeus Press, 2003.

———. *The New York Philharmonic: From Bernstein to Maazel*. New York: Amadeus Press, 2010.

———. *Uncle Sam's Orchestra: Memories of the Seventh Army Symphony*. Rochester, NY: University of Rochester Press, 1998.

Charry, Michael. *George Szell: A Life of Music*. Urbana: University of Illinois Press, 2011.

Del Mar, Norman. *Anatomy of the Orchestra*. Berkeley: University of California Press, 1981.

———. *Conducting Beethoven*. Vol. 1, *The Symphonies*. Oxford: Clarendon Press; New York: Oxford University Press, 1992–1993.

———. *Conducting Beethoven*. Vol. 2, *Overtures, Concertos, Missa solemnis*. Oxford: Clarendon Press; New York: Oxford University Press, 1992–1993.

———. *Conducting Berlioz*. Oxford: Clarendon Press; New York: Oxford University Press, 1997.

———. *Conducting Brahms*. Oxford: Clarendon Press; New York, Oxford University Press, 1993.

———. *Conducting Elgar*. Oxford: Clarendon Press; New York: Oxford University Press, 1998.

———. *Mahler's Sixth Symphony: A Study*. London: Eulenberg Books, 1980.

———. *Orchestral Variations: Confusion and Error in the Orchestral Repertoire*. London: Eulenberg Books, 1981.

Doráti, Antol. *Notes of Seven Decades*. Detroit, MI: Wayne State University Press, 1981.

Fennell, Frederick. *The Drummer's Heritage: A Collection of Popular Airs and Official U.S. Army Music for Fifes and Drums Combined with Similar Pieces for Field Trumpets, Cymbals, and Drums*. Rochester, NY: Eastman School of Music, 1956.

———. *Time and the Winds: A Short History of the Use of Wind Instruments in the Orchestra, Band, and the Wind Ensemble*. Huntersville, NC: Northland Music Publishers, 2007.

Glover, Jane. *Mozart's Women: His Family, His Friends, His Music*. New York: HarperCollins, 2005.

Gardiner, Sir John Elliot. *Bach: Music in the Castle of Heaven*. New York: Alfred A. Knopf, 2013.

Goldovsky, Boris. *Accents on Opera: A Series of Brief essays Stressing Known and Little Known Facts and Facets of a Familiar Art*. Freeport, NY: Books for Libraries Press, 1953.

———. *Bringing Opera to Life: Operatic Acting and Stage Direction*. Englewood Cliffs, NJ: Prentice-Hall, 1968.

———. *My Road to Opera: The Recollections of Boris Goldovsky as Told to Curtis Cate*. Boston: Houghton Mifflin, 1979.

Hogwood, Christopher. *Handel*. London: Thames and Hudson, 2007.

———. *Haydn's Visits to London*. London: Thames and Hudson, 1980.

———, ed. *The Keyboard in Baroque Europe*. Cambridge: Cambridge University Press, 2003.

———. *Music at Court*. London: Victor Gollancz, 1980.

———. *"Our Old Great Favourite": Burney, Bach, and the Bachists*. Cambridge: Cambridge University Press, 2006.

Hogwood, Christopher, and Richard Luckett, ed. *Music in the Eighteenth-Century England*. Cambridge: Cambridge University Press, 1983.

Klemperer, Otto. *Klemperer on Music: shavings from a musician's workbench*. Edited by Martin Andersen. London: Toccata Press, 1986.

———. *Minor Recollections*. London: Dobson Books, 1964.

Kostelanetz, André, and Gloria Hammond. *Echoes: Memoirs of André Kostelanetz*. New York: Harcourt, Brace, Jovanovich, 1981.

Leinsdorf, Erich. *Cadenza: A Musical Career*. Boston: Houghton Mifflin, 1976.

———. *The Composer's Advocate*. New Haven, CT: Yale University Press, 1981.

———. *On Music*. Portland, OR: Amadeus Press, 1997.

Malko, Nikolai. *The Conductor and His Baton: Fundamentals of the Technic of Conducting*. Copenhagen: Hansen, 1950.

Munch, Charles. *I Am a Conductor*. Translated by Leonard Burkat. New York: Oxford University Press, 1955.

Muti, Riccardo. *Riccardo Muti: An autobiography—First the Music, Then the Words*. Edited by Marco Grondona. New York: Rizzoli, 2011. English translation by Alta L. Price.

Penderecki, Krzysztof. *Labyrinth of Time: Five Addresses for the End of the Millenium*. Chapel Hill, NC: Hinshaw Music, 1998.

Seaman, Christopher. *Inside Conducting*. Rochester, NY: University of Rochester, 2013.

Schuller, Gunther. *A Life in Pursuit of Music and Beauty*. Rochester, NY: University of Rochester Press, 2011. An autobiography that includes many detailed and vivid descriptions of his experiences working with some of the twentieth century's greatest conductors.

———. *The Complete Conductor*. New York: Oxford University Press, 1997.

Slatkin, Leonard. *Conducting Business: Unveiling the Mystery behind the Maestro*. Milwaukee, WI: Amadeus Press, 2012.

Spohr, Louis. *Autobiography*. London, 1865; repr. New York by Da Capo Press, 1969.

Walter, Bruno. *Of Music and Music-Making*. Translated by Paul Hamburger. New York: W. W. Norton & Co., 1961.

———. *Theme and Variations*. New York: A. A. Knopf, 1946.

Weisberg, Arthur. *The Art of Wind Playing*. New York: Schirmer Books, 1975.

———. *Performing 20th Century Music—a Handbook for Conductors and Instrumentalists*. New Haven, CT: Yale University Press, 1993.

Wittry, Diane. *Beyond the Baton: What Every Conductor Needs to Know*. New York: Oxford University Press, 2007.

———. *Baton Basics: Communicating Music through Gesture*. New York: Oxford University Press, 2014.

ORCHESTRATION

Adler, Samuel. *The Study of Orchestration*. 4th ed. New York: W. W. Norton & Co., 2015.

Berlioz, Hector. *Treatise on Instrumentation*. Enlarged and edited by Richard Strauss. Translated by Theodore Front. New York: Kalmus, 1948.

Blatter, Alfred. *Instrumentation and Orchestration*. New York: Schirmer Books, 1997.

Forsyth, Cecil. *Orchestration*. Reprint of the 2nd ed. (1935). New York: Dover, 1982.

Kennan, Kent W., and Donald Grantham. *The Technique of Orchestration*. 5th ed. Englewood Cliffs, NJ: Prentice-Hall, 1997.

Piston, Walter. *Orchestration*. London: Victor Gollancz Ltd, 1973.

Rimsky-Korsakov, Nicolai. *Principles of Orchestration*. Translated by Edward Agate. New York: Dover, 1953.

THE ORCHESTRA AND ITS INSTRUMENTS

Bartolozzi, Bruno. *New Sounds for Woodwind*. Translated and edited by Reginald Smith Brindle. London: Oxford University Press, 1967. 2nd ed., 1982.

Beck, John H. *Encyclopedia of Percussion*. New York: Routledge, 2007.

Blades, James. *Percussion Instruments and Their History*. London: Faber and Faber, 1984.

Carroll, Raynor. *Symphonic Repertoire Guide for Timpani and Percussion*. Pasadena, CA: Batterie Music, 2005. Carroll, principal percussionist of the Los Angeles Philharmonic, has collected an exhaustive list of orchestral literature from the Baroque to Contemporary and the percussion requirements of each piece.

Carse, Adam. *Musical Wind Instruments: A History of the Wind Instruments Used in European Orchestras and Wind Bands from the Later Middle Ages up to the Present Time*. Mineola, NY: Dover, 2002.

———. *The Orchestra from Beethoven to Berlioz: A History of the Orchestra in the First Half of the 19th Century, and of the Development of Orchestral Baton Conducting.* St Clair Shores, MI: Scholarly Press, 1976.

———. *The Orchestra in the 18th Century.* New York: Broude Bros., 1969.

Craven Robert R., ed. *Symphony Orchestras of the United States.* Westport, CT: Greenwood Press, 1986.

Del Mar, Norman. *The Anatomy of the Orchestra.* Berkeley: University of California Press, 1981.

Flesch, Carl. *The Art of Violin Playing.* Translated by Eric Rosenblith. New York: C. Fisher, 2000.

Galamian, Ivan. *Principles of Violin Playing & Teaching.* Englewood Cliffs, NJ: Prentice-Hall, 1985.

Geminiani, Francesco. *The Art of Playing on the Violin.* New York: Performer's Facsimiles, 2001.

Green, Elizabeth A. H. *The Dynamic Orchestra: Principles of Orchestral Performance for Instrumentalists, Conductors and Audiences.* Englewood Cliffs, NJ: Prentice-Hall, 1987.

———. *Orchestral Bowings and Routines.* Ann Arbor, MI: Campus Publishers, 1983.

Mozart, Leopold. *A Treatise on the Fundamental Principles of Violin Playing.* Translated by Editha Knocker. London, New York: Oxford University Press, 1972.

Mueller, John H. *The American Symphony Orchestra: A Social History of Musical Taste.* Bloomington: Indiana University Press, 1951.

Quantz, Johann Joachim. *On Playing the Flute [Versuch einer Anweisung die Flöte traversiere zu spielen].* Translated by Edward R. Reilly. Boston: Northeastern University Press, 2001. (Orig. 1792.) An excellent resource for performance practice issues of the Classical period.

Sabanovich, Dan. *Brazilian Percussion Manual.* Van Nuys, CA: Alfred Publishing Co., 1994.

Schick, Steven. *The Percussionist's Art—Same Bed, Different Dreams.* Rochester, NY: University of Rochester Press, 2006.

Solomon, Samuel Z. *How to Write for Percussion.* New York: S. Z. Solomon, 2002.

Spitzer, John, and Zaslow, Neal. *The Birth of the Orchestra: History of an Institution, 1650–1815.* New York: Oxford University Press, 2004.

Spohr, Louis. *Spohr's Grand Violin School.* Boston: O. Ditson, 1852.

THEORY AND ANALYSIS

Adorno, Theodor. *Introduction to the Sociology of Music.* Translated by E. B. Ashton. New York: Continuum, 1989. (Orig. 1962.)

Adorno, Theodor. *Philosophy of Modern Music.* Translated by Anne G. Mitchell and Wesley V. Blomster. New York: Continuum, 1994.

———. *Philosophy of New Music.* Translated and edited by Robert Hullot-Kentor. Minneapolis: University of Minnesota Press, 2006.

Babbitt, Milton. *The Collected Essays of Milton Babbitt.* Edited by Stephen Peles. Princeton, NJ: Princeton University Press, 2003.

Boretz, Benjamin, and Edward Cone. *Perspectives on Contemporary Music Theory.* New York: W. W. Norton and Co., 1972.

Boulez, Pierre. *Boulez on Music Today.* Translated by Susan Bradshaw and Richard Rodney Bennett. London: Faber and Faber, 1971.

———. *Notes of an Apprenticeship.* Translated by Herbert Weinstock. New York: A. A. Knopf, 1968.

———. *Points de repère.* Translated by Martin Cooper. Cambridge, MA: Harvard University Press, 1986.

Brinkmann, Reinhold. *Late Idyll: The Second Symphony of Johannes Brahms.* Translated by Peter Palmer. Cambridge, MA: Harvard University Press, 1995.

Cage, John. *Silence.* Cambridge, MA: MIT Press, 1970.

Dallin, Leon. *Techniques of Twentieth Century Composition.* 2nd ed. Dubuque, IA: William C. Brown, 1971.

Epstein, David. *Beyond Orpheus: Studies in Musical Structure.* Cambridge, MA: MIT Press, 1979. Includes a preface by Milton Babbitt.

Hanson, Howard. *The Harmonic Materials of Modern Music.* New York: Appleton-Century-Crofts, 1960. An important text for the study of twentieth-century music.

Kennan, Kent. *Counterpoint: Based on Eighteenth-Century Practice.* Upper Saddle River, NJ: Prentice Hall, 1999.

Kramer, Jonathan. *The Time of Music: New Meanings, New Temporalities, New Listening Strategies.* New York: Schirmer Books, 1988. Kramer analyses how the left and right sides of the brain process music.

Lendvaï, Ernö. *Béla Bartók: An Analysis of His Music.* London: Kahn and Averill, 1971.

Morris, Robert. *The Whistling Blackbird: Essays and Talks on New Music.* Rochester, NY: University of Rochester Press, 2010.

Keller, Gary. *The Jazz Chord/Scale Handbook.* Advance Music, GmbH, 1997.

Perle, George. *Serial Composition and Atonality.* Berkeley: University of California Press, 1991.

———. *Twelve-Tone Tonality.* Berkeley: University of California Press, 1996.

Piston Walter. *Harmony.* 5th ed. Revised by Mark DeVoto. New York: Norton, 1987.

Pollack, Howard. *Aaron Copland: The Life and Work of an Uncommon Man.* New York: Henry Holt and Co., 1999.

Rufer, Josef. *Composition with Twelve Notes Related Only to One Another.* New York: Macmillian, 1954.

Salzer, Felix. *Structural Hearing: Tonal Coherence in Music.* New York: Dover Publications, 1982.

Schenker, Heinrich. *Beethovens Neunte Sinfonie.* Translated by John Rothgeb. New Haven, CT: Yale University Press, 1992.

———. *Five Graphic Music Analyses [Fünf Urlinie-Tafeln].* New York: Dover Publications, 1969. Includes and introduction and glossary by Felix Salzer.

Schillinger, Joseph. *The Schillinger System of Musical Composition.* New York: Carl Fisher, 1946.

Schoenberg, Arnold. *Style and Idea: Selected Writings of Arnold Schonberg.* Edited by Leonard Stein. New York: St. Martin's Press, 1975.

———. *Theory of Harmony.* Translated Roy E. Carter. Berkeley and Los Angeles: University of California Press, 1978.

Slonimsky, Nicolas. *Thesaurus of Scales and Melodic Patterns.* Coleman-Ross, New York, 1947.

Straus, Joseph. *Introduction to Post-Tonal Theory.* Upper Saddle River, NJ: Prentice Hall, 2004.

Tovey, Donald Francis. *Essays in Musical Analysis.* Oxford: University Press, 1972. Multiple volumes on symphonies, concertos, and more.

REFERENCE

The Harvard Biographical Dictionary of Music. Edited by Don Michael Randel. Published by the Harvard University Press, 1996.

The Harvard Dictionary of Music. Edited by Willi Apel and published by Harvard University Press. A standard reference tool first published in 1944. The fourth edition, edited by Don Michael Randel, appeared in 2003.

Die Musik in Geschichte und Gegenwart [Music in History and the Present]. (*MGG*) The largest and most comprehensive German music encyclopedia available today. Published by Barenreiter, a CD-ROM version is available in a limited number of libraries.

The New Grove's Dictionary of Music and Musicians. Edited by Stanley Sadie and Nigel Fortune. New York: St. Martin's Press, 1980. Supplementary volumes include: *American Music,* 1984; *A Dictionary of Opera,* 1992; *A Dictionary of Musical Instruments,* 1984. A second edition was published in 2001 and accompanied by a web-based version known as *Grove Music Online.*

Oxford Companion to Music. Published by Oxford University Press. The original edition was written by Percy Scholes and published in 1938. The 2002 version is accessible on the Internet through Oxford Music Online.

MIND AND BODY TECHNIQUES

Alexander, F. Matthias. *The Alexander Technique: The Essential Writings of F. Matthias Alexander.* Selected and introduced by Edward Maisel. New York, New: Carol Communications, 1989.

Barlow, Wilfred. *The Alexander Technique.* New York: Warner Books, 1973.

Bartenieff, Irmgard, and Dori Lewis. *Body Movement: Coping with the Environment.* New York: Gordon and Breach, 1980.

Conable, Barbara, and William Conable. *How to Learn the Alexander Technique: A Manual for Students.* Columbus, OH: Andover Press, 1992.

Gelb, Michael J. *Body Learning: An Introduction to the Alexander Technique.* 2nd ed. New York: Henry Holt and Co., 1994.

Horvath, Janet. *Playing (LESS) Hurt: An Injury and Prevention Guide for Musicians.* New York: Hal Leonard Books, 2010.

Laban, Rudolf. *The Mastery of Movement.* 4th ed. Revised and extended by L. Ullmann. London: MacDonald and Evans, 1980.

THE RECORDING INDUSTRY

Lebrecht, Norman. *Maestros, Masterpieces and Madness: The Secret Life and Shameful Death of the Classical Recording Industry.* New York: Penguin Books, 2008.

Marmorstein, Gary. *The Label: The Story of Columbia Records.* New York: Thunder's Mouth Press, 2007.

Rust, Brian. *The American Record Label Book.* New Rochelle, NY: Da Capo Press, 1984.

Soames, Nicolas. *The Story of Naxos: The Extraordinary Story of the Independent Record Label That Changed Recording for Ever.* London: Piatkus, 1012.

Sutton, A. *Directory of American Disc Record Brands and Manufacturers, 1891–1943.* Westport, CT: Greenwood Press, 1994.

THIS AND THAT

Adams, John. *Hallelujah Junction: Composing an American Life.* New York: Picador, 2008.

Bloom, Peter, ed. *Music in Paris in the Eighteen Thirties.* Stuyvesant, NY: Pendragon Press, 1987. Includes essays about conductors and conducting.

Brinkmann, Reinhold, and Christoph Wolff, eds. *Driven into paradise: The Musical Migration from Nazi Germany to the United States.* Berkeley, CA: University of California Press, 1999.

Cheah, Elena. *An Orchestra Beyond Borders: Voices of the West-Eastern Divan Orchestra.* Brooklyn, NY: Verso, 2009. Includes a foreword by Daniel Barenboim.

Craft, Robert. *Stravinsky: Chronicle of a Friendship, 1948–1971.* New York: A. A. Knopf, 1972.

Freeman, John W. *The Metropolitan Opera Stories of the Great Operas.* New York: W. W. Norton and Co., 1984. A collection of articles on over 130 operas, including story lines, roles, and interesting facts.

Freeman, Robert. *The Crisis of Classical Music in America: Lessons from a Life in the Education of a Musician.* Lanham, MD: Roman and Littlefield, 2014.

Frisch, Walter. *Brahms and the Principle of Developing Variation.* Berkeley: University of California Press, 1984.

Grant, Mark N. *Maestros of the Pen: A History of Classical Music Criticism in America.* Boston: Northeastern University Press, 1998.

Helmholtz, Hermann. *On the Sensations of Tone: As a Physiological Basis for the Theory of Music* [*Die Lehre von den Tonempfindungen als physiologische Grundlage für die Theorie der Musik*]. Translated by A. J. Ellis. New York: Dover, 1954. (Orig. 1863)

Hiller, Johann Adam. *Treatise on Vocal Performance and Ornamentation.* Reissued in translation and with commentary by Suzanne J. Beicken, Cambridge: Cambridge University Press, 2001. (Orig. 1780.)

Hogwood, Christopher. *Handel.* London: Thames and Hudson, 1984.

———. *Haydn's Visits to London.* London: Thames and Hudson, 1980.

———. *Music at Court.* London: Victor Gollancz, 1977.

Hogwood, Christopher, and R. Luckett: *Music in the Eighteenth-Century England.* Cambridge: Cambridge University Press, 1983.

Jacobson, Bernard. *A Polish Renaissance.* London: Phaidon Press, 1996. Includes chapters on composers Andrej Panufnik, Witold Lutosławski, Krzysztof Penderecki, and Henryk Górecki.

Kelly, Forrest. *First Nights: Five Musical Premieres.* New Haven, CT: Yale University Press, 2000.

Kramer, Jonathan D. *Listen to the Music: A Self-Guided Tour through the Orchestral Repertoire.* New York: Schirmer Books, 1988.

Landon, H. C. Robbins. *Essays on Viennese Classical Style: Gluck, Haydn, Mozart, Beethoven.* New York: Macmillan, 1970.

———. *Haydn: Chronicle and Works.* London: Thames and Hudson, 1976-1994.

———. *1791: Mozart's Last Year.* London and New York: Thames and Hudson, 1988.

———. *Mozart: the Golden Years, 1781–1791.* London and New York: Thames and Hudson, 1989.

———. *The Symphonies of Joseph Haydn.* New York: Macmillan, 1956.

Luening, Otto. *The Odyssey of an American Composer.* New York: Scribner, 1980.

Penderecki, Krzysztof. *Labyrinth of Time: Five Addresses for the End of the Millenium.* Chapel Hill, NC: Hinshaw Music, 1998.

Polisi, Joseph. *American Muse: The Life and Times of William Schuman.* New York: Amadeus Press, 2008.

———. *The Artist as Citizen.* Pompton Plains, NJ: Amadeus Press, 2005

Prausnitz, Frederik. *Roger Sessions: How a "Difficult" Composer Got That Way.* Oxford, New York: Oxford University Press, 2002.

Ratner, Leonard G. *Classic Music: Expression, Form and Style.* New York: Schirmer Books, 1980.

Rickards, Guy. *Hindemith, Hartmann and Henze.* London: Phaidon Press, 1995.

Robert, Grace. *The Borzoi Book of Ballets.* New York: Alfred A. Knopf, 1947. A book of sixty-three essays in alphabetical order about ballets beginning with *The Afternoon of a Faun,* music by Claude Debussy, and ending with *Voices of Spring,* music by Johann Strauss, and a glossary of terms with drawings of all the classic ballet positions.

Rosen, Charles. *The Classical Style: Haydn, Mozart, Beethoven.* London: Faber and Faber, 1971.

Ross, Alex. *The Rest Is Noise: Listening to the Twentieth Century.* New York: Farrar, Straus, and Giroux, 2007.

Slonimsky, Nicolas. *Lexicon of Musical Invective: Critical Assaults on Composers since Beethoven's Time.* 2nd ed. Seattle and London: University of Washington Press, 1965.

———. *Perfect Pitch: A Life Story.* New York: Schirmer Trade Books, 2002.

Spitzer, John, ed. *American Orchestras in the Nineteenth Century.* Chicago: University of Chicago Press, 2009.

Stephenson, Lesley. *Symphony of Dreams: The Conductor and Patron Paul Sacher.* Lanham, MD: Scarecrow Press, 2003.

Stravinsky, Igor. *Poetics of Music.* New York: Vintage Books, 1956.

Thayer, Alexander Wheelock. *Thayer's Life of Beethoven.* Revised and edited by Elliot Forbes. Princeton, NJ: Princeton University Press, 1967.

Tunstall, Tricia. *Changing Lives, Gustavo Dudamel, El Sistema, and the Transformative Power of Music.* New York: W. W. Norton and Co., 2012.

About the Author

Emily Freeman Brown is director of orchestral activities, professor of conducting, and music director of opera theater at Bowling Green State University. The first woman to receive a doctor of musical arts in orchestral conducting at the Eastman School of Music, she has appeared as a frequent guest conductor with orchestras throughout the world, including Europe, North and South America, and Asia. Under her direction, the Bowling Green Philharmonia has released numerous recordings in a series titled The Voice of the Composer: New Music from Bowling Green on Albany Records and syndicated internationally on National Public Radio. Other recordings have appeared on Naxos and Opus One Records.

Brown has conducted all-state orchestras in several states, including Washington, Missouri, Minnesota, Iowa, and Ohio, and has been a clinician at the Mid-West Band and Orchestra Clinic and for the Conductors Guild, where she also served as president. In that position, she organized numerous conducting workshops across the United States. Articles have been published in the *Journal of the Conductors Guild*, *Bach*, *Women of Note*, and the publication of the City University of London's International Conference on Jewish Music.

Brown has given conducting master classes in Berlin, Germany; Riga, Latvia; Cluj-Napoca, Romania; Astana and Almaty, Kazakhstan; Santiago, Chile; and at the Beijing China Central Conservatory. She served as a member of the jury for the Eduardo Mata Conducting Competition in Mexico.